Arithmetic Operations:

$$ab + ac = a(b+c)$$

$$\frac{a}{b} + \frac{c}{d} = \frac{ad+bc}{bd}$$

$$\frac{a+b}{c} = \frac{a}{c} + \frac{b}{c}$$

$$\frac{\left(\frac{a}{b}\right)}{\left(\frac{c}{d}\right)} = \frac{ad}{bc}$$

$$a\left(\frac{b}{c}\right) = \frac{ab}{c}$$

$$\frac{a-b}{c-d} = \frac{b-a}{d-c}$$

$$\frac{ab+ac}{a} = b+c, \; a \neq 0$$

$$\frac{\left(\frac{a}{b}\right)}{c} = \frac{a}{bc}$$

$$\frac{a}{\left(\frac{b}{c}\right)} = \frac{ac}{b}$$

Exponents and Radicals:

$$a^0 = 1, \; a \neq 0$$

$$\frac{a^x}{a^y} = a^{x-y}$$

$$\left(\frac{a}{b}\right)^x = \frac{a^x}{b^x}$$

$$\sqrt[n]{a^m} = a^{m/n} = \left(\sqrt[n]{a}\right)^m$$

$$a^{-x} = \frac{1}{a^x}$$

$$(a^x)^y = a^{xy}$$

$$\sqrt{a} = a^{1/2}$$

$$\sqrt[n]{ab} = \sqrt[n]{a}\sqrt[n]{b}$$

$$a^x a^y = a^{x+y}$$

$$(ab)^x = a^x b^x$$

$$\sqrt[n]{a} = a^{1/n}$$

$$\sqrt[n]{\left(\frac{a}{b}\right)} = \frac{\sqrt[n]{a}}{\sqrt[n]{b}}$$

Algebraic Errors to Avoid:

$\dfrac{a}{x+b} \neq \dfrac{a}{x} + \dfrac{a}{b}$ (To see this error, let $a = b = x = 1$.)

$\sqrt{x^2+a^2} \neq x + a$ (To see this error, let $x = 3$ and $a = 4$.)

$a - b(x-1) \neq a - bx - b$ (Remember to distribute negative signs. The equation should be $a - b(x-1) = a - bx + b$.)

$\dfrac{\left(\frac{x}{a}\right)}{b} \neq \dfrac{bx}{a}$ (To divide fractions, invert and multiply. The equation should be

$$\frac{\frac{x}{a}}{b} = \frac{\frac{x}{a}}{\frac{b}{1}} = \left(\frac{x}{a}\right)\left(\frac{1}{b}\right) = \frac{x}{ab}.)$$

$\sqrt{-x^2+a^2} \neq -\sqrt{x^2-a^2}$ (We can't factor a negative sign outside of the square root.)

$\dfrac{\cancel{a}+bx}{\cancel{a}} \neq 1+bx$ (This is one of many examples of incorrect cancellation. The equation should be $\dfrac{a+bx}{a} = \dfrac{a}{a} + \dfrac{bx}{a} = 1 + \dfrac{bx}{a}$.)

$\dfrac{1}{x^{1/2}-x^{1/3}} \neq x^{-1/2}-x^{-1/3}$ (This error is a sophisticated version of the first error.)

$(x^2)^3 \neq x^5$ (The equation should be $(x^2)^3 = x^2 x^2 x^2 = x^6$.)

Conversion Table:

1 centimeter = 0.394 inches	1 joule = 0.738 foot-pounds	1 mile = 1.609 kilometers
1 meter = 39.370 inches	1 gram = 0.035 ounces	1 gallon = 3.785 liters
= 3.281 feet	1 kilogram = 2.205 pounds	1 pound = 4.448 newtons
1 kilometer = 0.621 miles	1 inch = 2.540 centimeters	1 foot-lb = 1.356 joules
1 liter = 0.264 gallons	1 foot = 30.480 centimeters	1 ounce = 28.350 grams
1 newton = 0.225 pounds	= 0.305 meters	1 pound = 0.454 kilograms

GRAPHS OF COMMON FUNCTIONS

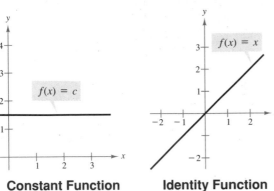

Constant Function — $f(x) = c$

Identity Function — $f(x) = x$

Absolute Value Function — $f(x) = |x|$

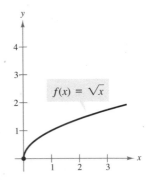

Square Root Function — $f(x) = \sqrt{x}$

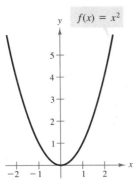

Squaring Function — $f(x) = x^2$

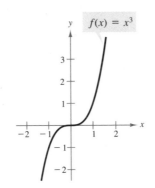

Cubing Function — $f(x) = x^3$

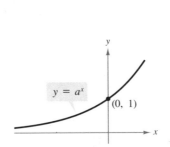

Exponential Function — $y = a^x$, $(0, 1)$

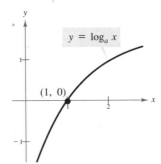

Logarithmic Function — $y = \log_a x$, $(1, 0)$

SYMMETRY

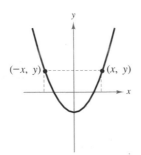

$(-x, y)$ (x, y)

y-Axis Symmetry

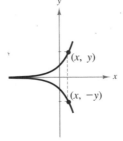

(x, y)
$(x, -y)$

x-Axis Symmetry

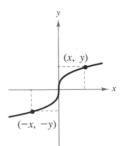

(x, y)
$(-x, -y)$

Origin Symmetry

Precalculus

THIRD EDITION

Roland E. Larson

Robert P. Hostetler

The Pennsylvania State University
The Behrend College

with the assistance of
David E. Heyd
The Pennsylvania State University
The Behrend College

D.C. Heath and Company
Lexington, Massachusetts   Toronto

Address editorial correspondence to:

D. C. Heath and Company
125 Spring Street
Lexington, MA 02173

Acquisitions Editor: Ann Marie Jones
Senior Development Editor: Cathy Cantin
Production Editor: Sarah Doyle
Designer and Art Editor: Sally Steele
Production Coordinator: Lisa Merrill
Composition: Jonathan Peck Typographers
Technical Art: Folium
Cover: Lance Hidy

Published simultaneously in Canada.

Printed in the United States of America.

International Standard Book Number: 0-669-28310-X

Library of Congress Catalog Card Number: 92-73025

10 9 8 7 6 5 4 3 2 1

Preface

Success in college-level mathematics courses begins with a good understanding of algebra, and one goal of *Precalculus, Third Edition* is to help students develop this understanding. Another goal is to show students how algebra can be used as a modeling language for real-life problems. Although we review some of the basic concepts of algebra, we assume that most students in this course have completed two years of high school algebra.

New to the Third Edition

Many users of the second edition of the text have given us suggestions for improving the text. We appreciate this type of input very much and have incorporated most of the suggestions into the Third Edition. Every section in the text was revised or considered for revision, and some sections were completely rewritten. Many new examples and exercises were added throughout the text. In addition, examples, exercises, and applications were revised and updated to expand the students' opportunities to practice their algebra skills. There is increased emphasis on the proper use of scientific and graphics calculators and graphing utilities in problem solving. Many examples and exercises now contain real data with credited source lines. Discussion problems were added to every section of the text. Each chapter now includes a two-page technology feature, and an introduction to graphics calculators was added to the appendix. New cumulative tests offer additional review after every three chapters.

Features

The features of this text are designed to help students develop their algebra and problem-solving skills, as well as acquire an understanding of mathematical concepts. To do this, the text has several key features.

Graphics

The ability to visualize a problem is a critical part of a student's ability to solve the problem. To encourage the development of this skill, the text has many figures in examples and exercise sets and in answers to odd-numbered exercises in the back of the text. Various types of graphics show geometric representations, including graphs of functions, geometric figures, symmetry, displays of statistical information, and screen outputs from graphing technology. All graphs are computer-generated for accuracy.

Applications

Numerous pertinent applications, many new to the Third Edition, are integrated throughout every section of the text, both as solved examples and as exercises. This encourages students to use and review their problem-solving skills. The text applications are current, and students learn to apply the process of mathematical modeling to real-world situations in many areas, such as business, economics, biology, engineering, chemistry, and physics. Many applications in the text use real-world data, and source lines are included to help motivate student interest.

Examples

For the Third Edition, many examples were revised and several new ones, including real-life applications, were added. Each was carefully chosen to illustrate a particular concept or problem-solving technique.

Discussion Problems

New to the Third Edition, the discussion problems offer students the opportunity for thinking, reasoning, and communicating about mathematics in different ways. Individually or in teams, for in-class discussion, writing assignments, or class presentations, students are encouraged to draw new conclusions about the concepts presented. The problem might ask for further explanation, synthesis, experimentation, or extension of the section concepts. Discussion problems appear at the end of each text section.

Exercise Sets

The exercise sets were extensively revised for the Third Edition. Many sets include a group of exercises that provide the graphs of functions involved. More exploratory and conceptual questions and questions involving geometry were added to the exercises to enhance their effectiveness. Each exercise set is carefully graded in difficulty to allow students to gain confidence as they progress. Exercise sets, including warm-up exercises, appear at the end of each text section. Review exercises are included at the end of each chapter, and now cumulative tests are included to review what students have learned from the three preceding chapters. The opportunity to use calculators is available with several topics to show patterns, experiment, calculate, or create graphic models.

Problem Solving Using Technology

Every chapter contains an optional feature that shows how graphics calculators and computer graphing utilities can be used to solve applications. New to the Third Edition, these features enhance and expand the range of problem-solving techniques using real data, computer-generated art, and graphing-technology screen output to simulate real-life problem-solving situations. Many of the problems discussed in these features are previews of classic problems in calculus, helping students develop an intuitive foundation for further study. In addition, there are opportunities throughout the text to use graphing technology in problems and applications in section exercises.

Enhanced Presentation

The Third Edition incorporates the use of additional colors to strengthen the text as a pedagogical tool. Color is used consistently to aid both reading and reference. For instance, definitions are highlighted by tan boxes, and equation side comments are given in red. Color in the art helps students visualize relationships.

These and other features of the text are described in greater detail on the following pages.

Features of the Text

Chapter Opener

Each chapter begins with a list of the topics to be covered and a brief overview. This provides a survey of the contents of the chapter, showing students how the topics fit into the overall development of algebra. Each section begins with a list of important topics covered in that section.

Definitions

All of the important rules, formulas, and definitions are boxed for emphasis. Each is also titled for easy reference.

Algebra of Calculus

Special emphasis has been given to algebraic skills that are needed in calculus. In addition to the material in Section 1.7 shown here, many other examples in the Third Edition discuss algebraic techniques that are used in calculus. These examples are clearly identified.

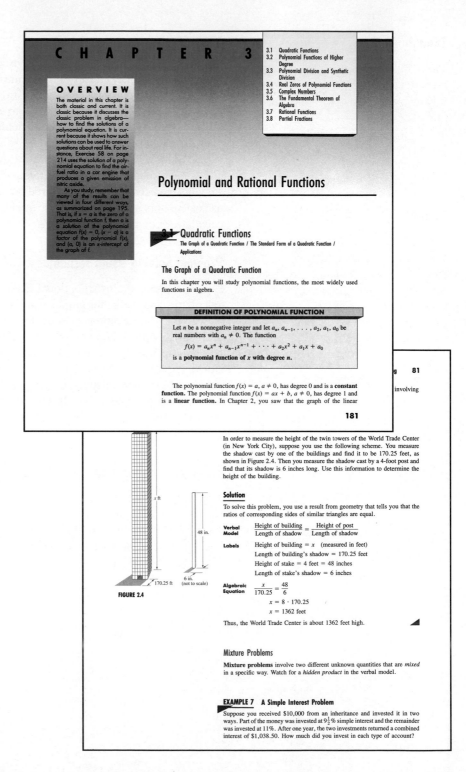

CHAPTER 3

3.1 Quadratic Functions
3.2 Polynomial Functions of Higher Degree
3.3 Polynomial Division and Synthetic Division
3.4 Real Zeros of Polynomial Functions
3.5 Complex Numbers
3.6 The Fundamental Theorem of Algebra
3.7 Rational Functions
3.8 Partial Fractions

OVERVIEW
The material in this chapter is both classic and current. It is classic because it discusses the classic problem in algebra—how to find the solutions of a polynomial equation. It is current because it shows how such solutions can be used to answer questions about real life. For instance, Exercise 58 on page 214 uses the solution of a polynomial equation to find the air-fuel ratio in a car engine that produces a given emission of nitric oxide.
 As you study, remember that many of the results can be viewed in four different ways, as summarized on page 195. That is, if $x = a$ is the zero of a polynomial function f, then a is a solution of the polynomial equation $f(x) = 0$, $(x - a)$ is a factor of the polynomial $f(x)$, and $(a, 0)$ is an x-intercept of the graph of f.

Polynomial and Rational Functions

3.1 Quadratic Functions
The Graph of a Quadratic Function / The Standard Form of a Quadratic Function / Applications

The Graph of a Quadratic Function

In this chapter you will study polynomial functions, the most widely used functions in algebra.

DEFINITION OF POLYNOMIAL FUNCTION

Let n be a nonnegative integer and let $a_n, a_{n-1}, \ldots, a_2, a_1, a_0$ be real numbers with $a_n \neq 0$. The function

$$f(x) = a_n x^n + a_{n-1} x^{n-1} + \cdots + a_2 x^2 + a_1 x + a_0$$

is a **polynomial function of x with degree n.**

The polynomial function $f(x) = a$, $a \neq 0$, has degree 0 and is a **constant function.** The polynomial function $f(x) = ax + b$, $a \neq 0$, has degree 1 and is a **linear function.** In Chapter 2, you saw that the graph of the linear

181

In order to measure the height of the twin towers of the World Trade Center (in New York City), suppose you use the following scheme. You measure the shadow cast by one of the buildings and find it to be 170.25 feet, as shown in Figure 2.4. Then you measure the shadow cast by a 4-foot post and find that its shadow is 6 inches long. Use this information to determine the height of the building.

Solution

To solve this problem, you use a result from geometry that tells you that the ratios of corresponding sides of similar triangles are equal.

Verbal Model

$$\frac{\text{Height of building}}{\text{Length of shadow}} = \frac{\text{Height of post}}{\text{Length of shadow}}$$

Labels

Height of building = x (measured in feet)
Length of building's shadow = 170.25 feet
Height of stake = 4 feet = 48 inches
Length of stake's shadow = 6 inches

Algebraic Equation

$$\frac{x}{170.25} = \frac{48}{6}$$
$$x = 8 \cdot 170.25$$
$$x = 1362 \text{ feet}$$

Thus, the World Trade Center is about 1362 feet high.

FIGURE 2.4

Mixture Problems

Mixture problems involve two different unknown quantities that are *mixed* in a specific way. Watch for a *hidden product* in the verbal model.

EXAMPLE 7   A Simple Interest Problem

Suppose you received $10,000 from an inheritance and invested it in two ways. Part of the money was invested at $9\frac{1}{2}\%$ simple interest and the remainder was invested at 11%. After one year, the two investments returned a combined interest of $1,038.50. How much did you invest in each type of account?

Examples

The Third Edition contains more than 775 text examples. They are titled for easy reference, and many include side comments that explain or justify steps in the solution. Students are encouraged to check their solutions.

Remarks

Special instructional notes to students appear with definitions, theorems, rules, and examples. Anticipating students' needs, they give additional insight, help avoid common errors, and describe generalizations.

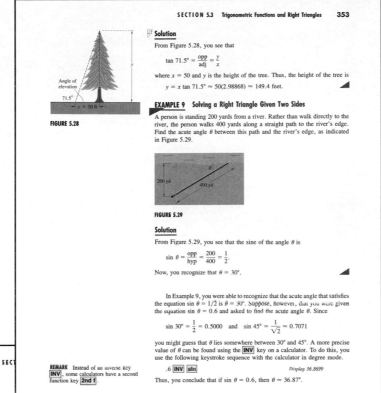

SECTION 5.3   Trigonometric Functions and Right Triangles   **353**

Solution

From Figure 5.28, you see that

$$\tan 71.5° = \frac{\text{opp}}{\text{adj}} = \frac{y}{x}$$

where $x = 50$ and y is the height of the tree. Thus, the height of the tree is

$$y = x \tan 71.5° \approx 50(2.98868) \approx 149.4 \text{ feet.}$$

EXAMPLE 9   Solving a Right Triangle Given Two Sides

A person is standing 200 yards from a river. Rather than walk directly to the river, the person walks 400 yards along a straight path to the river's edge. Find the acute angle θ between this path and the river's edge, as indicated in Figure 5.29.

FIGURE 5.28

FIGURE 5.29

Solution

From Figure 5.29, you see that the sine of the angle θ is

$$\sin \theta = \frac{\text{opp}}{\text{hyp}} = \frac{200}{400} = \frac{1}{2}.$$

Now, you recognize that $\theta = 30°$.

In Example 9, you were able to recognize that the acute angle that satisfies the equation $\sin \theta = 1/2$ is $\theta = 30°$. Suppose, however, that you were given the equation $\sin \theta = 0.6$ and asked to find the acute angle θ. Since

$$\sin 30° = \frac{1}{2} = 0.5000 \quad \text{and} \quad \sin 45° = \frac{1}{\sqrt{2}} \approx 0.7071$$

you might guess that θ lies somewhere between 30° and 45°. A more precise value of θ can be found using the ⟨INV⟩ key on a calculator. To do this, you use the following keystroke sequence with the calculator in degree mode.

.6 ⟨INV⟩ ⟨sin⟩   *Display 36.8699*

Thus, you conclude that if $\sin \theta = 0.6$, then $\theta \approx 36.87°$.

REMARK   Instead of an inverse key ⟨INV⟩, some calculators have a second function key ⟨2nd f⟩.

SEC

Solution

a. For $f(x) = 2^x$, we make a table

x	-2	-1	0	1	2	3
$f(x) = 2^x$	$\frac{1}{4}$	$\frac{1}{2}$	1	2	4	8

By plotting these points and connecting them with a smooth curve, we have the graph shown in Figure 4.10.
b. Since $g(x) = \log_2 x$ is the inverse of $f(x) = 2^x$, the graph of g is obtained by reflecting the graph of f in the line $y = x$, as shown in Figure 4.10.

FIGURE 4.10

EXAMPLE 4   Sketching the Graph of a Logarithmic Function

Sketch the graph of the logarithmic function $f(x) = \log_{10} x$.

Solution

We begin by making a table of values. Note that some of the values can be obtained without a calculator, while others require a calculator. We plot the corresponding points and sketch the graph in Figure 4.11.

FIGURE 4.11

	Without a calculator				With a calculator		
x	$\frac{1}{100}$	$\frac{1}{10}$	1	10	2	5	8
$\log_{10} x$	-2	-1	0	1	0.301	0.699	0.903

The nature of the graph in Figure 4.11 is typical of functions of the form $f(x) = \log_a x$, $a > 1$. They have one x-intercept and one vertical asymptote, and their domains are all positive numbers, $(0, \infty)$. We summarize the basic characteristics of logarithmic graphs in Figure 4.12.

REMARK   In Figure 4.12, note that the vertical asymptote occurs at $x = 0$, where $\log_a x$ is *undefined*.

FIGURE 4.12

Graph of $y = \log_a x$, $a > 1$
- Domain: $(0, \infty)$
- Range: $(-\infty, \infty)$
- Intercept: $(1, 0)$
- Increasing

- y-axis is a vertical asymptote ($\log_a x \to -\infty$ as $x \to 0^+$)
- Continuous
- Reflection of graph of $y = a^x$ about the line $y = x$

Calculators and Computer Graphing Utilities

To broaden the range of teaching and learning options, hints and instructions for working with calculators occur in many places in the Third Edition. If your students have access to graphics calculators or graphing utilities, they can solve exercises both graphically and analytically beginning with Chapter 3. Additionally, some exercises require a graphing utility, including Problem Solving Using Technology items.

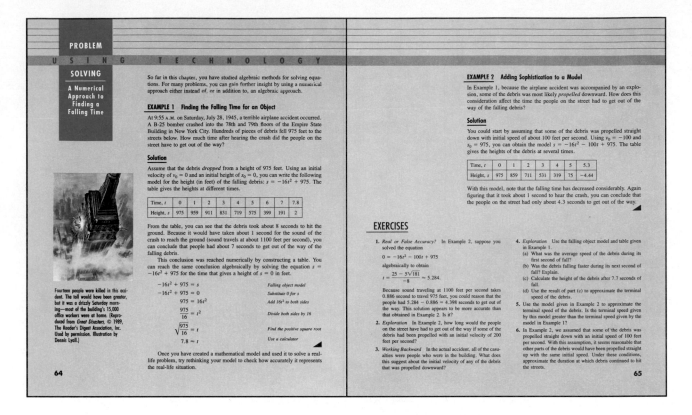

Problem Solving Using Technology

This optional feature in each chapter examines applications using graphing technology. As the basis for discussion, class demonstration, or student assignment, a variety of problems are explored, many of which use real data. Many of the problems discussed in these features are previews of classic problems in calculus.

Problem Solving Strategies

Throughout the text, a consistent strategy for solving problems is emphasized: analyze the problem, create a verbal model, construct an algebraic model, solve, and check the answer in the statement of the original problem. This problem-solving process has wide applicability and can be used with analytical, graphical, and numerical approaches.

Discussion Problems

A discussion problem appears at the end of each section. Each one encourages students to think, reason, and write about mathematics, individually or in groups. Examining the mathematics in a different way from that presented in the section, these problems emphasize synthesis and experimentation.

Warm Ups

Each section (except Sections 1.1 and 1.7) contains a set of 10 warm-up exercises for students to review and practice the previously learned skills that are necessary to master the new skills and concepts presented in the section. All warm-up exercises are answered in the back of the text.

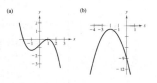

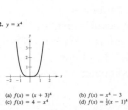

Exercises

The approximately 6000 exercises include computational, conceptual, exploratory, and applied problems. These are designed to build competence, skill, and understanding. Each exercise set is graded in difficulty to allow students to gain confidence as they progress. Some exercises require the use of a graphing utility. Answers to odd-numbered exercises are in the back of the text. Boxed numbers indicate exercises that are solved in detail in the *Study and Solutions Guide*.

Applications

Real-world applications are integrated throughout the text both in examples and exercises. This offers students insight about the usefulness of algebra, develops strategies for solving problems, and emphasizes the relevance of the mathematics. Many of the applications use current real data, and all are titled for reference.

---

308 CHAPTER 4 Exponential and Logarithmic Functions

Compound Interest In Exercises 71 and 72, find the time required for a $1000 investment to double at interest rate *r*, compounded continuously.

71. *r* = 0.085 **72.** *r* = 0.12

Compound Interest In Exercises 73 and 74, find the time required for a $1000 investment to triple at interest rate *r*, compounded continuously.

73. *r* = 0.085 **74.** *r* = 0.12

75. *Demand Function* The demand equation for a certain product is given by

$$p = 500 - 0.5(e^{0.004x}).$$

Find the demand *x* for a price of (a) *p* = $350 and (b) *p* = $300.

76. *Demand Function* The demand equation for a certain product is given by

$$p = 5000\left(1 - \frac{4}{4 + e^{-0.002x}}\right).$$

Find the demand *x* for a price of (a) *p* = $600 and (b) *p* = $400.

77. *Forest Yield* The yield *V* (in millions of cubic feet per acre) for a forest at age *t* years is given by

$$V = 6.7e^{-48.1/t}.$$

Find the time necessary to have a yield of (a) 1.3 million cubic feet and (b) 2 million cubic feet.

78. *Human Memory Model* In a group project in learning theory, a mathematical model for the proportion *P* of correct responses after *n* trials was found to be

$$P = \frac{0.83}{1 + e^{-0.2n}}.$$

After how many trials will 60% of the responses be correct?

79. *Average Heights* The percentage of American males between the ages of 18 and 24 who are no more than *x* inches tall is given by

$$m(x) = \frac{100}{1 + e^{-0.6114(x - 69.71)}}$$

where *m* is the percentage and *x* is the height in inches (see figure). (*Source:* U.S. National Center for Health Statistics) The function giving the percentages *f* for females for the same ages is given by

$$f(x) = \frac{100}{1 + e^{-0.66607(x - 64.51)}}.$$

What is the median height of each sex?

Figure for 79

80. *Trees per Acre* The number of trees per acre *N* of a certain species is approximated by the model

$$N = 68 \cdot 10^{-0.04x}, \qquad 5 \le x \le 40$$

where *x* is the average diameter (in inches) of the trees three feet above the ground. Use the model to approximate the average diameter of the trees in a test plot when *N* = 21.

SECTION 7.1 Exercises 481

38. *Distance* A boat is sailing due east parallel to the shoreline at a speed of 10 miles per hour. At a given time, the bearing to the lighthouse is S 72° E, and 15 minutes later the bearing is S 66° E (see figure). Find the distance from the boat to the shoreline if the lighthouse is at the shoreline.

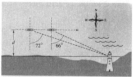

Figure for 38

39. *Distance* A family is traveling due west on a road that passes a famous landmark. At a given time, the bearing to the landmark is N 62° W, and after traveling 5 miles farther the bearing is N 38° W. What is the closest the family will come to the landmark while on the road?

40. *Engine Design* The connecting rod in a certain engine is 6 inches long and the radius of the crankshaft is $1\frac{1}{2}$ inches (see figure). The spark plug fires at 5° before top dead center. How far is the piston from the top of its stroke at this time?

Figure for 40

41. *Verification of Testimony* The following information about a triangular parcel of land is given at a zoning board meeting: "One side is 450 feet long and another is 120 feet long. The angle opposite the shorter side is 30°." Could this information be correct?

42. *Distance* The angles of elevation to an airplane, θ and φ, are being continuously monitored at two observation points *A* and *B*, which are two miles apart (see figure). Write an equation giving the distance *d* between the plane and point *B* in terms of θ and φ.

Figure for 42

Geometry

Geometric formulas and concepts are reviewed throughout the text. For easy reference, common formulas are given inside the back cover.

Graphics

The ability to visualize problems is a critical skill that students need in order to solve problems. To encourage the development of this skill and to reinforce concepts, the text has nearly 1100 figures, with every graph computer-generated for accuracy.

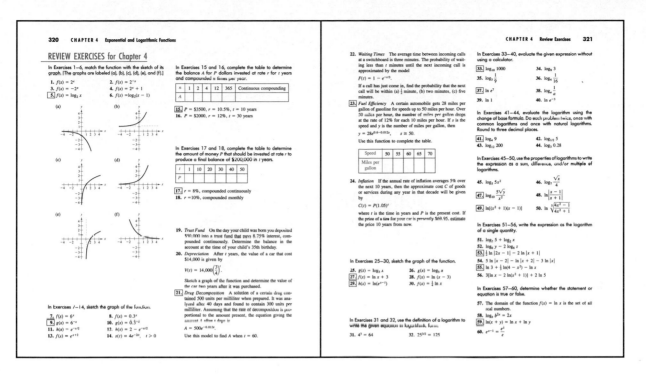

Review Exercises

A set of review exercises at the end of each chapter gives students an opportunity for additional practice. The review exercises include both computational and applied problems covering a wide range of topics.

Cumulative Test

Cumulative tests appear after Chapters 3, 7, and 11. These tests help students judge their mastery of previously covered concepts. They also help students maintain the knowledge-base they have been building throughout the text, preparing them for other exams and future courses.

Supplements

Precalculus, Third Edition by Larson and Hostetler is accompanied by a comprehensive supplements package for maximum teaching effectiveness and efficiency.

Instructor's Annotated Edition

Complete Solutions Guide

Study and Solutions Guide by Dianna L. Zook, Indiana University–Purdue University at Fort Wayne

Test Item File and Resource Guide by Meredythe M. Burrows, The Pennsylvania State University, The Behrend College

Precalculus Videotapes by Dana Mosely

Precalculus Tutor by Timothy R. Larson, Paula M. Sibeto, and John R. Musser

Test-Generating Software

Transparency Package

BestGrapher Software by George Best

Computer Activities for Precalculus Software
by Technology Training Associates

Precalculus Experiments with the Casio Graphics Calculator
by Lawrence G. Gilligan, OMI College of Applied Science,
University of Cincinnati

Precalculus Experiments with the TI-81 Graphics Calculator
by Lawrence G. Gilligan, OMI College of Applied Science,
University of Cincinnati

The Algebra of Calculus with Trigonometry and Analytic Geometry
by Eric Braude

Derive* Software by Soft Warehouse

This complete supplements package offers ancillary materials for students,
for instructors, and for classroom resources. Most items are keyed directly to
the textbook for easy use. For the convenience of software users, a technical
support telephone number is available with all D. C. Heath software
products: (617) 860-1218. The components of this comprehensive teaching
and learning package are outlined on the following pages.

* *Derive* is available to adopters at a discounted price.

INSTRUCTORS

Complete Solutions Guide
Solutions to warm ups, text exercises, discussion problems, technology features, and cumulative tests

Instructor's Annotated Edition
•Answers to warm ups, exercises, discussion problems, technology features, and cumulative tests
•Teaching strategies
•Additional examples and exercises

Test Item File and Resource Guide
•Printed test bank
•Approximately 2400 test items
•Open-ended and multiple-choice test items
•Available as test-generating software
•Sample tests
•Survey of assessment methods

STUDENTS

Study and Solutions Guide
•Solutions to selected odd-numbered text exercises
•Solutions match methods of text
•Summaries of key concepts in each text chapter
•Self-tests
•Study strategies

The Algebra of Calculus
•Reviews the algebra, trigonometry, and analytic geometry that students will encounter in calculus
•Over 200 examples
•Pretests and exercise sets

Precalulus Experiments with the TI-81 Graphics Calculator
•More than 20 labs
•Worktext format: includes numerous screen displays
•Examples, exercises, and cumulative exercise sets

Precalculus Experiments with the Casio Graphics Calculator
•More than 20 labs
•Worktext format: includes numerous screen displays
•Examples, exercises, and cumulative exercise set

CLASSROOM RESOURCES

Instructor's Annotated Edition
•Answers to warm ups, exercises, discussion problems, technology features, and cumulative tests
•Teaching strategies
•Additional examples and exercises

Transparency Package
•50 color transparencies
•Color-coded by text topic

Software		VIDEOTAPES

Computerized Testing Software
- Test-generating software
- Approximately 2400 test items
- Also available as a printed test item file

Derive
- Computer Algebra System (CAS)
- Discount available to adopters

Bestgrapher
- Function grapher
- Screen simultaneously displays equation, graph, and table of values
- Some features anticipate calculus
- Includes zoom and print features for use on assignments

Tutor
- Interactive tutorial software follows text section by section
- Diagnostic feedback
- Additional practice
- Chapter warm-ups and self-tests
- Glossary

Derive
- Computer Algebra System (CAS)
- Discount available to adopters

Bestgrapher
- Function grapher
- Screen simultaneously displays equation, graph, and table of values
- Some features anticipate calculus
- Includes zoom and print features for use on assignments

Computer Activities for Precalculus
- Function grapher
- Directed tutorial on selected topics

Videotapes
- Comprehensive coverage
- Computer-generated animation
- For media/resource centers
- Additional explanation of concepts, sample problems, and applications

---

Tutor
- Interactive tutorial software follows text section by section
- Diagnostic feedback
- Additional practice
- Chapter self-tests
- Glossary
- Guided exercises provide step-by-step solutions; can be useful for class demonstration

Derive
- Computer Algebra System (CAS)
- Discount available to adopters

Bestgrapher
- Function grapher
- Screen simultaneously displays equation, graph, and table of values
- Includes zoom

Computer Activities for Precalculus
- Function grapher
- Directed tutorial

Videotapes
- Comprehensive coverage
- Computer-generated animation
- Additional explanation of concepts, sample problems, and applications

INTEGRATED LEARNING PACKAGE

Computer Activities for Precalculus

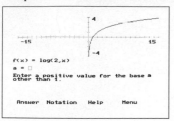

$f(x) = \log(2,x)$
$a = \square$
Enter a positive value for the base a
other than 1.

Answer   Notation   Help   Menu

Instructor's Annotated Edition

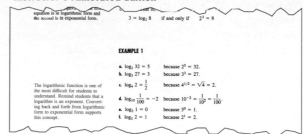

equation is in logarithmic form and
the second is in exponential form.

$3 = \log_2 8$ if and only if $2^3 = 8$.

EXAMPLE 1

The logarithmic function is one of the most difficult for students to understand. Remind students that a logarithm is an exponent. Converting back and forth from logarithmic form to exponential form supports this concept.

a. $\log_2 32 = 5$ because $2^5 = 32$.
b. $\log_3 27 = 3$ because $3^3 = 27$.
c. $\log_4 2 = \frac{1}{2}$ because $4^{1/2} = \sqrt{4} = 2$.
d. $\log_{10} \frac{1}{100} = -2$ because $10^{-2} = \frac{1}{10^2} = \frac{1}{100}$.
e. $\log_3 1 = 0$ because $3^0 = 1$.
f. $\log_2 2 = 1$ because $2^1 = 2$.

Precalculus Experiments with the TI-81 Graphics Calculator

In questions 1 through 4, graph the given logarithmic function and state its domain and range.

1. $y = \log(x+1)$ 2. $y = 4 + \ln x$

   Domain: _____   Domain: _____
   Range: _____   Range: _____

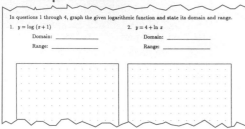

Precalculus Experiments with the Casio Graphics Calculator

<u>Procedure 1.</u> We graph the common logarithm, $y = \log x$ in Figure 8.1. Note the Casio range settings and the domain and range. (The domain and range correspond, of course, to the range and domain of the function $y = 10^x$.)

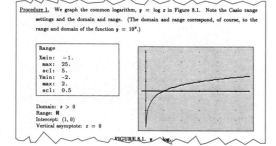

```
Range
 Xmin:  -1.
  max:  25.
  scl:   5.
 Ymin:  -2.
  max:   2.
  scl:  0.5
```

Domain: $x > 0$
Range: **R**
Intercept: $(1, 0)$
Vertical asymptote: $x = 0$

FIGURE 8.1. $y = \log x$

Transparency Package

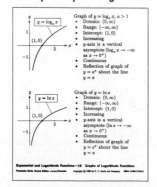

Graph of $y = \log_a x$, $a > 1$
- Domain: $(0, \infty)$
- Range: $(-\infty, \infty)$
- Intercept: $(1, 0)$
- Increasing
- y-axis is a vertical asymptote ($\log_a x \to -\infty$ as $x \to 0^+$)
- Continuous
- Reflection of graph of $y = a^x$ about the line $y = x$

Graph of $y = \ln x$
- Domain: $(0, \infty)$
- Range: $(-\infty, \infty)$
- Intercept: $(1, 0)$
- Increasing
- y-axis is a vertical asymptote ($\ln x \to -\infty$ as $x \to 0^+$)
- Continuous
- Reflection of graph of $y = e^x$ about the line $y = x$

Exponential and Logarithmic Functions—19 Graphs of Logarithmic Functions
Transparency Series, Second Edition, Larson/Hostetler Copyright © 1989 by D. C. Heath and Company ISBN: 0-669-17340-5

4.2 Logarithmic Functions
Introduction / The Common Logarithmic Function / Graphs of Logarithmic Functions / The Natural Logarithmic Function / Applications

Introduction

In Section 2.7 we discussed the concept of the inverse of a function. If a function has the property that no horizontal line intersects the graph of a function more than once, then the function must have an inverse. In Section 4.1, every function of the form $f(x) = a^x$ passes the "horizontal line test," and therefore must have an inverse. This inverse function is the **logarithmic function with base a** (see Figure 4.9).

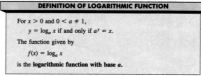

$f(x) = a^x$, $a > 1$

(0, 1)

(1, 0)

$f^{-1}(x) = \log_a x$

Inverse Functions
Domain of $\log_a x$ is Range of a^x.

FIGURE 4.9

DEFINITION OF LOGARITHMIC FUNCTION

For $x > 0$ and $0 < a \neq 1$,
$$y = \log_a x \text{ if and only if } a^y = x.$$
The function given by
$$f(x) = \log_a x$$
is the **logarithmic function with base a**.

REMARK The equations $y = \log_a x$ and $a^y = x$ are equivalent. The first equation is in logarithmic form and the second is in exponential form.

When evaluating logarithms, remember that *a logarithm is an exponent.* This means that $\log_a x$ is the exponent to which a must be raised to obtain x. For instance, $\log_2 8 = 3$ because 2 must be raised to the third power to obtain 8. That is,

$$3 = \log_2 8 \quad \text{if and only if} \quad 2^3 = 8.$$

Base

Logarithm is an exponent

EXAMPLE 1   Evaluating Logarithms

a. $\log_2 32 = 5$ because $2^5 = 32$.
b. $\log_3 27 = 3$ because $3^3 = 27$.
c. $\log_4 2 = \frac{1}{2}$ because $4^{1/2} = \sqrt{4} = 2$.
d. $\log_{10} \frac{1}{100} = -2$ because $10^{-2} = \frac{1}{10^2} = \frac{1}{100}$.
e. $\log_3 1 = 0$ because $3^0 = 1$.
f. $\log_2 2 = 1$ because $2^1 = 2$.

Videotapes

Derive

Complete Solutions Guide

r	0.005	0.010	0.015	0.020	0.025	0.030
t	138.6	69.3	46.2	34.7	27.7	23.1

60. $t = \dfrac{\ln K}{0.095}$

(a)

K	1	2	4	6	8	10	12
t	0	7.3	14.6	18.9	21.9	24.2	26.2

(b)

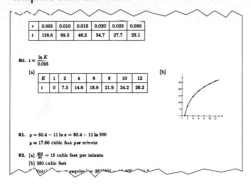

61. $y = 80.4 - 11 \ln x = 80.4 - 11 \ln 300$

$y \approx 17.66$ cubic feet per minute

62. (a) $\frac{450}{30} = 15$ cubic feet per minute

(b) 380 cubic feet

Study and Solutions Guide

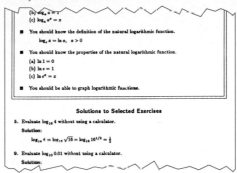

(b) $\log_a a = 1$

(c) $\log_a a^x = x$

■ You should know the definition of the natural logarithmic function.

$\log_e x = \ln x, \quad x > 0$

■ You should know the properties of the natural logarithmic function.

(a) $\ln 1 = 0$

(b) $\ln e = 1$

(c) $\ln e^x = x$

■ You should be able to graph logarithmic functions.

Solutions to Selected Exercises

5. Evaluate $\log_{16} 4$ without using a calculator.

Solution:

$$\log_{16} 4 = \log_{16} \sqrt{16} = \log_{16} 16^{1/2} = \tfrac{1}{2}$$

9. Evaluate $\log_{10} 0.01$ without using a calculator.

Solution:

---

292   CHAPTER 4   Exponential and Logarithmic Functions

In Exercises 39–44, use the graph of $y = \ln x$ to match the given function to its graph. [The graphs are labeled (a), (b), (c), (d), (e), and (f).]

39. $f(x) = \ln x + 2$
40. $f(x) = -\ln x$
41. $f(x) = -\ln(x + 2)$
42. $f(x) = \ln(x - 1)$
43. $f(x) = \ln(1 - x)$
44. $f(x) = -\ln(-x)$

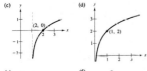

(a)   (b)

(c)   (d)

(e)   (f)

In Exercises 45–56, find the domain, vertical asymptote, and x-intercept of the logarithmic function and sketch its graph.

45. $f(x) = \log_4 x$
46. $g(x) = \log_6 x$
47. $h(x) = \log_4(x - 3)$
48. $f(x) = -\log_6(x + 2)$
49. $y = -\log_6 x + 2$
50. $y = \log_5(x - 1) + 4$
51. $y = \log_{10}\left(\dfrac{x}{5}\right)$
52. $y = \log_{10}(-x)$
53. $f(x) = \ln(x - 2)$
54. $h(x) = \ln(x + 1)$
55. $g(x) = \ln(-x)$
56. $f(x) = \ln(3 - x)$

57. *Human Memory Model*   Students in a mathematics class were given an exam and then tested monthly with an equivalent exam. The average score for the class was given by the human memory model

$$f(t) = 80 - 17 \log_{10}(t + 1), \quad 0 \le t \le 12$$

where t is the time in months.

(a) What was the average score on the original exam $(t = 0)$?

(b) What was the average score after 4 months?

(c) What was the average score after 10 months?

58. *Population Growth*   The population of a town will double in

$$t = \dfrac{10 \ln 2}{\ln 67 - \ln 50}$$

years. Find t.

59. *World Population Growth*   The time in years for the world population to double if it is increasing at a continuous rate of r is given by

$$t = \dfrac{\ln 2}{r}$$

Complete the table.

r	0.005	0.010	0.015	0.020	0.025	0.030
t						

60. *Investment Time*   A principal P invested at $9\frac{1}{2}\%$ and compounded continuously increases to an amount K times the original principal after t years, where t is given by

$$t = \dfrac{\ln K}{0.095}.$$

(a) Complete the table.

K	1	2	4	6	8	10	12
t							

(b) Use the table in part (a) to graph this function.

Ventilation Rates   In Exercises 61 and 62, use the model

$$y = 80.4 - 11 \ln x$$

which approximates the minimum required ventilation rate in terms of the air space per child in a public school classroom. In the model, x is the air space per child in cubic feet and y is the ventilation rate in cubic feet per minute (see figure).

Test Item File and Resource Guide

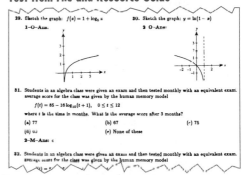

29. Sketch the graph: $f(x) = 1 + \log_5 x$

1-O-Ans.

30. Sketch the graph: $y = \ln(1 - x)$

2 O-Ans.

31. Students in an algebra class were given an exam and then tested monthly with an equivalent exam. average score for the class was given by the human memory model

$$f(t) = 85 - 16 \log_{10}(t + 1), \quad 0 \le t \le 12$$

where t is the time in months. What is the average score after 3 months?

(a) 77   (b) 67   (c) 75

(d) 65   (e) None of these

2-M-Ans: c

32. Students in an algebra class were given an exam and then tested monthly with an equivalent exam. average score for the class was given by the human memory model

Tutor

Computerized Testing Software

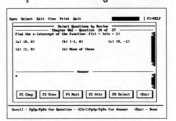

Acknowledgments

We would like to thank the many people who have helped us prepare the text and supplements package. Their encouragement, criticisms, and suggestions have been invaluable to us.

Third Edition Reviewers

Dennis Alber, Palm Beach Community College; Randall Allbritton, Daytona Beach Community College; Paul J. Allen, University of Alabama; Catherine C. Aust, Clayton State College; Judith Barclay, Cuesta College; Derek Bloomfield, Orange County Community College; Gene Clegg, Johnson County Community College; Maria Cossio, LaGuardia Community College; Margaret D. Dolgas, University of Delaware; Gregory Dotseth, University of Northern Iowa; Don A. Edwards, Houston Community College; Iris B. Fetta, Clemson University; Dewey Furness, Ricks College; James A. Gauthier, Louisiana State University; Nancy Henry, Indiana University at Kokomo; Marlene F. Hubbard, University of Arizona; Norma F. James, New Mexico State University; Moana Karsteter, Tallahassee Community College; Gary Ling, City College of San Francisco; Sheila D. McNicholas, University of Illinois at Chicago; Karla Neal, Louisiana State University; Mary Ellen O'Leary, University of South Carolina; Michael Perkowski, University of Missouri; Beverly B. Phillips, Thomas Nelson Community College; Beverly M. Reed, Kent State University; Mary Ellen Rivers, Grand Valley State University; Patricia B. D. Shure, University of Michigan; Burla J. Sims, University of Arkansas at Little Rock; Michel Smith, Auburn University; Theresa Stalder, University of Illinois at Chicago; Greg St. George, University of Montana; Arthur Szylewicz, Moorpark College; Mohan Tikoo, Southeast Missouri State University; Marvel D. Townsend, University of Florida.

Reviewers, First and Second Editions

Hollie Baker, Norfolk State University; Derek Bloomfield, Orange County Community College; Ben P. Bockstage, Broward Community College; Daniel D. Bonar, Denison University; John E. Bruha, University of Northern Iowa; Richard Cutts, University of Wisconsin–Stout; H. Eugene Hall, DeKalb Community College; Randal Hoppens, Blinn College; E. John Hornsby, Jr., University of New Orleans; William B. Jones, University of Colorado; Jimmie D. Lawson, Louisiana State University; Peter J. Livorsi, Oakton Community College; Wade T. Macey, Appalachian State University; Jerome L. Paul, University of Cincinnati; Marilyn Schiermeier, North Carolina State University; George W. Schultz, St. Petersburg Junior College; Edith Silver, Mercer County Community College; Shirley C. Sorensen, University of Maryland; Charles Stone, DeKalb Community College; Bruce Williamson, University of Wisconsin–River Falls.

Survey Respondents, Second Edition

Holli Adams, Portland Community College; Marion Baumler, Niagara County Community College; Diane Blansett, Delta State University; Derek Bloomfield, Orange County Community College; Daniel D. Bonar, Denison University; John E. Bruha, University of Northern Iowa; William L. Campbell, University of Wisconsin–Platteville; John Caraluzzo, Orange County Community College; William E. Chatfield, University of Wisconsin–Platteville; Robert P. Finley, Mississippi State University; August J. Garver, University of Missouri–Rolla; Sue Goodman, University of North Carolina; Louis Hoelzle, Bucks County Community College; Randal Hoppens, Blinn College; Moana Karsteter, Tallahassee Community College; Robert C. Limburg, St. Louis Community College at Florissant Valley; Peter J. Livorsi, Oakton Community College; John Locker, University of North Alabama; Wade T. Macey, Appalachian State University; J. Kent Minichiello, Howard University; Terry Mullen, Carroll College; Richard Nation, Palomar College; William Paul, Appalachian State University; Richard A. Quint, Ventura College; Charles T. Scarborough, Mississippi State University; Shannon Schumann, University of Wyoming; Arthur E. Schwartz, Mercer County Community College; Joseph Sharp , West Georgia College; Burla J. Sims, University of Arkansas at Little Rock; James R. Smith, Appalachian State University; B. Louise Whisler, San Bernardino Valley College; Bruce Williamson, University of Wisconsin–River Falls.

A special thanks to all the people at D. C. Heath and Company who worked with us in the development and production of the text, especially Ann Marie Jones, Mathematics Acquisitions Editor; Cathy Cantin, Senior Developmental Editor; Sarah Doyle, Production Editor; Elizabeth Gale, Editorial Assistant; Sally Steele, Designer and Art Editor; Carolyn Johnson, Editorial Associate; Mike O'Dea, Production Manager; and Lisa Merrill, Production Supervisor.

Several other people worked on this project. David E. Heyd assisted us in writing the text and solved the exercises; Dianna L. Zook wrote the *Study and Solutions Guide*; Meredythe Burrows wrote the *Test Item File* and checked the manuscript for accuracy; and Helen Medley checked the manuscript for accuracy. The following people also worked on the project: Richard J. Bambauer, Lisa K. Bickel, Linda M. Bollinger, Laurie A. Brooks, Patti Jo Campbell, Darin P. Johnson, Linda L. Kifer, Deanna G. Larson, Patricia S. Larson, Timothy R. Larson, Amy L. Marshall, John R. Musser, R. Scott O'Neil, Louis R. Rieger, Paula M. Sibeto, and Evelyn A. Wedzikowski.

On a personal level, we are grateful to our wives, Deanna Gilbert Larson and Eloise Hostetler, for their love, patience, and support. Also, a special thanks goes to R. Scott O'Neil.

If you have suggestions for improving the text, please feel free to write to us. Over the past two decades, we have received many useful comments from both instructors and students, and we value these very much.

Roland E. Larson
Robert P. Hostetler

The Larson and Hostetler Precalculus Series

College Algebra, Third Edition

This text is designed for a one-term course covering standard topics such as algebraic functions and their graphs, exponential and logarithmic functions, systems of equations, matrices, determinants, sequences, series, and probability.

Trigonometry, Third Edition

This text is for use in a one-term course covering the trigonometric functions and their graphs, exponential and logarithmic functions, and analytic geometry (including polar coordinates and parametric equations).

Algebra and Trigonometry, Third Edition

This book combines the contents of the two texts mentioned above (with the exception of polar coordinates and parametric equations). It is comprehensive enough for a two-term course or may be used selectively in a one-term course.

Precalculus, Third Edition

With this book, students cover the algebraic, exponential, logarithmic, and trigonometric functions and their graphs, as well as analytic geometry in preparation for a course in calculus. This text may be used in a one- or two-term course.

Also available :

College Algebra: Concepts and Models by Larson, Hostetler, and Munn
College Algebra: A Graphing Approach by Larson, Hostetler, and Edwards
Precalculus: A Graphing Approach by Larson, Hostetler, and Edwards

Contents

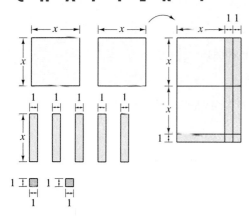
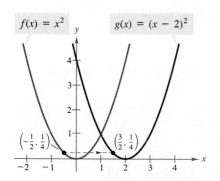

C H A P T E R 3

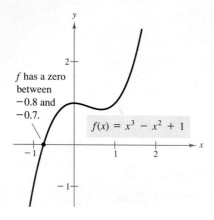

f has a zero between -0.8 and -0.7.

$f(x) = x^3 - x^2 + 1$

C H A P T E R 4

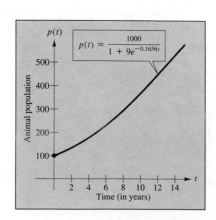

$$p(t) = \frac{1000}{1 + 9e^{-0.1656t}}$$

Animal population

Time (in years)

C H A P T E R 5

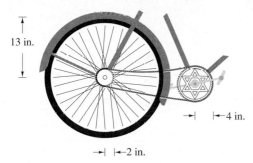

C H A P T E R 6

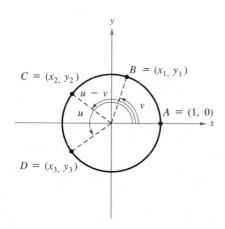

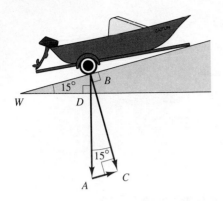
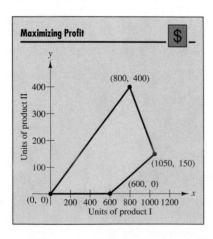

CHAPTER 9

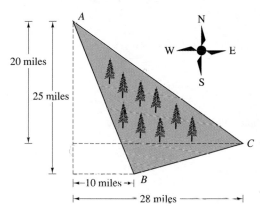

CHAPTER 10

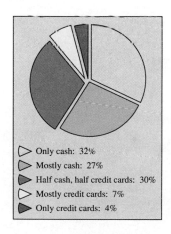

Only cash: 32%
Mostly cash: 27%
Half cash, half credit cards: 30%
Mostly credit cards: 7%
Only credit cards: 4%

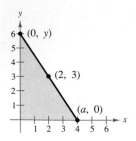

Introduction to Calculators

This text includes several examples and exercises that require the use of a calculator, thus enabling you to relate concepts that are closer to the way they are used in the workplace and in real-life applications. As each new calculator application is encountered, it is accompanied with instructions for efficient calculator use. These instructions, however, are general in nature and may not agree precisely with the steps required by your calculator.

Scientific Calculators

For use with this text, a scientific calculator with the following features will be helpful.

1. At least 8-digit display

2. Four arithmetic operations: $\boxed{+}$, $\boxed{-}$, $\boxed{\times}$, $\boxed{\div}$

3. Change sign key or Negation key: $\boxed{+/-}$ or $\boxed{(-)}$

4. Memory key and Recall key: $\boxed{\text{STO}}$, $\boxed{\text{RCL}}$

5. Parentheses: $\boxed{(}$, $\boxed{)}$

6. Exponent key: $\boxed{y^x}$, $\boxed{e^x}$, $\boxed{\wedge}$

7. Logarithm key: $\boxed{\ln x}$, $\boxed{\log x}$

8. Pi and Degree-Radian conversion: $\boxed{\pi}$, $\boxed{\text{DRG}}$

9. Inverse, reciprocal, square root: $\boxed{\text{INV}}$, $\boxed{1/x}$, $\boxed{\sqrt{x}}$

   One of the basic differences in calculators is their order of operations. Some calculators use an order of operations called RPN (for Reverse Polish Notation). In this text, however, all calculator steps are given using algebraic order of operations. For example, the calculation

$$4.69[5 + 2(6.87 - 3.042)]$$

can be performed with the following steps.

$$4.69 \;\boxed{\times}\; \boxed{(}\; 5 \;\boxed{+}\; 2 \;\boxed{\times}\; \boxed{(}\; 6.87 \;\boxed{-}\; 3.042 \;\boxed{)}\;\boxed{)}\;\boxed{=}$$

This yields the value of 59.35664. Without parentheses, you could enter the expression from the inside out with the sequence

6.87 $\boxed{-}$ 3.042 $\boxed{=}$ $\boxed{\times}$ 2 $\boxed{+}$ 5 $\boxed{=}$ $\boxed{\times}$ 4.69 $\boxed{=}$

to obtain the same result.

Graphing Calculators

A graphing calculator expands the features of a scientific calculator to include graphs of functions and programming. If you have access to such a calculator, you should consult its user's manual to see how to enter and evaluate expressions. You should also practice using its graphing features. To help you become familiar with the graphing features, we have included Appendix A, Graphing Utilities. Be sure to read the examples in Appendix A and work the exercises. Answers to odd-numbered exercises in Appendix A are given in the back of the book.

Rounding Numbers

For all their usefulness, calculators do have a problem representing numbers because they are limited to a finite number of digits. For instance, what does your calculator display when you compute 2 ÷ 3? Some calculators simply truncate (drop) the digits that exceed their display range and display .66666666. Others will round the number and display .66666667. Although the second display is more accurate, both of these decimal representations of 2/3 contain a rounding error.

When rounding decimals, we suggest the following guidelines.

1. Determine the number of digits of accuracy you want to keep. The digit in the last position you keep is the **rounding digit,** and the digit in the first position you discard is the **decision digit.**

2. If the decision digit is 5 or greater, round up by adding 1 to the rounding digit.

3. If the decision digit is 4 or less, round down by leaving the rounding digit unchanged.

Here are some examples. Note that you round down in the first example because the decision digit is 4 or less, and you round up in the other two examples because the decison digit is 5 or greater.

Number	*Rounded to three decimal places*	
a. $\sqrt{2} = 1.4142136...$	1.414	*Round down*
b. $\pi = 3.1415927...$	3.142	*Round up*
c. $\frac{7}{9} = 0.7777777...$	0.778	*Round up*

One of the best ways to minimize error due to rounding is to leave numbers in your calculator until your calculations are complete. If you want to save a number for future use, store it in your calculator's memory.

Remember that once you (or your calculator) have rounded a number, a round-off error has been introduced. For instance, if a number is rounded to $x \approx 27.3$, then the actual value of x can lie anywhere between 27.25 and 27.35, or at 27.25 exactly. That is, $27.25 \le x < 27.35$.

Problem Solving Using a Calculator

Here are some guidelines to consider when using any type of calculator in problem solving.

1. Be sure you understand the operation of your own calculator. You need to be skilled at entering expressions in a way that will guarantee that your calculator is performing the operations correctly.

2. Focus first on analyzing the problem. After you have developed a strategy, you may be able to use your calculator to help implement the strategy. Write down your steps in an organized way to clearly outline the strategy used and the results.

3. Most problems can be solved in a variety of ways. If you choose to solve a problem using a table, try checking the solution with an analytic (or algebraic) approach. Or, if you choose to solve a problem using algebra, try checking the solution with a graphing approach.

4. If you have access to a graphing calculator or other graphing utility, you will find many uses for it beginning with Chapter 3.

5. After obtaining a solution with a calculator, be sure to ask yourself if the solution is reasonable (within the context of the problem).

6. To lessen the chance of errors, clear the calculator display (and check the settings) before beginning a new problem.

CHAPTER 1

OVERVIEW

The rules of algebra reviewed in this chapter are generalizations of arithmetic rules. For instance, the rule for adding fractional expressions is a generalization of the rule for adding numerical fractions.

Rules for operations are an important feature of algebra. The *most* important feature of algebra, however, is that it is a language that can be used to answer questions about real life. For instance, Example 1 on page 40 uses algebra to model the volume of an open box. In the exercises that follow Example 1, you are asked to experiment with the model to find the maximum possible volume of the box.

Pay special attention to the terminology and notation used in the chapter. The meaning of such words as *term, factor,* and *expression* must be clear.

Review of Basic Algebra

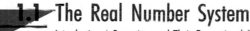

1.1 The Real Number System

Introduction / Operations and Their Properties / Equations / The Real Number Line / Ordering the Real Numbers / The Absolute Value of a Real Number / The Distance Between Two Real Numbers

Introduction

The **real number system** includes the set of real numbers, the basic operations of addition, subtraction, multiplication, and division, and the properties of these operations. The set of real numbers contains important subsets of numbers that are used to describe quantities such as temperature, age, miles per gallon, area, volume, population, and so on. These subsets of real numbers and their relationship to each other are shown in Figure 1.1.

1

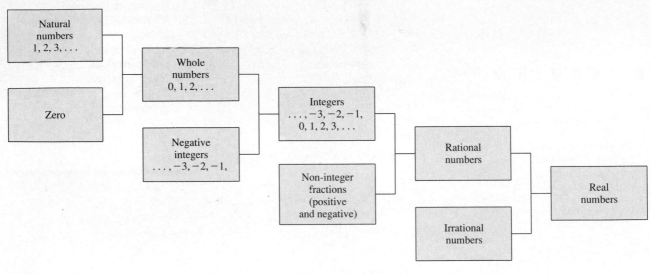

FIGURE 1.1   Subsets of the Real Numbers

A **rational number** is a real number that can be written as the ratio p/q of two integers, where $q \neq 0$. Rational numbers have decimal representations that either terminate or repeat a sequence of digits indefinitely. Here are some examples.

$$\frac{1}{5} = 0.2 \qquad\qquad \textit{Terminating decimal representation}$$

$$\frac{1}{8} = 0.125 \qquad\qquad \textit{Terminating decimal representation}$$

$$\frac{1}{3} = 0.3333\ldots = 0.\overline{3} \qquad \textit{Repeating decimal representation}$$

$$\frac{8}{55} = 0.14545\ldots = 0.1\overline{45} \quad \textit{Repeating decimal representation}$$

An **irrational number** is a real number that cannot be written as the ratio of two integers. Decimal representations of irrational numbers neither terminate nor repeat. Here are some examples.

$$\sqrt{2} = 1.4142135624\ldots \qquad \textit{Nonterminating and nonrepeating}$$

$$\pi = 3.1415926536\ldots \qquad \textit{Nonterminating and nonrepeating}$$

$$e = 2.7182818285\ldots \qquad \textit{Nonterminating and nonrepeating}$$

$$\frac{\sqrt{5}}{2} = 1.1180339887\ldots \qquad \textit{Nonterminating and nonrepeating}$$

You can check these decimal representations on a calculator. However, remember that a calculator gives only a limited number of digits. Hence, for many real numbers, the decimal values shown by a calculator are only approximations of the exact value. For such approximations, we use the symbol $\approx$, as follows.

$$\sqrt{2} \approx 1.4142 \quad \textit{Rounded to four decimal places}$$

Operations and Their Properties

There are four arithmetic operations with real numbers: **addition, multiplication, subtraction,** and **division,** denoted by the symbols $+$, $\times$ (or $\cdot$), $-$, and $\div$. Of these, addition and multiplication are the two primary operations. Subtraction and division are the inverse operations of addition and multiplication.

Subtraction	*Division*
$a - b = a + (-b)$	If $b \neq 0$, then $a \div b = a\left(\dfrac{1}{b}\right) = \dfrac{a}{b}$.

In these definitions, $-b$ is the **additive inverse** (or opposite) of b, and $1/b$ is the **multiplicative inverse** (or reciprocal) of b. In place of $a \div b$, we often use the fraction symbol a/b. In this fractional form, a is the **numerator** of the fraction and b is the **denominator.**

Be sure you see that the following properties, which we call the **basic rules of algebra,** are true for variables and algebraic expressions as well as for real numbers.

BASIC RULES OF ALGEBRA

Let a, b, and c be *real numbers, variables, or algebraic expressions.*

1. Closure: $a + b$ is a real number.   *Addition*
                  $a \cdot b$ is a real number.   *Multiplication*
2. Commutative: $a + b = b + a$ *Addition*
                  $a \cdot b = b \cdot a$ *Multiplication*
3. Associative: $(a + b) + c = a + (b + c)$ *Addition*
                  $(a \cdot b) \cdot c = a \cdot (b \cdot c)$ *Multiplication*
4. Identity: $a + 0 = a = 0 + a$ *0 is the additive identity*
                  $a \cdot 1 = a = 1 \cdot a$ *1 is the multiplicative identity*
5. Inverse: $a + (-a) = 0 = (-a) + a$ *$-a$ is the additive inverse of a*
                  $a\left(\dfrac{1}{a}\right) = 1 = \left(\dfrac{1}{a}\right)a, \qquad a \neq 0$ *$\dfrac{1}{a}$ is the multiplicative inverse of a*
6. Distributive: $a(b + c) = ab + ac$ *Left Distributive Property*
                  $(a + b)c = ac + bc$ *Right Distributive Property*

REMARK Multiplication is implied when no symbol is used between two letters or groups of letters. For instance, you can write ab instead of $a \cdot b$, and $a(b + c)$ instead of $a \cdot (b + c)$.

EXAMPLE 1   Properties of Addition and Multiplication

a. The statement

$$(3 + 6) + 8 = 3 + (6 + 8)$$

is justified by the Associative Property of Addition, which tells you that parentheses are not needed when writing the sum of several real numbers. In other words, you can write this sum as $3 + 6 + 8$ without ambiguity because you obtain the same sum whether you add 3 and 6 first, or 6 and 8 first.

b. The statement

$$2(5 + 3) = 2 \cdot 5 + 2 \cdot 3$$

is justified by the Distributive Property, or more formally by the *left* distributive property of *multiplication over addition*.

The following three lists summarize the basic properties of negation, zero, and fractions. We suggest that you not only *learn* a verbal description of each property, but that you also try to gain an *intuitive feeling* for the validity of each.

PROPERTIES OF NEGATION

Let a and b be real numbers, variables, or algebraic expressions.

Property	*Example*
1. $(-1)(a) = -a$	$(-1)7 = -7$
2. $-(-a) = a$	$-(-6) = 6$
3. $(-a)b = -(ab) = a(-b)$	$(-5)3 = -(5 \cdot 3) = 5(-3)$
4. $(-a)(-b) = ab$	$(-2)(-6) = 12$
5. $-(a + b) = (-a) + (-b)$	$-(3 + 8) = (-3) + (-8)$

Be sure you see the difference between the *opposite of a number* and a *negative number*. If a is already negative, then its opposite, $-a$, is positive. For instance, if $a = -5$, then $-a = -(-5) = 5$.

PROPERTIES OF ZERO

Let a and b be real numbers, variables, or algebraic expressions.

1. $a + 0 = a$ and $a - 0 = a$
2. $a \cdot 0 = 0$
3. $\dfrac{0}{a} = 0$, $a \neq 0$
4. $\dfrac{a}{0}$ is undefined.
5. Zero-Factor Property: If $ab = 0$, then $a = 0$ or $b = 0$.

The "or" in the Zero-Factor Property includes the possibilities that either or both factors may be zero. This is an **inclusive or,** and it is the way the word "or" is generally used in mathematics.

PROPERTIES OF FRACTIONS

Let a, b, c, and d be real numbers, variables, or algebraic expressions such that $b \neq 0$ and $d \neq 0$.

1. Equivalent Fractions: $\dfrac{a}{b} = \dfrac{c}{d}$ if and only if $ad = bc$.

2. Rules of Signs: $-\dfrac{a}{b} = \dfrac{-a}{b} = \dfrac{a}{-b}$ and $\dfrac{-a}{-b} = \dfrac{a}{b}$

3. Generate Equivalent Fractions: $\dfrac{a}{b} = \dfrac{ac}{bc}$, $c \neq 0$

4. Add or Subtract with Like Denominators: $\dfrac{a}{b} \pm \dfrac{c}{b} = \dfrac{a \pm c}{b}$

5. Add or Subtract with Unlike Denominators:
   $\dfrac{a}{b} \pm \dfrac{c}{d} = \dfrac{ad \pm bc}{bd}$

6. Multiply Fractions: $\dfrac{a}{b} \cdot \dfrac{c}{d} = \dfrac{ac}{bd}$

7. Divide Fractions: $\dfrac{a}{b} \div \dfrac{c}{d} = \dfrac{a}{b} \cdot \dfrac{d}{c} = \dfrac{ad}{bc}$, $c \neq 0$

In Property 1 (equivalent fractions) the phrase "if and only if" implies two statements. One statement is: If $a/b = c/d$, then $ad = bc$. The other statement is: If $ad = bc$, where $b \neq 0$ and $d \neq 0$, then $a/b = c/d$.

EXAMPLE 2 Properties of Zero and Properties of Fractions

a. $x - \dfrac{0}{5} = x - 0 = x$ *Properties 3 and 1 of zero*

b. $\dfrac{x}{5} = \dfrac{3 \cdot x}{3 \cdot 5} = \dfrac{3x}{15}$ *Generate equivalent fractions*

c. $\dfrac{x}{3} + \dfrac{2x}{5} = \dfrac{5 \cdot x + 3 \cdot 2x}{15}$ *Add fractions with unlike denominators*

d. $\dfrac{7}{x} \div \dfrac{3}{2} = \dfrac{7}{x} \cdot \dfrac{2}{3} = \dfrac{14}{3x}$ *Divide fractions*

If a, b, and c are integers such that $ab = c$, then a and b are **factors** or **divisors** of c. For example, 2 and 3 are factors of 6. A **prime number** is a positive integer that has exactly two factors: itself and 1. For example, 2, 3, 5, 7, and 11 are prime numbers. The numbers 4, 6, 8, 9, and 10 are **composite** because they can be written as the product of two or more prime numbers. The number 1 is neither prime nor composite. The **Fundamental Theorem of Arithmetic** states that every positive integer greater than 1 can be written as the product of prime numbers in precisely one way (disregarding order). For instance, the *prime factorization* of 24 is $24 = 2 \cdot 2 \cdot 2 \cdot 3$.

When adding or subtracting fractions with unlike denominators, you have two options. You could use Property 5 of fractions, as in Example 2(c). Alternatively, you could use Property 4 of fractions by rewriting both fractions so that they have the same denominator. We call this the **least common denominator** (LCD) method. For adding or subtracting *two* fractions, Property 5 is often more convenient. For *three or more* fractions, the LCD method is usually preferred.

EXAMPLE 3 The LCD Method of Adding or Subtracting Fractions

Evaluate the following.

$$\frac{2}{15} - \frac{5}{9} + \frac{4}{5}$$

Solution

By prime factorization of the denominators ($15 = 3 \cdot 5$, $9 = 3 \cdot 3$, and $5 = 5$), you can see that the LCD is $3 \cdot 3 \cdot 5 = 45$. Therefore, it follows that

$$\frac{2}{15} - \frac{5}{9} + \frac{4}{5} = \frac{2(3)}{15(3)} - \frac{5(5)}{9(5)} + \frac{4(9)}{5(9)} = \frac{6 - 25 + 36}{45} = \frac{17}{45}.$$

Equations

An **equation** is a statement of equality between two expressions. Thus, the statement

$$a + b = c + d$$

means that the expressions $a + b$ and $c + d$ represent the same number.

PROPERTIES OF EQUALITY

Let a, b, and c be real numbers, variables, or algebraic expressions.

1. Reflexive: $\qquad\qquad$ $a = a$
2. Symmetric: $\qquad\qquad$ If $a = b$, then $b = a$.
3. Transitive: $\qquad\qquad$ If $a = b$ and $b = c$, then $a = c$.
4. Substitution Principle: $\quad$ If $a = b$, then a can be replaced by b in any expression involving a.
5. Addition/Subtraction: $\quad$ If $a = b$, then $a + c = b + c$.
   $\qquad\qquad\qquad\qquad$ If $a = b$, then $a - c = b - c$.
6. Multiplication/Division: $\quad$ If $a = b$, then $ac = bc$.
   $\qquad\qquad\qquad\qquad$ If $a = b$, then $\dfrac{a}{c} = \dfrac{b}{c}$, $c \neq 0$.
7. Cancellation: $\qquad\qquad$ If $a + c = b + c$, then $a = b$.
   $\qquad\qquad\qquad\qquad$ If $ac = bc$ and $c \neq 0$, then $a = b$.

EXAMPLE 4　Using Properties of Equality

Solve for w in the perimeter formula $2w + 2l = p$.

Solution

$$2w + 2l = p \qquad\qquad\qquad \textit{Given formula}$$

$$2w + 2l - 2l = p - 2l \qquad\qquad \textit{Subtract 2l from both sides}$$

$$2w = p - 2l$$

$$\frac{2w}{2} = \frac{p - 2l}{2} \qquad\qquad\qquad \textit{Divide both sides by 2}$$

$$w = \frac{p - 2l}{2}$$

One-to-One Correspondence

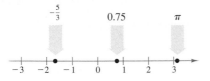

Every real number corresponds to exactly one point on the real number line.

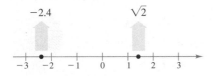

Every point on the real number line corresponds to exactly one real number.

FIGURE 1.3

The Real Number Line

The **real number line** is a visual model of the set of real numbers. The point that corresponds to 0 is the **origin.** Points to the right of the origin correspond to positive numbers, and points to the left of the origin correspond to negative numbers, as shown in Figure 1.2. The term *nonnegative* describes a number that is either positive or zero.

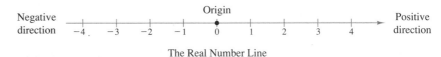

The Real Number Line

FIGURE 1.2

Each point on the real number line corresponds to one and only one real number and *each real number corresponds to one and only one point on the real number line.* The number associated with a point on the real number line is called the **coordinate** of the point. Because of the **one-to-one correspondence** between real numbers and points on the real number line, however, it usually isn't necessary to distinguish between a point and its coordinate. (See Figure 1.3.)

Ordering the Real Numbers

One important property of real numbers is that they are **ordered.**

DEFINITION OF ORDER ON THE REAL NUMBER LINE

If a and b are real numbers, then a is **less than** b if $b - a$ is positive. We denote this order by the **inequality**

$a < b$.

This relationship can also be described by saying that b is **greater than** a and writing $b > a$. The inequality $a \le b$ means that a is **less than or equal to** b and the inequality $b \ge a$ means that b is **greater than or equal to** a. The symbols $<$, $>$, $\le$, and $\ge$ are called **inequality symbols.**

$a < b$ if and only if a lies to the left of b.

FIGURE 1.4

Geometrically, this definition implies that $a < b$ if and only if a lies to the *left* of b on the real number line, as shown in Figure 1.4.

EXAMPLE 5   Interpreting Inequalities

a. The inequality $x \leq 2$ denotes all real numbers less than or equal to 2, as shown in Figure 1.5(a).

b. The inequality $-2 \leq x < 3$ means that $x \geq -2$ *and* $x < 3$. This "double" inequality denotes all real numbers between -2 and 3, including -2 but *not* including 3, as shown in Figure 1.5(b).

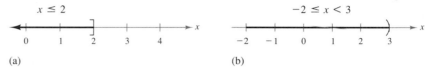

(a)   (b)

FIGURE 1.5

EXAMPLE 6   Using Inequalities to Represent Sets of Real Numbers

Use inequality notation to describe each of the following.

a. c is nonnegative.   **b.** d is negative and greater than -3.

Solution

a. "c is nonnegative" means that c is greater than or equal to zero, which can be written as $c \geq 0$.

b. "d is negative" can be written as $d < 0$, and "d is greater than -3" can be written as $-3 < d$. Combining these two inequalities produces the *double inequality* $-3 < d < 0$.

The **Law of Trichotomy** states that for any two real numbers a and b, *precisely* one of three relationships is possible.

$$a = b, \quad a < b, \quad \text{or} \quad a > b \qquad \text{\textit{Law of Trichotomy}}$$

The Absolute Value of a Real Number

The **absolute value** of a real number is its value, disregarding its sign.

DEFINITION OF ABSOLUTE VALUE

If a is a real number, then the **absolute value** of a is

$$|a| = \begin{cases} a, & \text{if } a \geq 0 \\ -a, & \text{if } a < 0. \end{cases}$$

REMARK The absolute value of a real number is either positive or zero. Moreover, 0 is the only real number whose absolute value is zero. Thus, $|0| = 0$.

Be sure you see that the absolute value of a real number is never negative. For instance, if $a = -5$, then $|-5| = -(-5) = 5$.

EXAMPLE 7   Evaluating the Absolute Value of a Number

Evaluate the fraction

$$\frac{|x|}{x}$$

for (a) $x > 0$ and (b) $x < 0$.

Solution

a. If $x > 0$, then $|x| = x$ and $\frac{|x|}{x} = \frac{x}{x} = 1$.

b. If $x < 0$, then $|x| = -x$ and $\frac{|x|}{x} = \frac{-x}{x} = -1$.

Try to formulate verbal descriptions of the following properties—they are easier to remember. For instance, the third property states that the absolute value of a product of two numbers is equal to the product of the absolute values of the two numbers.

PROPERTIES OF ABSOLUTE VALUES

Let a and b be real numbers.

1. $|a| \geq 0$ 2. $|-a| = |a|$

3. $|ab| = |a||b|$ 4. $\left|\dfrac{a}{b}\right| = \dfrac{|a|}{|b|}, \quad b \neq 0$

5. $|a + b| \leq |a| + |b|$, which is the Triangle Inequality

---

The Distance Between Two Real Numbers

Absolute value can be used to define the distance between two numbers on the real number line. For instance, the distance between -3 and 4 is

$$|4 - (-3)| = |7| = 7.$$

See Figure 1.6.

The distance between -3 and 4 is 7.

FIGURE 1.6

DISTANCE BETWEEN TWO POINTS ON THE REAL LINE

Let a and b be real numbers. The **distance between a and b** is

$$d(a, b) = |b - a| = |a - b|.$$

EXAMPLE 8 Distance and Absolute Value

REMARK From Example 8(a), we can reason that the distance between any real number x and the origin is $|x - 0| = x$.

a. The distance between -4 and the origin is given by

$$d(-4, 0) = |-4 - 0| = |-4| = 4.$$

b. The statement "the distance between c and -2 is at least 7" can be written as

$$d(c, -2) = |c - (-2)| = |c + 2| \geq 7.$$

DISCUSSION PROBLEM

Decimal Approximations of Irrational Numbers

At the beginning of this section we noted that $\sqrt{2}$ is not a rational number. There are, however, rational numbers whose squares are very close to 2. For instance, if you square the rational number

$$\frac{140}{99}$$

you obtain 1.9998. Can you find another rational number whose square is even closer to 2? Write a short paragraph explaining how you obtained this number.

EXERCISES for Section 1.1

In Exercises 1–4, determine which numbers are (a) natural numbers, (b) integers, (c) rational numbers, and (d) irrational numbers.

1. $-9, -\frac{7}{2}, 5, \frac{2}{3}, \sqrt{2}, 0, 1$ **2.** $\sqrt{5}, -7, -\frac{7}{3}, 0, 3.12, \frac{5}{4}$

* **3.** $-\pi, -\frac{1}{3}, \frac{6}{3}, \frac{1}{2}\sqrt{2}, -7.5$

4. $25, -17, -\frac{12}{5}, \sqrt{9}, 3.12, \frac{1}{2}\pi$

In Exercises 5–14, identify the property (or properties) illustrated in the equation.

5. $x + 9 = 9 + x$ **6.** $(x + 3) - (x + 3) = 0$

7. $\dfrac{1}{h + 6}(h + 6) = 1, \ h \neq -6$

8. $h + 0 = h$

9. $2(x + 3) = 2x + 6$ **10.** $1 \cdot (1 + x) = 1 + x$

*A boxed number indicates that a detailed solution can be found in the *Study and Solutions Guide*.

11. $x + (y + 10) = (x + y) + 10$

12. $4 + (-4 + x) = (4 - 4) + x = 0 + x = x$

13. $x(3y) = (x \cdot 3)y = (3x)y$

14. $\frac{1}{7}(7 \cdot 12) = \left(\frac{1}{7} \cdot 7\right)12 = 1 \cdot 12 - 12$

In Exercises 15–18, use the properties of zero to evaluate, if possible, the expression.

15. $\dfrac{81 - (90 - 9)}{5}$

16. $10(23 - 30 + 7)$

17. $\dfrac{8}{-9 + (6 + 3)}$

18. $15 - \dfrac{3 - 3}{5}$

In Exercises 19–30, perform the indicated operation(s). Reduce all fractions to lowest terms.

19. $10 - 6 - 2$

20. $-3(5 - 2)$

21. $2\left(\frac{77}{-11}\right)$

22. $-3\left(-\frac{8}{15}\right)$

23. $\frac{6}{7} - \frac{4}{7}$

24. $\frac{3}{16} + \frac{5}{16}$

25. $\frac{3}{8} - \frac{1}{4} + \frac{5}{6}$

26. $\frac{10}{11} + \frac{6}{33} - \frac{13}{66}$

27. $\frac{4}{5} \times \frac{1}{2} \times \frac{3}{4}$

28. $\frac{2}{3} \times \frac{5}{8} \times \frac{3}{4}$

29. $12 \div \frac{1}{4}$

30. $\left(\frac{3}{5} \div 3\right) - \left(6 \times \frac{4}{8}\right)$

In Exercises 31 and 32, identify the property used in each step of the solution process of the equation.

31.
$$3x + 15 = 0$$
$$3x + 15 - 15 = 0 - 15$$
$$3x = -15$$
$$\frac{3x}{3} = \frac{-15}{3}$$
$$x = -5$$

32.
$$25 - 3x = 10$$
$$25 - 3x + 3x = 10 + 3x$$
$$25 = 10 + 3x$$
$$25 - 10 = 10 + 3x - 10$$
$$15 = 3x$$
$$\frac{15}{3} = \frac{3x}{3}$$
$$5 = x$$

In Exercises 33–38, plot the two real numbers on the real number line and place the appropriate inequality sign ($<$ or $>$) between them.

33. $\frac{3}{2}, 7$

34. $-3.5, 1$

35. $-4, -8$

36. $1, \frac{16}{3}$

37. $\frac{5}{6}, \frac{2}{3}$

38. $-\frac{8}{7}, -\frac{3}{7}$

In Exercises 39–44, describe the subset of real numbers that is represented by the inequality and sketch the subset on the real number line.

39. $x \leq 5$

40. $x \geq -2$

41. $x < 2$

42. $0 \leq x \leq 5$

43. $-1 \leq x < 0$

44. $0 < x \leq 6$

In Exercises 45–50, use inequality notation to describe the set of real numbers.

45. x is negative.

46. z is at least 10.

47. y is no more than 25.

48. y is greater than 5 and less than or equal to 12.

49. The annual rate of inflation, r, is expected to be at least 3.5%, but no more than 6%.

50. The price, p, of unleaded gasoline is not expected to go above $1.35 per gallon during the coming year.

In Exercises 51–54, evaluate the expression.

51. (a) $|-10|$ (b) $|0|$

52. (a) $|3 - \pi|$ (b) $|4 - \pi|$

53. (a) $\frac{-5}{|-5|}$ (b) $-3 - |-3|$

54. (a) $-3|-3|$ (b) $|-1| - |-2|$

In Exercises 55 and 56, place the correct symbol ($<$, $>$, or $=$) between the pair of real numbers.

55. (a) $|-3| \;\blacksquare\; -|-3|$ (b) $|-4| \;\blacksquare\; |4|$

56. (a) $-5 \;\blacksquare\; -|5|$ (b) $-|-6| \;\blacksquare\; |-6|$

In Exercises 57–64, find the distance between a and b.

57.
$a = -1 \qquad b = 3$

58.
$a = -4 \qquad b = -\frac{3}{2}$

59.
$a = -\frac{5}{2} \qquad b = 0$

60.
$a = \frac{1}{4} \qquad b = \frac{11}{4}$

61. $a = 126, b = 75$

62. $a = -126, b = -75$

63. $a = 9.34, b = -5.65$

64. $a = \frac{16}{5}, b = \frac{112}{75}$

In Exercises 65–70, use absolute value notation to describe the situation.

65. The distance between x and 5 is no more than 3.

66. The distance between x and -10 is at least 6.

67. While traveling, you remember passing milepost 7, then milepost 18. How far did you travel during that time period?

68. While traveling, you remember passing milepost 103, then milepost 86. How far did you travel during that time period?

69. y is at least six units from 0.

70. y is at most two units from a.

Budget Variance In Exercises 71–74, the accounting department of a company is checking to see whether the actual expenses of a department differ from the budgeted expenses by more than $500 or over 5%. Complete the missing parts of the table, and determine whether the actual expense passes the "budget variance test."

		Budgeted Expense, b	Actual Expense, a	$|a - b|$	$0.05b$
71.	Wages	$112,700.00	$113,356.52		
72.	Utilities	$9,400.00	$9,772.59		
73.	Taxes	$37,640.00	$37,335.80		
74.	Insurance	$2,575.00	$2,613.15		

Federal Deficit In Exercises 75–78, the bar graph shows the receipts of the federal government (in billions of dollars) for selected years from 1960 through 1989. In each exercise, you are given the expenses of the federal government. Find the absolute value of the surplus or deficit for the year. (*Source:* U.S. Treasury Department)

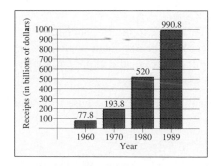

Figure for 75–78

		Income, y	Expenses, x	$|y - x|$	Surplus or Deficit
75.	1960		$92.2 billion		
76.	1970		$195.6 billion		
77.	1980		$590.2 billion		
78.	1989		$1142.9 billion		

79. *Work* One worker can assemble a component in 7 days and a second worker can do the same task in 5 days. If they work together, what fraction of the component can they assemble in 2 days?

80. *Copper Wire* One foot of copper wire weighs one ounce. What is the weight of $\frac{5}{8}$ mile of this wire?

In Exercises 81 and 82, use a calculator to order the given numbers from smallest to largest.

81. $\frac{7071}{5000}, \frac{584}{413}, \sqrt{2}, \frac{47}{33}, \frac{127}{90}$

82. $\frac{26}{15}, \sqrt{3}, 1.7320, \frac{381}{220}, \sqrt{10} - \sqrt{2}$

In Exercises 83–86, use a calculator to find the decimal form of the rational number. If it is a nonterminating decimal, write the repeating pattern.

83. $\frac{5}{8}$

84. $\frac{1}{3}$

85. $\frac{41}{333}$

86. $\frac{6}{11}$

In Exercises 87–90, determine whether the statement is true or false.

87. The reciprocal of a nonzero integer is an integer.

88. The reciprocal of a nonzero rational number is rational.

89. Every real number is either rational or irrational.

90. The absolute value of a real number is positive.

1.2 Exponents and Radicals

Exponents / Radicals and Properties of Radicals / Simplifying Radicals /
Rationalizing Denominators and Numerators / Rational Exponents / Scientific Notation /
Exponents and Calculators

Exponents

Repeated *multiplications* can be written in **exponential form.** Here are some examples.

Repeated Multiplication	*Exponential Form*
$7 \cdot 7$	7^2
$a \cdot a \cdot a \cdot a \cdot a$	a^5
$(-4)(-4)(-4)$	$(-4)^3$
$(2x)(2x)(2x)(2x)$	$(2x)^4$

EXPONENTIAL NOTATION

Let a be a real number, a variable, or an algebraic expression, and let n be a positive integer. Then

$$a^n = \underbrace{a \cdot a \cdot a \cdots a}_{n \text{ factors}}$$

where n is the **exponent** and a is the **base.** The expression a^n is read "a to the nth **power.**"

It is important to recognize the difference between expressions such as $(-2)^4$ and -2^4. In $(-2)^4$, the parentheses indicate that the exponent applies to the negative sign as well as to the 2, but in $-2^4 = -(2^4)$, the exponent applies only to the 2.

When multiplying exponential expressions with the same base, you *add* exponents.

$$a^m \cdot a^n = a^{m+n} \qquad \text{\textit{Add exponents when multiplying}}$$

When dividing exponential expressions, you *subtract* exponents. That is,

$$\frac{a^m}{a^n} = a^{m-n}, \qquad a \neq 0. \quad \text{\textit{Subtract exponents when dividing}}$$

There are two special cases involving division of exponential expressions. If $m = n$, then

$$\frac{a^n}{a^n} = a^{n-n} = a^0 = 1, \qquad a \neq 0$$

and we say that *any nonzero number raised to the zero power is 1*. If n is a positive integer, then

$$\frac{1}{a^n} = a^{-n}, \qquad a \neq 0.$$

PROPERTIES OF EXPONENTS

Let a and b be real numbers, variables, or algebraic expressions, and let m and n be integers. Then the following properties are true. (Assume all denominators and bases are nonzero.)

Property	*Example*
1. $a^m a^n = a^{m+n}$	$3^2 \cdot 3^4 = 3^{2+4} = 3^6$
2. $\dfrac{a^m}{a^n} = a^{m-n}$	$\dfrac{x^7}{x^4} = x^{7-4} = x^3$
3. $a^{-n} = \dfrac{1}{a^n} = \left(\dfrac{1}{a}\right)^n$	$y^{-4} = \dfrac{1}{y^4}$
4. $a^0 = 1, \qquad a \neq 0$	$(x^2 + 1)^0 = 1$
5. $(ab)^m = a^m b^m$	$(5x)^3 = 5^3 x^3 = 125 x^3$
6. $(a^m)^n = a^{mn}$	$(y^3)^{-4} = y^{3(-4)} = y^{-12} = \dfrac{1}{y^{12}}$
7. $\left(\dfrac{a}{b}\right)^m = \dfrac{a^m}{b^m}$	$\left(\dfrac{2}{x}\right)^3 = \dfrac{2^3}{x^3} = \dfrac{8}{x^3}$
8. $\lvert a^2 \rvert = \lvert a \rvert^2 = a^2$	$\lvert (-2)^2 \rvert = \lvert -2 \rvert^2 = (-2)^2 = 4$

These properties of exponents apply for *all* integers m and n, not just positive ones. For instance, by Property 2,

$$\frac{3^4}{3^{-5}} = 3^{4-(-5)} = 3^{4+5} = 3^9.$$

EXAMPLE 1   Using Properties of Exponents

a. $(-3ab^4)(4ab^{-3}) = -12(a)(a)(b^4)(b^{-3}) = -12a^2 b$

b. $(2xy^2)^3 = 2^3(x)^3(y^2)^3 = 8x^3 y^6$ *Apply exponent to coefficient*

c. $3a(-4a^2)^0 = 3a(1) = 3a, \qquad a \neq 0$

d. $\left(\dfrac{5x^3}{y}\right)^2 = \dfrac{5^2(x^3)^2}{y^2} = \dfrac{25x^6}{y^2}$ *Apply exponent to coefficient*

EXAMPLE 2   Rewriting with Positive Exponents

a. $x^{-1} = \dfrac{1}{x}$ *Property 3:* $a^{-n} = \dfrac{1}{a^n}$

b. $\dfrac{1}{3x^{-2}} = \dfrac{1(x^2)}{3} = \dfrac{x^2}{3}$ -2 *exponent does not apply to 3*

c. $\dfrac{12a^3b^{-4}}{4a^{-2}b} = \dfrac{12a^3 \cdot a^2}{4b \cdot b^4} = \dfrac{3a^5}{b^5}$

d. $\left(\dfrac{3x^2}{y}\right)^{-2} = \dfrac{3^{-2}(x^2)^{-2}}{y^{-2}} = \dfrac{3^{-2}x^{-4}}{y^{-2}} = \dfrac{y^2}{3^2x^4} = \dfrac{y^2}{9x^4}$

Radicals and Properties of Radicals

You already know how to square a number—raise it to the second power by using the number *twice* as a factor. For instance, 5 squared is $5 \cdot 5 = 5^2 = 25$. Conversely, a **square root of a number** is one of its two equal factors. For example, 5 is a square root of 25 because 5 is one of the two equal factors of 25. In a similar way, a **cube root** of a number is one of its three equal factors. Consider the following examples.

Number	Equal Factors	Root
$25 = (-5)^2$	$(-5)(-5)$	-5 (square root)
$-64 = (-4)^3$	$(-4)(-4)(-4)$	-4 (cube root)
$81 = 3^4$	$3 \cdot 3 \cdot 3 \cdot 3$	3 (fourth root)

DEFINITION OF *n*th ROOT OF A NUMBER

Let a and b be real numbers and let $n \geq 2$ be a positive integer. If

$$a = b^n$$

then b is an ***n*th root of a.** If $n = 2$, then the root is a **square root.** If $n = 3$, then the root is a **cube root.**

Some numbers have more than one *n*th root. For example, both 5 and -5 are square roots of 25. The **principal *n*th root** of a number is defined as follows.

PRINCIPAL *n*th ROOT OF A NUMBER

Let a be a real number that has at least one nth root. The **principal nth root of a** is the nth root that has the same sign as a. It is denoted by a **radical symbol**

$$\sqrt[n]{a}.$$ *Principal nth root*

The positive integer n is the **index** of the radical, and the number a is the **radicand.** If $n = 2$, we omit the index and write $\sqrt{a}$ rather than $\sqrt[2]{a}$.

REMARK The plural of index is *indices*.

EXAMPLE 3   Evaluating Expressions Involving Radicals

a. $\sqrt{49} = 7$ because $7^2 = 49$.

b. $-\sqrt{49} = -7$ because $7^2 = 49$.

c. $\sqrt[3]{\dfrac{125}{64}} = \dfrac{5}{4}$ because $\left(\dfrac{5}{4}\right)^3 = \dfrac{5^3}{4^3} = \dfrac{125}{64}$.

d. $\sqrt[5]{-32} = -2$ because $(-2)^5 = -32$.

e. $\sqrt[4]{-81}$ is not a real number because no real number can be raised to the fourth power to produce -81.

Here are some generalizations about the nth roots of a real number.

1. If a is a positive real number and n is a positive *even* integer, then a has exactly two (real) nth roots: $\sqrt[n]{a}$ and $-\sqrt[n]{a}$. (See Examples 3(a) and 3(b).)
2. If a is any real number and n is an *odd* integer, then a has only one (real) nth root: $\sqrt[n]{a}$. (See Examples 3(c) and 3(d).)
3. If a is a negative real number and n is an *even* integer, then a has no (real) nth root. (See Example 3(e).)
4. $\sqrt[n]{0} = 0$.

Integers such as 1, 4, 9, 16, 25, and 36 are **perfect squares** because they have integer square roots. Similarly, integers such as 1, 8, 27, 64, and 125 are called **perfect cubes** because they have integer cube roots.

To simplify or evaluate expressions involving radicals, we use the following properties.

PROPERTIES OF RADICALS

Let a and b be real numbers, variables, or algebraic expressions such that the indicated roots are real numbers, and let m and n be positive integers.

Property	*Example*
1. $\sqrt[n]{a^m} = (\sqrt[n]{a})^m$	$\sqrt[3]{8^2} = (\sqrt[3]{8})^2 = (2)^2 = 4$
2. $\sqrt[n]{a} \cdot \sqrt[n]{b} = \sqrt[n]{ab}$	$\sqrt{5} \cdot \sqrt{7} = \sqrt{5 \cdot 7} = \sqrt{35}$
3. $\dfrac{\sqrt[n]{a}}{\sqrt[n]{b}} = \sqrt[n]{\dfrac{a}{b}},\quad b \neq 0$	$\dfrac{\sqrt[4]{27}}{\sqrt[4]{9}} = \sqrt[4]{\dfrac{27}{9}} = \sqrt[4]{3}$
4. $\sqrt[m]{\sqrt[n]{a}} = \sqrt[mn]{a}$	$\sqrt[3]{\sqrt{10}} = \sqrt[6]{10}$
5. $(\sqrt[n]{a})^n = a$	$(\sqrt{3})^2 = 3$
6. For n even, $\sqrt[n]{a^n} = \lvert a \rvert$.	$\sqrt{(-12)^2} = \lvert -12 \rvert = 12$
$\quad$ For n odd, $\sqrt[n]{a^n} = a$.	$\sqrt[3]{(-12)^3} = -12$

REMARK   A common special case of Property 6 is $\sqrt{a^2} = \lvert a \rvert$.

Simplifying Radicals

An expression involving radicals is in **simplest form** when the following conditions are satisfied.

1. All possible factors have been removed from the radical.
2. All fractions have radical-free denominators (accomplished by a process called *rationalizing the denominator*).
3. The index of the radical is reduced.

   To simplify a radical, we factor the radicand into factors whose exponents are multiples of the index. The roots of these factors are written outside the radical and the "leftover" factors make up the new radicand.

EXAMPLE 4   Simplifying Even Roots

REMARK   In Example 4(b) we included absolute value in the answer because $\sqrt[4]{x^4} = \lvert x \rvert$.

a. $\sqrt[4]{48} = \sqrt[4]{16 \cdot 3} = \sqrt[4]{2^4 \cdot 3} = \sqrt[4]{2^4}\,\sqrt[4]{3} = 2\sqrt[4]{3}$

b. $\sqrt[4]{(5x)^4} = \lvert 5x \rvert = 5\lvert x \rvert$

EXAMPLE 5   Simplifying Odd Roots

a. $\sqrt[3]{24a^4} = \sqrt[3]{8a^3 \cdot 3a} = \sqrt[3]{(2a)^3 \cdot 3a} = 2a\sqrt[3]{3a}$

b. $\sqrt[3]{-40x^6} = \sqrt[3]{(-8x^6) \cdot 5} = \sqrt[3]{(-2x^2)^3 \cdot 5} = -2x^2\sqrt[3]{5}$

Radical expressions can be combined (added or subtracted) if they are **like radicals**—that is, if they have the same index and radicand. For instance, $2\sqrt{3x}$, $-\sqrt{3x}$, and $\sqrt{3x}/2$ are like radicals but $\sqrt[3]{3x}$ and $2\sqrt{3x}$ are not like radicals. To determine whether two radicals are like radicals, you should first simplify each radical.

EXAMPLE 6   Combining Radicals

a. $2\sqrt{48} - 3\sqrt{27} = 2\sqrt{16 \cdot 3} - 3\sqrt{9 \cdot 3}$ *Find square factors*

$\qquad\qquad\qquad = 8\sqrt{3} - 9\sqrt{3}$ *Find square roots*

$\qquad\qquad\qquad = (8 - 9)\sqrt{3}$ *Combine like terms*

$\qquad\qquad\qquad = -\sqrt{3}$

b. $\sqrt[3]{16x} - \sqrt[3]{54x^4} = \sqrt[3]{8 \cdot 2x} - \sqrt[3]{27 \cdot x^3 \cdot 2x}$

$\qquad\qquad\qquad = 2\sqrt[3]{2x} - 3x\sqrt[3]{2x}$

$\qquad\qquad\qquad = (2 - 3x)\sqrt[3]{2x}$

Rationalizing Denominators and Numerators

To rationalize a denominator or numerator of the form $a - b\sqrt{m}$ (or $a + b\sqrt{m}$), multiply both numerator and denominator by a **conjugate:** $a + b\sqrt{m}$ and $a - b\sqrt{m}$ are conjugates of each other. If $a = 0$, then the rationalizing factor for $\sqrt{m}$ is itself, $\sqrt{m}$.

EXAMPLE 7   Rationalizing Single-Term Denominators

a. $\dfrac{5}{2\sqrt{3}} = \dfrac{5}{2\sqrt{3}} \cdot \dfrac{\sqrt{3}}{\sqrt{3}} = \dfrac{5\sqrt{3}}{2(3)} = \dfrac{5\sqrt{3}}{6}$

b. $\dfrac{2}{\sqrt[3]{5}} = \dfrac{2}{\sqrt[3]{5}} \cdot \dfrac{\sqrt[3]{5^2}}{\sqrt[3]{5^2}} = \dfrac{2\sqrt[3]{5^2}}{\sqrt[3]{5^3}} = \dfrac{2\sqrt[3]{25}}{5}$

EXAMPLE 8   Rationalizing a Denominator with Two Terms

$\dfrac{2}{3 + \sqrt{7}} = \dfrac{2}{3 + \sqrt{7}} \cdot \dfrac{3 - \sqrt{7}}{3 - \sqrt{7}}$ *Multiply numerator and denominator by conjugate*

$\qquad = \dfrac{2(3 - \sqrt{7})}{(3)^2 - (\sqrt{7})^2}$

$\qquad = \dfrac{2(3 - \sqrt{7})}{9 - 7}$

$\qquad = \dfrac{\cancel{2}(3 - \sqrt{7})}{\cancel{2}}$ *Divide like factors*

$\qquad = 3 - \sqrt{7}$

EXAMPLE 9   **Rationalizing a Numerator**

$$\frac{\sqrt{5} - \sqrt{7}}{2} = \frac{\sqrt{5} - \sqrt{7}}{2} \cdot \frac{\sqrt{5} + \sqrt{7}}{\sqrt{5} + \sqrt{7}}$$

Multiply numerator and denominator by conjugate

$$= \frac{5 - 7}{2(\sqrt{5} + \sqrt{7})}$$

$$= \frac{-2}{2(\sqrt{5} + \sqrt{7})}$$

$$= \frac{-1}{\sqrt{5} + \sqrt{7}}$$

Simplify

Do not confuse an expression like $\sqrt{5} + \sqrt{7}$ with the expression $\sqrt{5 + 7}$. In general,

$$\sqrt{x + y} \quad \text{DOES NOT EQUAL} \quad \sqrt{x} + \sqrt{y}.$$

Similarly,

$$\sqrt{x^2 + y^2} \quad \text{DOES NOT EQUAL} \quad x + y.$$

Rational Exponents

Up to this point, our work with exponents has been restricted to *integer* exponents. In the following definition, note how radicals are used to define **rational exponents.**

DEFINITION OF RATIONAL EXPONENTS

If a is a real number and n is a positive integer such that the principal nth root of a exists, we define $a^{1/n}$ to be

$$a^{1/n} = \sqrt[n]{a}.$$

Moreover, if m is a positive integer that has no common factor with n, then

$$a^{m/n} = (a^{1/n})^m = (\sqrt[n]{a})^m \quad \text{and} \quad a^{m/n} = (a^m)^{1/n} = \sqrt[n]{a^m}.$$

The numerator of a rational exponent denotes the *power* to which the base is raised, and the denominator denotes the *index* or the *root* to be taken, as shown below.

$$b^{\overset{\text{Power}}{m}/\underset{\text{Index}}{n}} = (\sqrt[n]{b})^m = \sqrt[n]{b^m}$$

When working with rational exponents, the properties of integer exponents still apply. For instance,

$$2^{1/2}2^{1/3} = 2^{(1/2)+(1/3)} = 2^{5/6}.$$

EXAMPLE 10   Changing from Radical to Exponential Form

a. $\sqrt{3} = 3^{1/2}$

b. $\sqrt{(3xy)^5} = (3xy)^{(5/2)}$

c. $2x\sqrt[4]{x^3} = (2x)(x^{3/4}) = 2x^{1+(3/4)} = 2x^{7/4}$ ◢

EXAMPLE 11   Changing from Exponential to Radical Form

a. $(x^2 + y^2)^{3/2} = (\sqrt{x^2 + y^2})^3 = \sqrt{(x^2 + y^2)^3}$

b. $2y^{3/4}z^{1/4} = 2(y^3z)^{1/4} = 2\sqrt[4]{y^3z}$

c. $a^{-3/2} = \dfrac{1}{a^{3/2}} = \dfrac{1}{\sqrt{a^3}}$

d. $x^{0.2} = x^{1/5} = \sqrt[5]{x}$ ◢

REMARK   Rational exponents can be tricky, and you must remember that the expression $b^{m/n}$ is not defined unless $\sqrt[n]{b}$ is a real number. This restriction produces some unusual-looking results. For instance, the number $(-8)^{1/3}$ is defined because $\sqrt[3]{-8} = -2$, but the number $(-8)^{2/6}$ is undefined because $\sqrt[6]{-8}$ is not a real number.

Rational exponents are particularly useful for evaluating roots of numbers on a calculator, for reducing the index of a radical, and for simplifying expressions encountered in calculus.

EXAMPLE 12   Simplifying with Rational Exponents

a. $\sqrt[6]{27^2} = (27)^{2/6} = (27)^{1/3} = \sqrt[3]{27} - 3$

b. $(-32)^{-4/5} = \left(\sqrt[5]{(-32)}\right)^{-4} = (-2)^{-4} = \dfrac{1}{(-2)^4} = \dfrac{1}{16}$

c. $(-5x^{5/3})(3x^{-3/4}) = -15x^{(5/3)-(3/4)} = -15x^{11/12}, \; x \neq 0$ ◢

EXAMPLE 13   Simplifying Algebraic Expressions

a. $(2x - 1)^{4/3}(2x - 1)^{-1/3} = (2x - 1)^{(4/3)-(1/3)}$

$$= (2x - 1)^1$$

$$= 2x - 1, \; x \neq \frac{1}{2}$$

b. $\dfrac{x - 1}{(x - 1)^{-1/2}} \cdot \dfrac{(x - 1)^{1/2}}{(x - 1)^{1/2}} = \dfrac{(x - 1)^{3/2}}{(x - 1)^0} = (x - 1)^{3/2}, \; x \neq 1$ ◢

Scientific Notation

Exponents provide an efficient way of writing and computing with very large (or very small) numbers. For instance, a drop of water contains more than 33 billion billion molecules—33 followed by 18 zeros.

$$33,000,000,000,000,000,000$$

It is convenient to write such numbers in **scientific notation.** This notation has the form $c \times 10^n$, where $1 \le c < 10$ and n is an integer. Thus, the number of molecules in a drop of water can be written in scientific notation as

$$3.3 \times 10,000,000,000,000,000,000 = 3.3 \times 10^{19}.$$

The *positive* exponent 19 indicates that the number is *large* (10 or more) and that the decimal point has been moved 19 places. A *negative* exponent in scientific notation indicates that the number is *small* (less than 1). For instance, the mass (in grams) of one electron is approximately

$$9.0 \times 10^{-28} = 0.0000000000000000000000000009.$$

$$\underbrace{\qquad\qquad\qquad\qquad\qquad\qquad}_{28 \text{ decimal places}}$$

Most scientific calculators automatically switch to scientific notation when they are showing large (or small) numbers that exceed the display range. Try multiplying $86,500,000 \times 6000$. If your calculator follows standard conventions, its display should be $\boxed{\textbf{5.19 11}}$ or $\boxed{\textbf{5.19 E 11}}$. This means that $c = 5.19$ and the exponent of 10 is $n = 11$, which implies that the number is 5.19×10^{11}.

Exponents and Calculators

Scientific calculators are capable of evaluating exponential expressions using the $\boxed{\boldsymbol{y^x}}$ key. To use this key, remember that y is the base and x is the exponent. Here are three examples.

Expression	*Keystrokes*	*Display*
3^6	3 $\boxed{\boldsymbol{y^x}}$ 6 $\boxed{=}$	729
$\left(1 + \dfrac{0.09}{12}\right)^{12}$	.09 $\boxed{\div}$ 12 $\boxed{+}$ 1 $\boxed{=}$ $\boxed{\boldsymbol{y^x}}$ 12 $\boxed{=}$	1.0938069
27^{-6}	27 $\boxed{\boldsymbol{y^x}}$ 6 $\boxed{+/-}$ $\boxed{=}$	2.5812 −09

Note that negative exponents are entered into a calculator by pressing the change-sign key $\boxed{+/-}$ immediately after entering the exponent.

There are two methods of evaluating radicals on most calculators. For square roots, you use the *square root key* $\boxed{\sqrt{}}$. For other roots, you should first convert the radical to exponential form and then use the *exponential key* $\boxed{\boldsymbol{y^x}}$.

EXAMPLE 14   Evaluating Radicals with a Calculator

Use a calculator to evaluate $\sqrt[3]{56}$. (Round your answers to three decimal places.)

Solution

First you write $\sqrt[3]{56}$ in exponential form: $\sqrt[3]{56} = 56^{1/3}$. Now there are several options.

Calculator Steps

(i) 1 $\boxed{\div}$ 3 $\boxed{=}$ $\boxed{\text{STO}}$ 56 $\boxed{y^x}$ $\boxed{\text{RCL}}$ $\boxed{=}$ *Use memory key*

(ii) 56 $\boxed{y^x}$ $\boxed{(}$ 1 $\boxed{\div}$ 3 $\boxed{)}$ $\boxed{=}$ *Use parentheses*

(iii) 56 $\boxed{y^x}$ 3 $\boxed{1/x}$ $\boxed{=}$ *Use reciprocal key*

For each of these three keystroke sequences, the answer is $\sqrt[3]{56} \approx 3.8258624$.

EXAMPLE 15   Evaluating Radicals with a Calculator

Use a calculator to evaluate the following expressions. (Round your answers to three decimal places.)

a. $\sqrt[3]{-4}$ **b.** $(1.2)^{-1/6}$

Solution

a. Since

$$\sqrt[3]{-4} = \sqrt[3]{(-1)(4)} = \sqrt[3]{-1} \cdot \sqrt[3]{4} = -\sqrt[3]{4}$$

you can attach the negative sign of the radicand at the end of the keystroke sequence as follows.

4 $\boxed{y^x}$ $\boxed{(}$ 1 $\boxed{\div}$ 3 $\boxed{)}$ $\boxed{=}$ $\boxed{+/-}$ *Display: −1.5874011*

Thus, rounded to three decimal places, you have $\sqrt[3]{-4} \approx -1.587$.

b. 1.2 $\boxed{y^x}$ $\boxed{(}$ 1 $\boxed{\div}$ 6 $\boxed{+/-}$ $\boxed{)}$ $\boxed{=}$ *Display: 0.97007012*

Rounded to three decimal places, you have $(1.2)^{-1/6} \approx 0.970$.

Johannes Kepler (1571–1630), the well-known German astronomer, discovered a relationship between the average distance of a planet from the sun and the time (or period) it takes the planet to orbit the sun. At the time, people knew that planets that are closer to the sun take less time to complete an orbit than planets that are farther from the sun, as indicated in Figure 1.7. What Kepler discovered was that the distance and period are related by an exact mathematical formula. The following table shows the average distance (in astronomical units) and period (in years) for the six planets that are closest to the sun. By completing the table, can you rediscover Kepler's relationship? Discuss your conclusions.

Planet	Mercury	Venus	Earth	Mars	Jupiter	Saturn
Average Distance, x	0.387	0.723	1.0	1.523	5.203	9.541
$\sqrt{x}$						
Period, y	0.241	0.615	1.0	1.881	11.861	29.457
$\sqrt[3]{y}$						

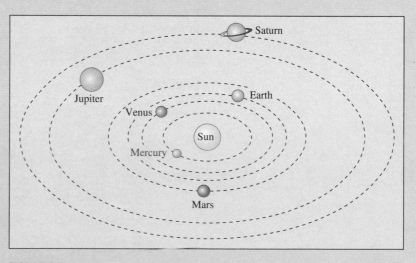

FIGURE 1.7

WARM UP

The following warm-up exercises involve skills that were covered in earlier sections. You will use these skills in the exercise set for this section.

In Exercises 1 and 2, place the correct inequality symbol ($<$ or $>$) between the numbers.

1. $4 \quad -2$ **2.** $-\pi \quad -3$

In Exercises 3 and 4, find the distance between the numbers.

3. $0, -5$ **4.** $-1, 3$

In Exercises 5–10, perform the indicated operations and simplify.

5. $\left(\frac{2}{3}\right)\left(\frac{3}{2}\right)$ **6.** $\frac{1}{2} \div 2$

7. $\frac{1}{3} + \frac{1}{2} - \frac{5}{6}$ **8.** $\frac{1}{12} - \frac{1}{3} + \frac{1}{8}$

9. $11\left(\frac{1}{4}\right) + \frac{5}{4}$ **10.** $\left(\frac{1}{2} - \frac{1}{3}\right) \div \frac{1}{6}$

EXERCISES for Section 1.2

In Exercises 1–6, evaluate the expression for the value of x.

Expression	Value
1. $-3x^3$	2
2. $\dfrac{x^2}{2}$	6
3. $4x^{-3}$	2
4. $7x^{-2}$	4
5. $6x^0 - (6x)^0$	10
6. $5(-x)^3$	3

In Exercises 7–22, simplify the expression.

7. $(-5z)^3$ **8.** $(4x^3)^2$

9. $6y^2(2y^4)^2$ **10.** $(-z)^3(3z^4)$

11. $\dfrac{7x^2}{x^3}$ **12.** $\dfrac{r^4}{r^6}$

13. $\dfrac{12(x + y)^3}{9(x + y)}$ **14.** $(2x^5)^0, \quad x \neq 0$

15. $(-2x^2)^3(4x^3)^{-1}$ **16.** $(4y^{-2})(8y^4)$

17. $\left(\dfrac{3z^2}{x}\right)^{-2}$ **18.** $\left(\dfrac{x^{-3}y^4}{5}\right)^{-3}$

19. $(4a^{-2}b^3)^{-3}$ **20.** $[(x^2y^{-2})^{-1}]^{-1}$

21. $(2x^2 + y^2)^4(2x^2 + y^2)^{-4}$ **22.** $\dfrac{x^2 \cdot x^{2n}}{x^3 \cdot x^n}$

In Exercises 23–26, evaluate the expression. (Do not use a calculator.)

23. (a) $\sqrt{\frac{9}{4}}$ (b) $\sqrt[3]{\frac{27}{8}}$

24. (a) $\sqrt{225}$ (b) $\sqrt[3]{0.064}$

25. (a) $(\sqrt[3]{-125})^3$ (b) $\sqrt[4]{562^4}$

26. (a) $\dfrac{4}{\sqrt{64}}$ (b) $\dfrac{\sqrt[4]{81}}{3}$

In Exercises 27–32, use the properties of radicals to simplify each expression.

27. (a) $\sqrt{8}$ (b) $\sqrt[3]{\frac{16}{27}}$

28. (a) $\sqrt[3]{16x^5}$ (b) $\sqrt[4]{(3x^2)^4}$

29. (a) $\sqrt{75x^2y^{-4}}$ (b) $\sqrt{5(x - y)^3}$

30. (a) $\sqrt[5]{96x^5y^3}$ (b) $\sqrt{72(x + 1)^4}$

31. (a) $\sqrt{5x^2y}\sqrt{3y}$ (b) $\dfrac{\sqrt{54a^2}}{\sqrt{2a^4}}$

32. (a) $\sqrt[3]{\frac{4z^2}{y^5}}\sqrt[3]{\frac{2z}{y}}$ (b) $\dfrac{\sqrt[4]{16b}}{\sqrt[4]{2b^5}}$

In Exercises 33–36, combine and/or simplify each expression.

33. (a) $5\sqrt{x} - 3\sqrt{x}$ (b) $6\sqrt{2} + 7\sqrt{2}$

34. (a) $4\sqrt{27} - \sqrt{75}$ (b) $5\sqrt[3]{2} + \sqrt[3]{54}$

35. (a) $2\sqrt{4y} - 2\sqrt{9y} + 10\sqrt{y}$
    (b) $6\sqrt[3]{32a} + 5\sqrt[3]{500a}$

36. (a) $2\sqrt{80x} + \sqrt{125x} - \sqrt{100x}$
    (b) $4\sqrt[3]{54z} - 2\sqrt[3]{40z} + \sqrt[3]{2z}$

In Exercises 37–42, rewrite each expression by rationalizing the denominator. Simplify your answer.

37. (a) $\dfrac{5}{\sqrt{10}}$ (b) $\dfrac{21}{\sqrt{7}}$

38. (a) $\dfrac{8}{\sqrt[3]{2}}$ (b) $\dfrac{1}{\sqrt[3]{12}}$

39. (a) $\dfrac{5}{\sqrt[3]{(5x)^2}}$ (b) $\dfrac{3}{\sqrt[4]{(3x)^3}}$

40. (a) $\dfrac{2x}{5 - \sqrt{3}}$ (b) $\dfrac{13}{6 + \sqrt{10}}$

41. (a) $\dfrac{3}{\sqrt{5} + \sqrt{6}}$ (b) $\dfrac{8}{\sqrt{2} - 2\sqrt{3}}$

42. (a) $\dfrac{5}{2\sqrt{10} - 5}$ (b) $\dfrac{34}{5\sqrt{2} - 4}$

In Exercises 43–46, rewrite each expression by rationalizing the numerator. Simplify your answer.

43. (a) $\dfrac{\sqrt{8}}{2}$ (b) $\dfrac{\sqrt{2}}{3}$

44. (a) $\dfrac{\sqrt{26}}{2}$ (b) $\dfrac{\sqrt{y}}{6y}$

45. (a) $\dfrac{\sqrt{3} - \sqrt{2}}{x}$ (b) $\dfrac{\sqrt{15} + \sqrt{3}}{12}$

46. (a) $\dfrac{1 + \sqrt{6}}{4}$ (b) $\dfrac{2\sqrt{3} + \sqrt{3}}{3}$

In Exercises 47–56, fill in the missing description.

Radical Form	*Rational Exponent Form*
47. $\sqrt{9} = 3$	
48. $\sqrt[3]{64} = 4$	
49.	$196^{1/2} = 14$
50. $\sqrt[3]{614.125} = 8.5$	
51. $\sqrt[3]{-216} = -6$	
52.	$(-243)^{1/5} = -3$
53.	$27^{2/3} = 9$
54. $(\sqrt[4]{81})^3 = 27$	
55. $\sqrt[4]{81^3} = 27$	
56.	$16^{5/4} = 32$

In Exercises 57–60, evaluate each expression without using a calculator.

57. (a) $36^{1/2}$ (b) $16^{3/2}$

58. (a) $121^{1/2}$ (b) $32^{-3/5}$

59. (a) $64^{-2/3}$ (b) $\left(\frac{9}{4}\right)^{-1/2}$

60. (a) $\left(-\frac{27}{8}\right)^{-1/3}$ (b) $\left(-\frac{1}{64}\right)^{-1/3}$

In Exercises 61–64, use fractional exponents to verify the reduction of the index.

61. $\sqrt[4]{x^2} = \sqrt{x}$, $x \geq 0$ 62. $\sqrt[6]{x^3} = \sqrt{x}$

63. $\sqrt[6]{(x + 1)^4} = \sqrt[3]{(x + 1)^2}$

64. $\sqrt[8]{(3x^2y^3)^2} = \sqrt[4]{3x^2y^3}$, $y \geq 0$

In Exercises 65–68, write the expression as a single radical.

65. $\sqrt{50}\sqrt[3]{2}$ 66. $\sqrt{40}\sqrt[3]{10}$

67. $\dfrac{\sqrt{x}}{\sqrt[3]{x}}$ 68. $\sqrt{\sqrt{\sqrt{32}}}$

In Exercises 69 and 70, use a calculator to approximate each number. (Round to four decimal places.)

69. (a) $\sqrt{57}$ (b) $\sqrt[5]{562}$
    (c) $225^{-2/3}$ (d) $\sqrt[5]{-65}$

70. (a) $\sqrt{3.95}$ (b) $\sqrt[4]{12.8}$
    (c) $\sqrt{75 + 3\sqrt{8}}$ (d) $(15.25)^{-1.4}$

In Exercises 71–74, write the number in scientific notation.

71. Land Area of the Earth: 57,500,000 square miles

72. Light Year: 9,461,000,000,000,000 kilometers

73. Relative Density of Hydrogen: 0.0000899

74. One Micron (Millionth of Meter): 0.00003937 inch

In Exercises 75–78, write the number in decimal form.

75. U.S. Daily Coca-Cola Consumption: 5.24×10^8 servings
76. Interior Temperature of Sun: 1.3×10^7 degrees Celsius
77. Charge of Electron: 4.8×10^{-10} electrostatic units
78. Width of Human Hair: 9.0×10^{-4} meters

In Exercises 79 and 80, use a calculator to evaluate the expression. (Round to three decimal places.)

79. (a) $2400(1 + 0.06)^{20}$ (b) $750\left(1 + \dfrac{0.11}{365}\right)^{800}$

  (c) $\dfrac{(2.414 \times 10^4)^6}{(1.68 \times 10^5)^5}$ (d) $(9.3 \times 10^6)^3(6.1 \times 10^{-4})^4$

80. (a) $\dfrac{3000}{[1 + (0.05)/4]^4}$ (b) $\dfrac{(3.28 \times 10^{-6})^{10}}{(5.34 \times 10^{-3})^{25}}$

  (c) $(0.000345)(8,980,000,000)$

  (d) $\dfrac{67,000,000 + 93,000,000}{0.0052}$

81. *Speed of Light* The speed of light is 11,160,000 miles per minute. The distance from the sun to the earth is 93,000,000 miles. Find the time for light to travel from the sun to the earth.

82. *Per Capita Debt* The per capita debt is defined to be the total debt divided by the population. Find the per capita debt of the federal government in 1990 if the gross debt was $3.2 trillion and the population was 250 million. (*Source:* U.S. Treasury Department)

83. *Compound Interest* The balance A after t years in an account earning an annual interest rate of r compounded n times per year is

$$A = P\left(1 + \frac{r}{n}\right)^{nt}$$

where P is the original deposit. Complete the table for $500 deposited in an account earning 12% compounded daily. (Note that $r = 0.12$ implies an interest rate of 12%.)

Number of Years	5	10	20	30	40	50
Balance						

84. *Erosion* A stream of water moving at the rate of v feet per second can carry particles of size $0.03\sqrt{v}$ inches. Find the size particle that can be carried by a stream flowing at $\frac{3}{4}$ feet per second.

Declining Balances Depreciation In Exercises 85 and 86, find the annual depreciation rate r. To find the annual depreciation rate by the **declining balances method**, use the formula

$$r = 1 - \left(\frac{S}{C}\right)^{1/n}$$

where n is the useful life of the item (in years), S is the salvage value (in dollars), and C is the original cost (in dollars).

85.

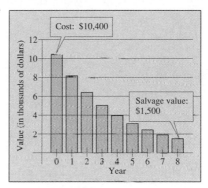

86.

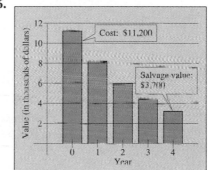

87. *Funnel Flow Rate* A funnel is filled with water to a height of h (see figure). The time t it takes for the funnel to empty is

$$t = 0.03[12^{5/2} - (12 - h)^{5/2}], \qquad 0 \le h \le 12.$$

Find t for $h = 7$ centimeters.

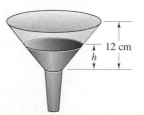

Figure for 87

88. *Period of a Pendulum*   The period T in seconds of a pendulum is

$$T = 2\pi\sqrt{\frac{L}{32}}$$

where L is the length of the pendulum in feet (see figure). Find the period of a pendulum whose length is 2 feet.

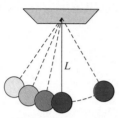

Figure for 88

89. *Calculator Experiment*   Enter any positive real number in your calculator and repeatedly take the square root. What real number does the display appear to be approaching?

90. *Calculator Experiment*   Square the real number $2/\sqrt{5}$ and note that the radical is eliminated from the denominator. Is this equivalent to rationalizing the denominator? Why or why not?

91. List all possible unit digits of the square of a positive integer. Use that list to determine whether $\sqrt{5233}$ is an integer.

1.3 Polynomials: Special Products and Factoring

Polynomials / Operations with Polynomials / Special Products / Factoring / Factoring Special Polynomial Forms / Trinomials with Binomial Factors / Factoring by Grouping

Polynomials

An **algebraic expression** is a collection of letters called **variables** and real numbers organized in some manner by using addition, subtraction, multiplication, division, or radicals. The simplest and most common kind of algebraic expression is the **polynomial.** Some examples are

$$2x + 5, \qquad 3x^4 - 7x^2 + 2x + 4, \qquad \text{and} \qquad 5x^2y^2 - xy + 3.$$

The first two are *polynomials in x* and the third one is a *polynomial in x and y*. The **terms** of a polynomial in x have the form ax^k, where a is the **coefficient** and k is the **degree** of the term. For instance, the third degree polynomial

$$2x^3 - 5x^2 + 1 = 2x^3 + (-5)x^2 + (0)x + 1$$

has coefficients 2, -5, 0, and 1.

DEFINITION OF A POLYNOMIAL IN x

Let $a_0, a_1, a_2, \ldots, a_n$ be *real numbers* and let n be a *nonnegative integer*. A **polynomial in x** is an expression of the form

$$a_n x^n + a_{n-1} x^{n-1} + \cdots + a_1 x + a_0$$

where $a_n \neq 0$. The polynomial is of **degree** n, a_n is the **leading coefficient,** and a_0 is the **constant term.**

REMARK Polynomials with one, two, or three terms are called **monomials, binomials,** or **trinomials,** respectively.

In **standard form,** a polynomial is written with descending powers of x.

EXAMPLE 1   Writing Polynomials in Standard Form

Polynomial	Standard Form	Degree
a. $4x^2 - 5x^7 - 2 + 3x$	$-5x^7 + 4x^2 + 3x - 2$	7
b. $4 - 9x^2$	$-9x^2 + 4$	2
c. 8	$8 \quad (8 = 8x^0)$	0

A polynomial that has all zero coefficients is the **zero polynomial,** denoted by 0. We do not assign a degree to the zero polynomial.

For polynomials in more than one variable, the degree of a *term* is the sum of the exponents of the variables in the term. The degree of the *polynomial* is the highest degree of its terms. For instance, the polynomial $5x^3 y - x^2 y^2 + 2xy - 5$ has two terms of degree 4, one term of degree 2, and one term of degree 0. The degree of the polynomial is 4.

Operations with Polynomials

You can **add** and **subtract** polynomials in much the same way you add and subtract real numbers. Simply add or subtract the *like terms* (terms having the same variables to the same powers) by adding their coefficients. For instance, $-3xy^2$ and $5xy^2$ are like terms and their sum is

$$-3xy^2 + 5xy^2 = (-3 + 5)xy^2 = 2xy^2.$$

EXAMPLE 2 Sums and Differences of Polynomials

a. $(5x^3 - 7x^2 - 3) + (x^3 + 2x^2 - x + 8)$

$$= (5x^3 + x^3) + (2x^2 - 7x^2) - x + (8 - 3) \qquad \text{\textit{Group like terms}}$$

$$= 6x^3 - 5x^2 - x + 5 \qquad \text{\textit{Combine like terms}}$$

b. $(7x^4 - x^2 - 4x + 2) - (3x^4 - 4x^2 + 3x)$

$$= 7x^4 - x^2 - 4x + 2 - 3x^4 + 4x^2 - 3x$$

$$= (7x^4 - 3x^4) + (4x^2 - x^2) + (-3x - 4x) + 2 \quad \text{\textit{Group like terms}}$$

$$= 4x^4 + 3x^2 - 7x + 2 \qquad \text{\textit{Combine like terms}}$$

REMARK A common mistake is to fail to change the sign of *each* term inside parentheses preceded by a negative sign. For instance, note that

$$-(3x^4 - 4x^2 + 3x) = -3x^4 + 4x^2 - 3x$$

and

$$-(3x^4 - 4x^2 + 3x) \neq -3x^4 - 4x^2 + 3x. \qquad \text{\textit{Common mistake}}$$

To find the **product** of two polynomials, use the left and right Distributive Properties, as shown in Example 3.

EXAMPLE 3 Multiplying Polynomials: The FOIL Method

Multiply $(3x - 2)$ by $(5x + 7)$.

Solution

By treating $(5x + 7)$ as a single quantity, we can perform the multiplication as follows.

$$(3x - 2)(5x + 7) = 3x(5x + 7) - 2(5x + 7)$$

$$= (3x)(5x) + (3x)(7) - (2)(5x) - (2)(7)$$

$$= 15x^2 + 21x - 10x - 14$$

Product of **F**irst terms	Product of **O**uter terms	Product of **I**nner terms	Product of **L**ast terms

$$= 15x^2 + 11x - 14$$

With practice, you should be able to multiply two binomials without writing all of the above steps. In fact, the four products in the boxes above suggest a single step: the **FOIL Method.**

When multiplying two polynomials, multiply *each* term of one polynomial by *each* term of the other. A vertical arrangement is helpful.

Special Products

SPECIAL PRODUCTS

Let u and v be real numbers, variables, or algebraic expressions.

Special Product	*Example*
Sum and Difference of Same Terms	
$\quad (u + v)(u - v) = u^2 - v^2$	$(x + 4)(x - 4) = x^2 - 16$
Square of a Binomial	
$\quad (u + v)^2 = u^2 + 2uv + v^2$	$(x + 3)^2 = x^2 + 2(x)(3) + 3^2$
	$\qquad\qquad = x^2 + 6x + 9$
$\quad (u - v)^2 = u^2 - 2uv + v^2$	$(3x - 2)^2 = (3x)^2 - 2(3x)(2) + 2^2$
	$\qquad\qquad = 9x^2 - 12x + 4$
Cube of a Binomial	
$\quad (u + v)^3 = u^3 + 3u^2v + 3uv^2 + v^3$	$(x + 2)^3 = x^3 + 3x^2(2) + 3x(2^2) + 2^3$
	$\qquad\qquad = x^3 + 6x^2 + 12x + 8$
$\quad (u - v)^3 = u^3 - 3u^2v + 3uv^2 - v^3$	$(x - 1)^3 = x^3 - 3(x^2)(1) + 3(x)(1^2) - 1^3$
	$\qquad\qquad = x^3 - 3x^2 + 3x - 1$

Occasionally, the formulas for special products can be extended to cover products of two trinomials, as demonstrated in the following example.

EXAMPLE 4   The Product of Two Trinomials

Find the product of $(x + y - 2)$ and $(x + y + 2)$.

Solution

By grouping $x + y$ in parentheses, you can write

$$(x + y - 2)(x + y + 2) = [(x + y) - 2][(x + y) + 2]$$
$$= (x + y)^2 - 2^2$$
$$= x^2 + 2xy + y^2 - 4.$$

Factoring

We just reviewed how to multiply polynomials to obtain a new polynomial. We now review how to find factors whose product yields a given polynomial. The process of writing a polynomial as a product is called **factoring.** It is an important tool for solving equations and reducing fractional expressions.

Unless noted otherwise, we will limit our discussion of factoring to polynomials whose factors have integer coefficients. If a polynomial cannot be factored using integer coefficients, it is called **prime** or **irreducible over the integers.** For instance, the polynomial $x^2 - 3$ is irreducible over the integers. [Over the *real numbers*, this polynomial can be factored as $x^2 - 3 = (x + \sqrt{3})(x - \sqrt{3})$.]

A polynomial is said to be **completely factored** when each of its factors is prime. For instance,

$$x^3 - x^2 + 4x - 4 = (x - 1)(x^2 + 4)$$

is completely factored, but

$$x^3 - x^2 - 4x + 4 = (x - 1)(x^2 - 4)$$

is not completely factored. Its complete factorization would be

$$x^3 - x^2 - 4x + 4 = (x - 1)(x + 2)(x - 2).$$

We start with polynomials that can be written as the product of a monomial and another polynomial. The technique used here is the distributive property, $a(b + c) = ab + ac$, in the *reverse* direction.

$$ab + ac = a(b + c) \qquad \qquad \textit{a is a common factor}$$

Removing (factoring out) a common factor is the first step in completely factoring polynomials.

EXAMPLE 5   Removing Common Factors

$$6x^3 - 4x = 2x(3x^2) - 2x(2)$$
$$= 2x(3x^2 - 2)$$

$$(x - 2)(2x) + (x - 2)(3) = (x - 2)(2x + 3)$$

Factoring Special Polynomial Forms

FACTORING SPECIAL POLYNOMIAL FORMS

Factored Form	*Example*
Difference of Two Squares	
$u^2 - v^2 = (u + v)(u - v)$	$9x^2 - 4 = (3x)^2 - 2^2$
	$\qquad\qquad = (3x + 2)(3x - 2)$
Perfect Square Trinomial	
$u^2 + 2uv + v^2 = (u + v)^2$	$x^2 + 6x + 9 = x^2 + 2(x)(3) + 3^2$
	$\qquad\qquad\quad = (x + 3)^2$
$u^2 - 2uv + v^2 = (u - v)^2$	$x^2 - 6x + 9 = x^2 - 2(x)(3) + 3^2$
	$\qquad\qquad\quad = (x - 3)^2$
Sum or Difference of Two Cubes	
$u^3 + v^3 = (u + v)(u^2 - uv + v^2)$	$x^3 + 8 = x^3 + 2^3$
	$\qquad\quad = (x + 2)(x^2 - 2x + 4)$
$u^3 - v^3 = (u - v)(u^2 + uv + v^2)$	$27x^3 - 1 = (3x)^3 - 1^3$
	$\qquad\qquad = (3x - 1)(9x^2 + 3x + 1)$

One of the easiest special polynomial forms to factor is the difference of two squares. Think of the form as follows.

$$u^2 \ominus v^2 \;=\; (u + v)(u - v) \qquad\qquad \textit{Factors are a conjugate pair}$$

Difference   Opposite signs

To recognize perfect square terms, look for coefficients that are squares of integers and variables raised to *even powers*.

REMARK In Example 6, note that the first step in factoring a polynomial is to check for common factors. Once the common factor is removed, it is often possible to recognize patterns that were not immediately obvious.

EXAMPLE 6   Removing a Common Factor First

$$3 - 12x^2 = 3(1 - 4x^2) \qquad\qquad \textit{Common factor}$$
$$= 3[1^2 - (2x)^2] \qquad\qquad \textit{Difference of squares}$$
$$= 3(1 + 2x)(1 - 2x)$$

EXAMPLE 7   Factoring the Difference of Two Squares

a. $(x + 2)^2 - y^2 = [(x + 2) + y][(x + 2) - y]$

$$= (x + 2 + y)(x + 2 - y)$$

$$= (x + y + 2)(x - y + 2)$$

b. Apply the difference of two squares formula twice.

$$16x^4 - 81 = (4x^2)^2 - 9^2$$

$$= (4x^2 + 9)(4x^2 - 9) \qquad \textit{First application}$$

$$= (4x^2 + 9)[(2x)^2 - 3^2]$$

$$= (4x^2 + 9)(2x + 3)(2x - 3) \quad \textit{Second application}$$

A perfect square trinomial is the square of a binomial, and has the following form.

$$u^2 + 2uv + v^2 = (u + v)^2 \qquad \text{or} \qquad u^2 - 2uv + v^2 = (u - v)^2$$

Same sign   Same sign

Note that the first and last terms are squares and the middle term is twice the product of u and v.

EXAMPLE 8   Factoring Perfect Square Trinomials

a. $16x^2 + 8x + 1 = (4x)^2 + 2(4x)(1) + 1^2$

$$= (4x + 1)^2$$

b. $x^2 - 10x + 25 = x^2 - 2(x)(5) + 5^2$

$$= (x - 5)^2$$

The next two formulas show sums and differences of cubes. Pay special attention to the signs of the terms.

Like signs   Like signs

$$u^3 + v^3 = (u + v)(u^2 - uv + v^2) \qquad u^3 - v^3 = (u - v)(u^2 + uv + v^2)$$

Unlike signs   Unlike signs

EXAMPLE 9   Factoring the Difference of Cubes

$$x^3 - 27 = x^3 - 3^3 = (x - 3)(x^2 + 3x + 9)$$

EXAMPLE 10   Factoring the Sum of Cubes

$$3x^3 + 192 = 3(x^3 + 64)$$

$$3(x^3 + 64) = 3(x^3 + 4^3) = 3(x + 4)(x^2 - 4x + 16)$$

Trinomials with Binomial Factors

To factor a trinomial of the form $ax^2 + bx + c$, use the following pattern.

$$\overset{\text{Factors of } a}{ax^2 + bx + c = (\ \ x + \ \ )(\ \ x + \ \ )}$$

$$\underset{\text{Factors of } c}{}$$

The goal is to find a combination of factors of a and c so that the outer and inner products add up to the middle term bx. For instance, in the trinomial $6x^2 + 17x + 5$, you can write

$$\overset{F \quad O \quad I \quad L}{(2x + 5)(3x + 1) = 6x^2 + 2x + 15x + 5 = 6x^2 + 17x + 5.}$$

Note that the outer (O) and inner (I) products add up to $17x$.

EXAMPLE 11   Factoring a Trinomial: Leading Coefficient Is 1

Factor the trinomial $x^2 - 7x + 12$.

Solution

The possible factorizations are $(x - 2)(x - 6)$, $(x - 1)(x - 12)$, and $(x - 3)(x - 4)$.

Testing the middle term, you will find the correct factorization is

$$x^2 - 7x + 12 = (x - 3)(x - 4). \quad \blacktriangle$$

EXAMPLE 12   Factoring a Trinomial: Leading Coefficient Is Not 1

Factor the trinomial $2x^2 + x - 15$.

Solution

The eight possible factorizations are as follows.

$$(2x - 1)(x + 15) \qquad (2x + 1)(x - 15)$$
$$(2x - 15)(x + 1) \qquad (2x + 15)(x - 1)$$
$$(2x - 3)(x + 5) \qquad (2x + 3)(x - 5)$$
$$(2x - 5)(x + 3) \qquad (2x + 5)(x - 3)$$

Testing the middle term, you will find the correct factorization is

$$2x^2 + x - 15 = (2x - 5)(x + 3). \quad \blacktriangle$$

Factoring by Grouping

Sometimes polynomials with more than three terms can be factored by a method called **factoring by grouping.** It is not always obvious which terms to group, and sometimes several different groupings will work.

EXAMPLE 13   Factoring by Grouping

$$x^3 - 2x^2 - 3x + 6 = (x^3 - 2x^2) - (3x - 6) \qquad \textit{Group terms}$$
$$= x^2(x - 2) - 3(x - 2) \qquad \textit{Factor groups}$$
$$= (x - 2)(x^2 - 3) \qquad \textit{Common factor}$$

As general guidelines for completely factoring polynomials, consider, in order, the following factorizations.

Guidelines for Factoring Polynomials

1. Factor out any common factors.
2. Factor according to one of the special polynomial forms.
3. Factor as $ax^2 + bx + c = (mx + r)(nx + s)$.
4. Factor by grouping.

DISCUSSION
PROBLEM
A Three-Dimensional View of a Special Product

Figure 1.8 shows two cubes: a large cube whose volume is a^3 and a smaller cube whose volume is b^3. If the smaller cube is removed from the larger, the remaining solid has a volume of $a^3 - b^3$ and is composed of three rectangular boxes, labeled Box 1, Box 2, and Box 3. Find the volume of each box and describe how these results are related to the following special product formula.

$$a^3 - b^3 = (a - b)(a^2 + ab + b^2)$$
$$= (a - b)a^2 + (a - b)ab + (a - b)b^2$$

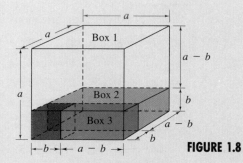

FIGURE 1.8

WARM UP

The following warm-up exercises involve skills that were covered in earlier sections. You will use these skills in the exercise set for this section.

In Exercises 1–10, perform the indicated operations.

1. $(7x^2)(6x)$

2. $(10z^3)(-2z^{-1})$

3. $(-3x^2)^3$

4. $-3(x^2)^3$

5. $\dfrac{27z^5}{12z^2}$

6. $\sqrt{24} \cdot \sqrt{2}$

7. $\left(\dfrac{2x}{3}\right)^{-2}$

8. $16^{3/4}$

9. $\dfrac{4}{\sqrt{8}}$

10. $\sqrt[3]{-27x^3}$

EXERCISES for Section 1.3

In Exercises 1–4, write the polynomial in standard form and determine the degree and leading coefficient.

1. $2x^2 - x + 1$
2. $5 + 2x^2 - 3x^4$
3. $1 - \frac{1}{2}x^5$
4. 3

In Exercises 5–26, perform the indicated operations and write the result in standard form.

5. $(6x + 5) - (8x + 15)$
6. $(2x^7 + 1) - (x^2 - 2x + 1)$
7. $-(x^3 - 2) + (4x^3 - 2x)$
8. $-(5x^2 - 1) - (-3x^2 + 5)$
9. $(15x^2 - 6) - (-8x^3 - 14x^2 - 17)$
10. $(15x^4 - 18x - 19) - (13x^4 - 5x + 15)$
11. $5z - [3z - (10z + 8)]$
12. $(y^3 + 1) - [(y^2 + 1) + (3y - 7)]$
13. $-5z(3z - 1)$
14. $-4x(3 - 6x^3)$
15. $(-2x)(-3x)(5x + 2)$
16. $(1 - x^3)(4x)$
17. $(x^3 - 2x + 1)(x - 5)$
18. $(x + 1)(x^2 - 1)$
19. $(x + 3)(x^2 - 3x + 9)$
20. $(2x^2 + 3)(4x^4 - 6x^2 + 9)$
21. $(x^2 + 1)(x + 1)(x - 1)$
22. $(x^2 + x - 2)(x^2 - x + 2)$
23. $5z(x + 1) - 3z(2x - 4)$
24. $(2x - y)(x + 3y) + 3(2x - y)$
25. $(x + \sqrt{5})(x - \sqrt{5})(x + 4)$
26. $\sqrt{x}(3\sqrt{x} - 4)$

In Exercises 27–40, use the special product formulas to find the product.

27. $(2x - 5y)^2$
28. $(5 - 8x)^2$
29. $[(x - 3) + y]^2$
30. $[(x + 1) - y]^2$
31. $(x + 2y)(x - 2y)$
32. $(2x + 3y)(2x - 3y)$
33. $[(m - 3) + n][(m - 3) - n]$
34. $[(x + y) + 1][(x + y) - 1]$
35. $(2r^2 - 5)(2r^2 + 5)$
36. $(3a^3 - 4b^2)(3a^3 + 4b^2)$
37. $(x + 1)^3$
38. $(x - 2)^3$
39. $(2x - y)^3$
40. $(3x + 2y)^3$

In Exercises 41–44, remove the common factor.

41. $2x^3 - 6x$
42. $4x^3 - 6x^2 + 12x$
43. $(x - 1)^2 + 6(x - 1)$
44. $3x(x + 2) - 4(x + 2)$

In Exercises 45–48, factor the difference of two squares.

45. $16y^2 - 9$
46. $x^2 - \frac{4}{25}$
47. $(x - 1)^2 - 4$
48. $25 - (z + 5)^2$

In Exercises 49–52, factor the perfect square trinomial.

49. $x^2 - 4x + 4$
50. $x^2 + 10x + 25$
51. $25y^2 - 10y + 1$
52. $z^2 + z + \frac{1}{4}$

In Exercises 53–60, factor the trinomial.

53. $s^2 - 5s + 6$ **54.** $t^2 - t - 6$
55. $x^2 - 30x + 200$ **56.** $x^2 - 13x + 42$
57. $9z^2 - 3z - 2$ **58.** $12x^2 + 7x + 1$
59. $5x^2 + 26x + 5$ **60.** $5u^2 + 13u - 6$

In Exercises 61–64, factor the sum or difference of cubes.

61. $x^3 - 8$
62. $z^3 + 125$
63. $27x^3 + 8$
64. $8t^3 - 1$

In Exercises 65–70, factor by grouping.

65. $x^3 - x^2 + 2x - 2$
66. $x^3 + 5x^2 - 5x - 25$
67. $2x^3 - x^2 - 6x + 3$
68. $5x^3 - 10x^2 + 3x - 6$
69. $6 + 2x - 3x^3 - x^4$
70. $x^5 + 2x^3 + x^2 + 2$

In Exercises 71–86, completely factor the expression.

71. $x^3 - 4x^2$
72. $6x^2 - 54$
73. $1 - 4x + 4x^2$
74. $1 - 6x + 9x^2$
75. $9x^2 + 10x + 1$
76. $13x + 6 + 5x^2$
77. $4x(2x - 1) + (2x - 1)^2$
78. $5(3 - 4x)^2 - 8(3 - 4x)(5x - 1)$
79. $2(x + 1)(x - 3)^2 - 3(x + 1)^2(x - 3)$
80. $7(3x + 2)^2(1 - x)^2 + (3x + 2)(1 - x)^3$
81. $3x^3 + x^2 + 15x + 5$
82. $5 - x + 5x^2 - x^3$
83. $25 - (z + 5)^2$
84. $(t - 1)^2 - 49$
85. $2t^3 - 16$
86. $5x^3 + 40$

87. *Stopping Distance*   The stopping distance of an automobile is the distance traveled during the driver's reaction time plus the distance traveled after the brakes are applied. In an experiment, these distances were measured (in feet) when the automobile was traveling at a speed of x miles per hour (see figure). The distance traveled during the reaction time is $R = 1.1x$ and the braking distance is $B = 0.14x^2 - 4.43x + 58.40$. Determine the polynomial for the stopping distance of this automobile. Use this polynomial to estimate the total stopping distance when $x = 30$, $x = 40$, and $x = 55$.

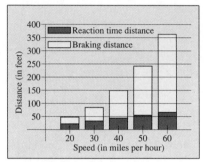

Figure for 87

88. *Compound Interest*   After 3 years an investment of $1200 compounded annually at an interest rate r will yield

$1200(1 + r)^3$.

Write this polynomial in standard form.

89. *Volume of a Box*   A closed box is constructed by cutting along the solid lines and folding along the broken lines of the rectangular piece of metal shown in the accompanying figure. Find the volume of the box in terms of x if the length and width of the rectangle are 45 inches and 15 inches, respectively. Find the volume when $x = 3$, $x = 5$, and $x = 7$.

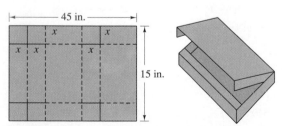

Figure for 89

90. *Floor Space*   Find a polynomial that represents the total number of square feet for the following floor plan.

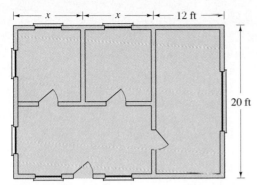

Figure for 90

91. *Volume*   The cylindrical shell shown in the accompanying figure has a volume of

$$\pi R^2 h - \pi r^2 h.$$

(a) Factor the expression for the volume.

(b) From the result of part (a) show that the volume can be expressed as

$$2\pi(\text{average radius})(\text{thickness of the shell})h.$$

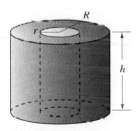

Figure for 91

92. *Autocatalytic Reaction*   The rate of change of an auto-catalytic chemical reaction is given by $kQx - kx^2$ where Q is the amount of the original substance, x is the amount of the substance formed, and k is a constant of proportionality. Factor the expression for this rate of change.

In Exercises 93–96, construct a "geometric factoring model" to represent the given factorization. For instance, a factoring model for $2x^2 + 5x + 2 = (2x + 1)(x + 2)$ is shown in the accompanying figure.

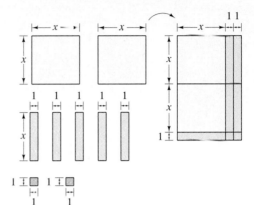

Figure for 93–96

93. $3x^2 + 7x + 2 = (3x + 1)(x + 2)$

94. $x^2 + 4x + 3 = (x + 3)(x + 1)$

95. $2x^2 + 7x + 3 = (2x + 1)(x + 3)$

96. $x^2 + 3x + 2 = (x + 2)(x + 1)$

97. Determine the degree of the product of two polynomials of degree m and n.

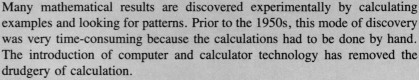
SOLVING

A Numerical Approach to Maximizing a Volume

Many mathematical results are discovered experimentally by calculating examples and looking for patterns. Prior to the 1950s, this mode of discovery was very time-consuming because the calculations had to be done by hand. The introduction of computer and calculator technology has removed the drudgery of calculation.

Using technology to conduct mathematical experiments usually involves creating an algebraic **model** to represent the quantity under question. For instance, the following example shows how to create a model for the volume of a rectangular box.

EXAMPLE 1   Creating a Model for the Volume of a Box

Consider a rectangular box with a square base and a surface area of 216 square inches. Let x represent the length (in inches) of each side of the base. Use the variable x to write a model, or expression, for the volume of the box.

Solution

You can begin by writing a model for the height h (in inches) in terms of x.

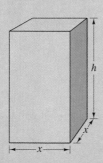

$$\boxed{\begin{array}{c}Surface \\ area\end{array}} = \boxed{\begin{array}{c}Area\ of \\ base\end{array}} + \boxed{\begin{array}{c}Area\ of \\ top\end{array}} + 4 \boxed{\begin{array}{c}Area\ of \\ side\end{array}}$$

$$216 = x^2 + x^2 + 4xh$$

$$216 = 2x^2 + 4xh$$

$$216 - 2x^2 = 4xh$$

$$\frac{216 - 2x^2}{4x} = h$$

$$\frac{54}{x} - \frac{x}{2} = h$$

Now, having written the height in terms of x, you can write the following model for the volume in terms of x.

$$\boxed{\begin{array}{c}Volume \\ of\ box\end{array}} = \boxed{\begin{array}{c}Length \\ of\ box\end{array}} \cdot \boxed{\begin{array}{c}Width \\ of\ box\end{array}} \cdot \boxed{\begin{array}{c}Height \\ of\ box\end{array}}$$

$$V = (x)(x)\left(\frac{54}{x} - \frac{x}{2}\right)$$

$$= 54x - \frac{1}{2}x^3, \quad 0 < x \le \sqrt{108}$$

Now, suppose you wanted to answer the following question. "Of all rectangular boxes with square bases and surface areas of 216 square inches, which has the largest volume?" You can use the model created in Example 1 to experimentally answer the question.

EXAMPLE 2 Finding the Maximum Volume of a Box

Of all rectangular boxes with a square base and a surface area of 216 square inches, which has the largest volume?

Solution

To answer the question experimentally, you can calculate several volumes. For instance, you could let x vary between 1.0 inches and 10 inches and calculate the resulting volume.

Base, x	Height	Surface Area	Volume of Box
1.0	53.5	216.0	53.5
1.5	35.3	216.0	79.3
2.0	26.0	216.0	104.0
2.5	20.4	216.0	127.2
3.0	16.5	216.0	148.5
3.5	13.7	216.0	167.6
4.0	11.5	216.0	184.0
4.5	9.8	216.0	197.4
5.0	8.3	216.0	207.5
5.5	7.1	216.0	213.8
6.0	6.0	216.0	216.0
6.5	5.1	216.0	213.7
7.0	4.2	216.0	206.5
7.5	3.5	216.0	194.1
8.0	2.8	216.0	176.0
8.5	2.1	216.0	151.9
9.0	1.5	216.0	121.5
9.5	0.9	216.0	84.3
10.0	0.4	216.0	40.0

From the results of the experiment, it appears that the *cube* (the box whose dimensions are 6 by 6 by 6) has the greatest volume. (In Chapter 3 on page 203, we look at a graphical approach to solving this problem.) ◢

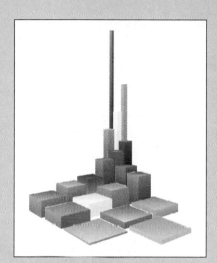

The diagram shows the 19 different boxes whose volumes were calculated in Example 2.

EXERCISES

(*See also: Discussion Problem, page 36; Exercise 89, Section 1.3*)

1. *Exploration* In Example 2, what happens to the height of the boxes as x gets closer and closer to 0? Of all boxes with a square base and a surface area of 216 square inches, is there a tallest?

2. *Exploration* In Example 2, what happens to the height of the boxes as x gets closer and closer to $\sqrt{108}$? Is there a shortest box that has a square base and a surface area of 216 square inches?

3. *Exploration* Complete the table. Why does this table lend further support to the conclusion obtained in Example 2?

Base, x	5.9	5.99	5.999	6.1	6.01	6.001
Volume, V	?	?	?	?	?	?

4. Of all rectangular boxes with a surface area of 216 square inches and a base that is x inches by $2x$ inches, which has the maximum volume?

41

Fractional Expressions

Domain of an Algebraic Expression / Simplifying Rational Expressions /
Operations with Rational Expressions / Compound Fractions

Domain of an Algebraic Expression

The set of real numbers for which an expression is defined is the **domain** of
the expression. We will not usually state the domain of a given algebraic
expression, but it will be implied. Two algebraic expressions are said to be
equivalent if they yield the same value for all numbers in their domain. For
instance, the expressions $[(x + 1) + (x + 2)]$ and $2x + 3$ are equivalent.

EXAMPLE 1   Finding the Domain of an Algebraic Expression

a. The domain of the polynomial

$$2x^3 + 3x + 4$$

is the set of all real numbers. In fact, the domain of any polynomial is the
set of all real numbers (unless the domain is specifically restricted).

b. The domain of the radical expression

$$\sqrt{x - 2}$$

is the set of real numbers greater than or equal to 2, because the square
root of a negative number is not a real number.

c. The domain of the expression

$$\frac{x + 2}{x - 3}$$

is the set of all real numbers except $x = 3$, which would produce an
undefined division by zero.   ◢

The quotient of two algebraic expressions is a **fractional expression**.
Moreover, the quotient of two *polynomials* such as

$$\frac{1}{x}, \qquad \frac{2x - 1}{x + 1}, \qquad \text{or} \qquad \frac{x^2 - 1}{x^2 + 1}$$

is a **rational expression.** Recall that a fraction is in reduced form if its numerator and denominator have no factors in common aside from ± 1. To write a fraction in reduced form, apply the following rule.

$$\frac{a \cdot \cancel{c}}{b \cdot \cancel{c}} = \frac{a}{b}, \qquad b \neq 0 \quad \text{and} \quad c \neq 0$$

The key to success in simplifying rational expressions lies in your ability to *factor* polynomials.

EXAMPLE 2   Reducing a Rational Expression

Write the following rational expression in reduced form.

$$\frac{x^2 + 4x - 12}{3x - 6}$$

Solution

Factoring both numerator and denominator, and then reducing, produces the following.

$$\frac{x^2 + 4x - 12}{3x - 6} = \frac{(x + 6)\cancel{(x - 2)}}{3\cancel{(x - 2)}} \qquad \textit{Factor completely}$$

$$= \frac{x + 6}{3}, \quad x \neq 2 \qquad \textit{Reduce}$$

Note that the original expression is undefined when $x = 2$ (because division by zero is undefined). To make sure that the reduced expression is *equivalent* to the original expression, you must restrict the domain of the reduced expression by excluding the value $x = 2$. ◢

REMARK   In Example 2, do not make the mistake of trying to reduce further by dividing *terms*.

$$\frac{x + 6}{3} \qquad \text{DOES NOT EQUAL} \qquad \frac{x + \cancel{6}}{\cancel{3}} \quad \text{or} \quad x + 2.$$

Remember that to reduce fractions, divide common *factors*, not terms. ◢

Simplifying Rational Expressions

When simplifying rational expressions, be sure to factor each polynomial completely before concluding that the numerator and denominator have no factors in common. Moreover, changing the sign of a factor may allow further reduction, as seen in part (b) of the next example.

EXAMPLE 3   Reducing Rational Expressions

a. $\dfrac{x^3 - 4x}{x^2 + x - 2} = \dfrac{x(x^2 - 4)}{(x + 2)(x - 1)}$

$\qquad\qquad = \dfrac{x(x + 2)(x - 2)}{(x + 2)(x - 1)}$ *Factor completely*

$\qquad\qquad = \dfrac{x(x - 2)}{x - 1}, \qquad x \neq -2$ *Reduce*

Note that the implied domain excludes $x = 1$ in both the original and the reduced expressions.

b. $\dfrac{12 + x - x^2}{2x^2 - 9x + 4} = \dfrac{(4 - x)(3 + x)}{(2x - 1)(x - 4)}$ *Factor completely*

$\qquad\qquad = \dfrac{-(x - 4)(3 + x)}{(2x - 1)(x - 4)}$ $(4 - x) = -(x - 4)$

$\qquad\qquad = -\dfrac{3 + x}{2x - 1}, \qquad x \neq 4$ *Reduce*

Operations with Rational Expressions

To multiply or divide rational expressions, use the properties of fractions. Recall that to divide fractions we invert the divisor and multiply.

EXAMPLE 4   Multiplying Rational Expressions

$\dfrac{2x^2 + x - 6}{x^2 + 4x - 5} \cdot \dfrac{x^3 - 3x^2 + 2x}{4x^2 - 6x} = \dfrac{(2x - 3)(x + 2)}{(x + 5)(x - 1)} \cdot \dfrac{x(x - 2)(x - 1)}{2x(2x - 3)}$

$\qquad\qquad\qquad\qquad\qquad = \dfrac{(x + 2)(x - 2)}{2(x + 5)}, \quad x \neq 0, x \neq 1, x \neq \dfrac{3}{2}$

EXAMPLE 5 Dividing Rational Expressions

$$\frac{x^3 - 8}{x^2 - 4} \div \frac{x^2 + 2x + 4}{x^3 + 8} = \frac{x^3 - 8}{x^2 - 4} \cdot \frac{x^3 + 8}{x^2 + 2x + 4} \quad \textit{Invert and multiply}$$

$$= \frac{\cancel{(x - 2)}\cancel{(x^2 + 2x + 4)}}{\cancel{(x + 2)}\cancel{(x - 2)}} \cdot \frac{\cancel{(x + 2)}(x^2 - 2x + 4)}{\cancel{x^2 + 2x + 4}}$$

$$= x^2 - 2x + 4, \quad x \neq \pm 2 \qquad \blacktriangleleft$$

To add or subtract rational expressions, use the familiar LCD (least common denominator) method or the basic definition

$$\frac{a}{b} \pm \frac{c}{d} = \frac{ad \pm bc}{bd}, \quad b \neq 0 \text{ and } d \neq 0.$$

This definition provides an efficient way of adding or subtracting *two* fractions that have no common factors in their denominators.

EXAMPLE 6 Subtracting Rational Expressions Using the Basic Definition

$$\frac{x}{x - 3} - \frac{2}{3x + 4} = \frac{x(3x + 4) - 2(x - 3)}{(x - 3)(3x + 4)}$$

$$= \frac{3x^2 + 4x - 2x + 6}{(x - 3)(3x + 4)} \qquad \textit{Remove parentheses}$$

$$= \frac{3x^2 + 2x + 6}{(x - 3)(3x + 4)} \qquad \textit{Combine like terms} \qquad \blacktriangleleft$$

For three or more fractions, or for fractions with a repeated factor in the denominator, the LCD method works well. Recall that the LCD of several fractions consists of the product of all prime factors in the denominators, with each factor given the highest power of its occurrence in any denominator.

EXAMPLE 7 The LCD Method for Combining Rational Expressions

Perform the given operations and simplify.

$$\frac{3}{x - 1} - \frac{2}{x} + \frac{x + 3}{x^2 - 1}$$

Solution

Using the factored denominators $(x - 1)$, x, and $(x + 1)(x - 1)$, you can see that the LCD is $x(x + 1)(x - 1)$.

$$\frac{3}{x - 1} - \frac{2}{x} + \frac{x + 3}{(x + 1)(x - 1)}$$

$$= \frac{3(x)(x + 1)}{x(x + 1)(x - 1)} - \frac{2(x + 1)(x - 1)}{x(x + 1)(x - 1)} + \frac{(x + 3)(x)}{x(x + 1)(x - 1)}$$

$$= \frac{3(x)(x + 1) - 2(x + 1)(x - 1) + (x + 3)(x)}{x(x + 1)(x - 1)}$$

$$= \frac{3x^2 + 3x - 2x^2 + 2 + x^2 + 3x}{x(x + 1)(x - 1)}$$

$$= \frac{2x^2 + 6x + 2}{x(x + 1)(x - 1)} = \frac{2(x^2 + 3x + 1)}{x(x + 1)(x - 1)}$$

REMARK Sometimes the numerator of the answer has a factor in common with the denominator. In such cases the answer should be reduced.

Compound Fractions

So far in this section we have limited our operations to simple fractional expressions. Fractional expressions with fractions in the numerator, denominator, or both, are called **compound fractions.** A compound fraction can be simplified by first combining both its numerator and its denominator into single fractions, then inverting the denominator and multiplying.

EXAMPLE 8   Simplifying a Compound Fraction

$$\frac{\left(\dfrac{2}{x} - 3\right)}{\left(1 - \dfrac{1}{x - 1}\right)} = \frac{\left(\dfrac{2 - 3(x)}{x}\right)}{\left(\dfrac{1(x - 1) - 1}{x - 1}\right)} \qquad \textit{Combine fractions}$$

$$= \frac{\left(\dfrac{2 - 3x}{x}\right)}{\left(\dfrac{x - 2}{x - 1}\right)} \qquad \textit{Simplify}$$

$$= \frac{2 - 3x}{x} \cdot \frac{x - 1}{x - 2} \qquad \textit{Invert and multiply}$$

$$= \frac{(2 - 3x)(x - 1)}{x(x - 2)}, \quad x \neq 1$$

Another way to simplify a compound fraction is to multiply each term in its numerator and denominator by the LCD of all fractions in both its numerator and denominator. Each product is then reduced to obtain a single fraction.

EXAMPLE 9 **Simplifying a Compound Fraction by Multiplying by the LCD**

Use the LCD to simplify the following compound fraction.

$$\frac{\left(\dfrac{1}{x^2} - \dfrac{1}{y^2}\right)}{\left(\dfrac{1}{x} + \dfrac{1}{y}\right)}$$

Solution

For the four fractions in the numerator and denominator, the LCD is x^2y^2. Multiplying each term of the numerator and denominator by this LCD yields the following.

$$\frac{\left(\dfrac{1}{x^2} - \dfrac{1}{y^2}\right)x^2y^2}{\left(\dfrac{1}{x} + \dfrac{1}{y}\right)x^2y^2} = \frac{\left(\dfrac{1}{x^2}\right)x^2y^2 - \left(\dfrac{1}{y^2}\right)x^2y^2}{\left(\dfrac{1}{x}\right)x^2y^2 + \left(\dfrac{1}{y}\right)x^2y^2}$$

$$- \frac{y^2 - x^2}{xy^2 + x^2y} = \frac{(y - x)\cancel{(y + x)}}{xy\cancel{(y + x)}} = \frac{y - x}{xy}$$

The next two examples illustrate some methods for simplifying expressions involving radicals and negative exponents. (These types of expressions occur frequently in calculus.)

EXAMPLE 10 **Simplifying an Expression with Negative Exponents**

Simplify the expression

$$x(1 - 2x)^{-3/2} + (1 - 2x)^{-1/2}.$$

Solution

By rewriting the given expression with positive exponents, we obtain

$$\frac{x}{(1 - 2x)^{3/2}} + \frac{1}{(1 - 2x)^{1/2}}$$

which could then be combined by the LCD method. However, by first removing the common factor with the *smaller exponent*, the process is simpler.

$$x(1 - 2x)^{-3/2} + (1 - 2x)^{-1/2} = (1 - 2x)^{-3/2}[x + (1 - 2x)^{(-1/2)-(-3/2)}]$$

$$= (1 - 2x)^{-3/2}[x + (1 - 2x)^1]$$

$$= \frac{1 - x}{(1 - 2x)^{3/2}}$$

Note that when factoring, we subtract exponents.

EXAMPLE 11   **Simplifying a Compound Fraction: LCD Method**

Simplify the expression

$$\frac{\sqrt{4 - x^2} + \dfrac{x^2}{\sqrt{4 - x^2}}}{4 - x^2}.$$

Solution

$$\frac{\sqrt{4 - x^2} + \dfrac{x^2}{\sqrt{4 - x^2}}}{4 - x^2} = \frac{\sqrt{4 - x^2} + \dfrac{x^2}{\sqrt{4 - x^2}}}{4 - x^2} \cdot \frac{\sqrt{4 - x^2}}{\sqrt{4 - x^2}}$$

$$= \frac{(4 - x^2) + x^2}{(4 - x^2)^{3/2}}$$

$$= \frac{4}{\sqrt{(4 - x^2)^3}}$$

DISCUSSION PROBLEM

Comparing Domains of Two Expressions

Complete the following table by evaluating the expressions

$$\frac{x^2 - 3x + 2}{x - 2} \quad \text{and} \quad x - 1$$

at the indicated values of x. Write a short paragraph describing the equivalence or nonequivalence of the two expressions.

x	-3	-2	-1	0	1	2	3
$\dfrac{x^2 - 3x + 2}{x - 2}$							
$x - 1$							

WARM UP

The following warm-up exercises involve skills that were covered in earlier sections. You will use these skills in the exercise set for this section.

In Exercises 1–10, completely factor the polynomials.

1. $5x^2 - 15x^3$ **2.** $16x^2 - 9$ **3.** $9x^2 - 6x + 1$

4. $9 + 12y + 4y^2$ **5.** $z^2 + 4z + 3$ **6.** $x^2 - 15x + 50$

7. $3 + 8x - 3x^2$ **8.** $3x^2 - 46x + 15$ **9.** $s^3 + s^2 - 4s - 4$

10. $y^3 + 64$

EXERCISES for Section 1.4

In Exercises 1–10, find the domain.

1. $3x^2 - 4x + 7$

2. $2x^2 + 5x - 2$

3. $4x^3 + 5x + 3, \quad x \geq 0$

4. $6x^2 + 7x - 9, \quad x > 0$

5. $\dfrac{1}{x - 2}$

6. $\dfrac{x + 1}{2x + 1}$

7. $\dfrac{x - 1}{x^2 - 4x}$

8. $\dfrac{2x + 1}{x^2 - 9}$

9. $\sqrt{x + 1}$

10. $\dfrac{1}{\sqrt{x + 1}}$

In Exercises 11–16, find the factor that makes the two fractions equivalent.

11. $\dfrac{5}{2x} = \dfrac{5(\rule{1cm}{0.15cm})}{6x^2}$

12. $\dfrac{3}{4} = \dfrac{3(\rule{1cm}{0.15cm})}{4(x + 1)}$

13. $\dfrac{x + 1}{x} = \dfrac{(x + 1)(\rule{1cm}{0.15cm})}{x(x - 2)}$

14. $\dfrac{3y - 4}{y + 1} = \dfrac{(3y - 4)(\rule{1cm}{0.15cm})}{y^2 \quad 1}$

15. $\dfrac{3x}{x - 3} - \dfrac{3x(\rule{1cm}{0.15cm})}{x^2 - x - 6}$

16. $\dfrac{1 - z}{z^2} = \dfrac{(1 - z)(\rule{1cm}{0.15cm})}{z^3 + z^2}$

In Exercises 17–30, write in reduced form.

17. $\dfrac{15x^2}{10x}$

18. $\dfrac{18y^2}{60y^5}$

19. $\dfrac{3xy}{xy + x}$

20. $\dfrac{9x^2 + 9x}{2x + 2}$

21. $\dfrac{x - 5}{10 - 2x}$

22. $\dfrac{x^2 - 25}{5 - x}$

23. $\dfrac{x^3 + 5x^2 + 6x}{x^2 - 4}$

24. $\dfrac{x^2 + 8x - 20}{x^2 + 11x + 10}$

25. $\dfrac{y^2 - 7y + 12}{y^2 + 3y - 18}$

26. $\dfrac{3 - x}{x^2 - 5x + 6}$

27. $\dfrac{2 - x + 2x^2 - x^3}{x - 2}$

28. $\dfrac{x^2 - 9}{x^3 + x^2 - 9x - 9}$

29. $\dfrac{z^3 - 8}{z^2 + 2z + 4}$

30. $\dfrac{y^3 - 2y^2 - 3y}{y^3 + 1}$

In Exercises 31–56, perform the indicated operations and simplify.

31. $\dfrac{5}{x - 1} \cdot \dfrac{x - 1}{25(x - 2)}$

32. $\dfrac{(x + 5)(x - 3)}{x + 2} \cdot \dfrac{1}{(x + 5)(x + 2)}$

33. $\dfrac{(x - 9)(x + 7)}{x + 1} \cdot \dfrac{x}{9 - x}$

34. $\dfrac{x + 13}{x^3(3 - x)} \cdot \dfrac{x(x - 3)}{5}$

35. $\dfrac{r}{r - 1} \cdot \dfrac{r^2 - 1}{r^2}$

36. $\dfrac{4y - 16}{5y + 15} \cdot \dfrac{2y + 6}{4 - y}$

37. $\dfrac{t^2 - t - 6}{t^2 + 6t + 9} \cdot \dfrac{t + 3}{t^2 - 4}$

38. $\dfrac{y^3 - 8}{2y^3} \cdot \dfrac{4y}{y^2 - 5y + 6}$

39. $\dfrac{x^2 + xy - 2y^2}{x^3 + x^2y} \cdot \dfrac{x}{x^2 + 3xy + 2y^2}$

40. $\dfrac{x^3 - 1}{x + 1} \cdot \dfrac{x^2 + 1}{x^2 - 1}$

41. $\dfrac{3(x + y)}{4} \div \dfrac{x + y}{2}$

42. $\dfrac{x + 2}{5(x - 3)} \div \dfrac{x - 2}{5(x - 3)}$

43. $\dfrac{\left(\dfrac{x^2}{(x + 1)^2}\right)}{\left(\dfrac{x}{(x + 1)^3}\right)}$

44. $\dfrac{\left(\dfrac{x^2 - 1}{x}\right)}{\left(\dfrac{(x - 1)^2}{x}\right)}$

45. $\dfrac{5}{x - 1} + \dfrac{x}{x - 1}$

46. $\dfrac{2x - 1}{x + 3} + \dfrac{1 - x}{x + 3}$

47. $6 - \dfrac{5}{x + 3}$

48. $\dfrac{3}{x - 1} - 5$

49. $\dfrac{3}{x - 2} + \dfrac{5}{2 - x}$

50. $\dfrac{2x}{x - 5} - \dfrac{5}{5 - x}$

51. $\dfrac{2}{x^2 - 4} - \dfrac{1}{x^2 - 3x + 2}$

52. $\dfrac{x}{x^2 + x - 2} - \dfrac{1}{x + 2}$

53. $\dfrac{1}{x^2 - x - 2} - \dfrac{x}{x^2 - 5x + 6}$

54. $\dfrac{2}{x^2 - x - 2} + \dfrac{10}{x^2 + 2x - 8}$

55. $-\dfrac{1}{x} + \dfrac{2}{x^2 + 1} + \dfrac{1}{x^3 + x}$

56. $\dfrac{2}{x + 1} + \dfrac{2}{x - 1} + \dfrac{1}{x^2 - 1}$

In Exercises 57–70, simplify the compound fraction.

57. $\dfrac{\left(\dfrac{x}{2} - 1\right)}{(x - 2)}$

58. $\dfrac{(x - 4)}{\left(\dfrac{x}{4} - \dfrac{4}{x}\right)}$

59. $\dfrac{\left(\dfrac{1}{x} - \dfrac{1}{x + 1}\right)}{\left(\dfrac{1}{x + 1}\right)}$

60. $\dfrac{\left(\dfrac{5}{y} - \dfrac{6}{2y + 1}\right)}{\left(\dfrac{5}{y} + 4\right)}$

61. $\dfrac{\left(\dfrac{x + 3}{x - 3}\right)^2}{\dfrac{1}{x + 3} + \dfrac{1}{x - 3}}$

62. $\dfrac{\left(\dfrac{x + 4}{x + 5} - \dfrac{x}{x + 1}\right)}{4}$

63. $\dfrac{\left(\dfrac{1}{(x + h)^2} - \dfrac{1}{x^2}\right)}{h}$

64. $\dfrac{\left(\dfrac{x + h}{x + h + 1} - \dfrac{x}{x + 1}\right)}{h}$

65. $\dfrac{\left(\sqrt{x} - \dfrac{1}{2\sqrt{x}}\right)}{\sqrt{x}}$

66. $\dfrac{3x^{1/3} - x^{-2/3}}{3x^{-2/3}}$

67. $\dfrac{\left(\dfrac{t^2}{\sqrt{t^2 + 1}} - \sqrt{t^2 + 1}\right)}{t^2}$

68. $\dfrac{-x^3(1 - x^2)^{-1/2} - 2x(1 - x^2)^{1/2}}{x^4}$

69. $\dfrac{x(x + 1)^{-3/4} - (x + 1)^{1/4}}{x^2}$

70. $\dfrac{(2x + 1)^{1/3} - \dfrac{4x}{3(2x + 1)^{2/3}}}{(2x + 1)^{2/3}}$

In Exercises 71 and 72, rationalize the numerator.

71. $\dfrac{\sqrt{x + 2} - \sqrt{x}}{2}$

72. $\dfrac{\sqrt{z - 3} - \sqrt{z}}{3}$

73. *Rate*   A photocopier copies at a rate of 16 pages per minute.
(a) Find the time required to copy one page.
(b) Find the time required to copy x pages.
(c) Find the time required to copy 60 pages.

74. *Rate*   After two people work together for t hours on a common task, the fractional part of the job done by each of the two workers is $t/3$ and $t/5$. What fractional part of the task has been completed?

75. *Average*   Find the average of $x/3$ and $2x/5$.

76. *Partition into Equal Parts*   Find three real numbers that divide the real number line between $x/3$ and $3x/4$ into four equal parts.

Monthly Payment   In Exercises 77 and 78, use the following formula, which gives the approximate annual percentage rate r of a monthly installment loan

$$r = \dfrac{\left(\dfrac{24(NM - P)}{N}\right)}{\left(P + \dfrac{NM}{12}\right)}$$

where N is the total number of payments, M is the monthly payment, and P is the amount financed.

77. (a) Approximate the annual percentage rate for a four-year car loan of $15,000 that has monthly payments of $400.
(b) Simplify the expression for the annual percentage rate r, and then rework part (a).

78. (a) Approximate the annual percentage rate for a five-year car loan of $18,000 that has monthly payments of $400.

    (b) Simplify the expression for the annual percentage rate r, and then rework part (a).

79. *Electronics* When two resistors are connected in parallel, the total resistance is given by

$$\frac{1}{\frac{1}{R_1} + \frac{1}{R_2}}.$$

Simplify this compound fraction.

80. *Refrigeration* When food (at room temperature) is placed in a refrigerator, the time required for the food to cool depends on the amount of food, the air circulation in the refrigerator, the original temperature of the food, and the temperature of the refrigerator. Consider the following model, which gives the temperature of food that is 75°F and is placed in a 40°F refrigerator

$$T = 10\left(\frac{4t^2 + 16t + 75}{t^2 + 4t + 10}\right)$$

where T is the temperature in degrees Fahrenheit and t is the time in hours. Sketch a bar graph showing the temperature of the food when $t = 0, 1, 2, 3, 4,$ and 5 hours.

1.5 Solving Equations

Equations and Solutions of Equations / Linear Equations / Quadratic Equations / Polynomial Equations of Higher Degree / Equations Involving Radicals / Equations Involving Absolute Value

Equations and Solutions of Equations

In the first four sections of this chapter, we reviewed the fundamentals of algebra. We now *use* these fundamentals to solve problems that can be expressed in the form of equations or inequalities. Such problems are common in science, business, industry, and government.

    An **equation** is a statement that the two algebraic expressions are equal. For example, $3x - 5 = 7$, $x^2 - x - 6 = 0$, and $\sqrt{2x} = 4$ are equations. To **solve** an equation in x means that you find all values of x for which the equation is true. Such values are **solutions.** For instance, $x = 4$ is a solution of the equation $3x - 5 = 7$, because $3(4) - 5 = 7$ is a true statement.

    The solutions of an equation depend upon the kinds of numbers being considered. For instance, in the set of rational numbers, the equation $x^2 = 10$ has no solution because there is no rational number whose square is 10. However, in the set of real numbers this equation has two solutions, $\sqrt{10}$ and $-\sqrt{10}$, because $(\sqrt{10})^2 = 10$ and $(-\sqrt{10})^2 = 10$.

    An equation that is true for *every* real number in the domain of the variable is an **identity.** For example, $x^2 - 9 = (x + 3)(x - 3)$ is an identity because it is a true statement for any real value of x, and $x/3x^2 = 1/3x$ where $x \neq 0$ is an identity because it is true for any nonzero real value of x.

    An equation that is true for just *some* (or even none) of the real numbers in the domain of the variable is a **conditional equation.** For example, the equation $x^2 - 9 = 0$ is conditional because $x = 3$ and $x = -3$ are the only values in the domain that satisfy the equation. Learning to solve conditional equations is the primary focus of this chapter.

    To solve a conditional equation in x we attempt to isolate x on one side of the equation by a sequence of **equivalent** (and usually simpler) equations, each having the same solution(s) as the original equation.

GENERATING EQUIVALENT EQUATIONS

An equation can be transformed into an *equivalent equation* by one or more of the following steps.

	Given Equation	*Equivalent Equation*
1. Remove symbols of grouping, combine like terms, or reduce fractions on one or both sides of the equation.	$2x - x = 4$	$x = 4$
2. Add (or subtract) the same quantity to *both* sides of the equation.	$x + 1 = 6$	$x = 5$
3. Multiply (or divide) *both* sides of the equation by the same *nonzero* quantity.	$2x = 6$	$x = 3$
4. Interchange the two sides of the equation.	$2 = x$	$x = 2$

Linear Equations

The most common type of conditional equation is a linear equation. A **linear equation** in one variable x is an equation that can be written in the standard form

$$ax + b = 0$$

where a and b are real numbers with $a \neq 0$.

EXAMPLE 1   Solving a Linear Equation

$6(x - 1) + 4 = 7x + 1$	*Given equation*
$6x - 6 + 4 = 7x + 1$	*Remove parentheses*
$6x - 2 = 7x + 1$	*Simplify*
$-x = 3$	*Add 2 and subtract 7x*
$x = -3$	*Multiply by −1*

Check

Check this solution by substituting in the original equation.

$6(x - 1) + 4 = 7x + 1$	*Given equation*
$6(-3 - 1) + 4 \overset{?}{=} 7(-3) + 1$	*Replace x by −3*
$6(-4) + 4 \overset{?}{=} -21 + 1$	*Add fractions*
$-24 + 4 \overset{?}{=} -21 + 1$	
$-20 = -20$	*Solution checks*

To solve an equation involving fractional expressions, we find the least common denominator of all terms in the equation and multiply every term by this LCD. This procedure clears the equation of fractions.

EXAMPLE 2 Solving an Equation Involving Fractional Expressions

$$\frac{x}{3} + \frac{3x}{4} = 2 \qquad \qquad \textit{Given equation}$$

$$(12)\frac{x}{3} + (12)\frac{3x}{4} = (12)2 \qquad \qquad \textit{Multiply by the LCD}$$

$$4x + 9x = 24 \qquad \qquad \textit{Reduce and multiply}$$

$$13x = 24 \qquad \qquad \textit{Combine like terms}$$

$$x = \frac{24}{13} \qquad \qquad \textit{Divide by 13}$$

The equation has one solution: $\frac{24}{13}$. Check this solution in the original equation. ◀

When multiplying or dividing an equation by a *variable* quantity, it is possible to introduce an **extraneous** solution that does not satisfy the original equation.

EXAMPLE 3 An Equation with an Extraneous Solution

Solve the equation for x.

$$\frac{1}{x - 2} = \frac{3}{x + 2} - \frac{6x}{x^2 - 4}$$

Solution

The LCD is $x^2 - 4 = (x + 2)(x - 2)$. Multiply every term by this LCD and reduce.

$$\frac{1}{x - 2}(x + 2)(x - 2) = \frac{3}{x + 2}(x + 2)(x - 2) - \frac{6x}{x^2 - 4}(x + 2)(x - 2)$$

$$x + 2 = 3(x - 2) - 6x, \quad x \neq \pm 2$$

$$x + 2 = 3x - 6 - 6x$$

$$4x = -8$$

$$x = -2$$

We know that in the original equation, $x = -2$ yields a denominator of zero. Therefore, $x = -2$ is an extraneous solution, and the equation has *no solution*. ◀

Quadratic Equations

A **quadratic equation** in x is an equation that can be written in the standard form

$$ax^2 + bx + c = 0$$

where a, b, and c are real numbers with $a \neq 0$. A quadratic equation in x is also known as a **second-degree polynomial equation in x.**

You should be familiar with the following four methods for solving quadratic equations.

SOLVING A QUADRATIC EQUATION

Method	Example
Factoring	
If $ab = 0$, then $a = 0$ or $b = 0$.	$x^2 - x - 6 = 0$
	$(x - 3)(x + 2) = 0$
	$x - 3 = 0 \;\rightarrow\; x = 3$
	$x + 2 = 0 \;\rightarrow\; x = -2$
Square Root Principle	
If $u^2 = c$, where $c > 0$,	$(x + 3)^2 = 16$
then $u = \pm\sqrt{c}$.	$x + 3 = \pm 4$
	$x = -3 \pm 4$
	$x = 1 \;\; \text{or} \;\; -7$
Completing the Square	
If $x^2 + bx = c$, then	$x^2 - 6x = 5$
$x^2 + bx + \left(\dfrac{b}{2}\right)^2 = c + \left(\dfrac{b}{2}\right)^2$	$x^2 - 6x + 3^2 = 5 + 3^2$
	$(x + 3)^2 = 14$
$\left(x + \dfrac{b}{2}\right)^2 = c + \dfrac{b^2}{4}$	$x + 3 = \pm\sqrt{14}$
	$x = -3 \pm \sqrt{14}$
Quadratic Formula	
If $ax^2 + bx + c = 0$, then	$2x^2 + 3x - 1 = 0$
$x = \dfrac{-b \pm \sqrt{b^2 - 4ac}}{2a}$	$x = \dfrac{-3 \pm \sqrt{3^2 - 4(2)(-1)}}{2(2)}$
	$= \dfrac{-3 \pm \sqrt{17}}{4}$

REMARK The Quadratic Formula can be derived by completing the square with the general form $ax^2 + bx + c = 0$ (see Exercise 96).

EXAMPLE 4   Solving a Quadratic Equation by Factoring

Solve the following quadratic equations.

a. $6x^2 = 3x$ **b.** $9x^2 - 6x + 1 = 0$

Solution

a.

$6x^2 = 3x$	*Given equation*
$6x^2 - 3x = 0$	*Standard form*
$3x(2x - 1) = 0$	*Factored form*
$3x = 0 \quad \rightarrow \quad x = 0$	*Set 1st factor equal to 0*
$2x - 1 = 0 \quad \rightarrow \quad x = \dfrac{1}{2}$	*Set 2nd factor equal to 0*

b.

$9x^2 - 6x + 1 = 0$	*Standard form*
$(3x - 1)^2 = 0$	*Factored form*
$3x - 1 = 0$	*Set repeated factor equal to 0*
$x - \dfrac{1}{3}$	*Solution*

REMARK Throughout the text, when you are finding solutions of equations, be sure to check your solutions in the *original* equations.

EXAMPLE 5   Solving a Quadratic Equation by Extracting Square Roots

Solve the following quadratic equations.

a. $4x^2 = 12$ **b.** $(x - 2)^2 = 5$

Solution

a. $4x^2 = 12$	*Given equation*
$x^2 = 3$	*Divide both sides by 4*
$x = \pm\sqrt{3}$	*Extract square roots*
b. $(x - 2)^2 = 5$	*Given equation*
$x - 2 = \pm\sqrt{5}$	*Extract square roots*
$x = 2 \pm \sqrt{5}$	*Add 2 to both sides*

EXAMPLE 6   Completing the Square

$x^2 - 6x + 2 = 0$	*Given equation*
$x^2 - 6x = -2$	*Subtract 2 from both sides*
$x^2 - \underbrace{6x + 3^2}_{(\text{half})^2} = -2 + 3^2$	*Add 3^2 to both sides*

$$x^2 - 6x + 9 = 7 \qquad \textit{Simplify}$$
$$(x - 3)^2 = 7 \qquad \textit{Perfect square trinomial}$$
$$x - 3 = \pm\sqrt{7} \qquad \textit{Extract square roots}$$
$$x = 3 \pm \sqrt{7} \qquad \textit{Solutions}$$

If the leading coefficient of a quadratic is not 1, you must divide both sides of the equation by this coefficient *before* completing the square. For instance, to complete the square for the equation $3x^2 - 4x = 5$, we first divide by 3 to obtain

$$x^2 - \frac{4}{3}x = \frac{5}{3}.$$

We then complete the square in the manner shown in Example 6.

EXAMPLE 7   Using the Quadratic Formula: Two Distinct Solutions

Use the Quadratic Formula to solve $x^2 + 3x = 9$.

Solution

To begin, write the equation in standard form, $ax^2 + bx + c = 0$. Then, determine the values of a, b, and c. Finally, substitute these values into the Quadratic Formula to obtain the solutions.

$$x^2 + 3x = 9 \qquad \textit{Given equation}$$
$$x^2 + 3x - 9 = 0 \qquad \textit{Standard form with } a = 1, b = 3, c = -9$$
$$x = \frac{-b \pm \sqrt{b^2 - 4ac}}{2a} \qquad \textit{Quadratic Formula}$$
$$x = \frac{-3 \pm \sqrt{(3)^2 - 4(1)(-9)}}{2(1)} \qquad \textit{Substitute}$$
$$x = \frac{-3 \pm \sqrt{45}}{2}$$
$$x = \frac{-3 \pm 3\sqrt{5}}{2} \qquad \textit{Solutions}$$

Therefore, the equation has two solutions:

$$x = \frac{-3 + 3\sqrt{5}}{2} \quad \text{and} \quad x = \frac{-3 - 3\sqrt{5}}{2}.$$

EXAMPLE 8   Using the Quadratic Formula: One Repeated Solution

Use the Quadratic Formula to solve the following equation.

$$8x^2 - 24x + 18 = 0$$

Solution

Note that this equation has a common factor of 2. To simplify things, first divide both sides of the equation by 2.

$8x^2 - 24x + 18 = 0$	*Common factor of 2*
$4x^2 - 12x + 9 = 0$	*Standard form with* $a = 4, b = -12, c = 9$

$x = \dfrac{-b \pm \sqrt{b^2 - 4ac}}{2a}$	*Quadratic Formula*
$x = \dfrac{-(-12) \pm \sqrt{(-12)^2 - 4(4)(9)}}{2(4)}$	*Substitute*
$x = \dfrac{12 \pm \sqrt{0}}{8} \quad \dfrac{3}{2}$	*Repeated solution*

Therefore, this quadratic equation has one repeated solution: $\frac{3}{2}$. Note that we could have used factoring to obtain the same result.   ◢

Polynomial Equations of Higher Degree

The methods used to solve quadratic equations can sometimes be extended to polynomial equations of higher degree, as shown in the next two examples.

EXAMPLE 9   Solving an Equation of Quadratic Type

$x^4 - 3x^2 + 2 = 0$	*Given equation*
$(x^2)^2 - 3x^2 + 2 = 0$	*Quadratic in* x^2
$(x^2 - 2)(x^2 - 1) = 0$	*Factor*
$x^2 - 2 = 0 \quad \rightarrow \quad x = \pm\sqrt{2}$	*Set 1st factor equal to 0*
$x^2 - 1 = 0 \quad \rightarrow \quad x = \pm 1$	*Set 2nd factor equal to 0*

◢

EXAMPLE 10   Solving a Polynomial Equation by Factoring

$x^3 - 3x^2 - 3x + 9 = 0$	*Given equation*
$x^2(x - 3) - 3(x - 3) = 0$	*Group terms*
$(x - 3)(x^2 - 3) = 0$	*Factor by grouping*
$x - 3 = 0 \quad \rightarrow \quad x = 3$	*Set 1st factor equal to 0*
$x^2 - 3 = 0 \quad \rightarrow \quad x = \pm\sqrt{3}$	*Set 2nd factor equal to 0*

◢

Equations Involving Radicals

An equation involving a radical expression can often be cleared of radicals by raising both sides of the equation to an appropriate power. This is demonstrated in the next example. When using this procedure, remember that it can introduce extraneous solutions—so be sure to check each solution in the original equation.

EXAMPLE 11   An Equation Involving a Radical

$$\sqrt{2x + 7} - x = 2 \qquad \text{\textit{Given equation}}$$
$$\sqrt{2x + 7} = x + 2 \qquad \text{\textit{Add x to both sides}}$$
$$2x + 7 = x^2 + 4x + 4 \qquad \text{\textit{Square both sides}}$$
$$0 = x^2 + 2x - 3 \qquad \text{\textit{Standard form}}$$
$$0 = (x + 3)(x - 1) \qquad \text{\textit{Factor}}$$
$$x + 3 = 0 \ \rightarrow \ x = -3 \qquad \text{\textit{Set 1st factor equal to 0}}$$
$$x - 1 = 0 \ \rightarrow \ x = 1 \qquad \text{\textit{Set 2nd factor equal to 0}}$$

By substituting these two x-values in the original equation, we find that $x = -3$ is *not* a solution. Thus, the given equation has only one solution: 1. ◢

For equations with two or more radicals, it may be necessary to repeat the "isolate a radical and square both sides" routine demonstrated in the preceding example. Remember to include the middle term when squaring a binomial.

EXAMPLE 12   An Equation Involving Two Radicals

$$\sqrt{2x + 6} - \sqrt{x + 4} = 1 \qquad \text{\textit{Given equation}}$$
$$\sqrt{2x + 6} = 1 + \sqrt{x + 4} \qquad \text{\textit{Isolate radical}}$$
$$2x + 6 = 1 + 2\sqrt{x + 4} + (x + 4) \qquad \text{\textit{Square both sides}}$$
$$x + 1 = 2\sqrt{x + 4} \qquad \text{\textit{Isolate radical}}$$
$$x^2 + 2x + 1 = 4(x + 4) \qquad \text{\textit{Square both sides}}$$
$$x^2 - 2x - 15 = 0 \qquad \text{\textit{Standard form}}$$
$$(x - 5)(x + 3) = 0 \qquad \text{\textit{Factor}}$$
$$x - 5 = 0 \ \rightarrow \ x = 5 \qquad \text{\textit{Set 1st factor equal to 0}}$$
$$x + 3 = 0 \ \rightarrow \ x = -3 \qquad \text{\textit{Set 2nd factor equal to 0}}$$

By substituting these two x-values in the original equation we see that $x = -3$ does not satisfy the given equation. Thus, the equation has only one solution: 5. ◢

Equations Involving Absolute Value

To solve an equation involving an absolute value, consider the fact that the expression inside the absolute value can be positive or negative. This consideration results in *two* separate equations, each of which must be solved. For instance, the equation

$$|x - 2| = 3$$

results in the two equations

$$x - 2 = 3 \quad \text{and} \quad -(x - 2) = 3$$

which implies that the equation has two solutions: 5 and -1.

EXAMPLE 13   An Equation Involving Absolute Value

Solve $|x^2 - 3x| = -4x + 6$.

Solution

Since the variable expression inside the absolute value signs can be positive or negative, we must solve two equations.

First Equation

$x^2 - 3x = -4x + 6$	*Use positive expression*
$x^2 + x - 6 = 0$	*Standard form*
$(x + 3)(x - 2) = 0$	*Factor*
$x + 3 = 0 \quad \rightarrow \quad x = -3$	*Set 1st factor equal to 0*
$x - 2 = 0 \quad \rightarrow \quad x = 2$	*Set 2nd factor equal to 0*

Second Equation

$-(x^2 - 3x) = -4x + 6$	*Use negative expression*
$x^2 - 7x + 6 = 0$	*Standard form*
$(x - 1)(x - 6) = 0$	*Factor*
$x - 1 = 0 \quad \rightarrow \quad x = 1$	*Set 1st factor equal to 0*
$x - 6 = 0 \quad \rightarrow \quad x = 6$	*Set 2nd factor equal to 0*

Check

$|(-3)^2 - 3(-3)| = -4(-3) + 6$	*-3 checks*
$|2^2 - 3(2)| \neq -4(2) + 6$	*2 does not check*
$|1^2 - 3(1)| = -4(1) + 6$	*1 checks*
$|6^2 - 3(6)| \neq -4(6) + 6$	*6 does not check*

Thus, the equation has only two solutions: -3 and 1.

DISCUSSION
PROBLEM

A
Mathematical
Fallacy

A mathematical **fallacy** is an argument that appears to prove something that we know is incorrect. For instance, the following argument appears to prove that $1 = 0$. Can you find the error in this argument?

$$x = 1 \qquad \textit{Given equation}$$

$$x - 1 = 0 \qquad \textit{Subtract 1 from both sides}$$

$$x(x - 1) = 0 \qquad \textit{Multiply both sides by } x$$

$$\frac{x(x - 1)}{x - 1} = \frac{0}{x - 1} \qquad \textit{Divide both sides by } x - 1$$

$$\frac{x\cancel{(x - 1)}}{\cancel{x - 1}} = 0 \qquad \textit{Reduce}$$

$$x = 0 \qquad \textit{Solution}$$

WARM UP

The following warm-up exercises involve skills that were covered in earlier sections. You will use these skills in the exercise set for this section.

In Exercises 1–10, perform the indicated operations and simplify your answer.

1. $(2x - 4) - (5x + 6)$

2. $(3x - 5) + (2x - 7)$

3. $2(x + 1) - (x + 2)$

4. $-3(2x - 4) + 7(x + 2)$

5. $\dfrac{x}{3} + \dfrac{x}{5}$

6. $x - \dfrac{x}{4}$

7. $\dfrac{1}{x + 1} - \dfrac{1}{x}$

8. $\dfrac{2}{x} + \dfrac{3}{x}$

9. $\dfrac{4}{x} + \dfrac{3}{x - 2}$

10. $\dfrac{1}{x + 1} - \dfrac{1}{x - 1}$

EXERCISES for Section 1.5

In Exercises 1–6, determine whether the equation is an identity or a conditional equation.

1. $2(x - 1) = 2x - 2$ **2.** $3(x + 2) = 5x + 4$

3. $-6(x - 3) + 5 = -2x + 10$

4. $3(x + 2) - 5 = 3x + 1$

5. $3x^2 - 8x + 5 = (x - 4)^2 - 11$

6. $x^2 + 2(3x - 2) = x^2 + 6x - 4$

In Exercises 7–12, determine whether the value of x is a solution of the equation.

Equation	Values	
7. $5x - 3 = 3x + 5$	(a) $x = 0$	(b) $x = -5$
	(c) $x = 4$	(d) $x = 10$
8. $7 - 3x = 5x - 17$	(a) $x = -3$	(b) $x = 0$
	(c) $x = 8$	(d) $x = 3$
9. $3x^2 + 2x - 5$	(a) $x = -3$	(b) $x = 1$
$= 2x^2 - 2$	(c) $x = 4$	(d) $x = -5$
10. $5x^3 + 2x - 3$	(a) $x = 2$	(b) $x = -2$
$= 4x^3 + 2x - 11$	(c) $x = 0$	(d) $x = 10$
11. $\dfrac{5}{2x} - \dfrac{4}{x} - 3$	(a) $x = -\frac{1}{2}$	(b) $x = 4$
	(c) $x = 0$	(d) $x = \frac{1}{4}$
12. $\sqrt[3]{x - 8} = 3$	(a) $x = 2$	(b) $x = -5$
	(c) $x = 35$	(d) $x = 8$

In Exercises 13–34, solve the equation (if possible) and check your answer.

13. $2(x + 5) - 7 = 3(x - 2)$

14. $2(13t - 15) + 3(t - 19) = 0$

15. $\dfrac{5x}{4} + \dfrac{1}{2} = x - \dfrac{1}{2}$ **16.** $\dfrac{x}{5} - \dfrac{x}{2} = 3$

17. $0.25x + 0.75(10 - x) = 3$

18. $0.60x + 0.40(100 - x) = 50$

19. $x + 8 = 2(x - 2) - x$ **20.** $3(x + 3) = 3(1 - x) - 1$

21. $\dfrac{100 - 4u}{3} = \dfrac{5u + 6}{4} + 6$

22. $\dfrac{17 + y}{y} + \dfrac{32 + y}{y} = 100$

23. $\dfrac{5x - 4}{5x + 4} = \dfrac{2}{3}$

24. $\dfrac{10x + 3}{5x + 6} = \dfrac{1}{2}$

25. $10 - \dfrac{13}{x} = 4 + \dfrac{5}{x}$

26. $\dfrac{15}{x} - 4 = \dfrac{6}{x} + 3$

27. $\dfrac{1}{x - 3} + \dfrac{1}{x + 3} = \dfrac{10}{x^2 - 9}$

28. $\dfrac{1}{x - 2} + \dfrac{3}{x + 3} = \dfrac{4}{x^2 + x - 6}$

29. $\dfrac{7}{2x + 1} - \dfrac{8x}{2x - 1} = -4$

30. $\dfrac{4}{u - 1} + \dfrac{6}{3u + 1} = \dfrac{15}{3u + 1}$

31. $(x + 2)^2 + 5 = (x + 3)^2$

32. $(x + 1)^2 + 2(x - 2) = (x + 1)(x - 2)$

33. $4 - 2(x - 2b) = ax + 3$

34. $5 + ax = 12 - bx$

In Exercises 35–42, solve the quadratic equation by factoring.

35. $6x^2 + 3x = 0$ **36.** $9x^2 - 1 = 0$

37. $x^2 - 2x - 8 = 0$ **38.** $x^2 + 10x + 25 = 0$

39. $16x^2 + 56x + 49 = 0$ **40.** $3 + 5x - 2x^2 = 0$

41. $2x^2 = 19x + 33$ **42.** $(x + a)^2 - b^2 = 0$

In Exercises 43–46, solve the equation by extracting square roots.

43. $3x^2 = 36$ **44.** $9x^2 = 25$

45. $(x - 12)^2 = 18$ **46.** $(x + 13)^2 = 21$

In Exercises 47–50, solve the quadratic equation by completing the square.

47. $x^2 + 4x - 32 = 0$ **48.** $x^2 - 2x - 3 = 0$

49. $9x^2 - 18x + 3 = 0$ **50.** $9x^2 - 12x - 14 = 0$

In Exercises 51–64, use the Quadratic Formula to solve the equation.

51. $2x^2 + x - 1 = 0$ **52.** $2x^2 - x - 1 = 0$

53. $16x^2 + 8x - 3 = 0$ **54.** $25x^2 - 20x + 3 = 0$

55. $2 + 2x - x^2 = 0$ **56.** $x^2 - 10x + 22 = 0$

57. $12x - 9x^2 = -3$ **58.** $16x^2 + 22 = 40x$

59. $4x^2 + 4x = 7$ **60.** $16x^2 - 40x + 5 = 0$

61. $(y - 5)^2 = 2y$ **62.** $(z + 6)^2 = -2z$

63. $\dfrac{1}{x} - \dfrac{1}{x + 1} = 3$ **64.** $\dfrac{x}{x^2 - 4} + \dfrac{1}{x + 2} = 3$

In Exercises 65–80, find all solutions of the equation. Check your answers in the original equation.

65. $x^3 - 2x^2 - 3x = 0$

66. $2x^4 - 15x^3 + 18x^2 = 0$

67. $x^3 - 3x^2 - x + 3 = 0$

68. $x^3 + 2x^2 + 3x + 6 = 0$

69. $x^4 + 5x^2 - 36 = 0$

70. $36t^4 + 29t^2 - 7 = 0$

71. $\sqrt{x + 1} - 3x = 1$

72. $\sqrt{x + 5} = \sqrt{x - 5}$

73. $\sqrt{x} + \sqrt{x - 20} = 10$

74. $\sqrt{x} - \sqrt{x - 5} = 1$

75. $2\sqrt{x + 1} - \sqrt{2x + 3} = 1$

76. $3\sqrt{x} - \dfrac{4}{\sqrt{x}} = 4$

77. $|2x - 1| = 5$

78. $|3x + 2| = 7$

79. $|x| = x^2 + x - 3$

80. $|x - 10| = x^2 - 10x$

In Exercises 81 and 82, complete the square on the quadratic portion of the algebraic expression.

81. $\dfrac{1}{x^2 - 4x - 12}$

82. $\dfrac{4}{4x^2 + 4x - 3}$

In Exercises 83 and 84, use your calculator to solve the given equation for x and round your answer to three decimal places.

83. $0.275x + 0.725(500 - x) = 300$

84. $5.1x^2 - 1.7x - 3.2 = 0$

Negative Income Tax   In Exercises 85 and 86, use the following information about a possible negative income tax for a family of two adults and two children. The plan would guarantee the poor a minimum income while encouraging families to increase their private income (see figure).

Family's earned income: $I = x$

Government payment: $G = 8000 - \frac{1}{2}x, \quad 0 \le x \le 16{,}000$

Spendable income: $S = I + G$

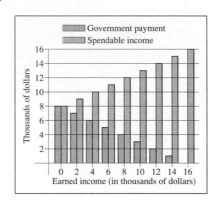

Figure for 85 and 86

85. The spendable income is \$11,800. Find the earned income x.

86. The spendable income is \$10,500. Find the government payment G.

87. *Depth of a Submarine*   The sonar of a navy cruiser detects a submarine that is 3000 feet from the cruiser. The angle between the water level and the submarine is $45°$ (see figure). How deep is the submarine?

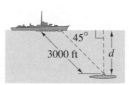

Figure for 87

88. *Dimensions of a Corral*   A rancher has 200 feet of fencing to enclose two adjacent rectangular corrals (see figure). Find the dimensions that would create an enclosed area of 1400 square feet.

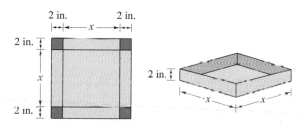

$4x + 3y = 200$

Figure for 88

89. *Dimensions of a Box*   An open box is to be made from a square piece of material by cutting 2-inch squares from each corner and turning up the sides (see figure). The volume of the finished box is to be 200 cubic inches. Find the size of the original piece of material.

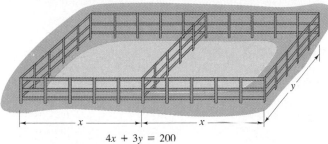

2 in.   2 in.

2 in.

x

2 in.

2 in.

Figure for 89

90. *Sharing the Cost*   A college charters a bus for $1700 to take a group of students to a museum. When six more students join the trip, the cost per student drops by $7.50. How many students were in the original group?

91. *Airspeed*   An airline runs a commuter flight between two cities that are 720 miles apart. If the average speed of the plane is increased by 40 miles per hour, the travel time is decreased by 12 minutes. What speed is required to obtain this decrease in travel time?

92. *Market Research*   The demand equation for a certain product is given by

$$p = 40 - \sqrt{0.01x + 1}$$

where x is the number of units demanded per day and p is the price per unit. Find the demand if the price is set at $37.55.

93. *Cost*   The cost for producing x units of a product is given by

$$C = 0.125x^2 + 20x + 5000.$$

Determine the number of units produced if the cost is $14,000.

94. *Surface Area*   The surface area of a cone is $S = \pi r \sqrt{r^2 + h^2}$. Solve this equation for h.

95. *Power Line*   A power station is on one side of a river that is $\frac{1}{2}$ mile wide. A factory is 6 miles downstream on the other side of the river. It costs $18 per foot to run power lines overland and $24 per foot to run them underwater. The total cost of the project is $616,877.27. Find the length x as labeled in the figure.

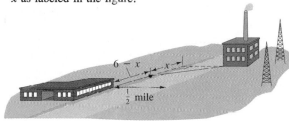

$6 - x$ x

$\frac{1}{2}$ mile

Figure for 95

96. Complete the square of the general quadratic equation $ax^2 + bx + c = 0$ to derive the Quadratic Formula

$$x = \frac{-b \pm \sqrt{b^2 - 4ac}}{2a}.$$

SOLVING

A Numerical Approach to Finding a Falling Time

So far in this chapter, you have studied algebraic methods for solving equations. For many problems, you can gain further insight by using a numerical approach either instead of, or in addition to, an algebraic approach.

EXAMPLE 1   Finding the Falling Time for an Object

At 9:55 A.M. on Saturday, July 28, 1945, a terrible airplane accident occurred. A B-25 bomber crashed into the 78th and 79th floors of the Empire State Building in New York City. Hundreds of pieces of debris fell 975 feet to the streets below. How much time after hearing the crash did the people on the street have to get out of the way?

Solution

Assume that the debris *dropped* from a height of 975 feet. Using an initial velocity of $v_0 = 0$ and an initial height of $s_0 = 0$, you can write the following model for the height (in feet) of the falling debris: $s = -16t^2 + 975$. The table gives the heights at different times.

Time, t	0	1	2	3	4	5	6	7	7.8
Height, s	975	959	911	831	719	575	399	191	2

From the table, you can see that the debris took about 8 seconds to hit the ground. Because it would have taken about 1 second for the sound of the crash to reach the ground (sound travels at about 1100 feet per second), you can conclude that people had about 7 seconds to get out of the way of the falling debris.

This conclusion was reached numerically by constructing a table. You can reach the same conclusion algebraically by solving the equation $s = -16t^2 + 975$ for the time that gives a height of $s = 0$ in feet.

Fourteen people were killed in this accident. The toll would have been greater, but it was a drizzly Saturday morning—most of the building's 15,000 office workers were at home. (Reproduced from *Great Disasters*, © 1989, The Reader's Digest Association, Inc. Used by permission. Illustration by Dennis Lyall.)

$-16t^2 + 975 = s$	*Falling object model*
$-16t^2 + 975 = 0$	*Substitute 0 for s*
$975 = 16t^2$	*Add $16t^2$ to both sides*
$\dfrac{975}{16} = t^2$	*Divide both sides by 16*
$\sqrt{\dfrac{975}{16}} = t$	*Find the positive square root*
$7.8 \approx t$	*Use a calculator*

Once you have created a mathematical model and used it to solve a real-life problem, try rethinking your model to check how accurately it represents the real-life situation.

EXAMPLE 2　Adding Sophistication to a Model

In Example 1, because the airplane accident was accompanied by an explosion, some of the debris was most likely *propelled* downward. How does this consideration affect the time the people on the street had to get out of the way of the falling debris?

Solution

You could start by assuming that some of the debris was propelled straight down with initial speed of about 100 feet per second. Using $v_0 = -100$ and $s_0 = 975$, you can obtain the model $s = -16t^2 - 100t + 975$. The table gives the heights of the debris at several times.

Time, t	0	1	2	3	4	5	5.3
Height, s	975	859	711	531	319	75	-4.44

With this model, note that the falling time has decreased considerably. Again figuring that it took about 1 second to hear the crash, you can conclude that the people on the street had only about 4.3 seconds to get out of the way.

◢

EXERCISES

1. *Real or False Accuracy?*　In Example 2, suppose you solved the equation

   $$0 = -16t^2 - 100t + 975$$

   algebraically to obtain

   $$t = \frac{25 - 5\sqrt{181}}{-8} \approx 5.284.$$

   Because sound traveling at 1100 feet per second takes 0.886 second to travel 975 feet, you could reason that the people had $5.284 - 0.886 = 4.398$ seconds to get out of the way. This solution appears to be more accurate than that obtained in Example 2. Is it?

2. *Exploration*　In Example 2, how long would the people on the street have had to get out of the way if some of the debris had been propelled with an initial velocity of 200 feet per second?

3. *Working Backward*　In the actual accident, all of the casualties were people who were in the building. What does this suggest about the initial velocity of any of the debris that was propelled downward?

4. *Exploration*　Use the falling object model and table given in Example 1.
   (a) What was the average speed of the debris during its first second of fall?
   (b) Was the debris falling faster during its next second of fall? Explain.
   (c) Calculate the height of the debris after 7.7 seconds of fall.
   (d) Use the result of part (c) to approximate the terminal speed of the debris.

5. Use the model given in Example 2 to approximate the terminal speed of the debris. Is the terminal speed given by this model greater than the terminal speed given by the model in Example 1?

6. In Example 2, we assumed that some of the debris was propelled straight down with an initial speed of 100 feet per second. With this assumption, it seems reasonable that other parts of the debris would have been propelled straight up with the same initial speed. Under these conditions, approximate the duration at which debris continued to hit the streets.

Solving Inequalities

Inequalities and Intervals on the Real Number Line / Solving Inequalities /
Inequalities Involving Absolute Value / Other Types of Inequalities

Inequalities and Intervals on the Real Number Line

Simple inequalities were introduced in Section 1.1 to *order* the real numbers.
There, inequality symbols $<$, $\leq$, $>$, and $\geq$ were used to compare two numbers
and to denote subsets of real numbers. For instance, the simple inequality

$x \geq 3$

denotes all real numbers x that are greater than or equal to 3.

In this section we expand our work with inequalities to include more
involved statements such as

$5x - 7 < 3x + 9$ and $-3 \leq 6x - 1 < 3$.

As with an equation, we **solve an inequality** in the variable x by finding all
values of x for which the inequality is true. These values are **solutions** and
the solutions **satisfy** the inequality. The set of all real numbers that are solutions
of an inequality is the **solution set** of the inequality.

The set of all points on the real number line that represents the solution
set is the **graph** of the inequality. Graphs of many types of inequalities consist
of intervals on the real number line.

BOUNDED INTERVALS ON THE REAL NUMBER LINE

Let a and b be real numbers such that $a < b$. The following intervals
on the real number line are **bounded intervals.** The numbers a and
b are the **endpoints** of each interval.

Notation	Interval Type	Inequality	Graph
$[a, b]$	Closed	$a \leq x \leq b$	
(a, b)	Open	$a < x < b$	
$[a, b)$	Half-open	$a \leq x < b$	
$(a, b]$	Half-open	$a < x \leq b$	

Note that a closed interval contains both of its endpoints, a half-open interval contains only one of its endpoints, and an open interval contains neither of its endpoints. Often, the solution of an inequality is an interval on the real line that is **unbounded.** For instance, the interval consisting of all positive numbers is unbounded.

UNBOUNDED INTERVALS ON THE REAL NUMBER LINE

Let a and b be real numbers. The following intervals on the real number line are **unbounded intervals.**

Notation	Interval Type	Inequality	Graph
$[a, \infty)$	Half open	$x \geq a$	
(a, ∞)	Open	$x > a$	
$(-\infty, b]$	Half-open	$x \leq b$	
$(-\infty, b)$	Open	$x < b$	
$(-\infty, \infty)$	Entire real line		

The symbols ∞ (**positive infinity**) and $-\infty$ (**negative infinity**) do not represent real numbers. They are simply convenient symbols used to describe the unboundedness of an interval such as $(1, \infty)$.

EXAMPLE 1   Intervals and Inequalities

Write an inequality to represent each of the following intervals and state whether the interval is bounded or unbounded.

a. $(-3, 5]$ **b.** $(-3, \infty)$ **c.** $[0, 2]$

Solution

a. $(-3, 5]$ corresponds to $-3 < x \leq 5$.   *Bounded*

b. $(-3, \infty)$ corresponds to $-3 < x$.   *Unbounded*

c. $[0, 2]$ corresponds to $0 \leq x \leq 2$.   *Bounded*

Solving Inequalities

The procedures for solving linear inequalities in one variable are much like those for solving linear equations. To isolate the variable we use **properties of inequalities.** These properties are similar to the properties of equality, but there are two important exceptions. When both sides of an inequality are multiplied or divided by a negative number, the direction of the inequality symbol must be reversed.

$$-2 < 5 \qquad\qquad \textit{Given inequality}$$

$$(-3)(-2) > (-3)(5) \qquad\qquad \textit{Multiply both sides by } -3$$
$$\textit{and reverse the inequality}$$

$$6 > -15$$

Two inequalities that have the same solution set are **equivalent.** The following list describes operations that can be used to create equivalent inequalities.

PROPERTIES OF INEQUALITIES

Let a, b, c, and d be real numbers.

Property	*Example*
1. Transitive Property: $a < b$ and $b < c \;\rightarrow\; a < c$	Since $-2 < 5$ and $5 < 7$, it follows that $-2 < 7$.
2. Addition of Inequalities: $a < b$ and $c < d \;\rightarrow\; a + c < b + d$	Since $2 < 4$ and $3 < 5$, it follows that $2 + 3 < 4 + 5$.
3. Addition of a Constant: $a < b \;\rightarrow\; a + c < b + c$	Since $-3 < 7$, it follows that $-3 + 2 < 7 + 2$.
4. Multiplying by a Constant: i. For $c > 0$, $\quad a < b \;\rightarrow\; ac < bc$ ii. For $c < 0$, $\quad a < b \;\rightarrow\; ac > bc$	Since $5 > 0$ and $3 < 9$, it follows that $3(5) < 9(5)$. Since $-5 < 0$ and $3 < 9$, it follows that $3(-5) > 9(-5)$.

REMARK Each of the properties of inequalities is true if the symbol $<$ is replaced by $\leq$.

As you read through the examples, pay special attention to the steps in which the inequality symbol is reversed. Remember that when you multiply or divide an inequality by a negative number, you must reverse the inequality symbol.

EXAMPLE 2 Solving a Linear Inequality

$$5x - 7 > 3x + 9 \qquad \text{\textit{Given inequality}}$$
$$5x > 3x + 16 \qquad \text{\textit{Add 7 to both sides}}$$
$$5x - 3x > 16 \qquad \text{\textit{Subtract 3x from both sides}}$$
$$2x > 16 \qquad \text{\textit{Combine terms}}$$
$$x > 8 \quad (\text{or } 8 < x) \qquad \text{\textit{Divide both sides by 2}}$$

Thus, the solution set consists of all real numbers that are greater than 8. The interval notation for this solution set is $(8, \infty)$. The graph of this solution set is shown in Figure 1.9.

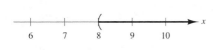

Solution interval: $(8, \infty)$

FIGURE 1.9

REMARK The five inequalities forming the solution steps of Example 2 are all **equivalent** in the sense that each has the same solution set. Moreover, the solution set can be denoted in three ways—by an inequality, by an interval, or by a graph.

Checking the solution set of an inequality is not as simple as checking the solution of an equation. (There are usually too many x-values to substitute back into the original inequality.) We can, however, get an indication of the validity of a solution set by substituting a few convenient values of x. For instance, in Example 2 we found the solution of $5x - 7 > 3x + 9$ to be $x > 8$. Check to see that $x = 9$ satisfies the original inequality, whereas $x = 7$ does not.

EXAMPLE 3 Solving a Linear Inequality

$$1 - \frac{3x}{2} \geq x - 4 \qquad \text{\textit{Given inequality}}$$
$$2 - 3x \geq 2x - 8 \qquad \text{\textit{Multiply both sides by LCD}}$$
$$-3x \geq 2x - 10 \qquad \text{\textit{Subtract 2 from both sides}}$$
$$-5x \geq -10 \qquad \text{\textit{Subtract 2x from both sides}}$$
$$x \leq 2 \qquad \text{\textit{Divide both sides by -5 and reverse inequality}}$$

Thus, the solution set consists of all real numbers that are less than or equal to 2. The interval notation for this solution set is $(-\infty, 2]$. The graph of this solution set is shown in Figure 1.10.

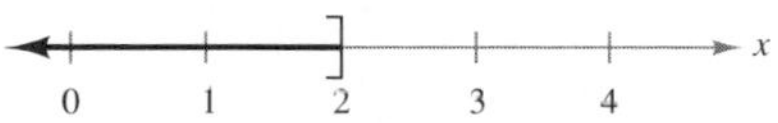

Sometimes it is convenient to write two inequalities as a **double inequality**. For instance, you can write the two inequalities $-4 \leq 5x - 2$ and $5x - 2 < 7$ more simply as

$$-4 \leq 5x - 2 < 7.$$

This form allows you to solve the two given inequalities together.

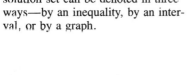

Solution interval: $(-\infty, 2]$

FIGURE 1.10

EXAMPLE 4 Solving a Double Inequality

Solve the double inequality and sketch the graph of its solution set.

$$-3 \leq 6x - 1 < 3$$

Solution

To solve this double inequality, isolate x as the middle term.

$$-3 \leq 6x - 1 < 3 \qquad \textit{Given inequality}$$

$$-2 \leq 6x < 4 \qquad \textit{Add 1 to all three parts}$$

$$-\frac{1}{3} \leq x < \frac{2}{3} \qquad \textit{Divide by 6 and reduce}$$

The solution set consists of all real numbers that are greater than or equal to $-\frac{1}{3}$ and less than $\frac{2}{3}$. Thus, the solution consists of all real numbers that are in the interval $\left[-\frac{1}{3}, \frac{2}{3}\right)$. The graph of this solution set is shown in Figure 1.11.

◄

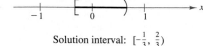

Solution interval: $\left[-\frac{1}{3}, \frac{2}{3}\right)$

FIGURE 1.11

The double inequality in Example 4 could have been solved in two parts.

$$-3 \leq 6x - 1 \quad \text{and} \quad 6x - 1 < 3$$

$$-2 \leq 6x \qquad\qquad 6x < 4$$

$$-\frac{1}{3} \leq x \qquad\qquad x < \frac{2}{3}$$

The solution set consists of all real numbers that satisfy *both* inequalities. In other words, the solution set is the set of all values of x for which $-\frac{1}{3} \leq x < \frac{2}{3}$.

When combining two inequalities to form a double inequality, be sure that the inequalities satisfy the Transitive Property. For instance, it is *incorrect* to combine the inequalities $3 < x$ and $x \leq -1$ as $3 < x \leq -1$. This "inequality" is obviously wrong because 3 is not less than -1.

Inequalities Involving Absolute Value

To see how to solve inequalities involving absolute values, consider the following comparisons.

Equation or Inequality	Geometric Solution	Graph
$\lvert x \rvert = 2$	Values of x that lie 2 units from 0	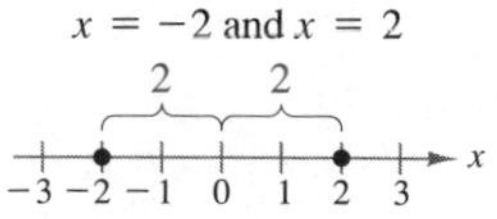 $x = -2$ and $x = 2$
$\lvert x \rvert < 2$	Values of x that lie *less than* 2 units from 0	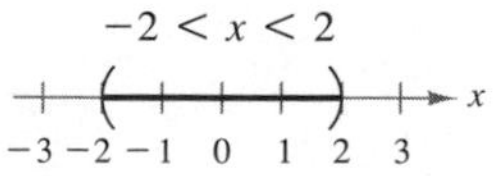 $-2 < x < 2$
$\lvert x \rvert > 2$	Values of x that lie *more than* 2 units from 0	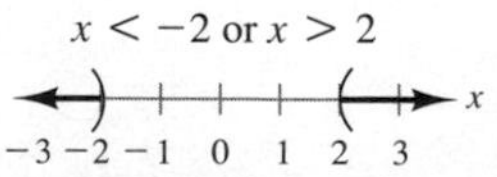 $x < -2$ or $x > 2$

SOLVING AN ABSOLUTE VALUE INEQUALITY

Let x be a variable or an algebraic expression and let a be a real number such that $a \geq 0$.

$$|x| < a \quad \text{if and only if} \quad -a < x < a.$$
$$|x| > a \quad \text{if and only if} \quad x < -a \text{ or } x > a.$$

Inequality	Interpretation	Graph
$|x| < a$	All numbers x whose distance from 0 is *less than a.*	$-a < x < a$
$|x| > a$	All numbers x whose distance from 0 is *greater than a.*	$x < -a \qquad x > a$

These two rules are also valid if $<$ is replaced by $\leq$ and $>$ is replaced by $\geq$.

REMARK Note that $-a < x < a$ means that $-a < x$ and $x < a$. ◢

EXAMPLE 5 Solving an Absolute Value Inequality

$|x - 5| < 2$	*Given inequality*
$-2 < x - 5 < 2$	*Equivalent inequalities*
$-2 + 5 < x - 5 + 5 < 2 + 5$	*Add 5 to all three parts*
$3 < x < 7$	*Solution set*

Thus, the solution set consists of all real numbers that are greater than 3 and less than 7. The interval notation for this solution set is (3, 7). The graph of this solution set is shown in Figure 1.12. ◢

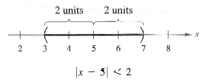

2 units   2 units

$|x - 5| < 2$

FIGURE 1.12

EXAMPLE 6 Solving an Absolute Value Inequality

$|x + 3| \geq 7$		*Given inequality*
$x + 3 \leq -7$	or $\qquad x + 3 \geq 7$	*Equivalent inequalities*
$x + 3 - 3 \leq -7 - 3$	$x + 3 - 3 \geq 7 - 3$	*Subtract 3 from both sides*
$x \leq -10$	$x \geq 4$	*Solution set*

Thus, the solution set consists of all real numbers that are less than or equal to -10 or greater than or equal to 4. This means that the solution set consists of all real numbers that are in the interval $(-\infty, -10]$ *or* in the interval $[4, \infty)$. The graph of this solution set is shown in Figure 1.13. ◢

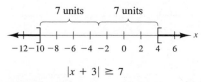

7 units   7 units

$|x + 3| \geq 7$

FIGURE 1.13

Other Types of Inequalities

To solve a polynomial inequality like

$$x^2 - 2x - 3 < 0$$

we use the fact that a polynomial can change signs only at its zeros (the x-values that make the polynomial zero). Between two consecutive zeros a polynomial must be entirely positive or entirely negative. This means that when the real zeros of a polynomial are put in order, they divide the real line into intervals in which the polynomial has no sign changes. These zeros are the **critical numbers** of the inequality, and the resulting intervals are the **test intervals** for the inequality. For example, the polynomial

$$x^2 - 2x - 3 = (x + 1)(x - 3)$$

has two zeros, $x = -1$ and $x = 3$, and these zeros divide the real line into three test intervals:

$$(-\infty, -1), \quad (-1, 3), \quad \text{and} \quad (3, \infty).$$

Thus, to solve the inequality $x^2 - 2x - 3 < 0$, we only need to test one value from each of these test intervals.

EXAMPLE 7   Solving a Quadratic Inequality

$$x^2 < x + 6 \qquad \textit{Given inequality}$$
$$x^2 - x - 6 < 0 \qquad \textit{Standard form}$$
$$(x - 3)(x + 2) < 0 \qquad \textit{Factor}$$

Critical Numbers $x = -2, x = 3$
Test Intervals $(-\infty, -2), (-2, 3), (3, \infty)$
Test   Is $(x - 3)(x + 2) < 0$?

To test an interval, we choose a convenient number in the interval and compute the sign of $(x - 3)(x + 2)$. The results are shown in Figure 1.14.

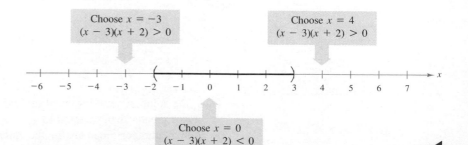

Choose $x = -3$
$(x - 3)(x + 2) > 0$

Choose $x = 4$
$(x - 3)(x + 2) > 0$

Choose $x = 0$
$(x - 3)(x + 2) < 0$

FIGURE 1.14

In Example 7, note that the first step in solving a polynomial *inequality* is to write the inequality in standard form (with the polynomial on the left and zero on the right).

EXAMPLE 8 Solving a Polynomial Inequality

$$2x^3 + 5x^2 > 12x \qquad \textit{Given inequality}$$

$$2x^3 + 5x^2 - 12x > 0 \qquad \textit{Write in standard form}$$

$$x(x + 4)(2x - 3) > 0 \qquad \textit{Factor}$$

Critical Numbers $\quad x = -4, \; x = 0, \; x = \dfrac{3}{2}$

Test Intervals $\quad (-\infty, -4), \; (-4, 0), \; \left(0, \dfrac{3}{2}\right), \; \left(\dfrac{3}{2}, \infty\right)$

Test $\qquad\qquad$ Is $x(x + 4)(2x - 3) > 0$?

FIGURE 1.15

After testing these intervals, as shown in Figure 1.15, we see that the polynomial $2x^3 + 5x^2 - 12x$ is positive in the interval $(-4, 0)$ and in the interval $\left(\frac{3}{2}, \infty\right)$. Therefore, the solution set of the inequality consists of all real numbers that are in the interval $(-4, 0)$ *or* in the interval $\left(\frac{3}{2}, \infty\right)$.

The concepts of critical numbers and test intervals can be extended to inequalities involving rational expressions. To do this, we use the fact that the value of a rational expression can change sign only at its *zeros* (the x-values for which its numerator is zero) and its *undefined values* (the x-values for which its denominator is zero). These two types of numbers make up the **critical numbers** of a rational inequality. For instance, the critical numbers of the inequality

$$\frac{x - 1}{(x - 2)(x + 3)} < 0$$

are $x = 1$ (the numerator is zero), and $x = 2$ and $x = -3$ (the denominator is zero). From these three critical numbers we see that the given inequality has *four* test intervals:

$$(-\infty, -3), \qquad (-3, 1), \qquad (1, 2), \quad \text{and} \quad (2, \infty).$$

EXAMPLE 9 Solving a Rational Inequality

$$\frac{2x - 7}{x - 5} \le 3 \qquad \textit{Given inequality}$$

$$\frac{2x - 7}{x - 5} - 3 \le 0 \qquad \textit{Standard form}$$

$$\frac{2x - 7 - 3x + 15}{x - 5} \le 0 \qquad \textit{Add fractions}$$

$$\frac{-x + 8}{x - 5} \le 0 \qquad \textit{Simplify}$$

Now, in standard form we see that the critical numbers are 5 and 8.

Critical Numbers $x = 5, x = 8$ *Denominator is zero*
                                               when x − 5

Test Intervals $(-\infty, 5), (5, 8), (8, \infty)$

Test   Is $\dfrac{-x + 8}{x - 5} \leq 0$?

After testing these intervals, as shown in Figure 1.16, we see that the rational expression $(-x + 8)/(x - 5)$ is negative in the open intervals $(-\infty, 5)$ and $(8, \infty)$. Moreover, since $(-x + 8)/(x - 5) = 0$ when $x = 8$, we conclude that the solution set of the inequality consists of all real numbers that are in the interval $(-\infty, 5)$ *or* in the interval $[8, \infty)$.

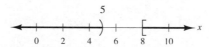

FIGURE 1.16

EXAMPLE 10   An Inequality Involving Fractions

$$\frac{x}{x - 2} > \frac{1}{x + 3}$$ *Given inequality*

$$\frac{x}{x - 2} - \frac{1}{x + 3} > 0$$ *Standard form*

$$\frac{x^2 + 3x - x + 2}{(x - 2)(x + 3)} > 0$$ *Combine fractions*

$$\frac{x^2 + 2x + 2}{(x - 2)(x + 3)} > 0$$ *Simplify*

The discriminant $b^2 - 4ac = 4 - 8 = -4 < 0$ indicates that the numerator has no zeros. Therefore, $x = 2$ and $x = -3$ are the only critical numbers.

Critical Numbers $x = -3, x = 2$

Test Intervals $(-\infty, -3), (-3, 2), (2, \infty)$

Test   Is $\dfrac{x^2 + 2x + 2}{(x - 2)(x + 3)} > 0$?

After testing these intervals, as shown in Figure 1.17, we see that the rational expression $(x^2 + 2x + 2)/[(x - 2)(x + 3)]$ is positive in the open intervals $(-\infty, -3)$ and $(2, \infty)$. Therefore, the solution set of the inequality consists of all real numbers that are in the interval $(-\infty, -3)$ *or* in the interval $(2, \infty)$.

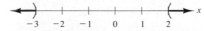

FIGURE 1.17

DISCUSSION

PROBLEM

Verbal
Statements of
Properties

You may find that it is easier to learn a verbal statement than to learn a mathematical formula. For instance, you can remember the Pythagorean Theorem, $a^2 + b^2 = c^2$, as "the sum of the squares of the two sides is equal to the square of the hypotenuse."

At the beginning of this section four properties of inequalities were given. Translate each of these mathematical statements into *verbal statements*.

WARM UP

The following warm-up exercises involve skills that were covered in earlier sections. You will use these skills in the exercise set for this section.

In Exercises 1–4, determine which of the two numbers is larger.

1. $-\frac{1}{2}, -7$

2. $-\frac{1}{3}, -\frac{1}{6}$

3. $-\pi, -3$

4. $-6, \frac{13}{2}$

In Exercises 5–8, use inequality notation to denote the statement.

5. x is nonnegative.

6. z is strictly between -3 and 10.

7. P is no more than 2.

8. W is at least 200.

In Exercises 9 and 10, evaluate the expression for the given values of x.

9. $|x - 10|, x = 12, x = 3$

10. $|2x - 3|, x = \frac{3}{2}, x = 1$

EXERCISES for Section 1.6

In Exercises 1–4, write an inequality to represent the interval and state whether the interval is bounded or unbounded.

1. $[-1, 3]$

2. $(4, 10]$

3. $(10, \infty)$

4. $[-6, \infty)$

In Exercises 5–8, determine whether the values of x are solutions of the inequality.

Inequality	Values	
5. $5x - 12 > 0$	(a) $x = 3$	(b) $x = -3$
	(c) $x = \frac{5}{2}$	(d) $x = \frac{3}{2}$
6. $x + 1 < \frac{2x}{3}$	(a) $x = 0$	(b) $x = 4$
	(c) $x = -4$	(d) $x = -3$

Inequality	Values	
7. $0 < \dfrac{x - 2}{4} < 2$	(a) $x = 4$	(b) $x = 10$
	(c) $x = 0$	(d) $x = \frac{7}{2}$
8. $-1 < \dfrac{3 - x}{2} \le 1$	(a) $x = 0$	(b) $x = \sqrt{5}$
	(c) $x = 1$	(d) $x = 5$

In Exercises 9–40, solve the inequality and sketch the solution on the real number line.

9. $4x < 12$

10. $2x > 3$

11. $-10x < 40$

12. $-6x > 15$

13. $x - 5 \ge 7$

14. $x + 7 \le 12$

15. $4(x + 1) < 2x + 3$

16. $2x + 7 < 3$

17. $4 - 2x < 3$

18. $6x - 4 \le 2$

19. $1 < 2x + 3 < 9$

20. $-8 \le 1 - 3(x - 2) < 13$

21. $-4 < \dfrac{2x - 3}{3} < 4$

22. $0 \le \dfrac{x + 3}{2} < 5$

23. $\frac{3}{4} > x + 1 > \frac{1}{4}$ **24.** $-1 < -\frac{x}{3} < 1$

25. $|x| < 5$ **26.** $|2x| < 6$

27. $\left|\frac{x}{2}\right| > 3$ **28.** $|5x| > 10$

29. $|x - 20| \leq 4$ **30.** $|x - 7| < 6$

31. $|x - 20| \geq 4$ **32.** $|x + 14| + 3 > 17$

33. $\left|\frac{x - 3}{2}\right| \geq 5$ **34.** $|1 - 2x| < 5$

35. $|9 - 2x| - 2 < -1$ **36.** $\left|1 - \frac{2x}{3}\right| < 1$

37. $2|x + 10| \geq 9$ **38.** $3|4 - 5x| \leq 9$

39. $|x - 5| < 0$ **40.** $|x - 5| \geq 0$

In Exercises 41–44, use absolute value notation to define the interval (or pair of intervals) on the real line.

41.

42.

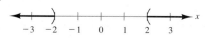

43.

44.

In Exercises 45–66, solve the inequality and give the answers in interval notation.

45. $x^2 \leq 9$ **46.** $x^2 < 5$

47. $x^2 > 4$ **48.** $(x - 3)^2 \geq 1$

49. $(x + 2)^2 < 25$ **50.** $(x + 6)^2 \leq 8$

51. $x^2 + 4x + 4 \geq 9$ **52.** $x^2 - 6x + 9 < 16$

53. $3(x - 1)(x + 1) > 0$ **54.** $6(x + 2)(x - 1) < 0$

55. $x^2 + 2x - 3 < 0$ **56.** $x^2 - 4x - 1 > 0$

57. $4x^3 - 6x^2 < 0$ **58.** $4x^3 - 12x^2 > 0$

59. $x^3 - 4x \geq 0$ **60.** $2x^3 - x^4 \leq 0$

61. $\frac{1}{x} > x$ **62.** $\frac{1}{x} < 4$

63. $\frac{x + 6}{x + 1} < 2$ **64.** $\frac{x + 12}{x + 2} \geq 3$

65. $\frac{4}{x + 5} > \frac{1}{2x + 3}$ **66.** $\frac{5}{x - 6} > \frac{3}{x + 2}$

In Exercises 67–74, find the interval(s) on the real number line for which the radicand is nonnegative (greater than or equal to zero).

67. $\sqrt{x - 5}$ **68.** $\sqrt{x - 10}$

69. $\sqrt{x + 3}$ **70.** $\sqrt[4]{6x + 15}$

71. $\sqrt[4]{4 - x^2}$ **72.** $\sqrt{x^2 - 4}$

73. $\sqrt{x^2 - 7x + 12}$ **74.** $\sqrt{144 - 9x^2}$

In Exercises 75–78, use a calculator to solve the inequality. (Round each number in your answer to two decimal places.)

75. $0.4x^2 + 5.26 < 10.2$ **76.** $-1.3x^2 + 3.78 > 2.12$

77. $\frac{1}{2.3x - 5.2} > 3.4$ **78.** $\frac{2}{3.1x - 3.7} > 5.8$

79. *Simple Interest* In order for an investment of $1000 to grow to *more than* $1250 in two years, what must the interest rate be? $[A = P(1 + rt)]$

80. *Comparative Shopping* Suppose you can rent a midsize car from Company A for $250 per week with no extra charge for mileage. A similar car can be rented from Company B for $150 per week plus $0.25 cents for each mile driven. How many miles must you drive in a week to make the rental fee for Company B *greater than* that for Company A?

81. *Break-Even Analysis* The revenue for selling x units of a product is

$R = 115.95x.$

The cost of producing x units is

$C = 95x + 750.$

In order to obtain a profit, the revenue must be *greater than* the cost. For what values of x will this product return a profit?

82. *Daily Sales* A doughnut shop sells a dozen doughnuts for $2.95. Beyond the fixed costs (for rent, utilities, and insurance) of $150 per day, it costs $1.45 for enough materials (flour, sugar, and so on) and labor to produce a dozen doughnuts. If the daily profit varies between $50 and $200, between what levels (in dozens) do the daily sales vary?

83. *Height* The heights, h, of two-thirds of the members of a certain population satisfy the inequality

$$\left| \frac{h - 68.5}{2.7} \right| \leq 1$$

where h is measured in inches. Determine the interval on the real line in which these heights lie.

84. *Relative Humidity* A certain electronic device is to be operated in an environment with relative humidity h in the interval defined by

$$|h - 50| \leq 30.$$

What are the minimum and maximum relative humidities for the operation of this device?

85. *Dimensions of a Field* A rectangular playing field with a perimeter of 100 meters is to have an area of at least 500 square meters. Within what bounds must the length of the rectangle lie?

86. *Compound Interest* P dollars, invested at interest rate r compounded annually, increases to an amount

$$A = P(1 + r)^2$$

in two years. If an investment of $1000 is to increase to an amount greater than $1200 in two years, then the interest rate must be greater than what percentage?

87. *Resistors* When two resistors of resistance R_1 and R_2 are connected in parallel (see figure), the total resistance R satisfies the equation

$$\frac{1}{R} = \frac{1}{R_1} + \frac{1}{R_2}.$$

Find R_1 for a parallel circuit in which $R_2 = 2$ ohms and R must be at least 1 ohm.

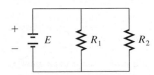

Figure for 87

88. *Percent of College Graduates* The percentage of the American population that graduated from college between 1940 and 1987 is approximated by the model

Percent of graduates $= 5.136 + 0.69t^2$

where the time t represents the calendar year with $t = 0$ corresponding to 1940, $t = 1$ corresponding to 1950, and so on (see figure). According to this model, when will the percentage of college graduates exceed 25% of the population? (*Source:* U.S. Bureau of the Census)

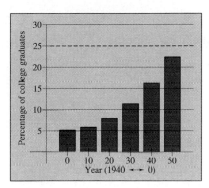

Figure for 88

89. *Safe Beam Loads* The maximum safe load uniformly distributed over a 1-foot section of a 2-inch-wide wooden beam is approximated by the model

Load $= 168.5d^2 - 472.1$

where d is the depth of the beam. Use this model to determine the depth of the beam that will safely support a load of 2000 pounds (see figure).

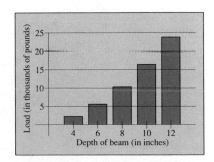

Figure for 89

1.7 Algebraic Errors and Some Algebra of Calculus

Algebraic Errors to Avoid / Some Algebra of Calculus

Algebraic Errors to Avoid

Before wrapping up our review of the fundamental concepts of algebra, we list some common algebraic errors. Many of these errors are made because they seem to be the *easiest* things to do.

Errors Involving Parentheses

Potential Error		Correct Form	Comment
$a - (x - b)$	DOES NOT EQUAL $a - x - b$	$a - (x - b) = a - x + b$	*Change all signs when distributing negative sign through parentheses.*
$(a + b)^2$	DOES NOT EQUAL $a^2 + b^2$	$(a + b)^2 = a^2 + 2ab + b^2$	*Remember the middle term when squaring binomials.*
$\left(\frac{1}{2}a\right)\left(\frac{1}{2}b\right)$	DOES NOT EQUAL $\frac{1}{2}(ab)$	$\left(\frac{1}{2}a\right)\left(\frac{1}{2}b\right) = \frac{1}{4}(ab) = \frac{ab}{4}$	$\frac{1}{2}$ *occurs twice as a factor.*
$(3x + 6)^2$	DOES NOT EQUAL $3(x + 2)^2$	$(3x + 6)^2 = [3(x + 2)]^2$ $= 3^2(x + 2)^2$	*When factoring, apply exponents to all factors.*
$6(3x + 4)^5$	DOES NOT EQUAL $(18x + 24)^5$	No simpler form	*Exponent 5 does not apply to 6.*

Errors Involving Fractions

Potential Error		Correct Form	Comment
$\dfrac{a}{x + b}$	DOES NOT EQUAL $\dfrac{a}{x} + \dfrac{a}{b}$	Leave as $\dfrac{a}{x + b}$	*Do not add denominators when adding fractions.*
$\dfrac{\left(\frac{x}{a}\right)}{b}$	DOES NOT EQUAL $\dfrac{bx}{a}$	$\dfrac{\left(\frac{x}{a}\right)}{b} = \left(\frac{x}{a}\right)\left(\frac{1}{b}\right) = \dfrac{x}{ab}$	*Multiply by the reciprocal when dividing fractions.*
$\dfrac{1}{a} + \dfrac{1}{b}$	DOES NOT EQUAL $\dfrac{1}{a + b}$	$\dfrac{1}{a} + \dfrac{1}{b} = \dfrac{a + b}{ab}$	*Use the definition for adding fractions.*
$\dfrac{1}{3x}$	DOES NOT EQUAL $\dfrac{1}{3}x$	$\dfrac{1}{3x} = \dfrac{1}{3} \cdot \dfrac{1}{x}$	*Use the definition for multiplying fractions.*
$(1/3)x$	DOES NOT EQUAL $\dfrac{1}{3x}$	$(1/3)x = \dfrac{1}{3} \cdot x = \dfrac{x}{3}$	*Be careful when using a slash to denote division.*
$(1/x) + 2$	DOES NOT EQUAL $\dfrac{1}{x + 2}$	$(1/x) + 2 = \dfrac{1}{x} + 2 = \dfrac{1 + 2x}{x}$	*Be careful when using a slash to denote division.*

Errors Involving Exponents and Radicals

Potential Error			Correct Form	Comment
$(x^2)^3$	DOES NOT EQUAL	x^5	$(x^2)^3 = x^{2 \cdot 3} = x^6$	Multiply exponents when raising an exponential form to a power.
$x^2 \cdot x^3$	DOES NOT EQUAL	x^6	$x^2 \cdot x^3 = x^{2+3} = x^5$	Add exponents when multiplying exponential forms with like bases.
$-2x^3$	DOES NOT EQUAL	$(-2x)^3$	$-2x^3 = -2(x^3)$	Exponents have priority over multiplication.
$3x^{-5}$	DOES NOT EQUAL	$\dfrac{1}{3x^5}$	$3x^{-5} = \dfrac{3}{x^5}$	Negative exponent does not apply to coefficient.
$\dfrac{1}{x^{1/2} - x^{1/3}}$	DOES NOT EQUAL	$x^{-1/2} - x^{-1/3}$	Leave as $\dfrac{1}{x^{1/2} - x^{1/3}}$	Do not move term-by-term from denominator to numerator.
$\sqrt{5x}$	DOES NOT EQUAL	$5\sqrt{x}$	$\sqrt{5x} = \sqrt{5}\sqrt{x}$	Radicals apply to every factor inside the radical.
$\sqrt{x^2 + a^2}$	DOES NOT EQUAL	$x + a$	Leave as $\sqrt{x^2 + a^2}$	Do not apply radicals term-by-term.
$\sqrt{-x^2 + a^2}$	DOES NOT EQUAL	$-\sqrt{x^2 - a^2}$	Leave as $\sqrt{-x^2 + a^2}$	Do not factor negative signs out of square roots.

Errors Involving Cancellation

Potential Error			Correct Form	Comment
$\dfrac{a + bx}{a}$	DOES NOT EQUAL	$1 + bx$	$\dfrac{a + bx}{a} = \dfrac{a}{a} + \dfrac{bx}{a} = 1 + \dfrac{b}{a}x$	Reduce common factors, not common terms.
$\dfrac{a + ax}{a}$	DOES NOT EQUAL	$a + x$	$\dfrac{a + ax}{a} = \dfrac{a(1 + x)}{a} = 1 + x$	Factor before reducing.
$1 + \dfrac{x}{2x}$	DOES NOT EQUAL	$1 + \dfrac{1}{x}$	$1 + \dfrac{x}{2x} = 1 + \dfrac{1}{2} = \dfrac{3}{2}$	Reduce common factors.

Some Algebra of Calculus

In calculus it is often necessary to take a simplified algebraic expression and "unsimplify" it. See the following list, taken from a standard calculus text.

Unusual Factoring

Expression	*Useful Calculus Form of Expression*	*Comment*
$\dfrac{5x^4}{8}$	$\dfrac{5}{8}x^4$	*Write with fractional coefficient.*
$\dfrac{x^2 + 3x}{-6}$	$-\dfrac{1}{6}(x^2 + 3x)$	*Write with fractional coefficient.*
$2x^2 - x - 3$	$2\left(x^2 - \dfrac{x}{2} - \dfrac{3}{2}\right)$	*Factor out the leading coefficient.*
$\dfrac{x}{2}(x + 1)^{-1/2} + (x + 1)^{1/2}$	$\dfrac{(x + 1)^{-1/2}}{2}[x + 2(x + 1)]$	*Factor out factor with least power.*

Inserting Factors or Terms

Expression	*Useful Calculus Form of Expression*	*Comment*
$(2x - 1)^3$	$\dfrac{1}{2}(2x - 1)^3(2)$	*Multiply and divide by 2.*
$7x^2(4x^3 - 5)^{1/2}$	$\dfrac{7}{12}(4x^3 - 5)^{1/2}(12x^2)$	*Multiply and divide by 12.*
$\dfrac{4x^2}{9} - 4y^2 = 1$	$\dfrac{x^2}{9/4} - \dfrac{y^2}{1/4} = 1$	*Write with fractional denominators.*
$\dfrac{x}{x + 1}$	$\dfrac{x + 1 - 1}{x + 1} = 1 - \dfrac{1}{x + 1}$	*Add and subtract the same term.*

Writing a Fraction as a Sum

Expression	Useful Calculus Form of Expression	Comment
$\dfrac{x + 2x^2 + 1}{\sqrt{x}}$	$x^{1/2} + 2x^{3/2} + x^{-1/2}$	Divide each term by $x^{1/2}$.
$\dfrac{1 + x}{x^2 + 1}$	$\dfrac{1}{x^2 + 1} + \dfrac{x}{x^2 + 1}$	Rewrite the fraction as the sum of fractions.
$\dfrac{2x}{x^2 + 2x + 1}$	$\dfrac{2x + 2 - 2}{x^2 + 2x + 1}$	Add and subtract a term to the numerator.
	$= \dfrac{2x + 2}{x^2 + 2x + 1} - \dfrac{2}{(x + 1)^2}$	Rewrite the fraction as the difference of fractions.
$\dfrac{x^2 - 2}{x + 1}$	$x - 1 - \dfrac{1}{x + 1}$	Use long division. (See Section 3.3.)
$\dfrac{x + 7}{x^2 - x - 6}$	$\dfrac{2}{x - 3} - \dfrac{1}{x + 2}$	Use the method of partial fractions. (See Section 3.8.)

Rewriting with Negative Exponents

Expression	Useful Calculus Form of Expression	Comment
$\dfrac{9}{5x^3}$	$\dfrac{9}{5}x^{-3}$	Move the factor to numerator and change the sign of the exponent.
$\dfrac{7}{\sqrt{2x - 3}}$	$7(2x - 3)^{-1/2}$	Move the factor to numerator and change the sign of the exponent

EXAMPLE 1   Rewriting Fractions

Explain the following.

$$\frac{4x^2}{9} - 4y^2 = \frac{x^2}{9/4} - \frac{y^2}{1/4}$$

Solution

To write the expression on the left side of the equation in the form given on the right, multiply the numerator and denominator of both terms by $\frac{1}{4}$.

$$\frac{4x^2}{9} - 4y^2 = \frac{4x^2}{9}\left(\frac{1/4}{1/4}\right) - 4y^2\left(\frac{1/4}{1/4}\right)$$

$$= \frac{x^2}{9/4} - \frac{y^2}{1/4}$$

EXAMPLE 2   Rewriting with Negative Exponents

Rewrite the expression using negative exponents.

$$\frac{2}{5x^3} - \frac{1}{\sqrt{x}} + \frac{3}{16x^2}$$

Solution

$$\frac{2}{5x^3} - \frac{1}{\sqrt{x}} + \frac{3}{16x^2} = \frac{2}{5x^3} - \frac{1}{x^{1/2}} + \frac{3}{(4x)^2}$$

$$= \frac{2}{5}x^{-3} - x^{-1/2} + 3(4x)^{-2}$$

◢

EXAMPLE 3   Factors Involving Negative Exponents

Factor $x(x + 1)^{-1/2} + (x + 1)^{1/2}$.

Solution

When multiplying factors with like bases, you add exponents. When factoring, you are undoing multiplication, and so you *subtract* exponents.

$$x(x + 1)^{-1/2} + (x + 1)^{1/2} = (x + 1)^{-1/2}[x(x + 1)^0 + (x + 1)^1]$$

$$= (x + 1)^{-1/2}[x + (x + 1)]$$

$$= (x + 1)^{-1/2}(2x + 1)$$

◢

EXAMPLE 4   Writing a Fraction as a Sum of Terms

Rewrite the fraction as the sum of three terms.

$$\frac{x + 2x^2 + 1}{\sqrt{x}}$$

Solution

$$\frac{x + 2x^2 + 1}{\sqrt{x}} = \frac{x}{x^{1/2}} + \frac{2x^2}{x^{1/2}} + \frac{1}{x^{1/2}}$$

$$= x^{1/2} + 2x^{3/2} + x^{-1/2}$$

◢

DISCUSSION PROBLEM

Algebra and Calculus

Suppose you are taking a course in calculus, and for one of the homework problems you obtain the following answer.

$$\frac{1}{10}(2x - 1)^{5/2} + \frac{1}{6}(2x - 1)^{3/2}$$

The answer in the back of the book is

$$\frac{1}{15}(2x - 1)^{3/2}(3x + 1).$$

Are these two answers equivalent? If so, show how the second answer can be obtained from the first.

EXERCISES for Section 1.7

In Exercises 1–24, find and correct any errors.

1. $2x - (3y + 4) = 2x - 3y + 4$

2. $\dfrac{4}{16x - (2x + 1)} = \dfrac{4}{14x + 1}$

3. $5z + 3(x - 2) = 5z + 3x - 2$

4. $x(yz) = (xy)(xz)$

5. $-\dfrac{x - 3}{x - 1} = \dfrac{3}{1 - x}\dfrac{x}{}$

6. $\dfrac{x - 1}{(5 - x)(-x)} = \dfrac{1 - x}{x(5 - x)}$

7. $a\left(\dfrac{x}{y}\right) = \dfrac{ax}{ay}$

8. $(5z)(6z) = 30z$

9. $(4x)^2 = 4x^2$

10. $\left(\dfrac{x}{y}\right)^3 = \dfrac{x^3}{y}$

11. $\sqrt{x + 9} = \sqrt{x} + 3$

12. $\sqrt{25 - x^2} = 5 - x$

13. $\dfrac{6x + y}{6x - y} = \dfrac{x + y}{x - y}$

14. $\dfrac{2x^2 + 1}{5x} = \dfrac{2x + 1}{5}$

15. $\dfrac{1}{x + y^{-1}} = \dfrac{y}{x + 1}$

16. $\dfrac{1}{a^{-1} + b^{-1}} = \left(\dfrac{1}{a + b}\right)^{-1}$

17. $x(2x - 1)^2 = (2x^2 - x)^2$

18. $x(x + 5)^{1/2} = (x^2 + 5x)^{1/2}$

19. $\sqrt[3]{x^3 + 7x^2} = x^2\sqrt[3]{x + 7}$

20. $(3x^2 - 6x)^3 = 3x(x - 2)^3$

21. $\dfrac{3}{x} + \dfrac{4}{y} = \dfrac{7}{x + y}$

22. $\dfrac{7 + 5(x + 3)}{x + 3} = 12$

23. $\dfrac{1}{2y} = \left(\dfrac{1}{2}\right)y$

24. $\dfrac{2x + 3x^2}{4x} = \dfrac{2 + 3x^2}{4}$

In Exercises 25–44, insert the required factor in the parentheses.

25. $\dfrac{3x + 2}{5} = \dfrac{1}{5}(\rule{1cm}{0.4pt})$

26. $\frac{3}{4}x + \frac{1}{2} = \frac{1}{4}(\rule{1cm}{0.4pt})$

27. $\frac{1}{3}x^3 + 5 = (\rule{1cm}{0.4pt})(x^3 + 15)$

28. $\frac{5}{2}z^2 - \frac{1}{4}z + 2 = (\rule{1cm}{0.4pt})(10z^2 - z + 8)$

29. $x(1 - 2x^2)^3 = (\rule{1cm}{0.4pt})(1 - 2x^2)^3(-4x)$

30. $5x\sqrt[3]{1 + x^2} - (\rule{1cm}{0.4pt})\sqrt[3]{1 + x^2}(2x)$

31. $\dfrac{1}{\sqrt{x}(1 + \sqrt{x})^2} = (\rule{1cm}{0.4pt})\dfrac{1}{(1 + \sqrt{x})^2}\left(\dfrac{1}{2\sqrt{x}}\right)$

32. $\dfrac{4x + 6}{(x^2 + 3x + 7)^3} = (\rule{1cm}{0.4pt})\dfrac{1}{(x^2 + 3x + 7)^3}(2x + 3)$

33. $\dfrac{x + 1}{(x^2 + 2x - 3)^2} = (\rule{1cm}{0.4pt})\dfrac{1}{(x^2 + 2x - 3)^2}(2x + 2)$

34. $\dfrac{1}{(x - 1)\sqrt{(x - 1)^4 - 4}} = \dfrac{(\rule{1cm}{0.4pt})}{(x - 1)^2\sqrt{(x - 1)^4 - 4}}$

35. $\dfrac{3}{x} + \dfrac{5}{2x^2} - \dfrac{3}{2}x = (\rule{1cm}{0.4pt})(6x + 5 - 3x^3)$

36. $\dfrac{(x - 1)^2}{169} + (y + 5)^2 = \dfrac{(x - 1)^3}{169(\rule{1cm}{0.4pt})} + (y + 5)^2$

37. $\dfrac{x^2}{1/12} - \dfrac{y^2}{2/3} = \dfrac{12x^2}{(\rule{1cm}{0.4pt})} - \dfrac{3y^2}{(\rule{1cm}{0.4pt})}$

38. $\dfrac{x^2}{4/9} + \dfrac{y^2}{7/8} = \dfrac{9x^2}{(\rule{1cm}{0.4pt})} + \dfrac{8y^2}{(\rule{1cm}{0.4pt})}$

39. $\sqrt{x} + (\sqrt{x})^3 = \sqrt{x}(\rule{1cm}{0.4pt})$

40. $(1 - 3x)^{4/3} - 4x(1 - 3x)^{1/3} = (1 - 3x)^{1/3}(\rule{1cm}{0.4pt})$

41. $\dfrac{x^2}{\sqrt{x^2+1}} - \sqrt{x^2+1} = \dfrac{1}{\sqrt{x^2+1}}(\blacksquare)$

42. $\dfrac{1}{2\sqrt{x}} + 5x^{3/2} - 10x^{5/2} = \dfrac{1}{2\sqrt{x}}(\blacksquare)$

43. $\dfrac{1}{10}(2x+1)^{5/2} - \dfrac{1}{6}(2x+1)^{3/2} = \dfrac{(2x+1)^{3/2}}{15}(\blacksquare)$

44. $\dfrac{3}{7}(t+1)^{7/3} - \dfrac{3}{4}(t+1)^{4/3} = \dfrac{3(t+1)^{4/3}}{28}(\blacksquare)$

In Exercises 45–50, write the fraction as a sum of two or more terms.

45. $\dfrac{16 - 5x - x^2}{x}$

46. $\dfrac{x^3 - 5x^2 + 4}{x^2}$

47. $\dfrac{4x^3 - 7x^2 + 1}{x^{1/3}}$

48. $\dfrac{2x^5 - 3x^3 + 5x - 1}{x^{3/2}}$

49. $\dfrac{3 - 5x^2 - x^4}{\sqrt{x}}$

50. $\dfrac{x^3 - 5x^4}{3x^2}$

In Exercises 51–58, simplify the expression.

51. $\dfrac{-2(x^2-3)^{-3}(2x)(6x+1)^3 - 3(6x+1)^2(6)(x^2-3)^{-2}}{[(6x+1)^3]^2}$

52. $\dfrac{(3x+2)^5(-3)(x^2+1)^{-4}(2x) - (x^2+1)^{-3}(5)(3x+2)^4(3)}{[(3x+2)^5]^2}$

53. $\dfrac{(6x+1)^3(27x^2+2) - (9x^3+2x)(3)(6x+1)^2(6)}{[(6x+1)^3]^2}$

54. $\dfrac{(4x^2+9)^{1/2}(2) - (2x+3)\left(\frac{1}{2}\right)(4x^2+9)^{-1/2}(8x)}{[(4x^2+9)^{1/2}]^2}$

55. $\dfrac{(3x+2)^{3/4}(2x+3)^{-2/3}(2) - (2x+3)^{1/3}(3x+2)^{-1/4}(3)}{[(3x+2)^{3/4}]^2}$

56. $\dfrac{\sqrt{2x-1} - \dfrac{x+2}{\sqrt{2x-1}}}{2x-1}$

57. $\dfrac{2(3x-1)^{1/3} - (2x+1)\left(\frac{1}{3}\right)(3x-1)^{-2/3}(3)}{(3x-1)^{2/3}}$

58. $\dfrac{(x+1)\left(\frac{1}{2}\right)(2x-3x^2)^{-1/2}(2-6x) - (2x-3x^2)^{1/2}}{(x+1)^2}$

REVIEW EXERCISES for Chapter 1 *See the Instructor's Complete Answers at the front of the text.*

In Exercises 1 and 2, determine which numbers in the set are (a) natural numbers, (b) integers, (c) rational numbers, and (d) irrational numbers.

1. $11, -14, -\frac{8}{9}, \frac{5}{2}, \sqrt{6}, 0.4$

2. $\sqrt{15}, -22, -\frac{10}{3}, 0, 5.2, \frac{3}{7}$

In Exercises 3 and 4, use absolute value notation to describe the expression.

3. The distance between x and 7 is at least 4.

4. The distance between x and 25 is no more than 10.

In Exercises 5–12, perform the indicated operations without the aid of a calculator.

5. $\sqrt{5} \cdot \sqrt{125}$

6. $\dfrac{\sqrt{72}}{\sqrt{2}}$

7. $\left(\dfrac{3^2}{5^2}\right)^{-3}$

8. $6^{-4}(-3)^5$

9. $2(-27)^{2/3}$

10. $\left(\frac{25}{16}\right)^{-1/2}$

11. $(3 \times 10^4)^2$

12. $(4 \times 10^{-2})^3$

In Exercises 13 and 14, write the number in scientific notation.

13. Daily U.S. Consumption of Dunkin' Donuts: 2,740,000

14. Number of Meters in One Foot: 0.3048

In Exercises 15 and 16, write the number in decimal form.

15. Distance Between Sun and Jupiter: 4.833×10^8 miles

16. Ratio of Day to Year: 2.74×10^{-3}

In Exercises 17 and 18, use a calculator to evaluate the expression. (Round to three decimal places.)

17. (a) $1800(1 + 0.08)^{24}$ (b) $0.0024(7,658,400)$

18. (a) $50,000\left(1 + \dfrac{0.075}{12}\right)^{48}$

(b) $\dfrac{28,000,000 + 34,000,000}{87,000,000}$

In Exercises 19–26, describe the error and then make the necessary correction.

19. $\left(\frac{1}{3}x\right)\left(\frac{1}{3}y\right) = \frac{1}{3}xy$

20. $\frac{2}{9} \times \frac{4}{9} = \frac{8}{9}$

21. $\frac{x-1}{1-x} = 1$

22. $(-x)^6 = -x^6$

23. $-x^2(-x^2 + 3) = x^4 + 3x^2$

24. $(5 + 8)^2 = 5^2 + 8^2$

25. $\sqrt{3^2 + 4^2} = 3 + 4$

26. $\sqrt{10x} = 10\sqrt{x}$

In Exercises 27 and 28, simplify by removing all possible factors from the radical.

27. $\sqrt{4x^4}$

28. $\sqrt[3]{\frac{2x^3}{27}}$

In Exercises 29 and 30, simplify the expression.

29. $\sqrt{50} - \sqrt{18}$

30. $\sqrt{8x^3} + \sqrt{2x}$

In Exercises 31 and 32, rewrite the expression by rationalizing the denominator. Simplify your answer.

31. $\dfrac{1}{2 - \sqrt{3}}$

32. $\dfrac{1}{\sqrt{x} - 1}$

In Exercises 33–46, perform the required operations and/or simplify your answer.

33. $(x^2 - 2x + 1)(x^3 - 1)$

34. $(x^3 - 3x)(2x^2 + 3x + 5)$

35. $\dfrac{x^2 - 4}{x^4 - 2x^2 - 8} \cdot \dfrac{x^2 + 2}{x^2}$

36. $\dfrac{2x - 1}{x + 1} \cdot \dfrac{x^2 - 1}{2x^2 - 7x + 3}$

37. $\dfrac{x^2(5x - 6)}{2x + 3} \div \dfrac{5x}{2x + 3}$

38. $\dfrac{4x - 6}{(x - 1)^2} \div \dfrac{2x^2 - 3x}{x^2 + 2x - 3}$

39. $\dfrac{1}{x - 1} - \dfrac{1}{x + 2}$

40. $\dfrac{2}{x} - \dfrac{3}{x - 1} + \dfrac{4}{x + 1}$

41. $x - 1 + \dfrac{1}{x + 2} + \dfrac{1}{x - 1}$

42. $2x + \dfrac{3}{2(x - 4)} - \dfrac{1}{2(x + 2)}$

43. $\dfrac{1}{x} - \dfrac{x - 1}{x^2 + 1}$

44. $\dfrac{1}{x - 1} + \dfrac{1 - x}{x^2 + x + 1}$

45. $\dfrac{1}{x - 2} + \dfrac{1}{(x - 2)^2} + \dfrac{1}{x + 2}$

46. $\dfrac{1}{L}\left(\dfrac{1}{y} - \dfrac{1}{L - y}\right)$, where L is a constant

In Exercises 47–50, simplify the compound fraction.

47. $\dfrac{\left(\dfrac{1}{x} - \dfrac{1}{y}\right)}{(x^2 - y^2)}$

48. $\dfrac{\left(\dfrac{1}{x} - \dfrac{1}{y}\right)}{\left(\dfrac{1}{x} + \dfrac{1}{y}\right)}$

49. $\dfrac{\left(\dfrac{3a}{(a^2/x) - 1}\right)}{\left(\dfrac{a}{x} - 1\right)}$

50. $\dfrac{\left(\dfrac{1}{2x - 3} - \dfrac{1}{2x + 3}\right)}{\left(\dfrac{1}{2x} - \dfrac{1}{2x + 3}\right)}$

In Exercises 51–56, insert the missing factor.

51. $x^3 - x^2 + 2x - 2 = (x - 1)(\ \rule{1cm}{0.4pt}\ )$

52. $3x^2 + 14x + 8 = (x + 4)(\ \rule{1cm}{0.4pt}\ )$

53. $x^3 - 1 = (x - 1)(\ \rule{1cm}{0.4pt}\ )$

54. $\frac{3}{4}x^2 - \frac{5}{6}x + 4 = \frac{1}{12}(\ \rule{1cm}{0.4pt}\ )$

55. $\dfrac{t}{\sqrt{t + 1}} - \sqrt{t + 1} = \dfrac{1}{\sqrt{t + 1}}(\ \rule{1cm}{0.4pt}\ )$

56. $2x(x^2 - 3)^{1/3} - 5(x^2 - 3)^{4/3} = (x^2 - 3)^{1/3}(\ \rule{1cm}{0.4pt}\ )$

In Exercises 57–74, solve the equation (if possible) and check your answer.

57. $3x - 2(x + 5) = 10$

58. $\frac{1}{2}(x - 3) - 2(x + 1) = 5$

59. $3\left(1 - \dfrac{1}{5t}\right) = 0$

60. $\dfrac{1}{x - 2} = 3$

61. $6x = 3x^2$

62. $3x^2 + 1 = 0$

63. $6x^2 = 5x + 4$

64. $x^2 + 6x - 3 = 0$

65. $5x^4 - 12x^3 = 0$

66. $12t^3 - 84t^2 + 120t = 0$

67. $2 - x^{-2} = 0$

68. $\dfrac{4}{x - 3} - \dfrac{4}{x} = 1$

69. $\sqrt{x + 4} = 3$

70. $\sqrt{x - 2} - 8 = 0$

71. $\sqrt{2x + 3} + \sqrt{x - 2} = 2$

72. $5\sqrt{x} - \sqrt{x - 1} = 6$

73. $|x - 5| = 10$

74. $|x^2 - 3| = 2x$

In Exercises 75–82, solve the inequality.

75. $\frac{1}{2}(3 - x) > \frac{1}{3}(2 - 3x)$

76. $\dfrac{x}{5} - 6 \le -\dfrac{x}{2} + 6$

77. $x^2 - 4 \le 0$

78. $x^2 - 2x \ge 3$

79. $\dfrac{x - 5}{3 - x} < 0$

80. $\dfrac{2}{x + 1} \le \dfrac{3}{x - 1}$

81. $\left|x - \frac{3}{2}\right| \ge \frac{3}{2}$

82. $|x - 2| < 1$

In Exercises 83 and 84, find the domain of the expression by finding the interval(s) on the real number line for which the radicand is nonnegative.

83. $\sqrt{2x - 10}$

84. $\sqrt{x(x - 4)}$

85. *Surface Area* The inside and outside radii of a thrust washer are r inches and R inches, respectively (see figure). Find an algebraic expression for the surface area of one side of the washer. Factor the expression if possible.

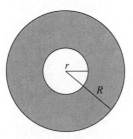

Figure for 85

86. *Discount Rate* The price of a television set has been discounted $85. The sale price is $340. What was the percent discount?

87. *Mixture Problem* A car radiator contains 10 quarts of a 30% antifreeze solution. How many quarts will have to be replaced with pure antifreeze if the resulting solution is to be 50% antifreeze?

88. *Starting Position* A fitness center has two running tracks around a rectangular playing floor. The tracks are 3 feet wide and form semicircles at the narrow end of the rectangular floor (see figure). Determine the distance between the starting positions if two runners must run the same distance to the finish line in one lap around the track.

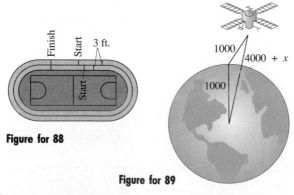

Figure for 88

Figure for 89

89. *Altitude* The distance from a spacecraft to the horizon is 1000 miles. Find x, the altitude of the craft (see figure). Assume that the radius of the earth is 4000 miles.

90. *Average Speed* Each week you must make a 180-mile trip to pick up supplies for your business. If you were to increase your average speed by 5 miles per hour, the trip would take 24 minutes less than usual. Find the usual average speed.

91. *Cost Sharing* A group of farmers agree to share equally in the cost of a $48,000 piece of machinery. If they could find two more farmers to join the group, each person's share of the cost would decrease by $4000. How many farmers are presently in the group?

92. *Market Research* The demand equation for a product is given by

$$p = 42 - \sqrt{0.001x + 2}$$

where x is the number of units demanded per day and p is the price per unit. Find the demand if the price is set at $29.95.

93. *Break-Even Analysis* The revenue for selling x units of a product is

$$R = 125.95x.$$

The cost of producing x units is

$$C = 92x + 1200.$$

In order to obtain a profit, the revenue must be greater than the cost. For what values of x will this product return a profit?

94. *Pendulum* The period of a pendulum is given by

$$T = 2\pi\sqrt{\frac{L}{32}}$$

where T is the time in seconds and L is the length of the pendulum in feet. If the period is to be at least 2 seconds, determine the minimum length of the pendulum.

C H A P T E R 2

OVERVIEW

In this chapter, you will learn how a graph can be used to visualize relationships between two variables. For instance, in Exercises 59 and 60 on page 98, a graph shows the changing cost of a Super Bowl ad from 1967 through 1991.

You will also learn that many of the equations used to model real-life relationships between two variables are *functions*. For instance, in Exercise 49 on page 158, the stopping distance of a car is a function of the speed of the car.

As you study the chapter, you should know that algebra is *not* a static branch of mathematics—it changes. Modern algebra employs technology, estimation, problem-solving strategies, functions, and their graphs to provide a deeper understanding of traditional algebraic concepts.

Functions and Graphs

2.1 The Cartesian Plane

Introduction / The Distance Between Two Points in the Plane / The Midpoint Formula

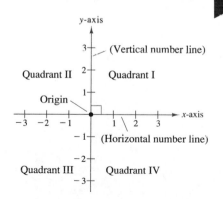

Cartesian Plane

FIGURE 2.1

Introduction

Just as we can represent real numbers by points on the real line, we can represent ordered pairs of real numbers by points in a plane. This plane is a **rectangular coordinate system** or the **Cartesian plane,** after the French mathematician René Descartes (1596–1650).

The Cartesian plane is formed by two real number lines intersecting at right angles, as shown in Figure 2.1. The horizontal number line is usually called the **x-axis** and the vertical number line is usually called the **y-axis.** (The plural of axis is *axes*.) The point of intersection of the two axes is the **origin.** The axes separate the plane into four regions called **quadrants.**

Each point in the plane corresponds to an **ordered pair** (x, y) of real numbers x and y, called **coordinates** of the point. The first number (**x-**

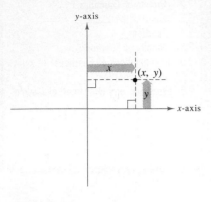

FIGURE 2.2

coordinate) tells how far to the left or right the point is from the vertical axis, and the second number (**y-coordinate**) tells how far up or down the point is from the horizontal axis, as shown in Figure 2.2.

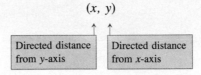

REMARK   It is customary to use the notation (x, y) to denote both a point in the plane and an open interval on the real number line. The nature of a specific problem will show which of the two we are talking about.   ◢

EXAMPLE 1   Plotting Points in the Cartesian Plane

Plot the points $(-1, 2)$, $(3, 4)$, $(0, 0)$, $(3, 0)$, and $(-2, -3)$ in the Cartesian plane.

Solution

To plot the point $(-1, 2)$ we envision a vertical line through -1 on the x-axis and a horizontal line through 2 on the y-axis. The intersection of these two lines is the point $(-1, 2)$, as shown in Figure 2.3. The other four points can be plotted in a similar way.

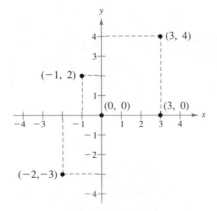

FIGURE 2.3   ◢

Shifting points in the Cartesian plane is a technique used in computer graphics.

EXAMPLE 2   Shifting Points in the Plane

The triangle shown in Figure 2.4(a) has vertices at the points $(-1, 2)$, $(1, -4)$, and $(2, 3)$. Shift the triangle three units to the right and two units up and find the vertices of the shifted triangle.

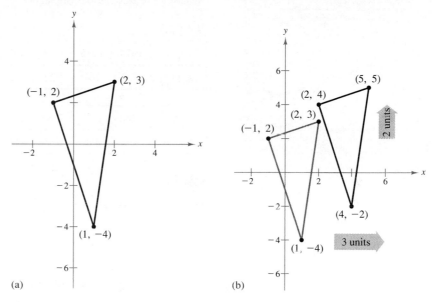

(a)   (b)

FIGURE 2.4

Solution

To shift the vertices three units to the right, we add 3 to each of the x-coordinates. To shift the vertices two units up, we add 2 to each of the y-coordinates. The coordinates of the shifted vertices are as follows.

Original Vertices	*Shifted Vertices*
$(-1, 2)$	$(-1 + 3, 2 + 2) = (2, 4)$
$(1, -4)$	$(1 + 3, -4 + 2) = (4, -2)$
$(2, 3)$	$(2 + 3, 3 + 2) = (5, 5)$

The original and shifted triangles are shown in Figure 2.4(b).

The rectangular coordinate system allows you to visualize relationships between variables x and y. Today, Descartes's ideas are commonly used in virtually every scientific and business-related field.

EXAMPLE 3   Number of Doctor's Degrees in Mathematics

The number of doctor's degrees in mathematics granted to United States citizens by universities in the United States from 1974 to 1989 is given in Table 2.1. Plot these points in a rectangular coordinate system. (*Source:* American Mathematical Society)

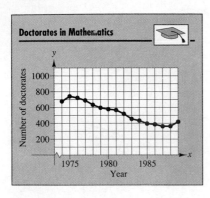

FIGURE 2.5

TABLE 2.1

Year	1974	1975	1976	1977	1978	1979	1980	1981
Degrees	677	741	722	689	634	596	578	567

Year	1982	1983	1984	1985	1986	1987	1988	1989
Degrees	519	455	433	396	386	362	363	419

Solution

The points are shown in Figure 2.5. Note that the break in the *x*-axis indicates that we have omitted the numbers between 0 and 1973. ◄

The Distance Between Two Points in the Plane

We know from Section 1.1 that the distance d between two points a and b on the real number line is simply $d = |b - a|$. The same "absolute value rule" is used to find the distance between two points that lie on the same *vertical* or *horizontal* line in the plane.

EXAMPLE 4   Finding Horizontal and Vertical Distances

a. Find the distance between the points $(1, -1)$, and $(1, 4)$.
b. Find the distance between the points $(-3, -1)$ and $(1, -1)$.

Solution

a. Because the *x*-coordinates are equal, we envision a vertical line through the points $(1, -1)$ and $(1, 4)$, as shown in Figure 2.6. The distance between these two points is the absolute value of the difference of their *y*-coordinates. That is,

$$\text{Vertical distance} = |4 - (-1)| = 5. \qquad \textit{Subtract y-coordinates}$$

b. Because the *y*-coordinates are equal, we envision a horizontal line through the points $(-3, -1)$ and $(1, -1)$, as shown in Figure 2.6. The distance between these two points is the absolute value of the difference of their *x*-coordinates. That is,

$$\text{Horizontal distance} = |1 - (-3)| = 4. \qquad \textit{Subtract x-coordinates} ◄$$

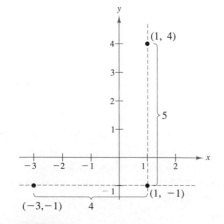

FIGURE 2.6

The technique shown in Example 4 can be used to develop a general formula for finding the distance between two points in a plane. This formula will work for any two points, even if they do not lie on the same vertical or horizontal line. To develop the formula, use the Pythagorean Theorem, which states that for a right triangle, the hypotenuse c and sides a and b are related by the formula $a^2 + b^2 = c^2$, as shown in Figure 2.7. (The converse is also true: If $a^2 + b^2 = c^2$, then the triangle is a right triangle.)

To develop a general formula for the distance between two points, let (x_1, y_1) and (x_2, y_2) represent two points in the plane (that do not lie on the same horizontal or vertical line). With these two points, a right triangle can be formed, as shown in Figure 2.8. Note that the third vertex of the triangle is (x_1, y_2). Since (x_1, y_1) and (x_1, y_2) lie on the same vertical line, the length of the vertical side of the triangle is $|y_2 - y_1|$. Similarly, the length of the horizontal side is $|x_2 - x_1|$. Thus, by the Pythagorean Theorem, the distance between (x_1, y_1) and (x_2, y_2) is

$$d^2 = |x_2 - x_1|^2 + |y_2 - y_1|^2.$$

Since the distance d must be positive, we choose the positive square root and write

$$d = \sqrt{|x_2 - x_1|^2 + |y_2 - y_1|^2}.$$

Finally, replacing $|x_2 - x_1|^2$ and $|y_2 - y_1|^2$ by the equivalent expressions $(x_2 - x_1)^2$ and $(y_2 - y_1)^2$ gives the following formula for the distance between two points in a rectangular coordinate plane.

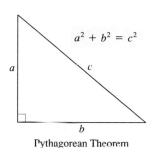

$$a^2 + b^2 = c^2$$

Pythagorean Theorem

FIGURE 2.7

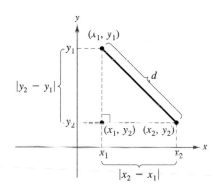

Distance Between Two Points

FIGURE 2.8

THE DISTANCE FORMULA

The distance d between the two points (x_1, y_1) and (x_2, y_2) in the coordinate plane is

$$d = \sqrt{(x_2 - x_1)^2 + (y_2 - y_1)^2}.$$

REMARK Note that for the special case in which the two points lie on the same vertical or horizontal line, the Distance Formula still works. For instance, applying the Distance Formula to the points $(1, -1)$ and $(1, 4)$ produces

$$d = \sqrt{(1 - 1)^2 + [4 - (-1)]^2} = \sqrt{5^2} = 5,$$

which is the same result obtained in Example 4.

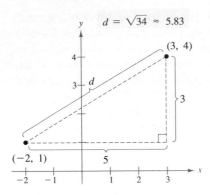

FIGURE 2.9

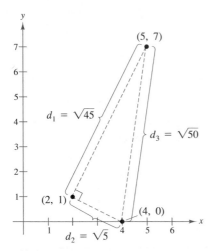

FIGURE 2.10

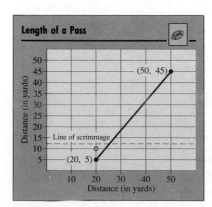

FIGURE 2.11

EXAMPLE 5 Finding the Distance Between Two Points

Find the distance between the points $(-2, 1)$ and $(3, 4)$.

Solution

Letting $(x_1, y_1) = (-2, 1)$ and $(x_2, y_2) = (3, 4)$, apply the Distance Formula to obtain

$$d = \sqrt{[3 - (-2)]^2 + (4 - 1)^2}$$
$$= \sqrt{5^2 + 3^2} = \sqrt{25 + 9} = \sqrt{34} \approx 5.83.$$

See Figure 2.9.

In Example 5, the figure provided was not essential to the solution of the problem. *Nevertheless*, we recommend that you include graphs with your problem solutions.

EXAMPLE 6 An Application of the Distance Formula

Show that the points $(2, 1)$, $(4, 0)$, and $(5, 7)$ are vertices of a right triangle.

Solution

The three points are plotted in Figure 2.10. Using the Distance Formula, you can find the lengths of the three sides of the triangle.

$$d_1 = \sqrt{(5 - 2)^2 + (7 - 1)^2} = \sqrt{9 + 36} = \sqrt{45}$$
$$d_2 = \sqrt{(4 - 2)^2 + (0 - 1)^2} = \sqrt{4 + 1} = \sqrt{5}$$
$$d_3 = \sqrt{(5 - 4)^2 + (7 - 0)^2} = \sqrt{1 + 49} = \sqrt{50}$$

Since $d_1{}^2 + d_2{}^2 = 45 + 5 = 50 = d_3{}^2$, you can conclude from the Pythagorean Theorem that the triangle is a right triangle.

EXAMPLE 7 An Application of the Distance Formula

In a football game, a quarterback throws a pass from the 5-yard line, 20 yards from the sideline. The pass is caught by a wide receiver on the 45-yard line, 50 yards from the same sideline, as shown in Figure 2.11. How long was the pass?

Solution

$$d = \sqrt{(50 - 20)^2 + (45 - 5)^2} \qquad \textit{Distance Formula}$$
$$= \sqrt{900 + 1600}$$
$$= \sqrt{2500}$$
$$= 50 \text{ yards}$$

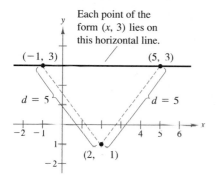

Each point of the form $(x, 3)$ lies on this horizontal line.

FIGURE 2.12

EXAMPLE 8 Finding Points at a Specified Distance from a Given Point

Find x so that the distance between $(x, 3)$ and $(2, -1)$ is 5.

Solution

$$\sqrt{(x - 2)^2 + (3 + 1)^2} = 5 \qquad \textit{Distance Formula}$$
$$(x^2 - 4x + 4) + 16 = 25 \qquad \textit{Square both sides}$$
$$x^2 - 4x - 5 = 0 \qquad \textit{Standard form}$$
$$(x - 5)(x + 1) = 0 \qquad \textit{Factor}$$
$$x - 5 = 0 \;\rightarrow\; x = 5 \qquad \textit{Set 1st factor equal to 0}$$
$$x + 1 = 0 \;\rightarrow\; x = -1 \qquad \textit{Set 2nd factor equal to 0}$$

There are two solutions: Each of the points $(5, 3)$ and $(-1, 3)$ lies five units from the point $(2, -1)$, as shown in Figure 2.12.

The Midpoint Formula

Next you will consider a formula for finding the midpoint of a line segment joining two points. The coordinates of the midpoint are the average values of the corresponding coordinates of the two endpoints.

THE MIDPOINT FORMULA

The **midpoint** of the line segment joining the points (x_1, y_1) and (x_2, y_2) in the coordinate plane is

$$\left(\frac{x_1 + x_2}{2}, \frac{y_1 + y_2}{2} \right).$$

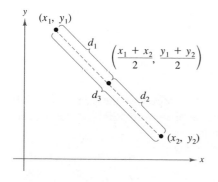

Midpoint Formula

FIGURE 2.13

Proof

Using Figure 2.13, you must show that

$$d_1 = d_2 \qquad \text{and} \qquad d_1 + d_2 = d_3.$$

By the Distance Formula, you obtain

$$d_1 = \sqrt{\left(\frac{x_1 + x_2}{2} - x_1 \right)^2 + \left(\frac{y_1 + y_2}{2} - y_1 \right)^2} = \frac{1}{2}\sqrt{(x_2 - x_1)^2 + (y_2 - y_1)^2}$$

$$d_2 = \sqrt{\left(x_2 - \frac{x_1 + x_2}{2} \right)^2 + \left(y_2 - \frac{y_1 + y_2}{2} \right)^2} = \frac{1}{2}\sqrt{(x_2 - x_1)^2 + (y_2 - y_1)^2}$$

$$d_3 = \sqrt{(x_2 - x_1)^2 + (y_2 - y_1)^2}.$$

Thus, it follows that $d_1 = d_2$ and $d_1 + d_2 = d_3$.

EXAMPLE 9 Finding the Midpoint of a Line Segment

Find the midpoint of the line segment joining the points $(-5, -3)$ and $(9, 3)$.

Solution

Figure 2.14 shows the two given points and their midpoint. By the Midpoint Formula,

$$\text{Midpoint} = \left(\frac{-5 + 9}{2}, \frac{-3 + 3}{2}\right) = (2, 0).$$

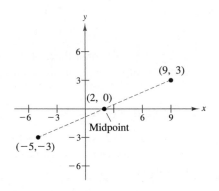

FIGURE 2.14

Although you have used the Midpoint Formula in the context of geometry, it can also be applied to problems that don't appear to be geometrical.

EXAMPLE 10 An Application: Retail Sales

A business had annual retail sales of \$240,000 in 1986 and \$312,000 in 1992. Find the sales for 1989, assuming that the annual increase in sales followed a *linear* pattern.

Solution

To make the computations simpler, let $t = 0$ represent the year 1986 and $t = 6$ represent the year 1992. Then, the retail sales in 1000s of dollars for 1986 and 1992 are represented by the points

$(0, 240)$ and $(6, 312)$.

1986 sales   1992 sales

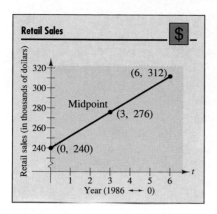

FIGURE 2.15

Since 1989 is midway between 1986 and 1992, and since the growth pattern is linear, you can use the Midpoint Formula to find the 1989 sales.

$$\text{Midpoint} = \left(\frac{0 + 6}{2}, \frac{240 + 312}{2} \right) = (3, 276)$$

1989 sales

Thus, the 1989 sales were approximately \$276,000, as indicated in Figure 2.15.

DISCUSSION

PROBLEM

A
Misleading
Graph

While graphs can help you visualize relationships between two variables, they can also mislead people. The graphs shown in Figure 2.16 represent the *same* data points. Which of the two graphs is misleading, and why?

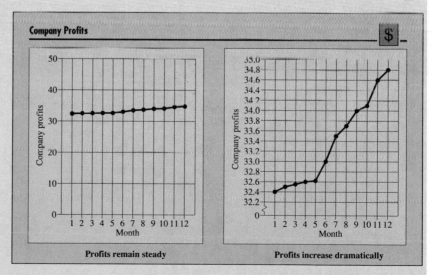

FIGURE 2.16

WARM UP

The following warm-up exercises involve skills that were covered in earlier sections. You will use these skills in the exercise set for this section.

In Exercises 1–6, simplify the expression.

1. $\sqrt{(2 - 6)^2 + [1 - (-2)]^2}$ **2.** $\sqrt{(1 - 4)^2 + (-2 - 1)^2}$

3. $\dfrac{4 + (-2)}{2}$ **4.** $\dfrac{-1 + (-3)}{2}$

5. $\sqrt{18} + \sqrt{45}$ **6.** $\sqrt{12} + \sqrt{44}$

In Exercises 7–10, solve for x or y.

7. $\sqrt{(4 - x)^2 + (5 - 2)^2} = \sqrt{58}$ **8.** $\sqrt{(8 - 6)^2 + (y - 5)^2} = 2\sqrt{5}$

9. $\dfrac{x + 3}{2} = 7$ **10.** $\dfrac{-2 + y}{2} = 1$

EXERCISES for Section 2.1

In Exercises 1–4, sketch the polygon with the indicated vertices.

1. Triangle: $(-1, 1)$, $(2, -1)$, $(3, 4)$
2. Triangle: $(0, 3)$, $(-1, -2)$, $(4, 8)$
3. Square: $(2, 4)$, $(5, 1)$, $(2, -2)$, $(-1, 1)$
4. Parallelogram: $(5, 2)$, $(7, 0)$, $(1, -2)$, $(-1, 0)$

In Exercises 5 and 6, the figure is shifted to a new position in the plane. Find the coordinates of the vertices of the figure in its *new* position.

5.

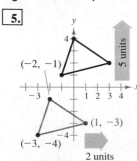

6. $(-5, 2)$

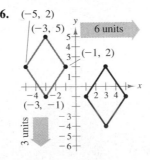

In Exercises 7–10, find the distance between the points. (*Note:* In each case the two points lie on the same horizontal or vertical line.)

7. $(6, -3)$, $(6, 5)$ **8.** $(1, 4)$, $(8, 4)$
9. $(-3, -1)$, $(2, -1)$ **10.** $(-3, -4)$, $(-3, 6)$

In Exercises 11–14, (a) find the length of the two sides of the right triangle and use the Pythagorean Theorem to find the length of the hypotenuse, and (b) use the Distance Formula to find the length of the hypotenuse of the triangle.

11.

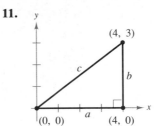

12.

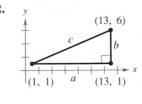

13.

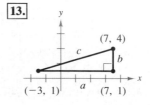

14.

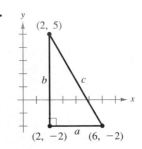

In Exercises 15–26, (a) plot the points, (b) find the distance between the points, and (c) find the midpoint of the line segment joining the points.

15. (1, 1), (9, 7)　　　　　　**16.** (1, 12), (6, 0)

17. (−4, 10), (4, −5)　　　　**18.** (−7, −4), (2, 8)

19. (−1, 2), (5, 4)　　　　　**20.** (2, 10), (10, 2)

21. $\left(\frac{1}{2}, 1\right), \left(-\frac{5}{2}, \frac{4}{3}\right)$　　　**22.** $\left(-\frac{1}{3}, -\frac{1}{3}\right), \left(-\frac{1}{6}, -\frac{1}{2}\right)$

23. (6.2, 5.4), (−3.7, 1.8)　　**24.** (−16.8, 12.3), (5.6, 4.9)

25. (−36, −18), (48, −72)

26. (1.451, 3.051), (5.906, 11.360)

In Exercises 27 and 28, use the Midpoint Formula to estimate the sales of a company for 1991. Assume the sales followed a linear pattern.

27.

Year	1989	1993
Sales	$520,000	$740,000

28.

Year	1989	1993
Sales	$4,200,000	$5,650,000

In Exercises 29–32, show that the points form the vertices of the indicated polygon.

29. Right triangle: (4, 0), (2, 1), (−1, −5)

30. Isosceles triangle: (1, −3), (3, 2), (−2, 4)

31. Rhombus: (0, 0), (1, 2), (2, 1), (3, 3)
(A rhombus is a parallelogram whose sides are all of the same length.)

32. Parallelogram: (0, 1), (3, 7), (4, 4), (1, −2)

In Exercises 33 and 34, find x so that the distance between the points is 13.

33. (1, 2), (x, −10)　　　　**34.** (−8, 0), (x, 5)

In Exercises 35 and 36, find y so that the distance between the points is 17.

35. (0, 0), (8, y)　　　　　**36.** (−8, 4), (7, y)

In Exercises 37 and 38, find a relationship between x and y so that (x, y) is equidistant from the two points.

37. (4, −1), (−2, 3)　　　　**38.** $\left(3, \frac{5}{2}\right), (−7, 1)$

In Exercises 39–48, determine the quadrant(s) in which (x, y) is located so that the conditions are satisfied.

39. $x > 0$ and $y < 0$　　　**40.** $x < 0$ and $y < 0$

41. $x > 0$ and $y > 0$　　　**42.** $x < 0$ and $y > 0$

43. $x = -4$ and $y > 0$　　**44.** $x > 2$ and $y = 3$

45. $y < -5$　　　　　　　**46.** $x > 4$

47. $(x, -y)$ is in the second quadrant.

48. $(-x, y)$ is in the fourth quadrant.

49. A line segment has (x_1, y_1) as one endpoint and (x_m, y_m) as its midpoint. Find the other endpoint (x_2, y_2) of the line segment in terms of $x_1, y_1, x_m,$ and y_m.

50. Use the result of Exercise 49 to find the coordinates of one endpoint of a line segment if the coordinates of the other endpoint and midpoint are, respectively,
(a) (1, −2), (4, −1)　　　(b) (−5, 11), (2, 4).

51. Use the Midpoint Formula twice to find the three points that divide the line segment joining (x_1, y_1) and (x_2, y_2) into four parts.

52. Use the result of Exercise 51 to find the points that divide the line segment joining the points into four equal parts.
(a) (1, −2), (4, −1)　　　(b) (−2, −3), (0, 0)

53. *Football Pass* In a football game, a quarterback throws a pass from the 15-yard line, 10 yards from the sideline. The pass is caught on the 40-yard line, 45 yards from the same sideline. How long was the pass? (Assume the pass and the reception are on the same side of midfield.)

54. *Flying Distance* A plane flies in a straight line to a city that is 100 miles east and 150 miles north of the point of departure. How far did it fly?

In Exercises 55 and 56, plot the points whose coordinates are given in the table.

55. *Normal Temperatures* The normal temperature y (Fahrenheit) for Duluth, Minnesota for each month of the year is given in the table. The months are numbered 1 through 12, with 1 corresponding to January. (*Source:* NOAA)

x	1	2	3	4	5	6	7	8	9	10	11	12
y	6	12	23	38	50	59	65	63	54	44	28	14

56. *Stock Price*   The price *y* per common share of stock on December 31 for the years 1984 through 1989 is given in the table. The time in years is given by *x*. (*Source:* Ameritech Annual Report for 1989)

x	1984	1985	1986	1987	1988	1989
y	$25.50	$35.50	$44.125	$42.25	$47.875	$68.00

Milk Prices   In Exercises 57 and 58, refer to the figure. (*Source:* U.S. Department of Agriculture and the National Milk Producers Federation)

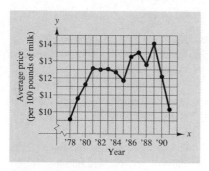

Figure for 57 and 58

57. What is the highest price of milk shown in the graph? When did this occur?

58. Find the percentage drop in the price of milk from the highest price shown in the graph to the price paid to farmers in January 1991.

TV Advertising   In Exercises 59 and 60, refer to the figure. (*Source:* Nielson Media Research)

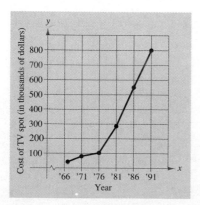

Figure for 59 and 60

59. Find the percentage increase in the cost of a 30-second spot from Super Bowl I to Super Bowl XXV.

60. Estimate the increase in the cost of a 30-second spot (a) from Super Bowl V to Super Bowl XV, and (b) from Super Bowl XV to Super Bowl XXV.

61. Plot the points $(2, 1)$, $(-3, 5)$, and $(7, -3)$ on the rectangular coordinate system. Now plot the corresponding points when the sign of the *x*-coordinate is reversed. What can you infer about the result of the location of a point when the sign of the *x*-coordinate is changed?

62. Plot the points $(2, 1)$, $(-3, 5)$, and $(7, -3)$ on the rectangular coordinate system. Now plot the corresponding points when the sign of the *y*-coordinate is reversed. What can you infer about the result of the location of a point when the sign of the *y*-coordinate is changed?

63. Prove that the diagonals of the parallelogram in the figure bisect each other.

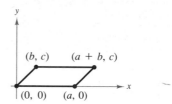

Figure for 63

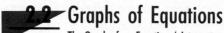Graphs of Equations

The Graph of an Equation / Intercepts of a Graph / Symmetry / The Equation of a Circle

The Graph of an Equation

News magazines often show graphs comparing the rate of inflation, the federal deficit, wholesale prices, or the unemployment rate to the time of year. Industrial firms and businesses use graphs to report their monthly production and sales statistics. Such graphs provide a simple geometric picture of the way one quantity changes with respect to another.

Frequently, the relationship between two quantities is expressed in the form of an equation. In this section, we introduce the basic procedure for determining the geometric picture associated with an algebraic equation.

For an equation in variables x and y, a point (a, b) is a **solution point** if the substitution of $x = a$ and $y = b$ satisfies the equation. Most equations have *infinitely* many solution points. For example, the equation $3x + y = 5$ has solution points $(0, 5)$, $(1, 2)$, $(2, -1)$, $(3, -4)$, and so on. The set of all solution points of a given equation is the **graph** of the equation.

The Point-Plotting Method of Graphing

To sketch the graph of an equation by point plotting, use the following method.

1. If possible, rewrite the equation so that one of the variables is isolated on the left side of the equation.
2. Make up a table of several solution points.
3. Plot these points in the coordinate plane.
4. Connect the points with a smooth curve.

EXAMPLE 1   Sketching the Graph of an Equation

Sketch a graph of the equation $3x + y = 5$.

Solution

Isolate the variable y.

$$y = 5 - 3x$$

Use negative, zero, and positive values for x to obtain a table of values (solution points).

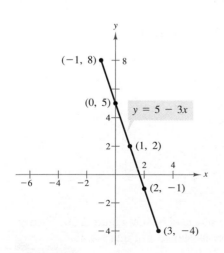

x	-1	0	1	2	3
$y = 5 - 3x$	8	5	2	-1	-4

Next, plot these points and connect them as shown in Figure 2.17. It appears that the graph is a straight line. (You will study lines extensively in Section 2.3.)

FIGURE 2.17

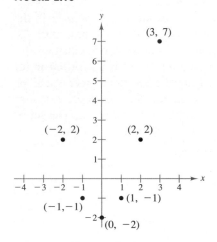

FIGURE 2.18

Step 4 of the point-plotting method can be difficult. For instance, how would you connect the four points in Figure 2.18? Without further information about the equation, any one of the three graphs in Figure 2.19 would be reasonable.

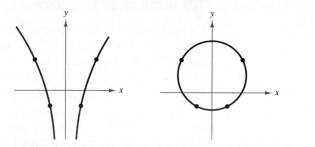

FIGURE 2.19

With too few solution points, you could grossly misrepresent the graph of an equation. Just how many points should be plotted? For straight-line graphs, two points are sufficient. For more complicated graphs, you need many more points, enough to reveal the essential behavior of the graph. A programmable calculator is useful for determining the many solution points needed for an accurate graph.

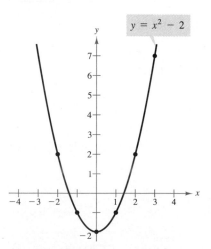

Plot several points.

FIGURE 2.20

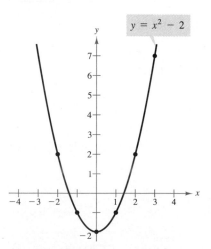

Connect points with a smooth curve.

FIGURE 2.21

EXAMPLE 2   Sketching the Graph of an Equation

Sketch the graph of the equation $y = x^2 - 2$.

Solution

First, make a table of values.

x	-2	-1	0	1	2	3
$y = x^2 - 2$	2	-1	-2	-1	2	7

Next, plot the corresponding solution points, as shown in Figure 2.20. Finally, connect the points with a smooth curve, as shown in Figure 2.21.

Intercepts of a Graph

Two types of points that are especially useful when sketching a graph are those for which either the y-coordinate or the x-coordinate is zero. These points are called **intercepts** because they are points at which the graph intersects the x- or y-axis.

DEFINITION OF INTERCEPTS

1. The point $(a, 0)$ is an **x-intercept** of the graph of an equation if it is a solution point of the equation. To find the x-intercepts, let y be zero and solve the equation for x.
2. The point $(0, b)$ is a **y-intercept** of the graph of an equation if it is a solution point of the equation. To find the y-intercepts, let x be zero and solve the equation for y.

REMARK Sometimes it is convenient to denote the x-intercept as simply the x-coordinate, a, of the point $(a, 0)$ rather than the point itself. The same is true with the y-intercept. Unless it is necessary to make a distinction, we will use "intercept" to mean either the point or the coordinate.

Of course, it is possible that a particular graph will have no intercepts or several intercepts. For instance, consider the three graphs in Figure 2.22.

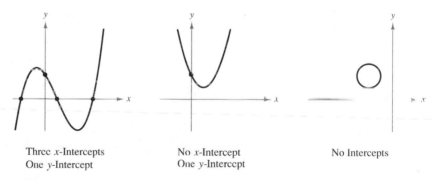

Three x-Intercepts
One y-Intercept

No x-Intercept
One y-Intercept

No Intercepts

FIGURE 2.22

EXAMPLE 3   Finding the x- and y-Intercepts of a Graph

Find the x- and y-intercepts of the graph of $x = y^2 - 3$.

Solution

To find the x-intercept, let $y = 0$. This produces $x = -3$, which implies that the graph has one x-intercept, which occurs at the point

$(-3, 0).$ *x-intercept*

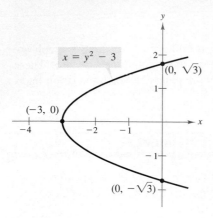

FIGURE 2.23

To find the y-intercept, let $x = 0$. This produces $0 = y^2 - 3$, which has two solutions: $y = \pm\sqrt{3}$. Thus, the equation has two y-intercepts, which occur at the points

$$(0, \sqrt{3}) \quad \text{and} \quad (0, -\sqrt{3}). \qquad \textit{y-intercepts}$$

See Figure 2.23.

EXAMPLE 4 Finding the *x*- and *y*-Intercepts of a Graph

Find the x- and y-intercepts of the graph of $y = x^3 - 4x$.

Solution

To find the x-intercepts, let $y = 0$.

$$0 = x^3 - 4x = x(x^2 - 4)$$

Set each factor equal to zero and solve for x to obtain $x = 0$ and $x = \pm 2$. Thus, the equation has three x-intercepts, which occur at the points

$$(0, 0), \quad (2, 0), \quad \text{and} \quad (-2, 0). \qquad \textit{x-intercepts}$$

Let $x = 0$ to obtain $y = 0$, which tells us that the y-intercept is

$$(0, 0). \qquad \textit{y-intercept}$$

See Figure 2.24.

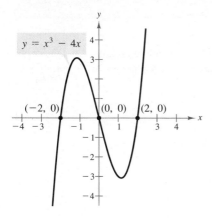

FIGURE 2.24

Symmetry

The graphs shown in Figures 2.21, 2.23, and 2.24 each have a type of **symmetry** with respect to one of the coordinate axes or with respect to the origin.

Figure 2.21	$y = x^2 - 2$	*y-axis symmetry*
Figure 2.23	$x = y^2 - 3$	*x-axis symmetry*
Figure 2.24	$y = x^3 - 4x$	*Origin symmetry*

Symmetry with respect to the x-axis means that if the Cartesian plane were folded along the x-axis, the portion of the graph above the x-axis would coincide with the portion below the x-axis. Symmetry with respect to the y-axis or to the origin is described in a similar manner, as shown in Figure 2.25.

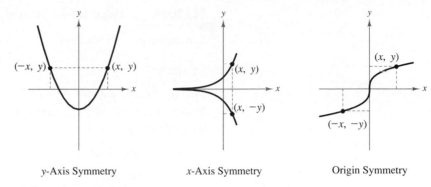

y-Axis Symmetry   x-Axis Symmetry   Origin Symmetry

FIGURE 2.25

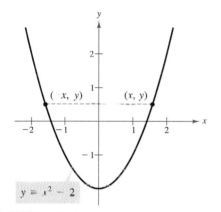

y-Axis Symmetry

FIGURE 2.26

Knowing the symmetry of a graph *before* attempting to sketch it is helpful, because then you need only half as many solution points to sketch the graph. There are three basic types of symmetry. (See Exercises 29–32.) A graph is **symmetric with respect to the y-axis** if, whenever (x, y) is on the graph, $(-x, y)$ is also on the graph. A graph is **symmetric with respect to the x-axis** if, whenever (x, y) is on the graph, $(x, -y)$ is also on the graph. A graph is **symmetric with respect to the origin** if, whenever (x, y) is on the graph, $(-x, -y)$ is also on the graph.

The graph of $y = x^2 - 2$ is symmetric with respect to the y-axis because the point $(-x, y)$ satisfies the equation.

$y = x^2 - 2$ *Given equation*

$y = (-x)^2 - 2$ *Substitute $(-x, y)$ for (x, y)*

$y = x^2 - 2$ *Replacement yields equivalent equation*

See Figure 2.26.

The graph of $y = x^3 - 4x$ (see Figure 2.24) is symmetric with respect to the origin because the point $(-x, -y)$ satisfies the equation.

$y = x^3 - 4x$ *Given equation*

$-y = (-x)^3 - 4(-x)$ *Substitute $(-x, -y)$ for (x, y)*

$-y = x^3 + 4x$ *Equation is equivalent to given equation*

A similar test can be made for symmetry with respect to the x-axis.

Tests for Symmetry

1. The graph of an equation is symmetric with respect to the *y-axis* if replacing x with $-x$ yields an equivalent equation.
2. The graph of an equation is symmetric with respect to the *x-axis* if replacing y with $-y$ yields an equivalent equation.
3. The graph of an equation is symmetric with respect to the *origin* if replacing x with $-x$ and y with $-y$ yields an equivalent equation.

EXAMPLE 5   Using Intercepts and Symmetry as Sketching Aids

Use intercepts and symmetry to sketch the graph of $x - y^2 = 1$.

Solution

Letting $x = 0$, you see that $-y^2 = 1$ or $y^2 = -1$ has no real solutions. Hence, there are no y-intercepts. Let $y = 0$ to obtain $x = 1$. Thus, the x-intercept is $(1, 0)$.

> y-intercept: None
>
> x-intercept: $(1, 0)$

Of the three tests for symmetry, the only one that is satisfied by this equation is the test for x-axis symmetry.

$$x - y^2 = 1 \qquad \textit{Given equation}$$
$$x - (-y)^2 = 1 \qquad \textit{Replace } y \textit{ with } -y$$
$$x - y^2 = 1 \qquad \textit{Replacement yields equivalent equation}$$

Thus, the graph is symmetric with respect to the x-axis. Using symmetry, you need only to find solution points above the x-axis and then reflect them to obtain the desired graph, as shown in Figure 2.27.

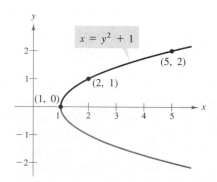

FIGURE 2.27

y	0	1	2
$x = y^2 + 1$	1	2	5

EXAMPLE 6   Sketching the Graph of an Equation

Sketch the graph of $y = |4x - x^2|$.

Solution

Intercepts: Letting $x = 0$ yields $y = 0$, which means that $(0, 0)$ is a y-intercept. Letting $y = 0$ yields $x = 0$ and $x = 4$, which means that $(0, 0)$ and $(4, 0)$ are x-intercepts.

Symmetry: This equation fails all three tests for symmetry and consequently its graph is not symmetric with respect to either axis or the origin.

The absolute value sign indicates that y is always nonnegative.

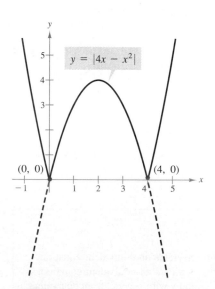

FIGURE 2.28

x	-1	0	1	2	3	4	5
$y = |4x - x^2|$	5	0	3	4	3	0	5

The graph is shown in Figure 2.28. The dotted portion of the figure shows how the graph would differ if no absolute value signs were used.

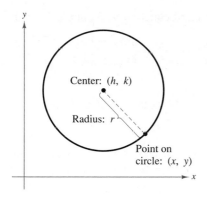

FIGURE 2.29

The Equation of a Circle

Thus far you have studied the point-plotting method and two additional concepts (intercepts and symmetry) that can be used to streamline the graphing procedure. Another graphing aid is *equation recognition*, the ability to recognize the general shape of a graph simply by looking at its equation. A circle is one type of graph that is easily recognized.

Figure 2.29 shows a circle of radius r with center at the point (h, k). The point (x, y) is on this circle if and only if its distance from the center (h, k) is r. This means that a **circle** in the plane consists of all points (x, y) that are a given positive distance r from a fixed point (h, k). Using the Distance Formula, you can express this relationship by saying that the point (x, y) lies on the circle if and only if

$$\sqrt{(x - h)^2 + (y - k)^2} = r.$$

You can square both sides of this equation to obtain the **standard form of the equation of a circle.**

STANDARD FORM OF THE EQUATION OF A CIRCLE

The **standard form of the equation of a circle** is

$$(x - h)^2 + (y - k)^2 = r^2.$$

The point (h, k) is the **center** of the circle and the positive number r is the **radius** of the circle.

REMARK The standard form of the equation of a circle whose center is the origin is simply $x^2 + y^2 = r^2$.

EXAMPLE 7 Finding an Equation of a Circle

The point $(3, 4)$ lies on a circle whose center is at $(-1, 2)$, as shown in Figure 2.30. Find an equation for the circle.

Solution

The radius r of the circle is the distance between $(-1, 2)$ and $(3, 4)$.

$$r = \sqrt{[3 - (-1)]^2 + (4 - 2)^2}$$
$$= \sqrt{16 + 4}$$
$$= \sqrt{20}$$

Thus, the center of the circle is $(h, k) = (-1, 2)$ and the radius is $r = \sqrt{20}$. Now, write the standard form of the equation of the circle.

$$(x - h)^2 + (y - k)^2 = r^2 \qquad \textit{Standard form}$$
$$[x - (-1)]^2 + (y - 2)^2 = (\sqrt{20})^2 \quad \textit{Let } h = -1, k = 2, \textit{ and } r = \sqrt{20}$$
$$(x + 1)^2 + (y - 2)^2 = 20 \qquad \textit{Equation of circle}$$

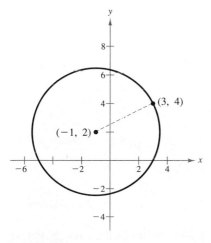

FIGURE 2.30

Removing the parentheses in the standard equation in Example 7 yields

$$(x + 1)^2 + (y - 2)^2 = 20 \qquad \textit{Standard form}$$
$$x^2 + 2x + 1 + y^2 - 4y + 4 = 20 \qquad \textit{Expand terms}$$
$$x^2 + y^2 + 2x - 4y - 15 = 0. \qquad \textit{General form}$$

The last equation is in the **general form of the equation of a circle.**

$$Ax^2 + Ay^2 + Dx + Ey + F = 0, \qquad A \neq 0$$

The general form of the equation of a circle is less useful than the standard form. For instance, it is not immediately apparent from the general equation of the circle in Example 7

$$x^2 + y^2 + 2x - 4y - 15 = 0$$

that the center is $(-1, 2)$ and the radius is $\sqrt{20}$. To graph the equation of a circle, it is best to write the equation in standard form. You can do this by **completing the square.**

EXAMPLE 8   Completing the Square to Sketch a Circle

Identify the center and radius of the circle given by the equation and sketch the circle.

$$4x^2 + 4y^2 + 20x - 16y + 37 = 0$$

Solution

To write the given equation in standard form, you must complete the square for both the x-terms *and* the y-terms.

$$4x^2 + 4y^2 + 20x - 16y + 37 = 0 \qquad \textit{General form}$$
$$x^2 + y^2 + 5x - 4y + \frac{37}{4} = 0 \qquad \textit{Divide by 4}$$
$$(x^2 + 5x + \quad) + (y^2 - 4y + \quad) = -\frac{37}{4} \qquad \textit{Group terms}$$
$$\left(x^2 + 5x + \left(\frac{5}{2}\right)^2\right) + (y^2 - 4y + 2^2) = -\frac{37}{4} + \frac{25}{4} + 4 \qquad \textit{Complete square}$$
$$\underbrace{\qquad}_{(\text{half})^2} \qquad\qquad \underbrace{\qquad}_{(\text{half})^2}$$
$$\left(x + \frac{5}{2}\right)^2 + (y - 2)^2 = 1 \qquad \textit{Standard form}$$

Thus, the center of the circle is $\left(-\frac{5}{2}, 2\right)$ and the radius of the circle is 1. Use this information to sketch the circle shown in Figure 2.31. ◣

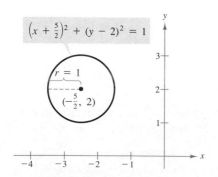

$\left(x + \frac{5}{2}\right)^2 + (y - 2)^2 = 1$

FIGURE 2.31

The general equation $Ax^2 + Ay^2 + Dx + Ey + F = 0$ may not always represent a circle. Such an equation will have no solution points if the procedure of completing the square yields the *impossible* result

$$(x - h)^2 + (y - k)^2 = \text{(negative number)}.$$

Moreover, the general equation $Ax^2 + Ay^2 + Dx + Ey + F = 0$ will have exactly one solution point if the procedure of completing the square yields the result $(x - h)^2 + (y - k)^2 = 0$. The point (h, k) is the only solution point for this equation.

Which of the following equations has no solution and which has exactly one solution? Discuss your reasons.

1. $x^2 + y^2 + 1 = 0$ 2. $x^2 + y^2 = 0$

WARM UP

The following warm-up exercises involve skills that were covered in earlier sections. You will use these skills in the exercise set for this section.

In Exercises 1 and 2, solve for y in terms of x.

1. $3x - 5y = 2$ **2.** $x^2 - 4x + 2y - 5 = 0$

In Exercises 3–6, solve for x.

3. $x^2 - 4x + 4 = 0$ **4.** $(x - 1)(x + 5) = 0$

5. $x^3 - 9x = 0$ **6.** $x^4 - 8x^2 + 16 = 0$

In Exercises 7–10, simplify the equations.

7. $-y = (-x)^3 + 4(-x)$ **8.** $(-x)^2 + (-y)^2 = 4$

9. $y = 4(-x)^2 + 8$ **10.** $(-y)^2 = 3(-x) + 4$

EXERCISES for Section 2.2

In Exercises 1–6, determine whether the indicated points lie on the graph of the equation.

Equation	Points	
1. $y = \sqrt{x + 4}$	(a) $(0, 2)$	(b) $(5, 3)$
2. $y = x^2 - 3x + 2$	(a) $(2, 0)$	(b) $(-2, 8)$
3. $2x - y - 3 = 0$	(a) $(1, 2)$	(b) $(1, -1)$
4. $x^2 + y^2 = 20$	(a) $(3, -2)$	(b) $(-4, 2)$
5. $x^2y - x^2 + 4y = 0$	(a) $\left(1, \frac{1}{5}\right)$	(b) $\left(2, \frac{1}{2}\right)$
6. $y = \dfrac{1}{x^2 + 1}$	(a) $(0, 0)$	(b) $(3, 0.1)$

In Exercises 7–10, find the constant C such that the ordered pair is a solution point of the equation.

7. $y = x^2 + C$, $(2, 6)$

8. $y = Cx^3$, $(-4, 8)$

9. $y = C\sqrt{x + 1}$, $(3, 8)$

10. $x + C(y + 2) = 0$, $(4, 3)$

In Exercises 11 and 12, complete the table. Use the solution points to sketch the graph of the equation.

11. $2x + y = 3$

x	-4			2	4
y		7	3		
(x, y)					

12. $y = 4 - x^2$

x		-1		2	
y	0		4		-5
(x, y)					

In Exercises 13–20, find the x- and y-intercepts of the graph of the equation.

13. $y = x - 5$

14. $y = (x - 1)(x - 3)$

15. $y = x^2 + x - 2$

16. $y = 4 - x^2$

17. $y = x\sqrt{x + 2}$

18. $xy = 4$

19. $xy - 2y - x + 1 = 0$

20. $x^2y - x^2 + 4y = 0$

In Exercises 21–28, check for symmetry with respect to both axes and the origin.

21. $x^2 - y = 0$

22. $xy^2 + 10 = 0$

23. $x - y^2 = 0$

24. $y = \sqrt{9 - x^2}$

25. $y = x^3$

26. $xy = 4$

27. $y = \dfrac{x}{x^2 + 1}$

28. $y = x^4 - x^2 + 3$

In Exercises 29–32, use symmetry to sketch the complete graph of the equation.

29.

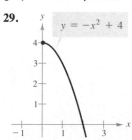

$y = -x^2 + 4$

y-Axis Symmetry

30.

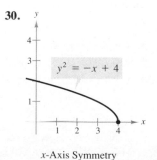

$y^2 = -x + 4$

x-Axis Symmetry

31.

$y = -x^3 + x$

Origin Symmetry

32.

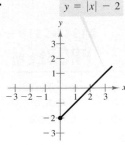

$y = |x| - 2$

y-Axis Symmetry

In Exercises 33–38, match the equation with its graph. [The graphs are labeled (a), (b), (c), (d), (e), and (f).]

33. $y = 4 - x$

34. $y = x^2 + 2x$

35. $y = \sqrt{4 - x^2}$

36. $y = \sqrt{x}$

37. $y = x^3 - x$

38. $y = |x| - 2$

(a)

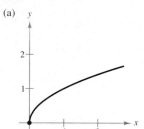

(b)

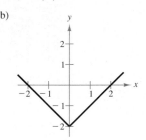

(c)

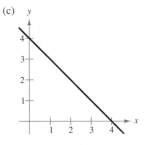

(d)

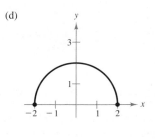

(e)

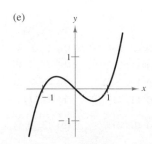

(f)

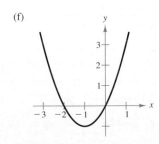

In Exercises 39–58, sketch the graph of the equation. Identify any intercepts and test for symmetry.

39. $y = -3x + 2$ **40.** $y = 2x - 3$

41. $y = 1 - x^2$ **42.** $y = x^2 - 1$

43. $y = x^2 - 4x + 3$ **44.** $y = -x^2 - 4x$

45. $y = x^3 + 2$ **46.** $y = x^3 - 1$

47. $y = x(x - 2)^2$ **48.** $y = \dfrac{4}{x^2 + 1}$

49. $y = \sqrt{x - 3}$ **50.** $y = \sqrt{1 - x}$

51. $y = \sqrt[3]{x}$ **52.** $y = \sqrt[3]{x + 1}$

53. $y = |x - 2|$ **54.** $y = 4 - |x|$

55. $x = y^2 - 1$ **56.** $x = y^2 - 4$

57. $x^2 + y^2 = 4$ **58.** $x^2 + y^2 = 16$

In Exercises 59–66, find the standard form of the equation of the specified circle.

59. Center: $(0, 0)$; radius: 3

60. Center: $(0, 0)$; radius: 5

61. Center: $(2, -1)$; radius: 4

62. Center: $\left(0, \frac{1}{3}\right)$; radius: $\frac{1}{3}$

63. Center: $(-1, 2)$; passing through: $(0, 0)$

64. Center: $(3, -2)$; passing through: $(-1, 1)$

65. Endpoints of a diameter: $(0, 0)$, $(6, 8)$

66. Endpoints of a diameter: $(-4, -1)$, $(4, 1)$

In Exercises 67–74, find the center and radius, and sketch the graph of the equation.

67. $x^2 + y^2 - 2x + 6y + 6 = 0$

68. $x^2 + y^2 - 2x + 6y - 15 = 0$

69. $x^2 + y^2 - 2x + 6y + 10 = 0$

70. $3x^2 + 3y^2 - 6y - 1 = 0$

71. $2x^2 + 2y^2 - 2x - 2y - 3 = 0$

72. $4x^2 + 4y^2 - 4x + 2y - 1 = 0$

73. $16x^2 + 16y^2 + 16x + 40y - 7 = 0$

74. $x^2 + y^2 - 4x + 2y + 3 = 0$

75. *Depreciation*   A manufacturing plant purchases a new molding machine for $225,000. The depreciated value y after t years is

$$y = 225{,}000 - 20{,}000t, \qquad 0 \le t \le 8.$$

Sketch the graph of the equation over the given interval for t.

76. *Dimensions of a Rectangle*   A rectangle of length l and width w has a perimeter of 12 meters.
(a) Show that the width of the rectangle is $w = 6 - l$ and its area is $A = l(6 - l)$.
(b) Sketch the graph of the equation for the area.
(c) From the graph of part (b), estimate the dimensions of the rectangle that yield maximum area.

In Exercises 77 and 78, (a) sketch a graph to compare the given data and the model for that data, (b) use the model to predict y for the year 1994, and (c) for the year 2000.

77. *Federal Debt*   The table gives the per capita federal debt for the United States for selected years from 1950 to 1990. (*Source:* U.S. Treasury Department)

Year	1950	1960	1970
Per capita debt	$1688	$1572	$1807

Year	1980	1985	1990
Per capita debt	$3981	$7614	$12,848

A mathematical model for the per capita debt during this period is

$$y = 0.40t^3 - 9.42t^2 + 1053.24$$

where y represents the per capita debt and t is the time in years with $t = 0$ corresponding to 1950.

78. *Life Expectancy*   The following table gives the life expectancy of a child (at birth) for selected years from 1920 to 1989. (*Source:* Department of Health and Human Services)

Year	1920	1930	1940	1950
Life expectancy	54.1	59.7	62.9	68.2

Year	1960	1970	1980	1989
Life expectancy	69.7	70.8	73.7	75.2

A mathematical model for the life expectancy during this period is

$$y = \frac{t + 66.94}{0.01t + 1}$$

where y represents the life expectancy and t represents the time in years with $t = 0$ corresponding to 1950.

79. Earnings Per Share The earnings per share for Eli Lilly Corporation from 1980 to 1986 can be approximated by the mathematical model

$$y = 1.097t + 0.15, \qquad 0 \le t \le 6$$

where y is the earnings and t represents the calendar year with $t = 0$ corresponding to 1980. Sketch the graph of this equation. (*Source:* NYSE Stock Reports)

80. Copper Wire The resistance y in ohms of 1000 feet of solid copper wire at 77 degrees Fahrenheit can be approximated by the mathematical model

$$y = \frac{10,770}{x^2} - 0.37, \qquad 5 \le x \le 100$$

where x is the diameter of the wire in mils (0.001 in.). Use the model to estimate the resistance when $x = 50$. (*Source:* American Wire Gage)

81. Find a and b if the x-intercept of the graph of $y = \sqrt{ax + b}$ is (5, 0). (The answer is not unique.)

82. Find a and b if the graph of $y = ax^2 + bx^3$ is symmetric to (a) the y-axis and (b) the origin. (The answer is not unique.)

2.3 Lines in the Plane

The Slope of a Line / The Point-Slope Form of the Equation of a Line / Sketching Graphs of Lines / Parallel and Perpendicular Lines

The Slope of a Line

In this section, we study lines and their equations. Throughout this text, we use the term **line** to mean a *straight* line.

The **slope** of a nonvertical line represents the number of units a line rises or falls vertically for each unit of horizontal change from left to right. For instance, consider the two points (x_1, y_1) and (x_2, y_2) on the line shown in Figure 2.32. As we move from left to right along this line, a change of $(y_2 - y_1)$ units in the vertical direction corresponds to a change of $(x_2 - x_1)$ units in the horizontal direction. That is,

$$y_2 - y_1 = \text{the change in } y$$

and

$$x_2 - x_1 = \text{the change in } x.$$

The slope of the line is given by the ratio of these two changes.

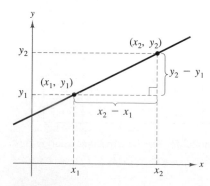

FIGURE 2.32

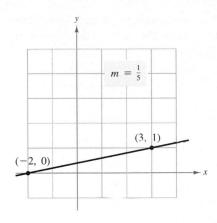

(a)

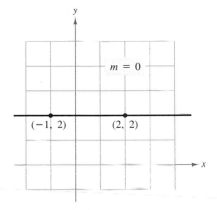

(b)

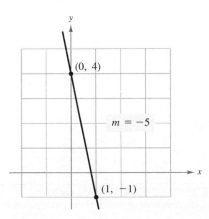

(c)

FIGURE 2.33

> ### DEFINITION OF THE SLOPE OF A LINE
>
> The **slope** m of the nonvertical line passing through the points (x_1, y_1) and (x_2, y_2) is
>
> $$m = \frac{y_2 - y_1}{x_2 - x_1} = \frac{\text{change in } y}{\text{change in } x}$$
>
> where $x_1 \neq x_2$.

When this formula is used, the *order of subtraction* is important. Given two points on a line, you are free to label either one of them as (x_1, y_1), and the other as (x_2, y_2). However, once this is done, you must form the numerator and denominator using the same order of subtraction.

$$\underbrace{m = \frac{y_2 - y_1}{x_2 - x_1}}_{\text{Correct}} \qquad \underbrace{m = \frac{y_1 - y_2}{x_1 - x_2}}_{\text{Correct}} \qquad \underbrace{m = \frac{y_2 - y_1}{x_1 - x_2}}_{\text{Incorrect}}$$

EXAMPLE 1   Finding the Slope of a Line Passing Through Two Points

Find the slopes of the lines passing through the pairs of points.

a. $(-2, 0)$ and $(3, 1)$
b. $(-1, 2)$ and $(2, 2)$
c. $(0, 4)$ and $(1, -1)$

Solution

a. $m = \dfrac{y_2 - y_1}{x_2 - x_1}$ ← *Difference in y-values*
  ← *Difference in x-values*

$$= \frac{1 - 0}{3 - (-2)}$$

$$= \frac{1}{3 + 2}$$

$$= \frac{1}{5}$$

b. $m = \dfrac{2 - 2}{2 - (-1)} = \dfrac{0}{3} = 0$

c. $m = \dfrac{-1 - 4}{1 - 0} = \dfrac{-5}{1} = -5$

The graphs of the three lines are shown in Figure 2.33.

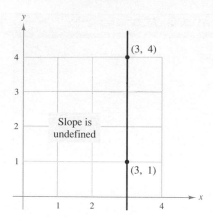

FIGURE 2.34

Note that the definition of slope does not apply to vertical lines. For instance, consider the points $(3, 4)$ and $(3, 1)$ on the vertical line shown in Figure 2.34. Applying the formula for slope,

$$m = \frac{4 - 1}{3 - 3}.$$ *Undefined division by zero*

Because division by zero is not defined, we do not define the slope of a vertical line.

From the slopes of the lines shown in Figures 2.33 and 2.34, you can make the following generalizations about the slope of a line.

1. A line with positive slope ($m > 0$) *rises* from left to right.
2. A line with negative slope ($m < 0$) *falls* from left to right.
3. A line with zero slope ($m = 0$) is *horizontal*.
4. A line with undefined slope is *vertical*.

Any two points on a line can be used to calculate its slope. This can be verified from the similar triangles shown in Figure 2.35. Recall that the ratios of corresponding sides of similar triangles are equal.

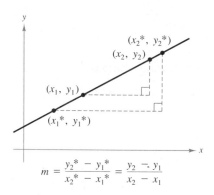

$$m = \frac{y_2{}^* - y_1{}^*}{x_2{}^* - x_1{}^*} = \frac{y_2 - y_1}{x_2 - x_1}$$

Any two points on a line can be used to determine the slope of the line.

FIGURE 2.35

The Point-Slope Form of the Equation of a Line

If you know the slope of a line *and* the coordinates of one point on the line, then you can find an equation for the line. For instance, in Figure 2.36, let (x_1, y_1) be a given point on the line whose slope is m. If (x, y) is any *other* point on the line, then it follows that

$$\frac{y - y_1}{x - x_1} = m.$$

This equation in variables x and y can be rewritten in the form

$$y - y_1 = m(x - x_1)$$

which is the **point-slope form** of the equation of a line.

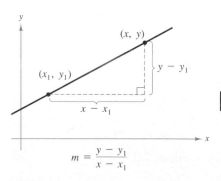

$$m = \frac{y - y_1}{x - x_1}$$

FIGURE 2.36

POINT-SLOPE FORM OF THE EQUATION OF A LINE

The **point-slope** form of the equation of the line that passes through the point (x_1, y_1) and has a slope of m is

$$y - y_1 = m(x - x_1).$$

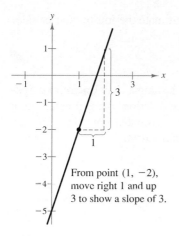

From point $(1, -2)$, move right 1 and up 3 to show a slope of 3.

FIGURE 2.37

EXAMPLE 2 The Point-Slope Form of the Equation of a Line

Find an equation of the line that passes through the point $(1, -2)$ and has a slope of 3.

Solution

$$y - y_1 = m(x - x_1) \quad \textit{Point-slope form}$$
$$y - (-2) = 3(x - 1) \quad \textit{Substitute } y_1 = -2, x_1 = 1, \textit{ and } m = 3$$
$$y + 2 = 3x - 3$$
$$y = 3x - 5 \quad \textit{Equation of line}$$

The graph of this line is shown in Figure 2.37.

The point-slope form can be used to find the equation of a line passing through two points (x_1, y_1) and (x_2, y_2). First, use the formula for the slope of the line passing through two points.

$$m = \frac{y_2 - y_1}{x_2 - x_1}$$

Then, once you know the slope, use the point-slope form to obtain the equation

$$y - y_1 = \frac{y_2 - y_1}{x_2 - x_1}(x - x_1).$$

This is sometimes called the **two-point form** of the equation of a line.

EXAMPLE 3 A Linear Model for Sales Prediction

During the first two quarters of the year, a company had total sales of $3.4 million and $3.7 million, respectively.

a. Write a linear equation giving the total sales y in terms of the quarter x.
b. Use the equation to predict the total sales during the fourth quarter.

Solution

a. In Figure 2.38 let $(1, 3.4)$ and $(2, 3.7)$ be two points on the line representing the total sales. The slope of the line passing through these two points is

$$m = \frac{3.7 - 3.4}{2 - 1} = 0.3.$$

By the point-slope form, the equation of the line is as follows.

$$y - y_1 = m(x - x_1)$$
$$y - 3.4 = 0.3(x - 1)$$
$$y = 0.3x - 0.3 + 3.4$$
$$y = 0.3x + 3.1$$

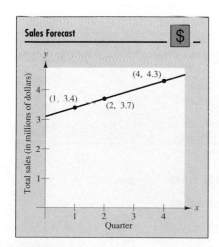

FIGURE 2.38

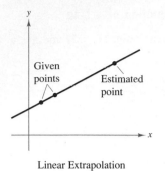

Linear Extrapolation

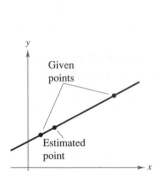

Linear Interpolation

FIGURE 2.39

b. Using the equation from part (a), you can estimate the fourth-quarter sales
($x = 4$).

$$y = 0.3(4) + 3.1 = 4.3 \text{ million dollars}$$

The approximation method illustrated in Example 3 is **linear extrapolation.** Note in Figure 2.39 that for linear extrapolation, the estimated point lies to the right of the given points. When the estimated point lies *between* two given points, the procedure is **linear interpolation.**

Sketching Graphs of Lines

Many problems in coordinate (or analytic) geometry can be classified in two basic categories.

1. Given a graph (or parts of it), find its equation.
2. Given an equation, find its graph.

For lines, the first problem is solved easily by using the point-slope form. This formula, however, is not particularly useful for solving the second type of problem. The form that is better suited to graphing linear equations is the **slope-intercept form** of the equation of a line. To derive the slope-intercept form, we write the following.

$$y - y_1 = m(x - x_1) \qquad \text{\textit{Point-slope form}}$$
$$y = mx - mx_1 + y_1 \qquad \text{\textit{Distributive Property}}$$
$$y = mx + b \qquad \text{\textit{$b = -mx_1 + y_1$, a constant}}$$

SLOPE-INTERCEPT FORM OF THE EQUATION OF A LINE

The graph of the equation

$$y = mx + b$$

is a line whose slope is m and y-intercept is $(0, b)$.

EXAMPLE 4   Using the Slope-Intercept Form

Sketch the graph of each of the linear equations.

a. $y = 2x + 1$ **b.** $y = 2$ **c.** $x + y = 2$

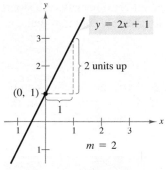

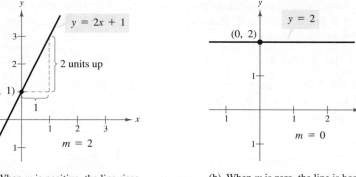

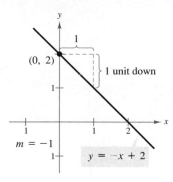

(a) When m is positive, the line rises.

(b) When m is zero, the line is horizontal.

(c) When m is negative, the line falls.

FIGURE 2.40

Solution

a. Since $b = 1$, the y-intercept is $(0, 1)$. Moreover, since the slope is $m = 2$, this line *rises* two units for each unit the line moves to the right, as shown in Figure 2.40(a).

b. By writing the equation $y = 2$ in the form $y = (0)x + 2$, you see that the y-intercept is $(0, 2)$ and the slope is zero. A zero slope implies that the line is horizontal, as shown in Figure 2.40(b).

c. By writing the equation $x + y = 2$ in slope-intercept form, $y = -x + 2$, you see that the y-intercept is $(0, 2)$. Moreover, since the slope is $m = -1$, this line *falls* one unit for each unit the line moves to the right, as shown in Figure 2.40(c).

◢

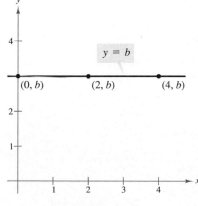

Horizontal Line

FIGURE 2.41

From the slope-intercept form of the equation of a line, you see that a horizontal line ($m = 0$) has an equation of the form

$$y = (0)x + b \quad \text{or} \quad y = b. \qquad \textit{Horizontal line}$$

This is consistent with the fact that each point on a horizontal line through $(0, b)$ has a y-coordinate of b, as shown in Figure 2.41.

Similarly, each point on a vertical line through $(a, 0)$ has an x-coordinate of a, as shown in Figure 2.42. Hence, a vertical line has an equation of the form

$$x = a. \qquad \textit{Vertical line}$$

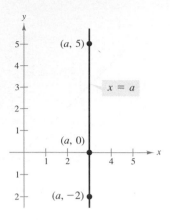

Vertical Line

FIGURE 2.42

This equation cannot be written in the slope-intercept form because the slope of a vertical line is undefined. However, *every* line has an equation that can be written in the **general form**

$$Ax + By + C = 0 \qquad \textit{General form}$$

where A and B are not *both* zero. If $A = 0$ (and $B \neq 0$), the equation can be reduced to the form $y = b$, a horizontal line. If $B = 0$ (and $A \neq 0$), the general equation can be reduced to the form $x = a$, a vertical line.

SUMMARY OF EQUATIONS OF LINES

1. General form: $\qquad Ax + By + C = 0$
2. Vertical line: $\qquad x = a$
3. Horizontal line: $\qquad y = b$
4. Slope-intercept form: $\quad y = mx + b$
5. Point-slope form: $\qquad y - y_1 = m(x - x_1)$

Parallel and Perpendicular Lines

PARALLEL LINES

Two distinct nonvertical lines are **parallel** if and only if their slopes are equal.

EXAMPLE 5 Equations of Parallel Lines

Find an equation of the line that passes through the point $(2, -1)$ and is parallel to the line $2x - 3y = 5$, as shown in Figure 2.43.

Solution

Write the given equation in slope-intercept form.

$$2x - 3y = 5 \qquad \textit{Given equation}$$
$$3y = 2x - 5$$
$$y = \frac{2}{3}x - \frac{5}{3} \qquad \textit{Slope-intercept form}$$

Therefore, the given line has a slope of $m = \frac{2}{3}$. Since any line parallel to the given line must also have a slope of $\frac{2}{3}$, the required line through $(2, -1)$ has the following equation.

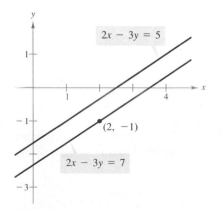

FIGURE 2.43

$$y - (-1) = \frac{2}{3}(x - 2) \qquad \textit{Point-slope form}$$

$$y = \frac{2}{3}x - \frac{4}{3} - 1$$

$$y = \frac{2}{3}x - \frac{7}{3} \qquad \textit{Slope-intercept form}$$

Notice the similarity between the slope-intercept form of the original equation and the slope-intercept form of the parallel equation.

PERPENDICULAR LINES

Two nonvertical lines are **perpendicular** if and only if their slopes are negative reciprocals of each other. That is,

$$m_1 = -\frac{1}{m_2}.$$

Proof

Recall that the phrase "if and only if" is a way of stating two rules in one. One rule says, "If two nonvertical lines are perpendicular, then their slopes must be negative reciprocals." The other rule is the converse, which says, "If two lines have slopes that are negative reciprocals, they must be perpendicular." We will prove the first of these two rules.

Assume that you are given two nonvertical perpendicular lines L_1 and L_2 with slopes m_1 and m_2. For simplicity's sake, let these two lines intersect at the origin, as shown in Figure 2.44. The vertical line $x = 1$ will intersect L_1 and L_2 at the respective points $(1, m_1)$ and $(1, m_2)$. Since L_1 and L_2 are perpendicular, the triangle formed by these two points and the origin is a right triangle. Thus, you can apply the Pythagorean Theorem and conclude that

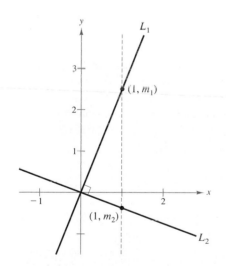

FIGURE 2.44

$$\left(\begin{array}{c}\text{Distance between} \\ (0, 0) \text{ and } (1, m_1)\end{array}\right)^2 + \left(\begin{array}{c}\text{Distance between} \\ (0, 0) \text{ and } (1, m_2)\end{array}\right)^2 = \left(\begin{array}{c}\text{Distance between} \\ (1, m_1) \text{ and } (1, m_2)\end{array}\right)^2$$

Using the Distance Formula,

$$(\sqrt{1 + m_1^2})^2 + (\sqrt{1 + m_2^2})^2 = (\sqrt{0^2 + (m_1 - m_2)^2})^2$$
$$1 + m_1^2 + 1 + m_2^2 = (m_1 - m_2)^2$$
$$2 + m_1^2 + m_2^2 = m_1^2 - 2m_1m_2 + m_2^2$$
$$2 = -2m_1m_2$$
$$-1 = m_1m_2$$
$$-\frac{1}{m_2} = m_1.$$

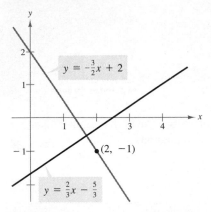

FIGURE 2.45

EXAMPLE 6   Equations of Perpendicular Lines

Find an equation of the line that passes through the point $(2, -1)$ and is perpendicular to the line $2x - 3y = 5$.

Solution

By writing the given line in the form $y = \frac{2}{3}x - \frac{5}{3}$ you see that the line has a slope of $\frac{2}{3}$. Hence, any line that is perpendicular to this line must have a slope of $-\frac{3}{2}$ (because $-\frac{3}{2}$ is the negative reciprocal of $\frac{2}{3}$). Therefore, the required line through the point $(2, -1)$ has the following equation:

$$y - (-1) = -\frac{3}{2}(x - 2) \qquad \textit{Point-slope form}$$

$$y = -\frac{3}{2}x + 3 - 1$$

$$y = -\frac{3}{2}x + 2. \qquad \textit{Slope-intercept form}$$

The graphs of both equations are shown in Figure 2.45.

DISCUSSION
PROBLEM
Linear
Interpolation

Linear interpolation can be used to approximate the x-intercept of the graph of an equation. For example, consider the graph of $y = x^3 + x + 1$ as shown in Figure 2.46. When $x = -0.69$ the value of y is negative, and when $x = -0.68$ the value of y is positive. This implies that the graph must have an x-intercept whose x-coordinate is between -0.69 and -0.68. Write a short paragraph describing how you could use linear interpolation with the following two points on the graph of $y = x^3 + x + 1$ to approximate the x-intercept of the graph.

$$(-0.69, -0.018509) \qquad \text{and} \qquad (-0.68, 0.005568)$$

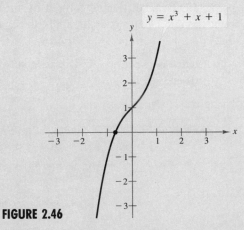

FIGURE 2.46

WARM UP

The following warm-up exercises involve skills that were covered in earlier sections. You will use these skills in the exercise set for this section.

In Exercises 1–4, simplify the expressions.

1. $\dfrac{4-(-5)}{-3-(-1)}$

2. $\dfrac{-5-8}{0-(-3)}$

3. Find $\dfrac{-1}{m}$ for $m = \dfrac{4}{5}$.

4. Find $\dfrac{-1}{m}$ for $m = -2$.

In Exercises 5–10, solve for y in terms of x.

5. $2x - 3y = 5$

6. $4x + 2y = 0$

7. $y - (-4) = 3[x - (-1)]$

8. $y - 7 = \frac{2}{3}(x - 3)$

9. $y - (-1) = \dfrac{3-(-1)}{2-4}(x - 4)$

10. $y - 5 = \dfrac{3-5}{0-2}(x - 2)$

EXERCISES for Section 2.3

In Exercises 1–6, estimate the slope of the line from its graph.

1.

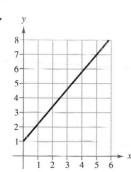

2.

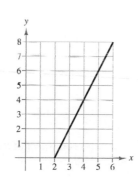

5.

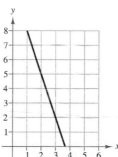

6.

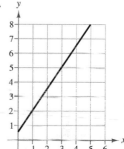

3.

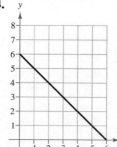

4.

In Exercises 7 and 8, sketch the graph of the lines through the given point with the indicated slope. Make the sketches on the same set of coordinate axes.

Point	Slopes
7. (2, 3)	(a) 0 (b) 1 (c) 2 (d) −3
8. (−4, 1)	(a) 3 (b) −3 (c) $\frac{1}{2}$ (d) Undefined

In Exercises 9–14, plot the points and find the slope of the line passing through each pair of points.

9. $(-3, -2)$, $(1, 6)$

10. $(2, 4)$, $(4, -4)$

11. $(-6, -1)$, $(-6, 4)$

12. $(0, -10)$, $(-4, 0)$

13. $(1, 2)$, $(-2, -2)$

14. $\left(\frac{7}{8}, \frac{3}{4}\right)$, $\left(\frac{5}{4}, -\frac{1}{4}\right)$

In Exercises 15–20, use the given point on the line and the slope of the line to find three additional points through which the line passes. (The solution is not unique.)

Point	Slope
15. (2, 1)	$m = 0$
16. (−4, 1)	m is undefined.
17. (5, −6)	$m = 1$
18. (10, −6)	$m = -1$
19. (−8, 1)	m is undefined.
20. (−3, −1)	$m = 0$

In Exercises 21–24, determine if the lines L_1 and L_2 passing through the pairs of points are parallel, perpendicular, or neither.

21. L_1: (0, −1), (5, 9)
L_2: (0, 3), (4, 1)

22. L_1: (−2, −1), (1, 5)
L_2: (1, 3), (5, −5)

23. L_1: (3, 6), (−6, 0)
L_2: (0, −1), $\left(5, \frac{7}{3}\right)$

24. L_1: (4, 8), (−4, 2)
L_2: (3, −5), $\left(-1, \frac{1}{3}\right)$

25. *Mountain Driving*   When driving down a mountain road, you notice signs warning of a "12% grade." This means that the slope of the road is $-\frac{12}{100}$. Determine the amount of horizontal change in your position if you note from elevation markers that you have descended 2000 feet vertically.

26. *Attic Height*   The "rise to run" in determining the steepness of the roof on a house is 3 to 4. Determine the maximum height in the attic of the house if the house is 30 feet wide (see figure).

Figure for 26

In Exercises 27–32, find the slope and y-intercept (if possible) of the line specified by the equation. Sketch a graph of the line.

27. $5x - y + 3 = 0$

28. $2x + 3y - 9 = 0$

29. $5x - 2 = 0$

30. $3y + 5 = 0$

31. $7x + 6y - 30 = 0$

32. $x - y - 10 = 0$

In Exercises 33–40, find an equation for the line passing through the points.

33. (5, −1,), (−5, 5)

34. (4, 3), (−4, −4)

35. $\left(2, \frac{1}{2}\right), \left(\frac{1}{2}, \frac{5}{4}\right)$

36. (−1, 4), (6, 4)

37. (−8, 1), (−8, 7)

38. (1, 1), $\left(6, -\frac{2}{3}\right)$

39. (1, 0.6), (−2, −0.6)

40. (−8, 0.6), (2, −2.4)

In Exercises 41–50, find an equation of the line that passes through the given point and has the indicated slope. Sketch the graph of the line.

Point	Slope
41. (0, −2)	$m = 3$
42. (0, 10)	$m = -1$
43. (−3, 6)	$m = -2$
44. (0, 0)	$m = 4$
45. (4, 0)	$m = -\frac{1}{3}$
46. (−2, −5)	$m = \frac{3}{4}$
47. (6, −1)	m is undefined.
48. (−10, 4)	$m = 0$
49. $\left(4, \frac{5}{2}\right)$	$m = 0$
50. $\left(-\frac{1}{2}, \frac{3}{2}\right)$	m is undefined.

The **intercept** form of the equation of a line with intercepts $(a, 0)$ and $(0, b)$ is

$$\frac{x}{a} + \frac{y}{b} = 1, \qquad a \neq 0, b \neq 0.$$

In Exercises 51–56, use the intercept form to find the equation of the line with the given intercepts.

51. x-intercept: (2, 0)
y-intercept: (0, 3)

52. x-intercept: (−3, 0)
y-intercept: (0, 4)

53. x-intercept: $\left(-\frac{1}{6}, 0\right)$
y-intercept: $\left(0, -\frac{2}{3}\right)$

54. x-intercept: $\left(\frac{2}{3}, 0\right)$
y-intercept: (0, −2)

55. Point on line: (1, 2)
x-intercept: $(a, 0)$
y-intercept: $(0, a)$
$(a \neq 0)$

56. Point on line: (−3, 4)
x-intercept: $(a, 0)$
y-intercept: $(0, a)$
$(a \neq 0)$

In Exercises 57–62, write an equation of the line through the given point (a) parallel to the given line, and (b) perpendicular to the given line.

	Point	Line
57.	$(2, 1)$	$4x - 2y = 3$
58.	$(-3, 2)$	$x + y = 7$
59.	$(-6, 4)$	$3x + 4y = 7$
60.	$\left(\frac{7}{8}, \frac{3}{4}\right)$	$5x + 3y = 0$
61.	$(-1, 0)$	$y = -3$
62.	$(2, 5)$	$x = 4$

In Exercises 63–66, you are given the dollar value of a product in 1990 *and* the rate at which the value of the item is expected to change during the next five years. Write a linear equation for the dollar value V of the product in terms of the year t. (Let $t = 0$ represent 1990.)

	1990 Value	Rate
63.	$2,540	$125 increase per year
64.	$156	$4.50 increase per year
65.	$20,400	$2,000 increase per year
66.	$245,000	$5,600 increase per year

In Exercises 67–70, match the description with a graph. Determine the slope and how it is interpreted in the situation. [The graphs are labeled (a), (b), (c), and (d).]

(a)
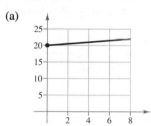

(b)
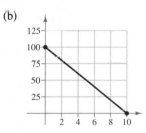

(c)
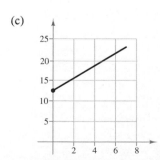

(d)
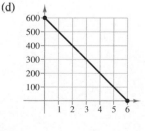

67. A person is paying $10 per week to a friend to repay a $100 loan.

68. An employee is paid $12.50 per hour plus $1.50 for each unit produced per hour.

69. A sales representative receives $20 per day for food plus $0.25 for each mile traveled.

70. A typewriter purchased for $600 depreciates $100 per year.

71. *Temperature*   Find the equation of the line giving the relationship between the temperature in degrees Celsius, C, and degrees Fahrenheit, F. Remember that water freezes at 0° Celsius (32° Fahrenheit) and boils at 100° Celsius (212° Fahrenheit).

72. *Temperature*   Use the result of Exercise 71 to complete the table.

C		-10°	10°			177°
F	0°			68°	90°	

73. *Annual Salary*   Suppose your salary was $28,500 in 1990 and $32,900 in 1992. If your salary follows a linear growth pattern, what will it be in 1995?

74. *College Enrollment*   A small college had 2546 students in 1990 and 2702 students in 1992. If the enrollment follows a linear growth pattern, how many students will the college have in 1997?

75. *Straight-Line Depreciation*   A small business purchases a piece of equipment for $875. After five years the equipment will be outdated and have no value. Write a linear equation giving the value V of the equipment during the five years it will be used.

76. *Straight-Line Depreciation*   A small business purchases a piece of equipment for $25,000. After 10 years the equipment will have to be replaced. Its value at that time is expected to be $2,000. Write a linear equation giving the value V of the equipment during the 10 years it will be used.

77. *Sales Price and List Price*   A store is offering a 15% discount on all items in its inventory. Write a linear equation giving the sale price S for an item with a list price L.

78. *Hourly Wages*   A manufacturer pays its assembly line workers $11.50 per hour plus $0.75 per unit produced. Write a linear equation for the hourly wages W in terms of the number of units x produced per hour.

79. *Sales Commission*   A salesperson receives a monthly salary of $2500 plus a commission of 7% of her sales. Write a linear equation for the salesperson's monthly wage W in terms of her monthly sales S.

80. *Daily Cost*   A sales representative using his personal car receives $120 per day for lodging and meals plus $0.26 per mile driven. Write a linear equation giving the daily cost C to the company in terms of x, the number of miles driven.

81. *Contracting Purchase*   A contractor purchases a piece of equipment for $36,500. The equipment requires an average expenditure of $5.25 per hour for fuel and maintenance, and the operator is paid $11.50 per hour.

(a) Write a linear equation giving the total cost C of operating this equipment for t hours. (Include the purchase cost for the equipment.)

(b) If customers are charged $27 per hour of machine use, write an equation for the revenue R derived from t hours of use.

(c) Use the formula for profit $(P = R - C)$ to write an equation for the profit derived from t hours of use.

(d) *Break-even Point*   Use the result of part (c) to find the number of hours this equipment must be used to yield a profit of 0 dollars.

82. *Real Estate*   A real estate office handles an apartment complex with 50 units. When the rent per unit is $380 per month, all 50 units are occupied. However, when the rent is $425 per month, the average number of occupied units drops to 47. Assume that the relationship between the monthly rent p and the demand x is linear.

(a) Write the equation of the line giving the demand x in terms of the rent p.

(b) Use this equation to predict the number of units occupied if the rent is $455.

(c) Predict the number of units occupied if the rent is $395.

83. *Baseball Salaries*   The average annual salaries of major league baseball players (in 1000s of dollars) from 1979 to 1989 are shown in the scatter plot. Find the equation of the line that you think best fits this data. (Let y represent the average salary and let t represent the year with $t = 0$ corresponding to 1980.)(*Source:* Major League Baseball)

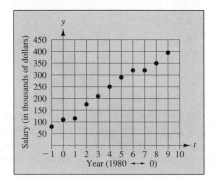

Figure for 83

84. *Quiz and Test Scores*   A mathematics instructor gives regular 20-point quizzes and 100-point exams. Average scores for six students, given as ordered pairs (x, y) where x is the average quiz score and y is the average test score, are $(18, 87), (10, 55), (19, 96), (16, 79), (13, 76)$ and $(15, 82)$.

(a) Plot the points.

(b) Use a straight edge to sketch the "best-fitting" line through the points.

(c) Find an equation for the line sketched in part (b).

(d) Use the equation of part (c) to estimate the average test score for a person with an average quiz score of 17.

[*Note:* The answers are not unique for parts (b)–(d).]

(e) If the instructor added four points to the average test score of everyone in the class, describe the change in the position of the plotted points and the change in the equation of the line.

2.4 Functions

Introduction to Functions / Function Notation / Finding the Domain of a Function / Applications

Introduction to Functions

Many everyday phenomena involve two quantities that are related to each other by some rule of correspondence. For example, the simple interest I earned on \$1000 for one year is related to the annual percentage rate r by the formula $I = 1000r$, and the distance d traveled on a bicycle in two hours is related to the speed s of the bicycle by the formula $d = 2s$.

Not all correspondences between two quantities have simple mathematical formulas. For instance, we commonly match up quantities such as NFL starting quarterbacks with touchdown passes and days of the year with the Dow-Jones Industrial Average. In both of these cases, however, there is some rule of correspondence that matches each item from one set with exactly one item from a different set. Such a rule of correspondence is a **function.**

DEFINITION OF A FUNCTION

A **function** f from a set A to a set B is a rule of correspondence that assigns to each element x in the set A exactly one element y in the set B. The set A is the **domain** (or set of inputs) of the function f, and the set B contains the **range** (or set of outputs).

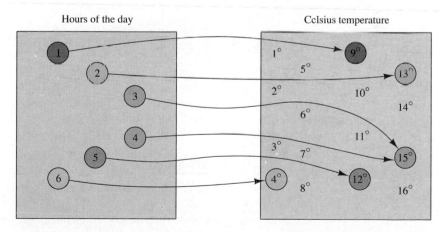

Hours of the day   Celsius temperature

Set A is the domain.
Input: 1, 2, 3, 4, 5, 6

Set B contains the range.
Output: $4°, 9°, 12°, 13°, 15°$

Function from Set A to Set B

FIGURE 2.47

The function in Figure 2.47 can be represented by the following set of ordered pairs.

$$\{(1, 9°), (2, 13°), (3, 15°), (4, 15°), (5, 12°), (6, 4°)\}$$

In each ordered pair, the first coordinate is the input and the second coordinate is the output. From this set and Figure 2.47, note the characteristics of a function.

1. Each element in A must be matched with an element of B.
2. Some elements in B may not be matched with any element in A.
3. Two or more elements of A may be matched with the same element of B.

The converse of the third statement is not true. That is, an element of A (the domain) cannot be matched with two different elements of B.

EXAMPLE 1   Testing for Functions

Let $A = \{a, b, c\}$ and $B = \{1, 2, 3, 4, 5\}$. Does the set of ordered pairs or figures represent a function from set A to set B?

a. $\{(a, 2), (b, 3), (c, 4)\}$ **b.** $\{(a, 4), (b, 5)\}$

c.

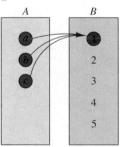

d.

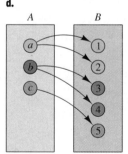

Solution

a. Yes, because each element of A is matched with exactly one element of B.
b. No, because not all elements of A are matched with an element of B.
c. Yes, because it does not matter that each element of A is matched with the same element of B.
d. No, because the element a in A is matched with *two* elements, 1 and 2, in B. This is also true of the element b.

Representing functions by sets of ordered pairs is a common practice in *discrete mathematics*. In algebra, however, it is more common to represent functions by equations or formulas involving two variables. For instance, the equation

$$y = x^2$$

represents the variable y as a function of the variable x. Here, x is the **independent variable** and y is the **dependent variable.** The **domain** of the function is the set of all values taken on by the independent variable x, and the **range** of the function is the set of all values taken on by the dependent variable y.

EXAMPLE 2   Testing for Functions Represented by Equations

Determine whether the equations represent y as a function of x.

a. $x^2 + y = 1$ **b.** $-x + y^2 = 1$

Solution

In each case, to determine whether y is a function of x, it is helpful to solve for y in terms of x.

a. $x^2 + y = 1$ *Given equation*

$\qquad\ y = 1 - x^2$ *Solve for y*

To each value of x there corresponds just one value for y. Therefore, y is a function of x.

b. $-x + y^2 = 1$ *Given equation*

$\qquad\quad y^2 = 1 + x$ *Add x to both sides*

$\qquad\quad\ y = \pm\sqrt{1 + x}$ *Solve for y*

The $\pm$ indicates that to a given value of x there correspond two values for y. Therefore, y is *not* a function of x.

Function Notation

When using an equation to represent a function, it is convenient to name the function so that it can be referenced easily. For example, you know that the equation $y = 1 - x^2$, Example 2(a), describes y as a function of x. Suppose you give this function the name "f." Then you can use **function notation.**

Input	*Output*	*Equation*
x	$f(x)$	$f(x) = 1 - x^2$

The symbol $f(x)$ is read as the **value of f at x** or simply "f of x." This corresponds to the y-value for a given x. Thus, you can write $y = f(x)$.

Keep in mind that f is the *name* of the function, while $f(x)$ is the *value* of the function at x. For instance, the function

$$f(x) = 3 - 2x$$

has *function values* denoted by $f(-1)$, $f(0)$, $f(2)$, and so on. To find these values, substitute the specified input values into the equation.

For $x = -1$, $\quad f(-1) = 3 - 2(-1) = 3 + 2 = 5$.

For $x = 0$, $\qquad f(0) = 3 - 2(0) = 3 + 0 = 3$.

For $x = 2$, $\qquad f(2) = 3 - 2(2) = 3 - 4 = -1$.

Although f is generally used as a convenient function name and x as the independent variable, you can use other letters. For instance, $f(x) = x^2 - 4x + 7$, $f(t) = t^2 - 4t + 7$, and $f(s) = s^2 - 4s + 7$ all define the same function. In fact, the role of the independent variable in a function is simply that of a "placeholder." Consequently, the above function could be described by the form

$$f(\blacksquare) = (\blacksquare)^2 - 4(\blacksquare) + 7$$

where the parentheses are used in place of a letter. To evaluate $f(-2)$, simply place -2 in each set of parentheses.

$$f(\blacksquare) = (\blacksquare)^2 - 4(\blacksquare) + 7$$
$$f(-2) = (-2)^2 - 4(-2) + 7 \quad \text{\textit{Place} -2 \textit{in each set of parentheses}}$$
$$= 4 + 8 + 7 \qquad\qquad \text{\textit{Evaluate each term}}$$
$$= 19 \qquad\qquad\qquad \text{\textit{Simplify}}$$

Similarly, the value of $f(3x)$ is obtained as follows.

$$f(\blacksquare) = (\blacksquare)^2 - 4(\blacksquare) + 7$$
$$f(3x) = (3x)^2 - 4(3x) + 7 \quad \text{\textit{Place} $3x$ \textit{in each set of parentheses}}$$
$$= 9x^2 - 12x + 7 \qquad \text{\textit{Simplify}}$$

EXAMPLE 3 Evaluating a Function

Let $g(x) = -x^2 + 4x + 1$ and find the following.

a. $g(2)$ **b.** $g(t)$ **c.** $g(x + 2)$

Solution

a. Replacing x with 2 in $g(x) = -x^2 + 4x + 1$ yields

$$g(2) = -(2)^2 + 4(2) + 1 = -4 + 8 + 1 = 5.$$

b. Replacing x with t yields

$$g(t) = -(t)^2 + 4(t) + 1 = -t^2 + 4t + 1.$$

REMARK Example 3 shows that $g(x + 2) \neq g(x) + g(2)$ because $-x^2 + 5 \neq (-x^2 + 4x + 1) + 5$. In general, $g(u + v) \neq g(u) + g(v)$.

c. Replacing x with $x + 2$ yields

$$g(x + 2) = -(x + 2)^2 + 4(x + 2) + 1$$
$$= -(x^2 + 4x + 4) + 4x + 8 + 1$$
$$= -x^2 - 4x - 4 + 4x + 8 + 1$$
$$= -x^2 + 5.$$

Sometimes a function is defined using more than one equation.

EXAMPLE 4   A Function Defined by Two Equations

Evaluate the function

$$f(x) = \begin{cases} x^2 + 1, & x < 0 \\ x - 1, & x \geq 0 \end{cases}$$

at $x = -1$, 0, and 1.

Solution

Since $x = -1$ is less than 0, use $f(x) = x^2 + 1$ to obtain

$$f(-1) = (-1)^2 + 1 = 2.$$

For $x = 0$, use $f(x) = x - 1$ to obtain

$$f(0) = (0) - 1 = -1.$$

For $x - 1$, use $f(x) = x - 1$ to obtain

$$f(1) = (1) - 1 = 0.$$

Finding the Domain of a Function

The domain of a function may be explicitly described along with the function, or it may be *implied* by the expression used to define the function. The **implied domain** is the set of all real numbers for which the expression is defined. For instance, the function

$$f(x) = \frac{1}{x^2 - 4}$$

has an implied domain that consists of all real x other than $x = \pm 2$. These two values are excluded from the domain because division by zero is undefined. Another common type of implied domain is used to avoid even roots of negative numbers. For example, the function

$$f(x) = \sqrt{x}$$

is defined only for $x \geq 0$. Hence, its implied domain is the interval $[0, \infty)$. In general, the domain of a function *excludes* values that would cause division by zero *or* result in the even root of a negative number.

The *range* of a function is more difficult to find, and can best be obtained from the graph of the function (see Section 2.5).

EXAMPLE 5 Finding the Domain of a Function

Find the domain of each of the functions.

a. f: $\{(-3, 0), (-1, 4), (0, 2), (2, 2), (4, -1)\}$

b. Volume of a sphere: $V = \frac{4}{3}\pi r^3$

c. $g(x) = \dfrac{1}{x + 5}$

d. $h(x) = \sqrt{4 - x^2}$

REMARK In Example 5(b), note that the domain of a function may be implied by the physical context. For instance, from the equation $V = \frac{4}{3}\pi r^3$, you would have no reason to restrict r to nonnegative values, but the physical context tells you that a sphere cannot have a negative radius.

Solution

a. The domain of f consists of all first coordinates in the set of ordered pairs, and is therefore the set

$$\text{Domain} = \{-3, -1, 0, 2, 4\}.$$

b. For the volume of a sphere you must choose nonnegative values for the radius r. Thus, the domain is the set of all real numbers r such that $r \geq 0$.

c. Excluding x-values that yield zero in the denominator, the domain of g is the set of all real numbers $x \neq -5$.

d. Choose x-values for which $4 - x^2 \geq 0$. Using the methods described in Section 1.6, you can conclude that $-2 \leq x \leq 2$. Thus, the domain is the interval $[-2, 2]$.

Applications

EXAMPLE 6 The Dimensions of a Container

A standard soft-drink can has a height of about 4.75 inches and a radius of about 1.3 inches. For this standard can, the ratio of the height to the radius is about 3.65. Suppose you worked in the marketing department of a soft-drink company and were experimenting with a new soft-drink can that was slightly narrower and taller. For your experimental can, the ratio of the height to the radius is 4, as shown in Figure 2.48.

a. Express the volume of the can as a function of the radius r.

b. Express the volume of the can as a function of the height h.

$\dfrac{h}{r} = 4$

FIGURE 2.48

Solution

The volume of a right circular cylinder is

$$V = \pi(\text{radius})^2(\text{height}) = \pi r^2 h.$$

Since the ratio of the height to the radius is 4, you can write $h = 4r$.

a. To write the volume as a function of the radius, use the fact that $h = 4r$.

$$V = \pi r^2 h = \pi r^2(4r) = 4\pi r^3$$

b. To write the volume as a function of the height, use the fact that $r = h/4$.

$$V = \pi\left(\frac{h}{4}\right)^2 h = \frac{\pi h^3}{16}$$

EXAMPLE 7   The Path of a Baseball

A baseball is hit 3 feet above ground at a velocity of 100 feet per second and at an angle of 45° with respect to the ground. The path of the baseball is given by the function

$$y = -0.0032x^2 + x + 3$$

where y and x are measured in feet, as shown in Figure 2.49. (From this equation, note that the height of the baseball is a function of the distance from home plate.) Will the baseball clear a 10-foot fence located 300 feet from home plate?

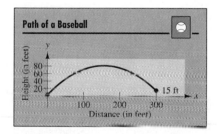

FIGURE 2.49

Solution

When $x = 300$, the height of the baseball is

$$y = -0.0032(300^2) + 300 + 3 = 15 \text{ feet.}$$

Thus, the ball will clear the fence.

One of the basic definitions in calculus employs the ratio

$$\frac{f(x + h) - f(x)}{h}, \quad h \neq 0$$

called a **difference quotient.**

EXAMPLE 8   Evaluating a Difference Quotient

For the function given by $f(x) = x^2 - 4x + 7$, find

$$\frac{f(x + h) - f(x)}{h}.$$

Solution

$$\begin{aligned}
\frac{f(x + h) - f(x)}{h} &= \frac{[(x + h)^2 - 4(x + h) + 7] - [x^2 - 4x + 7]}{h} \\
&= \frac{x^2 + 2xh + h^2 - 4x - 4h + 7 - x^2 + 4x - 7}{h} \\
&= \frac{2xh + h^2 - 4h}{h} \\
&= \frac{h(2x + h - 4)}{h} \\
&= 2x + h - 4
\end{aligned}$$

Summary of Function Terminology

Function:
   A **function** is a relationship between two variables such that to each value of the independent variable there corresponds exactly one value of the dependent variable.

Function Notation: $y = f(x)$
   f is the **name** of the function.
   y is the **dependent variable.**
   x is the **independent variable.**
   $f(x)$ is the **value of the function at x.**

Domain:
   The **domain** of a function is the set of all values (inputs) of the independent variable for which the function is defined. If x is in the domain of f, f is **defined** at x. If x is not in the domain of f, f is **undefined** at x.

Range:
   The **range** of a function is the set of all values (outputs) assumed by the dependent variable (that is, the set of all function values).

Implied Domain:
   If f is defined by an algebraic expression and the domain is not specified, then the **implied domain** consists of all real numbers for which the expression is defined.

DISCUSSION
PROBLEM

Determining
Relationships
That Are
Functions

Write (or discuss) two statements describing relationships in everyday life that *are* functions and two that are *not* functions. Here are two examples.

1. The statement "Your happiness is a function of the grade you receive in this course" is *not* a correct mathematical use of the word function. One problem is that the word "happiness" is ambiguous, and the other problem is that a person's happiness is affected by many more events than simply the grade the person receives in a single course.

2. The statement "Your federal income tax is a function of your adjusted gross income" *is* a correct mathematical use of the word function. Once you have determined your adjusted gross income, then your income tax can be determined.

WARM UP

The following warm-up exercises involve skills that were covered in earlier sections. You will use these skills in the exercise set for this section.

In Exercises 1–4, simplify the expression.

1. $2(-3)^3 + 4(-3) - 7$ **2.** $4(-1)^2 - 5(-1) + 4$

3. $(x + 1)^2 + 3(x + 1) - 4 - (x^2 + 3x - 4)$

4. $(x - 2)^2 - 4(x - 2) - (x^2 - 4)$

In Exercises 5 and 6, solve for y in terms of x.

5. $2x + 5y - 7 = 0$ **6.** $y^2 = x^2$

In Exercises 7–10, solve the inequality.

7. $x^2 - 4 \geq 0$ **8.** $9 - x^2 \geq 0$

9. $x^2 + 2x + 1 \geq 0$ **10.** $x^2 - 3x + 2 \geq 0$

EXERCISES for Section 2.4

In Exercises 1 and 2, determine which of the sets of ordered pairs represents a function from A to B. Give reasons for your answers.

1. $A = \{0, 1, 2, 3\}$ and $B = \{-2, -1, 0, 1, 2\}$
  (a) $\{(0, 1), (1, -2), (2, 0), (3, 2)\}$
  (b) $\{(0, -1), (2, 2), (1, -2), (3, 0), (1, 1)\}$
  (c) $\{(0, 0), (1, 0), (2, 0), (3, 0)\}$
  (d) $\{(0, 2), (3, 0), (1, 1)\}$

2. $A = \{a, b, c\}$ and $B = \{0, 1, 2, 3\}$
  (a) $\{(a, 1), (c, 2), (c, 3), (b, 3)\}$
  (b) $\{(a, 1), (b, 2), (c, 3)\}$
  (c) $\{(1, a), (0, a), (2, c), (3, b)\}$
  (d) $\{(c, 0), (b, 0), (a, 3)\}$

In Exercises 3–10, identify the equations that determine y as a function of x.

3. $x^2 + y^2 = 4$
4. $x = y^2$
5. $x^2 + y = 4$
6. $x + y^2 = 4$
7. $2x + 3y = 4$
8. $x^2 + y^2 - 2x - 4y + 1 = 0$
9. $y^2 = x^2 - 1$
10. $y = \sqrt{x + 5}$

In Exercises 11 and 12, fill in the blanks using the specified function and the value of the independent variable. (The symbol Δx represents a single variable and is read "delta x." This symbol is commonly used in calculus to denote a small change in x.)

11. $f(s) = \dfrac{1}{s + 1}$

  (a) $f(4) = \dfrac{1}{(\blacksquare) + 1}$

  (b) $f(0) = \dfrac{1}{(\blacksquare) + 1}$

  (c) $f(4x) = \dfrac{1}{(\blacksquare) + 1}$

  (d) $f(x + h) = \dfrac{1}{(\blacksquare) + 1}$

12. $g(x) = x^2 - 2x$
  (a) $g(2) = (\blacksquare)^2 - 2(\blacksquare)$
  (b) $g(-3) = (\blacksquare)^2 - 2(\blacksquare)$
  (c) $g(t + 1) = (\blacksquare)^2 - 2(\blacksquare)$
  (d) $g(x + \Delta x) = (\blacksquare)^2 - 2(\blacksquare)$

In Exercises 13–24, evaluate the function at the specified value of the independent variable and simplify.

13. $f(x) = 2x - 3$
  (a) $f(1)$ (b) $f(-3)$ (c) $f(x - 1)$

14. $g(y) = 7 - 3y$
  (a) $g(0)$ (b) $g\left(\tfrac{7}{3}\right)$ (c) $g(s + 2)$

15. $h(t) = t^2 - 2t$
  (a) $h(2)$ (b) $h(1.5)$ (c) $h(x + 2)$

16. $V(r) = \tfrac{4}{3}\pi r^3$
  (a) $V(3)$ (b) $V\left(\tfrac{3}{2}\right)$ (c) $V(2r)$

17. $f(y) = 3 - \sqrt{y}$
  (a) $f(4)$ (b) $f(0.25)$ (c) $f(4x^2)$

18. $f(x) = \sqrt{x + 8} + 2$
  (a) $f(-8)$ (b) $f(1)$ (c) $f(x - 8)$

19. $q(x) = \dfrac{1}{x^2 - 9}$
  (a) $q(0)$ (b) $q(3)$ (c) $q(y + 3)$

20. $q(t) = \dfrac{2t^2 + 3}{t^2}$
  (a) $q(2)$ (b) $q(0)$ (c) $q(-x)$

21. $f(x) = \dfrac{|x|}{x}$
  (a) $f(2)$ (b) $f(-2)$ (c) $f(x - 1)$

22. $f(x) = |x| + 4$
  (a) $f(2)$ (b) $f(-2)$ (c) $f(x^2)$

23. $f(x) = \begin{cases} 2x + 1, & x < 0 \\ 2x + 2, & x \geq 0 \end{cases}$
  (a) $f(-1)$ (b) $f(0)$ (c) $f(2)$

24. $f(x) = \begin{cases} x^2 + 2, & x \leq 1 \\ 2x^2 + 2, & x > 1 \end{cases}$
  (a) $f(-2)$ (b) $f(1)$ (c) $f(2)$

In Exercises 25–28, find all real values of x such that $f(x) = 0$.

25. $f(x) = 15 - 3x$

26. $f(x) = \dfrac{3x - 4}{5}$

27. $f(x) = x^2 - 9$

28. $f(x) = x^3 - x$

In Exercises 29–38, find the domain of the function.

29. $f(x) = 5x^2 + 2x - 1$ _any real #_

30. $g(x) = 1 - 2x^2$

31. $h(t) = \dfrac{4}{t}$

32. $s(y) = \dfrac{3y}{y + 5}$

33. $g(y) = \sqrt{y - 10}$

34. $f(t) = \sqrt[3]{t + 4}$ _All R_

35. $f(x) = \sqrt[4]{1 - x^2}$

36. $h(x) = \dfrac{10}{x^2 - 2x}$

37. $g(x) = \dfrac{1}{x} - \dfrac{3}{x + 2}$

38. $f(s) = \dfrac{\sqrt{s - 1}}{s - 4}$ _$s \neq 4$_ $[1, 4) \cup (4, \infty)$

In Exercises 39–42, assume that the domain of f is the set $A = \{-2, -1, 0, 1, 2\}$. Determine the set of ordered pairs representing the function f.

39. $f(x) = x^2$

40. $f(x) = \dfrac{2x}{x^2 + 1}$

41. $f(x) = \sqrt{x + 2}$

42. $f(x) = |x + 1|$

In Exercises 43–46, find the value(s) of x for which $f(x) = g(x)$.

43. $f(x) = x^2$, $g(x) = x + 2$

44. $f(x) = x^2 + 2x + 1$, $g(x) = 3x + 3$

45. $f(x) = \sqrt{3x} + 1$, $g(x) = x + 1$

46. $f(x) = x^4 - 2x^2$, $g(x) = 2x^2$

In Exercises 47–52, find the indicated difference quotient and simplify your answer.

47. $f(x) = x^2 - x + 1$
$$\dfrac{f(2 + h) - f(2)}{h}$$

48. $f(x) = 5x - x^2$
$$\dfrac{f(5 + h) - f(5)}{h}$$

49. $f(x) = x^3$
$$\dfrac{f(x + \Delta x) - f(x)}{\Delta x}$$

50. $f(x) = 2x$
$$\dfrac{f(x + \Delta x) - f(x)}{\Delta x}$$

51. $g(x) - 3x - 1$
$$\dfrac{g(x) - g(3)}{x - 3}$$

52. $f(t) = \dfrac{1}{t}$
$$\dfrac{f(t) - f(1)}{t - 1}$$

53. *Area of a Circle* Express the area A of a circle as a function of its circumference C.

54. *Area of a Triangle* Express the area A of an equilateral triangle as a function of the length s of its sides.

55. *Area of a Triangle* A right triangle is formed in the first quadrant by the x- and y-axes and a line through the point $(1, 2)$ (see figure). Write the area of the triangle as a function of x, and determine the domain of the function.

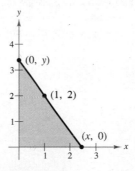

Figure for 55

56. *Area of a Rectangle*   A rectangle is bounded by the x-axis and the semicircle $y = \sqrt{25 - x^2}$ (see figure). Write the area of the rectangle as a function of x, and determine the domain of the function.

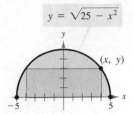

$y = \sqrt{25 - x^2}$

(x, y)

Figure for 56

57. *Volume of a Box*   An open box is made from a square piece of material 12 inches on a side by cutting equal squares from each corner and turning up the sides (see figure). Write the volume V of the box as a function of x. What is the domain of this function?

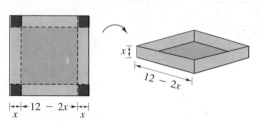

$12 - 2x$

Figure for 57

58. *Volume of a Package*   A rectangular package to be sent by a postal service can have a maximum combined length and girth (perimeter of a cross section) of 108 inches (see figure). Write the volume of such a package as a function of x. What is the domain of the function?

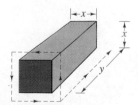

Figure for 58

59. *Height of a Balloon*   A balloon carrying a transmitter ascends vertically from a point 2000 feet from the receiving station (see figure). Let d be the distance between the balloon and the receiving station. Express the height of the balloon as a function of d. What is the domain of the function?

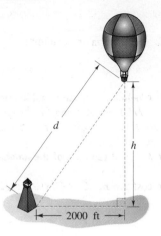

d

h

2000 ft

Figure for 59

60. *Price of Mobile Homes*   The average price of a new mobile home in the United States from 1974 to 1988 can be approximated by the model

$$p(t) = \begin{cases} 19.504 + 1.754t, & -6 \le t \le -1 \\ 19.839 + 0.081t^2, & 0 \le t \le 8 \end{cases}$$

where p is the price in thousands of dollars and t is the year with $t = 0$ corresponding to 1980 (see figure). Use this model to find the average price of a mobile home in 1978 and 1988. (*Source:* U.S. Bureau of Census, Construction Reports)

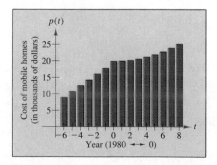

Figure for 60

61. *Cost, Revenue, and Profit*   A company produces a product for which the variable cost is $12.30 per unit and the fixed costs are $98,000. The product sells for $17.98. Let x be the number of units produced and sold.

(a) Write the total cost C as a function of the number of units produced.

(b) Write the revenue R as a function of the number of units sold.

(c) Write the profit P as a function of the number of units sold. (*Note: $P = R - C$.*)

62. The inventor of a game believes that the variable cost for producing the game is $0.95 per unit and the fixed costs are $6000. The inventor sells each game for $1.69. Let x be the number of games sold.

(a) Write the total cost C as a function of the number of games sold.

(b) Write the average cost per unit $\overline{C} = C/x$ as a function of x.

63. *Charter Bus Fares*   For groups of 80 or more people, a charter bus company determines the rate per person according to the formula

$$\text{Rate} = 8 - 0.05(n - 80), \quad n \geq 80$$

where the rate is given in dollars and n is the number of people.

(a) Express the revenue R for the bus company as a function of n.

(b) Use the function from part (a) to complete the table.

n	90	100	110	120	130	140	150
$R(n)$							

64. *Fluid Force*   The force F (in tons) of water against the face of a dam is the function

$$F(y) = 149.76\sqrt{10}y^{5/2}$$

where y is the depth of the water in feet. Complete the table.

y	5	10	20	30	40
$F(y)$					

SOLVING

A Graphical Approach to Finding a Maximum Revenue and Maximum Profit

In business, the **demand function** gives the price per unit p in terms of the number of units sold x. The demand function whose graph is shown below is

$$p = 40 - 5x^2, \quad 0 \le x \le \sqrt{8} \qquad \text{Demand function}$$

where x is measured in millions of units. Note that as the price decreases, the number of units sold increases.

The **revenue** R (in millions of dollars) is determined by multiplying the number of units sold by the price per unit. Thus,

$$R = xp = x(40 - 5x^2), \quad 0 \le x \le \sqrt{8}. \qquad \text{Revenue function}$$

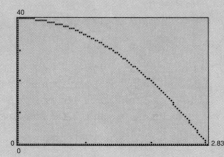

Graph of Demand Function

EXAMPLE 1   Finding the Maximum Revenue

Use a graphing utility to sketch the graph of the revenue function

$$R = 40x - 5x^3, \quad 0 \le x \le \sqrt{8}.$$

How many units should be sold to obtain a maximum revenue? What price per unit should be charged to obtain a maximum revenue?

Solution

To begin, you need to determine a viewing rectangle that will display the part of the graph that is important to this problem. The domain is given, so you can set the x boundaries of the graph between 0 and $\sqrt{8}$. To determine the y-boundaries, however, you need to experiment a little. After calculating several values of R, you could decide to use y boundaries between 0 and 50, as shown in the graph at left. Next, you can use the trace key to find that the maximum revenue of about $43.5 million occurs when x is approximately 1.64 million units.

To find the price per unit that corresponds to this maximum revenue, you can substitute $x = 1.64$ into the demand function to obtain

$$p = 40 - 5(1.64)^2 \approx \$26.55.$$

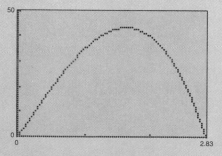

Graph of Revenue Function

EXAMPLE 2 Finding the Maximum Profit

Suppose the cost of producing each unit whose revenue function is discussed in Example 1 is $15. How many units should be sold to obtain a maximum profit? What price per unit should be charged to obtain a maximum profit?

Solution

The total cost C (in millions of dollars) of producing x million units is $C = 15x$. This implies that the profit P (in millions of dollars) obtained by selling x million units is

$$P = R - C$$
$$= (40x - 5x^3) - 15x$$
$$= -5x^3 + 25x.$$

As in Example 1, you can use a graphing utility to sketch the graph of this function. From the graph, you can approximate that the maximum profit of about $21.5 million occurs when x is approximately 1.28 million units. The price per unit that corresponds to this maximum profit is

$$p = 40 - 5(1.28)^2 = \$31.80.$$

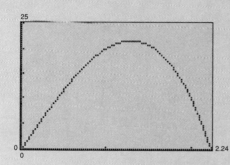

Graph of Profit Function

EXERCISES

(See also. Exercise 61, Section 2.4; Exercise 59, Section 2.5)

1. *Can't Give It Away!* For the demand function $p = 40 - 5x^2$, match the points $(0, 40)$ and $(\sqrt{8}, 0)$ with statement (a) or statement (b). Explain your reasoning.
   (a) At this price, no one is willing to buy the product.
   (b) You can't *give* more than this number of units away.

2. *Exploration* Use a graphing utility to *zoom in* on the maximum point of the revenue function in Example 1. (Use a setting of $1.62 \le x \le 1.65$ and $43.5 \le y \le 43.6$.) Use the trace feature of the graphing utility to improve the accuracy of the approximation obtained in Example 1. Do you think this improved accuracy is appropriate to the context of this particular problem? (Did it change the price?)

3. *Exploration* Find a setting that allows you to graphically improve the accuracy of the solution in Example 2.

4. *Exploration* In Example 2, suppose that, in addition to the cost of $15 per unit, there is an initial cost of $250,000. How does this change the profit function? Does this affect the *price* that corresponds to a maximum profit? Does it affect the *amount* of the maximum profit? Explain.

5. *Maximum Volume of a Box* In the Problem Solving with Technology feature on page 41, you were asked to maximize the volume of a box that has a square base and a surface area of 216 square inches. In that problem, x represents the length (in inches) of each side of the base and

   $$V = 54x - \tfrac{1}{2}x^3$$

   represents the volume (in cubic inches). Use a graphing calculator to approximate the dimensions that produce a box of maximum volume. (Use a graph setting that yields an accuracy of 0.0001.)

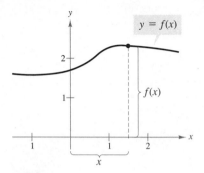

FIGURE 2.50

2.5 Graphs of Functions

The Graph of a Function / Increasing and Decreasing Functions / Even and Odd Functions / Summary of Graphs of Common Functions / Shifting, Reflecting, and Stretching Graphs / Step Functions

The Graph of a Function

In Section 2.4 we discussed functions from an algebraic point of view. Here, we look at functions from a geometric perspective. The **graph of a function** f is the collection of ordered pairs $(x, f(x))$ such that x is in the domain of f. As you study this section, remember that

$$x = \text{the directed distance from the } y\text{-axis}$$
$$f(x) = \text{the directed distance from the } x\text{-axis}$$

as shown in Figure 2.50.

You learned in Section 2.4 that the *range* (the set of values assumed by the dependent variable) of a function is often more easily determined from the graph of the function.

EXAMPLE 1   Finding Domain and Range from the Graph of a Function

Use the graph of the function f, shown in Figure 2.51, to find the following.

a. The domain of f
b. The function values $f(-1)$ and $f(2)$
c. The range of f

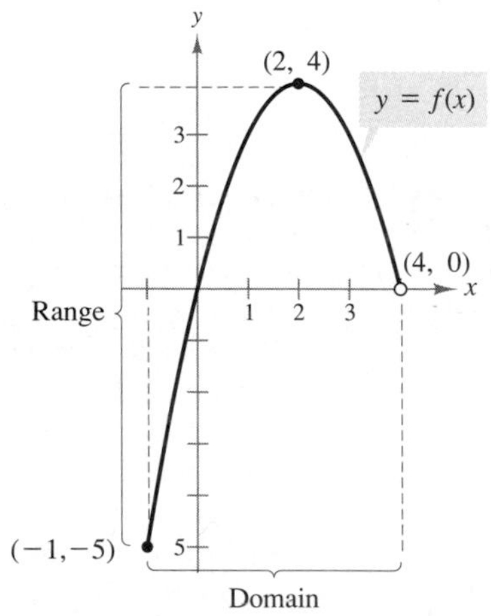

Solution

a. The closed dot (on the left) indicates that $x = -1$ is in the domain of f, whereas the open dot (on the right) indicates $x = 4$ is not in the domain. Thus, the domain of f is all x in the interval $[-1, 4)$.
b. Since $(-1, -5)$ is a point on the graph of f, it follows that $f(-1) = -5$. Similarly, since $(2, 4)$ is a point on the graph of f, it follows that $f(2) = 4$.
c. Because the graph does not extend below $f(-1) = -5$ nor above $f(2) = 4$, the range of f is the interval $[-5, 4]$.

FIGURE 2.51

REMARK The use of dots (open or closed) at the extreme left and right points of a graph indicates that the graph does not extend beyond these points. If no such dots are shown, assume that the graph extends beyond these points.

By the definition of a function, at most one y-value corresponds to a given x-value. It follows, then, that a vertical line can intersect the graph of a function at most once. This observation provides us with a convenient visual test for functions.

> ## VERTICAL LINE TEST FOR FUNCTIONS
>
> A set of points in a coordinate plane is the graph of y as a function of x if and only if no vertical line intersects the graph at more than one point.

EXAMPLE 2   Vertical Line Test for Functions

Do the graphs in Figure 2.52 represent y as a function of x?

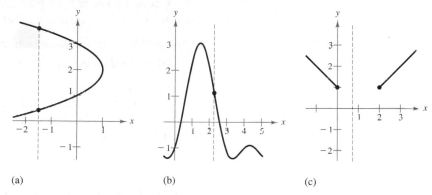

(a)   (b)   (c)

FIGURE 2.52

Solution

a. No, because you can find a vertical line that intersects the graph twice.

b. Yes, because every vertical line intersects the graph at most once.

c. Yes. (Note that if a vertical line does not intersect the graph, it simply means that the function is undefined for this particular value of x.)

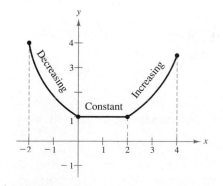

FIGURE 2.53

Increasing and Decreasing Functions

The more you know about the graph of a function, the more you know about the function itself. Consider the graph shown in Figure 2.53. Moving from *left to right*, this graph falls from $x = -2$ to $x = 0$, is constant from $x = 0$ to $x = 2$, and rises from $x = 2$ to $x = 4$. These observations indicate that the function has the following characteristics.

1. The function is **decreasing** on the interval $(-2, 0)$.
2. The function is **constant** on the interval $(0, 2)$.
3. The function is **increasing** on the interval $(2, 4)$.

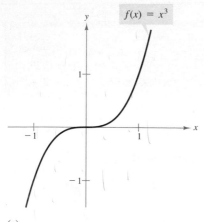

(a)

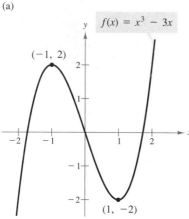

(b)

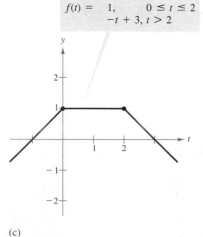

(c)

FIGURE 2.54

INCREASING, DECREASING, AND CONSTANT FUNCTIONS

A function f is **increasing** on an interval if, for any x_1 and x_2 in the interval,

$$x_1 < x_2 \quad \text{implies} \quad f(x_1) < f(x_2).$$

A function f is **decreasing** on an interval if, for any x_1 and x_2 in the interval,

$$x_1 < x_2 \quad \text{implies} \quad f(x_1) > f(x_2).$$

A function f is **constant** on an interval if, for any x_1 and x_2 in the interval,

$$f(x_1) = f(x_2).$$

EXAMPLE 3   Increasing and Decreasing Functions

In Figure 2.54, determine the open intervals on which each function is increasing, decreasing, or constant.

Solution

a. Although it might appear that there is an interval about zero over which this function is constant, you see that if $x_1 < x_2$, then $f(x_1) = x_1{}^3 < x_2{}^3 = f(x_2)$, and conclude that the function is increasing for all real numbers.

b. This function is increasing and decreasing on the following intervals.

Increasing on the interval $(-\infty, -1)$

Decreasing on the interval $(-1, 1)$

Increasing on the interval $(1, \infty)$

c. This function is increasing, constant, and decreasing on the following intervals.

Increasing on the interval $(-\infty, 0)$

Constant on the interval $(0, 2)$

Decreasing on the interval $(2, \infty)$

Even and Odd Functions

In Section 2.2, you learned about the different types of symmetry that a graph can possess. A function is **even** if its graph is symmetric with respect to the y-axis, and a function is **odd** if its graph is symmetric with respect to the origin. Thus, the symmetry tests given in Section 2.2 yield the following tests for even and odd functions.

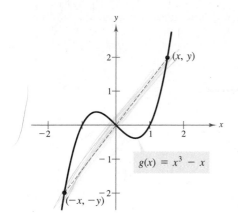

(a)

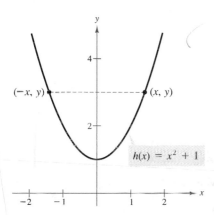

(b)

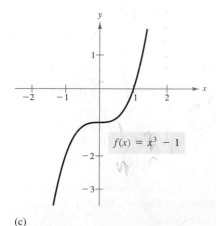

(c)

FIGURE 2.55

TESTS FOR EVEN AND ODD FUNCTIONS

A function given by $y = f(x)$ is **even** if, for each x in the domain of f,

$$f(-x) = f(x).$$

A function given by $y = f(x)$ is **odd** if, for each x in the domain of f,

$$f(-x) = -f(x).$$

REMARK The points at which a function changes its increasing, decreasing, or constant behavior are especially important in producing an accurate graph of the function. These points often identify *maximum* or *minimum* values of the function. Techniques for finding the exact location of these special points are developed in calculus. ◢

EXAMPLE 4 Even and Odd Functions

Are the functions even, odd, or neither?

a. $g(x) = x^3 - x$ **b.** $h(x) = x^2 + 1$ **c.** $f(x) = x^3 - 1$

Solution

a. Odd, because

$$g(-x) = (-x)^3 - (-x) = -x^3 + x = -(x^3 - x) = -g(x).$$

b. Even, because

$$h(-x) = (-x)^2 + 1 = x^2 + 1 = h(x).$$

c. Substituting $-x$ for x,

$$f(-x) = (-x)^3 - 1 = -x^3 - 1.$$

Since $f(x) = x^3 - 1$ and $-f(x) = -x^3 + 1$, then $f(-x) \neq f(x)$ and $f(-x) \neq -f(x)$. Hence, the function is neither even nor odd.

The graphs of the three functions are shown in Figure 2.55. ◢

Summary of Graphs of Common Functions

[handwritten: PARENT FUNCTIONS]

Figure 2.56 shows the graphs of six common functions. You should be familiar with these graphs.

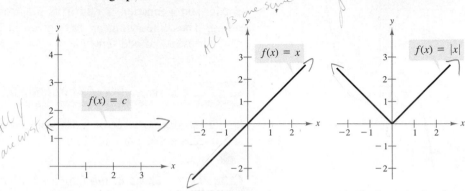

[handwritten: ACC 1/3 one Same]

[handwritten: ACC Y are const]

(a) Constant function $f(x) = c$

(b) Identity function $f(x) = x$

(c) Absolute value function $f(x) = |x|$

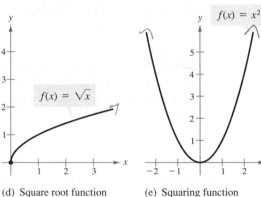
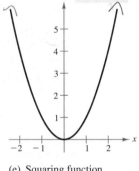
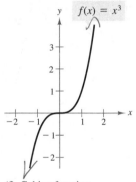

(d) Square root function $f(x) = \sqrt{x}$

(e) Squaring function $f(x) = x^2$

(f) Cubing function $f(x) = x^3$

FIGURE 2.56

$h(x) = x^2 + 2$

$(1, 3)$

$(1, 1)$ $f(x) = x^2$

Vertical shift upward: 2 units

FIGURE 2.57

Shifting, Reflecting, and Stretching Graphs

Many functions have graphs that are simple transformations of the common graphs summarized in Figure 2.56. For example, you can obtain the graph of $h(x) = x^2 + 2$ by shifting the graph of $f(x) = x^2$ *up* two units, as shown in Figure 2.57. In function notation, h and f are related as follows.

$$h(x) = x^2 + 2 = f(x) + 2 \qquad \text{\textit{Upward shift of 2}}$$

Similarly, you can obtain the graph of $g(x) = (x - 2)^2$ by shifting the graph of $f(x) = x^2$ to the *right* two units, as shown in Figure 2.58. In this case, the functions g and f have the following relationship.

$$g(x) = (x - 2)^2 = f(x - 2) \qquad \text{\textit{Right shift of 2}}$$

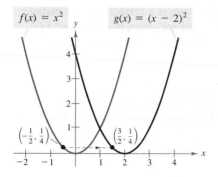

$f(x) = x^2$ $g(x) = (x - 2)^2$

Horizontal shift to the right: 2 units

FIGURE 2.58

REMARK In part (c) of Figure 2.59, note that the same result is obtained if the vertical shift precedes the horizontal shift.

FIGURE 2.59

VERTICAL AND HORIZONTAL SHIFTS

Let c be a positive real number. **Vertical** and **horizontal shifts** in the graph of $y = f(x)$ are represented as follows.

1. Vertical shift c units **upward:** $h(x) = f(x) + c$
2. Vertical shift c units **downward:** $h(x) = f(x) - c$
3. Horizontal shift c units to the **right:** $h(x) = f(x - c)$
4. Horizontal shift c units to the **left:** $h(x) = f(x + c)$

Some graphs can be obtained from a sequence of vertical and horizontal shifts. This is demonstrated in part (c) of Example 5.

EXAMPLE 5   Shifts in the Graph of a Function

Use the graph of $f(x) = x^3$ to sketch the graph of each of the functions.

a. $g(x) = x^3 + 1$ **b.** $h(x) = (x - 1)^3$ **c.** $k(x) = (x + 2)^3 + 1$

Solution

See Figure 2.59. Relative to the graph of $f(x) = x^3$, the graph of $g(x) = x^3 + 1$ is an upward shift of one unit, the graph of $h(x) = (x - 1)^3$ is a right shift of one unit, and the graph of $k(x) = (x + 2)^3 + 1$ involves a left shift of two units *and* an upward shift of one unit.

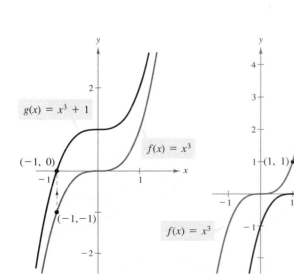

(a) Vertical shift: 1 unit up

(b) Horizontal shift: 1 unit right

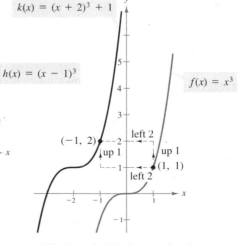

(c) Horizontal shift: 2 units left
    Vertical shift: 1 unit up

Step Functions

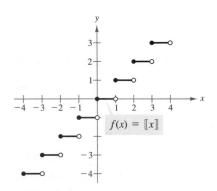

Greatest Integer Function

FIGURE 2.63

EXAMPLE 8   The Greatest Integer Function

The **greatest integer function** is denoted by $[\![x]\!]$ and is defined by

$$f(x) = [\![x]\!] = \text{the greatest integer less than or equal to } x.$$

The graph of this function is shown in Figure 2.63. Note that the graph of the greatest integer function jumps vertically one unit at each integer and is constant (a horizontal line segment) between each pair of consecutive integers. Because of the jumps in its graph, the greatest integer function is an example of a **step function.** Some values of the greatest integer function are as follows.

$$[\![-1]\!] = -1 \qquad [\![-0.5]\!] = -1$$
$$[\![0]\!] = 0 \qquad\quad [\![0.5]\!] = 0$$
$$[\![1]\!] = 1 \qquad\quad [\![1.5]\!] = 1$$

The range of the greatest integer function is the set of all integers.   ◢

EXAMPLE 9   The Cost of a Telephone Call

Suppose that the cost of a telephone call between Los Angeles and San Francisco is $0.50 for the first minute and $0.36 for each additional minute. The greatest integer function can be used to create a model for the cost of this call.

$$C = 0.50 + 0.36[\![t]\!]$$

where C is the total cost of the call in dollars and t is the length of the call in minutes. Sketch the graph of this function.

Solution

For calls up to one minute, the cost is $0.50. For calls between one and two minutes, the cost is $0.86, and so on.

Length of Call	$0 \le t < 1$	$1 \le t < 2$	$2 \le t < 3$	$3 \le t < 4$	$4 \le t < 5$
Cost of Call	$0.50	$0.86	$1.22	$1.58	$1.94

Using these values, you can sketch the graph shown in Figure 2.64.   ◢

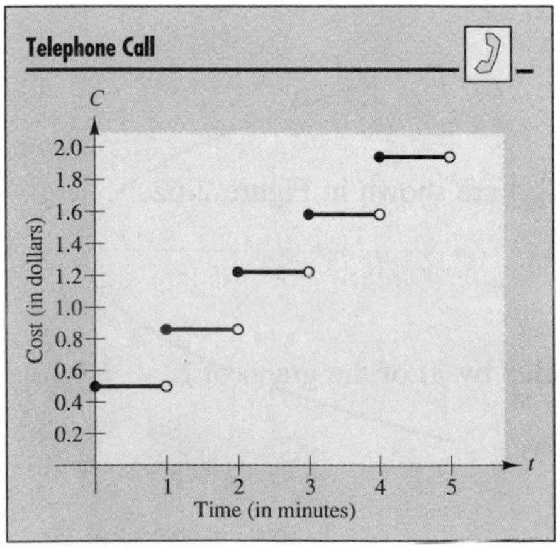

Telephone Call

Cost (in dollars)
Time (in minutes)

FIGURE 2.64

PROBLEM

Increasing and Decreasing Functions

Use your school's library or some other reference source to find examples of three different functions that represent data between 1980 and 1990. Find one that decreased during the decade, one that increased, and one that was constant. For instance, the value of the dollar decreased, the population of the United States increased, and the land size of the United States remained constant. Can you find three other examples? Present your results graphically.

WARM UP

The following warm-up exercises involve skills that were covered in earlier sections. You will use these skills in the exercise set for this section.

1. Find $f(2)$ for $f(x) = -x^3 + 5x$.

2. Find $f(6)$ for $f(x) = x^2 - 6x$.

3. Find $f(-x)$ for $f(x) = \dfrac{3}{x}$.

4. Find $f(-x)$ for $f(x) = x^2 + 3$.

In Exercises 5 and 6, solve for x.

5. $x^3 - 16x = 0$

6. $2x^2 - 3x + 1 = 0$

In Exercises 7–10, find the domain of the function.

7. $g(x) = \dfrac{4}{x - 4}$

8. $f(x) = \dfrac{2x}{x^2 - 9x + 20}$

9. $h(t) = \sqrt[4]{5 - 3t}$

10. $f(t) = t^3 + 3t - 5$

EXERCISES for Section 2.5

In Exercises 1–6, find the domain and range of the function.

1. $f(x) = \sqrt{x - 1}$

2. $f(x) = 4 - x^2$

3. $f(x) = \sqrt{x^2 - 4}$

4. $f(x) = |x - 2|$

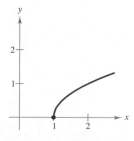

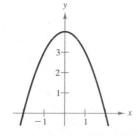

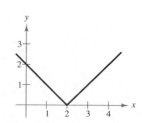

5. $f(x) = \sqrt{25 - x^2}$

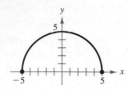

6. $f(x) = \dfrac{|x|}{x}$

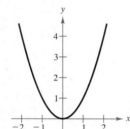

In Exercises 7–12, use the vertical line test to determine if y is a function of x.

7. $y = x^2$

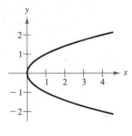

8. $y = x^3 - 1$

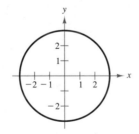

9. $x - y^2 = 0$

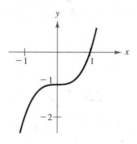

10. $x^2 + y^2 = 9$

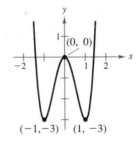

11. $x^2 = xy - 1$

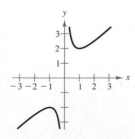

12. $x = |y|$

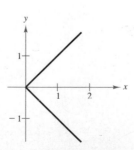

In Exercises 13–20, (a) determine the open intervals over which the function is increasing, decreasing, or constant, and (b) determine if the function is even, odd, or neither.

13. $f(x) = 2x$

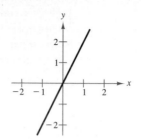

14. $f(x) = x^2 - 2x$

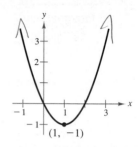

$(1, -1)$

15. $f(x) = x^3 - 3x^2$

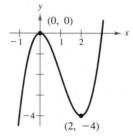

$(0, 0)$

$(2, -4)$

16. $f(x) = \sqrt{x^2 - 4}$

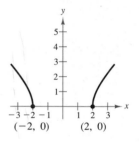

$(-2, 0)$ $(2, 0)$

17. $f(x) = 3x^4 - 6x^2$

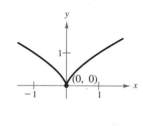

$(0, 0)$

$(-1, -3)$ $(1, -3)$

18. $f(x) = x^{2/3}$

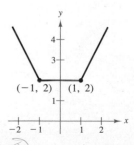

$(0, 0)$

19. $f(x) = x\sqrt{x + 3}$

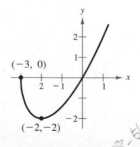

$(-3, 0)$

$(-2, -2)$

20. $f(x) = |x + 1| + |x - 1|$

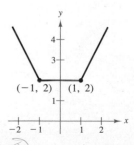

$(-1, 2)$ $(1, 2)$

In Exercises 21–26, determine whether the function is even, odd, or neither.

21. $f(x) = x^6 - 2x^2 + 3$　　**22.** $h(x) = x^3 - 5$

23. $g(x) = x^3 - 5x$　　**24.** $f(x) = x\sqrt{1 - x^2}$

25. $f(t) = t^2 + 2t - 3$　　**26.** $g(s) = 4s^{2/3}$

In Exercises 27–40, sketch the graph of the function and determine whether the function is even, odd, or neither.

27. $f(x) = 3$　　**28.** $g(x) = x$

29. $f(x) = 5 - 3x$　　**30.** $h(x) = x^2 - 4$

31. $g(s) = \dfrac{s^3}{4}$　　**32.** $f(t) = -t^4$

33. $f(x) = \sqrt{1 - x}$　　**34.** $f(x) = \sqrt{x + 2} - 1$

35. $g(t) = (t - 1)^2 + 2$　　**36.** $f(x) = |x + 2|$

37. $f(x) = \begin{cases} x + 3, & x \le 0 \\ 3, & 0 < x \le 2 \\ 2x - 1, & x > 2 \end{cases}$

38. $f(x) = \begin{cases} 2x + 1, & x \le -1 \\ x^2 - 2, & x > -1 \end{cases}$

39. $s(x) = 2[\![x - 1]\!]$　　**40.** $g(x) = 6 - [\![x]\!]$

In Exercises 41–50, sketch the graph of the function and determine the interval(s) (if any) on the real axis for which $f(x) \ge 0$.

41. $f(x) = 4 - x$　　**42.** $f(x) = 4x + 2$

43. $f(x) = x^2 - 9$　　**44.** $f(x) = x^2 - 4x$

45. $f(x) = 1 - x^4$　　**46.** $f(x) = \sqrt{x + 2}$

47. $f(x) = x^2 + 1$　　**48.** $f(x) = -(1 + |x|)$

49. $f(x) = -5$　　**50.** $f(x) = \frac{1}{2}(2 + |x|)$

51. Sketch (on the same set of coordinate axes) a graph of f for $c = -2, 0,$ and 2.
  (a) $f(x) = \frac{1}{2}x + c$
  (b) $f(x) = \frac{1}{2}(x - c)$
  (c) $f(x) = \frac{1}{2}(cx)$

52. Sketch (on the same set of coordinate axes) a graph of f for $c = -2, 0,$ and 2.
  (a) $f(x) = x^3 + c$
  (b) $f(x) = (x - c)^3$
  (c) $f(x) = (x - 2)^3 + c$

53. Use the graph of f to sketch the graphs.
  (a) $y = f(x) + 2$　　(b) $y = -f(x)$
  (c) $y = f(x - 2)$　　(d) $y = f(x + 3)$
  (e) $y = f(2x)$　　(f) $y = f(-x)$

54. Use the graph of f to sketch the graphs.
  (a) $y = f(x) - 1$　　(b) $y = f(x + 1)$
  (c) $y = f(x - 1)$　　(d) $y = -f(x - 2)$
  (e) $y = f(-x)$　　(f) $y = \frac{1}{2}f(x)$

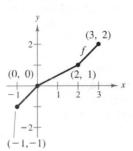

Figure for 53

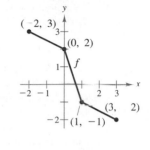

Figure for 54

55. Use the graph of $f(x) = x^2$ (see Figure 2.56(e)) to write formulas for the functions whose graphs are shown in parts (a) and (b) of the figure shown here.

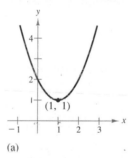

(a)

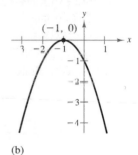

(b)

Figure for 55

56. Use the graph of $f(x) = x^3$ (see Figure 2.56(f)) to write formulas for the functions whose graphs are shown in parts (a) and (b) of the figure shown here.

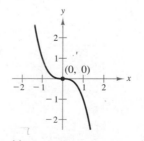

(a)

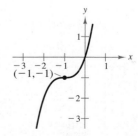

(b)

Figure for 56

57. *Cost of a Telephone Call* The cost of a telephone call between two cities is $0.65 for the first minute and $0.42 for each additional minute (or portion thereof). Use the greatest integer function to create a model for the cost C of a telephone call between the two cities lasting t minutes. Sketch the graph of the function.

58. *Cost of Overnight Delivery* Suppose the cost of sending an overnight package from New York to Atlanta is $9.80 for the first pound and $2.50 for each additional pound (or portion thereof). Use the greatest integer function to create a model for the cost C of overnight delivery of a package weighing x pounds. Sketch the graph of the function.

59. *Maximum Profit* The marketing department for a company estimates that the demand for a product is given by $p = 100 - 0.0001x$ where p is the price per unit and x is the number of units. The cost of producing x units is given by $C = 350,000 + 30x$, and the profit for producing and selling x units is given by

$$P = R - C = xp - C.$$

Sketch the graph of the profit function and estimate the number of units that would produce a maximum profit.

60. *Fluorescent Lamp* The number of lumens (time rate of flow of light) L from a fluorescent lamp can be approximated by the model

$$L = -0.294x^2 + 97.744x - 664.875, \quad 20 \le x \le 90$$

where x is the wattage of the lamp. Sketch a graph of the function and estimate the wattage of a bulb necessary to obtain 2000 lumens.

In Exercises 61–64, write the height h of the rectangle as a function of x.

61.

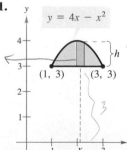

$y = 4x - x^2$

(1, 3) (3, 3)

62.

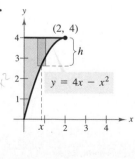

(2, 4)

$y = 4x - x^2$

63.

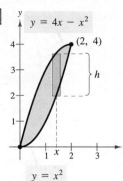

$y = 4x - x^2$

(2, 4)

h

$y = x^2$

64.

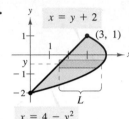

(8, 4)

h

$y = \sqrt{2x}$

In Exercises 65 and 66, write the length L of the rectangle as a function of y.

65.

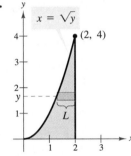

$x = y + 2$

(3, 1)

L

$x = 4 - y^2$

66.

$x = \sqrt{y}$

(2, 4)

L

67. Prove that a function of the following form is odd.

$$f(x) = a_{2n+1}x^{2n+1} + a_{2n-1}x^{2n-1} + \ldots + a_3x^3 + a_1x$$

68. Prove that a function of the following form is even.

$$f(x) = a_{2n}x^{2n} + a_{2n-2}x^{2n-2} + \ldots + a_2x^2 + a_0$$

69. The intake pipe of a 100-gallon tank has a flow rate of 10 gallons per minute, and two drain pipes have a flow rate of 5 gallons per minute each. The figure shows the volume V of fluid in the tank as a function of time t. Determine the pipes in which the fluid is flowing in specific subintervals of the 1 hour of time shown on the graph. (There is more than one correct answer.)

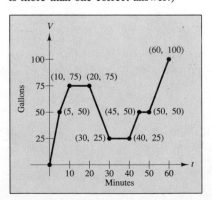

Figure for 69

2.6 Combinations of Functions

Arithmetic Combinations of Functions / Composition of Functions / Applications

Arithmetic Combinations of Functions

Just as two real numbers can be combined by the operations of addition, subtraction, multiplication, and division to form other real numbers, two *functions* can be combined to create new functions. For example, if

$$f(x) = 2x - 3 \quad \text{and} \quad g(x) = x^2 - 1$$

we can form the sum, difference, product, and quotient of f and g as follows.

$$f(x) + g(x) = (2x - 3) + (x^2 - 1) = x^2 + 2x - 4 \qquad \textit{Sum}$$

$$f(x) - g(x) = (2x - 3) - (x^2 - 1) = -x^2 + 2x - 2 \qquad \textit{Difference}$$

$$f(x)g(x) = (2x - 3)(x^2 - 1) = 2x^3 - 3x^2 - 2x + 3 \qquad \textit{Product}$$

$$\frac{f(x)}{g(x)} = \frac{2x - 3}{x^2 - 1}, \quad x \neq \pm 1 \qquad\qquad \textit{Quotient}$$

The domain of an arithmetic combination of functions f and g consists of all real numbers that are common to the domains of f and g. In the case of the quotient $f(x)/g(x)$, there is the further restriction that $g(x) \neq 0$.

SUM, DIFFERENCE, PRODUCT, AND QUOTIENT OF FUNCTIONS

Let f and g be two functions with overlapping domains. Then, for all x common to both domains,

1. Sum: $(f + g)(x) = f(x) + g(x)$
2. Difference: $(f - g)(x) = f(x) - g(x)$
3. Product: $(fg)(x) = f(x) \cdot g(x)$
4. Quotient: $\left(\dfrac{f}{g}\right)(x) = \dfrac{f(x)}{g(x)}, \quad g(x) \neq 0.$

EXAMPLE 1   Finding the Sum of Two Functions

Given $f(x) = 2x + 1$ and $g(x) = x^2 + 2x - 1$, find $(f + g)(x)$. Then evaluate this sum when $x = 2$.

Solution

The sum of the functions f and g is

$$(f + g)(x) = f(x) + g(x)$$
$$= (2x + 1) + (x^2 + 2x - 1)$$
$$= x^2 + 4x.$$

When $x = 2$, the value of this sum is

$$(f + g)(2) = 2^2 + 4(2) = 12.$$ ◢

EXAMPLE 2 Finding the Difference of Two Functions

Given $f(x) = 2x + 1$ and $g(x) = x^2 + 2x - 1$, find $(f - g)(x)$. Then evaluate this difference when $x = 2$.

Solution

The difference of the functions f and g is

$$\begin{aligned}
(f - g)(x) &= f(x) - g(x) \\
&= (2x + 1) - (x^2 + 2x - 1) \\
&= -x^2 + 2.
\end{aligned}$$

When $x = 2$, the value of this difference is

$$(f - g)(2) = -(2)^2 + 2 = -2.$$ ◢

In Examples 1 and 2, both f and g have domains that consist of all real numbers. Thus, the domain of both $(f + g)$ and $(f - g)$ is also the set of all real numbers. Remember that any restrictions on the domains of f or g must be taken into account when forming the sum, difference, product, or quotient of f and g. For instance, the domain of $f(x) = 1/x$ is all $x \neq 0$, and the domain of $g(x) = \sqrt{x}$ is $[0, \infty)$. This implies that the domain of $f + g$ is $(0, \infty)$.

EXAMPLE 3 Finding the Product and Quotient of Two Functions

Find $(fg)(x)$, $(f/g)(x)$, and $(g/f)(x)$ for the functions

$$f(x) = \sqrt{x} \quad \text{and} \quad g(x) = \sqrt{4 - x^2}.$$

Then find the domains of f/g and g/f.

Solution

$$(fg)(x) = f(x)g(x) = \sqrt{x}\sqrt{4 - x^2} = \sqrt{x(4 - x^2)} \quad \textit{Product, } f \cdot g$$

$$\left(\frac{f}{g}\right)(x) = \frac{f(x)}{g(x)} = \frac{\sqrt{x}}{\sqrt{4 - x^2}} \quad \textit{Quotient, } f/g$$

$$\left(\frac{g}{f}\right)(x) = \frac{g(x)}{f(x)} = \frac{\sqrt{4 - x^2}}{\sqrt{x}} \quad \textit{Quotient, } g/f$$

The domain of f is $[0, \infty)$ and the domain of g is $[-2, 2]$. The intersection of these two domains is $[0, 2]$. Thus, we have the following domains for f/g and g/f.

Domain of $\dfrac{f}{g}$: [0, 2)   Domain of $\dfrac{g}{f}$: (0, 2]

Can you see why these two domains differ slightly?   ◢

Composition of Functions

Another way of combining two functions is to form the **composition** of one with the other. For instance, if $f(x) = x^2$ and $g(x) = x + 1$, then the composition of f with g ($f \circ g$) is

$$f(g(x)) = f(x + 1) = (x + 1)^2.$$

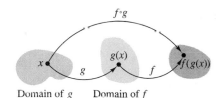

Domain of g Domain of f

FIGURE 2.65

DEFINITION OF COMPOSITION OF TWO FUNCTIONS

The **composition** of the functions f and g is

$$(f \circ g)(x) = f(g(x)).$$

The domain of $f \circ g$ is the set of all x in the domain of g such that $g(x)$ is in the domain of f. (See Figure 2.65.)

EXAMPLE 4   Forming the Composition of *f* with *g*

Find $(f \circ g)(x)$ for $f(x) = \sqrt{x}$, $x \ge 0$, and $g(x) = x - 1$, where $x \ge 1$. If possible, find $(f \circ g)(2)$ and $(f \circ g)(0)$.

Solution

$$
\begin{aligned}
(f \circ g)(x) &= f(g(x)) & &\textit{Definition of } f \circ g \\
&= f(x - 1) & &\textit{Definition of } g(x) \\
&= \sqrt{x - 1}, \quad x \ge 1 & &\textit{Definition of } f(x)
\end{aligned}
$$

The domain of $f \circ g$ is $[1, \infty)$. Thus,

$$(f \circ g)(2) = \sqrt{2 - 1} = 1$$

is defined, but $(f \circ g)(0)$ is not defined because 0 is not in the domain of $f \circ g$.   ◢

The composition of f with g is generally *not* the same as the composition of g with f.

EXAMPLE 5   Composition of Functions

Given $f(x) = x + 2$ and $g(x) = 4 - x^2$, find the following.

a. $(f \circ g)(x)$

b. $(g \circ f)(x)$

Solution

a. $(f \circ g)(x) = f(g(x))$ *Definition of $f \circ g$*

$\qquad\qquad\quad = f(4 - x^2)$ *Definition of $g(x)$*

$\qquad\qquad\quad = (4 - x^2) + 2$ *Definition of $f(x)$*

$\qquad\qquad\quad = -x^2 + 6$

b. $(g \circ f)(x) = g(f(x))$ *Definition of $g \circ f$*

$\qquad\qquad\quad = g(x + 2)$ *Definition of $f(x)$*

$\qquad\qquad\quad = 4 - (x + 2)^2$ *Definition of $g(x)$*

$\qquad\qquad\quad = 4 - (x^2 + 4x + 4)$

$\qquad\qquad\quad = -x^2 - 4x$

Note in this case that $(f \circ g)(x) \neq (g \circ f)(x)$.

EXAMPLE 6   A Case in Which $f \circ g = g \circ f$

Given $f(x) = 2x + 3$ and $g(x) = \frac{1}{2}(x - 3)$, find the following.

a. $(f \circ g)(x)$

b. $(g \circ f)(x)$

Solution

REMARK In Example 6, note that the two composite functions $f \circ g$ and $g \circ f$ are equal, and both represent the identity function—$(f \circ g)(x) = (g \circ f)(x) = x$.

a. $(f \circ g)(x) = f(g(x)) = f\left(\frac{1}{2}(x - 3)\right) = 2\left[\frac{1}{2}(x - 3)\right] + 3$

$\qquad\qquad\quad = x - 3 + 3 = x$

b. $(g \circ f)(x) = g(f(x)) = g(2x + 3) = \frac{1}{2}[(2x + 3) - 3] = \frac{1}{2}(2x) = x$

In Examples 4, 5, and 6, we formed the composite of two given functions. In calculus, it is also important to be able to identify two functions that *make up a given* composite function. For instance, the function h given by $h(x) = (3x - 5)^3$ is the composite of f with g, where $f(x) = x^3$ and $g(x) = 3x - 5$. That is,

$$h(x) = (3x - 5)^3 = [g(x)]^3 = f(g(x)).$$

To "decompose" a composite function, we look for an "inner" and an "outer" function. In the function h above, $g(x) = 3x - 5$ is the inner function and $f(x) = x^3$ is the outer function.

EXAMPLE 7   Identifying a Composite Function

Express the function $h(x) = 1/(x - 2)^2$ as a composition of two functions f and g.

Solution

Take the inner function to be

$$g(x) = x - 2$$

and the outer function to be

$$f(x) = \frac{1}{x^2} = x^{-2}.$$

Then you can write

$$h(x) = \frac{1}{(x - 2)^2} = (x - 2)^{-2} = f(x - 2) = f(g(x)).$$

Applications

EXAMPLE 8   Bacteria Count

The number of bacteria in a refrigerated food is given by

$$N(T) = 20T^2 - 80T + 500, \qquad 2 \leq T \leq 14$$

where T is the temperature of the food. When the food is removed from refrigeration, the temperature is given by

$$T(t) = 4t + 2, \qquad 0 \leq t \leq 3$$

where t is the time in hours. Find the following.

a. The composite function $N(T(t))$
b. The number of bacteria in the food when $t = 2$ hours
c. The time when the bacteria count reaches 2000

Solution

a. $N(T(t)) = 20(4t + 2)^2 - 80(4t + 2) + 500$

$\qquad\quad = 20(16t^2 + 16t + 4) - 320t - 160 + 500$

$\qquad\quad = 320t^2 + 320t + 80 - 320t - 160 + 500$

$\qquad\quad = 320t^2 + 420$

b. When $t = 2$, the number of bacteria is

$$N = 320(2)^2 + 420 = 1280 + 420 = 1700.$$

c. The bacteria count will reach $N = 2000$ when $320t^2 + 420 = 2000$.

$$320t^2 + 420 = 2000$$

$$320t^2 = 1580$$

$$t^2 = \frac{1580}{320} = \frac{79}{16}$$

$$t = \frac{\sqrt{79}}{4} \approx 2.2 \text{ hours}$$

DISCUSSION

PROBLEM

The Composition
of Two Functions

You learned in this section that the composite functions $(f \circ g)(x)$ and $(g \circ f)(x)$ are generally not equal to each other. Mathematically, you can say that in general the operation of forming the composition of two functions is *not commutative*. Discuss some examples of real-life situations in which the order of operations is commutative and some that are not commutative. For instance, the operations of "turning on a calculator" and "pressing the keys 2 $\boxed{+}$ 3 $\boxed{=}$" are not commutative, whereas the operations of "taking off your left shoe" and "taking off your right shoe" would generally be thought of as being commutative (because they produce the same results).

WARM UP

The following warm-up exercises involve skills that were covered in earlier sections. You will use these skills in the exercise set for this section.

In Exercises 1–10, perform the indicated operations and simplify the result.

1. $\dfrac{1}{x} + \dfrac{1}{1 - x}$

2. $\dfrac{2}{x + 3} - \dfrac{2}{x - 3}$

3. $\dfrac{3}{x - 2} - \dfrac{2}{x(x - 2)}$

4. $\dfrac{x}{x - 5} + \dfrac{1}{3}$

5. $(x - 1)\left(\dfrac{1}{\sqrt{x^2 - 1}}\right)$

6. $\left(\dfrac{x}{x^2 - 4}\right)\left(\dfrac{x^2 - x - 2}{x^2}\right)$

7. $(x^2 - 4) \div \left(\dfrac{x + 2}{5}\right)$

8. $\left(\dfrac{x}{x^2 + 3x - 10}\right) \div \left(\dfrac{x^2 + 3x}{x^2 + 6x + 5}\right)$

9. $\dfrac{\left(\dfrac{1}{x}\right) + 5}{3 - \left(\dfrac{1}{x}\right)}$

10. $\dfrac{\left(\dfrac{x}{4}\right) - \left(\dfrac{4}{x}\right)}{x - 4}$

EXERCISES for Section 2.6

In Exercises 1–8, find (a) $(f + g)(x)$, (b) $(f - g)(x)$, (c) $(fg)(x)$, and (d) $(f/g)(x)$. What is the domain of f/g?

1. $f(x) = x + 1,$ $g(x) = x - 1$
2. $f(x) = 2x - 5,$ $g(x) = 1 - x$
3. $f(x) = x^2,$ $g(x) = 1 - x$
4. $f(x) = 2x - 5,$ $g(x) = 5$
5. $f(x) = x^2 + 5,$ $g(x) = \sqrt{1 - x}$
6. $f(x) = \sqrt{x^2 - 4},$ $g(x) = \dfrac{x^2}{x^2 + 1}$
7. $f(x) = \dfrac{1}{x},$ $g(x) = \dfrac{1}{x^2}$
8. $f(x) = \dfrac{x}{x + 1},$ $g(x) = x^3$

In Exercises 9–20, evaluate the indicated function for $f(x) = x^2 + 1$ and $g(x) = x - 4$.

9. $(f + g)(3)$ **10.** $(f - g)(-2)$
11. $(f - g)(0)$ **12.** $(f + g)(1)$
13. $(f - g)(2t)$ **14.** $(f + g)(t - 1)$
15. $(fg)(4)$ **16.** $(fg)(-6)$
17. $\left(\dfrac{f}{g}\right)(5)$ **18.** $\left(\dfrac{f}{g}\right)(0)$
19. $\left(\dfrac{f}{g}\right)(-1) - g(3)$ **20.** $(2f)(5)$

In Exercises 21–24, find (a) $f \circ g$, (b) $g \circ f$, and (c) $f \circ f$.

21. $f(x) = x^2,$ $g(x) = x - 1$
22. $f(x) = \sqrt[3]{x - 1},$ $g(x) = x^3 + 1$
23. $f(x) = 3x + 5,$ $g(x) = 5 - x$
24. $f(x) = x^3,$ $g(x) = \dfrac{1}{x}$

In Exercises 25–32, find (a) $f \circ g$ and (b) $g \circ f$.

25. $f(x) = \sqrt{x + 4},$ $g(x) = x^2$
26. $f(x) = 3x + 2,$ $g(x) = x^2 - 8$
27. $f(x) = \frac{1}{3}x - 3,$ $g(x) = 3x + 1$
28. $f(x) = x^4,$ $g(x) = x^4$
29. $f(x) = \sqrt{x},$ $g(x) = \sqrt{x}$
30. $f(x) = 2x - 3,$ $g(x) = 2x - 3$

31. $f(x) = |x|,$ $g(x) = x + 6$
32. $f(x) = x^{2/3},$ $g(x) = x^6$

In Exercises 33–36, use the graphs of f and g (see figure) to evaluate the indicated functions.

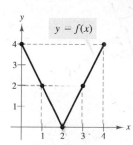
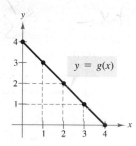

Figures for 33–36

33. (a) $(f + g)(3)$ (b) $\left(\dfrac{f}{g}\right)(2)$
34. (a) $(f - g)(1)$ (b) $(fg)(4)$
35. (a) $(f \circ g)(2)$ (b) $(g \circ f)(2)$
36. (a) $(f \circ g)(1)$ (b) $(g \circ f)(3)$

In Exercises 37–44, find two functions f and g such that $(f \circ g)(x) = h(x)$. (There are many correct answers to these exercises.)

37. $h(x) = (2x + 1)^2$ **38.** $h(x) = (1 - x)^3$
39. $h(x) = \sqrt[3]{x^2 - 4}$ **40.** $h(x) = \sqrt{9 - x}$
41. $h(x) = \dfrac{1}{x + 2}$ **42.** $h(x) = \dfrac{4}{(5x + 2)^2}$
43. $h(x) = (x + 4)^2 + 2(x + 4)$
44. $h(x) = (x + 3)^{3/2}$

In Exercises 45–48, determine the domain of (a) f, (b) g, and (c) $f \circ g$.

45. $f(x) = \sqrt{x},$ $g(x) = x^2 + 1$
46. $f(x) = \dfrac{1}{x},$ $g(x) = x + 3$
47. $f(x) = \dfrac{3}{x^2 - 1},$ $g(x) = x + 1$
48. $f(x) = 2x + 3,$ $g(x) = \dfrac{x}{2}$

$(x^2 + 5)(\sqrt{1 - x})$

49. *Stopping Distance* While traveling in a car at x miles per hour, you are required to stop quickly to avoid an accident. The distance the car travels during your reaction time is given by $R(x) = \frac{3}{4}x$. The distance traveled while braking is given by $B(x) = \frac{1}{15}x^2$. Find the function giving total stopping distance T. Graph the functions R, B, and T on the same set of coordinate axes for $0 \le x \le 60$.

50. *Comparing Sales* Suppose you own two fast-food restaurants in town. From 1985 to 1990, the sales for one restaurant have been decreasing according to the function

$$R_1 = 500 - 0.8t^2, \quad t = 5, 6, 7, 8, 9, 10$$

where R_1 represents the sales for the first restaurant (in thousands of dollars) and t represents the calendar year with $t = 5$ corresponding to 1985. During the same six-year period, the sales for the second restaurant have been increasing according to the function

$$R_2 = 250 + 0.78t, \quad t = 5, 6, 7, 8, 9, 10.$$

Write a function that represents the total sales for the two restaurants. Use the *stacked bar graph* in the figure, which represents the total sales during the six-year period, to determine whether the total sales have been increasing or decreasing.

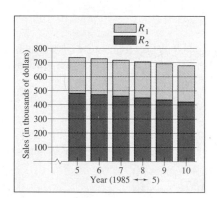

Figure for 50

51. *Ripples* A pebble is dropped into a calm pond, causing ripples in the form of concentric circles (see figure). The radius (in feet) of the outer ripple is given by $r(t) = 0.6t$, where t is the time in seconds after the pebble strikes the water. The area of the circle is given by the function $A(r) = \pi r^2$. Find and interpret $(A \circ r)(t)$.

Figure for 51

52. *Area* A square concrete foundation was prepared as a base for a large cylindrical gasoline tank (see figure).
  (a) Express the radius r of the tank as a function of the length x of the sides of the square.
  (b) Express the area A of the circular base of the tank as a function of the radius r.
  (c) Find and interpret $(A \circ r)(x)$.

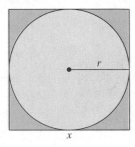

Figure for 52

53. *Cost* The weekly cost of producing x units in a manufacturing process is given by the function $C(x) = 60x + 750$. The number of units produced in t hours is given by $x(t) = 50t$. Find and interpret $(C \circ x)(t)$.

54. *Air Traffic Control* An air traffic controller spots two planes at the same altitude flying toward the same point (see figure). Their flight paths form a right angle at point P. One plane is 150 miles from point P and is moving at 450 miles per hour. The second plane is 200 miles from point P and is moving at 450 miles per hour. Write the distance s between the planes as a function of time t.

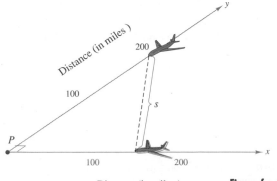

Distance (in miles)   **Figure for 54**

55. Prove that the product of two odd functions is an even function.

56. Prove that the product of two even functions is an even function.

57. Prove that the product of an odd function and an even function is odd.

2.7 Inverse Functions

The Inverse of a Function / The Existence of an Inverse Function /
Finding the Inverse of a Function

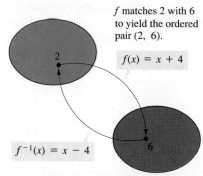

f matches 2 with 6
to yield the ordered
pair (2, 6).

$f(x) = x + 4$

2

6

$f^{-1}(x) = x - 4$

f^{-1} matches 6 with 2 to yield
the ordered pair (6, 2).

FIGURE 2.66

REMARK   Don't be confused by the
use of -1 to denote the inverse function f^{-1}. In this book f^{-1} will *always*
refer to the inverse of the function f
and *not* to the reciprocal of $f(x)$.

The Inverse of a Function

You know (from Section 2.4) that one way to represent a function is by a set
of ordered pairs. For instance, the function $f(x) = x + 4$ from the set $A = \{1, 2, 3, 4\}$ to the set $B = \{5, 6, 7, 8\}$ can be written as follows.

$$f(x) = x + 4: \{(1, 5), (2, 6), (3, 7), (4, 8)\}$$

By interchanging the first and second coordinates of each of these ordered
pairs, you can form the **inverse function** of f, denoted f^{-1}. This is a function
from the set B to the set A, and can be written

$$f^{-1}(x) = x - 4: \{(5, 1,), (6, 2), (7, 3), (8, 4)\}.$$

Note that the domain of f is equal to the range of f^{-1}, and vice versa, as
shown in Figure 2.66. Also note that the functions f and f^{-1} have the effect
of "undoing" each other. In other words, when you form the composition of
f with f^{-1} or the composition of f^{-1} with f, you obtain the identity function.

$$f(f^{-1}(x)) = f(x - 4) = (x - 4) + 4 = x$$
$$f^{-1}(f(x)) = f^{-1}(x + 4) = (x + 4) - 4 = x$$

EXAMPLE 1   Finding Inverse Functions Informally

Find the inverse of the following functions.

a. $f(x) = 4x$

b. $f(x) = x - 6$

Verify that both $f(f^{-1}(x))$ and $f^{-1}(f(x))$ are equal to the identity function.

Solution

a. The given function *multiplies* each input by 4. To "undo" this function,
divide each input by 4. Thus, the inverse function of $f(x) = 4x$ is

$$f^{-1}(x) = \frac{x}{4}.$$

You can verify that both $f(f^{-1}(x))$ and $f^{-1}(f(x))$ are equal to the identity
function.

$$f(f^{-1}(x)) = f\left(\frac{x}{4}\right) = 4\left(\frac{x}{4}\right) = x$$

$$f^{-1}(f(x)) = f^{-1}(4x) = \frac{4x}{4} = x$$

b. The given function *subtracts* 6 from each input. To "undo" this function, *add* 6 to each input. Thus, the inverse function of $f(x) = x - 6$ is

$$f^{-1}(x) = x + 6.$$

You can verify that both $f(f^{-1}(x))$ and $f^{-1}(f(x))$ are equal to the identity function.

$$f(f^{-1}(x)) = f(x + 6) = (x + 6) - 6 = x$$
$$f^{-1}(f(x)) = f^{-1}(x - 6) = (x - 6) + 6 = x$$

DEFINITION OF THE INVERSE OF A FUNCTION

Let f and g be two functions such that

$$f(g(x)) = x \qquad \text{for every } x \text{ in the domain of } g$$

and

$$g(f(x)) = x \qquad \text{for every } x \text{ in the domain of } f.$$

Then, the function g is the **inverse** of the function f, denoted f^{-1} (read "f-inverse"). Thus, $f(f^{-1}(x)) = x$ and $f^{-1}(f(x)) = x$. The domain of f must be equal to the range of f^{-1}, and vice versa.

Note from this definition that if the function g is the inverse of the function f, then it must also be true that the function f is the inverse of the function g. Thus, the functions f and g are *inverses of each other*.

EXAMPLE 2   Verifying Inverse Functions

Show that the following functions are inverses of each other.

$$f(x) = 2x^3 - 1$$

and

$$g(x) = \sqrt[3]{\frac{x + 1}{2}}$$

Solution

Note that the domain (and the range) of both functions is the entire set of real numbers. To show that f and g are inverses of each other, you need to show that $f(g(x)) = x$ and $g(f(x)) = x$.

$$f(g(x)) = f\left(\sqrt[3]{\frac{x+1}{2}}\right) = 2\left(\sqrt[3]{\frac{x+1}{2}}\right)^3 - 1$$

$$= 2\left(\frac{x+1}{2}\right) - 1$$

$$= x + 1 - 1 = x$$

$$g(f(x)) = g(2x^3 - 1) = \sqrt[3]{\frac{(2x^3 - 1) + 1}{2}}$$

$$= \sqrt[3]{\frac{2x^3}{2}}$$

$$= \sqrt[3]{x^3} = x$$

You can see that the two functions f and g "undo" each other: the function f first cubes the input x, multiplies by 2, and then subtracts 1, whereas the function g first adds 1, then divides by 2, and then takes the cube root of the result.

EXAMPLE 3 Verifying Inverse Functions

Which of the following functions

$$g(x) = \frac{x-2}{5} \quad \text{and} \quad h(x) = \frac{5}{x} + 2$$

is the inverse of the function

$$f(x) = \frac{5}{x-2}?$$

Solution

$$f(g(x)) = f\left(\frac{x-2}{5}\right) = \frac{5}{\left(\dfrac{x-2}{5}\right) - 2} \qquad \textit{Composition of f with g}$$

$$= \frac{25}{(x-2) - 10}$$

$$= \frac{25}{x - 12}$$

$$\neq x$$

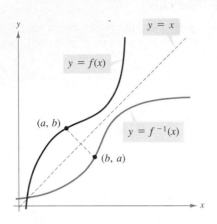

The graph of f^{-1} is a reflection of the graph of f in the line $y = x$.

FIGURE 2.67

Because this composition is not equal to the identity function x, g is *not* the inverse of f.

$$f(h(x)) = f\left(\frac{5}{x} + 2\right) = \frac{5}{\left(\frac{5}{x}\right) + 2 - 2} \qquad \textit{Composition of f with h}$$

$$= \frac{5}{\left(\frac{5}{x}\right)}$$

$$= x$$

Thus, it appears that h is the inverse of f. Confirm this by showing that the composition of h with f is also equal to the identity function. ◢

The graphs of f and f^{-1} are related to each other in the following way. If the point (a, b) lies on the graph of f, then the point (b, a) lies on the graph of f^{-1} and vice versa. This means that the graph of f^{-1} is a reflection of the graph of f in the line $y = x$, as shown in Figure 2.67.

The Existence of an Inverse Function

A function need not have an inverse function. For instance, the function $f(x) = x^2$ has no inverse [assuming a domain of $(-\infty, \infty)$]. To have an inverse, a function must be **one-to-one,** which means that no two elements in the domain of f correspond to the same element in the range of f.

DEFINITION OF ONE-TO-ONE FUNCTION

A function f is **one-to-one** if, for a and b in its domain,

$$f(a) = f(b) \qquad \text{implies that} \qquad a = b.$$

The function $f(x) = x + 1$ *is* one-to-one because $a + 1 = b + 1$ implies that a and b must be equal. However, the function $f(x) = x^2$ is *not* one-to-one because $a^2 = b^2$ does not imply that $a = b$. For instance, $(-1)^2 = 1^2$ and yet $-1 \neq 1$.

EXISTENCE OF AN INVERSE FUNCTION

A function f has an inverse function f^{-1} if and only if f is one-to-one.

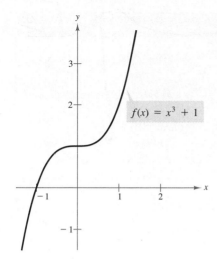

(a) f is one-to-one.

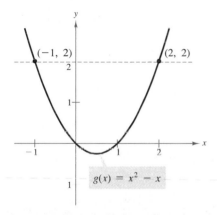

(b) g is not one-to-one.

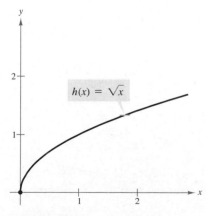

(c) h is one-to-one.

FIGURE 2.68

EXAMPLE 4 Testing for One-to-One Functions

Which functions are one-to-one and have an inverse function?

a. $f(x) = x^3 + 1$ **b.** $g(x) = x^2 - x$ **c.** $h(x) = \sqrt{x}$

Solution

a. Let a and b be real numbers with $f(a) = f(b)$. Then

$$a^3 + 1 = b^3 + 1 \qquad\qquad \textit{Set } f(a) = f(b)$$
$$a^3 = b^3$$
$$a = b.$$

Therefore, $f(a) = f(b)$ implies that $a = b$. The function $f(x) = x^3 + 1$ *is* one-to-one and it has an inverse function.

b. Since

$$g(-1) = (-1)^2 - (-1) = 2 \qquad \text{and} \qquad g(2) = 2^2 - 2 = 2$$

we have two distinct inputs matched with the same output. Therefore, g is *not* a one-to-one function and has no inverse function.

c. Let a and b be nonnegative real numbers with $h(a) = h(b)$. Then

$$\sqrt{a} = \sqrt{b} \qquad\qquad \textit{Set } h(a) = h(b)$$
$$a = b.$$

Therefore, $h(a) = h(b)$ implies that $a = b$. The function $h(x) = \sqrt{x}$ *is* one-to-one and it has an inverse function.

From its graph, it is easy to tell whether a function of x is one-to-one. Simply check to see that every *horizontal* line intersects the graph of the function at most once. For instance, Figure 2.68 shows the graphs of the three functions given in Example 4. For the graph of $g(x) = x^2 - x$ you can find a horizontal line that intersects the graph twice.

Two special types of functions that pass the **horizontal line test** are those that are increasing or decreasing on their entire domains.

1. If f is *increasing* on its entire domain, then f is one-to-one.
2. If f is *decreasing* on its entire domain, then f is one-to-one.

Finding the Inverse of a Function

For simple functions (like the ones in Example 1) you can find inverse functions by inspection. For instance, the inverse of $f(x) = 8x$ is equal to $f^{-1}(x) = x/8$. For more complicated functions, however, it is best to use the following procedure for finding the inverse of a function.

FINDING THE INVERSE OF A FUNCTION

To find the inverse of f, use the following procedure.

1. Test to see that f is one-to-one.
2. Write the function in the form $y = f(x)$ and interchange the roles of x and y.
3. Solve for y in terms of x, and then replace y by $f^{-1}(x)$.
4. Check to see that the domain of f is the range of f^{-1}, and that the domain of f^{-1} is the range of f.

EXAMPLE 5   Finding the Inverse of a Function

Find the inverse (if it exists) of $f(x) = \dfrac{5 - 3x}{2}$.

Solution

From Figure 2.69 you can see that f is one-to-one, and therefore has an inverse.

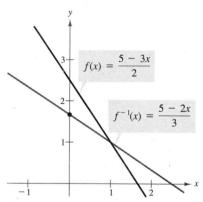

FIGURE 2.69

$$y = \frac{5 - 3x}{2} \qquad \textit{Write in form } y = f(x)$$

$$x = \frac{5 - 3y}{2} \qquad \textit{Interchange } x \textit{ and } y$$

$$2x = 5 - 3y$$

$$3y = 5 - 2x$$

$$y = \frac{5 - 2x}{3} \qquad \textit{Solve for } y$$

$$f^{-1}(x) = \frac{5 - 2x}{3} \qquad \textit{Replace } y \textit{ by } f^{-1}(x)$$

The domain and range of both f and f^{-1} consist of all real numbers. You can check your work by verifying that $f(f^{-1}(x)) = f^{-1}(f(x))$.

EXAMPLE 6 Finding the Inverse of a Function

Find the inverse of the function $f(x) = \sqrt{2x - 3}$ and sketch the graphs of f and f^{-1}.

Solution

$$y = \sqrt{2x - 3} \qquad\qquad \textit{Write } y = f(x)$$

$$x = \sqrt{2y - 3}, \quad y \geq \frac{3}{2}, \, x \geq 0 \qquad \textit{Interchange } x \textit{ and } y$$

$$x^2 + 3 = 2y \qquad\qquad \textit{Square both sides}$$

$$\frac{x^2 + 3}{2} = y \qquad\qquad \textit{Solve for } y$$

$$f^{-1}(x) = \frac{x^2 + 3}{2}, \quad x \geq 0 \qquad \textit{Replace } y \textit{ by } f^{-1}(x)$$

The graph of f^{-1} is the reflection of the graph of f in the line $y = x$, as shown in Figure 2.70. Note that the domain of f is the interval $\left[\frac{3}{2}, \infty\right)$ and the range of f is the interval $[0, \infty)$. Moreover, the domain of f^{-1} is the interval $[0, \infty)$ and the range of f^{-1} is the interval $\left[\frac{3}{2}, \infty\right)$.

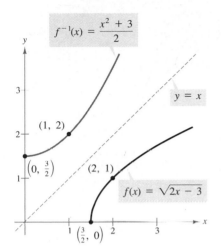

$f^{-1}(x) = \dfrac{x^2 + 3}{2}$

$y = x$

$(1, 2)$

$\left(0, \frac{3}{2}\right)$ $(2, 1)$

$f(x) = \sqrt{2x - 3}$

$\left(\frac{3}{2}, 0\right)$

FIGURE 2.70

The problem of finding the inverse of a function can be difficult (or even impossible) for two reasons. First, after interchanging x and y in $y = f(x)$, it may be algebraically difficult to solve for y in terms of x. Second, if f is not one-to-one, then f^{-1} does not exist.

DISCUSSION

PROBLEM

The Existence of an Inverse Function

Write a short paragraph describing why the following functions do or do not possess inverse functions.

1. Let x represent the retail price of an item (in dollars), and let $f(x)$ represent the sales tax on the item. Assume that the sales tax is 7% of the retail price *and* that the sales tax is rounded to the nearest cent. Does this function possess an inverse? (*Hint:* Can you undo this function? For instance, if you know that the sales tax is $0.14, can you determine *exactly* what the retail price is?)

2. Let x represent the temperature in degrees Celsius, and $f(x)$ represent the temperature in degrees Fahrenheit. Does this function possess an inverse? (*Hint:* The formula for converting from degrees Celsius to degrees Fahrenheit is $F = \frac{9}{5}C + 32$.)

WARM UP

The following warm-up exercises involve skills that were covered in earlier sections. You will use these skills in the exercise set for this section.

In Exercises 1–4, find the domain of each function.

1. $f(x) = \sqrt[3]{x + 1}$

2. $f(x) = \sqrt{x + 1}$

3. $g(x) = \dfrac{2}{x^2 - 2x}$

4. $h(x) = \dfrac{x}{3x + 5}$

In Exercises 5–8, simplify the expressions.

5. $2\left(\dfrac{x + 5}{2}\right) - 5$

6. $7 - 10\left(\dfrac{7 - x}{10}\right)$

7. $\sqrt[3]{2\left(\dfrac{x^3}{2} - 2\right) + 4}$

8. $(\sqrt[5]{x + 2})^5 - 2$

In Exercises 9 and 10, solve for x in terms of y.

9. $y = \dfrac{2x - 6}{3}$

10. $y = \sqrt[3]{2x - 4}$

EXERCISES for Section 2.7

In Exercises 1–6, find the inverse f^{-1} of the function f informally. Verify that $f(f^{-1}(x))$ and $f^{-1}(f(x))$ are equal to the identity function.

1. $f(x) = 8x$

2. $f(x) = \frac{1}{5}x$

3. $f(x) = x + 10$

4. $f(x) = x - 5$

5. $f(x) = \sqrt[3]{x}$

6. $f(x) = x^5$

In Exercises 7–16, (a) show that f and g are inverse functions by showing that $f(g(x)) = x$ and $g(f(x)) = x$, and (b) graph f and g on the same set of coordinate axes.

7. $f(x) = 2x$, $\qquad g(x) = \dfrac{x}{2}$

8. $f(x) = x - 5$, $\qquad g(x) = x + 5$

9. $f(x) = 5x + 1$, $\qquad g(x) = \dfrac{x - 1}{5}$

10. $f(x) = 3 - 4x$, $\qquad g(x) = \dfrac{3 - x}{4}$

11. $f(x) = x^3$, $\qquad g(x) = \sqrt[3]{x}$

12. $f(x) = \dfrac{1}{x}$, $\qquad g(x) = \dfrac{1}{x}$

13. $f(x) = \sqrt{x - 4}$, $\qquad g(x) = x^2 + 4$, $\quad x \ge 0$

14. $f(x) = 9 - x^2$, $\quad x \ge 0$, $\qquad g(x) = \sqrt{9 - x}$, $\quad x \le 9$

15. $f(x) = 1 - x^3$, $\qquad g(x) = \sqrt[3]{1 - x}$

16. $f(x) = \dfrac{1}{1 + x}$, $\quad x \ge 0$, $\qquad g(x) = \dfrac{1 - x}{x}$, $\quad 0 < x \le 1$

In Exercises 17–26, determine whether the function is one-to-one.

17.

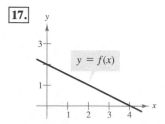

18.

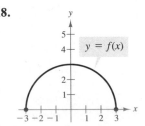

19.

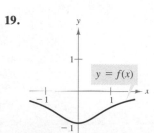

20.

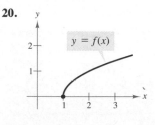

21. $g(x) = \dfrac{4 - x}{6}$

22. $f(x) = 10$

23. $h(x) = |x + 4|$

24. $g(x) = (x + 5)^3$

25. $f(x) = -\sqrt{16 - x^2}$

26. $f(x) = (x + 2)^2$

In Exercises 27–36, find the inverse of the one-to-one function f. Then graph both f and f^{-1} on the same coordinate plane.

27. $f(x) = 2x - 3$

28. $f(x) = 3x$

29. $f(x) = x^5$

30. $f(x) = x^3 + 1$

31. $f(x) = \sqrt{x}$

32. $f(x) = x^2, \quad x \geq 0$

33. $f(x) = \sqrt{4 - x^2}, \quad 0 \leq x \leq 2$

34. $f(x) = \dfrac{4}{x}$

35. $f(x) = \sqrt[3]{x - 1}$

36. $f(x) = x^{3/5}$

In Exercises 37–52, determine whether the given function is one-to-one. If it is, find its inverse.

37. $f(x) = x^4$

38. $f(x) = \dfrac{1}{x^2}$

39. $g(x) = \dfrac{x}{8}$

40. $f(x) = 3x + 5$

41. $p(x) = -4$

42. $f(x) = \dfrac{3x + 4}{5}$

43. $f(x) = (x + 3)^2, \quad x \geq -3$

44. $q(x) = (x - 5)^2$

45. $h(x) = \dfrac{1}{x}$

46. $f(x) = |x - 2|, \quad x \leq 2$

47. $f(x) = \sqrt{2x + 3}$

48. $f(x) = \sqrt{x - 2}$

49. $g(x) = x^2 - x^4$

50. $f(x) = \dfrac{x^2}{x^2 + 1}$

51. $f(x) = 25 - x^2, \quad x \leq 0$

52. $f(x) = ax + b, \quad a \neq 0$

In Exercises 53–56, delete part of the graph of the function so that the part that remains is one-to-one. Find the inverse of the remaining part and give the domain of the inverse. (*Note:* The answer is not unique.)

53. $f(x) = (x - 3)^2$

54. $f(x) = 16 - x^4$

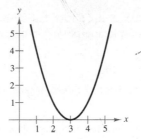

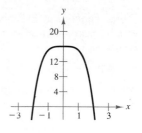

55. $f(x) = |x + 3|$

56. $f(x) = |x - 3|$

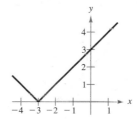

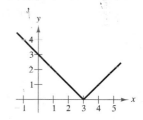

In Exercises 57 and 58, use the graph of the function f to complete the table and to sketch the graph of f^{-1}.

57.

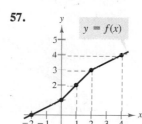

x	0	1	2	3	4
$f^{-1}(x)$					

58.

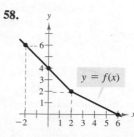

x	0	2	4	6
$f^{-1}(x)$				

In Exercises 59–64, use the functions $f(x) = \frac{1}{8}x - 3$ and $g(x) = x^3$ to find the indicated value.

59. $(f^{-1} \circ g^{-1})(1)$

60. $(g^{-1} \circ f^{-1})(-3)$

61. $(f^{-1} \circ f^{-1})(6)$

62. $(g^{-1} \circ g^{-1})(-4)$

63. $(f \circ g)^{-1}$

64. $g^{-1} \circ f^{-1}$

Diesel Engine In Exercises 65 and 66, use the function which approximates the exhaust temperature y in degrees Fahrenheit

$$y = 0.03x^2 + 254.50, \quad 0 < x < 100$$

where x is the percentage load for a diesel engine (see figure).

65. (a) Find the inverse of the function and state what the variables x and y represent in the inverse function.

(b) Sketch the graph of the inverse function.

66. Determine the percentage load interval if the exhaust temperature of the engine must not exceed 500 degrees Fahrenheit.

In Exercises 67–70, determine if the statement is true or false.

67. If f is an even function, then f^{-1} exists.

68. If the inverse of f exists, then the y-intercept of f is an x-intercept of f^{-1}.

69. If $f(x) = x^n$ where n is odd, then f^{-1} exists.

70. There exists no function f such that $f = f^{-1}$.

71. Prove that if f is a one-to-one odd function, then f^{-1} is an odd function.

72. Prove that if f and g are one-to-one functions, then $(f \circ g)^{-1}(x) = (g^{-1} \circ f^{-1})(x)$.

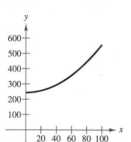

Figure for 65 and 66

2.8 Variation and Mathematical Models

Direct Variation / Direct Variation as *n*th Power / Inverse Variation / Joint Variation

Direct Variation

One of the goals of applied mathematics is to find equations, called **mathematical models,** that describe real-world phenomena. They can be developed in two basic ways: experimentally and theoretically. For models that are developed experimentally, we usually have a collection of x- and y-values and then try to *fit a curve* (or line) to the points (x, y). You used a simple form of curve fitting in Section 2.3, when you studied a method for finding the equation of a line through two points.

In this section you will study models related to **variation.**

DIRECT VARIATION
The following statements are equivalent.
1. *y* **varies directly** as *x*.
2. *y* is **directly proportional** to *x*.
3. $y = kx$ for some constant *k*.
k is the **constant of variation** or the **constant of proportionality.**

In the mathematical model for direct variation, *y* is a *linear* function of *x*. That is,

$$y = kx.$$

To set up a mathematical model, you use specific values of *x* and *y* to find the value of the constant *k*.

EXAMPLE 1 Direct Variation

Hooke's Law for a spring states that the distance a spring is stretched (or compressed) varies directly as the force on the spring. A force of 20 pounds stretches the spring 4 inches. (See Figure 2.71.)

a. Write an equation relating the distance stretched to the force applied.
b. How far will a force of 30 pounds stretch the spring?

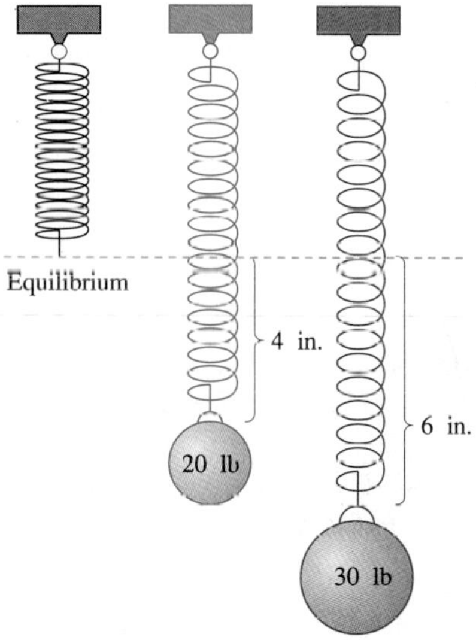

Solution

a. Let

$$d = \text{distance spring is stretched (in inches)}$$
$$F = \text{force (in pounds).}$$

Since distance varies directly as force,

$$d = kF.$$

To find the value of the constant *k*, use the fact that $d = 4$ when $F = 20$.

$$\begin{array}{cc} d & F \\ \downarrow & \downarrow \\ 4 & = k(20) \end{array}$$

which implies that $k = \frac{4}{20} = \frac{1}{5}$. Thus, the equation relating distance and force is

$$d = \frac{1}{5}F.$$

b. When $F = 30$, the distance is

$$d = \frac{1}{5}F = \frac{1}{5}(30) = 6 \text{ inches.}$$

Equilibrium

20 lb

30 lb

4 in.

6 in.

FIGURE 2.71

Direct Variation as *n*th Power

Another type of direct variation relates one variable to a *power* of another variable. For example, in the formula for the area of a circle

$$A = \pi r^2$$

the area A is directly proportional to the square of the radius r. Note that for this formula, π is the constant of proportionality.

DIRECT VARIATION AS *n*TH POWER

The following statements are equivalent.

1. y **varies directly as the *n*th power** of x.
2. y is **directly proportional to the *n*th power** of x.
3. $y = kx^n$ for some constant k.

EXAMPLE 2 Direct Variation as a Power

The distance a ball rolls down an inclined plane is directly proportional to the square of the time it rolls. During the first second the ball rolls 8 feet. (See Figure 2.72.)

a. Write an equation relating the distance traveled to the time.
b. How far will the ball roll during the first 3 seconds?

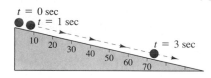

$t = 0$ sec
$t = 1$ sec
10 20 30 40 50 60 70
$t = 3$ sec

FIGURE 2.72

Solution

a. Letting d be the distance (in feet) the ball rolls and t be the time (in seconds),

$$d = kt^2.$$

Now, since $d = 8$ when $t = 1$, you can see that $k = 8$. Thus, the equation relating distance to time is

$$d = 8t^2.$$

b. When $t = 3$, the distance traveled is

$$d = 8(3^2) = 8(9) = 72 \text{ feet.}$$

In Examples 1 and 2 the direct variations were such that an *increase* in one variable corresponded to an *increase* in the other variable. For example, in the model

$$d = \frac{1}{5}F, \quad F > 0$$

an increase in F results in an increase in d. You should not, however, assume that this always occurs with direct variation. For example, in the model

$$y = -3x$$

an increase in x results in a *decrease* in y, and yet we say that y varies directly as x.

Inverse Variation

A third type of variation is **inverse variation.**

INVERSE VARIATION

The following statements are equivalent.

1. y **varies inversely** as x.
2. y is **inversely proportional** to x.
3. $y = \dfrac{k}{x}$ for some constant k.

EXAMPLE 3   Inverse Variation

A gas law states that the volume of an enclosed gas varies directly as the temperature *and* inversely as the pressure. The pressure of a gas is 0.75 kilograms per square centimeter when the temperature is 294° K and the volume is 8000 cubic centimeters.

a. Write an equation relating the pressure, temperature, and volume of this gas.
b. Find the pressure when the temperature is 300° K and the volume is 7000 cubic centimeters.

Solution

a. Let

$$V = \text{volume (in cubic centimeters)}$$
$$P = \text{pressure (in kilograms per square centimeter)}$$
$$T = \text{temperature (in degrees Kelvin)}.$$

Since V varies directly as T *and* inversely as P,

$$V = \frac{kT}{P}.$$

REMARK   If x and y are related by an equation of the form

$$y = \frac{k}{x^n}$$

then y varies inversely as the nth power of x (or y is inversely proportional to the nth power of x).

Note that the same constant of proportionality can be used for the direct variation of T and the inverse variation of P. Now, since $P = 0.75$ when $T = 294$ and $V = 8000$,

$$8000 = \frac{k(294)}{0.75}$$

$$\frac{8000(0.75)}{294} = k$$

$$k = \frac{6000}{294} = \frac{1000}{49}.$$

Thus, the equation relating pressure, temperature, and volume is

$$V = \frac{1000}{49}\left(\frac{T}{P}\right).$$

b. When $T = 300$ and $V = 7000$, the pressure is

$$P = \frac{1000}{49}\left(\frac{300}{7000}\right) = \frac{300}{343} \approx 0.87 \text{ kilogram per square centimeter.}$$

Joint Variation

In Example 3, note that when direct and inverse variation occur in the same statement, we couple them with the word "and." To describe two different *direct* variations in the same statement, you can use the word **jointly.**

JOINT VARIATION

The following statements are equivalent.

1. z **varies jointly** as x and y.
2. z is **jointly proportional** to x and y.
3. $z = kxy$ for some constant k.

EXAMPLE 4   Joint Variation

The *simple* interest for a certain savings account is jointly proportional to the time and the principal. After one quarter (three months), the interest on a principal of $5000 is $106.25.

a. Write an equation relating the interest, principal, and time.
b. Find the interest after three quarters.

REMARK If x, y, and z are related by an equation of the form

$$z = kx^n y^m$$

then z varies jointly as the nth power of x and the mth power of y.

Solution

a. Let I = interest (in dollars), P = principal (in dollars), and t = time (in years). Since I is jointly proportional to P and t,

$$I = kPt.$$

For $I = 106.25$, $P = 5000$, and $t = \frac{1}{4}$,

$$106.25 = k(5000)\left(\frac{1}{4}\right), \text{ which implies that } k = \frac{4(106.25)}{5000} = 0.085.$$

Thus, the equation relating interest, principal, and time is

$$I = 0.085Pt$$

which is the familiar equation for simple interest where the constant of proportionality, 0.085, represents an annual percentage rate of 8.5%.

b. When $P = \$5000$ and $t = \frac{3}{4}$, the interest is

$$I = (0.085)(5000)\left(\frac{3}{4}\right) = \$318.75.$$

DISCUSSION

PROBLEM

Mathematical
Models

In this section, you have learned about four basic types of variation: direct variation, direct variation as nth power, inverse variation, and joint variation. Find a model for each of the following situations and classify the model as one of the four basic types of variation. In each case identify the constant of proportionality.

1. Let A represent the area of a rectangle and let l and w represent the length and width of the rectangle. Find a model that gives A in terms of l and w.
2. Let k represent the speed of an automobile in kilometers per hour and let m represent the speed in miles per hour. Find a model that gives k in terms of m.
3. Let V represent the volume of a sphere and let r represent the radius of the sphere. Find a model that gives V in terms of r.
4. Let t represent the time required for an automobile that is traveling a constant rate of r to complete a 50-mile trip. Find a model that gives t in terms of r.

Can you find four other examples like these—one for each of the basic types of variation?

WARM UP

The following warm-up exercises involve skills that were covered in earlier sections. You will use these skills in the exercise set for this section.

In Exercises 1–6, solve for k.

1. $15 = k(45)$

2. $9 = k(4^2)$

3. $20 = \dfrac{k(15)}{32}$

4. $30 = \dfrac{k(0.2)}{0.5}$

5. $110 = k(27)(0.4)$

6. $210 = k(4^2)(16)$

In Exercises 7–10, find the indicated value.

7. Let $d = 2.7r$. Find d when $r = 10$.

8. Let $s = 3tp^3$. Find s when $t = 2$ and $p = \frac{1}{3}$.

9. Let $R = 4t/h$. Find R when $t = 7$ and $h = 13$.

10. Let $M = 14rst$. Find M when $r = 0.01$, $s = 150$, and $t = 7.5$.

EXERCISES for Section 2.8

In Exercises 1–14, find a mathematical model for the verbal statement.

1. A varies directly as the square of r.

2. V varies directly as the cube of e.

3. y varies inversely as the square of x.

4. h varies inversely as the square root of s.

5. z is proportional to the cube root of u.

6. x is inversely proportional to $t + 1$.

7. z varies jointly as u and v.

8. V varies jointly as l, w, and h.

9. F varies directly as g and inversely as the square of r.

10. z is jointly proportional to the square of x and the cube of y.

11. *Boyle's Law* For constant temperature, the pressure P of a gas is inversely proportional to the volume V of the gas.

12. *Newton's Law of Cooling* The rate of change R of the temperature of an object is proportional to the difference between the temperature T of the object and the temperature T_e of the environment in which the object is placed.

13. *Newton's Law of Universal Gravitation* The gravitational attraction F between two objects of masses m_1 and m_2 is proportional to the product of the masses and inversely proportional to the square of the distance r between the objects.

14. *Logistics Growth* The rate of growth R of a population is jointly proportional to the size S of the population and the difference between S and the maximum size L that the environment can support.

In Exercises 15–20, write a sentence using variation terminology to describe the formula.

15. Area of a Triangle: $A = \frac{1}{2}bh$

16. Surface Area of a Sphere: $S = 4\pi r^2$

17. Volume of a Sphere: $V = \frac{4}{3}\pi^3$

18. Volume of a Right Circular Cylinder: $V = \pi r^2 h$

19. Average Speed: $r = \dfrac{d}{t}$

20. Free Vibrations: $\omega = \sqrt{\dfrac{kg}{W}}$

In Exercises 21–36, find a mathematical model representing the statement. (In each case determine the constant of proportionality.)

21. y varies directly as x. ($y = 25$ when $x = 10$.)

22. y is directly proportional to x. ($y = 8$ when $x = 24$.)

23. A varies directly as the square of r. ($A = 9\pi$ when $r = 3$.)

24. s is directly proportional to the square of t. ($s = 64$ when $t = 2$.)

25. y varies inversely as x. ($y = 3$ when $x = 25$.)

26. y is inversely proportional to x. ($y = 7$ when $x = 4$.)

27. h is inversely proportional to the third power of t. ($h = \frac{3}{16}$ when $t = 4$.)

28. R varies inversely as the square of s. ($R = 80$ when $s = \frac{1}{5}$.)

29. z varies jointly as x and y. ($z = 64$ when $x = 4$ and $y = 8$.)

30. z is jointly proportional to x and y. ($z = 32$ when $x = 10$ and $y = 16$.)

31. F is jointly proportional to r and the third power of s. ($F = 4158$ when $r = 11$ and $s = 3$.)

32. P varies directly as x and inversely as the square of y. ($P = \frac{28}{3}$ when $x = 42$ and $y = 9$.)

33. z varies directly as the square of x and inversely as y. ($z = 6$ when $x = 6$ and $y = 4$.)

34. v varies jointly as p and q and inversely as the square of s. ($v = 1.5$ when $p = 4.1$, $q = 6.3$, and $s = 1.2$.)

35. S varies directly as L and inversely as $L - S$. ($S = 4$ when $L = 6$.)

36. P is jointly proportional to S and $L - S$. ($P = 10$ when $S = 4$ and $L = 6$.)

Hooke's Law In Exercises 37–40, use Hooke's Law as stated in Example 1 of this section.

37. A force of 50 pounds stretches a spring 5 inches (see figure).
    (a) How far will a force of 20 pounds stretch the spring?
    (b) What force is required to stretch the spring 1.5 inches?

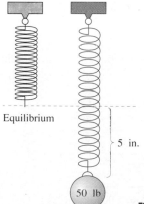

Equilibrium

5 in.

50 lb

Figure for 37

38. A force of 50 pounds stretches a spring 3 inches.
    (a) How far will a force of 20 pounds stretch the spring?
    (b) What force is required to stretch the spring 1.5 inches?

39. The coiled spring of a toy supports the weight of a child. The spring compresses a distance of 1.9 inches under the weight of a 25-pound child. The toy will not work properly if its spring is compressed more than 3 inches. What is the weight of the heaviest child who should be allowed to use the toy?

40. An overhead garage door has two springs, one on each side of the door (see figure). A force of 15 pounds is required to stretch each spring 1 foot. A pulley system allows the springs to stretch only one-half the distance the door travels. The door moves a total of 8 feet and the springs are at their natural length when the door is open. Find the combined lifting force applied to the door by the springs when the door is in the closed position.

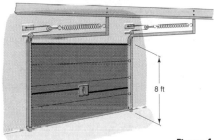

8 ft

Figure for 40

Erosion In Exercises 41 and 42, use the fact that the diameter of a particle moved by a stream varies approximately as the square of the velocity of the stream.

41. A stream with a velocity of $\frac{1}{4}$ mile per hour can move coarse sand particles of about 0.02 inch diameter. What must the velocity be to carry particles with a diameter of 0.12 inch?

42. A stream of velocity v can move particles of diameter d or less. By what factor does d increase when the velocity is doubled?

Electrical Resistance In Exercises 43 and 44, use the fact that the resistance of a wire carrying electrical current is directly proportional to its length and inversely proportional to its cross-sectional area.

43. If #28 copper wire (which has a diameter of 0.0126 inch) has a resistance of 66.17 ohms per thousand feet, what length of #28 copper wire will produce a resistance of 33.5 ohms?

44. A 14-foot piece of copper wire produces a resistance of 0.05 ohms. Use the constant of proportionality of Exercise 43 to find the diameter of the wire.

45. *Free Fall*   Neglecting air resistance, the distance *s* that an object falls varies directly as the square of the time *t* it has been falling. An object falls a distance of 144 feet in 3 seconds. How far will it fall in 5 seconds?

46. *Stopping Distance*   The stopping distance *d* of an automobile is directly proportional to the square of its speed *s*. A car required 75 feet to stop when its speed was 30 miles per hour. Estimate the stopping distance if the brakes are applied when the car is traveling at 50 miles per hour.

47. *Comparative Shopping*   The prices of 9-inch, 12-inch, and 15-inch diameter pizzas are $6.78, $9.78, and $12.18, respectively. One would expect that the price of a pizza of a certain size would be directly proportional to its surface area. Is that the case for these pizzas? If not, which pizza is the best buy?

48. *Demand for a Product*   A company has found that the demand for its product varies inversely as the price of the product. When the price is $3.75, the demand is 500 units. Approximate the demand for a price of $4.25.

49. *Illumination of a Light*   The illumination from a light source varies inversely as the square of the distance from the light source. When the distance from a light source is doubled, how does the illumination change?

50. *Safe Load of a Beam*   The load that can be safely supported by a horizontal beam varies jointly as the width of the beam and the square of its depth and inversely as the length of the beam. Determine what happens to the safe load under the following conditions.
(a) The width and length of the beam are doubled.
(b) The width and depth of the beam are doubled.
(c) All three of the dimensions are doubled.
(d) The depth of the beam is halved.

51. *Fluid Flow*   The velocity *v* of a fluid flowing in a conduit is inversely proportional to the cross-sectional area of the conduit. (Assume the volume of the flow per unit of time is held constant.) Determine the change of velocity of water flowing from a hose when a person places a finger over the end of the hose to decrease its cross-sectional area by 25%.

52. *Fluid Flow*   Use the fluid velocity model of Exercise 51 to determine the effect on the velocity of a stream when it is dredged to increase its cross-sectional area by one-third.

In Exercises 53–56, use the given value of *k* to complete the table for the direct variation model $y = kx^2$. Plot the points on the rectangular coordinate system.

x	2	4	6	8	10
$y = kx^2$					

53. $k = 1$ **54.** $k = 2$
55. $k = \frac{1}{2}$ **56.** $k = \frac{1}{4}$

In Exercises 57–60, use the given value of *k* to complete the table for the inverse variation model $y = k/x^2$. Plot the points on the rectangular coordinate system.

x	2	4	6	8	10
$y = \dfrac{k}{x^2}$					

57. $k = 2$ **58.** $k = 5$
59. $k = 10$ **60.** $k = 20$

REVIEW EXERCISES for Chapter 2

In Exercises 1–6, find (a) the distance between the two points, (b) the coordinates of the midpoint of the line segment between the two points, (c) an equation of the line through the two points, and (d) an equation of the circle whose diameter is the line segment between the two points.

1. (0, 0), (0, 10)   **2.** (−1, 4), (2, 0)
3. (2, 1), (14, 6)   **4.** (−2, 2), (3, −10)
5. (−1, 0), (6, 2)   **6.** (1, 6), (4, 2)

In Exercises 7 and 8, use the Midpoint Formula to estimate the sales of a company for 1991. Assume the sales followed a linear growth pattern.

7.

Year	1989	1993
Sales	640,000	810,000

8.

Year	1989	1993
Sales	3,250,000	5,690,000

In Exercises 9–12, find t so that the three points are collinear.

9. $(-2, 5)$, $(0, t)$, $(1, 1)$ **10.** $(-6, 1)$, $(1, t)$, $(10, 5)$
11. $(1, -4)$, $(t, 3)$, $(5, 10)$ **12.** $(-3, 3)$, $(t, -1)$, $(8, 6)$

In Exercises 13–16, show that the points form the vertices of the indicated polygon.

13. Parallelogram: $(1, 1)$, $(8, 2)$, $(9, 5)$, $(2, 4)$
14. Isosceles triangle: $(4, 5)$, $(1, 0)$, $(-1, 2)$
15. Right triangle: $(-1, -1)$, $(10, 7)$, $(2, 18)$
16. Square: $(-4, 0)$, $(1, -3)$, $(4, 2)$, $(-1, 5)$

In Exercises 17–26, find the intercepts of the graph and check for symmetry with respect to each of the coordinate axes and the origin.

17. $2y^2 = x^3$ **18.** $x^2 + (y + 2)^2 = 4$

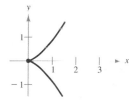   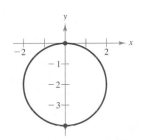

19. $y = \frac{1}{4}x^4 - 2x^2$ **20.** $y - \frac{1}{4}x^3 - 3x$

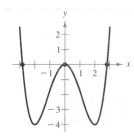   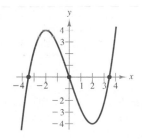

21. $y = x\sqrt{4 - x^2}$ **22.** $y = x\sqrt{x + 3}$

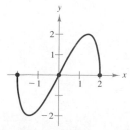   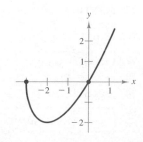

23. $y = x^3 - 3x^2$ **24.** $x^3 + y^3 - 3xy = 0$

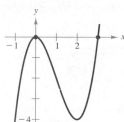   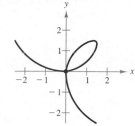

25. $y^2 = \dfrac{x^3}{4 - x}$ **26.** $x^{2/3} + y^{2/3} = 4^{2/3}$

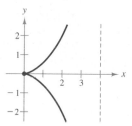   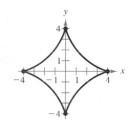

In Exercises 27–30, determine the center and radius of the circle and sketch its graph.

27. $x^2 + y^2 - 12x - 8y + 43 = 0$
28. $x^2 + y^2 - 20x - 10y + 100 = 0$
29. $4x^2 + 4y^2 - 4x - 40y + 92 = 0$
30. $5x^2 + 5y^2 - 14y = 0$

In Exercises 31–44, sketch a graph of the equation.

31. $y - 2x - 3 = 0$ **32.** $3x + 2y + 6 = 0$
33. $x - 5 - 0$ **34.** $y = 8 - |x|$
35. $y = \sqrt{5 - x}$ **36.** $y = \sqrt{x + 2}$
37. $y + 2x^2 = 0$ **38.** $y = x^2 - 4x$
39. $y = \sqrt{25 - x^2}$ **40.** $y = |x^2 - 4x|$
41. $y = |25 - x^2|$ **42.** $y = -(x - 4)^2$
43. $y = \frac{1}{4}(x + 1)^3$ **44.** $y = 4 - (x - 4)^2$

In Exercises 45–48, find an equation of the line that passes through the given point and has the specified slope. Sketch the graph of the line.

Point	Slope
45. $(0, -5)$	$m = \frac{3}{2}$
46. $(-2, 6)$	$m = 0$
47. $(3, 0)$	$m = -\frac{2}{3}$
48. $(5, 4)$	m is undefined.

In Exercises 49 and 50, write an equation of the line through the point (a) parallel to the given line, and (b) perpendicular to the given line.

Point	Line
49. $(3, -2)$	$5x - 4y = 8$
50. $(-8, 3)$	$2x + 3y = 5$

51. *Fourth Quarter Sales* During the second and third quarters of the year, a business had sales of $160,000 and $185,000, respectively. If the growth of sales follows a linear pattern, estimate sales during the fourth quarter.

52. *Dollar Value* The dollar value of a product in 1990 was $85. The item will increase in value at an expected rate of $3.75 per year. Write a linear equation that gives the dollar value V of the product in terms of the year t. (Let $t = 0$ represent 1990.) Use this model to estimate the dollar value of the product in 1995.

In Exercises 53–56, evaluate the function at the specified values of the independent variable. Simplify your answers.

53. $f(x) = x^2 + 1$
(a) $f(2)$ (b) $f(-4)$
(c) $f(t^2)$ (d) $-f(x)$

54. $g(x) = x^{4/3}$
(a) $g(8)$ (b) $g(t + 1)$
(c) $\dfrac{g(8) - g(1)}{8 - 1}$ (d) $g(-x)$

55. $h(x) = 6 - 5x^2$
(a) $h(2)$ (b) $h(x + 3)$
(c) $\dfrac{h(4) - h(2)}{4 - 2}$ (d) $\dfrac{h(x + \Delta x) - h(x)}{\Delta x}$

56. $f(t) = \sqrt[4]{t}$
(a) $f(16)$ (b) $f(t + 5)$
(c) $\dfrac{f(16) - f(0)}{16}$ (d) $f(t + \Delta t)$

In Exercises 57–62, determine the domain of the function.

57. $f(x) = \sqrt{25 - x^2}$

58. $f(x) = 3x + 4$

59. $g(s) = \dfrac{5}{3s - 9}$

60. $f(x) = \sqrt{x^2 + 8x}$

61. $h(x) = \dfrac{x}{x^2 - x - 6}$

62. $h(t) = |t + 1|$

In Exercises 63–68, (a) find f^{-1}, (b) sketch the graphs of f and f^{-1} on the same coordinate plane, and (c) verify that $f^{-1}(f(x)) = x = f(f^{-1}(x))$.

63. $f(x) = \frac{1}{2}x - 3$

64. $f(x) = 5x - 7$

65. $f(x) = \sqrt{x + 1}$

66. $f(x) = x^3 + 2$

67. $f(x) = x^2 - 5, \quad x \geq 0$

68. $f(x) = \sqrt[3]{x + 1}$

In Exercises 69–72, restrict the domain of the function f to an interval where the function is increasing and determine f^{-1} over that interval.

69. $f(x) = 2(x - 4)^2$

70. $f(x) = |x - 2|$

71. $f(x) = \sqrt{x^2 - 4}$

72. $f(x) = x^{4/3}$

In Exercises 73–80, let $f(x) = 3 - 2x$, $g(x) = \sqrt{x}$ and $h(x) = 3x^2 + 2$, and find the indicated value.

73. $(f - g)(4)$

74. $(f + h)(5)$

75. $(fh)(1)$

76. $\left(\dfrac{g}{h}\right)(1)$

77. $(h \circ g)(7)$

78. $(g \circ f)(-2)$

79. $g^{-1}(3)$

80. $(h \circ f^{-1})(1)$

81. *Vertical Motion*   The velocity of a ball thrown vertically upward from ground level is

$$v(t) = -32t + 48$$

where t is the time in seconds and v is the velocity in feet per second.
(a) Find the velocity when $t = 1$.
(b) Find the time when the ball reaches its maximum height. (*Hint:* Find the time when $v(t) = 0$.)
(c) Find the velocity when $t = 2$.

82. *Cost and Profit*   A company produces a product for which the variable cost is \$5.35 per unit and the fixed costs are \$16,000. The company sells the product for \$8.20, and can sell all that it produces.
(a) Find the total cost as a function of the number of units produced x.
(b) Find the profit as a function of x.

83. *Dimensions of a Rectangle*   A wire 24 inches long is cut into four pieces to form a rectangle whose shortest side has length x. Express the area A of the rectangle as a function of x. Determine the domain of the function and sketch its graph over that domain.

84. *Cost of a Phone Call*   Suppose the cost of a telephone call between Dallas and Philadelphia is \$0.70 for the first minute and \$0.38 for each additional minute (or portion thereof). A model for the total cost of the phone call is

$$C = 0.70 + 0.38[\![x]\!]$$

where C is the total cost of the call in dollars and x is the length of the call in minutes. Sketch the graph of this function.

In Exercises 85–88, find a mathematical model representing the statement. (In each case determine the constant of proportionality.)

85. F is jointly proportional to x and the square root of y. ($F = 6$ when $x = 9$ and $y = 4$.)

86. R varies inversely as the cube of x. ($R = 128$ when $x = 2$.)

87. z varies directly as the square of x and inversely as y. ($z = 16$ when $x = 5$ and $y = 2$.)

88. w varies jointly as x and y and inversely as the cube of z. ($w = \frac{44}{9}$ when $x = 12$, $y = 11$, and $z = 6$.)

89. *Wind Power*   The power P produced by a wind turbine is proportional to the cube of the wind speed S. A wind speed of 27 miles per hour produces a power output of 750 kilowatts. Find the output for a wind speed of 40 miles per hour.

90. *Frictional Force*   The frictional force F between the tires and the road required to keep a car on a curved section of a highway is directly proportional to the square of the speed s of the car. If the speed of the car is doubled, the force will change by what factor?

CHAPTER 3

OVERVIEW

The material in this chapter is both classic and current. It is classic because it discusses the classic problem in algebra— how to find the solutions of a polynomial equation. It is current because it shows how such solutions can be used to answer questions about real life. For instance, Exercise 58 on page 214 uses the solution of a polynomial equation to find the air-fuel ratio in a car engine that produces a given emission of nitric oxide.

As you study, remember that many of the results can be viewed in four different ways, as summarized on page 195. That is, if $x = a$ is the zero of a polynomial function f, then a is a *solution* of the polynomial equation $f(x) = 0$, $(x - a)$ is a *factor* of the polynomial $f(x)$, and $(a, 0)$ is an *x-intercept* of the graph of f.

Polynomial and Rational Functions

3.1 Quadratic Functions

The Graph of a Quadratic Function / The Standard Form of a Quadratic Function / Applications

The Graph of a Quadratic Function

In this chapter you will study polynomial functions, the most widely used functions in algebra.

DEFINITION OF POLYNOMIAL FUNCTION

Let n be a nonnegative integer and let $a_n, a_{n-1}, \ldots, a_2, a_1, a_0$ be real numbers with $a_n \neq 0$. The function

$$f(x) = a_n x^n + a_{n-1} x^{n-1} + \cdots + a_2 x^2 + a_1 x + a_0$$

is a **polynomial function of x with degree n**.

The polynomial function $f(x) = a$, $a \neq 0$, has degree 0 and is a **constant function**. The polynomial function $f(x) = ax + b$, $a \neq 0$, has degree 1 and is a **linear function**. In Chapter 2, you saw that the graph of the linear

181

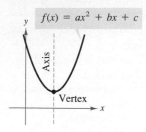

$f(x) = ax^2 + bx + c$

$a > 0$: Parabola opens upward.

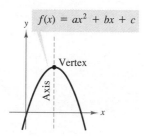

$f(x) = ax^2 + bx + c$

$a < 0$: Parabola opens downward.

FIGURE 3.1

function $f(x) = ax + b$ is a line whose slope is a and whose y-intercept is $(0, b)$. In this section we look at second-degree polynomial functions (**quadratic functions**).

DEFINITION OF QUADRATIC FUNCTION

Let a, b, and c be real numbers with $a \neq 0$. The function of x given by

$$f(x) = ax^2 + bx + c$$

is a **quadratic function.** The graph of a quadratic function is a **parabola.**

All parabolas are symmetric with respect to a line called the **axis of symmetry,** or simply the **axis** of the parabola. The point where the axis intersects the parabola is the **vertex** of the parabola, as shown in Figure 3.1. If the leading coefficient is positive, then the graph of $f(x) = ax^2 + bx + c$ is a parabola that opens upward, and if the leading coefficient is negative, then the graph is a parabola that opens downward.

The simplest type of quadratic function is $f(x) = ax^2$. Its graph is a parabola whose vertex is $(0, 0)$. If $a > 0$, then the vertex is the *minimum* point on the graph, and if $a < 0$, then the vertex is the *maximum* point on the graph, as shown in Figure 3.2. When sketching the graph of $f(x) = ax^2$, it is helpful to use the graph of $y = x^2$ as a reference, as discussed in Section 2.5.

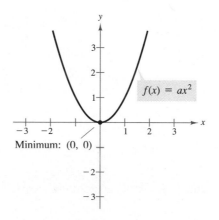

$a > 0$: Parabola opens upward.

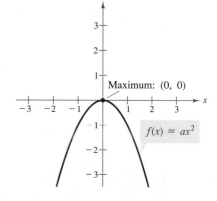

$a < 0$: Parabola opens downward.

FIGURE 3.2

EXAMPLE 1   Sketching the Graphs of Simple Quadratic Functions

Sketch the graphs of the functions.

a. $f(x) - \frac{1}{3}x^2$

b. $g(x) = 2x^2$

REMARK In Example 1, note that the coefficient a determines how widely the parabola given by $f(x) = ax^2$ opens. If $|a|$ is small, the parabola opens more widely than if $|a|$ is large.

Solution

a. Compared with $y = x^2$, each output of f "shrinks" by a factor of $\frac{1}{3}$. The result is a parabola that opens upward and is broader than the parabola represented by $y = x^2$, as shown in Figure 3.3.

b. Each output of g "stretches" by a factor of 2, creating the more narrow parabola shown in Figure 3.4.

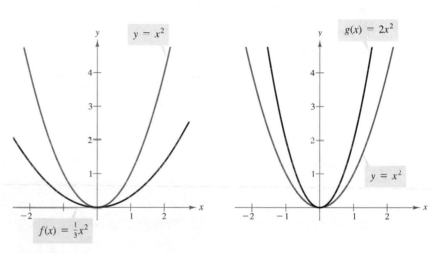

FIGURE 3.3   **FIGURE 3.4**

Recall from Section 2.5 that the graphs of $y = f(x \pm c)$, $y = f(x) \pm c$, and $y = -f(x)$ are rigid transformations of the graph of $y = f(x)$.

$y = f(x \pm c)$	*Horizontal shift*
$y = f(x) \pm c$	*Vertical shift*
$y = -f(x)$	*Reflection*

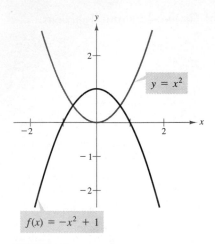

$f(x) = -x^2 + 1$

FIGURE 3.5

EXAMPLE 2 Sketching a Parabola

Sketch the graphs of the quadratic functions.

a. $f(x) = -x^2 + 1$ **b.** $g(x) = (x + 2)^2 - 3$

Solution

a. With respect to the graph of $y = x^2$, the negative coefficient in $f(x) = -x^2 + 1$ reflects the graph *downward* and the positive constant term shifts the vertex *up one unit*. The graph of f is shown in Figure 3.5. Note that the axis of the parabola is the y-axis and the vertex is $(0, 1)$.

b. With respect to the graph of $y = x^2$, the graph of $g(x) = (x + 2)^2 - 3$ is obtained by a horizontal shift two units *to the left* and a vertical shift three units *down,* as shown in Figure 3.6. Note that the axis of the parabola is the vertical line $x = -2$ and the vertex is $(-2, -3)$.

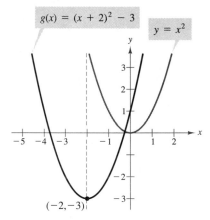

$g(x) = (x + 2)^2 - 3$

$y = x^2$

$(-2, -3)$

FIGURE 3.6

The Standard Form of a Quadratic Function

The equation in Example 2(b) is written in **standard form:**

$$f(x) = a(x - h)^2 + k.$$

This form is especially convenient for sketching a parabola because it identifies the vertex of the parabola.

STANDARD FORM OF A QUADRATIC FUNCTION

The quadratic function

$$f(x) = a(x - h)^2 + k, \quad a \neq 0$$

is said to be in **standard form.** The graph of f is a parabola whose axis is the vertical line $x = h$ and whose vertex is the point (h, k). If $a > 0$, the parabola opens upward and if $a < 0$, the parabola opens downward.

EXAMPLE 3 Writing a Quadratic Function in Standard Form

Sketch the graph of $f(x) = 2x^2 + 8x + 7$ and identify the vertex and x-intercepts.

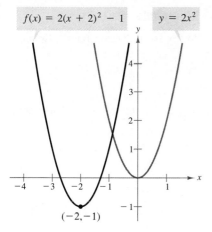

$f(x) = 2(x + 2)^2 - 1$ $y = 2x^2$

$(-2, -1)$

FIGURE 3.7

REMARK When completing the square to write a function, $f(x)$, in standard form, bear in mind that you are rewriting an *expression*, not an equation (as was the case with circles in Section 2.2). Thus, you must do all algebraic steps on *one* side of the equal sign and no factors can be divided out.

Solution

Write the quadratic function in standard form by completing the square. Notice that the first step is to factor out any coefficient of x^2 that is different from 1.

$$f(x) = 2x^2 + 8x + 7 \qquad \text{\textit{Given form}}$$
$$= 2(x^2 + 4x) + 7 \qquad \text{\textit{Factor 2 out of x terms}}$$
$$= 2(x^2 + 4x + 4 - 4) + 7 \qquad \text{\textit{Add and subtract 4 within parentheses}}$$
$$\underset{2^2}{\underbrace{\qquad}}$$
$$= 2(x^2 + 4x + 4) - 2(4) + 7 \qquad \text{\textit{Regroup terms}}$$
$$= 2(x^2 + 4x + 4) - 8 + 7 \qquad \text{\textit{Simplify}}$$
$$= 2(x + 2)^2 - 1 \qquad \text{\textit{Standard form}}$$

From the standard form, you can see that the graph of f is a parabola that opens upward with vertex $(-2, -1)$. This corresponds to a left shift of two units and a downward shift of one unit relative to the graph of $y = 2x^2$, as shown in Figure 3.7. The x-intercepts can be found by using the quadratic formula to solve $2x^2 + 8x + 7 = 0$ or by extracting square roots for the equation $2(x + 2)^2 - 1 = 0$. In either case, $x = -2 \pm (\sqrt{2}/2)$.

EXAMPLE 4   Writing a Quadratic Function in Standard Form

Sketch the graph of $f(x) = -x^2 + 6x - 8$ and identify the vertex.

Solution

As in Example 3, we begin by writing the quadratic function in standard form.

$$f(x) = -x^2 + 6x - 8 \qquad \text{\textit{Given form}}$$
$$= -(x^2 - 6x) - 8 \qquad \text{\textit{Factor −1 out of x terms}}$$
$$= -(x^2 - 6x + 9 - 9) - 8 \qquad \text{\textit{Add and subtract 9 within parentheses}}$$
$$\underset{3^2}{\underbrace{\qquad}}$$
$$= -(x^2 - 6x + 9) - (-9) - 8 \qquad \text{\textit{Regroup terms}}$$
$$= -(x - 3)^2 + 1 \qquad \text{\textit{Standard form}}$$

Thus, the graph of f is a parabola that opens downward with vertex at $(3, 1)$, as shown in Figure 3.8.

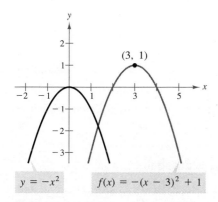

$(3, 1)$

$y = -x^2$ $f(x) = -(x - 3)^2 + 1$

FIGURE 3.8

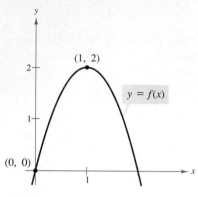

FIGURE 3.9

EXAMPLE 5 Finding the Equation of a Parabola

Find an equation for the parabola whose vertex is (1, 2) and passes through the point (0, 0), as shown in Figure 3.9.

Solution

Since the parabola has a vertex at $(h, k) = (1, 2)$, the equation must have the form

$$\overset{\overset{\displaystyle h}{\downarrow}}{f(x) = a(x} - \overset{\overset{\displaystyle k}{\downarrow}}{1)^2 + 2}.$$
                                                              Standard form

Because the parabola passes through the point (0, 0), it follows that $f(0) = 0$. Thus,

$$0 = a(0 - 1)^2 + 2 \quad \rightarrow \quad a = -2$$

which implies that the equation is

$$f(x) = -2(x - 1)^2 + 2 = -2x^2 + 4x.$$

Applications

We know that the vertex (h, k) of a parabola is either its lowest point (Example 3) or its highest point (Example 4) and that $k = f(h)$ is the corresponding minimum or maximum value of f. Many applications involve finding the maximum or minimum value of a quadratic function. By writing the quadratic function $f(x) = ax^2 + bx + c$ in standard form

$$f(x) = a\left(x + \frac{b}{2a}\right)^2 + \left(c - \frac{b^2}{4a}\right)$$

you can see that the vertex occurs at $x = -b/2a$, and you can determine the following.

1. If $a > 0$, then the quadratic function $f(x) = ax^2 + bx + c$ has a *minimum* that occurs at $x = -b/2a$.
2. If $a < 0$, then the quadratic function $f(x) = ax^2 + bx + c$ has a *maximum* that occurs at $x = -b/2a$.

In either case, you can find the minimum or maximum by evaluating the function at $x = -b/2a$.

EXAMPLE 6 The Maximum Height of a Baseball

A baseball is hit 3 feet above ground at a velocity of 100 feet per second and at an angle of 45 degrees with respect to the ground. The path of the baseball is given by the function

$$f(x) = -0.0032x^2 + x + 3$$

where $f(x)$ is the height of the baseball (in feet) and x is the distance from home plate (in feet). What is the maximum height reached by the baseball?

Solution

For this quadratic function,

$$f(x) = ax^2 + bx + c$$
$$= -0.0032x^2 + x + 3.$$

Thus, $a = -0.0032$ and $b = 1$. Since the function has a maximum when $x = -b/2a$, you can conclude that the baseball reaches its maximum height when it is

$$x = -\frac{b}{2a} = -\frac{1}{2(-0.0032)} = 156.25 \text{ feet}$$

from home plate. At this distance, the maximum height is

$$f(156.25) = -0.0032(156.25)^2 + 156.25 + 3 = 81.125 \text{ feet.}$$

The path of the baseball is shown in Figure 3.10.

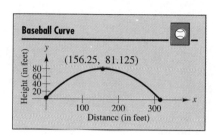

FIGURE 3.10

EXAMPLE 7   Charitable Contributions

According to a survey conducted in 1990 by *Independent Sector*, the percent of their income that Americans give to charities is related to their household income. For families with an annual income of $100,000 or less, the percent is approximately

$$P = 0.0014x^2 - 0.1529x + 5.855, \qquad 5 \le x \le 100$$

where P is the percentage of annual income given and x is the annual income in 1000s of dollars. According to this model, what income level corresponds to the least percentage of charitable contributions?

Solution

There are two ways to answer this question. One is to sketch the graph of the quadratic function, as shown in Figure 3.11. From this graph, it appears that the minimum percentage corresponds to an income level of about $55,000. The other way to answer the question is to use the fact that the minimum point of the parabola occurs when $x = -b/2a$. For this function, you have $a = 0.0014$ and $b = -0.1529$. Thus,

$$x = -\frac{b}{2a} = -\frac{-0.1529}{2(0.0014)} \approx 54.6.$$

From this x-value, you can conclude that the minimum percentage corresponds to an income level of about $54,600.

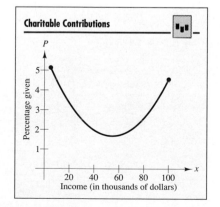

FIGURE 3.11

DISCUSSION

PROBLEM

Finding an Equation for a Curve

The parabola in Figure 3.12 has an equation of the form $y = x^2 + bx + c$. Try to find the equation for this parabola, and write a short paragraph about (or discuss) the method you used.

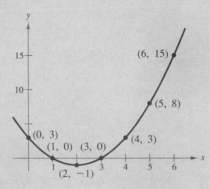

FIGURE 3.12

WARM UP

The following warm-up exercises involve skills that were covered in earlier sections. You will use these skills in the exercise set for this section.

In Exercises 1–4, solve the quadratic equations by factoring.

1. $2x^2 + 11x - 6 = 0$ **2.** $5x^2 - 12x - 9 = 0$

3. $3 + x - 2x^2 = 0$ **4.** $x^2 + 20x + 100 = 0$

In Exercises 5–8, solve the quadratic equations by completing the square.

5. $x^2 - 6x + 4 = 0$ **6.** $x^2 + 4x + 1 = 0$

7. $2x^2 - 16x + 25 = 0$ **8.** $3x^2 + 30x + 74 = 0$

In Exercises 9 and 10, use the Quadratic Formula to solve the quadratic equations.

9. $x^2 + 3x + 3 = 0$ **10.** $x^2 + 3x - 3 = 0$

EXERCISES for Section 3.1

In Exercises 1–6, match the given quadratic function with the correct graph. [The graphs are labeled (a), (b), (c), (d), (e), and (f).]

1. $f(x) = (x - 3)^2$
2. $f(x) = (x + 5)^2$
3. $f(x) = x^2 - 4$
4. $f(x) = 5 - x^2$
5. $f(x) = 4 - (x - 1)^2$
6. $f(x) = (x + 2)^2 - 2$

(a)
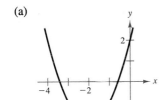

(b)
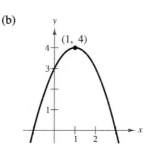

(c)
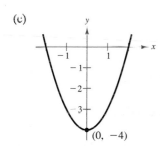

(d)
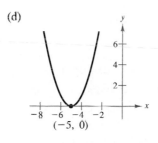

(e)
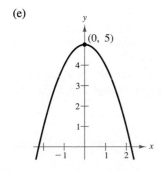

(f)
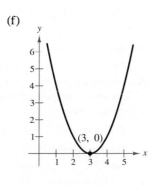

In Exercises 7–12, find an equation for the parabola.

7.
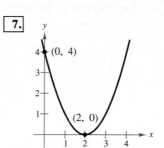

8.
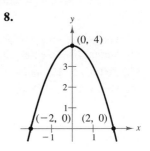

9.
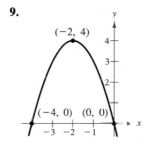

10.
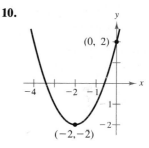

11.
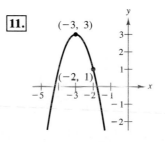

12.
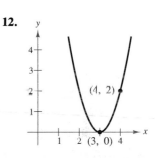

In Exercises 13–30, sketch the graph of the quadratic function. Identify the vertex and intercepts.

13. $f(x) = x^2 - 5$
14. $f(x) = \frac{1}{2}x^2 - 4$
15. $f(x) = 16 - x^2$
16. $h(x) = 25 - x^2$
17. $f(x) = (x + 5)^2 - 6$
18. $f(x) = (x - 6)^2 + 3$
19. $h(x) = x^2 - 8x + 16$
20. $g(x) = x^2 + 2x + 1$
21. $f(x) = -(x^2 + 2x - 3)$
22. $g(x) = x^2 + 8x + 11$
23. $f(x) = x^2 - x + \frac{5}{4}$
24. $f(x) = x^2 + 3x + \frac{1}{4}$
25. $f(x) = -x^2 + 2x + 5$
26. $f(x) = -x^2 - 4x + 1$
27. $h(x) = 4x^2 - 4x + 21$
28. $f(x) = 2x^2 - x + 1$
29. $f(x) = 2x^2 - 16x + 31$
30. $g(x) = \frac{1}{2}(x^2 + 4x - 2)$

In Exercises 31–34, find the quadratic function that has the indicated vertex and whose graph passes through the given point.

31. Vertex: $(3, 4)$; point: $(1, 2)$
32. Vertex: $(2, 3)$; point: $(0, 2)$
33. Vertex: $(5, 12)$; point: $(7, 15)$
34. Vertex: $(-2, -2)$; point: $(-1, 0)$

In Exercises 35–40, find two quadratic functions whose graphs have the given x-intercepts. (One function has a graph that opens upward and the other has a graph that opens downward.)

35. $(-1, 0), (3, 0)$ **36.** $\left(-\frac{5}{2}, 0\right), (2, 0)$
37. $(0, 0), (10, 0)$ **38.** $(4, 0), (8, 0)$
39. $(-3, 0), \left(-\frac{1}{2}, 0\right)$ **40.** $(-5, 0), (5, 0)$

In Exercises 41–44, find two positive real numbers that satisfy the requirements.

41. The sum is 110 and the product is a maximum.
42. The sum is S and the product is a maximum.
43. The sum of the first and twice the second is 24 and the product is a maximum.
44. The sum of two numbers is 50 and the product is a maximum.

Maximum Area   In Exercises 45 and 46, consider a rectangle of length x and perimeter P (see figure). (a) Express the area A as a function of x and determine the domain of the function. (b) Sketch the graph of the area function. (c) Find the length and width of the rectangle of maximum area.

Figure for 45 and 46

45. $P = 100$ feet   **46.** $P = 36$ meters

47. *Maximum Area*   A rancher has 200 feet of fencing to enclose two adjacent rectangular corrals (see figure). What dimensions will produce a maximum enclosed area?

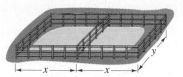

Figure for 47

48. *Maximum Area*   An indoor physical fitness room consists of a rectangular region with a semicircle on each end (see figure). The perimeter of the room is to be a 200-meter running track. What dimensions will produce a maximum area of the rectangle?

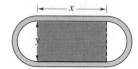

Figure for 48

49. *Maximum Revenue*   Find the number of units that produce a maximum revenue

$$R = 900x - 0.1x^2$$

where R is the total revenue in dollars and x is the number of units sold.

50. *Maximum Revenue*   Find the number of units that produce a maximum revenue

$$R = 100x - 0.0002x^2$$

where R is the total revenue in dollars and x is the number of units sold.

51. *Minimum Cost*   A manufacturer of lighting fixtures has daily production costs of

$$C = 800 - 10x + 0.25x^2$$

where C is the total cost in dollars and x is the number of units produced. How many fixtures should be produced each day to yield a minimum cost?

52. *Maximum Profit*   Let x be the amount (in hundreds of dollars) a company spends on advertising, and let P be the profit, where

$$P = 230 + 20x - 0.5x^2.$$

What expenditure for advertising gives the maximum profit?

53. *Trajectory of a Ball* The height y (in feet) of a ball thrown by a child is

$$y = -\tfrac{1}{12}x^2 + 2x + 4$$

where x is the horizontal distance (in feet) from where the ball is thrown (see figure).
(a) Sketch the path of the ball.
(b) How high was the ball when it left the child's hand? (*Note:* Find y when $x = 0$.)
(c) How high was the ball when it was at its maximum height?
(d) How far from the child did the ball strike the ground?

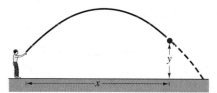

Figure for 53

54. *Maximum Height of a Dive* The path of a dive is

$$y = -\tfrac{4}{9}x^2 + \tfrac{24}{9}x + 10$$

where y is the height in feet and x is the horizontal distance from the end of the diving board in feet (see figure). What is the maximum height of the dive?

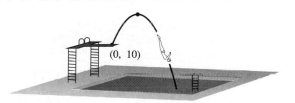

(0, 10)

Figure for 54

55. *Forestry* The number of board feet in a 16-foot log is approximated by the model

$$V = 0.77x^2 - 1.32x - 9.31, \qquad 5 \le x \le 40$$

where V is the number of board feet and x is the diameter of the log at the small end in inches. (One board foot is

a measure of volume equivalent to a board that is 12 inches wide, 12 inches long, and 1 inch thick.)
(a) Sketch a graph of the function.
(b) Estimate the number of board feet in a 16-foot log with a diameter of 16 inches.
(c) Estimate the diameter of a 16-foot log that scaled 500 board feet when the lumber was sold.

56. *Automobile Aerodynamics* The amount of horsepower y required to overcome wind drag on a certain automobile is approximated by

$$y = 0.002x^2 + 0.005x - 0.029, \qquad 0 \le x \le 100$$

where x is the speed of the car in miles per hour.
(a) Sketch a graph of the function.
(b) Estimate the maximum speed of the car if the power required to overcome wind drag is not to exceed 10 horsepower.

57. Complete the square for the quadratic function $f(x) = ax^2 + bx + c$ ($a \ne 0$) and show that the vertex is at

$$\left(-\frac{b}{2a}, -\frac{b^2 - 4ac}{4a} \right).$$

58. Use Exercise 57 to verify the vertices found in Exercises 19 and 20.

59. Assume that the function $f(x) = ax^2 + bx + c$ ($a \ne 0$) has two real zeros. Show that the x-coordinate of the vertex of the graph is the average of the zeros of f. (*Hint:* Use the Quadratic Formula.)

60. Create a quadratic function with zeros at $x = -4$ and $x = 2$. (The answer is not unique.)

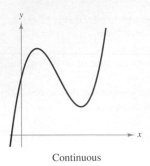

Continuous

Discontinuous

FIGURE 3.13

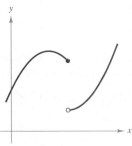

Polynomial functions have
smooth, rounded graphs.

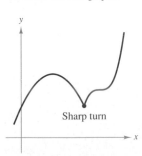

Sharp turn

The graph of a polynomial function
cannot have a sharp pointed turn.

FIGURE 3.14

Polynomial Functions of Higher Degree

Graphs of Polynomial Functions / The Leading Coefficient Test /
Zeros of Polynomial Functions / The Intermediate Value Theorem

Graphs of Polynomial Functions

At this point you should be able to sketch an accurate graph of polynomial functions of degrees 0, 1, and 2.

Function	Graph
$f(x) = a$	Horizontal line
$f(x) = ax + b$	Line of slope a
$f(x) = ax^2 + bx + c$	Parabola

The graphs of polynomial functions of degree greater than 2 are more difficult to sketch. However, in this section you will learn how to recognize some of the basic features of the graphs of polynomial functions. Using these features and point-plotting, intercepts, and symmetry, you should be able to make reasonably accurate sketches *by hand*. Of course, if you have a graphing facility such as a graphing calculator or graphing software for a computer, then the task is easier.

The graph of a polynomial function is **continuous.** Essentially, this means that the graph of a polynomial function has no breaks, as shown in Figure 3.13.

Another feature of the graph of a polynomial function is that it has only smooth, rounded turns, as shown in Figure 3.14. Notice that the graph of a polynomial function cannot have a sharp turn. (For instance, the graph of $f(x) = |x|$ has a sharp turn at the point (0, 0).)

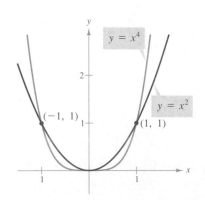

If n is even, the graph of $y = x^n$
touches axis at x-intercept.

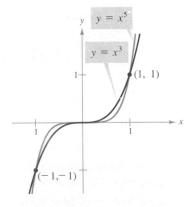

If n is odd, the graph of $y = x^n$
crosses axis at x-intercept.

FIGURE 3.15

The polynomial functions that have the simplest graphs are monomials of the form

$$f(x) = x^n$$

where n is an integer greater than zero. From Figure 3.15, we see that when n is *even* the graph is similar to the graph of $f(x) = x^2$, and when n is *odd* the graph is similar to the graph of $f(x) = x^3$. Moreover, the greater the value of n, the flatter the graph is on the interval $[-1, 1]$. You can check this by plotting a few points in this interval.

EXAMPLE 1   Sketching Transformations of Monomial Functions

Sketch the graphs of the polynomial functions.

a. $f(x) = -x^5$ **b.** $g(x) = x^4 + 1$ **c.** $h(x) = (x + 1)^4$

Solution

a. Since the degree of f is odd, the graph is similar to the graph of $y = x^3$. Moreover, the negative coefficient reflects the graph in the x-axis. Plotting the intercept $(0, 0)$ and the points $(1, -1)$ and $(-1, 1)$, we obtain the graph shown in Figure 3.16.

b. In this case, the graph of g is an upward shift, by one unit, of the graph of $y = x^4$ (see Figure 3.15). Thus, we obtain the graph shown in Figure 3.17.

c. The graph of h is a left shift, by one unit, of the graph of $y = x^4$ and it is shown in Figure 3.18.

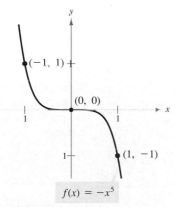

FIGURE 3.16

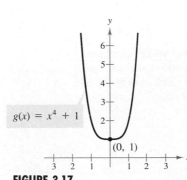

FIGURE 3.17

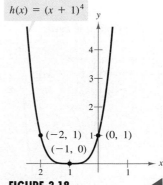

FIGURE 3.18

The Leading Coefficient Test

In Example 1, note that the three graphs eventually rise or fall without bound as x moves to the right or left. Symbolically, we write

$$f(x) \to \infty \qquad \text{as} \qquad x \to \infty$$

to mean that $f(x)$ increases without bound as x moves to the right without bound. (The infinity symbol ∞ indicates unboundedness.) Whether the graph of a polynomial eventually rises or falls can be determined by the function's degree (even or odd) and by its leading coefficient, as indicated by the **Leading Coefficient Test.**

Leading Coefficient Test

As x moves without bound to the left or to the right, the graph of the polynomial function $f(x) = a_n x^n + \cdots + a_1 x + a_0$ eventually rises or falls in the following manner. (*Note:* The dashed portions of the graphs indicate that the test determines *only* the right and left behavior of the graph.)

1. **When n is *odd*:**

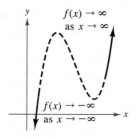

If the leading coefficient is positive ($a_n > 0$), then the graph falls to the left and rises to the right.

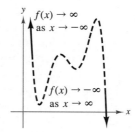

If the leading coefficient is negative ($a_n < 0$), then the graph rises to the left and falls to the right.

2. **When n is *even*:**

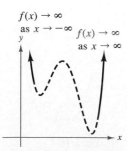

If the leading coefficient is positive ($a_n > 0$), then the graph rises to the left and right.

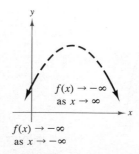

If the leading coefficient is negative ($a_n < 0$), then the graph falls to the left and right.

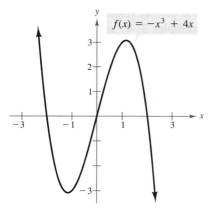

$f(x) = -x^3 + 4x$

FIGURE 3.19

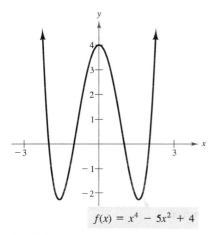

$f(x) = x^4 - 5x^2 + 4$

FIGURE 3.20

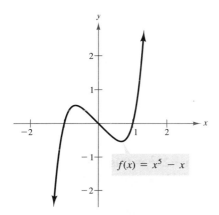

$f(x) = x^5 - x$

FIGURE 3.21

EXAMPLE 2 Applying the Leading Coefficient Test

Use the Leading Coefficient Test to determine the right and left behavior of the graphs of the polynomial functions.

a. $f(x) = -x^3 + 4x$ **b.** $f(x) = x^4 - 5x^2 + 4$ **c.** $f(x) = x^5 - x$

Solution

a. Because the degree is odd and the leading coefficient is negative, the graph rises to the left and falls to the right, as shown in Figure 3.19.
b. Because the degree is even and the leading coefficient is positive, the graph rises to the left and right, as shown in Figure 3.20.
c. Because the degree is odd and the leading coefficient is positive, the graph falls to the left and rises to the right, as shown in Figure 3.21. ◢

Zeros of Polynomial Functions

A **zero** of a function f is a number x for which $f(x) = 0$. For instance, 2 is a zero for the function $f(x) = x - 2$ because $f(2) = 2 - 2 = 0$. Similarly, 0 and -3 are zeros of the function $f(x) = x^2 + 3x$ because $f(0) = 0^2 + 3(0) = 0$ and $f(-3) = (-3)^3 + 3(-3) = 0$.

It can be shown that for a polynomial function f of degree n, the following statements are true.

1. The graph of f has, at most, $n - 1$ turning points. (Turning points are points at which the graph changes from increasing to decreasing or vice versa.)
2. The function f has, at most, n real zeros. (We will discuss this result in detail in Section 3.6 when we present the Fundamental Theorem of Algebra.)

Finding the zeros of polynomial functions is one of the most important problems in algebra. There is a strong interplay between graphical and algebraic approaches to this problem. Sometimes you can use information about the graph of a function to help find its zeros, and in other cases you can use information about the zeros of a function to help sketch its graph.

REAL ZEROS OF POLYNOMIAL FUNCTIONS

If f is a polynomial function and a is a real zero of f, then the following statements are equivalent.

1. $x = a$ is a *zero* of the function f.
2. $x = a$ is a *solution* of the polynomial equation $f(x) = 0$.
3. $(x - a)$ is a *factor* of the polynomial $f(x)$.
4. $(a, 0)$ is an *x-intercept* of the graph of f.

SOLVING

A Graphical
Approach to
Finding the
Zeros of a
Function

You can use the *zoom* feature of a graphing utility to approximate a function's real zeros (the *x*-intercepts of its graph) to any desired accuracy. The four graphs below show four steps in approximating the positive zero of $f(x) = x^2 - 5$ to be $x \approx 2.236$. (The actual zero is $x = \sqrt{5} \approx 2.236068$.) By repeated zooming, you can obtain whatever accuracy you need.

1.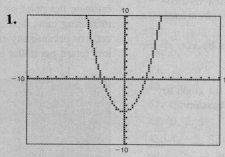

Sketch the graph of $y = x^2 - 5$.

SETTING: Xmin = -10 Ymin=-10
          Xmax=10 Ymax=10
          Xscl=1 Yscl=1

2.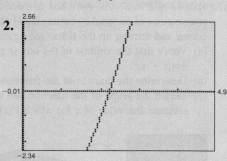

Zoom once to get a closer view of the positive *x*-intercept. (The *x*- and *y*-settings will change automatically.

3.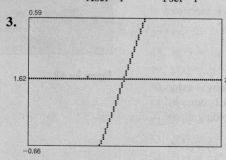

Zoom a second time to get an even better view. Use the cursor keys to determine that the *x*-intercept is about 2.2.

4.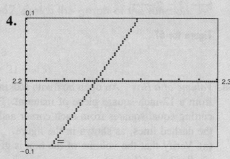

Set *x*-values to vary from 2.2 to 2.3, with an *x*-scale of 0.01. Using the trace key, you can approximate the *x*-intercept to be 2.236.

SETTING: Xmin = 2.2 Ymin=$-.1$
          Xmax=2.3 Ymax=.1
          Xscl=.01 Yscl=0.01

The equation $x^2 - 5 = 0$ that is solved graphically above is, of course, easy to solve algebraically. Example 1 uses a graphic approach to solving an equation that would be difficult to solve algebraically.

EXAMPLE 1   Finding Points of Intersection of Two Graphs

Find the points of intersection of the circle and parabola given by

$$x^2 + y^2 - 3x + 5y - 11 = 0 \quad \text{and} \quad y = x^2 - 4x + 5.$$

Solution

To begin, you can sketch the graph of both equations on the same graphing utility screen. If you are using a graphing utility that graphs *functions*, rather than *relations*, you should begin by writing the circle as the union of two functions.

$$y = \tfrac{1}{2}(-5 + \sqrt{69 + 12x - 4x^2})$$ *Top half of circle*

$$y = \tfrac{1}{2}(-5 - \sqrt{69 + 12x - 4x^2})$$ *Bottom half of circle*

$$y = x^2 - 4x + 5$$ *Parabola*

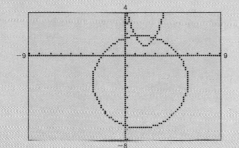

From the graph, you can see that the parabola intersects the circle twice. The coordinates of the points of intersection are roughly (1, 1.9) and (2.8, 1.7). To obtain a more accurate approximation of the points of intersection, you could use the zoom feature of the graphing utility. (See Exercise 1 below.)

Another approach is to substitute $x^2 - 4x + 5$ for y in the equation of the circle. This produces a fourth-degree polynomial equation that can be solved for x.

$$x^2 + y^2 - 3x + 5y - 11 = 0$$
$$x^2 + (x^2 - 4x + 5)^2 - 3x + 5(x^2 - 4x + 5) - 11 = 0$$
$$x^4 - 8x^3 + 32x^2 - 63x + 39 = 0$$

Using a graphing utility, you can approximate the solutions of this equation to be $x \approx 1.055$ and $x \approx 2.841$.

EXERCISES

(See also: Exercises 63–66, Section 3.2)

1. *Exploration* Using a setting of $1.05 \le x \le 1.06$ and $1.89 \le y \le 1.90$, sketch the graphs of the top half of the circle and the parabola on the same screen. Then use the trace feature to approximate (accurate to 3 decimal places) the y-coordinate of the point of the intersection that is shown on the screen.

2. *Exploration*
   (a) Find a graphing utility setting that will allow you to approximate the solution $x = 1.055$ to two more decimal places of accuracy.
   (b) Find a graphing utility setting that will allow you to approximate the solution $x = 2.841$ to two more decimal places of accuracy.

3. *It Doesn't Look Like a Circle* The graphs of

$$y = \sqrt{36 - x^2} \quad \text{and} \quad y = -\sqrt{36 - x^2}$$

   form the top and bottom halves of a circle. Use a graphing utility to sketch both graphs on the same display screen. Which of the following produces a result that "looks" like a circle? Describe a general rule that can be used with your graphing utility to make the circles look like circles.

   (a) SETTING Xmin=−10   Ymin=−10
               Xmax=10   Ymax=10
               Xscl=1   Yscl=1

   (b) SETTING Xmin=−9   Ymin=−6
               Xmax=9   Ymax=6
               Xscl=1   Yscl=1

205

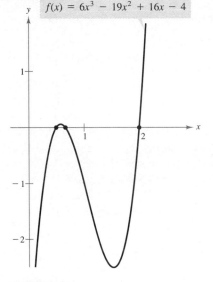

$f(x) = 6x^3 - 19x^2 + 16x - 4$

FIGURE 3.31

Long Division of Polynomials / Synthetic Division / The Remainder and Factor Theorems

Long Division of Polynomials

Up to this point in the text we have added, subtracted, and multiplied polynomials. In this section, we look at a procedure for *dividing* polynomials. This procedure has many important applications and is especially valuable in factoring and finding the zeros of polynomial functions.

To begin, consider the graph of

$$f(x) = 6x^3 - 19x^2 + 16x - 4,$$

shown in Figure 3.31. Notice that a zero of f occurs at $x = 2$. [Try verifying this by evaluating $f(x)$ at $x = 2$.] Since $x = 2$ is a zero of the polynomial function f, $(x - 2)$ is a factor of $f(x)$. This means that there exists a second-degree polynomial $q(x)$ such that

$$f(x) = (x - 2) \cdot q(x).$$

To find $q(x)$, we use **long division of polynomials.** Study the following example to see how this process works.

EXAMPLE 1   Long Division of Polynomials

Divide the polynomial

$$f(x) = 6x^3 - 19x^2 + 16x - 4$$

by $x - 2$, and use the result to factor $f(x)$ completely.

Solution

$$
\begin{array}{r}
6x^2 - 7x + 2 \\
x - 2 \overline{)6x^3 - 19x^2 + 16x - 4} \\
\underline{6x^3 - 12x^2} \\
-7x^2 + 16x \\
\underline{-7x^2 + 14x} \\
2x - 4 \\
\underline{2x - 4} \\
0
\end{array}
$$

Partial quotients

Multiply: $6x^2(x - 2)$

Subtract

Multiply: $-7x(x - 2)$

Subtract

Multiply: $2(x - 2)$

Subtract

We see that

$$6x^3 - 19x^2 + 16x - 4 = (x - 2)(6x^2 - 7x + 2)$$

and, factoring the quadratic $6x^2 - 7x + 2$,

$$6x^3 - 19x^2 + 16x - 4 = (x - 2)(2x - 1)(3x - 2).$$

Note that this factorization agrees with the graph of f (Figure 3.31) in that the three x-intercepts occur at

$$x = 2, \qquad x = \frac{1}{2}, \qquad \text{and} \qquad x = \frac{2}{3}.$$

◢

In Example 1, $x - 2$ is a factor of the polynomial $6x^3 - 19x^2 + 16x - 4$, and the long division process produced a remainder of zero. Often, long division will produce a nonzero remainder. For instance, if we divide $x^2 + 3x + 5$ by $x + 1$, we obtain the following.

$$
\begin{array}{r}
x + 2 \quad \leftarrow \text{Quotient} \\
\text{Divisor} \rightarrow x + 1 \overline{\smash{)}\, x^2 + 3x + 5} \quad \leftarrow \text{Dividend} \\
\underline{x^2 + x} \\
2x + 5 \\
\underline{2x + 2} \\
3 \quad \leftarrow \text{Remainder}
\end{array}
$$

We write this result as

$$
\underbrace{\frac{\overbrace{x^2 + 3x + 5}^{\text{Dividend}}}{\underbrace{x + 1}_{\text{Divisor}}}}_{} = \overbrace{x + 2}^{\text{Quotient}} + \frac{\overbrace{3}^{\text{Remainder}}}{\underbrace{x + 1}_{\text{Divisor}}}
$$

or

$$x^2 + 3x + 5 = (x + 2)(x + 1) + 3.$$

This example illustrates the well-known theorem, the **Division Algorithm.**

THE DIVISION ALGORITHM

If $f(x)$ and $d(x)$ are polynomials such that $d(x) \neq 0$, and the degree of $d(x)$ is less than or equal to the degree of $f(x)$, then there exist unique polynomials $q(x)$ and $r(x)$ such that

$$f(x) = d(x)q(x) + r(x)$$

Dividend Divisor Quotient Remainder

where $r(x) = 0$ or the degree of $r(x)$ is less than the degree of $d(x)$. If the remainder $r(x)$ is zero, then $d(x)$ **divides evenly** into $f(x)$.

REMARK The Division Algorithm can also be written as
$$\frac{f(x)}{d(x)} = q(x) + \frac{r(x)}{d(x)}.$$

In the Division Algorithm the rational expression $f(x)/d(x)$ is **improper** because the degree of $f(x)$ is greater than or equal to the degree of $d(x)$. On the other hand, the rational expression $r(x)/d(x)$ is **proper** because the degree of $r(x)$ is less than the degree of $d(x)$.

EXAMPLE 2 Long Division of Polynomials

Divide $x^3 - 1$ by $x - 1$.

Solution

Because there is no x^2-term or x-term in the dividend, we line up the subtraction by using zero coefficients (or leaving a space) for the missing terms.

$$
\begin{array}{r}
x^2 + x + 1 \\
x - 1 \overline{)x^3 + 0x^2 + 0x - 1} \\
\underline{x^3 - x^2} \\
x^2 \\
\underline{x^2 - x} \\
x - 1 \\
\underline{x - 1} \\
0
\end{array}
$$

Thus, $x - 1$ divides evenly into $x^3 - 1$ and we can write

$$\frac{x^3 - 1}{x - 1} = x^2 + x + 1.$$

EXAMPLE 3 Long Division of Polynomials

$$
\begin{array}{r}
2x^2 + 1 \\
x^2 + 2x - 3 \overline{)2x^4 + 4x^3 - 5x^2 + 3x - 2} \\
\underline{2x^4 + 4x^3 - 6x^2} \\
x^2 + 3x - 2 \\
\underline{x^2 + 2x - 3} \\
x + 1
\end{array}
$$

Note that the first subtraction eliminated two terms from the dividend. When this happens, the quotient skips a term. Thus, we can write

$$\frac{2x^4 + 4x^3 - 5x^2 + 3x - 2}{x^2 + 2x - 3} = 2x^2 + 1 + \frac{x + 1}{x^2 + 2x - 3}.$$

Synthetic Division

Synthetic division is a shortcut for long division by polynomials of the form $x - k$. To see how it works, take another look at Example 1.

$$
\begin{array}{r}
6x^2 - 7x + 2 \\
x - 2 \overline{\smash{)}6x^3 - 19x^2 + 16x - 4} \\
\underline{6x^3 - 12x^2} \\
-7x^2 + 16x \\
\underline{-7x^2 + 14x} \\
2x - 4 \\
\underline{2x - 4} \\
0
\end{array}
$$

You can retain the essential steps of this division tableau by using only the coefficients, as follows.

$$
\begin{array}{r}
6 \quad -7 \quad 2 \\
-2 \overline{\smash{)}6 \quad -19 \quad 16 \quad -4} \\
\underline{6 \quad -12} \\
-7 \quad 16 \\
\underline{-7 \quad 14} \\
2 \quad -4 \\
\underline{2 \quad -4} \\
0
\end{array}
$$

Since the coefficients shown in color are duplicates of those in the quotient or the dividend, you can omit them and condense vertically.

$$
\begin{array}{r}
6 \quad -7 \quad 2 \\
-2 \overline{\smash{)}6 \quad -19 \quad 16 \quad -4} \\
\underline{-12 \quad 14 \quad -4} \\
0
\end{array}
$$

Now, move the quotient to the bottom row.

$$
\begin{array}{r}
-2 \overline{\smash{)}6 \quad -19 \quad 16 \quad -4} \\
\underline{-12 \quad 14 \quad -4} \\
6 \quad -7 \quad 2 \quad 0
\end{array}
$$

Finally, change from subtraction to addition (and reduce the likelihood of errors) by changing the sign of the divisor and of row two. This produces the following synthetic division array.

$$
\begin{array}{r|rrrr}
2 & 6 & -19 & 16 & -4 \\
& & 12 & -14 & 4 \\
\hline
& 6 & -7 & 2 & 0
\end{array}
$$

We summarize the pattern for synthetic division of a cubic polynomial as follows. (The pattern for higher-degree polynomials is similar.)

SYNTHETIC DIVISION (FOR A CUBIC POLYNOMIAL)

To divide $ax^3 + bx^2 + cx + d$ by $x - k$, use the following pattern.

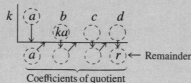

Coefficients of quotient

Vertical Pattern: Add terms.
Diagonal Pattern: Multiply by k.

REMARK Synthetic division works *only* for divisors of the form $x - k$. You cannot use synthetic division to divide a polynomial by a quadratic such as $x^2 - 3$.

EXAMPLE 4 Using Synthetic Division

Use synthetic division to divide $x^4 - 10x^2 - 2x + 4$ by $x + 3$.

Solution

You can set up the array as follows. (Note that you must include a zero for each missing term in the dividend.)

Divisor: $x - (-3)$ Dividend: $x^4 - 10x^2 - 2x + 4$

$$
\begin{array}{r|rrrrr}
-3 & 1 & 0 & -10 & -2 & 4 \\
   &   & -3 & 9 & 3 & -3 \\
\hline
   & 1 & -3 & -1 & 1 & 1 \\
\end{array}
$$
← Remainder: 1

Quotient: $x^3 - 3x^2 - x + 1$

Thus, you have

$$\frac{x^4 - 10x^2 - 2x + 4}{x + 3} = x^3 - 3x^2 - x + 1 + \frac{1}{x + 3}.$$

The Remainder and Factor Theorems

The remainder obtained in the synthetic division process has an important interpretation, as given in the **Remainder Theorem.**

THE REMAINDER THEOREM

If a polynomial $f(x)$ is divided by $x - k$, then the remainder is

$$r = f(k).$$

Proof

From the Division Algorithm, we have

$$f(x) = (x - k)q(x) + r(x)$$

and since either $r(x) = 0$ or the degree of $r(x)$ is less than the degree of $x - k$, we know that $r(x)$ must be a constant. That is, $r(x) = r$. Now, by evaluating $f(x)$ at $x = k$, we have

$$f(k) = (k - k)q(k) + r = (0)q(k) + r = r.$$ ◣

EXAMPLE 5   Evaluating a Polynomial by the Remainder Theorem

Use the Remainder Theorem to evaluate the following function at $x = -2$.

$$f(x) = 3x^3 + 8x^2 + 5x - 7$$

Solution

Using synthetic division, we obtain the following.

$$
\begin{array}{r|rrrr}
-2 & 3 & 8 & 5 & -7 \\
   &   & -6 & -4 & -2 \\
\hline
   & 3 & 2 & 1 & -9
\end{array}
$$

Since the remainder is $r = -9$, we conclude that

$$f(-2) = -9.$$

This means that $(-2, -9)$ is a point on the graph of f. Check this by substituting $x = -2$ in the original function. ◣

FACTOR THEOREM
A polynomial $f(x)$ has a factor $(x - k)$ if and only if $f(k) = 0$.

Proof

Using the Division Algorithm with the factor $(x - k)$, we have

$$f(x) = (x - k)q(x) + r(x).$$

By the Remainder Theorem, $r(x) = r = f(k)$, and we have

$$f(x) = (x - k)q(x) + f(k)$$

where $q(x)$ is a polynomial of lesser degree than $f(x)$. If $f(k) = 0$, then

$$f(x) = (x - k)q(x)$$

and we see that $(x - k)$ is a factor of $f(x)$. Conversely, if $(x - k)$ is a factor of $f(x)$, then division of $f(x)$ by $(x - k)$ yields a remainder of 0. Hence, by the Remainder Theorem, we have $f(k) = 0$. ◣

EXAMPLE 6 Using Synthetic Division to Find Factors of a Polynomial

Show that $(x - 2)$ and $(x + 3)$ are factors of the polynomial

$$f(x) = 2x^4 + 7x^3 - 4x^2 - 27x - 18.$$

Then find the remaining factors of $f(x)$.

Solution

Use synthetic division with 2 and -3 *successively* to obtain the following.

$$
\begin{array}{r|rrrrl}
2 & 2 & 7 & -4 & -27 & -18 \\
  &   & 4 & 22 & 36 & 18 & \text{0 remainder}\\
\hline
  & 2 & 11 & 18 & 9 & 0 \rightarrow (x-2) \text{ is a factor}
\end{array}
$$

$$
\begin{array}{r|rrrrl}
-3 & 2 & 11 & 18 & 9 & \text{Use new coefficients}\\
   &   & -6 & -15 & -9 & \text{0 remainder}\\
\hline
   & 2 & 5 & 3 & 0 & \rightarrow (x+3) \text{ is a factor}
\end{array}
$$

Since the resulting quadratic factors as

$$2x^2 + 5x + 3 = (2x + 3)(x + 1)$$

the complete factorization of $f(x)$ is

$$f(x) = (x - 2)(x + 3)(2x + 3)(x + 1).$$

This factorization implies that f has four real zeros: 2, -3, $-\frac{3}{2}$, and -1.

In summary, the remainder r, obtained in the synthetic division of $f(x)$ by $x - k$, provides the following information.

1. The remainder r gives the value of f at $x = k$. That is, $r = f(k)$.
2. If $r = 0$, then $(x - k)$ is a factor of $f(x)$.
3. If $r = 0$, then $(k, 0)$ is an x-intercept of the graph of f.

DISCUSSION

PROBLEM

Finding Patterns in Polynomial Division

Complete the polynomial divisions.

1. $\dfrac{x^2 - 1}{x - 1} = $ ▨

2. $\dfrac{x^3 - 1}{x - 1} = $ ▨

3. $\dfrac{x^4 - 1}{x - 1} = $ ▨

Describe the pattern that you obtain and use your result to find a formula for the polynomial division

$$\frac{x^n - 1}{x - 1}.$$

WARM UP

The following warm-up exercises involve skills that were covered in earlier sections. You will use these skills in the exercise set for this section.

In Exercises 1–4, write the expression in standard polynomial form.

1. $(x - 1)(x^2 + 2) + 5$ **2.** $(x^2 - 3)(2x + 4) + 8$

3. $(x^2 + 1)(x^2 - 2x + 3) - 10$ **4.** $(x + 6)(2x^3 - 3x) - 5$

In Exercises 5 and 6, factor the polynomials.

5. $x^2 - 4x + 3$ **6.** $4x^3 - 10x^2 + 6x$

In Exercises 7–10, find a polynomial function that has the given zeros.

7. $0, 3, 4$ **8.** $-6, 1$

9. $-3, 1 + \sqrt{2}, 1 \ \sqrt{2}$ **10.** $1, -2, 2 + \sqrt{3}, 2 - \sqrt{3}$

EXERCISES for Section 3.3

In Exercises 1–14, divide by long division.

Dividend	Divisor
1. $2x^2 + 10x + 12$	$x + 3$
2. $5x^2 - 17x - 12$	$x - 4$
3. $4x^3 \ \ 7x^2 - 11x + 5$	$4x + 5$
4. $6x^3 - 16x^2 + 17x - 6$	$3x - 2$
5. $x^4 + 5x^3 + 6x^2 - x - 2$	$x + 2$
6. $x^3 + 4x^2 - 3x - 12$	$x^2 - 3$
7. $7x + 3$	$x + 2$
8. $8x - 5$	$2x + 1$
9. $6x^3 + 10x^2 + x + 8$	$2x^2 + 1$
10. $x^3 - 9$	$x^2 + 1$
11. $x^4 + 3x^2 + 1$	$x^2 - 2x + 3$
12. $x^5 + 7$	$x^3 - 1$
13. $2x^3 - 4x^2 - 15x + 5$	$(x - 1)^2$
14. x^4	$(x - 1)^3$

Dividend	Divisor
20. $3x^3 - 16x^2 - 72$	$x - 6$
21. $5x^3 - 6x^2 + 8$	$x - 4$
22. $5x^3 + 6x + 8$	$x + 2$
23. $10x^4 - 50x^3 - 800$	$x - 6$
24. $x^5 - 13x^4 - 120x + 80$	$x + 3$
25. $x^3 + 512$	$x + 8$
26. $5x^3$	$x + 3$
27. $-3x^4$	$x - 2$
28. $-3x^4$	$x + 2$
29. $5 - 3x + 2x^2 - x^3$	$x + 1$
30. $180x - x^4$	$x - 6$
31. $4x^3 + 16x^2 - 23x - 15$	$x + \frac{1}{2}$
32. $3x^3 - 4x^2 + 5$	$x - \frac{3}{2}$

In Exercises 15–32, divide by synthetic division.

Dividend	Divisor
15. $3x^3 - 17x^2 + 15x - 25$	$x - 5$
16. $5x^3 + 18x^2 + 7x - 6$	$x + 3$
17. $4x^3 - 9x + 8x^2 - 18$	$x + 2$
18. $9x^3 - 16x - 18x^2 + 32$	$x - 2$
19. $-x^3 + 75x - 250$	$x + 10$

In Exercises 33–40, use synthetic division to show that x is a solution of the third-degree polynomial equation, and use the result to factor the polynomial completely.

Polynomial Equation	Value of x
33. $x^3 - 7x + 6 = 0$	$x = 2$
34. $x^3 - 28x - 48 = 0$	$x = -4$
35. $2x^3 - 15x^2 + 27x - 10 = 0$	$x = \frac{1}{2}$
36. $48x^3 - 80x^2 + 41x - 6 = 0$	$x = \frac{2}{3}$

Polynomial Equation	Value of x
37. $x^3 + 2x^2 - 3x - 6 = 0$	$x = \sqrt{3}$
38. $x^3 + 2x^2 - 2x - 4$	$x = \sqrt{2}$
39. $x^3 - 3x^2 + 2 = 0$	$x = 1 + \sqrt{3}$
40. $x^3 - x^2 - 13x - 3 = 0$	$x = 2 - \sqrt{5}$

In Exercises 41–44, express the function in the form $f(x) = (x - k)q(x) + r$ for the given value of k, and demonstrate that $f(k) = r$.

Function	Value of k
41. $f(x) = x^3 - x^2 - 14x + 11$	$k = 4$
42. $f(x) = \frac{1}{3}(15x^4 + 10x^3 - 6x^2 + 17x + 14)$	$k = -\frac{2}{3}$
43. $f(x) = x^3 + 3x^2 - 2x - 14$	$k = \sqrt{2}$
44. $f(x) = 4x^3 - 6x^2 - 12x - 4$	$k = 1 - \sqrt{3}$

In Exercises 45–50, use synthetic division to find the required function values.

45. $f(x) = 4x^3 - 13x + 10$
   (a) $f(1)$ (b) $f(-2)$ (c) $f\left(\frac{1}{2}\right)$ (d) $f(8)$

46. $g(x) = x^6 - 4x^4 + 3x^2 + 2$
   (a) $g(2)$ (b) $g(-4)$ (c) $g(3)$ (d) $g(-1)$

47. $h(x) = 3x^3 + 5x^2 - 10x + 1$
   (a) $h(3)$ (b) $h\left(\frac{1}{3}\right)$ (c) $h(-2)$ (d) $h(-5)$

48. $f(x) = 0.4x^4 - 1.6x^3 + 0.7x^2 - 2$
   (a) $f(1)$ (b) $f(-2)$ (c) $f(5)$ (d) $f(-10)$

49. $f(x) = x^3 - 2x^2 - 11x + 52$
   (a) $f(5)$ (b) $f(-4)$ (c) $f(1.2)$ (d) $f(2)$

50. $g(x) = x^3 - x^2 + 25x - 25$
   (a) $g(5)$ (b) $g\left(\frac{1}{5}\right)$ (c) $g(-1.5)$ (d) $g(-1)$

In Exercises 51–56, simplify the rational expression.

51. $\dfrac{4x^3 - 8x^2 + x + 3}{2x - 3}$

52. $\dfrac{x^3 + x^2 - 64x - 64}{x + 8}$

53. $\dfrac{x^3 + 3x^2 - x - 3}{x + 1}$

54. $\dfrac{2x^3 + 3x^2 - 3x - 2}{x - 1}$

55. $\dfrac{x^4 + 6x^3 + 11x^2 + 6x}{x^2 + 3x + 2}$

56. $\dfrac{x^4 + 9x^3 - 5x^2 - 36x + 4}{x^2 - 4}$

57. *Power of an Engine*   The horsepower y developed by a compact car engine is approximated by the model

$$y = -1.42x^3 + 5.04x^2 + 32.45x - 0.75, \quad 1 \le x \le 5$$

where x is the engine speed in thousands of revolutions

per minute. Note on the graph that there are two engine speeds that develop 110 horsepower, one of which is 5000 rpm. Approximate the other engine speed.

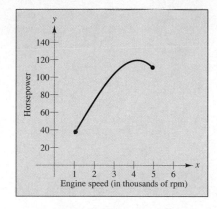

Figure for 57

58. *Automobile Emissions*   The number of parts per million of nitric oxide emissions y from a certain car engine is approximated by the model

$$y = -5.05x^3 + 3857x - 38,411.25, \quad 13 \le x \le 18$$

where x is the air-fuel ratio. Note on the graph that there are two air-fuel ratios that produce 2400 parts per million of nitric oxide, one of which is 15. Approximate the other air-fuel mixture.

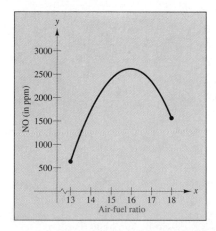

Figure for 58

59. Use the form $f(x) = (x - k)q(x) + r$ to create a cubic function that (a) passes through the point $(2, 5)$ and rises to the right, and (b) passes through the point $(-3, 1)$ and falls to the right. (The answers are not unique.)

3.4 Real Zeros of Polynomial Functions

Descartes's Rule of Signs / The Rational Zero Test /
Bounds for Real Zeros of Polynomial Functions

Descartes's Rule of Signs

In this and the following section we will present some additional aids for
finding zeros of polynomial functions.

In Section 3.2, we noted that an nth degree polynomial function can have
at most n real zeros. Of course, many nth degree polynomials do not have
that many real zeros. For instance, $f(x) = x^2 + 1$ has no real zeros, and $f(x)$
$= x^3 + 1$ has only one real zero. **Descartes's Rule of Signs** sheds more light
on the number of real zeros that a polynomial can have.

DESCARTES'S RULE OF SIGNS

Let $f(x) = a_n x^n + a_{n-1} x^{n-1} + \cdots + a_2 x^2 + a_1 x + a_0$ be a
polynomial with real coefficients and $a_0 \neq 0$.

1. The number of *positive real zeros* of f is either equal to the number
   of variations in sign of $f(x)$ or is less than that number by an even
   integer.
2. The number of *negative real zeros* of f is either equal to the
   number of variations in sign of $f(-x)$ or is less than that number
   by an even integer.

REMARK When there is only one variation in sign, Descartes's Rule of Signs guarantees the existence of exactly one positive (or negative) real zero.

Variation in sign means that two consecutive coefficients have opposite signs.
For example, the polynomial

$$
\begin{array}{cccc}
+ \text{ to } - & & + \text{ to } - \\
\downarrow \quad \downarrow & & \downarrow \quad \downarrow
\end{array}
$$
$$
f(x) = 3x^3 - 5x^2 + 6x - 4
$$
$$
\begin{array}{cc}
\uparrow \qquad \uparrow \\
- \text{ to } +
\end{array}
$$

has *three* variations in sign, whereas

$$f(-x) = 3(-x)^3 - 5(-x)^2 + 6(-x) - 4$$
$$= -3x^3 - 5x^2 - 6x - 4$$

has no variations in sign. Thus, from Descartes's Rule of Signs, the polynomial $f(x) = 3x^3 - 5x^2 + 6x - 4$ has either three positive real zeros or
one positive real zero, and has no negative real zeros. From the graph of f
shown in Figure 3.32, you can see that the function has only one positive
real zero.

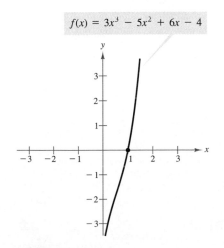

$f(x) = 3x^3 - 5x^2 + 6x - 4$

FIGURE 3.32

EXAMPLE 1 Using Descartes's Rule of Signs

Apply Descartes's Rule of Signs to the polynomial function

$$f(x) = 2x^4 + 7x^3 - 4x^2 - 27x - 18.$$

Solution

Because $f(x)$ has only *one* variation in sign, f must have *exactly one* positive real zero. Moreover, because

$$f(-x) = 2(-x)^4 + 7(-x)^3 - 4(-x)^2 - 27(-x) - 18$$
$$= 2x^4 - 7x^3 - 4x^2 + 27x - 18$$

has *three* variations in sign, f has either three negative zeros or one negative zero. This result agrees with Example 6 in Section 3.3, where the zeros of f were determined to be 2, -3, $-\frac{3}{2}$, and -1.

EXAMPLE 2 Using Descartes's Rule of Signs

Apply Descartes's Rule of Signs to the polynomial function

$$f(x) = x^3 - x + 1.$$

Solution

Because $f(x)$ has two variations in sign, it follows that f can have either two or no positive real zeros. Moreover, because

$$f(-x) = -x^3 + x + 1$$

has one variation in sign, f has exactly one negative real zero. The graph of f in Figure 3.33 shows that f actually has only one real zero (it is a negative number between -2 and -1).

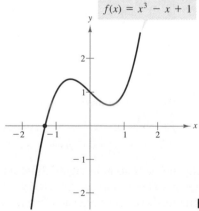

$$f(x) = x^3 - x + 1$$

FIGURE 3.33

The Rational Zero Test

The **Rational Zero Test** relates the possible rational zeros of a polynomial (having integer coefficients) to the leading coefficient and to the constant term of the polynomial.

THE RATIONAL ZERO TEST

If the polynomial $f(x) = a_n x^n + a_{n-1} x^{n-1} + \cdots + a_2 x^2 + a_1 x + a_0$ has *integer* coefficients, then every rational zero of f has the form

$$\text{Rational zero} = \frac{p}{q}$$

where p and q have no common factors other than 1, and

p = a factor of the constant term a_0

q = a factor of the leading coefficient a_n.

The feasibility of this theorem can be seen by exploring a special case. Consider a third-degree polynomial $P(x)$ having $\frac{2}{3}$ as a zero.

$$
\begin{aligned}
P(x) &= (3x - 2)(ax^2 + bx + c) && \textit{Factored form} \\
&= 3ax^3 - 2ax^2 + 3bx^2 - 2bx + 3cx - 2c \\
&= 3ax^3 + (3b - 2a)x^2 + (3c - 2b)x - 2c && \textit{Standard form}
\end{aligned}
$$

Note that the numerator of $\frac{2}{3}$ is a factor of the constant term, $-2c$, and that the denominator is a factor of the leading coefficient, $3a$, as specified by the theorem.

To use the Rational Zero Test, we first list all rational numbers whose numerators are factors of the constant term and whose denominators are factors of the leading coefficient.

$$\text{Possible rational zeros} = \frac{\text{factors of constant term}}{\text{factors of leading coefficient}}$$

Having formed this list of *possible rational zeros*, we use a trial-and-error method to determine which, if any, are actual zeros of the polynomial. Note that when the leading coefficient is 1, then the possible rational zeros are simply the factors of the constant term.

EXAMPLE 3   **Rational Zero Test with Leading Coefficient of 1**

Find the rational zeros of $f(x) = x^3 + x + 1$.

Solution

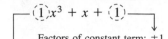

$$(1)x^3 + x + (1)$$

Factors of constant term: ± 1

Factors of leading coefficient: ± 1

Since 1 and -1 are the only factors of the leading coefficient, the possible rational zeros are simply the factors of the constant term, ± 1.

By testing these possible zeros, you can see that neither works.

$$f(1) = (1)^3 + 1 + 1 = 3$$
$$f(-1) = (-1)^3 + (-1) + 1 = -1$$

Thus, the given polynomial has *no* rational zeros. Note from the graph of f in Figure 3.34 that f does have one real zero (between -1 and 0). However, by the Rational Zero Test, you know that this real zero is *not* a rational number.

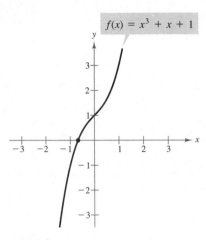

FIGURE 3.34

EXAMPLE 4   **Rational Zero Test with Leading Coefficient of 1**

Find the rational zeros of $f(x) = x^4 - x^3 + x^2 - 3x - 6$.

Solution

For $f(x) = x^4 - x^3 + x^2 - 3x - 6$, the leading coefficient is 1. Hence, the possible rational zeros are the factors of the constant term.

$$\pm 1, \ \pm 2, \ \pm 3, \ \pm 6$$

A test of these possible zeros would show that $x = -1$ and $x = 2$ are the only two that work. Check the others to be sure.

If the leading coefficient of a polynomial is not 1, the list of possible rational zeros can increase dramatically. In such cases the search can be shortened in several ways. (1) A programmable calculator can be used to speed up the calculations. (2) A rough sketch, possibly with a graphics calculator or graphing software, may give a good estimate of the location of the zeros. (3) Synthetic division can be used to test the possible rational zeros.

To see how to use synthetic division to test the possible rational zeros, let's take another look at the function

$$f(x) = x^4 - x^3 + x^2 - 3x - 6$$

given in Example 4. To test that $x = -1$ and $x = 2$ are zeros of f, you can apply synthetic division.

$$
\begin{array}{r|rrrrr}
-1 & 1 & -1 & 1 & -3 & -6 \\
   &   & -1 & 2 & -3 & 6 \\
\hline
   & 1 & -2 & 3 & -6 & 0
\end{array}
$$

$$
\begin{array}{r|rrrr}
2 & 1 & -2 & 3 & -6 \\
  &   & 2 & 0 & 6 \\
\hline
  & 1 & 0 & 3 & 0
\end{array}
$$

Thus,

$$f(x) = (x + 1)(x - 2)(x^2 + 3).$$

Since the factor $(x^2 + 3)$ produces no real zeros, $x = -1$ and $x = 2$ are the *only* real zeros of f.

Finding the first zero is often the most difficult part. After that, the search is simplified by working with the lower-degree polynomial obtained in synthetic division.

EXAMPLE 5   Using the Rational Zero Test

Find the rational zeros of $f(x) = 2x^3 + 3x^2 - 8x + 3$.

Solution

Since the leading coefficient is 2 and the constant term is 3, the possible rational zeros are as follows.

$$\frac{\text{Factors of } 3}{\text{Factors of } 2} = \frac{\pm 1, \pm 3}{\pm 1, \pm 2} = \pm 1, \pm 3, \pm\frac{1}{2}, \pm\frac{3}{2}$$

By synthetic division, we determine that $x = 1$ is a zero.

$$
\begin{array}{r|rrrr}
1 & 2 & 3 & -8 & 3 \\
  &   & 2 & 5 & -3 \\
\hline
  & 2 & 5 & -3 & 0
\end{array}
$$

Thus, $f(x)$ factors as

$$
\begin{aligned}
f(x) &= (x - 1)(2x^2 + 5x - 3) \\
     &= (x - 1)(2x - 1)(x + 3)
\end{aligned}
$$

and we conclude that the zeros of f are $x = 1$, $x = \frac{1}{2}$ and $x = -3$. ◄

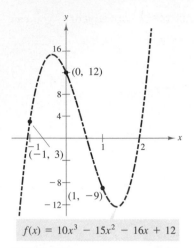

$f(x) = 10x^3 - 15x^2 - 16x + 12$

FIGURE 3.35

EXAMPLE 6   Using the Rational Zero Test

Find all the real zeros of $f(x) = 10x^3 - 15x^2 - 16x + 12$.

Solution

Since the leading coefficient is 10 and the constant term is 12, we have a long list of possible rational zeros.

$$\frac{\text{Factors of 12}}{\text{Factors of 10}} = \frac{\pm 1, \ \pm 2, \ \pm 3, \ \pm 4, \ \pm 6, \ \pm 12}{\pm 1, \ \pm 2, \ \pm 5, \ \pm 10}$$

With so many possibilities (32, in fact), it is worth our time to stop and make a rough sketch of this function. From Figure 3.35, it looks like three reasonable choices would be $x = -\frac{6}{5}$, $x = \frac{1}{2}$, and $x = 2$. Testing these by synthetic division shows that only $x = 2$ works. Thus, we have

$$f(x) = (x - 2)(10x^2 + 5x - 6).$$

Using the Quadratic Formula, we find that the two additional zeros are irrational numbers:

$$x = \frac{-5 + \sqrt{265}}{20} \approx 0.5639 \quad \text{and} \quad x = \frac{-5 - \sqrt{265}}{20} \approx -1.0639.$$

Bounds for Real Zeros of Polynomial Functions

The final test for zeros of a polynomial function is related to the sign pattern in the last row of the synthetic division tableau. This test can give us an upper or a lower bound of the real zeros of f. A real number b is an **upper bound** for the real zeros of f if no zeros are greater than b. Similarly, b is a **lower bound** if no real zeros of f are less than b.

LOWER AND UPPER BOUND RULE

Let $f(x)$ be a polynomial with real coefficients and a positive leading coefficient. Suppose $f(x)$ is divided by $x - c$, using synthetic division.

1. If $c > 0$ and each number in the last row is either positive or zero, then c is an *upper bound* for the real zeros of f.
2. If $c < 0$ and the numbers in the last row are alternatively positive and negative (zero entries count as positive or negative), then c is a *lower bound* for the real zeros of f.

Note in Example 7 that we use all three tests presented in this section to search for the real zeros of a polynomial function. In addition, we show how to handle rational coefficients by factoring out the reciprocal of their least common denominator.

EXAMPLE 7   A Polynomial Function with Rational Coefficients

Find the real zeros of

$$f(x) = x^3 - \frac{2}{3}x^2 + \frac{1}{2}x - \frac{1}{3}.$$

Solution

To find the rational zeros, rewrite $f(x)$ by factoring out the reciprocal of the least common denominator of the coefficients.

$$f(x) = \frac{6}{6}x^3 - \frac{4}{6}x^2 + \frac{3}{6}x - \frac{2}{6} = \frac{1}{6}(6x^3 - 4x^2 + 3x - 2)$$

Now, for the purpose of finding the zeros of f, you can drop the factor $\frac{1}{6}$. This is legitimate because the zeros of f are the same as the zeros of

$$g(x) = 6x^3 - 4x^2 + 3x - 2$$

which has the following possible rational zeros.

$$\frac{\text{Factors of 2}}{\text{Factors of 6}} = \frac{\pm 1, \pm 2}{\pm 1, \pm 2, \pm 3, \pm 6} = \pm 1, \pm\frac{1}{2}, \pm\frac{1}{3}, \pm\frac{1}{6}, \pm\frac{2}{3}, \pm 2$$

Since $f(x)$ has three variations in sign and $f(-x)$ has none, we conclude by Descartes's Rule of Signs that there are three positive real zeros or one positive real zero, and no negative zeros. Trying $x = 1$, we obtain the following.

$$
\begin{array}{r|rrrr}
1 & 6 & -4 & 3 & -2 \\
  &   & 6 & 2 & 5 \\
\hline
  & 6 & 2 & 5 & 3 \end{array} \leftarrow \text{All positive entries}
$$

Thus, $x = 1$ is not a zero, but because the last row has all positive entries, $x = 1$ is an upper bound for the real zeros. Thus, we restrict our search to zeros between 0 and 1. Choosing $x = \frac{2}{3}$, we obtain the following.

$$
\begin{array}{r|rrrr}
\frac{2}{3} & 6 & -4 & 3 & -2 \\
  &   & 4 & 0 & 2 \\
\hline
  & 6 & 0 & 3 & 0 \end{array}
$$

Thus, $f(x)$ factors as

$$f(x) = \frac{1}{6}\left(x - \frac{2}{3}\right)(6x^2 + 3)$$

$$= \frac{1}{6}\left(\frac{1}{3}\right)(3x - 2)(3)(2x^2 + 1)$$

$$= \frac{1}{6}(3x - 2)(2x^2 + 1).$$

Since $2x^2 + 1$ has no real zeros, we conclude that $x = \frac{2}{3}$ is the only real zero of f.

Additional Hints for Finding Zeros of Polynomials

1. If the terms of $f(x)$ have a common monomial factor, it should be factored out before applying the tests in this section. For instance, by writing

$$f(x) = x^4 - 5x^3 + 3x^2 + x$$
$$= x(x^3 - 5x^2 + 3x + 1)$$

   you can see that $x = 0$ is a zero of f and the remaining zeros can be obtained by analyzing the cubic factor.

2. If you are able to find all but two zeros of $f(x)$, then you are home free because you can always use the Quadratic Formula on the remaining quadratic factor. For instance, if you succeeded in writing

$$f(x) = x^4 - 5x^3 + 3x^2 + x$$
$$= x(x - 1)(x^2 - 4x - 1)$$

   then you can apply the Quadratic Formula to $x^2 - 4x - 1$ to find the two remaining zeros.

DISCUSSION

PROBLEM

Comparing Real
Zeros and
Rational Zeros

Compare the *real* zeros of a polynomial function with the *rational* zeros of a polynomial function. Then answer the following questions.

1. Is it possible for a polynomial function to have no rational zeros but to have real zeros? If so, give an example.
2. If a polynomial function has three real zeros, and only one of them is a rational number, then must the other two zeros be irrational numbers?
3. Consider a cubic polynomial function, $f(x) = ax^3 + bx^2 + cx + d$, where $a \neq 0$. Is it possible that f has no real zeros? If so, give an example. Is it possible that f has no rational zeros? If so, give an example.

WARM UP

The following warm-up exercises involve skills that were covered in earlier sections. You will use these skills in the exercise set for this section.

In Exercises 1 and 2, find a polynomial function with integer coefficients having the given zeros.

1. $-1, \frac{2}{3}, 3$

2. $-2, 0, \frac{3}{4}, 2$

In Exercises 3 and 4, divide by synthetic division.

3. $\dfrac{x^5 - 9x^3 + 5x + 18}{x + 3}$

4. $\dfrac{3x^4 + 17x^3 + 10x^2 - 9x - 8}{x + (2/3)}$

In Exercises 5–8, use the given zero to find all the real zeros of f.

Polynomial Equation	Value of x
5. $f(x) = 2x^3 + 11x^2 + 2x - 4$	$x = \frac{1}{2}$
6. $f(x) = 6x^3 - 47x^2 - 124x - 60$	$x = 10$
7. $f(x) = 4x^3 - 13x^2 - 4x + 6$	$x = -\frac{3}{4}$
8. $f(x) = 10x^3 + 51x^2 + 48x - 28$	$x = \frac{2}{5}$

In Exercises 9 and 10, find all real solutions of the polynomial equation.

9. $x^4 - 3x^2 + 2 = 0$

10. $x^4 - 7x^2 + 12 = 0$

EXERCISES for Section 3.4

In Exercises 1–10, use Descartes's Rule of Signs to determine the possible number of positive and negative zeros of the function.

1. $f(x) = x^3 + 3$

2. $g(x) = x^3 + 3x^2$

3. $h(x) = 3x^4 + 2x^2 + 1$

4. $h(x) = 2x^4 - 3x + 2$

5. $g(x) = 2x^3 - 3x^2 - 3$

6. $f(x) = 4x^3 - 3x^2 + 2x - 1$

7. $f(x) = -5x^3 + x^2 - x + 5$

8. $g(x) = 5x^5 + 10x$

9. $h(x) = 4x^2 - 8x + 3$

10. $f(x) = 3x^3 + 2x^2 + x + 3$

In Exercises 11–16, use the Rational Zero Test to list all possible rational zeros of f. Verify that the zeros of f on the graph are contained in the list.

11. $f(x) = x^3 + x^2 - 4x - 4$

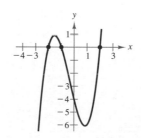

12. $f(x) = -3x^3 + 20x^2 - 36x + 16$

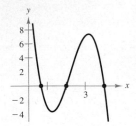

16. $f(x) = 4x^4 - 17x^2 + 4$

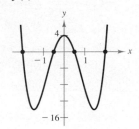

13. $f(x) = -4x^3 + 15x^2 - 8x - 3$

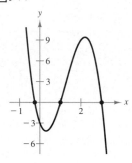

In Exercises 17–20, use synthetic division to determine if the x-value is an upper bound of the zeros of f, a lower bound of the zeros of f, or neither.

17. $f(x) = x^4 - 4x^3 + 15$
  (a) $x = 4$ (b) $x = -1$ (c) $x = 3$

18. $f(x) = 2x^3 - 3x^2 - 12x + 8$
  (a) $x = 2$ (b) $x = 4$ (c) $x = -1$

19. $f(x) = x^4 - 4x^3 + 16x - 16$
  (a) $x = -1$ (b) $x = -3$ (c) $x = 5$

20. $f(x) = 2x^4 - 8x + 3$
  (a) $x = 1$ (b) $x = 3$ (c) $x = -4$

14. $f(x) = 4x^3 - 12x^2 - x + 15$

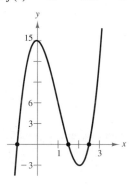

In Exercises 21–36, find the real zeros of the function.

21. $f(x) = x^3 - 6x^2 + 11x - 6$
22. $f(x) = x^3 - 7x - 6$
23. $g(x) = x^3 - 4x^2 - x + 4$
24. $h(x) = x^3 - 9x^2 + 20x - 12$
25. $h(t) = t^3 + 12t^2 + 21t + 10$
26. $f(x) = x^3 + 6x^2 + 12x + 8$
27. $f(x) = x^3 - 4x^2 + 5x - 2$
28. $p(x) = x^3 - 9x^2 + 27x - 27$
29. $C(x) = 2x^3 + 3x^2 - 1$
30. $f(x) = 3x^3 - 19x^2 + 33x - 9$
31. $f(x) = 4x^3 - 3x - 1$
32. $f(z) = 12z^3 - 4z^2 - 27z + 9$
33. $f(y) = 4y^3 + 3y^2 + 8y + 6$
34. $g(x) = 3x^3 - 2x^2 + 15x - 10$
35. $f(x) = x^4 - 3x^2 + 2$
36. $P(t) = t^4 - 7t^2 + 12$

15. $f(x) = -2x^4 + 13x^3 - 21x^2 + 2x + 8$

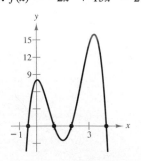

In Exercises 37–44, find all real solutions of the polynomial equation.

37. $z^4 - z^3 - 2z - 4 = 0$

38. $x^4 - x^3 - 29x^2 - x - 30 = 0$

39. $x^4 - 13x^2 - 12x = 0$

40. $2y^4 + 7y^3 - 26y^2 + 23y - 6 = 0$

41. $2x^4 - 11x^3 - 6x^2 + 64x + 32 = 0$

42. $x^5 - x^4 - 3x^3 + 5x^2 - 2x = 0$

43. $x^5 - 7x^4 + 10x^3 + 14x^2 - 24x = 0$

44. $6x^4 - 11x^3 - 51x^2 + 99x - 27 = 0$

In Exercises 45–48, (a) list the possible rational zeros of f, (b) sketch the graph of f so that some of the possible zeros in part (a) can be disregarded, and then (c) determine all real zeros of f.

45. $f(x) = 32x^3 - 52x^2 + 17x + 3$

46. $f(x) = 6x^3 - x^2 - 13x + 8$

47. $f(x) = 4x^3 + 7x^2 - 11x - 18$

48. $f(x) = 2x^3 + 5x^2 - 21x - 10$

In Exercises 49–52, find the rational zeros of the polynomial function.

49. $P(x) = x^4 - \frac{25}{4}x^2 + 9$

50. $f(x) = x^3 - \frac{3}{2}x^2 - \frac{23}{2}x + 6$

51. $f(x) = x^3 - \frac{1}{4}x^2 - x + \frac{1}{4}$

52. $f(z) = z^3 + \frac{11}{6}z^2 - \frac{1}{2}z - \frac{1}{3}$

In Exercises 53–56, match the cubic equation with the number of rational and irrational zeros (a), (b), (c), or (d).

53. $f(x) = x^3 - 1$ **54.** $f(x) = x^3 - 2$

55. $f(x) = x^3 - x$ **56.** $f(x) = x^3 - 2x$

  (a) Rational zeros: 0   (b) Rational zeros: 3
        Irrational zeros: 1   Irrational zeros: 0

  (c) Rational zeros: 1   (d) Rational zeros: 1
        Irrational zeros: 2   Irrational zeros: 0

57. *Dimensions of a Box* An open box is made from a rectangular piece of material, 9 inches by 5 inches, by cutting equal squares from each corner and turning up the sides (see figure). Find the dimensions of the box, given that the volume is to be 18 cubic inches.

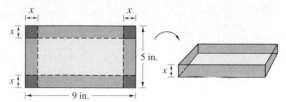

Figure for 57

58. *Dimensions of a Box* An open box is made from a rectangular piece of material, 12 inches by 10 inches, by cutting equal squares from each corner and turning up the sides. Find the dimensions of the box, given that the volume is to be 96 cubic inches.

59. *Dimensions of a Package* A rectangular package to be sent by a postal service can have a maximum combined length and girth (perimeter of a cross section) of 108 inches (see figure). Find the dimensions of the package, given that the volume is to be 11,664 cubic inches.

60. *Dimensions of a Package* A rectangular package to be sent by a postal service can have a maximum combined length and girth (perimeter of a cross section) of 120 inches (see figure). Find the dimensions of the package, given that the volume is to be 16,000 cubic inches.

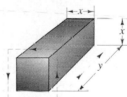

Figure for 59 and 60

3.5 Complex Numbers

The Imaginary Unit i / Operations with Complex Numbers /
Complex Conjugates and Division / Complex Solutions of Quadratic Equations

The Imaginary Unit i

When we introduced the Quadratic Formula in Section 1.5, we noted that some quadratic equations have no real solutions. For instance, the quadratic equation $x^2 + 1 = 0$ has no real solution because there is no real number x that can be squared to produce -1. To overcome this deficiency, mathematicians created an expanded system of numbers using the **imaginary unit i,** defined as

$$i = \sqrt{-1}$$

where $i^2 = -1$. Adding real numbers to real multiples of this imaginary unit gives the set of **complex numbers.** Each complex number can be written in the **standard form,** $a + bi$.

DEFINITION OF A COMPLEX NUMBER

For real numbers a and b, the number

$$a + bi$$

is a **complex number.** If $a = 0$ and $b \neq 0$, then the complex number bi is an **imaginary number.**

The set of real numbers is a subset of the set of complex numbers because every real number a can be written as a complex number using $b = 0$. That is, for every real number a, we can write $a = a + 0i$.

Two complex numbers $a + bi$ and $c + di$, written in standard form, are **equal** to each other

$$a + bi = c + di \qquad \textit{Equality of two complex numbers}$$

if and only if $a = c$ and $b = d$. For instance, $a + 3i = -2 + 3i$ only if $a = -2$.

Operations with Complex Numbers

To add (or subtract) two complex numbers, add (or subtract) the real and imaginary parts of the numbers separately.

ADDITION AND SUBTRACTION OF COMPLEX NUMBERS

If $a + bi$ and $c + di$ are two complex numbers written in standard form, then their sum and difference are defined as follows.

Sum $\qquad (a + bi) + (c + di) = (a + c) + (b + d)i$

Difference $\quad (a + bi) - (c + di) = (a - c) + (b - d)i$

The **additive identity** in the complex number system is zero (the same as in the real number system). Furthermore, the **additive inverse** of the complex number $a + bi$ is

$$-(a + bi) = -a - bi. \qquad\qquad \textit{Additive inverse}$$

Thus, we have

$$(a + bi) + (-a - bi) = 0 + 0i = 0.$$

EXAMPLE 1 Adding and Subtracting Complex Numbers

Write the sums and differences in standard form.

REMARK Note in Example 1(b) that the sum of two complex numbers can be a real number.

a. $(3 - i) + (2 + 3i)$
b. $2i + (-4 - 2i)$
c. $3 - (-2 + 3i) + (-5 + i)$

Solution

a. $(3 - i) + (2 + 3i) = 3 - i + 2 + 3i$ $\qquad$ *Remove parentheses*

$\qquad\qquad\qquad\qquad = 3 + 2 - i + 3i$ $\qquad$ *Group real and imaginary terms*

$\qquad\qquad\qquad\qquad = (3 + 2) + (-1 + 3)i$

$\qquad\qquad\qquad\qquad = 5 + 2i$ $\qquad\qquad$ *Standard form*

b. $2i + (-4 - 2i) = 2i - 4 - 2i$ $\qquad$ *Remove parentheses*

$\qquad\qquad\qquad\qquad = -4 + 2i - 2i$ $\qquad$ *Group real and imaginary terms*

$\qquad\qquad\qquad\qquad = -4$ $\qquad\qquad$ *Standard form*

c. $3 - (-2 + 3i) + (-5 + i) = 3 + 2 - 3i - 5 + i$

$\qquad\qquad\qquad\qquad\qquad = 3 + 2 - 5 - 3i + i$

$\qquad\qquad\qquad\qquad\qquad = 0 - 2i \quad = -2i$

Many of the properties of real numbers are valid for complex numbers as well. For example:

Associative Property of Addition and Multiplication,
Commutative Property of Addition and Multiplication, and
Distributive Property of Multiplication over Addition.

65. *Cost of Clean Water* The cost in millions of dollars for removing $p\%$ of the industrial and municipal pollutants discharged into a river is

$$C = \frac{255p}{100 - p}, \qquad 0 \le p < 100.$$

(a) Find the cost of removing 10% of the pollutants.
(b) Find the cost of removing 40%.
(c) Find the cost of removing 75%.
(d) According to this model, would it be possible to remove 100% of the pollutants?

66. *Recycling Costs* In a pilot project, a rural township was given recycling bins for separating and storing recyclable products. The cost in dollars for giving bins to $p\%$ of the population is

$$C = \frac{25,000p}{100 - p}, \qquad 0 \le p < 100.$$

(a) Find the cost of 15% of the population receiving the bins.
(b) Find the cost of 50% receiving the bins.
(c) Find the cost of 90% receiving the bins.
(d) According to this model, would it be possible to give bins to 100% of the residents?

67. *Deer Population* The game commission introduces 50 deer into newly acquired state game lands. The population of the herd is

$$N = \frac{10(5 + 3t)}{1 + 0.04t}, \qquad 0 \le t$$

where t is the time in years (see figure).
(a) Find the population when t is 5, 10, and 25.
(b) What is the limiting size of the herd as time increases?

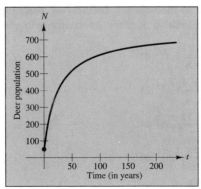

Figure for 67

68. *Food Consumption* A biology class performs an experiment comparing the quantity of food consumed by a certain kind of moth with the quantity supplied (see figure). The model for their experimental data is given by

$$y = \frac{1.568x - 0.001}{6.360x + 1}$$

where x is the quantity (mg) of food supplied and y is the quantity (mg) eaten. At what level of consumption will the moth become satiated?

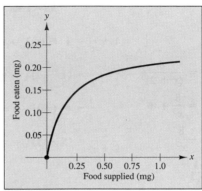

Figure for 68

69. *Average Cost* The cost of producing x units of a product is $C = 150,000 + 0.25x$, and therefore the average cost per unit is

$$\overline{C} = \frac{C}{x} = \frac{150,000 + 0.25x}{x}, \qquad 0 < x.$$

Sketch the graph of this average cost function and find the average cost for producing $x = 1000$, $x = 10,000$, and $x = 100,000$ units.

70. *Average Cost* The cost of producing x units of a product is $C = 0.2x^2 + 10x + 5$, and therefore the average cost per unit is

$$\overline{C} = \frac{C}{x} = \frac{0.2x^2 + 10x + 5}{x}, \qquad 0 < x.$$

Sketch the graph of the average cost function, and estimate the number of units that should be produced to minimize the average cost per unit.

71. *Minimum Area* A right triangle is formed in the first quadrant by the *x*-axis, the *y*-axis, and a line segment through the point (2, 3) (see figure).

(a) Show that an equation of the line segment is

$$y = \frac{3(x - a)}{2 - a}, \qquad 0 \leq x \leq a.$$

(b) Show that the area of the triangle is

$$A = \frac{-3a^2}{2(2 - a)}.$$

(c) Sketch the graph of the area function of part (b), and from the graph estimate the value of *a* that yields a minimum area.

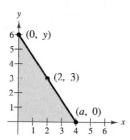

Figure for 71

72. *Human Memory Model* Psychologists have developed mathematical models to predict performance as a function of the number of trials *n* for a certain task. Consider the learning curve given by

$$P = \frac{0.5 + 0.9(n - 1)}{1 + 0.9(n - 1)}, \qquad 0 < n$$

where *P* is the percentage of correct responses after *n* trials.

(a) Complete the following table for this model.

n	1	2	3	4	5	6	7	8	9	10
P										

(b) According to this model, what is the limiting percentage of correct responses as *n* increases?

A graphing utility can be used to investigate asymptotic behavior. For instance, the following example shows how to use a graphing utility to visualize how the average cost of producing a product changes as the number of units produced increases.

EXAMPLE 1   Finding the Average Cost of a Product

You have started a small business to produce copies of compact discs. Your initial investment is $250,000 and the cost of producing each disc is $0.32. Describe the *average cost per unit* of producing each disc as a function of x (the number of units produced).

Solution

The total cost C of producing x units is

$$C = \boxed{\begin{array}{c}\textit{Initial}\\\textit{cost}\end{array}} + \boxed{\begin{array}{c}\textit{Cost per}\\\textit{unit}\end{array}} \cdot \boxed{\begin{array}{c}\textit{Number}\\\textit{of units}\end{array}}$$

$$= 250{,}000 + 0.32x.$$

To obtain the average cost per unit $\overline{C}$ of producing x units, divide the total cost by x.

$$\overline{C} = \frac{C}{x} = \frac{250{,}000 + 0.32x}{x} = \frac{250{,}000}{x} + 0.32$$

The following table shows the average cost per unit for several different levels of production.

$\overline{C}$

Average cost (in dollars)

Number of units (in millions)

Number of units, x	100	1000	10,000	100,000	1,000,000	10,000,000
Total cost, C	$250,032	$250,320	$253,200	$282,000	$570,000	$3,450,000
Average cost, $\overline{C}$	$2500.32	$250.32	$25.32	$2.82	$0.57	$0.345

The graph of the average cost function is shown at the left together with the graph of the horizontal line $y = 0.32$. Notice that as the number of units produced increases, the average cost per unit gets closer and closer to the unit cost of $0.32.

In Example 1, it is assumed that the production level can continue to increase without having to invest additional capital. Example 2 shows how the problem changes when additional capital investments are required.

EXAMPLE 2 Finding the Minimum Average Cost

As the production level in Example 1 increases and the business grows, suppose that you must invest additional capital to buy more equipment, hire more employees, advertise, build new offices, and so on. You have determined that the additional investments are proportional to the square of the number of units produced, and you have derived the following model for the total cost of producing x units.

$$C = 250,000 + 0.32x + 0.00001x^2.$$

Describe the average cost per unit as a function of the number of units produced.

Solution

With this model for the total cost, the average cost function is

$$\overline{C} = \frac{250,000 + 0.32x + 0.00001x^2}{x} = \frac{250,000}{x} + 0.32 + 0.00001x.$$

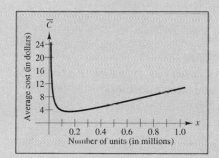

The graph of the average cost function is shown at the left. With this model, notice that the average cost decreases until the production level reaches about 150,000 or 160,000 units. Then, with increased production, the average cost per unit increases.

EXERCISES

(See also: Exercises 67–70, Section 3.7)

1. *Exploration* In Example 1, would it be possible to produce enough units so that the average cost is exactly $0.32? Would it be possible to produce enough units so that the average cost is arbitrarily close to $0.32? Explain.

2. *Exploration* In Example 1, how many units should be produced to obtain an average cost per unit of $0.33? To answer this question, did you use a numerical approach, an algebraic approach, or a graphical approach? Explain why you chose the approach you used.

3. *Exploration* In Example 2, use the zoom feature of a graphing utility to approximate the *minimum* average cost. At what production level does this minimum average cost occur?

4. *Slant Asymptote* The graph shown in Example 2 has a slant asymptote. Find its equation, sketch its graph, and interpret it in the context of the problem.

5. *Economy of Scale* In business, the expression *economy of scale* means that the average cost per unit tends to decrease as the production level increases. Judging from Examples 1 and 2 *and* your own knowledge of business, what factors could temper an economy of scale in a business?

6. *Testing a Hypothesis* Which graph has the x-axis as an asymptote? Which has a horizontal asymptote that is not the x-axis? Which has a slant asymptote?

(a) $y = \dfrac{3}{2x + 1},\quad 0 \le x$

(b) $y = \dfrac{3x}{2x + 1},\quad 0 \le x$

(c) $y = \dfrac{3x^2}{2x + 1},\quad 0 \le x$

Form a hypothesis about the horizontal or slant asymptotes of the graph of

$$y = \frac{ax^n}{bx + 1}.$$

Test your hypothesis with examples.

257

 Partial Fractions

Introduction / Partial Fraction Decomposition

Introduction

In Section 1.4, you learned how to combine two or more rational expressions using a least common denominator (LCD). In this section, we reverse the problem (a useful procedure in calculus) and write a given rational expression as the sum of two or more simpler rational expressions. For example, the rational expression $(x + 7)/(x^2 - x - 6)$ can be written as the sum of two fractions with first-degree denominators. That is,

$$\frac{x + 7}{x^2 - x - 6} = \frac{2}{x - 3} + \frac{-1}{x + 2}.$$

Each fraction on the right side of the equation is a **partial fraction,** and together they make up the **partial fraction decomposition** of the left side.

Earlier, we noted that it is theoretically possible to write any polynomial as the product of linear and irreducible quadratic factors. For instance,

$$x^5 + x^4 - x - 1 = (x - 1)(x + 1)^2(x^2 + 1)$$

where $(x - 1)$ is a linear factor, $(x + 1)$ is a repeated linear factor, and $(x^2 + 1)$ is an irreducible quadratic factor.

We can use this factorization to find the partial fraction decomposition of any rational expression having $x^5 + x^4 - x - 1$ as its denominator. Specifically, if $N(x)$ is a polynomial of degree 4 or less, then the partial fraction decomposition of $N(x)/(x^5 + x^4 - x - 1)$ has the form

$$\frac{N(x)}{x^5 + x^4 - x - 1} = \frac{N(x)}{(x - 1)(x + 1)^2(x^2 + 1)}$$
$$= \frac{A}{x - 1} + \frac{B}{x + 1} + \frac{C}{(x + 1)^2} + \frac{Dx + F}{x^2 + 1}.$$

Note that the factor $(x + 1)^2$ results in *two* fractions: one for $(x + 1)$ and one for $(x + 1)^2$. If $(x + 1)^3$ were a factor, then we would use three fractions: one for $(x + 1)$, one for $(x + 1)^2$, and one for $(x + 1)^3$. In general, the number of fractions resulting from a repeated factor is equal to the exponent of the factor. Note also that an irreducible quadratic factor like $x^2 + 1$ must have a linear numerator.

Decomposition of $N(x)/D(x)$ into Partial Fractions

1. *Divide if improper:* If $N(x)/D(x)$ is an improper fraction, then divide the denominator into the numerator to obtain

$$\frac{N(x)}{D(x)} = \text{(polynomial)} + \frac{N_1(x)}{D(x)}$$

and apply Steps 2, 3, and 4 (below) to the proper rational expression $N_1(x)/D(x)$.

2. *Factor denominator:* Completely factor the denominator into factors of the form

$$(px + q)^m \quad \text{and} \quad (ax^2 + bx + c)^n$$

where $(ax^2 + bx + c)$ is irreducible.

3. *Linear factors:* For *each* factor the form $(px + q)^m$, the partial fraction decomposition must include the following sum of m fractions.

$$\frac{A_1}{(px + q)} + \frac{A_2}{(px + q)^2} + \cdots + \frac{A_m}{(px + q)^m}$$

4. *Quadratic factors:* For *each* factor of the form $(ax^2 + bx + c)^n$, the partial fraction decomposition must include the following sum of n fractions.

$$\frac{B_1 x + C_1}{ax^2 + bx + c} + \frac{B_2 x + C_2}{(ax^2 + bx + c)^2} + \cdots + \frac{B_n x + C_n}{(ax^2 + bx + c)^n}$$

Partial Fraction Decomposition

Algebraic techniques for determining the constants in the numerators of the partial fractions are demonstrated in the examples that follow. Note that the techniques vary slightly, depending on the type of factors of the denominator: linear or quadratic, distinct or repeated.

EXAMPLE 1   Distinct Linear Factors

Write the partial fraction decomposition for

$$\frac{x + 7}{x^2 - x - 6}.$$

Solution

Since $x^2 - x - 6 = (x - 3)(x + 2)$, we include one partial fraction with a constant numerator for each linear factor of the denominator and write

$$\frac{x + 7}{x^2 - x - 6} = \frac{A}{x - 3} + \frac{B}{x + 2}.$$

Multiplying both sides of this equation by the least common denominator, $(x - 3)(x + 2)$, leads to the **basic equation**

$$x + 7 = A(x + 2) + B(x - 3).\qquad \textit{Basic equation}$$

Because this equation is true for all x, you can substitute any *convenient* values of x which will help determine the constants A and B. Values of x that are especially convenient are ones that make the factors $(x + 2)$ and $(x - 3)$ equal to zero. For instance, let $x = -2$. Then

$$-2 + 7 = A(0) + B(-5)\qquad \textit{Substitute convenient value of x}$$
$$5 = -5B$$
$$-1 = B.$$

To solve for A, let $x = 3$ to obtain

$$3 + 7 = A(5) + B(0)\qquad \textit{Substitute convenient value of x}$$
$$10 = 5A$$
$$2 = A.$$

Therefore, the decomposition is

$$\frac{x + 7}{x^2 - x - 6} = \frac{2}{x - 3} - \frac{1}{x + 2}$$

as indicated at the beginning of this section. Check this result by combining the two partial fractions on the right side of the equation.   ◢

EXAMPLE 2   Repeated Linear Factors

Write the partial fraction decomposition for

$$\frac{5x^2 + 20x + 6}{x^3 + 2x^2 + x}.$$

Solution

Since the denominator factors as

$$x^3 + 2x^2 + x = x(x^2 + 2x + 1) = x(x + 1)^2$$

we include one fraction with a constant numerator for each power of x and $(x + 1)$ and write

$$\frac{5x^2 + 20x + 6}{x(x + 1)^2} = \frac{A}{x} + \frac{B}{x + 1} + \frac{C}{(x + 1)^2}.$$

Multiplying by the LCD, $x(x + 1)^2$, leads to the basic equation

$$5x^2 + 20x + 6 = A(x + 1)^2 + Bx(x + 1) + Cx.\quad \textit{Basic equation}$$

Letting $x = -1$ eliminates the A and B terms and yields

$$5 - 20 + 6 = 0 + 0 - C \qquad \textit{Substitute convenient value of x}$$
$$C = 9.$$

Letting $x = 0$ eliminates the B and C terms and yields

$$6 = A(1) + 0 + 0 \qquad \textit{Substitute convenient value of x}$$
$$6 = A.$$

At this point, we have exhausted the most convenient choices for x, so to find the value of B, use *any other value* for x along with the known values of A and C. Thus, using $x = 1$, $A = 6$, and $C = 9$,

$$5 + 20 + 6 = A(4) + B(2) + C$$
$$31 = 6(4) + 2B + 9$$
$$-2 = 2B$$
$$-1 = B.$$

Therefore, the partial fraction decomposition is

$$\frac{5x^2 + 20x + 6}{x(x + 1)^2} = \frac{6}{x} - \frac{1}{x + 1} + \frac{9}{(x + 1)^2}.$$

The procedure used to solve for the constants $A, B, C, \ldots$ in Examples 1 and 2 works well when the factors of the denominator are linear. However, when the denominator contains irreducible quadratic factors, we use a different procedure, which involves writing the right side of the basic equation in polynomial form and *equating the coefficients* of like terms.

EXAMPLE 3   Distinct Linear and Quadratic Factors

Write the partial fraction decomposition for

$$\frac{3x^2 + 4x + 4}{x^3 + 4x}.$$

Solution

Since the denominator factors as

$$x^3 + 4x = x(x^2 + 4)$$

we include one partial fraction with a constant numerator and one partial fraction with a linear numerator and write

$$\frac{3x^2 + 4x + 4}{x^3 + 4x} = \frac{A}{x} + \frac{Bx + C}{x^2 + 4}.$$

Multiplying by the LCD, $x(x^2 + 4)$, yields the basic equation

$$3x^2 + 4x + 4 = A(x^2 + 4) + (Bx + C)x. \qquad \textit{Basic equation}$$

Expanding this basic equation and collecting like terms produces

$$3x^2 + 4x + 4 = Ax^2 + 4A + Bx^2 + Cx$$
$$= (A + B)x^2 + Cx + 4A. \qquad \textit{Polynomial form}$$

Finally, because two polynomials are equal if and only if the coefficients of like terms are equal,

$$3x^2 + 4x + 4 = (A + B)x^2 + Cx + 4A \qquad \textit{Equate coefficients} \\ \textit{of like terms}$$

we obtain the following equations.

$$3 = A + B, \qquad 4 = C, \qquad \text{and} \qquad 4 = 4A$$

Thus, $A = 1$ and $C = 4$. Moreover, substituting $A = 1$ in the equation $3 = A + B$ yields

$$3 = 1 + B$$
$$2 = B.$$

Therefore, the partial fraction decomposition is

$$\frac{3x^2 + 4x + 4}{x^3 + 4x} = \frac{1}{x} + \frac{2x + 4}{x^2 + 4}.$$

EXAMPLE 4   Repeated Quadratic Factors

Write the partial fraction decomposition for

$$\frac{8x^3 + 13x}{(x^2 + 2)^2}.$$

Solution

We include one partial fraction with a linear numerator for each power of $(x^2 + 2)$, and write

$$\frac{8x^3 + 13x}{(x^2 + 2)^2} = \frac{Ax + B}{x^2 + 2} + \frac{Cx + D}{(x^2 + 2)^2}.$$

Multiplying by the LCD, $(x^2 + 2)^2$, yields the basic equation

$$8x^3 + 13x = (Ax + B)(x^2 + 2) + Cx + D \qquad \textit{Basic equation}$$
$$= Ax^3 + 2Ax + Bx^2 + 2B + Cx + D$$
$$= Ax^3 + Bx^2 + (2A + C)x + (2B + D). \quad \textit{Polynomial form}$$

REMARK By equating coefficients of like terms in Examples 3 and 4, you obtained several equations involving A, B, C, and D, which were solved by *substitution*. In Chapter 8 we will discuss a more general method for solving systems of equations.

Equating coefficients of like terms,

$$8x^3 + 0x^2 + 13x + 0 = Ax^3 + Bx^2 + (2A + C)x + (2B + D)$$

produces

$$8 = A, \quad 0 = B, \quad 13 = 2A + C, \quad \text{and} \quad 0 = 2B + D. \quad \textit{Equate coefficients}$$

Finally, use the values $A = 8$ and $B = 0$ to obtain the following.

$$13 = 2A + C = 2(8) + C \qquad 0 = 2B + D = 2(0) + D$$
$$-3 = C \qquad\qquad\qquad\qquad 0 = D$$

Therefore,

$$\frac{8x^3 + 13x}{(x^2 + 2)^2} = \frac{8x}{x^2 + 2} + \frac{-3x}{(x^2 + 2)^2}.$$

Guidelines for Solving the Basic Equation

Linear Factors

1. Substitute the *zeros* of the distinct linear factors into the basic equation.
2. For repeated linear factors, use the coefficients determined above to rewrite the basic equation. Then substitute *other* convenient values for x and solve for the remaining coefficients.

Quadratic Factors

1. Expand the basic equation.
2. Collect terms according to powers of x.
3. Equate the coefficients of like terms to obtain equations involving A, B, C, and so on.
4. Use substitution to solve for A, B, C, ...

Keep in mind that for *improper* rational expressions like

$$\frac{N(x)}{D(x)} = \frac{2x^3 + x^2 - 7x + 7}{x^2 + x - 2}$$

you must first divide to obtain the form

$$\frac{N(x)}{D(x)} = (\text{polynomial}) + \frac{N_1(x)}{D(x)}.$$

The proper rational expression $N_1(x)/D(x)$ is then decomposed into its partial fractions by the usual methods.

DISCUSSION

PROBLEM

You Be
the
Instructor

Suppose you were tutoring a student in algebra. In trying to find a partial fraction decomposition, your student wrote the following.

$$\frac{x^2 + 1}{x(x - 1)} = \frac{A}{x} + \frac{B}{x - 1}$$

$$\frac{x^2 + 1}{x(x - 1)} = \frac{A(x - 1)}{x(x - 1)} + \frac{Bx}{x(x - 1)}$$

$$x^2 + 1 = A(x - 1) + Bx \qquad\qquad \textit{Basic equation}$$

By substituting $x = 0$ and $x = 1$ into the basic equation, your student concluded that $A = -1$ and $B = 2$. However, in checking this solution, your student obtained

$$\frac{-1}{x} + \frac{2}{x - 1} = \frac{(-1)(x - 1) + 2(x)}{x(x - 1)} = \frac{x + 1}{x(x - 1)} \neq \frac{x^2 + 1}{x(x - 1)}.$$

What went wrong?

WARM UP

The following warm-up exercises involve skills that were covered in earlier sections. You will use these skills in the exercise set for this section.

In Exercises 1–10, find the sum and simplify.

1. $\dfrac{2}{x} + \dfrac{3}{x + 1}$

2. $\dfrac{5}{x + 2} + \dfrac{3}{x}$

3. $\dfrac{7}{x - 2} - \dfrac{3}{2x - 1}$

4. $\dfrac{2}{x + 5} - \dfrac{5}{x + 12}$

5. $\dfrac{1}{x - 3} + \dfrac{3}{(x - 3)^2} - \dfrac{5}{(x - 3)^3}$

6. $\dfrac{-5}{x + 2} + \dfrac{4}{(x + 2)^2}$

7. $\dfrac{-3}{x} + \dfrac{3x - 1}{x^2 + 3}$

8. $\dfrac{5}{x + 1} - \dfrac{x - 6}{x^2 + 5}$

9. $\dfrac{3}{x^2 + 1} + \dfrac{x - 3}{(x^2 + 1)^2}$

10. $\dfrac{x}{x^2 + x + 1} - \dfrac{x - 1}{(x^2 + x + 1)^2}$

EXERCISES for Section 3.8

In Exercises 1–36, write the partial fraction decomposition for the rational expression.

1. $\dfrac{1}{x^2 - 1}$

2. $\dfrac{1}{4x^2 - 9}$

3. $\dfrac{1}{x^2 + x}$

4. $\dfrac{3}{x^2 - 3x}$

5. $\dfrac{1}{2x^2 + x}$

6. $\dfrac{5}{x^2 + x - 6}$

7. $\dfrac{3}{x^2 + x - 2}$

8. $\dfrac{x + 1}{x^2 + 4x + 3}$

9. $\dfrac{5 - x}{2x^2 + x - 1}$

10. $\dfrac{3x^2 - 7x - 2}{x^3 - x}$

11. $\dfrac{x^2 + 12x + 12}{x^3 - 4x}$

12. $\dfrac{x + 2}{x(x - 4)}$

13. $\dfrac{4x^2 + 2x - 1}{x^2(x + 1)}$

14. $\dfrac{2x - 3}{(x - 1)^2}$

15. $\dfrac{x - 1}{x^3 + x^2}$

16. $\dfrac{4x^2 - 1}{2x(x + 1)^2}$

17. $\dfrac{3x}{(x - 3)^2}$

18. $\dfrac{6x^2 + 1}{x^2(x - 1)^3}$

19. $\dfrac{x^2 - 1}{x(x^2 + 1)}$

20. $\dfrac{x}{(x - 1)(x^2 + x + 1)}$

21. $\dfrac{x^2}{x^4 - 2x^2 - 8}$

22. $\dfrac{2x^2 + x + 8}{(x^2 + 4)^2}$

23. $\dfrac{x}{16x^4 - 1}$

24. $\dfrac{x^2 - 4x + 7}{(x + 1)(x^2 - 2x + 3)}$

25. $\dfrac{x^2 + x + 2}{(x^2 + 2)^2}$

26. $\dfrac{x^3}{(x + 2)^2(x - 2)^2}$

27. $\dfrac{x^2 + 5}{(x + 1)(x^2 - 2x + 3)}$

28. $\dfrac{x + 1}{x^3 + x}$

29. $\dfrac{2x^3 - 4x^2 - 15x + 5}{x^2 - 2x - 8}$

30. $\dfrac{x^3 - x + 3}{x^2 + x - 2}$

31. $\dfrac{x^4}{(x - 1)^3}$

32. $\dfrac{x^2 - x}{x^2 + x + 1}$

33. $\dfrac{1}{a^2 - x^2}$, a is a constant

34. $\dfrac{1}{x(x + a)}$, a is a constant

35. $\dfrac{1}{y(L - y)}$, L is a constant

36. $\dfrac{1}{(x + 1)(n - x)}$, n is a positive integer

REVIEW EXERCISES for Chapter 3

In Exercises 1–4, sketch the graph of the quadratic function. Identify the vertex and the intercepts.

1. $f(x) = \left(x + \frac{3}{2}\right)^2 + 1$

2. $f(x) = (x - 4)^2 - 4$

3. $f(x) = \frac{1}{3}(x^2 + 5x - 4)$

4. $f(x) = 3x^2 - 12x + 11$

In Exercises 5 and 6, find the quadratic function that has the indicated vertex and whose graph passes through the given point.

5. Vertex: $(1, -4)$; point: $(2, -3)$

6. Vertex: $(2, 3)$; point: $(-1, 6)$

In Exercises 7–14, find the maximum or minimum value of the quadratic function.

7. $g(x) = x^2 - 2x$

8. $f(x) = x^2 + 8x + 10$

9. $f(x) = 6x - x^2$

10. $f(x) = 3 + 4x - x^2$

11. $f(t) = -2t^2 + 4t + 1$

12. $h(x) = 4x^2 + 4x + 13$

13. $h(x) = x^2 + 5x - 4$

14. $f(x) = 4x^2 + 4x + 5$

15. *Maximum Area* A rectangle is inscribed in the region bounded by the x-axis, the y-axis, and the graph of $x + 2y - 6 = 0$ (see figure). Find the coordinates (x, y) that yield a maximum area for the rectangle.

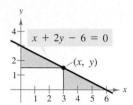

Figure for 15

16. *Maximum Area* The perimeter of a rectangle is 200 feet. Let x represent the width of the rectangle and write a quadratic function that expresses the area of the rectangle in terms of x. Of all possible rectangles with a perimeter of 200 feet, find the dimensions of the one that has the greatest area.

17. *Maximum Revenue* Find the number of units x that produce a maximum revenue R, where
$$R = 900x - 0.1x^2.$$

18. *Maximum Profit* Let x be the amount (in hundreds of dollars) that a company spends on advertising, and let P be the profit, where
$$P = 230 + 20x - \tfrac{1}{2}x^2.$$
What amount of advertising will yield a maximum profit?

19. *Maximum Profit* A real estate office handles 50 apartment units. When the rent is $540 per month, all units are occupied. However, for each $30 increase in rent, one unit becomes vacant. Each occupied unit requires an average of $18 per month for service and repairs. What rent should be charged to realize the most profit?

20. *Minimum Cost* A manufacturer has daily production costs of
$$C = 20,000 - 120x + 0.055x^2$$
where C is the total cost in dollars and x is the number of units produced. How many units should be produced each day to yield a minimum cost?

In Exercises 21–24, determine the right-hand and left-hand behavior of the graph of the polynomial function.

21. $f(x) = -x^2 + 6x + 9$

22. $f(x) = \tfrac{1}{2}x^3 + 2x$

23. $g(x) = \tfrac{3}{4}(x^4 + 3x^2 + 2)$

24. $h(x) = -x^5 - 7x^2 + 10x$

In Exercises 25–32, sketch the graph of the function.

25. $f(x) = -(x - 2)^3$

26. $f(x) = (x + 1)^3$

27. $g(x) = x^4 - x^3 - 2x^2$

28. $h(x) = -2x^3 - x^2 + x$

29. $f(t) = t^3 - 3t$

30. $f(x) = -x^3 + 3x - 2$

31. $f(x) = x(x + 3)^2$

32. $f(t) = t^4 - 4t^2$

In Exercises 33–40, perform the indicated division.

33. $\dfrac{24x^2 - x - 8}{3x - 2}$

34. $\dfrac{4x + 7}{3x - 2}$

35. $\dfrac{x^4 + x^3 - x^2 + 2x}{x^2 + 2x}$

36. $\dfrac{5x^3 - 13x^2 - x + 2}{x^2 - 3x + 1}$

37. $\dfrac{x^4 - 3x^2 + 2}{x^2 - 1}$

38. $\dfrac{3x^4}{x^2 - 1}$

39. $\dfrac{x^4 - 3x^3 + 4x^2 - 6x + 3}{x^2 + 2}$

40. $\dfrac{6x^4 + 10x^3 + 13x^2 - 5x + 2}{2x^2 - 1}$

In Exercises 41–50, perform the indicated operations and write the result in standard form.

41. $\left(\dfrac{\sqrt{2}}{2} - \dfrac{\sqrt{2}}{2}i\right) - \left(\dfrac{\sqrt{2}}{2} + \dfrac{\sqrt{2}}{2}i\right)$

42. $(13 - 8i) - 5i$

43. $5i(13 - 8i)$

44. $(1 + 6i)(5 - 2i)$

45. $(10 - 8i)(2 - 3i)$

46. $i(6 + i)(3 - 2i)$

47. $\dfrac{6 + i}{i}$

48. $\dfrac{3 + 2i}{5 + i}$

49. $\dfrac{4}{-3i}$

50. $\dfrac{1}{(2 + i)^4}$

In Exercises 51–56, use synthetic division to perform the indicated division.

51. $\dfrac{0.25x^4 - 4x^3}{x - 2}$

52. $\dfrac{2x^3 + 2x^2 - x + 2}{x - (1/2)}$

53. $\dfrac{6x^4 - 4x^3 - 27x^2 + 18x}{x - (2/3)}$

54. $\dfrac{0.1x^3 + 0.3x^2 - 0.5}{x - 5}$

55. $\dfrac{2x^3 - 5x^2 + 12x - 5}{x - (1 + 2i)}$

56. $\dfrac{9x^3 - 15x^2 + 11x - 5}{x - [(1/3) + (2/3)i]}$

In Exercises 57–60, use synthetic division to determine whether the given values of x are zeros of the function.

57. $f(x) = 2x^3 + 3x^2 - 20x - 21$
  (a) $x = 4$
  (b) $x = -1$
  (c) $x = -\frac{7}{2}$
  (d) $x = 0$

58. $f(x) = 20x^4 + 9x^3 - 14x^2 - 3x$
  (a) $x = -1$
  (b) $x = \frac{3}{4}$
  (c) $x = 0$
  (d) $x = 1$

59. $f(x) = 2x^3 + 7x^2 - 18x - 30$
  (a) $x = 1$
  (b) $x = \frac{5}{2}$
  (c) $x = -3 + \sqrt{3}$
  (d) $x = 0$

60. $f(x) = 3x^3 - 26x^2 + 364x - 232$
  (a) $x = 4 - 10i$
  (b) $x = 4$
  (c) $x = \frac{2}{3}$
  (d) $x = -1$

In Exercises 61–64, use synthetic division to find the specified value of the function.

61. $g(x) = 2x^4 - 17x^3 + 58x^2 - 77x + 26$
  (a) $g(-2)$
  (b) $g(\frac{1}{2})$

62. $h(x) = 5x^5 - 2x^4 - 45x + 18$
  (a) $h(2)$
  (b) $h(\sqrt{3})$

63. $f(x) = x^4 + 10x^3 - 24x^2 + 20x + 44$
  (a) $f(-3)$
  (b) $f(\sqrt{2}i)$

64. $g(t) = 2t^5 - 5t^4 - 8t + 20$
  (a) $g(-4)$
  (b) $g(\sqrt{2})$

In Exercises 65–68, find a polynomial with integer coefficients that has the given zeros.

65. $-1, -1, \frac{1}{3}, -\frac{1}{2}$

66. $5, 1 - \sqrt{2}, 1 + \sqrt{2}$

67. $\frac{2}{3}, 4, \sqrt{3}i, -\sqrt{3}i$

68. $2, -3, 1 - 2i, 1 + 2i$

In Exercises 69–74, find all the zeros of the function.

69. $f(x) = 4x^3 - 11x^2 + 10x - 3$

70. $f(x) = 10x^3 + 21x^2 - x - 6$

71. $f(x) = 6x^3 - 5x^2 + 24x - 20$

72. $f(x) = x^3 - 1.3x^2 - 1.7x + 0.6$

73. $f(x) = 6x^4 - 25x^3 + 14x^2 + 27x - 18$

74. $f(x) = 5x^4 + 126x^2 + 25$

In Exercises 75–84, sketch the graph of the rational function. As sketching aids, check for intercept, symmetry, vertical asymptotes, horizontal asymptotes, and slant asymptotes.

75. $g(x) = \dfrac{2 + x}{1 - x}$

76. $h(x) = \dfrac{x - 3}{x - 2}$

77. $f(x) = \dfrac{x}{x^2 + 1}$

78. $f(x) = \dfrac{2x}{x^2 + 4}$

79. $P(x) = \dfrac{x^2}{x^2 + 1}$

80. $s(x) = \dfrac{2x^2}{x^2 + 4}$

81. $y = \dfrac{x}{x^2 - 1}$

82. $y = \dfrac{2x}{x^2 - 4}$

83. $y = \dfrac{2x^2}{x^2 - 4}$

84. $g(x) = \dfrac{x^2 + 1}{x + 1}$

85. *Seizure of Illegal Drugs* The cost in millions of dollars for the federal government to seize $p\%$ of an illegal drug as it enters the country is given by

$$C = \frac{528p}{100 - p}, \qquad 0 \le p < 100.$$

(a) Find the cost of seizing 25%.

(b) Find the cost of seizing 50%.

(c) Find the cost of seizing 75%.

(d) According to this model, would it be possible to seize 100% of the drug?

86. *Average Cost* A business has a cost of $C = 0.5x + 500$ for producing x units. The average cost per unit is

$$\bar{C} = \frac{C}{x} = \frac{0.5x + 500}{x}, \qquad 0 < x.$$

Determine the average cost per unit as x increases without bound. (Find the horizontal asymptote.)

87. *Capillary Attraction* The rise of distilled water in tubes x inches in diameter is approximated by the model

$$y = \left(\frac{0.80 - 0.54x}{1 + 2.72x}\right)^2, \qquad 0 < x$$

where y is measured in inches (see figure). Approximate the diameter of the tube that will cause the water to rise 0.1 inch.

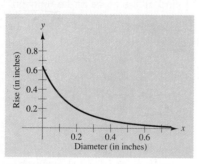

Figure for 87

88. *Population of Fish* The Parks and Wildlife Commission introduces 80,000 fish into a large manmade lake. The population of the fish in thousands is given by

$$N = \frac{20(4 + 3t)}{1 + 0.05t}, \qquad 0 \le t$$

where t is the time in years.

(a) Find the population when t is 5, 10, and 25.

(b) What is the limiting number of fish in the lake as time increases?

In Exercises 89–94, write the partial fraction decomposition for the rational expression.

89. $\dfrac{4 - x}{x^2 + 6x + 8}$

90. $\dfrac{9}{x^2 - 9}$

91. $\dfrac{x^2 + 2x}{x^3 - x^2 + x - 1}$

92. $\dfrac{4x - 2}{3(x - 1)^2}$

93. $\dfrac{3x^3 + 4x}{(x^2 + 1)^2}$

94. $\dfrac{4x^2}{(x - 1)(x^2 + 1)}$

CUMULATIVE TEST for Chapters 1–3

Take this test as you would take a test in class. After you are done, check your work with the answers given in the back of the book.

1. Simplify: $\dfrac{8x^2y^{-3}}{30x^{-1}y^2}$

2. Simplify: $\sqrt{24x^4y^3}$

3. Factor completely: $x - 5x^2 - 6x^3$

4. Subtract and simplify: $\dfrac{2}{s + 3} - \dfrac{1}{s + 1}$

5. Simplify: $\dfrac{\dfrac{2x + 1}{2\sqrt{x}} - \sqrt{x}}{2x + 1}$

6. Solve: $-5(x + 3) + 2x = 3(2x - 7)$

7. Solve: $2\left(x + \dfrac{10}{x}\right) = 13$

8. Solve: $x^2 + 4x + 5 = 0$

9. Solve: $\sqrt{9x + 7} - x = 3$

10. Solve and sketch the solution on the real number line: $\left|\dfrac{x - 2}{3}\right| < 1$

11. Given the points $(-1, 3)$ and $(5, 0)$, find (a) the distance between them and (b) an equation of a line through them.

12. Sketch a graph of the equation $2x - 3y - 6 = 0$.

13. Sketch a graph of the equation $x^2 + y^2 - 6y = 0$.

14. Given the function $f(x) = 3 - x^2$, evaluate and/or simplify each of the following

    (a) $f(3)$ (b) $\dfrac{f(1 + h) - f(1)}{h}$

15. Find $f \circ g$ if $f(x) = \sqrt{x}$ and $g(x) = x^2 + 3$.

16. Find the inverse of the function $F(x) = 2x + 5$

17. Three gallons of a mixture is 60% water by volume. Determine the number of gallons of water that must be added to bring the mixture to 75% water.

18. Let x be the amount (in hundreds of dollars) that a company spends on advertising, and let P be the profit, where

    $P = 230 + 20x - \frac{1}{2}x^2$.

    What amount of advertising will yield maximum profit?

19. Use synthetic division to perform the division: $\dfrac{3x^3 - 5x + 4}{x - 2}$

20. Find all the zeros of the function $f(x) = x^3 + 2x^2 + 4x + 8$.

21. Use the Bisection Method to approximate the real zero of the function $g(x) = x^3 + 3x^2 - 6$ to the nearest hundredth.

22. Sketch a graph of the function $g(s) = \dfrac{2s^2}{s - 3}$.

C H A P T E R 4

OVERVIEW

This chapter discusses two types of functions—exponential and logarithmic functions.

A quantity is said to grow or decay *exponentially* if its rate of growth is proportional to its size. Many real-life quantities grow or decay exponentially. For instance, the balance in a savings account *grows* exponentially (see Example 9 on page 278), and the amount of a radioactive material *decays* exponentially (see Example 10 on page 279).

In the chapter, you will study two uses of logarithmic functions. First, you will study real-life situations that can be modeled with logarithmic functions. Second, you will learn how to use the inverse relationship between exponential and logarithmic functions to solve exponential and logarithmic equations.

Exponential and Logarithmic Functions

4.1 Exponential Functions

Introduction / Graphs of Exponential Functions / The Natural Base *e* / Compound Interest / Other Applications

Introduction

Thus far in the text, we have dealt only with **algebraic functions,** which include polynomial functions and rational functions. In this chapter you will study two types of nonalgebraic functions—*exponential* functions and *logarithmic* functions. These functions are **transcendental functions.**

Exponential functions are widely used in describing economic and physical phenomena such as compound interest, population growth, memory retention, and decay of radioactive material. Exponential functions involve a *constant base* and a *variable exponent* such as

$$f(x) = 2^x \quad \text{or} \quad g(x) = 3^{-x}.$$

DEFINITION OF EXPONENTIAL FUNCTION

The **exponential function** f **with base** a is denoted by

$$f(x) = a^x$$

where $a > 0$, $a \neq 1$, and x is any real number.

271

REMARK   We exclude the base $a = 1$ because it yields $f(x) = 1^x = 1$, which is a constant function, not an exponential function.

In Section 1.2 you learned to evaluate a^x for integer and rational values of x. For example, we know that

$$8^3 = 8 \cdot 8 \cdot 8 = 512 \qquad \text{and} \qquad 8^{2/3} = (\sqrt[3]{8})^2 = (2)^2 = 4.$$

However, to evaluate 8^x for any real number x, we need to interpret forms with *irrational* exponents, such as $8^{\sqrt{2}}$ and 8^{π}. A technical definition of such forms is beyond the scope of this text. For our purposes, it is sufficient to think of

$$a^{\sqrt{2}} \qquad (\text{where } \sqrt{2} \approx 1.414214)$$

as that value which has the successively closer approximations

$$a^{1.4}, \ a^{1.41}, \ a^{1.414}, \ a^{1.4142}, \ a^{1.41421}, \ a^{1.414214}, \ \ldots \ .$$

Consequently, we assume in this text that a^x exists for all real x and that the properties of exponents (Section 1.3) can be extended to cover exponential functions. For instance,

$$a^{-x} = \frac{1}{a^x} = \left(\frac{1}{a}\right)^x.$$

EXAMPLE 1   Using a Calculator to Evaluate Exponential Expressions

Number	Keystrokes	Display
$(1.085)^3$	1.085 $\boxed{y^x}$ 3 $\boxed{=}$	1.277289
$12^{5/7}$	12 $\boxed{y^x}$ $\boxed{(}$ 5 $\boxed{\div}$ 7 $\boxed{)}$ $\boxed{=}$	5.899888
$2^{-\pi}$	2 $\boxed{y^x}$ π $\boxed{+/-}$ $\boxed{=}$	0.1133147

Graphs of Exponential Functions

EXAMPLE 2   Graphs of $y = a^x$

On the same coordinate plane, sketch the graphs of the following functions.

a. $f(x) = 2^x$ **b.** $g(x) = 4^x$

Solution

Table 4.1 lists some values for each function, and Figure 4.1 shows their graphs. Note that both graphs are increasing. Moreover, the graph of $g(x) = 4^x$ is increasing more rapidly than the graph of $f(x) = 2^x$.

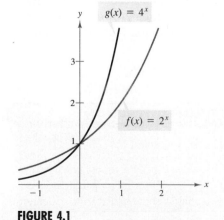

FIGURE 4.1

TABLE 4.1

x	-2	-1	0	1	2	3
a. $f(x) = 2^x$	$\frac{1}{4}$	$\frac{1}{2}$	1	2	4	8
b. $g(x) = 4^x$	$\frac{1}{16}$	$\frac{1}{4}$	1	4	16	64

EXAMPLE 3   Graphs of $y = a^{-x}$

On the same coordinate plane, sketch the graphs of the following functions.

a. $F(x) = 2^{-x}$ **b.** $G(x) = 4^{-x}$

Solution

Table 4.2 lists some values for each function, and Figure 4.2 shows their graphs. Note that both graphs are decreasing. Moreover, the graph of $G(x) = 4^{-x}$ is decreasing more rapidly than the graph of $F(x) = 2^{-x}$.

TABLE 4.2

x	-3	-2	-1	0	1	2
a. $F(x) = 2^{-x}$	8	4	2	1	$\frac{1}{2}$	$\frac{1}{4}$
b. $G(x) = 4^{-x}$	64	16	4	1	$\frac{1}{4}$	$\frac{1}{16}$

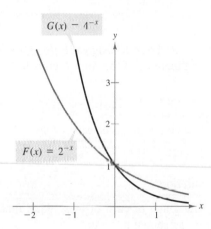

FIGURE 4.2

Comparing the functions in Examples 2 and 3, observe that

$$F(x) = 2^{-x} = f(-x) \qquad \text{and} \qquad G(x) = 4^{-x} = g(-x).$$

Consequently, the graph of F is a reflection (in the y-axis) of the graph of f. The graphs of G and g have the same relationship. This is verified by a comparison of the graphs in Figures 4.1 and 4.2.

The graphs in Figures 4.1 and 4.2 are typical of the exponential functions a^x and a^{-x}. They have one y-intercept and one horizontal asymptote (the x-axis), and they are continuous. The basic characteristics of these exponential functions are summarized in Figure 4.3.

REMARK   Since $2^{-x} = \left(\frac{1}{2}\right)^x$, Examples 2 and 3 show that the function $f(x) = a^x$ *increases* if $a > 1$ and *decreases* if $0 < a < 1$.

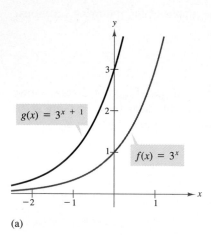

$g(x) = 3^{x+1}$

$f(x) = 3^x$

(a)

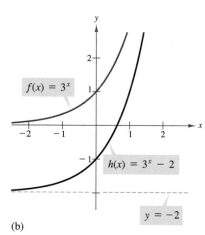

$f(x) = 3^x$

$h(x) = 3^x - 2$

$y = -2$

(b)

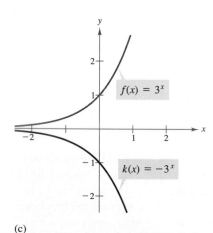

$f(x) = 3^x$

$k(x) = -3^x$

(c)

FIGURE 4.4

FIGURE 4.3

Graph of $y = a^x$
- Domain: $(-\infty, \infty)$
- Range: $(0, \infty)$
- Intercept: $(0, 1)$
- Increasing
- x-axis is a horizontal asymptote
  ($a^x \to 0$ as $x \to -\infty$)
- Continuous

Graph of $y = a^{-x}$
- Domain: $(-\infty, \infty)$
- Range: $(0, \infty)$
- Intercept: $(0, 1)$
- Decreasing
- x-axis is a horizontal asymptote
  ($a^{-x} \to 0$ as $x \to \infty$)
- Continuous
- Reflection of graph of
  $y = a^x$ about y-axis

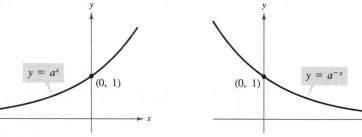

$y = a^x$ $(0, 1)$

$(0, 1)$ $y = a^{-x}$

Characteristics of the Exponential Functions a^x and $a^{-x}(a > 1)$

In the following example, we use the graph of a^x to sketch the graphs of functions of the form $f(x) = b \pm a^{x+c}$.

EXAMPLE 4   Sketching Graphs of Exponential Functions

Sketch the graph of each of the following.

a. $g(x) = 3^{x+1}$ **b.** $h(x) = 3^x - 2$ **c.** $k(x) = -3^x$

Solution

The graph of each of these three functions is similar to the graph of $f(x) = 3^x$, as shown in Figure 4.4.

a. Because $g(x) = 3^{x+1} = f(x + 1)$, the graph of g can be obtained by shifting the graph of f one unit to the left.
b. Because $h(x) = 3^x - 2 = f(x) - 2$, the graph of h can be obtained by shifting the graph of f down two units. The horizontal asymptote is $y = -2$.
c. Because $k(x) = -3^x = -f(x)$, the graph of k can be obtained by reflecting the graph of f in the x-axis.   ◢

The Natural Base e

We used an unspecified base a to introduce exponential functions. It happens that in many applications the convenient choice for a base is the irrational number

$$e \approx 2.71828 \ldots$$

called the **natural base.** The function $f(x) = e^x$ is the **natural exponential function.** Its graph is shown in Figure 4.5. Be sure you see that for the exponential function $f(x) = e^x$, e is the constant 2.71828 . . . , whereas x is the variable.

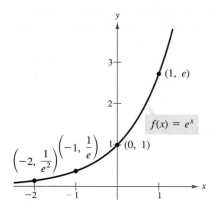

FIGURE 4.5

EXAMPLE 5   Evaluating the Natural Exponential Function

Number	Keystrokes	Display
$3e^2$	3 $\boxed{\times}$ 2 $\boxed{e^x}$ $\boxed{=}$	22.1671683
e^{-1}	1 $\boxed{+/-}$ $\boxed{e^x}$	0.3678794
$e^{0.12(4)}$	.12 $\boxed{\times}$ 4 $\boxed{=}$ $\boxed{e^x}$	1.6160744

Some calculators have a natural exponential key $\boxed{e^x}$. On such a calculator you can evaluate e^2 by entering the sequence 2 $\boxed{e^x}$. Other calculators require the two-key sequence $\boxed{INV}$ $\boxed{\ln x}$ to evaluate exponential functions. On such a calculator you can evaluate e^2 using the following sequence.

2 $\boxed{INV}$ $\boxed{\ln x}$ *Display: 7.3890561*

Similarly, to evaluate e^{-1}, enter the sequence

1 $\boxed{+/-}$ $\boxed{INV}$ $\boxed{\ln x}$.   *Display: 0.3678794*

EXAMPLE 6   Sketching the Graph of a Natural Exponential Function

Sketch the graphs of the following natural exponential functions.

a. $f(x) = 2e^{0.24x}$ **b.** $g(x) = \dfrac{1}{2}e^{-0.58x}$

Solution

To sketch these two graphs, we use a calculator to plot several points on each graph, as shown in Table 4.3. Then we connect the points with a smooth curve, as shown in Figure 4.6. Note that the graph in part (a) is increasing whereas the graph in part (b) is decreasing.

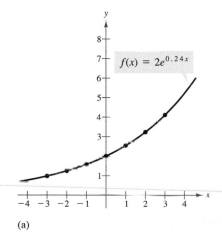

(a)

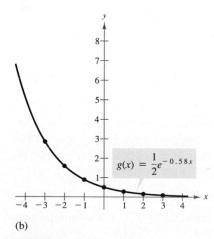

(b)

FIGURE 4.6

TABLE 4.3

x	-3	-2	-1	0	1	2	3
a. $f(x) = 2e^{0.24x}$	0.974	1.238	1.573	2.000	2.542	3.232	4.109
b. $g(x) = \frac{1}{2}e^{-0.58x}$	2.849	1.595	0.893	0.500	0.280	0.157	0.088

Example 7 gives an indication of how the irrational number e arises in applications. We will refer to this example when we develop the formula for continuous compounding of interest.

EXAMPLE 7   Approximation of the Number e

Evaluate the expression

$$\left(1 + \frac{1}{n}\right)^n$$

for several large values of n to see that the values approach $e \approx 2.71828$ as n increases without bound.

Solution

Using the keystroke sequence

$$n \boxed{1/x} \boxed{+} 1 \boxed{=} \boxed{y^x} n \boxed{=}$$

we obtain the values shown in the table.

n	10	100	1,000	10,000	100,000	1,000,000
$\left(1 + \frac{1}{n}\right)^n$	2.59374	2.70481	2.71692	2.71815	2.71827	2.71828

From this table, it seems reasonable to conclude that

$$\left(1 + \frac{1}{n}\right)^n \to e \quad \text{as} \quad n \to \infty.$$

Compound Interest

One of the most familiar examples of exponential growth is an investment earning *continuously compounded interest*. Suppose a principal P is invested at an annual percentage rate r, compounded once a year. If the interest is added to the principal at the end of the year, then the balance is

$$P_1 = P + Pr = P(1 + r).$$

This pattern of multiplying the previous principal by $1 + r$ is then repeated each successive year, as shown in Table 4.4.

TABLE 4.4

Time in years	Balance after each compounding
0	$P = P$
1	$P_1 = P(1 + r)$
2	$P_2 = P_1(1 + r) = P(1 + r)(1 + r) = P(1 + r)^2$
3	$P_3 = P_2(1 + r) = P(1 + r)^2(1 + r) = P(1 + r)^3$
$\vdots$	$\vdots$
n	$P_n = P(1 + r)^n$

To accommodate more frequent (quarterly, monthly, or daily) compounding of interest, we let n be the number of compoundings per year and t be the number of years. Then the rate per compounding is r/n and the account balance after t years is

$$A = P\left(1 + \frac{r}{n}\right)^{nt}. \quad \textit{Amount with n compoundings per year}$$

If we let the number of compoundings, n, increase without bound, we approach **continuous compounding.** In the formula for n compoundings per year, let $m = n/r$. This produces

$$A = P\left(1 + \frac{r}{n}\right)^{nt} = P\left(1 + \frac{1}{m}\right)^{mrt} = P\left[\left(1 + \frac{1}{m}\right)^m\right]^{rt}.$$

As m increases without bound, we know from Example 7 that

$$\left(1 + \frac{1}{m}\right)^m \to e.$$

Hence, for continuous compounding, it follows that

$$P\left[\left(1 + \frac{1}{m}\right)^m\right]^{rt} \to P[e]^{rt}$$

and we write $A = Pe^{rt}$.

FORMULAS FOR COMPOUND INTEREST

After t years, the balance A in an account with principal P and annual percentage rate r (expressed as a decimal) is given by the following formulas.

1. For n compoundings per year: $A = P\left(1 + \frac{r}{n}\right)^{nt}$
2. For continuous compounding: $A = Pe^{rt}$

EXAMPLE 8   **Finding the Balance for Compound Interest**

A sum of $9,000 is invested at an annual percentage rate of 8.5%, compounded annually. Find the balance in the account after three years.

Solution

In this case, $P = 9,000$, $r = 8.5\% = 0.085$, $n = 1$, and $t = 3$. Using the formula

$$A = P\left(1 + \frac{r}{n}\right)^{nt}$$

we have

$$A = 9,000(1 + 0.085)^3 = 9,000(1.085)^3 \approx \$11,495.60.$$

EXAMPLE 9   **Compounding n Times and Compounding Continuously**

A total of $12,000 is invested at an annual percentage rate of 9%. Find the balance after five years if it is compounded

a. quarterly   **b.** continuously.

Solution

a. For quarterly compoundings, we have $n = 4$. Thus, in five years at 9%, the balance is

$$A = P\left(1 + \frac{r}{n}\right)^{nt} = 12,000\left(1 + \frac{0.09}{4}\right)^{4(5)} = \$18,726.11.$$

b. Compounding continuously, the balance is

$$A = Pe^{rt} = 12,000e^{0.09(5)} = \$18,819.75.$$

Note that continuous compounding yields

$$\$18,819.75 - \$18,726.11 = \$93.64$$

more than quarterly compounding.

Other Applications

You have already seen that exponential functions can be used as models for continuously compounded interest. Throughout this chapter you will also encounter several other types of applications that have exponential models.

EXAMPLE 10   An Application Involving Radioactive Decay

Let y represent the mass of a particular radioactive element whose half-life is 25 years. After t years, the mass (in grams) is given by

$$y = 10\left(\frac{1}{2}\right)^{t/25}$$

a. What is the initial mass (when $t = 0$)?
b. How much of the initial mass is present after 80 years?

Solution

a. When $t = 0$, the mass is

$$y = 10\left(\frac{1}{2}\right)^{0} - 10(1) = 10 \text{ grams.}$$

b. When $t = 80$, the mass is

$$y = 10\left(\frac{1}{2}\right)^{80/25} = 10(0.5)^{3.2} \approx 1.088 \text{ grams.}$$

The graph of this function is shown in Figure 4.7.

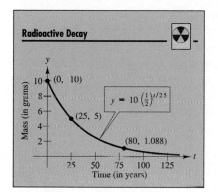

FIGURE 4.7

EXAMPLE 11   Population Growth

The number of fruit flies in an experimental population after t hours is given by

$$Q(t) = 20e^{0.03t}, \qquad t \geq 0.$$

a. Find the initial number of fruit flies in the population.
b. How large is the population of fruit flies after 72 hours?
c. Sketch the graph of Q.

Solution

a. To find the initial population, we evaluate $Q(t)$ at $t = 0$.

$$Q(0) = 20e^{0.03(0)} = 20e^{0} = 20(1) = 20 \text{ flies}$$

b. After 72 hours, the population size is

$$Q(72) = 20e^{(0.03)(72)} = 20e^{2.16} \approx 173 \text{ flies.}$$

c. To sketch the graph of Q, we evaluate $Q(t)$ for several values of t (rounded to the nearest integer) and plot the corresponding points, as shown in Figure 4.8.

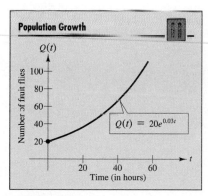

FIGURE 4.8

REMARK   Many animal populations have a growth pattern described by the function $Q(t) = ce^{kt}$ where c is the original population, $Q(t)$ is the population at time t, and k is a constant determined by the rate of growth. Informally, we can write this as $(Then) = (Now)(e^{kt})$.

t	0	5	10	20	40	60
$20e^{0.03t}$	20	23	27	36	66	121

DISCUSSION
PROBLEM
Exponential
Growth

Consider the following sequences of numbers.

Sequence 1   2, 4, 6, 8, 10, 12, . . .

Sequence 2   2, 4, 8, 16, 32, 64, . . .

The first sequence is given by $f(n) = 2n$, $n = 1, 2, 3, 4, \ldots$. This type of growth is **linear growth.** The second sequence is given by $f(n) = 2^n$, $n = 1, 2, 3, 4, \ldots$. This type of growth is **exponential growth.** Which of the following sequences represents linear growth and which represents exponential growth? Can you find a linear function and an exponential function that represent the sequences?

1. 3, 6, 9, 12, 15, . . .
2. 3, 9, 27, 81, 243, . . .

We will say more about these two types of growth later. At that time, we will see that sequences that represent linear growth are called *arithmetic sequences* and sequences that represent exponential growth are called *geometric sequences.*

WARM UP

The following warm-up exercises involve skills that were covered in earlier sections. You will use these skills in the exercise set for this section.

In Exercises 1–10, use the properties of exponents to simplify the expressions.

1. $5^{2x}(5^{-x})$

2. $3^{-x}(3^{3x})$

3. $\dfrac{4^{5x}}{4^{2x}}$

4. $\dfrac{10^{2x}}{10^x}$

5. $(4^x)^2$

6. $(4^{2x})^5$

7. $\left(\dfrac{2^x}{3^x}\right)^{-1}$

8. $(4^{6x})^{1/2}$

9. $(2^{3x})^{-1/3}$

10. $(16^x)^{1/4}$

EXERCISES for Section 4.1

In Exercises 1–14, use a calculator to evaluate the given quantity. Round your answers to three decimal places.

1. $(3.4)^{5.6}$

2. $(1.005)^{400}$

3. $1000(1.06)^{-5}$

4. $5000(2^{-1.5})$

5. $\sqrt[4]{763}$

6. $\sqrt[3]{4395}$

7. $8^{2\pi}$

8. $5^{-\pi}$

9. $100^{\sqrt{2}}$

10. $0.6^{\sqrt{3}}$

11. e^2

12. $e^{1/2}$

13. $e^{-3/4}$

14. $e^{3.2}$

In Exercises 15–22, match the exponential function with its graph. [The graphs are labeled (a), (b), (c), (d), (e), (f), (g), and (h).]

15. $f(x) = 3^x$

16. $f(x) = -3^x$

17. $f(x) = 3^{-x}$

18. $f(x) = -3^{-x}$

19. $f(x) = 3^x - 4$

20. $f(x) = 3^x + 1$

21. $f(x) = -3^{x-2}$

22. $f(x) = 3^{x-2}$

(a)
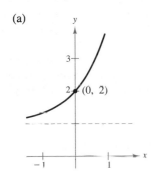

(b)
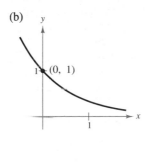

(c)
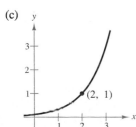

(d)
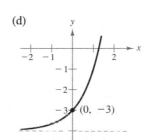

(e)
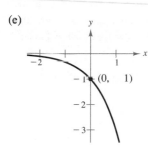

(f)
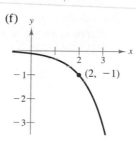

(g)
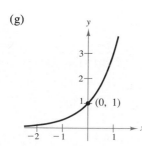

(h)
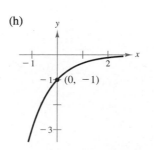

In Exercises 23–40, sketch the graph of the given exponential function.

23. $g(x) = 5^x$

24. $f(x) = \left(\frac{3}{2}\right)^x$

25. $f(x) = \left(\frac{1}{5}\right)^x = 5^{-x}$

26. $h(x) = \left(\frac{3}{2}\right)^{-x}$

27. $h(x) = 5^{x-2}$

28. $g(x) = \left(\frac{3}{2}\right)^{x+2}$

29. $g(x) = 5^{-x} - 3$

30. $f(x) = \left(\frac{3}{2}\right)^{-x} + 2$

31. $f(x) = 3^{x-2} + 1$

32. $f(x) = 4^{x+1} - 2$

33. $y = -e^{-x}$

34. $y = e^{x/2}$

35. $s(t) = 2e^{0.12t}$

36. $s(t) = 3e^{-0.2t}$

37. $f(x) = e^{2x}$

38. $h(x) = e^{x-2}$

39. $g(x) = 1 + e^{-x}$

40. $N(t) = 1000e^{-0.2t}$

In Exercises 41–44, complete the table to determine the balance A for P dollars invested at rate r for t years and compounded n times per year.

n	1	2	4	12	365	Continuous compounding
A						

41. $P = \$2500$, $r = 12\%$, $t = 10$ years

42. $P = \$1000$, $r = 10\%$, $t = 10$ years

43. $P = \$2500$, $r = 12\%$, $t = 20$ years

44. $P = \$1000$, $r = 10\%$, $t = 40$ years

In Exercises 45–48, complete the following table to determine the amount of money P that should be invested at rate r to produce a final balance of $\$100,000$ in t years.

t	1	10	20	30	40	50
P						

45. $r = 9\%$, compounded continuously

46. $r = 12\%$, compounded continuously

47. $r = 10\%$, compounded monthly

48. $r = 7\%$, compounded daily

49. *Trust Fund* On the day of your grandchild's birth, you deposited $\$25,000$ in a trust fund that pays 8.75% interest, compounded continuously. Determine the balance in this account on your grandchild's 25th birthday.

50. *Trust Fund* Suppose you deposited $5000 in a trust fund that pays 7.5% interest, compounded continuously. In the trust fund, you specify that the balance will be given to the college from which you graduated after the money has earned interest for 50 years. How much will your college receive after 50 years?

51. *Demand Function* The demand equation for a certain product is given by

$$p = 500 - 0.5e^{0.004x}.$$

Find the price p for a demand of (a) $x = 1000$ units and (b) $x = 1500$ units.

52. *Demand Function* The demand equation for a certain product is given by

$$p = 5000\left(1 - \frac{4}{4 + e^{-0.002x}}\right).$$

Find the price p for a demand of (a) $x = 100$ units and (b) $x = 500$ units.

53. *Bacteria Growth* A certain type of bacteria increases according to the model

$$P(t) = 100e^{0.2197t}$$

where t is the time in hours. Find (a) $P(0)$, (b) $P(5)$, and (c) $P(10)$.

54. *Population Growth* The population of a town increases according to the model

$$P(t) = 2500e^{0.0293t}$$

where t is the time in years, with $t = 0$ corresponding to 1990. Use the model to approximate the population in (a) 1995, (b) 2000, and (c) 2010.

55. *Radioactive Decay* Let Q represent the mass of radium (Ra^{226}) whose half-life is 1620 years. The quantity of radium present after t years is given by

$$Q = 25\left(\frac{1}{2}\right)^{t/1620}.$$

(a) Determine the initial quantity (when $t = 0$).
(b) Determine the quantity present after 1000 years.
(c) Sketch the graph of this function over the interval $t = 0$ to $t = 5000$.

56. *Radioactive Decay* Let Q represent the mass of carbon 14 (C^{14}) whose half-life is 5,730 years. The quantity of carbon 14 present after t years is given by

$$Q = 10\left(\frac{1}{2}\right)^{t/5730}.$$

(a) Determine the initial quantity (when $t = 0$).
(b) Determine the quantity present after 2,000 years.
(c) Sketch the graph of this function over the interval $t = 0$ to $t = 10,000$.

57. *Forest Defoliation* To estimate the amount of defoliation caused by the gypsy moth during a given year, a forester counts the number of egg masses on $\frac{1}{40}$ of an acre the preceding fall. The percentage of defoliation y is approximated by

$$y = \frac{300}{3 + 17e^{-1.57x}}$$

where x is the number of egg masses in thousands. Estimate the percentage of defoliation if 2000 egg masses are counted. (*Source:* Department of Environmental Resources)

58. *Inflation* If the annual rate of inflation averages 5% over the next 10 years, then the approximate cost C of goods or services during any year in that decade will be given by

$$C(t) = P(1.05)^t$$

where t is the time in years and P is the present cost. If the price of an oil change for your car is presently $19.95, estimate the price 10 years from now.

59. *Depreciation* After t years, the value of a car that cost you $20,000 is given by

$$V(t) = 20,000\left(\frac{3}{4}\right)^t.$$

Sketch a graph of the function and determine the value of the car two years after it was purchased.

60. Create two exponential functions of the form $f(x) = C2^{kx}$ with y-intercepts $(0, 10)$. (The answer is not unique.)

61. Given the exponential function $f(x) = a^x$, show that
(a) $f(u + v) = f(u) \cdot f(v)$, and (b) $f(2x) = [f(x)]^2$.

SOLVING

A Graphical Approach to Compound Interest.

A graphing utility can be used to investigate the rate of growth of different types of compound interest.

EXAMPLE 1   Comparing Balances

You are depositing $1000 into a savings account. Which of the following will produce a larger balance?

a. 6% annual percentage rate, compounded annually
b. 6% annual percentage rate, compounded continuously
c. 6.25% annual percentage rate, compounded quarterly

Solution

Option (b) is better than option (a) because, for a given annual percentage rate, continuous compounding yields a larger balance than compounding n times per year. Distinguishing between the second and third options is not as straightforward—the higher percentage rate favors option (c), but the "more frequent" compounding favors option (b). One way to compare all three options is to sketch their graphs on the same display screen.

Option (a)	*Option* (b)	*Option* (c)
$A = 1000(1 + 0.06)^t$	$A = 1000e^{0.06t}$	$A = 1000\left(1 + \frac{0.0625}{4}\right)^{4t}$

The graphs of all three functions are shown at the left. On the graph, the t-values vary from 0 years through 100 years. Note that for the first 50 years, there is little difference in the graphs. Between 50 and 100 years, however, the balances obtained with the three options begin to differ significantly. At the end of 100 years, the balances are (a) $339,302, (b) $403,429, and (c) $493,575.

Thus, your conclusion could be that for any length of time, option (c) is better than option (b), and option (b) is better than option (a). Moreover, as the time increases, the difference between the three options increases. ◢

To help distinguish between different interest rates and different types of compounding, banks use the concept of *effective yield*. The **effective yield** of a savings plan is the percentage increase in the balance at the end of *one* year. For instance, in Example 1 the balances at the end of one year are (a) $1060.00, (b) $1061.84, and (c) $1063.98. The effective yields are below.

Effective Yield (a)	*Effective Yield* (b)	*Effective Yield* (c)
6.000%	6.184%	6.398%

Because option (c) has the largest effective yield, it is the best option and will yield the highest balance.

283

If you were to create a retirement plan with a regular savings account, the income tax on the interest would be due each year. With a *tax deferred* retirement plan, the interest is allowed to build without being taxed until the account reaches its maturity.

EXAMPLE 2 To Defer or Not to Defer

You deposit $25,000 in an account to accrue interest for 40 years. The account pays 8% compounded annually. Assume that the income tax on the earned interest is 30%. Which of the following plans produces a larger balance after all income tax is paid?

a. *Deferred* The income tax on the interest that is earned is paid in one lump sum at the end of 40 years.

b. *Not Deferred* The income tax on the interest that is earned each year is paid at the end of that year.

Solution

a. The untaxed balance at the end of 40 years is

$$A = 25{,}000(1 + 0.08)^{40} = \$543{,}113.04.$$

The income tax due is $0.3(518{,}113.04) = \$155{,}433.91$, so you are left with a balance of $387,579.13.

b. You can reason that only 70% of the earned interest will remain in the account each year. The taxed balance at the end of t years is $A = 25{,}000[1 + 0.08(0.7)]^t$, which implies that the balance at the end of 40 years is

$$A = 25{,}000[1 + 0.08(0.7)]^{40} = \$221{,}053.16.$$

Thus, the tax deferred plan will produce a significantly larger balance at the end of 40 years. The balances of the two plans are compared at left. ◢

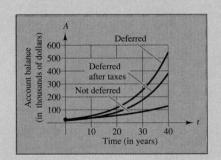

EXERCISES

(See also: Exercises 41–50, Section 4.1)

1. *Comparing Savings Plans* Which would produce a larger balance: an annual percentage rate of 8.05% compounded monthly, or an annual percentage rate of 8% compounded continuously? Explain.

2. *Exploration* You deposit $1000 into each of two savings accounts. The interest for the accounts is paid according to the two options described in Exercise 1. How long would it take for the balance in one of the accounts to exceed the balance in the other account by $100? By $100,000?

3. No income tax is due on the interest earned in some types of investments. You deposit $25,000 into an account. Which plan produces a larger balance in 40 years (after taxes)?

(a) *Tax-free* The account pays 5% compounded annually. There is no income tax due on the earned interest.

(b) *Tax-deferred* The account pays 7% compounded annually. At maturity, the earned interest is taxable at a rate of 40%.

284

4.2 Logarithmic Functions

Introduction / The Common Logarithmic Function / Graphs of Logarithmic Functions / The Natural Logarithmic Function / Applications

Introduction

In Section 2.7 we discussed the concept of the inverse of a function. If a function has the property that no horizontal line intersects the graph of a function more than once, then the function must have an inverse. In Section 4.1, every function of the form $f(x) = a^x$ passes the "horizontal line test," and therefore must have an inverse. This inverse function is the **logarithmic function with base** a (see Figure 4.9).

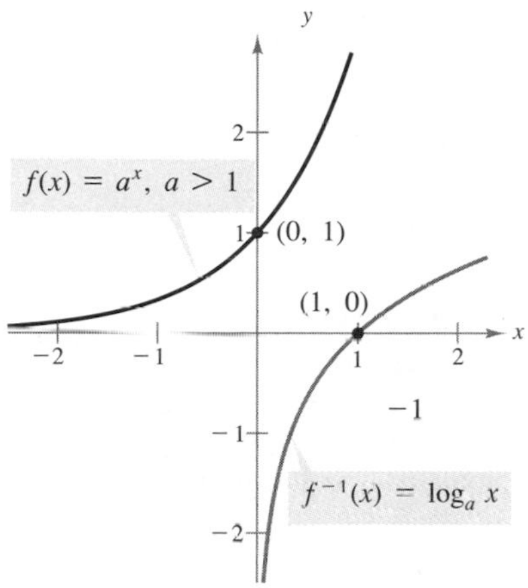

$f(x) = a^x, a > 1$

$(0, 1)$

$(1, 0)$

$f^{-1}(x) = \log_a x$

Inverse Functions
Domain of $\log_a x$ is Range of a^x.

FIGURE 4.9

DEFINITION OF LOGARITHMIC FUNCTION

For $x > 0$ and $0 < a \neq 1$,

$$y = \log_a x \text{ if and only if } a^y = x.$$

The function given by

$$f(x) = \log_a x$$

is the **logarithmic function with base** a.

REMARK The equations $y = \log_a x$ and $a^y = x$ are equivalent. The first equation is in logarithmic form and the second is in exponential form.

When evaluating logarithms, remember that *a logarithm is an exponent.* This means that $\log_a x$ is the exponent to which a must be raised to obtain x. For instance, $\log_2 8 = 3$ because 2 must be raised to the third power to obtain 8. That is,

$$3 = \log_2 8 \quad \text{if and only if} \quad 2^3 = 8.$$

Base

Logarithm is an exponent

EXAMPLE 1 Evaluating Logarithms

a. $\log_2 32 = 5$ because $2^5 = 32$.

b. $\log_3 27 = 3$ because $3^3 = 27$.

c. $\log_4 2 = \dfrac{1}{2}$ because $4^{1/2} = \sqrt{4} = 2$.

d. $\log_{10} \dfrac{1}{100} = -2$ because $10^{-2} = \dfrac{1}{10^2} = \dfrac{1}{100}$.

e. $\log_3 1 = 0$ because $3^0 = 1$.

f. $\log_2 2 = 1$ because $2^1 = 2$.

The Common Logarithmic Function

The logarithmic function with base 10 is the **common logarithmic function.** On most calculators, this function is denoted by **log** . You can tell whether this key denotes base 10 by entering 10 **log** . The display should be 1. The common logarithmic function is often written as log x, without denoting the base 10.

EXAMPLE 2   Evaluating Logarithms on a Calculator

Number	Keystrokes	Display
$\log_{10} 10$	10 **log**	1
$2 \log_{10} 2.5$	2.5 **log** **×** 2 **=**	0.7958800
$\log_{10} (-2)$	2 **+/−** **log**	ERROR

Note that the calculator displays an error message when you try to evaluate $\log_{10} (-2)$. The reason for this is that the domain of every logarithmic function is the set of *positive real numbers*.

The following properties follow directly from the definition of the logarithmic function with base a.

PROPERTIES OF LOGARITHMS

1. $\log_a 1 = 0$ because 0 is the power to which a must be raised to obtain 1.
2. $\log_a a = 1$ because 1 is the power to which a must be raised to obtain a.
3. $\log_a a^x = x$ because x is the power to which a must be raised to obtain a^x.

Graphs of Logarithmic Functions

To sketch the graph of $y = \log_a x$, we can use the fact that the graphs of inverse functions are reflections of each other in the line $y = x$.

EXAMPLE 3   Graphs of Exponential and Logarithmic Functions

Show graphically and algebraically that the logarithmic function is the inverse of the exponential function.

On the same coordinate plane, sketch the graphs of the following functions.

a. $f(x) = 2^x$ **b.** $g(x) = \log_2 x$

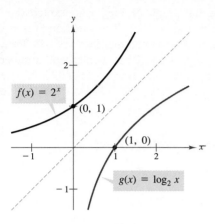

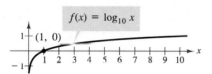

Inverse Functions

FIGURE 4.10

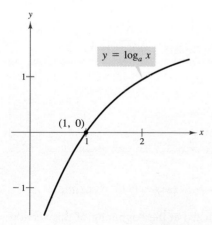

FIGURE 4.11

Solution

a. For $f(x) = 2^x$, we make a table of values.

x	-2	-1	0	1	2	3
$f(x) = 2^x$	$\frac{1}{4}$	$\frac{1}{2}$	1	2	4	8

By plotting these points and connecting them with a smooth curve, we have the graph shown in Figure 4.10.

b. Since $g(x) = \log_2 x$ is the inverse of $f(x) = 2^x$, the graph of g is obtained by reflecting the graph of f in the line $y = x$, as shown in Figure 4.10.

EXAMPLE 4 Sketching the Graph of a Logarithmic Function

Sketch the graph of the logarithmic function $f(x) = \log_{10} x$.

Solution

We begin by making a table of values. Note that some of the values can be obtained without a calculator, while others require a calculator. We plot the corresponding points and sketch the graph in Figure 4.11.

x	Without a calculator				With a calculator		
	$\frac{1}{100}$	$\frac{1}{10}$	1	10	2	5	8
$\log_{10} x$	-2	-1	0	1	0.301	0.699	0.903

The nature of the graph in Figure 4.11 is typical of functions of the form $f(x) = \log_a x$, $a > 1$. They have one x-intercept and one vertical asymptote, and their domains are all positive numbers, $(0, \infty)$. We summarize the basic characteristics of logarithmic graphs in Figure 4.12.

REMARK In Figure 4.12, note that the vertical asymptote occurs at $x = 0$, where $\log_a x$ is *undefined*.

Graph of $y = \log_a x$, $a > 1$
- Domain: $(0, \infty)$
- Range: $(-\infty, \infty)$
- Intercept: $(1, 0)$
- Increasing

- y-axis is a vertical asymptote ($\log_a x \to -\infty$ as $x \to 0^+$)
- Continuous
- Reflection of graph of $y = a^x$ about the line $y = x$

FIGURE 4.12

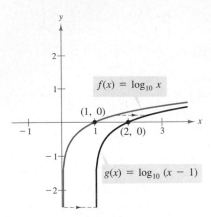

(a) Right Shift of 1 Unit
Vertical Asymptote is $x = 1$.

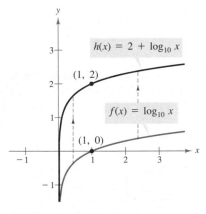

(b) Upward shift of 2 units
Vertical asympote remains $x = 0$.

FIGURE 4.13

In the following example we use the graph of $\log_a x$ to sketch the graphs of functions of the form $y = b \pm \log_a(x + c)$. The function $f(x) = \log_a(bx + c)$ has a domain which consists of all x such that $bx + c > 0$. The vertical asymptote occurs when $bx + c = 0$, and the x-intercept occurs when $bx + c = 1$.

EXAMPLE 5 Sketching the Graphs of Logarithmic Functions

Sketch the graphs of the following functions.

a. $g(x) = \log_{10}(x - 1)$ **b.** $h(x) = 2 + \log_{10} x$

Solution

The graph of each of these functions is similar to the graph of $f(x) = \log_{10} x$, as shown in Figure 4.13.

a. Because $g(x) = \log_{10}(x - 1) = f(x - 1)$, the graph of g can be obtained by shifting the graph of f one unit to the right.
b. Because $h(x) = 2 + \log_{10} x = 2 + f(x)$, the graph of h can be obtained by shifting the graph of f two units up.

The Natural Logarithmic Function

As with exponential functions, the most widely used base for logarithmic functions is the number e. The logarithmic function with base e is the **natural logarithmic function,** denoted by the special symbol $\ln x$, read as "el en of x."

THE NATURAL LOGARITHMIC FUNCTION

The function defined by

$$f(x) = \log_e x = \ln x, \qquad x > 0$$

is the **natural logarithmic function.**

The three properties of logarithms listed at the beginning of this section are also valid for natural logarithms.

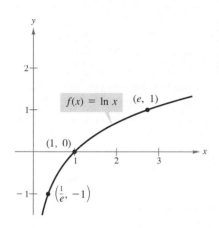

FIGURE 4.14

PROPERTIES OF NATURAL LOGARITHMS

1. $\ln 1 = 0$ because 0 is the power to which e must be raised to obtain 1.
2. $\ln e = 1$ because 1 is the power to which e must be raised to obtain e.
3. $\ln e^x = x$ because x is the power to which e must be raised to obtain e^x.

The graph of the natural logarithmic function is shown in Figure 4.14.

EXAMPLE 6   Evaluating the Natural Logarithmic Function

a. $\ln \dfrac{1}{e} = \ln e^{-1} = -1$ *Property 3*

b. $\ln e^2 = 2$ *Property 3*

On most calculators, the natural logarithm is denoted by $\boxed{\text{ln } x}$.

EXAMPLE 7   Evaluating the Natural Logarithmic Function

Number	Calculator Steps	Display
$\ln 2$	2 $\boxed{\text{ln } x}$	0.6931472
$\ln 0.3$	.3 $\boxed{\text{ln } x}$	-1.2039728
$\ln(-1)$	1 $\boxed{+/-}$ $\boxed{\text{ln } x}$	ERROR

Be sure you see that $\ln(-1)$ gives an error. This occurs because the domain of $\ln x$ is the set of positive real numbers. (See Figure 4.14.) Hence, $\ln(-1)$ is undefined.

EXAMPLE 8   Finding the Domain of Logarithmic Functions

Find the domain of the following functions.

a. $f(x) = \log_3(x - 2)$ **b.** $g(x) = \ln(2 - x)$
c. $h(x) = \log_{10}(x^2 - 1)$

Solution

a. Because $\log_3(x - 2)$ is defined only if $x - 2 > 0$, it follows that the domain of f is $(2, \infty)$.
b. Because $\ln(2 - x)$ is defined only if $2 - x > 0$, it follows that the domain of g is $(-\infty, 2)$. The graph of g is shown in Figure 4.15.
c. Because $\log_{10}(x^2 - 1)$ is defined only if $x^2 - 1 > 0$, it follows that the domain of h is all real numbers in the interval $(-\infty, -1)$ or the interval $(1, \infty)$.

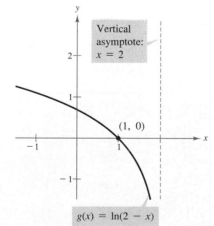

FIGURE 4.15

Applications

EXAMPLE 9   Human Memory Model

Students participating in a psychological experiment attended several lectures on a subject. Every month for a year after that, the students were tested to see how much of the material they remembered. The average scores for the group were given by the *human memory model*

$$f(t) = 75 - 6\ln(t + 1), \qquad 0 \le t \le 12$$

where t is the time in months.

a. What was the average score on the original ($t = 0$) exam?
b. What was the average score at the end of $t = 2$ months?
c. What was the average score at the end of $t = 6$ months?
d. Sketch the graph of f.

Solution

a. The original average score was

$$f(0) = 75 - 6\ln(0 + 1) = 75 - 6(0) = 75.$$

b. After two months, the average score was

$$f(2) = 75 - 6\ln 3 \approx 75 - 6(1.0986) \approx 68.4.$$

c. After six months, the average score was

$$f(6) = 75 - 6\ln 7 \approx 75 - 6(1.9459) \approx 63.3.$$

d. Several points are shown in the following table, and the graph of f is shown in Figure 4.16.

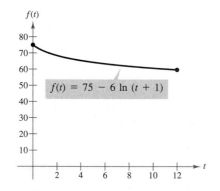

FIGURE 4.16

t	0	1	2	6	8	12
$f(t)$	75	70.8	68.4	63.3	61.8	59.6

DISCUSSION

PROBLEM

The Graph of a
Logarithmic
Function

In the summary of the characteristics of the logarithmic function $f(x) = \log_a x$, we stated that the range of the function is $(-\infty, \infty)$. From this, we can conclude that the value of $\log_a x$ can be made as large as we want. Can you find values of x that satisfy the following equations?

1. $\log_{10} x = 10$ 2. $\log_{10} x = 1{,}000$ 3. $\log_{10} x = 10{,}000{,}000$

WARM UP

The following warm-up exercises involve skills that were covered in earlier sections. You will use these skills in the exercise set for this section.

In Exercises 1–4, solve for x.

1. $2^x = 8$ **2.** $4^x = 1$

3. $10^x = 0.1$ **4.** $e^x = e$

In Exercises 5 and 6, evaluate the given expressions. Round to three decimal places.

5. e^2 **6.** e^{-1}

In Exercises 7–10, describe how the graph of g is related to the graph of f.

7. $g(x) = f(x + 2)$ **8.** $g(x) - -f(x)$

9. $g(x) = -1 + f(x)$ **10.** $g(x) = f(-x)$

EXERCISES for Section 4.2

In Exercises 1–16, evaluate the given expression without using a calculator.

1. $\log_2 16$ **2.** $\log_4 64$

3. $\log_5\left(\frac{1}{25}\right)$ **4.** $\log_2\left(\frac{1}{8}\right)$

5. $\log_{16} 4$ **6.** $\log_{27} 9$

7. $\log_7 1$ **8.** $\log_{10} 1000$

9. $\log_{10} 0.01$ **10.** $\log_{10} 10$

11. $\ln e^3$ **12.** $\ln \frac{1}{e}$

13. $\ln e^{-2}$ **14.** $\ln 1$

15. $\log_a a^2$ **16.** $\log_a \frac{1}{a}$

In Exercises 17–26, use the definition of a logarithm to write the given equation in logarithmic form. For instance, the logarithmic form of $2^3 = 8$ is $\log_2 8 = 3$.

17. $5^3 = 125$ **18.** $8^2 = 64$

19. $81^{1/4} = 3$ **20.** $9^{3/2} = 27$

21. $6^{-2} = \frac{1}{36}$ **22.** $10^{-3} = 0.001$

23. $e^3 = 20.0855 \ldots$ **24.** $e^0 = 1$

25. $e^x = 4$ **26.** $u^v = w$

In Exercises 27–34, use a calculator to evaluate the logarithm. Round to three decimal places.

27. $\log_{10} 345$

28. $\log_{10}\left(\frac{4}{5}\right)$

29. $\log_{10} (0.48)$

30. $\log_{10} 12.5$

31. $\ln 18.42$

32. $\ln \sqrt{42}$

33. $\ln(1 + \sqrt{3})$

34. $\ln(\sqrt{5} - 2)$

In Exercises 35–38, sketch the graphs of f and g on the same coordinate plane to demonstrate that one is the inverse of the other.

35. $f(x) = 3^x$, $g(x) = \log_3 x$

36. $f(x) = 5^x$, $g(x) = \log_5 x$

37. $f(x) = e^x$, $g(x) = \ln x$

38. $f(x) = 10^x$, $g(x) = \log_{10} x$

In Exercises 39–44, use the graph of $y = \ln x$ to match the given function to its graph. [The graphs are labeled (a), (b), (c), (d), (e), and (f).]

39. $f(x) = \ln x + 2$

40. $f(x) = -\ln x$

41. $f(x) = -\ln(x + 2)$

42. $f(x) = \ln(x - 1)$

43. $f(x) = \ln(1 - x)$

44. $f(x) = -\ln(-x)$

(a)

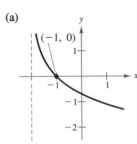

(b)

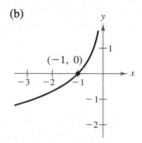

(c)

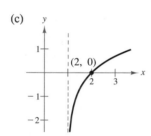

(d)

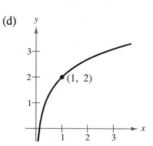

(e)

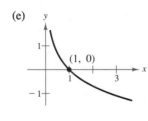

(f)

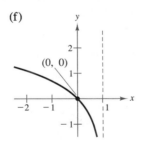

In Exercises 45–56, find the domain, vertical asymptote, and x-intercept of the logarithmic function and sketch its graph.

45. $f(x) = \log_4 x$

46. $g(x) = \log_6 x$

47. $h(x) = \log_4(x - 3)$

48. $f(x) = -\log_6(x + 2)$

49. $y = -\log_3 x + 2$

50. $y = \log_5(x - 1) + 4$

51. $y = \log_{10}\left(\dfrac{x}{5}\right)$

52. $y = \log_{10}(-x)$

53. $f(x) = \ln(x - 2)$

54. $h(x) = \ln(x + 1)$

55. $g(x) = \ln(-x)$

56. $f(x) = \ln(3 - x)$

57. *Human Memory Model*   Students in a mathematics class were given an exam and then tested monthly with an equivalent exam. The average score for the class was given by the human memory model

$$f(t) = 80 - 17 \log_{10}(t + 1), \qquad 0 \le t \le 12$$

where t is the time in months.
(a) What was the average score on the original exam ($t = 0$)?
(b) What was the average score after 4 months?
(c) What was the average score after 10 months?

58. *Population Growth*   The population of a town will double in

$$t = \frac{10 \ln 2}{\ln 67 - \ln 50}$$

years. Find t.

59. *World Population Growth*   The time in years for the world population to double if it is increasing at a continuous rate of r is given by

$$t = \frac{\ln 2}{r}.$$

Complete the table.

r	0.005	0.010	0.015	0.020	0.025	0.030
t						

60. *Investment Time*   A principal P invested at $9\frac{1}{2}\%$ and compounded continuously increases to an amount K times the original principal after t years, where t is given by

$$t = \frac{\ln K}{0.095}.$$

(a) Complete the table.

K	1	2	4	6	8	10	12
t							

(b) Use the table in part (a) to graph this function.

Ventilation Rates   In Exercises 61 and 62, use the model

$$y = 80.4 - 11 \ln x$$

which approximates the minimum required ventilation rate in terms of the air space per child in a public school classroom. In the model, x is the air space per child in cubic feet and y is the ventilation rate in cubic feet per minute (see figure).

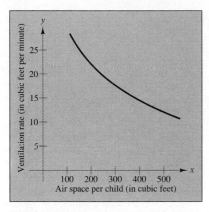

Figure for 61 and 62

61. Use the model to approximate the required ventilation rate if there are 300 cubic feet of air space per child.

62. A classroom is designed for 30 students, and the air-conditioning system in the room has the capacity to move 450 cubic feet of air per minute.
    (a) Determine the ventilation rate per child assuming the room is filled to capacity.
    (b) Use the figure to estimate the air space required per child.
    (c) Determine the minimum number of square feet of floor space required for the room if the ceiling height is 30 feet.

Monthly Payment   In Exercises 63–66, use the model

$$t = \frac{5.315}{-6.7968 + \ln x}, \quad 1000 < x$$

which approximates the length of a home mortgage of $120,000 at 10% in terms of the monthly payment. In the model, t is the length of the mortgage in years and x is the monthly payment in dollars (see figure).

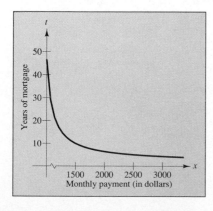

Figure for 63–66

63. Use the model to approximate the length of a home mortgage (for $120,000 at 10%) that has a monthly payment of $1167.41.

64. Use the model to approximate the length of a home mortgage (for $120,000 at 10%) that has a monthly payment of $1068.45.

65. Approximate the total amount paid over the term of a mortgage with a monthly payment of $1167.41.

66. Approximate the total amount paid over the term of a mortgage with a monthly payment of $1068.45.

67. *Work*   The work (in foot-pounds) done in compressing an initial volume of 9 cubic feet at a pressure of 15 pounds per square inch to a volume of 3 cubic feet is

$$W = 19,440(\ln 9 - \ln 3).$$

Find W.

68. *Sound Intensity*   The relationship between the number of decibels β and the intensity of a sound I in watts per meter squared is given by

$$\beta = 10 \log_{10}\left(\frac{I}{10^{-16}}\right).$$

Determine the number of decibels of a sound with an intensity of 10^{-4} watts per meter squared.

69. (a) Use a calculator to complete the table for the function

$$f(x) = \frac{\ln x}{x}.$$

x	1	5	10	10^2	10^4	10^6
$f(x)$						

(b) Use the table in part (a) to determine what $f(x)$ approaches as x increases without bound.

70. Answer the following for the function $f(x) = \log_{10} x$. Do not use a calculator.
    (a) What is the domain of f?
    (b) Find f^{-1}.
    (c) If x is a real number between 1000 and 10,000, then determine the interval in which $f(x)$ will be found.
    (d) Determine the interval in which x will be found if $f(x)$ is negative.
    (e) If $f(x)$ is increased by one unit, then x must have been increased by what factor?
    (f) If $f(x_1) = 3n$ and $f(x_2) = n$, then find the ratio of x_1 to x_2.

Properties of Logarithms

Change of Base / Properties of Logarithms / Rewriting Logarithmic Expressions

Change of Base

Most calculators have only two types of "log keys," one for common logarithms (base 10) and one for natural logarithms (base e). Although common logs and natural logs are the most frequently used, we occasionally need to evaluate logarithms to other bases. To do this, the *change of base formula* is useful. (This formula is derived in Example 10 in Section 4.4.)

CHANGE OF BASE FORMULA

Let a, b, and x be positive real numbers such that $a \neq 1$ and $b \neq 1$. Then $\log_a x$ is given by

$$\log_a x = \frac{\log_b x}{\log_b a}.$$

REMARK One way to look at the change of base formula is that logarithms to base a are simply *constant multiples* of logarithms to base b. The constant multiplier is $1/(\log_b a)$.

EXAMPLE 1 Changing Bases

Use *common* logarithms to evaluate the following.

a. $\log_4 30$ **b.** $\log_2 14$

Solution

a. Using the change of base formula with $a = 4$, $b = 10$, and $x = 30$, we convert to common logarithms and obtain

$$\log_4 30 = \frac{\log_{10} 30}{\log_{10} 4} \approx \frac{1.47712}{0.60206} \approx 2.4534.$$

b. Using the change of base formula with $a = 2$, $b = 10$, and $x = 14$, we convert to common logarithms and obtain

$$\log_2 14 = \frac{\log_{10} 14}{\log_{10} 2} \approx \frac{1.14613}{0.30103} \approx 3.8074.$$

EXAMPLE 2 Changing Bases

Use *natural* logarithms to evaluate the following.

a. $\log_4 30$ **b.** $\log_2 14$

Solution

a. Using the change of base formula with $a = 4$, $b = e$, and $x = 30$, we convert to natural logarithms and obtain

$$\log_4 30 = \frac{\ln 30}{\ln 4} \approx \frac{3.40120}{1.38629} \approx 2.4534.$$

b. Using the change of base formula with $a = 2$, $b = e$, and $x = 14$, we convert to natural logarithms and obtain

$$\log_2 14 = \frac{\ln 14}{\ln 2} \approx \frac{2.63906}{0.693147} \approx 3.8074.$$

Note that the results agree with those obtained in Example 1 using common logarithms.　◀

Properties of Logarithms

We know from the previous section that the logarithmic function with base a is the *inverse* of the exponential function with base a. Thus, it makes sense that the properties of exponents should have corresponding properties involving logarithms. For instance, the exponential property

$$a^0 = 1$$

has the corresponding logarithmic property

$$\log_a 1 = 0.$$

In this section we will show how to use the logarithmic properties that correspond to the following three exponential properties.

1. $a^n a^m = a^{n+m}$　　　2. $\dfrac{a^n}{a^m} = a^{n-m}$　　　3. $(a^n)^m = a^{nm}$

PROPERTIES OF LOGARITHMS

Let a be a positive number such that $a \neq 1$, and let n be a real number. If u and v are positive real numbers, then the following properties are true.

Base a Logarithm	*Natural Logarithm*
1. $\log_a(uv) = \log_a u + \log_a v$	1. $\ln(uv) = \ln u + \ln v$
2. $\log_a \dfrac{u}{v} = \log_a u - \log_a v$	2. $\ln \dfrac{u}{v} = \ln u - \ln v$
3. $\log_a u^n = n \log_a u$	3. $\ln u^n = n \ln u$

Proof

We give a proof of Property 1 and leave the other two proofs for you. To prove Property 1, let

$$x = \log_a u \quad \text{and} \quad y = \log_a v.$$

The corresponding exponential forms of these two equations are

$$a^x = u \quad \text{and} \quad a^y = v.$$

Multiplying u and v produces $uv = a^x a^y = a^{x+y}$. The corresponding logarithmic form of $uv = a^{x+y}$ is

$$\log_a(uv) = x + y.$$

Hence, $\log_a(uv) = \log_a u + \log_a v$.   ◢

REMARK   There is no general property that can be used to rewrite $\log_a(u \pm v)$. Specifically

$$\log_a(x + y) \quad \text{DOES NOT EQUAL} \quad \log_a x + \log_a y.$$

("The log of a sum does *not* equal the sum of the logs.")   ◢

EXAMPLE 3   Using Properties of Logarithms

Given $\log_b 2 \approx 0.693$, $\log_b 3 \approx 1.099$, and $\log_b 7 \approx 1.946$, use the properties of logarithms to approximate the following.

a. $\log_b 6$ **b.** $\log_b \dfrac{7}{27}$

Solution

a. $\log_b 6 = \log_b(2 \cdot 3)$

$\quad\quad\quad\; = \log_b 2 + \log_b 3$ *Property 1*

$\quad\quad\quad\; \approx 0.693 + 1.099$

$\quad\quad\quad\; = 1.792$

b. $\log_b \dfrac{7}{27} = \log_b 7 - \log_b 27$ *Property 2*

$\quad\quad\quad\; = \log_b 7 - \log_b 3^3$

$\quad\quad\quad\; = \log_b 7 - 3 \log_b 3$ *Property 3*

$\quad\quad\quad\; \approx 1.946 - 3(1.099)$

$\quad\quad\quad\; = -1.351$ ◢

EXAMPLE 4 Using Properties of Logarithms

Use the properties of logarithms to verify that

$$-\ln \frac{1}{a} = \ln a.$$

Solution

$$-\ln \frac{1}{a} = -\ln(a^{-1}) = -(-1) \ln a = \ln a$$

Try verifying this result on your calculator using $a = 2$. ◢

Rewriting Logarithmic Expressions

The properties of logarithms are useful for rewriting logarithmic expressions in forms that simplify the operations of algebra. This is true because they convert complicated products, quotients, and exponential forms into simpler sums, differences, and products, respectively.

EXAMPLE 5 Rewriting the Logarithm of a Product

Use the properties of logarithms to rewrite

$$\log_{10} 5x^3 y$$

as the sum of logarithms.

Solution

$$\log_{10} 5x^3 y = \log_{10} 5 + \log_{10} x^3 y$$
$$= \log_{10} 5 + \log_{10} x^3 + \log_{10} y$$
$$= \log_{10} 5 + 3 \log_{10} x + \log_{10} y$$ ◢

EXAMPLE 6 Rewriting the Logarithm of a Quotient

Use the properties of logarithms to rewrite

$$\ln \frac{\sqrt{3x - 5}}{7}$$

as the sum and/or difference of logarithms.

Solution

$$\ln \frac{\sqrt{3x - 5}}{7} = \ln(3x - 5)^{1/2} - \ln 7$$

$$= \frac{1}{2}\ln(3x - 5) - \ln 7$$ ◢

In Examples 5 and 6, we used the properties of logarithms to *expand* logarithmic expressions. In Examples 7 and 8, we reverse the procedure and use the properties of logarithms to *condense* logarithmic expressions.

EXAMPLE 7   Condensing a Logarithmic Expression

Rewrite as the logarithm of a single quantity.

$$\frac{1}{2} \log_{10} x - 3 \log_{10}(x + 1)$$

Solution

$$\frac{1}{2} \log_{10} x - 3 \log_{10}(x + 1) = \log_{10} x^{1/2} - \log_{10}(x + 1)^3 \qquad \textit{Property 3}$$

$$= \log_{10} \frac{\sqrt{x}}{(x + 1)^3} \qquad \textit{Property 2}$$

EXAMPLE 8   Condensing a Logarithmic Expression

Rewrite as the logarithm of a single quantity.

$$2 \ln(x + 2) + \ln x$$

Solution

$$2 \ln(x + 2) + \ln x = \ln(x + 2)^2 + \ln x \qquad \textit{Property 3}$$

$$= \ln x(x + 2)^2 \qquad \textit{Property 1}$$

When applying the properties of logarithms to a logarithmic function, you should take note of the domain of the function. For example, the domain of $f(x) = \ln x^2$ is all real $x \neq 0$, whereas the domain of $g(x) = 2 \ln x$ is all real $x > 0$.

DISCUSSION

PROBLEM

Demonstrating
Properties of
Logarithms

For each of the following statements: (a) If it is *true*, state a property of logarithms to support your answer. (b) If it is *false*, use your calculator to support your answer.

1. $\log(3 + 5) = \log 3 + \log 5$ 2. $\log 9 = \log 36 - \log 4$

3. $\dfrac{\log 3}{\log 2} = \log \dfrac{3}{2}$ 4. $\log 28 = \log 4 \cdot \log 7$

5. $\log 3^5 = 3 \log 5$ 6. $\log 81 = 4 \log 3$

WARM UP

The following warm-up exercises involve skills that were covered in earlier sections. You will use these skills in the exercise set for this section.

In Exercises 1–4, evaluate the expressions without using a calculator.

1. $\log_7 49$

2. $\log_2\left(\frac{1}{32}\right)$

3. $\ln \frac{1}{e^2}$

4. $\log_{10} 0.001$

In Exercises 5–8, simplify the expressions.

5. e^2e^3

6. $\dfrac{e^2}{e^3}$

7. $(e^2)^3$

8. $(e^2)^0$

In Exercises 9 and 10, rewrite the expressions in exponential form.

9. $\dfrac{1}{x^2}$

10. $\sqrt{x}$

EXERCISES for Section 4.3

In Exercises 1–4, use the change of base formula to write the given logarithm as a multiple of a common logarithm. For instance, $\log_2 3 = (1/\log_{10} 2)\log_{10} 3$.

1. $\log_3 5$

2. $\log_4 10$

3. $\log_2 x$

4. $\ln 5$

In Exercises 5–8, use the change of base formula to write the given logarithm as a multiple of a natural logarithm. For instance, $\log_2 3 = (1/\ln 2)\ln 3$.

5. $\log_3 5$

6. $\log_4 10$

7. $\log_2 x$

8. $\log_{10} 5$

In Exercises 9–16, evaluate the logarithm using the change of base formula. Do the problem twice, once with common logarithms and once with natural logarithms. Round to three decimal places.

9. $\log_3 7$

10. $\log_7 4$

11. $\log_{1/2} 4$

12. $\log_4(0.55)$

13. $\log_9(0.4)$

14. $\log_{20} 125$

15. $\log_{15} 1250$

16. $\log_{1/3}(0.015)$

In Exercises 17–36, use the properties of logarithms to write the expression as a sum, difference, and/or multiple of logarithms.

17. $\log_{10} 5x$

18. $\log_{10} 10z$

19. $\log_{10} \dfrac{5}{x}$

20. $\log_{10} \dfrac{y}{2}$

21. $\log_8 x^4$

22. $\log_6 z^{-3}$

23. $\ln \sqrt{z}$

24. $\ln \sqrt[3]{t}$

25. $\ln xyz$

26. $\ln \dfrac{xy}{z}$

27. $\ln \sqrt{a-1}$

28. $\ln\left(\dfrac{x^2-1}{x^3}\right)$

29. $\ln z(z-1)^2$

30. $\ln \sqrt{\dfrac{x^2}{y^3}}$

31. $\ln \sqrt[3]{\dfrac{x}{y}}$

32. $\ln \dfrac{x}{\sqrt{x^2+1}}$

33. $\ln \dfrac{x^4\sqrt{y}}{z^5}$

34. $\ln \sqrt{x^2(x+2)}$

35. $\log_b \dfrac{x^2}{y^2z^3}$

36. $\log_b \dfrac{\sqrt{xy^4}}{z^4}$

In Exercises 37–56, write the expression as the logarithm of a single quantity.

37. $\ln x + \ln 2$

38. $\ln y + \ln z$

39. $\log_4 z - \log_4 y$

40. $\log_5 8 - \log_5 t$

41. $2 \log_2(x + 4)$

42. $-4 \log_6 2x$

43. $\frac{1}{3} \log_3 5x$

44. $\frac{3}{2} \log_7(z - 2)$

45. $\ln x - 3 \ln(x + 1)$

46. $2 \ln 8 + 5 \ln z$

47. $\ln(x - 2) - \ln(x + 2)$

48. $3 \ln x + 2 \ln y - 4 \ln z$

49. $\ln x - 2[\ln(x + 2) + \ln(x - 2)]$

50. $4[\ln z + \ln(z + 5)] - 2 \ln(z - 5)$

51. $\frac{1}{3}[2 \ln(x + 3) + \ln x - \ln(x^2 - 1)]$

52. $2[\ln x - \ln(x + 1) - \ln(x - 1)]$

53. $\frac{1}{3}[\ln y + 2 \ln(y + 4)] - \ln(y - 1)$

54. $\frac{1}{2}[\ln(x + 1) + 2 \ln(x - 1)] + 3 \ln x$

55. $2 \ln 3 - \frac{1}{2} \ln(x^2 + 1)$

56. $\frac{3}{2} \ln 5t^6 - \frac{3}{4} \ln t^4$

In Exercises 57–70, approximate the logarithm using the properties of logarithms, given $\log_b 2 \approx 0.3562$, $\log_b 3 \approx 0.5646$, and $\log_b 5 \approx 0.8271$.

57. $\log_b 6$

58. $\log_b 15$

59. $\log_b\left(\frac{3}{2}\right)$

60. $\log_b\left(\frac{5}{3}\right)$

61. $\log_b 25$

62. $\log_b 18 \quad (18 = 2 \cdot 3^2)$

63. $\log_b \sqrt{2}$

64. $\log_b\left(\frac{9}{2}\right)$

65. $\log_b \frac{1}{4}$

66. $\log_b \sqrt[3]{75}$

67. $\log_b \sqrt{5b}$

68. $\log_b(3b^2)$

69. $\log_b \dfrac{(4.5)^3}{\sqrt{3}}$

70. $\log_b 1$

In Exercises 71–76, find the exact value of the logarithm.

71. $\log_3 9$

72. $\log_6 \sqrt[3]{6}$

73. $\log_4 16^{1.2}$

74. $\log_5\left(\frac{1}{125}\right)$

75. $\ln e^{4.5}$

76. $\ln \sqrt[4]{e^3}$

In Exercises 77–84, use the properties of logarithms to simplify the given logarithmic expression.

77. $\log_4 8$

78. $\log_5\left(\frac{1}{15}\right)$

79. $\log_7 \sqrt{70}$

80. $\log_2(4^2 \cdot 3^4)$

81. $\log_5\left(\frac{1}{250}\right)$

82. $\log_{10}\left(\frac{9}{300}\right)$

83. $\ln(5e^6)$

84. $\ln \dfrac{6}{e^2}$

85. *Sound Intensity*   The relationship between the number of decibels β and the intensity of a sound I in watts per meter squared is given by

$$\beta = 10 \log_{10}\left(\frac{I}{10^{-16}}\right).$$

Use properties of logarithms to write the formula in simpler form, and determine the number of decibels of a sound with an intensity of 10^{-10} watts per meter squared.

86. Approximate the natural logarithm of as many integers as possible between 1 and 20 given that $\ln 2 \approx 0.6931$, $\ln 3 \approx 1.0986$, and $\ln 5 \approx 1.6094$.

87. Prove that $\log_b \dfrac{u}{v} = \log_b u - \log_b v$.

88. Prove that $\log_b u^n = n \log_b u$.

4.4 Solving Exponential and Logarithmic Equations

Introduction / Solving Exponential Equations / Solving Logarithmic Equations / Applications

Introduction

So far in this chapter, you have studied the definitions, graphs, and properties of exponential and logarithmic functions. Now we will concentrate on procedures for *solving equations* involving these exponential and logarithmic functions. The solution procedures are based on the fact that the exponential and logarithmic functions are inverses of each other.

PROPERTIES OF EXPONENTIAL AND LOGARITHMIC FUNCTIONS

Let $f(x) = a^x$ and $g(x) = \log_a x$, with $a > 1$.

Inverse Properties	*Reason*
1. $\log_a a^x = x$	$(g \circ f)(x) = x$
$\quad \ln e^x = x$	Replace base a by base e
2. $a^{\log_a x} = x$	$(f \circ g)(x) = x$
$\quad e^{\ln x} = x$	Replace base a by base e

One-to-One Properties	*Reason*
3. $x = y$ if and only if $\log_a x = \log_a y$	g is one-to-one
4. $x = y$ if and only if $a^x = a^y$	f is one-to-one

To solve a simple equation like $2^x = 32$, we can rewrite it as $2^x = 2^5$ and use Property 4 to conclude that $x = 5$. However, to solve for x in the equation $e^x = 7$, we use two different properties.

$$e^x = 7 \qquad \qquad \text{\textit{Given equation}}$$
$$\ln e^x = \ln 7 \qquad \text{\textit{Take logarithm of both sides}}$$
$$x = \ln 7 \qquad \qquad \text{\textit{Property 1}}$$

This example suggests that to solve an exponential equation, you take the logarithms of both sides. On the other hand, to solve a logarithmic equation you rewrite it in exponential form.

Guidelines for Solving Exponential and Logarithmic Equations

1. *To solve an exponential equation*, first isolate the exponential expression, then take the logarithm of both sides and solve for the variable.
2. *To solve a logarithmic equation*, rewrite the equation in exponential form and solve for the variable.

Solving Exponential Equations

EXAMPLE 1   Solving an Exponential Equation

$$e^x = 72 \qquad \qquad \text{\textit{Given equation}}$$
$$\ln e^x = \ln 72 \qquad \text{\textit{Take log of both sides}}$$
$$x = \ln 72 \qquad \quad \text{\textit{Inverse property of logs and exponents}}$$
$$x \approx 4.277$$

A check, using your calculator, will show that $e^{4.277} \approx 72$.

EXAMPLE 2   Solving an Exponential Equation

$$4e^{2x} = 5 \qquad \textit{Given equation}$$

$$e^{2x} = \frac{5}{4} \qquad \textit{Divide both sides by 4}$$

$$\ln e^{2x} = \ln \frac{5}{4} \qquad \textit{Take log of both sides}$$

$$2x = \ln \frac{5}{4} \qquad \textit{Inverse property of logs and exponents}$$

$$x = \frac{1}{2} \ln \frac{5}{4} \qquad \textit{Divide both sides by 2}$$

$$x \approx 0.112$$

Thus, the solution is $x = \frac{1}{2} \ln \frac{5}{4}$. Check this solution in the original equation.

When an equation involves two or more exponential expressions, we can still use a procedure similar to that demonstrated in the first two examples. However, the algebra is a bit more complicated. Study the next example carefully.

EXAMPLE 3   Solving an Exponential Equation

$$e^{2x} - 3e^x + 2 = 0 \qquad \textit{Given equation}$$

$$(e^x)^2 - 3e^x + 2 = 0 \qquad \textit{Quadratic form}$$

$$(e^x - 2)(e^x - 1) = 0 \qquad \textit{Factor}$$

$$e^x - 2 = 0 \qquad e^x - 1 = 0 \qquad \textit{Set factors to zero}$$

$$e^x = 2 \qquad \qquad e^x = 1$$

$$x = \ln 2 \qquad \qquad x = 0 \qquad \textit{Solutions}$$

Thus, the equation has two solutions: $x = \ln 2$ and $x = 0$. Check each solution in the original equation.

Examples 1 through 3 all deal with exponential equations in which the base is e. The same approach can be used to solve exponential equations involving other bases.

EXAMPLE 4 A Base Other Than e

$2^x = 10$	*Given equation*
$\ln 2^x = \ln 10$	*Take log of both sides*
$x \ln 2 = \ln 10$	*Property of logarithms*
$x = \dfrac{\ln 10}{\ln 2}$	*Divide both sides by ln 2*

Thus, the equation has one solution: $x = \ln 10/\ln 2 \approx 3.32$. Try checking this solution in the original equation. (*Note:* Using the change of base formula, this solution could be written as $x = \log_2 10$.)

EXAMPLE 5 A Base Other Than e

$4^{x+3} = 7^x$	*Given equation*
$\ln 4^{x+3} = \ln 7^x$	*Take ln of both sides*
$(x + 3)\ln 4 = x \ln 7$	*Property 3*
$x \ln 4 + 3 \ln 4 = x \ln 7$	*Distributive Property*
$x \ln 4 - x \ln 7 = -3 \ln 4$	*Collect like terms*
$x(\ln 4 - \ln 7) = -3 \ln 4$	*Factor out x*
$x = \dfrac{-3 \ln 4}{\ln 4 - \ln 7}$	*Divide*
$x \approx 7.432$	

Solving Logarithmic Equations

To solve a logarithmic equation, convert it to an equivalent exponential equation by using the definition $\log_a x = y$ if and only if $x = a^y$. For example,

$\ln x = 3$	*Logarithmic form*
$x = e^3.$	*Exponential form (by definition)*

Such a conversion to exponential form encompasses two properties of exponential functions.

$\ln x = 3$	*Given equation*
$e^{\ln x} = e^3$	*Exponentiate both sides (Property 4)*
$x = e^3$	*Exponential form (Property 2)*

This latter procedure is sometimes called *exponentiating* both sides of an equation.

EXAMPLE 6 Solving a Logarithmic Equation

$\ln x = 2$	*Given equation*
$x = e^2$	*Exponential form*
$x \approx 7.389$	

Thus, the solution is $x = e^2$. Check this solution in the original equation. ◢

EXAMPLE 7 Solving a Logarithmic Equation

$5 + 2 \ln x = 4$	*Given equation*
$2 \ln x = -1$	*Subtract 5 from both sides*
$\ln x = -\dfrac{1}{2}$	*Divide both sides by 2*
$x = e^{-1/2}$	*Exponential form*
$x \approx 0.607$	

Thus, the equation has one solution: $x = e^{-1/2}$. Check this solution in the original equation. ◢

EXAMPLE 8 Solving a Logarithmic Equation

$2 \ln 3x = 4$	*Given equation*
$\ln 3x = 2$	*Divide both sides by 2*
$3x = e^2$	*Exponential form*
$x = \dfrac{1}{3}e^2$	*Divide both sides by 3*
$x \approx 2.463$	

Thus, the equation has one solution: $x = \frac{1}{3}e^2$. Check this solution in the original equation. ◢

The techniques used to solve the equations involving logarithmic expressions can produce extraneous solutions.

EXAMPLE 9   Solving a Logarithmic Equation

$$\ln(x - 2) + \ln(2x - 3) = 2 \ln x \qquad \textit{Given equation}$$

$$\ln(x - 2)(2x - 3) = \ln x^2 \qquad \textit{Properties of logarithms}$$

$$\ln(2x^2 - 7x + 6) = \ln x^2$$

$$2x^2 - 7x + 6 = x^2 \qquad \textit{One-to-one property of exponentials}$$

$$x^2 - 7x + 6 = 0 \qquad \textit{Quadratic form}$$

$$(x - 6)(x - 1) = 0 \qquad \textit{Factor}$$

$$x - 6 = 0 \ \rightarrow \ x = 6 \qquad \textit{Set 1st factor equal to 0}$$

$$x - 1 = 0 \ \rightarrow \ x = 1 \qquad \textit{Set 2nd factor equal to 0}$$

Finally, by checking these two "solutions" in the original equation, we find that $x = 1$ is not valid. Do you see why? Thus, the only solution is $x = 6$.

EXAMPLE 10   The Change of Base Formula

Prove the change of base formula given in Section 4.3.

$$\log_a x = \frac{\log_b x}{\log_b a}$$

Solution

We begin by letting

$$y = \log_a x$$

and writing the equivalent exponential form

$$a^y = x.$$

Now, taking the logarithm *with base b* of both sides, we have

$$\log_b a^y = \log_b x$$

$$y \log_b a = \log_b x$$

$$y = \frac{\log_b x}{\log_b a}$$

$$\log_a x = \frac{\log_b x}{\log_b a}.$$

Applications

EXAMPLE 11   Waste Processed for Energy Recovery

The amount of municipal waste processed for energy recovery in the United States from 1960 to 1986 can be approximated by the equation

$$y = 0.00643e^{0.00533t^2}$$

where y is the amount of waste (in pounds per person) that was processed for energy recovery and t represents the calendar year with $t = 0$ corresponding to 1960 (see Figure 4.17). According to this model, during which year did the amount of waste reach 0.2 pounds? (*Source:* Franklin Associates, *Characterization of Municipal Solid Waste in U.S.*)

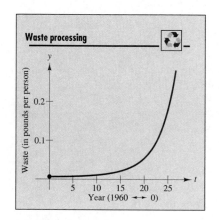

Waste processing

Waste (in pounds per person)

Year (1960 ⟷ 0)

FIGURE 4.17

Solution

$$0.00643e^{0.00533t^2} = y \qquad \textit{Given model}$$
$$0.00643e^{0.00533t^2} = 0.2 \qquad \textit{Let y equal 0.2}$$
$$e^{0.00533t^2} \approx 31.104 \qquad \textit{Divide both sides by 0.00643}$$
$$\ln e^{0.00533t^2} \approx \ln 31.104 \qquad \textit{Take log of both sides}$$
$$0.00533t^2 \approx 3.437 \qquad \textit{Inverse property of logs and exponents}$$
$$t^2 \approx 644.905 \qquad \textit{Divide both sides by 0.00533}$$
$$t \approx 25.4 \qquad \textit{Extract positive square root}$$

Thus, the solution is $t \approx 25.4$ years. Since $t = 0$ represents 1960, it follows that the amount of waste would have reached 0.2 pounds per person in 1985.

DISCUSSION
PROBLEM

Verifying
Inverse
Relationships

If you have a graphics calculator or other graphing facility (such as computer software), use it to verify the following inverse relationships between logarithmic and exponential functions.

Base 10	Base e
1. $\log_{10} 10^x = x$	$\ln e^x = x$
2. $10^{\log_{10} x} = x$	$e^{\ln x} = x$

You can do this by sketching the graph of each relationship. For instance, to verify that $\ln e^x = x$, try sketching the graph of $y = \ln e^x$ and $y = x$. The two graphs should be identical.

WARM UP

The following warm-up exercises involve skills that were covered in earlier sections. You will use these skills in the exercise set for this section.

In Exercises 1–6, solve for x.

1. $x \ln 2 = \ln 3$
2. $(x - 1)\ln 4 = 2$
3. $2xe^2 = e^3$
4. $4xe^{-1} = 8$
5. $x^2 - 4x + 5 = 0$
6. $2x^2 - 3x + 1 = 0$

In Exercises 7–10, simplify the expressions.

7. $\log_{10} 100^x$
8. $\log_4 64^x$
9. $\ln e^{2x}$
10. $\ln e^{-x^2}$

EXERCISES for Section 4.4

In Exercises 1–10, solve for x without the aid of a calculator.

1. $4^x = 16$
2. $3^x = 243$
3. $7^x = \frac{1}{49}$
4. $8^x = 4$
5. $\left(\frac{3}{4}\right)^x = \frac{27}{64}$
6. $3^{x-1} = 27$
7. $\log_4 x = 3$
8. $\log_5 5x = 2$
9. $\log_{10} x = -1$
10. $\ln(2x - 1) = 0$

In Exercises 11–16, apply the inverse properties of $\ln x$ and e^x to simplify the given expression.

11. $\ln e^{x^2}$
12. $\ln e^{2x-1}$
13. $e^{\ln(5x+2)}$
14. $-1 + \ln e^{2x}$
15. $e^{\ln x^2}$
16. $-8 + e^{\ln x^3}$

In Exercises 17–50, solve the given exponential equation. Round to three decimal places.

17. $e^x = 10$
18. $e^x = 6500$
19. $2e^x = 39$
20. $4e^x = 91$
21. $e^x - 5 = 10$
22. $e^x + 6 = 38$
23. $7 - 2e^x = 5$
24. $-14 + 3e^x = 11$
25. $e^{3x} = 12$
26. $e^{2x} = 50$
27. $500e^{-x} = 300$
28. $1000e^{-4x} = 75$
29. $3e^{3x/2} = 962$
30. $6e^{1-x} = 25$
31. $e^{2x} - 4e^x - 5 = 0$
32. $e^{2x} - 5e^x + 6 = 0$
33. $3(1 + e^{2x}) = 4$
34. $20(100 - e^{x/2}) = 500$

35. $\dfrac{400}{1 + e^{-x}} = 200$
36. $\dfrac{3000}{2 + e^{-2x}} - 1200$
37. $10^x = 42$
38. $10^x = 570$
39. $3^{2x} = 80$
40. $6^{5x} = 3000$
41. $5^{-t/2} = 0.20$
42. $4^{-3t} = 0.10$
43. $\frac{1}{3}(10^{2x}) = 12$
44. $8(10^{3x}) = 12$
45. $3(5^{x-1}) = 21$
46. $2^{3-x} = 565$
47. $5^{x+2} = 3^{2x-1}$
48. $6^{3x-5} = 2^{7x}$
49. $\left(1 + \dfrac{0.10}{12}\right)^{12t} = 2$
50. $\left(1 + \dfrac{0.065}{365}\right)^{365t} = 4$

In Exercises 51–70, solve the given logarithmic equation. Round to three decimal places.

51. $\ln x = 5$
52. $\ln x = -4.5$
53. $\ln 2x = 2.4$
54. $\ln 4x = 1$
55. $2 \log_6 4x = 0$
56. $3 \log_2 5x = 10$
57. $\ln \sqrt{x + 2} = 1$
58. $\ln(x + 1)^2 = 2$
59. $\ln x + \ln(x - 2) = 1$
60. $\ln x + \ln(x + 3) = 1$
61. $\log_{10}(z - 3) = 2$
62. $\log_{10} x^2 = 6$
63. $\log_{10}(x + 4) - \log_{10} x = \log_{10}(x + 2)$
64. $\log_2 x + \log_2(x + 2) = \log_2(x + 6)$
65. $\log_3 x + \log_3(x^2 - 8) = \log_3 8x$
66. $\ln(x + 1) - \ln(x - 2) = \ln x^2$
67. $\ln(x + 5) = \ln(x - 1) - \ln(x + 1)$
68. $\log_{10} x - \log_{10}(2x - 1) = 0$
69. $\log_2(x + 5) - \log_2(x - 2) = 3$
70. $\log_4 x - \log_4(x - 1) = \frac{1}{2}$

Compound Interest   In Exercises 71 and 72, find the time required for a $1000 investment to double at interest rate r, compounded continuously.

71. $r = 0.085$ **72.** $r = 0.12$

Compound Interest   In Exercises 73 and 74, find the time required for a $1000 investment to triple at interest rate r, compounded continuously.

73. $r = 0.085$ **74.** $r = 0.12$

75. *Demand Function*   The demand equation for a certain product is given by

$$p = 500 - 0.5(e^{0.004x}).$$

Find the demand x for a price of (a) $p = \$350$ and (b) $p = \$300$.

76. *Demand Function*   The demand equation for a certain product is given by

$$p = 5000\left(1 - \frac{4}{4 + e^{-0.002x}}\right).$$

Find the demand x for a price of (a) $p = \$600$ and (b) $p = \$400$.

77. *Forest Yield*   The yield V (in millions of cubic feet per acre) for a forest at age t years is given by

$$V = 6.7e^{-48.1/t}.$$

Find the time necessary to have a yield of (a) 1.3 million cubic feet and (b) 2 million cubic feet.

78. *Human Memory Model*   In a group project in learning theory, a mathematical model for the proportion P of correct responses after n trials was found to be

$$P = \frac{0.83}{1 + e^{-0.2n}}.$$

After how many trials will 60% of the responses be correct?

79. *Average Heights*   The percentage of American males between the ages of 18 and 24 who are no more than x inches tall is given by

$$m(x) = \frac{100}{1 + e^{-0.6114(x-69.71)}}$$

where m is the percentage and x is the height in inches (see figure). (*Source:* U.S. National Center for Health Statistics) The function giving the percentages f for females for the same ages is given by

$$f(x) = \frac{100}{1 + e^{-0.66607(x-64.51)}}.$$

What is the median height of each sex?

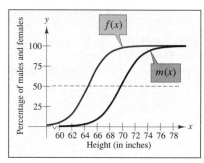

Figure for 79

80. *Trees per Acre*   The number of trees per acre N of a certain species is approximated by the model

$$N = 68 \cdot 10^{-0.04x}, \qquad 5 \le x \le 40$$

where x is the average diameter (in inches) of the trees three feet above the ground. Use the model to approximate the average diameter of the trees in a test plot when $N = 21$.

4.5 Exponential and Logarithmic Applications

Compound Interest / Growth and Decay / Logistics Growth Models / Logarithmic Models

Compound Interest

The behavior of many physical, economic, and social phenomena can be described by exponential and logarithmic functions. In this section, we look at four basic types of applications: (1) compound interest, (2) growth and decay, (3) logistics models, and (4) intensity models. The problems presented in this section require the full range of solution techniques studied in this chapter.

From Section 4.1, recall the following two compound interest formulas, where A is the account balance, P is the principal, r is the annual percentage rate, and t is the time in years.

n Compoundings per Year   *Continuous Compounding*

$$A = P\left(1 + \frac{r}{n}\right)^{nt} \qquad\qquad A = Pe^{rt}$$

EXAMPLE 1 Doubling Time for an Investment

An investment is made in a trust fund at an annual percentage rate of 9.5%, compounded quarterly. How long will it take for the investment to double in value?

Solution

For quarterly compounding, we use the formula

$$A = P\left(1 + \frac{r}{4}\right)^{4t}.$$

Using $r = 0.095$, the time required for the investment to double is given by solving for t in the equation $2P = A$.

$$2P = P\left(1 + \frac{0.095}{4}\right)^{4t} \qquad\qquad 2P = A$$

$$2 = (1.02375)^{4t} \qquad\qquad \textit{Divide both sides by P}$$

$$\ln 2 = \ln(1.02375)^{4t} \qquad\qquad \textit{Take ln of both sides}$$

$$\ln 2 = 4t \ln(1.02375)$$

$$t = \frac{\ln 2}{4 \ln(1.02375)} \approx 7.4$$

Therefore, it will take approximately 7.4 years for the investment to double in value with quarterly compounding. ◢

Try reworking Example 1 using continuous compounding. To do this you will need to solve the equation

$$2P = Pe^{0.095t}.$$

The solution is $t \approx 7.3$ years, which makes sense because the principal should double more quickly with continuous compounding than with quarterly compounding.

From Example 1, we see that the time required for an investment to double in value is independent of the amount invested. In general, the **doubling time** is as follows.

n Compoundings per Year	*Continuous Compounding*
$t = \dfrac{\ln 2}{n \ln[1 + (r/n)]}$	$t = \dfrac{\ln 2}{r}$

EXAMPLE 2   Finding an Annual Percentage Rate

An investment of $10,000 is compounded continuously. What annual percentage rate will produce a balance of $25,000 in 10 years?

Solution

We use the formula

$$A = Pe^{rt}$$

with $P = 10,000$, $A = 25,000$, and $t = 10$, and solve the following equation for r.

$$10,000e^{10r} = 25,000$$
$$e^{10r} = 2.5$$
$$10r = \ln 2.5$$
$$r = \frac{1}{10} \ln 2.5 \approx 0.0916$$

Thus, the annual percentage rate must be approximately 9.16%.

EXAMPLE 3   The Effective Yield for an Investment

A deposit is compounded continuously at an annual percentage rate of 7.5%. Find the simple interest rate that would yield the same balance at the end of one year (**effective yield**).

Solution

Using the formula $A = Pe^{rt}$ with $r = 0.075$ and $t = 1$, the balance at the end of one year is

$$A = Pe^{0.075(1)}$$
$$\approx P(1.0779)$$
$$= P(1 + 0.0779).$$ $A = P(1 + r)$

Since the formula for simple interest after one year is

$$A = P(1 + r)$$

we conclude that the effective yield is approximately 7.79%.   ◀

Growth and Decay

The balance in an account earning *continuously compounded* interest is one example of a quantity that increases over time according to the **exponential growth model**

$$Q(t) = Ce^{kt}.$$

In this model, $Q(t)$ is the size of the population (balance, weight, and so forth) at any time t, C is the original population (when $t = 0$), and k is a constant determined by the rate of growth. If $k > 0$, the population *grows* (increases) over time, and if $k < 0$ it *decays* (decreases) over time. Example 11 of Section 4.1 is an example of population growth. Recall from Section 4.1 that we can remember this growth model as *(Then)* $= (Now)(e^{kt})$.

EXAMPLE 4   Exponential Decay

Radioactive iodine is a by-product of some types of nuclear reactors. Its half-life is 60 days. That is, after 60 days, a given amount of radioactive iodine will have decayed to half the original amount. Suppose a contained nuclear accident occurs and gives off an initial amount C of radioactive iodine.

a. Write an equation for the amount of radioactive iodine present at any time t following the accident.
b. How long will it take for the radioactive iodine to decay to a level of 20% of the original amount?

Solution

a. We first need to find the rate k, in the exponential model $Q(t) = Ce^{kt}$. Knowing that half the original amount remains after $t = 60$ days, we obtain

$$Q(60) = Ce^{k(60)} = \frac{1}{2}C$$

$$e^{60k} = \frac{1}{2}$$

$$60k = -\ln 2$$

$$k = \frac{-\ln 2}{60} \approx -0.0116.$$

Thus, the exponential model is

$$Q(t) = Ce^{-0.0116t}.$$

b. The time required to decay to 20% of the original amount is given by

$$Q(t) = Ce^{-0.0116t} = (0.2)C$$

$$e^{-0.0116t} = 0.2$$

$$-0.0116t = \ln 0.2$$

$$t = \frac{\ln 0.2}{-0.0116} \approx 139 \text{ days.}$$

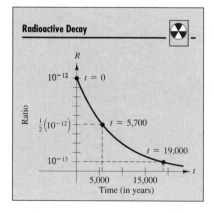

Radioactive Decay

FIGURE 4.18

In living organic material the ratio of radioactive carbon isotopes (Carbon 14) to the number of nonradioactive carbon isotopes (Carbon 12) is about 1 to 10^{12}. When organic material dies, its Carbon 12 content remains fixed, whereas its radioactive Carbon 14 begins to decay with a half-life of about 5700 years. To estimate the age of dead organic material, scientists use the following formula, which denotes the ratio of Carbon 14 to Carbon 12 present at any time t (in years).

$$R = \frac{1}{10^{12}}e^{-t/8223}$$

The graph of R is shown in Figure 4.18. Note that R decreases as the time t increases.

EXAMPLE 5   Carbon Dating

Suppose the Carbon 14/Carbon 12 ratio of a newly discovered fossil is

$$R = \frac{1}{10^{13}}.$$

Estimate the age of the fossil.

Solution

In the carbon dating model, we substitute the given value of R to obtain

$$\frac{1}{10^{12}}e^{-t/8223} = R \qquad \textit{Given model}$$

$$\frac{e^{-t/8223}}{10^{12}} = \frac{1}{10^{13}} \qquad \textit{Let R equal } 1/10^{13}$$

$$e^{-t/8223} = \frac{1}{10} \qquad \textit{Multiply both sides by } 10^{12}$$

$$\ln e^{-t/8223} = \ln \frac{1}{10} \qquad \textit{Take log of both sides}$$

$$-\frac{t}{8223} \approx -2.3026 \qquad \textit{Inverse property of logs and exponents}$$

$$t \approx 18,934. \qquad \textit{Multiply both sides by 8223}$$

Thus, to the nearest thousand years, we estimate the age of the fossil to be 19,000 years. ▲

REMARK The carbon dating model in Example 5 assumed that the Carbon 14/Carbon 12 ratio was one part in 10,000,000,000,000. Suppose an error in measurement occurred and the actual ratio was only one part in 8,000,000,000,000. The fossil age corresponding to the actual ratio would then be approximately 17,000 years. Check this result.

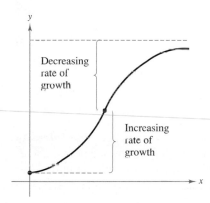

Logistic Curve

FIGURE 4.19

Logistics Growth Models

Some populations initially have rapid growth, followed by a declining rate of growth, as indicated by the graph in Figure 4.19. One model for describing this type of growth pattern is the **logistics curve** given by the function

$$y = \frac{a}{1 + be^{(-(x-c)/d)}}$$

where y is the population size and x is the time. An example would be a bacteria culture allowed to grow initially under ideal conditions, followed by less favorable conditions that inhibit growth. A logistics growth curve is also called a **sigmoidal curve**.

EXAMPLE 6 Spread of a Virus

On a college campus of 5000 students, one student returned from vacation with a contagious flu virus. The spread of the virus through the student body is given by

$$y = \frac{5000}{1 + 4999e^{-0.8t}}$$

where y is the total number infected after t days. The college will cancel classes when 40% or more of the students are ill.

a. How many students are infected after five days?
b. After how many days will the college cancel classes?

Solution

a. After five days, the number of students infected is

$$y = \frac{5000}{1 + 4999e^{-0.8(5)}} = \frac{5000}{1 + 4999e^{-4}} \approx 54.$$

b. In this case, the number of students infected is $(0.40)(5000) = 2000$. Therefore, we solve for t in the following equation.

$$2000 = \frac{5000}{1 + 4999e^{-0.8t}}$$

$$1 + 4999e^{-0.8t} = 2.5$$

$$e^{-0.8t} \approx 0.0003$$

$$\ln(e^{-0.8t}) \approx \ln 0.0003$$

$$-0.8t \approx -8.1115$$

$$t \approx 10.1$$

Hence, after 10 days, at least 40% of the students will be infected, and the college will cancel classes. The graph of the function is shown in Figure 4.20. ◢

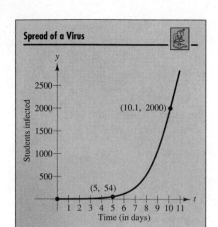

Spread of a Virus

FIGURE 4.20

Logarithmic Models

Sound and shock waves can be measured by the **intensity model**

$$S = K \log_{10} \frac{I}{I_0}$$

where I is the intensity of the stimulus wave, I_0 is the **threshold intensity** (the smallest value of I that can be detected by the listening device), and K determines the units in which S is measured. Sound heard by the human ear is measured in decibels. One **decibel** is considered to be the smallest detectable difference in the loudness of two sounds.

EXAMPLE 7 Magnitude of Earthquakes

On the Richter Scale, the magnitude R of an earthquake of intensity I is given by

$$R = \log_{10} \frac{I}{I_0}$$

where $I_0 = 1$ is the minimum intensity used for comparison. Find the intensity per unit of area for the following earthquakes. (Intensity is a measure of the wave energy of an earthquake.)

a. San Francisco in 1906, $R = 8.6$
b. Mexico City in 1978, $R = 7.85$
c. San Francisco Bay Area in 1989, $R = 7.1$

Solution

a. Since $I_0 = 1$ and $R = 8.6$, we have

$$8.6 = \log_{10} I$$
$$I = 10^{8.6} \approx 398,107,171.$$

b. For Mexico City, we have $7.85 = \log_{10} I$, and

$$I = 10^{7.85} \approx 70,795,000.$$

c. For $R = 7.1$, we have $7.1 = \log_{10} I$, and

$$I = 10^{7.1} \approx 12,589,254.$$

Note that an increase of 1.5 units on the Richter Scale (from 7.1 to 8.6) represents an intensity change by a factor of

$$\frac{398,107,171}{12,589,254} \approx 31.6.$$

In other words, the "great San Francisco earthquake" in 1906 had a magnitude that was about 32 times more than the one in 1989.

DISCUSSION

PROBLEM

Comparing
Population
Models

The population of the United States from 1800 to 1990 is given (in millions) in the table .

t	0	1	2	3	4	5	6	7	8	9
Year	1800	1810	1820	1830	1840	1850	1860	1870	1880	1890
Population	5.31	7.23	9.64	12.87	17.07	23.19	31.44	39.82	50.16	62.95

t	10	11	12	13	14	15	16	17	18	19
Year	1900	1910	1920	1930	1940	1950	1960	1970	1980	1990
Population	75.99	91.97	105.71	122.78	131.67	151.33	179.32	203.30	226.55	250.00

Using the statistical procedure *least squares regression analysis*, we found the best quadratic and exponential models for this data. Which of the following two equations is a better model for the population of the United States between 1800 and 1990? Describe the method you used to reach your conclusion.

Quadratic Model

$$P = 0.662t^2 + 0.211t + 6.165$$

Exponential Model

$$P = 7.7899e^{0.2013t}$$

WARM UP

The following warm-up exercises involve skills that were covered in earlier sections. You will use these skills in the exercise set for this section.

In Exercises 1–6, sketch the graph of the equation.

1. $y = 2^{0.25x}$

2. $y = 2^{-0.25x}$

3. $y = 4 \log_2 x$

4. $y = \ln(x - 3)$

5. $y = e^{-x^2/5}$

6. $y = \dfrac{2}{1 + e^{-x}}$

In Exercises 7–10, solve the equation for x. Round to three decimal places.

7. $3e^{2x} = 7$

8. $2e^{-0.2x} = 0.002$

9. $4 \ln 5x = 14$

10. $6 \ln 2x = 12$

EXERCISES for Section 4.5

Compound Interest In Exercises 1–10, complete the table for a savings account in which interest is compounded continuously.

	Initial investment	Annual % rate	Effective yield	Time to double	Amount after 10 years
1.	$1,000	12%			
2.	$20,000	$10\frac{1}{2}\%$			
3.	$750			$7\frac{3}{4}$ yr	
4.	$10,000			5 yr	
5.	$500				$1,292.85
6.	$2,000		4.5%		
7.		11%			$19,205.00
8.		8%			$20,000.00
9.	$5,000		8.33%		
10.	$250		12.19%		

Compound Interest In Exercises 11 and 12, determine the principal P which must be invested at rate r, compounded monthly, so that $500,000 will be available for retirement in t years.

11. $r = 7\frac{1}{2}\%$, $t = 20$

12. $r = 12\%$, $t = 40$

Compound Interest In Exercises 13 and 14, determine the time necessary for $1000 to double if it is invested at interest rate r compounded (a) annually, (b) monthly, (c) daily, and (d) continuously.

13. $r = 11\%$

14. $r = 10\frac{1}{2}\%$

15. *Compound Interest* Complete the following table for the time t necessary for P dollars to triple if interest is compounded continuously at rate r.

r	2%	4%	6%	8%	10%	12%
t						

16. *Compound Interest* Complete the following table for the time t necessary for P dollars to triple if interest is compounded annually at rate r.

r	2%	4%	6%	8%	10%	12%
t						

In Exercises 17–22, complete the table for the given radioactive isotope.

Isotope	Half-life (years)	Initial quantity	Amount after 1000 years	Amount after 10,000 years
17. Ra^{226}	1,620	10 g		
18. Ra^{226}	1,620		1.5 g	
19. C^{14}	5,730			2 g
20. C^{14}	5,730	3 g		
21. Pu^{230}	24,360		2.1 g	
22. Pu^{230}	24,360			0.4 g

In Exercises 23–26, find the constant k such that the exponential function $y = Ce^{kt}$ passes through the given points on the graph.

23.
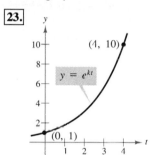

24.
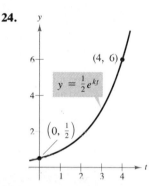

25.
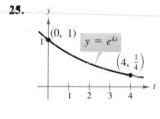

26.
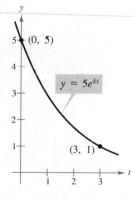

27. *Population*   The population P of a city is given by

$$P = 105,300e^{0.015t}$$

where t is the time in years, with $t = 0$ corresponding to 1990. According to this model, in what year will the city have a population of 150,000?

28. *Population*   The population P of a city is given by

$$P = 240,360e^{0.012t}$$

where t is the time in years, with $t = 0$ corresponding to 1990. According to this model, in what year will the city have a population of 250,000?

29. *Population*   The population P of a city is given by

$$P = 2500e^{kt}$$

where t is the time in years, with $t = 0$ corresponding to the year 1990. In 1945, the population was 1350. Find the value of k and use this result to predict the population in the year 2010.

30. *Population*   The population P of a city is given by

$$P = 140,500e^{kt}$$

where t is the time in years, with $t = 0$ corresponding to the year 1990. In 1960, the population was 100,250. Find the value of k and use this result to predict the population in the year 2000.

31. *Population*   The population of Dhaka, Bangladesh was 4.22 million in 1990, and its projected population for the year 2000 is 6.49 million. (*Source:* U.S Bureau of the Census) Find the exponential growth model $y = Ce^{kt}$ for the population growth of Dhaka by letting $t = 0$ correspond to 1990. Use the model to predict the population of the city in 2010.

32. *Population*   The population of Houston, Texas was 2.30 million in 1990, and its projected population for the year 2000 is 2.65 million. (*Source:* U.S. Bureau of the Census) Find the exponential growth model $y = Ce^{kt}$ for the population growth of Houston by letting $t = 0$ correspond to 1990. Use the model to predict the population of the city in 2010.

33. *Bacteria Growth*   The number of bacteria N in a culture is given by the model

$$N = 100e^{kt}$$

where t is the time in hours, with $t = 0$ corresponding to the time when $N = 100$. When $t = 5$, $N = 300$. How long will it take the population to double in size?

34. *Bacteria Growth*   The number of bacteria N in a culture is given by the model

$$N = 250e^{kt}$$

where t is the time in hours, with $t = 0$ corresponding to the time when $N = 250$. When $t = 10$, $N = 280$. How long will it take the population to double in size?

35. *Radioactive Decay*   The half-life of radioactive radium (Ra^{226}) is 1620 years. What percentage of a present amount of radioactive radium will remain after 100 years?

36. *Radioactive Decay* C^{14} dating assumes that the carbon dioxide on earth today has the same radioactive content as it did centuries ago. If this is true, then the amount of C^{14} absorbed by a tree that grew several centuries ago should be the same as the amount of C^{14} absorbed by a tree growing today. A piece of ancient charcoal contains only 15% as much of the radioactive carbon as a piece of modern charcoal. How long ago was the tree burned to make the ancient charcoal if the half-life of C^{14} is 5730 years?

37. *Depreciation*   A certain car that cost $22,000 new has a depreciated value of $16,500 after one year. Find the value of the car when it is three years old by using the exponential model $y = Ce^{kt}$.

38. *Depreciation*   A computer that cost $4600 new has a depreciated value of $3000 after two years. Find the value of the computer after three years by using the exponential model $y = Ce^{kt}$.

39. *Sales*   The sales S (in thousands of units) of a new product after it has been on the market t years are given by

$$S(t) = 100(1 - e^{kt}).$$

(a) Find S as a function of t if 15,000 units have been sold after one year.

(b) How many units will be sold after five years?

40. *Learning Curve*   The management at a factory has found that the maximum number of units a worker can produce in a day is 30. The learning curve for the number of units N produced per day after a new employee has worked t days is given by

$$N = 30(1 - e^{kt}).$$

After 20 days on the job, a worker produced 19 units per day.

(a) Find the learning curve for this worker (first, find the value of k).

(b) How many days should pass before this worker is producing 25 units per day?

41. *Stocking a Lake with Fish*   A certain lake was stocked with 500 fish and the fish population increased according to the logistics curve

$$p(t) = \frac{10,000}{1 + 19e^{-t/5}}$$

where t is measured in months (see figure).

(a) Estimate the fish population after five months.

(b) After how many months will the fish population be 2000?

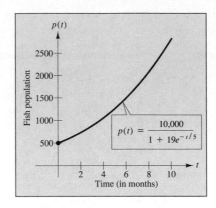

$$p(t) = \frac{10,000}{1 + 19e^{-t/5}}$$

Fish population / Time (in months)

Figure for 41

42. *Endangered Species*   A conservation organization releases 100 animals of an endangered species into a game preserve. The organization believes that the preserve has a carrying capacity of 1000 animals and that the growth of the herd will be modeled by the logistics curve

$$p(t) = \frac{1000}{1 + 9e^{-0.1656t}}$$

where t is measured in years (see figure).

(a) Estimate the population after five years.

(b) After how many years will the population be 500?

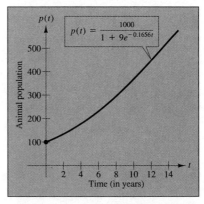

$$p(t) = \frac{1000}{1 + 9e^{-0.1656t}}$$

Animal population / Time (in years)

Figure for 42

43. *Sales and Advertising*   The sales S (in thousands of units) of a product after spending x hundred dollars in advertising is given by

$$S = 10(1 - e^{kx}).$$

(a) Find S as a function of x if 2500 units are sold when $500 is spent on advertising.

(b) Estimate the number of units that will be sold if advertising expenditures are raised to $700.

44. *Sales and Advertising*   After discontinuing all advertising for a certain product in 1988, the manufacturer noted that sales began to drop according to the model

$$S - \frac{500,000}{1 + 0.6e^{kt}}$$

where S represents the number of units sold and t represents the calendar year with $t = 0$ corresponding to 1988.
(a) Find k if the company sold 300,000 units in 1990.
(b) According to this model, what will sales be in 1993?

Earthquake Magnitudes   In Exercises 45 and 46, use the Richter Scale (Example 7) for measuring the magnitude of earthquakes.

45. Find the magnitude R of an earthquake of intensity I (let $I_0 = 1$).
(a) $I = 80,500,000$ (b) $I = 48,275,000$

46. Find the intensity I of an earthquake measuring R on the Richter Scale (let $I_0 = 1$).
(a) Colombia in 1906, $R = 8.6$
(b) Los Angeles in 1971, $R = 6.7$

Intensity of Sound   In Exercises 47–50 use the following information to determine the level of sound (in decibels) for the given sound intensity. The level of sound β, in decibels, with an intensity of I is given by

$$\beta(I) = 10 \log_{10} \frac{I}{I_0}$$

where I_0 is an intensity of 10^{-16} watts per square centimeter, corresponding roughly to the faintest sound that can be heard.

47. (a) $I = 10^{-14}$ watts per square centimeter (faint whisper)
(b) $I = 10^{-9}$ watts per square centimeter (busy street corner)
(c) $I = 10^{-6.5}$ watts per square centimeter (air hammer)
(d) $I = 10^{-4}$ watts per square centimeter (threshold of pain)

48. (a) $I = 10^{-13}$ watts per square centimeter (whisper)
(b) $I = 10^{-7.5}$ watts per square centimeter (DC-8 four miles from takeoff)
(c) $I = 10^{-7}$ watts per square centimeter (diesel truck at 25 feet)
(d) $I = 10^{-4.5}$ watts per square centimeter (auto horn at three feet)

49. *Noise Level*   Due to the installation of noise suppression materials, the noise level in an auditorium was reduced from 93 to 80 decibels. Find the percentage decrease in the intensity level of the noise because of the installation of these materials.

50. *Noise Level*   Due to the installation of a muffler, the noise level in an engine was reduced from 88 to 72 decibels. Find the percentage decrease in the intensity level of the noise because of the installation of the muffler.

Acidity   In Exercises 51–56, use the acidity model given by

$$pH = -\log_{10}[H^+]$$

where acidity (pH) is a measure of the hydrogen ion concentration $[H^+]$ (measured in moles of hydrogen per liter) of a solution.

51. Find the pH if $[H^+] = 2.3 \times 10^{-5}$.

52. Find the pH if $[H^+] = 11.3 \times 10^{-6}$.

53. Compute $[H^+]$ for a solution in which pH $= 5.8$.

54. Compute $[H^+]$ for a solution in which pH $= 3.2$.

55. A certain fruit has a pH of 2.5 and an antacid tablet has a pH of 9.5. The hydrogen ion concentration of the fruit is how many times the concentration of the tablet?

56. If the pH of a solution is decreased by one unit, the hydrogen ion concentration is increased by what factor?

57. *Estimating the Time of Death*   At 8:30 A.M., a coroner was called to the home of a person who had died during the night. In order to estimate the time of death, the coroner took the person's temperature twice. At 9:00 A.M. the temperature was 85.7°, and at 9:30 A.M. the temperature was 82.8°. From these two temperatures the coroner was able to determine that the time elapsed since death and the body temperature were related by the formula

$$t = -2.5 \ln \frac{T - 70}{98.6 - 70}$$

where t is the time in hours that has elapsed since the person died and T is the temperature (in degrees Fahrenheit) of the person's body at 9:00 A.M. Assume that the person had a normal body temperature of 98.6° at death, and that the room temperature was a constant 70°. (This formula is derived from a general cooling principle called Newton's Law of Cooling.) Use this formula to estimate the time of death of the person.

58. *Population Growth*   From Exercises 31 and 32, it is obvious that the populations of the two different cities are growing at different rates. What constant in the equation $y = Ce^{kt}$ is affected by those different growth rates? Discuss the relationship between the different growth rates and the magnitude of the constant.

In Exercises 61–64, approximate the logarithm using the properties of logarithms given $\log_b 2 \approx 0.3562$, $\log_b 3 \approx 0.5646$, and $\log_b 5 \approx 0.8271$.

61. $\log_b 25$

62. $\log_b\left(\frac{25}{9}\right)$

63. $\log_b \sqrt{3}$

64. $\log_b 30$

65. *Snow Removal* The number of miles s of roads cleared of snow is approximated by the model

$$s = 25 - \frac{13 \ln(h/12)}{\ln 3}, \quad 2 \le h \le 15$$

where h is the depth of the snow in inches. Use this model to find s when $h = 10$ inches.

66. *Climb Rate* The time t, in minutes, for a small plane to climb to an altitude of h feet is given by

$$t = 50 \log_{10} \frac{18,000}{18,000 - h}$$

where 18,000 feet is its absolute ceiling. Find the time for the plane to climb to an altitude of 4000 feet.

In Exercises 67–72, solve the exponential equation. Round to three decimal places.

67. $e^x = 12$

68. $e^{3x} = 25$

69. $3e^{-5x} = 132$

70. $14e^{3x+2} = 560$

71. $e^{2x} - 7e^x + 10 = 0$

72. $e^{2x} - 6e^x + 8 = 0$

In Exercises 73–76, solve the logarithmic equation. Round to three decimal places.

73. $\ln 3x = 8.2$

74. $2 \ln 4x = 15$

75. $\ln x - \ln 3 = 2$

76. $\ln \sqrt{x + 1} = 2$

In Exercises 77–80, find the exponential function $y = Ce^{kt}$ that passes through the two points.

77. $(0, 2)$, $(4, 3)$

78. $\left(0, \frac{1}{2}\right)$, $(5, 5)$

79. $(0, 4)$, $\left(5, \frac{1}{2}\right)$

80. $(0, 2)$, $(5, 1)$

81. *Demand Function* The demand equation for a certain product is given by

$$p = 500 - 0.5e^{0.004x}.$$

Find the demand x for a price of (a) $p = \$450$ and (b) $p = \$400$.

82. *Typing Speed* In a typing class, the average number of words per minute typed after t weeks of lessons was found to be

$$N = \frac{157}{1 + 5.4e^{-0.12t}}.$$

Find the time necessary to type (a) 50 words per minute and (b) 75 words per minute.

83. *Compound Interest* A deposit of \$750 is made in a savings account for which the interest is compounded continuously. The balance will double in $7\frac{3}{4}$ years.
(a) What is the annual percentage rate for this account?
(b) Find the balance in the account after 10 years.
(c) Find the effective yield.

84. *Compound Interest* A deposit of \$10,000 is made in a savings account for which the interest is compounded continuously. The balance will double in five years.
(a) What is the annual percentage rate for this account?
(b) Find the balance after one year.
(c) Find the effective yield.

85. *Sound Intensity* The relationship between the number of decibels β and the intensity of a sound I in watts per centimeter squared is given by

$$\beta = 10 \log_{10}\left(\frac{I}{10^{-16}}\right).$$

Determine the intensity of a sound in watts per centimeter squared if the decibel level is 125.

86. *Earthquake Magnitudes* On the Richter Scale, the magnitude R of an earthquake of intensity I is given by

$$R = \log_{10} \frac{I}{I_0}$$

where $I_0 = 1$ is the minimum intensity used for comparison. Find the intensity per unit of area for the following R.
(a) $R = 8.4$ (b) $R = 6.85$ (c) $R = 9.1$

C H A P T E R 5

OVERVIEW

Trigonometry can be studied from two points of view. In the first, trigonometry is used to find relationships between the sides and angles of triangles. For instance, Example 8 on page 352 uses trigonometry to find the height of a tree. This type of "right-triangle" trigonometry is used in surveying and other sciences that involve measurements of length.

The second approach uses the trigonometric functions as models of real-life quantities that are periodic. For instance, Exercise 34 on page 396 shows how to use trigonometric functions to model the normal high and low temperatures throughout a year. In this chapter, you will study several other real-life models that are periodic—sales patterns, oscillating springs, sound waves, and many others.

Trigonometry

 ## 5.1 Radian and Degree Measure

Introduction / Angles / Radian Measure / Degree Measure / Degrees, Minutes, and Seconds / Applications

Introduction

As derived from the Greek language, the word **trigonometry** means "measurement of triangles." Initially, trigonometry dealt with relationships among the sides and angles of triangles, and was used in the development of astronomy, navigation, and surveying. With the development of calculus and the physical sciences in the 17th century, a different perspective arose—one that viewed the classic trigonometric relationships as *functions* with the set of real numbers as their domains. Consequently, the applications of trigonometry expanded to include a vast number of physical phenomena involving rotations, or vibrations. These include sound waves, light rays, planetary orbits, vibrating strings, pendulums, and orbits of atomic particles.

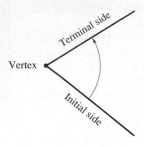

FIGURE 5.1

Angles

An **angle** is determined by rotating a ray (half-line) about its endpoint. The starting position of the ray is the **initial side** of the angle, and the position after rotation is the **terminal side,** as shown in Figure 5.1. The endpoint of the ray is the **vertex** of the angle. This perception of an angle fits a coordinate system in which the origin is the vertex and the initial side coincides with the positive *x*-axis. Such an angle is in **standard position,** as shown in Figure 5.2. **Positive angles** are generated by counterclockwise rotation, and **negative angles** by clockwise rotation, as shown in Figures 5.3 and 5.4. To label angles in trigonometry, we use the Greek letters α (alpha), β (beta), and θ (theta), as well as uppercase letters A, B, and C.

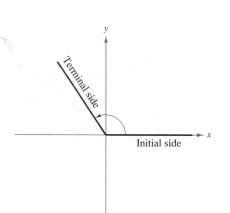

Standard Position of an Angle

FIGURE 5.2

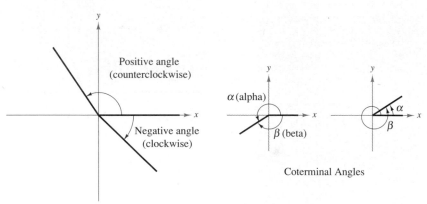

FIGURE 5.3

FIGURE 5.4

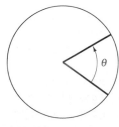

Central Angle θ

FIGURE 5.5

Radian Measure

The **measure of an angle** is determined by the amount of rotation from the initial to the terminal side. One way to measure angles is in radians. This type of measure is needed in calculus. To define a radian we use a **central angle** of a circle, one whose vertex is the center of the circle, as shown in Figure 5.5.

DEFINITION OF A RADIAN

One **radian** is the measure of a central angle θ that subtends (intercepts) an arc s equal in length to the radius r of the circle. [See Figure 5.6(a).]

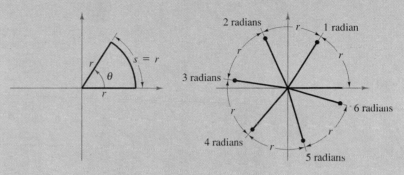

arc length = radius when θ = 1 radian

(a)   (b)

FIGURE 5.6

Since the circumference of a circle is $2\pi r$, it follows that a central angle of one full revolution (counterclockwise) corresponds to an arc length of $s = 2\pi r$. Moreover, because each radian intercepts an arc of length r, we conclude that one full revolution corresponds to an angle of $(2\pi r)/r = 2\pi$ radians. Note that since $2\pi \approx 6.28$, there are a little more than six radius lengths in a full circle, as shown in Figure 5.6(b).

In general, the radian measure of a central angle θ is obtained by dividing the arc length s by r. That is,

$$\frac{s}{r} = \theta$$

where θ *is measured in radians*. Because the units of measure for s and r are the same, this ratio is unitless—it is simply a real number.

Since the radian measure of an angle of one full revolution is 2π, it follows that

$$\frac{1}{2} \text{ revolution} = \frac{2\pi}{2} = \pi \text{ radians}$$

$$\frac{1}{4} \text{ revolution} = \frac{2\pi}{4} = \frac{\pi}{2} \text{ radians}$$

$$\frac{1}{6} \text{ revolution} = \frac{2\pi}{6} = \frac{\pi}{3} \text{ radians}.$$

These and other common angles are shown in Figure 5.7.

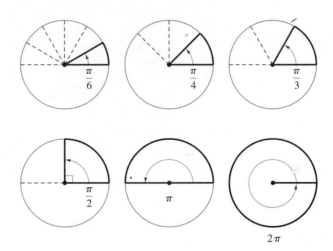

Radian Measure for Several Common Angles

FIGURE 5.7

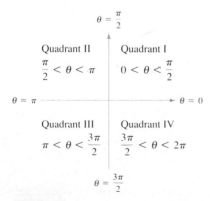

FIGURE 5.8

Recall that the four quadrants in a coordinate system are numbered counterclockwise as I, II, III, and IV. Figure 5.8 shows which angles between 0 and 2π lie in each of the four quadrants.

We can find an angle that is coterminal to a given angle θ by adding or subtracting 2π (one revolution), as demonstrated in Example 1. (Note that a given angle has many coterminal angles. For instance, $\theta = \pi/6$ is coterminal with both $13\pi/6$ and $-11\pi/6$.)

EXAMPLE 1 Sketching and Finding Coterminal Angles

Sketch each of the following angles in standard position and find a coterminal angle for each.

a. $\theta = \dfrac{13\pi}{6}$ b. $\theta = \dfrac{3\pi}{4}$ c. $\theta = -\dfrac{2\pi}{3}$

Solution

a. For the positive angle $\theta = 13\pi/6$, we subtract 2π and obtain the coterminal angle

$$\frac{13\pi}{6} - 2\pi = \frac{\pi}{6}.$$

Thus, the terminal side of θ lies in Quadrant I. Its sketch is shown in Figure 5.9(a).

b. Again subtracting 2π, an angle coterminal with $3\pi/4$ is

$$\frac{3\pi}{4} - 2\pi = -\frac{5\pi}{4}.$$

Since $\pi/2 < \theta < \pi$, the terminal side of θ lies in Quadrant II. Moreover, since $\theta = 3\pi/4$ is $\pi/4$ less than π, it follows that θ lies in Quadrant II, $\pi/4$ radians up from the horizontal axis. A sketch is shown in Figure 5.9(b).

c. For the negative angle $\theta = -2\pi/3$, we add 2π to obtain the coterminal angle

$$\theta = -\frac{2\pi}{3} + 2\pi = \frac{4\pi}{3}$$

as shown in Figure 5.9(c).

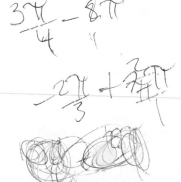

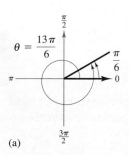

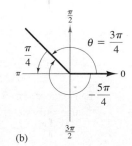

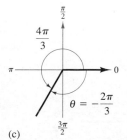

(a)   (b)   (c)

FIGURE 5.9

Figure 5.10 shows several common angles with their radian measures. Note that we classify angles between 0 and $\pi/2$ radians as **acute** and angles between $\pi/2$ and π as **obtuse**.

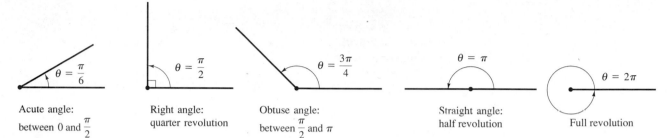

Acute angle:
between 0 and $\dfrac{\pi}{2}$

Right angle:
quarter revolution

Obtuse angle:
between $\dfrac{\pi}{2}$ and π

Straight angle:
half revolution

Full revolution

FIGURE 5.10

Two *positive* angles α and β are said to be **complementary** (or complements of each other) if their sum is $\pi/2$. For example, $\pi/6$ and $\pi/3$ are complementary angles because $(\pi/6) + (\pi/3) = \pi/2$. Two positive angles are **supplementary** (or supplements of each other) if their sum is π. For example, $2\pi/3$ and $\pi/3$ are supplementary angles because $(2\pi/3) + (\pi/3) = \pi$.

(a) Complementary Angle

(b) Supplementary Angle

FIGURE 5.11

EXAMPLE 2 Complementary and Supplementary Angles

If possible, find the complementary and the supplementary angles for (a) $2\pi/5$ and (b) $4\pi/5$. (See Figure 5.11.)

Solution

a. The complement of $2\pi/5$ is

$$\frac{\pi}{2} - \frac{2\pi}{5} = \frac{5\pi}{10} - \frac{4\pi}{10} = \frac{\pi}{10}.$$

The supplement of $2\pi/5$ is

$$\pi - \frac{2\pi}{5} = \frac{3\pi}{5}.$$

b. Because $4\pi/5$ is greater than $\pi/2$, it has no complement. (Remember, we use only *positive* angles for complements.) The supplement of $\theta = 4\pi/5$ is

$$\pi - \frac{4\pi}{5} = \frac{\pi}{5}.$$

Degree Measure

A second way to measure angles is in terms of degrees. A measure of **one degree (1°)** is equivalent to a rotation 1/360 of a complete revolution about the vertex. To measure angles in degrees, it is convenient to mark degrees on the circumference of a circle as shown in Figure 5.12. Thus, a full revolution (counterclockwise) corresponds to 360°, a half revolution to 180°, and a quarter revolution to 90°.

Since 2π radians is the measure of an angle of one complete revolution, degrees and radians are related by the equations

$$360° = 2\pi \text{ rad} \quad \text{and} \quad 180° = \pi \text{ rad}.$$

From the latter equation, we obtain

$$1° = \frac{\pi}{180} \text{ rad} \quad \text{and} \quad 1 \text{ rad} = \left(\frac{180}{\pi}\right)°$$

which leads to the following conversion rules.

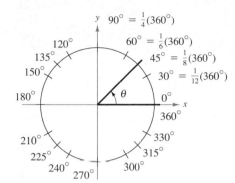

y $90° = \frac{1}{4}(360°)$

$60° = \frac{1}{6}(360°)$

$45° = \frac{1}{8}(360°)$

$30° = \frac{1}{12}(360°)$

Degree Measure of an Angle

FIGURE 5.12

CONVERSIONS: DEGREES ⟷ RADIANS

1. To convert degrees to radians, multiply degrees by $\dfrac{\pi \text{ rad}}{180°}$. *divide by 180*

2. To convert radians to degrees, multiply radians by $\dfrac{180°}{\pi \text{ rad}}$.

To apply these two conversion rules, you simply need to remember the basic relationship π rad $= 180°$, as demonstrated in Examples 3 and 4.

EXAMPLE 3 **Converting from Degrees to Radians**

a. $135° = (135 \text{ deg})\left(\dfrac{\pi \text{ rad}}{180 \text{ deg}}\right) = \dfrac{3\pi}{4} \text{ rad}$

b. $540° = (540 \text{ deg})\left(\dfrac{\pi \text{ rad}}{180 \text{ deg}}\right) = 3\pi \text{ rad}$

c. $-270° = (-270 \text{ deg})\left(\dfrac{\pi \text{ rad}}{180 \text{ deg}}\right) = -\dfrac{3\pi}{2} \text{ rad}$

EXAMPLE 4 **Converting from Radians to Degrees**

a. $-\dfrac{\pi}{2}$ rad $= \left(-\dfrac{\pi}{2} \text{ rad}\right)\left(\dfrac{180 \text{ deg}}{\pi \text{ rad}}\right) = -90°$

b. $\dfrac{9\pi}{2}$ rad $= \left(\dfrac{9\pi}{2} \text{ rad}\right)\left(\dfrac{180 \text{ deg}}{\pi \text{ rad}}\right) = 810°$

c. 2 rad $= (2 \text{ rad})\left(\dfrac{180 \text{ deg}}{\pi \text{ rad}}\right) = \dfrac{360}{\pi}$ deg $\approx 114.59°$

don't worry about multiplying π unless the original unit doesn't contain π

If you have a calculator with a radian-to-degree conversion key, try using it to verify these results. Note that when no units of angle measure are specified, *radian measure is implied.* For instance, if we write $\theta = \pi$ or $\theta = 2$, we mean $\theta = \pi$ radians or $\theta = 2$ radians.

Degrees, Minutes, and Seconds

With calculators it is convenient to use *decimal* degrees to denote fractional parts of degrees. Historically, however, fractional parts of degrees were expressed in *minutes* and *seconds*, using the prime (') and double prime (") notations, respectively. That is,

$$1' = \text{one minute} = \frac{1}{60}(1°)$$

$$1'' = \text{one second} = \frac{1}{60}(1') = \frac{1}{3600}(1°).$$

Consequently, an angle of 64 degrees, 32 minutes, and 47 seconds is represented by $\theta = 64° \, 32' \, 47''$.

Many calculators have special keys for converting an angle in degrees, minutes, and seconds (D°M'S″) into decimal degree form, and conversely. If your calculator does not have these special keys, you can use the techniques demonstrated in the next example to make the conversions.

EXAMPLE 5 **Converting an Angle from D°M'S″ to Decimal Form**

Convert $152°15'29''$ to decimal degree form.

Solution

Since $1' = \left(\frac{1}{60}\right)°$ and $1'' = \left(\frac{1}{60}\right)\left(\frac{1}{60}\right)° = \left(\frac{1}{3600}\right)°$, we have

$$152°15'29'' = 152° + \left(\frac{15}{60}\right)° + \left(\frac{29}{3600}\right)°$$

$$\approx 152° + 0.25° + 0.00806°$$

$$= 152.25806°.$$

Applications

The *radian measure* formula, $\theta = s/r$, can be used to measure arc length along a circle. Specifically, for a circle of radius r, a central angle θ subtends an arc of length s given by

$$s = r\theta$$ *Length of circular arc*

where θ is measured in radians.

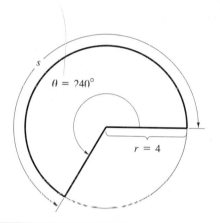

FIGURE 5.13

EXAMPLE 6   Finding Arc Length

A circle has a radius of 4 inches. Find the length of the arc cut off (subtended) by a central angle of 240°, as shown in Figure 5.13.

Solution

To use the formula $s = r\theta$, you must first convert 240° to radian measure.

$$240° = (240 \text{ deg})\left(\frac{\pi \text{ rad}}{180 \text{ deg}}\right) = \frac{4\pi}{3} \text{ rad}$$

Then, using a radius of $r = 4$ inches, you find the arc length to be

$$s = r\theta = 4\left(\frac{4\pi}{3}\right) - \frac{16\pi}{3} \approx 16.76 \text{ inches}.$$

Note that the units for $r\theta$ are determined by the units for r because θ has no units.

The formula for the length of a circular arc can be used to analyze the motion of a particle moving at a *constant speed* along a circular path. Assume that the particle is moving at a constant speed along a circular path (of radius r). If s is the length of the arc traveled in time t, then the **speed** of the particle is

$$\text{Speed} = \frac{\text{Distance}}{\text{Time}} = \frac{s}{t}.$$

Moreover, if θ is the angle (in radian measure) corresponding to the arc length s, then the **angular speed** of the particle is

$$\text{Angular speed} = \frac{\theta}{t}.$$

FIGURE 5.14

EXAMPLE 7   Finding the Speed of an Object

The second hand on a clock is 4 inches long, as shown in Figure 5.14. Find the speed of the tip of this second hand.

Solution

The time required for the second hand to make one full revolution is

$$t = 60 \text{ seconds} = 1 \text{ minute}.$$

The distance traveled by the tip of the second hand in one revolution is

$$s = 2\pi(\text{radius}) = 2\pi(4) = 8\pi \text{ inches}.$$

Therefore, the speed of the tip of the second hand is

$$\text{Speed} = \frac{s}{t} = \frac{8\pi \text{ inches}}{60 \text{ seconds}} \approx 0.419 \text{ in./sec.}$$

EXAMPLE 8   Finding Angular Speed and Speed

A lawn roller 30 inches in diameter makes 1.2 revolutions per second, as shown in Figure 5.15.

a. Find the angular speed of the roller in radians per second.
b. How fast is the roller moving across the lawn?

Solution

a. Since each revolution generates 2π radians, it follows that the roller turns $(1.2)(2\pi) = 2.4\pi$ radians per second. Thus, the angular speed is

$$\text{Angular speed} = \frac{\theta}{t} = \frac{2.4\pi \text{ radians}}{1 \text{ second}} = 2.4\pi \text{ rad/sec.}$$

b. To find the speed of the roller, we use the fact that its diameter is 30 inches. Thus, its radius is 15 inches and we have $s = 2\pi r = 2\pi(15) = 30\pi$ inches. Since the roller makes 1.2 revolutions per second, its speed is

$$\text{Speed} = \left(\frac{1.2 \text{ rev}}{1 \text{ sec}}\right)\left(\frac{30\pi \text{ in.}}{1 \text{ rev}}\right) = 36\pi \text{ in./sec} \approx 113.1 \text{ in./sec.}$$

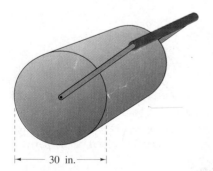

FIGURE 5.15

|←—— 30 in. ——→|

DISCUSSION
PROBLEM
___
Converting to
Degrees-Minutes-
Seconds

In Example 5, we demonstrated a procedure for converting an angle in degrees, minutes, and seconds to decimal degrees. Write a paragraph describing how you could reverse this procedure, and then apply your technique to write the following angle measures in degree-minute-second form.

a. $31.2635°$ **b.** $54.5125°$

WARM UP

The following warm-up exercises involve skills that were covered in earlier sections. You will use these skills in the exercise set for this section.

In Exercises 1–10, solve for x.

1. $x + 135 = 180$

2. $790 = 720 + x$

3. $\pi = \dfrac{5\pi}{6} + x$

4. $2\pi - x = \dfrac{5\pi}{3}$

5. $\dfrac{45}{180} = \dfrac{x}{\pi}$

6. $\dfrac{240}{180} = \dfrac{x}{\pi}$

7. $\dfrac{\pi}{180} = \dfrac{x}{20}$

8. $\dfrac{180}{\pi} = \dfrac{330}{x}$

9. $\dfrac{x}{60} = \dfrac{3}{4}$

10. $\dfrac{x}{3600} = 0.0125$

EXERCISES for Section 5.1

In Exercises 1–4, determine the quadrant in which the terminal side of the angle lies. (The angle is given in radians.)

1. (a) $\dfrac{\pi}{5}$ *1st*   (b) $\dfrac{7\pi}{5}$

2. (a) $-\dfrac{\pi}{12}$ (b) $-\dfrac{11\pi}{9}$

3. (a) -1 *1st*   (b) -2 *2nd Actually work out the # is when its Neg, you go counterclockwise start in Quad II*

4. (a) 5.63 (b) -2.25

In Exercises 5 and 6, determine the quadrant in which the terminal side of the angle lies.

5. (a) $130°$ (b) $285°$

6. (a) $-260°$ (b) $-3.4°$

In Exercises 7–10, sketch the angle in standard position.

7. (a) $\dfrac{5\pi}{4}$ *(180)*
   (b) $\dfrac{2\pi}{3}$

Convert radians to degrees 1st

8. (a) $-\dfrac{7\pi}{4}$
   (b) $-\dfrac{5\pi}{2}$

9. (a) $30°$
   (b) $150°$

10. (a) $405°$
   (b) $-480°$

In Exercises 11 and 12, determine two coterminal angles (one positive and one negative) for the angle. Give the answers in radians.

11. (a) $\theta = \dfrac{\pi}{9}$

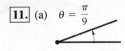

(b) $\theta = \dfrac{4\pi}{3}$

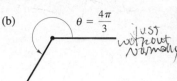

12. (a) $\theta = -\dfrac{9\pi}{4}$

(b) $\theta = -\dfrac{2\pi}{15}$

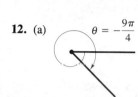

In Exercises 13–16, determine two coterminal angles (one positive and one negative) for the angle. Give the answers in degrees.

13. (a)

$\theta = 36°$

(b)

$\theta = -45°$

14. (a)

$\theta = -120°$

(b) $\theta = 390°$

15. (a) $\theta = 300°$

(b)

$\theta = 740°$

16. (a) $\theta = -420°$

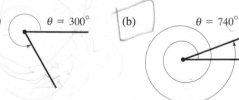

(b)

$\theta = 230°$

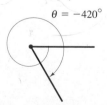

In Exercises 17–20, find (if possible) the positive angle complement and the positive angle supplement of the angle.

17. (a) $\dfrac{\pi}{3}$ (b) $\dfrac{3\pi}{4}$

18. (a) 1   (b) 2

19. (a) 18°   (b) 115°

20. (a) 79°   (b) 150°

In Exercises 21–24, express the angle in degree measure. (Do not use a calculator.)

21. (a) $\dfrac{3\pi}{2}$ (b) $\dfrac{7\pi}{6}$

22. (a) $-\dfrac{7\pi}{12}$ (b) $\dfrac{\pi}{9}$

23. (a) $\dfrac{7\pi}{3}$ (b) $-\dfrac{11\pi}{30}$

24. (a) $\dfrac{11\pi}{6}$ (b) $\dfrac{34\pi}{15}$

In Exercises 25–28, express the angle in radian measure as a multiple of π. (Do not use a calculator.)

25. (a) 30°   (b) 150°

26. (a) 315°   (b) 120°

27. (a) −20°   (b) −240°

28. (a) −270°   (b) 144°

In Exercises 29–32, convert the angle from degrees to radian measure. List your answers to three decimal places.

29. (a) 115°   (b) 87.4°

30. (a) −216.35°   (b) −48.27°

31. (a) 532°   (b) 0.54°

32. (a) −0.83°   (b) 345°

In Exercises 33–36, convert the angle from radian to degree measure. List your answers to three decimal places.

33. (a) $\dfrac{\pi}{7}$ (b) $\dfrac{5\pi}{11}$

34. (a) $\dfrac{15\pi}{8}$ (b) 6.5π

35. (a) -4.2π (b) 4.8

36. (a) −2   (b) −0.57

In Exercises 37 and 38, convert the angle measurement to decimal form.

37. (a) 245° 10′   (b) 2° 12′
38. (a) −135° 36″   (b) −408° 16′ 25″

In Exercises 39–42, convert the angle measurement to D° M′ S″ form.

since .6 is A part of a Minute its 6 to 36

39. (a) 240.6°   (b) −145.8°
40. (a) −345.12°   (b) 0.45
41. (a) 2.5   (b) −3.58
42. (a) −0.355   (b) 0.7865

In Exercises 43–46, find the radian measure of the central angle of a circle of radius r that intercepts an arc of length s.

Radius	Arc Length
43. 15 inches	4 inches
44. 16 feet	10 feet
45. 14.5 centimeters	25 centimeters
46. 80 kilometers	160 kilometers

In Exercises 47–50, on the circle of radius r find the length of the arc intercepted by the central angle θ.

Radius	Central Angle
47. 15 inches	180°
48. 9 feet	60°
49. 6 meters	2 radians
50. 40 centimeters	$\dfrac{3\pi}{4}$ radians

37° 15′ 22″ conv. to dec form

$$37° + \left(\frac{15}{60}\right)° + \left(\frac{22}{3600}\right)° = 37.256°$$

Distance Between Cities   In Exercises 51–54, find the distance between the two cities. Assume that the earth is a sphere of radius 4000 miles and that the cities are on the same meridian (one city is due north of the other).

City		Latitude
51.	Dallas	32° 47′ 9″ N
	Omaha	41° 15′ 42″ N
52.	San Francisco	37° 46′ 39″ N
	Seattle	47° 36′ 32″ N
53.	Miami	25° 46′ 37″ N
	Erie	42° 7′ 15″ N
54.	Johannesburg, South Africa	26° 10′ S
	Jerusalem, Israel	31° 47′ N

Convert to degrees subtract Convert to radius use S = rθ

55. *Difference in Latitudes*   Assuming that the earth is a sphere of radius 4000 miles, what is the difference in latitude of two cities, one of which is 325 miles due north of the other?

56. *Difference in Latitudes*   Assuming that the earth is a sphere of radius 4000 miles, what is the difference in latitude of two cities, one of which is 500 miles due north of the other?

57. *Instrumentation*   The pointer on a voltmeter is 2 inches long (see figure). Find the angle through which the pointer rotates when it moves $\frac{1}{2}$ inch on the scale.

Figure for 57

58. *Electric Hoist*   An electric hoist is used to lift a piece of equipment (see figure). The diameter of the drum on the hoist is 8 inches and the equipment must be raised one foot. Find the number of degrees through which the drum must rotate.

8 in.

1 ft

Figure for 58

59. *Angular Speed*   A car is moving at the rate of 50 miles per hour, and the diameter of each wheel is 2.5 feet. (a) Find the number of revolutions per minute of the rotating wheels. (b) Find the angular speed of the wheels in radians per minute.

60. *Angular Speed*   A truck is moving at the rate of 50 miles per hour, and the diameter of each wheel is 3 feet. (a) Find the number of revolutions per minute the wheels are rotating. (b) Find the angular speed of the wheels in radians per minute.

61. *Angular Speed*   A 2-inch-diameter pulley on an electric motor that runs at 1700 revolutions per minute is connected by a belt to a 4-inch-diameter pulley on a saw arbor. (a) Find the angular speed (in radians per minute) of each pulley. (b) Find the revolutions per minute of the saw.

62. *Angular Speed*   How long will it take a pulley rotating at 12 radians per second to make 100 revolutions?

63. *Circular Saw Speed*   The circular blade on a saw has a diameter of 7.5 inches and the blade rotates at 2400 revolutions per minute (see figure). (a) Find the angular speed in radians per second. (b) Find the speed of the saw teeth (in feet per second) as they contact the wood being cut.

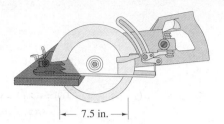

7.5 in.

Figure for 63

64. *Speed of a Bicycle*   The radii of the sprocket assemblies and the wheel of the bicycle in the figure are 4 inches, 2 inches, and 13 inches, respectively. If the cyclist is pedaling at the rate of 1 revolution per second, find the speed of the bicycle in (a) feet per second and (b) miles per hour.

13 in.

4 in.

2 in.

Figure for 64

The Trigonometric Functions and the Unit Circle

The Unit Circle / The Trigonometric Functions / Domain and Period of Sine and Cosine /
Evaluating Trigonometric Functions with a Calculator

The Unit Circle

The two historical perspectives of trigonometry incorporate different methods for introducing the trigonometric functions. Our first introduction to these functions is based on the unit circle.

Consider the **unit circle** given by $x^2 + y^2 = 1$, as shown in Figure 5.16. Imagine that the real number line is wrapped around this circle, with positive numbers corresponding to a counterclockwise wrapping and negative numbers corresponding to a clockwise wrapping, as shown in Figure 5.17.

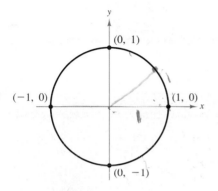

Unit Circle: $x^2 + y^2 = 1$

FIGURE 5.16

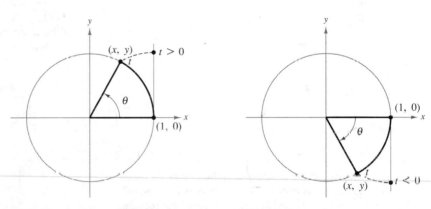

(a) Positive numbers   (b) Negative numbers

FIGURE 5.17

As the real number line is wrapped around the unit circle, each real number t will correspond with a point (x, y) on the circle. For example, the real number 0 corresponds to the point $(1, 0)$. Moreover, because the unit circle has a circumference of 2π, the real number 2π will also correspond to the point $(1, 0)$.

In general, each real number t also corresponds to a central angle θ (in standard position) whose radian measure is t. With this interpretation of t, the arc length formula $s = r\theta$ (with $r = 1$) indicates that the real number t is the length of the arc subtended by the angle θ, given in radians.

The Trigonometric Functions

From the preceding discussion, it follows that the coordinates x and y are two functions of the real variable t. We use these coordinates to define the six trigonometric functions of t.

> **sine**   **cosecant**
> **cosine**   **secant**
> **tangent**   **cotangent**

These six functions are normally abbreviated as sin, csc, cos, sec, tan, and cot, respectively.

DEFINITION OF TRIGONOMETRIC FUNCTIONS

Let t be a real number and (x, y) the point on the unit circle corresponding to t.

$$\sin t = y \qquad\qquad \csc t = \frac{1}{y}, \qquad y \neq 0$$

$$\cos t = x \qquad\qquad \sec t = \frac{1}{x}, \qquad x \neq 0$$

$$\tan t = \frac{y}{x}, \qquad x \neq 0 \qquad \cot t = \frac{x}{y}, \qquad y \neq 0$$

REMARK   The functions in the second column are the *reciprocals* of the corresponding functions in the first column.

◀

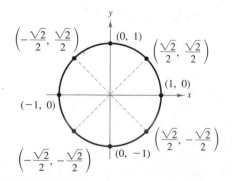

$$\left(-\frac{\sqrt{2}}{2}, \frac{\sqrt{2}}{2}\right) \quad (0, 1) \quad \left(\frac{\sqrt{2}}{2}, \frac{\sqrt{2}}{2}\right)$$

$$(-1, 0) \qquad (1, 0)$$

$$\left(-\frac{\sqrt{2}}{2}, -\frac{\sqrt{2}}{2}\right) \quad (0, -1) \quad \left(\frac{\sqrt{2}}{2}, -\frac{\sqrt{2}}{2}\right)$$

Unit Circle Divided into 8 Equal Arcs

FIGURE 5.18

In the definition of the trigonometric functions, note that we do not define the tangent or secant if $x = 0$. For instance, because $t = \pi/2$ corresponds to $(x, y) = (0, 1)$, it follows that $\tan(\pi/2)$ and $\sec(\pi/2)$ are *undefined*. Similarly, we do not define the cotangent or cosecant if $y = 0$. For instance, because $t = 0$ corresponds to $(x, y) = (1, 0)$, cot 0 and csc 0 are *undefined*.

In Figure 5.18, the unit circle has been divided into eight equal arcs, corresponding to t-values of

$$0, \frac{\pi}{4}, \frac{\pi}{2}, \frac{3\pi}{4}, \pi, \frac{5\pi}{4}, \frac{3\pi}{2}, \frac{7\pi}{4}, \text{ and } 2\pi.$$

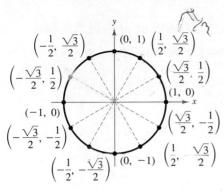

$\left(-\frac{1}{2}, \frac{\sqrt{3}}{2}\right)$ (0, 1) $\left(\frac{1}{2}, \frac{\sqrt{3}}{2}\right)$

$\left(-\frac{\sqrt{3}}{2}, \frac{1}{2}\right)$ $\left(\frac{\sqrt{3}}{2}, \frac{1}{2}\right)$

(−1, 0) (1, 0)

$\left(-\frac{\sqrt{3}}{2}, -\frac{1}{2}\right)$ $\left(\frac{\sqrt{3}}{2}, -\frac{1}{2}\right)$

$\left(-\frac{1}{2}, -\frac{\sqrt{3}}{2}\right)$ (0, −1) $\left(\frac{1}{2}, \frac{\sqrt{3}}{2}\right)$

Unit Circle Divided into 12 Equal Arcs

FIGURE 5.19

Similarly, in Figure 5.19, the unit circle has been divided into 12 equal arcs, corresponding to *t*-values of

$$0, \frac{\pi}{6}, \frac{\pi}{3}, \frac{\pi}{2}, \frac{2\pi}{3}, \frac{5\pi}{6}, \pi, \frac{7\pi}{6}, \frac{4\pi}{3}, \frac{3\pi}{2}, \frac{5\pi}{3}, \frac{11\pi}{6}, \text{ and } 2\pi.$$

Using the (*x*, *y*) coordinates in Figures 5.18 and 5.19, we can easily evaluate the trigonometric functions for common *t*-values. This procedure is demonstrated in Examples 1, 2, and 3.

EXAMPLE 1   Evaluating Trigonometric Functions of Real Numbers

Evaluate the six trigonometric functions at the following real numbers.

a. $t = \frac{\pi}{6}$

b. $t = \frac{5\pi}{4}$

Solution

a. Since $t = \pi/6$ corresponds to the first quadrant point $(x, y) = (\sqrt{3}/2, 1/2)$, we can write the following.

$$\sin \frac{\pi}{6} = y = \frac{1}{2} \qquad\qquad \csc \frac{\pi}{6} = 2$$

$$\cos \frac{\pi}{6} = x = \frac{\sqrt{3}}{2} \qquad\qquad \sec \frac{\pi}{6} = \frac{2}{\sqrt{3}} = \frac{2\sqrt{3}}{3}$$

$$\tan \frac{\pi}{6} = \frac{y}{x} = \frac{1/2}{\sqrt{3}/2} = \frac{1}{\sqrt{3}} \qquad \cot \frac{\pi}{6} = \sqrt{3}$$

b. Since $t = 5\pi/4$ corresponds to the third quadrant point $(x, y) = (-\sqrt{2}/2, -\sqrt{2}/2)$, we can write the following.

$$\sin \frac{5\pi}{4} = y = -\frac{\sqrt{2}}{2} \qquad\qquad \csc \frac{5\pi}{4} = -\frac{2}{\sqrt{2}} = -\sqrt{2}$$

$$\cos \frac{5\pi}{4} = x = -\frac{\sqrt{2}}{2} \qquad\qquad \sec \frac{5\pi}{4} = -\frac{2}{\sqrt{2}} = -\sqrt{2}$$

$$\tan \frac{5\pi}{4} = \frac{y}{x} = \frac{-\sqrt{2}/2}{-\sqrt{2}/2} = 1 \qquad \cot \frac{5\pi}{4} = 1$$

EXAMPLE 2 Evaluating Trigonometric Functions of Real Numbers

Evaluate the six trigonometric functions at the following real numbers.

a. $t = 0$ **b.** $t = \pi$

Solution

a. Since $t = 0$ corresponds to the point $(x, y) = (1, 0)$ on the unit circle, we have the following.

$$\sin 0 = y = 0 \qquad\qquad\qquad \csc 0 \text{ is undefined}$$

$$\cos 0 = x = 1 \qquad\qquad\qquad \sec 0 = 1$$

$$\tan 0 = \frac{y}{x} = 0 \qquad\qquad\qquad \cot 0 \text{ is undefined}$$

b. Since $t = \pi$ corresponds to the point $(x, y) = (-1, 0)$, we can write the following.

$$\sin \pi = y = 0 \qquad\qquad\qquad \csc \pi \text{ is undefined}$$

$$\cos \pi = x = -1 \qquad\qquad\qquad \sec \pi = -1$$

$$\tan \pi = \frac{y}{x} = \frac{0}{-1} = 0 \qquad\qquad \cot \pi \text{ is undefined}$$

EXAMPLE 3 Evaluating Trigonometric Functions of Real Numbers

Evaluate the six trigonometric functions at the following real numbers.

a. $t = -\dfrac{\pi}{3}$ **b.** $t = \dfrac{5\pi}{2}$

Solution

a. Moving *clockwise* around the unit circle, we find that $t = -\pi/3$ corresponds to the point $(x, y) = (1/2, -\sqrt{3}/2)$. Hence, we have the following.

$$\sin\left(-\frac{\pi}{3}\right) = -\frac{\sqrt{3}}{2} \qquad \csc\left(-\frac{\pi}{3}\right) = -\frac{2}{\sqrt{3}}$$

$$\cos\left(-\frac{\pi}{3}\right) = \frac{1}{2} \qquad \sec\left(-\frac{\pi}{3}\right) = 2$$

$$\tan\left(-\frac{\pi}{3}\right) = -\sqrt{3} \qquad \cot\left(-\frac{\pi}{3}\right) = -\frac{1}{\sqrt{3}}$$

b. Moving *counterclockwise* around the unit circle one and a quarter revolutions, we find that $t = 5\pi/2$ corresponds to the point $(x, y) = (0, 1)$. Hence, we can write the following.

$$\sin \frac{5\pi}{2} = y = 1 \qquad\qquad \csc \frac{5\pi}{2} = 1$$

$$\cos \frac{5\pi}{2} = x = 0 \qquad\qquad \sec \frac{5\pi}{2} \text{ is undefined}$$

$$\tan \frac{5\pi}{2} = \frac{y}{x} \text{ is undefined} \qquad \cot \frac{5\pi}{2} = \frac{x}{y} = 0$$

Domain and Period of Sine and Cosine

The *domain* of the sine and cosine functions is the set of all real numbers. To determine the *range* of these two functions, consider the unit circle shown in Figure 5.20. Since $r = 1$, it follows that $\sin t = y$ and $\cos t = x$. Moreover, because (x, y) is on the unit circle we know that $-1 \leq y \leq 1$ and $-1 \leq x \leq 1$, and it follows that the values of the sine and cosine also range between -1 and 1.

$$-1 \leq y \leq 1 \qquad\qquad -1 \leq x \leq 1$$
$$-1 \leq \sin t \leq 1 \qquad \text{and} \qquad -1 \leq \cos t \leq 1$$

Suppose we add 2π to each value of t in the interval $[0, 2\pi]$, thus completing a second revolution around the unit circle, as shown in Figure 5.21. The values of $\sin(t + 2\pi)$ and $\cos(t + 2\pi)$ correspond to those of $\sin t$ and $\cos t$. Similar results can be obtained for repeated revolutions (positive or negative) on the unit circle. This leads to the general result

$$\sin(t + 2\pi n) = \sin t \qquad \text{and} \qquad \cos(t + 2\pi n) = \cos t$$

for any integer n and real number t. Functions that behave in such a repetitive (or cyclic) manner are **periodic.**

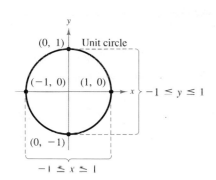

y

(0, 1) | Unit circle

(−1, 0) | (1, 0) | x | $-1 \leq y \leq 1$

(0, −1)

$-1 \leq x \leq 1$

FIGURE 5.20

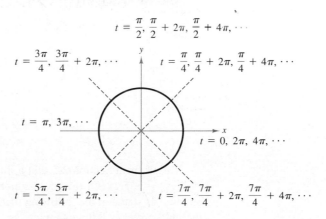

$$t = \frac{\pi}{2}, \frac{\pi}{2} + 2\pi, \frac{\pi}{2} + 4\pi, \cdots$$

$$t = \frac{3\pi}{4}, \frac{3\pi}{4} + 2\pi, \cdots$$

$$t = \frac{\pi}{4}, \frac{\pi}{4} + 2\pi, \frac{\pi}{4} + 4\pi, \cdots$$

$$t = \pi, 3\pi, \cdots$$

$$t = 0, 2\pi, 4\pi, \cdots$$

$$t = \frac{5\pi}{4}, \frac{5\pi}{4} + 2\pi, \cdots$$

$$t = \frac{7\pi}{4}, \frac{7\pi}{4} + 2\pi, \frac{7\pi}{4} + 4\pi, \cdots$$

Repeated Revolutions on the Unit Circle

FIGURE 5.21

REMARK In Figure 5.21 we added *positive* multiples of 2π to the *t*-values. We could just as well have added *negative* multiples. For instance, $\pi/4 - 2\pi$ and $\pi/4 - 4\pi$ are also coterminal to $\pi/4$.

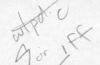

DEFINITION OF A PERIODIC FUNCTION

A function f is **periodic** if there exists a positive real number c such that

$$f(t + c) = f(t)$$

for all t in the domain of f. The least number c for which f is periodic is the **period** of f.

From this definition it follows that the sine and cosine functions are periodic and have a period of 2π. The other four trigonometric functions are also periodic, and we will say more about that in Section 5.6.

EXAMPLE 4 Using the Period to Evaluate the Sine and Cosine

a. Since

$$\frac{13\pi}{6} = 2\pi + \frac{\pi}{6}$$

we have

$$\sin \frac{13\pi}{6} = \sin\left(2\pi + \frac{\pi}{6}\right) = \sin \frac{\pi}{6} = \frac{1}{2}.$$

b. Since

$$-\frac{7\pi}{2} = -4\pi + \frac{\pi}{2}$$

we have

$$\cos\left(-\frac{7\pi}{2}\right) = \cos\left(-4\pi + \frac{\pi}{2}\right) = \cos \frac{\pi}{2} = 0.$$ ◀

Recall from Section 2.5 that a function f is *even* if $f(-t) = f(t)$ and *odd* if $f(-t) = -f(t)$. Of the six trigonometric functions, two are even and four are odd, as stated in the following theorem. Verification of this theorem, using the unit circle, is left as an exercise.

EVEN AND ODD TRIGONOMETRIC FUNCTIONS

The cosine and secant functions are *even*.

$$\cos(-t) = \cos t \qquad \sec(-t) = \sec t$$

The sine, cosecant, tangent, and cotangent functions are *odd*.

$$\sin(-t) = -\sin t \qquad \csc(-t) = -\csc t$$

$$\tan(-t) = -\tan t \qquad \cot(-t) = -\cot t$$

Evaluating Trigonometric Functions with a Calculator

At the beginning of this section, we mentioned that each real number t can be viewed as a central angle θ given in radian measure. Thus, when we are evaluating trigonometric functions, *it doesn't make any difference whether we consider t to be a real number or an angle given in radians.*

A scientific calculator can be used to obtain decimal approximations of the values of the trigonometric functions of any real number. Before entering the number and function, we need to set a switch to the desired *mode* of measurement (degrees or radians). For instance, to find the value of $\tan(\pi/12)$, use the following keystroke sequence.

Radian Mode π ÷ 12 = tan   *Display 0.2679492*

Most calculators do not have keys for cosecant, secant, or cotangent. To evaluate these functions, we use the 1/x key with their respective reciprocal functions sine, cosine, and tangent. For example, to evaluate $\csc(\pi/8)$, we use the fact that

$$\csc \frac{\pi}{8} = \frac{1}{\sin(\pi/8)}$$

and enter the following keystroke sequence.

Radian Mode π ÷ 8 = sin 1/x   *Display 2.6131259*

EXAMPLE 5   Using a Calculator to Evaluate Trigonometric Functions

Use a calculator to evaluate each of the following.

a. $\sin \dfrac{\pi}{6}$ **b.** $\cot 1.5$ **c.** $\sec 0.7$

Solution

Function	Mode	Keystrokes	Display
a. $\sin \dfrac{\pi}{6}$	Radian	π ÷ 6 = sin	0.5
b. $\cot 1.5$	Radian	1.5 tan 1/x	0.0709148
c. $\sec 0.7$	Radian	0.7 cos 1/x	1.3074593

DISCUSSION PROBLEM
You Be the Instructor

Suppose you are tutoring a student in trigonometry. Your student is asked to evaluate the cosine of 2 radians and, using a calculator, obtains the following.

Keystrokes	Display
2 cos	0.999390827

You know that 2 radians lie in the second quadrant. You also know that this implies that the cosine of 2 radians should be negative. What did your student do wrong?

WARM UP

The following warm-up exercises involve skills that were covered in earlier sections. You will use these skills in the exercise set for this section.

In Exercises 1 and 2, simplify the expression.

1. $\dfrac{1/2}{-\sqrt{3}/2}$

2. $\dfrac{\sqrt{2}/2}{-\sqrt{2}/2}$

In Exercises 3 and 4, find an angle θ in the interval $[0, 2\pi]$ that is coterminal with the given angle.

3. $\dfrac{8\pi}{3}$

4. $-\dfrac{\pi}{4}$

In Exercises 5 and 6, convert the angle to radian measure.

5. $30°$

6. $135°$

In Exercises 7 and 8, convert the angle to degree measure.

7. $\dfrac{\pi}{3}$ radians

8. $-\dfrac{3\pi}{2}$ radians

9. Determine the circumference of a circle with radius 1.

10. Determine the arc length of a semicircle with radius 1.

EXERCISES for Section 5.2

In Exercises 1–8, find the point (x, y) on the unit circle that corresponds to the real number t (see Figures 5.18 and 5.19).

1. $t = \dfrac{\pi}{4}$ 2. $t = \dfrac{\pi}{3}$

3. $t = \dfrac{5\pi}{6}$ 4. $t = \dfrac{5\pi}{4}$

5. $t = \dfrac{4\pi}{3}$ 6. $t = \dfrac{11\pi}{6}$

7. $t = \dfrac{3\pi}{2}$ 8. $t = \pi$

In Exercises 9–16, evaluate the sine, cosine, and tangent of the real number.

9. $t = \dfrac{\pi}{4}$ 10. $t = -\dfrac{\pi}{4}$

11. $t = -\dfrac{5\pi}{4}$ 12. $t = -\dfrac{5\pi}{6}$

13. $t - \dfrac{11\pi}{6}$ 14. $t = \dfrac{2\pi}{3}$

15. $t = \dfrac{4\pi}{3}$ 16. $t = \dfrac{7\pi}{4}$

In Exercises 17–22, evaluate (if possible) the six trigonometric functions of the real number.

17. $t = \dfrac{3\pi}{4}$

18. $t = -\dfrac{2\pi}{3}$

19. $t = \dfrac{\pi}{2}$

20. $t = \dfrac{3\pi}{2}$

21. $t = -\dfrac{4\pi}{3}$

22. $t = -\dfrac{11\pi}{6}$

In Exercises 23–30, evaluate the trigonometric function using its period as an aid.

23. $\sin 3\pi$ $(1, 0)$

24. $\cos 3\pi$

25. $\cos \dfrac{8\pi}{3}$

26. $\sin \dfrac{9\pi}{4}$

27. $\cos \dfrac{19\pi}{6}$

28. $\sin\left(-\dfrac{13\pi}{6}\right)$

29. $\sin\left(-\dfrac{9\pi}{4}\right)$

30. $\cos\left(-\dfrac{8\pi}{3}\right)$

In Exercises 31–36, use the value of the trigonometric function to evaluate the indicated functions.

31. $\sin t = \tfrac{1}{3}$
   (a) $\sin(-t)$ (b) $\csc(-t)$

32. $\sin(-t) = \tfrac{2}{5}$
   (a) $\sin t$ (b) $\csc t$

33. $\cos(-t) = -\tfrac{7}{8}$
   (a) $\cos t$ (b) $\sec(-t)$

34. $\cos t = -\tfrac{3}{4}$
   (a) $\cos(-t)$ (b) $\sec(-t)$

35. $\sin t = \tfrac{4}{5}$
   (a) $\sin(\pi - t)$ (b) $\sin(t + \pi)$

36. $\cos t = \tfrac{4}{5}$
   (a) $\cos(\pi - t)$ (b) $\cos(t + \pi)$

In Exercises 37–44, use a calculator to evaluate the trigonometric function. (Set your calculator in radian mode and round your answer to four decimal places.)

37. $\sin \dfrac{\pi}{4}$

38. $\tan \pi$

39. $\cos(-3)$

40. $\cot 1$

41. $\cos(-1.7)$

42. $\sec 1.8$

43. $\csc 0.8$

44. $\sin(-0.9)$

In Exercises 45 and 46, use the accompanying figure and a straightedge to approximate the value of the trigonometric function. In Exercises 47 and 48, approximate the solution of the equation. Use $0 \le t \le 2\pi$.

45. (a) $\sin 5$ (b) $\cos 2$

46. (a) $\sin 0.75$ (b) $\cos 2.5$

47. (a) $\sin t = 0.25$ (b) $\cos t = -0.25$

48. (a) $\sin t = -0.75$ (b) $\cos t = 0.75$

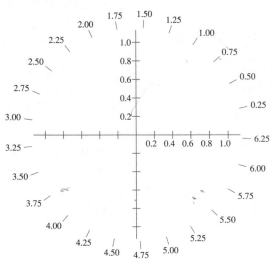

Figure for 45–48

51. *Electric Circuits* The initial current and charge in the electrical circuit shown in the accompanying figure is zero. The current when 100 volts is applied to the circuit is given by

$$I = 5e^{-2t} \sin t$$

if the resistance, inductance, and capacitance are 80 ohms, 20 henrys, and 0.01 farads, respectively. Approximate the current $t = 0.7$ seconds after the voltage is applied.

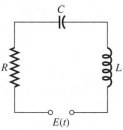

Figure for 51

52. Use the unit circle to verify that the cosine and secant functions are even and the sine, secant, tangent, and cotangent functions are odd.

49. *Harmonic Motion* The displacement from equilibrium of an oscillating weight suspended by a spring is

$$y(t) = \tfrac{1}{4} \cos 6t$$

where y is the displacement in feet and t is the time in seconds. Find the displacement when (a) $t = 0$, (b) $t = \tfrac{1}{4}$, and (c) $t = \tfrac{1}{2}$.

50. *Harmonic Motion* The displacement from equilibrium of an oscillating weight suspended by a spring and subject to the damping effect of friction is

$$y(t) = \tfrac{1}{4}e^{-t} \cos 6t$$

where y is the displacement in feet and t is the time in seconds. Find the displacement when (a) $t = 0$, (b) $t = \tfrac{1}{4}$, and (c) $t = \tfrac{1}{2}$.

5.3 Trigonometric Functions and Right Triangles

Trigonometric Functions of an Acute Angle / Trigonometric Identities /
Evaluating Trigonometric Functions with a Calculator / Applications Involving Right Triangles

Trigonometric Functions of an Acute Angle

Our second look at the trigonometric functions is from a *right triangle* perspective. Note that the three sides of the right triangle shown in Figure 5.22 are labeled the **hypotenuse,** the **opposite side** (the side opposite the angle θ), and the **adjacent side** (the side adjacent to the angle θ). Using the lengths of these three sides, we can form six ratios that define the six trigonometric functions of the acute angle θ.

In the following definition it is important to see that $0° < \theta < 90°$, and for such angles the value of each of the six trigonometric functions is *positive*.

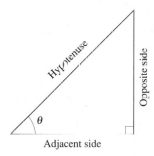

FIGURE 5.22

RIGHT TRIANGLE DEFINITION OF TRIGONOMETRIC FUNCTIONS

Let θ be an *acute* angle of a right triangle. Then the six trigonometric functions of the angle θ are defined as follows.

$$\sin \theta = \frac{\text{opp}}{\text{hyp}} \qquad \csc \theta = \frac{\text{hyp}}{\text{opp}}$$

$$\cos \theta = \frac{\text{adj}}{\text{hyp}} \qquad \sec \theta = \frac{\text{hyp}}{\text{adj}}$$

$$\tan \theta = \frac{\text{opp}}{\text{adj}} \qquad \cot \theta = \frac{\text{adj}}{\text{opp}}$$

The abbreviations opp, adj, and hyp represent the lengths of the three sides of the right triangle, as follows.

opp = the length of the side *opposite* θ

adj = the length of the side *adjacent* to θ

hyp = the length of the *hypotenuse*

EXAMPLE 1   Evaluating Trigonometric Functions

Find the values of the six trigonometric functions of θ as shown in Figure 5.23.

Solution

By the Pythagorean Theorem $(\text{hyp})^2 = (\text{opp})^2 + (\text{adj})^2$, it follows that

$$\text{hyp} = \sqrt{3^2 + 4^2} = \sqrt{25} = 5.$$

Thus, you have adj = 3, opp = 4, and hyp = 5, and the six trigonometric functions of θ have the following values.

$$\sin \theta = \frac{\text{opp}}{\text{hyp}} = \frac{4}{5} \qquad \csc \theta = \frac{\text{hyp}}{\text{opp}} = \frac{5}{4}$$

$$\cos \theta = \frac{\text{adj}}{\text{hyp}} = \frac{3}{5} \qquad \sec \theta = \frac{\text{hyp}}{\text{adj}} = \frac{5}{3}$$

$$\tan \theta = \frac{\text{opp}}{\text{adj}} = \frac{4}{3} \qquad \cot \theta = \frac{\text{adj}}{\text{opp}} = \frac{3}{4}$$

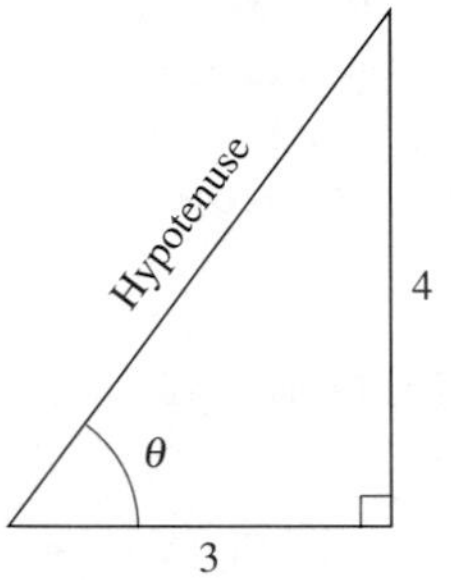

In Example 1, we were given the lengths of the sides of the right triangle, but not the angle θ. A much more common problem in trigonometry is to be asked to find the trigonometric functions for a *given* acute angle θ. To do this, we construct a right triangle having θ as one of its angles.

EXAMPLE 2   Evaluating Trigonometric Functions of 45°

Find the value of sin 45°, cos 45°, and tan 45°.

Solution

Construct a right triangle having 45° as one of its acute angles, as shown in Figure 5.24. Arbitrarily choose the length of the adjacent side to be 1. From geometry, you know that the other acute angle is also 45° and therefore the triangle is isosceles. Hence, the length of the opposite side is also 1. Then, using the Pythagorean Theorem, find the length of the hypotenuse to be

$$\text{hyp} = \sqrt{1^2 + 1^2} = \sqrt{2}.$$

Finally, you have the following.

$$\sin 45° = \frac{\text{opp}}{\text{hyp}} = \frac{1}{\sqrt{2}} = \frac{\sqrt{2}}{2}$$

$$\cos 45° = \frac{\text{adj}}{\text{hyp}} = \frac{1}{\sqrt{2}} = \frac{\sqrt{2}}{2}$$

$$\tan 45° = \frac{\text{opp}}{\text{adj}} = \frac{1}{1} = 1$$

FIGURE 5.23

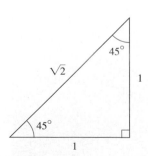

FIGURE 5.24

EXAMPLE 3   Evaluating Trigonometric Functions of 30° and 60°

Use the equilateral triangle shown in Figure 5.25 to find the value of sin 60°, cos 60°, sin 30°, and cos 30°.

Solution

Try using the Pythagorean Theorem and the 60° − 60° − 60° equilateral triangle to verify the lengths of the sides given in Figure 5.25. For $\theta = 60°$, you have adj = 1, opp = $\sqrt{3}$, and hyp = 2. Therefore,

$$\sin 60° = \frac{\text{opp}}{\text{hyp}} = \frac{\sqrt{3}}{2}$$

and

$$\cos 60° = \frac{\text{adj}}{\text{hyp}} = \frac{1}{2}.$$

For $\theta = 30°$, you have adj = $\sqrt{3}$, opp = 1, and hyp = 2. Therefore,

$$\sin 30° = \frac{\text{opp}}{\text{hyp}} = \frac{1}{2}$$

and

$$\cos 30° = \frac{\text{adj}}{\text{hyp}} = \frac{\sqrt{3}}{2}.$$

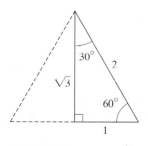

FIGURE 5.25

Because the angles 30°, 45°, and 60° ($\pi/6$, $\pi/4$, and $\pi/3$) occur frequently in trigonometry, we suggest that you learn to construct the triangles shown in Figures 5.24 and 5.25.

SINE, COSINE, AND TANGENT OF SPECIAL ANGLES

$$\sin 30° = \sin \frac{\pi}{6} = \frac{1}{2} \qquad \cos 30° = \cos \frac{\pi}{6} = \frac{\sqrt{3}}{2} \qquad \tan 30° = \tan \frac{\pi}{6} = \frac{\sqrt{3}}{3}$$

$$\sin 45° = \sin \frac{\pi}{4} = \frac{\sqrt{2}}{2} \qquad \cos 45° = \cos \frac{\pi}{4} = \frac{\sqrt{2}}{2} \qquad \tan 45° = \tan \frac{\pi}{4} = 1$$

$$\sin 60° = \sin \frac{\pi}{3} = \frac{\sqrt{3}}{2} \qquad \cos 60° = \cos \frac{\pi}{3} = \frac{1}{2} \qquad \tan 60° = \tan \frac{\pi}{3} = \sqrt{3}$$

Trigonometric Identities

In the preceding box, note that for the angles 30° and 60°, we have $\sin 30° = \frac{1}{2} = \cos 60°$. This occurs because 30° and 60° are complementary angles, and, in general, it can be shown from the right triangle definitions that *cofunctions of complementary angles are equal*. That is, if θ is an acute angle, then the following relationships are true.

$$\sin(90° - \theta) = \cos \theta \qquad \cos(90° - \theta) = \sin \theta$$
$$\tan(90° - \theta) = \cot \theta \qquad \cot(90° - \theta) = \tan \theta$$
$$\sec(90° - \theta) = \csc \theta \qquad \csc(90° - \theta) = \sec \theta$$

For instance, since 10° and 80° are complementary angles, it follows that $\sin 10° = \cos 80°$ and $\tan 10° = \cot 80°$.

In trigonometry, a great deal of time is spent studying relationships between trigonometric functions. We begin with some basic identities you should know and that are easily established from the unit circle definitions of the six trigonometric functions (see Exercise 57).

FUNDAMENTAL TRIGONOMETRIC IDENTITIES

Reciprocal Identities

$$\sin \theta = \frac{1}{\csc \theta} \qquad \sec \theta = \frac{1}{\cos \theta} \qquad \tan \theta = \frac{1}{\cot \theta}$$

$$\csc \theta = \frac{1}{\sin \theta} \qquad \cos \theta = \frac{1}{\sec \theta} \qquad \cot \theta = \frac{1}{\tan \theta}$$

Quotient Identities

$$\tan \theta = \frac{\sin \theta}{\cos \theta} \qquad \cot \theta = \frac{\cos \theta}{\sin \theta}$$

Pythagorean Identities

$$\sin^2 \theta + \cos^2 \theta = 1 \qquad 1 + \tan^2 \theta = \sec^2 \theta$$
$$1 + \cot^2 \theta = \csc^2 \theta$$

REMARK   We use $\sin^2 \theta$ to represent $(\sin \theta)^2$, $\cos^2 \theta$ to represent $(\cos \theta)^2$, and so on.

EXAMPLE 4   Applying Trigonometric Identities

Let θ be the acute angle such that $\cos \theta = \frac{1}{5}$. Find $\sec \theta$.

Solution

Using one of the reciprocal identities, you have

$$\sec \theta = \frac{1}{\cos \theta} = \frac{1}{1/5} = 5.$$

EXAMPLE 5 Applying Trigonometric Identities

Let θ be the acute angle such that $\sin \theta = 0.6$. Find the values of (a) $\cos \theta$ and (b) $\tan \theta$ using trigonometric identities.

Solution

a. To find the value of $\cos \theta$, we use the Pythagorean Identity for sine and cosine. Thus, you have

$$(0.6)^2 + \cos^2 \theta = 1$$
$$\cos^2 \theta = 1 - (0.6)^2 = 0.64$$
$$\cos \theta = \sqrt{0.64} = 0.8.$$

b. Now, knowing the sine and cosine of θ, find the tangent of θ to be

$$\tan \theta = \frac{\sin \theta}{\cos \theta} = \frac{0.6}{0.8} = 0.75.$$

Try using the definitions of $\cos \theta$ and $\tan \theta$, and the triangle shown in Figure 5.26 to check these results.

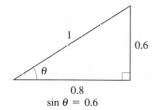

$\sin \theta = 0.6$

FIGURE 5.26

REMARK The triangle shown in Figure 5.26 was obtained from the fact that

$$\sin \theta = 0.6 = \frac{0.6}{1} = \frac{\text{opp}}{\text{hyp}}.$$

Thus, opp $= 0.6$, hyp $= 1$, and by the Pythagorean Theorem, it follows that

$$\text{adj} = \sqrt{1^2 - (0.6)^2} = \sqrt{0.64} = 0.8$$

EXAMPLE 6 Applying Trigonometric Identities

Let θ be an acute angle such that $\tan \theta = 3$. Find the values of (a) $\cot \theta$ and (b) $\sec \theta$ using trigonometric identities.

Solution

a. Using the reciprocal identity $\cot \theta = 1/\tan \theta$, you have

$$\cot \theta = \frac{1}{3}.$$

b. Using the Pythagorean Identity $1 + \tan^2 \theta = \sec^2 \theta$, you have

$$\sec^2 \theta = 1 + 3^2 = 10$$
$$\sec \theta = \sqrt{10}.$$

Try using the definitions of $\cot \theta$ and $\sec \theta$, and the triangle shown in Figure 5.27 to check these results.

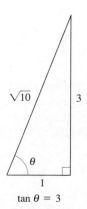

$\tan \theta = 3$

FIGURE 5.27

Evaluating Trigonometric Functions with a Calculator

To use a calculator to evaluate trigonometric functions of angles measured in degrees, first set the calculator in *degree mode* and then proceed as demonstrated in the previous section. For instance, you can find the values of cos 28° and sec 28° as follows.

Function	Mode	Keystrokes	Display
cos 28°	Degree	28 $\boxed{\text{cos}}$	0.8829476
sec 28°	Degree	28 $\boxed{\text{cos}}$ $\boxed{1/x}$	1.1325701

Throughout this text, we follow the convention that angles are assumed to be measured in radians unless noted otherwise. For example, when we write sin 1, we will always mean the sine of 1 *radian*. When we want to denote the sine of 1 degree, we will write sin 1°.

EXAMPLE 7   Using a Calculator to Evaluate Trigonometric Functions

Use a calculator to evaluate sec(5° 40′ 12″).

Solution

Converting first to decimal form, you have

$$5° \ 40′ \ 12″ = 5° + \left(\frac{40}{60}\right)° + \left(\frac{12}{3600}\right)° = 5.67°.$$

Hence, it follows that

$$\sec(5° \ 40′ \ 12″) = \sec 5.67° = \frac{1}{\cos 5.67°} \approx 1.00492.$$

Applications Involving Right Triangles

Many applications of trigonometry involve a process called **solving right triangles.** In this type of application, we are usually given one side of a right triangle and one of the acute angles and asked to find one of the other sides, *or* we are given two sides and asked to find one of the acute angles.

EXAMPLE 8   Solving a Right Triangle Given an Angle and One Side

A surveyor is standing 50 feet from the base of a large tree, as shown in Figure 5.28. The surveyor measures the angle of elevation to the top of the tree as 71.5°. How tall is the tree?

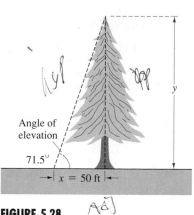

FIGURE 5.28

Solution

From Figure 5.28, you see that

$$\tan 71.5° = \frac{\text{opp}}{\text{adj}} = \frac{y}{x}$$

where $x = 50$ and y is the height of the tree. Thus, the height of the tree is

$$y = x \tan 71.5° \approx 50(2.98868) \approx 149.4 \text{ feet.}$$

EXAMPLE 9   Solving a Right Triangle Given Two Sides

A person is standing 200 yards from a river. Rather than walk directly to the river, the person walks 400 yards along a straight path to the river's edge. Find the acute angle θ between this path and the river's edge, as indicated in Figure 5.29.

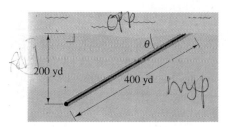

FIGURE 5.29

Solution

From Figure 5.29, you see that the sine of the angle θ is

$$\sin \theta = \frac{\text{opp}}{\text{hyp}} = \frac{200}{400} = \frac{1}{2}.$$

Now, you recognize that $\theta = 30°$.

In Example 9, you were able to recognize that the acute angle that satisfies the equation $\sin \theta = 1/2$ is $\theta = 30°$. Suppose, however, that you were given the equation $\sin \theta = 0.6$ and asked to find the acute angle θ. Since

$$\sin 30° = \frac{1}{2} = 0.5000 \quad \text{and} \quad \sin 45° = \frac{1}{\sqrt{2}} \approx 0.7071$$

you might guess that θ lies somewhere between 30° and 45°. A more precise value of θ can be found using the **INV** key on a calculator. To do this, you use the following keystroke sequence with the calculator in degree mode.

REMARK Instead of an inverse key **INV** , some calculators have a second function key **2nd f** .

.6 **INV** **sin**   *Display 36.8699*

Thus, you conclude that if $\sin \theta = 0.6$, then $\theta \approx 36.87°$.

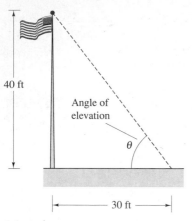

40 ft

Angle of
elevation

θ

30 ft

FIGURE 5.30

EXAMPLE 10   Solving a Right Triangle Given Two Sides

A 40-foot flagpole casts a 30-foot shadow, as shown in Figure 5.30. Find θ, the angle of elevation of the sun.

Solution

From Figure 5.30, you see that the *opposite* and *adjacent* sides are known. Thus, we write

$$\tan \theta = \frac{\text{opp}}{\text{adj}} = \frac{40}{30}.$$

With a calculator in degree mode, you use the keystrokes

40 ÷ 30 = INV tan

to obtain $\theta \approx 53.13°$.

DISCUSSION

PROBLEM

Comparing
Definitions of
Trigonometric
Functions

In Sections 5.2 and 5.3, we presented two different definitions of trigonometric functions. One was the "unit-circle definition" and the other was the "right-triangle definition." Write a short paper that compares the two definitions. Then use both definitions to find the values of the six trigonometric functions at $\theta = 30°$. For this value of θ, which definition do you prefer? For $\theta = 3\pi$, which do you prefer and why?

WARM UP

The following warm-up exercises involve skills that were covered in earlier sections. You will use these skills in the exercise set for this section.

In Exercises 1–4, find the distance between each pair of points.

1. (3, 8), (1, 4)

2. (5, 2), (2, −7)

3. (−4, 0), (2, 8)

4. (−3, −3), (0, 0)

In Exercises 5–10, perform the indicated operations. (Round to two decimal places.)

5. 0.300×4.125

6. 7.30×43.50

7. $\dfrac{151.5}{2.40}$

8. $\dfrac{3740}{28.0}$

9. $\dfrac{19,500}{0.007}$

10. $\dfrac{(10.5)(3401)}{1240}$

EXERCISES for Section 5.3

In Exercises 1–4, find the exact value of the six trigonometric functions of the angle θ given in the accompanying figure. (Use the Pythagorean Theorem to find the third side of the triangle.)

1.

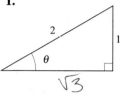

$1^2 + B^2 = 2^2$
$1 + B^2 = 4$

2.

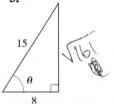

3.

$\sqrt{161}$

4.

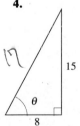

In Exercises 5–8, sketch a right triangle corresponding to the trigonometric function of the acute angle θ. Use the Pythagorean Theorem to determine the third side and then find the other five trigonometric functions of θ.

5. $\sin \theta = \frac{2}{3}$

6. $\sec \theta = 2$

7. $\tan \theta = 3$

8. $\cot \theta = \frac{3}{2}$

In Exercises 9–12, use the given functional values and trigonometric identities (including the relationship between a trigonometric function and its cofunction of a complementary angle) to find the trigonometric functions.

9. $\sin 60° = \dfrac{\sqrt{3}}{2}$, $\cos 60° = \dfrac{1}{2}$

   (a) $\tan 60°$ (b) $\sin 30°$
   (c) $\cos 30°$ (d) $\cot 60°$

10. $\sin 30° = \dfrac{1}{2}$, $\tan 30° = \dfrac{\sqrt{3}}{3}$

   (a) $\csc 30°$ (b) $\cot 60°$
   (c) $\cos 30°$ (d) $\cot 30°$

11. $\csc \theta = 3$, $\sec \theta = \dfrac{3\sqrt{2}}{4}$

   (a) $\sin \theta$ (b) $\cos \theta$
   (c) $\tan \theta$ (d) $\sec(90° - \theta)$

12. $\sec \theta = 5$, $\tan \theta = 2\sqrt{6}$

   (a) $\cos \theta$ (b) $\cot \theta$
   (c) $\cot(90° - \theta)$ (d) $\sin \theta$

In Exercises 13–16, evaluate the trigonometric function by memory or by constructing an appropriate triangle for the special angles.

13. (a) $\cos 60°$ (b) $\tan \dfrac{\pi}{6}$

14. (a) $\csc 30°$ (b) $\sin \dfrac{\pi}{4}$

15. (a) $\cot 45°$ (b) $\cos 45°$

16. (a) $\sin \dfrac{\pi}{3}$ (b) $\csc 45°$

In Exercises 17–22, use a calculator to evaluate each function. Round to four decimal places. (Be sure the calculator is in the correct mode.)

17. (a) $\sin 16.35°$ (b) $\csc 16.35°$

18. (a) $\tan 23.5°$ (b) $\cot 66.5°$

19. (a) $\cot \dfrac{\pi}{16}$ (b) $\tan \dfrac{\pi}{16}$

20. (a) $\cos 4° \, 50' \, 15''$ (b) $\sec 4° \, 50' \, 15''$

21. (a) $\csc 1$ (b) $\sec\left(\dfrac{\pi}{2} - 1\right)$

22. (a) $\sec 0.75$ (b) $\cos 0.75$

In Exercises 23–28, find the value of θ in degrees $(0° < \theta < 90°)$ and radians $(0 < \theta < \pi/2)$ without the aid of a calculator.

23. (a) $\sin \theta = \frac{1}{2}$ (b) $\csc \theta = 2$

24. (a) $\cos \theta = \frac{\sqrt{2}}{2}$ (b) $\tan \theta = 1$

25. (a) $\sec \theta = 2$ (b) $\cot \theta = 1$

26. (a) $\tan \theta = \sqrt{3}$ (b) $\cos \theta = \frac{1}{2}$

27. (a) $\csc \theta = \frac{2\sqrt{3}}{3}$ (b) $\sin \theta = \frac{\sqrt{2}}{2}$

28. (a) $\cot \theta = \frac{\sqrt{3}}{3}$ (b) $\sec \theta = \sqrt{2}$

In Exercises 29–32, find the value of θ in degrees $(0° < \theta < 90°)$ and radians $(0 < \theta < \pi/2)$ by using the inverse key on a calculator.

29. (a) $\sin \theta = 0.8191$ (b) $\cos \theta = 0.0175$

30. (a) $\cos \theta = 0.9848$ (b) $\cos \theta = 0.8746$

31. (a) $\tan \theta = 1.1920$ (b) $\tan \theta = 0.4663$

32. (a) $\sin \theta = 0.3746$ (b) $\cos \theta = 0.3746$

33. Solve for y.   **34.** Solve for x.

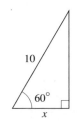

35. Solve for x.   **36.** Solve for r.

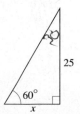

37. Solve for r.   **38.** Solve for x.

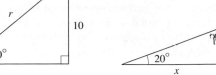

39. Solve for y.   **40.** Solve for r.

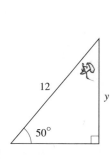

41. *Height*   A 6-foot person standing 12 feet from a streetlight casts an 8-foot shadow (see figure). What is the height of the streetlight?

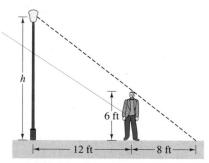

Figure for 41

42. *Height*   A 6-foot man walked from the base of a broadcasting tower directly toward the tip of the shadow cast by the tower. When 132 feet from the tower, his shadow started to appear beyond the tower's shadow. What is the height of the tower if he is 3 feet from the tip of the shadow?

43. *Length*   A 20-foot ladder leaning against the side of a house makes a 75° angle with the ground (see figure). How far up the side of the house does the ladder reach?

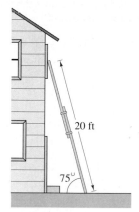

20 ft

75°

Figure for 43

44. *Width of a River*   A biologist wants to know the width w of a river in order to properly set instruments for studying the pollutants in the water. From point A, the biologist walks downstream 100 feet and sights to point C. From this sighting, it is determined that $\theta = 50°$ (see figure). How wide is the river?

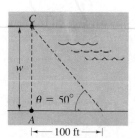

w

$\theta = 50°$

A

|← 100 ft →|

Figure for 44

45. *Distance*   From a 150-foot observation tower on the coast, a Coast Guard officer sights a boat in difficulty. The angle of depression of the boat is 4° (see figure). How far is the boat from the shoreline?

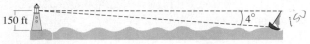

150 ft   4°

Figure for 45

46. *Angle of Elevation*   A ramp $17\frac{1}{2}$ feet in length rises to a loading platform that is $3\frac{1}{3}$ feet off the ground (see figure). Find the angle θ that the ramp makes with the ground.

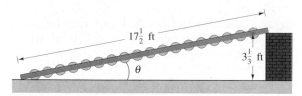

$17\frac{1}{2}$ ft

$3\frac{1}{3}$ ft

θ

Figure for 46

47. *Machine Shop Calculations*   A steel plate has the form of $\frac{1}{4}$ of a circle with a radius of 24 inches. Two $\frac{3}{8}$-inch holes are to be drilled in the plate positioned as shown in the figure. Find the coordinates of the center of each hole.

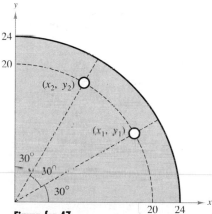

y

24

20

(x_2, y_2)

(x_1, y_1)

30°

30°

30°

20   24 x

Figure for 47

48. *Machine Shop Calculations*   A tapered shaft has a diameter of 2 inches at the small end and is 6 inches long (see figure). If the taper is 3°, find the diameter d of the large end of the shaft.

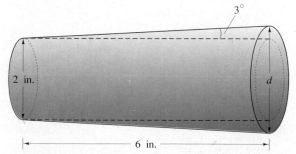

3°

2 in.

d

|← 6 in. →|

Figure for 48

49. *Trigonometric Functions by Actual Measurement* Use a compass to sketch a quarter of a circle of radius 10 centimeters. Using a protractor, construct an angle of 25° in standard position (see figure). Drop a perpendicular line from the point of intersection of the terminal side of the angle and the arc of the circle. By actual measurement, calculate the coordinates (x, y) of the point of intersection and use these measurements to approximate the six trigonometric functions of a 25° angle.

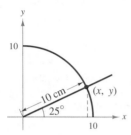

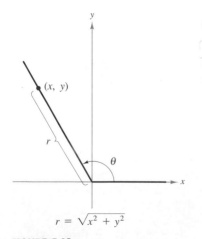

Figure for 49

50. *Trigonometric Functions by Actual Measurement* Repeat Exercise 49 using an angle of 75°.

In Exercises 51–56, determine whether the statement is true or false, and give a reason for your answer.

51. $\sin 60° \csc 60° = 1$

52. $\sec 30° = \csc 60°$

53. $\sin 45° + \cos 45° = 1$

54. $\cot^2 10° - \csc^2 10° = -1$

55. $\dfrac{\sin 60°}{\sin 30°} = \sin 2°$

56. $\tan[(0.8)^2] = \tan^2(0.8)$

57. Use the unit circle to verify the fundamental trigonometric identities given in this section.

5.4 Trigonometric Functions of Any Angle

Introduction / Reference Angles

Introduction

In Section 5.3, we restricted the evaluation of trigonometric functions to acute angles. In this section, we expand our evaluation techniques to include any angle θ.

FIGURE 5.31

$r = \sqrt{x^2 + y^2}$

TRIGONOMETRIC FUNCTIONS OF ANY ANGLE

Let θ be an angle in standard position with (x, y) any point (except the origin) on the terminal side of θ and $r = \sqrt{x^2 + y^2}$, as shown in Figure 5.31.

$$\sin \theta = \frac{y}{r} \qquad\qquad \csc \theta = \frac{r}{y}, \quad y \neq 0$$

$$\cos \theta = \frac{x}{r} \qquad\qquad \sec \theta = \frac{r}{x}, \quad x \neq 0$$

$$\tan \theta = \frac{y}{x}, \quad x \neq 0 \qquad \cot \theta = \frac{x}{y}, \quad y \neq 0$$

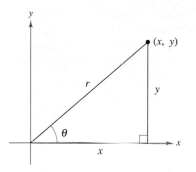

FIGURE 5.32

This result can be easily derived from the unit circle definition of the six trigonometric functions. By referring back to Section 5.2, you will see that the only difference is that, in the unit circle definition, the point (x, y) lies on the unit circle (which implies that $1 = \sqrt{x^2 + y^2}$), whereas, in the above description, (x, y) can be *any* point in the plane (other than the origin) and the positive number r is given by $r = \sqrt{x^2 + y^2}$.

Moreover, if θ is an *acute* angle, then the six ratios listed above coincide with those given in the previous section. To see this, note in Figure 5.32 that for an acute angle θ, $x = $ adj, $y = $ opp, and $r = $ hyp.

EXAMPLE 1 Evaluating Trigonometric Functions

Let $(-3, 4)$ be a point on the terminal side of θ. Find the sine, cosine, and tangent of θ.

Solution

Referring to Figure 5.33, you see that $x = -3$, $y = 4$, and

$$r = \sqrt{x^2 + y^2} = \sqrt{(-3)^2 + 4^2} = \sqrt{25} = 5.$$

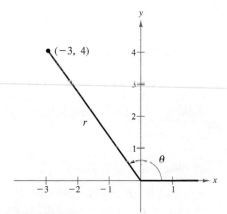

FIGURE 5.33

Thus, we have

$$\sin \theta = \frac{y}{r} = \frac{4}{5}$$

$$\cos \theta = \frac{x}{r} = \frac{-3}{5} = -\frac{3}{5}$$

$$\tan \theta = \frac{y}{x} = \frac{4}{-3} = -\frac{4}{3}.$$

The *signs* of the trigonometric function values in the four quadrants can be easily determined from the definitions of the functions. For instance, since $\cos \theta = x/r$, it follows that $\cos \theta$ is positive whenever $x > 0$, which is in Quadrants I and IV (r is always positive). In a similar manner you can verify the results shown in Figure 5.34.

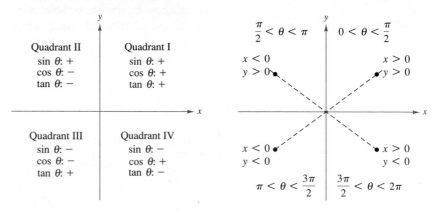

Quadrant II	Quadrant I
$\sin \theta$: +	$\sin \theta$: +
$\cos \theta$: −	$\cos \theta$: +
$\tan \theta$: −	$\tan \theta$: +

Quadrant III	Quadrant IV
$\sin \theta$: −	$\sin \theta$: −
$\cos \theta$: −	$\cos \theta$: +
$\tan \theta$: +	$\tan \theta$: −

Signs of Trigonometric Functions

FIGURE 5.34

EXAMPLE 2 Evaluating Trigonometric Functions

Given $\tan \theta = -5/4$ and $\cos \theta > 0$, find $\sin \theta$ and $\sec \theta$.

Solution

Note that θ lies in Quadrant IV because that is the only quadrant in which the tangent is negative and the cosine is positive. Moreover, using

$$\tan \theta = \frac{y}{x} = -\frac{5}{4}$$

and the fact that y is negative in Quadrant IV, you can let $y = -5$ and $x = 4$. Hence, $r = \sqrt{25 + 16} = \sqrt{41}$ and you have

$$\sin \theta = \frac{y}{r} = \frac{-5}{\sqrt{41}} \approx -0.7809$$

$$\sec \theta = \frac{r}{x} = \frac{\sqrt{41}}{4} \approx 1.6008.$$

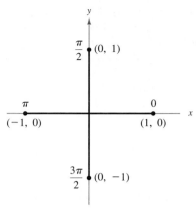

FIGURE 5.35

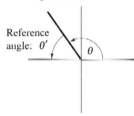

Quadrant II

Reference angle: θ'

$\theta' = \pi - \theta$ (radians)
$\theta' = 180° - \theta$ (degrees)

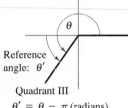

Reference angle: θ'

Quadrant III
$\theta' = \theta - \pi$ (radians)
$\theta' = \theta - 180°$ (degrees)

Reference angle: θ'

Quadrant IV
$\theta' = 2\pi - \theta$ (radians)
$\theta' = 360° - \theta$ (degrees)

FIGURE 5.36

EXAMPLE 3 Trigonometric Functions of Quadrant Angles

Evaluate the sine function at the four quadrant angles 0, $\pi/2$, π, and $3\pi/2$.

Solution

First choose a point on the terminal side of each angle, as shown in Figure 5.35. For each of the four given points, $r = 1$, so that you have

$$\sin 0 = \frac{y}{r} = \frac{0}{1} = 0 \qquad\qquad (x, y) = (1, 0)$$

$$\sin \frac{\pi}{2} = \frac{y}{r} = \frac{1}{1} = 1 \qquad\qquad (x, y) = (0, 1)$$

$$\sin \pi = \frac{y}{r} = \frac{0}{1} = 0 \qquad\qquad (x, y) = (-1, 0)$$

$$\sin \frac{3\pi}{2} = \frac{y}{r} - \frac{-1}{1} = -1. \qquad\qquad (x, y) = (0, -1)$$

Try using Figure 5.35 to evaluate some of the other **trigonometric functions** at the four quadrant angles.

Reference Angles

The values of the trigonometric functions of angles greater than 90° (or less than 0°) can be determined from their values at corresponding acute angles **(reference angles).**

To help with *graphm back*

DEFINITION OF REFERENCE ANGLES
Let θ be an angle in standard position. Its **reference angle** is the acute angle θ' formed by the terminal side of θ and the horizontal axis.

Figure 5.36 illustrates the reference angle for θ in Quadrants II–IV.

EXAMPLE 4 Finding Reference Angles

Find the reference angle θ'.

a. $\theta = 300°$
b. $\theta = 2.3$
c. $\theta = -135°$

Solution

a. Since $\theta = 300°$ lies in Quadrant IV, the angle it makes with the x-axis is

$$\theta' = 360° - 300° = 60°. \qquad \textit{Degrees}$$

b. Since $\theta = 2.3$ lies between $\pi/2 \approx 1.5708$ and $\pi \approx 3.1416$, it follows that θ is in Quadrant II and its reference angle is

$$\theta' = \pi - 2.3 \approx 0.8416. \qquad \textit{Radians}$$

c. First, determine that $-135°$ is coterminal with $225°$, which lies in Quadrant III. Hence, the reference angle is

$$\theta' = 225° - 180° = 45°. \qquad \textit{Degrees}$$

Figure 5.37 shows each angle θ and its reference angle θ'.

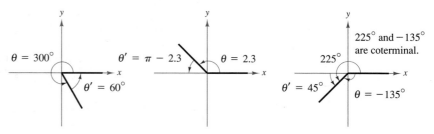

(a) θ in Quadrant IV   (b) θ in Quadrant II   (c) θ in Quadrant III

FIGURE 5.37

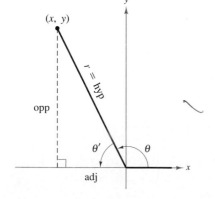

$$\text{opp} = |y|, \text{ adj} = |x|$$

FIGURE 5.38

To see how a reference angle is used to *evaluate* a trigonometric function, consider the point (x, y) on the terminal side of θ, as shown in Figure 5.38. We know that

$$\sin \theta = \frac{y}{r} \quad \text{and} \quad \tan \theta = \frac{y}{x}.$$

For the triangle with acute angle θ' and sides of lengths $|x|$ and $|y|$, we have

$$\sin \theta' = \frac{\text{opp}}{\text{hyp}} = \frac{|y|}{r} \quad \text{and} \quad \tan \theta' = \frac{\text{opp}}{\text{adj}} = \frac{|y|}{|x|}.$$

Thus, it follows that $\sin \theta$ and $\sin \theta'$ are equal, *except possibly in sign.* The same is true for $\tan \theta$ and $\tan \theta'$ *and* for the other four trigonometric functions. In all cases, the sign of the function value can be determined by the quadrant in which θ lies.

Evaluating Trigonometric Functions of Any Angle

To find the value of a trigonometric function of any angle θ, use the following steps.

1. Determine the function value for the associated reference angle θ'.
2. Depending on the quadrant in which θ lies, prefix the appropriate sign to the function value.

By using reference angles together with the special angles discussed in the previous section, we can greatly extend our scope of *exact* trigonometric values. For instance, knowing the function values of 30° means that we know the function values of all angles for which 30° is a reference angle. For convenience, Table 5.1 gives the exact values of the trigonometric functions of special angles and quadrant angles.

TABLE 5.1

θ(degrees)	0°	30°	45°	60°	90°	180°	270°
θ(radians)	0	$\dfrac{\pi}{6}$	$\dfrac{\pi}{4}$	$\dfrac{\pi}{3}$	$\dfrac{\pi}{2}$	π	$\dfrac{3\pi}{2}$
$\sin \theta$	0	$\dfrac{1}{2}$	$\dfrac{\sqrt{2}}{2}$	$\dfrac{\sqrt{3}}{2}$	1	0	-1
$\cos \theta$	1	$\dfrac{\sqrt{3}}{2}$	$\dfrac{\sqrt{2}}{2}$	$\dfrac{1}{2}$	0	-1	0
$\tan \theta$	0	$\dfrac{\sqrt{3}}{3}$	1	$\sqrt{3}$	undef.	0	undef.

memorize

EXAMPLE 5   Trigonometric Functions of Nonacute Angles

Evaluate the following.

a. $\cos \dfrac{4\pi}{3}$ **b.** $\tan(-210°)$ **c.** $\csc \dfrac{11\pi}{4}$

Solution

a. Since $\theta = 4\pi/3$ lies in Quadrant III, the reference angle is $\theta' = (4\pi/3) - \pi = \pi/3$, as shown in Figure 5.39(a). Moreover, the cosine is negative in Quadrant III, so that

$$\cos \frac{4\pi}{3} = (-)\cos \frac{\pi}{3} = -\frac{1}{2}. \qquad \text{Special angle, } \tfrac{\pi}{3}$$

b. Since $-210° + 360° = 150°$, it follows that $-210°$ is coterminal with the second-quadrant angle $150°$. Therefore, the reference angle is $\theta' = 180° - 150° = 30°$, as shown in Figure 5.39(b). Finally, since the tangent is negative in Quadrant II, you have

$$\tan(-210°) = (-)\tan 30° = -\frac{\sqrt{3}}{3}. \qquad \text{Special angle, } 30°$$

c. Since $(11\pi/4) - 2\pi = 3\pi/4$, it follows that $11\pi/4$ is coterminal with the second-quadrant angle $3\pi/4$. Therefore, the reference angle is $\theta' = \pi - (3\pi/4) = \pi/4$, as shown in Figure 5.39(c). Because the cosecant is positive in Quadrant II, you have

$$\csc \frac{11\pi}{4} = (+)\csc \frac{\pi}{4} = \frac{1}{\sin(\pi/4)} = \sqrt{2}. \qquad \text{Special angle, } \tfrac{\pi}{4}$$

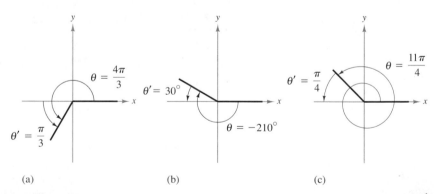

(a)	(b)	(c)

FIGURE 5.39

The fundamental trigonometric identities listed in the previous section (for an acute angle θ) are also valid when θ is any angle in the domain of the functions.

EXAMPLE 6   Using Identities to Evaluate Trigonometric Functions

Let θ be an angle in Quadrant II such that $\sin \theta = 1/3$. Find (a) $\cos \theta$ and (b) $\tan \theta$ by using trigonometric identities.

Solution

a. Since $\sin \theta = 1/3$, use the Pythagorean Identity $\sin^2 \theta + \cos^2 \theta = 1$ to obtain

$$\left(\frac{1}{3}\right)^2 + \cos^2 \theta = 1$$

$$\cos^2 \theta = 1 - \frac{1}{9} = \frac{8}{9}.$$

Since $\cos \theta < 0$ in Quadrant II, use the negative root

$$\cos \theta = -\frac{\sqrt{8}}{\sqrt{9}} = -\frac{2\sqrt{2}}{3}.$$

b. Using the result from part (a) and the trigonometric identity $\tan \theta = \sin \theta / \cos \theta$, you obtain

$$\tan \theta = \frac{1/3}{-2\sqrt{2}/3} = -\frac{1}{2\sqrt{2}} = -\frac{\sqrt{2}}{4}.$$

EXAMPLE 7   Finding Function Values and Angles with a Calculator

a. Use a calculator to approximate the values of $\cot 410°$ and $\sin(-7)$.
b. Use the INV or 2nd f key on a calculator to solve the equations

$$\cos \theta = -0.3522 \quad (0° \leq \theta < 360°) \quad \text{and}$$
$$\tan \theta = 4.812 \quad (0 \leq \theta < 2\pi).$$

Solution

Function	Mode	Keystrokes	Display
a. $\cot 410°$	Degree	410 `tan` `1/x`	0.839099631
$\sin(-7)$	Radian	7 `+/-` `sin`	−0.656986598

Equation	Mode	Keystrokes	Display
b. $\cos \theta = -0.3522$	Degree	0.3522 `+/-` `INV` `cos`	110.6219361
$\tan \theta = 4.812$	Radian	4.812 `INV` `tan`	1.365898912

For the cosine equation, $\theta \approx 111°$ (to nearest degree) and lies in Quadrant II with a reference angle of $\theta' = 180° - 111° = 69°$. A second value of θ lies in Quadrant III (cos is negative) and is $\theta = 180° + \theta' = 180° + 69° = 249°$.

For the tangent equation, $\theta \approx 1.366$ (to three decimal places) and lies in Quadrant I. A second value of θ lies in Quadrant III (tan is positive) and is $\theta = \pi + 1.366 \approx 4.508$. ◢

We have now completed our introduction to basic trigonometry. We have measured angles in both radians and degrees. We have defined the six trigonometric functions from a right triangle perspective and as functions of real numbers. In our remaining work with trigonometry, we will continue to rely on both perspectives. For instance, in the next three sections on graphing techniques we will think of the trigonometric functions as functions of real numbers. Later, in Chapter 7, we will look at applications involving angles and triangles.

For your convenience, we have included on the inside back cover of this text a summary of basic trigonometry.

DISCUSSION
PROBLEM
Patterns in Trigonometric Functions

Complete the following table. Then write a paragraph describing any inherent patterns in the trigonometric functions.

Function	Domain	Range	Even/Odd	Period	Zeros
sine					
cosine					
tangent					
cosecant					
secant					
cotangent					

WARM UP

The following warm-up exercises involve skills that were covered in earlier sections. You will use these skills in the exercise set for this section.

In Exercises 1–6, evaluate the trigonometric function from memory.

1. $\sin 30°$

2. $\tan 45°$

3. $\cos \dfrac{\pi}{4}$

4. $\cot \dfrac{\pi}{3}$

5. $\sec \dfrac{\pi}{6}$

6. $\csc \dfrac{\pi}{4}$

In Exercises 7–10, use the given trigonometric function of an acute angle θ to find the values of the remaining trigonometric functions.

7. $\tan \theta = \dfrac{3}{2}$

8. $\cos \theta = \dfrac{2}{3}$

9. $\sin \theta = \dfrac{1}{5}$

10. $\sec \theta = 3$

EXERCISES for Section 5.4

In Exercises 1–4, determine the exact value of the six trigonometric functions of the angle θ.

1. (a)   (b)

2. (a)   (b)

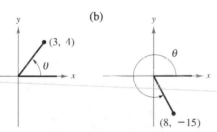

3. (a)   (b)

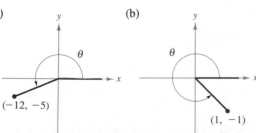

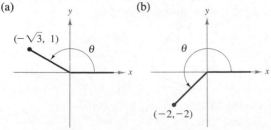

4. (a)   (b)

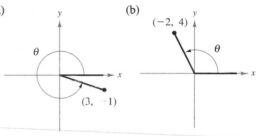

In Exercises 5–8, the point is on the terminal side of an angle in standard position. Determine the exact value of the six trigonometric functions of the angle.

5. (a) $(7, 24)$ (b) $(7, -24)$

6. (a) $(8, 15)$ (b) $(-9, -40)$

7. (a) $(-4, 10)$ (b) $(3, -5)$

8. (a) $(-5, -2)$ (b) $(-3/2, 3)$

In Exercises 9–12, use the two similar triangles in the accompanying figure to find (a) the unknown sides of the triangles and (b) the six trigonometric functions of the angles α_1 and α_2.

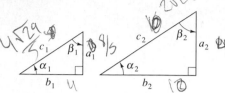

Figure for 9–12

9. $a_1 = 3$, $\quad b_1 = 4$, $\quad a_2 = 9$
10. $b_1 = 12$, $\quad c_1 = 13$, $\quad c_2 = 26$
11. $a_1 = 1$, $\quad c_1 = 2$, $\quad b_2 = 5$
12. $b_1 = 4$, $\quad a_2 = 4$, $\quad b_2 = 10$

In Exercises 13–16, determine the quadrant in which θ lies.

13. (a) $\sin \theta < 0$ and $\cos \theta < 0$
     (b) $\sin \theta > 0$ and $\cos \theta < 0$
14. (a) $\sin \theta > 0$ and $\cos \theta > 0$
     (b) $\sin \theta < 0$ and $\cos \theta > 0$
15. (a) $\sin \theta > 0$ and $\tan \theta < 0$
     (b) $\cos \theta > 0$ and $\tan \theta < 0$
16. (a) $\sec \theta > 0$ and $\cot \theta < 0$
     (b) $\csc \theta < 0$ and $\tan \theta > 0$

In Exercises 17–26, find the values (if possible) of the six trigonometric functions of θ using the given functional value and constraint.

Functional Value	*Constraint*
17. $\sin \theta = \frac{3}{5}$	θ lies in Quadrant II
18. $\cos \theta = -\frac{4}{5}$	θ lies in Quadrant III
19. $\tan \theta = -\frac{15}{8}$	$\sin \theta < 0$
20. $\cos \theta = \frac{8}{17}$	$\tan \theta < 0$
21. $\sec \theta = -2$	$\sin \theta > 0$
22. $\cot \theta$ is undefined	$\frac{\pi}{2} \le \theta \le \frac{3\pi}{2}$
23. $\sin \theta = 0$	$\sec \theta = -1$
24. $\tan \theta$ is undefined	$\pi \le \theta \le 2\pi$

25. The terminal side of θ is in Quadrant III and lies on the line $y = 2x$.
26. The terminal side of θ is in Quadrant IV and lies on the line $4x + 3y = 0$.

In Exercises 27–34, find the reference angle θ', and sketch θ and θ' in standard position.

27. (a) $\theta = 203°$ (b) $\theta = 127°$
28. (a) $\theta = 309°$ (b) $\theta = 226°$
29. (a) $\theta = -245°$ (b) $\theta = -72°$
30. (a) $\theta = -145°$ (b) $\theta = -239°$
31. (a) $\theta = \frac{2\pi}{3}$ (b) $\theta = \frac{7\pi}{6}$
32. (a) $\theta = \frac{7\pi}{4}$ (b) $\theta = \frac{8\pi}{9}$
33. (a) $\theta = 3.5$ (b) $\theta = 5.8$
34. (a) $\theta = \frac{11\pi}{3}$ (b) $\theta = -\frac{7\pi}{10}$

In Exercises 35–44, evaluate the sine, cosine, and tangent of the angles without using a calculator.

35. (a) $225°$ (b) $-225°$
36. (a) $300°$ (b) $330°$
37. (a) $750°$ (b) $510°$
38. (a) $-405°$ (b) $-120°$
39. (a) $\frac{4\pi}{3}$ (b) $\frac{2\pi}{3}$
40. (a) $\frac{\pi}{4}$ (b) $\frac{5\pi}{4}$
41. (a) $-\frac{\pi}{6}$ (b) $\frac{5\pi}{6}$
42. (a) $-\frac{\pi}{2}$ (b) $\frac{\pi}{2}$
43. (a) $\frac{11\pi}{4}$ (b) $-\frac{13\pi}{6}$
44. (a) $\frac{10\pi}{3}$ (b) $\frac{17\pi}{3}$

In Exercises 45–52, use a calculator to evaluate the trigonometric functions to four decimal places. (Be sure the calculator is set in the correct mode.)

45. (a) $\sin 10°$ (b) $\csc 10°$
46. (a) $\sec 225°$ (b) $\sec 135°$
47. (a) $\cos(-110°)$ (b) $\cos 250°$
48. (a) $\csc 330°$ (b) $\csc 150°$
49. (a) $\tan 240°$ (b) $\cot 210°$
50. (a) $\cot 1.35$ (b) $\tan 1.35$

51. (a) $\tan \dfrac{\pi}{9}$ (b) $\tan \dfrac{10\pi}{9}$

52. (a) $\sin(-0.65)$ (b) $\sin 5.63$

In Exercises 53–58, find two values of θ that satisfy the equation. Give your answers in degrees $(0° \le \theta < 360°)$ and radians $(0 \le \theta < 2\pi)$. Do not use a calculator.

53. (a) $\sin \theta = \frac{1}{2}$ (b) $\sin \theta = -\frac{1}{2}$

54. (a) $\cos \theta = \dfrac{\sqrt{2}}{2}$ (b) $\cos \theta = -\dfrac{\sqrt{2}}{2}$

55. (a) $\csc \theta = \dfrac{2\sqrt{3}}{3}$ (b) $\cot \theta = -1$

56. (a) $\sec \theta = 2$ (b) $\sec \theta = -2$

57. (a) $\tan \theta = 1$ (b) $\cot \theta = -\sqrt{3}$

58. (a) $\sin \theta = \dfrac{\sqrt{3}}{2}$ (b) $\sin \theta = -\dfrac{\sqrt{3}}{2}$

In Exercises 59 and 60, use a calculator to approximate two values of θ $(0° \le \theta < 360°)$ that satisfy the equation. Round to two decimal places.

59. (a) $\sin \theta = 0.8191$ (b) $\sin \theta = -0.2589$

60. (a) $\cos \theta = 0.8746$ (b) $\cos \theta = -0.2419$

In Exercises 61–64, use a calculator to approximate two values of θ $(0 \le \theta < 2\pi)$ that satisfy the equation. Round to three decimal places.

61. (a) $\cos \theta = 0.9848$ (b) $\cos \theta = -0.5890$

62. (a) $\sin \theta = 0.0175$ (b) $\sin \theta = -0.6691$

63. (a) $\tan \theta = 1.192$ (b) $\tan \theta = -8.144$

64. (a) $\cot \theta = 5.671$ (b) $\cot \theta = -1.280$

In Exercises 65–68, use the value of the given trigonometric function and trigonometric identities to find the required trigonometric function of the angle θ in the specified quadrant.

Given Function	Quadrant	Find
65. $\sin \theta = -\frac{3}{5}$	IV	$\cos \theta$
66. $\tan \theta = \frac{3}{2}$	III	$\sec \theta$
67. $\csc \theta = -2$	IV	$\cot \theta$
68. $\sec \theta = -\frac{9}{4}$	III	$\tan \theta$

In Exercises 69 and 70, evaluate the expression without using a calculator.

69. $\sin^2 2 + \cos^2 2$ **70.** $\tan^2 20° - \sec^2 20°$

71. *Average Temperature*   The average daily temperature T (in degrees Fahrenheit) for a city is

$$T = 45 - 23 \cos\left[\frac{2\pi}{365}(t - 32)\right]$$

where t is the time in days with $t = 1$ corresponding to January 1. Find the average daily temperature on the following days.
(a) January 1   (b) July 4 $(t = 185)$
(c) October 18 $(t = 291)$

72. *Sales*   A company that produces a seasonal product forecasts monthly sales over the next two years to be

$$S = 23.1 + 0.442t + 4.3 \sin \frac{\pi t}{6}$$

where S is measured in thousands of units and t is the time in months with $t = 1$ representing January 1991. Predict sales for the following months.
(a) February 1991   (b) February 1992
(c) September 1991   (d) September 1992

73. *Distance*   An airplane flying at an altitude of five miles is on a flight path that passes directly over an observer (see figure). If θ is the angle of elevation from the observer to the plane, find the distance from the observer to the plane when (a) $\theta = 30°$, (b) $\theta = 75°$, and (c) $\theta = 90°$.

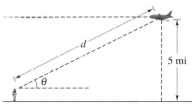

Figure for 73

74. Consider an angle in standard position with $r = 10$ cm as shown in the figure. Write a short paragraph describing the change in the magnitude of x, y, $\sin \theta$, $\cos \theta$, and $\tan \theta$, as θ increases continuously from $0°$ to $90°$.

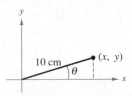

Figure for 74

Graphs of Sine and Cosine Functions

Basic Sine and Cosine Curves / Key Points on Basic Sine and Cosine Curves /
Amplitude and Period of Sine and Cosine Curves / Translations of Sine and Cosine Curves

Basic Sine and Cosine Curves

In this section we look at techniques for sketching the graphs of the sine and cosine functions. To accommodate the familiar xy-coordinate system, we use the variable x in place of θ or t. For example, $y = \sin x$ and $y = \cos x$.

The graph of the sine function is a **sine curve.** In Figure 5.40, the solid portion of the graph represents one period of the function and is called **one cycle** of the sine curve. The gray portion of the graph indicates that the basic sine wave repeats indefinitely to the right and left. The graph of the cosine function is shown in Figure 5.41.

Recall from Section 5.3 that the domain of the sine and cosine function is the set of all real numbers. Moreover, the range of each function is the interval $[-1, 1]$, and each function has a period of 2π. Do you see how this information is consistent with the basic graphs in Figures 5.40 and 5.41?

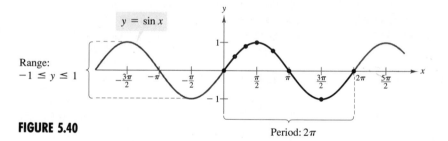

Range: $-1 \le y \le 1$

FIGURE 5.40

x	0	$\dfrac{\pi}{6}$	$\dfrac{\pi}{3}$	$\dfrac{\pi}{2}$	$\dfrac{3\pi}{4}$	π	$\dfrac{3\pi}{2}$	2π
$\sin x$	0	$\dfrac{1}{2}$	$\dfrac{\sqrt{3}}{2}$	1	$\dfrac{\sqrt{2}}{2}$	0	-1	0

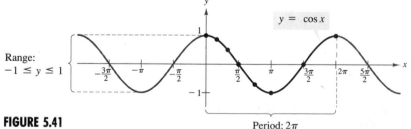

Range: $-1 \le y \le 1$

FIGURE 5.41

x	0	$\dfrac{\pi}{6}$	$\dfrac{\pi}{3}$	$\dfrac{\pi}{2}$	$\dfrac{3\pi}{4}$	π	$\dfrac{3\pi}{2}$	2π
$\cos x$	1	$\dfrac{\sqrt{3}}{2}$	$\dfrac{1}{2}$	0	$-\dfrac{\sqrt{2}}{2}$	-1	0	1

Note from Figures 5.40 and 5.41 that the sine graph is symmetric with respect to the *origin,* whereas the cosine graph is symmetric with respect to the y-axis. These properties of symmetry follow from the fact that the sine function is odd

$$\sin(-x) = -\sin x \qquad \textit{Origin symmetry}$$

whereas the cosine function is even

$$\cos(-x) = \cos x. \qquad \textit{y-axis symmetry}$$

Key Points on Basic Sine and Cosine Curves

To help you construct the graphs of the basic sine and cosine functions, we note five **key points** in one period of each graph: the *intercepts, maximum points*, and *minimum points*. For the sine function, the key points are

| Intercept | Maximum | Intercept | Minimum | | Intercept |

$$(0, 0), \quad \left(\frac{\pi}{2}, 1\right), \quad (\pi, 0), \quad \left(\frac{3\pi}{2}, -1\right), \quad \text{and} \quad (2\pi, 0).$$

For the cosine function, the key points are

| Maximum | Intercept | Minimum | Intercept | | Maximum |

$$(0, 1), \quad \left(\frac{\pi}{2}, 0\right), \quad (\pi, -1) \quad \left(\frac{3\pi}{2}, 0\right), \quad \text{and} \quad (2\pi, 1).$$

Note how the *x*-coordinates of these points divide the period of sin *x* and cos *x* into *four* equal parts, as indicated in Figure 5.42.

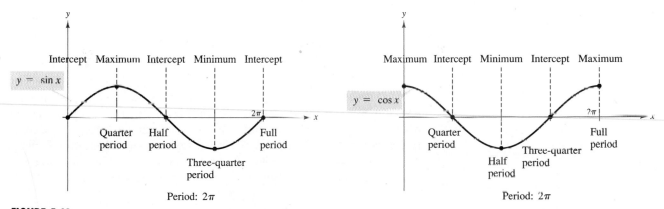

FIGURE 5.42

EXAMPLE 1   Using Key Points to Sketch a Sine Curve

Sketch the graph of $y = 2 \sin x$ on the interval $[-\pi, 4\pi]$.

Solution

Note that $y = 2 \sin x = 2(\sin x)$ indicates that the *y*-values for the key points will have twice the magnitude of the graph of $y = \sin x$. Divide the period 2π into four equal parts to get the following key points for $y = 2 \sin x$.

$$(0, 0), \quad \left(\frac{\pi}{2}, 2\right), \quad (\pi, 0), \quad \left(\frac{3\pi}{2}, -2\right), \quad \text{and} \quad (2\pi, 0)$$

By connecting these key points with a smooth curve and extending the curve in both directions over the interval $[-\pi, 4\pi]$, you obtain the graph in Figure 5.43.

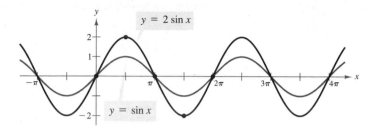

FIGURE 5.43

Amplitude and Period of Sine and Cosine Curves

In the rest of this section we look at variations in the graphs of the basic functions $y = \sin x$ and $y = \cos x$. In particular, we want to investigate the graphic effect of each of the constants a, b, c, and d in equations of the forms

$$y = d + a \sin(bx - c) \qquad \text{and} \qquad y = d + a \cos(bx - c).$$

A quick review of the transformations studied in Section 2.5 should help in this investigation.

The constant factor a in $y = a \sin x$ acts as a *scaling factor*—a *vertical stretch* or *vertical shrink* of the basic sine curve. (If $|a| > 1$, the basic sine curve is stretched, and if $|a| < 1$, the basic sine curve is shrunk.) The result is that the graph of $y = a \sin x$ ranges between $-a$ and a instead of between -1 and 1. The absolute value of a is the **amplitude** of the function $y = a \sin x$. The range of the function $y = a \sin x$ is $-a \leq y \leq a$.

DEFINITION OF AMPLITUDE OF SINE AND COSINE CURVES

The **amplitude** of $y = a \sin x$ and $y = a \cos x$ is the largest value of y and is given by

Amplitude $= |a|$.

EXAMPLE 2   Scaling: Vertical Shrinking and Stretching

On the same coordinate axes, sketch the graphs of

$$y = \frac{1}{2} \cos x \qquad \text{and} \qquad y = 3 \cos x.$$

Solution

Since the amplitude of $y = \frac{1}{2} \cos x$ is $\frac{1}{2}$, the maximum value is $\frac{1}{2}$ and the minimum value is $-\frac{1}{2}$. Divide one cycle, $0 \le x \le 2\pi$, into four equal parts to get the key points

$$\left(0, \frac{1}{2}\right), \quad \left(\frac{\pi}{2}, 0\right), \quad \left(\pi, -\frac{1}{2}\right), \quad \left(\frac{3\pi}{2}, 0\right), \quad \text{and} \quad \left(2\pi, \frac{1}{2}\right).$$

A similar analysis shows that the amplitude of $y = 3 \cos x$ is 3, and the key points are

$$(0, 3), \quad \left(\frac{\pi}{2}, 0\right), \quad (\pi, -3), \quad \left(\frac{3\pi}{2}, 0\right), \quad \text{and} \quad (2\pi, 3).$$

The graphs of these two functions are shown in Figure 5.44.

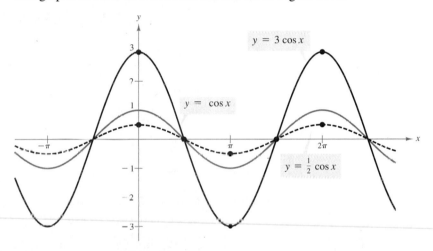

Amplitude Determines Vertical Stretch or Shrink

FIGURE 5.44

We know from Section 2.5 that the graph of $y = -f(x)$ is a **reflection** (in the x-axis) of the graph of $y = f(x)$. For instance, the graph of $y = -3 \cos x$ is a reflection of the graph of $y = 3 \cos x$, as shown in Figure 5.45.

Next, we consider the effect of the *positive* constant b on the graphs of

$$y = a \sin bx \qquad \text{and} \qquad y = a \cos bx.$$

Because $y = a \sin x$ completes one cycle from $x = 0$ to $x = 2\pi$, it follows that $y = a \sin bx$ completes one cycle from $bx = 0$ to $bx = 2\pi$. Since

$$bx = 0 \qquad \rightarrow \qquad x = 0$$

$$bx = 2\pi \qquad \rightarrow \qquad x = \frac{2\pi}{b}$$

it follows that $y = a \sin bx$ completes one cycle from $x = 0$ to $x = 2\pi/b$. Hence, the period of $y = a \sin bx$ is $2\pi/b$.

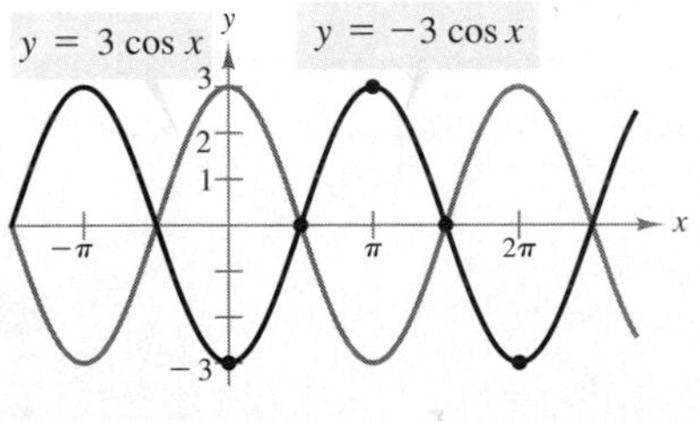

Reflection in the x -Axis

FIGURE 5.45

PERIOD OF SINE AND COSINE FUNCTIONS

Let b be a positive real number. The **period** of $y = a \sin bx$ and $y = a \cos bx$ is $2\pi/b$.

Note that if $0 < b < 1$, the period of $y = a \sin bx$ is greater than 2π and represents a *horizontal stretching* of the graph of $y = a \sin x$. Similarly, if $b > 1$, the period of $y = a \sin bx$ is less than 2π and represents a *horizontal shrinking* of the graph of $y = a \sin x$.

If b is negative, we use the identities $\sin(-x) = -\sin x$ and $\cos(-x) = \cos x$ to rewrite the function. For example, the period of $y = \sin(-2x) = -\sin 2x$ is $2\pi/2 = \pi$, and the period of $y = \cos(-3x) = \cos 3x$ is $2\pi/3$.

EXAMPLE 3   Scaling: Horizontal Stretching

Sketch the graph of $y = \sin \dfrac{x}{2}$.

Solution

The amplitude is 1. Moreover, since $b = \frac{1}{2}$, the period is

$$\frac{2\pi}{b} = \frac{2\pi}{\frac{1}{2}} = 4\pi.$$

Now, divide the period-interval $[0, 4\pi]$ into four equal parts with the values π, 2π, and 3π, to obtain the following key points on the graph.

$$(0, 0), \quad (\pi, 1), \quad (2\pi, 0), \quad (3\pi, -1), \quad \text{and} \quad (4\pi, 0)$$

The graph is shown in Figure 5.46.

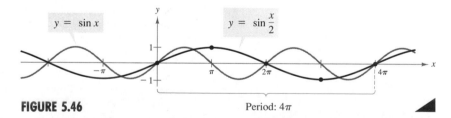

FIGURE 5.46   Period: 4π

In general, to divide a period-interval into four equal parts, successively add "period/4," starting with the left endpoint of the interval. For the period-interval $[-\pi/6, \pi/2]$ of length $2\pi/3$, we would successively add

$$\frac{2\pi/3}{4} = \frac{\pi}{6}$$

to get $-\pi/6$, 0, $\pi/6$, $\pi/3$ and $\pi/2$.

EXAMPLE 4   Horizontal Shrinking

Sketch the graph of $y = \sin 3x$.

Solution

The amplitude is 1, and since $b = 3$, the period is

$$\frac{2\pi}{b} = \frac{2\pi}{3}.$$

Dividing the period-interval $[0, 2\pi/3]$ into four equal parts, you obtain the following key points on the graph.

$$(0, 0), \quad \left(\frac{\pi}{6}, 1\right), \quad \left(\frac{\pi}{3}, 0\right), \quad \left(\frac{\pi}{2}, -1\right), \quad \text{and} \quad \left(\frac{2\pi}{3}, 0\right)$$

The graph is shown in Figure 5.47.   ◢

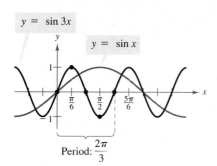

$y = \sin 3x$

$y = \sin x$

Period: $\dfrac{2\pi}{3}$

FIGURE 5.47

Translations of Sine and Cosine Curves

The constant c in the general equations

$$y = a \sin(bx - c) \qquad \text{and} \qquad y = a \cos(bx - c)$$

creates a horizontal translation (shift) of the basic sine and cosine curves. Comparing $y = a \sin bx$ with $y = a \sin(bx - c)$, we find that the graph of $y = a \sin(bx - c)$ completes one cycle from $bx - c = 0$ to $bx - c = 2\pi$. By solving for x, we find the interval for one cycle to be

Left endpoint

Right endpoint

$$\underbrace{\frac{c}{b}} \quad \leq x \leq \quad \underbrace{\frac{c}{b} + \frac{2\pi}{b}}_{\text{Period}}.$$

This implies that the period of $y - a \sin(bx - c)$ is $2\pi/b$, and the graph of $y = a \sin bx$ is translated by an amount c/b. The number c/b is the **phase shift.**

GRAPHS OF THE SINE AND COSINE FUNCTIONS

The graphs of $y = a \sin(bx - c)$ and $y = a \cos(bx - c)$ have the following characteristics. (Assume $b > 0$.)

$$\textbf{Amplitude} = |a| \qquad \textbf{Period} = 2\pi/b$$

The left and right endpoints corresponding to a one-cycle interval of the graphs can be determined by solving the equations $bx - c = 0$ and $bx - c = 2\pi$.

Note how we use this information to sketch graphs of the sine and cosine functions in Examples 5 and 6.

EXAMPLE 5   Horizontal Translation

Sketch the graph of

$$y = \frac{1}{2} \sin\left(x - \frac{\pi}{3}\right).$$

Solution

The amplitude is $\frac{1}{2}$ and the period is 2π. By solving the equations

$$x - \frac{\pi}{3} = 0 \qquad \text{and} \qquad x - \frac{\pi}{3} = 2\pi$$

$$x = \frac{\pi}{3} \qquad\qquad\qquad x = \frac{7\pi}{3}$$

you see that the interval $[\pi/3, 7\pi/3]$ corresponds to one cycle of the graph. Dividing this interval into four equal parts produces the following key points.

$$\left(\frac{\pi}{3}, 0\right), \quad \left(\frac{5\pi}{6}, \frac{1}{2}\right), \quad \left(\frac{4\pi}{3}, 0\right), \quad \left(\frac{11\pi}{6}, -\frac{1}{2}\right), \quad \text{and} \quad \left(\frac{7\pi}{3}, 0\right)$$

The graph is shown in Figure 5.48. ◢

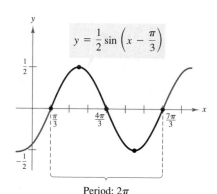

$$y = \frac{1}{2} \sin\left(x - \frac{\pi}{3}\right)$$

Period: 2π

FIGURE 5.48

EXAMPLE 6   Horizontal Translation

Sketch the graph of $y = -3 \cos(2\pi x + 4\pi)$.

Solution

For this function the amplitude is 3 and the period is $2\pi/2\pi = 1$. By solving the equations

$$2\pi x + 4\pi = 0 \qquad \text{and} \qquad 2\pi x + 4\pi = 2\pi$$
$$x = -2 \qquad\qquad\qquad x = -1$$

you see that one cycle corresponds to the interval $[-2, -1]$. Dividing this interval into four equal parts produces the following key points.

$$(-2, -3), \quad \left(-\frac{7}{4}, 0\right), \quad \left(-\frac{3}{2}, 3\right), \quad \left(-\frac{5}{4}, 0\right), \quad \text{and} \quad (-1, -3)$$

The graph is shown in Figure 5.49 ◢

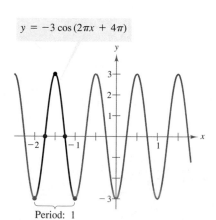

$$y = -3 \cos(2\pi x + 4\pi)$$

Period: 1

FIGURE 5.49

Our final type of transformation is the *vertical translation* caused by the constant d in the equations

$$y = d + a \sin(bx - c) \qquad \text{and} \qquad y = d + a \cos(bx - c).$$

The shift is d units upward for $d > 0$ and downward for $d < 0$. In other words, the graph oscillates about the horizontal line $y = d$ instead of the x-axis.

EXAMPLE 7 Vertical Translation

Sketch the graph of $y = 2 + 3 \sin 2x$.

Solution

The amplitude is 3 and the period is π. The key points over the interval $[0, \pi]$ are

$$(0, 2), \quad \left(\frac{\pi}{4}, 5\right), \quad \left(\frac{\pi}{2}, 2\right), \quad \left(\frac{3\pi}{4}, -1\right), \quad \text{and} \quad (\pi, 2).$$

The graph is shown in Figure 5.50.

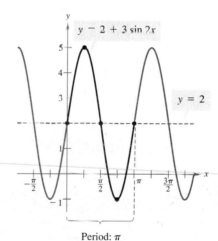

FIGURE 5.50   Period: π

EXAMPLE 8 Finding an Equation for a Given Graph

Find the amplitude, period, and phase shift for the *sine* function whose graph is shown in Figure 5.51. Write an equation for this graph.

Solution

The amplitude for this sine curve is 2. The period is 2π, and there is a right phase shift of $\pi/2$. Thus, you can write

$$y = 2 \sin\left(x - \frac{\pi}{2}\right).$$

Try finding a cosine function with this same graph.

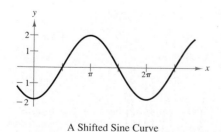

A Shifted Sine Curve

FIGURE 5.51

DISCUSSION PROBLEM

Comparing Sine and Cosine Curves

In Figure 5.52, note that you can obtain the graph of the sine function by translating the graph of the cosine function $\pi/2$ units to the right. What trigonometric identity can be used to verify this relationship between the graphs of the sine and cosine functions?

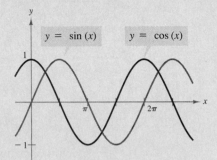

FIGURE 5.52

WARM UP

The following warm-up exercises involve skills that were covered in earlier sections. You will use these skills in the exercise set for this section.

In Exercises 1 and 2, simplify the expression.

1. $\dfrac{2\pi}{1/3}$

2. $\dfrac{2\pi}{4\pi}$

In Exercises 3–6, solve for x.

3. $2x - \dfrac{\pi}{3} = 0$

4. $2x - \dfrac{\pi}{3} = 2\pi$

5. $3\pi x + 6\pi = 0$

6. $3\pi x + 6\pi = 2\pi$

In Exercises 7–10, evaluate the trigonometric functions from memory.

7. $\sin \dfrac{\pi}{2}$

8. $\sin \pi$

9. $\cos 0$

10. $\cos \dfrac{\pi}{2}$

EXERCISES for Section 5.5

In Exercises 1–14, determine the period and amplitude of the given function.

1. $y = 2 \sin 2x$

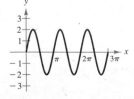

2. $y = 3 \cos 3x$

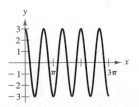

3. $y = \dfrac{3}{2} \cos \dfrac{x}{2}$

4. $y = -2 \sin \dfrac{x}{3}$

5. $y = \dfrac{1}{2} \sin \pi x$

6. $y = \dfrac{5}{2} \cos \dfrac{\pi x}{2}$

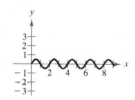
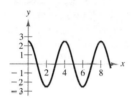

7. $y = 2 \sin x$

8. $y = -\cos \dfrac{2x}{3}$

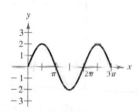
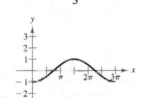

9. $y = 3 \sin 10x$

10. $y = \dfrac{1}{3} \sin 8x$

11. $y = \dfrac{1}{2} \cos \dfrac{2x}{3}$

12. $y = \dfrac{5}{2} \cos \dfrac{x}{4}$

13. $y = 3 \sin 4\pi x$

14. $y = \dfrac{2}{3} \cos \dfrac{\pi x}{10}$

In Exercises 15–22, describe the relationship between the graphs of f and g.

15. $f(x) = \sin x$
  $g(x) = \sin(x - \pi)$

16. $f(x) = \cos x$
  $g(x) = \cos(x + \pi)$

17. $f(x) = \cos 2x$
  $g(x) = -\cos 2x$

18. $f(x) = \sin 3x$
  $g(x) = \sin(-3x)$

19. $f(x) = \cos x$
  $g(x) = \cos 2x$

20. $f(x) = \sin x$
  $g(x) = \sin 3x$

21. $f(x) = \sin x$
  $g(x) = 2 + \sin x$

22. $f(x) = \cos 4x$
  $g(x) = -2 + \cos 4x$

In Exercises 23–30, sketch the graphs of the two functions on the same coordinate plane. (Include two full periods.) 2 q'5

23. $f(x) = -2 \sin x$
  $g(x) = 4 \sin x$

24. $f(x) = \sin x$
  $g(x) = \sin \dfrac{x}{3}$

25. $f(x) = \cos x$
  $g(x) = 1 + \cos x$

26. $f(x) = 2 \cos 2x$
  $g(x) = -\cos 4x$

27. $f(x) = -\dfrac{1}{2} \sin \dfrac{x}{2}$
  $g(x) = 3 - \dfrac{1}{2} \sin \dfrac{x}{2}$

28. $f(x) = 4 \sin \pi x$
  $g(x) = 4 \sin \pi x - 3$

29. $f(x) = 2 \cos x$
  $g(x) = 2 \cos(x + \pi)$

30. $f(x) = -\cos x$
  $g(x) = -\cos(x - \pi)$

In Exercises 31–34, sketch the graphs of f and g on the same coordinate axes and show that $f(x) = g(x)$ for all x. (Include two full periods.)

31. $f(x) = \sin x$
  $g(x) = \cos\left(x - \dfrac{\pi}{2}\right)$

32. $f(x) = \sin x$
  $g(x) = -\cos\left(x + \dfrac{\pi}{2}\right)$

33. $f(x) = \cos x$
  $g(x) = -\sin\left(x - \dfrac{\pi}{2}\right)$

34. $f(x) = \cos x$
  $g(x) = -\cos(x - \pi)$

In Exercises 35–60, sketch the graph of the function. (Include two full periods.)

35. $y = -2 \sin 6x$

36. $y = -3 \cos 4x$

37. $y = \cos 2\pi x$

38. $y = \dfrac{3}{2} \sin \dfrac{\pi x}{4}$

39. $y = -\sin \dfrac{2\pi x}{3}$

40. $y = 10 \cos \dfrac{\pi x}{6}$

41. $y = 2 - \sin \dfrac{2\pi x}{3}$

42. $y = 2 \cos x - 3$

43. $y = \sin\left(x - \dfrac{\pi}{4}\right)$

44. $y = \dfrac{1}{2} \sin(x - \pi)$

45. $y = 3 \cos(x + \pi)$

46. $y = 4 \cos\left(x + \dfrac{\pi}{4}\right)$

47. $y = 3 \cos(x + \pi) - 3$

48. $y = 4 \cos\left(x + \dfrac{\pi}{4}\right) + 4$

49. $y = \dfrac{2}{3} \cos\left(\dfrac{x}{2} - \dfrac{\pi}{4}\right)$

50. $y = -3 \cos(6x + \pi)$

51. $y = -2 \sin(4x + \pi)$ **52.** $y = -4 \sin\left(\dfrac{2}{3}x - \dfrac{\pi}{3}\right)$

53. $y = \cos\left(2\pi x - \dfrac{\pi}{2}\right) + 1$ **54.** $y = 3 \cos\left(\dfrac{\pi x}{2} + \dfrac{\pi}{2}\right) - 2$

55. $y = -0.1 \sin\left(\dfrac{\pi x}{10} + \pi\right)$ **56.** $y = 5 \sin(\pi - 2x) + 10$

57. $y = 5 \cos(\pi - 2x) + 2$ **58.** $y = -3 + 5 \cos\dfrac{\pi t}{12}$

59. $y = \frac{1}{10} \cos 60\pi x$ **60.** $y = \frac{1}{100} \sin 120\pi t$

In Exercises 61–64, use the graph of the trigonometric function to find all real numbers x in the interval $[-2\pi, 2\pi]$ that gives the specified functional value.

Function	Functional Value
61. $\sin x$	$-\dfrac{1}{2}$
62. $\cos x$	-1
63. $\cos x$	$\dfrac{\sqrt{2}}{2}$
64. $\sin x$	$\dfrac{\sqrt{3}}{2}$

In Exercises 65–68, find a, b, and c so that the graph of the function matches the graph in the figure.

65. $y = a \sin(bx - c)$

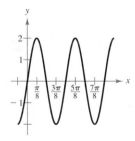

66. $y = a \sin(bx - c)$

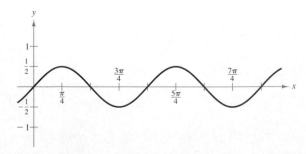

67. $y = a \cos(bx - c)$ **68.** $y = a \sin(bx - c)$

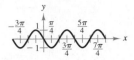
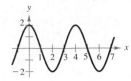

69. *Respiratory Cycle* For a person at rest, the velocity v (in liters per second) of air flow during a respiratory cycle is

$$v = 0.85 \sin\frac{\pi t}{3}$$

where t is the time in seconds. (Inhalation occurs when $v > 0$, and exhalation occurs when $v < 0$.)
(a) Find the time for one full respiratory cycle.
(b) Find the number of cycles per minute.
(c) Sketch the graph of the velocity function.

70. *Respiratory Cycle* After exercising for a few minutes, a person has a respiratory cycle for which the velocity of air flow is approximated by

$$v = 1.75 \sin\frac{\pi t}{2}.$$

Repeat Exercise 69 using this model.

71. *Piano Tuning* When tuning a piano, a technician strikes a tuning fork for the A above middle C and sets up wave motion that can be approximated by

$$y = 0.001 \sin 880\pi t$$

where t is the time in seconds.
(a) What is the period p of this function?
(b) The frequency f is given by $f = 1/p$. What is the frequency of this note?
(c) Sketch the graph of this function.

72. *Blood Pressure* The function

$$P = 100 - 20 \cos\frac{5\pi t}{3}$$

approximates the blood pressure P in millimeters of mercury at time t in seconds for a person at rest.
(a) Find the period of the function.
(b) Find the number of heartbeats per minute.
(c) Sketch the graph of the pressure function.

Sales In Exercises 73 and 74, sketch the graph of the sales function over one year where S is sales in thousands of units and t is the time in months, with $t = 1$ corresponding to January.

73. $S = 22.3 - 3.4 \cos \dfrac{\pi t}{6}$

74. $S = 74.50 + 43.75 \sin \dfrac{\pi t}{6}$

In Exercises 75–78, determine the relationship between the graphs of the functions f and g.

75.

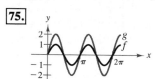

76.

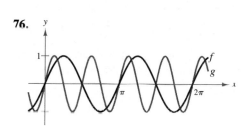

77.

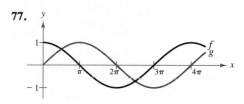

78.

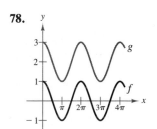

5.6 Graphs of Other Trigonometric Functions

Graph of the Tangent Function / Graph of the Cotangent Function /
Graphs of the Reciprocal Functions

Graph of the Tangent Function

In this section we continue our discussion of the graphs of the trigonometric functions, starting with the graph of the tangent function. Recall from Section 5.3 that the tangent function is odd. That is, $\tan(-x) = -\tan x$. Consequently, the graph of

$$y = \tan x$$

is symmetric with respect to the origin. We know also from the identity $\tan x = \sin x / \cos x$ that the tangent is undefined when $\cos x = 0$. Two such values are $x = \pm \pi/2 \approx \pm 1.5708$. We examine this in more detail in the following table.

x	$-\dfrac{\pi}{2}$	-1.57	-1.5	-1	0	1	1.5	1.57	$\dfrac{\pi}{2}$
$\tan x$	undef.	-1255.8	-14.1	-1.56	0	1.56	14.1	1255.8	undef.

$\tan x$ approaches $-\infty$ as x approaches $-\pi/2$ from the right

$\tan x$ approaches ∞ as x approaches $\pi/2$ from the left

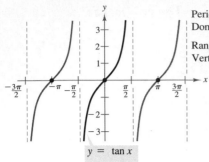

Period: π

Domain: all $x \neq \dfrac{\pi}{2} \pm n\pi$

Range: $(-\infty, \infty)$

Vertical asymptotes: $x = \dfrac{\pi}{2} \pm n\pi$

FIGURE 5.53

Tan x increases without bound as x approaches $\pi/2$ from the left, and decreases without bound as x approaches $-\pi/2$ from the right. Thus, the graph of $y = \tan x$ has *vertical asymptotes* at $x = \pi/2$ and $-\pi/2$, as shown in Figure 5.53. Moreover, because the period of the tangent function is π, vertical asymptotes also occur when $x = \pi/2 \pm n\pi$. The domain of the tangent function is the set of all real numbers other than $x = \pi/2 \pm n\pi$, and the range is the set of all real numbers.

Sketching the graph of a function with the form

$$y = a \tan(bx - c)$$

is similar to sketching the graph of $y = a \sin(bx - c)$ in that we locate key points which identify the intercepts and asymptotes. Two consecutive asymptotes can be found by solving the equations

$$bx - c = -\frac{\pi}{2} \quad \text{and} \quad bx - c = \frac{\pi}{2}.$$

REMARK The period of the function $y = a \tan(bx - c)$ is the distance between two consecutive asymptotes. The amplitude of a tangent function is not defined.

The midpoint between two consecutive asymptotes is an x-intercept of the graph. After plotting the asymptotes and the x-intercept, plot a few additional points between the two asymptotes and sketch one cycle. Finally, sketch one or two additional cycles to the left and right.

EXAMPLE 1   Sketching the Graph of a Tangent Function

Sketch the graph of $y = \tan \dfrac{x}{2}$.

$-\dfrac{\pi}{2} < x < \dfrac{\pi}{2}$

$-\dfrac{\pi}{2} < \dfrac{x}{2} < \dfrac{\pi}{2}$

$-\pi < x < \pi$

Solution

From the equations

$$\frac{x}{2} = -\frac{\pi}{2} \quad \text{and} \quad \frac{x}{2} = \frac{\pi}{2}$$

$$x = -\pi \qquad\qquad x = \pi$$

you see that two consecutive asymptotes occur at $x = -\pi$ and $x = \pi$. Between these two asymptotes plot a few points, including the x-intercept, as shown in the table. Three cycles of the graph are shown in Figure 5.54.

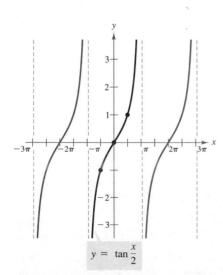

$y = \tan \dfrac{x}{2}$

FIGURE 5.54

x	$-\dfrac{\pi}{2}$	0	$\dfrac{\pi}{2}$
$\tan \dfrac{x}{2}$	-1	0	1

EXAMPLE 2 Sketching the Graph of a Tangent Function

Sketch the graph of $y = -3 \tan 2x$.

Solution

By solving the equations

$$2x = -\frac{\pi}{2} \quad \text{and} \quad 2x = \frac{\pi}{2}$$

$$x = -\frac{\pi}{4} \qquad\qquad x = \frac{\pi}{4}$$

you see that two consecutive asymptotes occur at $x = -\pi/4$ and $x = \pi/4$. Between these two asymptotes, plot a few points, as shown in the table, and complete one cycle.

x	$-\dfrac{\pi}{8}$	0	$\dfrac{\pi}{8}$
$-3 \tan 2x$	3	0	-3

Four cycles of the graph are shown in Figure 5.55. ◢

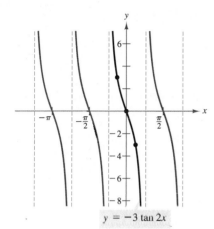

FIGURE 5.55

The caption on the figure reads: $y = -3 \tan 2x$

By comparing the graphs in Examples 1 and 2, you see that the graph of $y = a \tan(bx + c)$ is increasing between consecutive vertical asymptotes if $a > 0$ and decreasing between consecutive vertical asymptotes if $a < 0$. In other words, the graph for $a < 0$ is a reflection in the x-axis of the graph for $a > 0$.

Period: π
Domain: all $x \neq n\pi$
Range: $(-\infty, \infty)$
Vertical asymptotes: $x = n\pi$

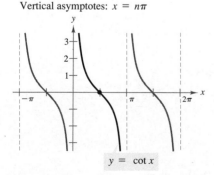

FIGURE 5.56

The caption on the figure reads: $y = \cot x$

Graph of the Cotangent Function

The graph of the cotangent function is similar to the graph of the tangent function. It also has a period of π. However, from the identity

$$y = \cot x = \frac{\cos x}{\sin x}$$

we can see that the cotangent function has vertical asymptotes at $x = n\pi$ because $\sin x$ is zero at these x-values. The graph of the cotangent function is shown in Figure 5.56.

EXAMPLE 3   Sketching the Graph of a Cotangent Function

Sketch the graph of $y = 2 \cot \dfrac{x}{3}$.

Solution

To locate two consecutive vertical asymptotes of the graph, solve

$$\frac{x}{3} = 0 \qquad \text{and} \qquad \frac{x}{3} = \pi$$
$$x = 0 \qquad\qquad\qquad x = 3\pi.$$

Then, between these two asymptotes, plot the points shown in the table and complete one cycle of the graph. (Note that the period is 3π, the distance between consecutive asymptotes.)

x	$\dfrac{3\pi}{4}$	$\dfrac{3\pi}{2}$	$\dfrac{9\pi}{4}$
$2 \cot \dfrac{x}{3}$	2	0	-2

Three cycles of the graph are shown in Figure 5.57.

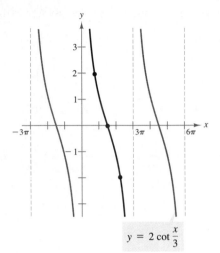

$$y = 2 \cot \frac{x}{3}$$

FIGURE 5.57

Graphs of the Reciprocal Functions

The graphs of the two remaining trigonometric functions can be obtained from the graphs of the sine and cosine functions using the reciprocal identities

$$\csc x = \frac{1}{\sin x} \qquad \text{and} \qquad \sec x = \frac{1}{\cos x}.$$

For instance, at a given value for x, the y-coordinate for $\sec x$ is the reciprocal of the y-coordinate for $\cos x$. Of course, when $\cos x = 0$, the reciprocal does not exist. Near such values for x, the behavior of the secant function is similar to that of the tangent function. In other words, the graphs of

$$\tan x = \frac{\sin x}{\cos x} \qquad \text{and} \qquad \sec x = \frac{1}{\cos x}$$

have vertical asymptotes at $x = (\pi/2) + n\pi$ because n is an integer and the cosine is zero at these x-values. Similarly,

$$\cot x = \frac{\cos x}{\sin x} \qquad \text{and} \qquad \csc x = \frac{1}{\sin x}$$

have vertical asymptotes where $\sin x = 0$, that is, at $x = n\pi$.

To sketch the graph of a secant or cosecant function we suggest that you first make a sketch of its reciprocal function. For instance, to sketch the graph of $y = \csc x$, first sketch the graph of $y = \sin x$. Then take reciprocals of the y-coordinates to obtain points on the graph of $y = \csc x$. We use this procedure to obtain the graphs shown in Figure 5.58.

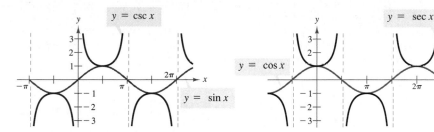

Period: 2π
Domain: all $x \neq n\pi$
Range: all y not in $(-1,\ 1)$
Vertical asymptotes: $x = n\pi$
Symmetry: origin

Period: 2π
Domain: all $x \neq \dfrac{\pi}{2} + n\pi$
Range: all y not in $(-1,\ 1)$
Vertical asymptotes: $x = \dfrac{\pi}{2} + n\pi$
Symmetry: y-axis

FIGURE 5.58

In comparing the graphs of the secant and cosecant functions with those of the sine and cosine functions, note that the "hills" and "valleys" are interchanged. For example, a hill (or maximum point) on the sine curve corresponds to a valley (a local minimum) on the cosecant curve. Similarly, a valley (or minimum point) on the sine curve corresponds to a hill (a local maximum) on the cosecant curve, as shown in Figure 5.59.

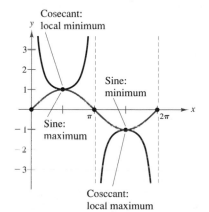

FIGURE 5.59

EXAMPLE 4   Sketching the Graph of a Cosecant Function

Sketch the graph of $y = 2 \csc \left(x + \dfrac{\pi}{4} \right)$.

Solution

Begin by sketching the graph of

$$y = 2 \sin \left(x + \frac{\pi}{4} \right).$$

For this function, the amplitude is 2 and the period is 2π. By solving the equations

$$x + \frac{\pi}{4} = 0 \qquad \text{and} \qquad x + \frac{\pi}{4} = 2\pi$$

$$x = -\frac{\pi}{4} \qquad\qquad\qquad x = \frac{7\pi}{4}$$

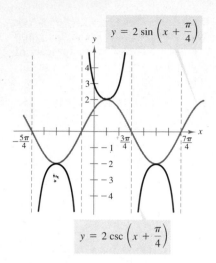

$y = 2 \sin\left(x + \dfrac{\pi}{4}\right)$

$y = 2 \csc\left(x + \dfrac{\pi}{4}\right)$

FIGURE 5.60

you can see that one cycle of the sine function corresponds to the interval from $x = -\pi/4$ to $x = 7\pi/4$. The graph of this sine function is represented by the gray curve in Figure 5.60. Because the sine function is zero at the endpoints of this interval, the corresponding cosecant function

$$y = 2 \csc\left(x + \frac{\pi}{4}\right) = 2\left(\frac{1}{\sin[x + (\pi/4)]}\right)$$

has vertical asymptotes at $x = -\pi/4$, $x = 3\pi/4$, and $7\pi/4$. The graph of the cosecant function is represented by the solid curve.

EXAMPLE 5 Sketching the Graph of a Secant Function

Sketch the graph of $y = \sec 2x$.

Solution

Begin by sketching the graph of $\cos 2x$ as indicated by the gray curve in Figure 5.61. Then, form the graph of $y = \sec 2x$ as the solid curve in the figure. Note that the x-intercepts of $\cos 2x$

$$\left(\frac{\pi}{4}, 0\right), \quad \left(\frac{3\pi}{4}, 0\right), \quad \left(\frac{5\pi}{4}, 0\right), \quad \cdots$$

correspond to the vertical asymptotes

$$x = \frac{\pi}{4}, \quad x = \frac{3\pi}{4}, \quad x = \frac{5\pi}{4}, \quad \cdots$$

of the graph of $y = \sec 2x$.

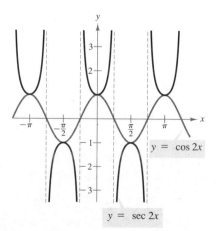

$y = \cos 2x$

$y = \sec 2x$

FIGURE 5.61

In Figure 5.62, we summarize the graphs, domains, ranges, and periods of the six basic trigonometric functions. Be sure you know this information.

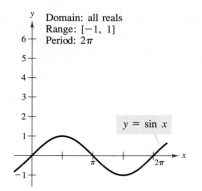

Domain: all reals
Range: $[-1, 1]$
Period: 2π

$y = \sin x$

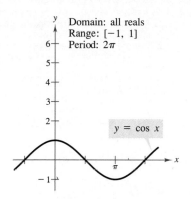

Domain: all reals
Range: $[-1, 1]$
Period: 2π

$y = \cos x$

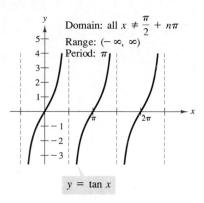

Domain: all $x \neq \dfrac{\pi}{2} + n\pi$
Range: $(-\infty, \infty)$
Period: π

$y = \tan x$

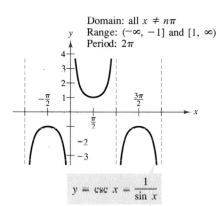

Domain: all $x \neq n\pi$
Range: $(-\infty, -1]$ and $[1, \infty)$
Period: 2π

$y = \csc x = \dfrac{1}{\sin x}$

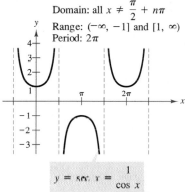

Domain: all $x \neq \dfrac{\pi}{2} + n\pi$
Range: $(-\infty, -1]$ and $[1, \infty)$
Period: 2π

$y = \sec x = \dfrac{1}{\cos x}$

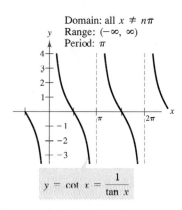

Domain: all $x \neq n\pi$
Range: $(-\infty, \infty)$
Period: π

$y = \cot x = \dfrac{1}{\tan x}$

FIGURE 5.62   Graphs of the Six Trigonometric Functions

DISCUSSION

PROBLEM

**Graphing
Facilities**

If you have access to a graphing calculator or a computer graphing facility, use it to sketch graphs of the following functions for varying values of a, b, c, and d.

$$y = d + a \sin(bx + c) \qquad y = d + a \cos(bx + c)$$
$$y = d + a \tan(bx + c) \qquad y = d + a \cot(bx + c)$$
$$y = d + a \sec(bx + c) \qquad y = d + a \csc(bx + c)$$

In a paper or a discussion, summarize the effects of the constants a, b, c, and d in these graphs.

EXERCISES for Section 5.6

In Exercises 1–8, match the trigonometric function with the correct graph and give the period of the function. [The graphs are labeled (a), (b),(c), (d), (e), (f), (g), and (h).]

1. $y = \sec 2x$ **2.** $y = \tan 3x$

3. $y = \tan \dfrac{x}{2}$ **4.** $y = 2 \csc \dfrac{x}{2}$

5. $y = \cot \pi x$ **6.** $y = \frac{1}{2} \sec \pi x$

7. $y = -\sec x$ **8.** $y = -2 \csc 2\pi x$

(a)

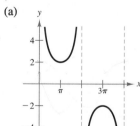

(b)

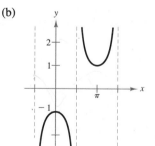

(c)

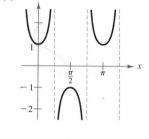

(d)

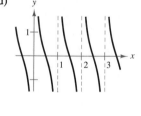

(e)

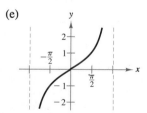

(f)

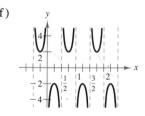

(g)

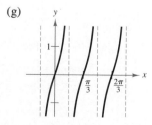

(h)

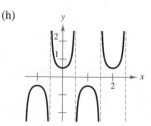

In Exercises 9–40, sketch the graph of the function through two periods.

9. $y = \frac{1}{3} \tan x$

10. $y = \frac{1}{4} \tan x$

11. $y = \tan 2x$

12. $y = -\tan 2x$

13. $y = \tan \dfrac{x}{3}$

14. $y = -3 \tan \pi x$

15. $y = -\frac{1}{2} \sec x$

16. $y = \frac{1}{4} \sec x$

17. $y = -2 \sec 4x$

18. $y = 2 \sec 4x$

19. $y = -\sec \pi x$

20. $y = \sec \pi x$

21. $y = \sec \pi x - 1$

22. $y = -2 \sec 4x + 2$

23. $y = \csc \dfrac{x}{2}$

24. $y = \csc \dfrac{x}{3}$

25. $y = \cot \dfrac{x}{2}$

26. $y = 3 \cot \dfrac{\pi x}{2}$

27. $y = \frac{1}{2} \sec 2x$

28. $y = -\frac{1}{2} \tan x$

29. $y = \tan\left(x - \dfrac{\pi}{4}\right)$

30. $y = \sec(x + \pi)$.

31. $y = \dfrac{1}{4} \csc\left(x + \dfrac{\pi}{4}\right)$

32. $y = -\csc(4x - \pi)$

33. $y = \dfrac{1}{4} \cot\left(x - \dfrac{\pi}{2}\right)$

34. $y = 2 \cot\left(x + \dfrac{\pi}{2}\right)$

35. $y = 2 \sec(2x - \pi)$

36. $y = \dfrac{1}{3} \sec\left(\dfrac{\pi x}{2} + \dfrac{\pi}{2}\right)$

37. $y = \tan \dfrac{\pi x}{4}$

38. $y = 0.1 \tan\left(\dfrac{\pi x}{4} + \dfrac{\pi}{4}\right)$

39. $y = \csc(\pi - x)$

40. $y = \sec(\pi - x)$

In Exercises 41–44, use the graph of the trigonometric function to find all real numbers x in the interval $[-2\pi, 2\pi]$ that gives the functional value.

Function	Functional Value
41. $\tan x$	1
42. $\cot x$	$-\sqrt{3}$
43. $\sec x$	-2
44. $\csc x$	$\sqrt{2}$

45. *Distance*   A plane flying at an altitude of six miles over level ground will pass directly over a radar antenna (see figure). Let d be the ground distance from the antenna to the point directly under the plane and let x be the angle of elevation to the plane from the antenna. Write d as a function of x and sketch the graph of the function over the interval $0 < x < \pi$.

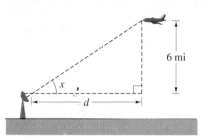

Figure for 45

46. *Television Coverage*   A television camera is on a reviewing platform 100 feet from the street on which a parade will be passing from left to right (see figure). Express the distance d from the camera to a particular unit in the parade as a function of the angle x and sketch the graph of the function over the interval

$$-\frac{\pi}{2} < x < \frac{\pi}{2}.$$

(Consider x as negative when a unit in the parade approaches from the left.)

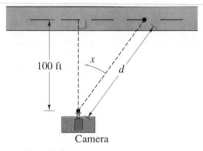

Figure for 46

5.7 Other Graphing Techniques

Addition of Ordinates / Damped Trigonometric Graphs

Addition of Ordinates

The behavior of some physical phenomena can be represented by more than one trigonometric function or by a combination of algebraic and trigonometric functions. We can use a technique called **addition of ordinates** (*y*-values) to sketch the graphs of functions like

$$y = \sin x - \cos 2x \quad \text{and} \quad y = x + \cos x.$$

For example, the graph of $y = x + \cos x$ can be obtained by first making sketches of $y = x$ and $y = \cos x$ on the same set of axes and then geometrically adding the ordinates (*y*-values) for several representative *x*-values. This addition of ordinates is aided by the use of a compass or ruler to measure the vertical displacements, as shown in Figure 5.63.

As with previous trigonometric graphs, the *key points* to plot are those for which one or both functions have an intercept, maximum point, or minimum point.

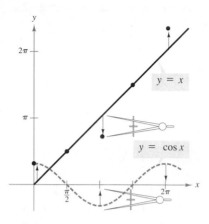

FIGURE 5.63

EXAMPLE 1   Graphing by Addition of Ordinates

Use addition of ordinates to sketch the graph of $f(x) = x + \cos x$ for $x \geq 0$.

Solution

First, make sketches of the graphs of

$$y = x \quad \text{and} \quad y = \cos x$$

on the same coordinate plane. For $y = \cos x$, the key points are

$$(0, 1), \quad \left(\frac{\pi}{2}, 0\right), \quad (\pi, -1), \quad \left(\frac{3\pi}{2}, 0\right), \quad \text{and} \quad (2\pi, 1).$$

The points lying on the graph of $y = x$ directly above (or below) these five points are

$$(0, 0), \quad \left(\frac{\pi}{2}, \frac{\pi}{2}\right), \quad (\pi, \pi), \quad \left(\frac{3\pi}{2}, \frac{3\pi}{2}\right), \quad \text{and} \quad (2\pi, 2\pi).$$

Geometrically add the *y*-values of the two functions at these key points

$$(0, 1), \quad \left(\frac{\pi}{2}, \frac{\pi}{2}\right), \quad (\pi, -1 + \pi), \quad \left(\frac{3\pi}{2}, \frac{3\pi}{2}\right), \quad \text{and} \quad (2\pi, 1 + 2\pi)$$

and plot the results. Then connect the resulting points by a smooth curve, obtaining the black graph shown in Figure 5.64. Note that the graph of

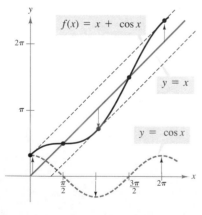

Addition of Ordinates

FIGURE 5.64

$f(x) = x + \cos x$ lies between the graphs of $y = 1 + x$ and $y = 1 - x$. That is,

$$x - 1 \leq x + \cos x \leq 1 + x.$$

Note that the function in Figure 5.64 is not periodic. However, the next example involves two trigonometric functions whose resulting difference is a periodic function.

EXAMPLE 2 Graphing by Addition of Ordinates

Sketch the graph of $g(x) = \sin x - \cos 2x$.

Solution

Make sketches of the graphs of

$$y = \sin x \quad \text{and} \quad y = -\cos 2x$$

noting that their respective periods are 2π and π. From the shorter period (the one for $-\cos 2x$), consider the key points given in the table.

x	0	$\dfrac{\pi}{4}$	$\dfrac{\pi}{2}$	$\dfrac{3\pi}{4}$	π	$\dfrac{5\pi}{4}$	$\dfrac{3\pi}{2}$	$\dfrac{7\pi}{4}$	2π
$-\cos 2x$	-1	0	1	0	-1	0	1	0	-1
$\sin x$	0	$\dfrac{\sqrt{2}}{2}$	1	$\dfrac{\sqrt{2}}{2}$	0	$-\dfrac{\sqrt{2}}{2}$	-1	$-\dfrac{\sqrt{2}}{2}$	0
$\sin x - \cos 2x$	1	$\dfrac{\sqrt{2}}{2}$	2	$\dfrac{\sqrt{2}}{2}$	1	$\dfrac{\sqrt{2}}{2}$	0	$\dfrac{\sqrt{2}}{2}$	1

By plotting the points indicated in the fourth row of the table and connecting them with a smooth curve, you obtain the graph shown in Figure 5.65. Note that the function has a period of 2π.

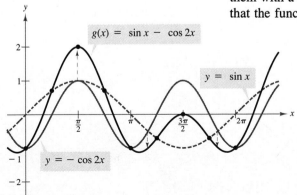

Addition of Ordinates

FIGURE 5.65

EXAMPLE 3   Graphing by Addition of Ordinates

Sketch the graph of $f(x) = \sin x + 2 \cos x$.

Solution

Make sketches of the graphs of

$$y = \sin x \quad \text{and} \quad y = 2 \cos x$$

noting that both have periods of 2π. Then consider the key points given in the table.

x	0	$\dfrac{\pi}{2}$	π	$\dfrac{3\pi}{2}$	2π
$2 \cos x$	2	0	-2	0	2
$\sin x$	0	1	0	-1	0
$\sin x + 2 \cos x$	2	1	-2	-1	2

By plotting the points indicated in the fourth row of the table and connecting them with a smooth curve, you obtain the graph shown in Figure 5.66. Note that this function has a period of 2π.

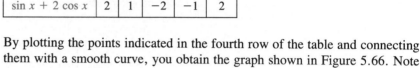

FIGURE 5.66

One of the simplest uses of addition of ordinates is in vertical translation like those in the graphs of

$$y = 2 + \sin 3x \quad \text{and} \quad y = 3 + \cos\left(x - \frac{\pi}{4}\right).$$

We know from Sections 2.5 and 5.5 that adding a constant does not change the shape (or period) of a trigonometric graph—it only changes its vertical location. For example, using the graph of $y = \sin 3x$, you can easily sketch the graph of

$$f(x) = 2 + \sin 3x$$

by adding 2 to each ordinate, as shown in Figure 5.67.

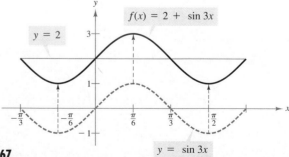

FIGURE 5.67

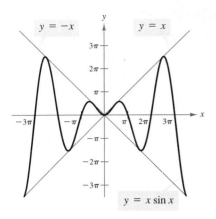

FIGURE 5.68

Damped Trigonometric Graphs

A *product* of two functions can be graphed using properties of the individual functions. For instance, consider the function

$$f(x) = x \sin x$$

as the product of the functions $y = x$ and $y = \sin x$. Using properties of absolute value and the fact that $|\sin x| \leq 1$, we have $0 \leq |x| \, |\sin x| \leq |x|$. Consequently,

$$-|x| \leq x \sin x \leq |x|$$

which means that the graph of $f(x) = x \sin x$ lies between the lines $y = -x$ and $y = x$. Furthermore, since

$$f(x) = x \sin x = \pm x \qquad \text{at} \qquad x = \frac{\pi}{2} + n\pi$$

$$f(x) = x \sin x = 0 \qquad \text{at} \qquad x = n\pi$$

the graph of f touches the line $y = -x$ or the line $y = x$ at $x = (\pi/2) + n\pi$ and has x-intercepts at $x = n\pi$. A sketch of f is shown in Figure 5.68.

In the function $f(x) = x \sin x$, the factor x is the **damping factor.** By changing the damping factor, we can change the graph significantly. For example, look in Figure 5.69 at the graphs of

$$y = \frac{1}{x} \sin x \qquad \text{and} \qquad y = e^{-x} \sin 3x.$$

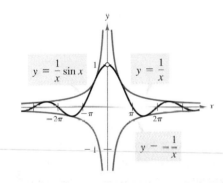

EXAMPLE 4 Damped Cosine Wave

Sketch the graph of $f(x) = 2^{-x/2} \cos x$.

Solution

Consider $f(x)$ as the product of the two functions

$$y = 2^{-x/2} \qquad \text{and} \qquad y = \cos x$$

each of which has the set of real numbers as its domain. For any real number x, we know that $2^{-x/2} \geq 0$ and $|\cos x| \leq 1$. Therefore, $|2^{-x/2}||\cos x| \leq 2^{-x/2}$, which means that

$$-2^{-x/2} \leq 2^{-x/2} \cos x \leq 2^{-x/2}.$$

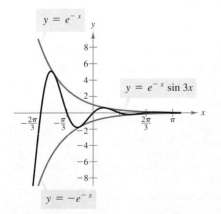

FIGURE 5.69

Furthermore, since

$$f(x) = 2^{-x/2} \cos x = \pm 2^{-x/2} \qquad \text{at} \qquad x = n\pi$$

and

$$f(x) = 2^{-x/2} \cos x = 0 \qquad \text{at} \qquad x = \frac{\pi}{2} + n\pi$$

the graph of f touches the curve $y = -2^{-x/2}$ or the curve $y = 2^{-x/2}$ at $x = n\pi$ and has x-intercepts at $x = (\pi/2) + n\pi$. A sketch is shown in Figure 5.70.

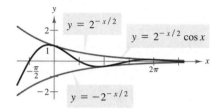

FIGURE 5.70

DISCUSSION

PROBLEM

Periodic
Functions as
Models

Trigonometric functions can be used as models for real-life situations that are periodic. For example, at most locations on the earth, the average temperature is periodic (it cycles from lower temperatures in winter to higher temperatures in summer). Here is a model for the average temperature (in degrees Fahrenheit) in Washington, D.C.

$$T = 57.44 + 21.88 \sin(0.522x + 4.110), \qquad \text{Jan.} = 1, \text{Feb.} = 2, \dots$$

Compare the temperatures given by this model with the actual average temperatures in Washington, D.C., shown in the table. (*Source:* P.C. U.S.A.)

x	1	2	3	4	5	6	7	8	9	10	11	12
T	35.2	37.5	45.8	56.7	66.0	74.5	78.9	77.6	71.1	59.3	48.7	38.9

Describe some other examples of periodic behavior that occur in real-life situations.

WARM UP

The following warm-up exercises involve skills that were covered in earlier sections. You will use these skills in the exercise set for this section.

In Exercises 1–4, find the x-values in the interval $[0, 2\pi]$ for which $f(x)$ is -1, 0, or 1.

1. $f(x) = \sin x$

2. $f(x) = \cos x$

3. $f(x) = \sin 2x$

4. $f(x) = \cos \dfrac{x}{2}$

In Exercises 5–8, sketch the graph of the function.

5. $y = |x|$

6. $y = e^{-x}$

7. $y = \sin \pi x$

8. $y = \cos 2x$

In Exercises 9 and 10, evaluate $f(x)$ when $x = 0$, $\pi/6$, $\pi/4$, $\pi/3$, and $\pi/2$.

9. $f(x) = x \cos x$

10. $f(x) = x + \sin x$

EXERCISES for Section 5.7

In Exercises 1–22, use addition of ordinates to sketch the graph of the function.

1. $y = 2 - 2 \sin \dfrac{x}{2}$

2. $y = -3 + \cos x$

3. $y = 4 - 2 \cos \pi x$

4. $y - 5 - \frac{1}{2} \sin 2\pi x$

5. $y = -1 + \cot x$

6. $y = 2 + \tan \pi x$

7. $y = 1 + \csc x$

8. $y = 1 - \sec x$

9. $y = x + \sin x$

10. $y = x + \cos x$

11. $y = \frac{1}{2}x - 2 \cos x$

12. $y = 2x - \sin x$

13. $y = \sin x + \cos x$

14. $y = \cos x + \cos 2x$

15. $y = 2 \sin x + \sin 2x$

16. $y - 2 \sin x + \cos 2x$

17. $y = \cos x - \cos \dfrac{x}{2}$

18. $y = \sin x - \dfrac{1}{2} \sin \dfrac{x}{2}$

19. $y = \sin x + \frac{1}{3} \sin 5x$

20. $y = \cos x - \frac{1}{4} \cos 2x$

21. $y = -3 + \cos x + 2 \sin 2x$

22. $y = \sin \pi x + \sin \dfrac{\pi x}{2}$

In Exercises 23–30, sketch the graph of the function.

23. $y = x \cos x$

24. $y = |x| \sin x$

25. $y = |x| \cos x$

26. $y = 2^{-x/4} \cos \pi x$

27. $y = e^{-x^2/2} \sin x$

28. $y = e^{-t} \cos t$

29. $y = \sin^2 x$

30. $y = \cos^2 \dfrac{\pi x}{2}$

31. *Sales*   The projected monthly sales S (in thousands of units) of a seasonal product is modeled by

$$S = 74 + 3t + 40 \sin \frac{\pi t}{6}$$

where t is the time in months, with $t = 1$ corresponding to January. Sketch the graph of this sales function over one year.

32. *Sales*   The projected monthly sales S (in thousands of units) of a seasonal product is modeled by

$$S = 25 + 2t + 20 \sin \frac{\pi t}{6}$$

where t is the time in months, with $t = 1$ corresponding to January. Sketch the graph of this sales function over one year.

33. *Predator-Prey Problem*   Suppose the population of a certain predator at time t (in months) in a given region is estimated to be

$$P = 10{,}000 + 3{,}000 \sin \frac{2\pi t}{24}$$

and the population of its primary food source (its prey) is estimated to be

$$p = 15{,}000 + 5{,}000 \cos \frac{2\pi t}{24}.$$

Sketch both of these functions on the same graph and explain the oscillations in the size of each population.

34. *Normal Temperatures*   The normal monthly high temperatures for Erie, Pennsylvania are approximated by

$$H(t) = 54.33 - 20.38 \cos \frac{\pi t}{6} - 15.69 \sin \frac{\pi t}{6}$$

and the normal monthly low temperatures are approximated by

$$L(t) = 39.36 - 15.70 \cos \frac{\pi t}{6} - 14.16 \sin \frac{\pi t}{6}$$

where t is the time in months with $t = 1$ corresponding to January. (*Source*: NOAA) Use the figure to answer the following questions.

(a) During what part of the year is the difference between the normal high and low temperatures greatest? When is it smallest?

(b) The sun is the farthest north in the sky around June 21, but the graph shows the warmest temperatures at a later date. Approximate the lag time of the temperatures relative to the position of the sun.

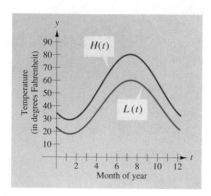

Figure for 34

35. *Harmonic Motion*   An object weighing W pounds is suspended from the ceiling by a steel spring (see figure). The weight is pulled downward (positive direction) from its equilibrium position and released. The resulting motion of the weight is described by the function

$$y = \tfrac{1}{2}e^{-t/4} \cos 4t, \qquad t > 0$$

where y is the distance in feet and t is the time in seconds. Sketch the graph of the function.

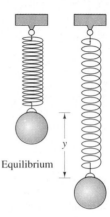

Figure for 35

36. Use a calculator to evaluate the function

$$f(x) = \frac{1 - \cos x}{x}$$

at several points in the interval $[-1, 1]$. Use these points to sketch the graph of f. From your graph, estimate the value that $f(x)$ is approaching as x approaches 0. (*Note*: The function is undefined when $x = 0$.)

x	-0.5	-0.4	-0.3	-0.2	-0.1
$\dfrac{1 - \cos x}{x}$					

x	0.1	0.2	0.3	0.4	0.5
$\dfrac{1 - \cos x}{x}$					

PROBLEM

U S I N G   T E C H N O L O G Y

SOLVING

Using Technology
to Analyze a
Complicated
Graph

Graphs of functions that are combinations of algebraic functions and trigonometric functions can be difficult to sketch by hand. A graphing utility such as computer graphing software or a graphics calculator can help.

EXAMPLE 1   Sketching the Graph of a Function

Since 1957, the Mauna Loa Climate Observatory in Hawaii has been collecting data on the carbon dioxide level of earth's atmosphere. A model that closely represents the data is given by

$$y = 316 + 0.654t + 0.0216t^2 + 2.5 \sin 2\pi t$$

where y represents the carbon dioxide concentration (in parts per million) and $t = 0$ represents 1960 (January 1). Sketch a graph of this function and explain the oscillations in the graph.

Solution

The graph of the function is shown below. From the graph, you can see that the carbon dioxide level fluctuates each year. The low level each year, which occurs toward the end of summer in the northern hemisphere, is caused by the intake of carbon dioxide into growing plants.

Mauna Loa
Climate Observatory

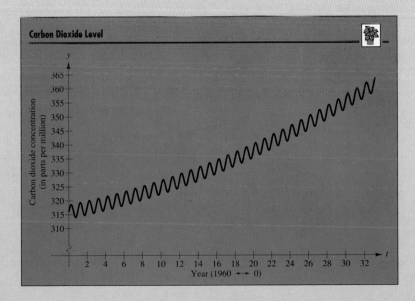

397

The ability of a graphing utility to sketch a complicated graph depends on the size of the screen and the resolution of the graphing utility. Large screens with high resolution can display much more detail than small screens with low resolution.

EXAMPLE 2   Sketching the Graph of a Function

Sketch the graph of $y = \sin \dfrac{1}{x}$. Describe the graph near the origin.

Solution

High resolution computer software was used to produce the graph shown below. Notice that as x approaches the origin from the left or the right, the graph oscillates more and more quickly.

EXERCISES

(See also: Exercises 23–36, Section 5.7)

In Exercises 1–6, use a graphing utility to sketch the graph of the function. Choose a viewing rectangle that you think produces a good representation of the important features of the graph.

1. $y = x^2 + \sin x$
2. $y = x^2 \sin x$
3. $y = |\cos x|$
4. $y = 2 \sin x - \cos 2x$
5. $y = \sin^2 x + \sin x$
6. $y = \dfrac{\sin x}{x}$

7. *Carbon Dioxide Levels*   Sketch the graph of the model given in Example 1 for $28 \le t \le 30$. Between January 1, 1988, and January 1, 1990, what were the highest and lowest levels of carbon dioxide? When did each occur?

8. *Throwing a Shot Put*   The path of a shot put can be modeled by

$$y = -\frac{16}{v^2 \cos^2 \theta} x^2 + (\tan \theta)x + h$$

where y is the height of the ball (in feet), x is the horizontal distance (in feet), v is the initial velocity (in feet per second), h is the initial height (in feet), and θ is the angle at which the ball is thrown. Choose several values of v, h and θ and sketch the corresponding path. Discuss your results.

Inverse Trigonometric Functions

Inverse Sine Function / Other Inverse Trigonometric Functions /
Compositions of Trigonometric and Inverse Trigonometric Functions

Inverse Sine Function

Up to this point, much of our time has been spent evaluating trigonometric functions at specified angles or real numbers. However, in Section 5.3 we introduced the *inverse* problem: *Given the value of sin x, find x.* There we used the calculator key INV or 2nd f and promised to explain the functions involved later. We now investigate these **inverse trigonometric functions.**

Recall from Section 2.7 that, in order for a function to have an inverse, it must be one-to-one. From Figure 5.71 it is obvious that $y = \sin x$ is not one-to-one because different values of x yield the same y-value. However, if we restrict the domain to the interval $-\pi/2 \le x \le \pi/2$ (corresponding to the solid portion of the graph in Figure 5.71), the following properties hold.

1. On the interval $[-\pi/2, \pi/2]$, the function $y = \sin x$ is increasing.
2. On the interval $[-\pi/2, \pi/2]$, $y = \sin x$ takes on its full range of values, $-1 \le \sin x \le 1$.
3. On the interval $[-\pi/2, \pi/2]$, $y = \sin x$ is a one-to-one function.

Thus, on the restricted domain $-\pi/2 \le x \le \pi/2$, $y = \sin x$ has a unique inverse called the **inverse sine function.** It is denoted by

$$y = \arcsin x \qquad \text{or} \qquad y = \sin^{-1} x.$$

The notation $\sin^{-1} x$ is consistent with the inverse function notation $f^{-1}(x)$ used in Section 2.7. The arcsin x notation (read as "the arc sine of x") comes from the association of a central angle with its subtended *arc length* on a unit circle. Thus, arcsin x means the angle (or arc) whose sine is x. Both notations, arcsin x and $\sin^{-1} x$, are commonly used in mathematics, so remember that $\sin^{-1} x$ denotes the *inverse* sine function rather than $1/\sin x$.

The values of arcsin x lie in the interval $-\pi/2 \le \arcsin x \le \pi/2$. The graph of $y = \arcsin x$ is shown in Example 2.

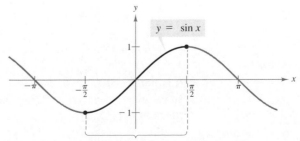

Sin x is one-to-one on this interval.

FIGURE 5.71

DEFINITION OF INVERSE SINE FUNCTION

The **inverse sine function** is defined by

$$y = \arcsin x \qquad \text{if and only if} \qquad \sin y = x$$

where $-1 \le x \le 1$ and $-\pi/2 \le y \le \pi/2$. The domain of $y = \arcsin x$ is $[-1, 1]$ and the range is $[-\pi/2, \pi/2]$.

REMARK   When evaluating the inverse sine function, it helps to remember the phrase "the arcsine of x is the angle (or number) whose sine is x."

As with the trigonometric functions, much of the work with the inverse trigonometric functions can be done by *exact* calculations rather than by calculator approximations. Exact calculations help to increase our understanding of the inverse functions by relating them to the triangle definitions of the trigonometric functions.

EXAMPLE 1   Evaluating the Inverse Sine Function

Find the values (if possible).

a. $\arcsin\left(-\dfrac{1}{2}\right)$ **b.** $\sin^{-1} \dfrac{\sqrt{3}}{2}$ **c.** $\sin^{-1} 2$

Solution

a. By definition, $y = \arcsin\left(-\frac{1}{2}\right)$ implies that

$$\sin y = -\frac{1}{2}, \qquad \text{for } -\frac{\pi}{2} \le y \le \frac{\pi}{2}.$$

Because $\sin(-\pi/6) = -\frac{1}{2}$, you conclude that $y = -\pi/6$ and

$$\arcsin\left(-\frac{1}{2}\right) = -\frac{\pi}{6}.$$

b. By definition, $y = \sin^{-1}(\sqrt{3}/2)$ implies that

$$\sin y = \frac{\sqrt{3}}{2}, \qquad \text{for } -\frac{\pi}{2} \le y \le \frac{\pi}{2}.$$

Because $\sin(\pi/3) = \sqrt{3}/2$, you conclude that $y = \pi/3$ and

$$\sin^{-1} \frac{\sqrt{3}}{2} = \frac{\pi}{3}.$$

c. It is not possible to evaluate $y = \sin^{-1} x$ when $x = 2$ because there is no angle whose sine is 2. Remember that the domain of the inverse sine function is $[-1, 1]$.

From Section 2.7 we know that graphs of inverse functions are reflections of each other in the line $y = x$.

EXAMPLE 2   Graphing the Arcsine Function

Sketch a graph of $y = \arcsin x$.

Solution

By definition, the equations

$$y = \arcsin x \qquad \text{and} \qquad \sin y = x$$

are equivalent for $-\pi/2 \le y \le \pi/2$. Hence, their graphs are the same. From the interval $[-\pi/2, \pi/2]$, we assign values to y in the second equation to make a table of values.

y	$-\dfrac{\pi}{2}$	$-\dfrac{\pi}{4}$	$-\dfrac{\pi}{6}$	0	$\dfrac{\pi}{6}$	$\dfrac{\pi}{4}$	$\dfrac{\pi}{2}$
$x = \sin y$	-1	$-\dfrac{\sqrt{2}}{2}$	$-\dfrac{1}{2}$	0	$\dfrac{1}{2}$	$\dfrac{\sqrt{2}}{2}$	1

The resulting graph for $y = \arcsin x$ is shown in Figure 5.72. Note that it is the reflection (in line $y = x$) of the solid part of Figure 5.71. Be sure you see that Figure 5.72 shows the *entire* graph of the inverse sine function. Remember that the range of $y = \arcsin x$ is the closed interval $[-\pi/2, \pi/2]$.

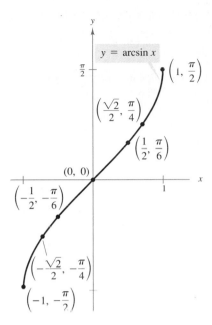

FIGURE 5.72

Other Inverse Trigonometric Functions

The cosine function is decreasing on the interval $0 \le x \le \pi$, as shown in Figure 5.73. Consequently, on this interval the cosine has an inverse function—the **inverse cosine function**   denoted by

$$y = \arccos x \qquad \text{or} \qquad y = \cos^{-1} x.$$

Similarly, we can define an **inverse tangent function** by restricting the domain of $y = \tan x$ to the interval $(-\pi/2, \pi/2)$. In the following list, we summarize the definitions of the three most common inverse trigonometric functions. The remaining three are discussed in the exercise set. (We summarize the graphs, domains, and ranges of *all six* inverse trigonometric functions in the Appendix.)

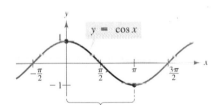

Cos x is one-to-one on this interval.

FIGURE 5.73

DEFINITION OF THE INVERSE TRIGONOMETRIC FUNCTIONS

Function	Domain	Range
$y = \arcsin x$ if and only if $\sin y = x$	$-1 \le x \le 1$	$-\dfrac{\pi}{2} \le y \le \dfrac{\pi}{2}$
$y = \arccos x$ if and only if $\cos y = x$	$-1 \le x \le 1$	$0 \le y \le \pi$
$y = \arctan x$ if and only if $\tan y = x$	$-\infty < x < \infty$	$-\dfrac{\pi}{2} < y < \dfrac{\pi}{2}$

The graphs of these three inverse trigonometric functions are shown in Figure 5.74.

Domain: [−1, 1]
Range: [−π/2, π/2]

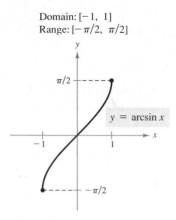

Domain: [−1, 1]
Range: [0 ,π]

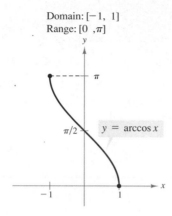

Domain: (−∞, ∞)
Range: (−π/2, π/2)

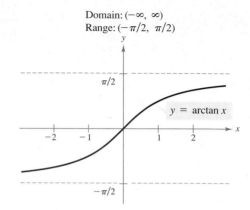

FIGURE 5.74

EXAMPLE 3   Evaluating Inverse Trigonometric Functions

Find the exact value.

a. $\arccos \dfrac{\sqrt{2}}{2}$ **b.** $\arccos(-1)$ **c.** $\arctan 0$

Solution

a. Because $\cos(\pi/4) = \sqrt{2}/2$ and $\pi/4$ lies in $[0, \pi]$, it follows that

$$\arccos \frac{\sqrt{2}}{2} = \frac{\pi}{4}.$$

b. Because $\cos \pi = -1$ and π lies in $[0, \pi]$, it follows that

$$\arccos(-1) = \pi.$$

c. Because $\tan 0 = 0$ and 0 lies in $(-\pi/2, \pi/2)$, it follows that

$$\arctan 0 = 0.$$

EXAMPLE 4   Evaluating Inverse Trigonometric Functions (Calculator)

Use a calculator to approximate the value (if possible).

a. $\arctan(-8.45)$ **b.** $\arcsin 0.2447$ **c.** $\arccos 2$

Solution

Function	Mode	Keystrokes	Display
a. arctan(−8.45)	Radian	8.45 $\boxed{+/-}$ $\boxed{INV}$ $\boxed{tan}$	−1.453001
b. arcsin 0.2447	Radian	0.2447 $\boxed{INV}$ $\boxed{sin}$	0.2472103
c. arccos 2	Radian	2 $\boxed{INV}$ $\boxed{cos}$	ERROR

REMARK In Example 4, if you had set the calculator to degree mode, the display would have been in degrees rather than radians. This convention is peculiar to calculators. By definition, the values of inverse trigonometric functions are always *in radians*.

Note that the *error* in part (c) occurs because the domain of the inverse cosine function is $[-1, 1]$.

Compositions of Trigonometric and Inverse Trigonometric Functions

Recall from Section 2.7 that inverse functions possess the properties

$$f(f^{-1}(x)) = x \quad \text{and} \quad f^{-1}(f(x)) = x.$$

The inverse trigonometric versions of these properties are given in the following list.

INVERSE PROPERTIES

If $-1 \leq x \leq 1$ and $-\pi/2 \leq y \leq \pi/2$, then

$$\sin(\arcsin x) = x \quad \text{and} \quad \arcsin(\sin y) = y.$$

If $1 \leq x \leq 1$ and $0 \leq y \leq \pi$, then

$$\cos(\arccos x) = x \quad \text{and} \quad \arccos(\cos y) = y.$$

If $-\pi/2 < y < \pi/2$, then

$$\tan(\arctan x) = x \quad \text{and} \quad \arctan(\tan y) = y.$$

REMARK Keep in mind that these inverse properties do not apply for arbitrary values of x and y. For instance,

$$\arcsin\left(\sin\frac{3\pi}{2}\right) = \arcsin(-1)$$

$$= -\frac{\pi}{2} \neq \frac{3\pi}{2}.$$

In other words, the property $\arcsin(\sin y) = y$ is not valid for values of y outside the interval $[-\pi/2, \pi/2]$.

EXAMPLE 5   Using Inverse Properties

If possible, find the exact value.

a. $\tan[\arctan(-5)]$ **b.** $\arcsin\left(\sin\dfrac{5\pi}{3}\right)$ **c.** $\cos(\cos^{-1}\pi)$

Solution

a. Since -5 lies in the domain of the arctan x, the inverse property applies, and you have

$$\tan[\arctan(-5)] = -5.$$

b. In this case, $5\pi/3$ does not lie within the range of the arcsine function, $-\pi/2 \leq x \leq \pi/2$. However, $5\pi/3$ is coterminal with

$$\frac{5\pi}{3} - 2\pi = -\frac{\pi}{3}$$

which does lie in the range of the arcsine function, and you have

$$\arcsin\left(\sin \frac{5\pi}{3} \right) = \arcsin\left[\sin\left(-\frac{\pi}{3}\right) \right] = -\frac{\pi}{3}.$$

c. The expression $\cos(\cos^{-1} \pi)$ is not defined because $\cos^{-1} \pi$ is not defined. Remember that the domain of the inverse cosine function is $[-1, 1]$.

In Example 6, we show how to use right triangles to find exact values of functions of inverse functions. Then, in Example 7, we show how to use triangles to convert a trigonometric expression into an algebraic one. This conversion technique is used frequently in calculus.

EXAMPLE 6 Evaluating Functions of Inverse Trigonometric Functions

Find the exact value.

a. $\tan\left(\arccos \frac{2}{3} \right)$ **b.** $\cos\left[\arcsin\left(-\frac{3}{5}\right) \right]$

Solution

a. If you let $u = \arccos \frac{2}{3}$, then $\cos u = \frac{2}{3}$. Because $\cos u$ is positive, u is a *first* quadrant angle. You can sketch and label angle u as shown in Figure 5.75. Consequently,

$$\tan\left(\arccos \frac{2}{3} \right) = \tan u = \frac{\text{opp}}{\text{adj}} = \frac{\sqrt{5}}{2}.$$

b. If you let $u = \arcsin -\frac{3}{5}$, then $\sin u = -\frac{3}{5}$. Because $\sin u$ is negative, u is a *fourth* quadrant angle. You can sketch and label u as shown in Figure 5.76. Consequently,

$$\cos\left[\arcsin\left(-\frac{3}{5}\right) \right] = \cos u = \frac{\text{adj}}{\text{hyp}} = \frac{4}{5}.$$

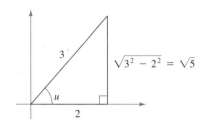

FIGURE 5.75

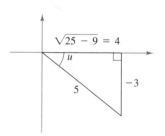

FIGURE 5.76

EXAMPLE 7 Some Problems from Calculus

Write each of the following as an algebraic expression in x.

a. $\sin(\arccos 3x)$, $0 \leq x \leq \frac{1}{3}$ **b.** $\cot(\arccos 3x)$, $0 \leq x \leq \frac{1}{3}$

Solution

If you let $u = \arccos 3x$, then $\cos u = 3x$. Because

$$\cos u = \frac{3x}{1} = \frac{\text{adj}}{\text{hyp}}$$

you can sketch a right triangle with acute angle u, as shown in Figure 5.77.

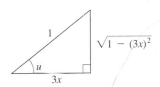

FIGURE 5.77

From this triangle, you can easily convert each expression to algebraic form.

REMARK   In Example 7, a similar argument can be made for x-values lying in the interval $\left[-\frac{1}{3}, 0\right]$.

a. $\sin(\arccos 3x) = \sin u = \dfrac{\text{opp}}{\text{hyp}} = \sqrt{1 - 9x^2}, \quad 0 \le x \le \dfrac{1}{3}$

b. $\cot(\arccos 3x) = \cot u = \dfrac{\text{adj}}{\text{opp}} = \dfrac{3x}{\sqrt{1 - 9x^2}}, \quad 0 \le x \le \dfrac{1}{3}$

DISCUSSION

PROBLEM

Inverse Functions

We have discussed inverse functions for several types of functions. Match each of the functions in the left column with its inverse function given in the right column.

1. $f(x) = x$

2. $f(x) = x^2, \quad 0 \le x$

3. $f(x) = x^3$

4. $f(x) = e^x$

5. $f(x) = \ln x$

6. $f(x) = \sin x, \quad -\dfrac{\pi}{2} \le x \le \dfrac{\pi}{2}$

7. $f(x) = \cot x, \quad 0 < x < \pi$

8. $f(x) = \tan x, \quad -\dfrac{\pi}{2} < x < \dfrac{\pi}{2}$

(a) $f^{-1}(x) = \arcsin x$

(b) $f^{-1}(x) = \ln x$

(c) $f^{-1}(x) = \sqrt{x}$

(d) $f^{-1}(x) = \arctan x$

(e) $f^{-1}(x) = \text{arccot } x$

(f) $f^{-1}(x) = \sqrt[3]{x}$

(g) $f^{-1}(x) = e^x$

(h) $f^{-1}(x) = x$

Provide reasons for your answers.

WARM UP

The following warm-up exercises involve skills that were covered in earlier sections. You will use these skills in the exercise set for this section.

In Exercises 1–4, evaluate the trigonometric function from memory.

1. $\sin\left(-\dfrac{\pi}{2}\right)$

2. $\cos \pi$

3. $\tan\left(-\dfrac{\pi}{4}\right)$

4. $\sin \dfrac{\pi}{4}$

In Exercises 5 and 6, find a real number x in the interval $[-\pi/2, \pi/2]$ that has the same sine value as the given value.

5. $\sin 2\pi$

6. $\sin \dfrac{5\pi}{6}$

In Exercises 7 and 8, find a real number x in the interval $[0, \pi]$ that has the same cosine value as the given value.

7. $\cos 3\pi$

8. $\cos\left(-\dfrac{\pi}{4}\right)$

In Exercises 9 and 10, find a real number x in the interval $[-\pi/2, \pi/2]$ that has the same tangent value as the given value.

9. $\tan 4\pi$

10. $\tan \dfrac{3\pi}{4}$

EXERCISES for Section 5.8

In Exercises 1–16, evaluate the given expression without the aid of a calculator.

1. $\arcsin \frac{1}{2}$

2. $\arcsin 0$

3. $\arccos \frac{1}{2}$

4. $\arccos 0$

5. $\arctan \dfrac{\sqrt{3}}{3}$

6. $\arctan(-1)$

7. $\arccos\left(-\dfrac{\sqrt{3}}{2}\right)$

8. $\arcsin\left(-\dfrac{\sqrt{2}}{2}\right)$

9. $\arctan(-\sqrt{3})$

10. $\arctan(\sqrt{3})$

11. $\arccos\left(-\dfrac{1}{2}\right)$

12. $\arcsin \dfrac{\sqrt{2}}{2}$

13. $\arcsin \dfrac{\sqrt{3}}{2}$

14. $\arctan\left(-\dfrac{\sqrt{3}}{3}\right)$

15. $\arctan 0$

16. $\arccos 1$

In Exercises 17–28, use a calculator to approximate the value. (Round your answers to two decimal places.)

17. $\arccos 0.28$

18. $\arcsin 0.45$

19. $\arcsin(-0.75)$

20. $\arccos(-0.8)$

21. $\arctan(-2)$

22. $\arctan 15$

23. $\arcsin 0.31$

24. $\arccos 0.26$

25. $\arccos(-0.41)$

26. $\arcsin(-0.125)$

27. $\arctan 0.92$

28. $\arctan 2.8$

In Exercises 29–34, use the properties of inverse trigonometric functions to evaluate the expression.

29. $\sin(\arcsin 0.3)$

30. $\tan(\arctan 25)$

31. $\cos[\arccos(-0.1)]$

32. $\sin[\arcsin(-0.2)]$

33. $\arcsin(\sin 3\pi)$

34. $\arccos\left(\cos \dfrac{7\pi}{2}\right)$

In Exercises 35–42, find the exact value of the expression without using a calculator. (*Hint*: Make a sketch of a right triangle, as illustrated in Example 6.)

35. $\sin\left(\arctan \frac{3}{4}\right)$

36. $\sec\left(\arcsin \frac{4}{5}\right)$

37. $\cos(\arctan 2)$

38. $\sin\left(\arccos \frac{\sqrt{5}}{5}\right)$

39. $\cos\left(\arcsin \frac{5}{13}\right)$

40. $\csc\left[\arctan\left(-\frac{5}{12}\right)\right]$

41. $\sec\left[\arctan\left(-\frac{3}{5}\right)\right]$

42. $\tan\left[\arcsin\left(-\frac{3}{4}\right)\right]$

In Exercises 43–52, write an algebraic expression that is equivalent to the expression. (*Hint*: Sketch a right triangle, as demonstrated in Example 7.)

43. $\cot(\arctan x)$

44. $\sin(\arctan x)$

45. $\cos(\arcsin 2x)$

46. $\sec(\arctan 3x)$

47. $\sin(\arccos x)$

48. $\cot\left(\arctan \frac{1}{x}\right)$

49. $\tan\left(\arccos \frac{x}{3}\right)$

50. $\sec[\arcsin(x - 1)]$

51. $\csc\left(\arctan \frac{x}{\sqrt{2}}\right)$

52. $\cos\left(\arcsin \frac{x - h}{r}\right)$

In Exercises 53–56, fill in the blanks.

53. $\arctan \frac{9}{x} = \arcsin\left(\boxed{}\right)$

54. $\arctan \frac{\sqrt{36 - x^2}}{x} = \arccos\left(\boxed{}\right), \quad |x| \le 6$

55. $\arccos \frac{3}{\sqrt{x^2 - 2x + 10}} = \arcsin\left(\boxed{}\right)$

56. $\arccos \frac{x - 2}{2} = \arctan\left(\boxed{}\right), \quad |x - 2| \le 2$

In Exercises 57–60, sketch the graph of the function.

57. $f(x) = \arcsin(x - 1)$

58. $f(x) = \frac{\pi}{2} + \arctan x$

59. $f(x) = \arctan 2x$

60. $f(x) = \arccos \frac{x}{4}$

61. *Photography*   A photographer is taking a picture of a four-foot-square painting hung in an art gallery. The camera lens is one foot below the lower edge of the painting (see figure). The angle β subtended by the camera lens x feet from the painting is

$$\beta = \arctan \frac{4x}{x^2 + 5}.$$

Find β when (a) $x = 3$ feet and (b) $x = 6$ feet.

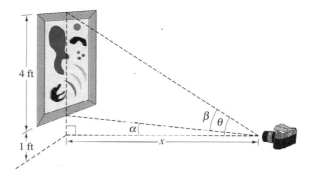

Figure for 61

62. *Photography*   A television camera at ground level is filming the lift-off of the space shuttle at a point 2000 feet from the launch pad (see figure). If θ is the angle of elevation to the shuttle and s is the height of the shuttle in feet, write θ as a function of s. Find θ when (a) $s = 1000$ and (b) $s = 4000$.

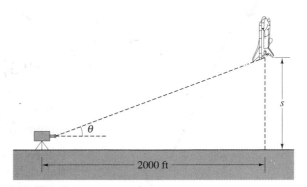

Figure for 62

Moreover, since the maximum displacement from zero is 10 and the period is 4, you have

$$\text{Amplitude} = |a| = 10$$

$$\text{Period} = \frac{2\pi}{\omega} = 4 \quad \rightarrow \quad \omega = \frac{\pi}{2}.$$

Consequently, the equation of motion is

$$d = 10 \sin \frac{\pi}{2}t.$$

Note that the choice of $a = 10$ or $a = -10$ depends on whether the ball initially moves up or down. The frequency is given by

$$\text{Frequency} = \frac{\omega}{2\pi} = \frac{\pi/2}{2\pi} = \frac{1}{4} \text{ cycle per second.}$$

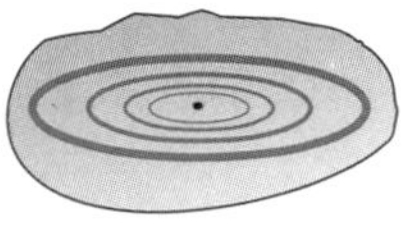

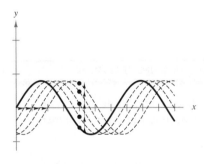

FIGURE 5.86

One illustration of the relationship between sine waves and harmonic motion is seen in the wave motion resulting from dropping a stone into a calm pool of water. The waves move outward in roughly the shape of sine (or cosine) waves, as shown in Figure 5.86. As an example, suppose you are fishing and your fishing bob is attached so that it does not move horizontally. As the waves move outward from the dropped stone, your fishing bob will move up and down in simple harmonic motion, as shown in Figure 5.87.

A fishing bob moves in a vertical direction as waves move to the right.

FIGURE 5.87

EXAMPLE 7   Simple Harmonic Motion

Given the equation for simple harmonic motion

$$d = 6 \cos \frac{3\pi}{4}t$$

find (a) the maximum displacement, (b) the frequency, (c) the value of d when $t = 4$, and (d) the least positive value of t for which $d = 0$.

Solution

The given equation has the form $d = a \cos \omega t$, with $a = 6$ and $\omega = 3\pi/4$.

a. The maximum displacement (from the point of equilibrium) is given by the amplitude. Thus, the maximum displacement is 6.

b. $\text{Frequency} = \dfrac{\omega}{2\pi} = \dfrac{3\pi/4}{2\pi} = \dfrac{3}{8}$ cycle per unit of time

c. $d = 6 \cos\left[\dfrac{3\pi}{4}(4)\right] = 6 \cos 3\pi = 6(-1) = -6$

d. To find the least positive value of t for which $d = 0$, solve the equation

$$d = 6 \cos \frac{3\pi}{4}t = 0$$

to obtain

$$\frac{3\pi}{4}t = \frac{\pi}{2}, \frac{3\pi}{2}, \frac{5\pi}{2}, \ldots$$

$$t = \frac{2}{3}, 2, \frac{10}{3}, \ldots .$$

Thus, the least positive value of t is $t = \frac{2}{3}$.

Many other physical phenomena can be characterized by wave motion. These include electromagnetic waves such as radio waves, television waves, and microwaves. Radio waves transmit sound in two different ways. For an AM station, the *amplitude* of the wave is modified to carry sound. (AM stands for **amplitude modulation.**) See Figure 5.88(a). An FM radio signal has its *frequency* modified in order to carry sound, hence the term **frequency modulation.** See Figure 5.88(b).

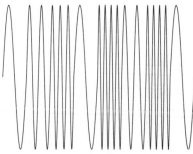

(a) AM: Amplitude modulation   (b) FM: Frequency modulation

FIGURE 5.88   Radio Waves

DISCUSSION

PROBLEM

You Be the
Instructor

Suppose you are teaching a class in trigonometry. Write two "right triangle problems" that you think would be reasonable to ask your students to solve (Assume that your students have five minutes to solve each problem., Explain why you chose these problems.

WARM UP

The following warm-up exercises involve skills that were covered in earlier sections. You will use these skills in the exercise set for this section.

In Exercises 1–4, evaluate the expression and round to two decimal places.

1. $20 \sin 25°$

2. $42 \tan 62°$

3. $\arcsin 0.8723$

4. $\arctan 2.8703$

In Exercises 5 and 6, solve for x and round to two decimal places.

5. $\cos 22° = \dfrac{x + 13 \sin 22°}{13 \sin 54°}$

6. $\tan 36° = \dfrac{x + 85 \tan 18°}{85}$

In Exercises 7–10, find the amplitude and period of the function.

7. $f(x) = -4 \sin 2x$

8. $f(x) = \frac{1}{2} \sin \pi x$

9. $g(x) = 3 \cos 3\pi x$

10. $g(x) = 0.2 \cos \dfrac{x}{4}$

EXERCISES for Section 5.9

In Exercises 1–10, solve the right triangle shown in the figure. (Round to two decimal places.)

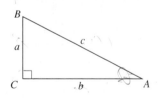

Figure for 1–10

1. $A = 20°$, $b = 10$

2. $B = 54°$, $c = 15$

3. $B = 71°$, $b = 24$

4. $A = 8.4°$, $a = 40.5$

5. $A = 12°15'$, $c = 430.5$

6. $B = 65°12'$, $a = 14.2$

7. $a = 6$, $b = 10$

8. $a = 25$, $c = 35$

9. $b = 16$, $c = 52$

10. $b = 1.32$, $c = 9.45$

In Exercises 11 and 12, find the altitude of the isosceles triangle shown in the figure. (Round to two decimal places.)

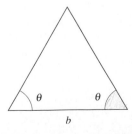

Figure for 11 and 12

11. $\theta = 52°$, $b = 4$ inches

12. $\theta = 18°$, $b = 10$ meters

13. *Length of a Shadow* The sun is 30° above the horizon. Find the length of a shadow cast by a silo that is 70 feet high.

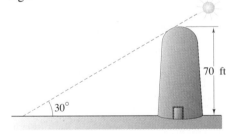

Figure for 13

14. *Length of a Shadow* If the sun is 20° above the horizon, find the length of a shadow cast by a building that is 600 feet high.

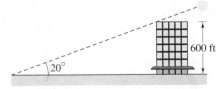

Figure for 14

15. *Height* A ladder of length 16 feet leans against the side of a house (see figure). Find the height h of the top of the ladder if the angle of elevation of the ladder is 74°.

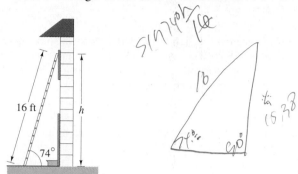

Figure for 15

16. *Height* The length of a shadow of a tree is 125 feet when the angle of elevation of the sun is 33° (see figure). Approximate the height h of the tree.

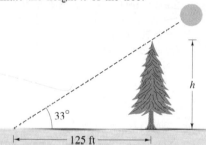

Figure for 16

17. *Angle of Elevation* An amateur radio operator erects a 75-foot vertical tower for his antenna. Find the angle of elevation to the top of the tower at a point on level ground 50 feet from the base.

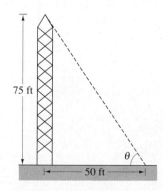

Figure for 17

18. *Angle of Elevation* The height of an outdoor basketball backboard is $12\frac{1}{2}$ feet, and the backboard casts a shadow $17\frac{1}{3}$ feet long (see figure). Find the angle of elevation of the sun.

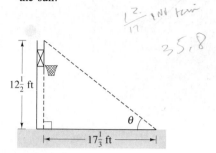

Figure for 18

19. *Angle of Depression* A spacecraft is traveling in a circular orbit 100 miles above the surface of the earth (see figure). Find the angle of depression from the spacecraft to the horizon. Assume that the radius of the earth is 4000 miles.

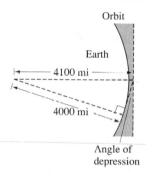

Figure for 19

20. *Angle of Depression* Find the angle of depression from the top of a lighthouse 250 feet above water level to the water line of a ship two miles offshore.

21. *Airplane Ascent* When an airplane leaves the runway, its angle of climb is 18° and its speed is 275 feet per second. Find the altitude of the plane after one minute.

Figure for 21

22. *Mountain Descent* A sign on the roadway at the top of a mountain indicates that for the next four miles the grade is 12.5° (see figure). Find the change in elevation for a car descending the mountain.

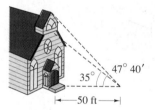

Figure for 22

23. *Height* From a point 50 feet in front of a church, the angles of elevation to the base of the steeple and the top of the steeple are 35° and 47° 40′, respectively (see figure). Find the height of the steeple.

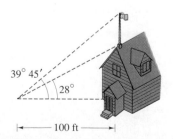

Figure for 23

24. *Height* From a point 100 feet in front of the public library, the angles of elevation to the base of the flagpole and the top of the pole are 28° and 39°45′, respectively. The flagpole is mounted on the front of the library's roof (see figure). Find the height of the pole.

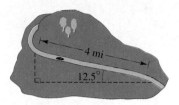

Figure for 24

25. *Navigation* An airplane flying at 550 miles per hour has a bearing of N 52° E. After flying 1.5 hours, how far north and how far east has the plane traveled from its point of departure?

26. *Navigation* A ship leaves port at noon and has a bearing of S 27° W. If the ship is sailing at 20 knots, how many nautical miles south and how many nautical miles west has the ship traveled by 6:00 P.M.?

27. *Navigation* A ship is 45 miles east and 30 miles south of port. If the captain wants to sail directly to port, what bearing should he take?

28. *Navigation* A plane is 120 miles north and 85 miles east of an airport. If the pilot wants to fly directly to the airport, what bearing should she take?

29. *Surveying* A surveyor wishes to find the distance across a swamp (see figure). The bearing from A to B is N 32° W. The surveyor walks 50 yards from A, and at the point C the bearing to B is N 68° W.
(a) Find the bearing from A to C.
(b) Find the distance from A to B.

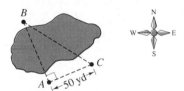

Figure for 29

30. *Location of a Fire* Two fire towers are 20 miles apart, tower A being due west of tower B. A fire is spotted from the towers, and the bearings from A and B are E 14° N and W 34° N (see figure). Find the distance *d* of the fire from the line segment AB. [*Hint*: Use the fact that *d* = 20/(cot 14° + cot 34°).]

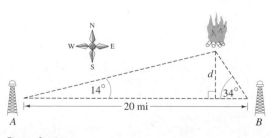

Figure for 30

31. *Distance Between Ships* An observer in a lighthouse 300 feet above sea level spots two ships directly offshore. The angles of depression to the ships are 4° and 6.5° (see figure). How far apart are the ships?

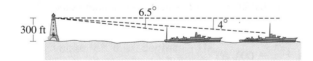

Figure for 31

32. *Distance Between Towns* A passenger in an airplane flying at a height of 30,000 feet sees two towns directly to the left of the airplane. The angles of depression to the towns are 28° and 55° (see figure). How far apart are the towns?

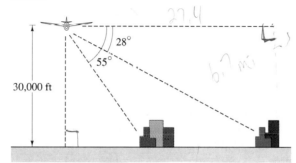

Figure for 32

33. *Altitude of a Plane* A plane is observed approaching your home, and you assume it is traveling at 550 miles per hour. If the angle of elevation of the plane is 16° at one time, and one minute later the angle is 57°, approximate the altitude.

34. *Height of a Mountain* In traveling across flat land, you notice a mountain directly in front of you. The angle of elevation (to the peak) is 3.5°. After you drive 13 miles closer to the mountain, the angle of elevation is 9°. Approximate the height of the mountain.

35. *Length* A regular pentagon is inscribed in a circle of radius 25 inches. Find the length of the sides of the pentagon.

36. *Length* A regular hexagon is inscribed in a circle of radius 25 inches. Find the length of the sides of the hexagon.

37. *Wrench Size* Use the figure to find the distance y across the flat sides of the hexagonal nut as a function of r.

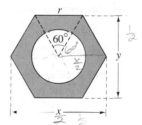

Figure for 37

38. *Bolt Circle* The figure shows a circular sheet of diameter 25 cm, containing 12 equally spaced bolt holes. Determine the straight-line distance between the centers of the adjacent bolt holes.

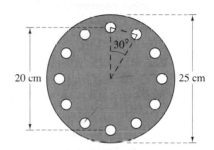

Figure for 38

Trusses In Exercises 39 and 40, find the length of all the unknown members of the truss.

39.

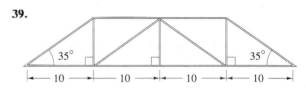

40.

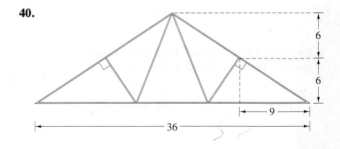

In Exercises 4
onometric fu

41. tan 33°

43. sec $\dfrac{12\pi}{5}$

In Exercises
($0° \le \theta \le 360$
a calculator.

45. cos $\theta = $

47. csc $\theta = $

In Exercises
($0° \le \theta < 36$
calculator.

49. sin $\theta = 0$
51. sec $\theta = $

In Exercises
expression.

53. sec[arcsin

55. sin$\left(\text{arcco}\right.$

In Exercises

57. $y = 3 \cos$

59. $f(x) = 5$

61. $f(x) = $

63. $g(t) = \frac{5}{2}$

65. $h(t) = $ ta

67. $f(t) = $ cs

69. $f(\theta) = $ c

70. $E(t) = 1$

Harm
harmo
tion, fi
and (c

41. d
43. d

45. T_t
in
F_i
fr

REV

In Exe
list on

1. 1̵

3. –

In Exe
imal f

5. 1̵

7. 5̵

In Ex_c
M' S'

9. 1̵

11. –

In Ex_c
radia

13. $\frac{5}{7}$

15. –

In Ex_c
degre

17. 4̵

19. –

FUNDAMENTAL TRIGONOMETRIC IDENTITIES

Reciprocal Identities

$$\sin u = \frac{1}{\csc u} \qquad \sec u = \frac{1}{\cos u} \qquad \tan u = \frac{1}{\cot u}$$

$$\csc u = \frac{1}{\sin u} \qquad \cos u = \frac{1}{\sec u} \qquad \cot u = \frac{1}{\tan u}$$

Quotient Identities

$$\tan u = \frac{\sin u}{\cos u} \qquad \cot u = \frac{\cos u}{\sin u}$$

Pythagorean Identities

$$\sin^2 u + \cos^2 u = 1 \qquad 1 + \tan^2 u = \sec^2 u \qquad 1 + \cot^2 u = \csc^2 u$$

Cofunction Identities

$$\sin\left(\frac{\pi}{2} - u\right) = \cos u \qquad \sec\left(\frac{\pi}{2} - u\right) = \csc u \qquad \tan\left(\frac{\pi}{2} - u\right) = \cot u$$

$$\cos\left(\frac{\pi}{2} - u\right) = \sin u \qquad \csc\left(\frac{\pi}{2} - u\right) = \sec u \qquad \cot\left(\frac{\pi}{2} - u\right) = \tan u$$

Even/Odd Identities

$$\sin(-u) = -\sin u \qquad \sec(-u) = \sec u \qquad \tan(-u) = -\tan u$$

$$\csc(-u) = -\csc u \qquad \cos(-u) = \cos u \qquad \cot(-u) = -\cot u$$

REMARK   Pythagorean identities are sometimes used in radical form such as

$$\sin u = \pm\sqrt{1 - \cos^2 u}$$

or

$$\tan u = \pm\sqrt{\sec^2 u - 1}$$

where the sign depends on the choice of u.

Using the Fundamental Identities

One of the most common uses of trigonometric identities is to use given values of one or more trigonometric functions to find the values of the other trigonometric functions.

EXAMPLE 1   Using Identities to Evaluate a Function

Use the given values

$$\sec u = -\frac{3}{2} \qquad \text{and} \qquad \tan u > 0$$

to find the values of all six trigonometric functions.

Solution

Using a reciprocal identity, you have

$$\cos u = \frac{1}{\sec u} = \frac{1}{-\frac{3}{2}} = -\frac{2}{3}.$$

By a Pythagorean identity, you obtain

$$\sin^2 u = 1 - \cos^2 u = 1 - \left(-\frac{2}{3}\right)^2 = 1 - \frac{4}{9} = \frac{5}{9}.$$

Because $\sec u < 0$ and $\tan u > 0$, it follows that u lies in Quadrant III. Moreover, because $\sin u$ is negative when u is in Quadrant III, you choose the negative root and obtain

$$\sin u = -\frac{\sqrt{5}}{3}.$$

Now, knowing the values of the sine and cosine, you can find the values of all six trigonometric functions, as follows.

$$\sin u = -\frac{\sqrt{5}}{3} \qquad\qquad \csc u = \frac{1}{\sin u} = -\frac{3}{\sqrt{5}}$$

$$\cos u = -\frac{2}{3} \qquad\qquad \sec u = -\frac{3}{2}$$

$$\tan u = \frac{\sin u}{\cos u} = \frac{-\dfrac{\sqrt{5}}{3}}{-\dfrac{2}{3}} = \frac{\sqrt{5}}{2} \qquad \cot u = \frac{1}{\tan u} = \frac{2}{\sqrt{5}}$$

◢

In the next four examples, we use algebraic techniques and fundamental identities to factor and/or simplify trigonometric *expressions* such as

$$\cot x - \cos x \sin x, \qquad \frac{1 - \sin x}{\cos^2 x}, \qquad \text{and} \qquad \frac{\tan x}{\sec x - 1}.$$

EXAMPLE 2   Simplifying a Trigonometric Expression

Simplify the expression $\sin x \cos^2 x - \sin x$.

Solution

First factor out a common monomial factor and then use a fundamental identity.

$$\sin x \cos^2 x - \sin x = \sin x(\cos^2 x - 1) \qquad \textit{Monomial factor}$$

$$= -\sin x(1 - \cos^2 x)$$

$$= -\sin x(\sin^2 x) \qquad \textit{Pythagorean identity}$$

$$= -\sin^3 x \qquad \textit{Multiply}$$

◢

EXAMPLE 3   Factoring Trigonometric Expressions

Factor the expressions.

a. $\sec^2 \theta - 1$ **b.** $4 \tan^2 \theta + \tan \theta - 3$

Solution

a. Here you have the difference of two squares, which factors as

$$\sec^2 \theta - 1 = (\sec \theta - 1)(\sec \theta + 1).$$

b. This expression has the polynomial form, $ax^2 + bx + c$, and it factors as

$$4 \tan^2 \theta + \tan \theta - 3 = (4 \tan \theta - 3)(\tan \theta + 1).$$

On occasion, factoring or simplifying can best be done by first rewriting the expression in terms of just *one* trigonometric function or in terms of *sine and cosine alone*.

EXAMPLE 4   Factoring a Trigonometric Expression

Factor the expression $\csc^2 x - \cot x - 3$.

Solution

As given, this expression cannot be factored, so you use the identity $\csc^2 x = 1 + \cot^2 x$ to rewrite the expression in terms of the cotangent alone.

$$
\begin{aligned}
\csc^2 x - \cot x - 3 &= (1 + \cot^2 x) - \cot x - 3 && \textit{Pythagorean identity} \\
&= \cot^2 x - \cot x - 2 && \textit{Combine terms} \\
&= (\cot x - 2)(\cot x + 1) && \textit{Factor}
\end{aligned}
$$

EXAMPLE 5   Simplifying a Trigonometric Expression

Simplify the expression $\sin t + \cot t \cos t$.

Solution

Since this expression is not factorable as given, convert all terms to sines and cosines to see what can be done.

$$
\begin{aligned}
\sin t + \cot t \cos t &= \sin t + \left(\frac{\cos t}{\sin t} \right) \cos t && \textit{Cotangent identity} \\
&= \frac{\sin^2 t + \cos^2 t}{\sin t} && \textit{Add fractions} \\
&= \frac{1}{\sin t} && \textit{Pythagorean identity} \\
&= \csc t && \textit{Reciprocal identity}
\end{aligned}
$$

EXAMPLE 6 Combining Fractional Expressions

$$\frac{\sin \theta}{1 + \cos \theta} + \frac{\cos \theta}{\sin \theta} = \frac{(\sin \theta)(\sin \theta) + (\cos \theta)(1 + \cos \theta)}{(1 + \cos \theta)(\sin \theta)} \qquad \frac{a}{b} + \frac{c}{d} = \frac{ad + bc}{bd}$$

$$= \frac{\sin^2 \theta + \cos^2 \theta + \cos \theta}{(1 + \cos \theta)\sin \theta} \qquad \textit{Multiply}$$

$$= \frac{1 + \cos \theta}{(1 + \cos \theta) \sin \theta} \qquad \textit{Pythagorean identity}$$

$$= \frac{1}{\sin \theta} \qquad \textit{Cancel common factor}$$

$$= \csc \theta \qquad \textit{Reciprocal identity}$$

The last two examples of this section involve techniques for rewriting expressions into forms that are useful in calculus.

EXAMPLE 7 Rewriting a Trigonometric Expression

Rewrite the following expression so that it is *not* in fractional form.

$$\frac{1}{1 + \sin x}$$

Solution

From the Pythagorean identity

$$\cos^2 x = 1 - \sin^2 x = (1 - \sin x)(1 + \sin x)$$

you can see that by multiplying both the numerator and the denominator by $(1 - \sin x)$ you will obtain a monomial denominator.

$$\frac{1}{1 + \sin x} = \frac{1}{1 + \sin x} \cdot \frac{1 - \sin x}{1 - \sin x} \qquad \textit{Multiply numerator and denominator by } (1 - \sin x)$$

$$= \frac{1 - \sin x}{1 - \sin^2 x} \qquad \textit{Multiply}$$

$$= \frac{1 - \sin x}{\cos^2 x} \qquad \textit{Pythagorean identity}$$

$$= \frac{1}{\cos^2 x} - \frac{\sin x}{\cos^2 x} \qquad \textit{Separate fractions}$$

$$= \frac{1}{\cos^2 x} - \frac{\sin x}{\cos x} \cdot \frac{1}{\cos x} \qquad$$

$$= \sec^2 x - \tan x \sec x \qquad \textit{Identities}$$

EXAMPLE 8   Trigonometric Substitution

Use the substitution $x = 2 \tan \theta$, $0 < \theta < \pi/2$, to express $\sqrt{4 + x^2}$ as a trigonometric function of θ.

Solution

Letting $x = 2 \tan \theta$, you have

$$
\begin{aligned}
\sqrt{4 + x^2} &= \sqrt{4 + (2 \tan \theta)^2} \\
&= \sqrt{4(1 + \tan^2 \theta)} \\
&= \sqrt{4 \sec^2 \theta} \qquad \text{\textit{Pythagorean identity}} \\
&= 2 \sec \theta. \qquad \textit{sec } \theta > 0 \textit{ for } 0 < \theta < \dfrac{\pi}{2}
\end{aligned}
$$

Figure 6.1 shows the right angle illustration of the trigonometric substitution in Example 8. For $0 < \theta < \pi/2$, we have opp $= x$, adj $= 2$, and hyp $= \sqrt{4 + x^2}$. Thus, we can write

$$
\sec \theta = \frac{\sqrt{4 + x^2}}{2} \quad \rightarrow \quad \sqrt{4 + x^2} = 2 \sec \theta.
$$

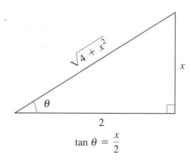

$$
\tan \theta = \frac{x}{2}
$$

FIGURE 6.1

DISCUSSION

PROBLEM

Remembering
Trigonometric
Identities

Most people find the Pythagorean identity involving sine and cosine to be fairly easy to remember: $\sin^2 u + \cos^2 u = 1$. The one involving tangent and secant, however, tends to give some people trouble. They can't remember if the identity is

$$
1 + \tan^2 u \overset{?}{=} \sec^2 u \qquad \text{or} \qquad 1 + \sec^2 u \overset{?}{=} \tan^2 u.
$$

Which of these two is the correct Pythagorean identity involving tangent and secant? Write a short paragraph describing how a person can remember (or derive) this identity.

WARM UP

The following warm-up exercises involve skills that were covered in earlier sections. You will use these skills in the exercise set for this section.

In Exercises 1 and 2, use a right triangle to evaluate the other five trigonometric functions of the acute angle θ.

1. $\tan \theta = \frac{3}{2}$ **2.** $\sec \theta = 3$

In Exercises 3 and 4, determine the exact value of the six trigonometric functions of θ. Assume the point is on the terminal side of an angle θ in standard position.

3. $(7, -3)$ **4.** $(-10, 5)$

In Exercises 5–8, simplify the expression.

5. $\sqrt{1 - \left(\frac{\sqrt{3}}{2}\right)^2}$ **6.** $\sqrt{\left(\frac{3}{4}\right)^2 + 1}$

7. $\sqrt{1 + \left(\frac{3}{8}\right)^2}$ **8.** $\sqrt{1 - \left(\frac{\sqrt{5}}{3}\right)^2}$

In Exercises 9 and 10, perform the indicated operations and simplify the result.

9. $\dfrac{4}{1 + x} + \dfrac{x}{4}$ **10.** $\dfrac{3}{1 - x} - \dfrac{5}{1 + x}$

EXERCISES for Section 6.1

In Exercises 1–14, use the fundamental identities to evaluate (if possible) the other trigonometric functions.

1. $\sin x = \frac{1}{2}$, $\cos x = \frac{\sqrt{3}}{2}$

2. $\tan x = \frac{\sqrt{3}}{3}$, $\cos x = -\frac{\sqrt{3}}{2}$

3. $\sec \theta = \sqrt{2}$; $\sin \theta = -\frac{\sqrt{2}}{2}$

4. $\csc \theta = \frac{5}{3}$, $\tan \theta = \frac{3}{4}$

5. $\tan x = \frac{5}{12}$, $\sec x = -\frac{13}{12}$

6. $\cot \phi = -3$, $\sin \phi = \frac{\sqrt{10}}{10}$

7. $\sec \phi = -1$, $\sin \phi = 0$

8. $\cos\left(\frac{\pi}{2} - x\right) = \frac{3}{5}$, $\cos x = \frac{4}{5}$

9. $\sin(-x) = -\frac{2}{3}$, $\tan x = -\frac{2\sqrt{5}}{5}$

10. $\csc x = 5$, $\cos x > 0$

11. $\tan \theta = 2$, $\sin \theta < 0$

12. $\sec \theta = -3$, $\tan \theta < 0$

13. $\sin \theta = -1$, $\cot \theta = 0$

14. $\tan \theta$ is undefined, $\sin \theta > 0$

In Exercises 15–20, match the trigonometric expression with one of the following.

(a) -1 (b) $\cos x$ (c) $\cot x$
(d) 1 (e) $-\tan x$ (f) $\sin x$

15. $\sec x \cos x$ **16.** $\dfrac{\sin(-x)}{\cos(-x)}$

17. $\tan^2 x - \sec^2 x$ **18.** $\dfrac{1 - \cos^2 x}{\sin x}$

19. $\cot x \sin x$ **20.** $\dfrac{\sin[(\pi/2) - x]}{\cos[(\pi/2) - x]}$

In Exercises 21–26, match the trigonometric expression with one of the following.

(a) $\csc x$ (b) $\tan x$ (c) $\sin^2 x$

(d) $\sin x \tan x$ (e) $\sec^2 x$ (f) $\sec^2 x + \tan^2 x$

21. $\sin x \sec x$ **22.** $\cos^2 x(\sec^2 x - 1)$

23. $\dfrac{\sec^2 x - 1}{\sin^2 x}$ **24.** $\cot x \sec x$

25. $\sec^4 x - \tan^4 x$ **26.** $\dfrac{\cos^2[(\pi/2) - x]}{\cos x}$

In Exercises 27–40, use the fundamental identities to simplify the expression.

27. $\tan \phi \csc \phi$ **28.** $\sin \phi(\csc \phi - \sin \phi)$

29. $\cos \beta \tan \beta$ **30.** $\sec \alpha \dfrac{\sin \alpha}{\tan \alpha}$

31. $\dfrac{\cot x}{\csc x}$ **32.** $\dfrac{\csc \theta}{\sec \theta}$

33. $\sec^2 x(1 - \sin^2 x)$ **34.** $\dfrac{1}{\tan^2 x + 1}$

35. $\dfrac{\sin(-x)}{\cos x}$ **36.** $\dfrac{\tan^2 \theta}{\sec^2 \theta}$

37. $\cos\left(\dfrac{\pi}{2} - x\right) \sec x$ **38.** $\cot\left(\dfrac{\pi}{2} - x\right) \cos x$

39. $\dfrac{\cos^2 y}{1 - \sin y}$ **40.** $\cos t(1 + \tan^2 t)$

In Exercises 41–48, factor the expression and use the fundamental identities to simplify the result.

41. $\tan^2 x - \tan^2 x \sin^2 x$ **42.** $\sec^2 x \tan^2 x + \sec^2 x$

43. $\sin^2 x \sec^2 x - \sin^2 x$ **44.** $\dfrac{\sec^2 x - 1}{\sec x - 1}$

45. $\tan^4 x + 2 \tan^2 x + 1$ **46.** $1 - 2 \cos^2 x + \cos^4 x$

47. $\sin^4 x - \cos^4 x$

48. $\csc^3 x - \csc^2 x - \csc x + 1$

In Exercises 49–52, perform the multiplication and use the fundamental identities to simplify the result.

49. $(\sin x + \cos x)^2$

50. $(\cot x + \csc x)(\cot x - \csc x)$

51. $(\sec x + 1)(\sec x - 1)$

52. $(3 - 3 \sin x)(3 + 3 \sin x)$

In Exercises 53–56, perform the addition or subtraction and use the fundamental identities to simplify the result.

53. $\dfrac{1}{1 + \cos x} + \dfrac{1}{1 - \cos x}$ **54.** $\dfrac{1}{\sec x + 1} - \dfrac{1}{\sec x - 1}$

55. $\dfrac{\cos x}{1 + \sin x} + \dfrac{1 + \sin x}{\cos x}$ **56.** $\tan x - \dfrac{\sec^2 x}{\tan x}$ $- \cot x$

In Exercises 57–60, rewrite the expression so that it is *not* in fractional form.

57. $\dfrac{\sin^2 y}{1 - \cos y}$ **58.** $\dfrac{5}{\tan x + \sec x}$ $5(\sec x - \tan x)$

59. $\dfrac{3}{\sec x - \tan x}$ **60.** $\dfrac{\tan^2 x}{\csc x + 1}$

In Exercises 61–70, use the specified trigonometric substitution to write the algebraic expression as a trigonometric function of θ, where $0 < \theta < \pi/2$.

61. $\sqrt{25 - x^2}$, $x = 5 \sin \theta$

62. $\sqrt{16 - 4x^2}$, $x = 2 \sin \theta$

63. $\sqrt{x^2 - 9}$, $x = 3 \sec \theta$

64. $\sqrt{x^2 - 4}$, $x = 2 \sec \theta$

65. $\sqrt{x^2 + 25}$, $x = 5 \tan \theta$

66. $\sqrt{x^2 + 100}$, $x = 10 \tan \theta$

67. $\sqrt{1 - (x - 1)^2}$, $x - 1 = \sin \theta$

68. $\sqrt{1 - e^{2x}}$, $e^x = \sin \theta$

69. $\sqrt{(9 + x^2)^3}$, $x = 3 \tan \theta$

70. $\sqrt{(x^2 - 16)^3}$, $x = 4 \sec \theta$

In Exercises 71 and 72, determine the values of θ, $0 \le \theta < 2\pi$, for which the equation is true.

71. $\sec \theta = \sqrt{1 + \tan^2 \theta}$ **72.** $\cos \theta = -\sqrt{1 - \sin^2 \theta}$

In Exercises 73–76, determine whether the equation is an identity, and give a reason for your answer.

73. $\dfrac{\sin k\theta}{\cos k\theta} = \tan \theta$, k is constant

74. $\dfrac{1}{5 \cos \theta} = 5 \sec \theta$

75. $\sin \theta \csc \theta = 1$ **76.** $\sin \theta \csc \phi = 1$

In Exercises 77–80, use a calculator to demonstrate the identity for the given values of θ.

77. $\csc^2 \theta - \cot^2 \theta = 1$

(a) $\theta = 132°$ (b) $\theta = \dfrac{2\pi}{7}$

78. $\tan^2 \theta + 1 = \sec^2 \theta$

(a) $\theta = 346°$ (b) $\theta = 3.1$

79. $\cos\left(\dfrac{\pi}{2} - \theta\right) = \sin \theta$

(a) $\theta = 80°$ (b) $\theta = 0.8$

80. $\sin(-\theta) = -\sin \theta$

(a) $\theta = 250°$ (b) $\theta = \frac{1}{2}$

81. Express each of the other trigonometric functions of θ in terms of $\sin \theta$.

82. Express each of the other trigonometric functions of θ in terms of $\cos \theta$.

6.2 Verifying Trigonometric Identities

Introduction / Verifying Trigonometric Identities

Introduction

In the previous section, we showed how to rewrite trigonometric expressions in equivalent forms. In this section, we will demonstrate methods for proving (or verifying) trigonometric identities. And in Section 6.3, we will show how to solve trigonometric equations. The key to verifying identities and solving equations is the ability to use the fundamental identities and the rules of algebra to rewrite trigonometric expressions.

Before going on, let's review some distinctions among trigonometric expressions, equations, and identities. An *expression* has no equal sign. It is merely a combination of functions. When simplifying expressions, we use an equal sign only to indicate the equivalence of the original expression and the new form. An *equation* is a statement containing an equal sign that is true for a specific set of values. In this sense, it is really a *conditional* equation. For example, the equation

$$\sin x = -1$$

is true only for $x = (3\pi/2) \pm 2n\pi$ and integer n. Hence, it is a conditional equation. On the other hand, an equation that is true for all real values in the domain of the variable is an *identity*. For example, the familiar equation

$$\sin^2 x = 1 - \cos^2 x$$

is true for all real numbers x. Hence, it is an identity.

Though there are similarities, proving that a trigonometric equation is an identity is quite different from solving an equation. There is no well-defined set of rules to follow in verifying trigonometric identities, and the process is best learned by practice.

Guidelines for Verifying Trigonometric Identities

1. Work with one side of the equation at a time. It is often better to work with the more complicated side first.
2. Look for opportunities to factor an expression, add fractions, square a binomial, or create a monomial denominator.
3. Look for opportunities to use the fundamental identities. Note which functions are in the final expression you want. Sines and cosines pair up well, as do secants and tangents, and cosecants and cotangents.
4. If the preceding guidelines do not help, try converting all terms to sines and cosines.
5. Do not just sit and stare at the problem. Try something! Even paths that lead to dead ends give you insights.

Verifying Trigonometric Identities

EXAMPLE 1   Verifying a Trigonometric Identity

Verify the identity

$$\frac{\sec^2 \theta - 1}{\sec^2 \theta} = \sin^2 \theta.$$

Solution

Because the left side is more complicated, we will work with it.

$$\frac{\sec^2 \theta - 1}{\sec^2 \theta} = \frac{(\tan^2 \theta + 1) - 1}{\sec^2 \theta} \qquad \textit{Pythagorean identity}$$

$$= \frac{\tan^2 \theta}{\sec^2 \theta} \qquad \textit{Simplify}$$

$$= \tan^2 \theta(\cos^2 \theta) \qquad \textit{Reciprocal identity}$$

$$= \frac{\sin^2 \theta}{\cos^2 \theta}(\cos^2 \theta) \qquad \textit{Tangent identity}$$

$$= \sin^2 \theta \qquad \textit{Reduce}$$

Alternative Solution

Sometimes it is helpful to separate a fraction into two parts. In this case, we have

$$\frac{\sec^2 \theta - 1}{\sec^2 \theta} = \frac{\sec^2 \theta}{\sec^2 \theta} - \frac{1}{\sec^2 \theta} \qquad \textit{Separate fractions}$$

$$= 1 - \cos^2 \theta \qquad \textit{Reciprocal identity}$$

$$= \sin^2 \theta. \qquad \textit{Pythagorean identity}$$

As you can see from Example 1, there can be more than one way to verify an identity. Your method may differ from that used by your instructor or fellow students. Here is a good chance to be creative and establish your own style, but try to be as efficient as possible.

EXAMPLE 2   Combining Fractions Before Using Identities

Verify the identity

$$\frac{1}{1 - \sin \alpha} + \frac{1}{1 + \sin \alpha} = 2 \sec^2 \alpha.$$

Solution

Add the two fractions and see where you can go from there.

$$\frac{1}{1 - \sin \alpha} + \frac{1}{1 + \sin \alpha} = \frac{1 + \sin \alpha + 1 - \sin \alpha}{(1 - \sin \alpha)(1 + \sin \alpha)} \qquad \textit{Add fractions}$$

$$= \frac{2}{1 - \sin^2 \alpha} \qquad \textit{Simplify}$$

$$= \frac{2}{\cos^2 \alpha} \qquad \textit{Pythagorean identity}$$

$$= 2 \sec^2 \alpha \qquad \textit{Reciprocal identity}$$

EXAMPLE 3   Verifying a Trigonometric Identity

Verify the identity

$$(\tan^2 x + 1)(\cos^2 x - 1) = -\tan^2 x.$$

Solution

By applying identities before multiplying, you obtain the following.

$$(\tan^2 x + 1)(\cos^2 x - 1) = (\sec^2 x)(-\sin^2 x) \qquad \textit{Pythagorean identities}$$

$$= -\frac{\sin^2 x}{\cos^2 x} \qquad \textit{Reciprocal identity}$$

$$= -\left(\frac{\sin x}{\cos x}\right)^2 \qquad \textit{Rule of exponents}$$

$$= -\tan^2 x \qquad \textit{Tangent identity}$$

EXAMPLE 4   Converting to Sines and Cosines

Verify the identity

$$\tan x + \cot x = \sec x \csc x.$$

Solution

In this case there appear to be no fractions to add, no products to find, and no opportunity to use one of the Pythagorean identities. Hence, try converting the left side into sines and cosines to see what happens.

$$\tan x + \cot x = \frac{\sin x}{\cos x} + \frac{\cos x}{\sin x} \qquad \textit{Identities}$$

$$= \frac{\sin^2 x + \cos^2 x}{\cos x \sin x} \qquad \textit{Add fractions}$$

$$= \frac{1}{\cos x \sin x} \qquad \textit{sin}^2 \textit{ x} + \textit{cos}^2 \textit{ x} = 1$$

$$= \frac{1}{\cos x} \cdot \frac{1}{\sin x} \qquad \textit{Product of fractions}$$

$$= \sec x \csc x \qquad \textit{Reciprocal identities}$$

Recall from algebra that *rationalizing the denominator* is, on occasion, a powerful simplification technique. A related form of this technique works for simplifying trigonometric expressions as well.

EXAMPLE 5   Verifying a Trigonometric Identity

Verify the identity

$$\sec y + \tan y = \frac{\cos y}{1 - \sin y}.$$

Solution

Work with the *right* side. Note that you can create a monomial denominator by multiplying the numerator and denominator by $(1 + \sin y)$.

$$\frac{\cos y}{1 - \sin y} = \frac{\cos y}{1 - \sin y}\left(\frac{1 + \sin y}{1 + \sin y}\right) \qquad \textit{Multiply numerator and denominator by (1 + sin y)}$$

$$= \frac{\cos y + \cos y \sin y}{1 - \sin^2 y}$$

$$= \frac{\cos y + \cos y \sin y}{\cos^2 y} \qquad \textit{Pythagorean identity}$$

$$= \frac{\cos y}{\cos^2 y} + \frac{\cos y \sin y}{\cos^2 y} \qquad \textit{Separate fractions}$$

$$= \frac{1}{\cos y} + \frac{\sin y}{\cos y} \qquad \textit{Reduce}$$

$$= \sec y + \tan y \qquad \textit{Identities}$$

So far in this section, we have been verifying trigonometric identities by working with one side of the equation and converting to the form given on the other side. On occasion it is practical to work with each side *separately* to obtain one common form equivalent to both sides.

EXAMPLE 6 Working with Each Side Separately

Verify the identity

$$\frac{\cot^2 \theta}{1 + \csc \theta} = \frac{1 - \sin \theta}{\sin \theta}.$$

Solution

Working with the left side, you have

$$\frac{\cot^2 \theta}{1 + \csc \theta} = \frac{\csc^2 \theta - 1}{1 + \csc \theta} \qquad \text{cot}^2 \theta = \csc^2 \theta - 1$$

$$= \frac{(\csc \theta - 1)\cancel{(\csc \theta + 1)}}{\cancel{1 + \csc \theta}} \qquad \text{Factor}$$

$$= \csc \theta - 1. \qquad \text{Reduce}$$

Now, simplifying the right side of the original equation, you have

$$\frac{1 - \sin \theta}{\sin \theta} = \frac{1}{\sin \theta} - \frac{\sin \theta}{\sin \theta} = \csc \theta - 1.$$

The identity is verified since both sides are equal to $\csc \theta - 1$. ◄

In Example 7, powers of trigonometric functions are rewritten as more complicated sums of products of trigonometric functions. This is a common procedure used in calculus.

EXAMPLE 7 Two Examples from Calculus

Verify the identities.

a. $\tan^4 x = \tan^2 x \sec^2 x - \tan^2 x$
b. $\sin^3 x \cos^4 x = (\cos^4 x - \cos^6 x)\sin x$

Solution

Note the use of the Pythagorean identities in the verifications.

a. $\tan^4 x = (\tan^2 x)(\tan^2 x)$ *Separate factors*

$\qquad = \tan^2 x(\sec^2 x - 1)$ *Pythagorean identity*

$\qquad = \tan^2 x \sec^2 x - \tan^2 x$ *Multiply*

b. $\sin^3 x \cos^4 x = \sin^2 x \cos^4 x \sin x$ *Separate factors*

$\qquad = (1 - \cos^2 x)\cos^4 x \sin x$ *Pythagorean identity*

$\qquad = (\cos^4 x - \cos^6 x)\sin x$ *Multiply* ◄

DISCUSSION

PROBLEM

You Be
the
Instructor

Suppose you are tutoring a student in trigonometry. After working several homework problems, your student becomes discouraged because he is unable to get his answers to agree with those in the back of the textbook. Which of the following answers does your student actually get right? Which are wrong? How would you help your student?

Student's answers	Text's answers
1. $\dfrac{1}{2 \csc x}$	$\dfrac{1}{2} \sin x$
2. $(1 - \cos x)(1 + \cos x)$	$\sin^2 x$
3. $\dfrac{\sin^2 x}{1 - \cos x}$	$1 + \cos x$
4. $\cot^2 x + 2$	$1 + \csc^2 x$
5. $(\sec x - \tan x)(\sec x + \tan x)$	1

WARM UP

The following warm-up exercises involve skills that were covered in earlier sections. You will use these skills in the exercise set for this section.

In Exercises 1–6, factor each expression and, if possible, simplify the results.

1. (a) $x^2 - x^2 y^2$
   (b) $\sin^2 x - \sin^2 x \cos^2 x$

2. (a) $x^2 + x^2 y^2$
   (b) $\cos^2 x + \cos^2 x \tan^2 x$

3. (a) $x^4 - 1$
   (b) $\tan^4 x - 1$

4. (a) $z^3 + 1$
   (b) $\tan^3 x + 1$

5. (a) $x^3 - x^2 + x - 1$
   (b) $\cot^3 x - \cot^2 x + \cot x - 1$

6. (a) $x^4 - 2x^2 + 1$
   (b) $\sin^4 x - 2 \sin^2 x + 1$

In Exercises 7–10, perform the additions or subtractions and, if possible, simplify the results.

7. (a) $\dfrac{y^2}{x} - x$
   (b) $\dfrac{\csc^2 x}{\cot x} - \cot x$

8. (a) $1 - \dfrac{1}{x^2}$
   (b) $1 - \dfrac{1}{\sec^2 x}$

9. (a) $\dfrac{y}{1 + z} + \dfrac{1 + z}{y}$
   (b) $\dfrac{\sin x}{1 + \cos x} + \dfrac{1 + \cos x}{\sin x}$

10. (a) $\dfrac{y}{z} - \dfrac{z}{1 + y}$
   (b) $\dfrac{\tan x}{\sec x} - \dfrac{\sec x}{1 + \tan x}$

EXERCISES for Section 6.2

In Exercises 1–56, verify the identity.

1. $\sin t \csc t = 1$ **2.** $\tan y \cot y = 1$

3. $(1 + \sin \alpha)(1 - \sin \alpha) = \cos^2 \alpha$

4. $\cot^2 y(\sec^2 y - 1) = 1$

5. $\cos^2 \beta - \sin^2 \beta = 1 - 2 \sin^2 \beta$

6. $\cos^2 \beta - \sin^2 \beta = 2 \cos^2 \beta - 1$

7. $\tan^2 \theta + 4 = \sec^2 \theta + 3$ **8.** $2 - \sec^2 z = 1 - \tan^2 z$

9. $\sin^2 \alpha - \sin^4 \alpha = \cos^2 \alpha - \cos^4 \alpha$

10. $\cos x + \sin x \tan x = \sec x$

11. $\dfrac{\sec^2 x}{\tan x} = \sec x \csc x$ **12.** $\dfrac{\cot^3 t}{\csc t} = \cos t(\csc^2 t - 1)$

13. $\dfrac{\cot^2 t}{\csc t} = \csc t - \sin t$ **14.** $\dfrac{1}{\sin x} - \sin x = \dfrac{\cos^2 x}{\sin x}$

15. $\sin^{1/2} x \cos x - \sin^{5/2} x \cos x = \cos^3 x\sqrt{\sin x}$

16. $\sec^6 x(\sec x \tan x) - \sec^4 x(\sec x \tan x) = \sec^5 x \tan^3 x$

17. $\dfrac{1}{\sec x \tan x} = \csc x - \sin x$

18. $\dfrac{\sec \theta - 1}{1 - \cos \theta} = \sec \theta$

19. $\csc x - \sin x = \cos x \cot x$

20. $\sec x - \cos x = \sin x \tan x$

21. $\cos x + \sin x \tan x = \sec x$

22. $\dfrac{\sec x + \tan x}{\sec x - \tan x} = (\sec x + \tan x)^2$

23. $\dfrac{1}{\tan x} + \dfrac{1}{\cot x} = \tan x + \cot x$

24. $\dfrac{1}{\sin x} - \dfrac{1}{\csc x} = \csc x - \sin x$

25. $\dfrac{\cos \theta \cot \theta}{1 - \sin \theta} - 1 = \csc \theta$

26. $\dfrac{1 + \sin \theta}{\cos \theta} + \dfrac{\cos \theta}{1 + \sin \theta} = 2 \sec \theta$

27. $\dfrac{1}{\cot x + 1} + \dfrac{1}{\tan x + 1} = 1$

28. $\cos x - \dfrac{\cos x}{1 - \tan x} = \dfrac{\sin x \cos x}{\sin x - \cos x}$

29. $2 \sec^2 x - 2 \sec^2 x \sin^2 x - \sin^2 x - \cos^2 x = 1$

30. $\csc x(\csc x - \sin x) + \dfrac{\sin x - \cos x}{\sin x} + \cot x = \csc^2 x$

31. $2 + \cos^2 x - 3 \cos^4 x = \sin^2 x(2 + 3 \cos^2 x)$

32. $4 \tan^4 x + \tan^2 x - 3 = \sec^2 x(4 \tan^2 x - 3)$

33. $\csc^4 x - 2 \csc^2 x + 1 = \cot^4 x$

34. $\sin x(1 - 2 \cos^2 x + \cos^4 x) = \sin^5 x$

35. $\sec^4 \theta - \tan^4 \theta = 1 + 2 \tan^2 \theta$

36. $\csc^4 \theta - \cot^4 \theta = 2 \csc^2 \theta - 1$

37. $\dfrac{\sin \beta}{1 - \cos \beta} = \dfrac{1 + \cos \beta}{\sin \beta}$

38. $\dfrac{\cot \alpha}{\csc \alpha - 1} = \dfrac{\csc \alpha + 1}{\cot \alpha}$

39. $\dfrac{\tan^3 \alpha - 1}{\tan \alpha - 1} = \tan^2 \alpha + \tan \alpha + 1$

40. $\dfrac{\sin^3 \beta + \cos^3 \beta}{\sin \beta + \cos \beta} = 1 - \sin \beta \cos \beta$

41. $\cos\left(\dfrac{\pi}{2} - x\right) \csc x = 1$ **42.** $\dfrac{\cos[(\pi/2) - x]}{\sin[(\pi/2) - x]} - \tan x$

43. $\dfrac{\csc(-x)}{\sec(-x)} - -\cot x$

44. $(1 + \sin y)[1 + \sin(-y)] = \cos^2 y$

45. $\dfrac{\cos(-\theta)}{1 + \sin(-\theta)} = \sec \theta + \tan \theta$

46. $\dfrac{1 + \sec(-\theta)}{\sin(-\theta) + \tan(-\theta)} = -\csc \theta$

47. $\dfrac{\sin x \cos y + \cos x \sin y}{\cos x \cos y - \sin x \sin y} = \dfrac{\tan x + \tan y}{1 - \tan x \tan y}$

48. $\dfrac{\tan x + \tan y}{1 - \tan x \tan y} = \dfrac{\cot x + \cot y}{\cot x \cot y - 1}$

49. $\dfrac{\tan x + \cot y}{\tan x \cot y} = \tan y + \cot x$

50. $\dfrac{\cos x - \cos y}{\sin x + \sin y} + \dfrac{\sin x - \sin y}{\cos x + \cos y} = 0$

51. $\sqrt{\dfrac{1 + \sin \theta}{1 - \sin \theta}} = \dfrac{1 + \sin \theta}{|\cos \theta|}$

52. $\sqrt{\dfrac{1 - \cos \theta}{1 + \cos \theta}} = \dfrac{1 - \cos \theta}{|\sin \theta|}$

53. $\sin^2 x + \sin^2\left(\dfrac{\pi}{2} - x\right) = 1$

54. $\sec^2 y - \cot^2\left(\dfrac{\pi}{2} - y\right) = 1$

55. $\csc x \cos\left(\dfrac{\pi}{2} - x\right) = 1$

56. $\sec^2\left(\dfrac{\pi}{2} - x\right) - 1 = \cot^2 x$

In Exercises 57–60, explain why the equation is *not* an identity and find one value of the variable for which the equation is not true.

57. $\sin \theta = \sqrt{1 - \cos^2 \theta}$ **58.** $\tan \theta = \sqrt{\sec^2 \theta - 1}$

59. $\sqrt{\tan^2 x} = \tan x$

60. $\sqrt{\sin^2 x + \cos^2 x} = \sin x + \cos x$

61. *Rate of Change* The rate of change of the function $f(x) = \sin x + \csc x$ with respect to change in the variable x is given by the expression $\cos x - \csc x \cot x$. Show that the expression for the rate of change can also be given by $-\cos x \cot^2 x$.

62. *Friction* The forces acting on an object weighing W units on an inclined plane positioned at an angle of θ with the horizontal is modeled by

$$\mu W \cos \theta = W \sin \theta$$

where μ is the coefficient of friction (see figure). Solve the equation for μ and simplify the result.

Figure for 62

6.3 Solving Trigonometric Equations

Introduction / Equations of Quadratic Type / Functions Involving Multiple Angles / Using Inverse Functions and a Calculator

Introduction

We now switch from *verifying* trigonometric identities to *solving* trigonometric equations. To see the difference, consider the following two equations.

$$\sin^2 x + \cos^2 x = 1 \quad \text{and} \quad \sin x = 1$$

The first equation is an identity because it is true for *all* real values of x. The second equation, however, is true only for *some* values of x. When we find these values, we say we are solving the equation. To solve a trigonometric equation, use standard algebraic techniques such as collecting like terms and factoring to isolate the trigonometric function involved in the equation.

EXAMPLE 1   Solving a Trigonometric Equation

$$2 \sin x - 1 = 0 \qquad \text{\textit{Given equation}}$$
$$2 \sin x = 1 \qquad \text{\textit{Add 1 to both sides}}$$
$$\sin x = \frac{1}{2} \qquad \text{\textit{Divide both sides by 2}}$$

Now, to solve for x, note that the equation $\sin x = \frac{1}{2}$ has solutions $x = \pi/6$ and $x = 5\pi/6$ in the interval $[0, 2\pi)$. Moreover, because $\sin x$ has a period of 2π, there are infinitely many other solutions, which can be written as

$$x = \frac{\pi}{6} + 2n\pi \quad \text{and} \quad x = \frac{5\pi}{6} + 2n\pi \quad \text{\textit{General solution}}$$

where n is an integer, as shown in Figure 6.2. This is the **general form** of the solution.

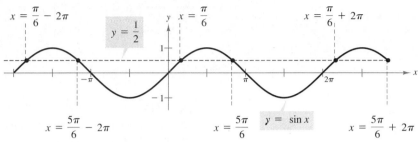

FIGURE 6.2

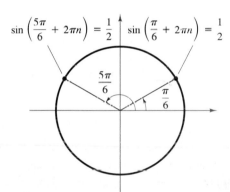

FIGURE 6.3

Another way to see that the equation $\sin x = \frac{1}{2}$ has infinitely many solutions is indicated in Figure 6.3. For $0 \le x < 2\pi$, the solutions are $x = \pi/6$ and $x = 5\pi/6$. Any angles that are coterminal with $\pi/6$ or $5\pi/6$ will also be solutions of the equation.

EXAMPLE 2   Collecting Like Terms

$$\sin x + \sqrt{2} = -\sin x \qquad \textit{Given equation}$$

$$\sin x + \sin x = -\sqrt{2} \qquad \textit{Add } \sin x \textit{ and subtract } \sqrt{2} \textit{ from both sides}$$

$$2 \sin x = -\sqrt{2} \qquad \textit{Collect like terms}$$

$$\sin x = -\frac{\sqrt{2}}{2} \qquad \textit{Divide both sides by 2}$$

Since $\sin x$ has a period of 2π, first find all solutions in the interval $[0, 2\pi)$. These are $x = 5\pi/4$ and $x = 7\pi/4$. Now add $2n\pi$ to each of these solutions to get the general form

$$x = \frac{5\pi}{4} + 2n\pi \qquad \text{and} \qquad x = \frac{7\pi}{4} + 2n\pi \qquad \textit{General solution}$$

where n is an integer.

$2\sqrt{3}$ $\sqrt{3}$

3

$\frac{\sin}{\cos}$ $\sqrt{3}$

$\sqrt{3}+3$

$\cdot\sqrt{12}$

$2\sqrt{3}$

$\sin \frac{\sqrt{3}}{2\sqrt{3}} \cdot \frac{2\sqrt{3}}{2\sqrt{3}} \frac{6}{4\cdot3} \frac{1}{2}$

EXAMPLE 3   Extracting Square Roots

$3\tan^2 x - 1 = 0$	*Given equation*
$3\tan^2 x = 1$	*Add 1 to both sides*
$\tan^2 x = \dfrac{1}{3}$	*Divide both sides by 3*
$\tan x = \pm\dfrac{1}{\sqrt{3}}$ $\frac{\sqrt{3}}{3}$	*Extract square roots*

Since $\tan x$ has a period of π, find all solutions in the interval $[0, \pi)$. These are $x = \pi/6$ and $x = 5\pi/6$. Finally, add $n\pi$ to each and obtain the following general form of the solution

$$x = \frac{\pi}{6} + n\pi \quad \text{and} \quad x = \frac{5\pi}{6} + n\pi \quad \text{\textit{General solution}}$$

where n is an integer.

The equations in Examples 1, 2, and 3 involved only one trigonometric function. When two or more functions occur in the same equation, collect all terms to one side and try to separate the functions by factoring or by using appropriate identities. This may produce factors that yield no solutions, as illustrated in Example 4.

EXAMPLE 4   Factoring

$\cot x \cos^2 x = 2\cot x$	*Given equation*
$\cot x \cos^2 x - 2\cot x = 0$	*Subtract 2 cot x from both sides*
$\cot x(\cos^2 x - 2) = 0$	*Factor left side*

By setting each of these factors to zero, you obtain the following.

$$\cot x = 0 \quad \text{and} \quad \cos^2 x - 2 = 0$$
$$x = \frac{\pi}{2} \qquad\qquad\qquad \cos^2 x = 2$$
$$\cos x = \pm\sqrt{2}$$

No solution is obtained from $\cos x = \pm\sqrt{2}$ because $\pm\sqrt{2}$ are outside the range of the cosine function. Therefore, the general form of the solution is obtained by adding multiples of π to $x = \pi/2$, to get

$$x = \frac{\pi}{2} \pm n\pi \qquad\qquad \text{\textit{General solution}}$$

where n is an integer.

Equations of Quadratic Type

Many trigonometric equations are of quadratic type. Here are a couple of examples.

Quadratic in sin x	*Quadratic in sec x*
$2 \sin^2 x - \sin x - 1 = 0$	$\sec^2 x - 3 \sec x - 2 = 0$
$2(\sin x)^2 - (\sin x) - 1 = 0$	$(\sec x)^2 - 3(\sec x) - 2 = 0$

To solve equations of this type, we factor the quadratic or, if that is not possible, we use the Quadratic Formula.

EXAMPLE 5   Factoring an Equation of Quadratic Type

Find all solutions of $2 \sin^2 x - \sin x - 1 = 0$ in the interval $[0, 2\pi)$.

Solution

Treating the equation as a quadratic in $\sin x$ and factoring, you obtain

$$2 \sin^2 x - \sin x - 1 = 0 \qquad \textit{Given equation}$$
$$(2 \sin x + 1)(\sin x - 1) = 0. \qquad \textit{Factor}$$

Setting each factor to zero, you obtain the following solutions.

$$2 \sin x + 1 = 0 \qquad \text{and} \qquad \sin x - 1 = 0$$
$$\sin x = -\frac{1}{2} \qquad\qquad\qquad \sin x = 1$$
$$x = \frac{7\pi}{6}, \frac{11\pi}{6} \qquad\qquad\qquad x = \frac{\pi}{2}$$

REMARK   In Example 5, the general solution would be

$$x = \frac{7\pi}{6} + 2n\pi,$$
$$x = \frac{11\pi}{6} + 2n\pi,$$
$$x = \frac{\pi}{2} + 2n\pi$$

where n is an integer.

When working with an equation of quadratic type, be sure that the equation involves a *single* trigonometric function, as shown in the next example.

EXAMPLE 6   Writing in Terms of a Single Trigonometric Function

$$2 \sin^2 x + 3 \cos x - 3 = 0 \qquad \textit{Given equation}$$
$$2(1 - \cos^2 x) + 3 \cos x - 3 = 0 \qquad \textit{Pythagorean identity}$$
$$2 \cos^2 x - 3 \cos x + 1 = 0 \qquad \textit{Multiply both sides by } -1$$
$$(2 \cos x - 1)(\cos x - 1) = 0 \qquad \textit{Factor}$$

By setting each factor equal to zero, you find the solutions in the interval $[0, 2\pi)$ to be $x = 0$, $x = \pi/3$, and $x = 5\pi/3$. The general solution is therefore

$$x = 2n\pi, \qquad x = \frac{\pi}{3} + 2n\pi, \qquad x = \frac{5\pi}{3} + 2n\pi \qquad \textit{General solution}$$

where n is an integer.

Sometimes we must square both sides of an equation to obtain a quadratic, as demonstrated in the next example. Because this procedure can introduce extraneous solutions, you should check any solutions in the original equation to see if they are valid or extraneous.

EXAMPLE 7 Squaring and Converting to Quadratic Type

Find all solutions of $\cos x + 1 = \sin x$ in the interval $[0, 2\pi)$.

Solution

It is not immediately clear how to rewrite this equation in terms of a single trigonometric function. See what happens when you square both sides of the equation.

$$\cos x + 1 = \sin x \qquad \textit{Given equation}$$
$$\cos^2 x + 2\cos x + 1 = \sin^2 x \qquad \textit{Square both sides}$$
$$\cos^2 x + 2\cos x + 1 = 1 - \cos^2 x \qquad \textit{Identity}$$
$$2\cos^2 x + 2\cos x = 0 \qquad \textit{Collect terms}$$
$$2\cos x(\cos x + 1) = 0 \qquad \textit{Factor}$$

Setting each factor to zero produces the following.

$$2\cos x = 0 \qquad \text{and} \qquad \cos x + 1 = 0$$
$$\cos x = 0 \qquad\qquad\qquad \cos x = -1$$
$$x = \frac{\pi}{2}, \frac{3\pi}{2} \qquad\qquad\qquad x = \pi$$

REMARK In Example 7, the general solution would be $x = \pi/2 + 2n\pi$ and $x = \pi + 2n\pi$ where n is an integer.

Because you squared the original equation, you must check for extraneous solutions. Of the three possible solutions, $x = 3\pi/2$ is extraneous. (Try checking this.) Thus, in the interval $[0, 2\pi)$, the only two solutions are $x = \pi/2$ and $x = \pi$.

Functions Involving Multiple Angles

For trigonometric functions of *multiple angles*, extra care is needed to determine all possible solutions.

EXAMPLE 8 Functions of Multiple Angles

Find all solutions of $2\cos 3t - 1 = 0$.

Solution

$$2\cos 3t - 1 = 0 \qquad \textit{Given equation}$$
$$2\cos 3t = 1 \qquad \textit{Add 1 to both sides}$$
$$\cos 3t = \frac{1}{2} \qquad \textit{Divide both sides by 2}$$

In the interval $[0, 2\pi)$, you know that $3t = \pi/3$ and $3t = 5\pi/3$ are the only solutions so that, in general,

$$3t = \frac{\pi}{3} + 2n\pi \quad \text{and} \quad 3t = \frac{5\pi}{3} + 2n\pi.$$

Dividing this result by 3, you obtain the general solution

$$t = \frac{\pi}{9} + \frac{2n\pi}{3} \quad \text{and} \quad t = \frac{5\pi}{9} + \frac{2n\pi}{3} \qquad \textit{General solution}$$

where n is an integer. ◢

EXAMPLE 9 Functions of Multiple Angles

Find all solutions of $3\tan(x/2) + 3 = 0$.

Solution

$$3\tan\frac{x}{2} + 3 = 0 \qquad \textit{Given equation}$$

$$3\tan\frac{x}{2} = -3 \qquad \textit{Subtract 3 from both sides}$$

$$\tan\frac{x}{2} = -1 \qquad \textit{Divide both sides by 3}$$

In the interval $[0, \pi)$, you know that $x/2 = 3\pi/4$ is the only solution so that, in general, you have

$$\frac{x}{2} = \frac{3\pi}{4} + n\pi.$$

Multiplication by 2 yields the general form

$$x = \frac{3\pi}{2} + 2n\pi \qquad \textit{General solution}$$

where n is an integer. ◢

Using Inverse Functions and a Calculator

So far in this section, we have chosen examples for which the solutions are special values like

$$0, \quad \pm\frac{\pi}{6}, \quad \pm\frac{\pi}{4}, \quad \pm\frac{\pi}{3}, \quad \pm\frac{\pi}{2}$$

and so on. In the remaining examples, we solve more general trigonometric equations by using inverse trigonometric functions or a calculator.

EXAMPLE 10   Using Inverse Functions

Find all solutions of $\sec^2 x - 2 \tan x = 4$.

Solution

$$
\begin{aligned}
\sec^2 x - 2 \tan x &= 4 & & \textit{Given equation} \\
1 + \tan^2 x - 2 \tan x - 4 &= 0 & & \textit{Pythagorean identity} \\
\tan^2 x - 2 \tan x - 3 &= 0 & & \textit{Combine like terms} \\
(\tan x - 3)(\tan x + 1) &= 0 & & \textit{Factor}
\end{aligned}
$$

Setting each factor equal to zero, you obtain two solutions in the interval $(-\pi/2, \pi/2)$. [Recall that the range of the inverse tangent function is $(-\pi/2, \pi/2)$.]

$$
\tan x = 3, \qquad \qquad \tan x = -1
$$

$$
x = \arctan 3 \qquad \quad x = -\frac{\pi}{4}
$$

Finally, by adding multiples of π (the period of the tangent), you obtain the general solution

$$
x = \arctan 3 + n\pi \qquad \text{and} \qquad x = -\frac{\pi}{4} + n\pi \quad \textit{General solution}
$$

where n is an integer.   ◢

If you have access to a computer or calculator with graphing capabilities, you might want to check your solutions graphically. For instance, the graph of the function

$$
f(x) = \tan^2 x - 2 \tan x - 3
$$

(shown in Figure 6.4) has the two x-intercepts

$$
x = \arctan 3 \approx 1.2490 \qquad \text{and} \qquad x = -\frac{\pi}{4} \approx -0.7854
$$

in the interval $(-\pi/2, \pi/2)$.

When using a calculator for $\arcsin x$, $\arccos x$, and $\arctan x$, the displayed solution may need to be adjusted to obtain solutions in the desired interval.

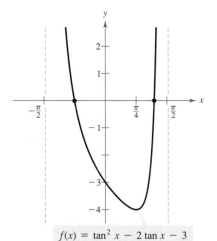

$f(x) = \tan^2 x - 2 \tan x - 3$

FIGURE 6.4

EXAMPLE 11   Using the Quadratic Formula

Find all solutions of $\sin^2 t - 3 \sin t - 2 = 0$ in the interval $[0, 2\pi)$.

Solution

$$\sin^2 t - 3 \sin t - 2 = 0 \qquad\qquad\qquad\qquad \textit{Given equation}$$

$$\sin t = \frac{-(-3) \pm \sqrt{(-3)^2 - 4(1)(-2)}}{2(1)} \qquad \textit{Quadratic Formula}$$

$$= \frac{3 \pm \sqrt{17}}{2} \qquad\qquad\qquad\qquad \textit{Simplify}$$

$$\approx 3.561553 \quad \text{or} \quad -0.5615528$$

Because the range of the sine function is $[-1, 1]$, the equation $\sin t = 3.561553$ has no solution. To solve the equation $\sin t = -0.5615528$, use a calculator and the inverse sine function as follows.

$$t \approx \arcsin(-0.5615528) \approx -0.5962613$$

Note that this solution is not in the interval $[0, 2\pi)$. To find the solutions in $[0, 2\pi)$, it is helpful to make a sketch of the graph of the sine function. From Figure 6.5, you see that the two solutions that lie in the interval $[0, 2\pi)$ are

$$t \approx \pi + 0.5962613 \approx 3.737854 \qquad\qquad \textit{Quadrant III}$$

and

$$t \approx 2\pi - 0.5962613 \approx 5.686924. \qquad\qquad \textit{Quadrant IV}$$

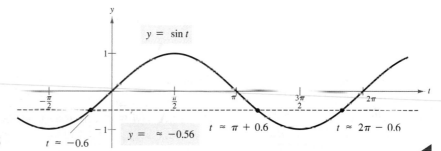

FIGURE 6.5

DISCUSSION

PROBLEM

Equations
with No
Solutions

One of these equations has solutions and the other two don't. Which equations do not have solutions?

1. $\sin^2 x - 5 \sin x + 6 = 0$
2. $\sin^2 x - 4 \sin x + 6 = 0$
3. $\sin^2 x - 5 \sin x - 6 = 0$

Can you find conditions involving the constants b and c that will guarantee that the equation

$$\sin^2 x + b \sin x + c = 0$$

has at least one solution on some interval of length 2π?

WARM UP

The following warm-up exercises involve skills that were covered in earlier sections. You will use these skills in the exercise set for this section.

In Exercises 1–6, find the values of θ in the interval $0 \leq \theta < 2\pi$ that satisfy the equation.

1. $\cos \theta = -\dfrac{1}{2}$

2. $\sin \theta = \dfrac{\sqrt{3}}{2}$

3. $\cos \theta = \dfrac{\sqrt{2}}{2}$

4. $\sin \theta = -\dfrac{\sqrt{2}}{2}$

5. $\tan \theta = \sqrt{3}$

6. $\tan \theta = -1$

In Exercises 7–10, solve for x.

7. $\dfrac{x}{3} + \dfrac{x}{5} = 1$

8. $2x(x + 3) - 5(x + 3) = 0$

9. $2x^2 - 4x - 5 = 0$

10. $\dfrac{1}{x} = \dfrac{x}{2x + 3}$

EXERCISES for Section 6.3

In Exercises 1–6, verify that the values of x are solutions of the equation.

1. $2 \cos x - 1 = 0$
   (a) $x = \dfrac{\pi}{3}$ (b) $x = \dfrac{5\pi}{3}$

2. $\csc x - 2 = 0$
   (a) $x = \dfrac{\pi}{6}$ (b) $x = \dfrac{5\pi}{6}$

3. $3 \tan^2 2x - 1 = 0$
   (a) $x = \dfrac{\pi}{12}$ (b) $x = \dfrac{5\pi}{12}$

4. $2 \cos^2 4x - 1 = 0$
   (a) $x = \dfrac{\pi}{16}$ (b) $x = \dfrac{3\pi}{16}$

5. $2 \sin^2 x - \sin x - 1 = 0$
   (a) $x = \dfrac{\pi}{2}$ (b) $x = \dfrac{7\pi}{6}$

6. $\sec^4 x - 4 \sec^2 x = 0$
   (a) $x = \dfrac{2\pi}{3}$ (b) $x = \dfrac{5\pi}{3}$

In Exercises 7–20, find all solutions of the equation without the aid of a calculator.

7. $2 \cos x + 1 = 0$

8. $2 \sin x - 1 = 0$

9. $\sqrt{3} \csc x - 2 = 0$

10. $\tan x + 1 = 0$

11. $2 \sin^2 x = 1$

12. $\tan^2 x = 3$

13. $3 \sec^2 x - 4 = 0$

14. $\csc^2 x - 2 = 0$

15. $\tan x(\tan x - 1) = 0$

16. $\cos x(2 \cos x + 1) = 0$

17. $\sin x(\sin x + 1) = 0$

18. $4 \sin^2 x - 3 = 0$

19. $\sin^2 x = 3 \cos^2 x$

20. $(3 \tan^2 x - 1)(\tan^2 x - 3) = 0$

In Exercises 21–40, find all solutions of the equation in the interval $[0, 2\pi)$. Do not use a calculator.

21. $\sec x \csc x - 2 \csc x = 0$

22. $\sec^2 x - \sec x - 2 = 0$

23. $2 \sin^2 x + 3 \sin x + 1 = 0$

24. $3 \tan^3 x - \tan x = 0$

25. $\cos^3 x = \cos x$

26. $4 \sin^3 x + 2 \sin^2 x - 2 \sin x - 1 = 0$

27. $\sec^2 x = (1 + \sqrt{3}) - (1 - \sqrt{3}) \tan x$

28. $\csc^2 x = (1 + \sqrt{3}) - (1 - \sqrt{3}) \cot x$

29. $2 \sec^2 x + \tan^2 x - 3 = 0$

30. $2 \sin^2 x = 2 + \cos x$

31. $2 \sin x + \csc x = 0$ 32. $\csc x + \cot x = 1$

33. $\sin 2x = -\dfrac{\sqrt{3}}{2}$ 34. $\tan 3x = 1$

35. $\cos \dfrac{x}{2} = \dfrac{\sqrt{2}}{2}$ 36. $\sec 4x = 2$

37. $\dfrac{1 + \cos x}{1 - \cos x} = 0$ 38. $\cos x + \sin x \tan x = 2$

39. $\dfrac{1 + \sin x}{\cos x} + \dfrac{\cos x}{1 + \sin x} = 4$

40. $\dfrac{\cos x \cot x}{1 - \sin x} = 3$

In Exercises 41–50, solve the algebraic and trigonometric equations. Restrict the solutions to the interval $[0, 2\pi)$.

41. $2y^2 + 7y - 15 = 0$
    $2 \tan^2 x + 7 \tan x - 15 = 0$

42. $12y^2 + 5y - 3 = 0$
    $12 \cos^2 x + 5 \cos x - 3 = 0$

43. $12y^2 - 13y + 3 = 0$
    $12 \sin^2 x - 13 \sin x + 3 = 0$

44. $3y^2 + 4y - 4 = 0$
    $3 \tan^2 x + 4 \tan x - 4 = 0$

45. $6y^2 - 13y + 6 = 0$
    $6 \cos^2 x - 13 \cos x + 6 = 0$

46. $y^2 + y - 20 = 0$
    $\sin^2 x + \sin x - 20 = 0$

47. $y^2 - 8y + 13 = 0$
    $\tan^2 x - 8 \tan x + 13 = 0$

48. $2y^2 + 6y - 1 = 0$
    $2 \cos^2 x + 6 \cos x - 1 = 0$

49. $y^2 + 2y - 1 = 0$
    $\sin^2 x + 2 \sin x - 1 = 0$

50. $4y^2 - 4y - 1 = 0$
    $4 \cos^2 x - 4 \cos x - 1 = 0$

51. *Extrema of a Function* The function $f(x) = \sin x + \cos x$ has maximum or minimum values at values of x for which

$\cos x - \sin x = 0$.

Find the exact solutions of this equation in the interval $[0, 2\pi)$ and find the coordinates of the maximum and minimum points on the graph of f shown in the figure.

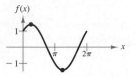

Figure for 51

52. *Extrema of a Function* The function $f(x) = 2 \sin x + \cos 2x$ has maximum or minimum values at values of x for which

$2 \cos x - 4 \sin x \cos x = 0$.

Find the exact solutions of this equation in the interval $[0, 2\pi)$ and find the coordinates of the maximum and minimum points on the graph of f shown in the figure.

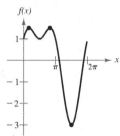

Figure for 52

53. *Harmonic Motion* A 5 pound weight is oscillating on the end of a spring. The position of the weight relative to the point of equilibrium is given by

$y = \frac{1}{4}(\cos 8t - 3 \sin 8t)$

where t is seconds (see figure). Find the times when the weight is at the point of equilibrium ($y = 0$) for $0 \le t \le 1$.

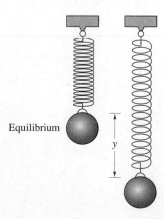

Figure for 53

54. *Sales* The monthly sales (in thousands of units) of a seasonal product are approximated by

$$S = 74.50 + 43.75 \sin \frac{\pi t}{6}$$

where t is the time in months, with $t = 1$ corresponding to January (see figure). Determine the months when sales exceed 100,000 units.

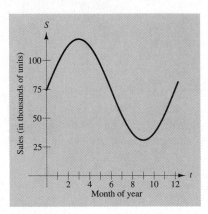

Figure for 54

55. *Projectile Motion* A batted baseball leaves the bat at an angle of θ with the horizontal and an initial velocity of $v_0 = 100$ feet per second. The ball is caught by an outfielder 300 feet from home plate (see figure). Find θ if the range r of a projectile is given by

$$r = \tfrac{1}{32} v_0{}^2 \sin 2\theta.$$

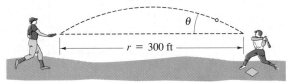

Figure for 55

56. *Projectile Motion* A marksman intends to hit a target at a distance of 1000 yards with a gun that has a muzzle velocity of 1200 feet per second (see figure). Neglecting air resistance, determine the minimum elevation of the gun if the range is given by

$$r = \tfrac{1}{32} v_0{}^2 \sin 2\theta.$$

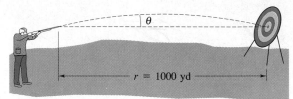

Figure for 56

SOLVING

Using Technology
to Solve a
Trigonometric
Equation

Equations that involve both algebraic and trigonometric expressions are often difficult to solve by analytic methods. For instance, how would you solve the following equation?

$$x = \cos x$$

None of the standard techniques such as factoring or using a trigonometric identity can be used to solve this equation. In such cases, technology can be used to approximate the solution, as shown in Example 1.

EXAMPLE 1   Approximating Solutions of an Equation

Approximate all solutions of $x = \cos x$.

Solution

There are two ways that a graphing utility can be used to solve this problem. One is to sketch the graphs of $y = x$ and $y = \cos x$ on the same screen and use the trace feature of the graphing utility to approximate the x-coordinate of the point at which the two graphs intersect. From the graph shown below on the left, you can see that the two graphs intersect when x is approximately 0.74. More accuracy can be obtained by using the zoom feature of the graphing utility.

Another way to solve the problem is to collect all nonzero terms on one side of the equation.

$$x - \cos x = 0$$

Then, use a graphing utility to sketch the graph of $y = x - \cos x$ and approximate the zeros of the function. By setting the minimum and maximum x- and y-values of the screen to $0.735 \leq x \leq 0.745$ and $-0.01 \leq y \leq 0.01$, you can obtain the graph shown on the right. From this graph, you can see that the solution is $x \approx 0.739$, which is accurate to three decimal places.

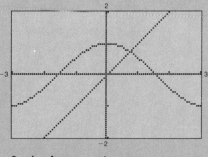

Graphs of $y = x$ and $y = \cos x$

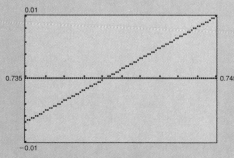

Graph of $y = x - \cos x$

EXAMPLE 2 Approximating Solutions of an Equation

Approximate all solutions of $0.5x + 1.13 = \cos x$.

Solution

By sketching the graphs of $y = 0.5x + 1.13$ and $y = \cos x$ on the same screen, it is clear that one solution occurs when $x \approx -3.8$. From the screen shown below on the left, however, it is unclear whether the two graphs have other points of intersection near $x = -0.5$. To determine whether there are other points of intersection, you use the zoom feature. After doing that, you can see that, for x-values near -0.5, the line lies above the cosine curve. Thus, there is only one point of intersection—it is $x \approx -3.819$.

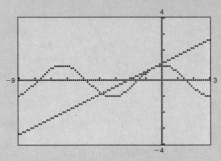

Graphs of $y = 0.5x + 1.13$ and $y = \cos x$

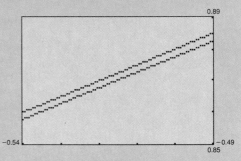

Graphs of $y = 0.5x + 1.13$ and $y = \cos x$

EXERCISES

(See also: Exercises 51–54, Section 6.3)

In Exercises 1–4, sketch the graphs of all three functions on the same display screen. Which two graphs are the same? What trigonometric identity have you discovered?

1. (a) $y = \sin^2 x$
   (b) $y = \frac{1}{2}(1 - \cos 2x)$
   (c) $y = \frac{1}{2}(1 + \cos 2x)$

2. (a) $y = 2\cos^2 x$
   (b) $y = 1 - \cos 2x$
   (c) $y = 1 + \cos 2x$

3. (a) $y = 2\sin x \cos 2x$
   (b) $y = \sin 3x + \sin x$
   (c) $y = \sin 3x - \sin x$

4. (a) $y = \sin 2x$
   (b) $y = 2\sin x$
   (c) $y = 2\sin x \cos x$

In Exercises 5–10, use a graphing utility to approximate all solutions of the equation. List the solutions correct to three decimal places.

5. $x + \sin x = 1$

6. $x^2 + \cos x = 2$

7. $5\cos \dfrac{1}{x^2 + 1} = 3$

8. $|x| + \sec \dfrac{1}{x^2 + 1} = 3$

9. $x + 1.25 = \arctan x$

10. $(x^2 + 1)\cos x = 1$

11. *Seasonal Sales* During 1991, the national monthly sales S (in thousands of units) of a lawn furniture company can be modeled by

$$S = 74.50 + 43.75 \sin \frac{1}{6}\pi t$$

where t represents the time in months, with $t = 0$ corresponding to January 1. Sketch the graph of this function for $0 \leq t \leq 12$. During which months did sales exceed 100,000 units?

6.4 Sum and Difference Formulas

Introduction / Using Sum and Difference Formulas

Introduction

In this and the following section, we show the derivations and uses of several trigonometric identities (or formulas) that are useful in mathematics and scientific applications.

We begin with six sum and difference formulas that express trigonometric functions of $(u \pm v)$ as functions of u and v alone.

SUM AND DIFFERENCE FORMULAS

$$\sin(u + v) = \sin u \cos v + \cos u \sin v \qquad \sin(u - v) = \sin u \cos v - \cos u \sin v$$

$$\cos(u + v) = \cos u \cos v - \sin u \sin v \qquad \cos(u - v) = \cos u \cos v + \sin u \sin v$$

$$\tan(u + v) = \frac{\tan u + \tan v}{1 - \tan u \tan v} \qquad \tan(u - v) = \frac{\tan u - \tan v}{1 + \tan u \tan v}$$

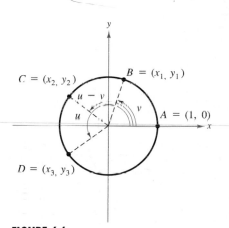

FIGURE 6.6

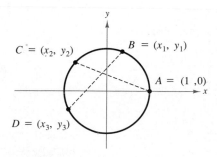

FIGURE 6.7

Proof

We prove only the formulas for $\cos(u \pm v)$. In Figure 6.6 we let A be the point $(1, 0)$ and then use u and v to locate the points $B = (x_1, y_1)$, $C = (x_2, y_2)$, and $D = (x_3, y_3)$ on the unit circle. Thus, $x_i^2 + y_i^2 = 1$ for $i = 1, 2, 3$. For convenience, we assume that $0 < v < u < 2\pi$. From Figure 6.7, note that arcs AC and BD have the same length. Hence, *line segments AC and BD* are also equal in length, which implies that

$$\sqrt{(x_2 - 1)^2 + (y_2 - 0)^2} = \sqrt{(x_3 - x_1)^2 + (y_3 - y_1)^2}$$

$$x_2^2 - 2x_2 + 1 + y_2^2 = x_3^2 - 2x_1x_3 + x_1^2 + y_3^2 - 2y_1y_3 + y_1^2$$

$$(x_2^2 + y_2^2) + 1 - 2x_2 = (x_3^2 + y_3^2) + (x_1^2 + y_1^2) - 2x_1x_3 - 2y_1y_3$$

$$1 + 1 - 2x_2 = 1 + 1 - 2x_1x_3 - 2y_1y_3$$

$$x_2 = x_3x_1 + y_3y_1.$$

Finally, by substituting the values $x_2 = \cos(u - v)$, $x_3 = \cos u$, $x_1 = \cos v$, $y_3 = \sin u$, and $y_1 = \sin v$, we obtain

$$\cos(u - v) = \cos u \cos v + \sin u \sin v.$$

The formula for $\cos(u + v)$ can be established by considering $u + v = u - (-v)$ and using the formula just derived to obtain

$$\cos(u + v) = \cos[u - (-v)]$$

$$= \cos u \cos(-v) + \sin u \sin(-v) = \cos u \cos v - \sin u \sin v.$$

Using Sum and Difference Formulas

In the remainder of this section, we show a variety of uses of sum and difference formulas. First, we show that sum and difference formulas can be used to find exact values of trigonometric functions involving sums or differences of special angles.

EXAMPLE 1   Evaluating a Trigonometric Function

Find the exact value of $\cos 75°$.

Solution

To find the *exact* value of $\cos 75°$, you use the fact that $75° = 30° + 45°$. Consequently, the formula for $\cos(u + v)$ yields

$$\cos 75° = \cos(30° + 45°)$$
$$= \cos 30° \cos 45° - \sin 30° \sin 45°$$
$$= \frac{\sqrt{3}}{2}\left(\frac{\sqrt{2}}{2}\right) - \frac{1}{2}\left(\frac{\sqrt{2}}{2}\right)$$
$$= \frac{\sqrt{6} - \sqrt{2}}{4}.$$

EXAMPLE 2   Evaluating a Trigonometric Function

Find the exact value of $\cos \dfrac{\pi}{12}$.

Solution

Using the fact that

$$\frac{\pi}{12} = \frac{\pi}{3} - \frac{\pi}{4}$$

together with the formula for $\cos(u - v)$, you obtain

$$\cos \frac{\pi}{12} = \cos\left(\frac{\pi}{3} - \frac{\pi}{4}\right)$$
$$= \cos \frac{\pi}{3} \cos \frac{\pi}{4} + \sin \frac{\pi}{3} \sin \frac{\pi}{4}$$
$$= \frac{1}{2}\left(\frac{\sqrt{2}}{2}\right) + \frac{\sqrt{3}}{2}\left(\frac{\sqrt{2}}{2}\right)$$
$$= \frac{\sqrt{2} + \sqrt{6}}{4}.$$

EXAMPLE 3   Evaluating a Trigonometric Expression

Find the exact value of $\sin 42° \cos 12° - \cos 42° \sin 12°$.

Solution

Recognizing that this expression fits the formula for $\sin(u - v)$, you can write

$$\sin 42° \cos 12° - \cos 42° \sin 12° = \sin(42° - 12°) = \sin 30° = \frac{1}{2}.$$

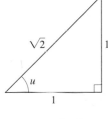

$u = \arctan 1$

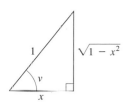

$v = \arccos x$

FIGURE 6.8

EXAMPLE 4   An Application of a Difference Formula

Evaluate $\cos(\arctan 1 + \arccos x)$.

Solution

This expression fits the formula for $\cos(u - v)$. Angles $u = \arctan 1$ and $v = \arccos x$ are shown in Figure 6.8. Therefore,

$$\cos(u - v) = \cos(\arctan 1) \cos(\arccos x) - \sin(\arctan 1) \sin(\arccos x)$$

$$= \frac{1}{\sqrt{2}} \cdot x - \frac{1}{\sqrt{2}} \cdot \sqrt{1 - x^2}$$

$$= \frac{x - \sqrt{1 - x^2}}{\sqrt{2}}.$$

EXAMPLE 5   Proving a Cofunction Identity

Use the formula for $\cos(u - v)$ to prove the cofunction identity

$$\cos\left(\frac{\pi}{2} - x\right) = \sin x.$$

Solution

Using the difference formula $\cos(u - v) = \cos u \cos v + \sin u \sin v$ you have

$$\cos\left(\frac{\pi}{2} - x\right) = \cos \frac{\pi}{2} \cos x + \sin \frac{\pi}{2} \sin x$$

$$= (0) \cos x + (1) \sin x$$

$$= \sin x.$$

Sum and difference formulas can be used to derive **reduction formulas** involving expressions like

$$\sin\left(\theta + \frac{n\pi}{2}\right) \quad \text{and} \quad \cos\left(\theta + \frac{n\pi}{2}\right)$$

where n is an integer.

EXAMPLE 6   Deriving Reduction Formulas

Simplify the expressions.

a. $\cos\left(\theta - \dfrac{3\pi}{2}\right)$ **b.** $\tan(\theta + 3\pi)$

Solution

a. Using the formula $\cos(u - v) = \cos u \cos v + \sin u \sin v$ you have

$$\cos\left(\theta - \frac{3\pi}{2}\right) = \cos \theta \cos \frac{3\pi}{2} + \sin \theta \sin \frac{3\pi}{2}$$

$$= (\cos \theta)(0) + (\sin \theta)(-1)$$

$$= -\sin \theta.$$

b. Using the formula for $\tan(u + v)$, you have

$$\tan(\theta + 3\pi) = \frac{\tan \theta + \tan 3\pi}{1 - \tan \theta \tan 3\pi}$$

$$= \frac{\tan \theta + 0}{1 - (\tan \theta)(0)}$$

$$= \tan \theta.$$

EXAMPLE 7   Solving a Trigonometric Equation

Find all solutions of

$$\sin\left(x + \frac{\pi}{4}\right) + \sin\left(x - \frac{\pi}{4}\right) = -1$$

in the interval $[0, 2\pi)$.

Solution

Using sum and difference formulas, we rewrite the given equation as follows.

$$\sin x \cos \frac{\pi}{4} + \cos x \sin \frac{\pi}{4} + \sin x \cos \frac{\pi}{4} - \cos x \sin \frac{\pi}{4} = -1$$

$$2 \sin x \cos \frac{\pi}{4} = -1$$

$$2(\sin x)\left(\frac{\sqrt{2}}{2}\right) = -1$$

$$\sin x = -\frac{1}{\sqrt{2}}$$

$$\sin x = -\frac{\sqrt{2}}{2}$$

Therefore, the only solutions in the interval $[0, 2\pi)$ are

$$x = \frac{5\pi}{4} \quad \text{and} \quad x = \frac{7\pi}{4}.$$

EXAMPLE 8 An Application from Calculus

Verify that

$$\frac{\sin(x + h) - \sin x}{h} = (\cos x)\left(\frac{\sin h}{h}\right) - (\sin x)\left(\frac{1 - \cos h}{h}\right)$$

where $h \neq 0$.

Solution

Using the formula for $\sin(u + v)$, you have

$$\frac{\sin(x + h) - \sin x}{h} = \frac{\sin x \cos h + \cos x \sin h - \sin x}{h}$$

$$= \frac{\cos x \sin h - \sin x(1 - \cos h)}{h}$$

$$= (\cos x)\left(\frac{\sin h}{h}\right) - (\sin x)\left(\frac{1 - \cos h}{h}\right).$$

DISCUSSION

PROBLEM

Verifying
a Sum
Formula

At the beginning of this section we listed a proof of the formulas for $\cos(u - v)$. Show how you can use this formula together with the identity

$$\sin x = \cos\left(\frac{\pi}{2} - x\right)$$

to prove the formula for $\sin(u + v)$. Start by writing

$$\sin(u + v) = \cos\left(\frac{\pi}{2} - (u + v)\right).$$

WARM UP

The following warm-up exercises involve skills that were covered in earlier sections. You will use these skills in the exercise set for this section.

In Exercises 1–4, use the given information to find $\sin \theta$.

1. $\tan \theta = \frac{1}{3}$, θ in Quadrant I

2. $\cot \theta = \frac{3}{5}$, θ in Quadrant III

3. $\cos \theta = \frac{3}{4}$, θ in Quadrant IV

4. $\sec \theta = -3$, θ in Quadrant II

In Exercises 5 and 6, find all solutions in the interval $[0, 2\pi)$.

5. $\sin x = \dfrac{\sqrt{2}}{2}$

6. $\cos x = 0$

In Exercises 7–10, simplify the expression.

7. $\tan x \sec^2 x - \tan x$

8. $\dfrac{\cos x \csc x}{\tan x}$

9. $\dfrac{\cos x}{1 - \sin x} - \tan x$

10. $\dfrac{\cos^4 x - \sin^4 x}{\cos^2 x}$

EXERCISES for Section 6.4

In Exercises 1–10, use the sum and difference identities to find the exact values of the sine, cosine, and tangent of the angle.

1. $75° = 30° + 45°$

2. $15° = 45° - 30°$

3. $105° = 60° + 45°$

4. $165° = 135° + 30°$

5. $195° = 225° - 30°$

6. $255° = 300° - 45°$

7. $\dfrac{11\pi}{12} = \dfrac{3\pi}{4} + \dfrac{\pi}{6}$

8. $\dfrac{7\pi}{12} = \dfrac{\pi}{3} + \dfrac{\pi}{4}$

9. $\dfrac{17\pi}{12} = \dfrac{9\pi}{4} - \dfrac{5\pi}{6}$

10. $-\dfrac{\pi}{12} = \dfrac{\pi}{6} - \dfrac{\pi}{4}$

In Exercises 11–20, use the sum and difference identities to write the expression as the sine, cosine, or tangent of an angle.

11. $\cos 25° \cos 15° - \sin 25° \sin 15°$

12. $\sin 140° \cos 50° + \cos 140° \sin 50°$

13. $\sin 230° \cos 30° - \cos 230° \sin 30°$

14. $\cos 20° \cos 30° + \sin 20° \sin 30°$

15. $\dfrac{\tan 325° - \tan 86°}{1 + \tan 325° \tan 86°}$

16. $\dfrac{\tan 140° - \tan 60°}{1 + \tan 140° \tan 60°}$

17. $\sin 3 \cos 1.2 - \cos 3 \sin 1.2$

18. $\cos \dfrac{\pi}{7} \cos \dfrac{\pi}{5} - \sin \dfrac{\pi}{7} \sin \dfrac{\pi}{5}$

19. $\dfrac{\tan 2x + \tan x}{1 - \tan 2x \tan x}$

20. $\cos 3x \cos 2y + \sin 3x \sin 2y$

In Exercises 21–24, find the exact value of the trigonometric function given that

$$\sin u = \frac{5}{13}, \ 0 < u < \frac{\pi}{2} \ \text{and} \ \cos v = -\frac{3}{5}, \ \frac{\pi}{2} < v < \pi.$$

21. $\sin(u + v)$

22. $\cos(v - u)$

23. $\cos(v + u)$

24. $\sin(u - v)$

In Exercises 25–28, find the exact value of the trigonometric function given that

$$\sin u = \frac{7}{25}, \frac{\pi}{2} < u < \pi \quad \text{and} \quad \cos v = \frac{4}{5}, \frac{3\pi}{2} < v < 2\pi.$$

25. $\cos(u + v)$

26. $\sin(u + v)$

27. $\sin(v - u)$

28. $\cos(u - v)$

In Exercises 47–50, use the formulas given in Exercises 45 and 46 to write the trigonometric expression in the following forms.

(a) $\sqrt{a^2 + b^2} \sin(B\theta + C)$ **(b)** $\sqrt{a^2 + b^2} \cos(B\theta - C)$

47. $\sin \theta + \cos \theta$

48. $3 \sin 2\theta + 4 \cos 2\theta$

49. $12 \sin 3\theta + 5 \cos 3\theta$

50. $\sin 2\theta - \cos 2\theta$

In Exercises 29–46, verify the identity.

29. $\sin\left(\frac{\pi}{2} + x\right) = \cos x$

30. $\sin(3\pi - x) = \sin x$

31. $\cos\left(\frac{3\pi}{2} - x\right) = -\sin x$

32. $\cos(\pi + x) = -\cos x$

33. $\sin\left(\frac{\pi}{6} + x\right) = \frac{1}{2}(\cos x + \sqrt{3} \sin x)$

34. $\cos\left(\frac{5\pi}{4} - x\right) = -\frac{\sqrt{2}}{2}(\cos x + \sin x)$

35. $\cos(\pi - \theta) + \sin\left(\frac{\pi}{2} + \theta\right) = 0$

36. $\sin\left(\frac{3\pi}{2} + \theta\right) + \sin(\pi - \theta) = \sin \theta - \cos \theta$

37. $\tan(\pi + \theta) = \tan \theta$

38. $\tan\left(\frac{\pi}{4} - \theta\right) = \frac{1 - \tan \theta}{1 + \tan \theta}$

39. $\cos(x + y) \cos(x - y) = \cos^2 x - \sin^2 y$

40. $\sin(x + y) \sin(x - y) = \sin^2 x - \sin^2 y$

41. $\sin(x + y) + \sin(x - y) = 2 \sin x \cos y$

42. $\cos(x + y) + \cos(x - y) = 2 \cos x \cos y$

43. $\cos(n\pi + \theta) = (-1)^n \cos \theta, \quad n$ is an integer

44. $\sin(n\pi + \theta) = (-1)^n \sin \theta, \quad n$ is an integer

45. $a \sin B\theta + b \cos B\theta = \sqrt{a^2 + b^2} \sin(B\theta + C)$, where $C = \arctan \frac{b}{a}, a > 0$

46. $a \sin B\theta + b \cos B\theta = \sqrt{a^2 + b^2} \cos(B\theta - C)$, where $C = \arctan \frac{a}{b}, b > 0$

In Exercises 51 and 52, use the formulas given in Exercises 45 and 46 to write the trigonometric expression in the form $a \sin B\theta + b \cos B\theta$.

51. $2 \sin\left(\theta + \frac{\pi}{4}\right)$

52. $5 \cos\left(\theta + \frac{3\pi}{4}\right)$

In Exercises 53 and 54, write the trigonometric expression as an algebraic expression.

53. $\sin(\arcsin x + \arccos x)$

54. $\sin(\arctan 2x - \arccos x)$

In Exercises 55–60, find all solutions in the interval $[0, 2\pi)$.

55. $\sin\left(x + \frac{\pi}{3}\right) + \sin\left(x - \frac{\pi}{3}\right) = 1$

56. $\sin\left(x + \frac{\pi}{6}\right) - \sin\left(x - \frac{\pi}{6}\right) = \frac{1}{2}$

57. $\cos\left(x + \frac{\pi}{4}\right) + \cos\left(x - \frac{\pi}{4}\right) = 1$

58. $\cos\left(x + \frac{\pi}{4}\right) - \cos\left(x - \frac{\pi}{4}\right) = 1$

59. $\tan(x + \pi) + 2 \sin(x + \pi) = 0$

60. $\tan(x + \pi) - \cos\left(x + \frac{\pi}{2}\right) = 0$

61. *Standing Waves*   The equation of a standing wave is obtained by adding the displacements of two waves traveling in opposite directions (see figure). Assume that each of the waves has amplitude A, period T, and wavelength λ. If the models for these waves are

$$y_1 = A \cos 2\pi\left(\frac{t}{T} - \frac{x}{\lambda}\right) \quad \text{and} \quad y_2 = A \cos 2\pi\left(\frac{t}{T} + \frac{x}{\lambda}\right)$$

show that

$$y_1 + y_2 = 2A \cos \frac{2\pi t}{T} \cos \frac{2\pi x}{\lambda}.$$

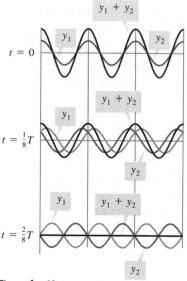

Figure for 61

62. *Harmonic Motion*   A weight is attached to a spring suspended vertically from the ceiling. When a driving force is applied to the system, the weight moves vertically from its equilibrium position. This motion is described by the model

$$y = \tfrac{1}{3}\sin 2t + \tfrac{1}{4}\cos 2t$$

where y is the distance from equilibrium measured in feet and t is the time in seconds.

(a) Write the model in the form

$$y = \sqrt{a^2 + b^2}\, \sin(Bt + C).$$

(See Exercise 45.)

(b) Find the amplitude of the oscillations of the weight.

(c) Find the frequency of the oscillations of the weight.

63. Verify the following identity used in calculus.

$$\frac{\cos(x + h) - \cos x}{h} = \cos x\left(\frac{\cos h - 1}{h}\right) - \sin x\left(\frac{\sin h}{h}\right)$$

64. Use the sum formulas for the sine and cosine to derive the formula

$$\tan(u + v) = \frac{\tan u + \tan v}{1 - \tan u \tan v}.$$

6.5 ▸ Multiple-Angle and Product-Sum Formulas

Multiple-Angle Formulas / Power-Reducing Formulas / Half-Angle Formulas / Product-to-Sum Formulas

Multiple-Angle Formulas

In this section we look at four other categories of trigonometric identities. The first category involves functions of multiple angles such as $\sin ku$ and $\cos ku$. The second category involves squares of trigonometric functions such as $\sin^2 u$. The third involves functions of half-angles such as $\sin u/2$, and the fourth category involves products of trigonometric functions such as $\sin u \cos v$.

The most commonly used multiple-angle formulas are the double-angle formulas. They are used often, so you should learn them.

DOUBLE-ANGLE FORMULAS

$$\sin 2u = 2 \sin u \cos u$$

$$\cos 2u = \cos^2 u - \sin^2 u = 2 \cos^2 u - 1 = 1 - 2 \sin^2 u$$

$$\tan 2u = \frac{2 \tan u}{1 - \tan^2 u}$$

Proof

To prove the first formula, we let $v = u$ in the formula for $\sin(u + v)$, and obtain

$$\sin 2u = \sin(u + u)$$

$$= \sin u \cos u + \cos u \sin u$$

$$= 2 \sin u \cos u.$$

REMARK Note that $\sin 2u \neq 2 \sin u$. Similar statements can be made for $\cos 2u$ and $\tan 2u$.

The other double-angle formulas can be proved in a similar way, and we leave their proofs for you to do. ◢

EXAMPLE 1 Solving a Trigonometric Equation

Find all solutions of $2 \cos x + \sin 2x = 0$.

Solution

Begin by rewriting the equation so that it involves functions of x (rather than $2x$). Then factor and solve as usual.

$$2 \cos x + \sin 2x = 0 \qquad \textit{Given equation}$$

$$2 \cos x + 2 \sin x \cos x = 0 \qquad \textit{Double-angle formula}$$

$$2 \cos x(1 + \sin x) = 0 \qquad \textit{Factor}$$

$$\cos x = 0, \qquad 1 + \sin x = 0 \qquad \textit{Set factors to zero}$$

$$x = \frac{\pi}{2}, \frac{3\pi}{2} \qquad\qquad x = \frac{3\pi}{2} \qquad \textit{Solutions in } [0, 2\pi)$$

Therefore, the general solution is

$$x = \frac{\pi}{2} + 2n\pi \qquad \text{and} \qquad x = \frac{3\pi}{2} + 2n\pi$$

where n is an integer. ◢

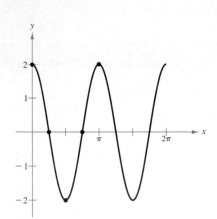

FIGURE 6.9

EXAMPLE 2   Using Double-Angle Formulas in Sketching Graphs

Sketch the graph of $y = 4 \cos^2 x - 2$ over the interval $[0, 2\pi]$.

Solution

Using a double angle identity, you can rewrite the given function as

$$y = 4 \cos^2 x - 2 = 2(2 \cos^2 - 1) = 2 \cos 2x.$$

Using the techniques discussed in Section 5.5, you will recognize that the graph of this function has an amplitude of 2 and a period of π. The key points in the interval $[0, \pi]$ are as follows.

Maximum	Intercept	Minimum	Intercept	Maximum
$(0, 2)$	$\left(\dfrac{\pi}{4}, 0\right)$	$\left(\dfrac{\pi}{2}, -2\right)$	$\left(\dfrac{3\pi}{4}, 0\right)$	$(\pi, 2)$

Two cycles of the graph are shown in Figure 6.9.

EXAMPLE 3   Evaluating Functions Involving Double Angles

Use the fact that

$$\cos \theta = \frac{5}{13}, \quad \frac{3\pi}{2} < \theta < 2\pi$$

to find $\sin 2\theta$, $\cos 2\theta$, and $\tan 2\theta$.

Solution

From Figure 6.10, you can see that $\sin \theta = y/r = -12/13$. Consequently, you can write the following.

$$\sin 2\theta = 2 \sin \theta \cos \theta = 2\left(\frac{-12}{13}\right)\left(\frac{5}{13}\right) = -\frac{120}{169}$$

$$\cos 2\theta = 2 \cos^2 \theta - 1 = 2\left(\frac{25}{169}\right) - 1 = -\frac{119}{169}$$

$$\tan 2\theta = \frac{\sin 2\theta}{\cos 2\theta} = \frac{120}{119}$$

The double-angle formulas are not restricted to angles 2θ and θ. Other *double* combinations like 4θ and 2θ or 6θ and 3θ are also valid. Here are a couple of examples.

$$\sin 4\theta = 2 \sin 2\theta \cos 2\theta \quad \text{and} \quad \cos 6\theta = \cos^2 3\theta - \sin^2 3\theta$$

By using double-angle formulas together with the sum formulas derived in the previous section, you can form other multiple-angle formulas.

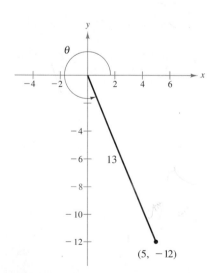

FIGURE 6.10

EXAMPLE 4   Deriving a Triple-Angle Formula

Express $\sin 3x$ in terms of $\sin x$.

Solution

$$
\begin{aligned}
\sin 3x &= \sin(2x + x) \qquad\qquad\qquad 3x = 2x + x\\
&= \sin 2x \cos x + \cos 2x \sin x\\
&= 2 \sin x \cos x \cos x + (1 - 2 \sin^2 x) \sin x\\
&= 2 \sin x \cos^2 x + \sin x - 2 \sin^3 x\\
&= 2 \sin x(1 - \sin^2 x) + \sin x - 2 \sin^3 x\\
&= 2 \sin x - 2 \sin^3 x + \sin x - 2 \sin^3 x\\
&= 3 \sin x - 4 \sin\ x
\end{aligned}
$$

Power-Reducing Formulas

The double-angle formulas can be used to obtain the following **power-reducing formulas**.

POWER-REDUCING FORMULAS

$$
\sin^2 u = \frac{1 - \cos 2u}{2} \qquad \cos^2 u = \frac{1 + \cos 2u}{2} \qquad \tan^2 u = \frac{1 - \cos 2u}{1 + \cos 2u}
$$

Proof

The first two formulas can be verified by solving for $\sin^2 u$ and $\cos^2 u$, respectively, in the double-angle formulas

$$
\cos 2u = 1 - 2 \sin^2 u \qquad \text{and} \qquad \cos 2u = 2 \cos^2 u - 1.
$$

The third formula can be verified using the fact that

$$
\tan^2 u = \frac{\sin^2 u}{\cos^2 u}.
$$

Example 5 shows a typical power reduction that is used in calculus.

EXAMPLE 5   Reducing the Power of a Trigonometric Function

Rewrite $\sin^4 x$ as a sum involving first powers of the cosine of multiple angles.

Solution

Note the repeated use of power-reducing formulas in the following procedure.

$$\sin^4 x = (\sin^2 x)^2 = \left(\frac{1 - \cos 2x}{2}\right)^2$$

$$= \frac{1}{4}(1 - 2\cos 2x + \cos^2 2x)$$

$$= \frac{1}{4}\left(1 - 2\cos 2x + \frac{1 + \cos 4x}{2}\right)$$

$$= \frac{1}{4} - \frac{1}{2}\cos 2x + \frac{1}{8} + \frac{1}{8}\cos 4x$$

$$= \frac{3}{8} - \frac{1}{2}\cos 2x + \frac{1}{8}\cos 4x$$

$$= \frac{1}{8}(3 - 4\cos 2x + \cos 4x)$$

Half-Angle Formulas

We can derive some useful alternative forms of the power-reducing formulas by replacing u with $u/2$. The results are **half-angle formulas.**

HALF-ANGLE FORMULAS

$$\sin\frac{u}{2} = \pm\sqrt{\frac{1 - \cos u}{2}}$$

$$\cos\frac{u}{2} = \pm\sqrt{\frac{1 + \cos u}{2}}$$

$$\tan\frac{u}{2} = \frac{1 - \cos u}{\sin u} = \frac{\sin u}{1 + \cos u}$$

The signs of $\sin u/2$ and $\cos u/2$ depend on the quadrant in which $u/2$ lies.

EXAMPLE 6   Using a Half-Angle Formula

Find the exact value of sin 105°.

Solution

Begin by noting that 105° is half of 210°. Then, using the half-angle formula for $\sin(u/2)$ and the fact that 105° lies in Quadrant II, you have

$$\sin 105° = \sqrt{\frac{1 - \cos 210°}{2}}$$

$$= \sqrt{\frac{1 - (-\cos 30°)}{2}}$$

$$= \sqrt{\frac{1 + (\sqrt{3}/2)}{2}}$$

$$= \frac{\sqrt{2 + \sqrt{3}}}{2}.$$

REMARK Use your calculator to verify the result obtained in Example 6. That is, evaluate sin 105° and $\sqrt{2 + \sqrt{3}}/2$ and you will see that both values are approximately 0.9659258.

We chose the positive square root because sin θ is positive in Quadrant II.

EXAMPLE 7   Solving a Trigonometric Equation

Find all solutions of $2 - \sin^2 x = 2 \cos^2 \frac{x}{2}$.

Solution

$$2 - \sin^2 x = 2 \cos^2 \frac{x}{2} \qquad \textit{Given equation}$$

$$2 - \sin^2 x = 2\left(\frac{1 + \cos x}{2}\right) \qquad \textit{Half angle formula}$$

$$2 - \sin^2 x = 1 + \cos x \qquad \textit{Simplify}$$

$$2 - (1 - \cos^2 x) = 1 + \cos x \qquad \textit{Pythagorean identity}$$

$$\cos^2 x - \cos x = 0 \qquad \textit{Simplify}$$

$$\cos x(\cos x - 1) = 0 \qquad \textit{Factor}$$

By setting the factor cos x and (cos $x - 1$) equal to zero, you find that the solutions in the interval $[0, 2\pi)$ are $x = \pi/2$, $x = 3\pi/2$, and $x = 0$. Therefore, the general solution is

$$x = 2n\pi, \qquad x = \frac{\pi}{2} + 2n\pi, \qquad \text{and} \qquad x = \frac{3\pi}{2} + 2n\pi$$

where n is an integer.

Product-to-Sum Formulas

Each of the following **product-to-sum formulas** are easily verified using the sum and difference formulas discussed in the preceding section.

PRODUCT-TO-SUM FORMULAS

$$\sin u \sin v = \frac{1}{2}[\cos(u - v) - \cos(u + v)]$$

$$\cos u \cos v = \frac{1}{2}[\cos(u - v) + \cos(u + v)]$$

$$\sin u \cos v = \frac{1}{2}[\sin(u + v) + \sin(u - v)]$$

$$\cos u \sin v = \frac{1}{2}[\sin(u + v) - \sin(u - v)]$$

EXAMPLE 8 Writing Products as Sums

Rewrite $\cos 5x \sin 4x$ as a sum or difference.

Solution

$$\cos 5x \sin 4x = \frac{1}{2}[\sin(5x + 4x) - \sin(5x - 4x)] = \frac{1}{2}\sin 9x - \frac{1}{2}\sin x$$

Occasionally, it is useful to reverse the procedure and write a sum of trigonometric functions as a product. This can be accomplished with the following **sum-to-product formulas.**

SUM-TO-PRODUCT FORMULAS

$$\sin x + \sin y = 2 \sin\left(\frac{x + y}{2}\right) \cos\left(\frac{x - y}{2}\right)$$

$$\sin x - \sin y = 2 \cos\left(\frac{x + y}{2}\right) \sin\left(\frac{x - y}{2}\right)$$

$$\cos x + \cos y = 2 \cos\left(\frac{x + y}{2}\right) \cos\left(\frac{x - y}{2}\right)$$

$$\cos x - \cos y = -2 \sin\left(\frac{x + y}{2}\right) \sin\left(\frac{x - y}{2}\right)$$

Proof

To prove the first formula, we let $x = u + v$ and $y = u - v$. Then, substituting $u = (x + y)/2$ and $v = (x - y)/2$ in the product-to-sum formula

$$\sin u \cos v = \frac{1}{2}[\sin(u + v) + \sin(u - v)]$$

we get

$$\sin\left(\frac{x+y}{2}\right)\cos\left(\frac{x-y}{2}\right) = \frac{1}{2}(\sin x + \sin y)$$

or equivalently,

$$\sin x + \sin y = 2\sin\left(\frac{x+y}{2}\right)\cos\left(\frac{x-y}{2}\right).$$

▲

EXAMPLE 9   Using a Sum-to-Product Formula

Find the exact value of $\cos 195° + \cos 105°$.

Solution

Using the appropriate sum-to-product formula, you obtain

$$\cos 195° + \cos 105° = 2\cos\left(\frac{195° + 105°}{2}\right)\cos\left(\frac{195° - 105°}{2}\right)$$

$$= 2\cos 150° \cos 45°$$

$$= 2\left(-\frac{\sqrt{3}}{2}\right)\left(\frac{\sqrt{2}}{2}\right) = -\frac{\sqrt{6}}{2}.$$

▲

EXAMPLE 10   Solving a Trigonometric Equation

Find all solutions of $\sin 5x + \sin 3x = 0$.

Solution

$$\sin 5x + \sin 3x = 0 \quad \text{\textit{Given equation}}$$

$$2\sin\left(\frac{5x + 3x}{2}\right)\cos\left(\frac{5x - 3x}{2}\right) = 0 \quad \text{\textit{Sum-to-product formula}}$$

$$2\sin 4x \cos x = 0 \quad \text{\textit{Simplify}}$$

By setting the factor $\sin 4x$ equal to zero, you find that the solutions in the interval $[0, 2\pi)$ are

$$x = 0, \frac{\pi}{4}, \frac{\pi}{2}, \frac{3\pi}{4}, \pi, \frac{5\pi}{4}, \frac{3\pi}{2}, \frac{7\pi}{4}.$$

Moreover, the equation $\cos x = 0$ yields no additional solutions, and you can conclude that the solutions are of the form

$$x = \frac{n\pi}{4}$$

where n is an integer.

▲

EXAMPLE 11   Verifying a Trigonometric Identity

Verify the identity

$$\frac{\sin t + \sin 3t}{\cos t + \cos 3t} = \tan 2t.$$

Solution

Using appropriate sum-to-product formulas, you have

$$\frac{\sin t + \sin 3t}{\cos t + \cos 3t} = \frac{2 \sin 2t \cos(-t)}{2 \cos 2t \cos(-t)} = \frac{\sin 2t}{\cos 2t} = \tan 2t.$$

DISCUSSION
PROBLEM

Deriving a
Triple-Angle
Formula

In Example 4, we showed how to derive a formula for $\sin 3x$. Show how you can derive a similar formula for $\cos 3x$. That is, find a formula that expresses $\cos 3x$ in terms of $\cos x$.

WARM UP

The following warm-up exercises involve skills that were covered in earlier sections. You will use these skills in the exercise set for this section.

In Exercises 1 and 2, factor the trigonometric expression.

1. $2 \sin x + \sin x \cos x$ **2.** $\cos^2 x - \cos x - 2$

In Exercises 3–6, find all solutions of the equation in the interval $[0, 2\pi)$.

3. $\sin 2x = 0$ **4.** $\cos 2x = 0$

5. $\cos \frac{x}{2} = 0$ **6.** $\sin \frac{x}{2} = 0$

In Exercises 7–10, simplify the expression.

7. $\frac{1 - \cos(\pi/4)}{2}$ **8.** $\frac{1 + \cos(\pi/3)}{2}$

9. $\frac{2 \sin 3x \cos x}{2 \cos 3x \cos x}$

10. $(1 - 2 \sin^2 x) \cos x - 2 \sin^2 x \cos x$

98. *Projectile Moti*
angle θ with the
v_0 feet per secon

$r = \frac{1}{32}v_0 \sin 2\theta$

where r is meas
the range in term

REVIEW EXER

In Exercises 1–10,

1. $\dfrac{1}{\cot^2 x + 1}$

3. $\dfrac{\sin^2 \alpha - \cos^2}{\sin^2 \alpha - \sin \alpha \,}$

5. $\cos^2 \beta + \cos^2 \beta$

6. $\dfrac{\sin \theta}{1 + \cos \theta} + \dfrac{1}{}$

7. $\tan^2 \theta(\csc^2 \theta -$

8. $\dfrac{2 \tan(x + 1)}{1 - \tan^2(x + 1)}$

9. $1 - 4 \sin^2 x \cos$

10. $\sqrt{\dfrac{1 - \cos^2 x}{1 + \cos x}}$

In Exercises 11–36,

11. $\tan x(1 - \sin^2 x)$

12. $\cos x(\tan^2 x + 1$

13. $\sec^2 x \cot x - c$

14. $\sin^3 \theta + \sin \theta \, c$

15. $\sin^5 x \cos^2 x = ($

16. $\cos^3 x \sin^2 x = ($

17. $\sin 3\theta \sin \theta = \frac{1}{2}$

18. $\sin 3x \cos 2x =$

19. $\sqrt{\dfrac{1 - \sin \theta}{1 + \sin \theta}} =$

20. $\sqrt{1 - \cos x} =$

21. $\cos 3x = 4 \cos^3$

22. $\sin 4x = 8 \cos^3$

23. $\sin\left(x - \dfrac{3\pi}{2}\right) =$

EXERCISES for Section 6.5

In Exercises 1–10, find all solutions of the equation in the interval $[0, 2\pi)$.

1. $\sin 2x - \sin x = 0$
2. $\sin 2x + \cos x = 0$
3. $4 \sin x \cos x = 1$
4. $\sin 2x \sin x = \cos x$
5. $\cos 2x - \cos x = 0$
6. $\cos 2x + \sin x = 0$
7. $\tan 2x - \cot x = 0$
8. $\tan 2x - 2 \cos x = 0$
9. $\sin 4x + 2 \sin 2x = 0$
10. $(\sin 2x + \cos 2x)^2 = 1$

In Exercises 11–14, use a double-angle identity to rewrite the function and sketch its graph.

11. $f(x) = 6 \sin x \cos x$
12. $g(x) = 4 \sin x \cos x + 2$
13. $g(x) = 4 - 8 \sin^2 x$
14. $f(x) = (\cos x + \sin x)(\cos x - \sin x)$

In Exercises 15–20, find the exact values of $\sin 2u$, $\cos 2u$, and $\tan 2u$ by using the double-angle formulas.

15. $\sin u = \dfrac{3}{5}, \quad 0 < u < \dfrac{\pi}{2}$

16. $\cos u = -\dfrac{2}{3}, \quad \dfrac{\pi}{2} < u < \pi$

17. $\tan u = \dfrac{1}{2}, \quad \pi < u < \dfrac{3\pi}{2}$

18. $\cot u = -4, \quad \dfrac{3\pi}{2} < u < 2\pi$

19. $\sec u = -\dfrac{5}{2}, \quad \dfrac{\pi}{2} < u < \pi$

20. $\csc u = 3, \quad \dfrac{\pi}{2} < u < \pi$

In Exercises 21–26, use the power-reducing formulas to write the expression in terms of the first power of the cosine.

21. $\cos^4 x$
22. $\sin^4 x$
23. $\sin^2 x \cos^2 x$
24. $\cos^6 x$
25. $\sin^2 x \cos^4 x$
26. $\sin^4 x \cos^2 x$

In Exercises 27–32, use the half-angle formulas to determine the exact values of the sine, cosine, and tangent of the given angle.

27. $105°$
28. $165°$
29. $112° \, 30'$
30. $67° \, 30'$
31. $\dfrac{\pi}{8}$
32. $\dfrac{\pi}{12}$

In Exercises 33–38, find the exact values of $\sin(u/2)$, $\cos(u/2)$, and $\tan(u/2)$ by using the half-angle formulas.

33. $\sin u = \dfrac{5}{13}, \quad \dfrac{\pi}{2} < u < \pi$

34. $\cos u = \dfrac{3}{5}, \quad 0 < u < \dfrac{\pi}{2}$

35. $\tan u = -\dfrac{5}{8}, \quad \dfrac{3\pi}{2} < u < 2\pi$

36. $\cot u = 3, \quad \pi < u < \dfrac{3\pi}{2}$

37. $\csc u = -\dfrac{5}{3}, \quad \pi < u < \dfrac{3\pi}{2}$

38. $\sec u = -\dfrac{7}{2}, \quad \dfrac{\pi}{2} < u < \pi$

In Exercises 39–42, use a half-angle formula or a power-reducing formula to simplify the expression.

39. $\sqrt{\dfrac{1 - \cos 6x}{2}}$
40. $\sqrt{\dfrac{1 + \cos 4x}{2}}$

41. $-\sqrt{\dfrac{1 - \cos 8x}{1 + \cos 8x}}$
42. $-\sqrt{\dfrac{1 - \cos(x - 1)}{2}}$

In Exercises 43–46, find all solutions of the equation in the interval $[0, 2\pi)$.

43. $\sin \dfrac{x}{2} + \cos x = 0$
44. $\sin \dfrac{x}{2} + \cos x = 1$

45. $\cos \dfrac{x}{2} - \sin x = 0$
46. $\tan \dfrac{x}{2} - \sin x = 0$

In Exercises 47–56, use the product-to-sum formulas to write the product as a sum.

47. $6 \sin \dfrac{\pi}{4} \cos \dfrac{\pi}{4}$
48. $4 \sin \dfrac{\pi}{3} \cos \dfrac{5\pi}{6}$

49. $\sin 5\theta \cos 3\theta$
50. $3 \sin 2\alpha \sin 3\alpha$

51. $5 \cos(-5\beta) \cos 3\beta$
52. $\cos 2\theta \cos 4\theta$

53. $\sin(x + y) \sin(x - y)$
54. $\sin(x + y) \cos(x - y)$

55. $\sin(\theta + \pi) \cos(\theta - \pi)$
56. $10 \cos 75° \cos 15°$

In Exercises 5
write the sum

57. sin 60° +

59. $\cos \dfrac{3\pi}{4} -$

61. $\cos 6x + $

63. $\sin(\alpha + \beta)$

64. $\cos\left(\theta + \dfrac{\pi}{2}\right.$

65. $\cos(\phi + 2$

66. $\sin\left(x + \dfrac{\pi}{2}\right.$

In Exercises 67
interval $[0, 2\pi$

67. $\sin 6x + $

69. $\dfrac{\cos 2x}{\sin 3x - }$

In Exercises 71

71. $\csc 2\theta = $

73. $\cos^2 2\alpha - $

74. $\cos^4 x - $

75. $(\sin x + c$

76. $\sin \dfrac{\alpha}{3} \cos $

77. $\cos 3\beta = $

78. $\sin 4\beta = 4$

79. $1 + \cos 1$

80. $\dfrac{\cos 3\beta}{\cos \beta} = $

81. $\sec \dfrac{u}{2} = \pm$

82. $\tan \dfrac{u}{2} = cs$

83. $\dfrac{\cos 4x + }{\sin 4x + }$

84. $\dfrac{\cos 3x - }{\sin 3x - }$

85. $\dfrac{\cos 4x - }{2 \sin 3}$

86. $\dfrac{\sin x \pm si}{\sin x + co}$

REMARK   The Law of Sines can also be written in the reciprocal form

$$\frac{\sin A}{a} = \frac{\sin B}{b} = \frac{\sin C}{c}.$$

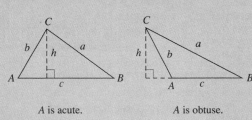

LAW OF SINES

If ABC is a triangle with sides a, b, and c, then

$$\frac{a}{\sin A} = \frac{b}{\sin B} = \frac{c}{\sin C}.$$

A is acute.   *A* is obtuse.

Oblique Triangles

Proof

Let h be the altitude of either triangle found in the figure showing oblique triangles, above. Then we have

$$\sin A = \frac{h}{b} \quad \text{or} \quad h = b \sin A$$

$$\sin B = \frac{h}{a} \quad \text{or} \quad h = a \sin B.$$

Equating these two values of h, we have

$$a \sin B = b \sin A \quad \text{or} \quad \frac{a}{\sin A} = \frac{b}{\sin B}.$$

Note that $\sin A \neq 0$ and $\sin B \neq 0$ because no angle of a triangle can have a measure of 0° or 180°. In a similar manner, by constructing an altitude from vertex B to side AC (extended), we can show that

$$\frac{a}{\sin A} = \frac{c}{\sin C}.$$

Hence, the Law of Sines is established.   ◢

When using a calculator with the Law of Sines, remember to store all intermediate calculations. By not rounding until the final result, you minimize the round-off error.

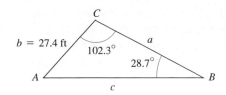

$b = 27.4$ ft

FIGURE 7.2

EXAMPLE 1   Given Two Angles and One Side—AAS

Given a triangle with $C = 102.3°$, $B = 28.7°$, and $b = 27.4$ feet, as shown in Figure 7.2, find the remaining angle and sides.

Solution

The third angle of the triangle is

$$A = 180° - B - C = 180° - 28.7° - 102.3° = 49.0°.$$

By the Law of Sines, you have

$$\frac{a}{\sin 49°} = \frac{b}{\sin 28.7°} = \frac{c}{\sin 102.3°}.$$

Because $b = 27.4$, you obtain

$$a = \frac{27.4}{\sin 28.7°}(\sin 49°) \approx 43.06 \text{ feet}$$

and

$$c = \frac{27.4}{\sin 28.7°}(\sin 102.3°) \approx 55.75 \text{ feet.}$$

Note that the ratio $(27.4)/(\sin 28.7°)$ occurs in both solutions, and you can save time by storing this result for repeated use.   ◢

When solving triangles, a careful sketch is useful as a quick test for the feasibility of an answer. Remember that the longest side lies opposite the largest angle, and the shortest side lies opposite the smallest angle of a triangle.

EXAMPLE 2   Given Two Angles and One Side—ASA

A pole tilts *toward* the sun at an 8° angle from vertical, and it casts a 22-foot shadow. The angle of elevation from the tip of the shadow to the top of the pole is 43°. How tall is the pole?

Solution

From Figure 7.3, note that $A = 43°$, and $B = 90° + 8° = 98°$. Thus, the third angle is

$$C = 180° - A - B = 180° - 43° - 98° = 39°.$$

By the Law of Sines, you have

$$\frac{a}{\sin 43°} = \frac{c}{\sin 39°}.$$

Because $c = 22$ feet, the length of the pole is

$$a = \frac{22}{\sin 39°}(\sin 43°) \approx 23.84 \text{ feet.}$$ ◢

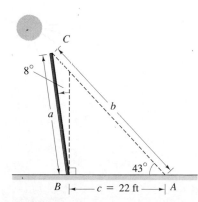

FIGURE 7.3

REMARK   For practice, try reworking Example 2 for a pole that tilts *away* from the sun under the same conditions.

The Ambiguous Case (SSA)

In Examples 1 and 2 you saw that two angles (whose sum is less than 180°) and one side determine a unique triangle. However, if two sides and one opposite angle are given, three possible situations can occur: (1) no such triangle exists, (2) one such triangle exists, or (3) two distinct triangles may satisfy the conditions. The possibilities in this *ambiguous* case (SSA) are summarized in the following table.

The ambiguous case (SSA) (given: *a*, *b*, and *A*)

	A Is Acute				A Is Obtuse	
Sketch ($h = b \sin A$)	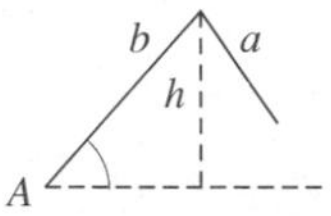	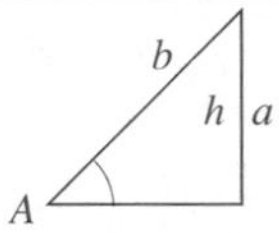	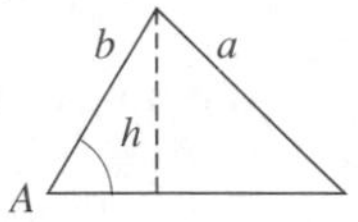	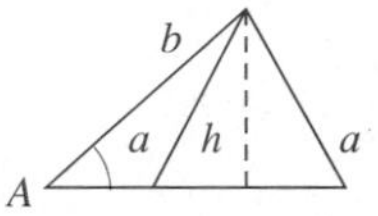	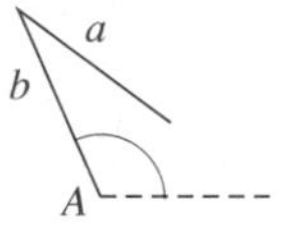	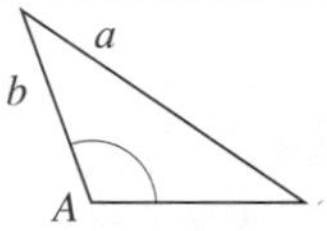
Necessary Condition	$a < h$	$a = h$	$a > b$	$h < a < b$	$a \le b$	$a > b$
Triangles Possible	None	One	One	Two	None	One

In order to determine which of the possibilities hold for a given pair of sides and opposite angles, we suggest that you make a sketch.

EXAMPLE 3   Single-Solution Case—SSA

Given a triangle with $a = 22$ inches, $b = 12$ inches, and $A = 42°$, find the remaining side and angles.

Solution

Since A is acute and $a > b$, you know that B is acute and there is only one triangle that satisfies the given conditions, as shown in Figure 7.4. Thus, by the Law of Sines, you have

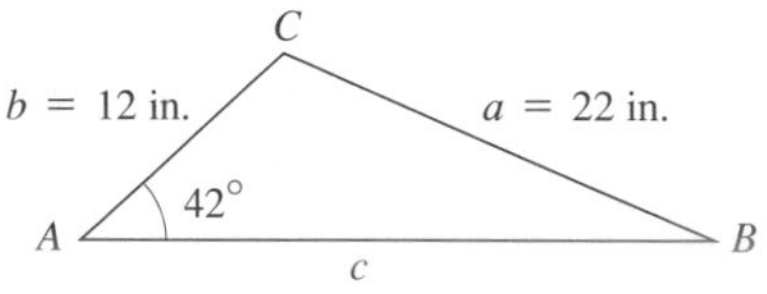

$$\frac{22}{\sin 42°} = \frac{12}{\sin B}$$

which implies that

$$\sin B = 12\left(\frac{\sin 42°}{22}\right) \approx 0.3649803$$

$$B \approx 21.41°. \qquad \qquad \textit{B is acute}$$

$b = 12$ in. $a = 22$ in.

$42°$

One solution: $a > b$

FIGURE 7.4

Now you can determine that $C \approx 180° - 42° - 21.41° = 116.59°$, and the remaining side is given by

$$\frac{c}{\sin 116.59°} = \frac{22}{\sin 42°}$$

$$c = \sin 116.59° \left(\frac{22}{\sin 42°}\right) \approx 29.40 \text{ inches.}$$

EXAMPLE 4   No-Solution Case—SSA

Show that there is no triangle that satisfies either of the following conditions.

a. $a = 15$, $b = 25$, $A = 85°$
b. $a = 15.2$, $b = 20$, $A = 110°$

Solution

a. Begin by making the sketch shown in Figure 7.5. From this figure it appears that no triangle is formed. You can verify this using the Law of Sines.

$$\frac{a}{\sin A} = \frac{b}{\sin B}$$

$$\frac{15}{\sin 85°} = \frac{25}{\sin B}$$

$$\sin B = 25\left(\frac{\sin 85°}{15}\right) \approx 1.660 > 1$$

This contradicts the fact that $|\sin B| \leq 1$. Hence, no triangle can be formed having sides $a = 15$ and $b = 25$ and an angle of $A = 85°$.

b. Because A is obtuse and $a = 15.2$ is less than $b = 20$, you conclude that there is *no solution*, as shown in Figure 7.6. Try using the Law of Sines to verify this.

EXAMPLE 5   Two-Solution Case—SSA

Find two triangles for which $a = 12$ meters, $b = 31$ meters, and $A = 20.5°$.

Solution

To begin, note that

$$h = b \sin A = 31(\sin 20.5°) \approx 10.86 \text{ meters.}$$

Hence, $h < a < b$ and you conclude that there are two possible triangles. By the Law of Sines, you obtain

$$\frac{a}{\sin A} = \frac{b}{\sin B}$$

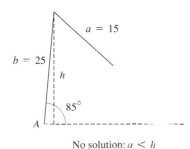

$a = 15$

$b = 25$

h

$85°$

A

No solution: $a < h$

FIGURE 7.5

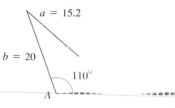

$a = 15.2$

$b = 20$

$110°$

A

No solution: $a < b$ and $A > 90°$

FIGURE 7.6

which implies that

$$\sin B = b\left(\frac{\sin A}{a}\right) = 31\left(\frac{\sin 20.5°}{12}\right) \approx 0.9047.$$

There are two angles $B_1 \approx 64.8°$ and $B_2 \approx 115.2°$ between $0°$ and $180°$ whose sine is 0.9047. For $B_1 \approx 64.8°$, you obtain

$$C \approx 180° - 20.5° - 64.8° = 94.7°$$

$$c = \frac{a}{\sin A}(\sin C) = \frac{12}{\sin 20.5°}(\sin 94.7°) \approx 34.15 \text{ meters.}$$

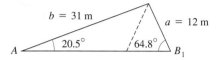

FIGURE 7.7

For $B_2 \approx 115.2°$, you obtain

$$C \approx 180° - 20.5° - 115.2° = 44.3°$$

$$c = \frac{a}{\sin A}(\sin C) = \frac{12}{\sin 20.5°}(\sin 44.3°) \approx 23.93 \text{ meters.}$$

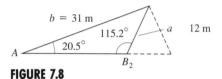

FIGURE 7.8

The resulting triangles are shown in Figures 7.7 and 7.8.   ◣

Applications

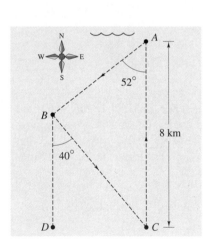

FIGURE 7.9

EXAMPLE 6   An Application of the Law of Sines

The course for a boat race starts at point A and proceeds in the direction S $52°$ W to point B, then in the direction S $40°$ E to point C, and finally back to A, as shown in Figure 7.9. The point C lies 8 kilometers directly south of point A. Approximate the total distance of the race course.

Solution

Because lines BD and AC are parallel, it follows that $\angle BCA = \angle DBC$. Consequently, triangle ABC has the measures shown in Figure 7.10. For angle B, you have

$$B = 180° - 52° - 40° = 88°.$$

Thus, using the Law of Sines,

$$\frac{a}{\sin 52°} = \frac{b}{\sin 88°} = \frac{c}{\sin 40°},$$

let $b = 8$ and obtain the following.

$$a = \frac{8}{\sin 88°}(\sin 52°) \approx 6.308$$

$$c = \frac{8}{\sin 88°}(\sin 40°) \approx 5.145$$

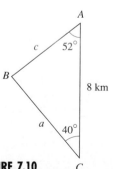

FIGURE 7.10

Finally, the total length of the course is approximately

$$\text{Length} \approx 8 + 6.308 + 5.145 = 19.453 \text{ kilometers.}$$ ◣

Area of an Oblique Triangle

The procedure used to prove the Law of Sines leads to a simple formula for the area of an oblique triangle. Referring to Figure 7.11, note that each triangle has a height of

$$h = b \sin A.$$

Consequently, the area of each triangle is given by

$$\text{Area} = \frac{1}{2}(\text{base})(\text{height}) = \frac{1}{2}(c)(b \sin A) = \frac{1}{2}bc \sin A.$$

By similar arguments, we can develop the formulas

$$\text{Area} = \frac{1}{2}ab \sin C = \frac{1}{2}ac \sin B.$$

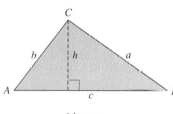

A is acute.   A is obtuse.

FIGURE 7.11

Oblique Triangles

REMARK Note that if angle A is 90°, then the formula gives the area for a right triangle as

$$\text{Area} = \frac{1}{2}bc = \frac{1}{2}(\text{base})(\text{height}).$$

Similar results are obtained for C and B equal to 90°.

AREA OF AN OBLIQUE TRIANGLE

The area of any triangle is given by one-half the product of the lengths of two sides times the sine of their included angle. That is,

$$\text{Area} = \frac{1}{2}bc \sin A = \frac{1}{2}ab \sin C = \frac{1}{2}ac \sin B.$$

EXAMPLE 7 Finding the Area of an Oblique Triangle

Find the area of a triangular lot having two sides of lengths 90 meters and 52 meters and an included angle of 102°.

Solution

Consider $a = 90$ m, $b = 52$ m, and angle $C = 102°$, as shown in Figure 7.12. Then the area of the triangle is

$$\text{Area} = \frac{1}{2}ab \sin C = \frac{1}{2}(90)(52)(\sin 102°) \approx 2289 \text{ square meters.}$$

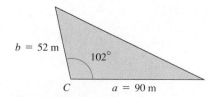

FIGURE 7.12

DISCUSSION
PROBLEM

Solving
Right
Triangles

In this section, we have been using the Law of Sines to solve *oblique* triangles. Can the Law of Sines also be used to solve a right triangle? If so, write a short paragraph explaining how to use the Law of Sines to solve the following two triangles. Is there an easier way to solve the triangles?

1. (AAS)

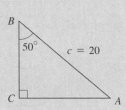

2. (ASA)

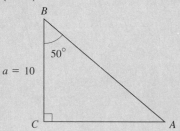

WARM UP

The following warm-up exercises involve skills that were covered in earlier sections. You will use these skills in the exercise set for this section.

In Exercises 1–6, solve the *right* triangle shown in the figure.

1. $a = 3$, $c = 6$

2. $a = 5$, $b = 5$

3. $b = 15$, $c = 17$

4. $A = 42°$, $a = 7.5$

5. $B = 10°$, $b = 4$

6. $B = 72° 15'$, $c = 150$

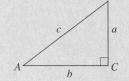

In Exercises 7 and 8, find the altitude of the triangle.

7.

8.

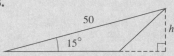

In Exercises 9 and 10, solve the equation for x.

9. $\dfrac{2}{\sin 30°} = \dfrac{9}{x}$

10. $\dfrac{100}{\sin 72°} = \dfrac{x}{\sin 60°}$

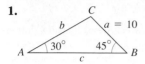

EXERCISES for Section 7.1

In Exercises 1–16, use the given information to find the remaining sides and angles of the triangle.

1.

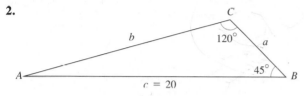

2.

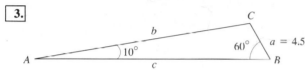

3.

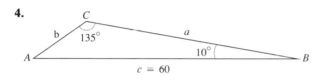

4.

5. $A = 36°$, $a = 8$, $b = 5$

6. $A = 60°$, $a = 9$, $c = 10$

7. $A = 150°$, $C = 20°$, $a = 200$

8. $A = 24.3°$, $C = 54.6°$, $c = 2.68$

9. $A = 83° 20'$, $C = 54.6°$, $c = 18.1$

10. $A = 5° 40'$, $B = 8° 15'$, $b = 4.8$

11. $B = 15° 30'$, $a = 4.5$, $b = 6.8$

12. $C = 85° 20'$, $a = 35$, $c = 50$

13. $C = 145°$, $b = 4$, $c = 14$

14. $A = 100°$, $a = 125$, $c = 10$

15. $A = 110° 15'$, $a = 48$, $b = 16$

16. $B = 2° 45'$, $b = 6.2$, $c = 5.8$

In Exercises 17–22, use the given information to find (if possible) the remaining sides and angles of the triangle. If two solutions exist, find both.

17. $A = 58°$, $a = 4.5$, $b = 12.8$

18. $A = 58°$, $a = 11.4$, $b = 12.8$

19. $A = 58°$, $a = 4.5$, $b = 5$

20. $A = 58°$, $a = 42.4$, $b = 50$

21. $A = 110°$, $a = 125$, $b = 200$

22. $A = 110°$, $a = 125$, $b = 100$

In Exercises 23 and 24, find a value for b such that the triangle has (a) one solution, (b) two solutions, and (c) no solution.

23. $A = 36°$, $a = 5$ **24.** $A = 60°$, $a = 10$

In Exercises 25–30, find the area of the triangle having the indicated sides and angles.

25. $C = 120°$, $a = 4$, $b = 6$

26. $B = 72° 30'$, $a = 105$, $c = 64$

27. $A = 43° 45'$, $b = 57$, $c = 85$

28. $A = 5° 15'$, $b = 4.5$, $c = 22$

29. $B = 130°$, $a = 62$, $c = 20$

30. $C = 84° 30'$, $a = 16$, $b = 20$

31. *Streetlight Design* Find the length d of the brace required to support the streetlight in the figure.

Figure for 31

32. *Height* Because of the prevailing winds, a tree grew so that it was leaning 6° from the vertical. At a point 100 feet away from the tree, the angle of elevation to the top of the tree is 22° 50' (see figure). Find the height h of the tree.

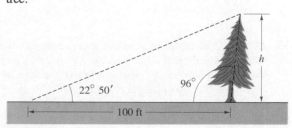

Figure for 32

33. *Bridge Design* A bridge is to be built across a small lake from *B* to *C* (see figure). The bearing from *B* to *C* is S 41° W. From a point *A*, 100 yards from *B*, the bearings to *B* and *C* are S 74° E and S 28° E, respectively. Find the distance from *B* to *C*.

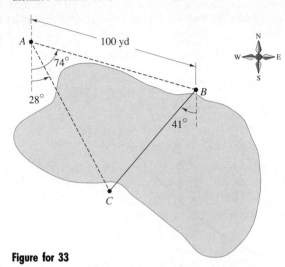

Figure for 33

34. *Railroad Track Design* The circular arc of a railroad curve has a chord of length 3000 feet and a central angle of 40° (see figure). Find (a) the radius *r* of the circular arc, and (b) the length *s* of the circular arc.

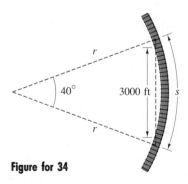

Figure for 34

35. *Altitude* The angles of elevation to an airplane from two points *A* and *B* on level ground are 51° and 68°, respectively. The points *A* and *B* are 6 miles apart, and the airplane is between those positions in the same vertical plane. Find the altitude of the airplane.

36. *Altitude* The angles of elevation to an airplane from two points *A* and *B* on level ground are 51° and 68°, respectively. The points *A* and *B* are 2.5 miles apart, and the airplane is east of both points in the same vertical plane. Find the altitude of the plane.

37. *Locating a Fire* Two fire towers *A* and *B* are 18.5 miles apart. The bearing from *A* to *B* is N 65° E. A fire is spotted by the ranger in each tower, and its bearings from *A* and *B* are N 28° E and N 16.5° W, respectively (see figure). Find the distance of the fire from each tower.

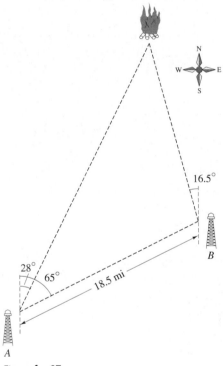

Figure for 37

38. *Distance*   A boat is sailing due east parallel to the shoreline at a speed of 10 miles per hour. At a given time, the bearing to the lighthouse is S 72° E, and 15 minutes later the bearing is S 66° E (see figure). Find the distance from the boat to the shoreline if the lighthouse is at the shoreline.

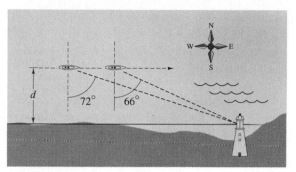

Figure for 38

39. *Distance*   A family is traveling due west on a road that passes a famous landmark. At a given time, the bearing to the landmark is N 62° W, and after traveling 5 miles farther the bearing is N 38° W. What is the closest the family will come to the landmark while on the road?

40. *Engine Design*   The connecting rod in a certain engine is 6 inches long and the radius of the crankshaft is $1\frac{1}{2}$ inches (see figure). The spark plug fires at 5° before top dead center. How far is the piston from the top of its stroke at this time?

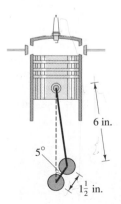

Figure for 40

41. *Verification of Testimony*   The following information about a triangular parcel of land is given at a zoning board meeting: "One side is 450 feet long and another is 120 feet long. The angle opposite the shorter side is 30°." Could this information be correct?

42. *Distance*   The angles of elevation to an airplane, θ and ϕ, are being continuously monitored at two observation points A and B, which are two miles apart (see figure). Write an equation giving the distance d between the plane and point B in terms of θ and ϕ.

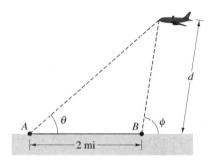

Figure for 42

7.2 Law of Cosines
Introduction / Heron's Formula

Introduction

Two cases remain in our list of conditions needed to solve an oblique triangle—SSS and SAS. The Law of Sines does not work in either of these cases. To see why, consider the three ratios given in the Law of Sines.

$$\frac{a}{\sin A} = \frac{b}{\sin B} = \frac{c}{\sin C}$$

To use the Law of Sines we must know at least one side and its opposite angle. If we are given three sides (SSS), or two sides and their included angle (SAS), none of the above ratios would be complete. In such cases we rely on the **Law of Cosines.**

LAW OF COSINES

If ABC is a triangle with sides a, b, and c, then the following equations are valid.

Standard Form	Alternative Form
$a^2 = b^2 + c^2 - 2bc \cos A$	$\cos A = \dfrac{b^2 + c^2 - a^2}{2bc}$
$b^2 = a^2 + c^2 - 2ac \cos B$	$\cos B = \dfrac{a^2 + c^2 - b^2}{2ac}$
$c^2 = a^2 + b^2 - 2ab \cos C$	$\cos C = \dfrac{a^2 + b^2 - c^2}{2ab}$

Proof

We prove only the first equation for a triangle that has three acute angles, as shown in Figure 7.13. In the figure, note that vertex B has coordinates $(c, 0)$. Furthermore, C has coordinates (x, y), where $x = b \cos A$ and $y = b \sin A$. Since a is the distance from vertex C to vertex B, it follows that

$$a = \sqrt{(x - c)^2 + (y - 0)^2}$$
$$a^2 = (b \cos A - c)^2 + (b \sin A)^2$$
$$= b^2 \cos^2 A - 2bc \cos A + c^2 + b^2 \sin^2 A$$
$$= b^2(\sin^2 A + \cos^2 A) + c^2 - 2bc \cos A.$$

Using the identity $\sin^2 A + \cos^2 A = 1$, we then obtain

$$a^2 = b^2 + c^2 - 2bc \cos A.$$

Similar arguments can be used to establish the other two equations. ◢

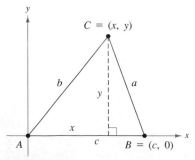

FIGURE 7.13

Note that if $A = 90°$ in Figure 7.13, then $\cos A = 0$ and the first form of the Law of Cosines becomes the Pythagorean Theorem.

$$a^2 = b^2 + c^2$$

Thus, the Pythagorean Theorem is actually just a special case of the more general Law of Cosines.

EXAMPLE 1   Given Three Sides of a Triangle—SSS

Find the three angles of the triangle whose sides have lengths $a = 8$ feet, $b = 19$ feet, and $c = 14$ feet.

Solution

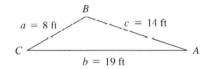

FIGURE 7.14

It is a good idea first to find the angle opposite the longest side—side b in this case (see Figure 7.14). Using the Law of Cosines, you find that

$$\cos B = \frac{a^2 + c^2 - b^2}{2ac} = \frac{8^2 + 14^2 - 19^2}{2(8)(14)} \approx -0.45089.$$

Since $\cos B$ is negative, you know B is an *obtuse* angle given by $B \approx 116.80°$. At this point you could use the Law of Cosines to find $\cos A$ and $\cos C$. However, knowing that $B \approx 116.80°$, it is simpler to use the Law of Sines to obtain the following.

$$\frac{b}{\sin B} = \frac{a}{\sin A}$$

$$\sin A = a\left(\frac{\sin B}{b}\right) \approx 8\left(\frac{\sin 116.80°}{19}\right) \approx 0.37582$$

Since B is obtuse, you know that A must be acute, because a triangle can have, at most, one obtuse angle. Thus, $A \approx 22.08°$ and

$$C \approx 180° - 22.08° - 116.80° = 41.12°.$$

Do you see why it was wise to find the largest angle *first* in Example 1? Knowing the cosine of an angle, we can determine whether the angle is acute or obtuse. That is,

$\cos \theta > 0$	for	$0° < \theta < 90°$	*Acute*
$\cos \theta < 0$	for	$90° < \theta < 180°.$	*Obtuse*

So, in Example 1, once you found that B was obtuse, you subsequently knew that angles A and C were both acute. If the largest angle is acute, then the remaining two angles will be acute also.

EXAMPLE 2   Given Two Sides and the Included Angle—SAS

The pitcher's mound on a softball field is 46 feet from home plate and the distance between the bases is 60 feet, as shown in Figure 7.15. How far is the pitcher's mound from first base? (Note that the pitcher's mound is *not* halfway between home plate and second base.)

Solution

In triangle HPF, $H = 45°$ (line HP bisects the right angle at H), $f = 46$, and $p = 60$. Using the Law of Cosines for this SAS case, you have

$$h^2 = f^2 + p^2 - 2fp \cos H$$
$$= 46^2 + 60^2 - 2(46)(60) \cos 45°$$
$$\approx 1812.8.$$

Therefore, the approximate distance from the pitcher's mound to first base is

$$h \approx \sqrt{1812.8} \approx 42.58 \text{ feet.}$$

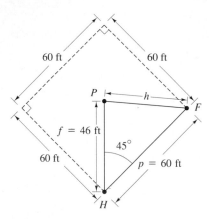

FIGURE 7.15

EXAMPLE 3   Given Two Sides and the Included Angle—SAS

A ship travels 60 miles due east, then adjusts its course 15° northward, as shown in Figure 7.16. After traveling 80 miles in that direction, how far is the ship from its point of departure?

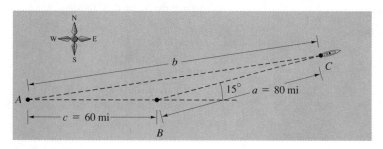

FIGURE 7.16

Solution

You have $c = 60$, $B = 180° - 15° = 165°$, and $a = 80$. Consequently, by the Law of Cosines, you find that

$$b^2 = a^2 + c^2 - 2ac \cos B = 80^2 + 60^2 - 2(80)(60) \cos 165° \approx 19{,}273.$$

Therefore, the distance b is

$$b \approx \sqrt{19{,}273} \approx 138.8 \text{ miles.}$$

Heron's Formula

The Law of Cosines can be used to establish the following formula for the area of a triangle. This formula is credited to the Greek mathematician Heron (c. 100 B.C.).

HERON'S AREA FORMULA

Given any triangle with sides of length a, b, and c, the area of the triangle is

$$\text{Area} = \sqrt{s(s-a)(s-b)(s-c)}$$

where $s = (a + b + c)/2$.

Proof

From the previous section, we know that

$$\text{Area} = \frac{1}{2}bc\sin A = \sqrt{\frac{1}{4}b^2c^2\sin^2 A} = \sqrt{\frac{1}{4}b^2c^2(1 - \cos^2 A)}$$

$$= \sqrt{\left[\frac{1}{2}bc(1 + \cos A)\right]\left[\frac{1}{2}bc(1 - \cos A)\right]}.$$

Using the Law of Cosines, we can show that

$$\frac{1}{2}bc(1 + \cos A) = \frac{a+b+c}{2} \cdot \frac{-a+b+c}{2}$$

and

$$\frac{1}{2}bc(1 - \cos A) = \frac{a-b+c}{2} \cdot \frac{a+b-c}{2}.$$

(See Exercises 47 and 48.) Letting $s = (a + b + c)/2$, these two equations can be rewritten as

$$\frac{1}{2}bc(1 + \cos A) = s(s-a)$$

and

$$\frac{1}{2}bc(1 - \cos A) = (s-b)(s-c).$$

Thus, we conclude that

$$\text{Area} = \sqrt{s(s-a)(s-b)(s-c)}.$$

EXAMPLE 4   Using Heron's Area Formula

Find the area of the triangular region having sides of lengths $a = 47$ yards, $b = 58$ yards, and $c = 78.6$ yards.

Solution

Since

$$s = \frac{1}{2}(a + b + c) = \frac{183.6}{2} = 91.8,$$

Heron's Formula yields

$$\begin{aligned} \text{Area} &= \sqrt{s(s - a)(s - b)(s - c)} \\ &= \sqrt{91.8(44.8)(33.8)(13.2)} \\ &\approx 1354.58 \text{ square yards.} \end{aligned}$$

DISCUSSION
PROBLEM

The Area of a Triangle

We have now discussed three different formulas for the area of a triangle.

Standard Formula $\text{Area} = \frac{1}{2}bh$

Oblique Triangle $\text{Area} = \frac{1}{2}bc \sin A = \frac{1}{2}ab \sin C = \frac{1}{2}ac \sin B$

Heron's Formula $\text{Area} = \sqrt{s(s - a)(s - b)(s - c)},$
$s = (a + b + c)/2$

Use the most appropriate formula to find the area of each of the following triangles. Show your work and give your reasons for choosing each formula.

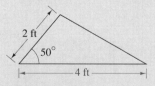

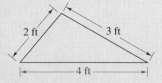

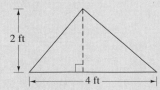

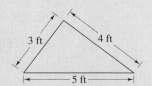

WARM UP

The following warm-up exercises involve skills that were covered in earlier sections. You will use these skills in the exercise set for this section.

In Exercises 1 and 2, simplify the expression.

1. $\sqrt{(7-3)^2 + [1-(-5)]^2}$

2. $\sqrt{[-2-(-5)]^2 + (12-6)^2}$

In Exercises 3 and 4, find the distance between the two points.

3. $(4, -2)$, $(8, 10)$

4. $(1, 3)$, $(7, 12)$

In Exercises 5 and 6, find the area of the triangle.

5.

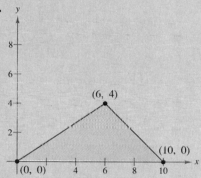

6.

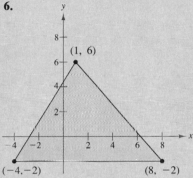

In Exercises 7–10, find (if possible) the remaining sides and angles of the triangle labeled as shown in Figure 7.1.

7. $A = 10°$, $C = 100°$, $b = 25$

8. $A = 20°$, $C = 90°$, $c = 100$

9. $B = 30°$, $b = 6.5$, $c = 15$

10. $A = 30°$, $b = 6.5$, $a = 10$

EXERCISES for Section 7.2

In Exercises 1–14, use the Law of Cosines to solve the given triangle.

1.

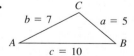

$b = 7$ $a = 5$ $c = 10$

2.

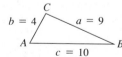

$b = 4$ $a = 9$ $c = 10$

3.

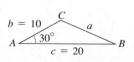

$b = 10$ a $30°$ $c = 20$

4.

$b = 4.5$ $a = 10$ $110°$ c

5. $a = 9$, $b = 12$, $c = 15$

6. $a = 55$, $b = 25$, $c = 72$ $A = 39.35°$ $B = 16.74°$ $C = 123.91°$

7. $a = 75.4$, $b = 52$, $c = 52$

8. $a = 1.42$, $b = 0.75$, $c = 1.25$

9. $A = 120°$, $b = 3$, $c = 10$

10. $A = 55°$, $b = 3$, $c = 10$

11. $B = 8° 45'$, $a = 25$, $c = 15$

12. $B = 75° 20'$, $a = 6.2$, $c = 9.5$ $b = 9.94$ $A = 37.1°$ $C = 67.6°$

13. $C = 125° 40'$, $a = 32$, $b = 32$

14. $C = 15°$, $a = 6.25$, $b = 2.15$

In Exercises 15–20, complete the table by solving the parallelogram shown in the figure. (The lengths of the diagonals are given by c and d.)

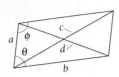

Figure for 15–20

	a	b	c	d	θ	ϕ
15.	4	6			30°	
16.	25	35				120°
17.	10	14	20			
18.	40	60	6	80	$104.5°$	$75.5°$
19.	10		18	12		
20.		25	50	35		

In Exercises 21–26, use Heron's Formula to find the area of the triangle.

21. $a = 5$, $b = 7$, $c = 10$
22. $a = 2.5$, $b = 10.2$, $c = 9$ 10.44
23. $a = 12$, $b = 15$, $c = 9$
24. $a = 75.4$, $b = 52$, $c = 52$
25. $a = 20$, $b = 20$, $c = 10$
26. $a = 4.25$, $b = 1.55$, $c = 3.00$

27. *Area*   The lengths of the sides of a triangular parcel of land are approximately 400 feet, 500 feet, and 700 feet. Approximate the area of the parcel.

28. *Area*   The lengths of two adjacent sides of a parallelogram are 4 yards and 6 yards. Find the area of the parallelogram if the angle between the two sides is 30°.

29. *Navigation*   A boat race occurs along a triangular course marked by buoys A, B, and C. The race starts with the boats heading in a westerly direction. The other two sides of the course lie to the north of the first side, and their lengths are 3500 feet and 6500 feet (see figure). Find the bearings for the last two legs of the race.

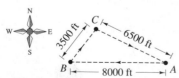

Figure for 29

30. *Navigation*   A plane flies 675 miles from A to B with a bearing of N 75° E. Then it flies 540 miles from B to C with a bearing of N 32° E (see figure). Find the straight-line distance and bearing from C to A.

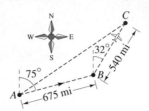

Figure for 30

31. *Distance*   Two ships leave a port at 9 A.M. One travels at a bearing of N 53° W at 12 miles per hour and the other at a bearing of S 67° W at 16 miles per hour. Approximately how far apart are they at noon that day?

32. *Distance*   A 100-foot vertical tower is to be erected on the side of a hill that makes an 8° angle with the horizontal (see figure). Find the length of each of the two guy wires that will be anchored 75 feet uphill and downhill from the base of the tower.

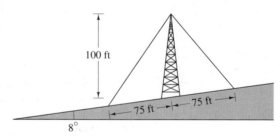

Figure for 32

33. *Surveying*   To approximate the length of a marsh, a surveyor walks 950 feet from point A to point B, then turns 80° and walks 800 feet to point C (see figure). Approximate the length $\overline{AC}$ of the marsh.

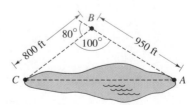

Figure for 33

34. *Surveying* A triangular parcel of land has 375 feet of frontage, and the other boundaries have lengths of 250 feet and 300 feet. What angles does the frontage make with the two other boundaries?

35. *Streetlight Design* Determine the angle θ in the design of the streetlight shown in the figure.

Figure for 35

36. *Aircraft Tracking* In order to determine the distance between two aircraft, a tracking station continuously determines the distance to each aircraft and the angle α between them. Determine the distance a between the planes when $\alpha = 42°$, $b = 35$ miles, and $c = 20$ miles.

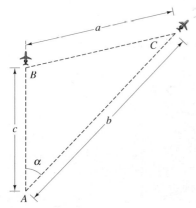

Figure for 36

37. *Engineering* If Q is the midpoint of the line segment $\overline{PR}$, find the lengths of the line segments $\overline{PQ}$, $\overline{QS}$, and $\overline{RS}$ on the truss rafter shown in the figure.

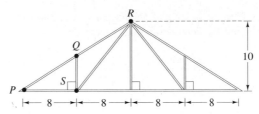

Figure for 37

38. *Paper Manufacturing* In a certain process with continuous paper, the paper passes across three rollers of radii 3 inches, 4 inches, and 6 inches (see figure). The centers of the 3-inch and 6-inch rollers are d inches apart, and the length of the arc in contact with the paper on the 4-inch roller is s inches. Complete the table.

d (inches)	9	10	12	13	14	15	16
θ (degrees)							
s (inches)							

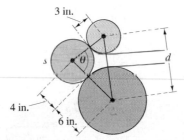

Figure for 38

39. *Navigation* On a certain map, Orlando is 7 inches due south of Niagara Falls, Denver is 10.75 inches from Orlando, and Denver is 9.25 inches from Niagara Falls (see figure).
(a) Find the bearing of Denver from Orlando.
(b) Find the bearing of Denver from Niagara Falls.

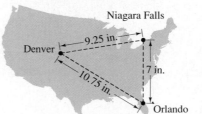

Figure for 39

40. *Navigation* On a certain map, Minneapolis is 6.5 inches due west of Albany, Phoenix is 8.5 inches from Minneapolis, and Phoenix is 14.5 inches from Albany (see figure).
(a) Find the bearing of Minneapolis from Phoenix.
(b) Find the bearing of Albany from Phoenix.

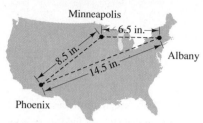

Figure for 40

41. *Baseball* In a (square) baseball diamond with 90-foot sides, the pitcher's mound is 60 feet from home plate.
(a) How far is it from the pitcher's mound to third base?
(b) When a runner is halfway from second to third, how far is the runner from the pitcher's mound?

42. *Baseball* The baseball player in center field is playing approximately 330 feet from the television camera that is behind home plate. A batter hits a fly ball that goes to the wall that is 420 feet from the camera (see figure). Approximate the number of feet that the center fielder had to run to make the catch if the camera turned 9° in following the play.

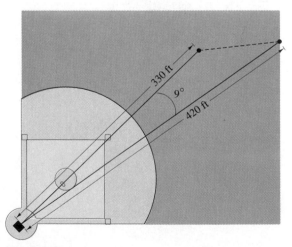

Figure for 42

43. *Awning Design* A retractable awning lowers at an angle of 50° from the top of a patio door that is 7 feet high (see figure). Find the length x of the awning if no direct sunlight is to enter the door when the angle of elevation of the sun is greater than 65°.

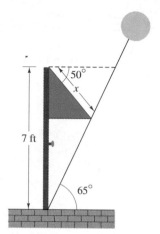

Figure for 43

44. *Circumscribed and Inscribed Circles* Let R and r be the radii of the circumscribed and inscribed circles of a triangle ABC, respectively, and let $s = (a + b + c)/2$ (see figure). Prove the following.

(a) $2R = \dfrac{a}{\sin A} = \dfrac{b}{\sin B} = \dfrac{c}{\sin C}$

(b) $r = \sqrt{\dfrac{(s - a)(s - b)(s - c)}{s}}$

R = radius of the
   large circle

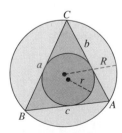

r = radius of the
   small circle

Figure for 44

Circumscribed and Inscribed Circles In Exercises 45 and 46, use the results of Exercise 44.

45. Given the triangle with $a = 25$, $b = 55$, and $c = 72$, find the area of (a) the triangle, (b) the circumscribed circle, and (c) the inscribed circle.

46. Find the length of the largest circular track that can be built on a triangular piece of property whose sides are 200 feet, 250 feet, and 325 feet.

47. Use the Law of Cosines to prove that

$$\frac{1}{2}bc(1 + \cos A) = \frac{a + b + c}{2} \cdot \frac{-a + b + c}{2}.$$

48. Use the Law of Cosines to prove that

$$\frac{1}{2}bc(1 - \cos A) = \frac{a - b + c}{2} \cdot \frac{a + b - c}{2}.$$

7.3 Vectors in the Plane

Introduction / Component Form of a Vector / Vector Operations / Unit Vectors / Direction Angles / Applications of Vectors

Introduction

Many quantities in geometry and physics, such as area, time, and temperature, can be represented by a single real number. Other quantities, such as force and velocity, involve both *magnitude* and *direction* and cannot be completely characterized by a single real number. To represent such a quantity, we use a **directed line segment,** as shown in Figure 7.17. The directed line segment $\overrightarrow{PQ}$ has **initial point** P and **terminal point** Q and we denote its **length** by $\|PQ\|$.

Two directed line segments that have the same length (or magnitude) and direction are **equivalent.** For example, the directed line segments in Figure 7.18 are all equivalent. The set of all directed line segments that are equivalent to a given directed line segment $\overrightarrow{PQ}$ is a **vector v in the plane,** written $\mathbf{v} = \overrightarrow{PQ}$. We denote vectors by lowercase, boldface letters such as **u, v,** and **w.**

Be sure you see that a vector in the plane can be represented by many different directed line segments.

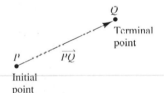

FIGURE 7.17

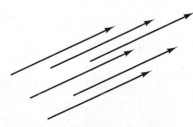

FIGURE 7.18   Equivalent Directed Line Segments

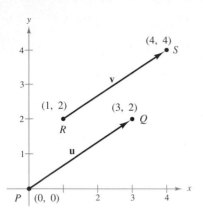

FIGURE 7.19

EXAMPLE 1   Vector Representation by Directed Line Segments

Let **u** be represented by the directed line segment from $P = (0, 0)$ to $Q = (3, 2)$, and let **v** be represented by the directed line segment from $R = (1, 2)$ to $S = (4, 4)$, as shown in Figure 7.19. Show that **u** = **v**.

Solution

From the distance formula, you see that $\overrightarrow{PQ}$ and $\overrightarrow{RS}$ have the *same length*.

$$\|\overrightarrow{PQ}\| = \sqrt{(3 - 0)^2 + (2 - 0)^2} = \sqrt{13}$$
$$\|\overrightarrow{RS}\| = \sqrt{(4 - 1)^2 + (4 - 2)^2} = \sqrt{13}$$

Moreover, both line segments have the *same direction* since they are both directed toward the upper right on lines having a slope of $\frac{2}{3}$. Thus, $\overrightarrow{PQ}$ and $\overrightarrow{RS}$ have the same length and direction, and you conclude that **u** = **v**. ◢

Component Form of a Vector

The directed line segment whose initial point is the origin is often the most convenient representative of a set of equivalent directed line segments. We say that this representative of the vector **v** is in **standard position.**

A vector whose initial point is at the origin $(0, 0)$ can be uniquely represented by the coordinates of its terminal point (v_1, v_2). This is the **component form of a vector v,** written

$$\mathbf{v} = \langle v_1, v_2 \rangle.$$

The coordinates v_1 and v_2 are the **components** of **v.** If both the initial point and the terminal point lie at the origin, then **v** is the **zero vector** and is denoted by $\mathbf{0} = \langle 0, 0 \rangle$. To convert directed line segments to component form we use the following procedure.

COMPONENT FORM OF A VECTOR

The component form of the vector with initial point $P = (p_1, p_2)$ and terminal point $Q = (q_1, q_2)$ is

$$\overrightarrow{PQ} = \langle q_1 - p_1, q_2 - p_2 \rangle = \langle v_1, v_2 \rangle = \mathbf{v}.$$

The **length** (or magnitude) of **v** is given by

$$\|\mathbf{v}\| = \sqrt{(q_1 - p_1)^2 + (q_2 - p_2)^2} = \sqrt{v_1^2 + v_2^2}.$$

If $\|\mathbf{v}\| = 1$, then **v** is a **unit vector.** Moreover, $\|\mathbf{v}\| = 0$ if and only if **v** is the zero vector **0.**

Two vectors $\mathbf{u} = \langle u_1, u_2 \rangle$ and $\mathbf{v} = \langle v_1, v_2 \rangle$ are **equal** if and only if $u_1 = v_1$ and $u_2 = v_2$. For instance, in Example 1, the vector $\mathbf{u}$ from $P = (0, 0)$, to $Q = (3, 2)$ is

$$\mathbf{u} = \overrightarrow{PQ} = \langle 3 - 0, 2 - 0 \rangle = \langle 3, 2 \rangle$$

and the vector $\mathbf{v}$ from $R = (1, 2)$ to $S = (4, 4)$ is

$$\mathbf{v} = \overrightarrow{RS} = \langle 4 - 1, 4 - 2 \rangle = \langle 3, 2 \rangle.$$

EXAMPLE 2   Finding the Component Form and Length of a Vector

Find the component form and length of the vector $\mathbf{v}$ that has initial point $(4, -7)$ and terminal point $(-1, 5)$.

Solution

Let $P = (4, -7) = (p_1, p_2)$ and $Q = (-1, 5) = (q_1, q_2)$. Then, the components of $\mathbf{v} = \langle v_1, v_2 \rangle$ are given by

$$v_1 = q_1 - p_1 = -1 - 4 = -5$$
$$v_2 = q_2 - p_2 = 5 - (-7) = 12.$$

Thus, $\mathbf{v} = \langle -5, 12 \rangle$ and the length of $\mathbf{v}$ is

$$\|\mathbf{v}\| = \sqrt{(-5)^2 + 12^2} = \sqrt{169} = 13$$

as shown in Figure 7.20.

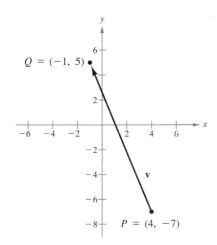

$Q = (-1, 5)$

$P = (4, -7)$

Component form of $\mathbf{v}$:
$\mathbf{v} = \langle -5, 12 \rangle$

FIGURE 7.20

Vector Operations

The two basic operations are **scalar multiplication** and **vector addition.** (In this text, we use the term **scalar** to mean a real number.) Geometrically, the product of a vector $\mathbf{v}$ and a scalar k is the vector that is $|k|$ times as long as $\mathbf{v}$. If k is positive, then $k\mathbf{v}$ has the same direction as $\mathbf{v}$, and if k is negative, then $k\mathbf{v}$ has the opposite direction of $\mathbf{v}$, as shown in Figure 7.21.

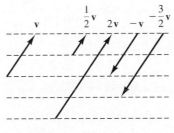

$\mathbf{v}$ $\dfrac{1}{2}\mathbf{v}$ $2\mathbf{v}$ $-\mathbf{v}$ $-\dfrac{3}{2}\mathbf{v}$

Scalar Multiplication of $\mathbf{v}$

FIGURE 7.21

To add two vectors geometrically, we position them (without changing length or direction) so that the initial point of one coincides with the terminal point of the other. The sum **u** + **v** is formed by joining the initial point of the second vector **v** with the terminal point of the first vector **u,** as shown in Figure 7.22. Since the vector **u** + **v** is the diagonal of a parallelogram having **u** and **v** as its adjacent sides, we call this the **parallelogram law** for vector addition.

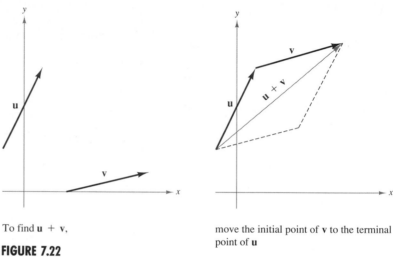

To find **u** + **v**,

move the initial point of **v** to the terminal point of **u**

FIGURE 7.22

Vector addition and scalar multiplication can also be defined using components of vectors.

DEFINITION OF VECTOR ADDITION & SCALAR MULTIPLICATION

Let $\mathbf{u} = \langle u_1, u_2 \rangle$ and $\mathbf{v} = \langle v_1, v_2 \rangle$ be vectors and let k be a scalar (a real number). Then the **sum** of **u** and **v** is the vector

$$\mathbf{u} + \mathbf{v} = \langle u_1 + v_1, u_2 + v_2 \rangle \quad \textit{Sum}$$

and the **scalar multiple** of k times **u** is the vector

$$k\mathbf{u} = k\langle u_1, u_2 \rangle = \langle ku_1, ku_2 \rangle. \quad \textit{Scalar multiple}$$

The **negative** of $\mathbf{v} = \langle v_1, v_2 \rangle$ is

$$-\mathbf{v} = (-1)\mathbf{v} = \langle -v_1, -v_2 \rangle \qquad \textit{Negative}$$

and the **difference** of **u** and **v** is

$$\mathbf{u} - \mathbf{v} = \mathbf{u} + (-\mathbf{v}) = \langle u_1 - v_1, u_2 - v_2 \rangle. \qquad \textit{Difference}$$

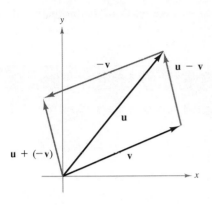

−v

u − v

u

u + (−v)

v

x

y

Vector Subtraction

FIGURE 7.23

To represent **u** − **v** graphically, we use directed line segments with the *same* initial points. The difference **u** − **v** is the vector from the terminal point of **v** to the terminal point of **u**, as shown in Figure 7.23.

EXAMPLE 3   Vector Operations

Let $\mathbf{v} = \langle -2, 5 \rangle$ and $\mathbf{w} = \langle 3, 4 \rangle$, and find the following vectors.

a. 2**v**   **b.** **w** − **v**   **c.** **v** + 2**w**

Solution

a. Since $\mathbf{v} = \langle -2, 5 \rangle$, you have

$$2\mathbf{v} = \langle 2(-2), 2(5) \rangle = \langle -4, 10 \rangle.$$

A sketch of 2**v** is shown in Figure 7.24(a).

b. The difference of **w** and **v** is given by

$$\mathbf{w} - \mathbf{v} = \langle 3 - (-2), 4 - 5 \rangle = \langle 5, -1 \rangle.$$

A sketch of **w** − **v** is shown in Figure 7.24(b).

c. Since $2\mathbf{w} = \langle 6, 8 \rangle$, it follows that

$$\mathbf{v} + 2\mathbf{w} = \langle -2, 5 \rangle + \langle 6, 8 \rangle$$
$$= \langle -2 + 6, 5 + 8 \rangle$$
$$= \langle 4, 13 \rangle.$$

A sketch of **v** + 2**w** is shown in Figure 7.24(c).

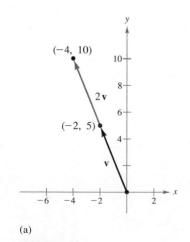

(a)

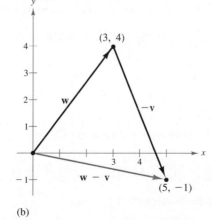

(b)

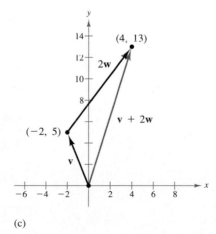

(c)

FIGURE 7.24

Vector addition and scalar multiplication share many of the properties of ordinary arithmetic.

PROPERTIES OF VECTOR ADDITION & SCALAR MULTIPLICATION

Let **u**, **v**, and **w** be vectors and let c and d be scalars. Then the following properties are true.

1. $\mathbf{u} + \mathbf{v} = \mathbf{v} + \mathbf{u}$
2. $(\mathbf{u} + \mathbf{v}) + \mathbf{w} = \mathbf{u} + (\mathbf{v} + \mathbf{w})$
3. $\mathbf{u} + \mathbf{0} = \mathbf{u}$
4. $\mathbf{u} + (-\mathbf{u}) = \mathbf{0}$
5. $c(d\mathbf{u}) = (cd)\mathbf{u}$
6. $(c + d)\mathbf{u} = c\mathbf{u} + d\mathbf{u}$
7. $c(\mathbf{u} + \mathbf{v}) = c\mathbf{u} + c\mathbf{v}$
8. $1(\mathbf{u}) = \mathbf{u}, \; 0(\mathbf{u}) = \mathbf{0}$
9. $\|c\mathbf{v}\| = |c| \, \|\mathbf{v}\|$

REMARK Property 9 can be stated as follows: The length of the vector $c\mathbf{v}$ is the absolute value of c times the length of **v**.

Unit Vectors

In many applications of vectors it is useful to find a unit vector that has the same direction as a given nonzero vector **v**. To do this, we divide **v** by its length to obtain

$$\mathbf{u} = \text{unit vector} = \frac{\mathbf{v}}{\|\mathbf{v}\|} = \left(\frac{1}{\|\mathbf{v}\|}\right)\mathbf{v}.$$

Note that **u** is a scalar multiple of **v**. The vector **u** has length 1 and the same direction as **v**. We call **u** a **unit vector in the direction of v**.

EXAMPLE 4   Finding a Unit Vector

Find a unit vector in the direction of $\mathbf{v} = \langle -2, 5 \rangle$ and verify that the result has length 1.

Solution

The unit vector in the direction of **v** is

$$\frac{\mathbf{v}}{\|\mathbf{v}\|} = \frac{\langle -2, 5 \rangle}{\sqrt{(-2)^2 + (5)^2}} = \frac{1}{\sqrt{29}}\langle -2, 5 \rangle = \left\langle \frac{-2}{\sqrt{29}}, \frac{5}{\sqrt{29}} \right\rangle.$$

This vector has length 1 because

$$\sqrt{\left(\frac{-2}{\sqrt{29}}\right)^2 + \left(\frac{5}{\sqrt{29}}\right)^2} = \sqrt{\frac{4}{29} + \frac{25}{29}} = \sqrt{\frac{29}{29}} = 1.$$

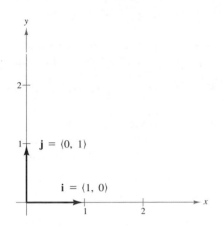

$j = \langle 0, 1 \rangle$

$i = \langle 1, 0 \rangle$

Standard Unit Vectors **i** and **j**

FIGURE 7.25

The unit vectors $\langle 1, 0 \rangle$ and $\langle 0, 1 \rangle$ are the **standard unit vectors** and are denoted by

$$\mathbf{i} = \langle 1, 0 \rangle \quad \text{and} \quad \mathbf{j} = \langle 0, 1 \rangle$$

as shown in Figure 7.25. (Note that the lowercase letter **i** is written in boldface to distinguish it from the imaginary number $i = \sqrt{-1}$.) These vectors can be used to represent any vector $\mathbf{v} = \langle v_1, v_2 \rangle$ as follows.

$$\mathbf{v} = \langle v_1, v_2 \rangle = v_1 \langle 1, 0 \rangle + v_2 \langle 0, 1 \rangle = v_1 \mathbf{i} + v_2 \mathbf{j}$$

The scalars v_1 and v_2 are the **horizontal** and **vertical components of v,** respectively. The vector sum $v_1 \mathbf{i} + v_2 \mathbf{j}$ is a **linear combination** of the vectors **i** and **j.** Any vector in the plane can be expressed as a linear combination of the standard unit vectors **i** and **j.**

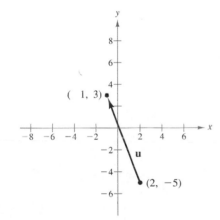

$(1, 3)$

u

$(2, -5)$

EXAMPLE 5 Writing a Linear Combination of Unit Vectors

Let **u** be the vector with initial point $(2, -5)$ and terminal point $(-1, 3)$. Write **u** as a linear combination of the standard unit vectors **i** and **j.**

Solution

$$\mathbf{u} = \langle -1 - 2, 3 + 5 \rangle$$
$$= \langle -3, 8 \rangle$$
$$= -3\mathbf{i} + 8\mathbf{j}$$

This result is shown graphically in Figure 7.26.

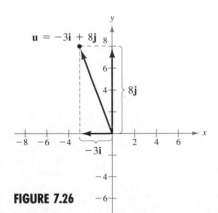

$\mathbf{u} = -3\mathbf{i} + 8\mathbf{j}$

$8\mathbf{j}$

$-3\mathbf{i}$

FIGURE 7.26

EXAMPLE 6 Vector Operations

Let $\mathbf{u} = 3\mathbf{i} + 8\mathbf{j}$ and $\mathbf{v} = 2\mathbf{i} - \mathbf{j}$. Find $2\mathbf{u} - 3\mathbf{v}$.

Solution

$$2\mathbf{u} - 3\mathbf{v} = 2(-3\mathbf{i} + 8\mathbf{j}) - 3(2\mathbf{i} - \mathbf{j})$$
$$= -6\mathbf{i} + 16\mathbf{j} - 6\mathbf{i} + 3\mathbf{j}$$
$$= -12\mathbf{i} + 19\mathbf{j}$$

Direction Angles

If **u** is a *unit vector* such that θ is the angle (measured counterclockwise) from the positive x-axis to **u**, then the terminal point of **u** lies on the unit circle and we have

$$\mathbf{u} = \langle \cos\theta, \sin\theta \rangle = (\cos\theta)\mathbf{i} + (\sin\theta)\mathbf{j}$$

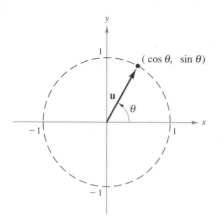

as shown in Figure 7.27. We call θ the **direction angle** of the vector **u.**

Suppose that **u** is a unit vector with direction angle θ. If **v** is any vector that makes an angle θ with the positive x-axis, then it has the same direction as **u** and we can write

$$\mathbf{v} = \|\mathbf{v}\| \langle \cos\theta, \sin\theta \rangle = \|\mathbf{v}\| (\cos\theta)\mathbf{i} + \|\mathbf{v}\| (\sin\theta)\mathbf{j}.$$

For instance, the vector **v** of length 3 making an angle of 30° with the positive x-axis is given by

$$\mathbf{v} = 3(\cos 30°)\mathbf{i} + 3(\sin 30°)\mathbf{j} = \frac{3\sqrt{3}}{2}\mathbf{i} + \frac{3}{2}\mathbf{j}$$

where $\|\mathbf{v}\| = 3$.

Since $\mathbf{v} = a\mathbf{i} + b\mathbf{j} = \|\mathbf{v}\| \cos\theta\mathbf{i} + \|\mathbf{v}\| \sin\theta\mathbf{j}$, it follows that the direction angle θ for **v** is determined from

$$\tan\theta = \frac{\sin\theta}{\cos\theta} = \frac{\|\mathbf{v}\| \sin\theta}{\|\mathbf{v}\| \cos\theta} = \frac{b}{a}.$$

FIGURE 7.27

EXAMPLE 7   Finding Direction Angles of Vectors

Find the direction angles of the vectors.

a. $\mathbf{u} = 3\mathbf{i} + 3\mathbf{j}$ **b.** $\mathbf{v} = 3\mathbf{i} - 4\mathbf{j}$

Solution

a. The direction angle is given by

$$\tan\theta = \frac{b}{a} = \frac{3}{3} = 1.$$

Therefore, $\theta = 45°$, as shown in Figure 7.28.

b. The direction angle is given by

$$\tan\theta = \frac{b}{a} = \frac{-4}{3}.$$

Moreover, since $\mathbf{v} = 3\mathbf{i} - 4\mathbf{j}$ lies in Quadrant IV, θ lies in Quadrant IV and its reference angle is

$$\theta = \left| \arctan\left(-\frac{4}{3}\right) \right| \approx |-53.13°| = 53.13°.$$

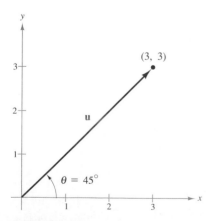

FIGURE 7.28

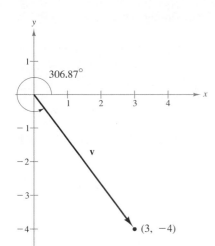

FIGURE 7.29

Therefore, it follows that

$$\theta \approx 360° - 53.13° = 306.87°$$

as shown in Figure 7.29.

Applications of Vectors

Many applications of vectors involve the use of triangles and trigonometry in their solutions.

EXAMPLE 8   Finding Component Form, Given Magnitude and Direction

Find the component form of the vector that represents the velocity of an airplane descending at a speed of 100 miles per hour at an angle 30° below horizontal, as shown in Figure 7.30.

Solution

The velocity vector **v** has a magnitude of 100 and a direction angle of $\theta = 210°$. Hence, the component form of **v** is

$$\mathbf{v} = \|\mathbf{v}\| (\cos \theta)\mathbf{i} + \|\mathbf{v}\| (\sin \theta)\mathbf{j}$$
$$= 100(\cos 210°)\mathbf{i} + 100(\sin 210°)\mathbf{j}$$
$$= 100\left(\frac{-\sqrt{3}}{2}\right)\mathbf{i} + 100\left(\frac{-1}{2}\right)\mathbf{j}$$
$$= -50\sqrt{3}\mathbf{i} - 50\mathbf{j}$$
$$= \langle -50\sqrt{3}, -50 \rangle.$$

You should check to see that $\|\mathbf{v}\| = 100$.

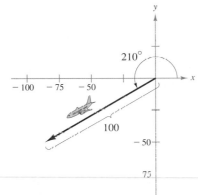

FIGURE 7.30

EXAMPLE 9   An Application

A force of 600 pounds is required to pull a boat and trailer up a ramp inclined at 15° from horizontal. Find the combined weight of the boat and trailer. (Assume no friction is involved.)

Solution

Based on Figure 7.31, you can make the following observations.

$$\|\overrightarrow{BA}\| = \text{force of gravity} = \text{combined weight of boat and trailer}$$

$$\|\overrightarrow{BC}\| = \text{force against ramp}$$

$$\|\overrightarrow{AC}\| = \text{force required to move boat up ramp} = 600 \text{ pounds}$$
$$\qquad\qquad (\text{Note that } AC \text{ is parallel to the ramp.})$$

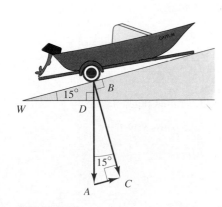

FIGURE 7.31

By construction, triangles *WBD* and *ABC* are similar. Hence, angle *ABC* is 15°. Therefore, in triangle *ABC* you have

$$\sin 15° = \frac{\|\overrightarrow{AC}\|}{\|\overrightarrow{BA}\|} = \frac{600}{\|\overrightarrow{BA}\|}$$

$$\|\overrightarrow{BA}\| = \frac{600}{\sin 15°} \approx 2318.$$

Consequently, the combined weight is approximately 2318 pounds. ◢

EXAMPLE 10   An Application

An airplane is traveling at a fixed altitude with a negligible wind factor. The airplane is headed N 30° W at a speed of 500 miles per hour, as shown in Figure 7.32. As the airplane reaches a certain point, it encounters a wind with a velocity of 70 miles per hour in the direction N 45° E. What are the resultant speed and direction of the airplane?

Solution

Using Figure 7.32, you can represent the velocity of the airplane by the vector

$$\mathbf{v}_1 = 500\langle \cos 120°, \sin 120° \rangle = \langle -250, 250\sqrt{3} \rangle$$

and the velocity of the wind by the vector

$$\mathbf{v}_2 = 70\langle \cos 45°, \sin 45° \rangle = \langle 35\sqrt{2}, 35\sqrt{2} \rangle.$$

Thus, the velocity of the airplane is given by the vector

$$\mathbf{v} = \mathbf{v}_1 + \mathbf{v}_2 = \langle -250 + 35\sqrt{2}, 250\sqrt{3} + 35\sqrt{2} \rangle \approx \langle -200.5, 482.5 \rangle$$

and the speed of the airplane is

$$\|\mathbf{v}\| = \sqrt{(-200.5)^2 + (482.5)^2} \approx 522.5 \text{ miles per hour.}$$

Finally, if θ is the direction angle of the flight path, you have

$$\tan \theta = \frac{482.5}{-200.5} \approx -2.4065$$

which implies that

$$\theta \approx 180° + \arctan(-2.4065) \approx 180° - 67.4° = 112.6°.$$ ◢

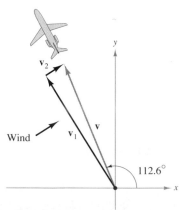

FIGURE 7.32

DISCUSSION PROBLEM

Comparing Velocity and Speed

In everyday conversation, the terms velocity and speed are often used as synonyms. In mathematics and science, however, we consider the terms to be different. *Velocity* is a vector quantity that has both magnitude and direction, whereas *speed* is a single-dimensional quantity that can be represented by nonnegative real numbers. Consider an object that has a velocity of **v** and a speed of *s*. How are these two quantities related to each other?

Which of the following statements is correct mathematically?

1. While driving to work, I did not exceed a velocity of 55 miles per hour.
2. While driving to work, I did not exceed a speed of 55 miles per hour.

Find another pair of quantities that are related to each other in a similar manner.

WARM UP

The following warm-up exercises involve skills that were covered in earlier sections. You will use these skills in the exercise set for this section.

In Exercises 1 and 2, find the distance between the points.

1. $(-2, 6)$, $(5, -15)$ **2.** $(0, 0)$, $(-3, -7)$

In Exercises 3 and 4, find an equation of the line through the two points.

3. $(3, 1)$, $(-2, 4)$ **4.** $(-2, -3)$, $(4, 5)$

In Exercises 5 and 6, find an angle θ $(0 \le \theta \le 360°)$ whose vertex is at the origin and whose terminal side passes through the point.

5. $(-2, 5)$ **6.** $(4, -3)$

In Exercises 7–10, find the sine and cosine of the angle θ.

7. $\theta = 30°$ **8.** $\theta = 120°$

9. $\theta = 300°$ **10.** $\theta = 210°$

EXERCISES for Section 7.3

In Exercises 1–6, use the figure to sketch a graph of the vector.

1. $-\mathbf{u}$ **2.** $3\mathbf{v}$

3. $\mathbf{u} + \mathbf{v}$ **4.** $\mathbf{u} + 2\mathbf{v}$

5. $\mathbf{u} - \mathbf{v}$ **6.** $\mathbf{v} - \frac{1}{2}\mathbf{u}$

Figure for 1–6

In Exercises 7–16, find the component form and the magnitude of the vector **v**.

7.

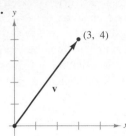

8.

$V = \langle -4, -2 \rangle$

$\|V\| = \sqrt{(4)^2 + (-2)^2}$

$= \sqrt{20}$

$= 2\sqrt{5}$

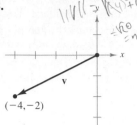

9.

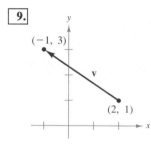

10.

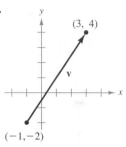

11.

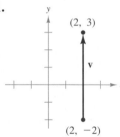

12.

$\langle 7, 0 \rangle$

$\|v\| = 7$

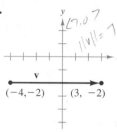

13. Initial point: $(-1, 5)$
Terminal point: $(15, 2)$

14. Initial point: $(1, 11)$
Terminal point: $(9, 3)$

15. Initial point: $(-3, -5)$
Terminal point: $(5, -1)$

16. Initial point: $(-3, 11)$
Terminal point: $(9, 40)$

In Exercises 17–26, find (a) $u + v$, (b) $u - v$, and (c) $2u - 3v$.

17. $u = \langle 1, 2 \rangle$, $v = \langle 3, 1 \rangle$
18. $u = \langle 2, 3 \rangle$, $v = \langle 4, 0 \rangle$
19. $u = \langle -2, 3 \rangle$, $v = \langle -2, 1 \rangle$
20. $u = \langle 0, 1 \rangle$, $v = \langle 0, -1 \rangle$
21. $u = \langle 4, -2 \rangle$, $v = \langle 0, 0 \rangle$
22. $u = \langle 0, 0 \rangle$, $v = \langle 2, 1 \rangle$
23. $u = i + j$, $v = 2i - 3j$
24. $u = 2i - j$, $v = -i + j$
25. $u = 2i$, $v = j$
26. $u = 3j$, $v = 2i$

In Exercises 27–30, find the magnitude and direction angle of the vector **v**.

27. $v = 5\langle \cos 30°, \sin 30° \rangle$
28. $v = 8\langle \cos 135°, \sin 135° \rangle$
29. $v = 6i - 6j$
30. $v = -2i + 5j$

In Exercises 31–38, sketch **v** and find its component form. (Assume θ is measured counterclockwise from the x-axis to the vector.)

31. $\|v\| = 3$, $\theta = 0°$
32. $\|v\| = 1$, $\theta = 45°$
33. $\|v\| = 1$, $\theta = 150°$
34. $\|v\| = \frac{5}{2}$, $\theta = 45°$
35. $\|v\| = 3\sqrt{2}$, $\theta = 150°$
36. $\|v\| = 8$, $\theta = 90°$
37. $\|v\| = 2$, v in the direction $i + 3j$
38. $\|v\| = 3$, v in the direction $3i + 4j$

In Exercises 39–44, find the component form of **v** and sketch the specified vector operations geometrically, where $u = 2i - j$ and $w = i + 2j$.

39. $v = \frac{3}{2}u$
40. $v = u + w$
41. $v = u + 2w$
42. $v = -u + w$
43. $v = \frac{1}{2}(3u + w)$
44. $v = u - 2w$

In Exercises 45–48, find the component form of the sum of the vectors **u** and **v** with direction angles θ_u and θ_v, respectively.

45. $\|u\| = 5$, $\theta_u = 0°$
$\|v\| = 5$, $\theta_v = 90°$
46. $\|u\| = 2$, $\theta_u = 30°$
$\|v\| = 2$, $\theta_v = 90°$
47. $\|u\| = 20$, $\theta_u = 45°$
$\|v\| = 50$, $\theta_v = 180°$
48. $\|u\| = 35$, $\theta_u = 25°$
$\|v\| = 50$, $\theta_v = 120°$

$\langle 9-(-3), 3(0-11) \rangle = \langle 12, 2.9 \rangle$ $\|u\| = \sqrt{144 + 841}$

$= \sqrt{985}$

In Exercises 49–52, find a unit vector in the direction of the vector.

49. $v = 4i - 3j$
50. $v = i + j$
51. $v = 2j$
52. $v = i - 2j$

In Exercises 53–56, use the Law of Cosines to find the angle α between the vectors. (Assume $0° \leq \alpha \leq 180°$.)

53. $v = i + j$, $w = 2(i - j)$
54. $v = 3i + j$, $w = 2i - j$
55. $v = i + j$, $w = 3i - j$
56. $v = i + 2j$, $w = 2i - j$

V

In Exercises 57 and 58, find the angle between the forces, given the magnitude of their resultant (vector sum). (*Hint:* Write one force as a vector in the direction of the positive *x*-axis and the other as a vector at an angle θ with the positive *x*-axis.)

57. Force one: 45 pounds
Force two: 60 pounds
Resultant force: 90 pounds

58. Force one: 3000 pounds
Force two: 1000 pounds
Resultant force: 3750 pounds

59. *Resultant Force*   Forces with magnitudes of 35 pounds and 50 pounds act on a hook (see figure). The angle between the two forces is 30°. Find the direction and magnitude of the resultant (vector sum) of these two forces.

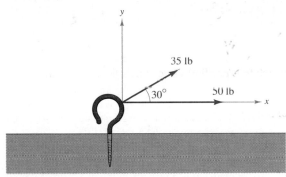

Figure for 59

60. *Resultant Force*   Forces with magnitudes of 500 pounds and 200 pounds act on a machine part at angles of 30° and −45°, respectively, with the *x*-axis (see figure). Find the direction and magnitude of the resultant (vector sum) of these forces.

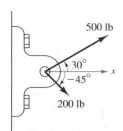

Figure for 60

61. *Resultant Force*   Three forces with magnitudes of 75 pounds, 100 pounds, and 125 pounds act on an object at angles of 30°, 45°, and 120°, respectively, with the positive *x*-axis. Find the direction and magnitude of the resultant of these forces.

62. *Resultant Force*   Three forces with magnitudes of 70 pounds, 40 pounds, and 60 pounds act on an object at angles of −30°, 45°, and 135°, respectively, with the positive *x*-axis. Find the direction and magnitude of the resultant of these forces.

63. *Horizontal and Vertical Components of Velocity*   A ball is thrown with an initial velocity of 80 feet per second at an angle of 50° with the horizontal (see figure). Find the vertical and horizontal components of the velocity.

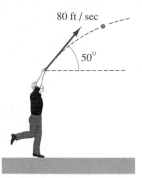

Figure for 63

64. *Horizontal and Vertical Components of Velocity*   A gun with a muzzle velocity of 1200 feet per second is fired at an angle of 6° with the horizontal. Find the vertical and horizontal components of the velocity.

Cable Tension   In Exercises 65 and 66, use the figure to determine the tension in each cable supporting the given load.

65.

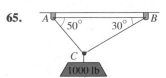

66.

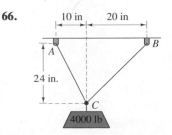

67. *Barge Towing* A loaded barge is being towed by two tugboats, and the magnitude of the resultant force is 6000 pounds directed along the axis of the barge (see figure). Find the tension in the towlines if they each make a 20° angle with the axis of the barge.

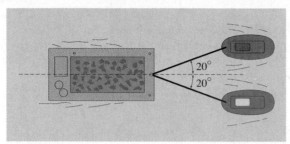

Figure for 67

68. *Shared Load* To carry a 100-pound cylindrical weight, two people lift on the ends of short ropes that are tied to an eyelet on the top center of the cylinder. Find the tension in the ropes if they each make a 30° angle with the vertical (see figure).

69. *Navigation* An airplane is flying in the direction S 32° E, with an airspeed of 540 miles per hour. Because of the wind, its groundspeed and direction are 500 miles per hour and S 40° E, respectively (see figure). Find the direction and speed of the wind.

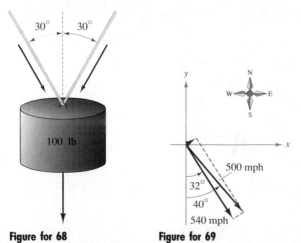

Figure for 68   **Figure for 69**

70. *Navigation* An airplane's velocity with respect to the air is 580 miles per hour, and it is headed N 58° W. The wind at the altitude of the plane is from the southwest and has a velocity of 60 miles per hour (see figure). What is the true direction of the plane, and what is its speed with respect to the ground?

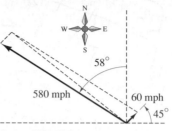

Figure for 70

71. *Work* A heavy implement is pulled 10 feet across the floor, using a force of 85 pounds. Find the work done if the direction of the force is 60° above the horizontal (see figure). (Use the formula for work, $W = FD$, where F is the component of the force in the direction of motion and D is the distance.)

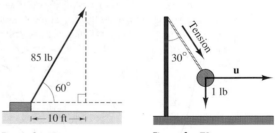

Figure for 71   **Figure for 72**

72. *Tether Ball* A tether ball weighing 1 pound is pulled outward from the pole by a horizontal force **u** until the rope makes a 30° angle with the pole (see figure). Determine the resulting tension in the rope and the magnitude of **u**.

PROBLEM

U S I N G T E C H N O L O G Y

SOLVING

Using Technology
to Sketch the
Sum of Two
Vectors

The following program is written for a Texas Instruments TI-81 graphing calculator. The program sketches two vectors $\mathbf{u} = a\mathbf{i} + b\mathbf{j}$ and $\mathbf{v} = c\mathbf{i} + d\mathbf{j}$ in standard position. Then, using the parallelogram law for vector addition, the program also sketches the vector sum $\mathbf{u} + \mathbf{v}$. *Before* running the program, you should set the range values to produce an appropriate viewing rectangle.

TI-81 Program

```
:Disp    "ENTER,(A,B)"       :Line(0,0,A,B)
:Disp    "ENTER,A"           :Line(0,0,C,D)
:Input   A                   :A+C→E
:Disp    "ENTER,B"           :B+D→F
:Input   B                   :Line(0,0,E,F)
:Disp    "ENTER,(C,D)"       :Line(A,B,E,F)
:Disp    "ENTER,C"           :Line(C,D,E,F)
:Input   C                   :Pause
:Disp    "ENTER,D"           :ClrDraw
:Input   D                   :End
```

EXAMPLE 1   Sketching a Vector Sum

Use the program listed above to sketch the sum of the vectors $\mathbf{u} = 5\mathbf{i} + 2\mathbf{j}$ and $\mathbf{v} = -4\mathbf{i} + 3\mathbf{j}$.

Solution

To show both vectors and their sum, you can use the viewing rectangle $-6 \leq x \leq 6$ and $-2 \leq y \leq 6$. Note that this setting is "square." That is, the spacing on the horizontal and vertical axes is the same. After running the program and entering $A = 5$, $B = 2$, $C = -4$, and $D = 3$, you will obtain the screen shown below. Note that the vector sum

$$\mathbf{u} + \mathbf{v} = \mathbf{i} + 5\mathbf{j}$$

appears as the diagonal of the parallelogram. The vectors $\mathbf{u}$ and $\mathbf{v}$ appear as two of the sides of the parallelogram.

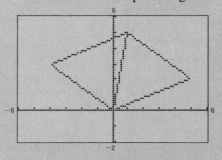

505

EXAMPLE 2 Finding the Speed and Direction of an Airplane

An airplane is headed N 60° W at a speed of 400 miles per hour. The airplane encounters a wind with a velocity of 75 miles per hour in the direction N 40° E. What is the resultant speed and direction of the airplane? (See Example 10, Section 7.3.)

Solution

The velocity of the airplane can be represented by the vector

$$\mathbf{v}_1 = 400\langle\cos 150°, \sin 150°\rangle$$

and the velocity of the wind by the vector

$$\mathbf{v}_2 = 75\langle\cos 50°, \sin 50°\rangle.$$

Thus, the resultant velocity of the airplane can be represented by $\mathbf{v}_1 + \mathbf{v}_2$. With the program given on page 585, you do not need to evaluate the numerical values of the vector coordinates. Simply enter the following.

$A = 400 \cos 150°$ $B = 400 \sin 150°$
$C = 75 \cos 50°$ $D = 75 \sin 50°$

Using $-400 \le x \le 200$ and $-100 \le y \le 300$, you will obtain the screen shown at the left.

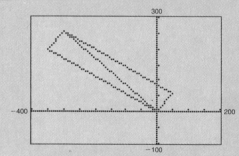

EXERCISES

(See also: Exercises 57–71, Section 7.3)

In Exercises 1–4, use the program on page 585 (or a comparable program on some other graphing utility) to sketch the sum of the two vectors. Use the result to graphically estimate the components of the sum. Then check your result algebraically. (Use $-9 \le x \le 9$ and $-6 \le y \le 6$.)

1. $\mathbf{u} = 3\mathbf{i} + 4\mathbf{j}, \mathbf{u} = -5\mathbf{i} + 1\mathbf{j}$
2. $\mathbf{u} = 5\mathbf{i} - 4\mathbf{j}, \mathbf{u} = 3\mathbf{i} + 2\mathbf{j}$
3. $\mathbf{u} = -4\mathbf{i} + 4\mathbf{j}, \mathbf{u} = -2\mathbf{i} - 6\mathbf{j}$
4. $\mathbf{u} = 7\mathbf{i} + 3\mathbf{j}, \mathbf{u} = -2\mathbf{i} - 6\mathbf{j}$

5. *Airplane Speed* Consider the airplane described in Example 2, headed N 60° W at a speed of 400 miles per hour. What wind velocity, in the direction N 40° E, will produce a resultant direction of N 50° W? Explain how to use the program given on page 585 to *experimentally* arrive at an answer. Then explain how to obtain the answer analytically.

6. *Airplane Speed* Consider the airplane described in Example 2, headed N 60° W at a speed of 400 miles per hour. What wind direction, at a velocity of 75 miles per hour, will produce a resultant direction of N 50° W? Explain how to use the program given on page 585 to *experimentally* arrive at an answer. Then explain how to obtain the answer analytically.

7. *Airplane Speed* After encountering the wind, is the airplane in Example 2 traveling at a faster speed or a slower speed? Explain.

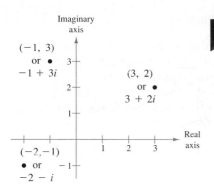

The Complex Plane

FIGURE 7.33

7.4 Trigonometric Form of a Complex Number

The Complex Plane / Trigonometric Form of a Complex Number /
Multiplication and Division of Complex Numbers

The Complex Plane

In this section we develop the trigonometric form of a complex number. The convenience of this form will not be fully apparent until we introduce DeMoivre's Theorem in Section 7.5.

Just as real numbers can be represented by points on the real number line, we can represent a complex number

$$z = a + bi$$

as the point (a, b) in a coordinate plane (the **complex plane**). In this context, we call the horizontal axis the **real axis** and the vertical axis the **imaginary axis,** as shown in Figure 7.33.

The **absolute value** of the complex number $a + bi$ is defined to be the distance between the origin $(0, 0)$ and the point (a, b), as shown in Figure 7.34.

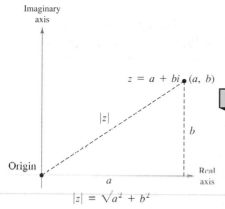

FIGURE 7.34

DEFINITION OF THE ABSOLUTE VALUE OF A COMPLEX NUMBER

The **absolute value** of the complex number $z = a + bi$ is given by

$$|a + bi| = \sqrt{a^2 + b^2}.$$

REMARK   Note that if the complex number $a + bi$ happens to be a real number (that is, if $b = 0$), then this definition agrees with that given for the absolute value of a real number. $|a + 0i| = \sqrt{a^2 + 0^2} = \sqrt{a^2} = |a|$ ◢

EXAMPLE 1   Finding the Absolute Value of a Complex Number

Plot the points corresponding to the following complex numbers and find the absolute value of each.

a. $z = -3i$ **b.** $z = -2 + 5i$

Solution

The points are shown in Figure 7.35.

a. The complex number $z = 0 + (-3)i$ has an absolute value of

$$|z| = \sqrt{0^2 + (-3)^2} = \sqrt{9} = 3.$$

b. The complex number $z = -2 + 5i$ has an absolute value of

$$|z| = \sqrt{(-2)^2 + 5^2} = \sqrt{29}.$$ ◢

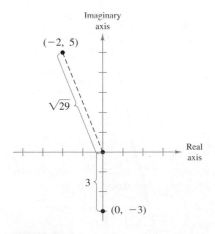

FIGURE 7.35

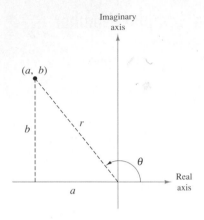

Complex Number: $a + bi$

FIGURE 7.36

Trigonometric Form of a Complex Number

In Section 3.5 we discussed how to add, subtract, multiply, and divide complex numbers. To work effectively with *powers* and *roots* of complex numbers, it is helpful to write complex numbers in **trigonometric form.** In Figure 7.36, consider the nonzero complex number $a + bi$. By letting θ be the angle from the positive x-axis (measured counterclockwise) to the line segment connecting the origin and the point (a, b), we can write

$$a = r \cos \theta \quad \text{and} \quad b = r \sin \theta$$

where $r = \sqrt{a^2 + b^2}$. Consequently, we have

$$a + bi = (r \cos \theta) + (r \sin \theta)i$$

from which we obtain the **trigonometric form of a complex number.**

TRIGONOMETRIC FORM OF A COMPLEX NUMBER

Let $z = a + bi$ be a complex number. The **trigonometric form** of z is

$$z = r(\cos \theta + i \sin \theta)$$

where $a = r \cos \theta$, $b = r \sin \theta$, $r = \sqrt{a^2 + b^2}$, and $\tan \theta = b/a$. The number r is the **modulus** of z, and θ is an **argument** of z.

REMARK The trigonometric form of a complex number is also called the **polar form.** Because there are infinitely many choices for θ, the trigonometric form of a complex number is not unique. Normally, we use θ values in the interval $0 \leq \theta < 2\pi$, though on occasion we may use $\theta < 0$.

EXAMPLE 2 Writing Complex Numbers in Trigonometric Form

Write the complex numbers in trigonometric form.

a. $z = -2 - 2\sqrt{3}i$ **b.** $z = 6 + 2i$

Use radian measure for part (a) and degree measure for part (b).

Solution

a. The absolute value of z is

$$r = |-2 - 2\sqrt{3}i| = \sqrt{(-2)^2 + (-2\sqrt{3})^2} = \sqrt{16} = 4$$

and the angle θ is given by

$$\tan \theta = \frac{b}{a} = \frac{-2\sqrt{3}}{-2} = \sqrt{3}.$$

Since $\tan \pi/3 = \sqrt{3}$ and $z = -2 - 2\sqrt{3}i$ lies in Quadrant III, you choose θ to be $\theta = \pi + \pi/3 = 4\pi/3$. Thus, the trigonometric form is

$$z = r(\cos \theta + i \sin \theta) = 4\left(\cos \frac{4\pi}{3} + i \sin \frac{4\pi}{3}\right).$$

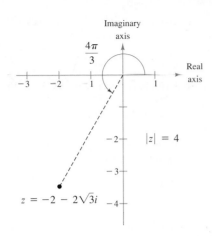

(a)

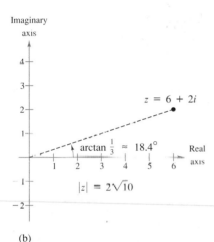

(b)

FIGURE 7.37

See Figure 7.37(a).

b. Here you have $r = |6 + 2i| = 2\sqrt{10}$ with θ given by

$$\tan \theta = \frac{2}{6} = \frac{1}{3} \qquad \qquad \theta \text{ in Quadrant I}$$

$$\theta = \arctan \frac{1}{3} \approx 18.4°.$$

Therefore, the trigonometric form of z is

$$z = r(\cos \theta + i \sin \theta)$$

$$= 2\sqrt{10}\left[\cos\left(\arctan \frac{1}{3}\right) + i \sin\left(\arctan \frac{1}{3}\right)\right]$$

$$\approx 2\sqrt{10}(\cos 18.4° + i \sin 18.4°).$$

See Figure 7.37(b).

EXAMPLE 3 **Writing a Complex Number in Standard Form**

Write the complex number in standard form $a + bi$.

$$z = \sqrt{8}\left[\cos\left(-\frac{\pi}{3}\right) + i \sin\left(-\frac{\pi}{3}\right)\right]$$

Solution

Since $\cos(-\pi/3) = 1/2$ and $\sin(-\pi/3) = -\sqrt{3}/2$, you can write

$$z = \sqrt{8}\left[\cos\left(-\frac{\pi}{3}\right) + i \sin\left(-\frac{\pi}{3}\right)\right]$$

$$= \sqrt{8}\left[\frac{1}{2} - \frac{\sqrt{3}}{2}i\right]$$

$$= 2\sqrt{2}\left[\frac{1}{2} - \frac{\sqrt{3}}{2}i\right]$$

$$= \sqrt{2} - \sqrt{6}i.$$

Multiplication and Division of Complex Numbers

The trigonometric form adapts nicely to multiplication and division of complex numbers. Suppose we are given two complex numbers

$$z_1 = r_1(\cos \theta_1 + i \sin \theta_1) \qquad \text{and} \qquad z_2 = r_2(\cos \theta_2 + i \sin \theta_2).$$

The product of z_1 and z_2 is

$$z_1 z_2 = r_1 r_2(\cos \theta_1 + i \sin \theta_1)(\cos \theta_2 + i \sin \theta_2)$$

$$= r_1 r_2[(\cos \theta_1 \cos\theta_2 - \sin \theta_1 \sin \theta_2) + i(\sin \theta_1 \cos\theta_2 + \cos\theta_1 \sin \theta_2)].$$

Using the sum and difference formulas for cosine and sine, you can rewrite this equation as

$$z_1 z_2 = r_1 r_2 [\cos(\theta_1 + \theta_2) + i \sin(\theta_1 + \theta_2)].$$

This establishes the first part of the following rule. The second part is left to you (see Exercise 55).

PRODUCT AND QUOTIENT OF TWO COMPLEX NUMBERS

Let $z_1 = r_1(\cos \theta_1 + i \sin \theta_1)$ and $z_2 = r_2(\cos \theta_2 + i \sin \theta_2)$ be complex numbers.

$$z_1 z_2 = r_1 r_2 [\cos(\theta_1 + \theta_2) + i \sin(\theta_1 + \theta_2)] \qquad \textit{Product}$$

$$\frac{z_1}{z_2} = \frac{r_1}{r_2}[\cos(\theta_1 - \theta_2) + i \sin(\theta_1 - \theta_2)], \ z_2 \neq 0 \quad \textit{Quotient}$$

Note that this rule says that to multiply two complex numbers we multiply moduli and add arguments, whereas to divide two complex numbers we divide moduli and subtract arguments.

EXAMPLE 4   Multiplying Complex Numbers in Trigonometric Form

Find the product of the complex numbers.

$$z_1 = 2\left(\cos \frac{2\pi}{3} + i \sin \frac{2\pi}{3}\right) \qquad z_2 = 8\left(\cos \frac{11\pi}{6} + i \sin \frac{11\pi}{6}\right)$$

Solution

$$z_1 z_2 = 2\left(\cos \frac{2\pi}{3} + i \sin \frac{2\pi}{3}\right) \cdot 8\left(\cos \frac{11\pi}{6} + i \sin \frac{11\pi}{6}\right)$$

$$= 16\left[\cos\left(\frac{2\pi}{3} + \frac{11\pi}{6}\right) + i \sin\left(\frac{2\pi}{3} + \frac{11\pi}{6}\right)\right]$$

$$= 16\left[\cos \frac{5\pi}{2} + i \sin \frac{5\pi}{2}\right]$$

$$= 16\left[\cos \frac{\pi}{2} + i \sin \frac{\pi}{2}\right]$$

$$= 16[0 + i(1)] = 16i$$

Check this result by first converting to the standard forms $z_1 = -1 + \sqrt{3}i$ and $z_2 = 4\sqrt{3} - 4i$ and then multiplying algebraically, as in Section 3.5.

EXAMPLE 5 **Dividing Complex Numbers in Trigonometric Form**

Find z_1/z_2 for the following two complex numbers.

$$z_1 = 24(\cos 300° + i \sin 300°) \qquad z_2 = 8(\cos 75° + i \sin 75°)$$

Solution

$$\frac{z_1}{z_2} = \frac{24(\cos 300° + i \sin 300°)}{8(\cos 75° + i \sin 75°)}$$

$$= \frac{24}{8}[\cos(300° - 75°) + i \sin(300° - 75°)]$$

$$= 3[\cos 225° + i \sin 225°]$$

$$= 3\left[\left(-\frac{\sqrt{2}}{2}\right) + i\left(-\frac{\sqrt{2}}{2}\right)\right]$$

$$= -\frac{3\sqrt{2}}{2} - \frac{3\sqrt{2}}{2}i$$

DISCUSSION

PROBLEM

Addition of Two Complex Numbers

In Section 7.3, we gave a graphical interpretation of addition of two vectors in the plane, which we called the parallelogram law for vector addition. A similar graphical interpretation can be given for addition of two complex numbers. Write a paragraph describing this interpretation and illustrate your result with the complex numbers $z_1 = 1 + 2i$ and $z_2 = 3 + i$.

WARM UP

The following warm-up exercises involve skills that were covered in earlier sections. You will use these skills in the exercise set for this section.

In Exercises 1–4, write the complex number in standard form.

1. $-5 - \sqrt{-100}$

2. $7 + \sqrt{-54}$

3. $-4i + i^2$

4. $3i^3$

In Exercises 5–10, perform the indicated operations and write the answers in standard form.

5. $(3 - 10i) - (-3 + 4i)$

6. $(2 + \sqrt{-50}) + (4 - \sqrt{2}i)$

7. $(4 - 2i)(-6 + i)$

8. $(3 - 2i)(3 + 2i)$

9. $\dfrac{1 + 4i}{1 - i}$

10. $\dfrac{3 - 5i}{2i}$

EXERCISES for Section 7.4

In Exercises 1–6, represent the complex number graphically and find its absolute value.

1. $-5i$

2. -5

3. $-4 + 4i$

4. $5 - 12i$

5. $6 - 7i$

6. $-8 + 3i$

In Exercises 7–10, express the complex number in trigonometric form.

7.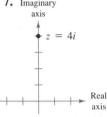

8.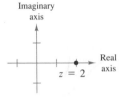

9.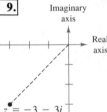

10.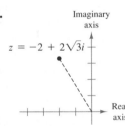

In Exercises 11–26, represent the complex numbers graphically, and find the trigonometric form of the number.

11. $3 - 3i$

12. $-2 - 2i$

13. $\sqrt{3} + i$

14. $-1 + \sqrt{3}i$

15. $-2(1 + \sqrt{3}i)$

16. $\frac{5}{2}(\sqrt{3} - i)$

17. $6i$

18. 4

19. $-7 + 4i$

20. $3 - i$

21. 7

22. $-2i$

23. $1 + 6i$

24. $2\sqrt{2} - i$

25. $-3 - i$

26. $1 + 3i$

In Exercises 27–36, represent the complex number graphically, and find the standard form of the number.

27. $2(\cos 150° + i \sin 150°)$

28. $5(\cos 135° + i \sin 135°)$

29. $\frac{3}{2}(\cos 300° + i \sin 300°)$

30. $\frac{3}{4}(\cos 315° + i \sin 315°)$

31. $3.75\left(\cos \frac{3\pi}{4} + i \sin \frac{3\pi}{4}\right)$

32. $8\left(\cos \frac{\pi}{12} + i \sin \frac{\pi}{12}\right)$

33. $4\left(\cos \frac{3\pi}{2} + i \sin \frac{3\pi}{2}\right)$

34. $7(\cos 0° + i \sin 0°)$

35. $3[\cos(18° \ 45') + i \sin(18° \ 45')]$

36. $6[\cos(230° \ 30') + i \sin (230° \ 30')]$

In Exercises 37–48, perform the indicated operation and leave the result in trigonometric form.

37. $[3(\cos \pi/3 + i \sin \pi/3)][4(\cos \pi/6 + i \sin \pi/6)]$

38. $[\frac{3}{2}(\cos \pi/2 + i \sin \pi/2)][6(\cos \pi/4 + i \sin \pi/4)]$

39. $[\frac{5}{3}(\cos 140° + i \sin 140°)][\frac{2}{3}(\cos 60° + i \sin 60°)]$

40. $[0.5(\cos 100° + i \sin 100°)][0.8(\cos 300° + i \sin 300°)]$

41. $[0.45(\cos 310° + i \sin 310°)][0.60(\cos 200° + i \sin 200°)]$

42. $(\cos 5° + i \sin 5°)(\cos 20° + i \sin 20°)$

43. $\dfrac{2(\cos 120° + i \sin 120°)}{4(\cos 40° + i \sin 40°)}$

44. $\dfrac{\cos 40° + i \sin 40°}{\cos 10° + i \sin 10°}$

45. $\dfrac{\cos(5\pi/3) + i \sin(5\pi/3)}{\cos \pi + i \sin \pi}$

46. $\dfrac{5(\cos 4.3 + i \sin 4.3)}{4(\cos 2.1 + i \sin 2.1)}$

47. $\dfrac{12(\cos 52° + i \sin 52°)}{3(\cos 110° + i \sin 110°)}$

48. $\dfrac{9(\cos 20° + i \sin 20°)}{5(\cos 75° + i \sin 75°)}$

In Exercises 49–54, (a) give the trigonometric form of the complex numbers, (b) perform the indicated operation using the trigonometric form, and (c) perform the indicated operation using the standard form and check your result with the answer to part (b).

49. $(2 + 2i)(1 - i)$

50. $(\sqrt{3} + i)(1 + i)$

51. $-2i(1 + i)$

52. $\dfrac{3 + 4i}{1 - \sqrt{3}i}$

53. $\dfrac{5}{2 + 3i}$

54. $\dfrac{4i}{-4 + 2i}$

55. Given two complex numbers, $z_1 = r_1(\cos \theta_1 + i \sin \theta_1)$ and $z_2 = r_2(\cos \theta_2 + i \sin \theta_2)$, $z_2 \neq 0$, prove that

$$\frac{z_1}{z_2} = \frac{r_1}{r_2}[\cos(\theta_1 - \theta_2) + i \sin(\theta_1 - \theta_2)].$$

56. Show that the complex conjugate of $z = r(\cos \theta + i \sin \theta)$ is $\bar{z} = r[\cos(-\theta) + i \sin(-\theta)]$.

57. Use the trigonometric form of z and $\bar{z}$ in Exercise 56 to find (a) $z\bar{z}$ and (b) $z/\bar{z}$, $z \neq 0$.

58. Show that the negative of $z = r(\cos \theta + i \sin \theta)$ is $-z = r[\cos(\theta + \pi) + i \sin(\theta + \pi)]$.

In Exercises 59 and 60, sketch the graph of all complex numbers z satisfying the given condition.

59. $|z| = 2$

60. $\theta = \pi/6$

7.5 DeMoivre's Theorem and *n*th Roots

Powers of Complex Numbers / Roots of Complex Numbers

Powers of Complex Numbers

In this section we will study procedures for finding powers and roots of complex numbers. To begin, consider the complex number (in trigonometric form), $z = r(\cos \theta + i \sin \theta)$. Repeated use of the multiplication rule from the previous section yields

$$z = r(\cos \theta + i \sin \theta)$$
$$z^2 = r(\cos \theta + i \sin \theta)r(\cos \theta + i \sin \theta)$$
$$= r^2(\cos 2\theta + i \sin 2\theta)$$
$$z^3 = z^2(z) = r^2(\cos 2\theta + i \sin 2\theta)r(\cos \theta + i \sin \theta)$$
$$= r^3(\cos 3\theta + i \sin 3\theta).$$

Similarly,

$$z^4 = r^4(\cos 4\theta + i \sin 4\theta)$$
$$z^5 = r^5(\cos 5\theta + i \sin 5\theta)$$
$$\vdots$$

This pattern leads to the following important theorem, which is named after the French mathematician Abraham DeMoivre (1667–1754).

DEMOIVRE'S THEOREM

If $z = r(\cos \theta + i \sin \theta)$ is a complex number and n is a positive integer, then

$$z^n = [r(\cos \theta + i \sin \theta)]^n = r^n(\cos n\theta + i \sin n\theta).$$

A proof of this theorem can be given using mathematical induction (see Section 10.4).

EXAMPLE 1   Finding Powers of a Complex Number

Use DeMoivre's Theorem to find $(-1 + \sqrt{3}i)^{12}$.

Solution

First convert to trigonometric form.

$$-1 + \sqrt{3}i = 2\left(\cos \frac{2\pi}{3} + i \sin \frac{2\pi}{3}\right)$$

Then, by DeMoivre's Theorem, you have

$$(-1 + \sqrt{3}i)^{12} = \left[2\left(\cos\frac{2\pi}{3} + i\sin\frac{2\pi}{3}\right)\right]^{12}$$

$$= 2^{12}\left[\cos(12)\frac{2\pi}{3} + i\sin(12)\frac{2\pi}{3}\right]$$

$$= 4096(\cos 8\pi + i\sin 8\pi)$$

$$= 4096(1 + 0)$$

$$= 4096.$$

Are you surprised to see a real number as the answer?

Roots of Complex Numbers

Recall that a consequence of the Fundamental Theorem of Algebra is that a polynomial equation of degree n has n solutions in the complex number system. Hence, an equation like $x^6 = 1$ has six solutions, and in this particular case we can find the six solutions by factoring and using the Quadratic Formula.

$$x^6 - 1 = (x^3 - 1)(x^3 + 1)$$
$$= (x - 1)(x^2 + x + 1)(x + 1)(x^2 - x + 1) = 0$$

Consequently, the solutions are

$$x = \pm 1, \quad x = \frac{-1 \pm \sqrt{3}i}{2}, \quad \text{and} \quad x = \frac{1 \pm \sqrt{3}i}{2}.$$

Each of these numbers is a sixth root of 1. In general, we define the **nth root** of a complex number as follows.

DEFINITION OF nTH ROOT OF A COMPLEX NUMBER

The complex number $u = a + bi$ is an **nth root** of the complex number z if

$$z = u^n = (a + bi)^n.$$

To find a formula for an nth root of a complex number, we let u be an nth root of z, where

$$u = s(\cos\beta + i\sin\beta) \quad \text{and} \quad z = r(\cos\theta + i\sin\theta).$$

By DeMoivre's Theorem and the fact that $u^n = z$, we have

$$s^n(\cos n\beta + i\sin n\beta) = r(\cos\theta + i\sin\theta).$$

Now, taking the absolute value of both sides of this equation, it follows that $s^n = r$. Substituting back into the previous equation and dividing by r, we get

$$\cos n\beta + i \sin n\beta = \cos \theta + i \sin \theta.$$

Thus, it follows that

$$\cos n\beta = \cos \theta \quad \text{and} \quad \sin n\beta = \sin \theta.$$

Since both sine and cosine have a period of 2π, these last two equations have solutions if and only if the angles differ by a multiple of 2π. Consequently, there must exist an integer k such that

$$n\beta = \theta + 2\pi k$$

$$\beta = \frac{\theta + 2\pi k}{n}.$$

REMARK Note that when k exceeds $n - 1$ the roots begin to repeat. For instance, if $k = n$, the angle

$$\frac{\theta + 2n\pi}{n} = \frac{\theta}{n} + 2\pi$$

is coterminal with θ/n, which is also obtained when $k = 0$.

By substituting this value for β into the trigonometric form of u, we get the result stated in the following theorem.

---

*n*TH ROOTS OF A COMPLEX NUMBER

For a positive integer n, the complex number $z = r(\cos \theta + i \sin \theta)$ has exactly n distinct nth roots given by

$$\sqrt[n]{r}\left(\cos \frac{\theta + 2\pi k}{n} + i \sin \frac{\theta + 2\pi k}{n}\right)$$

where $k = 0, 1, 2, \ldots, n - 1$.

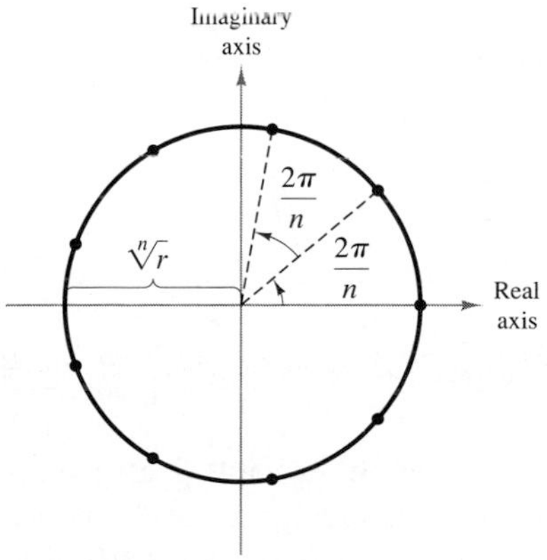

FIGURE 7.38

This formula for the nth roots of a complex number z has a nice geometrical interpretation, as shown in Figure 7.38. Note that because the nth roots of z all have the same magnitude $\sqrt[n]{r}$, they all lie on a circle of radius $\sqrt[n]{r}$ with center at the origin. Furthermore, the n roots are equally spaced along the circle, since successive nth roots have arguments that differ by $2n/\pi$.

We have already found the sixth roots of 1 by factoring and by using the Quadratic Formula. Now let's see how we can solve the same problem with the formula for nth roots.

EXAMPLE 2   Finding *n*th Roots of a Real Number

Find all the sixth roots of 1.

Solution

First write 1 in the trigonometric form $1 = 1(\cos 0 + i \sin 0)$. Then, by the *n*th root formula, with $n = 6$ and $r = 1$, the roots have the form

$$\sqrt[6]{1}\left(\cos \frac{0 + 2\pi k}{6} + i \sin \frac{0 + 2\pi k}{6}\right)$$

or simply $\cos (\pi k/3) + i \sin(\pi k/3)$. Thus, for $k = 0, 1, 2, 3, 4, 5$, the sixth roots are as follows.

$$\cos 0 + i \sin 0 = 1$$

$$\cos \frac{\pi}{3} + i \sin \frac{\pi}{3} = \frac{1}{2} + \frac{\sqrt{3}}{2}i$$

$$\cos \frac{2\pi}{3} + i \sin \frac{2\pi}{3} = -\frac{1}{2} + \frac{\sqrt{3}}{2}i$$

$$\cos \pi + i \sin \pi = -1$$

$$\cos \frac{4\pi}{3} + i \sin \frac{4\pi}{3} = -\frac{1}{2} - \frac{\sqrt{3}}{2}i$$

$$\cos \frac{5\pi}{3} + i \sin \frac{5\pi}{3} = \frac{1}{2} - \frac{\sqrt{3}}{2}i$$

See Figure 7.39.

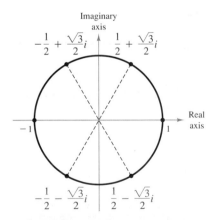

FIGURE 7.39

In Figure 7.39, notice that the roots obtained in Example 2 all have a magnitude of 1 and are equally spaced around this unit circle. Also, notice that the complex roots occur in conjugate pairs, as previously discussed in Section 3.6. We refer to the special case of the *n* distinct *n*th roots of 1 as the ***n*th roots of unity.**

EXAMPLE 3 Finding the *n*th Roots of a Complex Number

Find the three cube roots of $z = -2 + 2i$.

Solution

Because z lies in the second quadrant, the trigonometric form for z is

$$z = -2 + 2i = \sqrt{8}(\cos 135° + i \sin 135°).$$

By the formula for *n*th roots, the cube roots have the form

$$\sqrt[6]{8}\left(\cos \frac{135° + 360°k}{3} + i \sin \frac{135° + 360°k}{3}\right).$$

Finally, for $k = 0, 1, 2$, you obtain the roots

$$\sqrt{2}(\cos 45° + i \sin 45°) = 1 + i$$
$$\sqrt{2}(\cos 165° + i \sin 165°) \approx -1.3660 + 0.3660i$$
$$\sqrt{2}(\cos 285° + i \sin 285°) \approx 0.3660 - 1.3660i.$$

The *n*th roots of a complex number can be useful for solving polynomial equations.

EXAMPLE 4 Finding the Roots of a Polynomial Equation

Find all solutions to the equation $x^4 + 16 = 0$.

Solution

The given equation can be written as

$$x^4 = -16 = 16(\cos \pi + i \sin \pi)$$

which means that you can solve the equation by finding the four fourth roots of -16. Each of these roots has the form

$$\sqrt[4]{16}\left(\cos \frac{\pi + 2\pi k}{4} + i \sin \frac{\pi + 2\pi k}{4}\right).$$

Finally, using $k = 0, 1, 2, 3$, you obtain the roots

$$2\left(\cos \frac{\pi}{4} + i \sin \frac{\pi}{4}\right) = 2\left(\frac{\sqrt{2}}{2} + \frac{\sqrt{2}}{2}i\right) = \sqrt{2} + \sqrt{2}i$$
$$2\left(\cos \frac{3\pi}{4} + i \sin \frac{3\pi}{4}\right) = 2\left(-\frac{\sqrt{2}}{2} + \frac{\sqrt{2}}{2}i\right) = -\sqrt{2} + \sqrt{2}i$$
$$2\left(\cos \frac{5\pi}{4} + i \sin \frac{5\pi}{4}\right) = 2\left(-\frac{\sqrt{2}}{2} - \frac{\sqrt{2}}{2}i\right) = -\sqrt{2} - \sqrt{2}i$$
$$2\left(\cos \frac{7\pi}{4} + i \sin \frac{7\pi}{4}\right) = 2\left(\frac{\sqrt{2}}{2} - \frac{\sqrt{2}}{2}i\right) = \sqrt{2} - \sqrt{2}i.$$

DISCUSSION

PROBLEM

A Famous
Mathematical
Formula

In this section we discussed DeMoivre's Theorem, which gives a formula for raising a complex number to a positive integer power. Another famous formula that involves complex numbers and powers is called Euler's Formula, after the German mathematician Leonhard Euler (1707–1783). This formula states that

$$e^{a+bi} = e^a(\cos b + i \sin b).$$

While the interpretation of this formula is beyond the scope of this text, we decided to include it because it gives rise to one of the most wonderful equations in mathematics.

$$e^{\pi i} + 1 = 0$$

This elegant equation relates the five most famous numbers in mathematics—0, 1, π, e, and i—in a single equation. Show how Euler's Formula can be used to derive the equation.

WARM UP

The following warm-up exercises involve skills that were covered in earlier sections. You will use these skills in the exercise set for this section.

In Exercises 1 and 2, simplify the expression.

1. $\sqrt[3]{54}$ **2.** $\sqrt[4]{16 + 48}$

In Exercises 3–6, write the complex numbers in trigonometric form.

3. $-5 + 5i$ **4.** $-3i$

5. -12 **6.** 12

In Exercises 7–10, perform the indicated operation. Leave the result in trigonometric form.

7. $\left(\cos \dfrac{\pi}{4} + i \sin \dfrac{\pi}{4}\right)\left(\cos \dfrac{\pi}{2} + i \sin \dfrac{\pi}{2}\right)$

8. $\left(\cos \dfrac{\pi}{12} + i \sin \dfrac{\pi}{12}\right)\left(\cos \dfrac{5\pi}{6} + i \sin \dfrac{5\pi}{6}\right)$

9. $\dfrac{6[\cos(2\pi/3) + i \sin(2\pi/3)]}{3[\cos(\pi/6) + i \sin(\pi/6)]}$ **10.** $\dfrac{2(\cos 55° + i \sin 55°)}{3(\cos 10° + i \sin 10°)}$

EXERCISES for Section 7.5

In Exercises 1–12, use DeMoivre's Theorem to find the indicated powers of the complex number. Express the result in standard form.

1. $(1 + i)^5$ **2.** $(2 + 2i)^6$

3. $(-1 + i)^{10}$ **4.** $(1 - i)^{12}$

5. $2(\sqrt{3} + i)^7$ **6.** $4(1 - \sqrt{3}i)^3$

7. $[5(\cos 20° + i \sin 20°)]^3$ **8.** $[3(\cos 150° + i\sin 150°)]^4$

9. $\left(\cos \dfrac{5\pi}{4} + i \sin \dfrac{5\pi}{4}\right)^{10}$ **10.** $\left[2\left(\cos \dfrac{\pi}{2} + i \sin \dfrac{\pi}{2}\right)\right]^8$

11. $[5(\cos 3.2 + i \sin 3.2)]^4$ **12.** $(\cos 0 + i \sin 0)^{20}$

In Exercises 13–24, (a) use DeMoivre's Theorem to find the indicated roots of the complex number, (b) represent each of the roots graphically, and (c) express each of the roots in standard form.

13. Square roots of:
$9(\cos 120° + i \sin 120°)$

14. Square roots of:
$16(\cos 60° + i \sin 60°)$

15. Fourth roots of:
$16\left(\cos \dfrac{4\pi}{3} + i \sin \dfrac{4\pi}{3}\right)$

16. Fifth roots of:
$32\left(\cos \dfrac{5\pi}{6} + i \sin \dfrac{5\pi}{6}\right)$

17. Square roots of:
$-25i$

18. Fourth roots of:
$625i$

19. Cube roots of:
$-\frac{125}{2}(1 + \sqrt{3}i)$

20. Cube roots of:
$-4\sqrt{2}(1 - i)$

21. Cube roots of:
8

22. Fourth roots of:
i

23. Fifth roots of:
1

24. Cube roots of:
1000

In Exercises 25–32, find all the solutions of the equation and represent the solutions graphically.

25. $x^4 - i = 0$

26. $x^3 + 1 = 0$

27. $x^5 + 243 = 0$

28. $x^4 - 81 = 0$

29. $x^3 + 64i = 0$

30. $x^6 - 64i = 0$

31. $x^3 - (1 - i) = 0$

32. $x^4 + (1 + i) = 0$

REVIEW EXERCISES for Chapter 7

In Exercises 1–16, use the information to solve the triangle (if possible). If two solutions exist, list both.

1. $a = 5$, $b = 8$, $c = 10$

2. $a = 6$, $b = 9$, $C = 45°$

3. $A = 12°$, $B = 58°$, $a = 5$

4. $B = 110°$, $C = 30°$, $c = 10.5$

5. $B = 110°$, $a = 4$, $c = 4$

6. $a = 80$, $b = 60$, $c = 100$

7. $A = 75°$, $a = 2.5$, $b = 16.5$

8. $A = 130°$, $a = 50$, $b = 30$

9. $B = 115°$, $a = 7$, $b = 14.5$

10. $C = 50°$, $a = 25$, $c = 22$

11. $A = 15°$, $a = 5$, $b = 10$

12. $B = 150°$, $a = 64$, $b = 10$

13. $B = 150°$, $a = 10$, $c = 20$

14. $a = 2.5$, $b = 15.0$, $c = 4.5$

15. $B = 25°$, $a = 6.2$, $b = 4$

16. $B = 90°$, $a = 5$, $c = 12$

In Exercises 17–20, use the information to find the area of the triangle.

17. $a = 4$, $b = 5$, $c = 7$ **18.** $a = 15$, $b = 8$, $c = 10$

19. $A = 27°$, $b = 5$, $c = 8$

20. $B = 80°$, $a = 4$, $c = 8$

21. *Height of a Tree* Find the height of a tree that stands on a hillside of slope 32° (from the horizontal) if from a point 75 feet down the hill from the tree the angle of elevation to the top of the tree is 48° (see figure).

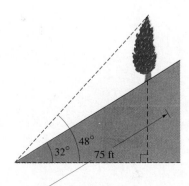

Figure for 21

22. *Surveying*   To approximate the length of a marsh, a surveyor walks 450 meters from point A to point B. Then the surveyor turns 65° and walks 325 meters to point C. Approximate the length AC of the marsh (see figure).

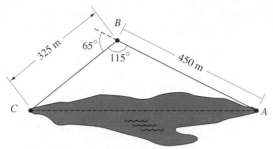

Figure for 22

23. *Height*   From a certain distance, the angle of elevation of the top of a building is 17°. At a point 50 meters closer to the building, the angle of elevation is 31°. Approximate the height of the building.

24. *River Width*   Determine the width of a river that flows due east, if a tree on the opposite bank has a bearing of N 22° 30′ E and, after walking 400 feet downstream, a surveyor finds the tree has a bearing of N 15° W.

25. *Navigation*   Two planes leave an airport at approximately the same time. One is flying at 425 miles per hour at a bearing of N 5° W, and the other is flying at 530 miles per hour at a bearing of N 67° E (see figure). How far apart are the planes after flying for 2 hours?

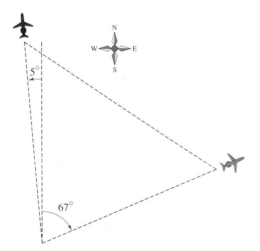

Figure for 25

26. *Geometry*   The lengths of the diagonals of a parallelogram are 10 feet and 16 feet. Find the lengths of the sides of the parallelogram if the diagonals intersect at an angle of 28°.

In Exercises 27–30, find the component form of the vector **v** satisfying the given conditions.

27. Initial point: (0, 10)
Terminal point: (7, 3)

28. Initial point: (1, 5)
Terminal point: (15, 9)

29. $\|\mathbf{v}\| = 8$, $\theta = 120°$

30. $\|\mathbf{v}\| = \frac{1}{2}$, $\theta = 225°$

In Exercises 31–34, find the component form of the specified vector and sketch its graph given that $\mathbf{u} = 6\mathbf{i} - 5\mathbf{j}$ and $\mathbf{v} = 10\mathbf{i} + 3\mathbf{j}$.

31. $\dfrac{1}{\|\mathbf{u}\|}\mathbf{u}$

32. $3\mathbf{v}$

33. $4\mathbf{u} - 5\mathbf{v}$

34. $\frac{1}{2}\mathbf{v}$

35. *Resultant Force*   Find the direction and magnitude of the resultant of the three forces shown in the figure.

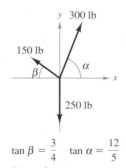

$$\tan \beta = \frac{3}{4} \qquad \tan \alpha = \frac{12}{5}$$

Figure for 35

36. *Resultant Force*   Forces of magnitude 85 pounds and 50 pounds act on a single point. Find the magnitude of the resultant if the angle between the forces is 15°.

37. *Rope Tension*   A 100-pound weight is supported by two ropes as shown in the figure. Find the tension in each rope.

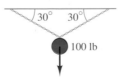

Figure for 37

38. *Braking Force*   A 500-pound motorcycle is headed up a hill inclined at 12°. What force is required to keep the motorcycle from rolling back down the hill when stopped at a red light?

39. *Navigation*   An airplane has an airspeed of 450 miles per hour at a bearing of N 30° E. If the wind velocity is 20 miles per hour from the west, find the ground speed and the direction of the plane.

40. *Angle Between Forces*   Forces of 60 pounds and 100 pounds have a resultant force of 125 pounds. Find the angle between the two given forces.

In Exercises 41–44, find the trigonometric form of the complex number.

41. $5 - 5i$

42. $-3\sqrt{3} + 3i$

43. $5 + 12i$

44. -7

In Exercises 45–48, write the complex number in standard form.

45. $100(\cos 240° + i \sin 240°)$

46. $24(\cos 330° + i \sin 330°)$

47. $13(\cos 0 + i \sin 0)$

48. $8\left(\cos \dfrac{5\pi}{6} + i \sin \dfrac{5\pi}{6}\right)$

In Exercises 49–52, (a) express the two complex numbers in trigonometric form, and (b) use the trigonometric form to find $z_1 z_2$ and $\dfrac{z_1}{z_2}$.

49. $z_1 = -5, \quad z_2 = 5i$

50. $z_1 = 2\sqrt{3} - 2i, \quad z_2 = -10i$

51. $z_1 = -3(1 + i), \quad z_2 = 2(\sqrt{3} + i)$

52. $z_1 = 5i, \quad z_2 = 2(1 - i)$

In Exercises 53–56, use DeMoivre's Theorem to find the indicated power of the complex number. Express the result in standard form.

53. $\left[5\left(\cos \dfrac{\pi}{12} + i \sin \dfrac{\pi}{12}\right)\right]^4$

54. $\left[2\left(\cos \dfrac{4\pi}{15} + i \sin \dfrac{4\pi}{15}\right)\right]^5$

55. $(2 + 3i)^6$

56. $(1 - i)^8$

In Exercises 57–60, use DeMoivre's Theorem to find the roots of the complex number.

57. Sixth roots of: $-729i$

58. Fourth roots of: 256

59. Cube roots of: -1

60. Fourth roots of: $-1 + i$

In Exercises 61–64, find all solutions to the equation and represent the solutions graphically.

61. $x^4 + 81 = 0$

62. $x^5 - 32 = 0$

63. $(x^3 - 1)(x^2 + 1) = 0$

64. $x^3 + 8i = 0$

CUMULATIVE TEST for Chapters 4–7

Take this test as you would take a test in class. After you are done, check your work with the answers given in the back of the book.

1. Sketch a graph of each of the functions.
   (a) $f(x) = 6(2^{-x})$ (b) $g(x) = \log_3 x$

2. Evaluate without the aid of a calculator: $\log_5 125$

3. Use the properties of logarithms to write the expression $2 \ln x - \frac{1}{2} \ln(x + 5)$ as the logarithm of a single quantity.

4. Solve the equation: $6e^{2x} = 72$

5. On the day a grandchild is born, a grandparent deposits $2500 into a fund earning 7.5% interest compounded continuously. Determine the balance in the account at the time of the grandchild's 25th birthday.

6. Consider the angle $\theta = -120°$.
   (a) Sketch the angle in standard position.
   (b) Give a coterminal angle in the interval $[0°, 360°)$.
   (c) Convert the angle to radian measure.
   (d) Find its reference angle θ'.
   (e) Find the exact values of the six trigonometric functions of θ.

7. Convert the angle of magnitude 2.35 radians to degrees. Round the answer to one decimal place.

8. Sketch the graphs of the functions (a) $f(x) = 3 - 2 \sin \pi x$ and (b) $g(x) = \frac{1}{2} \tan\left(x - \frac{\pi}{2}\right)$.

9. Write an algebraic expression that is equivalent to $\sin[\arccos(2x)]$.

10. Perform the following subtraction and simplify the result.
$$\frac{\sin \theta - 1}{\cos \theta} - \frac{\cos \theta}{\sin \theta - 1}$$

11. Prove the following identities.
    (a) $\cot^2 \alpha(\sec^2 \alpha - 1) = 1$,   (b) $\sin(x + y) \sin(x - y) = \sin^2 x - \sin^2 y$,   (c) $\sin^2 x \cos^2 x = \frac{1}{8}(1 - \cos 4x)$

12. Find all the solutions of the following equations in the interval $[0, 2\pi)$.
    (a) $2 \cos^2 \beta = 0$,   (b) $3 \tan \theta - \cot \theta = 0$

13. Find the remaining sides and angles of the triangle shown in the accompanying figure.
(a) $A = 30°$, $a = 9$, $b = 8$ (b) $A = 30°$, $b = 8$, $c = 10$

14. Find the trigonometric form of the complex number $-2 + 2i$.

15. Use DeMoivre's Theorem to find the three cube roots of 1.

16. From a point 200 feet from a flag pole, the angles of elevation to the bottom and top of the flag are $16°45'$ and $18°$, respectively. Approximate the height of the flag to the nearest foot.

17. An airplane's velocity with respect to the air is 500 miles per hour, and it is headed N 30° E. The wind at the altitude of the plane has a velocity of 50 miles per hour in the direction N 60° E. What is the true direction of the plane, and what is its speed relative to the ground?

C H A P T E R 8

OVERVIEW

In this chapter, you will study ways to solve systems of equations. A system of equations can be used to model many different types of real-life situations. For instance, Example 7 on page 531 uses a system of equations to compare the sales of compact disc players and turntables from 1983 through 1987. During these years, the sale of turntables decreased at a linear rate and the sale of compact disc players increased at a linear rate. The solution of the system represents the time at which the sale of compact disc players overtook the sale of turntables.

Solving a system of equations can involve many arithmetic steps. Because it is easy to make errors, be sure to check your solution(s) in the original system or problem statement.

Systems of Equations and Inequalities

8.1 Systems of Equations

The Method of Substitution / Graphical Approach to Finding Solutions / Applications

The Method of Substitution

Up to this point in the text most problems have involved either a function of one variable or a single equation in two variables. However, many problems in science, business, and engineering involve two or more equations in two or more variables. To solve such problems, you need to find solutions of a **system of equations.**

Here is an example of a system of two equations in x and y.

$$2x + y = 5 \qquad \textit{Equation 1}$$
$$3x - 2y = 4 \qquad \textit{Equation 2}$$

A **solution** of this system is an ordered pair that satisfies each equation in the system, and when you find the set of all solutions you are **solving the system of equations.** For instance, the ordered pair $(2, 1)$ is a solution of this system. To check this you can substitute 2 for x and 1 for y into *each* equation, as follows.

$$2(2) + 1 = 5 \qquad \textit{Equation 1 checks}$$
$$3(2) - 2(1) = 4 \qquad \textit{Equation 2 checks}$$

There are several different ways to solve systems of equations. In this chapter we will consider three of the most common techniques. We begin with the **method of substitution.** This method has five basic steps, which can be labeled *solve*, *substitute*, *solve*, *back-substitute*, and *check*. We illustrate these five steps in Example 1.

EXAMPLE 1   Solving a System of Two Equations in Two Variables

Solve the following system of equations.

$$x + y = 4 \qquad \qquad \text{Equation 1}$$
$$x - y = 2 \qquad \qquad \text{Equation 2}$$

Solution

Solving for y in Equation 1, you get

$$y = 4 - x.$$

Substituting $(4 - x)$ for y in Equation 2, you obtain a single-variable equation, which you then *solve* for x.

$$x - (4 - x) = 2$$
$$x - 4 + x = 2$$
$$2x = 6$$
$$x = 3$$

REMARK   The term *back-substitution* implies that you work *backwards*. First solve for one of the variables, and then substitute that value *back* into one of the equations in the system to find the value of the other variable.

Finally, by *back-substituting* $x = 3$ into the equation $y = 4 - x$, you obtain

$$y = 4 - x = 4 - 3 = 1.$$

Thus, the solution is the ordered pair (3, 1).

Check

Equation 1: $3 + 1 = 4$ *Check solution in each equation in the original system.*
Equation 2: $3 - 1 = 2$

Because many steps are required to solve a system of equations, it is very easy to make errors in arithmetic. Thus, we *strongly* suggest that you always *check your solution by substituting it into each equation in the original system.*

Method of Substitution

To solve a system of two equations in two variables, use the following process.

1. *Solve* one of the equations for one variable in terms of the other.
2. *Substitute* the expression found in Step 1 into the other equation to obtain an equation of one variable.
3. *Solve* the equation obtained in Step 2.
4. *Back-substitute* the solution in Step 3 into the expression obtained in Step 1 to find the value of the other variable.
5. *Check* the solution to see that it satisfies *each* of the original equations.

EXAMPLE 2   Solving a System by Substitution: One-Solution Case

A total of $12,000 is invested in two funds paying 9% and 11% simple interest. If the yearly interest is $1,180, how much of the $12,000 is invested at each rate?

Solution

Verbal Model

$$\frac{9\%}{\text{fund}} + \frac{11\%}{\text{fund}} = \frac{\text{Total}}{\text{investment}}$$

$$\frac{9\%}{\text{interest}} + \frac{11\%}{\text{interest}} = \frac{\text{Total}}{\text{interest}}$$

Labels

9% fund $= x$,   9% interest $= 0.09x$
11% fund $= y$,   11% interest $= 0.11y$
Total investment $= \$12,000$,   Total interest $= \$1,180$

System of Equations

$x + \quad y = 12,000$ *Equation 1*
$0.09x + 0.11y = \quad 1,180$ *Equation 2*

To begin, it is convenient to multiply both sides of the second equation by 100 to obtain $9x + 11y = 118,000$. This eliminates the need to work with decimals. Then the following steps are performed.

1. Solve for x in Equation 1.

$$x = 12,000 - y$$

2. Substitute this expression for x into the new Equation 2.

$$9(12,000 - y) + 11y = 118,000$$

3. Solve for y.

$$108,000 - 9y + 11y = 118,000$$
$$2y = 10,000$$
$$y = 5,000 \text{ (dollars)}$$

4. Back-substitute the value $y = 5{,}000$ to solve for x.

$$x = 12{,}000 - 5{,}000 = 7{,}000 \text{ (dollars)}$$

Therefore, the solution is the ordered pair (7000, 5000). Check to see that $x = 7{,}000$ and $y = 5{,}000$ satisfy each of the original equations.

Note that the equations in Examples 1 and 2 are linear. That is, the variables x and y occurred to the first power only. The method of substitution can also be used to solve systems in which one or both of the equations are nonlinear.

EXAMPLE 3   Solving a System by Substitution: Two-Solution Case

Solve the following system of equations.

$$x^2 - x - y = 1 \qquad\qquad \textit{Equation 1}$$
$$-x + y = -1 \qquad\qquad \textit{Equation 2}$$

Solution

1. Solve for y in Equation 2.

$$-x + y = -1$$
$$y = x - 1$$

2. Substitute this expression for y into Equation 1.

$$x^2 - x - (x - 1) = 1$$

3. Solve for x.

$$x^2 - 2x + 1 = 1$$
$$x^2 - 2x = 0$$
$$x(x - 2) = 0$$
$$x = 0, x = 2$$

4. Back-substitute these values of x to solve for the corresponding values of y.

For $x = 0$: $y = 0 - 1 = -1$
For $x = 2$: $y = 2 - 1 = 1$

Thus, there are two solutions: $(0, -1)$ and $(2, 1)$. Check these solutions in the original system to see that both work.

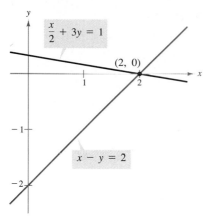

(a) One Point of Intersection

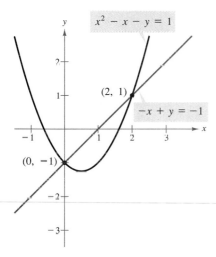

(b) Two Points of Intersection

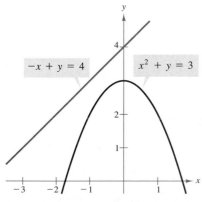

(c) No Points of Intersection

EXAMPLE 4   Solving a System by Substitution: No-Solution Case

Solve the following system of equations.

$$-x + y = 4 \qquad\qquad \textit{Equation 1}$$
$$x^2 + y = 3 \qquad\qquad \textit{Equation 2}$$

Solution

1. In this case, you solve for y in Equation 1.

$$y = x + 4$$

2. Substitute this expression for y into Equation 2.

$$x^2 + (x + 4) = 3$$

3. Solve for x.

$$x^2 + x + 4 = 3$$
$$x^2 + x + 1 = 0$$
$$x = \frac{-1 \pm \sqrt{1^2 - 4(1)(1)}}{2} \qquad \textit{Quadratic Formula}$$

Since the discriminant is negative, the equation $x^2 + x + 1 = 0$ has no (real) solution. Hence, this system has no (real) solution. ◢

Graphical Approach to Finding Solutions

From Examples 2, 3, and 4 you can see that a system of two equations in two unknowns can have exactly one solution, more than one solution, or no solution. In practice, you can gain insight about the location and number of solutions of a system of equations by graphing each of the equations on the same coordinate plane. The solutions of the system correspond to the **points of intersection** of the graphs. For instance, in Figure 8.1(a) the two equations graph as two lines with a *single point* of intersection. The two equations in Example 3 graph as a parabola and a line with *two points* of intersection, as shown in Figure 8.1(b). Moreover, the two equations in Example 4 graph as a line and a parabola that happen to have *no points* of intersection, as shown in Figure 8.1(c).

Occasionally, the graphical approach to solving a system of equations is easier than the method of substitution.

FIGURE 8.1

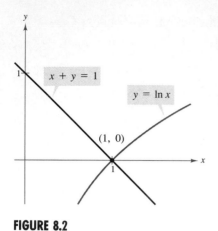

FIGURE 8.2

EXAMPLE 5   Solving a System of Equations

Solve the following system of equations.

$$y = \ln x \qquad \text{\textit{Equation 1}}$$
$$x + y = 1 \qquad \text{\textit{Equation 2}}$$

Solution

The graph of each equation is shown in Figure 8.2. From this sketch it is clear that there is only one point of intersection. Also, it appears that $(1, 0)$ is the solution point, and you can confirm this by checking these coordinates in *both* equations.

Check   Let $x = 1$ and $y = 0$.

$$0 = \ln 1 \qquad \text{\textit{Equation 1 checks}}$$
$$1 + 0 = 1 \qquad \text{\textit{Equation 2 checks}}$$

REMARK   Example 5 shows you the value of a graphical approach to solving systems of equations in two variables. Notice what would have happened if you had tried only the substitution method in Example 5. By substituting $y = \ln x$ into $x + y = 1$, you obtain $x + \ln x = 1$. It would be difficult to solve this equation for x using standard algebraic techniques.

Applications

The total cost C of producing x units of a product typically has two components—the initial cost and the cost per unit. When enough units have been sold so that the total revenue R equals the total cost, sales have reached the **break-even point.** The break-even point corresponds to the point of intersection of the cost and revenue curves.

EXAMPLE 6   An Application: Break-Even Analysis

A small business invests $10,000 in equipment to produce a product. Each unit of the product costs $0.65 to produce and is sold for $1.20. How many items must be sold before the business breaks even?

Solution

The total cost of producing x units is

$$\begin{array}{cc} \text{Cost per} & \text{Initial} \\ \text{unit} & \text{cost} \end{array}$$
$$C = \overbrace{0.65x} + \overbrace{10,000} \qquad \text{\textit{Equation 1}}$$

and the revenue obtained by selling x units is

$$\begin{array}{c} \text{Price} \\ \text{per unit} \end{array}$$
$$R = \overbrace{1.2x}. \qquad \text{\textit{Equation 2}}$$

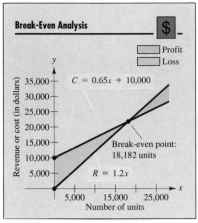
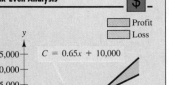

FIGURE 8.3

Since the break-even point occurs when $R = C$, we have

$$1.2x = 0.65x + 10,000 \qquad \textit{Solve for R and C}$$
$$0.55x = 10,000$$
$$x = \frac{10,000}{0.55} \approx 18,182 \text{ units.}$$

Note in Figure 8.3 that sales less than the break-even point correspond to an overall loss, while sales greater than the break-even point correspond to a profit.

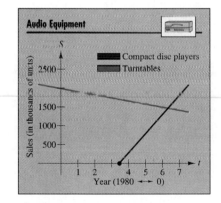

FIGURE 8.4

EXAMPLE 7 Compact Disc Players and Turntables

Between 1983 and 1987 the number of compact disc players sold each year in the United States was *increasing* and the number of turntables was *decreasing*. Two models that approximate the sales are

$$S = -1700 + 496t \qquad \textit{Compact disc players}$$
$$S = 1972 - 82t \qquad \textit{Turntables}$$

where S represents the annual sales in thousands of units and t represents the calendar year with $t = 3$ corresponding to 1983 (see Figure 8.4). According to these two models, when would you expect the sales of compact disc players to have exceeded the sales of turntables? (*Source:* Dealerscope Merchandising)

Solution

Since the first equation has already been solved for S in terms of t, substitute this value into the second equation and solve for t as follows.

$$-1700 + 496t = 1972 - 82t$$
$$496t + 82t = 1972 + 1700$$
$$578t = 3672$$
$$t \approx 6.4$$

Thus, from the given models, you would expect that the sales of compact disc players exceeded the sales of turntables sometime during 1986.

DISCUSSION
PROBLEM

Points of
Intersection of
Two Graphs

In this section, you learned that the graphs of two equations can intersect at zero, one, or more than one point. Sketch the graphs of the following systems. Which represents a system with no solution? Which represents a system with one solution? Which represents a system with two solutions?

1. $x^2 + y^2 = 4$
   $x + y = 2$

2. $x^2 + y^2 = 8$
   $x + y = 4$

3. $x^2 + y^2 = 4$
   $x + y = 6$

Find an example of three other systems of equations, one with no solution, one with one solution, and one with two solutions.

WARM UP

The following warm-up exercises involve skills that were covered in earlier sections. You will use these skills in the exercise set for this section.

In Exercises 1–4, sketch the graph of the equation.

1. $y = -\frac{1}{3}x + 6$

2. $y = 2(x - 3)$

3. $x^2 + y^2 = 4$

4. $y = 5 - (x - 3)^2$

In Exercises 5–8, perform the indicated operations and simplify.

5. $(3x + 2y) - 2(x + y)$

6. $(-10u + 3v) + 5(2u - 8v)$

7. $x^2 + (x - 3)^2 + 6x$

8. $y^2 - (y + 1)^2 + 2y$

In Exercises 9 and 10, solve the equation.

9. $3x + (x - 5) = 15 + 4$

10. $y^2 + (y - 2)^2 = 2$

EXERCISES for Section 8.1

In Exercises 1–10, solve the system by the method of substitution.

1. $2x + y = 4$
   $-x + y = 1$

   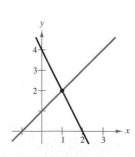

2. $x - y = -5$
   $x + 2y = 4$

   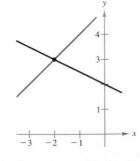

3. $x - y = -3$
   $x^2 - y = -1$

   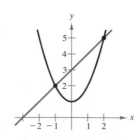

4. $3x - y = -2$
   $x^3 - y = 0$

   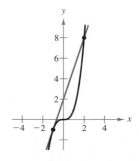

5. $x + 3y = 15$
$x^2 + y^2 = 25$

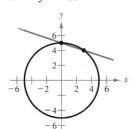

6. $x \quad - y = 0$
$x^3 - 5x + y = 0$

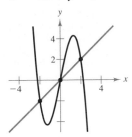

7. $x^2 - y = 0$
$x^2 - 4x + y = 0$

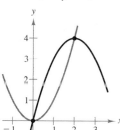

8. $y = \quad -x^2 + 1$
$y = x^4 - 2x^2 + 1$

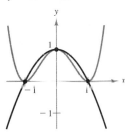

9. $x - 3y = -4$
$x^2 - y^3 - \quad 0$

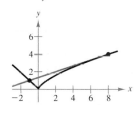

10. $y = x^3 - 3x^2 + 3$
$y - \quad - 2x + 3$

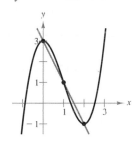

In Exercises 11–30, solve the system by the method of substitution.

11. $x - y = 0$
$5x - 3y = 10$

12. $x + 2y = 1$
$5x - 4y = -23$

13. $2x - y + 2 = 0$
$4x + y - 5 = 0$

14. $6x - 3y - 4 = 0$
$x + 2y - 4 = 0$

15. $30x - 40y - 33 = 0$
$10x + 20y - 21 = 0$

16. $1.5x + 0.8y = 2.3$
$0.3x - 0.2y = 0.1$

17. $\frac{1}{5}x + \frac{1}{2}y = 8$
$x + y = 20$

18. $\frac{1}{2}x + \frac{3}{4}y = 10$
$\frac{3}{2}x - y = 4$

19. $x - y = 0$
$2x + y = 0$

20. $x - 2y = 0$
$3x - y = 0$

21. $y = 2x$
$y = x^2 + 1$

22. $x + y = 4$
$x^2 - y = 2$

23. $3x - 7y + 6 = 0$
$x^2 - y^2 = 4$

24. $x^2 + y^2 = 25$
$2x + y = 10$

25. $x^2 + y^2 = 5$
$x - y = 1$

26. $y = x^3 - 2x^2 + x - 1$
$y = -x^2 + 3x - 1$

27. $y = x^4 - 2x^2 + 1$
$y = 1 - x^2$

28. $x^2 + y = 4$
$2x - y = 1$

29. $xy - 1 = 0$
$2x - 4y + 7 = 0$

30. $x - 2y = 1$
$y = \sqrt{x - 1}$

In Exercises 31–42, find all points of intersection of the graphs of the given pair of equations. [*Hint:* A graphical approach, as demonstrated in Example 5, may be helpful.]

31. $x + y = 4$
$x^2 + y^2 - 4x = 0$

32. $x - y + 3 = 0$
$x^2 - 4x + 7 = y$

33. $2x - y + 3 = 0$
$x^2 + y^2 - 4x = 0$

34. $3x - 2y = 0$
$x^2 - y^2 = 4$

35. $x^2 + y^2 = 25$
$(x - 8)^2 + y^2 = 41$

36. $x^2 + y^2 = 8$
$y = x^2$

37. $y = e^x$
$x - y + 1 = 0$

38. $x + 2y = 8$
$y = \log_2 x$

39. $y = \sqrt{x}$
$y = x$

40. $x - y = 3$
$x - y^2 - 1$

41. $x^2 + y^2 = 169$
$x^2 - 8y = 104$

42. $x^2 + y^2 = 4$
$2x^2 - y = 2$

Break-Even Analysis In Exercises 43–46, find the sales necessary to break even ($R = C$) for the given cost C of x units, and the given revenue R obtained by selling x units. (Round your answer to the nearest whole unit.)

43. $C = 8650x + 250{,}000,$ $R = 9950x$

44. $C = 5.5\sqrt{x} + 10{,}000,$ $R = 3.29x$

45. $C = 2.65x + 350{,}000,$ $R = 4.15x$

46. $C = 0.08x + 50{,}000,$ $R = 0.25x$

47. *Break-Even Point* Suppose you are setting up a small business and have invested \$16,000 to produce an item that will sell for \$5.95. If each unit can be produced for \$3.45, how many units must be sold to break even?

48. *Break-Even Point*   Suppose you are setting up a small business and have an initial investment of $5000. The unit cost of the product is $21.60, and the selling price is $34.10. How many units must be sold to break even?

49. *Investment Portfolio*   A total of $25,000 is invested in two funds paying 8% and 8.5% simple interest. If the yearly interest is $2,060, how much of the $25,000 is invested at each rate?

50. *Investment Portfolio*   A total of $18,000 is invested in two funds paying 7.75% and 8.25% simple interest. If the yearly interest is $1,455, how much of the $18,000 is invested at each rate?

51. *Choice of Two Jobs*   Suppose you are offered two different jobs selling dental supplies. One company offers a straight commission of 6% of sales. The other company offers a salary of $250 per week *plus* 3% of the sales. How much would you have to sell in a week in order to make the straight commission offer better?

52. *Choice of Two Jobs*   Suppose you are offered two different jobs selling college textbooks. One company offers an annual salary of $20,000 *plus* a year-end bonus of 1% of your total sales. The other company offers a salary of $15,000 *plus* a year-end bonus of 2% of your total sales. How much would you have to sell in a year in order to make the second offer better than the first?

53. *Log Volume*   You are offered two different rules for estimating the number of board feet in a log that is 16 feet long. One is the *Doyle Log Rule* and is modeled by

$$V = (D - 4)^2, \quad 5 \le D \le 40$$

and the other is the *Scribner Log Rule* and is modeled by

$$V = 0.79D^2 - 2D - 4, \quad 5 \le D \le 40$$

where D is the diameter of the log and V is its volume in board feet (see figure).
(a) For what diameter do the two scales agree?
(b) If you were selling large logs, which scale would you want to be used?

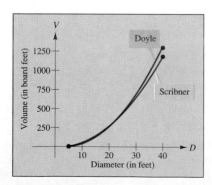

Figure for 53

54. *Market Equilibrium*   The supply and demand curves for a business dealing with wheat are given by

Supply: $p = 1.45 + 0.00014x^2$
Demand: $p = (2.388 - 0.007x)^2$

where p is the price in dollars per bushel and x is the quantity in bushels per day (see figure). Find the market equilibrium.

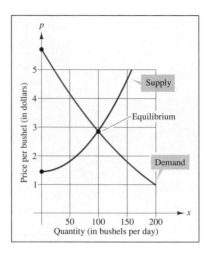

Figure for 54

55. *Area*   What are the dimensions of a rectangular tract of land if its perimeter is 40 miles and its area is 96 square miles?

56. *Area*   What are the dimensions of an isosceles right triangle with a 2-inch-long hypotenuse and an area of 1 square inch?

57. Find an equation of a line whose graph intersects the graph of the parabola $y = x^2$ at (a) two points, (b) one point, and (c) no points. (The answers are not unique.)

8.2 Systems of Linear Equations in Two Variables

The Method of Elimination / Graphical Interpretation of Solutions / Applications

The Method of Elimination

In Section 8.1, we discussed two methods of solving a system of equations (by substitution and by graphing). In this section, we discuss the **method of elimination.** The key step in the method of elimination is to obtain, for one of the variables, coefficients that differ only in sign so that by *adding* the two equations this variable will be eliminated. This is true for the following system.

$$
\begin{array}{ll}
3x + 5y = 7 & \text{\textit{Equation 1}} \\
-3x - 2y = -1 & \text{\textit{Equation 2}} \\
\hline
3y = 6 & \text{\textit{Add equations}}
\end{array}
$$

Note that by adding the two equations, you eliminated the variable x and obtained a single equation in y. Solving this equation for y produces $y = 2$, which you back-substitute into one of the original equations to solve for x.

EXAMPLE 1   The Method of Elimination

Solve the following system of linear equations.

$$
\begin{array}{ll}
3x + 2y = 4 & \text{\textit{Equation 1}} \\
5x - 2y = 8 & \text{\textit{Equation 2}}
\end{array}
$$

Solution

Begin by noting that the coefficients for y differ only in sign. Therefore, by adding the two equations, you can eliminate y.

$$
\begin{array}{ll}
3x + 2y = 4 & \text{\textit{Equation 1}} \\
5x - 2y = 8 & \text{\textit{Equation 2}} \\
\hline
8x = 12 & \text{\textit{Add equations}}
\end{array}
$$

Therefore, $x = \frac{3}{2}$. By back-substituting this value into the first equation, you can solve for y, as follows.

$$
\begin{array}{ll}
3x + 2y = 4 & \text{\textit{Equation 1}} \\
3\left(\dfrac{3}{2}\right) + 2y = 4 & \text{\textit{Replace x by }}\tfrac{3}{2} \\
y = -\dfrac{1}{4} & \text{\textit{Solve for y}}
\end{array}
$$

Therefore, the solution is $\left(\frac{3}{2}, -\frac{1}{4}\right)$. Check this solution in the original system of linear equations.

Try using the method of substitution to solve the system given in Example 1. Which method do you think is easier? Many people find that the method of elimination is more efficient.

The Method of Elimination

To use the **method of elimination** to solve a system of two linear equations in x and y, use the following steps.

1. Obtain coefficients for x (or y) that differ only in sign by multiplying all terms of one or both equations by suitably chosen constants.
2. Add the equations to eliminate one variable and solve the resulting equation.
3. Back-substitute the value obtained in Step 2 into either of the original equations and solve for the other variable.
4. Check your solution in both of the original equations.

To obtain coefficients (for one of the variables) that differ only in sign we often need to multiply one or both of the equations by a suitable constant.

EXAMPLE 2   The Method of Elimination

Solve the following system of linear equations.

$$2x - 3y = -7 \qquad \text{\textit{Equation 1}}$$
$$3x + y = -5 \qquad \text{\textit{Equation 2}}$$

Solution

For this system, you can obtain coefficients that differ only in sign by multiplying the second equation by 3.

$$
\begin{array}{llll}
2x - 3y = -7 & \rightarrow & 2x - 3y = -7 & \textit{Equation 1} \\
3x + y = -5 & \rightarrow & 9x + 3y = -15 & \textit{Multiply Equation 2 by 3} \\
\hline
& & 11x = -22 & \textit{Add equations}
\end{array}
$$

Thus, you see that $x = -2$. By back-substituting this value of x into the first equation, you can solve for y.

$$
\begin{array}{ll}
2x - 3y = -7 & \textit{Equation 1} \\
2(-2) - 3y = -7 & \textit{Replace x by} -2 \\
-3y = -3 & \textit{Add 4 to both sides} \\
y = 1 & \textit{Solve for y}
\end{array}
$$

Therefore, the solution is $(-2, 1)$. Check to see that it satisfies both original equations.

In Example 2, the two systems of linear equations

$$2x - 3y = -7 \quad \text{and} \quad 2x - 3y = -7$$
$$3x + y = -5 \qquad\qquad 9x + 3y = -15$$

are **equivalent** because they have precisely the same solution set. The operations that can be performed on a system of linear equations to produce an equivalent system are (1) interchange two equations, (2) multiply an equation by a nonzero constant, and (3) add a multiple of an equation to another equation.

EXAMPLE 3 The Method of Elimination: One-Solution Case

Solve the following system of linear equations.

$$5x + 3y = 9 \qquad\qquad \textit{Equation 1}$$
$$2x - 4y = 14 \qquad\qquad \textit{Equation 2}$$

Solution

You can obtain coefficients that differ only in sign by multiplying the first equation by 4 and the second equation by 3.

$$5x + 3y = 9 \quad \rightarrow \quad 20x + 12y = 36 \qquad \textit{Multiply Equation 1 by 4}$$
$$\underline{2x - 4y = 14} \quad \rightarrow \quad \underline{6x - 12y = 42} \qquad \textit{Multiply Equation 2 by 3}$$
$$26x \qquad = 78 \qquad \textit{Add equations}$$

From this equation, you can see that $x = 3$. By back-substituting this value of x into the second equation, you can solve for y, as follows.

$$2x - 4y = 14 \qquad\qquad \textit{Equation 2}$$
$$2(3) - 4y = 14 \qquad\qquad \textit{Replace x by 3}$$
$$-4y = 8$$
$$y = -2 \qquad\qquad \textit{Solve for y}$$

Therefore, the solution is $(3, -2)$. Check the solution in each of the original equations.

Graphical Interpretation of Solutions

As you observed in Section 8.1, it is possible for a *general* system of equations to have exactly one solution, two or more solutions, or no solution. For a system of *linear* equations you can strengthen this result somewhat. Specifically, if a system of linear equations has two different solutions, then it must have an infinite number of solutions! To see why this is true, consider the following graphical interpretations of a system of two linear equations in two variables. (Remember that the graph of a linear equation in two variables is a straight line.)

Graphical Interpretation of Solutions

For a system of two linear equations in two variables, the number of solutions is given by one of the following.

Number of Solutions	Graphical Interpretation
1. Exactly one solution	The two lines intersect at one point.
2. Infinitely many solutions	The two lines are identical.
3. No solution	The two lines are parallel.

These three possibilities are shown in Figure 8.5.

A system of linear equations is **consistent** if it has at least one solution, and it is **inconsistent** if it has no solution.

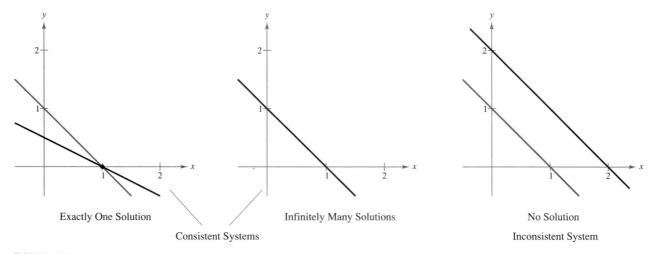

Exactly One Solution   Infinitely Many Solutions   No Solution

Consistent Systems   Inconsistent System

FIGURE 8.5

EXAMPLE 4   The Method of Elimination: No-Solution Case

Solve the following system of linear equations.

$$x - 2y = 3 \qquad \text{\textit{Equation 1}}$$
$$-2x + 4y = 1 \qquad \text{\textit{Equation 2}}$$

Solution

To obtain coefficients that differ only in sign, multiply the first equation by 2.

$$
\begin{array}{lll}
x - 2y = 3 & \rightarrow & 2x - 4y = 6 \qquad \textit{Multiply Equation 1 by 2} \\
-2x + 4y = 1 & \rightarrow & \underline{-2x + 4y = 1} \qquad \textit{Equation 2} \\
& & \qquad\quad 0 = 7 \qquad \textit{False statement}
\end{array}
$$

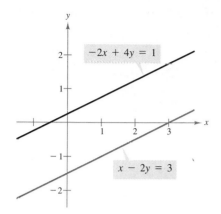

$-2x + 4y = 1$

$x - 2y = 3$

FIGURE 8.6

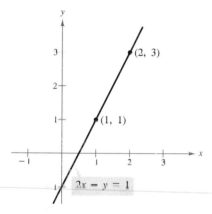

$(2, 3)$

$(1, 1)$

$2x - y = 1$

Infinite Number of Solutions

FIGURE 8.7

Since there are no values of x and y for which $0 = 7$, the system is inconsistent and has no solution. The lines corresponding to the two equations given in this system are shown in Figure 8.6. Note that the two lines are parallel, and therefore have no point of intersection. ◢

EXAMPLE 5 The Method of Elimination: Many-Solutions Case

Solve the following system of linear equations.

$$2x - y = 1 \qquad \text{Equation 1}$$
$$4x - 2y = 2 \qquad \text{Equation 2}$$

Solution

To obtain coefficients that differ only in sign, multiply the second equation by $-\frac{1}{2}$.

$$
\begin{array}{llll}
2x - y = 1 & \rightarrow & 2x - y = 1 & \textit{Equation 1} \\
4x - 2y = 2 & \rightarrow & -2x + y = -1 & \textit{Multiply Equation 2 by } -\frac{1}{2} \\
\hline
& & 0 = 0 & \textit{Add equations}
\end{array}
$$

Since the two equations turn out to be equivalent (have the same solution set), the system has infinitely many solutions. The solution set consists of all points (x, y) lying on the line $2x - y = 1$, as shown in Figure 8.7. ◢

In Example 5, you could have reached the same conclusion by multiplying the first equation by 2 to obtain

$$4x - 2y = 2 \qquad \textit{New Equation 1}$$
$$4x - 2y = 2. \qquad \textit{Equation 2}$$

EXAMPLE 6 Solving a Linear System Having Decimal Coefficients

Solve the following system of linear equations.

$$0.02x - 0.05y = -0.38 \qquad \textit{Equation 1}$$
$$0.03x + 0.04y = 1.04 \qquad \textit{Equation 2}$$

Solution

Because the coefficients in this system have two decimal places, we begin by multiplying each equation by 100. (This produces an equivalent system in which the coefficients are all integers.)

$$2x - 5y = -38 \qquad \textit{Revised Equation 1}$$
$$3x + 4y = 104 \qquad \textit{Revised Equation 2}$$

Now, to obtain coefficients that differ only in sign, we multiply the first equation by 3 and the second equation by -2.

$$2x - 5y = -38 \quad \rightarrow \quad 6x - 15y = -114 \qquad \textit{Multiply Equation 1 by 3}$$

$$\underline{3x + 4y = 104} \quad \rightarrow \quad \underline{-6x - 8y = -208} \qquad \textit{Multiply Equation 2 by } -2$$

$$-23y = -322 \qquad \textit{Add equations}$$

Thus, we find that

$$y = \frac{-322}{-23} = 14.$$

Back-substituting this value into Equation 2 produces the following.

$$3x + 4y = 104 \qquad\qquad\qquad \textit{Equation 2}$$

$$3x + 4(14) = 104 \qquad\qquad\qquad \textit{Replace y by 14}$$

$$3x = 48$$

$$x = 16 \qquad\qquad\qquad \textit{Solve for x}$$

Therefore, the solution is (16, 14). Check this solution in each of the original equations in the system. ◢

Applications

We stated at the beginning of this chapter that systems of linear equations have many applications in science, business, health services, and government. The question that may come to mind is, How can I tell which application problems can be solved using a system of linear equations? The answer comes from the following considerations.

1. Does the problem involve more than one unknown quantity?
2. Are there two (or more) equations or conditions to be satisfied?

If one or both of these conditions occur, then the appropriate mathematical model for the problem may be a system of linear equations. Example 7 shows how to construct such a model.

EXAMPLE 7   An Application of a Linear System

An airplane flying into a headwind travels the 2000-mile flying distance between two cities in 4 hours and 24 minutes. On the return flight, the same distance is traveled in 4 hours. Find the ground speed of the plane and the speed of the wind, assuming that both remain constant.

Solution

The two unknown quantities are the speeds of the wind and of the plane. If r_1 is the speed of the plane and r_2 is the speed of the wind, then

$$r_1 - r_2 = \text{speed of the plane } against \text{ the wind}$$
$$r_1 + r_2 = \text{speed of the plane } with \text{ the wind}$$

as shown in Figure 8.8. Using the formula

$$\text{Distance} = (\text{Rate})(\text{Time})$$

for these two speeds, you obtain the following equations.

$$2000 = (r_1 - r_2)\left(4 + \frac{24}{60}\right)$$
$$2000 = (r_1 + r_2)(4)$$

These two equations simplify as follows.

$$5000 = 11r_1 - 11r_2 \qquad\qquad \textit{Equation 1}$$
$$500 = r_1 + r_2 \qquad\qquad \textit{Equation 2}$$

By elimination, the solution is

$$r_1 = \frac{5250}{11} \approx 477.27 \text{ miles per hour}$$

$$r_2 = \frac{250}{11} \approx 22.73 \text{ miles per hour.}$$

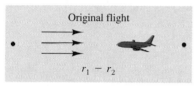

Original flight

$r_1 - r_2$

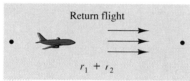

Return flight

$r_1 + r_2$

FIGURE 8.8

In a free market, the demand for many products is related to the price of the product. As the price of a product decreases, the demand by *consumers* increases. For *producers* the opposite is true. In other words, as the price of a product decreases, the supply tends to decrease.

EXAMPLE 8   Finding the Point of Equilibrium

Suppose the demand and supply functions for a certain type of calculator are given by

$$p = 150 - 10x \qquad\qquad \textit{Demand equation}$$
$$p = 60 + 20x \qquad\qquad \textit{Supply equation}$$

where p is the price in dollars and x represents the number of units in millions. Find the **point of equilibrium** for this market by solving this system of equations. (The point of equilibrium is the price p and the number of units x that satisfy both the demand and the supply equations.)

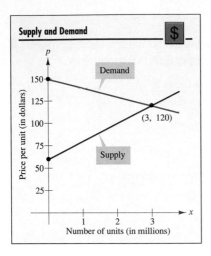

Supply and Demand $

FIGURE 8.9

Solution

For this system, you use the method of substitution (because the two equations are given in a form in which p is written in terms of x). By substituting the value of p given in the second equation into the first equation, you obtain the following.

$$p = 150 - 10x \quad \textit{First equation}$$
$$60 + 20x = 150 - 10x \quad \textit{Replace p by 60 + 20x}$$
$$30x = 90 \quad \textit{Add 10x and subtract 60}$$
$$x = 3 \quad \textit{Divide both sides by 30}$$

Thus, the point of equilibrium occurs when the demand and supply are each 3 million units. (See Figure 8.9.) The price that corresponds to this x-value is obtained by back-substituting $x = 3$ into either of the original equations. For instance, back-substituting into the first equation produces

$$p = 150 - 10(3) = 150 - 30 = \$120.$$

Try back-substituting $x = 3$ into the second equation to see that you obtain the same price. ◄

DISCUSSION

PROBLEM

Creating Consistent and Inconsistent Systems

Consider the following system of linear equations.

$$x - y = 4$$
$$-2x + 2y = k$$

1. Find the value of k so that the system has an infinite number of solutions.
2. Find one value of k so that the system has no solutions.
3. Can the system have a unique solution? Why or why not?

WARM UP

The following warm-up exercises involve skills that were covered in earlier sections. You will use these skills in the exercise set for this section.

In Exercises 1 and 2, sketch the graph of the equation.

1. $2x + y = 4$ **2.** $5x - 2y = 3$

In Exercises 3 and 4, find an equation of the line passing through the two points.

3. $(-1, 3)$, $(4, 8)$ **4.** $(2, 6)$, $(5, 1)$

In Exercises 5 and 6, determine the slope of the line.

5. $3x + 6y = 4$ **6.** $7x - 4y = 10$

In Exercises 7–10, determine whether the lines represented by the pair of equations are parallel, perpendicular, or neither.

7. $2x - 3y = -10$ **8.** $4x - 12y = 5$
     $3x + 2y = 11$ $-2x + 6y = 3$

9. $5x + y = 2$ **10.** $x - 3y = 2$
     $3x + 2y = 1$ $6x + 2y = 4$

EXERCISES for Section 8.2

In Exercises 1–10, solve the linear system by elimination. Label each line with the appropriate equation.

1. $2x + y = 4$
     $x - y = 2$

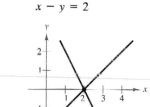

2. $x + 3y = 2$
     $-x + 2y = 3$

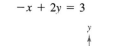

5. $x - y = 1$
   $-2x + 2y = 5$

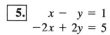

6. $3x + 2y = 2$
   $6x + 4y = 14$

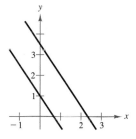

7. $3x - 2y = 6$
     $6x + 4y = -12$

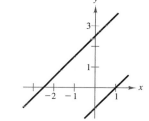

8. $x - 2y = 5$
     $6x + 2y = 7$

9. $9x - 3y = -1$
   $3x + 6y = -5$

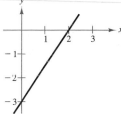

10. $5x + 3y = 18$
    $2x - 7y = -1$

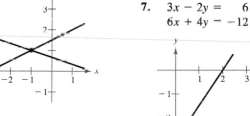

3. $x - y = 0$
     $3x - 2y = -1$

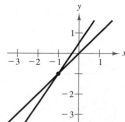

4. $2x - y = 2$
   $4x + 3y = 24$

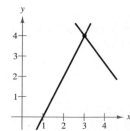

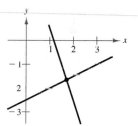

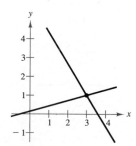

In Exercises 11–30, solve the system by elimination.

11. $x + 2y = 4$
$x - 2y = 1$

12. $3x - 5y = 2$
$2x + 5y = 13$

13. $2x + 3y = 18$
$5x - y = 11$

14. $x + 7y = 12$
$3x - 5y = 10$

15. $3x + 2y = 10$
$2x + 5y = 3$

16. $8r + 16s = 20$
$16r + 50s = 55$

17. $2u + v = 120$
$u + 2v = 120$

18. $5u + 6v = 24$
$3u + 5v = 18$

19. $6r - 5s = 3$
$10s - 12r = 5$

20. $1.8x + 1.2y = 4$
$9x + 6y = 3$

21. $\dfrac{x}{4} + \dfrac{y}{6} = 1$
$x - y = 3$

22. $\dfrac{2}{3}x + \dfrac{1}{6}y = \dfrac{2}{3}$
$4x + y = 4$

23. $\dfrac{x + 3}{4} + \dfrac{y - 1}{3} = 1$
$2x - y = 12$

24. $\dfrac{x - 1}{2} + \dfrac{y + 2}{3} = 4$
$x - 2y = 5$

25. $2.5x - 3y = 1.5$
$10x - 12y = 6$

26. $0.02x - 0.05y = -0.19$
$0.03x + 0.04y = 0.52$

27. $0.05x - 0.03y = 0.21$
$0.07x + 0.02y = 0.16$

28. $0.2x - 0.5y = -27.8$
$0.3x + 0.4y = 68.7$

29. $4b + 3m = 3$
$3b + 11m = 13$

30. $3b + 3m = 7$
$3b + 5m = 3$

In Exercises 31 and 32, the graphs of the two equations appear to be parallel. Yet, when the system is solved algebraically, we find that the system does have a solution. Find the solution and explain why it does not appear on the portion of the graph that is shown.

31. $200y - x = 200$
$199y - x = -198$

32. $25x - 24y = 0$
$13x - 12y = 120$

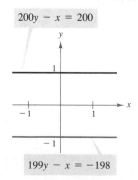

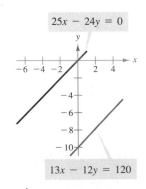

33. *Airplane Speed*   An airplane flying into a headwind travels the 1800-mile flying distance between two cities in 3 hours and 36 minutes. On the return flight, the distance is traveled in 3 hours. Find the ground speed of the plane and the speed of the wind, assuming that both remain constant.

34. *Airplane Speed*   Two planes start from the same airport and fly in opposite directions. The second plane starts one-half hour after the first plane, but its speed is 50 miles per hour faster. Find the ground speed of each plane if 2 hours after the first plane starts, the planes are 2000 miles apart.

35. *Acid Mixture*   Ten gallons of a 30% acid solution are obtained by mixing a 20% solution with a 50% solution. How much of each must be used?

36. *Fuel Mixture*   Five hundred gallons of 82-octane gasoline are obtained by mixing 80-octane gasoline with 86-octane gasoline. How much of each must be used?

37. *Investment Portfolio*   A total of $12,000 is invested in two corporate bonds that pay 10.5% and 12% simple interest. The annual interest is $1,380. How much is invested in each bond?

38. *Investment Portfolio*   A total of $32,000 is invested in two municipal bonds that pay 5.75% and 6.25% simple interest. The annual interest is $1,930. How much is invested in each bond?

39. *Ticket Sales*   Five hundred tickets were sold for a certain performance of a play. The tickets for adults and children sold for $7.50 and $4.00, respectively, and the receipts for the performance were $3312.50. How many of each kind of ticket were sold?

40. *Shoe Sales*   Suppose you are the manager of a shoe store. On Saturday night you are going over the receipts of the previous week's sales. Two hundred and forty pairs of tennis shoes were sold. One style sold for $66.95 and the other sold for $84.95. The total receipts were $17,652. The cash register that was supposed to record the number of each type of shoe sold malfunctioned. Can you recover the information? If so, how many shoes of each type were sold?

Supply and Demand   In Exercises 41–46, find the point of equilibrium for each pair of supply and demand equations.

Demand	Supply
41. $p = 50 - 0.5x$	$p = 0.125x$
42. $p = 60 - x$	$p = 10 + \frac{7}{3}x$

Demand	Supply
43. $p = 300 - x$	$p = 100 + x$
44. $p = 100 - 0.05x$	$p = 25 + 0.1x$
45. $p = 140 - 0.00002x$	$p = 80 + 0.00001x$
46. $p = 400 - 0.0002x$	$p = 225 + 0.0005x$

47. *Driving Distances* On a 300-mile trip two people do the driving. One person drives three times as far as the other. Find the distance that each person drives.

48. *Truck Scheduling* A contractor is hiring two trucking companies to haul 1600 tons of crushed stone for a highway construction project. The contracts state that one company is to haul four times as much as the other. Find the amount hauled by each.

Fitting a Line to Data In Exercises 49–56, find the *least squares regression line* $y = ax + b$ for the points

$(x_1, y_1), (x_2, y_2), \ldots, (x_n, y_n)$.

To find the line, solve the following system for a and b. (If you are unfamiliar with summation notation, look at the discussion in Section 10.1.)

$$nb + \left(\sum_{i=1}^{n} x_i\right)a = \sum_{i=1}^{n} y_i$$

$$\left(\sum_{i=1}^{n} x_i\right)b + \left(\sum_{i=1}^{n} x_i^2\right)a = \sum_{i=1}^{n} x_i y_i$$

49. $5b + 10a = 20.2$
$10b + 30a = 50.1$

50. $5b + 10a = 11.7$
$10b + 30a = 25.6$

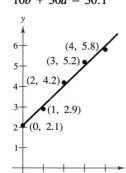

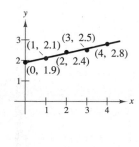

51. $7b + 21a = 35.1$
$21b + 91a = 114.2$

52. $6b + 15a = 23.6$
$15b + 55a = 48.8$

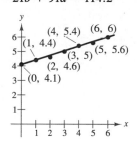

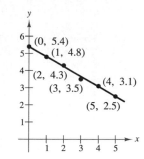

53. $(-2, 0), (0, 1), (2, 3)$

54. $(-3, 0), (-1, 1), (1, 1), (3, 2)$

55. $(0, 4), (1, 3), (1, 1), (2, 0)$

56. $(1, 0), (2, 0), (3, 0), (3, 1), (4, 1), (4, 2), (5, 2), (6, 2)$

57. *Demand Function* A store manager wants to know the demand of a certain product as a function of the price. The daily sales for the different prices of the product are given in the table.

Price (x)	$1.00	$1.25	$1.50
Demand (y)	450	375	330

Use the technique demonstrated in Exercises 49–56 to find the line that best fits the given data. Then use the line to predict the demand when the price is $1.40.

58. *Yield* A farmer used four test plots to determine the relationship between wheat yield in bushels per acre and the amount of fertilizer in hundreds of pounds per acre. The results are given in the table.

Fertilizer (x)	1.0	1.5	2.0	2.5
Yield (y)	32	41	48	53

Use the technique demonstrated in Exercises 49–56 to find the line that best fits the given data. Then use the line to estimate the yield for a fertilizer application of 160 pounds per acre.

In Exercises 59 and 60, find a system of linear equations having the given solution. (The answers are not unique.)

59. $\left(3, \frac{5}{2}\right)$

60. $(8, -2)$

SOLVING

Using Technology to Fit Models to Data

Many of the models in this text were created with a statistical method called *least squares regression analysis*. This procedure is tedious to perform by hand, but can be performed quite efficiently with a computer or graphing calculator.

EXAMPLE 1   Fitting a Line to Data

For 1978 through 1989, the numbers (in millions) of morning and evening newspapers sold each day in the United States are as shown in the table. Use the data to project the number of morning and evening newspapers that will be sold each day in 1995. In the table, $t = 0$ represents 1980. (*Source:* Editor and Publisher Company)

Year, t	-2	-1	0	1	2	3
Morning	27.7	28.6	29.4	30.6	33.2	33.8
Evening	34.3	33.6	32.8	30.9	29.3	28.8

Year, t	4	5	6	7	8	9
Morning	35.4	36.4	37.4	39.1	40.4	40.7
Evening	27.7	26.4	25.1	23.7	22.2	21.8

Solution

Begin by finding a computer or graphing calculator program that will perform linear regression analysis. (Such a program is a built-in feature of some calculators.) After entering the data and running the program, you should obtain the following models. (Both models have a correlation coefficient of $r^2 > 0.99$, which means that the models are very good fits for the data.)

$$y = 29.956 + 1.267t \qquad \textit{Morning paper circulation}$$
$$y = 32.243 - 1.198t \qquad \textit{Evening paper circulation}$$

With these models, you can project the 1995 newspaper sales. *If* the sales through 1995 continue to follow the pattern from 1978 through 1989, then the 1995 sales of morning papers should be about

$$y = 29.956 + 1.267(15) \approx 49.0 \text{ million} \qquad \textit{Morning}$$

and the sales of evening papers should be about

$$y = 32.243 - 1.198(15) \approx 14.3 \text{ million.} \qquad \textit{Evening}$$

The graphs of the data points and their models are shown at the left. ◢

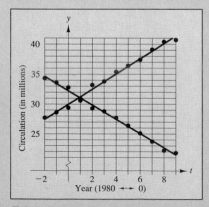

EXERCISES

(See also: Exercises 49–58, Section 8.2)

1. *Sunday Paper Circulation* The numbers (in millions) of Sunday newspapers sold each week in the United States from 1978 through 1989 are shown in the table below. Find a linear model that represents this data. Use your model to project the number of Sunday newspapers to be sold each week in 1995.

2. *Newspaper Companies* The numbers of morning, evening, and Sunday newspaper companies in the United States from 1978 through 1989 are shown in the table below. Find a linear model for each of these three sets of data.

3. *Average Sales* From 1978 through 1989, the circulation of morning newspapers increased. However, because the number of morning newspaper companies also increased, the competition for morning newspaper readers became keener. Did the average circulation per morning newspaper company increase or decrease? Explain.

4. *Average Sales* From 1978 through 1989, the circulation of evening newspapers decreased. However, because the number of evening newspaper companies also decreased,

the competition for evening newspaper readers became less keen. Did the average circulation per evening newspaper company increase or decrease? Explain.

5. *Average Sales* From 1978 through 1989, the circulation of Sunday newspapers increased. However, because the number of Sunday newspaper companies also increased, the competition for Sunday newspaper readers became keener. Did the average circulation per Sunday newspaper company increase or decrease? Explain.

6. *Which Would You Choose?* If you had the opportunity to invest in a company that produced only one type of newspaper (morning, evening, or Sunday), which would you choose? Explain your reasoning.

7. *Households and Population* For 1978 through 1989, the population and number of households in the United States (both in millions) are given in the table below. From this information, would you say that the percent of Americans who read newspapers was increasing or decreasing from 1978 through 1989? Explain your reasoning.

Year, t	−2	−1	0	1	2	3	4	5	6	7	8	9
Sunday	54.0	54.4	54.7	55.2	56.3	56.7	57.5	58.8	58.9	60.1	61.5	62.0

Table for Exercise 1

Year, t	−2	−1	0	1	2	3	4	5	6	7	8	9
Morning	355	382	387	408	434	446	458	482	499	511	529	530
Evening	1419	1405	1388	1352	1310	1284	1257	1220	1188	1166	1141	1125
Sunday	696	720	736	755	768	772	783	798	802	820	840	847

Table for Exercise 2

Year, t	−2	−1	0	1	2	3	4	5	6	7	8	9
Households	77.6	78.9	80.8	81.6	83.0	83.9	85.4	86.8	88.5	89.5	91.1	92.8
Population	222.6	225.1	227.7	229.9	232.2	234.3	236.3	238.5	240.7	242.8	245.1	247.4

Table for Exercise 3

8.3 Linear Systems in More Than Two Variables

Row-Echelon Form and Back-Substitution / Gaussian Elimination / Nonsquare Systems /
Applications

Row-Echelon Form and Back-Substitution

The method of elimination can be applied to a system of linear equations in
more than two variables. In fact, this method easily adapts to computer use
for solving linear systems with dozens of variables.

When using elimination to solve a system of linear equations, the goal
is to rewrite the system in a form to which back-substitution can be applied.
To see how this works, consider the following two systems of linear equations.

$$\begin{aligned} x - 2y + 3z &= 9 \\ -x + 3y &= -4 \\ 2x - 5y + 5z &= 17 \end{aligned} \qquad \begin{aligned} x - 2y + 3z &= 9 \\ y + 3z &= 5 \\ z &= 2 \end{aligned}$$

Clearly, the system on the right is easier to solve. This system is in **row-
echelon form,** which means that it follows a stair-step pattern and has leading
coefficients of 1. To solve such a system, use back-substitution, working from
the bottom equation to the top equation, as demonstrated in Example 1.

EXAMPLE 1   Back-Substitution to Solve a System in Row-Echelon Form

Solve the following system of linear equations.

$$\begin{aligned} x - 2y + 3z &= 9 && \textit{Equation 1} \\ y + 3z &= 5 && \textit{Equation 2} \\ z &= 2 && \textit{Equation 3} \end{aligned}$$

Solution

From Equation 3, you already know the value of z. To solve for y, substitute
$z = 2$ into Equation 2 to obtain

$$\begin{aligned} y + 3(2) &= 5 && \textit{Substitute } z = 2 \\ y &= -1. && \textit{Solve for } y \end{aligned}$$

Finally, substitute $y = -1$ and $z = 2$ into Equation 1 to obtain

$$\begin{aligned} x - 2(-1) + 3(2) &= 9 && \textit{Substitute } y = -1, z = 2 \\ x &= 1. && \textit{Solve for } x \end{aligned}$$

Thus, the solution is $x = 1$, $y = -1$, and $z = 2$.

Gaussian Elimination

Two systems of equations are **equivalent** if they have precisely the same solution set. To solve a system that is not in row-echelon form, first change it to an *equivalent* system that is in row-echelon form by using the following operations.

Operations that Lead to Equivalent Systems of Equations

Each of the following operations on a system of linear equations produce an *equivalent* system.

1. Interchange two equations.
2. Multiply one of the equations by a nonzero constant.
3. Add a multiple of an equation to another equation.

Rewriting a system of linear equations in row-echelon form usually involves a *chain* of equivalent systems, each of which is obtained by using one of the three basic operations. This process is called **Gaussian elimination,** after the German mathematician Carl Friedrich Gauss (1777–1855).

EXAMPLE 2   Using Elimination to Solve a Linear System

Solve the following system of linear equations.

$$\begin{aligned} x - 2y + 3z &= 9 \\ -x + 3y &= -4 \\ 2x - 5y + 5z &= 17 \end{aligned}$$

Solution

Although there are several ways to begin, the goal is to develop a systematic procedure that can be applied to large systems. Work from the upper left corner, saving the x in the upper left position and eliminating the other x's from the first column.

$$\begin{aligned} x - 2y + 3z &= 9 \\ y + 3z &= 5 \\ 2x - 5y + 5z &= 17 \end{aligned}$$

Adding the first equation to the second equation produces a new second equation.

$$\begin{aligned} x - 2y + 3z &= 9 \\ y + 3z &= 5 \\ -y - z &= -1 \end{aligned}$$

Adding -2 times the first equation to the third equation produces a new third equation.

Now that all but the first x has been eliminated from the first column, go to work on the second column. (You need to eliminate y from the third equation.)

$$\begin{aligned} x - 2y + 3z &= 9 \\ y + 3z &= 5 \\ 2z &= 4 \end{aligned}$$

> Adding the second equation to the third equation produces a a new third equation.

Finally, you need a coefficient of 1 for z in the third equation.

$$\begin{aligned} x - 2y + 3z &= 9 \\ y + 3z &= 5 \\ z &= 2 \end{aligned}$$

> Multiplying the third equation by $\frac{1}{2}$ produces a new third equation.

This is the same system you solved in Example 1, and, as in that example, the solution is

$$x = 1, \qquad y = -1, \qquad \text{and} \qquad z = 2.$$

The solution can also be written as the **ordered triple** $(1, -1, 2)$.

In Example 2, you can check the solution $x = 1$, $y = -1$, and $z = 2$ as follows.

Equation 1: $\qquad (1) - 2(-1) + 3(2) = \quad 9$ *Check solution in each equation of original system.*

Equation 2: $\quad -(1) + 3(-1) \qquad\qquad = -4$

Equation 3: $\qquad 2(1) - 5(-1) + 5(2) = \quad 17$

We now look at an inconsistent system—one that has no solution. The key to recognizing an inconsistent system is that at some stage in the elimination process, you obtain an absurdity such as $0 = 7$. This is demonstrated in Example 3.

EXAMPLE 3   An Inconsistent System

Solve the following system of linear equations.

$$\begin{aligned} x - 3y + z &= \quad 1 \\ 2x - y - 2z &= \quad 2 \\ x + 2y - 3z &= -1 \end{aligned}$$

Solution

$$x - 3y + z = 1$$
$$5y - 4z = 0 \quad \longleftarrow$$
$$x + 2y - 3z = -1$$

> Adding -2 times the first equation to the second equation produces a new second equation.

$$x - 3y + z = 1$$
$$5y - 4z = 0$$
$$5y - 4z = -2 \quad \longleftarrow$$

> Adding -1 times the first equation to the third equation produces a new third equation.

$$x - 3y + z = 1$$
$$5y - 4z = 0$$
$$0 = -2 \quad \longleftarrow$$

> Adding -1 times the second equation to the third equation produces a new third equation.

Because the third "equation" is absurd, this system is inconsistent and has no solution. Moreover, because this system is equivalent to the original system, the original system also has no solution.

◀

As with a system of linear equations in two variables, the solutions of a system of linear equations in more than two variables must fall into one and only one of the following categories.

1. There is exactly one solution.
2. There are infinitely many solutions.
3. There is no solution.

When a system of equations has no solution, you simply state that it is *inconsistent*. If a system has exactly one solution, you list the value of each variable. However, for systems that have infinitely many solutions, you encounter a certain awkwardness in listing the solutions. For example, you might give the solutions to a system in three variables as

$$(a, a + 1, 2a), \qquad \text{where } a \text{ is any real number.}$$

This means that for each real number a, you have a valid solution to the system. A few of the infinitely many possible solutions are found by letting $a = -1, 0, 1,$ and 2 to obtain $(-1, 0, -2)$, $(0, 1, 0)$, $(1, 2, 2)$, and $(2, 3, 4)$, respectively. Now consider the solutions represented by

$$(b - 1, b, 2b - 2), \qquad \text{where } b \text{ is any real number.}$$

Here again a few possible solutions are $(-1, 0, -2)$, $(0, 1, 0)$, $(1, 2, 2)$, and $(2, 3, 4)$, found by letting $b = 0, 1, 2,$ and 3, respectively. Note that both descriptions result in the same collection of solutions. Thus, when comparing descriptions of an infinite solution set, keep in mind that there is more than one way to describe the set.

EXAMPLE 4 A System with Infinitely Many Solutions

Solve the following system of linear equations.

$$x + y - 3z = -1 \qquad \text{\textit{Equation 1}}$$
$$y - z = 0 \qquad \text{\textit{Equation 2}}$$
$$-x + 2y = 1 \qquad \text{\textit{Equation 3}}$$

Solution

Begin by rewriting the system in row-echelon form, as follows.

$$x + y - 3z = -1$$
$$y - z = 0$$
$$3y - 3z = 0 \leftarrow$$

Adding the first equation to the third equation produces a new third equation.

$$x + y - 3z = -1$$
$$y - z = 0$$
$$0 = 0 \leftarrow$$

Adding -3 times the second equation to the third equation produces a new third equation.

This means that Equation 3 is *dependent* on Equations 1 and 2 in the sense that it gives no additional information about the variables. Thus, the original system is equivalent to the system

$$x + y - 3z = -1$$
$$y - z = 0.$$

In this last equation, you solve for y in terms of z to obtain $y = z$. Back-substituting for y into the previous equation, you find x in terms of z, as follows.

$$x + z - 3z = -1$$
$$x - 2z = -1$$
$$x = 2z - 1$$

Finally, letting $z = a$, the solutions to the given system are all of the form

$$x = 2a - 1, \qquad y = a, \qquad z = a$$

where a is a real number. Thus, every ordered triple of the form

$$(2a - 1, a, a), \qquad a \text{ is a real number}$$

is a solution of the system.

Nonsquare Systems

So far we have only considered **square** systems, for which the number of equations is equal to the number of variables. In a **nonsquare** system, the number of equations differs from the number of variables. It can be shown that a system of linear equations cannot have a unique solution unless there are at least as many equations as there are variables in the system.

EXAMPLE 5   A System with Fewer Equations than Variables

Solve the following system of linear equations.

$$x - 2y + z = 2 \qquad \qquad \textit{Equation 1}$$
$$2x \quad y - z = 1 \qquad \qquad \textit{Equation 2}$$

Solution

$$x - 2y + z = 2$$
$$3y - 3z = -3 \quad \longleftarrow$$

Adding -2 times the first equation to the second equation produces a new second equation.

$$x - 2y + z = 2$$
$$y - z = -1 \quad \longleftarrow$$

Multiplying the second equation by $\frac{1}{3}$ produces a new second equation.

Solving for y in terms of z, you get $y = z - 1$, and back-substitution into Equation 1 yields

$$x \quad 2(z - 1) + z = 2$$
$$x - \quad 2z + 2 + z - 2$$
$$x = z.$$

Finally, by letting $z = a$, you have the solution

$$x = a, \qquad y = a - 1, \qquad \text{and} \qquad z = a$$

where a is a real number. Thus, every ordered triple of the form

$$(a, a - 1, a), \qquad a \text{ is a real number}$$

is a solution of the system.

Applications

We conclude this section with three applications involving systems of linear equations in three variables.

In Example 6 we show how to fit a parabola through three given points in the plane. This procedure can be generalized to fit an nth degree polynomial function to $n + 1$ points in the plane. The only restriction to the procedure is that (since we are trying to fit a *function* to the points) every point must have a distinct x-coordinate.

EXAMPLE 6   An Application: Moving Object

The height at time t of an object that is moving in a (vertical) line with constant acceleration a is given by the **position equation**

$$s = \frac{1}{2}at^2 + v_0 t + s_0.$$

The height s is measured in feet, t is measured in seconds, v_0 is the initial velocity (at time $t = 0$), and s_0 is the initial height. Find the values of a, v_0, and s_0, if $s = 52$ feet at 1 second, $s = 52$ feet at 2 seconds, and $s = 20$ feet at 3 seconds.

Solution

By substituting the three values of t and s into the position equation, you obtain three linear equations in a, v_0, and s_0.

When $t = 1$: $\frac{1}{2}a(1^2) + v_0(1) + s_0 = 52$

When $t = 2$: $\frac{1}{2}a(2^2) + v_0(2) + s_0 = 52$

When $t = 3$: $\frac{1}{2}a(3^2) + v_0(3) + s_0 = 20$

By multiplying the first and third equations by 2, this system can be rewritten

$$a + 2v_0 + 2s_0 = 104$$
$$2a + 2v_0 + s_0 = 52$$
$$9a + 6v_0 + 2s_0 = 40$$

and you apply elimination as follows.

$$
\begin{aligned}
a + \quad 2v_0 + \quad 2s_0 &= \quad 104 \\
-2v_0 - \quad 3s_0 &= -156 \\
9a + \quad 6v_0 + \quad 2s_0 &= \quad 40
\end{aligned}
$$

> Adding -2 times the first equation to the second equation produces a new second equation.

$$
\begin{aligned}
a + \quad 2v_0 + \quad 2s_0 &= \quad 104 \\
-2v_0 - \quad 3s_0 &= -156 \\
-12v_0 - 16s_0 &= -896
\end{aligned}
$$

> Adding -9 times the first equation to the third equation produces a new third equation.

$$
\begin{aligned}
a + \quad 2v_0 + \quad 2s_0 &= \quad 104 \\
-2v_0 - \quad 3s_0 &= -156 \\
2s_0 &= \quad 40
\end{aligned}
$$

> Adding -6 times the second equation to the third equation produces a new third equation.

By back-substituting $s_0 = 20$ (obtained from the third equation), we find that $v_0 = 48$ and ultimately $a = -32$. Thus, the position equation for this object is

$$s = -16t^2 + 48t + 20.$$

EXAMPLE 7 An Application: Curve-Fitting

Find a quadratic function

$$f(x) = ax^2 + bx + c$$

whose graph passes through the points $(-1, 3)$, $(1, 1)$, and $(2, 6)$.

Solution

Since the graph of f passes through the points $(-1, 3)$, $(1, 1)$, and $(2, 6)$, you have

$$f(-1) = a(-1)^2 + b(-1) + c = 3$$
$$f(1) = a(1)^2 + b(1) + c = 1$$
$$f(2) = a(2)^2 + b(2) + c = 6.$$

This produces the following system of linear equations in the variables a, b, and c.

$$a - b + c = 3$$
$$a + b + c = 1$$
$$4a + 2b + c = 6$$

The solution to this system turns out to be

$$a = 2, \qquad b = -1, \qquad \text{and} \qquad c = 0.$$

Thus, the equation of the parabola passing through the three given points is

$$f(x) = 2x^2 - x$$

as shown in Figure 8.10.

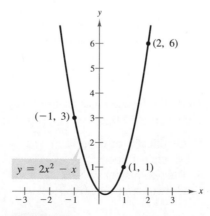

$$y = 2x^2 - x$$

FIGURE 8.10

EXAMPLE 8   An Investment Portfolio

Suppose an investor has a portfolio totaling $450,000, and wishes to allocate this amount to the following types of investments: (1) certificates of deposit, (2) municipal bonds, (3) blue-chip stocks, and (4) growth or speculative stocks. The certificates of deposit pay 9% annually, and the municipal bonds pay 6% annually. Over a five-year period the investor expects the blue-chip stocks to return 10% annually, and expects the growth stocks to return 15% annually. The investor wants a combined annual return of 8%, and also wants to have only one-third of the portfolio invested in stocks. How much should be allocated to each type of investment?

Solution

To solve this problem, let C, M, B, and G represent the amounts in the four types of investments. Because the total investment is $450,000, you can write the following equation.

$$C + M + B + G = 450{,}000$$

A second equation can be derived from the fact that the combined annual return should be 8%.

$$0.09C + 0.06M + 0.10B + 0.15G = 0.08(450{,}000)$$

Finally, because only one-third of the investment should be allocated to stocks, you can write

$$B + G = \frac{1}{3}(450{,}000).$$

These three equations make up the following system.

$$
\begin{aligned}
C + \quad M + \quad B + \quad G &= 450{,}000 \\
0.09C + 0.06M + 0.1B + 0.15G &= \quad 36{,}000 \\
B + \quad G &= 150{,}000
\end{aligned}
$$

Using elimination, you find that the system has infinitely many solutions, which can be written as follows.

$$C = -\frac{5}{3}a + 100{,}000, \quad M = \frac{5}{3}a + 200{,}000, \quad B = -a + 150{,}000, \quad G = a$$

Thus, the investor has many different options. One possible solution is to choose $a = 30{,}000$, which yields the following portfolio.

1. Certificates of deposit: $50,000
2. Municipal bonds: $250,000
3. Blue-chip stocks: $120,000
4. Growth or speculative stocks: $30,000

EXAMPLE 9 An Application: Partial Fractions

Write the partial fraction decomposition for

$$\frac{3x + 4}{x^3 - 2x - 4}.$$

Solution

Since

$$x^3 - 2x - 4 = (x - 2)(x^2 + 2x + 2)$$

you write

$$\frac{3x + 4}{x^3 - 2x - 4} = \frac{A}{x - 2} + \frac{Bx + C}{x^2 + 2x + 2}$$

$$3x + 4 = A(x^2 + 2x + 2) + (Bx + C)(x - 2) \qquad \textit{Basic equation}$$

$$3x + 4 = (A + B)x^2 + (2A - 2B + C)x + (2A - 2C).$$

By equating coefficients of like powers on opposite sides of the expanded equation, you obtain the following system of linear equations in A, B, and C.

$$
\begin{aligned}
A + B \qquad\quad &= 0 \\
2A - 2B + C &= 3 \\
2A \qquad - 2C &= 4
\end{aligned}
$$

The solution of this system is $A = 1$, $B = -1$, and $C = -1$. Therefore, the partial fraction decomposition is

$$\frac{3x + 4}{x^3 - 2x - 4} = \frac{1}{x - 2} + \frac{-x - 1}{x^2 + 2x + 2}$$

$$= \frac{1}{x - 2} - \frac{x + 1}{x^2 + 2x + 2}.$$

In addition to a graphing calculator, there are many computer software programs that will solve a system of linear equations. One is called MATRIXPAD and is available from D.C. Heath and Company. Use this software (or some other program) to solve the examples given in this section. For example, a screen from MATRIXPAD showing the solution to Example 7 is given below.

T register	3	3		0
Z register	3	3		0
Y register	3	4		0
	1	-1	1	3
	1	1	1	1
	4	2	1	6
X register	3	4		0
	1	0	0	2
	0	1	0	-1
	0	0	1	0

MATRIXPAD   © Copyright D.C. Heath and Company

Press ⟨H⟩ for Help   ⟨Q⟩ to Quit program

Try using this, or some other computer software, to solve some of the systems of linear equations that are given in this section.

WARM UP

The following warm-up exercises involve skills that were covered in earlier sections. You will use these skills in the exercise set for this section.

In Exercises 1–4, solve the system of linear equations.

1. $x + y = 25$
$\quad\quad y = 10$

2. $2x - 3y = 4$
$\quad 6x \quad\quad = -12$

3. $x + y = 32$
$\quad x - y = 24$

4. $2r - s = 5$
$\quad r + 2s = 10$

In Exercises 5–8, determine whether the ordered triple is a solution of the equation.

5. $5x - 3y + 4z = 2$
$(-1, -2, 1)$

6. $x - 2y + 12z = 9$
$(6, 3, 2)$

7. $2x - 5y + 3z = -9$
$(a - 2, a + 1, a)$

8. $-5x + y + z = 21$
$(a - 4, 4a + 1, a)$

In Exercises 9 and 10, solve for x in terms of a.

9. $x + 2y - 3z = 4$
$y = 1 - a, z = a$

10. $x - 3y + 5z = 4$
$y = 2a + 3, z = a$

EXERCISES for Section 8.3

In Exercises 1–26, solve the system of linear equations.

1. $x + y + z = 6$
$2x - y + z = 3$
$3x \quad - z = 0$

2. $x + y + z = 2$
$-x + 3y + 2z = 8$
$4x + y \quad = 4$

3. $4x + y - 3z = 11$
$2x - 3y + 2z = 9$
$x + y + z = -3$

4. $2x \quad + 2z = 2$
$5x + 3y \quad = 4$
$3y - 4z = 4$

5. $6y + 4z = -12$
$3x + 3y \quad = 9$
$2x \quad - 3z = 10$

6. $2x + 4y + z = -4$
$2x - 4y + 6z = 13$
$4x - 2y + z = 6$

7. $3x - 2y + 4z = 1$
$x + y - 2z = 3$
$2x - 3y + 6z = 8$

8. $5x - 3y + 2z = 3$
$2x + 4y - z = 7$
$x - 11y + 4z = 3$

9. $3x + 3y + 5z = 1$
$3x + 5y + 9z = 0$
$5x + 9y + 17z = 0$

10. $2x + y + 3z = 1$
$2x + 6y + 8z = 3$
$6x + 8y + 18z = 5$

11. $x + 2y - 7z = -4$
$2x + y + z = 13$
$3x + 9y - 36z = -33$

12. $2x + y - 3z = 4$
$4x \quad + 2z = 10$
$-2x + 3y - 13z = -8$

13. $x \quad + 4z = 13$
$4x - 2y + z = 7$
$2x - 2y - 7z = -19$

14. $4x - y + 5z = 11$
$x + 2y - z = 5$
$5x - 8y + 13z = 7$

15. $x - 2y + 5z = 2$
$3x + 2y - z = -2$

16. $x - 3y + 2z = 18$
$5x - 13y + 12z = 80$

17. $2x - 3y + z = -2$
$-4x + 9y \quad = 7$

18. $2x + 3y + 3z = 7$
$4x + 18y + 15z = 44$

19. $x \quad + 3w = 4$
$2y - z - w = 0$
$3y \quad - 2w = 1$
$2x \quad y + 4z \quad = 5$

20. $x + y + z + w = 6$
$2x + 3y \quad - w = 0$
$-3x + 4y + z + 2w = 4$
$x + 2y - z + w = 0$

21. $x \quad + 4z = 1$
$x + y + 10z = 10$
$2x - y + 2z = -5$

22. $3x - 2y - 6z = -4$
$-3x + 2y + 6z = 1$
$x - y - 5z = -3$

23. $4x + 3y + 17z = 0$
$5x + 4y + 22z = 0$
$4x + 2y + 19z = 0$

24. $2x + 3y \quad = 0$
$4x + 3y - z = 0$
$8x + 3y + 3z = 0$

25. $5x + 5y - z = 0$
$10x + 5y + 2z = 0$
$5x + 15y - 9z = 0$

26. $12x + 5y + z = 0$
$12x + 4y - z = 0$

In Exercises 27–30, find the equation of the parabola

$$y = ax^2 + bx + c$$

that passes through the given points.

27. $(0, -4), (1, 1), (2, 10)$

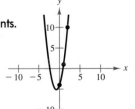

28. $(0, 5), (1, 6), (2, 5)$

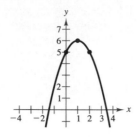

29. $(1, 0), (2, -1), (3, 0)$

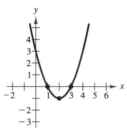

30. $(1, 2), (2, 1), (3, -4)$

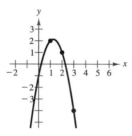

In Exercises 31–34, find the equation of the circle

$$x^2 + y^2 + Dx + Ey + F = 0$$

that passes through the given points.

31. $(0, 0), (2, -2), (4, 0)$

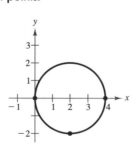

32. $(0, 0), (0, 6), (-3, 3)$

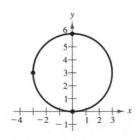

33. $(3, -1), (-2, 4), (6, 8)$

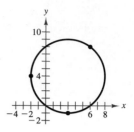

34. $(0, 0), (0, 2), (3, 0)$

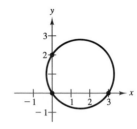

Vertical Motion   In Exercises 35–38, find the position equation

$$s = \tfrac{1}{2}at^2 + v_0t + s_0$$

for an object moving vertically and at the given heights at the specified times.

35. At $t = 1$ second, $s = 128$ feet
At $t = 2$ seconds, $s = 80$ feet
At $t = 3$ seconds, $s = 0$ feet

36. At $t = 1$ second, $s = 48$ feet
At $t = 2$ seconds, $s = 64$ feet
At $t = 3$ seconds, $s = 48$ feet

37. At $t = 1$ second, $s = 452$ feet
At $t = 3$ seconds, $s = 260$ feet
At $t = 4$ seconds, $s = 116$ feet

38. At $t = 2$ seconds, $s = 132$ feet
At $t = 3$ seconds, $s = 100$ feet
At $t = 4$ seconds, $s = 36$ feet

39. *Investments*   An inheritance of $16,000 was divided among three investments yielding a total of $990 in interest per year. The interest rates for the three investments were 5%, 6%, and 7%. Find the amount placed in each investment if the 5% and 6% investments were $3000 and $2000 less than the 7% investment, respectively.

40. *Investments*   Suppose you receive a total of $1520 a year in interest from three investments. The interest rates for the three investments are 5%, 7%, and 8%. The 5% investment is half of the 7% investment, and the 7% investment is $1500 less than the 8% investment. What is the amount of each investment?

41. *Borrowing*   A small corporation borrowed $775,000 to expand its product line. Some of the money was borrowed at 8%, some at 9%, and some at 10%. How much was borrowed at each rate if the annual interest was $67,500 and the amount borrowed at 8% was four times the amount borrowed at 10%?

42. *Borrowing*   A small corporation borrowed $800,000 to expand its product line. Some of the money was borrowed at 8%, some at 9%, and some at 10%. How much was borrowed at each rate if the annual interest was $67,000 and the amount borrowed at 8% was five times the amount borrowed at 10%?

Investment Portfolio   In Exercises 43 and 44, consider an investor with a portfolio totaling $500,000 that is to be allocated among the following types of investments: (1) certificates of deposit, (2) municipal bonds, (3) blue-chip stocks, and (4) growth or speculative stocks. How much should be allocated to each type of investment?

43. The certificates of deposit pay 10% annually, and the municipal bonds pay 8% annually. Over a five-year period, the investor expects the blue chip stocks to return 12% annually, and expects the growth stocks to return 13% annually. The investor wants a combined annual return of 10% and also wants to have only one-fourth of the portfolio invested in stocks.

44. The certificates of deposit pay 9% annually, and the municipal bonds pay 5% annually. Over a five-year period, the investor expects the blue-chip stocks to return 12% annually, and expects the growth stocks to return 14% annually. The investor wants a combined annual return of 10% and also wants to have only one-fourth of the portfolio invested in stocks.

45. *Crop Spraying*   A mixture of 12 gallons of chemical A, 16 gallons of chemical B, and 26 gallons of chemical C is required to kill a certain destructive crop insect. Commercial spray X contains 1, 2, and 2 parts, respectively, of these chemicals. Commercial spray Y contains only chemical C. Commercial spray Z contains only chemicals A and B in equal amounts. How much of each type of commercial spray is needed to get the desired mixture?

46. *Chemistry*   A chemist needs 10 liters of a 25% acid solution. The solution is to be mixed from three solutions whose concentrations are 10%, 20%, and 50%, respectively. How many liters of each solution should the chemist use to satisfy the following?

(a) Use as little as possible of the 50% solution.
(b) Use as much as possible of the 50% solution.
(c) Use two liters of the 50% solution.

47. *Truck Scheduling*   A small company that manufactures products A and B has an order for 15 units of product A and 16 units of product B. The company has trucks of three different sizes that can haul the products, as shown in the table.

	Product	
Truck	A	B
Large	6	3
Medium	4	4
Small	0	3

How many trucks of each size are needed to deliver the order? (Give *two* possible solutions.)

48. *Electrical Networks*   Applying Kirchhoff's Laws to the electrical network in the accompanying figure, the currents I_1, I_2, and I_3 must be the solution to the system

$$\begin{aligned} I_1 - I_2 + I_3 &= 0 \\ 3I_1 + 2I_2 &\quad= -7 \\ 2I_2 + 4I_3 &= 8 \end{aligned}$$

where the current is measured in amperes. Find the currents.

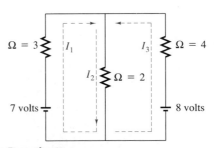

Figure for 48

49. *Pulley System* A system of pulleys that are assumed frictionless and without mass is loaded with 128-pound and 32-pound weights (see figure). The tensions t_1 and t_2 in the ropes and the acceleration a of the 32-pound weight are found by solving the system

$$t_1 - 2t_2 \qquad\qquad = \quad 0$$
$$t_1 \qquad\quad - 2a = 128$$
$$\qquad t_2 + \quad a = \quad 32$$

where t_1 and t_2 are measured in pounds and a is in feet per second squared. Solve the system.

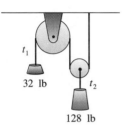

32 lb

128 lb

Figure for 49

50. *Pulley System* If the 32-pound weight is replaced by a 64-pound weight in the pulley system of Exercise 49, it is modeled by the following system of equations.

$$t_1 - 2t_2 \qquad\qquad = \quad 0$$
$$t_1 \qquad\quad - 2a = 128$$
$$\qquad t_2 + 2a = \quad 64$$

Solve the system and use your answer for the acceleration to describe what (if anything) is happening in the system.

Partial Fractions In Exercises 51–54, write the partial fraction decomposition for the rational fraction (see Example 9).

51. $\dfrac{1}{x^3 - x} = \dfrac{A}{x} + \dfrac{B}{x - 1} + \dfrac{C}{x + 1}$

52. $\dfrac{3}{x^2 + x - 2} = \dfrac{A}{x - 1} + \dfrac{B}{x + 2}$

53. $\dfrac{x^2 - 3x - 3}{x(x - 2)(x + 3)} = \dfrac{A}{x} + \dfrac{B}{x - 2} + \dfrac{C}{x + 3}$

54. $\dfrac{12}{x(x - 2)(x + 3)} = \dfrac{A}{x} + \dfrac{B}{x - 2} + \dfrac{C}{x + 3}$

Fitting a Parabola In Exercises 55–58, find the **least squares regression parabola** $y = ax^2 + bx + c$ for the points

$$(x_1, y_1), (x_2, y_2), \ldots, (x_n, y_n).$$

To find the parabola, solve the following system of linear equations for a, b, and c.

$$nc + \left(\sum_{i=1}^{n} x_i\right)b + \left(\sum_{i=1}^{n} x_i^2\right)a = \sum_{i=1}^{n} y_i$$

$$\left(\sum_{i=1}^{n} x_i\right)c + \left(\sum_{i=1}^{n} x_i^2\right)b + \left(\sum_{i=1}^{n} x_i^3\right)a = \sum_{i=1}^{n} x_i y_i$$

$$\left(\sum_{i=1}^{n} x_i^2\right)c + \left(\sum_{i=1}^{n} x_i^3\right)b + \left(\sum_{i=1}^{n} x_i^4\right)a = \sum_{i=1}^{n} x_i^2 y_i$$

55. $\begin{aligned} 4c \quad + 40a &= \quad 19 \\ 40b \quad\quad &= -12 \\ 40c \quad + 544a &= 160 \end{aligned}$

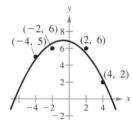

56. $\begin{aligned} 5c \quad + 10a &= \quad 8 \\ 10b \quad\quad &= 12 \\ 10c \quad + 34a &= 22 \end{aligned}$

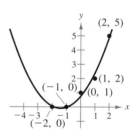

57. $\begin{aligned} 4c + 9b + 29a &= 20 \\ 9c + 29b + 99a &= 70 \\ 29c + 99b + 353a &= 254 \end{aligned}$

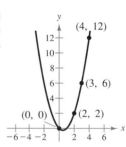

58. $\begin{aligned} 4c + 6b + 14a &= 25 \\ 6c + 14b + 36a &= 21 \\ 14c + 36b + 98a &= 33 \end{aligned}$

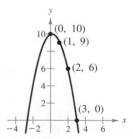

59. *Stopping Distances*   In testing the new braking system on an automobile, the speed in miles per hour and the stopping distance in feet were recorded (see table).

Speed (x)	20	30	40	50	60
Stopping distance (y)	25	55	105	188	300

(a) Plot the data on the rectangular coordinate system.
(b) Fit a least squares regression parabola to the data and sketch the graph of the parabola on the coordinate system of part (a).

60. *Reproduction*   A wildlife management team studied the reproduction rates of deer in five tracts of a wildlife preserve. Each tract contained five acres. In each tract the number of females and the percentage of females that had offspring the following year were counted. The results are given in the table.

Number (x)	80	100	120	140	160
Percentage (y)	80	75	68	55	30

(a) Plot the data on the rectangular coordinate system.
(b) Fit a least squares regression parabola to the data and sketch the graph of the parabola on the coordinate system of part (a).

In Exercises 61 and 62, find a system of linear equations having the given solution. (The answers are not unique.)

61. $(4, -1, 2)$ **62.** $\left(-\frac{3}{2}, 4, -7\right)$

8.4 Systems of Inequalities
The Graph of an Inequality / Systems of Inequalities / Applications

The Graph of an Inequality

The following statements are inequalities in two variables:

$$3x - 2y < 6 \quad \text{and} \quad 2x^2 + 3y^2 \geq 6.$$

An ordered pair (a, b) is a **solution of an inequality** in x and y if the inequality is true when a and b are substituted for x and y, respectively. The **graph** of an inequality is the collection of all solutions of the inequality. To sketch the graph of an inequality such as $3x - 2y < 6$, begin by sketching the graph of the *corresponding equation* $3x - 2y = 6$. This graph is made with a dashed line for the strict inequalities $<$ or $>$ and a solid line for the inequalities $\leq$ or $\geq$. The graph of the equation will normally separate the plane into two or more regions. In each such region, one of the following must be true.

1. *All* points in the region are solutions of the inequality.
2. *No* points in the region are solutions of the inequality.

Thus, you can determine whether the points in an entire region satisfy the inequality by simply testing *one* point in the region.

Sketching the Graph of an Inequality in Two Variables

1. Replace the inequality sign by an equal sign, and sketch the graph of the resulting equation. (Use a dashed line for $<$ or $>$ and a solid line for $\leq$ or $\geq$.)
2. Test one point in each of the regions formed by the graph in Step 1. If the point satisfies the inequality, then shade the entire region to denote that every point in the region satisfies the inequality.

EXAMPLE 1 Sketching the Graph of an Inequality

Sketch the graph of the inequality $y \geq x^2 - 1$.

Solution

The graph of the corresponding *equation* $y = x^2 - 1$ is a parabola, as shown in Figure 8.11. By testing a point *above* the parabola $(0, 0)$, and a point *below* the parabola $(0, -2)$, you see that the points that satisfy the inequality are those lying above (or on) the parabola.

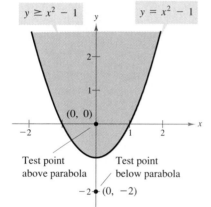

$y \geq x^2 - 1$

$y = x^2 - 1$

$(0, 0)$

Test point above parabola

Test point below parabola

$(0, -2)$

FIGURE 8.11

The inequality given in Example 1 is a nonlinear inequality in two variables. In this section, however, you will work primarily with **linear inequalities** of the form

$$ax + by < c \qquad ax + by \leq c$$
$$ax + by > c \qquad ax + by \geq c.$$

The graph of each of these linear inequalities is a half-plane lying on one side of the line $ax + by = c$.

The simplest linear inequalities are those corresponding to horizontal or vertical lines.

EXAMPLE 2 Sketching the Graph of a Linear Inequality

Sketch the graphs of the following linear inequalities.

a. $x > -2$
b. $y \leq 3$

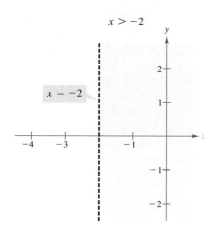

FIGURE 8.12

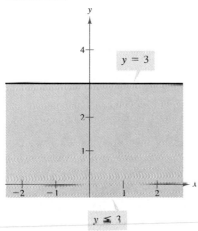

FIGURE 8.13

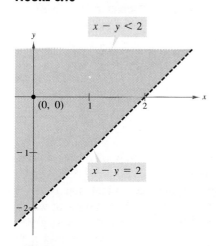

FIGURE 8.14

Solution

a. The graph of the corresponding equation $x = -2$ is a vertical line. The points that satisfy the inequality $x > -2$ are those lying to the right of this line, as shown in Figure 8.12.

b. The graph of the corresponding equation $y = 3$ is a horizontal line. The points that satisfy the inequality $y \leq 3$ are those lying below (or on) this line, as shown in Figure 8.13.

EXAMPLE 3 Sketching the Graph of a Linear Inequality

Sketch the graph of $x - y < 2$.

Solution

The graph of the corresponding equation $x - y = 2$ is a line, as shown in Figure 8.14. Since the origin $(0, 0)$ satisfies the inequality, the graph consists of the half-plane lying above the line. (Try checking a point below the line. Regardless of which point you choose, you will see that it does not satisfy the inequality.)

For a linear inequality in two variables, you can sometimes simplify the graphing procedure by writing the inequality in *slope-intercept* form. For instance, by writing $x - y < 2$ in the form

$$y > x - 2$$

you can see that the solution points lie *above* the line $y = x - 2$, as shown in Figure 8.14. Similarly, by writing the inequality $3x - 2y > 5$ in the form

$$y < \frac{3}{2}x - \frac{5}{2}$$

you see that the solutions lie *below* the line $y = \frac{3}{2}x - \frac{5}{2}$.

Systems of Inequalities

Many practical problems in business, science, and engineering involve systems of linear inequalities. Here are two examples of such systems.

$$2x - y \leq 5 \qquad x + y \leq 12$$
$$x + 2y > 2 \qquad 3x - 4y \leq 15$$
$$x \geq 0$$
$$y \geq 0$$

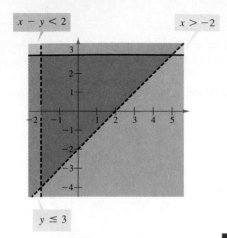

$x - y < 2$

$x > -2$

$y \leq 3$

A **solution** of a system of inequalities in x and y is an ordered pair (x, y) that satisfies each inequality in the system. For instance, $(2, 4)$ is a solution of the system on the right because $x = 2$ and $y = 4$ satisfy each of the four inequalities in the system.

To sketch the graph of a system of inequalities in two variables, first sketch the graph of each individual inequality (on the same coordinate system) and then find the region that is *common* to every graph in the system. For systems of linear inequalities, it is helpful to find the *vertices* of the solution region, as shown in the following example.

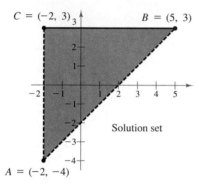

$C = (-2, 3)$ $B = (5, 3)$

Solution set

$A = (-2, -4)$

FIGURE 8.15

EXAMPLE 4   Solving a System of Inequalities

Sketch the graph (and label the vertices) of the solution set of the following system.

$$x - y < 2$$
$$x > -2$$
$$y \leq 3$$

Solution

You already sketched the graph of each inequality in Examples 2 and 3. The triangular region common to all three graphs can be found by superimposing the graphs on the same coordinate plane, as shown in Figure 8.15. To find the vertices of the region, solve the three systems of corresponding equations obtained by taking *pairs* of equations representing the boundaries of the individual regions.

Vertex A: $(-2, -4)$	Vertex B: $(5, 3)$	Vertex C: $(-2, 3)$
Obtained by solving the system	Obtained by solving the system	Obtained by solving the system
$x - y = 2$ $x = -2.$	$x - y = 2$ $y = 3.$	$x = -2$ $y = 3.$

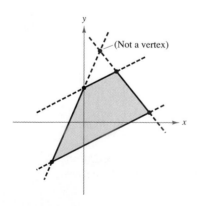

(Not a vertex)

Boundary lines can intersect at a point that is not a vertex.

FIGURE 8.16

For the triangular region shown in Figure 8.15, each point of intersection of a pair of boundary lines corresponds to a vertex. With more complicated regions, two border lines can sometimes intersect at a point that is not a vertex of the region, as shown in Figure 8.16. In order to keep track of which points of intersection are actually vertices of the region, we suggest that you make a careful sketch of the region and refer to your sketch as you find each point of intersection.

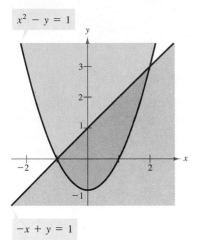

$x^2 - y = 1$

$-x + y = 1$

FIGURE 8.17

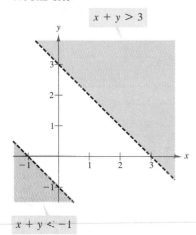

$x + y > 3$

$x + y < -1$

No solution

FIGURE 8.18

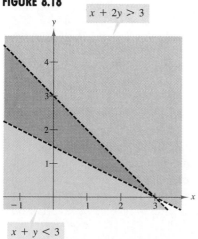

$x + 2y > 3$

$x + y < 3$

Unbounded region

EXAMPLE 5   Solving a System of Inequalities

Sketch the region containing all points that satisfy the following system.

$$x^2 - y \leq 1$$
$$-x + y \leq 1$$

Solution

As shown in Figure 8.17, the points that satisfy the inequality $x^2 - y \leq 1$ are the points lying above (or on) the parabola given by $y = x^2 - 1$. The points satisfying the inequality $-x + y \leq 1$ are the points lying on or below the line given by $y = x + 1$. To find the points of intersection of the parabola and the line, solve the following system of corresponding equations.

$$x^2 - y = 1$$
$$-x + y = 1$$

Using the method of substitution, you find the solutions to be $(-1, 0)$ and $(2, 3)$, as shown in Figure 8.17.

When solving a system of inequalities, you should be aware that the system might have no solution. For instance, the system

$$x + y > 3$$
$$x + y < -1$$

has no solution points, because the quantity $(x + y)$ cannot be both less than -1 and greater than 3, as shown in Figure 8.18.

Another possibility is that the solution set of a system of inequalities can be unbounded. For instance, the solution set of

$$x + y < 3$$
$$x + 2y > 3$$

forms an *infinite wedge*, as shown in Figure 8.19.

FIGURE 8.19

Applications

EXAMPLE 6 An Application of a System of Inequalities

The liquid portion of a diet is to provide at least 300 calories, 36 units of vitamin A, and 90 units of vitamin C daily. A cup of dietary drink X provides 60 calories, 12 units of vitamin A, and 10 units of vitamin C. A cup of dietary drink Y provides 60 calories, 6 units of vitamin A, and 30 units of vitamin C. Set up a system of linear inequalities that describes the minimum daily requirements for calories and vitamins.

Solution

Let

x = number of cups of dietary drink X

y = number of cups of dietary drink Y.

Then, to meet the minimum daily requirements, the following inequalities must be satisfied.

For Calories: $60x + 60y \geq 300$

For Vitamin A: $12x + 6y \geq 36$

For Vitamin C: $10x + 30y \geq 90$

$$x \geq 0$$
$$y \geq 0$$

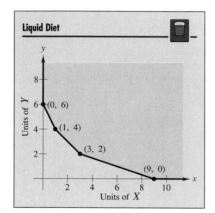

FIGURE 8.20

The last two inequalities are included because x and y cannot be negative. The graph of this system of inequalities is shown in Figure 8.20. (More is said about this application in Section 8.5, Example 6.)

In Example 8 in Section 8.2 we discussed the *point of equilibrium* for a demand and supply function. In the next example, we discuss two related concepts that economists call **consumer surplus** and **producer surplus.** As shown in Figure 8.21, the consumer surplus is defined to be the area of the region that lies *below* the demand curve, *above* the horizontal line passing through the equilibrium point, and to the right of the y-axis. Similarly, the producer surplus is defined to be the area of the region that lies *above* the supply curve, *below* the horizontal line passing through the equilibrium point, and to the right of the y-axis. In general terms, consumer surplus is a measure of the amount of money that consumers would have been willing to pay *above what they actually paid*. Similarly, producer surplus is a measure of the amount of money that producers would have been willing to receive *below what they actually received.*

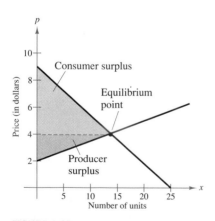

FIGURE 8.21

EXAMPLE 7   Consumer and Producer Surplus

Suppose the demand and supply functions for a certain type of calculator are given by

$$p = 150 - 10x \qquad \text{Demand equation}$$
$$p = 60 + 20x \qquad \text{Supply equation}$$

where p is the price in dollars and x represents the number of units in millions. Find the consumer and producer surplus for these two equations.

Solution

To begin, find the point of equilibrium by solving the equation

$$60 + 20x = 150 - 10x.$$

In Example 8 of Section 8.2, you found that the solution was $x = 3$, which corresponded to an equilibrium price of $p = \$120$. Thus, the consumer surplus and producer surplus are the areas of the triangular regions given by the following sets of inequalities.

Consumer Surplus	Producer Surplus
$p \leq 150 - 10x$	$p > 60 + 20x$
$p \geq 120$	$p \leq 120$
$x \geq 0$	$x \geq 0$

Using Figure 8.22 and the formula for the area of a triangle, you find that the consumer surplus is

$$\text{Consumer surplus} = \frac{1}{2}(\text{base})(\text{height}) = \frac{1}{2}(30)(3) = \$45 \text{ million}$$

and the producer surplus is

$$\text{Producer surplus} = \frac{1}{2}(\text{base})(\text{height}) = \frac{1}{2}(60)(3) = \$90 \text{ million}.$$

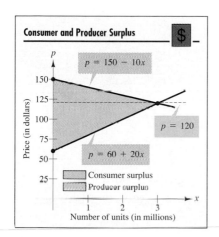

FIGURE 8.22

DISCUSSION

PROBLEM

**You Be
the
Instructor**

Suppose you are tutoring a student in algebra and want to construct some practice problems for your student. Write a paragraph describing how you could write a system of linear inequalities that had a given region as its solution. Then apply your procedure to find two systems of linear inequalities that have the following regions as solutions (see Figures 8.23 and 8.24).

1. Region with (0, 0), (0, 2), (3, 0), and (2, 1) as vertices.

2. Region with (0, 0), (0, 3), (4, 0), and (3, 2) as vertices.

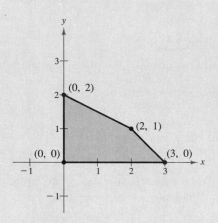

FIGURE 8.23

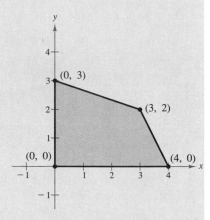

FIGURE 8.24

WARM UP

The following warm-up exercises involve skills that were covered in earlier sections. You will use these skills in the exercise set for this section.

In Exercises 1–6, identify the graph of each equation.

1. $x + y = 3$

2. $4x - y = 8$

3. $y = x^2 - 4$

4. $y = -x^2 + 1$

5. $x^2 + y^2 = 9$

6. $\dfrac{x^2}{4} + \dfrac{y^2}{9} = 1$

In Exercises 7–10, solve the system of equations.

7. $\begin{aligned} x + 2y &= 3 \\ 4x - 7y &= -3 \end{aligned}$

8. $\begin{aligned} 2x - 3y &= 4 \\ x + 5y &= 2 \end{aligned}$

9. $\begin{aligned} x^2 + y &= 5 \\ 2x - 4y &= 0 \end{aligned}$

10. $\begin{aligned} x^2 + y^2 &= 13 \\ x + y &= 5 \end{aligned}$

EXERCISES for Section 8.4

In Exercises 1–8, match the inequality with its graph. [The graphs are labeled (a), (b), (c), (d), (e), (f), (g), and (h).]

1. $x > 3$

2. $y \le 2$

3. $2x + 3y \le 6$

4. $2x - y \ge -2$

5. $x^2 + y^2 < 4$

6. $(x - 2)^2 + (y - 3)^2 > 4$

7. $xy > 2$

8. $y \le 4 - x^2$

(a)

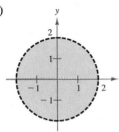

(b)

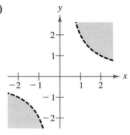

(c)

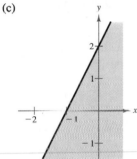

(d)

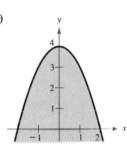

(e)

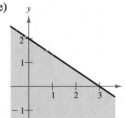

(f)

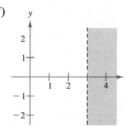

(g)

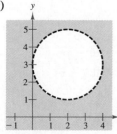

(h)

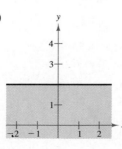

In Exercises 9–20, sketch the graph of the inequality.

9. $x \ge 2$

10. $x \le 4$

11. $y \ge -1$

12. $y \le 3$

13. $y < 2 - x$

14. $y > 2x - 4$

15. $2y - x \ge 4$

16. $5x + 3y \ge -15$

17. $(x + 1)^2 + (y - 2)^2 < 9$

18. $y^2 - x < 0$

19. $y \le \dfrac{1}{1 + x^2}$

20. $y < \ln x$

In Exercises 21–40, sketch the graph of the solution of the system of inequalities

21.
$$\begin{aligned} x + y &\le 1 \\ -x + y &\le 1 \\ y &\ge 0 \end{aligned}$$

22.
$$\begin{aligned} 3x + 2y &< 6 \\ x &> 0 \\ y &> 0 \end{aligned}$$

23.
$$\begin{aligned} x + y &< 5 \\ x &\ge 2 \\ y &\ge 0 \end{aligned}$$

24.
$$\begin{aligned} 2x + y &\ge 2 \\ x &\le 2 \\ y &\le 1 \end{aligned}$$

25.
$$\begin{aligned} -3x + 2y &< 6 \\ x + 4y &> -2 \\ 2x + y &< 3 \end{aligned}$$

26.
$$\begin{aligned} x - 7y &> -36 \\ 5x + 2y &> 5 \\ 6x - 5y &> 6 \end{aligned}$$

27.
$$\begin{aligned} 2x + y &> 2 \\ 6x + 3y &< 2 \end{aligned}$$

28.
$$\begin{aligned} x - 2y &< -6 \\ 5x - 3y &> -9 \end{aligned}$$

29.
$$\begin{aligned} x &\ge 1 \\ x - 2y &\le 3 \\ 3x + 2y &\ge 9 \\ x + y &\le 6 \end{aligned}$$

30.
$$\begin{aligned} x - y^2 &> 0 \\ x - y &< 2 \end{aligned}$$

31.
$$\begin{aligned} x^2 + y^2 &\le 9 \\ x^2 + y^2 &\ge 1 \end{aligned}$$

32.
$$\begin{aligned} x^2 + y^2 &\le 25 \\ 4x - 3y &\le 0 \end{aligned}$$

33.
$$\begin{aligned} x &> y^2 \\ x &< y + 2 \end{aligned}$$

34.
$$\begin{aligned} x &< 2y - y^2 \\ 0 &< x + y \end{aligned}$$

35.
$$\begin{aligned} y &\le \sqrt{3x} + 1 \\ y &\ge x + 1 \end{aligned}$$

36.
$$\begin{aligned} y &< -x^2 + 2x + 3 \\ y &> x^2 - 4x + 3 \end{aligned}$$

37.
$$\begin{aligned} y &< x^3 - 2x + 1 \\ y &> -2x \\ x &\le 1 \end{aligned}$$

38.
$$\begin{aligned} y &\ge x^4 - 2x^2 + 1 \\ y &\le 1 - x^2 \end{aligned}$$

39.
$$\begin{aligned} x^2 y &\ge 1 \\ 0 &< x \le 4 \\ y &\le 4 \end{aligned}$$

40.
$$\begin{aligned} y &\le e^{-x^2/2} \\ y &\ge 0 \\ -2 &\le x \le 2 \end{aligned}$$

In Exercises 41–46, derive a set of inequalities to describe the region.

41. Rectangular region with vertices at (2, 1), (5, 1), (5, 7), and (2, 7)

42. Parallelogram region with vertices at (0, 0), (4, 0), (1, 4), and (5, 4)

43. Triangular region with vertices at (0, 0), (5, 0), and (2, 3)

44. Triangular region with vertices at (−1, 0), (1, 0), and (0, 1)

45. Sector of a circle **46.** Sector of a circle

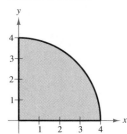 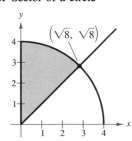

47. *Furniture Production* A furniture company can sell all the tables and chairs it produces. Each table requires 1 hour in the assembly center and $1\frac{1}{3}$ hours in the finishing center. Each chair requires $1\frac{1}{2}$ hours in the assembly center and $1\frac{1}{2}$ hours in the finishing center. The company's assembly center is available 12 hours per day, and its finishing center is available 15 hours per day. If x is the number of tables produced per day and y is the number of chairs produced per day, find a system of inequalities describing all possible production levels. Sketch the graph of the system.

48. *Computer Inventory* A store sells two models of a certain brand of computer. Because of the demand, it is necessary to stock twice as many units of model A as units of model B. The cost to the store for the two models is $800 and $1,200, respectively. The management does not want more than $20,000 in computer inventory at any one time, and it wants at least four model A computers and two model B computers in inventory at all times. Devise a system of inequalities describing all possible inventory levels, and sketch the graph of the system.

49. *Investment* A person plans to invest $20,000 in two different interest-bearing accounts. Each account is to contain at least $5,000. Moreover, one account should have at least twice the amount that is in the other account. Find a system of inequalities to describe the various amounts that can be deposited in each account, and sketch the graph of the system.

50. *Concert Ticket Sales* Two types of tickets are to be sold for a concert. One type costs $15 per ticket and the other type costs $25 per ticket. The promoter of the concert must sell at least 15,000 tickets, including 8,000 of the $15 tickets and 4,000 of the $25 tickets. Moreover, the gross receipts must total at least $275,000 in order for the concert to be held. Find a system of inequalities describing the different numbers of tickets that can be sold and sketch the graph of the system.

51. *Diet Supplement* A dietitian is asked to design a special diet supplement using two different foods. Each ounce of food X contains 20 units of calcium, 15 units of iron, and 10 units of vitamin B. Each ounce of food Y contains 10 units of calcium, 10 units of iron, and 20 units of vitamin B. The minimum daily requirements in the diet are 280 units of calcium, 160 units of iron, and 180 units of vitamin B. Find a system of inequalities describing the different amounts of food X and food Y that can be used in the diet and sketch the graph of the system.

52. *Diet Supplement* A dietitian is asked to design a special diet supplement using two different foods. Each ounce of food X contains 20 units of calcium, 15 units of iron, and 10 units of vitamin B. Each ounce of food Y contains 10 units of calcium, 10 units of iron, and 20 units of vitamin B. The minimum daily requirements in the diet are 300 units of calcium, 150 units of iron, and 200 units of vitamin B. Find a system of inequalities describing the different amounts of food X and food Y that can be used in the diet and sketch the graph of the system.

Consumer and Producer Surplus In Exercises 53–58, find the consumer surplus and producer surplus for the given pair of supply and demand equations.

Demand	Supply
53. $p = 50 - 0.5x$	$p = 0.125x$
54. $p = 60 - x$	$p = 10 + \frac{7}{3}x$
55. $p = 300 - x$	$p = 100 + x$
56. $p = 100 - 0.05x$	$p = 25 + 0.1x$
57. $p = 140 - 0.00002x$	$p = 80 + 0.00001x$
58. $p = 400 - 0.0002x$	$p = 225 + 0.0005x$

59. *Physical Fitness Facility*   An indoor running track is to be constructed with a space for body-building equipment inside the track (see figure). The inside track must be at least 125 meters long, and the body-building space must have an area of at least 500 square meters. Find a system of inequalities describing the various sizes of the track, and sketch the graph of the system.

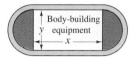

Figure for 59

The Graphical Approach to Linear Programming / Applications

The Graphical Approach to Linear Programming

Many applications in business and economics involve a process called **optimization,** in which we are required to find the minimum cost, the maximum profit, or the minimum use of resources. In this section we discuss one type of optimization problem called **linear programming.**

A two-dimensional linear programming problem consists of a linear **objective function** and a system of linear inequalities (**constraints**). The objective function gives the quantity that is to be maximized (or minimized), and the constraints determine the set of **feasible solutions.**

For example, consider a linear programming problem in which you are asked to maximize the value of

$$z = ax + by \qquad\qquad \textit{Objective function}$$

subject to a set of constraints that determine the region indicated in Figure 8.25. Because every point in the region satisfies each constraint, it is not clear how you should go about finding the point that yields a maximum value of z. Fortunately, it can be shown that if there is an optimal solution, it must occur at one of the vertices of the region. In other words, *you can find the maximum value by testing z at each of the vertices*, as shown in Example 1.

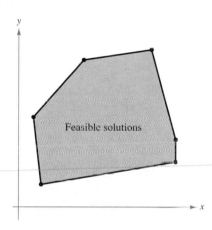

Feasible solutions

The objective function has its optimal value at one of the vertices of the region determined by the constraints.

FIGURE 8.25

Optimal Solution of Linear Programming Problem

If a linear programming problem has a solution, it must occur at a vertex of the set of feasible solutions. If the problem has more than one solution, then at least one of them must occur at a vertex of the set of feasible solutions. In either case, the value of the objective function is unique.

EXAMPLE 1 Solving a Linear Programming Problem

Find the maximum value of

$$z = 3x + 2y \qquad \textit{Objective function}$$

subject to the following constraints.

$$\left.\begin{array}{r} x \geq 0 \\ y \geq 0 \\ x + 2y \leq 4 \\ x - y \leq 1 \end{array}\right\} \quad \textit{Constraints}$$

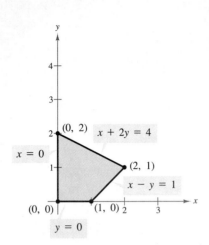

FIGURE 8.26

Solution

The constraints form the region shown in Figure 8.26. At the four vertices of this region, the objective function has the following values.

At $(0, 0)$: $z = 3(0) + 2(0) = 0$

At $(1, 0)$: $z = 3(1) + 2(0) = 3$

At $(2, 1)$: $z = 3(2) + 2(1) = 8$ *Maximum value of z*

At $(0, 2)$: $z = 3(0) + 2(2) = 4$

Thus, the maximum value of z is 8, and this occurs when $x = 2$ and $y = 1$.

REMARK In Example 1, try testing some of the *interior* points in the region. You will see that the corresponding values of z are less than 8.

To see why the maximum value of the objective function in Example 1 must occur at a vertex, consider writing the objective function in the form

$$y = -\frac{3}{2}x + \frac{z}{2}$$

where $z/2$ is the y-intercept of the objective function. This equation represents a family of lines, each of slope $-\frac{3}{2}$. Of these infinitely many lines, you want the one that has the largest z-value, while still intersecting the region determined by the constraints. In other words, of all the lines whose slope is $-\frac{3}{2}$, you want the one that has the largest y-intercept *and* intersects the given region, as shown in Figure 8.27. It should be clear that such a line will pass through one (or more) of the vertices of the region.

The steps used in Example 1 can be outlined as follows.

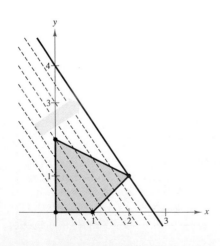

FIGURE 8.27

Graphical Method of Solving a Linear Programming Problem

To solve a linear programming problem involving two variables by the graphical method, use the following steps.

1. Sketch the region corresponding to the system of constraints. (The points inside or on the boundary of the region are called feasible solutions.)
2. Find the vertices of the region.
3. Test the objective function at each of the vertices and select the values of the variables that optimize the objective function. For a bounded region, both a minimum and maximum value will exist. (For an unbounded region, *if* an optimal solution exists, then it will occur at a vertex.)

These guidelines will work whether the objective function is to be maximized *or* minimized. For instance, in Example 1 the same test used to find the maximum value of z can be used to conclude that the minimum value of z is 0, and this occurs at the vertex $(0, 0)$.

EXAMPLE 2   Solving a Linear Programming Problem

Find the maximum value of the objective function

$$z = 4x + 6y \qquad \textit{Objective function}$$

where $x \geq 0$ and $y \geq 0$, subject to the following constraints.

$$\left. \begin{array}{r} -x + y \leq 11 \\ x + y \leq 27 \\ 2x + 5y \leq 90 \end{array} \right\} \quad \textit{Constraints}$$

Solution

The region bounded by the constraints is shown in Figure 8.28. By testing the objective function at each vertex, you obtain the following.

At $(0, 0)$: $z = 4(0) + 6(0) = 0$

At $(0, 11)$: $z = 4(0) + 6(11) = 66$

At $(5, 16)$: $z = 4(5) + 6(16) = 116$

At $(15, 12)$: $z = 4(15) + 6(12) = 132$ *Maximum value of z*

At $(27, 0)$: $z = 4(27) + 6(0) = 108$

Thus, the maximum value of z is 132 when $x = 15$ and $y = 12$.

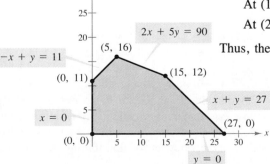

FIGURE 8.28

REMARK   In Example 3, note that the steps used to find the minimum value are precisely the same ones you would use to find the maximum value. In other words, once you have evaluated the objective function at the vertices of the feasible region, you simply choose the largest value as the maximum and the smallest value as the minimum.

EXAMPLE 3   Minimizing an Objective Function

Find the minimum value of the objective function

$$z = 5x + 7y \qquad \textit{Objective function}$$

where $x \geq 0$ and $y \geq 0$, subject to the following constraints.

$$\left.\begin{array}{r} 2x + 3y \geq 6 \\ 3x - y \leq 15 \\ -x + y \leq 4 \\ 2x + 5y \leq 27 \end{array}\right\} \quad \textit{Constraints}$$

Solution

The region bounded by the constraints is shown in Figure 8.29. By testing the objective function at each vertex, we obtain the following.

At $(0, 2)$: $z = 5(0) + 7(2) = 14$ *Minimum value of z*

At $(0, 4)$: $z = 5(0) + 7(4) = 28$

At $(1, 5)$: $z = 5(1) + 7(5) = 40$

At $(6, 3)$: $z = 5(6) + 7(3) = 51$

At $(5, 0)$: $z = 5(5) + 7(0) = 25$

At $(3, 0)$: $z = 5(3) + 7(0) = 15$

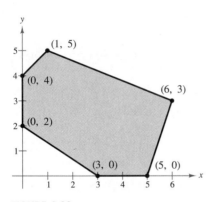

FIGURE 8.29

Thus, the minimum value of z is 14 when $x = 0$ and $y = 2$. ◢

When solving a linear programming problem, it is possible that the maximum (or minimum) value occurs at *two* different vertices. For instance, at the vertices of the region shown in Figure 8.30, the objective function

$$z = 2x + 2y \qquad \textit{Objective function}$$

has the following values.

At $(0, 0)$: $z = 2(0) + 2(0) = 0$

At $(0, 4)$: $z = 2(0) + 2(4) = 8$

At $(2, 4)$: $z = 2(2) + 2(4) = 12$ *Maximum value of z*

At $(5, 1)$: $z = 2(5) + 2(1) = 12$ *Maximum value of z*

At $(5, 0)$: $z = 2(5) + 2(0) = 10$

In this case, the objective function has a maximum value not only at the vertices $(2, 4)$ and $(5, 1)$; it also has a maximum value (of 12) at *any point on the line segment connecting these two vertices*. Note that the objective function, $y = -x + \frac{1}{2}z$, has the same slope as the line through the vertices $(2, 4)$ and $(5, 1)$.

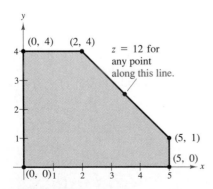

FIGURE 8.30

Some linear programming problems have no optimal solution. This can occur if the region determined by the constraint is *unbounded*. Example 4 illustrates such a problem.

EXAMPLE 4 An Unbounded Region

Find the maximum value of

$$z = 4x + 2y \qquad \text{\textit{Objective function}}$$

where $x \geq 0$ and $y \geq 0$, subject to the following constraints.

$$\left.\begin{array}{r} x + 2y \geq 4 \\ 3x + y \geq 7 \\ -x + 2y \leq 7 \end{array}\right\} \quad \text{\textit{Constraints}}$$

Solution

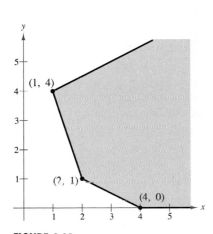

FIGURE 8.31

The region determined by the constraints is shown in Figure 8.31. For this unbounded region, there is no maximum value of z. Note that the point $(x, 0)$ lies in the region for all values of $x \geq 4$. By choosing x to be large, you can obtain values of $z = 4(x) + 2(0) = 4x$ to be as large as you want. Thus, there is no maximum value of z. For this problem, there *is* a minimum value of $z = 10$, which occurs at the vertex $(2, 1)$.

Applications

EXAMPLE 5 A Business Application: Maximum Profit

A manufacturer wants to maximize the profit for two products. The first product yields a profit of \$1.50 per unit, and the second product yields a profit of \$2.00 per unit. Market tests and available resources have indicated the following constraints.

1. The combined production level should not exceed 1200 units per month.
2. The demand for product II is less than or equal to half of the demand for product I.
3. The production level of product I is less than or equal to 600 units plus three times the production level of product II.

Solution

If x is the number of units of product I and y is the number of units of product II, then the objective function (for the combined profit) is given by

$$P = 1.5x + 2y. \qquad \text{\textit{Objective function}}$$

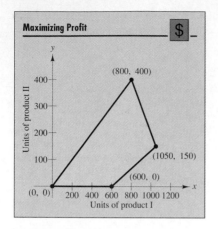

Maximizing Profit   💲

Units of product II (y-axis)

(800, 400)

400

300

200

100

(1050, 150)

(600, 0)

(0, 0)   200 400 600 800 1000 1200

Units of product I

FIGURE 8.32

The three constraints translate into the following linear inequalities.

1. $x + y \leq 1200$ $\rightarrow$ $x + y \leq 1200$
2. $y \leq \frac{1}{2}x$ $\rightarrow$ $x - 2y \geq 0$
3. $x \leq 3y + 600$ $\rightarrow$ $x - 3y \leq 600$

Since neither x nor y can be negative, you also have the two additional constraints of $x \geq 0$ and $y \geq 0$. Figure 8.32 shows the region determined by the constraints. To find the maximum profit, test the value of P at the vertices of the region.

At $(0, 0)$: $P = 1.5(0)$ $+ 2(0)$ $= 0$

At $(800, 400)$: $P = 1.5(800)$ $+ 2(400) = 2000$ *Maximum profit*

At $(1050, 150)$: $P = 1.5(1050) + 2(150) = 1875$

At $(600, 0)$: $P = 1.5(600)$ $+ 2(0)$ $= 900$

Thus, the maximum profit is \$2000, and it occurs when the monthly production consists of 800 units of product I and 400 units of product II. ◢

EXAMPLE 6   An Application: Minimum Cost

In Example 6 in Section 8.4, we set up a system of linear equations for the following problem. The liquid portion of a diet is to provide at least 300 calories, 36 units of vitamin A, and 90 units of vitamin C daily. A cup of dietary drink X provides 60 calories, 12 units of vitamin A, and 10 units of vitamin C. A cup of dietary drink Y provides 60 calories, 6 units of vitamin A, and 30 units of vitamin C. Now, suppose that dietary drink X costs \$0.12 per cup and drink Y costs \$0.15 per cup. How many cups of each drink should be consumed each day to minimize the cost and still meet the stated daily requirements?

Solution

Begin by letting x be the number of cups of dietary drink X and y be the number of cups of dietary drink Y. Moreover, to meet the minimum daily requirements, the following inequalities must be satisfied.

$$
\left.
\begin{array}{llr}
\textit{For Calories:} & 60x + 60y \geq & 300 \\
\textit{For Vitamin A:} & 12x + 6y \geq & 36 \\
\textit{For Vitamin C:} & 10x + 30y \geq & 90 \\
& x \geq & 0 \\
& y \geq & 0
\end{array}
\right\} \quad \textit{Constraints}
$$

The cost C is given by

$$C = 0.12x + 0.15y. \qquad \textit{Objective function}$$

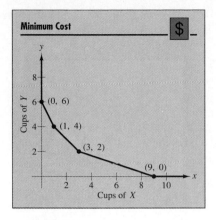

Minimum Cost $ —

Cups of Y

(0, 6)

(1, 4)

(3, 2)

(9, 0)

Cups of X

FIGURE 8.33

The graph of the region corresponding to the constraints is shown in Figure 8.33. To determine the minimum cost, test C at each vertex of the region as follows.

At $(0, 6)$: $C = 0.12(0) + 0.15(6) = 0.90$

At $(1, 4)$: $C = 0.12(1) + 0.15(4) = 0.72$

At $(3, 2)$: $C = 0.12(3) + 0.15(2) = 0.66$ *Minimum value of C*

At $(9, 0)$: $C = 0.12(9) + 0.15(0) = 1.08$

Thus, the minimum cost is \$0.66 per day, and this occurs when three cups of drink X and two cups of drink Y are consumed each day.

EXAMPLE 7   Maximum Profit

A small computer keyboard company makes two popular models, for which the demand is much greater than the current supply (both models have substantial back orders). Both models take 1 hour to assemble. However, Model TT1 requires only 7.5 minutes to test, whereas Model TT2 requires 30 minutes to test. With the company's current facilities, there are 45,000 hours per month available for assembly, and 15,000 hours per month available for testing. The profit for Model TT1 is \$50 per unit, and the profit for Model TT2 is \$80 per unit. What is the greatest monthly profit the company can make without increasing its current facilities?

Solution

To begin to solve this problem, it is helpful to organize the information in table form, as shown in Table 8.1.

TABLE 8.1

	Model TT1 (x units)	Model TT2 (y units)	Maximum Hours
Assembly time per unit	1 hour	1 hour	45,000
Test time per unit	$\frac{1}{8}$ hour	$\frac{1}{2}$ hour	15,000
Profit per unit	\$50	\$80	—

From the third row in the table, you see that the total profit for selling x units of Model TT1 and y units of Model TT2 is

$$P = 50x + 80y.$$ *Objective function*

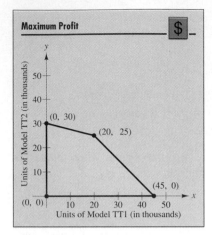

FIGURE 8.34

This equation represents the objective function that you need to maximize. The constraints under which you are allowed to work are given by the following two inequalities.

$$x + y \le 45,000$$
$$\frac{1}{8}x + \frac{1}{2}y \le 15,000$$

In addition, you further require that $x \ge 0$ and $y \ge 0$. Thus, the possible values of x and y are those that lie in (or on the boundary of) the region shown in Figure 8.34. At the four vertices, you obtain the following profits.

$$P = 50(0) + 80(0) = \$0$$
$$P = 50(0) + 80(30,000) = \$2,400,000$$
$$P = 50(20,000) + 80(25,000) = \$3,000,000 \quad \textit{Maximum value of P}$$
$$P = 50(45,000) + 80(0) = \$2,250,000$$

Therefore, the maximum profit can be obtained by producing 20,000 units of Model TT1 and 25,000 units of Model TT2.

DISCUSSION

PROBLEM

Creating
a
Linear
Programming
Problem

Consider the following linear programming problem.

Objective Function: $\qquad z = ax + by$

Constraints: $\qquad\qquad x \ge 0$
$$y \ge 0$$
$$x + 2y \le 8$$
$$x + y \le 5$$

The region determined by these constraints is shown in Figure 8.35. Find, if possible, an objective function that has a *maximum* at the indicated vertex of the region.

1. Maximum at (0, 4)
2. Maximum at (2, 3)
3. Maximum at (5, 0)
4. Maximum at (0, 0)

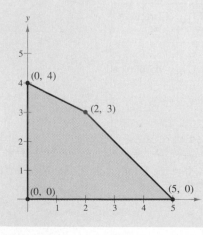

FIGURE 8.35

WARM UP

WARM UP

The following warm-up exercises involve skills that were covered in earlier sections. You will use these skills in the exercise set for this section.

In Exercises 1–4, sketch the graph of the linear equation.

1. $y + x = 3$

2. $y - x = 12$

3. $x = 0$

4. $y = 4$

In Exercises 5–8, solve the system of equations.

5. $x + y = 4$
$\quad x \quad\;\; = 0$

6. $x + 2y = 12$
$\quad\quad\quad\; y = 0$

7. $\;\; x + \;\; y = 4$
$\;\; 2x + 3y = 9$

8. $\;\; x + 2y = 12$
$\;\; 2x + \;\; y = 9$

In Exercises 9 and 10, sketch the graph of the inequality.

9. $2x + 3y \geq 18$

10. $4x + 3y \geq 12$

EXERCISES for Section 8.5

In Exercises 1–12, find the minimum and maximum values of the given objective function, subject to the indicated constraints. (For each exercise, the graph of the region determined by the constraints is provided.)

1. Objective function:
$z = 4x + 5y$
Constraints:
$$x \geq 0$$
$$y \geq 0$$
$$x + y \leq 6$$

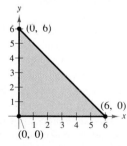

2. Objective function:
$z = 2x + 8y$
Constraints:
$$x \geq 0$$
$$y \geq 0$$
$$2x + y \leq 4$$

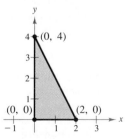

5. Objective function:
$z = 3x + 2y$
Constraints:
$$x \geq 0$$
$$y \geq 0$$
$$x + 3y \leq 15$$
$$4x + y \leq 16$$

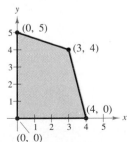

6. Objective function:
$z = 4x + 3y$
Constraints:
$$x \geq 0$$
$$2x + 3y \geq 6$$
$$3x - 2y \leq 9$$
$$x + 5y \leq 20$$

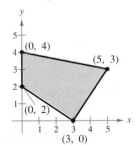

3. Objective function:
$z = 10x + 6y$
Constraints:
(See Exercise 1.)

4. Objective function:
$z = 7x + 3y$
Constraints:
(See Exercise 2.)

7. Objective function:
$z = 5x + 0.5y$
Constraints:
(See Exercise 5.)

8. Objective function:
$z = x + 6y$
Constraints:
(See Exercise 6.)

9. Objective function:
$z = 10x + 7y$
Constraints:
$$0 \le x \le 60$$
$$0 \le y \le 45$$
$$5x + 6y \le 420$$

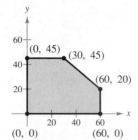

10. Objective function:
$z = 50x + 35y$
Constraints:
$$x \ge 0$$
$$y \ge 0$$
$$8x + 9y \le 7200$$
$$8x + 9y \ge 5400$$

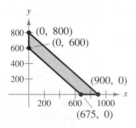

11. Objective function:
$z = 25x + 30y$
Constraints:
(See Exercise 9.)

12. Objective function:
$z = 16x + 18y$
Constraints:
(See Exercise 10.)

In Exercises 13–24, sketch the region determined by the constraints. Then find the minimum and maximum values of the objective function, subject to the constraints.

13. Objective function:
$z = 6x + 10y$
Constraints:
$$x \ge 0$$
$$y \ge 0$$
$$2x + 5y \le 10$$

14. Objective function:
$z = 7x + 8y$
Constraints:
$$x \ge 0$$
$$y \ge 0$$
$$x + \tfrac{1}{2}y \le 4$$

15. Objective function:
$z = 9x + 24y$
Constraints:
(See Exercise 13.)

16. Objective function:
$z = 7x + 2y$
Constraints:
(See Exercise 14.)

17. Objective function:
$z = 4x + 5y$
Constraints:
$$x \ge 0$$
$$y \ge 0$$
$$4x + 3y \ge 27$$
$$x + y \ge 8$$
$$3x + 5y \ge 30$$

18. Objective function:
$z = 4x + 5y$
Constraints:
$$x \ge 0$$
$$y \ge 0$$
$$2x + 2y \le 10$$
$$x + 2y \le 6$$

19. Objective function:
$z = 2x + 7y$
Constraints:
(See Exercise 17.)

20. Objective function:
$z = 2x - y$
Constraints:
(See Exercise 18.)

21. Objective function:
$z = 4x + y$
Constraints:
$$x \ge 0$$
$$y \ge 0$$
$$x + 2y \le 40$$
$$x + y \ge 30$$
$$2x + 3y \ge 72$$

22. Objective function:
$z = x$
Constraints:
$$x \ge 0$$
$$y \ge 0$$
$$2x + 3y \le 60$$
$$2x + y \le 28$$
$$4x + y \le 48$$

23. Objective function:
$z = x + 4y$
Constraints:
(See Exercise 21.)

24. Objective function:
$z = y$
Constraints:
(See Exercise 22.)

In Exercises 25–28, maximize the objective function subject to the constraints $3x + y \le 15$ and $4x + 3y \le 30$, where $x \ge 0$ and $y \ge 0$.

25. $z = 2x + y$

26. $z = 5x + y$

27. $z = x + y$

28. $z = 3x + y$

In Exercises 29–32, maximize the objective function subject to the constraints $x + 4y \le 20$, $x + y \le 8$, and $3x + 2y \le 21$, where $x \ge 0$ and $y \ge 0$.

29. $z = x + 5y$

30. $z = 2x + 4y$

31. $z = 4x + 5y$

32. $z = 4x + y$

33. *Maximum Profit*   A merchant plans to sell two models of home computers at costs of $250 and $400, respectively. The $250 model yields a profit of $45 and the $400 model yields a profit of $50. The merchant estimates that the total monthly demand will not exceed 250 units. Find the number of units of each model that should be stocked in order to maximize profit. Assume that the merchant does not want to invest more than $70,000 in computer inventory.

34. *Maximum Profit*   A fruit grower has 150 acres of land available to raise two crops, A and B. It takes one day to trim an acre of crop A and two days to trim an acre of crop B, and there are 240 days per year available for trimming. It takes 0.3 day to pick an acre of crop A and 0.1 day to pick an acre of crop B, and there are 30 days per year available for picking. Find the number of acres of each fruit that should be planted to maximize profit, assuming that the profit is $140 per acre for crop A and $235 per acre for crop B.

35. *Minimum Cost*   A farming cooperative mixes two brands of cattle feed. Brand X costs $25 per bag and contains 2 units of nutritional element A, 2 units of element B, and 2 units of element C. Brand Y costs $20 per bag and contains 1 unit of nutritional element A, 9 units of element

B, and 3 units of element C. Find the number of bags of each brand that should be mixed to produce a mixture having a minimum cost per bag. The minimum requirements of nutrients A, B, and C are 12 units, 36 units, and 24 units, respectively.

36. Minimum Cost Two gasolines, type A and type B, have octane ratings of 80 and 92, respectively. Type A costs $1.13 per gallon and type B costs $1.28 per gallon. Determine the blend of minimum cost with an octane rating of at least 90. (*Hint:* Let x be the fraction of each gallon that is type A and y be the fraction that is type B.)

37. Maximum Profit A manufacturer produces two models of bicycles. The time (in hours) required for assembling, painting, and packaging each model is as follows.

	Model A	Model B
Assembling	2	2.5
Painting	4	1
Packaging	1	0.75

The total time available for assembling, painting, and packaging is 4000 hours, 4800 hours, and 1500 hours, respectively. The profit per unit for each model is $45 (model A) and $50 (model B). How many of each type should be produced to obtain a maximum profit?

38. Maximum Profit A manufacturer produces two models of bicycles. The time (in hours) required for assembling, painting, and packaging each model is as follows.

	Model A	Model B
Assembling	2.5	3
Painting	2	1
Packaging	0.75	1.25

The total time available for assembling, painting, and packaging is 4000 hours, 2500 hours, and 1500 hours, respectively. The profit per unit for each model is $50 (model A) and $52 (model B). How many of each type should be produced to obtain a maximum profit?

39. Maximum Revenue An accounting firm has 900 hours of staff time and 100 hours of reviewing time available each week. It charges $2000 for an audit and $300 for a tax return. Each audit takes 100 hours of staff time and 10 hours of review time. Each tax return takes 12.5 hours of staff time and 2.5 hours of review time. What number of audits and tax returns will yield the maximum revenue?

40. Maximum Revenue The accounting firm in Exercise 39 lowers its charge for an audit to $1000. What number of audits and tax returns will yield the maximum revenue?

In Exercises 41–46, the given linear programming problem has an unusual characteristic. Sketch a graph of the solution region for the problem and describe the unusual characteristic. In each problem, the objective function is to be maximized.

41. Objective function:
$z = 2.5x + y$
Constraints:
$x \geq 0$
$y \geq 0$
$3x + 5y \leq 15$
$5x + 2y \leq 10$

42. Objective function:
$z = x + y$
Constraints:
$x \geq 0$
$y \geq 0$
$-x + y \leq 1$
$-x + 2y \leq 4$

43. Objective function:
$z = -x + 2y$
Constraints:
$x \geq 0$
$y \geq 0$
$x \leq 10$
$x + y \leq 7$

44. Objective function:
$z = x + y$
Constraints:
$x \geq 0$
$y \geq 0$
$-x + y \leq 0$
$-3x + y \geq 3$

45. Objective function:
$z = 3x + 4y$
Constraints:
$x \geq 0$
$y \geq 0$
$x + y \leq 1$
$2x + y \leq 4$

46. Objective function:
$z = x + 2y$
Constraints:
$x \geq 0$
$y \geq 0$
$x + 2y \leq 4$
$2x + y \leq 4$

In Exercises 47 and 48, determine the values of t such that the objective function has a maximum value at the indicated vertex.

47. Objective function:
$z = 3x + ty$
Constraints:
$x \geq 0$
$y \geq 0$
$x + 3y \leq 15$
$4x + y \leq 16$

(a) $(0, 5)$
(b) $(3, 4)$

48. Objective function:
$z = 3x + ty$
Constraints:
$x \geq 0$
$y \geq 0$
$x + 2y \leq 4$
$x - y \leq 1$

(a) $(2, 1)$
(b) $(0, 2)$

REVIEW EXERCISES for Chapter 8

In Exercises 1–8, solve the system by the method of substitution.

1. $x + y = 2$
$x - y = 0$

2. $2x = 3(y - 1)$
$y = x$

3. $x^2 - y^2 = 9$
$x - y = 1$

4. $x^2 + y^2 = 169$
$3x + 2y = 39$

5. $y = 2x^2$
$y = x^4 - 2x^2$

6. $x = y + 3$
$x = y^2 + 1$

7. $y^2 - 2y + x = 0$
$x + y = 0$

8. $y = 2x^2 - 4x + 1$
$y = x^2 - 4x + 3$

9. *Break-Even Point*   Suppose you are setting up a small business and have made an initial investment of $10,000. The unit cost of the product is $2.85 and the selling price is $4.95. How many units must you sell to break even? (Round your answer to the nearest whole unit.)

10. *Choice of Two Jobs*   You are offered two different jobs selling personal computers. One company offers an annual salary of $22,500 plus a year-end bonus of 1.5% of your total sales. The other company offers a salary of $20,000 plus a year-end bonus of 2% of your total sales. How much would you have to sell in order to make the second offer better than the first?

In Exercises 11–18, solve the system by elimination.

11. $2x - y = 2$
$6x + 8y = 39$

12. $40x + 30y = 24$
$20x - 50y = -14$

13. $0.2x + 0.3y = 0.14$
$0.4x + 0.5y = 0.20$

14. $12x + 42y = -17$
$30x - 18y = 19$

15. $3x - 2y = 0$
$3x + 2(y + 5) = 10$

16. $7x + 12y = 63$
$2x + 3y = 15$

17. $1.25x - 2y = 3.5$
$5x - 8y = 14$

18. $1.5x + 2.5y = 8.5$
$6x + 10y = 24$

19. *Acid Mixture*   One hundred gallons of a 60% acid solution are obtained by mixing a 75% solution with a 50% solution. How many gallons of each must be used to obtain the desired mixture?

20. *Cassette Tape Sales*   Suppose you are the manager of a music store. At the end of the week you are going over receipts for the previous week's sales. Six hundred and fifty cassette tapes were sold. One type of cassette sold for $9.95 and the other sold for $14.95. The total cassette receipts were $7717.50. The cash register that was supposed to record the number of each type of cassette sold malfunctioned. Can you recover the information? If so, how many of each type of cassette were sold?

21. *Flying Speeds*   Two planes leave Pittsburgh and Philadelphia at the same time, each going to the other city. Because of the wind, one plane flies 25 miles per hour faster than the other. Find the ground speed of each plane if the cities are 275 miles apart and the planes pass one another (at different altitudes) after 40 minutes of flying time.

22. *Dimensions of a Rectangle*   The perimeter of a rectangle is 480 meters, and its length is 150% of its width. Find the dimensions of the rectangle.

Supply and Demand   In Exercises 23 and 24, find the point of equilibrium for each pair of supply and demand equations.

Demand	Supply
23. $p = 37 - 0.0002x$	$p = 22 + 0.00001x$
24. $p = 120 - 0.0001x$	$p = 45 + 0.0002x$

In Exercises 25–30, solve the system of equations.

25. $x + 2y + 6z = 4$
$-3x + 2y - z = -4$
$4x + 2z = 16$

26. $x + 3y - z = 13$
$2x - 5z = 23$
$4x - y - 2z = 14$

27. $x - 2y + z = -6$
$2x - 3y = -7$
$-x + 3y - 3z = 11$

28. $2x + 6z = -9$
$3x - 2y + 11z = -16$
$3x - y + 7z = -11$

29. $2x + 5y - 19z = 34$
$3x + 8y - 31z = 54$

30. $2x + y + z + 2w = -1$
$5x - 2y + z - 3w = 0$
$-x + 3y + 2z + 2w = 1$
$3x + 2y + 3z - 5w = 12$

In Exercises 31 and 32, find the equation of the parabola
$y = ax^2 + bx + c$
that passes through the given points.

31. $(0, -6)$, $(1, -3)$, $(2, 4)$ **32.** $(-5, 0)$, $(1, -6)$, $(2, 14)$

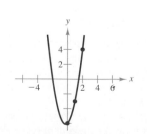

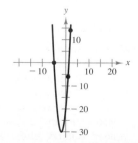

In Exercises 33 and 34, find the equation of the circle

$$x^2 + y^2 + Dx + Ey + F = 0$$

that passes through the given points.

33. $(2, 2), (5, -1), (-1, -1)$

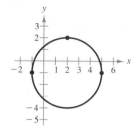

34. $(4, 2), (1, 3), (-2, -6)$

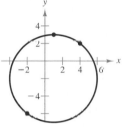

35. *Crop Spraying* A mixture of 6 gallons of chemical A, 8 gallons of chemical B, and 13 gallons of chemical C is required to kill a certain destructive crop insect. Commercial spray X contains 1, 2, and 2 parts, respectively, of these chemicals. Commercial spray Y contains only chemical C. Commercial spray Z contains chemicals A, B, and C in equal amounts. How much of each type of commercial spray is needed to get the desired mixture?

36. *Investments* An inheritance of $20,000 was divided among three investments yielding $1,780 in interest per year. The interest rates for the three investments were 7%, 9%, and 11%. Find the amount placed in each investment if the second and third were $3,000 and $1,000 less than the first, respectively.

37. *Fitting a Line to Data* Find the least squares regression line $y = ax + b$ for the points

$$(x_1, y_1), (x_2, y_2), \ldots, (x_n, y_n).$$

To find the line, solve the following system of linear equations for a and b.

$$5b + 10a = 17.8$$
$$10b + 30a = 45.7$$

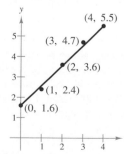

38. *Fitting a Parabola to Data* Find the least squares regression parabola $y = ax^2 + bx + c$ for the points

$$(x_1, y_1), (x_2, y_2), \ldots, (x_n, y_n).$$

To find the parabola, solve the following system of linear equations for a, b, and c.

$$5c + 10a = 9.1$$
$$10b = 8.0$$
$$10c + 34a = 19.8$$

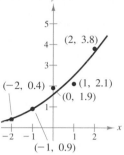

In Exercises 39–46, sketch a graph of the solution set of the system of inequalities.

39.
$$x + 2y \le 160$$
$$3x + y < 180$$
$$x \ge 0$$
$$y \ge 0$$

40.
$$2x + 3y \le 24$$
$$2x + y \le 16$$
$$x \ge 0$$
$$y \ge 0$$

41.
$$3x + 2y \ge 24$$
$$x + 2y \ge 12$$
$$2 \le x \le 15$$
$$y \le 15$$

42.
$$2x + y \ge 16$$
$$x + 3y \ge 18$$
$$0 \le x \le 25$$
$$0 \le y \le 25$$

43.
$$y < x + 1$$
$$y > x^2 - 1$$

44.
$$y \le 6 - 2x - x^2$$
$$y \ge x + 6$$

45.
$$2x - 3y \ge 0$$
$$2x - y \le 8$$
$$y \ge 0$$

46.
$$x^2 + y^2 \le 9$$
$$(x - 3)^2 + y^2 \le 9$$

In Exercises 47 and 48, derive a set of inequalities to describe the region.

47. Parallelogram with vertices at $(1, 5), (3, 1), (6, 10), (8, 6)$

48. Triangle with vertices at $(1, 2), (6, 7), (8, 1)$

In Exercises 49 and 50, determine a system of inequalities that models the description and sketch a graph of the solution of the system.

49. *Fruit Distribution* A Pennsylvania fruit grower has 1500 bushels of apples that are to be divided between markets in Harrisburg and Philadelphia. These two markets need at least 400 bushels and 600 bushels, respectively.

50. *Inventory Costs*   A warehouse operator has 24,000 square feet of floor space in which to store two products. Each unit of product I requires 20 square feet of floor space and costs $12 per day to store. Each unit of product II requires 30 square feet of floor space and costs $8 per day to store. The total storage cost per day cannot exceed $12,400.

In Exercises 51 and 52, find the consumer surplus and producer surplus for the pair of supply and demand equations.

Demand	*Supply*
51. $p = 160 - 0.0001x$	$p = 70 + 0.0002x$
52. $p = 130 - 0.0002x$	$p = 30 + 0.0003x$

In Exercises 53–56, find the required optimum value of the objective function subject to the indicated constraints.

53. Maximize the objective function:

$z = 3x + 4y$

Constraints:

$$x \geq 0$$
$$y \geq 0$$
$$2x + 5y \leq 50$$
$$4x + \ y \leq 28$$

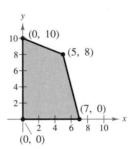

54. Minimize the objective function:

$z = 10x + 7y$

Constraints:

$$x \geq 0$$
$$y \geq 0$$
$$2x + y \geq 100$$
$$x + y \geq 75$$

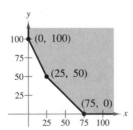

55. Minimize the objective function:

$z = 1.75x + 2.25y$

Constraints:

$$x \geq 0$$
$$y \geq 0$$
$$2x + \ y \geq 25$$
$$3x + 2y \geq 45$$

56. Maximize the objective function:

$z = 50x + 70y$

Constraints:

$$x \geq 0$$
$$y \geq 0$$
$$x + 2y \leq 1500$$
$$5x + 2y \leq 3500$$

57. *Maximum Profit*   A manufacturer produces products A and B yielding profits of $18 and $24, respectively. Each product must go through three processes with the required times per unit as shown in the following table.

Process	Hours for product A	Hours for product B	Hours available per day
I	4	2	24
II	1	2	9
III	1	1	8

Find the daily production level for each unit to maximize the profit.

58. *Maximum Revenue*   A student is working part-time as a cosmetologist to pay college expenses. The student may work no more than 21 hours per week. Haircuts cost $17 and require an average of 20 minutes; permanents cost $60 and require an average of 1 hour and 10 minutes. What combination of haircuts and/or perms will yield maximum revenue?

59. *Minimum Cost*   A pet supply company mixes two brands of dry dog food. Brand X costs $15 per bag and contains 8 units of nutritional element A, 1 unit of nutritional element B, and 2 units of nutritional element C. Brand Y costs $30 per bag and contains 2 units of nutritional element A, 1 unit of nutritional element B, and 7 units of nutritional element C. Each bag of dog food must contain at least 16 units, 5 units, and 20 units of nutritional elements A, B, and C, respectively. Find the number of bags of brands X and Y that should be mixed to produce a mixture meeting the minimum nutritional requirements and having a minimum cost per bag.

60. *Minimum Cost*   Two gasolines, type A and type B, have octane ratings of 80 and 92, respectively. Type A costs $1.25 per gallon and type B costs $1.55 per gallon. Determine the blend of minimum cost with an octane rating of at least 88. (*Hint:* Let x be the fraction of each gallon that is type A, and let y be the fraction that is type B.)

CHAPTER 9

OVERVIEW

This chapter shows how matrices can be used to model a variety of problems, beginning with their use in solving systems of linear equations.

The examples in the chapter tend to use matrices that have only a few rows or columns. You should realize, however, that matrices that model real life problems are often much larger. For instance, it is easy to imagine the need for very large matrices to model inventory levels, such as that described in Exercise 43 on page 612.

Adding, subtracting, and multiplying matrices can involve many arithmetic steps. Technology can minimize the tedium and the likelihood of calculation errors. If you have access to a calculator or computer software that performs matrix operations, you may want to use it.

Matrices and Determinants

9.1 Matrices and Systems of Linear Equations

Matrices / Elementary Row Operations / Gaussian Elimination with Back-Substitution / Gauss-Jordan Elimination

Matrices

In mathematics we always look for valid shortcuts to solving problems. In this section we look at a streamlined technique for solving systems of linear equations. This technique involves the use of a rectangular array of real numbers—a **matrix.**

DEFINITION OF A MATRIX

If m and n are positive integers, then an $m \times n$ **matrix** (read "m by n") is a rectangular array

$$\begin{bmatrix} a_{11} & a_{12} & a_{13} & \cdots & a_{1n} \\ a_{21} & a_{22} & a_{23} & \cdots & a_{2n} \\ a_{31} & a_{32} & a_{33} & \cdots & a_{3n} \\ \vdots & \vdots & \vdots & & \vdots \\ a_{m1} & a_{m2} & a_{m3} & \cdots & a_{mn} \end{bmatrix} \Bigg\} \; m \text{ rows}$$

$$\underbrace{\hphantom{a_{11} \quad a_{12} \quad a_{13} \quad \cdots \quad a_{1n}}}_{n \text{ columns}}$$

in which each **entry,** a_{ij}, of the matrix is a number. An $m \times n$ matrix has m **rows** (horizontal lines) and n **columns** (vertical lines).

REMARK   The plural of matrix is *matrices*.

The entry in the ith row and jth column is denoted by the *double subscript* notation a_{ij}. We call i the **row subscript** because it gives the position in the horizontal lines, and j the **column subscript** because it gives the position in the vertical lines.

A matrix having m rows and n columns is of **order $m \times n$.** If $m = n$, the matrix is **square** of order n. For a square matrix, the entries a_{11}, a_{22}, a_{33}, . . . are the **main diagonal** entries.

EXAMPLE 1   Examples of Matrices

The following matrices have the indicated orders.

a. Order: 1×4

$$\begin{bmatrix} 1 & -3 & 0 & \frac{1}{2} \end{bmatrix}$$

b. Order: 2×2

$$\begin{bmatrix} 0 & 0 \\ 0 & 0 \end{bmatrix}$$

c. Order: 2×3

$$\begin{bmatrix} -1 & 0 & 5 \\ 2 & 1 & -4 \end{bmatrix}$$

d. Order: 3×2

$$\begin{bmatrix} 5 & 0 \\ 2 & -2 \\ -7 & 4 \end{bmatrix}$$

A matrix that has only one row is a **row matrix** and a matrix that has only one column is a **column matrix.**

A matrix derived from a system of linear equations (each written in standard form with the constant term on the right) is the **augmented matrix** of the system. Moreover, the matrix derived from the coefficients of the system (but which does not include the constant terms) is the **coefficient matrix** of the system. Here is an example.

System	*Augmented Matrix*	*Coefficient Matrix*
$\begin{aligned} x - 4y + 3z &= 5 \\ -x + 3y - z &= -3 \\ 2x \quad\quad - 4z &= 6 \end{aligned}$	$\begin{bmatrix} 1 & -4 & 3 & \vdots & 5 \\ -1 & 3 & -1 & \vdots & -3 \\ 2 & 0 & -4 & \vdots & 6 \end{bmatrix}$	$\begin{bmatrix} 1 & -4 & 3 \\ -1 & 3 & -1 \\ 2 & 0 & -4 \end{bmatrix}$

REMARK Note the use of 0 for the missing y-variable in the third equation, and also note the fourth column of constant terms in the augmented matrix.

When forming either the coefficient matrix or the augmented matrix of a system, you should begin by vertically aligning the variables in the equations and using 0's for the missing variables.

Given System	*Line Up Variables*	*Form Augmented Matrix*
$\begin{aligned} x + 3y &= 9 \\ -y + 4z &= -2 \\ x - 5z &= 0 \end{aligned}$	$\begin{aligned} x + 3y \quad\quad &= 9 \\ -y + 4z &= -2 \\ x \quad\quad - 5z &= 0 \end{aligned}$	$\begin{bmatrix} 1 & 3 & 0 & \vdots & 9 \\ 0 & -1 & 4 & \vdots & -2 \\ 1 & 0 & -5 & \vdots & 0 \end{bmatrix}$

Elementary Row Operations

In Section 8.3 you studied three operations that can be used on a system of linear equations to produce an equivalent system.

1. Interchange two equations.
2. Multiply an equation by a nonzero constant.
3. Add a multiple of an equation to another equation.

In matrix terminology these three operations correspond to **elementary row operations.** An elementary row operation on an augmented matrix of a given system of linear equations produces a new augmented matrix corresponding to a new (but equivalent) system of linear equations. Two matrices are **row-equivalent** if one can be obtained from the other by a sequence of elementary row operations.

ELEMENTARY ROW OPERATIONS

1. Interchange two rows.
2. Multiply a row by a nonzero constant.
3. Add a multiple of a row to another row.

Although elementary row operations are simple to perform, they involve a lot of arithmetic. Because it is easy to make a mistake, we suggest that you get into the habit of noting the elementary row operations performed in each step so that you can go back and check your work.

EXAMPLE 2 Elementary Row Operations

a. Interchange the first and second rows.

Original Matrix

$$\begin{bmatrix} 0 & 1 & 3 & 4 \\ -1 & 2 & 0 & 3 \\ 2 & -3 & 4 & 1 \end{bmatrix}$$

New Row Equivalent Matrix

$$\begin{matrix} \curvearrowright R_2 \\ \curvearrowright R_1 \end{matrix} \begin{bmatrix} -1 & 2 & 0 & 3 \\ 0 & 1 & 3 & 4 \\ 2 & -3 & 4 & 1 \end{bmatrix}$$

b. Multiply the first row by $\frac{1}{2}$.

Original Matrix

$$\begin{bmatrix} 2 & -4 & 6 & -2 \\ 1 & 3 & -3 & 0 \\ 5 & -2 & 1 & 2 \end{bmatrix}$$

New Row Equivalent Matrix

$$\frac{1}{2}R_1 \rightarrow \begin{bmatrix} 1 & -2 & 3 & -1 \\ 1 & 3 & -3 & 0 \\ 5 & -2 & 1 & 2 \end{bmatrix}$$

c. Add -2 times the first row to the third row.

Original Matrix

$$\begin{bmatrix} 1 & 2 & -4 & 3 \\ 0 & 3 & -2 & -1 \\ 2 & 1 & 5 & -2 \end{bmatrix}$$

New Row Equivalent Matrix

$$-2R_1 + R_3 \rightarrow \begin{bmatrix} 1 & 2 & -4 & 3 \\ 0 & 3 & -2 & -1 \\ 0 & -3 & 13 & -8 \end{bmatrix}$$

Note that you write the elementary row operation beside the row that you are *changing*. ◀

In Section 8.3 you used Gaussian elimination with back-substitution to solve a system of linear equations. We now demonstrate the matrix version of Gaussian elimination. The two methods are essentially the same. The basic difference is that with matrices you do not need to keep writing the variables.

EXAMPLE 3 Using Elementary Row Operations to Solve a System

Linear System   *Associated Augmented Matrix*

$$
\begin{aligned}
x - 2y + 3z &= 9 \\
-x + 3y &= -4 \\
2x - 5y + 5z &= 17
\end{aligned}
\qquad
\left[\begin{array}{rrr:r}
1 & -2 & 3 & 9 \\
-1 & 3 & 0 & -4 \\
2 & -5 & 5 & 17
\end{array}\right]
$$

Add the first equation to the second equation.

Add the first row to the second row $(R_1 + R_2)$.

$$
\begin{aligned}
x - 2y + 3z &= 9 \\
y + 3z &= 5 \\
2x - 5y + 5z &= 17
\end{aligned}
\qquad
R_1 + R_2 \rightarrow
\left[\begin{array}{rrr:r}
1 & -2 & 3 & 9 \\
0 & 1 & 3 & 5 \\
2 & -5 & 5 & 17
\end{array}\right]
$$

Add -2 times the first equation to the third equation.

Add -2 times the first row to the third row $(-2R_1 + R_3)$.

$$
\begin{aligned}
x - 2y + 3z &= 9 \\
y + 3z &= 5 \\
-y - z &= -1
\end{aligned}
\qquad
-2R_1 + R_3 \rightarrow
\left[\begin{array}{rrr:r}
1 & -2 & 3 & 9 \\
0 & 1 & 3 & 5 \\
0 & -1 & -1 & -1
\end{array}\right]
$$

Add the second equation to the third equation.

Add the second row to the third row $(R_2 + R_3)$.

$$
\begin{aligned}
x - 2y + 3z &= 9 \\
y + 3z &= 5 \\
2z &= 4
\end{aligned}
\qquad
R_2 + R_3 \rightarrow
\left[\begin{array}{rrr:r}
1 & -2 & 3 & 9 \\
0 & 1 & 3 & 5 \\
0 & 0 & 2 & 4
\end{array}\right]
$$

Multiply the third equation by $\frac{1}{2}$.

Multiply the third row by $\frac{1}{2}$.

$$
\begin{aligned}
x - 2y + 3z &= 9 \\
y + 3z &= 5 \\
z &= 2
\end{aligned}
\qquad
\tfrac{1}{2}R_3 \rightarrow
\left[\begin{array}{rrr:r}
1 & -2 & 3 & 9 \\
0 & 1 & 3 & 5 \\
0 & 0 & 1 & 2
\end{array}\right]
$$

At this point, you can use back-substitution to find that the solution is $x = 1$, $y = -1$, and $z = 2$, as you did in Section 8.3. ◀

The last matrix in Example 3 is in **row-echelon form.** The term *echelon* refers to the stair-step pattern formed by the nonzero elements of the matrix. To be in this form, a matrix must have the following properties.

ROW-ECHELON FORM AND REDUCED ROW-ECHELON FORM

A matrix in **row-echelon form** has the following properties.

1. All rows consisting entirely of zeros occur at the bottom of the matrix.
2. For each row that does not consist entirely of zeros, the first nonzero entry is 1 (a **leading 1**).
3. For two successive (nonzero) rows, the leading 1 in the higher row is farther to the left than the leading 1 in the lower row.

A matrix in *row-echelon form* is in **reduced row-echelon form** if every column that has a leading 1 has zeros in every position above and below its leading 1.

EXAMPLE 4   Row-Echelon Form

The following matrices are in row-echelon form.

a. $\begin{bmatrix} 1 & 2 & -1 & 4 \\ 0 & 1 & 0 & 3 \\ 0 & 0 & 1 & -2 \end{bmatrix}$
b. $\begin{bmatrix} 0 & 1 & 0 & 5 \\ 0 & 0 & 1 & 3 \\ 0 & 0 & 0 & 0 \end{bmatrix}$

c. $\begin{bmatrix} 1 & -5 & 2 & -1 & 3 \\ 0 & 0 & 1 & 3 & -2 \\ 0 & 0 & 0 & 1 & 4 \\ 0 & 0 & 0 & 0 & 1 \end{bmatrix}$
d. $\begin{bmatrix} 1 & 0 & 0 & -1 \\ 0 & 1 & 0 & 2 \\ 0 & 0 & 1 & 3 \\ 0 & 0 & 0 & 0 \end{bmatrix}$

The matrices in (b) and (d) also happen to be in *reduced* row-echelon form. The following matrices are not in row-echelon form.

e. $\begin{bmatrix} 1 & 2 & -3 & 4 \\ 0 & 2 & 1 & -1 \\ 0 & 0 & 1 & -3 \end{bmatrix}$
f. $\begin{bmatrix} 1 & 2 & -1 & 2 \\ 0 & 0 & 0 & 0 \\ 0 & 1 & 2 & -4 \end{bmatrix}$

Every matrix is row equivalent to a matrix in row-echelon form. For instance, in Example 4, you can change the matrix in part (e) to row-echelon form by multiplying its second row by $\frac{1}{2}$.

Gaussian Elimination with Back-Substitution

Guidelines for using Gaussian elimination with back-substitution to solve a system of linear equations are summarized as follows.

Gaussian Elimination with Back-Substitution

1. Write the augmented matrix of the system of linear equations.
2. Use elementary row operations to rewrite the augmented matrix in row-echelon form.
3. Write the system of linear equations corresponding to the matrix in row-echelon form, and use back-substitution to find the solution.

Gaussian elimination with back-substitution works well for solving systems of linear equations with a computer. For this algorithm, the order in which the elementary row operations are performed is important. Operate from *left to right by columns*, using elementary row operations to obtain zeros in all entries directly below the leading 1's.

EXAMPLE 5   Gaussian Elimination with Back-Substitution

Solve the following system.

$$\begin{aligned}
y + z - 2w &= -3 \\
x + 2y - z &= 2 \\
2x + 4y + z - 3w &= -2 \\
x - 4y - 7z - w &= -19
\end{aligned}$$

Solution

The augmented matrix for this system is

$$\begin{bmatrix}
0 & 1 & 1 & -2 & \vdots & -3 \\
1 & 2 & -1 & 0 & \vdots & 2 \\
2 & 4 & 1 & -3 & \vdots & -2 \\
1 & -4 & -7 & -1 & \vdots & -19
\end{bmatrix}.$$

Begin by obtaining a leading 1 in the upper left corner by interchanging the first and second rows, and then proceed to obtain zeros elsewhere in the first column.

$$\begin{array}{c}
\curvearrowright R_2 \\
\curvearrowright R_1
\end{array}
\begin{bmatrix}
1 & 2 & -1 & 0 & \vdots & 2 \\
0 & 1 & 1 & -2 & \vdots & -3 \\
2 & 4 & 1 & -3 & \vdots & -2 \\
1 & -4 & -7 & -1 & \vdots & -19
\end{bmatrix}$$

First column has leading 1 in upper left corner.

$$\begin{array}{c}
\\
\\
-2R_1 + R_3 \rightarrow \\
-R_1 + R_4 \rightarrow
\end{array}
\begin{bmatrix}
1 & 2 & -1 & 0 & \vdots & 2 \\
0 & 1 & 1 & -2 & \vdots & -3 \\
0 & 0 & 3 & -3 & \vdots & -6 \\
0 & -6 & -6 & -1 & \vdots & -21
\end{bmatrix}$$

First column has zeros below its leading 1.

Now that the first column is in the desired form, change the second, third, and fourth columns as follows.

$$6R_2 + R_4 \rightarrow \begin{bmatrix} 1 & 2 & -1 & 0 & \vdots & 2 \\ 0 & 1 & 1 & -2 & \vdots & -3 \\ 0 & 0 & 3 & -3 & \vdots & -6 \\ 0 & 0 & 0 & -13 & \vdots & -39 \end{bmatrix}$$ *Second column has zeros below its leading 1.*

$$\tfrac{1}{3}R_3 \rightarrow \begin{bmatrix} 1 & 2 & -1 & 0 & \vdots & 2 \\ 0 & 1 & 1 & -2 & \vdots & -3 \\ 0 & 0 & 1 & -1 & \vdots & -2 \\ 0 & 0 & 0 & -13 & \vdots & -39 \end{bmatrix}$$ *Third column has zeros below its leading 1.*

$$-\tfrac{1}{13}R_4 \rightarrow \begin{bmatrix} 1 & 2 & -1 & 0 & \vdots & 2 \\ 0 & 1 & 1 & -2 & \vdots & -3 \\ 0 & 0 & 1 & -1 & \vdots & -2 \\ 0 & 0 & 0 & 1 & \vdots & 3 \end{bmatrix}$$ *Fourth column has a leading 1.*

The matrix is now in row-echelon form, and the corresponding system of linear equations is

$$\begin{aligned} x + 2y - z &= 2 \\ y + z - 2w &= -3 \\ z - w &= -2 \\ w &= 3. \end{aligned}$$

Using back-substitution, you can determine that the solution is

$$x = -1, \quad y = 2, \quad z = 1, \quad \text{and} \quad w = 3.$$

You can now check for errors in your elementary row operations by substituting these values in each equation in the *original* system. (If they don't check, then you know that you made an error in the back-substitution or one of the elementary row operations.) ◢

When solving a system of linear equations, remember that it is possible for the system to have no solution. If, in the elimination process, you obtain a row with zeros except for the last entry, it is unnecessary to continue the elimination process. You can simply conclude that the system is inconsistent. For instance, Gaussian elimination applied to the system

$$\begin{aligned} x - y + 2z &= 4 \\ x + z &= 6 \\ 2x - 3y + 5z &= 4 \\ 3x + 2y - z &= 1 \end{aligned}$$ yields the matrix $$\begin{bmatrix} 1 & -1 & 2 & \vdots & 4 \\ 0 & 1 & -1 & \vdots & 2 \\ 0 & 0 & 0 & \vdots & -2 \\ 0 & 5 & -7 & \vdots & -11 \end{bmatrix}.$$

Note that the third row of this matrix consists of zeros except for the last entry. This means that the original system of linear equations is *inconsistent*.

Gauss-Jordan Elimination

With Gaussian elimination, you apply elementary row operations to a matrix to obtain a (row-equivalent) row-echelon form. A second method of elimination, called **Gauss-Jordan elimination,** after Carl Friedrich Gauss and Wilhelm Jordan (1842–1899), continues the reduction process until a *reduced* row-echelon form is obtained. We demonstrate this procedure in the following example.

EXAMPLE 6   Gauss-Jordan Elimination

Use Gauss-Jordan elimination to solve the following system.

$$\begin{aligned} x - 2y + 3z &= 9 \\ -x + 3y &= -4 \\ 2x - 5y + 5z &= 17 \end{aligned}$$

Solution

In Example 3 you used Gaussian elimination to obtain the following row-echelon form.

$$\begin{bmatrix} 1 & -2 & 3 & \vdots & 9 \\ 0 & 1 & 3 & \vdots & 5 \\ 0 & 0 & 1 & \vdots & 2 \end{bmatrix}$$

Now, rather than using back-substitution, you will apply elementary row operations until you obtain a matrix in reduced row-echelon form. To do this, you must produce zeros above each of the leading 1's, as follows.

$$2R_2 + R_1 \rightarrow \begin{bmatrix} 1 & 0 & 9 & \vdots & 19 \\ 0 & 1 & 3 & \vdots & 5 \\ 0 & 0 & 1 & \vdots & 2 \end{bmatrix}$$

Second column has zeros above its leading 1.

$$\begin{aligned} -9R_3 + R_1 &\rightarrow \\ -3R_3 + R_2 &\rightarrow \end{aligned} \begin{bmatrix} 1 & 0 & 0 & \vdots & 1 \\ 0 & 1 & 0 & \vdots & -1 \\ 0 & 0 & 1 & \vdots & 2 \end{bmatrix}$$

Third column has zeros above its leading 1.

Now, converting back to a system of linear equations, you have

$$\begin{aligned} x &= 1 \\ y &= -1 \\ z &= 2. \end{aligned}$$

The beauty of Gauss-Jordan elimination is that, from the reduced row-echelon form, you can simply read the solution.

It is worth noting that the row-echelon form for a matrix is not unique. That is, two different sequences of elementary row operations may yield different row-echelon forms. For instance, the following sequence of elementary row operations on the matrix in Example 3 produces a slightly different row-echelon form.

$$\begin{bmatrix} 1 & -2 & 3 & \vdots & 9 \\ -1 & 3 & 0 & \vdots & -4 \\ 2 & -5 & 5 & \vdots & 17 \end{bmatrix} \quad \begin{matrix} \curvearrowright R_2 \\ \curvearrowright R_1 \end{matrix} \begin{bmatrix} -1 & 3 & 0 & \vdots & -4 \\ 1 & -2 & 3 & \vdots & 9 \\ 2 & -5 & 5 & \vdots & 17 \end{bmatrix}$$

$$-R_1 \rightarrow \begin{bmatrix} 1 & -3 & 0 & \vdots & 4 \\ 1 & -2 & 3 & \vdots & 9 \\ 2 & -5 & 5 & \vdots & 17 \end{bmatrix}$$

$$\begin{matrix} -R_1 + R_2 \rightarrow \\ -2R_1 + R_3 \rightarrow \end{matrix} \begin{bmatrix} 1 & -3 & 0 & \vdots & 4 \\ 0 & 1 & 3 & \vdots & 5 \\ 0 & 1 & 5 & \vdots & 9 \end{bmatrix}$$

$$-R_2 + R_3 \rightarrow \begin{bmatrix} 1 & -3 & 0 & \vdots & 4 \\ 0 & 1 & 3 & \vdots & 5 \\ 0 & 0 & 2 & \vdots & 4 \end{bmatrix}$$

$$\tfrac{1}{2}R_3 \rightarrow \begin{bmatrix} 1 & -3 & 0 & \vdots & 4 \\ 0 & 1 & 3 & \vdots & 5 \\ 0 & 0 & 1 & \vdots & 2 \end{bmatrix}$$

However, the *reduced* row-echelon form for a given matrix *is* unique. You should try applying Gauss-Jordan elimination to this matrix to see that you obtain the same reduced row-echelon form as in Example 6.

The elimination procedures described in this section employ an algorithmic approach that is easily adapted to computer use. However, the procedure makes no effort to avoid fractional coefficients. For instance, if the system given in Example 6 had been listed as

$$\begin{aligned} 2x - 5y + 5z &= 17 \\ x - 2y + 3z &= 9 \\ -x + 3y &= -4 \end{aligned}$$

the procedure would then have required multiplying the first row by $\tfrac{1}{2}$, which would have introduced fractions in the first row. For hand computations, fractions can sometimes be avoided by judiciously choosing the order in which the elementary row operations are applied.

The next example demonstrates how Gauss-Jordan elimination can be used to solve a system with an infinite number of solutions.

EXAMPLE 7   A System with an Infinite Number of Solutions

Solve the following system of linear equations.

$$2x + 4y - 2z = 0$$
$$3x + 5y \quad\;\; = 1$$

Solution

Using Gauss-Jordan elimination, the augmented matrix reduces as follows.

$$\begin{bmatrix} 2 & 4 & -2 & \vdots & 0 \\ 3 & 5 & 0 & \vdots & 1 \end{bmatrix} \qquad \tfrac{1}{2}R_1 \rightarrow \begin{bmatrix} 1 & 2 & -1 & \vdots & 0 \\ 3 & 5 & 0 & \vdots & 1 \end{bmatrix}$$

$$-3R_1 + R_2 \rightarrow \begin{bmatrix} 1 & 2 & -1 & \vdots & 0 \\ 0 & -1 & 3 & \vdots & 1 \end{bmatrix}$$

$$-R_2 \rightarrow \begin{bmatrix} 1 & 2 & -1 & \vdots & 0 \\ 0 & 1 & -3 & \vdots & -1 \end{bmatrix}$$

$$-2R_2 + R_1 \rightarrow \begin{bmatrix} 1 & 0 & 5 & \vdots & 2 \\ 0 & 1 & -3 & \vdots & -1 \end{bmatrix}$$

The corresponding system of equations is

$$x \;\; + 5z = \;\; 2$$
$$y - 3z = -1.$$

Solving for x and y in terms of z, you have $x = -5z + 2$ and $y = 3z - 1$. Then, letting $z = a$, the solution set has the form

$$(-5a + 2,\; 3a - 1,\; a), \qquad \text{where } a \text{ is a real number.}$$

You have looked at two elimination methods for solving a system of linear equations. Which is better? To some degree, it depends on personal preference. For hand computations, Gaussian elimination with back-substitution is often preferred. However, you will encounter other applications in which Gauss-Jordan elimination is better. Thus, you should know both methods.

DISCUSSION

PROBLEM

Comparing Gaussian Elimination with Gauss-Jordan Elimination

Solve the following system of linear equations in two ways: once with Gaussian elimination with back-substitution and once with Gauss-Jordan elimination. Then discuss, or write a short paragraph describing, the benefits of one method over the other.

$$3x - 2y + \;\; z = -6$$
$$-x + \;\; y - 2z = \;\; 1$$
$$2x + 2y - 3z = -1$$

WARM UP

The following warm-up exercises involve skills that were covered in earlier sections. You will use these skills in the exercise set for this section.

In Exercises 1–4, evaluate the given expression.

1. $2(-1) - 3(5) + 7(2)$

2. $-4(-3) + 6(7) + 8(-3)$

3. $11\left(\frac{1}{2}\right) - 7\left(-\frac{3}{2}\right) - 5(2)$

4. $\frac{2}{3}\left(\frac{1}{2}\right) + \frac{4}{3}\left(-\frac{1}{3}\right)$

In Exercises 5 and 6, determine whether $x = 1$, $y = 3$, and $z = -1$ is a solution of the system of linear equations.

5. $\begin{aligned} 4x - 2y + 3z &= -5 \\ x + 3y - z &= 11 \\ -x + 2y &= 5 \end{aligned}$

6. $\begin{aligned} -x + 2y + z &= 4 \\ 2x - 3z &= 5 \\ 3x + 5y - 2z &= 21 \end{aligned}$

In Exercises 7–10, use back-substitution to solve the system of linear equations.

7. $\begin{aligned} 2x - 3y &= 4 \\ y &= 2 \end{aligned}$

8. $\begin{aligned} 5x + 4y &= 0 \\ y &= -3 \end{aligned}$

9. $\begin{aligned} x - 3y + z &= 0 \\ y - 3z &= 8 \\ z &= 2 \end{aligned}$

10. $\begin{aligned} 2x - 5y + 3z &= -2 \\ y - 4z &= 0 \\ z &= 1 \end{aligned}$

EXERCISES for Section 9.1

In Exercises 1–6, determine the order of the matrix.

1. $\begin{bmatrix} 4 & -2 \\ 7 & 0 \\ 0 & 8 \end{bmatrix}$

2. $\begin{bmatrix} 5 & -3 & 8 & 7 \end{bmatrix}$

3. $\begin{bmatrix} -9 \\ 2 \\ 36 \\ 11 \\ 3 \end{bmatrix}$

4. $\begin{bmatrix} 11 & 0 & 8 & 5 & 5 \\ -3 & 7 & 15 & 0 & 10 \\ 0 & 6 & 3 & 3 & 9 \\ 12 & 4 & 16 & 9 & 0 \\ 1 & 1 & 6 & 7 & 8 \end{bmatrix}$

5. $\begin{bmatrix} 33 & 45 \\ -9 & 20 \end{bmatrix}$

6. $\begin{bmatrix} 4 \end{bmatrix}$

In Exercises 7–10, determine whether the matrix is in row-echelon form. If it is, determine if it is also in reduced row-echelon form.

7. $\begin{bmatrix} 1 & 0 & 0 & 0 \\ 0 & 1 & 1 & 5 \\ 0 & 0 & 0 & 0 \end{bmatrix}$

8. $\begin{bmatrix} 1 & 0 & 2 & 1 \\ 0 & 1 & -3 & 10 \\ 0 & 0 & 1 & 0 \end{bmatrix}$

9. $\begin{bmatrix} 2 & 0 & 4 & 0 \\ 0 & -1 & 3 & 6 \\ 0 & 0 & 1 & 5 \end{bmatrix}$

10. $\begin{bmatrix} 1 & 3 & 0 & 0 \\ 0 & 0 & 1 & 8 \\ 0 & 0 & 0 & 0 \end{bmatrix}$

In Exercises 11–14, fill in the blanks using the elementary row operations to form a row equivalent matrix.

11. $\begin{bmatrix} 1 & 4 & 3 \\ 2 & 10 & 5 \end{bmatrix}$

$\begin{bmatrix} 1 & 4 & 3 \\ 0 & \blacksquare & -1 \end{bmatrix}$

12. $\begin{bmatrix} 3 & 6 & 8 \\ 4 & -3 & 6 \end{bmatrix}$

$\begin{bmatrix} 1 & \blacksquare & \frac{8}{3} \\ 4 & -3 & 6 \end{bmatrix}$

13. $\begin{bmatrix} 1 & 1 & 4 & -1 \\ 3 & 8 & 10 & 3 \\ -2 & 1 & 12 & 6 \end{bmatrix}$

$\begin{bmatrix} 1 & 1 & 4 & -1 \\ 0 & 5 & \blacksquare & \blacksquare \\ 0 & 3 & \blacksquare & \blacksquare \end{bmatrix}$

$\begin{bmatrix} 1 & 1 & 4 & -1 \\ 0 & 1 & \blacksquare & \blacksquare \\ 0 & 3 & 20 & 4 \end{bmatrix}$

14. $\begin{bmatrix} 2 & 4 & 8 & 3 \\ 1 & -1 & -3 & 2 \\ 2 & 6 & 4 & 9 \end{bmatrix}$

$\begin{bmatrix} 1 & \blacksquare & \blacksquare & \blacksquare \\ 1 & -1 & -3 & 2 \\ 2 & 6 & 4 & 9 \end{bmatrix}$

$\begin{bmatrix} 1 & 2 & 4 & \frac{3}{2} \\ 0 & \blacksquare & -7 & \frac{1}{2} \\ 0 & 2 & \blacksquare & \blacksquare \end{bmatrix}$

15. Perform the indicated *sequence* of elementary row operations to write the given matrix in reduced row-echelon form.

$$\begin{bmatrix} 1 & 2 & 3 \\ 2 & -1 & -4 \\ 3 & 1 & -1 \end{bmatrix}$$

(a) Add (-2) times Row 1 to Row 2. (Only Row 2 should change.)

(b) Add (-3) times Row 1 to Row 3. (Only Row 3 should change.)

(c) Add (-1) times Row 2 to Row 3.

(d) Multiply Row 2 by $\left(-\frac{1}{5}\right)$.

(e) Add (-2) times Row 2 to Row 1.

16. Perform the indicated *sequence* of elementary row operations to write the given matrix in reduced row-echelon form.

$$\begin{bmatrix} 7 & 1 \\ 0 & 2 \\ -3 & 4 \\ 4 & 1 \end{bmatrix}$$

(a) Add Row 3 to Row 4. (Only Row 4 should change.)

(b) Interchange Rows 1 and 4. (Note that the first element in the matrix is now 1, and it was obtained without introducing fractions.)

(c) Add (3) times Row 1 to Row 3.

(d) Add (-7) times Row 1 to Row 4.

(e) Multiply Row 2 by $\frac{1}{2}$.

(f) Add the appropriate multiple of Row 2 to Rows 1, 3, and 4.

In Exercises 17–20, write the matrix in row-echelon form. Remember that the row-echelon form for a given matrix is not unique.

17. $\begin{bmatrix} 1 & 1 & 0 & 5 \\ -2 & -1 & 2 & -10 \\ 3 & 6 & 7 & 14 \end{bmatrix}$

18. $\begin{bmatrix} 1 & 2 & -1 & 3 \\ 3 & 7 & -5 & 14 \\ -2 & -1 & -3 & 8 \end{bmatrix}$

19. $\begin{bmatrix} 1 & -1 & -1 & 1 \\ 5 & -4 & 1 & 8 \\ -6 & 8 & 18 & 0 \end{bmatrix}$

20. $\begin{bmatrix} 1 & -3 & 0 & -7 \\ -3 & 10 & 1 & 23 \\ 4 & -10 & 2 & -24 \end{bmatrix}$

In Exercises 21–24, write the matrix in *reduced* row-echelon form.

21. $\begin{bmatrix} 3 & 3 & 3 \\ -1 & 0 & -4 \\ 2 & 4 & -2 \end{bmatrix}$

22. $\begin{bmatrix} 1 & 3 & 2 \\ 5 & 15 & 9 \\ 2 & 6 & 10 \end{bmatrix}$

23. $\begin{bmatrix} 1 & 2 & 3 & -5 \\ 1 & 2 & 4 & -9 \\ -2 & -4 & -4 & 3 \\ 4 & 8 & 11 & -14 \end{bmatrix}$

24. $\begin{bmatrix} 1 & -3 \\ -1 & 8 \\ 0 & 4 \\ -2 & 10 \end{bmatrix}$

In Exercises 25–28, write the system of linear equations represented by the augmented matrix.

25. $\begin{bmatrix} 4 & 3 & \vdots & 8 \\ 1 & -2 & \vdots & 3 \end{bmatrix}$

26. $\begin{bmatrix} 9 & -4 & \vdots & 0 \\ 6 & 1 & \vdots & -4 \end{bmatrix}$

27. $\begin{bmatrix} 1 & 0 & 2 & \vdots & -10 \\ 0 & 3 & -1 & \vdots & 5 \\ 4 & 2 & 0 & \vdots & 3 \end{bmatrix}$

28. $\begin{bmatrix} 5 & 8 & 2 & 0 & \vdots & -1 \\ -2 & 15 & 5 & 1 & \vdots & 9 \\ 1 & 6 & -7 & 0 & \vdots & -3 \end{bmatrix}$

In Exercises 29–32, write the system of linear equations represented by the augmented matrix. Then use back-substitution to find the solution. (Use variables x, y, and z.)

29. $\begin{bmatrix} 1 & -2 & \vdots & 4 \\ 0 & 1 & \vdots & -3 \end{bmatrix}$

30. $\begin{bmatrix} 1 & 5 & \vdots & 0 \\ 0 & 1 & \vdots & -1 \end{bmatrix}$

31. $\begin{bmatrix} 1 & -1 & 2 & \vdots & 4 \\ 0 & 1 & -1 & \vdots & 2 \\ 0 & 0 & 1 & \vdots & -2 \end{bmatrix}$

32. $\begin{bmatrix} 1 & 2 & -2 & \vdots & -1 \\ 0 & 1 & 1 & \vdots & 9 \\ 0 & 0 & 1 & \vdots & -3 \end{bmatrix}$

In Exercises 33–36, an augmented matrix that represents a system of linear equations (in variables x, y, and z) has been reduced using Gauss-Jordan elimination. Write the solution represented by the augmented matrix.

33. $\begin{bmatrix} 1 & 0 & \vdots & 7 \\ 0 & 1 & \vdots & -5 \end{bmatrix}$

34. $\begin{bmatrix} 1 & 0 & \vdots & -2 \\ 0 & 1 & \vdots & 4 \end{bmatrix}$

35. $\begin{bmatrix} 1 & 0 & 0 & \vdots & -4 \\ 0 & 1 & 0 & \vdots & -8 \\ 0 & 0 & 1 & \vdots & 2 \end{bmatrix}$

36. $\begin{bmatrix} 1 & 0 & 0 & \vdots & 3 \\ 0 & 1 & 0 & \vdots & -1 \\ 0 & 0 & 1 & \vdots & 0 \end{bmatrix}$

In Exercises 37–58, solve the system of equations. Use Gaussian elimination with back-substitution or Gauss-Jordan elimination.

37. $x + 2y = 7$
$2x + y = 8$

38. $2x + 6y = 16$
$2x + 3y = 7$

39. $-3x + 5y = -22$
$3x + 4y = 4$
$4x - 8y = 32$

40. $x + 2y = 0$
$x + y = 6$
$3x - 2y = 8$

41. $8x - 4y = 7$
$5x + 2y = 1$

42. $2x - y = -0.1$
$3x + 2y = 1.6$

43. $-x + 2y = 1.5$
$2x - 4y = 3$

44. $x - 3y = 5$
$-2x + 6y = -10$

45. $x - 3z = -2$
$3x + y - 2z = 5$
$2x + 2y + z = 4$

46. $2x - y + 3z = 24$
$2y - z = 14$
$7x - 5y = 6$

47. $x + y - 5z = 3$
$x - 2z = 1$
$2x - y - z = 0$

48. $2x + 3z = 3$
$4x - 3y + 7z = 5$
$8x - 9y + 15z = 9$

49. $x + 2y + z = 8$
$3x + 7y + 6z = 26$

50. $4x + 12y - 7z - 20w = 22$
$3x + 9y - 5z - 28w = 30$

51. $3x + 3y + 12z = 6$
$x + y + 4z = 2$
$2x + 5y + 20z = 10$
$-x + 2y + 8z = 4$

52. $2x + 10y + 2z = 6$
$x + 5y + 2z = 6$
$x + 5y + z = 3$
$-3x - 15y - 3z = -9$

53. $2x + y - z + 2w = -6$
$3x + 4y + w = 1$
$x + 5y + 2z + 6w = 3$
$5x + 2y - z - w = 3$

54. $x + 2y + 2z + 4w = 11$
$3x + 6y + 5z + 12w = 30$

55. $x + 2y = 0$
$-x - y = 0$

56. $x + 2y = 0$
$2x + 4y = 0$

57. $x + y + z = 0$
$2x + 3y + z = 0$
$3x + 5y + z = 0$

58. $x + 2y + z + 3w = 0$
$x - y + w = 0$
$y - z + 2w = 0$

59. *Borrowing Money* A small corporation borrowed $1,500,000—some of it at 8%, some at 9%, and some at 12%. How much was borrowed at each rate if the annual interest was $133,000 and the amount borrowed at 8% was four times the amount borrowed at 12%?

60. *Borrowing Money* A small corporation borrowed $500,000—some of it at 9%, some at 10%, and some at 12%. How much was borrowed at each rate if the annual interest was $52,000 and the amount borrowed at 10% was $2\frac{1}{2}$ times the amount borrowed at 9%?

In Exercises 61–64, find the specified equation that passes through the given points.

61. Parabola: $y = ax^2 + bx + c$

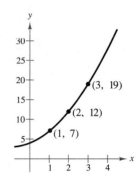

62. Parabola: $y = ax^2 + bx + c$

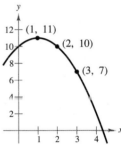

63. Circle: $x^2 + y^2 + Dx + Ey + F = 0$

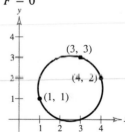

64. Cubic: $y = ax^3 + bx^2 + cx + d$

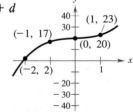

65. The given augmented matrix represents a system of linear equations (in variables x, y, and z) that has been reduced using Gauss-Jordan elimination. Write a system of equations with nonzero coefficients that is represented by the reduced matrix. (The answer is not unique.)

$$\begin{bmatrix} 1 & 0 & 3 & \vdots & -2 \\ 0 & 1 & 4 & \vdots & 1 \\ 0 & 0 & 0 & \vdots & 0 \end{bmatrix}$$

9.2 Operations with Matrices

Equality of Matrices / Matrix Addition and Scalar Multiplication / Matrix Multiplication / Applications

Equality of Matrices

In Section 9.1 you used matrices to solve systems of linear equations. Matrices, however, can do much more than that. There is a rich mathematical theory of matrices, and its applications are numerous. This section and the next introduce some fundamentals of matrix theory. It is standard mathematical convention to represent matrices in any of the following three ways.

1. A matrix can be denoted by an uppercase letter such as A, B, and C.
2. A matrix can be denoted by a representative element enclosed in brackets, such as $[a_{ij}]$, $[b_{ij}]$, and $[c_{ij}]$.
3. A matrix can be denoted by a rectangular array of numbers such as

$$A = [a_{ij}] = \begin{bmatrix} a_{11} & a_{12} & a_{13} & \cdots & a_{1n} \\ a_{21} & a_{22} & a_{23} & \cdots & a_{2n} \\ a_{31} & a_{32} & a_{33} & \cdots & a_{3n} \\ \vdots & \vdots & \vdots & & \vdots \\ a_{m1} & a_{m2} & a_{m3} & \cdots & a_{mn} \end{bmatrix}.$$

Two matrices are **equal** if their corresponding entries are equal.

DEFINITION OF EQUALITY OF MATRICES

Two matrices $A = [a_{ij}]$ and $B = [b_{ij}]$ are **equal** if they have the same order ($m \times n$) and

$$a_{ij} = b_{ij}$$

for $1 \le i \le m$ and $1 \le j \le n$.

EXAMPLE 1 Equality of Matrices

Solve for a_{11}, a_{12}, a_{21}, and a_{22} in the following matrix equation.

$$\begin{bmatrix} a_{11} & a_{12} \\ a_{21} & a_{22} \end{bmatrix} = \begin{bmatrix} 2 & -1 \\ -3 & 0 \end{bmatrix}$$

Solution

Because two matrices are equal only if corresponding entries are equal, you can conclude that

$$a_{11} = 2, \quad a_{12} = -1, \quad a_{21} = -3, \quad \text{and} \quad a_{22} = 0.$$

Matrix Addition and Scalar Multiplication

Add two matrices (of the same order) by adding their corresponding entries.

DEFINITION OF MATRIX ADDITION

If $A = [a_{ij}]$ and $B = [b_{ij}]$ are matrices of order $m \times n$, then their **sum** is the $m \times n$ matrix given by

$$A + B = [a_{ij} + b_{ij}].$$

The sum of two matrices of different orders is undefined.

EXAMPLE 2   Addition of Matrices

a. $\begin{bmatrix} -1 & 2 \\ 0 & 1 \end{bmatrix} + \begin{bmatrix} 1 & 3 \\ -1 & 2 \end{bmatrix} = \begin{bmatrix} -1+1 & 2+3 \\ 0-1 & 1+2 \end{bmatrix} = \begin{bmatrix} 0 & 5 \\ -1 & 3 \end{bmatrix}$

b. $\begin{bmatrix} 1 \\ -3 \\ -2 \end{bmatrix} + \begin{bmatrix} -1 \\ 3 \\ 2 \end{bmatrix} = \begin{bmatrix} 0 \\ 0 \\ 0 \end{bmatrix}$

c. The sum of

$$A = \begin{bmatrix} 2 & 1 & 0 \\ 4 & 0 & -1 \\ 3 & -2 & 2 \end{bmatrix} \quad \text{and} \quad B = \begin{bmatrix} 0 & 1 \\ -1 & 3 \\ 2 & 4 \end{bmatrix}$$

is undefined.

When working with matrices, we usually refer to numbers as **scalars.** In this text, scalars will always be real numbers. We multiply a matrix A by a scalar c by multiplying each entry in A by c.

DEFINITION OF SCALAR MULTIPLICATION

If $A = [a_{ij}]$ is an $m \times n$ matrix and c is a scalar, then the **scalar multiple** of A by c is the $m \times n$ matrix given by

$$cA = [ca_{ij}].$$

Use $-A$ to represent the scalar product $(-1)A$. Moreover, if A and B are of the same order, then $A - B$ represents the sum of A and $(-1)B$. That is,

$$A - B = A + (-1)B. \qquad \text{\textit{Subtraction of matrices}}$$

EXAMPLE 3 **Scalar Multiplication and Matrix Subtraction**

For the matrices

$$A = \begin{bmatrix} 1 & 2 & 4 \\ -3 & 0 & -1 \\ 2 & 1 & 2 \end{bmatrix} \quad \text{and} \quad B = \begin{bmatrix} 2 & 0 & 0 \\ 1 & -4 & 3 \\ -1 & 3 & 2 \end{bmatrix}$$

find the following.

a. $3A$ **b.** $3A - B$

Solution

a. $3A = 3\begin{bmatrix} 1 & 2 & 4 \\ -3 & 0 & -1 \\ 2 & 1 & 2 \end{bmatrix} = \begin{bmatrix} 3(1) & 3(2) & 3(4) \\ 3(-3) & 3(0) & 3(-1) \\ 3(2) & 3(1) & 3(2) \end{bmatrix} = \begin{bmatrix} 3 & 6 & 12 \\ -9 & 0 & -3 \\ 6 & 3 & 6 \end{bmatrix}$

b. $3A - B = \begin{bmatrix} 3 & 6 & 12 \\ -9 & 0 & -3 \\ 6 & 3 & 6 \end{bmatrix} - \begin{bmatrix} 2 & 0 & 0 \\ 1 & -4 & 3 \\ -1 & 3 & 2 \end{bmatrix} = \begin{bmatrix} 1 & 6 & 12 \\ -10 & 4 & -6 \\ 7 & 0 & 4 \end{bmatrix}$

◄

It is often convenient to rewrite the scalar multiple cA by factoring c out of every entry in the matrix. For instance, in the following example, the scalar $\frac{1}{2}$ has been factored out of the matrix.

$$\begin{bmatrix} \frac{1}{2} & -\frac{3}{2} \\ \frac{5}{2} & \frac{1}{2} \end{bmatrix} = \frac{1}{2}\begin{bmatrix} 1 & -3 \\ 5 & 1 \end{bmatrix}$$

The properties of matrix addition and scalar multiplication are similar to those of addition and multiplication of real numbers, and we summarize them in the following list.

MATRIX ADDITION AND SCALAR MULTIPLICATION

If A, B, and C are $m \times n$ matrices and c and d are scalars, then the following properties are true.

1. $A + B = B + A$ *Commutative Property of Addition*
2. $A + (B + C) = (A + B) + C$ *Associative Property of Addition*
3. $(cd)A = c(dA)$ *Associative Property of Scalar Multiplication*
4. $1A = A$ *Scalar Identity*
5. $c(A + B) = cA + cB$ *Distributive Property*
6. $(c + d)A = cA + dA$ *Distributive Property*

Note that the Associative Property of matrix addition allows you to write expressions like $A + B + C$ without ambiguity because the same sum occurs no matter how the matrices are grouped. In other words, you obtain the same sum whether you group $A + B + C$ as $(A + B) + C$ or as $A + (B + C)$. This same reasoning applies to sums of four or more matrices.

One important property of addition of real numbers is that the number 0 is the additive identity. That is, $c + 0 = c$ for any real number c. For matrices, a similar property holds. That is, if A is an $m \times n$ matrix and O is the $m \times n$ **zero matrix** consisting entirely of zeros, then

$$A + O = A.$$

In other words, O is the **additive identity** for the set of all $m \times n$ matrices. For example, the following matrix is the additive identity for the set of all 2×3 matrices.

$$O = \begin{bmatrix} 0 & 0 & 0 \\ 0 & 0 & 0 \end{bmatrix} \qquad \text{\textit{Zero 2 × 3 matrix}}$$

Similarly, the additive identity for the set of all 3×4 matrices is

$$O = \begin{bmatrix} 0 & 0 & 0 & 0 \\ 0 & 0 & 0 & 0 \\ 0 & 0 & 0 & 0 \end{bmatrix} \qquad \text{\textit{Zero 3 × 4 matrix}}$$

The algebra of real numbers and the algebra of matrices have many similarities.* For example, compare the following solutions.

Real Numbers *(Solve for x)*	*m × n Matrices* *(Solve for X)*
$x + a = b$	$X + A = B$
$x + a + (-a) = b + (-a)$	$X + A + (-A) = B + (-A)$
$x + 0 = b - a$	$X + O = B - A$
$x = b - a$	$X = B - A$

The process of solving a matrix equation is demonstrated in Example 4.

*There are also some important differences, which will be discussed later.

EXAMPLE 4   **Solving a Matrix Equation**

Solve for X in the equation $3X + A = B$, where

$$A = \begin{bmatrix} 1 & -2 \\ 0 & 3 \end{bmatrix} \quad \text{and} \quad B = \begin{bmatrix} -3 & 4 \\ 2 & 1 \end{bmatrix}.$$

Solution

Begin by solving the given equation for X to obtain

$$3X = B - A \quad \rightarrow \quad X = \frac{1}{3}(B - A).$$

Now, using the given matrices A and B, you have

$$X = \frac{1}{3}\left(\begin{bmatrix} -3 & 4 \\ 2 & 1 \end{bmatrix} - \begin{bmatrix} 1 & -2 \\ 0 & 3 \end{bmatrix} \right) = \frac{1}{3} \begin{bmatrix} -4 & 6 \\ 2 & -2 \end{bmatrix} = \begin{bmatrix} -\frac{4}{3} & 2 \\ \frac{2}{3} & -\frac{2}{3} \end{bmatrix}.$$

Matrix Multiplication

The third basic matrix operation is **matrix multiplication.** At first glance, the definition may seem unusual. You will see later, however, that this definition of the product of two matrices has many practical applications.

DEFINITION OF MATRIX MULTIPLICATION

If $A = [a_{ij}]$ is an $m \times n$ matrix and $B = [b_{ij}]$ is an $n \times p$ matrix, then the **product** AB is the $m \times p$ matrix

$$AB = [c_{ij}]$$

where $c_{ij} = a_{i1}b_{1j} + a_{i2}b_{2j} + a_{i3}b_{3j} + \cdots + a_{in}b_{nj}.$

This definition indicates a *row-by-column* multiplication, where the entry c_{ij} in the ith row and the jth column of the product AB is obtained by multiplying the entries in the ith row of A by the corresponding entries in the jth column of B and then adding the results. The following example illustrates the process.

EXAMPLE 5   **Finding the Product of Two Matrices**

Find the product AB where

$$A = \begin{bmatrix} -1 & 3 \\ 4 & -2 \\ 5 & 0 \end{bmatrix} \quad \text{and} \quad B = \begin{bmatrix} -3 & 2 \\ -4 & 1 \end{bmatrix}.$$

Solution

First note that the product AB is defined because the number of columns of A is equal to the number of rows of B. Moreover, the product AB has order 3×2 and will take the form

$$\begin{bmatrix} -1 & 3 \\ 4 & -2 \\ 5 & 0 \end{bmatrix} \begin{bmatrix} -3 & 2 \\ -4 & 1 \end{bmatrix} = \begin{bmatrix} c_{11} & c_{12} \\ c_{21} & c_{22} \\ c_{31} & c_{32} \end{bmatrix}.$$

To find c_{11} (the entry in the first row and first column of the product), multiply corresponding entries in the first row of A and the first column of B. That is,

$$c_{11} = (-1)(-3) + (3)(-4) = -9$$

$$\begin{bmatrix} -1 & 3 \\ 4 & -2 \\ 5 & 0 \end{bmatrix} \begin{bmatrix} -3 & 2 \\ -4 & 1 \end{bmatrix} = \begin{bmatrix} -9 & c_{12} \\ c_{21} & c_{22} \\ c_{31} & c_{32} \end{bmatrix}.$$

Similarly, to find c_{12}, multiply corresponding entries in the first row of A and the second column of B to obtain

$$c_{12} = (-1)(2) + (3)(1) = 1$$

$$\begin{bmatrix} -1 & 3 \\ 4 & -2 \\ 5 & 0 \end{bmatrix} \begin{bmatrix} -3 & 2 \\ -4 & 1 \end{bmatrix} = \begin{bmatrix} -9 & 1 \\ c_{21} & c_{22} \\ c_{31} & c_{32} \end{bmatrix}.$$

Continuing this pattern produces the following results.

$$\begin{aligned}
c_{21} &= (4)(-3) + (-2)(-4) = -4 \\
c_{22} &= (4)(2) + (-2)(1) = 6 \\
c_{31} &= (5)(-3) + (0)(-4) = -15 \\
c_{32} &= (5)(2) + (0)(1) = 10
\end{aligned}$$

Thus, the product is

$$\begin{aligned}
AB &= \begin{bmatrix} -1 & 3 \\ 4 & -2 \\ 5 & 0 \end{bmatrix} \begin{bmatrix} -3 & 2 \\ -4 & 1 \end{bmatrix} \\
&= \begin{bmatrix} (-1)(-3) + (3)(-4) & (-1)(2) + (3)(1) \\ (4)(-3) + (-2)(-4) & (4)(2) + (-2)(1) \\ (5)(-3) + (0)(-4) & (5)(2) + (0)(1) \end{bmatrix} \\
&= \begin{bmatrix} -9 & 1 \\ -4 & 6 \\ -15 & 10 \end{bmatrix}.
\end{aligned}$$

Be sure you understand that for the product of two matrices to be defined, the number of columns of the first matrix must equal the number of rows of the second matrix. That is, the middle two indices must be the same and the outside two indices give the order of the product, as shown in the following diagram.

$$\begin{array}{ccccc} A & & B & = & AB \\ m \times n & & n \times p & & m \times p \end{array}$$

The general pattern for matrix multiplication is as follows. To obtain the entry in the ith row and the jth column of the product AB, use the ith row of A and the jth column of B.

$$\begin{bmatrix} a_{11} & a_{12} & a_{13} & \cdots & a_{1n} \\ a_{21} & a_{22} & a_{23} & \cdots & a_{2n} \\ a_{31} & a_{32} & a_{33} & \cdots & a_{3n} \\ \vdots & \vdots & \vdots & & \vdots \\ a_{i1} & a_{i2} & a_{i3} & \cdots & a_{in} \\ \vdots & \vdots & \vdots & & \vdots \\ a_{m1} & a_{m2} & a_{m3} & \cdots & a_{mn} \end{bmatrix} \begin{bmatrix} b_{11} & b_{12} & \cdots & b_{1j} & \cdots & b_{1p} \\ b_{21} & b_{22} & \cdots & b_{2j} & \cdots & b_{2p} \\ b_{31} & b_{32} & \cdots & b_{3j} & \cdots & b_{3p} \\ \vdots & \vdots & & \vdots & & \vdots \\ b_{n1} & b_{n2} & \cdots & b_{nj} & \cdots & b_{np} \end{bmatrix} = \begin{bmatrix} c_{11} & c_{12} & \cdots & c_{1j} & \cdots & c_{1p} \\ c_{21} & c_{22} & & c_{2j} & \cdots & c_{2p} \\ \vdots & \vdots & & \vdots & & \vdots \\ c_{i1} & c_{i2} & \cdots & c_{ij} & \cdots & c_{ip} \\ \vdots & \vdots & & \vdots & & \vdots \\ c_{m1} & c_{m2} & \cdots & c_{mj} & \cdots & c_{mp} \end{bmatrix}$$

$$a_{i1}b_{1j} + a_{i2}b_{2j} + a_{i3}b_{3j} + \cdots + a_{in}b_{nj} = c_{ij}$$

EXAMPLE 6   Matrix Multiplication

a. $\begin{bmatrix} 1 & 0 & 3 \\ 2 & -1 & -2 \end{bmatrix} \begin{bmatrix} -2 & 4 & 2 \\ 1 & 0 & 0 \\ -1 & 1 & -1 \end{bmatrix} = \begin{bmatrix} -5 & 7 & -1 \\ -3 & 6 & 6 \end{bmatrix}$

$\quad\quad\quad 2 \times 3 \quad\quad\quad\quad\quad 3 \times 3 \quad\quad\quad\quad\quad 2 \times 3$

b. $[1 \quad -2 \quad -3] \begin{bmatrix} 2 \\ -1 \\ 1 \end{bmatrix} = [1]$

$\quad\quad 1 \times 3 \quad\quad\quad 3 \times 1 \quad\quad 1 \times 1$

REMARK In parts (b) and (c) of Example 6, note that the two products are different. Matrix multiplication is not, in general, commutative. That is, for most matrices, $AB \neq BA$.

c. $\begin{bmatrix} 2 \\ -1 \\ 1 \end{bmatrix} [1 \quad -2 \quad -3] = \begin{bmatrix} 2 & -4 & -6 \\ -1 & 2 & 3 \\ 1 & -2 & -3 \end{bmatrix}$

$\quad\quad 3 \times 1 \quad\quad 1 \times 3 \quad\quad\quad\quad 3 \times 3$

d. The product AB for

$$A = \begin{bmatrix} -2 & 1 \\ 1 & -3 \\ 1 & 4 \end{bmatrix} \quad \text{and} \quad B = \begin{bmatrix} -2 & 3 & 1 & 4 \\ 0 & 1 & -1 & 2 \\ 2 & -1 & 0 & 1 \end{bmatrix}$$

$$3 \times 2 \qquad\qquad\qquad 3 \times 4$$

is not defined (nor is the product BA).

◀

PROPERTIES OF MATRIX MULTIPLICATION

If A, B, and C are matrices and c is a scalar, then the following properties are true.

1. $A(BC) = (AB)C$ *Associative Property of Multiplication*
2. $A(B + C) = AB + AC$ *Left Distributive Property*
3. $(A + B)C = AC + BC$ *Right Distributive Property*
4. $c(AB) = (cA)B = A(cB)$

The $n \times n$ matrix that consists of 1's on its main diagonal and 0's elsewhere is the **identity matrix of order** n and is denoted by

$$I_n = \begin{bmatrix} 1 & 0 & 0 & \cdots & 0 \\ 0 & 1 & 0 & \cdots & 0 \\ 0 & 0 & 1 & \cdots & 0 \\ \vdots & \vdots & \vdots & & \vdots \\ 0 & 0 & 0 & \cdots & 1 \end{bmatrix}. \quad \textit{Identity matrix}$$

Note that an identity matrix must be *square*. When the order is understood to be n, I_n is often denoted simply by I. If A is an $n \times n$ matrix, then the identity matrix has the property that

$$AI_n = A \quad \text{and} \quad I_nA = A.$$

For example,

$$\begin{bmatrix} 3 & -2 & 5 \\ 1 & 0 & 4 \\ -1 & 2 & -3 \end{bmatrix}\begin{bmatrix} 1 & 0 & 0 \\ 0 & 1 & 0 \\ 0 & 0 & 1 \end{bmatrix} = \begin{bmatrix} 3 & -2 & 5 \\ 1 & 0 & 4 \\ -1 & 2 & -3 \end{bmatrix}$$

and

$$\begin{bmatrix} 1 & 0 & 0 \\ 0 & 1 & 0 \\ 0 & 0 & 1 \end{bmatrix}\begin{bmatrix} 3 & -2 & 5 \\ 1 & 0 & 4 \\ -1 & 2 & -3 \end{bmatrix} = \begin{bmatrix} 3 & -2 & 5 \\ 1 & 0 & 4 \\ -1 & 2 & -3 \end{bmatrix}.$$

Applications

EXAMPLE 7   An Application of Matrix Multiplication

Two softball teams submit equipment lists to their sponsors.

	Women's Team	*Men's Team*
Bats	12	15
Balls	45	38
Gloves	15	17

Each bat costs $21, each ball costs $4, and each glove costs $30. Use matrices to find the total cost of equipment for each team.

Solution

The equipment lists can be written in matrix form as

$$E = \begin{bmatrix} 12 & 15 \\ 45 & 38 \\ 15 & 17 \end{bmatrix}$$

and the cost per item can be written in matrix form as

$$C = [21 \quad 4 \quad 30].$$

The total cost of equipment for each team is given by the product

$$21(12) + 4(45) + 30(15) = 882 \quad \textit{(Women's team)}$$

$$CE = [21 \quad 4 \quad 30] \begin{bmatrix} 12 & 15 \\ 45 & 38 \\ 15 & 17 \end{bmatrix} = [\ 882 \quad 977\ ].$$

$$21(15) + 4(38) + 30(17) = 977 \quad \textit{(Men's team)}$$

Thus, the total cost of equipment for the women's team is $882, and the total cost of equipment for the men's team is $977.

Another useful application of matrix multiplication is in representing a system of linear equations. Note how the system

$$a_{11}x_1 + a_{12}x_2 + a_{13}x_3 = b_1$$

$$a_{21}x_1 + a_{22}x_2 + a_{23}x_3 = b_2$$

$$a_{31}x_1 + a_{32}x_2 + a_{33}x_3 = b_3$$

can be written as the matrix equation $AX = B$, where A is the *coefficient matrix* of the system, and X and B are column matrices.

$$\begin{bmatrix} a_{11} & a_{12} & a_{13} \\ a_{21} & a_{22} & a_{23} \\ a_{31} & a_{32} & a_{33} \end{bmatrix} \begin{bmatrix} x_1 \\ x_2 \\ x_3 \end{bmatrix} = \begin{bmatrix} b_1 \\ b_2 \\ b_3 \end{bmatrix}$$

$$\quad A \qquad\qquad X \;=\; B$$

EXAMPLE 8   Solving a System of Linear Equations

Solve the matrix equation $AX = B$ for X, where

Coefficient matrix   Constant matrix

$$A = \begin{bmatrix} 1 & -2 & 1 \\ 0 & 1 & 2 \\ 2 & 3 & -2 \end{bmatrix} \quad \text{and} \quad B = \begin{bmatrix} -4 \\ 4 \\ 2 \end{bmatrix}.$$

Solution

As a system of linear equations, $AX = B$ is as follows.

$$x_1 - 2x_2 + x_3 = -4$$
$$x_2 + 2x_3 = 1$$
$$2x_1 + 3x_2 - 2x_3 = 2$$

Using Gauss-Jordan elimination on the augmented matrix of this system, you obtain

$$\begin{bmatrix} 1 & 0 & 0 & \vdots & -1 \\ 0 & 1 & 0 & \vdots & 2 \\ 0 & 0 & 1 & \vdots & 1 \end{bmatrix}.$$

Thus, the solution of the system of linear equations is $x_1 = -1$, $x_2 = 2$, and $x_3 = 1$, and the solution of the matrix equation is

$$X = \begin{bmatrix} x_1 \\ x_2 \\ x_3 \end{bmatrix} = \begin{bmatrix} -1 \\ 2 \\ 1 \end{bmatrix}.$$

DISCUSSION PROBLEM

Diagonal Matrices

A square matrix is a **diagonal matrix** if each entry that is not on the main diagonal is zero. For instance,

$$A = \begin{bmatrix} -1 & 0 & 0 \\ 0 & 2 & 0 \\ 0 & 0 & 0 \end{bmatrix} \quad \text{and} \quad B = \begin{bmatrix} 2 & 0 & 0 & 0 \\ 0 & -1 & 0 & 0 \\ 0 & 0 & 3 & 0 \\ 0 & 0 & 0 & -2 \end{bmatrix}$$

are diagonal matrices. Describe a quick rule for multiplying a diagonal matrix by itself. Then illustrate your rule to find the matrices $A^2 = AA$ and $B^2 = BB$ for the given matrices A and B.

WARM UP

The following warm-up exercises involve skills that were covered in earlier sections. You will use these skills in the exercise set for this section.

In Exercises 1 and 2, evaluate the expressions.

1. $-3\left(-\frac{5}{6}\right) + 10\left(-\frac{3}{4}\right)$

2. $-22\left(\frac{5}{2}\right) + 6(8)$

In Exercises 3 and 4, determine whether the matrices are in *reduced* row-echelon form.

3. $\begin{bmatrix} 0 & 1 & 0 & -5 \\ 1 & 0 & 3 & 2 \\ 0 & 0 & 1 & 0 \end{bmatrix}$

4. $\begin{bmatrix} 1 & 0 & 0 & 2 & 3 \\ 0 & 0 & 0 & 0 & 0 \\ 0 & 1 & 1 & 3 & 10 \end{bmatrix}$

In Exercises 5 and 6, write the augmented matrix for each system of linear equations.

5. $\begin{aligned} -5x + 10y &= 12 \\ 7x - 3y &= 0 \\ -x + 7y &= 25 \end{aligned}$

6. $\begin{aligned} 10x + 15y - 9z &= 42 \\ 6x - 5y &= 0 \end{aligned}$

In Exercises 7–10, solve the systems of linear equations represented by the augmented matrices.

7. $\left[\begin{array}{cc:c} 1 & 0 & 0 \\ 0 & 1 & 2 \end{array}\right]$

8. $\left[\begin{array}{ccc:c} 1 & 0 & -1 & 2 \\ 0 & 1 & 1 & 3 \end{array}\right]$

9. $\left[\begin{array}{ccc:c} 1 & 2 & 1 & 0 \\ 0 & 0 & 1 & -1 \\ 0 & 0 & 0 & 0 \end{array}\right]$

10. $\left[\begin{array}{ccc:c} 1 & -1 & 0 & 3 \\ 0 & 1 & -2 & 1 \\ 0 & 0 & 1 & -1 \end{array}\right]$

EXERCISES for Section 9.2

In Exercises 1–4, find x and y.

1. $\begin{bmatrix} x & -2 \\ 7 & y \end{bmatrix} = \begin{bmatrix} -4 & -2 \\ 7 & 22 \end{bmatrix}$

2. $\begin{bmatrix} -5 & x \\ y & 8 \end{bmatrix} = \begin{bmatrix} -5 & 13 \\ 12 & 8 \end{bmatrix}$

3. $\begin{bmatrix} 16 & 4 & 5 & 4 \\ -3 & 13 & 15 & 6 \\ 0 & 2 & 4 & 0 \end{bmatrix} = \begin{bmatrix} 16 & 4 & 2x+1 & 4 \\ -3 & 13 & 15 & 3x \\ 0 & 2 & 3y-5 & 0 \end{bmatrix}$

4. $\begin{bmatrix} x+2 & 8 & -3 \\ 1 & 2y & 2x \\ 7 & -2 & y+2 \end{bmatrix} = \begin{bmatrix} 2x+6 & 8 & -3 \\ 1 & 18 & -8 \\ 7 & -2 & 11 \end{bmatrix}$

In Exercises 5–10, find (a) $A + B$, (b) $A - B$, (c) $3A$, and (d) $3A - 2B$.

5. $A = \begin{bmatrix} 1 & -1 \\ 2 & -1 \end{bmatrix}$, $\quad B = \begin{bmatrix} 2 & -1 \\ -1 & 8 \end{bmatrix}$

6. $A = \begin{bmatrix} 1 & 2 \\ 2 & 1 \end{bmatrix}$, $\quad B = \begin{bmatrix} -3 & -2 \\ 4 & 2 \end{bmatrix}$

7. $A = \begin{bmatrix} 6 & -1 \\ 2 & 4 \\ -3 & 5 \end{bmatrix}$, $\quad B = \begin{bmatrix} 1 & 4 \\ -1 & 5 \\ 1 & 10 \end{bmatrix}$

8. $A = \begin{bmatrix} 2 & 1 & 1 \\ -1 & -1 & 4 \end{bmatrix}$, $\quad B = \begin{bmatrix} 2 & -3 & 4 \\ -3 & 1 & -2 \end{bmatrix}$

9. $A = \begin{bmatrix} 2 & 2 & -1 & 0 & 1 \\ 1 & 1 & -2 & 0 & -1 \end{bmatrix}$,

$B = \begin{bmatrix} 1 & 1 & -1 & 1 & 0 \\ -3 & 4 & 9 & -6 & -7 \end{bmatrix}$

10. $A = \begin{bmatrix} 3 \\ 2 \\ -1 \end{bmatrix}$, $B = \begin{bmatrix} -4 \\ 6 \\ 2 \end{bmatrix}$

In Exercises 11–16, find (a) AB, (b) BA, and if possible
(c) A^2. (Note: $A^2 = AA$.)

11. $A = \begin{bmatrix} 1 & 2 \\ 4 & 2 \end{bmatrix}$, $B = \begin{bmatrix} 2 & -1 \\ -1 & 8 \end{bmatrix}$

12. $A = \begin{bmatrix} 2 & -1 \\ 1 & 4 \end{bmatrix}$, $B = \begin{bmatrix} 0 & 0 \\ 3 & -3 \end{bmatrix}$

13. $A = \begin{bmatrix} 3 & -1 \\ 1 & 3 \end{bmatrix}$, $B = \begin{bmatrix} 1 & -3 \\ 3 & 1 \end{bmatrix}$

14. $A = \begin{bmatrix} 1 & -1 \\ 1 & 1 \end{bmatrix}$, $B = \begin{bmatrix} 1 & 3 \\ -3 & 1 \end{bmatrix}$

15. $A = \begin{bmatrix} 1 & -1 & 7 \\ 2 & -1 & 8 \\ 3 & 1 & -1 \end{bmatrix}$, $B = \begin{bmatrix} 1 & 1 & 2 \\ 2 & 1 & 1 \\ 1 & -3 & 2 \end{bmatrix}$

16. $A = \begin{bmatrix} 3 & 2 & 1 \end{bmatrix}$, $B = \begin{bmatrix} 2 \\ 3 \\ 0 \end{bmatrix}$

In Exercises 17–24, find AB, if possible.

17. $A = \begin{bmatrix} 2 & 1 \\ -3 & 4 \\ 1 & 6 \end{bmatrix}$, $B = \begin{bmatrix} 0 & 1 & 0 \\ 4 & 0 & 2 \\ 8 & -1 & 7 \end{bmatrix}$

18. $A = \begin{bmatrix} 0 & -1 & 0 \\ 4 & 0 & 2 \\ 8 & -1 & 7 \end{bmatrix}$, $B = \begin{bmatrix} 2 & 1 \\ -3 & 4 \\ 1 & 6 \end{bmatrix}$

19. $A = \begin{bmatrix} -1 & 3 \\ 4 & -5 \\ 0 & 2 \end{bmatrix}$, $B = \begin{bmatrix} 1 & 2 \\ 0 & 7 \end{bmatrix}$

20. $A = \begin{bmatrix} 1 & 0 & 0 \\ 0 & 4 & 0 \\ 0 & 0 & -2 \end{bmatrix}$, $B = \begin{bmatrix} 3 & 0 & 0 \\ 0 & -1 & 0 \\ 0 & 0 & 5 \end{bmatrix}$

21. $A = \begin{bmatrix} 5 & 0 & 0 \\ 0 & -8 & 0 \\ 0 & 0 & 7 \end{bmatrix}$, $B = \begin{bmatrix} \frac{1}{5} & 0 & 0 \\ 0 & -\frac{1}{8} & 0 \\ 0 & 0 & \frac{1}{2} \end{bmatrix}$

22. $A = \begin{bmatrix} 0 & 0 & 5 \\ 0 & 0 & -3 \\ 0 & 0 & 4 \end{bmatrix}$, $B = \begin{bmatrix} 6 & -11 & 4 \\ 8 & 16 & 4 \\ 0 & 0 & 0 \end{bmatrix}$

23. $A = \begin{bmatrix} 6 \\ -2 \\ 1 \\ 6 \end{bmatrix}$, $B = \begin{bmatrix} 10 & 12 \end{bmatrix}$

24. $A = \begin{bmatrix} 1 & 0 & 3 & -2 & 4 \\ 6 & 13 & 8 & -17 & 10 \end{bmatrix}$,

$B = \begin{bmatrix} 1 & 6 \\ 4 & 2 \end{bmatrix}$

In Exercises 25–28, solve for X given

$$A = \begin{bmatrix} -2 & -1 \\ 1 & 0 \\ 3 & -4 \end{bmatrix} \quad \text{and} \quad B = \begin{bmatrix} 0 & 3 \\ 2 & 0 \\ -4 & -1 \end{bmatrix}.$$

25. $X = 3A - 2B$ **26.** $2X = 2A - B$

27. $2X + 3A = B$ **28.** $2A + 4B = -2X$

In Exercises 29–32, find matrices A, X, and B such that the
given system of linear equations can be written as the matrix
equation $AX = B$. Solve the system of equations.

29. $\begin{aligned} -x + y &= 4 \\ -2x + y &= 0 \end{aligned}$ **30.** $\begin{aligned} 2x + 3y &= 5 \\ x + 4y &= 10 \end{aligned}$

31. $\begin{aligned} x - 2y + 3z &= 9 \\ -x + 3y - z &= -6 \\ 2x - 5y + 5z &= 17 \end{aligned}$ **32.** $\begin{aligned} x + y + 3z &= -1 \\ -x + 2y &= 1 \\ -y + z &= 0 \end{aligned}$

In Exercises 33–36, find $f(A) = a_0 I_n + a_1 A + a_2 A^2 + \cdots + a_n A^n$.

33. $f(x) = x^2 - 5x + 2$, $A = \begin{bmatrix} 2 & 0 \\ 4 & 5 \end{bmatrix}$

34. $f(x) = x^2 - 7x + 6$, $A = \begin{bmatrix} 5 & 4 \\ 1 & 2 \end{bmatrix}$

35. $f(x) = x^3 - 10x^2 + 31x - 30$,

$A = \begin{bmatrix} 3 & 1 & 4 \\ 0 & 2 & 6 \\ 0 & 0 & 5 \end{bmatrix}$

36. $f(x) = x^2 - 10x + 24$, $A = \begin{bmatrix} 8 & -4 \\ 2 & 2 \end{bmatrix}$

Thus, from the "doubly augmented" matrix $[A \vdots I]$ you obtained the matrix $[I \vdots A^{-1}]$.

$$\begin{matrix} A & & I \\ \begin{bmatrix} 1 & 4 & \vdots & 1 & 0 \\ -1 & -3 & \vdots & 0 & 1 \end{bmatrix} \end{matrix} \rightarrow \begin{matrix} I & & A^{-1} \\ \begin{bmatrix} 1 & 0 & \vdots & -3 & -4 \\ 0 & 1 & \vdots & 1 & 1 \end{bmatrix} \end{matrix}$$

This procedure (or algorithm) works for an arbitrary square matrix that has an inverse.

Finding the Inverse of a Matrix by Gauss-Jordan Elimination

Let A be a square matrix of order n.

1. Write the $n \times 2n$ matrix that consists of the given matrix A on the left and the $n \times n$ identity matrix I on the right to obtain $[A \quad \vdots \quad I]$. Note that the matrices A and I are separated by a dotted line. We call this process **adjoining** the matrices A and I.
2. If possible, row reduce A to I using elementary row operations on the *entire* matrix $[A \quad \vdots \quad I]$. The result will be the matrix $[I \quad \vdots \quad A^{-1}]$. If this is not possible, then A is not invertible.
3. Check your work by multiplying to see that $AA^{-1} = I = A^{-1}A$.

EXAMPLE 3   Finding the Inverse of a Matrix

Find the inverse of the following matrix.

$$A = \begin{bmatrix} 1 & -1 & 0 \\ 1 & 0 & -1 \\ 6 & -2 & -3 \end{bmatrix}$$

Solution

Begin by adjoining the identity matrix to A to form the matrix

$$[A \quad \vdots \quad I] = \begin{bmatrix} 1 & -1 & 0 & \vdots & 1 & 0 & 0 \\ 1 & 0 & -1 & \vdots & 0 & 1 & 0 \\ 6 & -2 & -3 & \vdots & 0 & 0 & 1 \end{bmatrix}.$$

Now, use the elementary row operations to rewrite this matrix in the form $[I \quad \vdots \quad A^{-1}]$ as follows.

$$\begin{bmatrix} 1 & -1 & 0 & \vdots & 1 & 0 & 0 \\ 1 & 0 & -1 & \vdots & 0 & 1 & 0 \\ 6 & -2 & -3 & \vdots & 0 & 0 & 1 \end{bmatrix} \begin{matrix} \\ -R_1 + R_2 \rightarrow \\ -6R_1 + R_3 \rightarrow \end{matrix} \begin{bmatrix} 1 & -1 & 0 & \vdots & 1 & 0 & 0 \\ 0 & 1 & -1 & \vdots & -1 & 1 & 0 \\ 0 & 4 & -3 & \vdots & -6 & 0 & 1 \end{bmatrix}$$

$$\begin{matrix} R_2 + R_1 \rightarrow \\ \\ -4R_2 + R_3 \rightarrow \end{matrix} \begin{bmatrix} 1 & 0 & -1 & \vdots & 0 & 1 & 0 \\ 0 & 1 & -1 & \vdots & -1 & 1 & 0 \\ 0 & 0 & 1 & \vdots & -2 & -4 & 1 \end{bmatrix}$$

$$\begin{matrix} R_3 + R_1 \rightarrow \\ R_3 + R_2 \rightarrow \\ \end{matrix} \begin{bmatrix} 1 & 0 & 0 & \vdots & -2 & -3 & 1 \\ 0 & 1 & 0 & \vdots & -3 & -3 & 1 \\ 0 & 0 & 1 & \vdots & -2 & -4 & 1 \end{bmatrix}$$

Therefore, the matrix A is invertible and its inverse is

$$A^{-1} = \begin{bmatrix} -2 & -3 & \vdots & 1 \\ -3 & -3 & \vdots & 1 \\ -2 & -4 & \vdots & 1 \end{bmatrix}.$$

Try confirming this by multiplying A and A^{-1} to obtain I.

◢

The process shown in Example 3 applies to any $n \times n$ matrix A. If A has an inverse, this process will find it. On the other hand, if A does not have an inverse, the process will not lead to an identity matrix to the left of the dotted line.

Systems of Linear Equations

A system of linear equations can have exactly one solution, an infinite number of solutions, or no solution. If the coefficient matrix A of a *square* system (a system that has the same number of equations as variables) is invertible, the system has a unique solution, which is given as follows.

$$AX = B \qquad \textit{Given equation}$$
$$A^{-1}AX = A^{-1}B \qquad \textit{Multiply both sides by } A^{-1} \textit{ (on the left)}$$
$$X = A^{-1}B \qquad \textit{Solution}$$

A SYSTEM OF EQUATIONS WITH A UNIQUE SOLUTION

If A is an invertible matrix, then the system of linear equations represented by $AX = B$ has a unique solution given by

$$X = A^{-1}B.$$

Solving a system of linear equations by finding the inverse of the coefficient matrix is not very efficient. That is, it is usually more work to find A^{-1} and then multiply by B than simply to solve the system using Gaussian elimination with back-substitution. One case in which you might consider using an inverse matrix as a computational technique would be with *several* systems of linear equations, all of which have the same coefficient matrix A. In such a case, you could find the inverse matrix once and then solve each system by computing the product $A^{-1}B$. This is demonstrated in Example 4.

EXAMPLE 4 **Solving a System of Equations Using an Inverse**

Use an inverse matrix to solve the following systems.

a. $2x + 3y + z = -1$
 $3x + 3y + z = 1$
 $2x + 4y + z = -2$

b. $2x + 3y + z = 4$
 $3x + 3y + z = 8$
 $2x + 4y + z = 5$

Solution

First note that the coefficient matrix for each system is

$$A = \begin{bmatrix} 2 & 3 & 1 \\ 3 & 3 & 1 \\ 2 & 4 & 1 \end{bmatrix}.$$

Using Gauss-Jordan elimination, you find A^{-1} to be

$$A^{-1} = \begin{bmatrix} -1 & 1 & 0 \\ -1 & 0 & 1 \\ 6 & -2 & -3 \end{bmatrix}.$$

To solve each system, use matrix multiplication as follows.

a. $X = A^{-1}B = \begin{bmatrix} -1 & 1 & 0 \\ -1 & 0 & 1 \\ 6 & -2 & -3 \end{bmatrix} \begin{bmatrix} -1 \\ 1 \\ -2 \end{bmatrix} = \begin{bmatrix} 2 \\ -1 \\ -2 \end{bmatrix}$

The solution is $x = 2$, $y = -1$, and $z = -2$.

b. $X = A^{-1}B = \begin{bmatrix} -1 & 1 & 0 \\ -1 & 0 & 1 \\ 6 & -2 & -3 \end{bmatrix} \begin{bmatrix} 4 \\ 8 \\ 5 \end{bmatrix} = \begin{bmatrix} 4 \\ 1 \\ -7 \end{bmatrix}$

The solution is $x = 4$, $y = 1$, and $z = -7$.

DISCUSSION

PROBLEM

The Factorization Principle

For *real numbers* the Factorization Principle states that if $ab = 0$, then either $a = 0$ or $b = 0$. It is possible, however, to find nonzero matrices whose product is zero. For instance,

$$\begin{bmatrix} 2 & -1 \\ -4 & 2 \end{bmatrix} \begin{bmatrix} 3 & -3 \\ 6 & -6 \end{bmatrix} = \begin{bmatrix} 0 & 0 \\ 0 & 0 \end{bmatrix}.$$

In order to obtain a factorization principle for matrices, we must restrict ourselves to a certain type of matrix. Complete the following factorization principle for matrices by determining which type of matrix will make the statement true. Then write a short paragraph that justifies your conclusion.

"Let A and B be square matrices, each of order $n \times n$. If A and B are ▨▨▨ and $AB = O$ where O is the $n \times n$ zero matrix, then $A = O$ or $B = O$."

WARM UP

The following warm-up exercises involve skills that were covered in earlier sections. You will use these skills in the exercise set for this section.

In Exercises 1–8, perform the indicated matrix operations.

1. $4 \begin{bmatrix} 1 & 6 \\ 0 & -4 \\ 12 & 2 \end{bmatrix}$

2. $\dfrac{1}{2} \begin{bmatrix} 11 & 10 & 48 \\ 1 & 0 & 16 \\ 0 & 2 & 8 \end{bmatrix}$

3. $\begin{bmatrix} 1 & -10 & 3 \\ 4 & 1 & 0 \end{bmatrix} - 2 \begin{bmatrix} 3 & -4 & 8 \\ 0 & 7 & 1 \end{bmatrix}$

4. $\begin{bmatrix} 5 & 20 \\ -7 & 15 \end{bmatrix} - 3 \begin{bmatrix} 6 & 3 \\ 4 & -2 \end{bmatrix}$

5. $\begin{bmatrix} 1 & -2 \\ -1 & 3 \end{bmatrix} \begin{bmatrix} 3 & 2 \\ 1 & 1 \end{bmatrix}$

6. $\begin{bmatrix} 1 & 0 \\ 0 & 1 \end{bmatrix} \begin{bmatrix} 6 & 5 \\ 3 & -2 \end{bmatrix}$

7. $\begin{bmatrix} 2 & 0 & 0 \\ 0 & -1 & 0 \\ 0 & 0 & 3 \end{bmatrix} \begin{bmatrix} \frac{1}{2} & 0 & 0 \\ 0 & -1 & 0 \\ 0 & 0 & \frac{1}{3} \end{bmatrix}$

8. $\begin{bmatrix} 1 & -1 & 0 \\ 1 & 0 & -1 \\ 6 & -2 & -3 \end{bmatrix} \begin{bmatrix} -2 & -3 & 1 \\ -3 & -3 & 1 \\ -2 & -4 & 1 \end{bmatrix}$

In Exercises 9 and 10, rewrite the matrices in reduced row-echelon form.

9. $\begin{bmatrix} 3 & -2 & 1 & 0 \\ 4 & -3 & 0 & 1 \end{bmatrix}$

10. $\begin{bmatrix} 1 & 1 & 2 & 1 & 0 & 0 \\ -1 & 0 & 3 & 0 & 1 & 0 \\ 1 & 2 & 8 & 0 & 0 & 1 \end{bmatrix}$

EXERCISES for Section 9.3

In Exercises 1–8, show that B is the inverse of A.

1. $A = \begin{bmatrix} 2 & 1 \\ 5 & 3 \end{bmatrix}$, $\qquad B = \begin{bmatrix} 3 & -1 \\ -5 & 2 \end{bmatrix}$

2. $A = \begin{bmatrix} 1 & -1 \\ -1 & 2 \end{bmatrix}$, $\qquad B = \begin{bmatrix} 2 & 1 \\ 1 & 1 \end{bmatrix}$

3. $A = \begin{bmatrix} 1 & 2 \\ 3 & 4 \end{bmatrix}$, $\qquad B = \begin{bmatrix} -2 & 1 \\ \frac{3}{2} & -\frac{1}{2} \end{bmatrix}$

4. $A = \begin{bmatrix} 1 & -1 \\ 2 & 3 \end{bmatrix}$, $\qquad B = \begin{bmatrix} \frac{3}{5} & \frac{1}{5} \\ -\frac{2}{5} & \frac{1}{5} \end{bmatrix}$

5. $A = \begin{bmatrix} -2 & 2 & 3 \\ 1 & -1 & 0 \\ 0 & 1 & 4 \end{bmatrix}$, $\quad B = \dfrac{1}{3} \begin{bmatrix} -4 & -5 & 3 \\ -4 & -8 & 3 \\ 1 & 2 & 0 \end{bmatrix}$

6. $A = \begin{bmatrix} 2 & -17 & 11 \\ -1 & 11 & -7 \\ 0 & 3 & -2 \end{bmatrix}$, $\quad B = \begin{bmatrix} 1 & 1 & 2 \\ 2 & 4 & -3 \\ 3 & 6 & -5 \end{bmatrix}$

7. $A = \begin{bmatrix} 2 & 0 & 1 & 1 \\ 3 & 0 & 0 & 1 \\ -1 & 1 & -2 & 1 \\ 4 & -1 & 1 & 0 \end{bmatrix}$,

$\quad B = \begin{bmatrix} -1 & 2 & -1 & -1 \\ -4 & 9 & -5 & -6 \\ 0 & 1 & -1 & -1 \\ 3 & -5 & 3 & 3 \end{bmatrix}$

8. $A = \begin{bmatrix} -1 & 1 & 0 & -1 \\ 1 & -1 & 2 & 0 \\ -1 & 1 & 2 & 0 \\ 0 & -1 & 1 & 1 \end{bmatrix}$,

$\quad B = \dfrac{1}{3} \begin{bmatrix} -3 & 1 & 1 & -3 \\ -3 & -1 & 2 & -3 \\ 0 & 1 & 1 & 0 \\ -3 & -2 & 1 & 0 \end{bmatrix}$

Elementary Row Operations

It is not coincidental that the determinants of A and B are the same value. In fact, we obtained matrix B by performing elementary row operations on matrix A. (Try verifying this.) In this section, we consider the effect of elementary row (and column) operations on the value of a determinant. Here is an example.

EXAMPLE 1 The Effect of Elementary Row Operations on a Determinant

a. The matrix B was obtained from A by interchanging the rows of A.

$$|A| = \begin{vmatrix} 2 & -3 \\ 1 & 4 \end{vmatrix} = 11 \quad \text{and} \quad |B| = \begin{vmatrix} 1 & 4 \\ 2 & -3 \end{vmatrix} = -11$$

b. The matrix B was obtained from A by adding -2 times the first row of A to the second row of A.

$$|A| = \begin{vmatrix} 1 & -3 \\ 2 & 4 \end{vmatrix} = 10 \quad \text{and} \quad |B| = \begin{vmatrix} 1 & -3 \\ 0 & 10 \end{vmatrix} = 10$$

c. The matrix B was obtained from A by multiplying the first row of A by $\frac{1}{2}$.

$$|A| = \begin{vmatrix} 2 & -8 \\ -2 & 9 \end{vmatrix} = 2 \quad \text{and} \quad |B| = \begin{vmatrix} 1 & -4 \\ -2 & 9 \end{vmatrix} = 1$$

In Example 1, you saw that interchanging two rows of the matrix changed the sign of its determinant. Adding a multiple of one row to another did not change the determinant. Finally, multiplying a row by a nonzero constant multiplied the determinant by that same constant. The following theorem generalizes these observations.

ELEMENTARY ROW OPERATIONS AND DETERMINANTS

Let A and B be square matrices.

1. If B is obtained from A by interchanging two rows of A, then

$$|B| = -|A|.$$

2. If B is obtained from A by adding a multiple of a row of A to another row of A, then

$$|B| = |A|.$$

3. If B is obtained from A by multiplying a row of A to a nonzero constant C, then

$$|B| = c|A|.$$

REMARK Note that the third property allows us to take a common factor out of a row. For instance,

$$\begin{vmatrix} 2 & 4 \\ 1 & 3 \end{vmatrix} = 2 \begin{vmatrix} 1 & 2 \\ 1 & 3 \end{vmatrix}.$$ *Factor 2 out of the first row*

Moreover, the theorem is true if the word *row* is replaced by the word *column*. ◢

This theorem provides a practical way to evaluate determinants (especially determinants of large matrices). To find the determinant of a matrix A, use elementary row operations to obtain a triangular matrix B that is row equivalent to A. At each step in the elimination process, incorporate the effect of the elementary row operation on the determinant. Finally, find the determinant of B by forming the product of the entries on its main diagonal. This process is demonstrated in the next example.

EXAMPLE 2   Evaluating a Determinant

Find the determinant of

$$A = \begin{bmatrix} 2 & -3 & 10 \\ 1 & 2 & -2 \\ 0 & 1 & -3 \end{bmatrix}.$$

Solution

Using elementary row operations, rewrite A in triangular form as follows.

$$\begin{vmatrix} 2 & -3 & 10 \\ 1 & 2 & -2 \\ 0 & 1 & -3 \end{vmatrix} = -\begin{vmatrix} 1 & 2 & -2 \\ 2 & -3 & 10 \\ 0 & 1 & -3 \end{vmatrix}$$ Interchange the first two rows.

$$= -\begin{vmatrix} 1 & 2 & -2 \\ 0 & -7 & 14 \\ 0 & 1 & -3 \end{vmatrix}$$ Adding -2 times the first row to the second row produces a new second row.

$$= 7\begin{vmatrix} 1 & 2 & -2 \\ 0 & 1 & -2 \\ 0 & 1 & -3 \end{vmatrix}$$ Factor -7 out of the second row.

$$= 7\begin{vmatrix} 1 & 2 & -2 \\ 0 & 1 & -2 \\ 0 & 0 & -1 \end{vmatrix}$$ Adding -1 times the second row to the third row produces a new third row.

Now, because the final matrix is triangular, you may conclude that the determinant is

$$|A| = 7(1)(1)(-1) = -7.$$ ◢

Conditions that Yield a Zero Determinant

If A is a square matrix and any one of the following conditions is true, then $|A| = 0$.

1. An entire row (or an entire column) is zero.
2. Two rows (or two columns) are equal.
3. One row (or column) is a multiple of another row (or column).

Recognizing the conditions listed in this theorem can make evaluating a determinant much easier. For instance, consider the following three evaluations.

$$\begin{vmatrix} 0 & 0 & 0 \\ 2 & 4 & -5 \\ 3 & -5 & 2 \end{vmatrix} = 0 \qquad \begin{vmatrix} 1 & -2 & 4 \\ 0 & 1 & 2 \\ 1 & -2 & 4 \end{vmatrix} = 0 \qquad \begin{vmatrix} 1 & 2 & -3 \\ 2 & -1 & -6 \\ -2 & 0 & 6 \end{vmatrix} = 0$$

| First row has all zeros. | First and third rows are the same. | Third column is a multiple of first column. |

Do not conclude that the three conditions listed in this theorem are the *only* conditions that produce a determinant of zero. The theorem is often used indirectly. That is, you can begin with a matrix that does not satisfy any of the three conditions listed in the theorem, and through elementary row or column operations obtain a matrix that does satisfy one of the conditions. Then you may conclude that the original matrix has a determinant of zero.

EXAMPLE 3   A Matrix with a Zero Determinant

Find the determinant of

$$A = \begin{bmatrix} 1 & 4 & 1 \\ 2 & -1 & 0 \\ 0 & 18 & 4 \end{bmatrix}.$$

Solution

Adding -2 times the first row to the second row produces

$$|A| = \begin{vmatrix} 1 & 4 & 1 \\ 2 & -1 & 0 \\ 0 & 18 & 4 \end{vmatrix} = \begin{vmatrix} 1 & 4 & 1 \\ 0 & -9 & -2 \\ 0 & 18 & 4 \end{vmatrix}.$$

Because the second and third rows are multiples of each other, you conclude that the determinant is zero.

Determinants and the Inverse of a Matrix

We saw in Section 9.3 that some square matrices are not invertible. However, it can be difficult to tell simply by inspection whether a matrix possesses an inverse. For instance, can you tell which of the following two matrices is invertible?

$$A = \begin{bmatrix} 0 & 2 & -1 \\ 3 & -2 & 1 \\ 3 & 2 & -1 \end{bmatrix} \quad \text{or} \quad B = \begin{bmatrix} 0 & 2 & -1 \\ 3 & 2 & 1 \\ 3 & 2 & 1 \end{bmatrix}$$

The following theorem shows how determinants can be used to classify square matrices as invertible or noninvertible.

DETERMINANT OF AN INVERTIBLE MATRIX

A square matrix A is invertible (nonsingular) if and only if

$$|A| \neq 0.$$

EXAMPLE 4   Classifying Square Matrices as Singular or Nonsingular

Which of the following matrices possesses an inverse?

a. $\begin{bmatrix} 0 & 2 & -1 \\ 3 & -2 & 1 \\ 3 & 2 & -1 \end{bmatrix}$ b. $\begin{bmatrix} 0 & 2 & -1 \\ 3 & -2 & 1 \\ 3 & 2 & 1 \end{bmatrix}$

Solution

a. Because

$$\begin{vmatrix} 0 & 2 & -1 \\ 3 & -2 & 1 \\ 3 & 2 & -1 \end{vmatrix} = 0$$

this matrix has no inverse (it is singular).

b. Because

$$\begin{vmatrix} 0 & 2 & -1 \\ 3 & -2 & 1 \\ 3 & 2 & 1 \end{vmatrix} = -12 \neq 0$$

this matrix has an inverse (it is nonsingular).

DISCUSSION
PROBLEM

Systems of Linear Equations

In Example 4, you looked at two 3×3 matrices, one that had an inverse and one that didn't. Two systems of linear equations that have these matrices as coefficient matrices are as follows.

1.
$$\begin{aligned} 2y - z &= -5 \\ 3x - 2y + z &= 8 \\ 3x + 2y - z &= -2 \end{aligned}$$

2.
$$\begin{aligned} 2y - z &= -5 \\ 3x - 2y + z &= 8 \\ 3x + 2y + z &= 0 \end{aligned}$$

One of these two systems has a single solution and one has either infinitely many solutions or no solution. How can you use the result of Example 4 to determine which is which? Discuss, or write a short paragraph describing, the relationship between determinants and the number of solutions of a system of linear equations.

WARM UP

The following warm-up exercises involve skills that were covered in earlier sections. You will use these skills in the exercise set for this section.

In Exercises 1–4, write the matrices in row-echelon form.

1. $\begin{bmatrix} 2 & -6 \\ 5 & 20 \end{bmatrix}$

2. $\begin{bmatrix} -7 & 21 \\ 3 & 5 \end{bmatrix}$

3. $\begin{bmatrix} 1 & 3 & 4 \\ 0 & 1 & 1 \\ 2 & 4 & 6 \end{bmatrix}$

4. $\begin{bmatrix} 4 & 8 & 16 \\ 3 & -1 & 2 \\ -2 & 10 & 12 \end{bmatrix}$

In Exercises 5–10, evaluate the determinant.

5. $\begin{vmatrix} 4 & -3 \\ -2 & 1 \end{vmatrix}$

6. $\begin{vmatrix} 10 & -20 \\ -1 & 2 \end{vmatrix}$

7. $\begin{vmatrix} 4 & 0 \\ -3 & -2 \end{vmatrix}$

8. $\begin{vmatrix} x & x^2 \\ 1 & 2x \end{vmatrix}$

9. $\begin{vmatrix} 4 & 0 & -2 \\ 3 & 1 & 2 \\ -8 & 0 & 6 \end{vmatrix}$

10. $\begin{vmatrix} 3 & 2 & 5 \\ 0 & 0 & -4 \\ -6 & 1 & 1 \end{vmatrix}$

EXERCISES for Section 9.5

In Exercises 1–14, state the property of determinants that verifies the equation.

1. $\begin{vmatrix} 2 & -6 \\ 1 & -3 \end{vmatrix} = 0$

2. $\begin{vmatrix} -4 & 5 \\ 12 & -15 \end{vmatrix} = 0$

3. $\begin{vmatrix} 1 & 4 & 2 \\ 0 & 0 & 0 \\ 5 & 6 & -7 \end{vmatrix} = 0$

4. $\begin{vmatrix} -4 & 3 & 2 \\ 8 & 0 & 0 \\ -4 & 3 & 2 \end{vmatrix} = 0$

5. $\begin{vmatrix} 1 & 3 & 4 \\ -7 & 2 & -5 \\ 6 & 1 & 2 \end{vmatrix} = -\begin{vmatrix} 1 & 4 & 3 \\ -7 & -5 & 2 \\ 6 & 2 & 1 \end{vmatrix}$

6. $\begin{vmatrix} 1 & 3 & 4 \\ -2 & 2 & 0 \\ 1 & 6 & 2 \end{vmatrix} = -\begin{vmatrix} 1 & 6 & 2 \\ -2 & 2 & 0 \\ 1 & 3 & 4 \end{vmatrix}$

7. $\begin{vmatrix} 5 & 10 & 15 \\ 2 & -3 & 4 \\ 2 & -7 & 1 \end{vmatrix} - 5\begin{vmatrix} 1 & 2 & 3 \\ 2 & -3 & 4 \\ 2 & -7 & 1 \end{vmatrix}$

8. $\begin{vmatrix} 1 & 8 & -3 \\ 3 & -12 & 6 \\ 7 & 4 & 9 \end{vmatrix} = 12\begin{vmatrix} 1 & 2 & -1 \\ 3 & -3 & 2 \\ 7 & 1 & 3 \end{vmatrix}$

9. $\begin{vmatrix} 5 & 0 & 10 \\ 25 & -30 & 40 \\ -15 & 5 & 20 \end{vmatrix} = 5^3\begin{vmatrix} 1 & 0 & 2 \\ 5 & -6 & 8 \\ -3 & 1 & 4 \end{vmatrix}$

10. $\begin{vmatrix} 6 & 0 & 0 \\ 0 & 6 & 0 \\ 0 & 0 & 6 \end{vmatrix} = 6^3\begin{vmatrix} 1 & 0 & 0 \\ 0 & 1 & 0 \\ 0 & 0 & 1 \end{vmatrix}$

11. $\begin{vmatrix} 2 & -3 \\ 8 & 7 \end{vmatrix} = \begin{vmatrix} 2 & -3 \\ 0 & 19 \end{vmatrix}$

12. $\begin{vmatrix} 1 & -3 \\ 5 & 2 \end{vmatrix} = \begin{vmatrix} 1 & -3 \\ 0 & 17 \end{vmatrix}$

13. $\begin{vmatrix} 3 & 2 & 4 \\ -2 & 1 & 5 \\ 5 & -7 & -20 \end{vmatrix} = \begin{vmatrix} 7 & 2 & -6 \\ 0 & 1 & 0 \\ -9 & -7 & 15 \end{vmatrix}$

14. $\begin{vmatrix} 5 & 4 & 2 \\ 2 & -3 & 4 \\ 7 & 6 & 3 \end{vmatrix} = \begin{vmatrix} 1 & 10 & 6 \\ 2 & 3 & 4 \\ 7 & 6 & 3 \end{vmatrix}$

In Exercises 15–30, use elementary row (or column) operations as aids for evaluating the determinant.

15. $\begin{vmatrix} 1 & 2 & 5 \\ 1 & 4 & 2 \\ 0 & 3 & -4 \end{vmatrix}$

16. $\begin{vmatrix} 1 & 7 & -3 \\ 1 & 3 & 1 \\ 4 & 8 & 1 \end{vmatrix}$

17. $\begin{vmatrix} 3 & -1 & -3 \\ -1 & -4 & -2 \\ 3 & -1 & -1 \end{vmatrix}$

18. $\begin{vmatrix} 4 & 3 & -2 \\ 5 & 4 & 1 \\ -2 & 3 & 4 \end{vmatrix}$

19. $\begin{vmatrix} 3 & 8 & -7 \\ 0 & -5 & 4 \\ 8 & 1 & 6 \end{vmatrix}$

20. $\begin{vmatrix} 5 & -8 & 0 \\ 9 & 7 & 4 \\ -8 & 7 & 1 \end{vmatrix}$

21. $\begin{vmatrix} 2 & -1 & 3 \\ 1 & 2 & -1 \\ 3 & -4 & 7 \end{vmatrix}$

22. $\begin{vmatrix} 2 & 0 & 1 \\ 4 & -4 & 0 \\ -1 & 5 & 2 \end{vmatrix}$

23. $\begin{vmatrix} 7 & 0 & -14 \\ -2 & 5 & 4 \\ -6 & 2 & 12 \end{vmatrix}$

24. $\begin{vmatrix} 3 & 0 & 0 \\ -2 & 5 & 0 \\ 12 & 5 & 7 \end{vmatrix}$

25. $\begin{vmatrix} 4 & -8 & 5 & 0 \\ 8 & -5 & 3 & 0 \\ 8 & 5 & 2 & 0 \\ 1 & 7 & -5 & 1 \end{vmatrix}$

26. $\begin{vmatrix} 4 & -7 & 9 & 1 \\ 6 & 2 & 7 & 0 \\ 3 & 6 & -3 & 3 \\ 0 & 7 & 4 & -1 \end{vmatrix}$

27. $\begin{vmatrix} 0 & -3 & 8 & 2 \\ 8 & 1 & -1 & 6 \\ -4 & 6 & 0 & 9 \\ -7 & 0 & 0 & 14 \end{vmatrix}$

28. $\begin{vmatrix} 1 & -1 & 8 & 4 \\ 2 & 6 & 0 & -4 \\ 2 & 0 & 2 & 6 \\ 0 & 2 & 8 & 0 \end{vmatrix}$

29. $\begin{vmatrix} 3 & -2 & 4 & 3 & 1 \\ -1 & 0 & 2 & 1 & 0 \\ 5 & -1 & 0 & 3 & 2 \\ 4 & 7 & -8 & 0 & 0 \\ 1 & 2 & 3 & 0 & 2 \end{vmatrix}$

30. $\begin{vmatrix} 4 & 2 & -1 & 0 & 3 \\ 0 & 1 & 1 & 2 & -3 \\ 0 & 0 & -2 & 8 & 12 \\ 0 & 0 & 0 & 5 & 13 \\ 0 & 0 & 0 & 0 & 3 \end{vmatrix}$

In Exercises 31–36, use a determinant to ascertain whether the matrix is invertible.

31. $\begin{bmatrix} 5 & 4 \\ 10 & 8 \end{bmatrix}$

32. $\begin{bmatrix} 3 & -6 \\ 4 & 2 \end{bmatrix}$

33. $\begin{bmatrix} 14 & 7 & 0 \\ 2 & 3 & 0 \\ 1 & -5 & 2 \end{bmatrix}$

34. $\begin{bmatrix} 1 & 0 & 4 \\ 0 & 6 & 3 \\ 2 & -1 & 4 \end{bmatrix}$

35. $\begin{bmatrix} \frac{1}{2} & \frac{3}{2} & 2 \\ \frac{2}{3} & -\frac{1}{3} & 0 \\ 1 & 1 & 1 \end{bmatrix}$

36. $\begin{bmatrix} 2 & -1 & 6 \\ 1 & -3 & 4 \\ 4 & -2 & 12 \end{bmatrix}$

In Exercises 37 and 38, find the value(s) of k such that A is singular.

37. $\begin{bmatrix} k-1 & 3 \\ 2 & k-2 \end{bmatrix}$

38. $\begin{bmatrix} 1 & 0 & 3 \\ 2 & -1 & 0 \\ 4 & 2 & k \end{bmatrix}$

In Exercises 39–42, verify the equation.

39. $\begin{vmatrix} w & x \\ y & z \end{vmatrix} = -\begin{vmatrix} y & z \\ w & x \end{vmatrix}$ **40.** $\begin{vmatrix} w & cx \\ y & cz \end{vmatrix} = c\begin{vmatrix} w & x \\ y & z \end{vmatrix}$

41. $\begin{vmatrix} w & x \\ y & z \end{vmatrix} = \begin{vmatrix} w & x + cw \\ y & z + cy \end{vmatrix}$ **42.** $\begin{vmatrix} w & x \\ cw & cx \end{vmatrix} = 0$

In Exercises 43 and 44, evaluate the determinant to verify the equation.

43. $\begin{vmatrix} 1 & x & x^2 \\ 1 & y & y^2 \\ 1 & z & z^2 \end{vmatrix} = (y - x)(z - x)(z - y)$

44. $\begin{vmatrix} a + b & a & a \\ a & a + b & a \\ a & a & a + b \end{vmatrix} = b^2(3a + b)$

In Exercises 45–48, find (a) $|A|$, (b) $|B|$, (c) AB, and (d) $|AB|$.

45. $A = \begin{bmatrix} -1 & 0 \\ 0 & 3 \end{bmatrix}, \quad B = \begin{bmatrix} 2 & 0 \\ 0 & -1 \end{bmatrix}$

46. $A = \begin{bmatrix} -2 & 1 \\ 4 & -2 \end{bmatrix}, \quad B = \begin{bmatrix} 1 & 2 \\ 0 & -1 \end{bmatrix}$

47. $A = \begin{bmatrix} -1 & 2 & 1 \\ 1 & 0 & 1 \\ 0 & 1 & 0 \end{bmatrix}, \quad B = \begin{bmatrix} -1 & 0 & 0 \\ 0 & 2 & 0 \\ 0 & 0 & 3 \end{bmatrix}$

48. $A = \begin{bmatrix} 2 & 0 & 1 \\ 1 & -1 & 2 \\ 3 & 1 & 0 \end{bmatrix}, \quad B = \begin{bmatrix} 2 & -1 & 4 \\ 0 & 1 & 3 \\ 3 & -2 & 1 \end{bmatrix}$

49. Find the square matrices A and B to demonstrate that
$$|A + B| \neq |A| + |B|.$$

9.6 Applications of Determinants and Matrices

Cramer's Rule / Area of a Triangle / Lines in the Plane / Cryptography

Cramer's Rule

So far, we have discussed three methods for solving a system of linear equations: substitution, elimination (with equations), and elimination (with matrices). We now look at one more method, **Cramer's Rule,** named after Gabriel Cramer (1704–1752). This rule uses determinants to write the solution of a system of linear equations. To see how Cramer's Rule works, take another look at the solution described at the beginning of Section 9.4. There, we pointed out that the system

$$a_1 x + b_1 y = c_1$$
$$a_2 x + b_2 y = c_2$$

has a solution given by

$$x = \frac{c_1 b_2 - c_2 b_1}{a_1 b_2 - a_2 b_1} \quad \text{and} \quad y = \frac{a_1 c_2 - a_2 c_1}{a_1 b_2 - a_2 b_1}$$

provided $a_1 b_2 - a_2 b_1 \neq 0$. Each numerator and denominator in this solution can be expressed as a determinant, as follows.

$$x = \frac{c_1 b_2 - c_2 b_1}{a_1 b_2 - a_2 b_1} = \frac{\begin{vmatrix} c_1 & b_1 \\ c_2 & b_2 \end{vmatrix}}{\begin{vmatrix} a_1 & b_1 \\ a_2 & b_2 \end{vmatrix}}, \quad y = \frac{a_1 c_2 - a_2 c_1}{a_1 b_2 - a_2 b_1} = \frac{\begin{vmatrix} a_1 & c_1 \\ a_2 & c_2 \end{vmatrix}}{\begin{vmatrix} a_1 & b_1 \\ a_2 & b_2 \end{vmatrix}}$$

Relative to the original system, the denominator for x and y is simply the determinant of the *coefficient* matrix of the system. We denote this determinant by D. The numerators for x and y are denoted by D_x and D_y, respectively. They are formed by using the column of constants as replacements for the coefficients of x and y, as follows.

$$\begin{matrix} \text{Coefficient} \\ \text{Matrix} \end{matrix} \qquad D \qquad\qquad D_x \qquad\qquad D_y$$

$$\begin{bmatrix} a_1 & b_1 \\ a_2 & b_2 \end{bmatrix} \qquad \begin{vmatrix} a_1 & b_1 \\ a_2 & b_2 \end{vmatrix} \qquad \begin{vmatrix} c_1 & b_1 \\ c_2 & b_2 \end{vmatrix} \qquad \begin{vmatrix} a_1 & c_1 \\ a_2 & c_2 \end{vmatrix}$$

EXAMPLE 1   Using Cramer's Rule for a 2 × 2 System

Use Cramer's Rule to solve the following system of linear equations.

$$4x - 2y = 10$$
$$3x - 5y = 11$$

Solution

To begin, find the determinant of the coefficient matrix.

$$D = \begin{vmatrix} 4 & -2 \\ 3 & -5 \end{vmatrix} = -20 - (-6) = -14$$

Because this determinant is not zero, you can apply Cramer's Rule to find the solution, as follows.

$$x = \frac{D_x}{D} = \frac{\begin{vmatrix} 10 & -2 \\ 11 & -5 \end{vmatrix}}{-14} = \frac{(-50) - (-22)}{-14} = \frac{-28}{-14} = 2$$

$$y = \frac{D_y}{D} = \frac{\begin{vmatrix} 4 & 10 \\ 3 & 11 \end{vmatrix}}{-14} = \frac{44 - 30}{-14} = \frac{14}{-14} = -1$$

Therefore, the solution is $x = 2$ and $y = -1$. Check this solution in the original system of equations.

Cramer's Rule generalizes easily to systems of n equations in n variables. The value of each variable is given as the quotient of two determinants. The denominator is the determinant of the coefficient matrix, and the numerator is the determinant of the matrix formed by replacing the column corresponding to the variable (being solved for) with the column representing the constants. For example, the solution for x_3 in the system

$$a_{11}x_1 + a_{12}x_2 + a_{13}x_3 = b_1$$
$$a_{21}x_1 + a_{22}x_2 + a_{23}x_3 = b_2$$
$$a_{31}x_1 + a_{32}x_2 + a_{33}x_3 = b_3$$

is given by

$$x_3 = \frac{|A_3|}{|A|} = \frac{\begin{vmatrix} a_{11} & a_{12} & b_1 \\ a_{21} & a_{22} & b_2 \\ a_{31} & a_{32} & b_3 \end{vmatrix}}{\begin{vmatrix} a_{11} & a_{12} & a_{13} \\ a_{21} & a_{22} & a_{23} \\ a_{31} & a_{32} & a_{33} \end{vmatrix}}.$$

CRAMER'S RULE

If a system of n linear equations in n variables has a coefficient matrix A with a *nonzero* determinant $|A|$, then the solution of the system is given by

$$x_1 = \frac{|A_1|}{|A|}, \quad x_2 = \frac{|A_2|}{|A|}, \quad \ldots, \quad x_n = \frac{|A_n|}{|A|}$$

where the ith column of A_i is the column of constants in the system of equations. If the coefficient matrix is zero, then the system has either no solution *or* infinitely many solutions.

EXAMPLE 2 Using Cramer's Rule for a 3 × 3 System

Use Cramer's Rule to solve the following system of linear equations.

$$-x + 2y - 3z = 1$$
$$2x \qquad + z = 0$$
$$3x - 4y + 4z = 2$$

Solution

To begin, find the determinant of the coefficient matrix.

$$D = \begin{vmatrix} -1 & 2 & -3 \\ 2 & 0 & 1 \\ 3 & -4 & 4 \end{vmatrix} = -(2)\begin{vmatrix} 2 & -3 \\ -4 & 4 \end{vmatrix} + (0)\begin{vmatrix} -1 & -3 \\ 3 & 4 \end{vmatrix} - (1)\begin{vmatrix} -1 & 2 \\ 3 & -4 \end{vmatrix}$$

$$= -2(-4) + 0 - (-2)$$
$$= 10$$

Because this determinant is not zero, you can apply Cramer's Rule to find the solution, as follows.

$$x = \frac{D_x}{D} = \frac{\begin{vmatrix} 1 & 2 & -3 \\ 0 & 0 & 1 \\ 2 & -4 & 4 \end{vmatrix}}{10} = \frac{8}{10} = \frac{4}{5}$$

$$y = \frac{D_y}{D} = \frac{\begin{vmatrix} -1 & 1 & -3 \\ 2 & 0 & 1 \\ 3 & 2 & 4 \end{vmatrix}}{10} = \frac{-15}{10} = -\frac{3}{2}$$

$$z = \frac{D_z}{D} = \frac{\begin{vmatrix} -1 & 2 & 1 \\ 2 & 0 & 0 \\ 3 & -4 & 2 \end{vmatrix}}{10} = \frac{-16}{10} = -\frac{8}{5}$$

Therefore, the solution is $\left(\frac{4}{5}, -\frac{3}{2}, -\frac{8}{5}\right)$. Check this solution in the original system of equations. ◢

When using Cramer's Rule, remember that the method *does not* apply if the determinant of the coefficient matrix is zero.

Area of a Triangle

Throughout this chapter we have discussed several applications of matrices and determinants that involve a system of linear equations. In this section you will look at some *other* types of applications involving determinants and matrices.

The first gives a formula for finding the area of a triangle whose vertices are given by three points in a rectangular coordinate system.

AREA OF A TRIANGLE

The area of a triangle with vertices (x_1, y_1), (x_2, y_2), and (x_3, y_3) is given by

$$\text{Area} = \pm\frac{1}{2}\begin{vmatrix} x_1 & y_1 & 1 \\ x_2 & y_2 & 1 \\ x_3 & y_3 & 1 \end{vmatrix}$$

where the symbol ($\pm$) indicates that the appropriate sign should be chosen to yield a positive area.

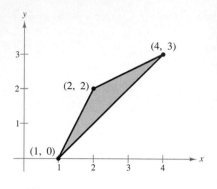

FIGURE 9.1

REMARK To see the benefit of the "determinant formula for area," you should try finding the area of the triangle in Example 3 using the standard formula: area $= \frac{1}{2}$(base)(height).

EXAMPLE 3   Finding the Area of a Triangle

Find the area of the triangle whose vertices are $(1, 0)$, $(2, 2)$, and $(4, 3)$, as shown in Figure 9.1.

Solution

Choose $(x_1, y_1) = (1, 0)$, $(x_2, y_2) = (2, 2)$, and $(x_3, y_3) = (4, 3)$. Then, to find the area of the triangle, evaluate the determinant

$$
\begin{vmatrix} x_1 & y_1 & 1 \\ x_2 & y_2 & 1 \\ x_3 & y_3 & 1 \end{vmatrix} = \begin{vmatrix} 1 & 0 & 1 \\ 2 & 2 & 1 \\ 4 & 3 & 1 \end{vmatrix}
$$

$$
= 1 \begin{vmatrix} 2 & 1 \\ 3 & 1 \end{vmatrix} - 0 \begin{vmatrix} 2 & 1 \\ 4 & 1 \end{vmatrix} + 1 \begin{vmatrix} 2 & 2 \\ 4 & 3 \end{vmatrix}
$$

$$
= 1(-1) - 0(-2) + 1(-2)
$$

$$
= -3.
$$

Using this value, you conclude that the area of the triangle is

$$
\text{Area} = -\frac{1}{2} \begin{vmatrix} 1 & 0 & 1 \\ 2 & 2 & 1 \\ 4 & 3 & 1 \end{vmatrix} = -\frac{1}{2}(-3) = \frac{3}{2}.
$$

Lines in the Plane

Suppose the three points in Example 3 had been on the same line. What would have happened had you applied the area formula to three such points? The answer is that the determinant would have been zero. Consider, for instance, the three collinear points $(0, 1)$, $(2, 2)$, and $(4, 3)$, as shown in Figure 9.2. The area of the "triangle" that has these three points as vertices is

$$
\frac{1}{2} \begin{vmatrix} 0 & 1 & 1 \\ 2 & 2 & 1 \\ 4 & 3 & 1 \end{vmatrix} = \frac{1}{2} \left(0 \begin{vmatrix} 2 & 1 \\ 3 & 1 \end{vmatrix} - 1 \begin{vmatrix} 2 & 1 \\ 4 & 1 \end{vmatrix} + 1 \begin{vmatrix} 2 & 2 \\ 4 & 3 \end{vmatrix} \right)
$$

$$
= \frac{1}{2}[0(-1) - 1(-2) + 1(-2)] = 0.
$$

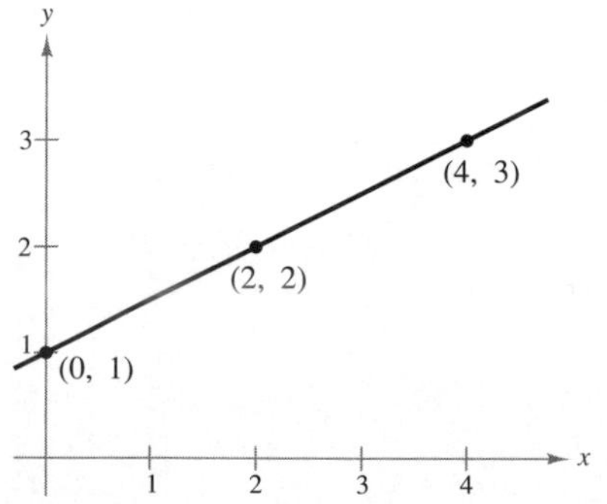

FIGURE 9.2

We generalize this result as follows.

TEST FOR COLLINEAR POINTS

Three points (x_1, y_1), (x_2, y_2), and (x_3, y_3) are collinear (lie on the same line), if and only if

$$\begin{vmatrix} x_1 & y_1 & 1 \\ x_2 & y_2 & 1 \\ x_3 & y_3 & 1 \end{vmatrix} = 0.$$

EXAMPLE 4 Testing for Collinear Points

Determine whether the points $(-2, -2)$, $(1, 1)$, and $(7, 5)$ lie on the same line. (See Figure 9.3.)

Solution

Letting $(x_1, y_1) = (-2, -2)$, $(x_2, y_2) = (1, 1)$, and $(x_3, y_3) = (7, 5)$, you have

$$\begin{vmatrix} x_1 & y_1 & 1 \\ x_2 & y_2 & 1 \\ x_3 & y_3 & 1 \end{vmatrix} = \begin{vmatrix} -2 & -2 & 1 \\ 1 & 1 & 1 \\ 7 & 5 & 1 \end{vmatrix}$$

$$= -2 \begin{vmatrix} 1 & 1 \\ 5 & 1 \end{vmatrix} - (-2) \begin{vmatrix} 1 & 1 \\ 7 & 1 \end{vmatrix} + 1 \begin{vmatrix} 1 & 1 \\ 7 & 5 \end{vmatrix}$$

$$= -2(-4) - (-2)(-6) + 1(-2)$$

$$= -6.$$

Because the value of this determinant is *not* zero, you conclude that the three points do not lie on the same line.

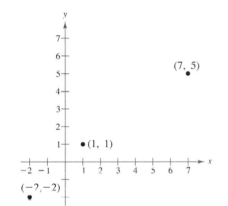

FIGURE 9.3

The test for collinear points can be adapted to another use. That is, if you are given two points in a rectangular coordinate system, then you can find the equation of the line passing through the two points as follows.

TWO-POINT FORM OF THE EQUATION OF A LINE

An equation of the line passing through the distinct points (x_1, y_1) and (x_2, y_2) is given by

$$\begin{vmatrix} x & y & 1 \\ x_1 & y_1 & 1 \\ x_2 & y_2 & 1 \end{vmatrix} = 0.$$

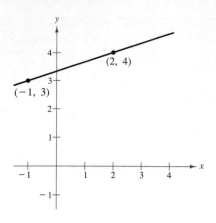

FIGURE 9.4

EXAMPLE 5 Finding an Equation of the Line Passing Through Two Points

Find an equation of the line passing through the two points (2, 4) and $(-1, 3)$, as shown in Figure 9.4.

Solution

Applying the determinant formula for the equation of the line passing through these two points produces

$$\begin{vmatrix} x & y & 1 \\ 2 & 4 & 1 \\ -1 & 3 & 1 \end{vmatrix} = 0.$$

To evaluate this determinant, expand by cofactors along the first row to obtain the following.

$$x \begin{vmatrix} 4 & 1 \\ 3 & 1 \end{vmatrix} - y \begin{vmatrix} 2 & 1 \\ -1 & 1 \end{vmatrix} + 1 \begin{vmatrix} 2 & 4 \\ -1 & 3 \end{vmatrix} = x - 3y + 10 = 0$$

Therefore, an equation of the line is

$$x - 3y + 10 = 0.$$

Cryptography

A **cryptogram** is a message written according to a secret code. (The Greek word "kryptos" means "hidden.") Next, we describe a method for using matrix multiplication to **encode** and **decode** messages.

We begin by assigning a number to each letter in the alphabet (with 0 assigned to a blank space) as follows.

0 = ▨	9 = I	18 = R
1 = A	10 = J	19 = S
2 = B	11 = K	20 = T
3 = C	12 = L	21 = U
4 = D	13 = M	22 = V
5 = E	14 = N	23 = W
6 = F	15 = O	24 = X
7 = G	16 = P	25 = Y
8 = H	17 = Q	26 = Z

Then the message is converted to numbers and partitioned into **uncoded row matrices,** each having n entries, as demonstrated in Example 6.

EXAMPLE 6 Forming Uncoded Row Matrices

Write the uncoded row matrices of order 1×3 for the message MEET ME MONDAY.

Solution

Partitioning the message (including blank spaces, but ignoring other punctuation) into groups of three produces the following uncoded row matrices.

[13 5 5] [20 0 13] [5 0 13] [15 14 4] [1 25 0]
M E E   T   M   E   M   O N D   A Y

Note that a blank space is used to fill out the last uncoded row matrix.

To **encode** a message you choose an $n \times n$ invertible matrix A and multiply the uncoded row matrices (on the right) by A to obtain **coded row matrices.** This process is demonstrated in Example 7.

EXAMPLE 7   Encoding a Message

Use the following matrix to encode the message MEET ME MONDAY.

$$A = \begin{bmatrix} 1 & -2 & 2 \\ -1 & 1 & 3 \\ 1 & -1 & -4 \end{bmatrix}$$

Solution

The coded row matrices are obtained by multiplying each of the uncoded row matrices found in Example 6 by the matrix A as follows.

Uncoded Row Matrix	Encoding Matrix A	Coded Row Matrix
$[13 \quad 5 \quad 5]$	$\begin{bmatrix} 1 & -2 & 2 \\ -1 & 1 & 3 \\ 1 & -1 & -4 \end{bmatrix}$	$= [13 \quad -26 \quad 21]$
$[20 \quad 0 \quad 13]$	$\begin{bmatrix} 1 & -2 & 2 \\ -1 & 1 & 3 \\ 1 & -1 & -4 \end{bmatrix}$	$= [33 \quad -53 \quad -12]$
$[5 \quad 0 \quad 13]$	$\begin{bmatrix} 1 & -2 & 2 \\ -1 & 1 & 3 \\ 1 & -1 & -4 \end{bmatrix}$	$= [18 \quad -23 \quad -42]$
$[15 \quad 14 \quad 4]$	$\begin{bmatrix} 1 & -2 & 2 \\ -1 & 1 & 3 \\ 1 & -1 & -4 \end{bmatrix}$	$= [5 \quad -20 \quad 56]$
$[1 \quad 25 \quad 0]$	$\begin{bmatrix} 1 & -2 & 2 \\ -1 & 1 & 3 \\ 1 & -1 & -4 \end{bmatrix}$	$= [-24 \quad 23 \quad 77]$

Thus, the sequence of coded row matrices is

$$[13 \quad -26 \quad 21][33 \quad -53 \quad -12][18 \quad -23 \quad -42][5 \quad -20 \quad 56][-24 \quad 23 \quad 77].$$

Finally, removing the matrix notation produces the following cryptogram.

$$13 \quad -26 \quad 21 \quad 33 \quad -53 \quad -12 \quad 18 \quad -23 \quad -42 \quad 5 \quad -20 \quad 56 \quad -24 \quad 23 \quad 77$$

For those who do not know the matrix A, decoding the cryptogram found in Example 7 is difficult. But for an authorized receiver who knows the matrix A, decoding is simple. The receiver need only multiply the coded row matrices by A^{-1} to retrieve the uncoded row matrices. In other words, if

$$X = [x_1 \quad x_2 \quad \cdots \quad x_n]$$

is an uncoded $1 \times n$ matrix, then $Y = XA$ is the corresponding encoded matrix. The receiver of the encoded matrix can decode Y by multiplying on the right by A^{-1} to obtain

$$YA^{-1} = (XA)A^{-1} = X.$$

This procedure is demonstrated in Example 8.

EXAMPLE 8   Decoding a Message

Use the inverse of the matrix

$$A = \begin{bmatrix} 1 & -2 & 2 \\ -1 & 1 & 3 \\ 1 & -1 & -4 \end{bmatrix}$$

to decode the cryptogram

$$13 \quad -26 \quad 21 \quad 33 \quad -53 \quad -12 \quad 18 \quad -23 \quad -42 \quad 5 \quad -20 \quad 56 \quad -24 \quad 23 \quad 77.$$

Solution

Begin by using Gauss-Jordan elimination to find A^{-1}.

$$[A \;\vdots\; I] \qquad\qquad\qquad [I \;\vdots\; A^{-1}]$$

$$\begin{bmatrix} 1 & -2 & 2 & \vdots & 1 & 0 & 0 \\ -1 & 1 & 3 & \vdots & 0 & 1 & 0 \\ 1 & -1 & -4 & \vdots & 0 & 0 & 1 \end{bmatrix} \rightarrow \begin{bmatrix} 1 & 0 & 0 & \vdots & -1 & -10 & -8 \\ 0 & 1 & 0 & \vdots & -1 & -6 & -5 \\ 0 & 0 & 1 & \vdots & 0 & -1 & -1 \end{bmatrix}$$

Now, to decode the message, partition the message into groups of three to form the coded row matrices

$$[13 \quad -26 \quad 21][33 \quad -53 \quad -12][18 \quad -23 \quad -42][5 \quad -20 \quad 56][-24 \quad 23 \quad 77].$$

Then multiply each coded row matrix by A^{-1} (on the right) to obtain the decoded row matrices.

Coded Row Matrix	Decoding Matrix A^{-1}	Decoded Row Matrix
$[13 \quad -26 \quad 21]$	$\begin{bmatrix} -1 & -10 & -8 \\ -1 & -6 & -5 \\ 0 & -1 & -1 \end{bmatrix}$	$= [13 \quad 5 \quad 5]$
$[33 \quad -53 \quad -12]$	$\begin{bmatrix} -1 & -10 & -8 \\ -1 & -6 & -5 \\ 0 & -1 & -1 \end{bmatrix}$	$= [20 \quad 0 \quad 13]$
$[18 \quad -23 \quad -42]$	$\begin{bmatrix} -1 & -10 & -8 \\ -1 & -6 & -5 \\ 0 & -1 & -1 \end{bmatrix}$	$= [5 \quad 0 \quad 13]$
$[5 \quad -20 \quad 56]$	$\begin{bmatrix} -1 & -10 & -8 \\ -1 & -6 & -5 \\ 0 & -1 & -1 \end{bmatrix}$	$= [15 \quad 14 \quad 4]$
$[-24 \quad 23 \quad 77]$	$\begin{bmatrix} -1 & -10 & -8 \\ -1 & -6 & -5 \\ 0 & -1 & -1 \end{bmatrix}$	$= [1 \quad 25 \quad 0]$

Thus, the sequence of decoded row matrices is

$$[13 \quad 5 \quad 5][20 \quad 0 \quad 13][5 \quad 0 \quad 13][15 \quad 14 \quad 4][1 \quad 25 \quad 0]$$

and the message is as follows.

$$[13 \quad 5 \quad 5] \quad [20 \quad 0 \quad 13] \quad [5 \quad 0 \quad 13] \quad [15 \quad 14 \quad 4] \quad [1 \quad 25 \quad 0]$$

M E E T ▨ M E ▨ M O N D A Y ▨

DISCUSSION

PROBLEM

Comparing Techniques

In Chapters 8 and 9, we have looked at several techniques for solving a system of linear equations.

1. Elimination method using equations (Section 8.3)
2. Gaussian elimination with back-substitution (Section 9.1)
3. Gauss-Jordan elimination (Section 9.1)
4. Inverse matrix method (Section 9.3)
5. Cramer's Rule (Section 9.6)

Write a short paper describing the advantages and disadvantages of each method. Include one example problem using all methods.

WARM UP

The following warm-up exercises involve skills that were covered in earlier sections. You will use these skills in the exercise set for this section.

In Exercises 1–4, solve the system of equations using Gaussian elimination with back-substitution or Gauss-Jordan elimination.

1. $\begin{aligned} x - 3y &= -2 \\ x + y &= 2 \end{aligned}$

2. $\begin{aligned} -x + 3y &= 5 \\ 4x - y &= 2 \end{aligned}$

3. $\begin{aligned} x + 2y - z &= 7 \\ -y - z &= 4 \\ 4x - z &= 16 \end{aligned}$

4. $\begin{aligned} 3x \quad + 6z &= 0 \\ -2x + y \quad &= 5 \\ y + 2z &= 3 \end{aligned}$

In Exercises 5–10, evaluate the determinant.

5. $\begin{vmatrix} 10 & 8 \\ -6 & -4 \end{vmatrix}$

6. $\begin{vmatrix} -7 & 14 \\ 2 & 3 \end{vmatrix}$

7. $\begin{vmatrix} 1 & 0 & -2 \\ 0 & 1 & 0 \\ -2 & 0 & 1 \end{vmatrix}$

8. $\begin{vmatrix} 0 & 3 & 1 \\ 5 & -2 & 1 \\ 1 & 6 & 1 \end{vmatrix}$

9. $\begin{vmatrix} 0 & -2 & 1 & 0 \\ -2 & 0 & 5 & -1 \\ 1 & 5 & 0 & 2 \\ 0 & -1 & 2 & 0 \end{vmatrix}$

10. $\begin{vmatrix} 1 & 0 & -2 & 1 \\ 0 & 2 & 5 & 1 \\ 3 & -3 & 2 & 1 \\ 0 & 0 & 4 & 1 \end{vmatrix}$

EXERCISES for Section 9.6

In Exercises 1–10, use Cramer's Rule to solve (if possible) the system of equations.

1. $\begin{aligned} x + 2y &= 5 \\ -x + y &= 1 \end{aligned}$

2. $\begin{aligned} 2x - y &= -10 \\ 3x + 2y &= -1 \end{aligned}$

3. $\begin{aligned} 3x + 4y &= -2 \\ 5x + 3y &= 4 \end{aligned}$

4. $\begin{aligned} 18x + 12y &= 13 \\ 30x + 24y &= 23 \end{aligned}$

5. $\begin{aligned} 20x + 8y &= 11 \\ 12x - 24y &= 21 \end{aligned}$

6. $\begin{aligned} 13x - 6y &= 17 \\ 26x - 12y &= 8 \end{aligned}$

7. $\begin{aligned} -0.4x + 0.8y &= 1.6 \\ 2x - 4y &= 5 \end{aligned}$

8. $\begin{aligned} -0.4x + 0.8y &= 1.6 \\ 0.2x + 0.3y &= 2.2 \end{aligned}$

9. $\begin{aligned} 3x + 6y &= 5 \\ 6x + 14y &= 11 \end{aligned}$

10. $\begin{aligned} 3x + 2y &= 1 \\ 2x + 10y &= 6 \end{aligned}$

In Exercises 11–20, use Cramer's Rule to solve (if possible) the given system for x. You do *not* have to solve the system for the other variables.

11. $\begin{aligned} 4x - y + z &= -5 \\ 2x + 2y + 3z &= 10 \\ 5x - 2y + 6z &= 1 \end{aligned}$

12. $\begin{aligned} 4x - 2y + 3z &= -2 \\ 2x + 2y + 5z &= 16 \\ 8x - 5y - 2z &= 4 \end{aligned}$

13. $\begin{aligned} 3x + 4y + 4z &= 11 \\ 4x - 4y + 6z &= 11 \\ 6x - 6y &= 3 \end{aligned}$

14. $\begin{aligned} 14x - 21y - 7z &= 10 \\ -4x + 2y - 2z &= 4 \\ 56x - 21y + 7z &= 5 \end{aligned}$

15. $\begin{aligned} 3x + 3y + 5z &= 1 \\ 3x + 5y + 9z &= 2 \\ 5x + 9y + 17z &= 4 \end{aligned}$

16. $\begin{aligned} 2x + 3y + 5z &= 4 \\ 3x + 5y + 9z &= 7 \\ 5x + 9y + 17z &= 13 \end{aligned}$

17. $5x - 3y + 2z = 2$
$2x + 2y - 3z = 3$
$x - 7y + 8z = -4$

18. $3x + 2y + 5z = 4$
$4x - 3y - 4z = 1$
$-8x + 2y + 3z = 0$

19. $7x - 3y \quad + 2w = 41$
$-2x + y \quad - w = -13$
$4x \quad + z - 2w = 12$
$-x + y \quad - w = -8$

20. $2x + 5y \quad + w = 11$
$x + 4y + 2z - 2w = -7$
$2x - 2y + 5z + w = 3$
$x \quad - 3w = 1$

21. **Circuit Analysis**   Consider the circuit in the figure. The currents I_1, I_2, and I_3 in amperes are given by the solution to the system of linear equations

$-4I_1 \quad + 10I_3 = 5$
$5I_2 + 10I_3 = 70$
$I_1 - I_2 + I_3 = 0.$

Use Cramer's Rule to find the three currents.

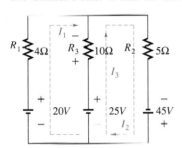

Figure for 21

22. **Circuit Analysis**   Consider the circuit in the figure. The currents I_1, I_2, and I_3 in amperes are given by the solution to the system of linear equations

$4I_1 \quad + 8I_3 - 2$
$2I_2 + 8I_3 = 6$
$I_1 + I_2 - I_3 = 0.$

Use Cramer's Rule to find the three currents.

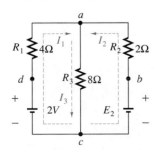

Figure for 22

23. **Maximum Social Security Contribution**   The maximum Social Security contributions for an employee between 1981 and 1989 are shown in the figure. (The figure shows the amount contributed by the *employee*. This amount is matched by the employer.) The least squares regression line $y = a + bt$ for this data is found by solving the system

$9a + 45b = 24.983$
$45a + 285b = 137.012$

where y is the contribution in 1000s of dollars and t is the calendar year with $t = 1$ corresponding to 1981. Use Cramer's Rule to solve this system, and use the result to approximate the maximum Social Security contribution in 1992. (*Source:* U.S. Social Security Administration)

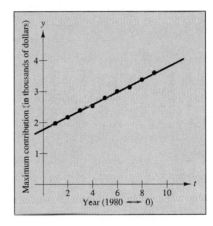

Figure for 23

24. **Pulley System**   A system of pulleys that is assumed frictionless and without mass is loaded with 192-pound and 64-pound weights (see figure). The tensions t_1 and t_2 in the ropes and the acceleration a of the 64-pound weight are found by solving the system

$t_1 - 2t_2 \quad = 0$
$t_1 \quad - 3a = 192$
$t_2 + 2a = 64$

where t_1 and t_2 are measured in pounds and a is in feet per second squared. Use Cramer's Rule to find the acceleration a of the system.

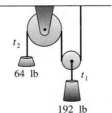

Figure for 24

In Exercises 25–34, use a determinant to find the area of the triangle with given vertices.

25. (0, 0), (3, 1), (1, 5)

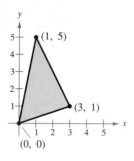

(1, 5)
(3, 1)
(0, 0)

26. (0, 0), (5, −2), (4, 5)

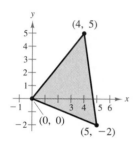

(4, 5)
(0, 0)
(5, −2)

27. (−2, −3), (2, −3), (0, 4)

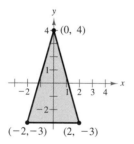

(0, 4)
(−2, −3)   (2, −3)

28. (−2, 1), (3, −1), (1, 6)

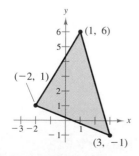

(1, 6)
(−2, 1)
(3, −1)

29. $\left(0, \frac{1}{2}\right)$, $\left(\frac{5}{2}, 0\right)$ (4, 3)

30. (−4, −5), (6, −1), (6, 10)

31. (−2, 4), (2, 3), (−1, 5)

32. (0, −2), (−1, 4), (3, 5)

33. (−3, 5), (2, 6), (3, −5)

34. (−2, 4), (1, 5), (3, −2)

35. *Area of a Region*   A large region of forest has been infested with gypsy moths. The region is roughly triangular, as shown in the figure. From the northernmost vertex *A* of the region, the distance to vertex *B* is 25 miles south and 10 miles east, and the distance to vertex *C* is 20 miles south and 28 miles east. Approximate the number of square miles in this region.

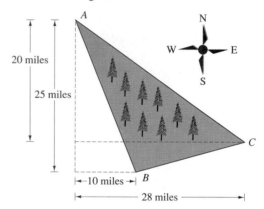

Figure for 35

36. *Area of a Region*   Suppose you purchased a triangular tract of land, as shown in the figure. To estimate the number of square feet in the tract, you start at one vertex and walk 65 feet east and 50 feet north to the second vertex. Then, from the second vertex you walk 85 feet west and 30 feet north to the third vertex. How many square feet are there in the tract of land?

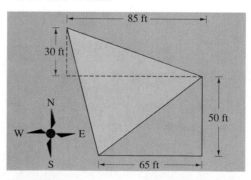

Figure for 36

In Exercises 37–42, use a determinant to ascertain if the points are collinear.

37. $(3, -1), (0, -3), (12, 5)$

38. $(-3, -5), (6, 1), (10, 2)$

39. $\left(2, -\tfrac{1}{2}\right), (-4, 4), (6, -3)$

40. $(0, 1), (4, -2), (-8, 7)$

41. $(0, 2), (1, 2.4), (-1, 1.6)$

42. $(2, 3), (3, 3.5), (-1, 2)$

In Exercises 43–48, use a determinant to find an equation of the line through the given points (x_1, y_1) and (x_2, y_2).

43. $(0, 0), (5, 3)$

44. $(0, 0), (-2, 2)$

45. $(-4, 3), (2, 1)$

46. $(10, 7), (-2, \ \ 7)$

47. $\left(-\tfrac{1}{2}, 3\right), \left(\tfrac{5}{2}, 1\right)$

48. $\left(\tfrac{2}{3}, 4\right) (6, 12)$

In Exercises 49–52, write a cryptogram for each message using the matrix

$$A = \begin{bmatrix} 1 & 2 & 2 \\ 3 & 7 & 9 \\ -1 & -4 & -7 \end{bmatrix}.$$

49. LANDING SUCCESSFUL

50. BEAM ME UP SCOTTY

51. HAPPY BIRTHDAY

52. OPERATION OVERLOAD

In Exercises 53 and 54, decode the cryptogram by using the inverse of matrix A from Exercises 49–52.

53. $20 \quad 17 \quad -15 \quad -12 \quad -56 \quad -104 \quad 1 \quad -25 \quad -65$
$62 \quad 143 \quad 181$

54. $13 \quad -9 \quad -59 \quad 61 \quad 112 \quad 106 \quad -17 \quad -73 \quad -131$
$11 \quad 24 \quad 29 \quad 65 \quad 144 \quad 172$

REVIEW EXERCISES for Chapter 9

In Exercises 1–12, use matrices and elementary row operations to solve the system of equations.

1. $5x + 4y = \ \ 2$
$-x + \ y = -22$

2. $2x - 5y = 2$
$3x - 7y = 1$

3. $0.2x - 0.1y = \ \ 0.07$
$0.4x - 0.5y = -0.01$

4. $2x + y = \ \ 0.3$
$3x - y = -1.3$

5. $-x + \ y + 2z = \ \ 1$
$2x + 3y + \ z = -2$
$5x + 4y + 2z = \ \ 4$

6. $2x + 3y + \ z = \ 10$
$2x - 3y - 3z = \ 22$
$4x - 2y + 3z = -2$

7. $2x + 3y + \ 3z = \ 3$
$6x + 6y + 12z = 13$
$12x + 9y - \ z = \ 2$

8. $4x + 4y + 4z = 5$
$4x - 2y - 8z = 1$
$5x + 3y + 8z = 6$

9. $2x + \ y + 2z = 4$
$2x + 2y \quad = 5$
$2x - \ y + 6z = 2$

10. $3x + 21y - 29z = -1$
$2x + 15y - 21z = \ \ 0$

11. $x + 2y + \ 6z = \ 1$
$2x + 5y + 15z = \ 4$
$3x + \ y + \ 3z = -6$

12. $x + 2y + \quad\quad w = 3$
$-3y + 3z \quad = 0$
$4x + 4y + \ z + 2w = 0$
$2x \quad\quad + \ z \quad = 3$

In Exercises 13–20, perform the indicated matrix operations (if possible).

13. $\begin{bmatrix} 2 & 1 & 0 \\ 0 & 5 & -4 \end{bmatrix} - 3\begin{bmatrix} 5 & 3 & -6 \\ 0 & -2 & 5 \end{bmatrix}$

14. $-2\begin{bmatrix} 1 & 2 \\ 5 & -4 \\ 6 & 0 \end{bmatrix} + 8\begin{bmatrix} 7 & 1 \\ 1 & 2 \\ 1 & 4 \end{bmatrix}$

15. $\begin{bmatrix} 1 & 2 \\ 5 & -4 \\ 6 & 0 \end{bmatrix}\begin{bmatrix} 6 & -2 & 8 \\ 4 & 0 & 0 \end{bmatrix}$

16. $\begin{bmatrix} 1 & 5 & 6 \\ 2 & -4 & 0 \end{bmatrix}\begin{bmatrix} 6 & -2 & 8 \\ 4 & 0 & 0 \end{bmatrix}$

17. $\begin{bmatrix} 1 & 5 & 6 \\ 2 & -4 & 0 \end{bmatrix}\begin{bmatrix} 6 & 4 \\ -2 & 0 \\ 8 & 0 \end{bmatrix}$

18. $\begin{bmatrix} 4 \\ 6 \end{bmatrix}[6 \ -2]$

19. $\begin{bmatrix} 1 & 3 & 2 \\ 0 & 2 & -4 \\ 0 & 0 & 3 \end{bmatrix}\begin{bmatrix} 4 & -3 & 2 \\ 0 & 3 & -1 \\ 0 & 0 & 2 \end{bmatrix}$

20. $\begin{bmatrix} 2 & 1 \\ 6 & 0 \end{bmatrix}\left(\begin{bmatrix} 4 & 2 \\ -3 & 1 \end{bmatrix} + \begin{bmatrix} -2 & 4 \\ 0 & 4 \end{bmatrix}\right)$

In Exercises 21–24, solve for X given

$$A = \begin{bmatrix} -4 & 0 \\ 1 & -5 \\ -3 & 2 \end{bmatrix} \quad \text{and} \quad B = \begin{bmatrix} 1 & 2 \\ -2 & 1 \\ 4 & 4 \end{bmatrix}.$$

21. $X = 3A - 2B$

22. $6X = 4A + 3B$

23. $3X + 2A = B$

24. $2A - 5B = 3X$

25. Write the system of linear equations represented by the matrix equation

$$\begin{bmatrix} 5 & 4 \\ -1 & 1 \end{bmatrix}\begin{bmatrix} x \\ y \end{bmatrix} = \begin{bmatrix} 2 \\ -22 \end{bmatrix}.$$

26. Write the matrix equation $AX = B$ for the following system of linear equations.

$$\begin{aligned} 2x + 3y + z &= 10 \\ 2x - 3y - 3z &= 22 \\ 4x - 2y + 3z &= -2 \end{aligned}$$

In Exercises 27–30, find the inverse of the matrix (if it exists).

27. $\begin{bmatrix} 2 & 6 \\ 3 & -6 \end{bmatrix}$

28. $\begin{bmatrix} 3 & -10 \\ 4 & 2 \end{bmatrix}$

29. $\begin{bmatrix} 2 & 0 & 3 \\ -1 & 1 & 1 \\ 2 & -2 & 1 \end{bmatrix}$

30. $\begin{bmatrix} 1 & 4 & 6 \\ 2 & -3 & 1 \\ -1 & 18 & 16 \end{bmatrix}$

In Exercises 31–34, evaluate the determinant.

31. $\begin{vmatrix} 50 & -30 \\ 10 & 5 \end{vmatrix}$

32. $\begin{vmatrix} 8 & 5 \\ 2 & -4 \end{vmatrix}$

33. $\begin{vmatrix} 3 & 0 & -4 & 0 \\ 0 & 8 & 1 & 2 \\ 6 & 1 & 8 & 2 \\ 0 & 3 & -4 & 1 \end{vmatrix}$

34. $\begin{vmatrix} -5 & 6 & 0 & 0 \\ 0 & 1 & -1 & 2 \\ -3 & 4 & -5 & 1 \\ 1 & 6 & 0 & 3 \end{vmatrix}$

In Exercises 35–42, solve (if possible) the system of linear equations using (a) the inverse of the coefficient matrix and (b) Cramer's Rule.

35. $\begin{aligned} x + 2y &= -1 \\ 3x + 4y &= -5 \end{aligned}$

36. $\begin{aligned} x + 3y &= 23 \\ -6x + 2y &= -18 \end{aligned}$

37. $\begin{aligned} -3x - 3y - 4z &= 2 \\ y + z &= -1 \\ 4x + 3y + 4z &= -1 \end{aligned}$

38. $\begin{aligned} x - 3y - 2z &= 8 \\ -2x + 7y + 3z &= -19 \\ x - y - 3z &= 3 \end{aligned}$

39. $\begin{aligned} x + 3y + 2z &= 2 \\ -2x - 5y - z &= 10 \\ 2x + 4y &= -12 \end{aligned}$

40. $\begin{aligned} 2x + 4y &= -12 \\ 3x + 4y - 2z &= -14 \\ -x + y + 2z &= -6 \end{aligned}$

41. $\begin{aligned} 2x + 3y - 4z &= 1 \\ x - y + 2z &= -4 \\ 3x + 7y - 10z &= 0 \end{aligned}$

42. $\begin{aligned} -x + y + z &= 6 \\ 4x - 3y + z &= 20 \\ 2x - y + 3z &= 8 \end{aligned}$

In Exercises 43–46, use a determinant to find the area of the triangle with the given vertices.

43. $(1, 0), (5, 0), (5, 8)$

44. $(-4, 0), (4, 0), (0, 6)$

45. $(1, 2), (4, -5), (3, 2)$

46. $\left(\frac{3}{2}, 1\right), \left(4, -\frac{1}{2}\right), (4, 2)$

In Exercises 47–50, use a determinant to find an equation of the line through the given points.

47. $(-4, 0), (4, 4)$

48. $(2, 5), (6, -1)$

49. $\left(-\frac{5}{2}, 3\right), \left(\frac{7}{2}, 1\right)$

50. $(-0.8, 0.2), (0.7, 3.2)$

51. *Mixture Problem*   A florist wants to arrange a dozen flowers consisting of two varieties—carnations and roses. Carnations cost $0.75 each and roses cost $1.50 each. How many of each should the florist use in order for the arrangement to cost $12.00?

52. *Mixture Problem*   One hundred gallons of a 60% acid solution are obtained by mixing a 75% solution with a 50% solution. How many gallons of each must be used to obtain the desired mixture?

53. *Fitting a Parabola to Three Points*   Find an equation of the parabola $y = ax^2 + bx + c$ passing through the points $(-1, 2), (0, 3),$ and $(1, 6)$.

54. *Break-Even Point*   A small business invests $25,000 in equipment to produce a product. Each unit of the product costs $3.75 to produce and is sold for $5.25. How many items must be sold before the business breaks even?

55. If A is a 3×3 matrix and $|A| = 2$, then what is the value of $|4A|$? Give the reason for your answer.

56. Verify that

$$\begin{vmatrix} a_{11} & a_{12} & a_{13} \\ a_{21} & a_{22} & a_{23} \\ a_{31} + c_1 & a_{32} + c_2 & a_{33} + c_3 \end{vmatrix}$$

$$= \begin{vmatrix} a_{11} & a_{12} & a_{13} \\ a_{21} & a_{22} & a_{23} \\ a_{31} & a_{32} & a_{33} \end{vmatrix} + \begin{vmatrix} a_{11} & a_{12} & a_{13} \\ a_{21} & a_{22} & a_{23} \\ c_1 & c_2 & c_3 \end{vmatrix}.$$

OVERVIEW

This chapter discusses four topics related to number patterns: sequences, mathematical induction, the binomial theorem, and probability.

In the first three sections, you will learn how sequences can be used to model real-life situations. For instance, Exercise 55 on page 687 uses a geometric sequence to model the profit earned by H. J. Heinz Company from 1980 through 1989.

The last two sections contain a brief introduction to probability. Even with such a brief presentation, however, you can get an idea of the broad applicability of this topic. For instance, Example 11 on page 725 shows how probability can be used in quality control, and Exercise 52 on page 730 shows how probability is used in market surveys.

Sequences, Counting Principles, and Probability

10.1 Sequences and Summation Notation

Sequences / Factorial Notation / Summation Notation / The Sum of a Sequence / Applications

Sequences

In mathematics, the word *sequence* is used in much the same way as it is in ordinary English. When we say that a collection of objects is listed *in sequence*, we usually mean that the collection is ordered so that it has a first member, a second member, a third member, and so on.

$$1, 3, 5, 7, \ldots \qquad \text{and} \qquad \frac{1}{2}, \frac{1}{4}, \frac{1}{8}, \frac{1}{16}, \ldots$$

A sequence is a *function* whose domain is the set of positive integers. However, we usually represent a sequence by subscript notation, rather than by the standard function notation. For instance, we write the terms of the sequence

$$f(1), f(2), f(3), f(4), \ldots, f(n), \ldots$$

as

$$a_1, a_2, a_3, a_4, \ldots, a_n, \ldots$$

Note that subscripts make up the domain of the sequence, and they serve to identify the location of a term within the sequence. For instance, a_4 is the 4th term of the sequence and a_n is the **nth term** of the sequence. The entire sequence is sometimes denoted by the short form $\{a_n\}$.

655

DEFINITION OF A SEQUENCE

An **infinite sequence** $\{a_n\}$ is a function whose domain is the set of positive integers. The function values

$$a_1, a_2, a_3, a_4, \ldots, a_n, \ldots$$

are the **terms** of the sequence. If the domain of the function consists of the first n positive integers only, then the sequence is a **finite sequence.**

On occasion it is convenient to begin subscripting a sequence with 0 instead of 1 so that the terms of the sequence become

$$a_0, a_1, a_2, a_3, a_4, \ldots, a_n, \ldots.$$

In such cases, we still call a_n the nth term of the sequence, even though it occupies the $(n + 1)$th position in the sequence.

EXAMPLE 1   Finding Terms in a Sequence

a. The first four terms of the sequence whose nth term is $a_n = 3n - 2$ are:

$$a_1 = 3(1) - 2 = 1$$
$$a_2 = 3(2) - 2 = 4$$
$$a_3 = 3(3) - 2 = 7$$
$$a_4 = 3(4) - 2 = 10.$$

b. The first four terms of the sequence whose nth term is $a_n = 3 + (-1)^n$ are:

$$a_1 = 3 + (-1)^1 = 3 - 1 = 2$$
$$a_2 = 3 + (-1)^2 = 3 + 1 = 4$$
$$a_3 = 3 + (-1)^3 = 3 - 1 = 2$$
$$a_4 = 3 + (-1)^4 = 3 + 1 = 4.$$

The terms of a sequence need not all be positive, as shown in part (b) of Example 2.

EXAMPLE 2   Finding Terms in a Sequence

a. The first four terms of the sequence whose nth term is $a_n = \dfrac{2n}{(1+n)}$ are:

$$a_1 = \frac{2(1)}{1+1} = \frac{2}{2} = 1$$

$$a_2 = \frac{2(2)}{1+2} = \frac{4}{3}$$

$$a_3 = \frac{2(3)}{1+3} = \frac{6}{4} = \frac{3}{2}$$

$$a_4 = \frac{2(4)}{1+4} = \frac{8}{5}.$$

b. The first four terms of the sequence whose nth term is $a_n = \dfrac{(-1)^n}{(2n-1)}$ are:

$$a_1 = \frac{(-1)^1}{2(1)-1} = \frac{-1}{2-1} = -1$$

$$a_2 = \frac{(-1)^2}{2(2)-1} = \frac{1}{4-1} = \frac{1}{3}$$

$$a_3 = \frac{(-1)^3}{2(3)-1} = \frac{-1}{6-1} = -\frac{1}{5}$$

$$a_4 = \frac{(-1)^4}{2(4)-1} = \frac{1}{8-1} = \frac{1}{7}.$$

REMARK   Try finding the first four terms of the sequence whose nth term is

$$a_n = \frac{(-1)^{n+1}}{2n-1}.$$

How do they differ from the first four terms of the sequence in Example 2(b)?

It is important to realize that simply listing the first few terms is not sufficient to define a unique sequence. Consider the following sequences, both of which have the same first three terms.

$$\frac{1}{2}, \frac{1}{4}, \frac{1}{8}, \frac{1}{16}, \dots, \frac{1}{2^n}, \dots$$

$$\frac{1}{2}, \frac{1}{4}, \frac{1}{8}, \frac{1}{15}, \dots, \frac{6}{(n+1)(n^2-n+6)}, \dots$$

When given the first few terms of a sequence, the best you can do is write an *apparent* nth term for the sequence. There are likely other nth terms.

EXAMPLE 3   Finding the *n*th Term of a Sequence

Write an expression for the apparent nth term (a_n) of each of the following sequences.

a. 1, 3, 5, 7, . . .   **b.** 2, 5, 10, 17, . . .   **c.** $\dfrac{2}{1}, \dfrac{3}{2}, \dfrac{4}{3}, \dfrac{5}{4}, \dots$

Solution

a. n: 1 2 3 4 . . . n

Terms: 1 3 5 7 . . . a_n

Apparent pattern: Each term is 1 less than twice n, which implies that

$$a_n = 2n - 1.$$

b. n: 1 2 3 4 . . . n

Terms: 2 5 10 17 . . . a_n

Apparent pattern: Each term is 1 more than the square of n, which implies that

$$a_n = n^2 + 1.$$

c. n: 1 2 3 4 . . . n

Terms: $\dfrac{2}{1}$ $\dfrac{3}{2}$ $\dfrac{4}{3}$ $\dfrac{5}{4}$ · · · a_n

Apparent pattern: Each term has a numerator that is greater than its denominator, which implies that

$$a_n = \frac{n + 1}{n}.$$

▲

Factorial Notation

Some very important sequences in mathematics involve terms that are defined with special types of products—**factorials.**

DEFINITION OF FACTORIAL

If n is a positive integer, then n **factorial** is defined by

$$n! = 1 \cdot 2 \cdot 3 \cdot 4 \cdots (n - 1) \cdot n.$$

As a special case, we define zero factorial to be $0! = 1$.

Here are some values of $n!$ for the first several nonnegative integers.

$0! = 1$

$1! = 1$

$2! = 1 \cdot 2 = 2$

$3! = 1 \cdot 2 \cdot 3 = 6$

$4! = 1 \cdot 2 \cdot 3 \cdot 4 = 24$

$5! = 1 \cdot 2 \cdot 3 \cdot 4 \cdot 5 = 120$

The value of n does not have to be very large before the value of $n!$ becomes huge. For instance, $10! = 3,628,800$. Many calculators have a factorial key, denoted by $\boxed{x!}$.

Factorials follow the same conventions for order of operations as do exponents. For instance,

$$2n! = 2(n!) = 2(1 \cdot 2 \cdot 3 \cdot 4 \cdots n)$$

whereas $(2n)! = 1 \cdot 2 \cdot 3 \cdot 4 \cdots 2n$.

EXAMPLE 4   Finding Terms of a Sequence Involving Factorials

List the first five terms of the sequence whose nth term is $a_n = 2^n/n!$. Begin with $n = 0$.

Solution

$$a_0 = \frac{2^0}{0!} = \frac{1}{1} = 1$$

$$a_1 = \frac{2^1}{1!} = \frac{2}{1} = 2$$

$$a_2 = \frac{2^2}{2!} = \frac{4}{2} = 2$$

$$a_3 = \frac{2^3}{3!} = \frac{8}{6} = \frac{4}{3}$$

$$a_4 = \frac{2^4}{4!} = \frac{16}{24} = \frac{2}{3}$$

When working with fractions involving factorials, you will often find that the fractions can be reduced.

$$\frac{n!}{(n-1)!} = \frac{1 \cdot 2 \cdot 3 \cdots (n-1) \cdot n}{1 \cdot 2 \cdot 3 \cdots (n-1)} = n$$

$$\frac{8!}{2! \cdot 6!} = \frac{1 \cdot 2 \cdot 3 \cdot 4 \cdot 5 \cdot 6 \cdot 7 \cdot 8}{1 \cdot 2 \cdot 1 \cdot 2 \cdot 3 \cdot 4 \cdot 5 \cdot 6} = \frac{7 \cdot 8}{2} = 28$$

Summation Notation

A convenient notation for the sum of the terms of a finite sequence is **summation notation** or **sigma notation** because it involves the use of the upper-case Greek letter sigma, written as Σ.

DEFINITION OF SUMMATION NOTATION

The sum of the first n terms of a sequence is represented by

$$\sum_{i=1}^{n} a_i = a_1 + a_2 + a_3 + a_4 + \cdots + a_n$$

where i is the **index of summation,** n is the **upper limit of summation,** and 1 is the **lower limit of summation.**

EXAMPLE 5   Summation Notation for Sums

a. $\displaystyle\sum_{i=1}^{5} 3i = 3(1) + 3(2) + 3(3) + 3(4) + 3(5)$

$$= 3(1 + 2 + 3 + 4 + 5)$$
$$= 3(15) = 45$$

b. $\displaystyle\sum_{i=1}^{4} 2 = 2 + 2 + 2 + 2 = 8$

c. $\displaystyle\sum_{k=3}^{6} (1 + k^2) = (1 + 3^2) + (1 + 4^2) + (1 + 5^2) + (1 + 6^2)$

$$= 10 + 17 + 26 + 37 = 90$$

d. $\displaystyle\sum_{i=0}^{8} \frac{1}{i!} = \frac{1}{0!} + \frac{1}{1!} + \frac{1}{2!} + \frac{1}{3!} + \frac{1}{4!} + \frac{1}{5!} + \frac{1}{6!} + \frac{1}{7!} + \frac{1}{8!}$

$$= 1 + 1 + \frac{1}{2} + \frac{1}{6} + \frac{1}{24} + \frac{1}{120} + \frac{1}{720} + \frac{1}{5,040} + \frac{1}{40,320}$$

$$\approx 2.71828$$

For this summation, note that the sum is very close to the irrational number $e \approx 2.718281828$. It can be shown that as more terms of the sequence whose nth term is $1/n!$ are added, the sum becomes closer and closer to e. ◢

REMARK   In Example 5, note that the lower index of a summation does not have to be 1. Also note that the index does not have to be the letter i. For instance, in part (c), the letter k is the index.

When working with summation notation, the following properties of sums are useful.

PROPERTIES OF SUMS

1. $\displaystyle\sum_{i=1}^{n} ca_i = c\sum_{i=1}^{n} a_i,$ $\quad c$ is any constant

2. $\displaystyle\sum_{i=1}^{n} (a_i + b_i) = \sum_{i=1}^{n} a_i + \sum_{i=1}^{n} b_i$

3. $\displaystyle\sum_{i=1}^{n} (a_i - b_i) = \sum_{i=1}^{n} a_i - \sum_{i=1}^{n} b_i$

Proof

Each of these properties follows directly from the associative property of addition, the commutative property of addition, and the distributive property of multiplication over addition. For example, note the use of the distributive property in the proof of Property 1.

$$\sum_{i=1}^{n} ca_i = ca_1 + ca_2 + ca_3 + \cdots + ca_n$$

$$= c(a_1 + a_2 + a_3 + \cdots + a_n) = c\sum_{i=1}^{n} a_i$$

◢

Variations in the upper and lower limits of summation can produce quite different-looking summation notations for *the same sum*. For example, consider the following two sums.

$$\sum_{i=1}^{5} 3(2^i) = 3\sum_{i=1}^{5} 2^i = 3(2^1 + 2^2 + 2^3 + 2^4 + 2^5)$$

$$\sum_{i=0}^{4} 3(2^{i+1}) = 3\sum_{i=0}^{4} 2^{i+1} = 3(2^1 + 2^2 + 2^3 + 2^4 + 2^5)$$

The Sum of a Sequence

The summation of the terms of a sequence is a **series.** For a finite sequence $a_1, a_2, a_3, \ldots, a_n$, the associated series is the summation

$$\sum_{i=1}^{n} a_i = a_1 + a_2 + a_3 + \cdots + a_n.$$

The summation

$$\sum_{i=1}^{\infty} a_i = a_1 + a_2 + a_3 + a_4 + \cdots$$

is an **infinite series.** Infinite series have important uses in calculus.

EXAMPLE 6 Finding the Sum of a Sequence

Write the sum of the sequence $1, \frac{1}{2}, \frac{1}{4}, \frac{1}{8}, \frac{1}{16}, \frac{1}{32}$ in sigma notation and evaluate the associated series.

Solution

Since the denominators of the terms of the sequence are powers of 2, the apparent ith term is $a_i = 1/2^i$, starting with $i = 0$. The associated series is

$$\sum_{i=0}^{5} \frac{1}{2^i} = 1 + \frac{1}{2} + \frac{1}{4} + \frac{1}{8} + \frac{1}{16} + \frac{1}{32}$$

and its value is

$$\sum_{i=0}^{5} \frac{1}{2^i} = 1 + \frac{16}{32} + \frac{8}{32} + \frac{4}{32} + \frac{2}{32} + \frac{1}{36} = 1 + \frac{31}{32} = 1.96895.$$

Applications

Sequences have many applications in business and science.

EXAMPLE 7 Population of the United States

The resident population of the United States from 1950 to 1989 can be approximated by the model

$$a_n = \sqrt{22{,}926 + 902.5n + 2.01n^2}, \qquad n = 0, 1, \ldots, 39$$

where a_n is the population in millions and n represents the calendar year with $n = 0$ corresponding to 1950. (*Source*: U.S. Bureau of Census) Find the last five terms of this finite sequence.

Solution

The last five terms of this finite sequence are:

$$a_{35} = \sqrt{22{,}926 + 902.5(35) + 2.01(35^2)} \approx 238.7 \qquad \textit{1985 population}$$
$$a_{36} = \sqrt{22{,}926 + 902.5(36) + 2.01(36^2)} \approx 240.9 \qquad \textit{1986 population}$$
$$a_{37} = \sqrt{22{,}926 + 902.5(37) + 2.01(37^2)} \approx 243.0 \qquad \textit{1987 population}$$
$$a_{38} = \sqrt{22{,}926 + 902.5(38) + 2.01(38^2)} \approx 245.2 \qquad \textit{1988 population}$$
$$a_{39} = \sqrt{22{,}926 + 902.5(39) + 2.01(39^2)} \approx 247.3. \qquad \textit{1989 population}$$

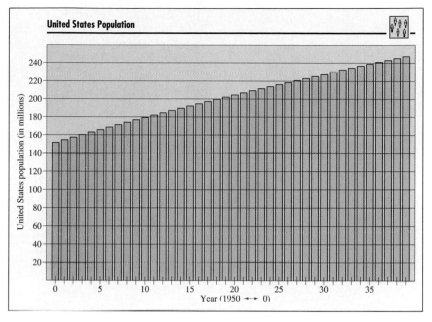

FIGURE 10.1

The bar graph in Figure 10.1 graphically represents the population given by this sequence for the entire 40-year period from 1950 to 1989.

DISCUSSION
PROBLEM

Finding the *n*th Term of a Sequence

Consider the following sequence.

$$a_1 = 1$$
$$a_2 = 1 \cdot 3$$
$$a_3 = 1 \cdot 3 \cdot 5$$
$$a_4 = 1 \cdot 3 \cdot 5 \cdot 7$$
$$\vdots$$
$$a_n = 1 \cdot 3 \cdot 5 \cdots (2n - 1)$$

Is it true that the *n*th term of this sequence can be written as

$$a_n = \frac{(2n)!}{2^n n!}?$$

Write a paragraph that justifies your answer.

WARM UP

The following warm-up exercises involve skills that were covered in earlier sections. You will use these skills in the exercise set for this section.

In Exercises 1 and 2, find the required value of the function.

1. $f(n) = \dfrac{2n}{n^2 + 1}$, $f(2)$ **2.** $f(n) = \dfrac{4}{3(n + 1)}$, $f(3)$

In Exercises 3–6, factor the expression.

3. $4n^2 - 1$ **4.** $4n^2 - 8n + 3$

5. $n^2 - 3n + 2$ **6.** $n^2 + 3n + 2$

In Exercises 7–10, perform the indicated operations and/or simplify.

7. $\left(\dfrac{2}{3}\right)\left(\dfrac{3}{4}\right)\left(\dfrac{4}{5}\right)\left(\dfrac{5}{6}\right)$ **8.** $\dfrac{2 \cdot 4 \cdot 6 \cdot 8}{2^4}$

9. $\dfrac{1}{2 \cdot 2} + \dfrac{1}{2 \cdot 3} + \dfrac{1}{2 \cdot 4}$ **10.** $\dfrac{1}{1 \cdot 2} + \dfrac{1}{2 \cdot 3} + \dfrac{1}{3 \cdot 4}$

EXERCISES for Section 10.1

In Exercises 1–18, write the first five terms of the indicated sequence. (Assume n begins with 1.)

1. $a_n = 2n + 1$ **2.** $a_n = 4n - 3$

3. $a_n = 2^n$ **4.** $a_n = \left(\dfrac{1}{2}\right)^n$

5. $a_n = (-2)^n$ **6.** $a_n = \left(-\dfrac{1}{2}\right)^n$

7. $a_n = \dfrac{1 + (-1)^n}{n}$ **8.** $a_n = \dfrac{n}{n + 1}$

9. $a_n = 3 - \dfrac{1}{2^n}$ **10.** $a_n = \dfrac{3^n}{4^n}$

11. $a_n = \dfrac{1}{n^{3/2}}$ **12.** $a_n = \dfrac{3n^2 - n + 4}{2n^2 + 1}$

13. $a_n = \dfrac{3^n}{n!}$ **14.** $a_n = \dfrac{n!}{n}$

15. $a_n = \dfrac{(-1)^n}{n^2}$ **16.** $a_n = (-1)^n\left(\dfrac{n}{n + 1}\right)$

17. $a_1 = 3$ and $a_{k+1} = 2(a_k - 1)$

18. $a_1 = 4$ and $a_{k+1} = \left(\dfrac{k + 1}{2}\right)a_k$

In Exercises 19–24, simplify the ratio of factorials.

19. $\dfrac{4!}{6!}$ **20.** $\dfrac{25!}{23!}$

21. $\dfrac{(n + 1)!}{n!}$ **22.** $\dfrac{(n + 2)!}{n!}$

23. $\dfrac{(2n - 1)!}{(2n + 1)!}$ **24.** $\dfrac{(2n + 2)!}{(2n)!}$

In Exercises 25–36, write an expression for the *most apparent* nth term of the sequence. (Assume n begins with 1.)

25. $1, 4, 7, 10, 13, \ldots$ **26.** $3, 7, 11, 15, 19, \ldots$

27. $0, 3, 8, 15, 24, \ldots$ **28.** $1, \dfrac{1}{4}, \dfrac{1}{9}, \dfrac{1}{16}, \dfrac{1}{25}, \ldots$

29. $\dfrac{1}{2}, \dfrac{-1}{4}, \dfrac{1}{8}, \dfrac{-1}{16}, \ldots$ **30.** $\dfrac{1}{3}, \dfrac{2}{9}, \dfrac{4}{27}, \dfrac{8}{81}, \ldots$

31. $1 + \dfrac{1}{1}, 1 + \dfrac{1}{2}, 1 + \dfrac{1}{3}, 1 + \dfrac{1}{4}, 1 + \dfrac{1}{5}, \ldots$

32. $1 + \dfrac{1}{2}, 1 + \dfrac{3}{4}, 1 + \dfrac{7}{8}, 1 + \dfrac{15}{16}, 1 + \dfrac{31}{32}, \ldots$

33. $1, \dfrac{1}{2}, \dfrac{1}{6}, \dfrac{1}{24}, \dfrac{1}{120}, \ldots$ **34.** $2, -4, 6, -8, 10, \ldots$

35. $1, -1, 1, -1, 1, \ldots$

36. $1, 2, \dfrac{2^2}{2}, \dfrac{2^3}{6}, \dfrac{2^4}{24}, \dfrac{2^5}{120}, \ldots$

In Exercises 37–50, find the given sum.

37. $\displaystyle\sum_{i=1}^{5}(2i + 1)$ **38.** $\displaystyle\sum_{i=1}^{6}(3i - 1)$

39. $\displaystyle\sum_{k=1}^{4} 10$ **40.** $\displaystyle\sum_{k=1}^{5} 6$

41. $\sum_{i=0}^{4} i^2$

42. $\sum_{i=0}^{5} 3i^2$

43. $\sum_{k=0}^{3} \dfrac{1}{k^2 + 1}$

44. $\sum_{j=3}^{5} \dfrac{1}{j}$

45. $\sum_{i=1}^{4} [(i - 1)^2 + (i + 1)^3]$

46. $\sum_{k=2}^{5} (k + 1)(k - 3)$

47. $\sum_{i=1}^{4} (9 + 2i)$

48. $\sum_{j=0}^{4} (-2)^j$

49. $\sum_{k=0}^{4} \dfrac{(-1)^k}{k + 1}$

50. $\sum_{k=0}^{4} \dfrac{(-1)^k}{k!}$

In Exercises 51–60, use sigma notation to write the given sum.

51. $\dfrac{1}{3(1)} + \dfrac{1}{3(2)} + \dfrac{1}{3(3)} + \cdots + \dfrac{1}{3(9)}$

52. $\dfrac{5}{1 + 1} + \dfrac{5}{1 + 2} + \dfrac{5}{1 + 3} + \cdots + \dfrac{5}{1 + 15}$

53. $\left[2\left(\tfrac{1}{8}\right) + 3\right] + \left[2\left(\tfrac{2}{8}\right) + 3\right] + \cdots + \left[2\left(\tfrac{8}{8}\right) + 3\right]$

54. $\left[1 - \left(\tfrac{1}{6}\right)^2\right] + \left[1 - \left(\tfrac{2}{6}\right)^2\right] + \cdots + \left[1 - \left(\tfrac{6}{6}\right)^2\right]$

55. $3 - 9 + 27 - 81 + 243 - 729$

56. $1 - \tfrac{1}{2} + \tfrac{1}{4} - \tfrac{1}{8} + \cdots - \tfrac{1}{128}$

57. $\dfrac{1}{1^2} - \dfrac{1}{2^2} + \dfrac{1}{3^2} - \dfrac{1}{4^2} + \cdots - \dfrac{1}{20^2}$

58. $\dfrac{1}{1 \cdot 3} + \dfrac{1}{2 \cdot 4} + \dfrac{1}{3 \cdot 5} + \cdots + \dfrac{1}{10 \cdot 12}$

59. $\tfrac{1}{4} + \tfrac{3}{8} + \tfrac{7}{16} + \tfrac{15}{32} + \tfrac{31}{64}$

60. $\tfrac{1}{2} + \tfrac{2}{4} + \tfrac{6}{8} + \tfrac{24}{16} + \tfrac{120}{32} + \tfrac{720}{64}$

61. *Compound Interest* A deposit of $5000 is made in an account that earns 8% interest compounded quarterly. The balance in the account after n quarters is given by

$$A_n = 5000\left(1 + \dfrac{0.08}{4}\right)^n, \qquad n = 1, 2, 3, \ldots.$$

(a) Compute the first eight terms of this sequence.

(b) Find the balance in this account after 10 years by computing the 40th term of the sequence.

62. *Compound Interest* A deposit of $100 is made *each* month in an account that earns 12% interest compounded monthly. The balance in the account after n months is given by

$$A_n = 100(101)[(1.01)^n - 1], \qquad n = 1, 2, 3, \ldots.$$

(a) Compute the first 6 terms of this sequence.

(b) Find the balance after 5 years by computing the 60th term of the sequence.

(c) Find the balance after 20 years by computing the 240th term of the sequence.

63. *Hospital Costs* The average cost of a day in a hospital from 1980 to 1987 is given by the model

$$a_n = 242.67 + 42.67n, \qquad n = 0, 1, 2, \ldots, 7$$

where a_n is the average cost in dollars and n is the year with $n = 0$ corresponding to 1980. (*Source:* American Hospital Association) Find the terms of this finite sequence and construct a bar graph that represents the sequence.

64. *Federal Debt* It took more than 200 years for the United States to accumulate a $1 trillion debt. Then it took just 8 years to get to $3 trillion. (*Source:* Treasury Department) The federal debt during the decade of the 1980s is approximated by the model

$$a_n = 0.1\sqrt{82 + 9n^2}, \qquad n = 0, 1, 2, \ldots, 10$$

where a_n is the debt in trillions and n is the year with $n = 0$ corresponding to 1980. Find the terms of this finite sequence and construct a bar graph that represents the sequence.

65. *Corporate Dividends* The dividends declared per share of common stock of Ameritech Corporation for the years 1985 through 1990 are shown in the figure. (*Source:* Ameritech 1990 Annual Report) These dividends can be approximated by the model

$$a_n = 0.20n + 1.17, \qquad n = 5, 6, 7, 8, 9, 10$$

where a_n is the dividend in dollars and n is the year with $n = 5$ corresponding to 1985. Approximate the sum of the dividends per share of common stock for the years 1985 through 1990 by evaluating

$$\sum_{5}^{10} (0.20n + 1.17).$$

Compare this sum with the result of adding the dividends as shown in the figure.

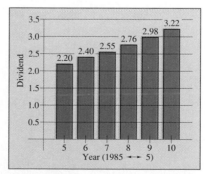

Figure for 65

66. *Total Revenue* The total annual sales for MCI Communications from 1980 through 1989 can be approximated by the model

$$a_n = 48.217n^2 + 228.1n + 311.28, \qquad n = 0, 1, 2, \ldots, 9$$

where a_n is the annual sales (in millions of dollars) and n is the year with $n = 0$ corresponding to 1980. (*Source:* MCI Communications) Find the total revenue from 1980 through 1989 by evaluating the sum

$$\sum_{0}^{9} (48.217n^2 + 228.1n + 311.28).$$

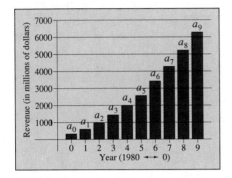

Figure for 66

In Exercises 67 and 68, use the following definition of the arithmetic mean $\bar{x}$ of a set of n measurements $x_1, x_2, x_3, \ldots, x_n$.

$$\bar{x} = \frac{1}{n} \sum_{i=1}^{n} x_i$$

67. Prove that $\sum_{i=1}^{n} (x_i - \bar{x}) = 0.$

68. Prove that $\sum_{i=1}^{n} (x_i - \bar{x})^2 = \sum_{i=1}^{n} x_i^2 - \frac{1}{n}\left(\sum_{i=1}^{n} x_i\right)^2.$

10.2 Arithmetic Sequences

Introduction / The Sum of an Arithmetic Sequence / Arithmetic Mean / Applications

Introduction

A sequence whose consecutive terms have a common difference is an **arithmetic sequence.**

DEFINITION OF AN ARITHMETIC SEQUENCE

A sequence is **arithmetic** if the differences between consecutive terms are the same. Thus, the sequence

$$a_1, a_2, a_3, a_4, \ldots, a_n, \ldots$$

is arithmetic if there is a number d such that

$$a_2 - a_1 = d, \qquad a_3 - a_2 = d, \qquad a_4 - a_3 = d,$$

and so on. The number d is the **common difference** of the arithmetic sequence.

EXAMPLE 1   Examples of Arithmetic Sequence

a. The sequence whose nth term is $4n + 3$ is arithmetic. For this sequence, the common difference between consecutive terms is 4.

$$\underbrace{7, 11,}_{11 - 7 = 4} 15, 19, \ldots, 4n + 3, \ldots$$

b. The sequence whose nth term is $7 - 5n$ is arithmetic. For this sequence, the common difference between consecutive terms is -5.

$$\underbrace{2, -3,}_{-3 - 2 = -5} -8, -13, \ldots, 7 - 5n, \ldots$$

c. The sequence whose nth term is $\frac{1}{4}(n + 3)$ is arithmetic. For this sequence, the common difference between consecutive terms is $\frac{1}{4}$.

$$\underbrace{1, \frac{5}{4},}_{\frac{5}{4} - 1 = \frac{1}{4}} \frac{3}{2}, \frac{7}{4}, \ldots, \frac{n + 3}{4}, \ldots$$

In Example 1, notice that each of the arithmetic sequences has an nth term that is of the form $dn + c$, where the common difference of the sequence is d. We summarize this result as follows.

THE nTH TERM OF AN ARITHMETIC SEQUENCE

The nth term of an arithmetic sequence has the form

$$a_n = dn + c$$

where d is the common difference between consecutive terms of the sequence and $c = a_1 - d$.

REMARK   An alternative form of the nth term of an arithmetic sequence is $a_n = a_1 + (n - 1)d$.

EXAMPLE 2   Finding the nth Term of an Arithmetic Sequence

Find a formula for the nth term of the arithmetic sequence whose common difference is 5 and whose *second* term is 12. What is the 18th term of this sequence?

Solution

You know that the formula for the nth term is of the form $a_n = dn + c$. Moreover, because the common difference is given to be $d = 5$, the formula must have the form

$$a_n = 5n + c.$$

Using the fact that the second term is

$$a_2 = 12 = 5(2) + c$$

it follows that $c = 2$. Thus, the formula for the nth term is

$$a_n = 5n + 2.$$

The sequence, therefore, has the form

$$7, 12, 17, 22, 27, \ldots, 5n + 2, \ldots$$

and the 18th term of the sequence is

$$a_{18} = 5(18) + 2 = 92.$$

▲

If you know the nth term of an arithmetic sequence *and* you know the common difference of the sequence, then you can find the $(n + 1)$th term by using the following **recursion formula.**

$$a_{n+1} = a_n + d$$

With such a formula, you can find any term of an arithmetic sequence, *provided* you know the previous term. For example, if you know the first term, then you can find the second term. Then, knowing the second term, you can find the third term, and so on.

EXAMPLE 3   Using a Recursion Formula

Find the ninth term of the arithmetic sequence whose first two terms are 2 and 9.

Solution

For this sequence you find that $a_1 = 2$ and $a_2 = 9$ so that the common difference is $d = 9 - 2 = 7$. There are two ways to find the ninth term. One way is to simply write out the first nine terms (by repeatedly adding 7):

$$2, 9, 16, 23, 30, 37, 44, 51, 58.$$

Another way to find the ninth term is to first find a formula for the nth term. Since the first term is 2, it follows that $c = a_1 - d = 2 - 7 = -5$. Therefore, a formula for the nth term of the sequence is $a_n = 7n - 5$, which implies that the ninth term is

$$a_9 = 7(9) - 5 = 58.$$

▲

EXAMPLE 4   Finding the *n*th Term of an Arithmetic Sequence

The fourth term of an arithmetic sequence is 20, and the thirteenth term is 65. Write the first several terms of this sequence.

Solution

To obtain the thirteenth term from the fourth term, you would have to add the common difference d to the fourth term nine times. That is,

$$a_{13} = a_4 + 9d.$$

Since you are given $a_4 = 20$ and $a_{13} = 65$, you can solve this equation for d as follows.

$$65 = 20 + 9d$$
$$45 = 9d$$
$$5 = d$$

Now, from the formula for the *n*th term of an arithmetic sequence, you have

$$a_n = dn + c$$
$$a_4 = 5(4) + c$$
$$20 = 20 + c$$
$$0 = c.$$

Thus, $a_n = 5_n$ and the first several terms of the sequence are as follows.

$$5, 10, 15, 20, 25, 30, 35, 40, 45, 50, 55, 60, 65, \ldots$$

The Sum of an Arithmetic Sequence

Now look at a formula for finding the *sum* of a finite arithmetic sequence.

THE SUM OF A FINITE ARITHMETIC SEQUENCE

The formula for the sum of a finite arithmetic sequence with n terms is

$$S = \frac{n}{2}(a_1 + a_n).$$

Proof

Begin by generating the terms of the arithmetic sequence in two ways. In the first way, repeatedly add d to the first term to obtain

$$S = a_1 + a_2 + a_3 + \cdots + a_{n-2} + a_{n-1} + a_n$$
$$= a_1 + [a_1 + d] + [a_1 + 2d] + \cdots + [a_1 + (n-1)d].$$

In the second way, repeatedly subtract d from the nth term to obtain

$$S = a_n + a_{n-1} + a_{n-2} + \cdots + a_3 + a_2 + a_1$$
$$= a_n + [a_n - d] + [a_n - 2d] + \cdots + [a_n - (n-1)d].$$

If you add these two versions of S, the multiples of d cancel and you obtain

$$\overbrace{2S = (a_1 + a_n) + (a_1 + a_n) + (a_1 + a_n) + \cdots + (a_1 + a_n)}^{n \text{ terms}}$$
$$= n(a_1 + a_n).$$

Thus, you have

$$S = \frac{n}{2}(a_1 + a_n).$$

REMARK   Be sure you see that this formula works only for *arithmetic* sequences.

EXAMPLE 5   Finding the Sum of an Arithmetic Sequence

Find the sum of the integers from 1 to 100.

Solution

The integers from 1 to 100 form an arithmetic sequence

$$1, 2, 3, 4, 5, 6, \ldots, 99, 100$$

that has 100 terms. Thus, you can use the formula for the sum of an arithmetic sequence, as follows.

$$S = 1 + 2 + 3 + 4 + 5 + 6 + \cdots + 99 + 100$$

$$= \frac{n}{2}(a_1 + a_n)$$

$$= \frac{100}{2}(1 + 100)$$

$$= 50(101)$$

$$= 5050$$

◢

EXAMPLE 6 Finding the Sum of an Arithmetic Sequence

Find the sum

$$\sum_{n=1}^{150} (11n - 6).$$

Solution

From the summation

$$\sum_{n=1}^{150} (11n - 6) = 5 + 16 + 27 + 38 + \cdots$$

you can conclude that $a_1 = 5$ and $a_n = 11n - 6$. Therefore, $a_{150} = 11(150) - 6 = 1644$ and the sum of the first 150 terms is

$$S = \frac{n}{2}(a_1 + a_n) = \frac{150}{2}(5 + 1644) = 75(1649) = 123{,}675.$$

◢

EXAMPLE 7 Finding the Sum of an Arithmetic Sequence

Verify the formula

$$S = 1 + 3 + 5 + \cdots + (2n - 1) = n^2.$$

Solution

Using the formula for the sum of a finite arithmetic sequence, you can write

$$S = 1 + 3 + 5 + \cdots + (2n - 1)$$

$$= \frac{n}{2}(a_1 + a_n)$$

$$= \frac{n}{2}[1 + (2n - 1)]$$

$$= \frac{n}{2}(2n)$$

$$= n^2.$$

◢

Arithmetic Mean

Recall that $(a + b)/2$ is the midpoint between the two numbers a and b on the real number line. As a result, the terms

$$a, \frac{a + b}{2}, b$$

have a common difference. We call $(a + b)/2$ the **arithmetic mean** of the numbers a and b. We can generalize this concept by finding k numbers m_1, m_2, m_3, . . . , m_k between a and b such that the terms

$$a, m_1, m_2, m_3, . . . , m_k, b$$

have a common difference. This process is referred to as **inserting k arithmetic means** between a and b.

EXAMPLE 8   Inserting Arithmetic Means Between Two Numbers

Insert three arithmetic means between 4 and 15.

Solution

You need to find three numbers m_1, m_2, and m_3 such that the terms

$$4, m_1, m_2, m_3, 15$$

have a common difference. In this case you have $a_1 = 4$, $n = 5$, and $a_5 = 15$. Therefore,

$$a_5 = 15 = a_1 + (n - 1)d = 4 + 4d.$$

Since $15 = 4 + 4d$, you find that $d = \frac{11}{4}$, and the three arithmetic means are as follows.

$$m_1 = a_1 + d = 4 + \frac{11}{4} = \frac{27}{4}$$

$$m_2 = m_1 + d = \frac{27}{4} + \frac{11}{4} = \frac{38}{4}$$

$$m_3 = m_2 + d = \frac{38}{4} + \frac{11}{4} = \frac{49}{4}$$

Applications

EXAMPLE 9 Seating Capacity

An auditorium has 20 rows of seats. There are 20 seats in the first row, 21 seats in the second row, 22 seats in the third row, and so on (see Figure 10.2). How many seats are there in all 20 rows?

Solution

The number of seats in the rows forms an arithmetic sequence in which the common difference is $d = 1$. Since $c = a_1 - d = 20 - 1 = 19$, you can determine that the formula for the nth term in the sequence is $a_n = n + 19$. Therefore, the 20th term in the sequence is $a_{20} = 20 + 19 = 39$, and the total number of seats is

$$S = 20 + 21 + 22 + \cdots + 39$$

$$= \frac{n}{2}(a_1 + a_{20})$$

$$= \frac{20}{2}(20 + 39)$$

$$= 10(59)$$

$$= 590.$$

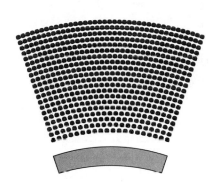

FIGURE 10.2

EXAMPLE 10 Total Sales

A small business sells $10,000 worth of products during its first year. The owner of the business has set a goal of increasing annual sales by $7,500 each year for 9 years. Assuming that this goal is met, find the total sales during the first 10 years this business is in operation.

Solution

The annual sales form an arithmetic sequence in which $a_1 = 10,000$ and $d = 7,500$. Thus, $c = a_1 - d = 10,000 - 7,500 = 2,500$ and the nth term of the sequence is

$$a_n = 7,500n + 2,500.$$

This implies that the 10th term of the sequence is $a_{10} = 77,500$. Therefore, the total sales for the first 10 years are as follows.

$$S = \frac{n}{2}(a_1 + a_{10})$$

$$= \frac{10}{2}(10,000 + 77,500)$$

$$= 5(87,500)$$

$$= \$437,500$$

The first five terms of each of the indicated sequences are 1, 3, 5, 7, 9.

1. $a_n = 2n - 1$ 2. $b_n = \sqrt{4n^2 - 4n + 1}$

3. $c_n = \dfrac{2n^2 + n - 1}{n + 1}$

Does this fact *alone* mean that each sequence is arithmetic? Is each sequence arithmetic? Write a paragraph justifying your answer. Here is another sequence whose first five terms are 1, 3, 5, 7, 9. Is it arithmetic?

$$d_n = n^6 - 15n^5 + 85n^4 - 225n^3 + 274n^2 - 118n - 1$$

WARM UP

The following warm-up exercises involve skills that were covered in earlier sections. You will use these skills in the exercise set for this section.

In Exercises 1 and 2, find the sum.

1. $\displaystyle\sum_{i=1}^{6} (2i - 1)$ **2.** $\displaystyle\sum_{i=1}^{10} (4i + 2)$

In Exercises 3 and 4, find the distance between the two real numbers.

3. $\frac{5}{2}$, 8   **4.** $\frac{4}{3}$, $\frac{14}{3}$

In Exercises 5 and 6, find the required value of the function.

5. $f(n) = 10 + (n - 1)4$, $f(3)$ **6.** $f(n) = 1 + (n - 1)\frac{1}{3}$, $f(10)$

In Exercises 7–10, evaluate the expression.

7. $\frac{11}{2}(1 + 25)$ **8.** $\frac{16}{2}(4 + 16)$

9. $\frac{20}{2}[2(5) + (12 - 1)3]$ **10.** $\frac{8}{2}[2(-3) + (15 - 1)5]$

EXERCISES for Section 10.2

In Exercises 1–10, determine whether the sequence is arithmetic. If it is, find the common difference.

1. 4, 7, 10, 13, 16, . . .   **2.** 10, 8, 6, 4, 2, . . .

3. 1, 2, 4, 8, 16, . . .   **4.** 3, $\frac{5}{2}$, 2, $\frac{3}{2}$, 1, . . .

5. $\frac{9}{4}$, 2, $\frac{7}{4}$, $\frac{3}{2}$, $\frac{5}{4}$, . . .   **6.** $-12, -8, -4, 0, 4, \ldots$

7. $\frac{1}{3}$, $\frac{2}{3}$, $\frac{4}{3}$, $\frac{8}{3}$, $\frac{16}{3}$, . . .

8. ln 1, ln 2, ln 3, ln 4, ln 5, . . .

9. 5.3, 5.7, 6.1, 6.5, 6.9, . . .

10. $1^2, 2^2, 3^2, 4^2, 5^2, \ldots$

In Exercises 11–18, write the first five terms of the specified sequence. Determine whether the sequence is arithmetic, and if it is, find the common difference.

11. $a_n = 5 + 3n$ **12.** $a_n = (2^n)n$

13. $a_n = \dfrac{1}{n + 1}$ **14.** $a_n = 1 + (n - 1)4$

15. $a_n = 100 - 3n$ **16.** $a_n = 2^{n-1}$

17. $a_1 = 1, a_2 = 1, a_n = a_{n-1} + a_{n-2}, \quad n \geq 3$

18. $a_n = (-1)^n$

In Exercises 19–30, find a formula for a_n for the given arithmetic sequence.

19. $a_1 = 1, d = 3$

20. $a_1 = 15, d = 4$

21. $a_1 = 100, d = -8$

22. $a_1 = 0, d = -\frac{2}{3}$

23. $a_1 = x, d = 2x$

24. $a_1 = -y, d = 5y$

25. $4, \frac{3}{2}, -1, -\frac{7}{2}, \ldots$

26. $10, 5, 0, -5, -10, \ldots$

27. $a_1 = 5, a_4 = 15$

28. $a_1 = -4, a_5 = 16$

29. $a_3 = 94, a_6 = 85$

30. $a_5 = 190, a_{10} = 115$

In Exercises 31–40, write the first five terms of the arithmetic sequence.

31. $a_1 = 5, d = 6$

32. $a_1 = 5, d = -\frac{3}{4}$

33. $a_1 = -2.6, d = -0.4$

34. $a_1 = 16.5, d = 0.25$

35. $a_1 = \frac{3}{2}, a_{k+1} = a_k - \frac{1}{4}$

36. $a_1 = 6, a_{k+1} = a_k + 12$

37. $a_1 = 2, a_{12} = 46$

38. $a_4 = 16, a_{10} = 46$

39. $a_8 = 26, a_{12} = 42$

40. $a_3 = 19, a_{15} = -1.7$

In Exercises 41–48, find the sum of the first n terms of the arithmetic sequence.

41. $8, 20, 32, 44, \ldots, \quad n = 10$

42. $2, 8, 14, 20, \ldots, \quad n = 25$

43. $-6, -2, 2, 6, \ldots, \quad n = 50$

44. $0.5, 0.9, 1.3, 1.7, \ldots, \quad n = 10$

45. $40, 37, 34, 31, \ldots, \quad n = 10$

46. $1.50, 1.45, 1.40, 1.35, \ldots, \quad n = 20$

47. $a_1 = 100, a_{25} = 220, \quad n = 25$

48. $a_1 = 15, a_{100} = 307, \quad n = 100$

In Exercises 49–60, find the indicated sum.

49. $\displaystyle\sum_{n=1}^{50} n$

50. $\displaystyle\sum_{n=1}^{100} 2n$

51. $\displaystyle\sum_{n=1}^{100} 5n$

52. $\displaystyle\sum_{n=51}^{100} 7n$

53. $\displaystyle\sum_{n=11}^{30} n - \sum_{n=1}^{10} n$

54. $\displaystyle\sum_{n=51}^{100} n - \sum_{n=1}^{50} n$

55. $\displaystyle\sum_{n=1}^{500} (n + 3)$

56. $\displaystyle\sum_{n=1}^{250} (1000 - n)$

57. $\displaystyle\sum_{n=1}^{20} (2n + 5)$

58. $\displaystyle\sum_{n=1}^{100} \frac{n + 4}{2}$

59. $\displaystyle\sum_{n=0}^{50} (1000 - 5n)$

60. $\displaystyle\sum_{n=0}^{100} \frac{8 - 3n}{16}$

In Exercises 61–64, insert k arithmetic means between the given pair of numbers.

61. $5, 17, \quad k = 2$

62. $24, 56, \quad k = 3$

63. $3, 6, \quad k = 3$

64. $2, 5, \quad k = 4$

65. Find the sum of the first 100 odd positive integers.

66. Find the sum of the integers from -10 to 50.

67. *Job Offer* A person accepts a position with a company at a salary of $27,500 for the first year. The person is guaranteed a raise of $1,500 per year for the first five years.
(a) Determine the person's salary during the sixth year of employment.
(b) Determine the person's total compensation from the company through six full years of employment.

68. *Job Offer* A person accepts a position with a company at a salary of $32,800 for the first year. The person is guaranteed a raise of $1,750 per year for the first five years.
(a) Determine the person's salary during the sixth year of employment.
(b) Determine the person's total compensation from the company through six full years of employment.

69. *Seating Capacity* Determine the seating capacity of an auditorium with 30 rows of seats if there are 20 seats in the first row, 24 seats in the second row, 28 seats in the third row, and so on.

70. *Seating Capacity* Determine the seating capacity of an auditorium with 36 rows of seats if there are 15 seats in the first row, 18 seats in the second row, 21 seats in the third row, and so on.

71. *Brick Pattern* A brick patio is roughly the shape of a trapezoid (see figure). The patio has 20 rows of bricks. The first row has 14 bricks and the 20th row has 33 bricks. How many bricks are in the patio?

Figure for 71

72. *Falling Object* An object (with negligible air resistance) is dropped from a plane. During the first second of its fall, the object falls 4.9 meters; during the second second, it falls 14.7 meters; during the third second, it falls 24.5 meters; and during the fourth second, it falls 34.3 meters. If this arithmetic pattern continues, how many meters will the object have fallen in 10 seconds?

When creating a mathematical model of a real-life situation, you often do not expect the model to fit the real-life data *exactly*. For instance, in the technology feature on page 546, we found linear models that approximately fit data for newspaper circulation. For that particular situation, there is no simple mathematical model that exactly fits the data.

Occasionally, however, real-life situations require mathematical models that do exactly fit the data. This often occurs in science and engineering, where you expect variables to be related by scientific or geometric principles.

EXAMPLE 1   Finding an Exact Mathematical Model

A polygon is *regular* if all its sides have the same length and all its angles have the same measure. The table gives the degree measures A_n of the interior angles of n-sided regular polygons for n equal to 3, 4, 5, 6, 7, and 8. Find a mathematical model for A_n in terms of n.

Number of Sides, n	3	4	5	6	7	8
Angle Measure, A_n	60°	90°	108°	120°	$128\frac{4}{7}°$	135°

Solution

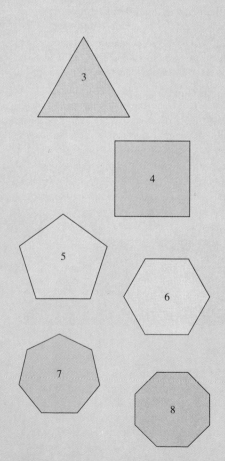

From the table, it is not clear what pattern the angle measures are following. When hunting for a mathematical model, performing an operation of the data can help to make the pattern more evident. For instance, you might take the natural logarithm of the angle measures, or square them, or take their square roots. For this particular data collection, multiplying A_n by n produces an easily recognized pattern.

Number of Sides, n	3	4	5	6	7	8
Product, nA_n	180°	360°	540°	720°	900°	1080°

From this result, you can see that the products nA_n form an arithmetic sequence whose nth term is

$$nA_n = 180(n - 2).$$

Thus, the model for the degree measure of the interior angle of an n-sided regular polygon is

$$A_n = \frac{180(n - 2)}{n}.$$

We have verified this model for values of n from 3 through 8. To verify that the model works for larger values of n would require further justification. ◢

EXERCISES

(*See also: Exercises 69–72, Section 10.2*)

1. *Stars* One way to form an *n*-pointed star is to begin with *n* equally spaced points on a circle and connect every second point. The angle measures of the star tips for *n* = 5, 6, 7, 8, 9, 10 are shown below. Find a mathematical model for these angle measures.

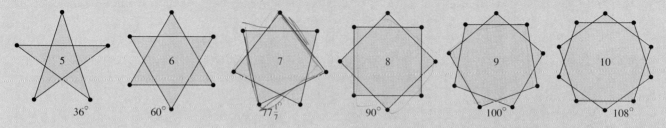

2. *More Stars* Another way to form an *n*-pointed star is to begin with *n* equally spaced points on a circle and connect every third point. The angle measures of the star tips for *n* = 7, 8, 9, 10, 11, 12 are shown below. Find a mathematical model for these angle measures.

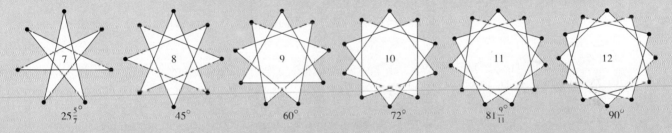

3. *Even More Stars* A regular polygon can be considered to be a "star" formed by connected adjacent points. Describe the pattern formed by the models in Example 1, Exercise 1, and Exercise 2.

> *Example 1:* Form star by connecting adjacent points.
> *Exercise 1:* Form star by connecting every second point.
> *Exercise 2:* Form star by connecting every third point.

The stars below are formed by connecting every *fourth* point on the circle. Find a model for the angle measures of these star tips. Explain your reasoning.

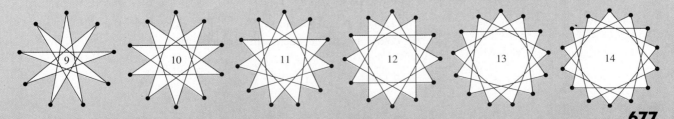

10.3 Geometric Sequences

Introduction / The Sum of a Geometric Sequence / Applications

Introduction

In Section 10.2 you saw that a sequence whose consecutive terms have a common *difference* is called an arithmetic sequence. In this section you will study another important type of sequence—a **geometric sequence.** Consecutive terms of a geometric sequence have a common *ratio*, as indicated in the following definition.

DEFINITION OF A GEOMETRIC SEQUENCE

A sequence is **geometric** if the ratios of consecutive terms are the same. Thus, the sequence

$$a_1, a_2, a_3, a_4, \ldots, a_n, \ldots$$

is geometric if there is a number r, $r \neq 0$, such that

$$\frac{a_2}{a_1} = r, \qquad \frac{a_3}{a_2} = r, \qquad \frac{a_4}{a_3} = r,$$

and so on. The number r is the **common ratio** of the geometric sequence.

EXAMPLE 1 Examples of Geometric Sequences

a. The sequence whose nth term is 2^n is geometric. For this sequence, the common ratio between consecutive terms is 2.

$$\underbrace{2, 4,}_{\frac{4}{2} = 2} 8, 16, \ldots, 2^n, \ldots$$

b. The sequence whose nth term is $4(3^n)$ is geometric. For this sequence, the common ratio between consecutive terms is 3.

$$\underbrace{12, 36,}_{\frac{36}{12} = 3} 108, 324, \ldots, 4(3^n), \ldots$$

c. The sequence whose nth term is $\left(-\frac{1}{3}\right)^n$ is geometric. For this sequence, the common ratio between consecutive terms is $-\frac{1}{3}$.

$$\underbrace{-\frac{1}{3}, \frac{1}{9},}_{\frac{1/9}{-1/3} = -\frac{1}{3}} -\frac{1}{27}, \frac{1}{81}, \ldots, \left(-\frac{1}{3}\right)^n, \ldots$$

In Example 1, notice that each of the geometric sequences has an nth term that is of the form ar^n, where the common ratio of the sequence is r. We summarize this result as follows.

THE nTH TERM OF A GEOMETRIC SEQUENCE

The nth term of a geometric sequence has the form

$$a_n = a_1 r^{n-1}$$

where r is the common ratio of consecutive terms of the sequence. Thus, every geometric sequence can be written in the following form.

$$a_1, \ a_2, \ a_3, \ a_4, \ a_5, \ldots, \ a_n, \ldots$$
$$\downarrow \ \downarrow \ \downarrow \ \downarrow \ \downarrow \ldots, \ \downarrow \ldots$$
$$a_1, a_1 r, a_1 r^2, a_1 r^3, a_1 r^4, \ldots, a_1 r^{n-1} \ldots$$

REMARK If you know the nth term of a geometric sequence, then the $(n + 1)$th term can be found by multiplying by r. That is,

$$a_{n+1} = r a_n.$$

EXAMPLE 2   Finding the Terms of a Geometric Sequence

Write the first five terms of the geometric sequence whose first term is $a_1 = 3$ and whose common ratio is $r = 2$.

Solution

Starting with 3, we repeatedly multiply by 2 to obtain the following.

$$a_1 = 3$$
$$a_2 = 3(2^1) = 6$$
$$a_3 = 3(2^2) = 12$$
$$a_4 = 3(2^3) = 24$$
$$a_5 = 3(2^4) = 48$$

▲

EXAMPLE 3   Finding a Term of a Geometric Sequence

Find the 15th term of the geometric sequence whose first term is 20 and whose common ratio is 1.05.

Solution

You can obtain the 15th term by multiplying the first term by r 14 times. Thus, since $a_1 = 20$ and $r = 1.05$, the 15th term ($n = 15$) is

$$a_{15} = a_1 r^{n-1} = 20(1.05)^{14} \approx 39.599.$$

▲

EXAMPLE 4   Finding a Term of a Geometric Sequence

Find the 12th term of the geometric sequence

5, 15, 45, ...

Solution

The common ratio of this sequence is $r = \frac{15}{5} = 3$. Therefore, since the first term is $a_1 = 5$, you determine the 12th term ($n = 12$) to be

$$a_{12} = a_1 r^{n-1} = 5(3)^{11} = 5(177,147) = 885,735.$$

EXAMPLE 5   Finding a Term of a Geometric Sequence

The 4th term of a geometric sequence is 125, and the 10th term is $\frac{125}{64}$. Find the 14th term.

Solution

To obtain the 10th term from the 4th term, you can multiply the 4th term by r^6. That is, $a_{10} = a_4 r^6$. Since $a_{10} = \frac{125}{64}$ and $a_4 = 125$, you have the following.

$$\frac{125}{64} = 125 r^6$$

$$\frac{1}{64} = r^6$$

$$\frac{1}{2} = r$$

Now you can obtain the 14th term by multiplying the 10th term by r^4. That is,

$$a_{14} = a_{10} r^4 = \frac{125}{64} \left(\frac{1}{2}\right)^4 = \frac{125}{1024}.$$

The Sum of a Geometric Sequence

The formula for the sum of a *finite* geometric sequence is as follows.

THE SUM OF A FINITE GEOMETRIC SEQUENCE

The sum of the finite geometric sequence

$$a_1, a_1 r, a_1 r^2, a_1 r^3, a_1 r^4, \ldots, a_1 r^{n-1}$$

with common ratio $r \neq 1$ is given by

$$S = a_1 \left(\frac{1 - r^n}{1 - r}\right).$$

Proof

Begin by writing out the nth partial sum.

$$S = a_1 + a_1 r + a_1 r^2 + \cdots + a_1 r^{n-2} + a_1 r^{n-1}$$

Multiplication by r yields

$$rS = a_1 r + a_1 r^2 + a_1 r^3 + \cdots + a_1 r^{n-1} + a_1 r^n.$$

Subtracting the second equation from the first yields

$$S - rS = a_1 - a_1 r^n.$$

Therefore, $S(1 - r) = a_1(1 - r^n)$, and since $r \neq 1$, you have

$$S = a_1 \left(\frac{1 - r^n}{1 - r} \right).$$

EXAMPLE 6   **Finding the Sum of a Finite Geometric Sequence**

Find the following sum.

$$\sum_{n=1}^{12} 4(0.3)^n$$

Solution

By writing out a few terms, you have

$$\sum_{n=1}^{12} 4(0.3)^n = 4(0.3) + 4(0.3)^2 + 4(0.3)^3 + \cdots + 4(0.3)^{12}.$$

Now, since $a_1 = 4(0.3)$, $r = 0.3$, and $n = 12$, apply the formula for the sum of a geometric sequence to obtain

$$\sum_{n=1}^{12} 4(0.3)^n = a_1 \left(\frac{1 - r^n}{1 - r} \right)$$

$$= 4(0.3) \left(\frac{1 - (0.3)^{12}}{1 - 0.3} \right)$$

$$\approx 1.714.$$

When using the formula for the sum of a finite geometric sequence, be careful to check that the index begins at $i = 1$. If the index begins at $i = 0$, you must adjust the formula for the nth partial sum, as demonstrated in the following example.

EXAMPLE 7 Finding the Sum of a Finite Geometric Sequence

Find the following sum.

$$\sum_{i=0}^{10} 10\left(-\frac{1}{2}\right)^i$$

Solution

By writing out a few terms, you have

$$\sum_{i=0}^{10} 10\left(-\frac{1}{2}\right)^i = 10 - 10\left(\frac{1}{2}\right) + 10\left(\frac{1}{2}\right)^2 - \cdots + 10\left(\frac{1}{2}\right)^{10}.$$

You can see that the *first term* is $a_1 = 10$ and $r = -\frac{1}{2}$. Moreover, by starting with $i = 0$ and ending with $i = 10$, you are adding $n = 11$ terms, which means that the partial sum is

$$\sum_{i=0}^{10} 10\left(-\frac{1}{2}\right)^i = a_1\left(\frac{1 - r^n}{1 - r}\right) = 10\left(\frac{1 - (-1/2)^{11}}{1 - (-1/2)}\right) \approx 6.670.$$

The formula for the sum of a *finite* geometric sequence can, depending on the value of r, be extended to find the sum of an *infinite* geometric sequence. Specifically, if the common ratio r has the property that $|r| < 1$, then it can be shown that r^n becomes arbitrarily close to zero as n increases without bound. Consequently,

$$S \to a_1\left(\frac{1 - 0}{1 - r}\right) = \frac{a_1}{1 - r} \quad \text{as} \quad n \to \infty.$$

We summarize this result as follows.

REMARK The summation $a_1 + a_1 r + a_1 r^2 + a_1 r^3 + \cdots$ is an **infinite geometric series.**

SUM OF AN INFINITE GEOMETRIC SEQUENCE

If $|r| < 1$, then the infinite geometric sequence

$$a_1, a_1 r, a_1 r^2, a_1 r^3, \ldots, a_1 r^{n-1}, \ldots$$

has the sum

$$S = \sum_{n=1}^{\infty} a_1 r^{n-1} = \frac{a_1}{1 - r}.$$

EXAMPLE 8   Finding the Sum of an Infinite Geometric Sequence

Find the sum of the following infinite geometric sequence.

$$4, 4(0.6), 4(0.6)^2, 4(0.6)^3, \ldots, 4(0.6)^{n-1}, \ldots$$

Solution

Since $a_1 = 4$, $r = 0.6$, and $|r| < 1$, you have

$$S = \sum_{n=1}^{\infty} 4(0.6)^{n-1}$$

$$= \frac{a_1}{1 - r}$$

$$= \frac{4}{1 - (0.6)}$$

$$= 10.$$

Applications

EXAMPLE 9   An Application: Compound Interest

A deposit of $50 is made the first day of each month in a savings account that pays 12% compounded monthly. What is the balance at the end of two years?

Solution

The formula for compound interest is

$$A = P\left(1 + \frac{r}{n}\right)^{tn}$$

where A is the balance of the account, P is the initial deposit, r is the annual percentage rate, n is the number of compoundings per year, and t is the time (in years). To find the balance in the account after 24 months, it is helpful to consider each of the 24 deposits separately. For example, the first deposit will gain interest for a full 24 months, and its balance will be

$$A_{24} = 50\left(1 + \frac{0.12}{12}\right)^{24} = 50(1.01)^{24}.$$

The second deposit will gain interest for 23 months, and its balance will be

$$A_{23} = 50\left(1 + \frac{0.12}{12}\right)^{23} = 50(1.01)^{23}.$$

The last (24th) deposit will gain interest for only 1 month, and its balance will be

$$A_1 = 50\left(1 + \frac{0.12}{12}\right)^1 = 50(1.01).$$

Finally, the total balance in the account will be the sum of the balances of the 24 deposits.

$$S = A_1 + A_2 + A_3 + \cdots + A_{23} + A_{24}$$

Using the formula for the sum of a geometric sequence, with $A_1 = 50(1.01)$ and $r = 1.01$, you have

$$S = 50(1.01)\left(\frac{1 - (1.01)^{24}}{1 - 1.01}\right) = \$1362.16.$$

DISCUSSION

PROBLEM

Comparing Two Sequences

The first several terms of the sequences whose nth terms are $a_n = (0.99)^{n-1}$ and $b_n = 1 - (n - 1)(0.01)$ are almost the same.

1. $a_1 = 1$
   $a_2 = 0.99$
   $a_3 = (0.99)^2 \approx 0.98$
   $a_4 = (0.99)^3 \approx 0.97$
   $a_5 = (0.99)^4 \approx 0.96$

2. $b_1 = 1$
   $b_2 = 1 - 0.01 = 0.99$
   $b_3 = 1 - 2(0.01) = 0.98$
   $b_4 = 1 - 3(0.01) = 0.97$
   $b_5 = 1 - 4(0.01) = 0.96$

Yet the two sequences have very basic differences. Discuss, or write a paragraph describing, some of the differences between the two sequences.

WARM UP

The following warm-up exercises involve skills that were covered in earlier sections. You will use these skills in the exercise set for this section.

In Exercises 1–4, evaluate the expression.

1. $\left(\frac{4}{5}\right)^3$

2. $\left(\frac{3}{4}\right)^2$

3. 2^{-4}

4. $\frac{5}{3^4}$

In Exercises 5–10, simplify the expression.

5. $(2n)(3n^2)$

6. $n(3n)^3$

7. $\frac{4n^5}{n^2}$

8. $\frac{(2n)^3}{8n}$

9. $[2(3)^{-4}]^n$

10. $3(4^2)^{-n}$

EXERCISES for Section 10.3

In Exercises 1–10, determine whether the sequence is geometric. If it is, find its common ratio.

1. 5, 15, 45, 135, . . .

2. 3, 12, 48, 192, . . .

3. 3, 12, 21, 30, . . .

4. 1, −2, 4, −8, . . .

5. $1, -\frac{1}{2}, \frac{1}{4}, -\frac{1}{8}, \dots$

6. 5, 1, 0.2, 0.04, . . .

7. $\frac{1}{2}, \frac{2}{3}, \frac{3}{4}, \frac{4}{5}, \dots$

8. $9, -6, 4, -\frac{8}{3}, \dots$

9. $1, \frac{1}{2}, \frac{1}{3}, \frac{1}{4}, \dots$

10. $\frac{1}{5}, \frac{2}{3}, \frac{3}{9}, \frac{4}{11}, \dots$

In Exercises 11–20, write the first five terms of the geometric sequence.

11. $a_1 = 2, r = 3$

12. $a_1 = 6, r = 2$

13. $a_1 = 1, r = \frac{1}{2}$

14. $a_1 = 1, r = \frac{1}{3}$

15. $a_1 = 5, r = -\frac{1}{10}$

16. $a_1 = 6, r = -\frac{1}{4}$

17. $a_1 = 1, r = e$

18. $a_1 = 2, r = \sqrt{3}$

19. $a_1 = 3, r = \dfrac{x}{2}$

20. $a_1 - 5, r = 2x$

In Exercises 21–32, find the nth term of the geometric sequence.

21. $a_1 = 4, r = \frac{1}{2}, n = 10$

22. $u_1 - 5, r = \frac{3}{2}, n = 8$

23. $a_1 = 6, r = -\frac{1}{3}, n = 12$

24. $a_1 = 8, r = \sqrt{5}, n = 9$

25. $a_1 - 100, r = e^x, n = 9$

26. $a_1 - 1, r = -\dfrac{x}{3}, n = 7$

27. $a_1 = 500, r = 1.02, n - 40$

28. $a_1 = 1000, r - 1.005, n - 60$

29. $a_1 = 16, a_4 = \frac{27}{4}, n = 3$

30. $a_2 = 3, a_5 = \frac{3}{64}, n = 1$

31. $a_2 = -18, a_5 = \frac{2}{3}, n = 6$

32. $a_3 = \frac{16}{3}, a_5 = \frac{64}{27}, n = 7$

33. *Compound Interest*   A principal of $1000 is invested at 10% interest. Find the amount after 10 years if the interest is compounded (a) annually, (b) semiannually, (c) quarterly, (d) monthly, and (e) daily.

34. *Compound Interest*   A principal of $2500 is invested at 12% interest. Find the amount after 20 years if the interest is compounded (a) annually, (b) semiannually, (c) quarterly, (d) monthly, and (e) daily.

35. *Depreciation*   A company buys a machine for $135,000 that depreciates at the rate of 30% per year. (In other words, at the end of each year the depreciated value is 70% of what it was at the beginning of the year.) Find the depreciated value of the machine after five full years.

36. *Population Growth*   A city of 250,000 people is growing at the rate of 1.3% per year. Estimate the population of the city 30 years from now.

In Exercises 37–46, find the indicated sum.

37. $\displaystyle\sum_{n=1}^{9} 2^{n-1}$

38. $\displaystyle\sum_{n=1}^{9} (-2)^{n-1}$

39. $\displaystyle\sum_{i=1}^{7} 64\left(-\tfrac{1}{2}\right)^{i-1}$

40. $\displaystyle\sum_{i=1}^{6} 32\left(\tfrac{1}{4}\right)^{i-1}$

41. $\displaystyle\sum_{i=1}^{10} 8\left(\tfrac{-1}{4}\right)^{i-1}$

42. $\displaystyle\sum_{i=1}^{10} 5\left(\tfrac{-1}{3}\right)^{i-1}$

43. $\displaystyle\sum_{n=0}^{20} 3\left(\tfrac{3}{2}\right)^{n}$

44. $\displaystyle\sum_{n=0}^{15} 2\left(\tfrac{4}{3}\right)^{n}$

45. $\displaystyle\sum_{n=0}^{5} 300(1.06)^{n}$

46. $\displaystyle\sum_{n=0}^{6} 500(1.04)^{n}$

47. *Compound Interest*   A deposit of $100 is made at the beginning of each month for five years in an account that pays 10%, compounded monthly. What is the balance A in the account at the end of five years?

$$A = 100\left(1 + \frac{0.10}{12}\right)^{1} + \cdots + 100\left(1 + \frac{0.10}{12}\right)^{60}$$

48. *Compound Interest*   A deposit of $50 is made at the beginning of each month for five years in an account that pays 12%, compounded monthly. What is the balance A in the account at the end of five years?

$$A = 50\left(1 + \frac{0.12}{12}\right)^{1} + \cdots + 50\left(1 + \frac{0.12}{12}\right)^{60}$$

49. *Compound Interest*   A deposit of P dollars is made at the beginning of each month in an account at an annual interest rate r, compounded monthly. The balance A after t years is

$$A = P\left(1 + \frac{r}{12}\right) + P\left(1 + \frac{r}{12}\right)^{2} + \cdots + P\left(1 + \frac{r}{12}\right)^{12t}.$$

Show that the balance is given by

$$A = P\left[\left(1 + \frac{r}{12}\right)^{12t} - 1\right]\left(1 + \frac{12}{r}\right).$$

50. *Compound Interest* A deposit of P dollars is made each month in an account at an annual interest rate r, compounded continuously. The balance A after t years is

$$A = Pe^{r/12} + Pe^{2r/12} + \cdots + Pe^{12tr/12}.$$

Show that the balance is given by

$$A = \frac{Pe^{r/12}(e^{rt} - 1)}{e^{r/12} - 1}.$$

Compound Interest In Exercises 51–54, consider making monthly deposits of P dollars into a savings account at an annual interest rate r. Use the results of Exercises 49 and 50 to find the balance A after t years if the interest is compounded (a) monthly and (b) continuously.

51. $P = \$50$, $r = 7\%$, $t = 20$ years
52. $P = \$75$, $r = 9\%$, $t = 25$ years
53. $P = \$100$, $r = 10\%$, $t = 40$ years
54. $P = \$20$, $r = 6\%$, $t = 50$ years

55. *Profit* The annual profit for the H.J. Heinz Company from 1980 through 1989 can be approximated by the model

$$a_n = 167.5e^{0.12n}, \qquad n = 0, 1, 2, \ldots, 9$$

where a_n is the annual profit in millions of dollars and n represents the year with $n = 0$ corresponding to 1980 (see figure). Use the formula for the sum of a geometric sequence to approximate the total profit earned during this 10-year period. (*Source:* H.J. Heinz Company)

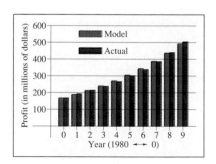

Figure for 55

56. *Would You Take This Job?* Suppose you went to work at a company that pays $0.01 for the first day, $0.02 for the second day, $0.04 for the third day, and so on. If the daily wage keeps doubling, what would your total income be for working (a) 29 days? (b) 30 days? (c) 31 days?

57. *Salary* You accept a job with a salary of $30,000 for the first year. Suppose that during the next 39 years you receive a 5% raise each year. What would your total compensation be over the 40-year period?

58. *Area* The sides of a square are 16 inches long. The square is divided into nine smaller squares, and the center square is shaded dark red (see figure). Each of the eight light red squares is then divided into nine smaller squares, and the center square of each is shaded dark red. If this process is repeated four more times, determine the area of the region shaded dark red.

 Figure for 58

In Exercises 59–68, find the sum of the infinite series.

59. $\displaystyle\sum_{n=0}^{\infty} \left(\tfrac{1}{2}\right)^n = 1 + \tfrac{1}{2} + \tfrac{1}{4} + \tfrac{1}{8} + \cdots$

60. $\displaystyle\sum_{n=0}^{\infty} 2\left(\tfrac{2}{3}\right)^n = 2 + \tfrac{4}{3} + \tfrac{8}{9} + \tfrac{16}{27} + \cdots$

61. $\displaystyle\sum_{n=0}^{\infty} \left(-\tfrac{1}{2}\right)^n = 1 - \tfrac{1}{2} + \tfrac{1}{4} - \tfrac{1}{8} + \cdots$

62. $\displaystyle\sum_{n=0}^{\infty} 2\left(-\tfrac{2}{3}\right)^n = 2 - \tfrac{4}{3} + \tfrac{8}{9} - \tfrac{16}{27} + \cdots$

63. $\displaystyle\sum_{n=0}^{\infty} 4\left(\tfrac{1}{4}\right)^n = 4 + 1 + \tfrac{1}{4} + \tfrac{1}{16} + \cdots$

64. $\displaystyle\sum_{n=0}^{\infty} \left(\tfrac{1}{10}\right)^n = 1 + 0.1 + 0.01 + 0.001 + \cdots$

65. $8 + 6 + \tfrac{9}{2} + \tfrac{27}{8} + \cdots$ **66.** $3 - 1 + \tfrac{1}{3} - \tfrac{1}{9} + \cdots$

67. $4 - 2 + 1 - \tfrac{1}{2} + \cdots$ **68.** $2 + \sqrt{2} + 1 + \dfrac{1}{\sqrt{2}} + \cdots$

69. *Distance* A ball is dropped 16 feet. Each time it drops h feet, it rebounds $0.81h$ feet. Find the total distance it travels.

70. *Time* The ball in Exercise 69 takes the following time for each fall.

$s_1 = -16t^2 + 16,$ $s_1 = 0$ if $t = 1$
$s_2 = -16t^2 + 16(0.81),$ $s_2 = 0$ if $t = 0.9$
$s_3 = -16t^2 + 16(0.81)^2,$ $s_3 = 0$ if $t = (0.9)^2$
$s_4 = -16t^2 + 16(0.81)^3,$ $s_4 = 0$ if $t = (0.9)^3$
$\vdots$ $\vdots$
$s_n = -16t^2 + 16(0.81)^{n-1},$ $s_n = 0$ if $t = (0.9)^{n-1}$

Beginning with s_2, the ball takes the same amount of time to bounce up as it does to fall, and thus the total time elapsed before it comes to rest is

$$t = 1 + 2\sum_{n=1}^{\infty} (0.9)^n.$$

Find this total.

10.4 Mathematical Induction

Introduction / Sums of Powers of Integers

Introduction

In this section we look at a form of mathematical proof, the principle of **mathematical induction.** It is important that you clearly see the logical need for this principle, so let's take a closer look at a problem we discussed earlier.

$$S_1 = 1 = 1^2$$
$$S_2 = 1 + 3 = 2^2$$
$$S_3 = 1 + 3 + 5 = 3^2$$
$$S_4 = 1 + 3 + 5 + 7 = 4^2$$
$$S_5 = 1 + 3 + 5 + 7 + 9 = 5^2$$

Judging from the pattern formed by these first five sums, it appears that the sum of the first n odd integers is

$$S_n = 1 + 3 + 5 + 7 + 9 + \cdots + 2n - 1 = n^2.$$

While this particular formula *is* valid, it is important for you to see that recognizing a pattern and then simply *jumping to the conclusion* that the pattern must be true for all values of n is *not* a logically valid method of proof. There are many examples in which a pattern appears to be developing for small values of n and then at some point the pattern fails. One of the most famous cases of this was the conjecture by the French mathematician Pierre de Fermat (1601–1655), who speculated that all numbers of the form

$$F_n = 2^{2^n} + 1, \qquad n = 0, 1, 2, \ldots$$

are prime. For $n = 0, 1, 2, 3,$ and 4, the conjecture is true.

$$F_0 = 3, \quad F_1 = 5, \quad F_2 = 17, \quad F_3 = 257, \quad F_4 = 65,537$$

The size of the next Fermat number ($F_5 = 4,294,967,297$) is so great that it was difficult for Fermat to determine whether it was prime or not. However, another well-known mathematician, Leonhard Euler (1707–1783), later found a factorization

$$F_5 = 4,294,967,297 = 641(6,700,417)$$

which proved that F_5 is not prime, and therefore Fermat's conjecture was false.

Just because a rule, pattern, or formula seems to work for several values of n, you cannot simply decide that it is valid for all values of n without going through a *legitimate proof*. Let's see how you prove such statements by the principle of **mathematical induction.**

THE PRINCIPLE OF MATHEMATICAL INDUCTION

Let P_n be a statement involving the positive integer n. If

1. P_1 is true, and
2. the truth of P_k implies the truth of P_{k+1}, for every positive integer k,

then P_n must be true for all positive integers n.

REMARK It is important to recognize that both parts of the Principle of Mathematical Induction are necessary.

To apply the Principle of Mathematical Induction you need to be able to determine the statement P_{k+1} for a given statement P_k.

EXAMPLE 1   A Preliminary Example

Find P_{k+1} for the following.

a. P_k: $S_k = \dfrac{k^2(k+1)^2}{4}$

b. P_k: $S_k = 1 + 5 + 9 + \cdots + [4(k-1)-3] + (4k-3)$

c. P_k: $3^k \geq 2k+1$

Solution

a. Substituting $k+1$ for k, you have

$$P_{k+1}: S_{k+1} = \frac{(k+1)^2(k+1+1)^2}{4} \qquad \textit{Replace k by k + 1}$$

$$= \frac{(k+1)^2(k+2)^2}{4}. \qquad \textit{Simplify}$$

b. In this case you have

$$P_{k+1}: S_{k+1} = 1 + 5 + 9 + \cdots + (4[(k+1)-1]-3) + [4(k+1)-3]$$

$$= 1 + 5 + 9 + \cdots + (4k-3) + (4k+1).$$

c. Replacing k by $k+1$ in the statement $3^k \geq 2k+1$, you have

$$P_{k+1}: 3^{k+1} \geq 2(k+1)+1$$

$$3^{k+1} \geq 2k+3.$$

EXAMPLE 2   Using Mathematical Induction

Use mathematical induction to prove the following formula.

$$S_n = 1 + 3 + 5 + 7 + \cdots + (2n-1) = n^2$$

Solution

Mathematical induction consists of two distinct parts. First, you must show that the formula is true when $n = 1$.

1. When $n = 1$, the formula is valid, since

$$S_1 = 1 = 1^2.$$

The second part of mathematical induction has two steps. The first step is to assume that the formula is valid for *some* integer k. The second step is to use this assumption to prove that the formula is valid for the next integer, $k + 1$.

2. Assuming that the formula

$$S_k = 1 + 3 + 5 + 7 + \cdots + (2k - 1) = k^2$$

is true, you must show that the formula $S_{k+1} = (k + 1)^2$ is true.

$$\begin{aligned} S_{k+1} &= 1 + 3 + 5 + 7 + \cdots + (2k - 1) + [2(k + 1) - 1] \\ &= [1 + 3 + 5 + 7 + \cdots + (2k - 1)] + (2k + 2 - 1) \\ &= S_k + (2k + 1) \\ &= k^2 + 2k + 1 \\ &= (k + 1)^2 \end{aligned}$$

REMARK When using mathematical induction to prove a *summation* formula (like the one in Example 2), it is helpful to think of S_{k+1} as $S_{k+1} = S_k + a_{k+1}$, where a_{k+1} is the $(k + 1)$ term of the original sum.

Combining the results of parts (1) and (2), you conclude by mathematical induction that the formula is valid for *all* positive integer values of n. ◢

A well-known illustration used to explain why the principle of mathematical induction works is the unending line of dominoes shown in Figure 10.3. If the line actually contains infinitely many dominoes, then it is clear that you could not knock the entire line down by knocking down only *one* domino at a time. However, suppose it were true that each domino would knock down the next one as it fell. Then you could knock them all down simply by pushing the first one and starting a chain reaction. Mathematical induction works in the same way. If the truth of P_k implies the truth of P_{k+1} and if P_1 is true, then the chain reaction proceeds as follows:

P_1 implies P_2
P_2 implies P_3
P_3 implies P_4

and so on.

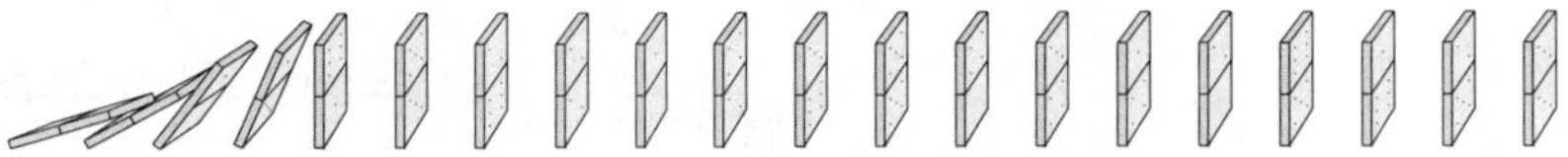

FIGURE 10.3

The first domino knocks over the second which knocks over the third which knocks over the fourth and so on.

It occasionally happens that a statement involving natural numbers is not true for the first $k - 1$ positive integers but is true for all values of $n \geq k$. In these instances, you use a slight variation of the principle of mathematical induction in which you verify P_k rather than P_1. This variation is called the **extended principle of mathematical induction.** To see the validity of this, note from Figure 10.3 that all but the first $k - 1$ dominoes can be knocked down by knocking over the kth domino. This suggests that you can prove a statement P_n to be true for $n \geq k$ by showing that P_k is true and that P_k implies P_{k+1}. In Exercises 29–32 of this section you are asked to apply this extension of mathematical induction.

EXAMPLE 3 Using Mathematical Induction

Use mathematical induction to prove the following formula.

$$S_n = 1^2 + 2^2 + 3^2 + 4^2 + \cdots + n^2 = \frac{n(n + 1)(2n + 1)}{6}$$

Solution

1. When $n = 1$, the formula is valid, because

$$S_1 = 1^2 = \frac{1(2)(3)}{6}.$$

2. Assuming that

$$S_k = 1^2 + 2^2 + 3^2 + 4^2 + \cdots + k^2 = \frac{k(k + 1)(2k + 1)}{6}$$

you must show that

$$S_{k+1} = \frac{(k + 1)(k + 2)(2k + 3)}{6}.$$

To do this, write the following.

$$
\begin{aligned}
S_{k+1} &= S_k + a_{k+1} \\
&= (1^2 + 2^2 + 3^2 + 4^2 + \cdots + k^2) + (k + 1)^2 \\
&= \frac{k(k + 1)(2k + 1)}{6} + (k + 1)^2 \\
&= \frac{k(k + 1)(2k + 1) + 6(k + 1)^2}{6} \\
&= \frac{(k + 1)[k(2k + 1) + 6(k + 1)]}{6} \\
&= \frac{(k + 1)[2k^2 + 7k + 6]}{6} \\
&= \frac{(k + 1)(k + 2)(2k + 3)}{6}
\end{aligned}
$$

Combining the results of parts (1) and (2), you conclude by mathematical induction that the formula is valid for *all* $n \geq 1$. ◢

Sums of Powers of Integers

The formula in Example 3 is one of a collection of useful summation formulas. We summarize this and other formulas dealing with the sum of various powers of the first n positive integers as follows.

SUMS OF POWERS OF INTEGERS

1. $1 + 2 + 3 + 4 + \cdots + n = \dfrac{n(n + 1)}{2}$

2. $1^2 + 2^2 + 3^2 + 4^2 + \cdots + n^2 = \dfrac{n(n + 1)(2n + 1)}{6}$

3. $1^3 + 2^3 + 3^3 + 4^3 + \cdots + n^3 = \dfrac{n^2(n + 1)^2}{4}$

4. $1^4 + 2^4 + 3^4 + 4^4 + \cdots + n^4$
$= \dfrac{n(n + 1)(2n + 1)(3n^2 + 3n - 1)}{30}$

5. $1^5 + 2^5 + 3^5 + 4^5 + \cdots + n^5 = \dfrac{n^2(n + 1)^2(2n^2 + 2n - 1)}{12}$

REMARK   Each of these formulas for sums can be proved by mathematical induction. (See Exercises 21–23, 25, 26.)

EXAMPLE 4   Finding a Sum of Powers of Integers

Find the following sum.

$$1^3 + 2^3 + 3^3 + 4^3 + 5^3 + 6^3 + 7^3$$

Solution

Using the formula for the sum of the cubes of the first n positive integers, you obtain the following.

$$1^3 + 2^3 + 3^3 + 4^3 + 5^3 + 6^3 + 7^3 = \frac{7^2(7 + 1)^2}{4}$$

$$= \frac{49(64)}{4}$$

$$= 784$$

Check this sum by adding the numbers 1, 8, 27, 64, 125, 216, and 343. ◢

EXAMPLE 5   **Proving an Inequality by Mathematical Induction**

Prove that $n < 2^n$ for all positive integers n.

Solution

1. For $n = 1$, the formula is true, since

    $$1 < 2^1.$$

2. Assuming that

    $$k < 2^k$$

    you need to show that $k + 1 < 2^{k+1}$. For $n = k$, you have

    $$2^{k+1} = 2(2^k) > 2(k) = 2k. \qquad \text{\textit{By assumption}}$$

    Since $2k = k + k > k + 1$ for all $k > 1$, it follows that

    $$2^{k+1} > 2k > k + 1$$

    or

    $$k + 1 < 2^{k+1}.$$

    Hence, $n < 2^n$ for all integers $n \geq 1$. ◢

DISCUSSION

PROBLEM

The Sum of the
Angles of a
Regular Polygon

A *regular* n-sided polygon is a polygon that has n equal sides and n equal angles. For instance, an equilateral triangle is a regular three-sided polygon. Each angle of an equilateral triangle measures 60°, and the sum of all three angles is 180°. Similarly, the sum of the four angles of a regular four-sided polygon (a square) is 360°. From the following four regular polygons (see Figure 10.4), find a formula for the sum of the angles of a regular n-sided polygon. Describe how you could *prove* that your formula is valid. Do you think that mathematical induction would be an appropriate technique to prove the validity of your formula?

(a) Equilateral   (b) Square   (c) Regular   (d) Regular
    Triangle   (360°)   Pentagon   Hexagon
    (180°)   (540°)   (720°)

FIGURE 10.4

WARM UP

The following warm-up exercises involve skills that were covered in earlier sections. You will use these skills in the exercise set for this section.

In Exercises 1–4, find the required sum.

1. $\displaystyle\sum_{k=3}^{6} (2k - 3)$

2. $\displaystyle\sum_{j=1}^{5} (j^2 - j)$

3. $\displaystyle\sum_{k=2}^{5} \frac{1}{k}$

4. $\displaystyle\sum_{i=1}^{2} \left(1 + \frac{1}{i}\right)$

In Exercises 5–10, simplify the expression.

5. $\dfrac{2(k + 1) + 3}{5}$

6. $\dfrac{3(k + 1) - 2}{6}$

7. $2 \cdot 2^{2(k+1)}$

8. $\dfrac{3^{2k}}{3^{2(k+1)}}$

9. $\dfrac{k + 1}{k^2 + k}$

10. $\dfrac{\sqrt{32}}{\sqrt{50}}$

EXERCISES for Section 10.4

In Exercises 1–10, find the indicated sum using the formulas for the sums of powers of integers.

1. $\displaystyle\sum_{n=1}^{20} n$

2. $\displaystyle\sum_{n=1}^{50} n$

3. $\displaystyle\sum_{n-1}^{6} n^2$

4. $\displaystyle\sum_{n=1}^{10} n^2$

5. $\displaystyle\sum_{n=1}^{5} n^3$

6. $\displaystyle\sum_{n=1}^{8} n^3$

7. $\displaystyle\sum_{n=1}^{6} n^4$

8. $\displaystyle\sum_{n=1}^{4} n^5$

9. $\displaystyle\sum_{n=1}^{6} (n^2 - n)$

10. $\displaystyle\sum_{n=1}^{10} (n^3 - n^2)$

In Exercises 11–14, find S_{k+1} for the given S_k.

11. $S_k = \dfrac{5}{k(k + 1)}$

12. $S_k = \dfrac{1}{(k + 1)(k + 3)}$

13. $S_k = \dfrac{k^2(k + 1)^2}{4}$

14. $S_k = \dfrac{k}{2}(3k - 1)$

In Exercises 15–28, use mathematical induction to prove the given formula for every positive integer n.

15. $2 + 4 + 6 + 8 + \cdots + 2n = n(n + 1)$

16. $3 + 7 + 11 + 15 + \cdots + (4n - 1) = n(2n + 1)$

17. $2 + 7 + 12 + 17 + \cdots + (5n - 3) = \dfrac{n}{2}(5n - 1)$

18. $1 + 4 + 7 + 10 + \cdots + (3n - 2) = \dfrac{n}{2}(3n - 1)$

19. $1 + 2 + 2^2 + 2^3 + \cdots + 2^{n-1} = 2^n - 1$

20. $2(1 + 3 + 3^2 + 3^3 + \cdots + 3^{n-1}) = 3^n - 1$

21. $1 + 2 + 3 + 4 + \cdots + n = \dfrac{n(n + 1)}{2}$

22. $1^2 + 2^2 + 3^2 + 4^2 + \cdots + n^2 = \dfrac{n(n + 1)(2n + 1)}{6}$

23. $1^3 + 2^3 + 3^3 + 4^3 + \cdots + n^3 = \dfrac{n^2(n + 1)^2}{4}$

24. $\left(1 + \dfrac{1}{1}\right)\left(1 + \dfrac{1}{2}\right)\left(1 + \dfrac{1}{3}\right) \cdots \left(1 + \dfrac{1}{n}\right) = n + 1$

25. $\displaystyle\sum_{i=1}^{n} i^5 = \dfrac{n^2(n + 1)^2(2n^2 + 2n - 1)}{12}$

26. $\sum_{i=1}^{n} i^4 = \dfrac{n(n+1)(2n+1)(3n^2+3n-1)}{30}$

27. $\sum_{i=1}^{n} i(i+1) = \dfrac{n(n+1)(n+2)}{3}$

28. $\sum_{i=1}^{n} \dfrac{1}{(2i-1)(2i+1)} = \dfrac{n}{2n+1}$

In Exercises 29–32, use mathematical induction to prove the given inequality for the indicated integer values of n.

29. $\left(\dfrac{4}{3}\right)^n > n, \quad n \geq 7$

30. $\dfrac{1}{\sqrt{1}} + \dfrac{1}{\sqrt{2}} + \dfrac{1}{\sqrt{3}} + \cdots + \dfrac{1}{\sqrt{n}} > \sqrt{n}, \quad n \geq 2$

31. $n! > 2^n, \quad n \geq 4$

32. $\left(\dfrac{x}{y}\right)^{n+1} < \left(\dfrac{x}{y}\right)^n, \quad$ if $n \geq 1$ and $0 < x < y$

In Exercises 33–42, use mathematical induction to prove the given property for all positive integers n.

33. $(ab)^n = a^n b^n$

34. $\left(\dfrac{a}{b}\right)^n = \dfrac{a^n}{b^n}$

35. If $x_1 \neq 0, x_2 \neq 0, \ldots, x_n \neq 0$, then
$$(x_1 x_2 x_3 \cdots x_n)^{-1} = x_1^{-1} x_2^{-1} x_3^{-1} \cdots x_n^{-1}.$$

36. If $x_1 > 0, x_2 > 0, \ldots, x_n > 0$, then
$$\ln(x_1 x_2 x_3 \cdots x_n)$$
$$= \ln x_1 + \ln x_2 + \ln x_3 + \cdots + \ln x_n.$$

37. Generalized Distributive Law:
$$x(y_1 + y_2 + \cdots + y_n) = xy_1 + xy_2 + \cdots + xy_n$$

38. $x^n - y^n = (x-y)(x^{n-1} + x^{n-2}y + \cdots + xy^{n-2} + y^{n-1})$
[*Hint*: $x^{n+1} - y^{n+1} = x^n(x-y) + y(x^n - y^n)$]

39. $(a+bi)^n$ and $(a-bi)^n$ are complex conjugates for all $n \geq 1$.

40. A factor of $(n^3 + 3n^2 + 2n)$ is 3.

41. A factor of $(2^{2n-1} + 3^{2n-1})$ is 5.

42. $\begin{vmatrix} a_{11} & 0 & 0 & \cdots & 0 \\ a_{21} & a_{22} & 0 & \cdots & 0 \\ \vdots & \vdots & & & \vdots \\ a_{n1} & a_{n2} & a_{n3} & \cdots & a_{nn} \end{vmatrix} = a_{11}a_{22}a_{33} \cdots a_{nn}$

10.5 The Binomial Theorem

Binomial Coefficients / Pascal's Triangle / Binomial Expansions

Binomial Coefficients

Recall that a **binomial** is a polynomial that has two terms. In this section, you will look at a formula that gives a quick method of raising a binomial to a power. To begin, look at the expansion of $(x + y)^n$ for several values of n.

$$(x + y)^0 = 1$$
$$(x + y)^1 = x + y$$
$$(x + y)^2 = x^2 + 2xy + y^2$$
$$(x + y)^3 = x^3 + 3x^2y + 3xy^2 + y^3$$
$$(x + y)^4 = x^4 + 4x^3y + 6x^2y^2 + 4xy^3 + y^4$$
$$(x + y)^5 = x^5 + 5x^4y + 10x^3y^2 + 10x^2y^3 + 5xy^4 + y^5$$

There are several observations you can make about these expansions of $(x + y)^n$.

1. In each expansion, there are $n + 1$ terms.
2. In each expansion, x and y have symmetrical roles. The powers of x decrease by 1 in successive terms, while the powers of y increase by 1.
3. The sum of the powers of each term in a binomial expansion is n. For example, in the expansion of $(x + y)^5$, the sum of the powers of each term is 5, as follows.

$$4 + 1 = 5 \qquad 3 + 2 = 5$$
$$(x + y)^5 = x^5 + 5x^4y^1 + 10x^3y^2 + 10x^2y^3 + 5xy^4 + y^5$$

4. The first term is x^n, the last term is y^n, and each of these terms has a coefficient of 1.
5. The coefficients increase and then decrease in a symmetrical pattern. For $(x + y)^5$, the pattern is

$$1 \quad 5 \quad 10 \quad 10 \quad 5 \quad 1.$$

The most difficult part of a binomial expansion is finding the coefficients of the interior terms. To find these **binomial coefficients,** we use a well-known theorem called the **Binomial Theorem.**

THE BINOMIAL THEOREM

In the expansion of $(x + y)^n$

$$(x + y)^n = x^n + nx^{n-1}y + \cdots + {}_nC_m x^{n-m}y^m + \cdots + nxy^{n-1} + y^n$$

the coefficient of $x^{n-m}y^m$ is given by

$$_nC_m = \frac{n!}{(n - m)!m!}.$$

Proof

The Binomial Theorem can be proved quite nicely using mathematical induction. The steps are straightforward but look a little messy, so we will present only an outline on the proof.

1. If $n = 1$, then you have

$$(x + y)^1 = x^1 + y^1 = {}_1C_0 x + {}_1C_1 y$$

and the formula is valid.

2. Assuming the formula is true for $n = k$, then the coefficient of $x^{k-m}y^m$ is given by

$$_kC_m = \frac{k!}{(k - m)!m!} = \frac{k(k - 1)(k - 2) \cdots (k - m + 1)}{m!}.$$

To show that the formula is true for $n = k + 1$, look at the coefficient of $x^{k+1-m}y^m$ in the expansion of

$$(x + y)^{k+1} = (x + y)^k (x + y).$$

From the right-hand side, you can determine that the term involving $x^{k+1-m}y^m$ is the sum of two products.

$$({}_kC_m x^{k-m}y^m)(x) + ({}_kC_{m-1} x^{k+1-m}y^{m-1})(y)$$

$$= \left[\frac{k!}{(k - m)!m!} + \frac{k!}{(k - m + 1)!(m - 1)!} \right] x^{k+1-m}y^m$$

$$= \left[\frac{(k + 1 - m)k!}{(k + 1 - m)!m!} + \frac{k!m}{(k + 1 - m)!m!} \right] x^{k+1-m}y^m$$

$$= \left[\frac{k!(k + 1 - m + m)}{(k + 1 - m)!m!} \right] x^{k+1-m}y^m$$

$$= \left[\frac{(k + 1)!}{(k + 1 - m)!m!} \right] x^{k+1-m}y^m$$

$$= {}_{k+1}C_m x^{k+1-m}y^m$$

REMARK The symbol $\binom{n}{m}$ is often used in place of $_nC_m$ to denote binomial coefficients.

Thus, by mathematical induction, the Binomial Theorem is valid for all positive integers n.

EXAMPLE 1 Finding Binomial Coefficients

Find the following binomial coefficients.

a. $_8C_2$ b. $_{10}C_3$
c. $_7C_3$ d. $_7C_4$

Solution

Note in parts (a) and (b) how the numerator factorial can be factored in order to cancel one of the denominator factorials.

a. $_8C_2 = \dfrac{8!}{6!2!} = \dfrac{(8 \cdot 7) \cdot 6!}{6! \cdot 2!} = \dfrac{8 \cdot 7}{2 \cdot 1} = 28$

b. $_{10}C_3 = \dfrac{10!}{7!3!} = \dfrac{(10 \cdot 9 \cdot 8) \cdot 7!}{7! \cdot 3!} = \dfrac{10 \cdot 9 \cdot 8}{3 \cdot 2 \cdot 1} = 120$

c. $_7C_3 = \dfrac{7 \cdot 6 \cdot 5}{3 \cdot 2 \cdot 1} = 35$

d. $_7C_4 = \dfrac{7 \cdot 6 \cdot 5 \cdot 4}{4 \cdot 3 \cdot 2 \cdot 1} = 35$

When $m \neq 0$ or $m \neq n$, as in the above example, there is a simple pattern for evaluating binomial coefficients.

$$\overbrace{}^{\text{2 factors}} \qquad\qquad \overbrace{}^{\text{3 factors}}$$

$$_8C_2 = \underbrace{\dfrac{8 \cdot 7}{2 \cdot 1}}_{\text{2 factorial}} \quad \text{and} \quad _{10}C_3 = \underbrace{\dfrac{10 \cdot 9 \cdot 8}{3 \cdot 2 \cdot 1}}_{\text{3 factorial}}$$

In general, you have the following.

$$_nC_m = \dfrac{\overbrace{n(n-1)(n-2) \cdots}^{m \text{ factors}}}{m!}, \qquad 0 < m < n$$

It is not a coincidence that the results in parts (c) and (d) of Example 1 are the same. In general, it is true that $_nC_m = {}_nC_{n-m}$. For instance,

$$_6C_0 = {}_6C_6 = 1, \qquad _6C_1 = {}_6C_5 = 6, \qquad \text{and} \qquad _6C_2 = {}_6C_4 = 15.$$

This shows the symmetric property of binomial coefficients that was identified earlier. By calculating $_6C_1$ and $_6C_5$, you can see that the simpler of the two symmetric coefficients to calculate is the one with the smaller number on the right.

Pascal's Triangle

There is a convenient way to remember a pattern for binomial coefficients. By arranging the coefficients in a triangular pattern, you obtain the following array, which is **Pascal's Triangle.** This triangle is named after the famous French mathematician Blaise Pascal (1623–1662).

$$
\begin{array}{ccccccccccccccc}
 & & & & & & & 1 & & & & & & & \\
 & & & & & & 1 & & 1 & & & & & & \\
 & & & & & 1 & & 2 & & 1 & & & & & \\
 & & & & 1 & & 3 & & 3 & & 1 & & & & \\
 & & & 1 & & 4 & & 6 & & 4 & & 1 & & & \\
 & & 1 & & 5 & & 10 & & 10 & & 5 & & 1 & & \\
 & 1 & & 6 & & 15 & & 20 & & 15 & & 6 & & 1 & \\
1 & & 7 & & 21 & & 35 & & 35 & & 21 & & 7 & & 1
\end{array}
$$

The first and last number in each row of Pascal's Triangle is 1. Every other number in each row is formed by adding the two numbers immediately above the number. For example, the two numbers above 35 are 15 and 20.

$$
\begin{array}{cc}
15 & 20 \\
 & \diagdown \!\! \diagup \\
 & 35
\end{array}
$$

$15 + 20 = 35$

Pascal noticed that numbers in this triangle are precisely the same numbers that are the coefficients of binomial expansions, as follows.

$$(x + y)^0 = 1$$
$$(x + y)^1 = 1x + 1y$$
$$(x + y)^2 = 1x^2 + 2xy + 1y^2$$
$$(x + y)^3 = 1x^3 + 3x^2y + 3xy^2 + 1y^3$$
$$(x + y)^4 = 1x^4 + 4x^3y + 6x^2y^2 + 4xy^3 + 1y^4$$
$$(x + y)^5 = 1x^5 + 5x^4y + 10x^3y^2 + 10x^2y^3 + 5xy^4 + 1y^5$$
$$(x + y)^6 = 1x^6 + 6x^5y + 15x^4y^2 + 20x^3y^3 + 15x^2y^4 + 6xy^5 + 1y^6$$
$$(x + y)^7 = 1x^7 + 7x^6y + 21x^5y^2 + 35x^4y^3 + 35x^3y^4 + 21x^2y^5 + 7xy^6 + 1y^6$$

Because the top row in Pascal's Triangle corresponds to the binomial expansion $(x + y)^0 = 1$, it is called the **zero row.** Similarly, the next row corresponds to the binomial expansion $(x + y)^1 = 1(x) + 1(y)$, and it is called the **first row.** In general, the *n*th **row** in Pascal's Triangle gives the coefficients of $(x + y)^n$.

EXAMPLE 2   Using Pascal's Triangle

Use Pascal's Triangle to find the following binomial coefficients.

$$_8C_0, \quad _8C_1, \quad _8C_2, \quad _8C_3, \quad _8C_4, \quad _8C_5, \quad _8C_6, \quad _8C_7, \quad _8C_8$$

Solution

These nine binomial coefficients represent the eighth row of Pascal's Triangle. Thus, using the seventh row of the triangle, you can calculate the numbers in the eighth row, as follows.

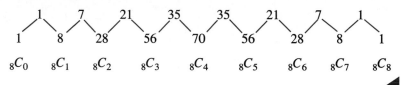

Binomial Expansions

As mentioned at the beginning of this section, when you write out the coefficients for a binomial that is raised to a power, you are **expanding a binomial.** The formulas for binomial coefficients give you an easy way to expand binomials, as demonstrated in the next three examples.

EXAMPLE 3 Expanding a Binomial

Write the expansion for the following expression.

$$(x + 1)^3$$

Solution

The binomial coefficients from the third row of Pascal's Triangle are 1, 3, 3, 1. Therefore, the expansion is as follows.

$$(x + 1)^3 = (1)x^3 + (3)x^2(1) + (3)x(1^2) + (1)(1^3)$$
$$= x^3 + 3x^2 + 3x + 1$$

To expand binomials representing *differences*, rather than sums, alternate signs.

$$(x - 1)^3 = x^3 - 3x^2 + 3x - 1$$
$$(x - 1)^4 = x^4 - 4x^3 + 6x^2 - 4x + 1$$

EXAMPLE 4 Expanding a Binomial

Write the expansion for the following expression.

$$(x + 3)^4$$

Solution

The binomial coefficients from the fourth row of Pascal's Triangle are 1, 4, 6, 4, 1. Therefore, the expansion is as follows.

$$(x + 3)^4 = (1)x^4 + (4)x^3(3) + (6)x^2(3^2) + (4)x(3^3) + (1)(3^4)$$
$$= x^4 + 12x^3 + 54x^2 + 108x + 81$$

◢

EXAMPLE 5   Expanding a Binomial

Write the expansion for the following expression.

$$(x - 2y)^4$$

Solution

The binomial coefficients from the fourth row of Pascal's Triangle are 1, 4, 6, 4, 1. Therefore, the expansion is as follows.

$$(x - 2y)^4 = (1)x^4 - (4)x^3(2y) + (6)x^2(2y)^2 - (4)x(2y)^3 + (1)(2y)^4$$
$$= x^4 - 8x^3y + 24x^2y^2 - 32xy^3 + 16y^4$$

◢

EXAMPLE 6   Finding a Specified Term in a Binomial Expansion

Find the sixth term in the expansion of $(3a + 2b)^{12}$.

Solution

Using the Binomial Theorem, let $x = 3a$ and $y = 2b$ and note that in the *sixth* term, the exponent of y is $m = 5$ and the exponent of x is $n - m = 12 - 5 = 7$. Consequently, the sixth term of the expansion is

$$_{12}C_5x^7y^5 = \frac{12 \cdot 11 \cdot 10 \cdot 9 \cdot 8}{5!}(3a)^7(2b)^5.$$

◢

By adding the terms in each of the rows of Pascal's Triangle, we obtain the following.

Row 0: $1 = 1$

Row 1: $1 + 1 = 2$

Row 2: $1 + 2 + 1 = 4$

Row 3: $1 + 3 + 3 + 1 = 8$

Row 4: $1 + 4 + 6 + 4 + 1 = 16$

Can you find a pattern for this sequence? Use this pattern to find the sum of the terms in the 10th row of Pascal's Triangle. Then check your answer by actually adding the terms of the 10th row.

WARM UP

The following warm-up exercises involve skills that were covered in earlier sections. You will use these skills in the exercise set for this section.

In Exercises 1–6, perform the indicated operations and/or simplify.

1. $5x^2(x^3 + 3)$ **2.** $(x + 5)(x^2 - 3)$

3. $(x + 4)^2$ **4.** $(2x - 3)^2$

5. $x^2y(3xy^{-2})$ **6.** $(-2z)^5$

In Exercises 7–10, evaluate the expression.

7. $5!$ **8.** $\dfrac{8!}{5!}$

9. $\dfrac{10!}{7!}$ **10.** $\dfrac{6!}{3!3!}$

EXERCISES for Section 10.5

In Exercises 1–10, evaluate $_nC_m$.

1. $_5C_3$ **2.** $_8C_6$

3. $_{12}C_0$ **4.** $_{20}C_{20}$

5. $_{20}C_{15}$ **6.** $_{12}C_5$

7. $_{100}C_{98}$ **8.** $_{10}C_4$

9. $_{100}C_2$ **10.** $_{10}C_6$

In Exercises 11–30, use the Binomial Theorem to expand and simplify the expression.

11. $(x + 1)^4$ **12.** $(x + 1)^6$

13. $(a + 2)^3$ **14.** $(a + 3)^4$

15. $(y - 2)^4$ **16.** $(y - 2)^5$

17. $(x + y)^5$ **18.** $(x + y)^6$

19. $(r + 3s)^6$ **20.** $(x + 2y)^4$

21. $(x - y)^5$ **22.** $(2x - y)^5$

23. $(1 - 2x)^3$

24. $(5 - 3y)^3$

25. $(x^2 + 5)^4$

26. $(x^2 + y^2)^6$

27. $\left(\dfrac{1}{x} + y\right)^5$

28. $\left(\dfrac{1}{x} + 2y\right)^6$

29. $2(x - 3)^4 + 5(x - 3)^2$

30. $3(x + 1)^5 - 4(x + 1)^3$

In Exercises 31–36, use the Binomial Theorem to expand the complex number. Simplify your answer by recalling that $i^2 = -1$.

31. $(1 + i)^4$

32. $(2 - i)^5$

33. $(2 - 3i)^6$

34. $(5 + \sqrt{-9})^3$

35. $\left(\dfrac{-1}{2} + \dfrac{\sqrt{3}}{2}i\right)^3$

36. $(5 - \sqrt{3}i)^4$

In Exercises 37–40, expand the binomial using Pascal's Triangle to determine the coefficients.

37. $(2t - s)^5$

38. $(x + 2y)^5$

39. $(3 - 2z)^4$

40. $(3y + 2)^5$

In Exercises 41–48, find the coefficient a of the given term in the expansion of the binomial.

Binomial	Term
41. $(x + 3)^{12}$	ax^5
42. $(x^2 + 3)^{12}$	ax^8
43. $(x - 2y)^{10}$	ax^8y^2
44. $(4x - y)^{10}$	ax^2y^8
45. $(3x - 2y)^9$	ax^4y^5
46. $(2x - 3y)^8$	ax^6y^2
47. $(x^2 + y)^{10}$	ax^8y^6
48. $(z^2 - 1)^{12}$	az^6

In Exercises 49–54, use the Binomial Theorem to expand the given expression. In the study of probability, it is sometimes necessary to use the expansion of $(p + q)^n$, where $p + q = 1$.

49. $\left(\dfrac{1}{2} + \dfrac{1}{2}\right)^7$

50. $\left(\dfrac{1}{4} + \dfrac{3}{4}\right)^{10}$

51. $\left(\dfrac{1}{3} + \dfrac{2}{3}\right)^8$

52. $(0.3 + 0.7)^{12}$

53. $(0.6 + 0.4)^5$

54. $(0.35 + 0.65)^6$

In Exercises 55–58, use the Binomial Theorem to approximate the given quantity accurate to three decimal places. For example, in Exercise 55 you have

$$(1.02)^8 = (1 + 0.02)^8 = 1 + 8(0.02) + 28(0.02)^2 + \ldots.$$

55. $(1.02)^8$

56. $(2.005)^{10}$

57. $(2.99)^{12}$

58. $(1.98)^9$

In Exercises 59–62, shift the graph of f to the right or left as indicated to form the graph of g. Then write the polynomial function g in standard form.

59. $f(x) = -x^2 + 3x + 2$

60. $f(x) = 2x^2 - 4x + 1$

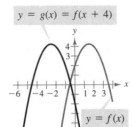
$y = g(x) = f(x + 4)$

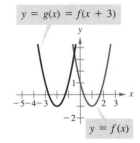
$y = g(x) = f(x + 3)$

61. $f(x) = x^3 - 4x$

62. $f(x) = -x^4 + 4x^2 - 1$

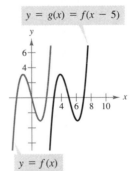
$y = g(x) = f(x - 5)$

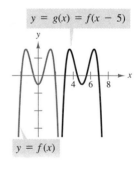
$y = g(x) = f(x - 5)$

63. *Life Insurance* The average amount of life insurance per household (in households that carry life insurance) from 1970 through 1988 can be approximated by the model

$$f(t) = 0.2187t^2 + 0.6715t + 26.67, \quad 0 \le t \le 18.$$

In this model, $f(t)$ represents the amount of life insurance (in 1000s of dollars) and t represents the calendar year with $t = 0$ corresponding to 1970 (see figure). You want to adjust this model so that $t = 0$ corresponds to 1980 rather than 1970. To do this, you shift the graph of f 10 units *to the left* and obtain

$g(t) = f(t + 10)$
$= 0.2187(t + 10)^2 + 0.6715(t + 10) + 26.67.$

Write this new polynomial function in standard form. (*Source*: American Council of Life Insurance)

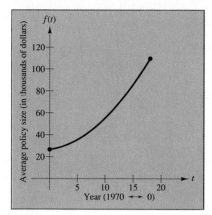

Figure for 63

64. *Health Maintenance Organizations*   The number of people enrolled in health maintenance organizations (HMOs) in the United States from 1976 through 1988 can be approximated by the model

$f(t) = 215t^2 - 470t + 6700, \qquad 0 \le t \le 12.$

In this model, $f(t)$ represents the number of people (in 1000s) and t represents the calendar year with $t = 0$ corresponding to 1976 (see figure). You want to adjust this model so that $t = 0$ corresponds to 1980 rather than 1976.

To do this, you shift the graph of f 4 units *to the left* and obtain

$g(t) = f(t + 4)$
$= 215(t + 4)^2 - 470(t + 4) + 6700.$

Write this new polynomial function in standard form. (*Source*: Group Health Insurance Association of America)

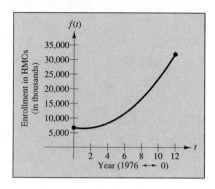

Figure for 64

In Exercises 65–68, prove the given property for all integers m and n where $0 \le m \le n$.

65. $_nC_m = {_nC_{n-m}}$

66. $_nC_0 - {_nC_1} + {_nC_2} - \cdots \pm {_nC_n} = 0$

67. $_{n+1}C_m = {_nC_m} + {_nC_{m-1}}$

68. $_{2n}C_n = (_nC_0)^2 + (_nC_1)^2 + (_nC_2)^2 + \cdots + (_nC_n)^2$

69. Prove that the sum of the numbers in the nth row of Pascal's Triangle is 2^n. (*Hint*: Consider $2^n = (1 + 1)^n$.)

Counting Principles, Permutations, Combinations

Simple Counting Problems / Counting Principles / Permutations / Combinations

Simple Counting Problems

In the last two sections of this chapter, we give a brief introduction to some of the basic counting principles and their application to probability. In the next section, you will see that much of probability has to do with counting the number of ways an event can occur. Examples 1, 2, and 3 describe some simple counting problems.

EXAMPLE 1 A Random Number Generator

A random number generator (on a computer) selects an integer from 1 to 40. Find the number of ways the following events can occur.

a. An even integer is selected.
b. A number less than 10 is selected.
c. A prime number is selected.

Solution

a. Since half of the numbers between 1 and 40 are even, this event can occur in 20 different ways.
b. The integers between 1 and 40 that are less than 10 are given in the following set.

$$\{1, 2, 3, 4, 5, 6, 7, 8, 9\}$$

Since this set has nine members, there are nine different ways this event can happen.
c. The prime numbers between 1 and 40 are given in the following set.

$$\{2, 3, 5, 7, 11, 13, 17, 19, 23, 29, 31, 37\}$$

Since this set has 12 members, there are 12 different ways this event can happen. ◢

EXAMPLE 2 Selecting Pairs of Numbers at Random

Eight pieces of paper are numbered from 1 to 8 and placed in a box. One piece of paper is drawn from the box, its number is written down, and the piece of paper is replaced in the box. Then a second piece of paper is drawn from the box, and its number is written down. Finally, the two numbers are added together. How many different ways can a total of 12 be obtained?

Solution

To solve this problem, you count the different ways that a total of 12 can be obtained using two numbers between 1 and 8.

| First number | + | Second number | = | 12 |

After considering the various possibilities, you see that this equation can be solved in the following five ways.

First Number	Second Number
4	8
5	7
6	6
7	5
8	4

Thus, a total of 12 can be obtained in five different ways.   ◢

Solving counting problems can be tricky. Often, seemingly minor changes in the statement of a problem can affect the answer. For instance, compare the counting problem in the next example with that given in Example 2.

EXAMPLE 3   Selecting Pairs of Numbers at Random

Eight pieces of paper are numbered from 1 to 8 and placed in a box. Two pieces of paper are drawn from the box, the number on each piece of paper is written down, and the two are totaled. How many different ways can a total of 12 be obtained?

Solution

To solve this problem, you count the different ways that a total of 12 can be obtained *using two different numbers* between 1 and 8.

REMARK   The difference between the counting problems in Examples 2 and 3 is that the random selection in Example 2 occurs **with replacement,** whereas the random selection in Example 3 occurs **without replacement,** which eliminates the possibility of choosing two 6's.

First Number	Second Number
4	8
5	7
7	5
8	4

Thus, a total of 12 can be obtained in four different ways.   ◢

Counting Principles

In the first three examples, we looked at simple counting problems in which we can *list* each possible way that an event can occur. When it is possible, this is always the best way to solve a counting problem. However, some events can occur in so many different ways that it is not feasible to write out the entire list. In such cases, we must rely on formulas and counting principles. The most important of these is the **Fundamental Counting Principle.**

REMARK The Fundamental Counting Principle can be extended to three or more events. For instance, the number of ways that three events E_1, E_2, and E_3 can occur is $m_1 \cdot m_2 \cdot m_3$.

FUNDAMENTAL COUNTING PRINCIPLE

Let E_1 and E_2 be two events. The first event E_1 can occur in m_1 different ways. After E_1 has occurred, E_2 can occur in m_2 different ways. The number of ways that the two events can occur is

$$m_1 \cdot m_2.$$

EXAMPLE 4   Applying the Fundamental Counting Principle

How many different pairs of letters from the English alphabet are possible? (Disregard the difference between uppercase and lowercase letters.)

Solution

This experiment has two events. The first event is the choice of the first letter, and the second event is the choice of the second letter. Since the English alphabet contains 26 letters, it follows that each event can occur in 26 ways.

Two-letter "words"

26   26

Thus, using the Fundamental Counting Principle, it follows that the number of two-letter "words" is

$$26 \cdot 26 = 676.$$

EXAMPLE 5   Applying the Fundamental Counting Principle

Telephone numbers in the United States have ten digits. The first three are the *area code* and the next seven are the *local telephone number*. How many different telephone numbers are possible within each area code? (Note that a local telephone number cannot begin with 0 or 1.)

Solution

Since the first digit cannot be 0 or 1, there are only eight choices for the first digit. For each of the other six digits, there are ten choices.

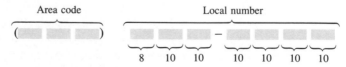

Area code   Local number

8   10   10   10   10   10   10

Thus, using the Fundamental Counting Principle, the number of local telephone numbers that are possible within each area code is

$$8 \cdot 10 \cdot 10 \cdot 10 \cdot 10 \cdot 10 \cdot 10 = 8{,}000{,}000.$$

Permutations

One important application of the Fundamental Counting Principle is in determining the number of ways that n elements can be arranged (in order). We call an ordering of n elements a **permutation** of the elements.

DEFINITION OF PERMUTATION

A **permutation** of n different elements is an ordering of the elements such that one element is first, one is second, one is third, and so on.

EXAMPLE 6 Listing Permutations

Write the different permutations of the letters A, B, and C.

Solution

These three letters can be arranged in the following six different ways.

A, B, C,   B, A, C,   C, A, B

A, C, B,   B, C, A,   C, B, A

Thus, you see that these three letters have six different permutations.

In Example 6, you were able to list the different permutations of three letters. However, you could also have used the Fundamental Counting Principle. To do this, you could reason that there are three choices for the first letter, two choices for the second, and only one choice for the third, as follows.

Permutations of three letters

3   2   1

Thus, the number of permutations of three letters is

$$3 \cdot 2 \cdot 1 = 3! = 6.$$

EXAMPLE 7 Finding the Number of Permutations of *n* Elements

How many different permutations are possible for the letters A, B, C, D, E, and F?

Solution

There are too many different permutations to list, so you use the following reasoning.

1st position: Any of the *six* letters.
2nd position: Any of the remaining *five* letters.
3rd position: Any of the remaining *four* letters.
4th position: Any of the remaining *three* letters.
5th position: Any of the remaining *two* letters.
6th position: The *one* remaining letter.

Thus, the number of choices for the six positions is as follows.

Permutations of six letters

6   5   4   3   2   1

Using the Fundamental Counting Principle, you find that the total number of permutations of the six letters is

$$6 \cdot 5 \cdot 4 \cdot 3 \cdot 2 \cdot 1 = 6! = 720.$$

The results obtained in Examples 6 and 7 can be generalized to conclude that the number of permutations of *n* different elements is *n*!.

NUMBER OF PERMUTATIONS OF *n* ELEMENTS

The number of permutations of *n* elements is given by

$$n \cdot (n - 1) \cdots 4 \cdot 3 \cdot 2 \cdot 1 = n!.$$

In other words, there are *n*! different ways that *n* elements can be ordered.

EXAMPLE 8 Finding the Number of Permutations

Suppose that you are a supervisor for 11 different employees. One of your responsibilities is to perform an annual evaluation for each employee, and then rank the 11 different performances. (In other words, one employee must be ranked as having the best performance, one must be ranked second, and so on.) How many different rankings are possible?

Solution

Since there are 11 different employees, you have 11 choices for first ranking. After choosing the first ranking, you can choose any of the remaining 10 for second ranking, and so on.

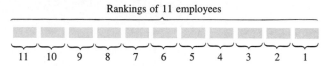

Rankings of 11 employees

11 10 9 8 7 6 5 4 3 2 1

Thus, the number of different rankings is

$11! = 39,916,800.$

Occasionally, you may be interested in ordering a *subset* of a collection of elements rather than the entire collection. For example, you might want to choose (and order) *m* elements out of a collection of *n* elements. Such an ordering is a **permutation of *n* elements taken *m* at a time.**

EXAMPLE 9 Permutations of *n* Elements Taken *m* at a Time

Eight horses are running in a race. In how many different ways can these horses come in first, second, and third? (Assume that there are no ties.)

Solution

You have the following possibilities.

Win   (1st position):   *Eight* choices
Place (2nd position):   *Seven* choices
Show   (3rd position):   *Six* choices

Using the Fundamental Counting Principle, multiply these three numbers together to obtain the following.

Different orders of horses

8   7   6

Thus, there are $8 \cdot 7 \cdot 6 = 336$ different orders.

The result of Example 9 can be generalized as follows.

PERMUTATIONS OF *n* ELEMENTS TAKEN *m* AT A TIME

The number of permutations of *n* elements taken *m* at a time is

$$_nP_m = \frac{n!}{(n-m)!} = n(n-1)(n-2)\cdots(n-m+1).$$

Using this formula, you can rework Example 9 to find that the number of permutations of eight horses taken three at a time is

$$_8P_3 = \frac{8!}{(8-3)!} = \frac{8!}{5!} = \frac{8\cdot7\cdot6\cdot5!}{5!} = 8\cdot7\cdot6 = 336$$

which is the same answer you obtained in the solution of Example 9.

Remember that for permutations, order is important. Thus, if you are looking at the possible permutations of the letters A, B, C, and D taken three at a time, the permutations (A, B, D) and (B, A, D) would be different (since the *order* of the elements is different).

Suppose, however, that you are asked to find the possible permutations of the letters A, A, B, and C. The total number of permutations of the four letters would be $_4P_4 = 4!$. However, not all of these arrangements would be *distinguishable* because there are two A's in the list. To find the number of distinguishable permutations, you can use the following formula.

DISTINGUISHABLE PERMUTATIONS

Suppose a set of *n* objects has n_1 of one kind of object, n_2 of a second kind, n_3 of a third kind, and so on, with $n = n_1 + n_2 + n_3 + \cdots + n_k$. Then the number of **distinguishable permutations** of the *n* objects is

$$\frac{n!}{n_1! \cdot n_2! \cdot n_3! \cdots n_k!}.$$

EXAMPLE 10   Distinguishable Permutations

In how many distinguishable ways can the letters in BANANA be written?

Solution

This word has six letters, of which three are A's, two are N's and one is a B. Thus, the number of distinguishable ways the letters can be written is

$$\frac{6!}{3! \cdot 2! \cdot 1!} = \frac{6\cdot5\cdot4\cdot3!}{3! \cdot 2!} = 60.$$

The 60 different "words" are as follows.

AAABNN	AAANBN	AAANNB	AABANN	AABNAN	AABNNA
AANABN	AANANB	AANBAN	AANBNA	AANNAB	AANNBA
ABAANN	ABANAN	ABANNA	ABNAAN	ABNANA	ABNNAA
ANAABN	ANAANB	ANABAN	ANABNA	ANANAB	ANANBA
ANBAAN	ANBANA	ANBNAA	ANNAAB	ANNABA	ANNBAA
BAAANN	BAANAN	BAANNA	BANAAN	BANANA	BANNAA
BNAAAN	BNAANA	BNANAA	BNNAAA	NAAABN	NAAANB
NAABAN	NAABNA	NAANAB	NAANBA	NABAAN	NABANA
NABNAA	NANAAB	NANABA	NANBAA	NBAAAN	NBAANA
NBANAA	NBNAAA	NNAAAB	NNAABA	NNABAA	NNBAAA

Combinations

When counting the number of possible permutations of a set of elements, *order* is important. As a final topic in this section, we look at a method of selecting subsets of a larger set in which order is *not important*. Such subsets are **combinations of *n* elements taken *m* at a time.** For instance, the combinations

$$\{A, B, C\} \quad \text{and} \quad \{B, A, C\}$$

are equivalent because both sets contain the same three elements, and the order in which the elements are listed is *not important*. Hence, we would count only one of the two sets. A common example of how a combination occurs is a card game in which the player is free to reorder the cards after they have been dealt.

EXAMPLE 11   Combination of *n* Elements Taken *m* at a Time

In how many different ways can three letters be chosen from the letters A, B, C, D, and E? (The order of the three letters is not important.)

Solution

The following subsets represent the different combinations of three letters that can be chosen from five letters.

$$\{A, B, C\} \quad \{A, B, D\}$$
$$\{A, B, E\} \quad \{A, C, D\}$$
$$\{A, C, E\} \quad \{A, D, E\}$$
$$\{B, C, D\} \quad \{B, C, E\}$$
$$\{B, D, E\} \quad \{C, D, E\}$$

From this list, you conclude that there are ten different ways that three letters can be chosen from five letters.

The formula for the number of *combinations* of *n* elements taken *m* at a time is as follows.

COMBINATIONS OF n ELEMENTS TAKEN m AT A TIME

The number of combinations of n elements taken m at a time is

$$_nC_m = \frac{n!}{(n-m)!m!}.$$

Note that the formula for $_nC_m$ is the same as the one given for binomial coefficients. To see how this formula is used, solve the counting problem given in Example 11. In that problem, you must find the number of combinations of five elements taken three at a time. Thus, $n = 5$, $m = 3$, and the number of combinations is

$$_5C_3 = \frac{5!}{2!3!} = \frac{5 \cdot 4 \cdot 3}{3 \cdot 2 \cdot 1} = 10$$

which is the same answer you obtained in Example 11.

EXAMPLE 12   Combinations of n Elements Taken m at a Time

A standard poker hand consists of five cards dealt from a deck of 52. How many different poker hands are possible? (After the cards are dealt, the player may reorder them, and therefore order is not important.)

Solution

Use the formula for the number of combinations of 52 elements taken five at a time, as follows.

$$_{52}C_5 = \frac{52!}{47!5!} = \frac{52 \cdot 51 \cdot 50 \cdot 49 \cdot 48}{5 \cdot 4 \cdot 3 \cdot 2 \cdot 1} = 2{,}598{,}960 \text{ different hands}$$

EXAMPLE 13   Combinations and the Fundamental Counting Principle

The traveling squad for a college basketball team consists of two centers, five forwards, and four guards. In how many ways can the coach select a starting team of one center, two forwards, and two guards?

Solution

The number of ways to select one center is

$$_2C_1 = \frac{2!}{1!(1!)} = 2.$$

The number of ways to select two forwards from among five is

$$_5C_2 = \frac{5!}{3!(2!)} = 10.$$

The number of ways to select two guards from among four is

$$_4C_2 = \frac{4!}{2!(2!)} = 6.$$

Therefore, the total number of ways to select a starting team is

$$_2C_1 \cdot {_5C_2} \cdot {_4C_2} = 2 \cdot 10 \cdot 6 = 120.$$

◢

DISCUSSION

PROBLEM

You Be
the
Instructor

Suppose you are teaching an algebra class and are writing a test for this chapter. Create two word problems that you think are appropriate for the test. One of the word problems should deal with permutations and the other should deal with combinations. (Assume that your students will have only five minutes to solve each problem.)

WARM UP

The following warm-up exercises involve skills that were covered in earlier sections. You will use these skills in the exercise set for this section.

In Exercises 1–4, evaluate the expression.

1. $13 \cdot 8^2 \cdot 2^3$

2. $10^2 \cdot 9^3 \cdot 4$

3. $\dfrac{12!}{2!(7!)(3!)}$

4. $\dfrac{25!}{22!}$

In Exercises 5 and 6, find the binomial coefficient.

5. $_{12}C_7$

6. $_{25}C_{22}$

In Exercises 7–10, simplify the expression.

7. $\dfrac{n!}{(n-4)!}$

8. $\dfrac{(2n)!}{4(2n-3)!}$

9. $\dfrac{2 \cdot 4 \cdot 6 \cdot 8 \cdots (2n)}{2^n}$

10. $\dfrac{3 \cdot 6 \cdot 9 \cdot 12 \cdots (3n)}{3^n}$

EXERCISES for Section 10.6

1. A bag contains 10 marbles numbered 1 through 10. A marble is selected, its number is recorded, and the marble is *replaced* in the bag. Then a second marble is drawn and its number recorded. Finally, the recorded numbers are added. How many different ways can a sum of 8 be obtained?

2. A bag contains 10 marbles numbered 1 through 10. Two marbles are selected and their numbers are recorded. Then the recorded numbers are added. How many different ways can a sum of 8 be obtained?

3. *Job Applicants* A small college needs two additional faculty members: a chemist and a statistician. In how many ways can these positions be filled if there are three applicants for the chemistry position and four for the position in statistics?

4. *Computer Systems* A customer in a computer store can choose one of three monitors, one of two keyboards, and one of four computers. If all the choices are compatible, how many different systems could be chosen?

5. *Toboggan Ride* Four people are lining up for a ride on a toboggan, but only two of the four are willing to take the first position. With that constraint, in how many ways can the four people be seated on the toboggan?

6. *Course Schedule* A college student is preparing a course schedule for the next semester. The student may select one of two mathematics courses, one of three science courses, and one of five courses from the social sciences and humanities. How many schedules are possible?

7. *License Plate Numbers* In a certain state the automobile license plates consist of two letters followed by a four-digit number. How many distinct license plate numbers can be formed?

8. *License Plate Numbers* In a certain state the automobile license plates consist of two letters followed by a four-digit number. To avoid confusion between "O" and "zero" and "I" and "one," the letters "O" and "I" are not used. How many distinct license plate numbers can be formed?

9. *True-False Exam* In how many ways can a six-question true-false exam be answered? (Assume that no questions are omitted.)

10. *Multiple Choice* In how many ways can a 10-question multiple choice exam be answered if there are four choices of answers for each question? (Assume that no questions are omitted.)

11. *Three-Digit Numbers* How many three-digit numbers can be formed under the following conditions?
(a) The leading digit cannot be zero.
(b) The leading digit cannot be zero and no repetition of digits is allowed.
(c) The leading digit cannot be zero and the number must be a multiple of 5.
(d) The number is at least 400.

12. *Four-Digit Numbers* How many four-digit numbers can be formed under the following conditions?
(a) The leading digit cannot be zero.
(b) The leading digit cannot be zero and no repetition of digits is allowed.

(c) The leading digit cannot be zero and the number must be less than 5000.
(d) The leading digit cannot be zero and the number must be even.

13. *Combination Lock* A combination lock will open when the right choice of three numbers (from 1 to 40, inclusive) is selected. How many different lock combinations are possible?

14. *Combination Lock* A combination lock will open when the right choice of three numbers (from 1 to 50, inclusive) is selected. How many different lock combinations are possible?

15. *Concert Seats* Three couples have reserved seats in a given row for a concert. In how many different ways can they be seated if
(a) there are no seating restrictions?
(b) the two members of each couple wish to sit together?

16. *Single File* In how many orders can three girls and two boys walk through a doorway single-file if
(a) there are no restrictions?
(b) the boys go before the girls?
(c) the girls go before the boys?

In Exercises 17–26, evaluate $_nP_m$.

17. $_4P_4$ **18.** $_5P_5$

19. $_8P_3$ **20.** $_{20}P_2$

21. $_{20}P_5$ **22.** $_{100}P_1$

23. $_{100}P_2$ **24.** $_{10}P_2$

25. $_5P_4$ **26.** $_7P_4$

27. Write all the permutations of the letters A, B, C, and D.

28. Write all the permutations of the letters A, B, C, and D if the letters B and C must remain between the letters A and D.

29. *Posing for a Photograph* In how many ways can five children line up in one row to have their picture taken?

30. *Riding in a Car* In how many ways can six people sit in a six-passenger car?

31. *Choosing Officers* From a pool of 12 candidates, the offices of president, vice-president, secretary, and treasurer will be filled. In how many different ways can the offices be filled, if each of the 12 candidates can hold any office?

32. *Assembly Line Production* There are four processes involved in assembling a certain product, and these can be performed in any order. The management wants to test each order to determine which is the least time-consuming. How many different orders will have to be tested?

In Exercises 33–38, find the number of distinguishable permutations of the given group of letters.

33. A, A, G, E, E, E, M

34. B, B, B, T, T, T, T, T

35. A, A, Y, Y, Y, Y, X, X, X

36. K, K, M, M, M, L, L, N, N

37. A, L, G, E, B, R, A

38. M, I, S, S, I, S, S, I, P, P, I

39. Write all the possible selections of two letters that can be formed from the letters A, B, C, D, E, and F. (The order of the two letters is not important.)

40. Write all the possible selections of three letters that can be formed from the letters A, B, C, D, E, and F. (The order of the three letters is not important.)

41. *Forming an Experimental Group* In order to conduct a certain experiment, four students are randomly selected from a class of 20. How many different groups of four students are possible?

42. *Test Questions* A student may answer any 10 questions from a total of 12 questions on an exam. In how many different ways can the student select the questions?

43. *Lottery Choices* There are 40 numbers in a particular state lottery. In how many ways can a player select six of the numbers? (The order of selection is not important.)

44. *Lottery Choices* There are 50 numbers in a particular state lottery. In how many ways can a player select six of the numbers? (The order of selection is not important.)

45. *Number of Subsets* How many subsets of four elements can be formed from a set of 100 elements?

46. *Number of Subsets* How many subsets of five elements can be formed from a set of 80 elements?

47. *Forming a Committee* A committee composed of three graduate students and two undergraduate students is to be selected from a group of eight graduates and five undergraduates. How many different committees can be formed?

48. *Defective Units* A shipment of 12 microwave ovens contains three defective units. In how many ways can a vending company purchase four of these units and receive (a) all good units, (b) two good units, and (c) at least two good units?

49. *Job Applicants* An employer interviews eight people for four openings in the company. Three of the eight people are women. If all eight are qualified, in how many ways could the employer fill the four positions if (a) the selection is random and (b) exactly two are women?

50. *Poker Hand* Five cards are selected from an ordinary deck of 52 playing cards. In how many ways can you get a full house? (A full house consists of three of one kind and two of another. For example, A-A-A-5-5 and K-K-K-10-10 are full houses.)

51. *Forming a Committee* Four people are to be selected at random from a group of four couples. In how many ways can this be done, given the following conditions?
(a) There are no restrictions.
(b) There is to be at least one couple in the group of four.
(c) The selection must include one member from each couple.

52. *Interpersonal Relationships* The complexity of the interpersonal relationships increases dramatically as the size of a group increases. Determine the number of two-person relationships in a group of people of size (a) 3, (b) 8, (c) 12, and (d) 20.

In Exercises 53–56, find the number of diagonals of the given polygon. (A line segment connecting any two non-adjacent vertices is called a *diagonal* of the polygon.)

53. Pentagon

54. Hexagon

55. Octagon

56. Decagon (10 sides)

In Exercises 57 and 58, solve for n.

57. $14 \cdot {}_nP_3 = {}_{n+2}P_4$

58. ${}_nP_5 = 18 \, {}_{n-2}P_4$

In Exercises 59–63, prove the identity.

59. ${}_nP_{n-1} = {}_nP_n$

60. ${}_nP_1 = {}_nC_1$

61. ${}_nC_{n-1} = {}_nC_1$

62. ${}_nC_n = {}_nC_0$

63. ${}_nC_m = \dfrac{{}_nP_m}{m!}$

10.7 Probability

Sample Spaces / The Probability of an Event / Mutually Exclusive Events / Independent Events / The Complement of an Event

Sample Spaces

As a member of a complex society, you are used to living with varying amounts of uncertainty. For example, you may be questioning the likelihood of getting a good job after graduation, of winning a state lottery, of having an accident on your next trip home, or of any of several other possibilities.

In assigning measurements to uncertainties in everyday life, we often use ambiguous terminology, such as *fairly certain*, *probable*, or *highly unlikely*. In mathematics, we attempt to remove this ambiguity by assigning a number to the likelihood of the occurrence of an event. We call this measurement the **probability** that the event will occur. For example, if we toss a fair coin, we say that the probability that it will land heads up is one-half, or 50%.

In the study of probability, any happening whose result is uncertain is an **experiment.** The various possible results of the experiment are **outcomes,** and the collection of all possible outcomes of an experiment is the **sample space** of the experiment. Finally, any subcollection of a sample space is an **event.** In this section we will deal only with sample spaces in which each outcome is equally likely, such as flipping a fair coin or tossing a fair die.

EXAMPLE 1   Finding the Sample Space

An experiment consists of tossing a six-sided die.

a. What is the sample space?
b. Describe the event corresponding to a number greater than 2 turning up.

Solution

a. The sample space consists of six outcomes, which you represent by the numbers 1 through 6. That is,

$$S = \{1, 2, 3, 4, 5, 6\}.$$

Note that each of the outcomes in the sample space is equally likely (assuming the die is balanced).
b. The *event* corresponding to a number greater than 2 turning up is the following subset of S.

$$A = \{3, 4, 5, 6\}$$

To describe sample spaces in such a way that each outcome is equally likely, we must sometimes distinguish between various outcomes in ways that appear artificial. The next example illustrates such a situation.

EXAMPLE 2   Finding the Sample Space

Find the sample spaces for the following.

a. One coin is tossed.
b. Two coins are tossed.
c. Three coins are tossed.

Solution

a. Since the coin will land either heads up (denoted by H) or tails up (denoted by T), the sample space is

$$S = \{H, T\}.$$

b. Since either coin can land heads up or tails up, the possible outcomes are as follows.

$HH = $ heads up on both coins

$HT = $ heads up on first coin and tails up on second coin

$TH = $ tails up on first coin and heads up on second coin

$TT = $ tails up on both coins

Thus, the sample space is

$$S = \{HH, HT, TH, TT\}.$$

Note that you must distinguish between the two cases HT and TH, even though these two outcomes appear to be similar.

c. Following the notation of part (b), the sample space is

$$S = \{HHH, HHT, HTH, HTT, THH, THT, TTH, TTT\}.$$

The Probability of an Event

To calculate the probability of an event, you count the number of outcomes in the event and in the sample space. The *number of outcomes* in event E is denoted by $n(E)$, and the number of outcomes in the sample space S is denoted by $n(S)$.

THE PROBABILITY OF AN EVENT

If an event E has $n(E)$ equally likely outcomes and its sample space S has $n(S)$ equally likely outcomes, then the **probability** of event E is

$$P(E) = \frac{n(E)}{n(S)}.$$

Because the number of outcomes in an event must be less than or equal to the number of outcomes in the sample space, you can see that the probability of an event must be a number between 0 and 1. That is, for any event E, it must be true that $0 \leq P(E) \leq 1$.

PROPERTIES OF THE PROBABILITY OF AN EVENT

Let E be an event that is a subset of a finite sample space S.

1. $0 \leq P(E) \leq 1$
2. If $P(E) = 0$, then the event E *cannot occur*, and E is an **impossible event.**
3. If $P(E) = 1$, then the event E *must occur*, and E is a **certain event.**

EXAMPLE 3   Finding the Probability of an Event

Find the probability of the following events.

a. Two coins are tossed. What is the probability that both land heads up?
b. A card is drawn from a standard deck of playing cards. What is the probability that it is an ace?

Solution

a. Following the procedure in Example 2(b), let

$$E = \{HH\} \qquad \text{and} \qquad S = \{HH, HT, TH, TT\}.$$

The probability of getting two heads is

$$P(E) = \frac{n(E)}{n(S)} = \frac{1}{4}.$$

b. Since there are 52 cards in a standard deck of playing cards and there are four aces (one in each suit), the probability of drawing an ace is

$$P(E) = \frac{n(E)}{n(S)} = \frac{4}{52} = \frac{1}{13}.$$

FIGURE 10.5

EXAMPLE 4   Finding the Probability of an Event

Two six-sided dice are tossed. What is the probability that the total of the two dice is 7? (See Figure 10.5.)

Solution

Since there are six possible outcomes on each die, you use the Fundamental Counting Principle to conclude that there are

$$6 \cdot 6 = 36 \text{ different outcomes}$$

when two dice are tossed. To find the probability of rolling a total of 7, you must first count the number of ways this can occur.

	Total of 7					
First die	1	2	3	4	5	6
Second die	6	5	4	3	2	1

Thus, a total of 7 can be rolled in six ways, which means that the probability of rolling a 7 is

$$P(E) = \frac{n(E)}{n(S)} = \frac{6}{36} = \frac{1}{6}.$$

You could have written out each sample space in Examples 3 and 4 and simply counted the outcomes in the desired events. For larger sample spaces, however, you must make more use of the counting principles discussed in the previous section.

EXAMPLE 5 Finding the Probability of an Event

Twelve-sided dice can be constructed (in the shape of regular dodecahedrons) so that each of the numbers from 1 to 6 appears twice on each die, as shown in Figure 10.6. Prove that these dice can be used in any game requiring ordinary six-sided dice without changing the probability of different outcomes.

Solution

For an ordinary six-sided die, each of the numbers 1, 2, 3, 4, 5, and 6 occurs only once, so the probability of any particular number coming up is

$$P(E) = \frac{n(E)}{n(S)} = \frac{1}{6}.$$

For one of the twelve-sided dice, each number occurs twice, so the probability of any particular number coming up is

$$P(E) = \frac{n(E)}{n(S)} = \frac{2}{12} = \frac{1}{6}.$$

Thus, the twelve-sided dice can be used in place of the six-sided dice without changing the probabilities.

FIGURE 10.6

EXAMPLE 6   The Probability of Winning a Lottery

A state lottery is set up so that each player chooses six different numbers from 1 to 40. If these six numbers match the six numbers drawn by the lottery commission, the player wins (or shares) the top prize. What is the probability of winning the top prize in this game?

Solution

Since the order of the numbers is not important, use the formula for the number of combinations of 40 elements taken six at a time to determine the size of the sample space.

$$n(S) = {}_{40}C_6 = \frac{40 \cdot 39 \cdot 38 \cdot 37 \cdot 36 \cdot 35}{6 \cdot 5 \cdot 4 \cdot 3 \cdot 2 \cdot 1} = 3{,}838{,}380$$

If a person buys only one ticket, the probability of winning is

$$P(E) = \frac{n(E)}{n(S)} = \frac{1}{3{,}838{,}380}.$$

EXAMPLE 7   Random Selection

The total number of colleges and universities in the United States in 1987 is shown in Figure 10.7. (*Source*: U.S. National Center for Education Statistics) Suppose one institution is selected at random. What is the probability that the institution is in one of three southern regions?

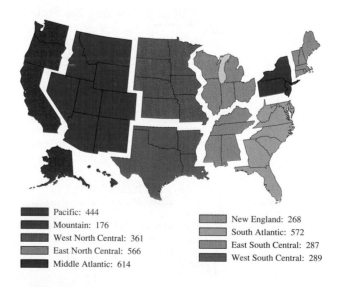

Pacific: 444
Mountain: 176
West North Central: 361
East North Central: 566
Middle Atlantic: 614

New England: 268
South Atlantic: 572
East South Central: 287
West South Central: 289

FIGURE 10.7

Solution

Begin by finding the total number of colleges and universities.

Total = 268 + 614 + 566 + 361 + 572 + 287 + 289 + 176 + 444 = 3577

Since there are 572 + 287 + 289 = 1148 colleges and universities in the three southern regions, the probability that the institution is from one of these regions is

$$P(E) = \frac{n(E)}{n(S)} = \frac{1148}{3577} \approx 0.321.$$

◢

Mutually Exclusive Events

Two events A and B (from the same sample space) are **mutually exclusive** if A and B have no outcomes in common. In the terminology of sets, we say that the **intersection of A and B** is the empty set, which implies that

$$P(A \cap B) = 0.$$

For instance, if two dice are tossed, the event A of rolling a total of six and the event B of rolling a total of nine are mutually exclusive. To find the probability that one or the other of two mutually exclusive events will occur, *add* their individual probabilities.

PROBABILITY OF THE UNION OF TWO EVENTS

If A and B are events in the same sample space, then the probability of A or B occurring is given by

$$P(A \cup B) = P(A) + P(B) - P(A \cap B).$$

If A and B are mutually exclusive, then $P(A \cap B) = 0$ and it follows that

$$P(A \cup B) = P(A) + P(B).$$

EXAMPLE 8   Finding the Probability of the Union of Two Events

One card is selected from a standard deck of 52 playing cards. What is the probability that the card is either a heart or a face card?

Solution

Since the deck has 13 hearts, the probability of selecting a heart (event A) is

$$P(A) = \frac{13}{52}.$$ *Selecting a heart*

Similarly, since the deck has 12 face cards, the probability of selecting a face card (event B) is

$$P(B) = \frac{12}{52}.$$ *Selecting a face card*

Now, because three of the cards are hearts and face cards (see Figure 10.8), it follows that

$$P(A \cap B) = \frac{3}{52}.$$

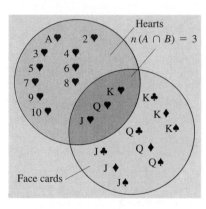

FIGURE 10.8

Finally, applying the formula for the probability of the union of two events, you conclude that the probability of selecting a heart or a face card is

$$P(A \cup B) = P(A) + P(B) - P(A \cap B)$$

$$= \frac{13}{52} + \frac{12}{52} - \frac{3}{52}$$

$$= \frac{22}{52} \approx 0.423.$$

Independent Events

Two events are **independent** if the occurrence of one has no effect on the occurrence of the other. To find the probability that two independent events will occur, *multiply* the probabilities of each. For instance, rolling a total of 12 with two-sided dice has no effect on the outcome for future rolls of the dice.

PROBABILITY OF INDEPENDENT EVENTS

If A and B are independent events, then the probability that both A and B will occur is

$$P(A \text{ and } B) = P(A) \cdot P(B).$$

EXAMPLE 9   Probability of Independent Events

A random number generator on a computer selects three integers from 1 to 20. What is the probability that all three numbers are less than or equal to 5?

Solution

If the random number generator is truly random, then you can conclude that the selection of any given number will not affect the selection of the next number. This means that the three choices represent independent events. Furthermore, since the probability of selecting a number from 1 to 5 is

$$P(A) = \frac{5}{20} = \frac{1}{4}$$

you can conclude that the probability of selecting all three numbers less than or equal to 5 is

$$P(A) \cdot P(A) \cdot P(A) = \left(\frac{1}{4}\right)\left(\frac{1}{4}\right)\left(\frac{1}{4}\right) = \frac{1}{64}.$$ ◢

EXAMPLE 10   Probability of Independent Events

In 1988, 54.2% of the population of the United States were 30 years old or older. Suppose that in a survey, 10 people were chosen at random from the population. What is the probability that all 10 are 30 years old or older?

Solution

Let A represent choosing a person who is 30 years old or older. Since the probability of choosing a person who is 30 years old or older is 0.542, you conclude that the probability that all 10 people are 30 years old or older is

$$P(A)^{10} = (0.542)^{10} \approx 0.0022.$$ ◢

The Complement of an Event

The **complement of an event** A is the collection of all outcomes in the sample space that are not in A. We denote the complement of event A by A'. Since $P(A \text{ or } A') = 1$ and since A and A' are mutually exclusive, we have $P(A) + P(A') = 1$. Therefore, the probability of A' is given by

$$P(A') = 1 - P(A).$$

For instance, if the probability of *winning* a certain game is

$$P(A) = \frac{1}{4}$$

then the probability of *losing* the game is

$$P(A') = 1 - \frac{1}{4} = \frac{3}{4}.$$

EXAMPLE 11   Finding the Probability of the Complement of an Event

A manufacturer has determined that a certain machine averages one faulty unit for every 1000 it produces. What is the probability that an order of 200 units will have one or more faulty units?

Solution

To solve this problem as stated, you would need to find the probability of having exactly one faulty unit, exactly two faulty units, exactly three faulty units, and so on. However, using complements, you can simply find the probability that all units are perfect and then subtract this value from 1. Since the probability that any given unit is perfect is $999/1000$, the probability that all 200 units are perfect is

$$P(A) = \left(\frac{999}{1000}\right)^{200} \approx 0.8186.$$

Therefore, the probability that at least one unit is faulty is

$$P(A') = 1 - P(A) \approx 0.1814.$$

In this section you have been finding probabilities from a *theoretical* point of view. Another way to find probabilities is from an *experimental* point of view. For instance, suppose you want to find the probability of obtaining a given total when two six-sided dice are tossed. The following BASIC program simulates the tossing of a pair of dice 5,000 times.

```
10   RANDOMIZE
20   DIM TALLY(12)
30   FOR I=1 TO 5000
40   ROLLONE=INT(6*RND)+1
50   ROLLTWO=INT(6*RND)+1
60   DICETOTAL=ROLLONE+ROLLTWO
70   TALLY(DICETOTAL)=TALLY(DICETOTAL)+1
80   NEXT
90   FOR I=2 TO 12
100  PRINT "TOTAL OF",I,"OCCURRED",TALLY(I),
     "TIMES"
110  NEXT
120  END
```

When you run this program, the printout is as follows.

```
TOTAL OF   2 OCCURRED 139 TIMES
TOTAL OF   3 OCCURRED 264 TIMES
TOTAL OF   4 OCCURRED 443 TIMES
TOTAL OF   5 OCCURRED 553 TIMES
TOTAL OF   6 OCCURRED 691 TIMES
TOTAL OF   7 OCCURRED 810 TIMES
TOTAL OF   8 OCCURRED 715 TIMES
TOTAL OF   9 OCCURRED 557 TIMES
TOTAL OF  10 OCCURRED 398 TIMES
TOTAL OF  11 OCCURRED 270 TIMES
TOTAL OF  12 OCCURRED 160 TIMES
```

In Example 4 you found that the theoretical probability of tossing a total of 7 on a pair of dice is $\frac{1}{6} \approx 0.167$. From this experiment, you find that the experimental probability of tossing a total of 7 on a pair of dice is $810/5,000 \approx 0.162$. Try this experiment on a computer that has the BASIC language. By increasing the number of trials from 5,000 to 10,000, does your experimental result get closer to the theoretical result?

WARM UP

The following warm-up exercises involve skills that were covered in earlier sections. You will use these skills in the exercise set for this section.

In Exercises 1–8, evaluate the expression.

1. $\dfrac{1}{4} + \dfrac{5}{8} - \dfrac{5}{16}$

2. $\dfrac{4}{15} + \dfrac{3}{5} - \dfrac{1}{3}$

3. $\dfrac{5 \cdot 4}{5!}$

4. $\dfrac{5!22!}{27!}$

5. $\dfrac{4!8!}{12!}$

6. $\dfrac{9 \cdot 8 \cdot 7 \cdot 6 \cdot 5}{9!}$

7. $\dfrac{{}_5C_3}{{}_{10}C_3}$

8. $\dfrac{{}_{10}C_2 \cdot {}_{10}C_2}{{}_{20}C_4}$

In Exercises 9 and 10, evaluate the expression. (Round to three decimal places.)

9. $\left(\dfrac{99}{100}\right)^{100}$

10. $1 - \left(\dfrac{89}{100}\right)^{50}$

EXERCISES for Section 10.7

In Exercises 1–6, determine the sample space for the given experiment.

1. A coin and a die are tossed.

2. A die is tossed twice and the sum of the points is recorded.

3. A taste tester has to rank three varieties of yogurt, A, B, and C, according to preference.

4. Two marbles are selected from a sack containing two red marbles, two blue marbles, and one black marble. The color of each marble is recorded.

5. Two county supervisors are selected from five supervisors, A, B, C, D, and E, to study a recycling plan.

6. A salesperson makes a presentation about a product in three homes per day. In each home there may be a sale (denote by S) or there may be no sale (denote by F).

Heads or Tails   In Exercises 7–10, find the required probability in the experiment of tossing a coin three times. Use the sample space $S = \{HHH, HHT, HTH, HTT, THH, THT, TTH, TTT\}$.

7. The probability of getting exactly one tail.

8. The probability of getting a head on the first toss.

9. The probability of getting at least one head.

10. The probability of getting at least two heads.

Drawing a Card   In Exercises 11–14, find the required probability in the experiment of selecting one card from a standard deck of 52 playing cards.

11. The probability of getting a face card.

12. The probability of not getting a face card.

13. The probability of getting a black card that is not a face card.

14. The probability that the card will be a 6 or less.

Tossing a Die   In Exercises 15–20, find the required probability in the experiment of tossing a six-sided die twice.

15. The probability that the sum is 4.

16. The probability that the sum is less than 11.

17. The probability that the sum is at least 7.

18. The probability that the total is 2, 3, or 12.

19. The probability that the sum is odd and no more than 7.

20. The probability that the sum is odd or a prime.

Drawing Marbles In Exercises 21–24, find the required probability in the experiment of drawing two marbles (the first is *not* replaced before the second is drawn) from a bag containing one green, two yellow, and three red marbles.

21. The probability of drawing two red marbles.

22. The probability of drawing two yellow marbles.

23. The probability of drawing neither yellow marble.

24. The probability of drawing marbles of different colors.

In Exercises 25 and 26, you are given the probability that an event *will* happen. Find the probability that the event *will not* happen.

25. $p = 0.7$ **26.** $p = 0.36$

In Exercises 27 and 28, you are given the probability that an event *will not* happen. Find the probability that the event *will* happen.

27. $p = 0.15$ **28.** $p = 0.84$

29. *Alumni Association* The alumni office of a college is sending a survey to selected members of the class of 1990. Of the 1254 people who graduated that year, 672 were women, 124 of whom went on to graduate school. Of the 582 male graduates, 198 went on to graduate school. If an alumni member is selected at random, what is the probability that the person is (a) female, (b) male, and (c) female and did not attend graduate school?

30. *Post High-School Education* In a high school graduating class of 72 students, 28 are on the honor roll. Of these 28, 18 are going on to college. Of the other 44 students, 12 are going on to college. If a student is selected at random from the class, what is the probability that the person chosen is (a) going to college, (b) not going to college, and (c) on the honor roll but not going to college?

31. *Winning an Election* Taylor, Moore, and Jenkins are candidates for public office. It is estimated that Moore and Jenkins have about the same probability of winning, and Taylor is believed to be twice as likely to win as either of the others. Find the probability of each candidate winning the election.

32. *Winning an Election* Three people have been nominated for president of a college class. From a small poll, it is estimated that the probability of the first candidate winning the election is 0.37, and the probability of the second candidate winning the election is 0.44. What is the probability that the third candidate will win?

33. *Preparing for a Test* An instructor gives her class a list of 20 study problems, from which she will select 10 to be answered on an exam. If a given student knows how to solve 15 of the problems, find the probability that the student will be able to answer (a) all 10 questions on the exam, (b) exactly eight questions on the exam, and (c) at least nine questions on the exam.

34. *Preparing for a Test* An instructor gives his class a list of eight study problems, from which he will select five to be answered on an exam. If a given student knows how to solve six of the problems, find the probability that the student will be able to answer (a) all five questions on the exam, (b) exactly four questions on the exam, and (c) at least four questions on the exam.

35. *Letter Mix-Up* Four letters and envelopes are addressed to four different people. If the letters are randomly inserted into the envelopes, what is the probability that (a) exactly one will be inserted in the correct envelope and (b) at least one will be inserted in the correct envelope?

36. *Payroll Mix-Up* Five paychecks and envelopes are addressed to five different people. If the paychecks are randomly inserted into the envelopes, what is the probability that (a) exactly one will be inserted in the correct envelope and (b) at least one will be inserted in the correct envelope?

37. *Game Show* On a game show you are given five digits to arrange in the proper order to give the price of a car. If you are correct, you win the car. What is the probability of winning, given the following conditions?
(a) You guess the position of each digit.
(b) You know the first digit, but must guess the remaining four.

38. *Game Show* On a game show you are given four digits to arrange in the proper order to give the price of a car. If you are correct, you win the car. What is the probability of winning, given the following conditions?
(a) You guess the position of each digit.
(b) You know the first digit, but must guess the remaining three.

39. *Drawing Cards from a Deck* Two cards are selected at random from an ordinary deck of 52 playing cards. Find the probability that two aces are selected, given the following conditions.
(a) The cards are drawn in sequence, with the first card being replaced and the deck reshuffled prior to the second drawing.
(b) The two cards are drawn consecutively, without replacement.

40. *Poker Hand* Five cards are drawn from an ordinary deck of 52 playing cards. What is the probability of getting a full house?

41. *Defective Units* A shipment of 12 microwave ovens contains three defective units. A vending company has ordered four of these 12 units, and since each is identically packaged, the selection will be random. What is the probability that (a) all four units are good, (b) exactly two units are good, and (c) at least two units are good?

42. *Defective Units* A shipment of 20 compact disc players contains four defective units. A retail outlet has ordered five of these units. What is the probability that (a) all five players are good, (b) exactly four of the players are good, and (c) at least one of the players is defective?

43. *Random Number Generator* Two integers (between 1 and 30 inclusive) are chosen by a random number generator on a computer. What is the probability that (a) the numbers are both even, (b) one number is even and one is odd, (c) both numbers are less than 10, and (d) the same number is chosen twice?

44. *Random Number Generator* Two integers (between 1 and 40 inclusive) are chosen by a random number generator on a computer. What is the probability that (a) the numbers are both even, (b) one number is even and one is odd, (c) both numbers are no more than 30, and (d) the same number is chosen twice?

45. *Backup System* A space vehicle has an independent backup system for one of its communication networks. The probability that either system will function satisfactorily for the duration of a flight is 0.985. What is the probability that during a given flight (a) both systems function satisfactorily, (b) at least one system functions satisfactorily, and (c) both systems fail?

46. *Backup Vehicle* A fire company keeps two rescue vehicles to serve the community. Because of the demand on the company's time and the chance of mechanical failure, the probability that a specific vehicle is available when needed is 90%. If the availability of one vehicle is *independent* of the other, find the probability that (a) both vehicles are available at a given time, (b) neither vehicle is available at a given time, and (c) at least one vehicle is available at a given time.

47. *Making a Sale* A sales representative makes a sale at a rate of approximately one-fourth of all calls. If, on a given day, the representative contacts five potential clients, what is the probability that a sale will be made with (a) all five contacts, (b) none of the contacts, and (c) at least one contact?

48. *Making a Sale* A sales representative makes a sale at a rate of approximately one-third of all calls. If, on a given day, the representative contacts four potential clients, what is the probability that a sale will be made with (a) all four contacts, (b) none of the contacts, and (c) at least one contact?

49. *A Boy or a Girl?* Assume that the probability of the birth of a child of a particular sex is 50%. In a family with four children, what is the probability that (a) all the children are boys, (b) all the children are the same sex, and (c) there is at least one boy?

50. *A Boy or a Girl?* Assume that the probability of the birth of a child of a particular sex is 50%. In a family with six children, what is the probability that (a) all the children are girls, (b) all the children are the same sex, and (c) there is at least one girl?

51. *Is That Cash or Charge?* According to a survey by *USA Today*, the method used by Christmas shoppers to pay for gifts is as shown in the pie chart. Suppose two Christmas shoppers are chosen at random. What is the probability that both shoppers paid for their gifts only in cash?

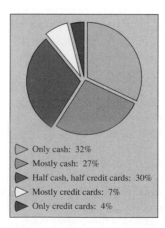

- ▷ Only cash: 32%
- ▷ Mostly cash: 27%
- ▶ Half cash, half credit cards: 30%
- ▷ Mostly credit cards: 7%
- ▶ Only credit cards: 4%

Figure for 51

52. *Flexible Work Hours*   In a survey by *Robert Hall International*, people were asked if they would prefer to work flexible hours—even if it meant slower career advancement—so they could spend more time with their family. The results of the survey are shown in the figure. Suppose three people from the survey were chosen at random. What is the probability that all three people would prefer flexible work hours?

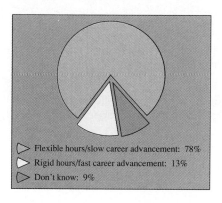

▷ Flexible hours/slow career advancement: 78%
▷ Rigid hours/fast career advancement: 13%
▷ Don't know: 9%

Figure for 52

REVIEW EXERCISES for Chapter 10

In Exercises 1–4, use sigma notation to write the given sum.

1. $\dfrac{1}{2(1)} + \dfrac{1}{2(2)} + \dfrac{1}{2(3)} + \cdots + \dfrac{1}{2(20)}$

2. $2(1^2) + 2(2^2) + 2(3^2) + \cdots + 2(9^2)$

3. $\frac{1}{2} + \frac{2}{3} + \frac{3}{4} + \cdots + \frac{9}{10}$

4. $1 - \frac{1}{3} + \frac{1}{9} - \frac{1}{27} + \cdots$

In Exercises 5–14, find the sum.

5. $\displaystyle\sum_{i=1}^{6} 5$

6. $\displaystyle\sum_{j=1}^{8} (20 - 3j)$

7. $\displaystyle\sum_{i=0}^{6} 2^i$

8. $\displaystyle\sum_{i=0}^{4} 3^i$

9. $\displaystyle\sum_{k=0}^{\infty} 4\left(\tfrac{2}{3}\right)^k$

10. $\displaystyle\sum_{k=0}^{\infty} 1.3\left(\tfrac{1}{10}\right)^k$

11. $\displaystyle\sum_{k=1}^{11} \left(\tfrac{2}{3}k + 4\right)$

12. $\displaystyle\sum_{k=1}^{25} \left(\dfrac{3k + 1}{4}\right)$

13. $\displaystyle\sum_{n=0}^{10} (n^2 + 3)$

14. $\displaystyle\sum_{n=1}^{100} \left(\dfrac{1}{n} - \dfrac{1}{n+1}\right)$

In Exercises 15–18, write the first five terms of the arithmetic sequence.

15. $a_1 = 3,\ d = 4$

16. $a_1 = 8,\ d = -2$

17. $a_4 = 10,\ a_{10} = 28$

18. $a_2 = 14,\ a_6 = 22$

In Exercises 19 and 20, write an expression for the *n*th term of the specified arithmetic sequence and find the sum of the first 20 terms of the sequence.

19. $a_1 = 100,\ d = -3$

20. $a_1 = 10,\ a_3 = 28$

21. Find the sum of the first 100 positive multiples of 5.

22. Find the sum of the integers from 20 to 80 (inclusive).

In Exercises 23–26, write the first five terms of the geometric sequence.

23. $a_1 = 4,\ r = -\tfrac{1}{4}$

24. $a_1 = 2,\ r = 2$

25. $a_1 = 9,\ a_3 = 4$

26. $a_1 = 2,\ a_3 = 12$

In Exercises 27 and 28, write an expression for the *n*th term of the specified geometric sequence and find the sum of the first 20 terms of the sequence.

27. $a_1 = 16,\ a_2 = -8$

28. $a_1 = 100,\ r = 1.05$

29. *Depreciation*   A company buys a machine for $120,000. During the next five years it will depreciate at the rate of 30% per year. (That is, at the end of each year, the depreciated value will be 70% of what it was at the beginning of the year.)

(a) Find the formula for the *t*th term of a geometric sequence that gives the value of the machine *t* full years after it was purchased.

(b) Find the depreciated value of the machine at the end of five full years.

30. *Total Compensation*   Suppose you accept a job that pays a salary of $32,000 the first year, and that you will receive a 5.5% raise for each of the next 39 years. What will your total salary be over the 40-year period?

31. *Compound Interest*   A deposit of $200 is made at the beginning of each month for two years into an account that pays 6%, compounded monthly. What is the balance in the account at the end of two years?

32. *Compound Interest* A deposit of $100 is made at the beginning of each month for 10 years into an account that pays 6.5%, compounded monthly. What is the balance in the account at the end of 10 years?

In Exercises 33–36, use mathematical induction to prove the given formula for every positive integer *n*.

33. $1 + 4 + \cdots + (3n - 2) = \dfrac{n}{2}(3n - 1)$

34. $1 + \dfrac{3}{2} + 2 + \dfrac{5}{2} + \cdots + \dfrac{1}{2}(n + 1) = \dfrac{n}{4}(n + 3)$

35. $\displaystyle\sum_{i=0}^{n-1} ar^i = \dfrac{a(1 - r^n)}{1 - r}$

36. $\displaystyle\sum_{k=0}^{n-1} (a + kd) = \dfrac{n}{2}[2a + (n - 1)d]$

In Exercises 37–40, evaluate the given expression.

37. $_6C_4$

38. $_{10}C_7$

39. $_8P_5$

40. $_{12}P_3$

In Exercises 41–46, use the Binomial Theorem to expand the binomial. Simplify your answer. (Remember that $i = \sqrt{-1}$.)

41. $\left(\dfrac{x}{2} + y\right)^4$

42. $(a - 3b)^5$

43. $\left(\dfrac{2}{x} - 3x\right)^6$

44. $(3x + y^2)^7$

45. $(5 + 2i)^4$

46. $(4 - 5i)^3$

47. *Interpersonal Relationships* The complexity of interpersonal relationships increases dramatically as the size of a group increases. Determine the number of different two-person relationships in a family of (a) 2, (b) 4, and (c) 6.

48. *Morse Code* In Morse Code, all characters are transmitted using a sequence of dits and dahs. How many different characters can be formed by a sequence of three dits and dahs? (These can be repeated. For example, dit-dit-dit represents the letter *s*.)

49. *Amateur Radio* A Novice Amateur Radio license consists of two letters, one digit, and then three more letters. How many different licenses can be issued if no restrictions are placed on the letters or digits?

50. *Connecting Points with Lines* How many different straight-line segments are determined by (a) five noncollinear points and (b) ten noncollinear points?

51. *Matching Socks* A man has five pairs of socks (no two pairs are the same color). If he randomly selects two socks from the drawer, what is the probability that he gets a matched pair?

52. *Bookshelf Order* A child carries a five-volume set of books to a bookshelf. The child is not able to read, and hence cannot distinguish one volume from another. What is the probability that the books are shelved in the correct order?

53. *Roll of the Dice* Are the chances of rolling a 3 with one die the same as the chances of rolling a total of 6 with two dice? If not, which has the higher probability?

54. *Roll of the Dice* A die is rolled six times. What is the probability that each side will appear exactly once?

55. *Tossing a Coin* Find the probability of obtaining at least one tail when a coin is tossed five times.

56. *Parental Independence* In the *Marriott Seniors' Attitudes Survey*, senior citizens were asked if they would live with their children when they reached the point of not being able to live alone. The results are shown in the figure. Suppose three senior citizens who could not live alone are randomly selected. What is the probability that all three are not living with their children?

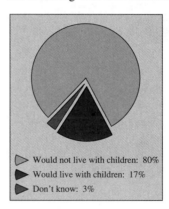

▷ Would not live with children: 80%
▶ Would live with children: 17%
▶ Don't know: 3%

Figure for 56

57. *Card Game* Five cards are drawn from an ordinary deck of 52 playing cards. Find the probability of getting two pairs. (For example, the hand could be A-A-5-5-Q or 4-4-7-7-K.)

58. *Birthday Problem*
(a) What is the probability that, in a group of 10 people, at least two have the same birthday? (Assume there are 365 different birthdays in a year.)
(b) How large must the group be before the probability that two have the same birthday is at least 50%?

C H A P T E R 11

OVERVIEW

This chapter discusses topics in analytic geometry: lines, conics, polar coordinates, and parametric equations.

In this chapter, you will see that conics are used as models for many real-life construction problems. For instance, Exercise 30 on page 746 uses a parabola as a model for constructing a solar heating unit, and Example 4 on page 752 uses an ellipse as a model for the moon's orbit about the earth.

Up to this point in the text, all graphs have been constructed on a rectangular coordinate plane. In this chapter, you will study a different type of coordinate plane that uses polar coordinates. For instance, in Example 4 on page 793, you will see how the orbit for Halley's comet can be modeled with a graph in a polar coordinate system.

Some Topics in Analytic Geometry

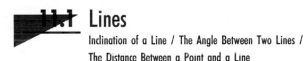

11.1 Lines

Inclination of a Line / The Angle Between Two Lines / The Distance Between a Point and a Line

Inclination of a Line

In Section 2.3 we saw that the graph of the linear equation $y = mx + b$ is a nonvertical line with slope m and y-intercept at $(0, b)$. There, we described the slope of a line as the rate of change in y with respect to x. In this section, we look at the slope of a line in terms of the angle of inclination of the line.

Every nonhorizontal line must intersect the x-axis. The angle formed by such an intersection determines the **inclination** of the line, as specified in the following definition.

DEFINITION OF INCLINATION

The **inclination** of a nonhorizontal line is the positive angle θ (less than 180°) measured counterclockwise from the x-axis to the line (see figure).

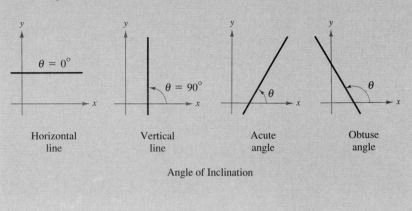

Horizontal line Vertical line Acute angle Obtuse angle

Angle of Inclination

The inclination of a line is related to its slope in the following manner.

INCLINATION AND SLOPE

If a nonvertical line has inclination θ and slope m, then

$$m = \tan \theta.$$

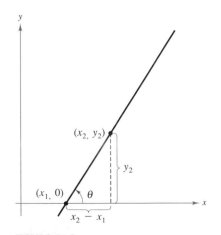

FIGURE 11.1

Proof

If $m = 0$, then the line is horizontal and $\theta = 0$. Thus, the result is true for horizontal lines because $m = 0 = \tan 0$.

If the line has a positive slope, then it will intersect the x-axis. We label this point $(x_1, 0)$, as shown in Figure 11.1. If (x_2, y_2) is a second point on the line, then the slope is given by

$$m = \frac{y_2 - 0}{x_2 - x_1} = \frac{y_2}{x_2 - x_1} = \tan \theta.$$

We leave the case in which the line has a negative slope for you to prove. ◢

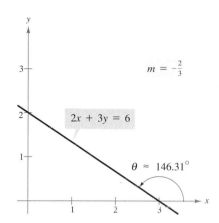

FIGURE 11.2

EXAMPLE 1   Finding the Inclination of a Line

Find the inclination of the line given by $2x + 3y = 6$.

Solution

The slope of this line is $m = -\frac{2}{3}$. Thus, its inclination is determined from the equation

$$\tan \theta = -\frac{2}{3}.$$

From Figure 11.2, we see that $90° < \theta < 180°$. This means that

$$\theta = 180° + \arctan\left(-\frac{2}{3}\right)$$

$$\approx 180° - 33.69°$$

$$\approx 146.31°.$$

The Angle Between Two Lines

Two distinct lines in a plane are either parallel or they intersect. If they intersect, then their intersection forms two pairs of opposing angles, as shown in Figure 11.3. The measure of the smaller of these is called the **angle between the two lines.** As shown in Figure 11.3, we can use the inclinations of the two lines to find the angle between the two lines. Specifically, if two lines have inclinations, θ_1 and θ_2, then the angle between the two lines is

$$\theta = \theta_2 - \theta_1$$

where $\theta_1 < \theta_2$.

We can use the formula for the tangent of the difference of two angles

$$\tan \theta = \tan(\theta_2 - \theta_1) = \frac{\tan \theta_2 - \tan \theta_1}{1 + \tan \theta_1 \tan \theta_2}$$

to obtain the following convenient formula for the angle between two lines.

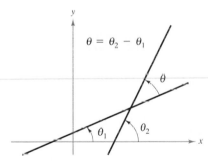

FIGURE 11.3

ANGLE BETWEEN TWO LINES

If two nonperpendicular lines have slopes m_1 and m_2, then the angle between the two lines is given by

$$\tan \theta = \left|\frac{m_2 - m_1}{1 + m_1 m_2}\right|.$$

EXAMPLE 2 Finding the Angle Between Two Lines

Find the angle between the following two lines.

Line 1: $2x - y - 4 = 0$
Line 2: $3x + 4y - 12 = 0$

Solution

The two lines have slopes of

$$m_1 = 2 \quad \text{and} \quad m_2 = -\frac{3}{4}$$

respectively. Thus, the angle between the two lines is given by

$$\tan \theta = \left| \frac{m_2 - m_1}{1 + m_1 m_2} \right|$$

$$= \left| \frac{(-3/4) - 2}{1 + (-3/4)(2)} \right|$$

$$= \left| \frac{-11/4}{-2/4} \right|$$

$$= \frac{11}{2}.$$

Finally, you conclude that the angle is

$$\theta = \arctan \frac{11}{2} \approx 79.70°$$

as shown in Figure 11.4.

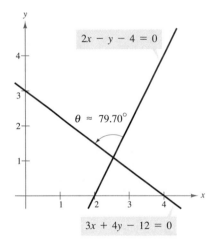

FIGURE 11.4

The Distance Between a Point and a Line

Finding the distance between a line and a point not on the line is an application of perpendicular lines. We define this distance to be the length of the perpendicular line segment joining the point to the given line, as shown in Figure 11.5.

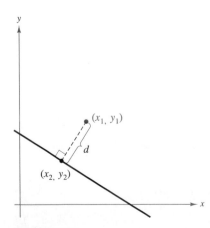

FIGURE 11.5

DISTANCE BETWEEN A POINT AND A LINE

The distance between the point (x_1, y_1) and the line given by $Ax + By + C = 0$ is

$$d = \frac{|Ax_1 + By_1 + C|}{\sqrt{A^2 + B^2}}.$$

Proof

For simplicity's sake, we assume that the given line is neither horizontal nor vertical. By writing the equation $Ax + By + C = 0$ in slope-intercept form

$$y = -\frac{A}{B}x - \frac{C}{B}$$

we see that the line has a slope of

$$m = -\frac{A}{B}.$$

Thus, the slope of the line passing through (x_1, y_1) and perpendicular to the given line is B/A, and its equation is

$$y - y_1 = \frac{B}{A}(x - x_1).$$

These two lines intersect at the point (x_2, y_2), where

$$x_2 = \frac{B(Bx_1 - Ay_1) - AC}{A^2 + B^2} \quad \text{and} \quad y_2 = \frac{A(-Bx_1 + Ay_1) - BC}{A^2 + B^2}.$$

Finally, the distance between (x_1, y_1) and (x_2, y_2) is

$$d = \sqrt{(x_2 - x_1)^2 + (y_2 - y_1)^2}$$

$$= \sqrt{\left(\frac{B^2x_1 - ABy_1 - AC}{A^2 + B^2} - x_1\right)^2 + \left(\frac{-ABx_1 + A^2y_1 - BC}{A^2 + B^2} - y_1\right)^2}$$

$$= \sqrt{\frac{A^2(Ax_1 + By_1 + C)^2 + B^2(Ax_1 + By_1 + C)^2}{(A^2 + B^2)^2}}$$

$$= \frac{|Ax_1 + By_1 + C|}{\sqrt{A^2 + B^2}}.$$

◀

EXAMPLE 3   Finding the Distance Between a Point and a Line

Find the distance between the point $(4, 1)$ and the line $y = 2x + 1$.

Solution

The general form of the given equation is

$$-2x + y - 1 = 0.$$

Hence, the distance between the point and the line is

$$d = \frac{|-2(4) + 1(1) - 1|}{\sqrt{(-2)^2 + 1^2}} = \frac{8}{\sqrt{5}} \approx 3.58.$$

◀

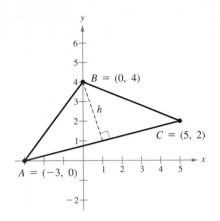

FIGURE 11.6

EXAMPLE 4   An Application of Two Distance Formulas

Figure 11.6 shows a triangle with vertices $A = (-3, 0)$, $B = (0, 4)$, and $C = (5, 2)$.

a. Find the altitude from vertex B to side AC.
b. Find the area of the triangle.

Solution

a. To find the altitude, you can use the formula for the distance between line AC and the point $(0, 4)$. The equation of line AC is obtained as follows.

Slope $m = \dfrac{2 - 0}{5 + 3} = \dfrac{1}{4}$

Equation $y - 0 = \dfrac{1}{4}(x + 3)$

$x - 4y + 3 = 0$

Therefore, the distance between this line and the point $(0, 4)$ is

$$\text{Altitude} = h = \frac{|1(0) - 4(4) + 3|}{\sqrt{1^2 + (-4)^2}} = \frac{13}{\sqrt{17}}.$$

b. Using the formula for the distance between two points, you find the length of the base AC to be

$$b = \sqrt{(5 + 3)^2 + (2 - 0)^2} = \sqrt{68} = 2\sqrt{17}.$$

Finally, the area of the triangle in Figure 11.6 is

$$A = \frac{1}{2}bh = \frac{1}{2}(2\sqrt{17})\left(\frac{13}{\sqrt{17}}\right) = 13.$$

DISCUSSION

PROBLEM

Inclination
and
the Angle
Between Two
Lines

Write a paragraph explaining why the inclination of a line can be an angle that is larger than 90°, but the angle between two lines cannot be larger than 90°. Explain whether the following statement is true or false: "The inclination of a line is the angle between the line and the x-axis."

WARM UP

The following warm-up exercises involve skills that were covered in earlier sections. You will use these skills in the exercise set for this section.

In Exercises 1 and 2, find the distance between the points.

1. $(-2, 0)$, $(3, 8)$ 2. $(0, 4)$, $(4, -2)$

In Exercises 3–6, find the slope of the line passing through the pair of points.

3. $(-5, 1)$, $(4, 10)$ 4. $(0, 2)$, $(7, 8)$
5. $(2, 12)$, $(10, 0)$ 6. $(-4, 4)$, $(6, -1)$

In Exercises 7–10, find an equation of the line passing through the point with the specified slope.

Point	Slope
7. $(0, 3)$	$m = \frac{2}{3}$
8. $(2, -5)$	$m = \frac{7}{2}$
9. $(3, 20)$	$m = -4$
10. $(-6, 4)$	$m = -\frac{3}{4}$

EXERCISES for Section 11.1

In Exercises 1–8, find the slope of the line with the given inclination θ.

5. $\theta = 38.2°$ 6. $\theta = 75.4°$
7. $\theta = 110°$ 8. $\theta = 145.5°$

1.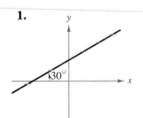

2.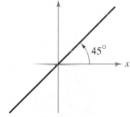

In Exercises 9–12, find the inclination, θ, of the line with given slope.

9. $m = -1$ 10. $m = 2$
11. $m = \frac{3}{4}$ 12. $m = -\frac{5}{2}$

3.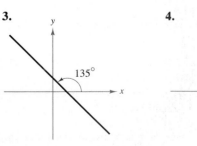

4.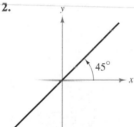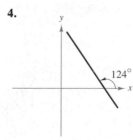

In Exercises 13–16, find the inclination, θ, of the line passing through the pair of points.

13. $(6, 1)$, $(10, 8)$ 14. $(-1, -4)$, $(7, 12)$
15. $(-2, 20)$, $(10, 0)$ 16. $(0, 100)$, $(50, 0)$

In Exercises 17–20, find the inclination, θ, of the given line.

17. $5x - y + 3 = 0$ 18. $4x + 5y - 9 = 0$
19. $5x + 3y = 0$ 20. $x - y - 10 = 0$

In Exercises 21–30, find the angle, θ, between the two lines.

21. $2x + y - 4 = 0$
$x - y - 2 = 0$

22. $x + 3y - 2 = 0$
$x - 2y + 3 = 0$

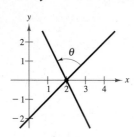

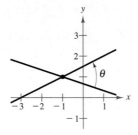

23. $x - y = 0$
$3x - 2y + 1 = 0$

24. $2x - y - 2 = 0$
$4x + 3y - 24 = 0$

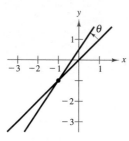

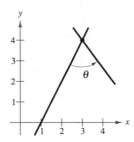

25. $x - 2y - 5 = 0$
$6x + 2y - 7 = 0$

26. $5x + 3y - 18 = 0$
$2x - 6y + 1 = 0$

27. $x + 2y - 4 = 0$
$x - 2y - 1 = 0$

28. $3x - 5y - 2 = 0$
$2x + 5y - 13 = 0$

29. $0.05x - 0.03y - 0.21 = 0$
$0.07x + 0.02y - 0.16 = 0$

30. $0.02x - 0.05y + 0.19 = 0$
$0.03x + 0.04y - 0.52 = 0$

In Exercises 31–38, find the distance between the point and the line.

Point	Line
31. $(0, 0)$	$4x + 3y - 10 = 0$
32. $(0, 0)$	$2x - y - 4 = 0$
33. $(2, 3)$	$4x + 3y - 10 = 0$
34. $(-2, 1)$	$x - y - 2 = 0$
35. $(6, 2)$	$x + 1 = 0$
36. $(10, 8)$	$y - 4 = 0$
37. $(0, 8)$	$6x - y = 0$
38. $(4, 2)$	$x - y - 20 = 0$

In Exercises 39 and 40, find the distance between the parallel lines. (*Hint*: Find the coordinates of any point on the one line and then find the distance between that point and the second line.)

39. $x + y - 1 = 0$
$x + y - 5 = 0$

40. $3x - 4y - 1 = 0$
$3x - 4y - 10 = 0$

41. *Grade of a Road*   A straight road rises with an inclination of 6.5° from the horizontal. Find the slope of the road and the change in elevation after driving 2 miles.

42. *Grade of a Road*   A straight road rises with an inclination of 4.5° from the horizontal. Find the slope of the road and the change in elevation after driving 3 miles.

43. *Mountain Climbing*   A group of mountain climbers are located in a mountain pass between two peaks (see figure). The angles of elevations to the two peaks are 48° and 63°. A range finder shows that the distances to the respective peaks are 3250 feet and 6700 feet.
(a) Find the angle between the two lines of sight to the peaks.
(b) Approximate the amount of vertical climb that is necessary to reach the summit of each peak.

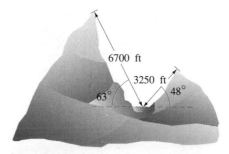

Figure for 43

44. *Conveyor Design*   A moving conveyor is built to rise 1 meter for each 3 meters of horizontal change.
(a) Find the inclination of the conveyor.
(b) Suppose the conveyor runs between two floors in a factory. Find the length of the conveyor if the vertical distance between floors is 10 feet.

45. *Pitch of a Roof*   There is a rise of 2 feet for every horizontal change of 3 feet on a roof. Find the inclination of the roof.

46. *Pitch of a Roof*   There is a rise of 3 feet for every horizontal change of 5 feet on a roof. Find the inclination of the roof.

Area   In Exercises 47–50, (a) find the altitude from vertex *B* of a triangle to the side *AC*, and (b) find the area of the triangle.

47. $A = (0, 0), B = (1, 5), C = (3, 1)$

48. $A = (0, 0), B = (4, 5), C = (5, -2)$

49. $A = \left(-\frac{1}{2}, \frac{1}{2}\right), B = (2, 3), C = \left(\frac{5}{2}, 0\right)$

50. $A = (-4, -5), B = (3, 10), C = (6, 10)$

Angle Measurement   In Exercises 51–54, find the slope of each side of the triangle and use the slopes to find the magnitude of the interior angles.

51.

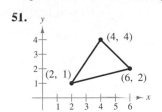

52.

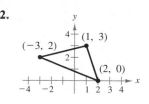

53.

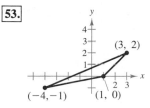

54.

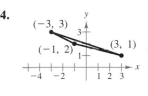

11.2 Introduction to Conics: Parabolas

Conics / Parabolas / Applications

Conics

Conic sections were discovered during the classical Greek period, 600 to 300 B.C. The early Greeks were concerned largely with the geometric properties of conics. It was not until the early 17th century that the broad applicability of conics became apparent, and then played a prominent role in the early development of calculus.

Each **conic section** (or simply **conic**) is the intersection of a plane and a double-napped cone. Notice from Figure 11.7 that in the formation of the four basic conics, the intersecting plane does not pass through the vertex of the cone. When the plane does pass through the vertex, the resulting figure is a **degenerate conic,** as shown in Figure 11.8.

Circle

Ellipse

Parabola

Hyperbola

Conic Sections

FIGURE 11.7

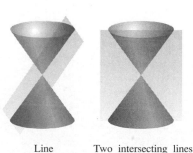

Point   Line   Two intersecting lines

Degenerate Conics

FIGURE 11.8

There are several ways to approach a study of conics. We could begin by defining conics in terms of the intersections of planes and cones, as the Greeks did, or we could define them algebraically in terms of the general second-degree equation

$$Ax^2 + Bxy + Cy^2 + Dx + Ey + F = 0.$$

However, we will use a third approach, in which each of the conics is defined as a **locus** (collection) of points satisfying a geometric property. For example, the definition of a circle as the collection of all points (x, y) that are equidistant from a fixed point (h, k) leads to the standard equation of a circle, $(x - h)^2 + (y - k)^2 = r^2$.

Parabolas

In this and the following two sections, we give similar definitions to the other three types of conics. We will also identify practical geometric properties of conics used in the construction of objects such as bridges, searchlights, telescopes, and radar detectors.

DEFINITION OF A PARABOLA

A **parabola** is the set of all points (x, y) that are equidistant from a fixed line (**directrix**) and a fixed point (**focus**) not on the line.

The midpoint between the focus and the directrix is the **vertex,** and the line passing through the focus and the vertex is the **axis** of the parabola. Note in Figure 11.9 that a parabola is symmetric with respect to its axis.

Using the definition of a parabola, we derive the following **standard form** of the equation of a parabola whose directrix is parallel to the x-axis or to the y-axis.

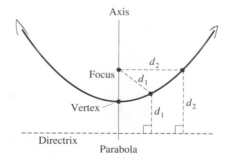

FIGURE 11.9

STANDARD EQUATION OF A PARABOLA

The **standard form** of the equation of a parabola with vertex at (h, k) is as follows.

$$(x - h)^2 = 4p(y - k), \, p \neq 0 \quad \textit{Vertical axis, directrix: } y = k - p$$
$$(y - k)^2 = 4p(x - h), \, p \neq 0 \quad \textit{Horizontal axis, directrix: } x = h - p$$

The focus lies on the axis p units (*directed distance*) from the vertex. If the vertex is at the origin $(0, 0)$, then the equation takes one of the following forms.

$$x^2 = 4py \quad \textit{Vertical axis}$$
$$y^2 = 4px \quad \textit{Horizontal axis}$$

See Figure 11.10.

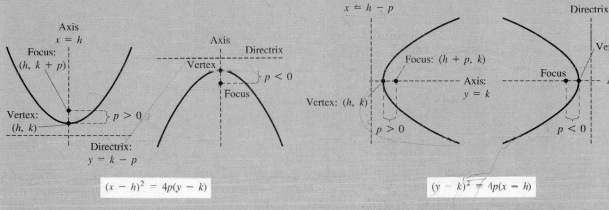

(a) Vertical axis: $p > 0$ (b) Vertical axis: $p < 0$ (c) Horizontal axis: $p > 0$ (d) Horizontal axis: $p < 0$

Parabolic Orientations

FIGURE 11.10

Proof

We prove only the case for which the directrix is parallel to the x-axis and the focus lies above the vertex, as shown in Figure 11.10(a). If (x, y) is any point on the parabola, then by definition it is equidistant from the focus $(h, k + p)$ and the directrix $y = k - p$, and we have

$$\sqrt{(x - h)^2 + [y - (k + p]^2} = y - (k - p)$$
$$(x - h)^2 + [y - (k + p)]^2 = [y - (k - p)]^2$$
$$(x - h)^2 + y^2 - 2y(k + p) + (k + p)^2 = y^2 - 2y(k - p) + (k - p)^2$$
$$(x - h)^2 - 2py + 2pk = 2py - 2pk$$
$$(x - h)^2 = 4p(y - k).$$

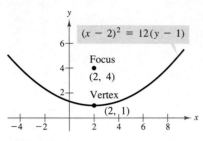

FIGURE 11.11

EXAMPLE 1   Finding the Standard Equation of a Parabola

Find the standard form of the equation of the parabola with vertex (2, 1) and focus (2, 4).

Solution

Since the axis of the parabola is vertical, consider the equation

$$(x - h)^2 = 4p(y - k)$$

where $h = 2$, $k = 1$, and $p = 4 - 1 = 3$. Thus, the standard form is

$$(x - 2)^2 = 12(y - 1).$$

The graph of this parabola is shown in Figure 11.11.

REMARK   By expanding the standard equation in Example 1, we obtain the more common quadratic form $y = \frac{1}{12}(x^2 - 4x + 16)$.

EXAMPLE 2   Finding the Focus of a Parabola

Find the focus of the parabola given by

$$y = -\frac{1}{2}x^2 - x + \frac{1}{2}.$$

Solution

To find the focus, convert to standard form by completing the square.

$$y = -\frac{1}{2}x^2 - x + \frac{1}{2} \qquad \textit{Given equation}$$

$$-2y = x^2 + 2x - 1 \qquad \textit{Multiply by } -2$$

$$1 - 2y = x^2 + 2x \qquad \textit{Group terms}$$

$$2 - 2y = x^2 + 2x + 1 \qquad \textit{Add 1 to both sides}$$

$$-2(y - 1) = (x + 1)^2 \qquad \textit{Standard form}$$

Comparing this equation to $(x - h)^2 = 4p(y - k)$, you conclude that $h = -1$, $k = 1$, and $p = -\frac{1}{2}$. Since p is negative, the parabola opens downward, as shown in Figure 11.12. Therefore, the focus of the parabola is

$$(h, k + p) = \left(-1, \frac{1}{2}\right). \qquad \textit{Focus}$$

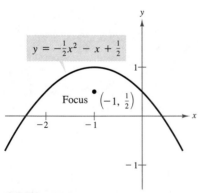

FIGURE 11.12

EXAMPLE 3   Vertex at the Origin

Find the standard equation of the parabola with vertex at the origin and focus at (2, 0).

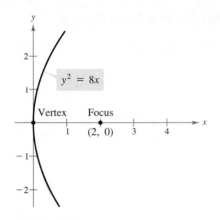

FIGURE 11.13

Solution

The axis of the parabola is horizontal, passing through $(0, 0)$ and $(2, 0)$ as shown in Figure 11.13. Thus, the standard form is

$$y^2 = 4px$$

where $h = k = 0$ and $p = 2$. Therefore, the equation is

$$y^2 = 8x.$$

Applications

A line segment that passes through the focus of a parabola and has endpoints on the parabola is called a **focal chord.** The specific focal chord perpendicular to the axis of the parabola is called the **latus rectum.**

Parabolas occur in a wide variety of applications. For instance, a parabolic reflector (Figure 11.14) can be formed by revolving a parabola around its axis. The resulting surface has the property that all incoming rays parallel to the axis are reflected through the focus of the parabola; this is the principle behind the construction of the parabolic mirrors used in reflecting telescopes. Conversely, the light rays emanating from the focus of a parabolic reflector used in a flashlight are all parallel to one another, as shown in Figure 11.14.

We say a line is **tangent** to a parabola at a point on the parabola if the line intersects, but does not cross, the parabola at the point. Tangent lines to parabolas have special properties related to the use of parabolas in constructing reflective surfaces.

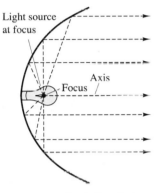

Parabolic reflector.
Light is reflected
in parallel rays.

FIGURE 11.14

REFLECTIVE PROPERTY OF A PARABOLA

The tangent line to a parabola at a point P makes equal angles with the following two lines (see figure).

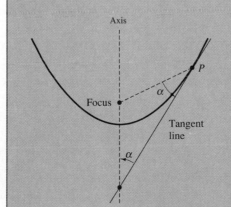

1. The line passing through P and the focus.

2. The axis of the parabola.

EXAMPLE 4   Finding the Tangent Line at a Point on a Parabola

Find the equation of the tangent line to the parabola given by $y = x^2$ at the point $(1, 1)$.

Solution

For this parabola, $p = \frac{1}{4}$ and the focus is $\left(0, \frac{1}{4}\right)$, as shown in Figure 11.15. You can find the y-intercept $(0, b)$ of the tangent line by equating the lengths of the two sides of the isosceles triangle

$$d_1 = \frac{1}{4} - b$$

and

$$d_2 = \sqrt{(1 - 0)^2 + [1 - (1/4)]^2} = \frac{5}{4}$$

shown in Figure 11.15. Setting $d_1 = d_2$ produces

$$\frac{1}{4} - b = \frac{5}{4}$$
$$b = -1.$$

Thus, the slope of the tangent line is

$$m = \frac{1 - (-1)}{1 - 0} = 2$$

and its slope-intercept equation is

$$y = 2x - 1.$$

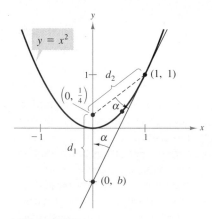

FIGURE 11.15

DISCUSSION

PROBLEM

Television
Antenna
Dishes

Cross sections of television antenna dishes are parabolic in shape. Write a paragraph describing why these dishes are parabolic.

WARM UP

The following warm-up exercises involve skills that were covered in earlier sections. You will use these skills in the exercise set for this section.

In Exercises 1–4, expand and simplify the expression.

1. $(x - 5)^2 - 20$ **2.** $(x + 3)^2 - 1$

3. $10 - (x + 4)^2$ **4.** $4 - (x - 2)^2$

In Exercises 5–8, complete the square on the quadratic expression.

5. $x^2 + 6x + 8$ **6.** $x^2 - 10x + 21$

7. $-x^2 + 2x + 1$ **8.** $-2x^2 + 4x - 2$

In Exercises 9 and 10, find an equation of the line passing through the given point with the specified slope.

9. $m = -\frac{2}{3}, (1, 6)$ **10.** $m = \frac{3}{4}, (3, -2)$

EXERCISES for Section 11.2

In Exercises 1–6, match the equation with its graph. [The graphs are labeled (a), (b), (c), (d), (e), and (f).]

1. $y^2 = 4x$ **2.** $x^2 = -2y$

3. $x^2 = 8y$ **4.** $y^2 = -12x$

5. $(y - 1)^2 = 4(x - 2)$ **6.** $(x + 3)^2 = -2(y - 2)$

(e)   (f)

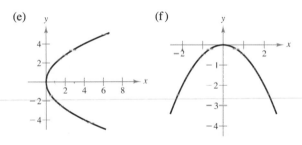

(a)   (b)

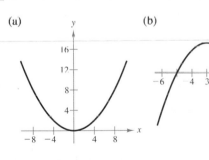

(c)   (d)

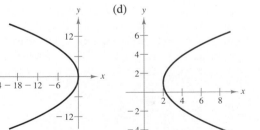

In Exercises 7–18, find the vertex, focus, and directrix of the parabola and sketch its graph.

7. $y = 4x^2$ **8.** $y^2 = -6x$

9. $x^2 + 8y = 0$ **10.** $y^2 - 8x = 0$

11. $(x - 1)^2 + 8(y + 2) = 0$ **12.** $\left(y + \frac{1}{2}\right)^2 = 2(x - 5)$

13. $y = \frac{1}{4}(x^2 - 2x + 5)$ **14.** $4x - y^2 - 2y - 33 = 0$

15. $y^2 + 6y + 8x + 25 = 0$ **16.** $y^2 - 4y - 4x = 0$

17. $y^2 - 4x - 4 = 0$ **18.** $y^2 + 4y + 8x - 12 = 0$

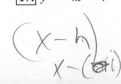

In Exercises 19–28, find an equation of the specified parabola.

19. Vertex: (0, 0)
Focus: $\left(0, -\frac{3}{2}\right)$

20. Vertex: (0, 0)
Focus: (−2, 0)

21. Vertex: (0, 0)
Directrix: $x = 3$

22. Vertex: (3, 2)
Focus: (1, 2)

23. Vertex: (0, 4)
Directrix: $y = 2$

24. Vertex: (0, 0)
Directrix: $y = 4$

25. Axis: Parallel to y-axis
Passes through the points:
(0, 3), (3, 4), (4, 11)

26. Axis: Parallel to x-axis
Passes through the points:
(4, −2), (0, 0), (3, −3)

27.

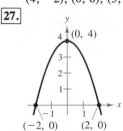

28.

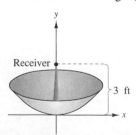

29. *Satellite Antenna* The receiver in a parabolic television dish antenna is 3 feet from the vertex and is located at the focus (see figure). Find an equation of a cross section of the reflector. (Assume that the dish is directed upward and the vertex is at the origin.)

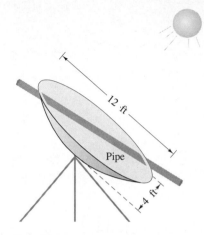

Figure for 29

30. *Solar Collector* A solar collector for heating water is constructed with a sheet of stainless steel that is formed into the shape of a parabola (see figure). The water flows through a pipe that passes through the focus of the parabola. At what distance is the pipe from the vertex?

Figure for 30

31. *Suspension Bridge* Each cable of a suspension bridge is suspended (in the shape of a parabola) between two towers that are 400 feet apart and 50 feet above the roadway (see figure). The cables touch the roadway midway between the towers.
(a) Find an equation for the parabolic shape of each cable.
(b) Find the length of the vertical supporting cable when $x = 100$.

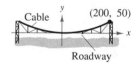

Figure for 31

32. *Beam Deflection* A simply supported beam that is 100 feet long has a load concentrated at its center (see figure). The deflection of the beam at its center is 3 inches. If the shape of the deflected beam is parabolic, find the equation of the parabola. (Assume the vertex is at the origin.)

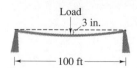

Figure for 32

33. *Escape Velocity* A satellite in a 100-mile-high circular orbit around the earth has a velocity of approximately 17,500 miles per hour. If this velocity is multiplied by $\sqrt{2}$, then the satellite will have the minimum velocity necessary to escape the earth's gravity and it will follow a parabolic path with the center of the earth as the focus (see figure).
(a) Find the escape velocity of the satellite.
(b) Find the equation of its path (assume that the radius of the earth is 4,000 miles).

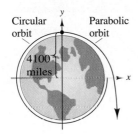

Circular orbit   Parabolic orbit

4100 miles

Figure for 33

34. *Highway Design* Highway engineers design a parabolic curve for an entrance ramp from a straight street to an interstate highway (see figure). Find an equation of the parabola.

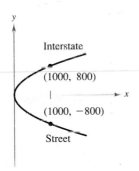

Interstate

(1000, 800)

(1000, −800)

Street

Figure for 34

Projectile Motion   In Exercises 35–37, consider the path of a projectile projected horizontally with a velocity of v feet per second at a height of s feet, where the model for the path is given by

$$y = -\frac{16}{v^2}x^2 + s.$$

In this model air resistance is disregarded and y is the height (in feet) of the projectile t seconds after its release.

35. A ball is thrown horizontally from the top of a 75-foot tower with a velocity of 32 feet per second.
(a) Find the equation of the parabolic path.
(b) How far does the ball travel horizontally before striking the ground?

36. A ball is thrown horizontally from the top of a 100-foot tower with a velocity of 32 feet per second.
(a) Find the equation of the parabolic path.
(b) How far does the ball travel horizontally before striking the ground?

37. A bomber flying due east at 550 miles per hour at an altitude of 42,000 feet releases a bomb. Determine how far the bomb travels horizontally before striking the ground.

38. Find the equation of the tangent line to the parabola $y = ax^2$ at $x = x_0$. Prove that the x-intercept of this tangent line is $(x_0/2, 0)$.

In Exercises 39–42, find an equation of the tangent line to the parabola at the given point and find the x-intercept of the line.

39. $y = \frac{1}{2}x^2$, $(4, 8)$ **40.** $y = \frac{1}{2}x^2$, $\left(-3, \frac{9}{2}\right)$

41. $y = -2x^2$, $(-1, -2)$ **42.** $y = -2x^2$, $(3, -18)$

11.3 Ellipses

Introduction / Applications / Eccentricity

Introduction

The second type of conic is called an **ellipse,** and is defined as follows.

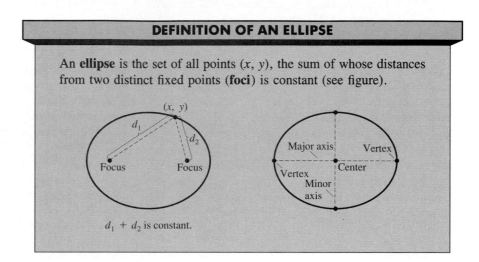

DEFINITION OF AN ELLIPSE

An **ellipse** is the set of all points (x, y), the sum of whose distances from two distinct fixed points (**foci**) is constant (see figure).

$d_1 + d_2$ is constant.

The line through the foci intersects the ellipse at two points (**vertices**). The chord joining the vertices is the **major axis,** and its midpoint is the **center** of the ellipse. The chord perpendicular to the major axis at the center is the **minor axis** of the ellipse.

You can visualize the definition of an ellipse by imagining two thumbtacks placed at the foci, as shown in Figure 11.16. If the ends of a fixed length of string are fastened to the thumbtacks and the string is drawn taut with a pencil, the path traced by the pencil will be an ellipse.

To derive the standard form of the equation of an ellipse, consider the ellipse in Figure 11.17 with the following points.

Center: (h, k) Vertices: $(h \pm a, k)$ Foci: $(h \pm c, k)$

The sum of the distances from any point on the ellipse to the two foci is constant. At a vertex, this constant sum is

$$(a + c) + (a - c) = 2a \qquad \textit{Length of major axis}$$

or simply the length of the major axis. Now, if we let (x, y) be *any* point on the ellipse, the sum of the distances between (x, y) and the two foci must also be $2a$. That is,

$$\sqrt{[x - (h - c)]^2 + (y - k)^2} + \sqrt{[x - (h + c)]^2 + (y - k)^2} = 2a.$$

FIGURE 11.16

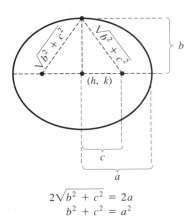

$$2\sqrt{b^2 + c^2} = 2a$$
$$b^2 + c^2 = a^2$$

FIGURE 11.17

Finally, in Figure 11.17, we can see that $b^2 = a^2 - c^2$, which implies that the equation of the ellipse is

$$b^2(x - h)^2 + a^2(y - k)^2 = a^2 b^2$$
$$\frac{(x - h)^2}{a^2} + \frac{(y - k)^2}{b^2} = 1.$$

Had we chosen a vertical major axis, we would have obtained a similar equation. Both results are summarized as follows.

STANDARD EQUATION OF AN ELLIPSE

The standard form of the equation of an ellipse, with center (h, k) and major and minor axes of lengths $2a$ and $2b$, where $0 < b < a$ is

$$\frac{(x - h)^2}{a^2} + \frac{(y - k)^2}{b^2} = 1 \qquad \text{Major axis is horizontal}$$

$$\frac{(x - h)^2}{b^2} + \frac{(y - k)^2}{a^2} = 1. \qquad \text{Major axis is vertical}$$

The foci lie on the major axis, c units from the center, with $c^2 = a^2 - b^2$. If the center is at the origin $(0, 0)$, then the equation takes one of the following forms.

$$\frac{x^2}{a^2} + \frac{y^2}{b^2} = 1 \qquad \text{Major axis is horizontal}$$

$$\frac{x^2}{b^2} + \frac{y^2}{a^2} = 1 \qquad \text{Major axis is vertical}$$

Figure 11.18 shows both the vertical and horizontal orientations for an ellipse.

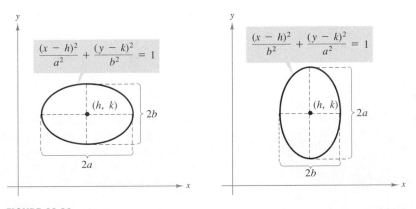

FIGURE 11.18

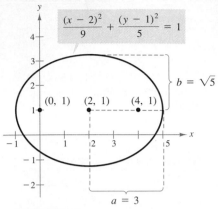

FIGURE 11.19

EXAMPLE 1   Finding the Standard Equation of an Ellipse

Find the standard form of the equation of the ellipse having foci at $(0, 1)$ and $(4, 1)$ and with a major axis of length 6, as shown in Figure 11.19.

Solution

Since the foci occur at $(0, 1)$ and $(4, 1)$, the center of the ellipse is $(2, 1)$. This implies that the distance from the center to one of the foci is $c = 2$, and since $2a = 6$ you know that $a = 3$. Now, from $c^2 = a^2 - b^2$, you have

$$b = \sqrt{a^2 - c^2} = \sqrt{9 - 4} = \sqrt{5}.$$

Since the major axis is horizontal, the standard equation is

$$\frac{(x - 2)^2}{9} + \frac{(y - 1)^2}{5} = 1.$$

EXAMPLE 2   Writing an Equation in Standard Form

Sketch the graph of the ellipse whose equation is

$$x^2 + 4y^2 + 6x - 8y + 9 = 0.$$

Solution

Begin by writing the given equation in standard form.

$$x^2 + 4y^2 + 6x - 8y + 9 = 0 \qquad \textit{Given equation}$$

$$(x^2 + 6x +) + (4y^2 - 8y +) = -9 \qquad \textit{Group terms}$$

$$(x^2 + 6x +) + 4(y^2 - 2y +) = -9 \qquad \textit{Factor 4 out of y-terms}$$

$$(x^2 + 6x + 9) + 4(y^2 - 2y + 1) = -9 + 9 + 4(1) \qquad \textit{Add 9 and 4 to both sides}$$

$$(x + 3)^2 + 4(y - 1)^2 = 4 \qquad \textit{Completed square form}$$

$$\frac{(x + 3)^2}{4} + \frac{(y - 1)^2}{1} = 1 \qquad \textit{Standard form}$$

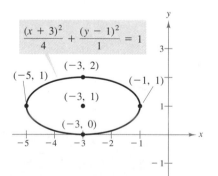

FIGURE 11.20

Now you see that the center occurs at $(h, k) = (-3, 1)$. Since the denominator of the x-term is $a^2 = 2^2$, we locate the endpoints of the major axis 2 units to the right and left of the center. Similarly, since the denominator of the y-term is $b^2 = 1^2$, we locate the endpoints of the minor axis 1 unit up and down from the center. The graph of this ellipse is shown in Figure 11.20.

EXAMPLE 3   Analyzing an Ellipse

Find the center, vertices, and foci of the ellipse given by

$$4x^2 + y^2 - 8x + 4y - 8 = 0.$$

Solution

By completing the square, you can write the given equation in standard form.

$$4x^2 + y^2 - 8x + 4y - 8 = 0$$

$$4(x^2 - 2x + 1) + (y^2 + 4y + 4) = 8 + 4 + 4$$

$$4(x - 1)^2 + (y + 2)^2 = 16$$

$$\frac{(x - 1)^2}{4} + \frac{(y + 2)^2}{16} = 1$$

Thus, the major axis is vertical, where $h = 1$, $k = -2$, $a = 4$, $b = 2$, and $c - \sqrt{16 - 4} = 2\sqrt{3}$. Therefore, you have the following.

Center: $(1, -2)$ Vertices: $(1, -6)$ Foci: $(1, -2 - 2\sqrt{3})$

$(1, 2)$ $(1, -2 + 2\sqrt{3})$

The graph of the ellipse is shown in Figure 11.21.

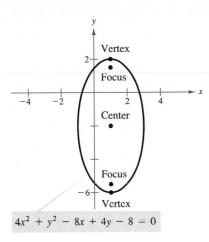

$$4x^2 + y^2 - 8x + 4y - 8 = 0$$

FIGURE 11.21

REMARK If the constant term in the equation in Example 3 had been $F \geq 8$, then we would have obtained one of the following degenerate cases.

1. Single point: $\dfrac{(x - 1)^2}{4} + \dfrac{(y + 2)^2}{16} = 0$ $F = 8$

2. No solution points: $\dfrac{(x - 1)^2}{4} + \dfrac{(y + 2)^2}{16} < 0$ $F > 8$

Applications

Ellipses have many practical and aesthetic uses. For instance, machine gears, supporting arches, and acoustical designs often involve elliptical shapes. The orbits of satellites and planets are also ellipses. In Example 4 we investigate the elliptical orbit of the moon about the earth.

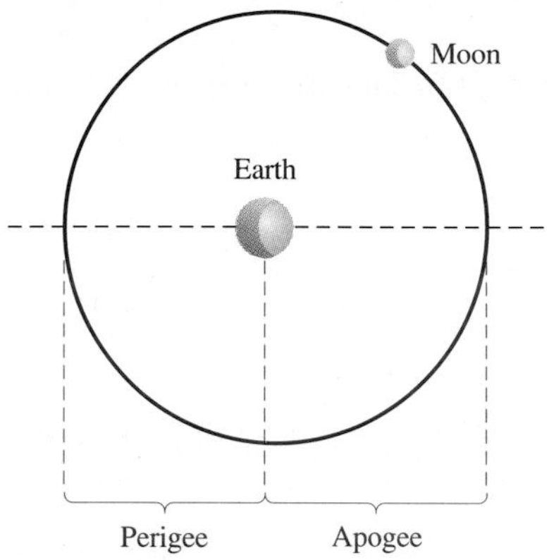

EXAMPLE 4 An Application Involving an Elliptical Orbit

The moon travels about the earth in an elliptical orbit with the earth at one focus, as shown in Figure 11.22. The major and minor axes of the orbit have lengths of 768,806 kilometers and 767,746 kilometers, respectively. Find the greatest and least distances (the apogee and perigee) from the earth's center to the moon's center.

Solution

Since $2a = 768,806$ and $2b = 767,746$, you have $a = 384,403$, $b = 383,873$, and $c = \sqrt{a^2 - b^2} \approx 20,179$.

Therefore, the greatest distance between the center of the earth and the center of the moon is

$$a + c \approx 404,582 \text{ km}$$

and the least distance is

$$a - c \approx 364,224 \text{ km.}$$

FIGURE 11.22

Eccentricity

One of the reasons it was difficult for early astronomers to detect that the orbits of the planets are ellipses is that the foci of the planetary orbits are relatively close to their centers, thus making the orbits nearly circular. To measure the ovalness of an ellipse, we use the concept of **eccentricity.**

DEFINITION OF ECCENTRICITY

The **eccentricity** e of an ellipse is given by the ratio

$$e = \frac{c}{a}.$$

To see how this ratio is used to describe the shape of an ellipse, note that since the foci of an ellipse are located along the major axis between the vertices and the center, it follows that

$$0 < c < a.$$

For an ellipse that is nearly circular, the foci are close to the center and the ratio c/a is small, as shown in Figure 11.23. On the other hand, for an elongated ellipse, the foci are close to the vertices, and the ratio c/a is close to 1.

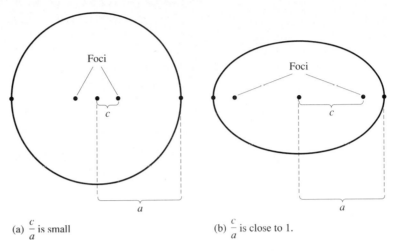

(a) $\dfrac{c}{a}$ is small   (b) $\dfrac{c}{a}$ is close to 1.

FIGURE 11.23

REMARK Note that $0 < e < 1$ for every ellipse.

The orbit of the moon has an eccentricity of $e = 0.0549$, and the eccentricities of the nine planetary orbits are as follows.

Mercury: $e = 0.2056$ Saturn: $e = 0.0543$
Venus: $e = 0.0068$ Uranus: $e = 0.0460$
Earth: $e = 0.0167$ Neptune: $e = 0.0082$
Mars: $e = 0.0934$ Pluto: $e = 0.2481$
Jupiter: $e = 0.0484$

DISCUSSION
PROBLEM

Halley's
Comet

Halley's comet, named after the English mathematician and physicist Edmund Halley (1656–1742), has an elliptical orbit with an eccentricity of $e \approx 0.97$ Write a paragraph describing how this large eccentricity is related to the infrequent occurrence of Halley's comet near the sun. (Halley's comet has a period of about 76 years. It passed near the sun in 1759, 1835, 1910, and 1986.)

WARM UP

The following warm-up exercises involve skills that were covered in earlier sections. You will use these skills in the exercise set for this section.

In Exercises 1–4, sketch a graph of the equation.

1. $x^2 = 9y$ **2.** $y^2 = 9x$

3. $y^2 = -9x$ **4.** $x^2 = -9y$

In Exercises 5–8, find the unknown in the equation $c^2 = a^2 - b^2$. (Assume a, b, and c are positive.)

5. $a = 13$, $b = 5$ **6.** $a = \sqrt{10}$, $c = 3$

7. $b = 6$, $c = 8$ **8.** $a = 7$, $b = 5$

In Exercises 9 and 10, simplify the compound fraction.

9. $\dfrac{x^2}{\frac{1}{4}} + \dfrac{y^2}{\frac{1}{3}}$ **10.** $\dfrac{(x-1)^2}{\frac{4}{9}} + \dfrac{(y+2)^2}{\frac{1}{9}}$

EXERCISES for Section 11.3

In Exercises 1–6, match the equation with its graph. [The graphs are labeled (a), (b), (c), (d), (e), and (f).]

1. $\dfrac{x^2}{1} + \dfrac{y^2}{9} = 1$ **2.** $\dfrac{x^2}{9} + \dfrac{y^2}{1} = 1$

3. $\dfrac{x^2}{9} + \dfrac{y^2}{4} = 1$ **4.** $\dfrac{y^2}{9} + \dfrac{x^2}{9} = 1$

5. $\dfrac{(x-2)^2}{16} + \dfrac{(y+1)^2}{4} = 1$ **6.** $\dfrac{(x+2)^2}{4} + \dfrac{(y+2)^2}{25} = 1$

(a)

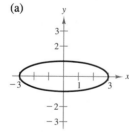

(b)

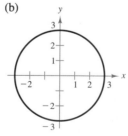

(c)

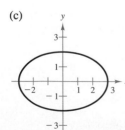

(d)

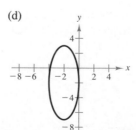

(e)

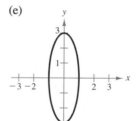

(f)

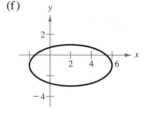

In Exercises 7–20, find the center, foci, vertices, and eccentricity of the ellipse and sketch its graph.

7. $\dfrac{x^2}{25} + \dfrac{y^2}{16} = 1$

8. $\dfrac{x^2}{16} + \dfrac{y^2}{25} = 1$

9. $\dfrac{x^2}{144} + \dfrac{y^2}{169} = 1$

10. $x^2 + 4y^2 = 4$

11. $3x^2 + 2y^2 = 6$

12. $4x^2 + y^2 = 1$

13. $\dfrac{(x-1)^2}{9} + \dfrac{(y-5)^2}{25} = 1$

14. $(x + 2)^2 + \dfrac{(y + 4)^2}{1/4} = 1$

15. $9x^2 + 4y^2 + 36x - 24y + 36 = 0$

16. $9x^2 + 4y^2 - 36x + 8y + 31 = 0$

17. $16x^2 + 25y^2 - 32x + 50y + 16 = 0$

18. $9x^2 + 25y^2 - 36x - 50y + 61 = 0$

19. $12x^2 + 20y^2 - 12x + 40y - 37 = 0$

20. $36x^2 + 9y^2 + 48x - 36y + 43 = 0$

In Exercises 21–28, find an equation of the specified ellipse.

21. Vertices: $(\pm 6, 0)$
Foci: $(\pm 5, 0)$

22. Vertices: $(0, \pm 8)$
Foci: $(0, \pm 4)$

23. Vertices: $(0, \pm 2)$
Minor axis of length 2

24. Vertices: $(0, 2), (4, 2)$
Minor axis of length 2

25. Foci: $(0, 0), (0, 8)$
Major axis of length 16

26. Vertices: $(0, \pm 5)$
Solution point: $(4, 2)$

27. Center: $(3, 2), a = 3c$
Foci: $(1, 2), (5, 2)$

28. Vertices: $(\pm 5, 0)$
Eccentricity: $\frac{3}{5}$

29. *Fireplace Arch*   A fireplace arch is to be constructed in the shape of a semi-ellipse. The opening is to have a height of 2 feet at the center and a width of 5 feet along the base (see figure). The contractor draws the outline of the ellipse by the method shown in Figure 11.16. Where should the tacks be placed and what should be the length of the piece of string?

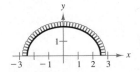

Figure for 29

30. *Mountain Tunnel*   A semi-elliptical arch over a tunnel for a road through a mountain has a major axis of 100 feet and its height at the center is 30 feet (see figure). Determine the height of the arch 5 feet from the edge of the tunnel.

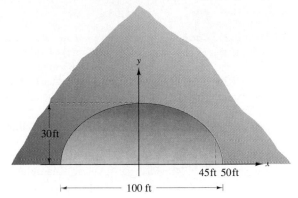

Figure for 30

31. Sketch a graph of the ellipse that consists of all points (x, y) such that the sum of the distances between (x, y) and two fixed points is 16 units and the foci are located at the centers of the two sets of concentric circles in the figure.

32. A line segment through a focus with endpoints on the ellipse and perpendicular to the major axis is called a **latus rectum** of the ellipse. Therefore, an ellipse has two latus recta. Knowing the length of the latus recta is helpful in sketching an ellipse because it yields other points on the curve (see figure). Show that the length of each latus rectum is $2b^2/a$.

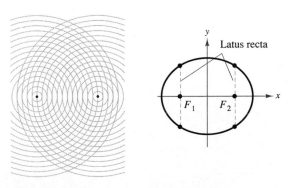

Figure for 31   **Figure for 32**

In Exercises 33–36, sketch the graph of the ellipse, making use of the latus recta (see Exercise 32).

33. $\dfrac{x^2}{4} + \dfrac{y^2}{1} = 1$ **34.** $\dfrac{x^2}{9} + \dfrac{y^2}{16} = 1$

35. $9x^2 + 4y^2 = 36$ **36.** $5x^2 + 3y^2 = 15$

37. *Orbit of the Earth*   The earth moves in an elliptical orbit with the sun at one of the foci (see figure). The length of half of the major axis is 92.957×10^6 miles and the eccentricity is 0.017. Find the smallest distance (*perihelion*) and the greatest distance (*aphelion*) of the earth from the sun.

38. *Orbit of Pluto*   The planet Pluto moves in an elliptical orbit with the sun at one of the foci (see figure). The length of half of the major axis is 3.666×10^9 miles and the eccentricity is 0.248. Find the smallest distance and the greatest distance of Pluto from the sun.

39. *Orbit of Saturn*   The planet Saturn moves in an elliptical orbit with the sun at one of the foci (see figure). The smallest distance and the greatest distance of the planet from the sun are 1.3495×10^9 kilometers and 1.5045×10^9, respectively. Find the eccentricity of the orbit.

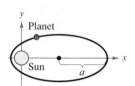

Figure for 37–39

40. *Satellite Orbit*   If the apogee and the perigee (see Example 4) of an elliptical orbit of an earth satellite are given by A and P, respectively, show that the eccentricity of the orbit is given by

$$e = \frac{A - P}{A + P}.$$

41. *Sputnik I*   The first artificial satellite to orbit the earth was Sputnik I (launched by the Soviet Union in 1957). Its highest point above the earth's surface was 583 miles, and its lowest point was 132 miles. Assume that the center of the earth is the focus of the elliptical orbit and the radius of the earth is 4000 miles. Find the eccentricity of the orbit.

42. *Explorer 18*   On November 26, 1963, the United States launched Explorer 18. Its low and high points over the surface of the earth were 119 miles and 122,000 miles, respectively. Find the eccentricity of its elliptical orbit.

43. Show that the equation of an ellipse can be written as

$$\frac{(x - h)^2}{a^2} + \frac{(y - k)^2}{a^2(1 - e^2)} = 1.$$

Note that as e approaches zero the ellipse approaches a circle of radius a.

11.4 Hyperbolas

Introduction / Asymptotes of a Hyperbola / Applications

Introduction

The definition of a hyperbola parallels that of an ellipse. The difference is that for an ellipse the *sum* of the distances between the foci and a point on the ellipse is fixed, while for a hyperbola the *difference* of these distances is fixed.

DEFINITION OF A HYPERBOLA

A **hyperbola** is the set of all points (x, y), the difference of whose distances from two distinct fixed points (foci) is constant (see figure).

$d_2 - d_1$ is constant.

Every hyperbola has two disconnected parts (**branches**). The lines through the two foci intersect a hyperbola at two points (**vertices**). The line segment connecting the vertices is the **transverse axis,** and the midpoint of the transverse axis is the **center** of the hyperbola.

The development of the standard form of the equation of a hyperbola is similar to that of an ellipse, and we list the following result without proof.

STANDARD EQUATION OF A HYPERBOLA

The standard form of the equation of a hyperbola with center at (h, k) is

$$\frac{(x - h)^2}{a^2} - \frac{(y - k)^2}{b^2} = 1 \qquad \textit{Transverse axis is horizontal}$$

$$\frac{(y - k)^2}{a^2} - \frac{(x - h)^2}{b^2} = 1. \qquad \textit{Transverse axis is vertical}$$

The vertices are a units from the center, and the foci are c units from the center. Moreover, $b^2 = c^2 - a^2$. If the center of the hyperbola is at the origin $(0, 0)$, then the equation takes one of the following forms.

$$\frac{x^2}{a^2} - \frac{y^2}{b^2} = 1 \qquad \textit{Transverse axis is horizontal}$$

$$\frac{y^2}{a^2} - \frac{x^2}{b^2} = 1 \qquad \textit{Transverse axis is vertical}$$

Figure 11.24 shows both the horizontal and vertical orientations for a hyperbola.

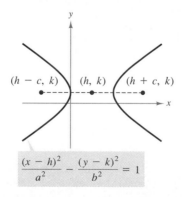

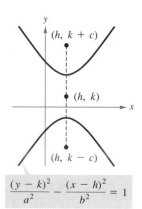

Standard Equations for Hyperbolas

FIGURE 11.24

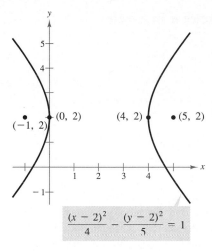

$$\frac{(x-2)^2}{4} - \frac{(y-2)^2}{5} = 1$$

FIGURE 11.25

EXAMPLE 1   Finding the Standard Equation of a Hyperbola

Find the standard form of the equation of the hyperbola with foci at $(-1, 2)$ and $(5, 2)$ and vertices at $(0, 2)$ and $(4, 2)$.

Solution

By the Midpoint Formula, the center of the hyperbola occurs at the point $(2, 2)$. Furthermore, $c = 3$ and $a = 2$, and it follows that

$$b^2 = 3^2 - 2^2 = 9 - 4 = 5.$$

Thus, the equation of the hyperbola is

$$\frac{(x-2)^2}{4} - \frac{(y-2)^2}{5} = 1.$$

Figure 11.25 shows the graph of the hyperbola.

Asymptotes of a Hyperbola

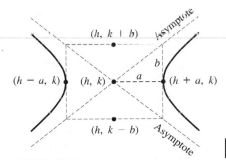

FIGURE 11.26

An important aid in sketching the graph of a hyperbola is the determination of its **asymptotes**, as shown in Figure 11.26. Each hyperbola has two asymptotes that intersect at the center of the hyperbola. The asymptotes pass through the vertices of a rectangle of dimension $2a$ by $2b$, with its center at (h, k). The line segment of length $2b$, joining $(h, k + b)$ and $(h, k - b)$, is the **conjugate axis** of the hyperbola. The following result identifies the equations for the asymptotes.

ASYMPTOTES OF A HYPERBOLA

For a *horizontal* transverse axis, the equations of the asymptotes are

$$y = k + \frac{b}{a}(x - h) \quad \text{and} \quad y = k - \frac{b}{a}(x - h).$$

For a *vertical* transverse axis, the equations of the asymptotes are

$$y = k + \frac{a}{b}(x - h) \quad \text{and} \quad y = k - \frac{a}{b}(x - h).$$

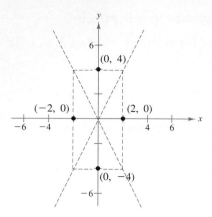

FIGURE 11.27

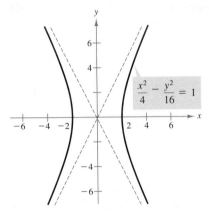

FIGURE 11.28

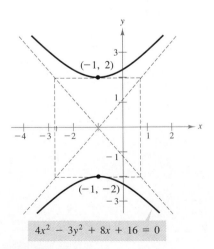

FIGURE 11.29

EXAMPLE 2 Using Asymptotes to Sketch a Hyperbola

Sketch the hyperbola whose equation is $4x^2 - y^2 = 16$.

Solution

$$4x^2 - y^2 = 16 \qquad \textit{Given equation}$$

$$\frac{4x^2}{16} - \frac{y^2}{16} = \frac{16}{16}$$

$$\frac{x^2}{4} - \frac{y^2}{16} = 1 \qquad \textit{Standard form}$$

From this, you conclude that the transverse axis is horizontal and the vertices occur at $(-2, 0)$ and $(2, 0)$. Moreover, the ends of the conjugate axis occur at $(0, -4)$ and $(0, 4)$, and you are able to sketch the rectangle shown in Figure 11.27. Finally, by drawing the asymptotes through the corners of this rectangle, complete the sketch, as shown in Figure 11.28.

EXAMPLE 3 Finding the Asymptotes of a Hyperbola

Sketch the hyperbola given by $4x^2 - 3y^2 + 8x + 16 = 0$ and find the equations of its asymptotes.

Solution

$$4x^2 - 3y^2 + 8x + 16 = 0 \qquad \textit{Given equation}$$

$$4(x^2 + 2x) - 3y^2 = -16$$

$$-4(x^2 + 2x + 1) + 3y^2 = 16 - 4$$

$$-4(x + 1)^2 + 3y^2 = 12$$

$$\frac{y^2}{4} - \frac{(x + 1)^2}{3} = 1 \qquad \textit{Standard form}$$

From this equation you conclude that the hyperbola is centered at $(-1, 0)$, has vertices at $(-1, 2)$ and $(-1, -2)$, and the ends of the conjugate axis occur at $(-1 - \sqrt{3}, 0)$ and $(-1 + \sqrt{3}, 0)$. To sketch the graph of the hyperbola, draw a rectangle through these four points. The asymptotes are the lines passing through the corners of the rectangle, as shown in Figure 11.29. Finally, using $a = 2$ and $b = \sqrt{3}$, you conclude that the equations of the asymptotes are

$$y = \frac{2}{\sqrt{3}}(x + 1)$$

and

$$y = -\frac{2}{\sqrt{3}}(x + 1).$$

REMARK If the constant term F in the equation in Example 3 had been $F = -4$ instead of 16, then we would have obtained the following degenerate case.

Two intersecting lines: $\quad \dfrac{y^2}{4} - \dfrac{(x+1)^2}{3} = 0$

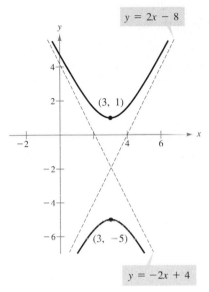

$y = 2x - 8$

$(3, 1)$

$(3, -5)$

$y = -2x + 4$

FIGURE 11.30

EXAMPLE 4   Using Asymptotes to Find the Standard Equation

Find the standard form of the equation of the hyperbola having vertices at $(3, -5)$ and $(3, 1)$ and with asymptotes $y = 2x - 8$ and $y = -2x + 4$, as shown in Figure 11.30.

Solution

By the Midpoint Formula, the center of the hyperbola is at $(3, -2)$. Furthermore, the hyperbola has a vertical transverse axis with $a = 3$. From the given equation, we determine the slopes of the asymptotes to be

$$m_1 = 2 = \frac{a}{b} \quad \text{and} \quad m_2 = -2 = -\frac{a}{b}$$

and since $a = 3$, we conclude that $b = \frac{3}{2}$. Thus, the standard equation is

$$\frac{(y+2)^2}{9} - \frac{(x-3)^2}{9/4} = 1.$$

As with ellipses, the **eccentricity** of a hyperbola is $e = c/a$, and because $c > a$ it follows that $e > 1$. If the eccentricity is large, then the branches of the hyperbola are nearly flat. If the eccentricity is close to 1, then the branches of the hyperbola are more pointed, as shown in Figure 11.31.

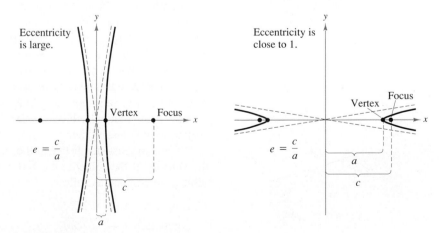

Eccentricity is large.

$e = \dfrac{c}{a}$

Vertex   Focus

Eccentricity is close to 1.

$e = \dfrac{c}{a}$

Vertex   Focus

FIGURE 11.31

Applications

The following application was developed during World War II. It shows how the properties of hyperbolas can be used in radar and other detection systems.

EXAMPLE 5 An Application Involving Hyperbolas

Two microphones, 1 mile apart, record an explosion. Microphone A received the sound 2 seconds before microphone B. Where was the explosion?

Solution

Assuming sound travels at 1100 feet per second, you know that the explosion took place 2200 feet farther from B than from A, as shown in Figure 11.32. The focus of all points that are 2200 feet closer to A than to B is one branch of the hyperbola $(x^2/a^2) - (y^2/b^2) = 1$, where

$$c = \frac{5280}{2} = 2640 \quad \text{and} \quad a = \frac{2200}{2} = 1100.$$

Thus, $b^2 = c^2 - a^2 = 5{,}759{,}600$ and you conclude that the explosion occurred somewhere on the right branch of the hyperbola given by

$$\frac{x^2}{1{,}210{,}000} - \frac{y^2}{5{,}759{,}600} = 1.$$

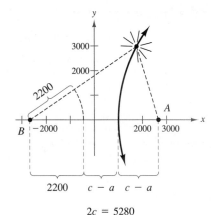

FIGURE 11.32

In Example 5, we were able to determine only the hyperbola on which the explosion occurred, but not the exact location of the explosion. If, however, we had received the sound from a third position C, then two other hyperbolas would have been determined. The exact location of the explosion would have been the point where these three hyperbolas intersected.

Another interesting application of conic sections involves the orbits of comets in our solar system. Of the 610 comets identified prior to 1970, 245 have elliptical orbits, 295 have parabolic orbits, and 70 have hyperbolic orbits. The center of the sun is a focus of each of these orbits, and each orbit has a vertex at the point where the comet is closest to the sun, as shown in Figure 11.33. Undoubtedly, there have been many comets with parabolic or hyperbolic orbits that were not identified. We only get to see such comets *once*. Comets with elliptical orbits, such as Halley's comet, are the only ones that remain in our solar system.

If p is the distance between the vertex and the focus in meters, and v is the velocity of the comet at the vertex in meters per second, then the type of orbit is determined as follows.

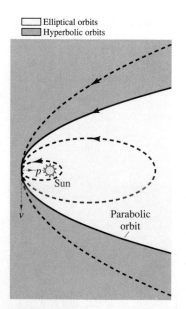

FIGURE 11.33

1. Ellipse: $v < \sqrt{2GM/p}$
2. Parabola: $v = \sqrt{2GM/p}$
3. Hyperbola: $v > \sqrt{2GM/p}$

In each of these equations, $M \approx 1.991 \times 10^{30}$ kilograms (the mass of the sun) and $G \approx 6.67 \times 10^{-11}$ cubic meters per gram-second squared.

We conclude this section with a procedure for classifying a conic using the coefficients in the general form of its equation.

CLASSIFYING A CONIC FROM ITS GENERAL EQUATION

The graph of $Ax^2 + Cy^2 + Dx + Ey + F = 0$ is one of the following (except in degenerate cases).

1. Circle: $A = C$
2. Parabola: $AC = 0$ *$A = 0$ or $C = 0$, but not both.*
3. Ellipse: $AC > 0$ *A and C have like signs.*
4. Hyperbola: $AC < 0$ *A and C have unlike signs.*

EXAMPLE 6   Classifying Conics from General Equations

a. For the general equation $4x^2 - 9x + y - 5 = 0$, we have $AC = 4(0) = 0$. Thus, the graph is a parabola.

b. For the general equation $4x^2 - y^2 + 8x - 6y + 4 = 0$, we have $AC = 4(-1) < 0$. Thus, the graph is a hyperbola.

c. For the general equation $2x^2 + 4y^2 - 4x + 12y = 0$, we have $AC = (2)(4) > 0$. Thus, the graph is an ellipse.

DISCUSSION

PROBLEM

Hyperbolas
in
Applications

At the beginning of Section 11.2, we mentioned that each type of conic section can be formed by the intersection of a plane and a double-napped cone. Figure 11.34 shows three examples of how such an intersection can occur in physical situations.

FIGURE 11.34

Identify the cone and hyperbola (or portion of a hyperbola) in each of the three situations. Can you think of other examples of physical situations in which hyperbolas are formed?

WARM UP

The following warm-up exercises involve skills that were covered in earlier sections. You will use these skills in the exercise set for this section.

In Exercises 1 and 2, find the distance between the two points.

1. $(4, 1)$, $(10, 6)$ **2.** $(-1, 5)$, $(3, -2)$

In Exercises 3–6, sketch the graph of the lines on the same set of coordinate axes.

3. $y = \pm\frac{1}{2}x$ **4.** $y = 3 \pm \frac{1}{2}x$

5. $y = 3 \pm \frac{1}{2}(x - 4)$ **6.** $y = \pm\frac{1}{2}(x - 4)$

In Exercises 7–10, identify the graph of the equation.

7. $x^2 + 4y = 4$ **8.** $x^2 + 4y^2 = 4$

9. $4x^2 + 4y^2 = 4$ **10.** $x + 4y^2 = 4$

EXERCISES for Section 11.4

In Exercises 1–6, match the equation with its graph. [The graphs are labeled (a), (b), (c), (d), (e), and (f).]

1. $\dfrac{x^2}{9} - \dfrac{y^2}{4} = 1$ **2.** $\dfrac{y^2}{9} - \dfrac{x^2}{4} = 1$

3. $\dfrac{y^2}{1} - \dfrac{x^2}{16} = 1$ **4.** $\dfrac{y^2}{16} - \dfrac{x^2}{1} = 1$

5. $\dfrac{(x - 2)^2}{9} - \dfrac{y^2}{4} = 1$ **6.** $\dfrac{(x + 1)^2}{16} - \dfrac{(y - 3)^2}{9} = 1$

(e)   (f)

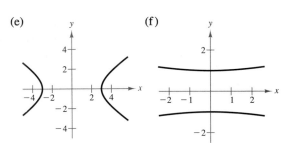

(a)   (b)

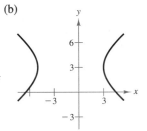

In Exercises 7–20, find the center, foci, and vertices of the hyperbola and sketch its graph using asymptotes as an aid.

7. $x^2 - y^2 = 1$ **8.** $\dfrac{y^2}{1} - \dfrac{x^2}{4} = 1$

9. $\dfrac{y^2}{25} - \dfrac{x^2}{144} = 1$ **10.** $2x^2 - 3y^2 = 6$

11. $5y^2 = 4x^2 + 20$

12. $\dfrac{(x + 1)^2}{144} - \dfrac{(y - 4)^2}{25} = 1$

13. $\dfrac{(x - 1)^2}{4} - \dfrac{(y + 2)^2}{1} = 1$

14. $\dfrac{(y - 1)^2}{1/4} - \dfrac{(x + 3)^2}{1/9} = 1$

15. $(y + 6)^2 - (x - 2)^2 = 1$

16. $9x^2 - y^2 - 36x - 6y + 18 = 0$

17. $9y^2 - x^2 + 2x + 54y + 62 = 0$

(c)   (d)

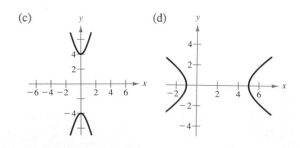

18. $16y^2 - x^2 + 2x + 64y + 63 = 0$

19. $x^2 - 9y^2 + 2x - 54y - 80 = 0$

20. $9x^2 - y^2 + 54x + 10y + 55 = 0$

In Exercises 21–30, find an equation of the specified hyperbola.

21. Vertices: $(0, \pm 2)$
Foci: $(0, \pm 4)$

22. Vertices: $(0, \pm 3)$
Asymptotes: $y = \pm 3x$

23. Vertices: $(\pm 1, 0)$
Asymptotes: $y = \pm 3x$

24. Vertices: $(0, \pm 3)$
Solution point: $(-2, 5)$

25. Vertices: $(2, 0)$, $(6, 0)$
Foci: $(0, 0)$, $(8, 0)$

26. Vertices: $(4, 1)$, $(4, 9)$
Foci: $(4, 0)$, $(4, 10)$

27. Vertices: $(2, \pm 3)$
Solution point: $(0, 5)$

28. Vertices: $(\pm 2, 1)$
Solution point: $(4, 3)$

29. Vertices: $(0, 2)$, $(6, 2)$
Asymptotes: $y = \frac{2}{3}x$
$y = 4 - \frac{2}{3}x$

30. Vertices: $(3, 0)$, $(3, 4)$
Asymptotes: $y = \frac{2}{3}x$
$y = 4 - \frac{2}{3}x$

31. *Sound Location* Three listening stations located at $(4400, 0)$, $(4400, 1100)$, and $(-4400, 0)$ monitor an explosion. If the latter two stations detect the explosion 1 second and 5 seconds after the first, respectively, determine the coordinates of the explosion. (Assume that the coordinate system is measured in feet and that sound travels at 1100 feet per second.)

32. *LORAN* Long-distance radio navigation for aircraft and ships uses synchronized pulses transmitted by widely separated transmitting stations. These pulses travel at the speed of light (186,000 miles per second). The difference in the times of arrival of these pulses at an aircraft or ship is constant on a hyperbola having the transmitting stations as foci. Assume that two stations, 300 miles apart, are positioned on the rectangular coordinate system at points with coordinates $(-150, 0)$ and $(150, 0)$ and that a ship is traveling on a path with coordinates $(x, 75)$ (see figure). Find the x-coordinate of the position of the ship if the time difference between the pulses from the transmitting stations is 1000 microseconds (0.001 second).

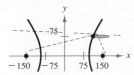

Figure for 32

33. *Hyperbolic Mirror* A hyperbolic mirror (used in some telescopes) has the property that a light ray directed at the focus will be reflected to the other focus (see figure). The focus of a hyperbolic mirror has coordinates $(12, 0)$. Find the vertex of the mirror if its mount has coordinates $(12, 12)$.

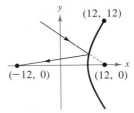

Figure for 33

34. Consider a hyperbola centered at the origin with a horizontal transverse axis. Use the definition of a hyperbola to derive its standard form.

In Exercises 35–42, classify the graph of each equation as a circle, a parabola, an ellipse, or a hyperbola.

35. $x^2 + y^2 - 6x + 4y + 9 = 0$

36. $x^2 + 4y^2 - 6x + 16y + 21 = 0$

37. $4x^2 - y^2 - 4x - 3 = 0$

38. $y^2 - 4y - 4x = 0$

39. $4x^2 + 3y^2 + 8x - 24y + 51 = 0$

40. $4y^2 - 2x^2 - 4y - 8x - 15 = 0$

41. $25x^2 - 10x - 200y - 119 = 0$

42. $4x^2 + 4y^2 - 16y + 15 = 0$

11.5 Rotation and General Second-Degree Equations

Rotation / Invariants under Rotation

Rotation

In the previous sections we have shown that the equation of a conic with axes parallel to one of the coordinate axes has a standard form that can be written in the general form

$$Ax^2 + Cy^2 + Dx + Ey + F = 0. \qquad \textit{Horizontal or vertical axes}$$

In this section we investigate the equations of conics whose axes are rotated so that they are not parallel to either the x-axis or the y-axis. The general equation for such conics contains an xy-term.

$$Ax^2 + Bxy + Cy^2 + Dx + Ey + F = 0 \qquad \textit{Equation in xy-plane}$$

To eliminate this xy-term, we use a procedure called **rotation of axes.** Our objective is to rotate the x- and y-axes until they are parallel to the axes of the conic. We denote the rotated axes as the x'-axis and the y'-axis, as shown in Figure 11.35. This having been accomplished, the equation of the conic in the new $x'y'$-plane will have the form

$$A'(x')^2 + C'(y')^2 + D'x' + E'y' + F' = 0. \qquad \textit{Equation in x'y'-plane}$$

Since this equation has no xy-term, we can obtain a standard form by completing the square.

The following theorem identifies how much to rotate the axes to eliminate the xy-term and also the equations for determining the new coefficients A', C', D', E', and F'.

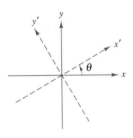

Rotated: x'-axis
y'-axis

FIGURE 11.35

ROTATION OF AXES TO ELIMINATE AN xy-TERM

The general second-degree equation $Ax^2 + Bxy + Cy^2 + Dx + Ey + F = 0$ can be rewritten as

$$A'(x')^2 + C'(y')^2 + D'x' + E'y' + F' = 0$$

by rotating the coordinate axes through an angle θ, where

$$\cot 2\theta = \frac{A - C}{B}.$$

The coefficients of the new equation are obtained by making the substitutions

$$x = x' \cos \theta - y' \sin \theta \quad \text{and} \quad y = x' \sin \theta + y' \cos \theta.$$

Proof

We need to discover how the coordinates in the xy-system are related to the coordinates in the $x'y'$-system. To do this, we choose a point $P = (x, y)$ in the original system and attempt to find its coordinates (x', y') in the rotated system. In either system, the distance r between the point P and the origin is the same; thus, the equations for x, y, x', and y' are those given in Figure 11.36. Using the formulas for the sine and cosine of the difference of two angles, we have the following.

$$x' = r \cos(\alpha - \theta)$$
$$= r(\cos \alpha \cos \theta + \sin \alpha \sin \theta)$$
$$= r \cos \alpha \cos \theta + r \sin \alpha \sin \theta$$
$$= x \cos \theta + y \sin \theta$$
$$y' = r \sin(\alpha - \theta)$$
$$= r(\sin \alpha \cos \theta - \cos \alpha \sin \theta)$$
$$= r \sin \alpha \cos \theta - r \cos \alpha \sin \theta$$
$$= y \cos \theta - x \sin \theta$$

Solving this system for x and y yields

$$x = x' \cos \theta - y' \sin \theta$$
$$y = x' \sin \theta + y' \cos \theta.$$

Finally, by substituting these values for x and y into the original equation and collecting terms, we obtain

$$A' = A \cos^2 \theta + B \cos \theta \sin \theta + C \sin^2 \theta$$
$$C' = A \sin^2 \theta - B \cos \theta \sin \theta + C \cos^2 \theta$$
$$D' = D \cos \theta + E \sin \theta$$
$$E' = -D \sin \theta + E \cos \theta$$
$$F' = F.$$

Now, in order to eliminate the $x'y'$-term, we must select θ so that $B' = 0$, as follows.

$$B' = 2(C - A) \sin \theta \cos \theta + B(\cos^2 \theta - \sin^2 \theta)$$
$$= (C - A) \sin 2\theta + B \cos 2\theta$$
$$= B(\sin 2\theta)\left(\frac{C - A}{B} + \cot 2\theta\right) = 0, \qquad \sin 2\theta \neq 0$$

If $B = 0$, no rotation is necessary since the xy-term is not present in the original equation. If $B \neq 0$, then the only way to make $B' = 0$ is to let

$$\cot 2\theta = \frac{A - C}{B}, \qquad B \neq 0.$$

Thus, we have established the desired results. ◢

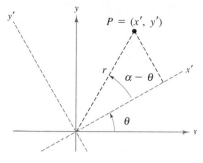

Rotated: $x' = r \cos(\alpha - \theta)$
$y' = r \sin(\alpha - \theta)$

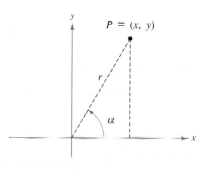

Original: $x = r \cos \alpha$
$y = r \sin \alpha$

FIGURE 11.36

EXAMPLE 1   Rotation of Axes for a Hyperbola

Write the equation $xy - 1 = 0$ in standard form.

Solution

Since $A = 0$, $B = 1$, and $C = 0$, you have

$$\cot 2\theta = \frac{A - C}{B} = 0 \quad \rightarrow \quad 2\theta = \frac{\pi}{2} \quad \rightarrow \quad \theta = \frac{\pi}{4}$$

which implies that

$$x = x' \cos \frac{\pi}{4} - y' \sin \frac{\pi}{4}$$

$$= x'\left(\frac{\sqrt{2}}{2}\right) - y'\left(\frac{\sqrt{2}}{2}\right) = \frac{x' - y'}{\sqrt{2}}$$

and

$$y = x' \sin \frac{\pi}{4} + y' \cos \frac{\pi}{4}$$

$$= x'\left(\frac{\sqrt{2}}{2}\right) + y'\left(\frac{\sqrt{2}}{2}\right) = \frac{x' + y'}{\sqrt{2}}.$$

The equation in the $x'y'$-system is obtained by substituting these expressions into the equation $xy - 1 = 0$.

$$\left(\frac{x' - y'}{\sqrt{2}}\right)\left(\frac{x' + y'}{\sqrt{2}}\right) - 1 = 0$$

$$\frac{(x')^2 - (y')^2}{2} - 1 = 0$$

$$\frac{(x')^2}{(\sqrt{2})^2} - \frac{(y')^2}{(\sqrt{2})^2} = 1 \qquad \qquad \textit{Standard form}$$

This is the equation of a hyperbola centered at the origin with vertices at $(\pm\sqrt{2}, 0)$ in the $x'y'$-system, as shown in Figure 11.37. To find the coordinates of the vertices in the xy-system, substitute the coordinates $(\pm\sqrt{2}, 0)$ into the equations

$$x = \frac{x' - y'}{\sqrt{2}} \quad \text{and} \quad y = \frac{x' + y'}{\sqrt{2}}.$$

This substitution yields the vertices $(1, 1)$ and $(-1, -1)$ in the xy-system. Note also that the asymptotes of the hyperbola have equations $y' = \pm x'$, which correspond to the original x- and y-axes.

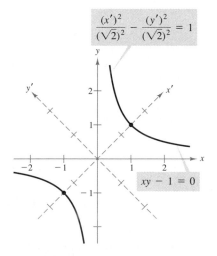

$$\frac{(x')^2}{(\sqrt{2})^2} - \frac{(y')^2}{(\sqrt{2})^2} = 1$$

$xy - 1 = 0$

Vertices:
In $x'y'$-system: $(\sqrt{2}, 0)$, $(-\sqrt{2}, 0)$
In xy-system: $(1, 1)$, $(-1, -1)$

FIGURE 11.37

EXAMPLE 2   Rotation of Axes for an Ellipse

Sketch the graph of $7x^2 - 6\sqrt{3}xy + 13y^2 - 16 = 0$.

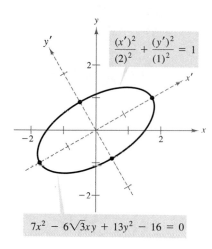

$$\frac{(x')^2}{(2)^2} + \frac{(y')^2}{(1)^2} = 1$$

$$7x^2 - 6\sqrt{3}xy + 13y^2 - 16 = 0$$

Vertices:
In $x'y'$ system: $(\pm 2, 0)$, $(0, \pm 1)$

In xy-system: $(\pm\sqrt{3}, \pm 1)$, $\left(\pm\frac{1}{2}, \mp\frac{\sqrt{3}}{2}\right)$

FIGURE 11.38

Solution

Since $A = 7$, $B = -6\sqrt{3}$, and $C = 13$, we have

$$\cot 2\theta = \frac{A - C}{B} = \frac{7 - 13}{-6\sqrt{3}} = \frac{1}{\sqrt{3}} \quad \rightarrow \quad \theta = \frac{\pi}{6}.$$

Therefore, the equation in the $x'y'$-system is obtained by making the substitutions

$$x = x' \cos\frac{\pi}{6} - y' \sin\frac{\pi}{6}$$

$$= x'\left(\frac{\sqrt{3}}{2}\right) - y'\left(\frac{1}{2}\right)$$

$$= \frac{\sqrt{3}x' - y'}{2}$$

and

$$y = x' \sin\frac{\pi}{6} + y' \cos\frac{\pi}{6}$$

$$= x'\left(\frac{1}{2}\right) + y'\left(\frac{\sqrt{3}}{2}\right)$$

$$= \frac{x' + \sqrt{3}y'}{2}$$

into the original equation. Thus, you have

$$7x^2 - 6\sqrt{3}xy + 13y^2 - 16 = 0$$

$$7\left(\frac{\sqrt{3}x' - y'}{2}\right)^2 - 6\sqrt{3}\left(\frac{\sqrt{3}x' - y'}{2}\right)\left(\frac{x' + \sqrt{3}y'}{2}\right) + 13\left(\frac{x' + \sqrt{3}y'}{2}\right)^2 - 16 = 0$$

which simplifies to

$$4(x')^2 + 16(y')^2 - 16 = 0$$

$$\frac{(x')^2}{4} + \frac{(y')^2}{1} = 1. \qquad \textit{Standard form}$$

This is the equation of an ellipse centered at the origin with vertices at $(\pm 2, 0)$ in the $x'y'$-system, as shown in Figure 11.38.

REMARK   Remember that the substitutions

$$x = x' \cos \theta - y' \sin \theta \quad \text{and} \quad y = x' \cos \theta + y' \sin \theta$$

were developed to eliminate the $x'y'$-term in the rotated system. You can use this as a check on your work. In other words, if your final equation contains an $x'y'$-term, you know that you made a mistake.   ◢

In constructing Examples 1 and 2 we carefully chose the equations so that θ would turn out to be one of the common angles 30°, 45°, and so forth. Of course, many second-degree equations do not yield such common solutions of the equation

$$\cot 2\theta = (A - C)/B.$$

Example 3 illustrates such a case.

EXAMPLE 3   Rotation of Axes for a Parabola

Sketch the graph of $x^2 - 4xy + 4y^2 + 5\sqrt{5}y + 1 = 0$.

Solution

Since $A = 1$, $B = -4$, and $C = 4$, you have

$$\cot 2\theta = \frac{A - C}{B} = \frac{1 - 4}{-4} = \frac{3}{4}.$$

Using the identity $\cot 2\theta = (\cot^2 \theta - 1)/(2 \cot \theta)$ produces

$$\cot 2\theta = \frac{3}{4} = \frac{\cot^2 \theta - 1}{2 \cot \theta}$$

from which you obtain the equation

$$4 \cot^2 \theta - 4 = 6 \cot \theta$$
$$4 \cot^2 \theta - 6 \cot \theta - 4 = 0$$
$$(2 \cot \theta - 4)(2 \cot \theta + 1) = 0.$$

Considering $0 < \theta < \pi/2$, we have $2 \cot \theta = 4$. Thus,

$$\cot \theta = 2 \quad \rightarrow \quad \theta \approx 26.6°.$$

From the triangle in Figure 11.39 you obtain $\sin \theta = 1/\sqrt{5}$ and $\cos \theta = 2/\sqrt{5}$. Consequently, you use the substitutions

$$x = x' \cos \theta - y' \sin \theta = x'\left(\frac{2}{\sqrt{5}}\right) - y'\left(\frac{1}{\sqrt{5}}\right) = \frac{2x' - y'}{\sqrt{5}}$$

$$y = x' \sin \theta + y' \cos \theta = x'\left(\frac{1}{\sqrt{5}}\right) + y'\left(\frac{2}{\sqrt{5}}\right) = \frac{x' + 2y'}{\sqrt{5}}.$$

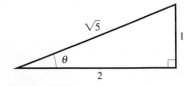

FIGURE 11.39

Substituting these expressions into the original equation, you have

$$x^2 - 4xy + 4y^2 + 5\sqrt{5}y + 1 = 0$$

$$\left(\frac{2x' - y'}{\sqrt{5}}\right)^2 - 4\left(\frac{2x' - y'}{\sqrt{5}}\right)\left(\frac{x' + 2y'}{\sqrt{5}}\right) + 4\left(\frac{x' + 2y'}{\sqrt{5}}\right)^2 + 5\sqrt{5}\left(\frac{x' + 2y'}{\sqrt{5}}\right) + 1 = 0$$

which simplifies as follows.

$$5(y')^2 + 5x' + 10y' + 1 = 0$$

$$5(y' + 1)^2 = -5x' + 4 \qquad \text{\textit{Complete the square}}$$

$$(y' + 1)^2 = (-1)\left(x' - \frac{4}{5}\right) \qquad \text{\textit{Standard form}}$$

The graph of this equation is a parabola with its vertex at $\left(\frac{4}{5}, -1\right)$. Its axis is parallel to the x'-axis in the $x'y'$-system, as shown in Figure 11.40.

Invariants under Rotation

In the rotation of axes theorem listed at the beginning of this section, note that the constant term $F' = F$ is the same in both equations, and we say that it is **invariant under rotation.** The next theorem lists some of the other rotation invariants.

$$x^2 - 4xy + 4y^2 + 5\sqrt{5}y + 1 = 0$$

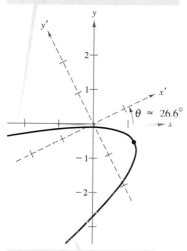

$$(y' + 1)^2 = 4\left(-\frac{1}{4}\right)\left(x' - \frac{4}{5}\right)$$

Vertex:

In $x'y'$-system: $\left(\frac{4}{5}, -1\right)$

In xy-system: $\left(\frac{13}{5\sqrt{5}}, -\frac{6}{5\sqrt{5}}\right)$

FIGURE 11.40

ROTATION INVARIANTS

The rotation of coordinate axes through an angle θ that transforms the equation $Ax^2 + Bxy + Cy^2 + Dx + Ey + F = 0$ into the form

$$A'(x')^2 + C'(y')^2 + D'x' + E'y' + F' = 0$$

has the following rotation invariants.

1. $F = F'$
2. $A + C = A' + C'$
3. $B^2 - 4AC = (B')^2 - 4A'C'$

We can use the results of this theorem to classify the graph of a second-degree equation *with* an xy-term in much the same way we did for second-degree equations *without* an xy-term. Note that since $B' = 0$, the invariant $B^2 - 4AC$ reduces to

$$B^2 - AC = -4A'C'. \qquad \text{\textit{Discriminant}}$$

We call this quantity the **discriminant** of the equation

$$Ax^2 + Bxy + Cy^2 + Dx + Ey + F = 0.$$

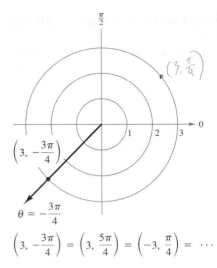

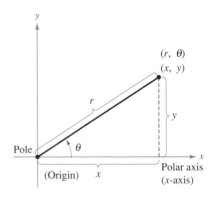

Relating Polar and Rectangular Coordinates

FIGURE 11.44

EXAMPLE 2   Multiple Representation of Points

Plot the point $(3, -3\pi/4)$ and find three additional polar representations of this point using $-2\pi < \theta < 2\pi$.

Solution

The point is shown in Figure 11.43. Three other representations are as follows.

$$\left(3, \frac{-3\pi}{4} + 2\pi\right) = \left(3, \frac{5\pi}{4}\right) \qquad \text{Add } 2\pi \text{ to } \theta$$

$$\left(-3, \frac{-3\pi}{4} - \pi\right) = \left(-3, \frac{-7\pi}{4}\right) \qquad \text{Replace } r \text{ by } -r; \text{ subtract } \pi \text{ from } \theta$$

$$\left(-3, \frac{-3\pi}{4} + \pi\right) = \left(-3, \frac{\pi}{4}\right) \qquad \text{Replace } r \text{ by } -r; \text{ add } \pi \text{ to } \theta$$

Coordinate Conversion

To establish the relationship between polar and rectangular coordinates, we let the polar axis coincide with the positive x-axis and the pole with the origin, as shown in Figure 11.44. Since (x, y) lies on a circle of radius r, it follows that $r^2 = x^2 + y^2$. Moreover, for $r > 0$, the definitions of the trigonometric functions imply that

$$\tan \theta = \frac{y}{x}, \qquad \cos \theta = \frac{x}{r}, \quad \text{and} \quad \sin \theta = \frac{y}{r}.$$

If $r < 0$, we can show that the same relationships hold. For example, consider the point (r, θ), where $r < 0$. Then, since $(-r, \theta + \pi)$ represents the same point and $-r > 0$, we have $-\sin \theta = \sin(\theta + \pi) = -y/r$, which implies that $\sin \theta = y/r$.

These relationships allow us to convert *coordinates* or *equations* from one system to the other as indicated in the following rule.

COORDINATE CONVERSION

The polar coordinates (r, θ) are related to the rectangular coordinates (x, y) as follows.

$$x = r \cos \theta \quad \text{and} \quad \tan \theta = \frac{y}{x}$$

$$y = r \sin \theta \qquad\qquad r^2 = x^2 + y^2$$

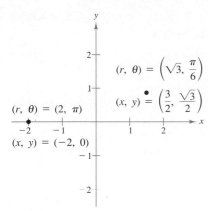

FIGURE 11.45

EXAMPLE 3 Polar-to-Rectangular Conversion

a. For the point $(r, \theta) = (2, \pi)$, we have

$$x = r \cos \theta = 2 \cos \pi = -2$$

and

$$y = r \sin \theta = 2 \sin \pi = 0.$$

Thus, the rectangular coordinates are $(x, y) = (-2, 0)$, as shown in Figure 11.45.

b. For the point $(r, \theta) = (\sqrt{3}, \pi/6)$, we have

$$x = \sqrt{3} \cos \frac{\pi}{6} = \sqrt{3}\left(\frac{\sqrt{3}}{2}\right) = \frac{3}{2}$$

and

$$y = \sqrt{3} \sin \frac{\pi}{6} = \sqrt{3}\left(\frac{1}{2}\right) = \frac{\sqrt{3}}{2}$$

and the rectangular coordinates are $(x, y) = (3/2, \sqrt{3}/2)$, as shown in Figure 11.45.

EXAMPLE 4 Rectangular-to-Polar Conversion

a. For the second quadrant point $(x, y) = (-1, 1)$, you have

$$\tan \theta = \frac{y}{x} = -1 \quad \rightarrow \quad \theta = \frac{3\pi}{4}.$$

Since θ lies in the same quadrant as (x, y), use positive r.

$$r = \sqrt{x^2 + y^2} = \sqrt{(-1)^2 + (1)^2} = \sqrt{2}$$

Thus, *one* set of polar coordinates is $(r, \theta) = (\sqrt{2}, 3\pi/4)$, as shown in Figure 11.46(a).

b. Since the point $(x, y) = (0, 2)$ lies on the positive y-axis, choose $\theta = \pi/2$ and $r = 2$, and one set of polar coordinates is $(r, \theta) = (2, \pi/2)$, as shown in Figure 11.46(b).

Equation Conversion

By comparing Examples 3 and 4, we see that point conversion from the polar to the rectangular system is straightforward, whereas point conversion from the rectangular to the polar system is more involved. For equations, the opposite is true. To convert a rectangular equation to polar form, we simply

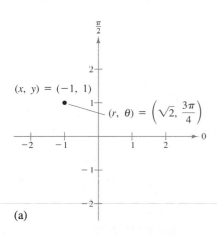

(a)

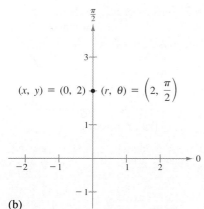

(b)

FIGURE 11.46

replace x by $r \cos \theta$ and y by $r \sin \theta$. For instance, the rectangular equation $y = x^2$ can be written in polar form as follows.

$$\underbrace{y = x^2}_{\text{Rectangular equation}} \quad \rightarrow \quad \underbrace{r \sin \theta = (r \cos \theta)^2}_{\text{Polar equation}}$$

On the other hand, converting a polar equation to rectangular form requires considerable ingenuity.

In the next example we demonstrate several polar-to-rectangular conversions that enable us to sketch the graphs of some polar equations.

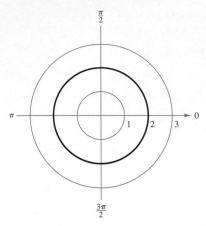

(a) Circle: $r = 2$

EXAMPLE 5   Converting Polar Equations to Rectangular Form

Describe the graphs of the following polar equations and find the corresponding rectangular equation.

a. $r = 2$ **b.** $\theta = \dfrac{\pi}{3}$ **c.** $r = \sec \theta$

Solution

a. The graph of the polar equation $r = 2$ consists of all points that are 2 units from the pole. In other words, this graph is a circle centered at the origin and having a radius of 2, as shown in Figure 11.47(a). You can confirm this by converting to rectangular coordinates, using the relationship $r^2 = x^2 + y^2$.

$$\underbrace{r = 2}_{\text{Polar equation}} \quad \rightarrow \quad r^2 = 2^2 \quad \rightarrow \quad \underbrace{x^2 + y^2 = 2^2}_{\text{Rectangular equation}}$$

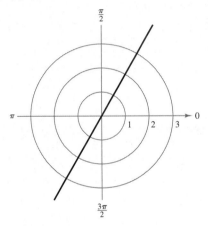

(b) Radial line: $\theta = \dfrac{\pi}{3}$

b. The graph of the polar equation $\theta = \pi/3$ consists of all points on the line that makes an angle of $\pi/3$ with the positive x-axis, as shown in Figure 11.47(b). To convert to rectangular form, make use of the relationship $\tan \theta = y/x$.

$$\underbrace{\theta = \dfrac{\pi}{3}}_{\text{Polar equation}} \quad \rightarrow \quad \tan \theta = \sqrt{3} \quad \rightarrow \quad \underbrace{y = \sqrt{3}x}_{\text{Rectangular equation}}$$

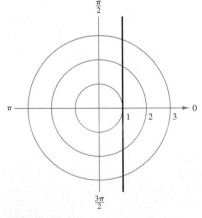

(c) Vertical line: $r = \sec \theta$

FIGURE 11.47

c. The graph of the polar equation $r = \sec \theta$ is not evident by simple inspection, so we convert to rectangular form by using the relationship $r \cos \theta = x$.

$$\underbrace{r = \sec \theta}_{\text{Polar equation}} \quad \rightarrow \quad r \cos \theta = 1 \quad \rightarrow \quad \underbrace{x = 1}_{\text{Rectangular equation}}$$

Now, you see that the graph is a vertical line, as shown in Figure 11.47(c).

Curve-sketching by converting to rectangular form is not always convenient. In the next section we demonstrate a straightforward point-plotting technique.

DISCUSSION

PROBLEM

Simplifying
a Polar
Equation

In the discussion before Example 5, we showed how to convert the rectangular equation $y = x^2$ to the polar equation

$$r \sin \theta = (r \cos \theta)^2.$$

If we simplify this equation by dividing both sides by r, we obtain

$$\sin \theta = r \cos^2 \theta \quad \text{or} \quad r = \frac{\sin \theta}{\cos^2 \theta}.$$

By doing this, we risk the possibility of losing the pole $(0, \theta)$ as a solution point. In this particular equation, however, division by r does not change the set of solution points because the pole is a solution point of the simplified equation. Can you find a polar equation for which division by r would change the set of solution points?

WARM UP

The following warm-up exercises involve skills that were covered in earlier sections. You will use these skills in the exercise set for this section.

In Exercises 1 and 2, find a positive angle coterminal with the angle.

1. $\dfrac{11\pi}{4}$ **2.** $-\dfrac{5\pi}{6}$

In Exercises 3 and 4, find the sine and cosine of the angle in standard position with its terminal side passing through the point.

3. $(2, 1)$ **4.** $(4, -3)$

In Exercises 5 and 6, find the magnitude (in radians) of an angle in standard position with its terminal side passing through the point.

5. $(-4, 4)$ **6.** $(3, 2)$

In Exercises 7 and 8, evaluate the trigonometric function without the aid of a calculator.

7. $\sin \dfrac{4\pi}{3}$ **8.** $\cos \dfrac{3\pi}{4}$

In Exercises 9 and 10, use a calculator to evaluate the trigonometric function.

9. $\cos \dfrac{3\pi}{5}$ **10.** $\sin 1.34$

EXERCISES for Section 11.6

In Exercises 1–10, plot the point given in polar coordinates and find the corresponding rectangular coordinates for the point.

1. $\left(4, \dfrac{3\pi}{6}\right)$ **2.** $\left(4, \dfrac{3\pi}{2}\right)$

3. $\left(-1, \dfrac{5\pi}{4}\right)$ **4.** $(0, -\pi)$

5. $\left(4, -\dfrac{\pi}{3}\right)$ **6.** $\left(-1, -\dfrac{3\pi}{4}\right)$

7. $\left(0, -\dfrac{7\pi}{6}\right)$ **8.** $\left(\dfrac{3}{2}, \dfrac{5\pi}{2}\right)$

9. $(\sqrt{2}, 2.36)$ **10.** $(-3, -1.57)$

In Exercises 11–20, the rectangular coordinates of a point are given. Plot the point and find *two* sets of polar coordinates for the point for $0 \le \theta < 2\pi$.

11. $(1, 1)$ **12.** $(0, -5)$
13. $(-6, 0)$ **14.** $(-3, -3)$
15. $(-3, 4)$ **16.** $(3, -1)$
17. $(-\sqrt{3}, -\sqrt{3})$ **18.** $(-2, 0)$
19. $(4, 6)$ **20.** $(5, 12)$

In Exercises 21–34, convert the rectangular equation to polar form.

21. $x^2 + y^2 = 9$ **22.** $x^2 + y^2 = a^2 \ \text{r} \le a$
23. $x^2 + y^2 - 2ax = 0$ **24.** $x^2 + y^2 - 2ay = 0$
25. $y = 4$ **26.** $y = b$
27. $x = 10$ **28.** $x = a$
29. $3x - y + 2 = 0$ **30.** $4x + 7y - 2 = 0$
31. $xy = 4$ **32.** $y = x$

33. $(x^2 + y^2)^2 - 9(x^2 - y^2) = 0$
34. $y^2 - 8x - 16 = 0$

In Exercises 35–44, convert the polar equation to rectangular form.

35. $r = 4 \sin \theta$ **36.** $r = 4 \cos \theta$

37. $\theta = \dfrac{\pi}{6}$ **38.** $r = 4$

39. $r = 2 \csc \theta$ **40.** $r^2 = \sin 2\theta$

41. $r = 2 \sin 3\theta$ **42.** $r = \dfrac{1}{1 - \cos \theta}$

43. $r = \dfrac{6}{2 - 3 \sin \theta}$ **44.** $r = \dfrac{6}{2 \cos \theta - 3 \sin \theta}$

In Exercises 45–50, convert the polar equation to rectangular form and sketch its graph.

45. $r = 3$ **46.** $r = 8$

47. $\theta = \dfrac{\pi}{4}$ **48.** $\theta = \dfrac{5\pi}{6}$

49. $r = 3 \sec \theta$ **50.** $r = 2 \csc \theta$

51. Show that the distance between the points (r_1, θ_1), and (r_2, θ_2) is given by
$$\sqrt{r_1^2 + r_2^2 - 2r_1r_2 \cos(\theta_1 - \theta_2)}.$$

52. Convert the polar equation
$$r = 2(h \cos \theta + k \sin \theta)$$

to rectangular form and verify that it is the equation of a circle. Find the radius and the rectangular coordinates of the center of the circle.

11.7 Graphs of Polar Equations

Introduction / Symmetry / Zeros and Maximum *r*-values / Special Polar Graphs

Introduction

In previous chapters we spent considerable time learning how to sketch graphs in rectangular coordinates. We began with the basic point-plotting method which was then enhanced by sketching aids such as symmetry, intercepts, asymptotes, periods, and shifts. We approach curve-sketching in the polar coordinate system similarly, beginning with a demonstration of point-plotting.

EXAMPLE 1   Graphing a Polar Equation by Point-Plotting

Sketch the graph of the polar equation $r = 4 \sin \theta$.

Solution

The sine function is periodic, so we can get a full range of r-values by considering values of θ in the interval $0 \le \theta \le 2\pi$, shown in the following table.

θ	0	$\dfrac{\pi}{6}$	$\dfrac{\pi}{3}$	$\dfrac{\pi}{2}$	$\dfrac{2\pi}{3}$	$\dfrac{5\pi}{6}$	π	$\dfrac{7\pi}{6}$	$\dfrac{3\pi}{2}$	$\dfrac{11\pi}{6}$	2π
r	0	2	$2\sqrt{3}$	4	$2\sqrt{3}$	2	0	-2	-4	-2	0

If you plot these points as shown in Figure 11.48, it appears that the graph is a circle of radius 2 whose center is at the point $(x, y) = (0, 2)$.

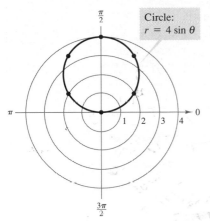

Circle: $r = 4 \sin \theta$

FIGURE 11.48

Symmetry

In Figure 11.48 note that as θ increases from 0 to 2π, the graph is traced out twice. Moreover, note that the graph is *symmetric with respect to the line* $\theta = \pi/2$. Had we known about this symmetry and retracing ahead of time, we could have reduced our table of points to half its size.

Symmetry with respect to the line $\theta = \pi/2$ is one of three important types of symmetry to consider in polar curve sketching. (See Figure 11.49.)

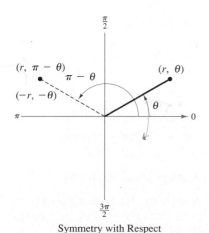

Symmetry with Respect
to the Line $\theta = \pi/2$

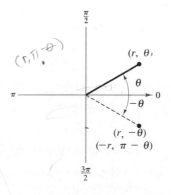

Symmetry with Respect
to the Polar Axis

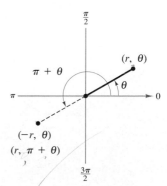

Symmetry with Respect
to the Pole

FIGURE 11.49

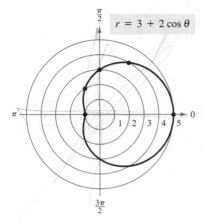

$r = 3 + 2 \cos \theta$

FIGURE 11.50

Test for Symmetry in Polar Coordinates

The graph of a polar equation is symmetric with respect to the following if the given substitution yields an equivalent equation.

1. The line $\theta = \pi/2$: Replace (r, θ) by $(r, \pi - \theta)$ or $(-r, -\theta)$.
2. The polar axis: Replace (r, θ) by $(r, -\theta)$ or $(-r, \pi - \theta)$.
3. The pole: Replace (r, θ) by $(r, \pi + \theta)$ or $(-r, \theta)$.

EXAMPLE 2   Using Symmetry to Sketch the Graph of a Polar Equation

Use symmetry to sketch the graph of $r = 3 + 2 \cos \theta$.

Solution

Replacing (r, θ) by $(r, -\theta)$ produces

$$r = 3 + 2 \cos(-\theta)$$
$$= 3 + 2 \cos \theta.$$

Thus, you conclude that the curve is symmetric with respect to the polar axis. Plotting the points in the table and using polar axis symmetry, you obtain the graph shown in Figure 11.50.

θ	0	$\pi/3$	$\pi/2$	$2\pi/3$	π
r	5	4	3	2	1

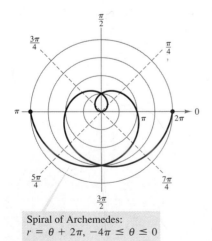

Spiral of Archemedes:
$r = \theta + 2\pi, \; -4\pi \le \theta \le 0$

FIGURE 11.51

These three tests for symmetry in polar coordinates are sufficient to guarantee symmetry, but they are not necessary. For instance, Figure 11.51 shows the graph of $r = \theta + 2\pi$ to be symmetric with respect to the line $\theta = \pi/2$. Yet the test fails to indicate symmetry because neither of the following replacements yields an equivalent equation.

Original Equation	*Replacement*	*New Equation*
$r = \theta + 2\pi$	(r, θ) by $(-r, -\theta)$	$-r = -\theta + 2\pi$
$r = \theta + 2\pi$	(r, θ) by $(r, \pi - \theta)$	$r = -\theta + 3\pi$

The equations discussed in Examples 1 and 2 are of the form

$$r = 4 \sin \theta = f(\sin \theta) \qquad \text{\textit{r is a function of} sin } \theta$$

and

$$r = 3 + \cos \theta = g(\cos \theta). \qquad \text{\textit{r is a function of} cos } \theta$$

The graph of the first equation is symmetric with respect to the line $\theta = \pi/2$, and the graph of the second equation is symmetric with respect to the polar axis. This observation can be generalized to yield the following *quick test for symmetry*.

1. The graph of $r = f(\sin \theta)$ is symmetric with respect to the line $\theta = \pi/2$.
2. The graph of $r = g(\cos \theta)$ is symmetric with respect to the polar axis.

Zeros and Maximum r-values

Two additional aids to sketching graphs of polar equations involve knowing the θ-values for which $|r|$ is maximum and knowing the θ-values for which $r = 0$. For instance, in Example 1, the maximum value of $|r|$ for $r = 4 \sin \theta$ is $|r| = 4$, and this occurs when $\theta = \pi/2$, as shown in Figure 11.48. Moreover, $r = 0$ when $\theta = 0$.

EXAMPLE 3   Sketching a Polar Graph

Sketch the graph of $r = 1 - 2 \cos \theta$.

Solution

From the equation $r = 1 - 2 \cos \theta$, you obtain the following information.

Symmetry	With respect to the polar axis
Maximum Value of $|r|$	$r = 3$ when $\theta = \pi$
Zero of r	$r = 0$ when $\theta = \pi/3$

Making a table for several θ-values in the interval $[0, \pi]$ and plotting the corresponding points produces the graph shown in Figure 11.52.

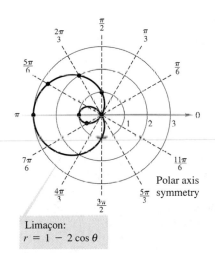

Limaçon:
$r = 1 - 2 \cos \theta$

FIGURE 11.52

θ	0	$\pi/6$	$\pi/3$	$\pi/2$	$2\pi/3$	$5\pi/6$	π
r	-1	-0.73	0	1	2	2.73	3

REMARK   Note how the negative r-values determine the *inner loop* of the graph in Figure 11.52. This type of graph is called a limaçon. ◢

Some curves reach their zeros and maximum r-values at more than one point. We show how to handle this situation in Example 4.

EXAMPLE 4   Sketching a Polar Graph

Sketch the graph of $r = 2 \cos 3\theta$.

Solution

Symmetry	With respect to the polar axis
Maximum Value of $|r|$	$|r| = 2$ when $3\theta = 0,\ \pi,\ 2\pi,\ 3\pi$
	or $\theta = 0,\ \pi/3,\ 2\pi/3,\ \pi$
Zeros of r	$r = 0$ when $3\theta = \pi/2,\ 3\pi/2,\ 5\pi/2$
	or $\theta = \pi/6,\ \pi/2,\ 5\pi/6$

θ	0	$\pi/12$	$\pi/6$	$\pi/4$	$\pi/3$	$5\pi/12$	$\pi/2$
r	2	$\sqrt{2}$	0	$-\sqrt{2}$	-2	$-\sqrt{2}$	0

By plotting these points and using the specified symmetry, zeros, and maximum values, we obtain the graph shown in Figure 11.53. Note how the entire curve is generated as θ increases from 0 to π.

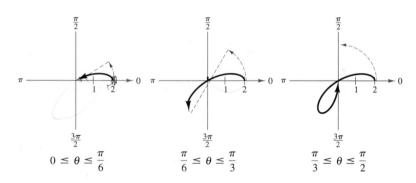

$$0 \le \theta \le \frac{\pi}{6} \qquad \frac{\pi}{6} \le \theta \le \frac{\pi}{3} \qquad \frac{\pi}{3} \le \theta \le \frac{\pi}{2}$$

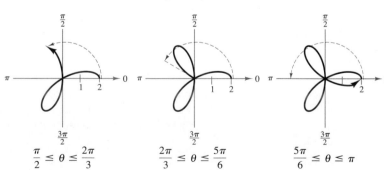

$$\frac{\pi}{2} \le \theta \le \frac{2\pi}{3} \qquad \frac{2\pi}{3} \le \theta \le \frac{5\pi}{6} \qquad \frac{5\pi}{6} \le \theta \le \pi$$

REMARK The graph shown in Figure 11.53 is called a **rose curve,** and each of the loops on the graph is called a *petal* of the rose curve.

FIGURE 11.53

Special Polar Graphs

Several important types of graphs have equations that are simpler in polar form than in rectangular form. For example, the circle $r = 4 \sin \theta$ in Example 1 has the more complicated rectangular equation $x^2 + (y - 2)^2 = 4$. The following list gives several other types of graphs that have simple polar equations.

Limaçons

$r = a \pm b \cos \theta$

$r = a \pm b \sin \theta$

$(0 < a, 0 < b)$

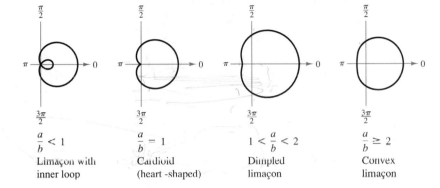

$\dfrac{a}{b} < 1$	$\dfrac{a}{b} = 1$	$1 < \dfrac{a}{b} < 2$	$\dfrac{a}{b} \geq 2$
Limaçon with inner loop	Cardioid (heart-shaped)	Dimpled limaçon	Convex limaçon

Rose Curves

n petals if n is odd

$2n$ petals if n is even

$(n \geq 2)$

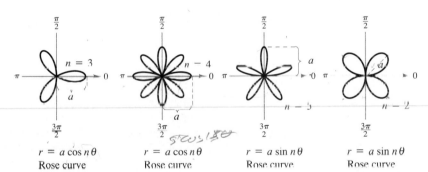

$r = a \cos n\theta$	$r = a \cos n\theta$	$r = a \sin n\theta$	$r = a \sin n\theta$
Rose curve	Rose curve	Rose curve	Rose curve

Circles and Lemniscates

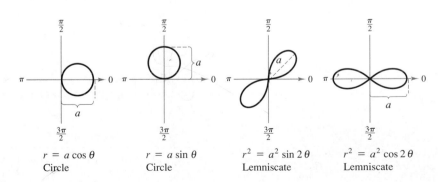

$r = a \cos \theta$	$r = a \sin \theta$	$r^2 = a^2 \sin 2\theta$	$r^2 = a^2 \cos 2\theta$
Circle	Circle	Lemniscate	Lemniscate

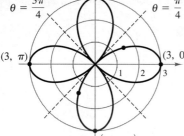

FIGURE 11.54

EXAMPLE 5 Sketching a Rose Curve

Sketch the graph of $r = 3 \cos 2\theta$.

Solution

Type of Curve	Rose curve with $2n = 4$ petals
Symmetry	With respect to polar axis and the line $\theta = \pi/2$
Maximum Value of $|r|$	$|r| = 3$ when $\theta = 0$, $\pi/2$, π, $3\pi/2$
Zeros of r	$r = 0$ when $\theta = \pi/4$, $3\pi/4$

Using this information together with the additional points shown in the table, you obtain the graph shown in Figure 11.54.

θ	0	$\pi/6$	$\pi/4$	$\pi/3$
r	3	$3/2$	0	$-3/2$

EXAMPLE 6 Sketching a Lemniscate

Sketch the graph of $r^2 = 9 \sin 2\theta$.

Solution

Type of Curve	Lemniscate
Symmetry	With respect to the pole
Maximum Value of $|r|$	$|r| = 3$ when $\theta = \pi/4$
Zeros of r	$r = 0$ when $\theta = 0$, $\pi/2$

If $\sin 2\theta < 0$, then this equation has no solution points. Thus, you restrict the values of θ to those for which $\sin 2\theta \geq 0$.

$$0 \leq \theta \leq \frac{\pi}{2} \quad \text{or} \quad \pi \leq \theta \leq \frac{3\pi}{2}$$

Moreover, using symmetry, you only need to consider the first of these two intervals. By finding a few additional points, we can obtain the graph shown in Figure 11.55.

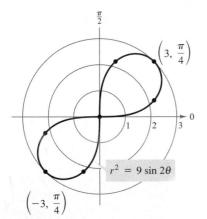

FIGURE 11.55

θ	0	$\pi/12$	$\pi/4$	$5\pi/12$	$\pi/2$
$r = \pm 3\sqrt{\sin 2\theta}$	0	$\pm 3/\sqrt{2}$	± 3	$\pm 3/\sqrt{2}$	0

DISCUSSION
PROBLEM
Computer
Software

If you have access to a graphing utility that will sketch graphs of polar equations, try using it to sketch several of the graphs in this section. One such software package is called *Computer Activities for Precalculus* and is available from D.C. Heath and Company.

WARM UP

The following warm up exercises involve skills that were covered in earlier sections. You will use these skills in the exercise set for this section.

In Exercises 1–4, determine the amplitude and period of the function.

1. $y = 5 \sin 4x$

2. $y = 3 \cos 2\pi x$

3. $y = -5 \cos \dfrac{5\pi}{2} x$

4. $y = -\dfrac{1}{2} \sin \dfrac{x}{2}$

In Exercises 5–8, sketch the graph of the function through two periods.

5. $y = 2 \sin x$

6. $y = 3 \cos x$

7. $y = 4 \cos 2x$

8. $y = 2 \sin \pi x$

In Exercises 9 and 10, use the sum and difference identities to simplify the trigonometric expression.

9. $\sin\left(x - \dfrac{\pi}{6}\right)$

10. $\sin\left(x + \dfrac{\pi}{4}\right)$

EXERCISES for Section 11.7

In Exercises 1–6, test for symmetry with respect to $\theta = \pi/2$, the polar axis, and the pole.

1. $r = 10 + 6 \cos \theta$

2. $r = 16 \cos 3\theta$

3. $r = \dfrac{2}{1 + \sin \theta}$

4. $r = 6 \sin \theta$

5. $r = 4 \sec \theta \csc \theta$

6. $r^2 = 25 \sin 2\theta$

In Exercises 7–10, find the maximum value of $|r|$ and any zeros of r.

7. $r = 5 \cos 3\theta$

8. $r = 3 \sin 2\theta$

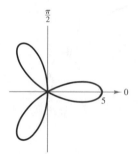
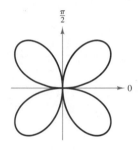

9. $r = 10(1 - \sin \theta)$

10. $r = 6 + 12 \cos \theta$

In Exercises 11–30, sketch the graph of the polar equation.

11. $r = 5$ circle $r=5$

12. $r = 2$ circle

13. $\theta = \dfrac{\pi}{6}$ line

14. $\theta = -\dfrac{\pi}{4}$ line

15. $r = 3 \sin \theta$ circle center with of 1.5

16. $r = 3(1 - \cos \theta)$

17. $r = 4(1 + \sin \theta)$

18. $r = 3 - 2 \cos \theta$ limp cnacon

19. $r = 4 + 3 \cos \theta$

20. $r = 2 + 4 \sin \theta$

21. $r = 3 - 4 \cos \theta$

22. $r = 2 \cos 3\theta$

23. $r = 3 \sin 2\theta$

24. $r = 2 \sec \theta$

25. $r = \dfrac{3}{\sin \theta - 2 \cos \theta}$

26. $r = \dfrac{6}{2 \sin \theta - 3 \cos \theta}$

27. $r^2 = 4 \cos 2\theta$

28. $r^2 = 4 \sin 2\theta$

29. $r = \dfrac{\theta}{2}$

30. $r = \theta$

In Exercises 31 and 32, convert the polar equation to rectangular form and show that the indicated line is an asymptote to the graph.

Polar Equation	Asymptote
31. $r = 2 - \sec \theta$	$x = -1$
32. $r = 2 + \csc \theta$	$y = 1$

33. The graph of $r = f(\theta)$ is rotated about the pole through an angle ϕ. Show that the equation for the rotated graph is $r = f(\theta - \phi)$.

34. Consider the graph of $r = f(\sin \theta)$.
   (a) Show that if the graph is rotated counterclockwise $\pi/2$ radians about the pole, then the equation for the rotated graph is $r = f(-\cos \theta)$.
   (b) Show that if the graph is rotated counterclockwise π radians about the pole, then the equation for the rotated graph is $r = f(-\sin \theta)$.
   (c) Show that if the graph is rotated counterclockwise $3\pi/2$ radians about the pole, then the equation for the rotated graph is $r = f(\cos \theta)$.

In Exercises 35–38, use the results of Exercises 33 and 34.

35. Write an equation for the limaçon $r = 2 - \sin \theta$ after it has been rotated by the given amount.
   (a) $\pi/4$ (b) $\pi/2$ (c) π (d) $3\pi/2$

36. Write an equation for the limaçon $r = 2 \sin 2\theta$ after it has been rotated by the given amount.
   (a) $\pi/6$ (b) $\pi/2$ (c) $2\pi/3$ (d) π

37. Sketch the graph of the equations.
   (a) $r = 1 - \sin \theta$ (b) $r = 1 - \sin\left(\theta - \dfrac{\pi}{4}\right)$

38. Sketch the graph of the equations.
   (a) $r = 3 \sec \theta$ (b) $r = 3 \sec\left(\theta - \dfrac{\pi}{4}\right)$
   (c) $r = 3 \sec\left(\theta + \dfrac{\pi}{3}\right)$ (d) $r = 3 \sec\left(\theta - \dfrac{\pi}{2}\right)$

15–22
29. rotation

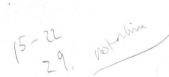

11.8 Polar Equations of Conics

Alternative Definition of Conics / Polar Equations of Conics / Applications

Alternative Definition of Conics

In Sections 11.3 and 11.4, we saw that the rectangular equations of ellipses and hyperbolas take simple forms when the origin lies at their *center*. As it happens, there are many important applications of conics in which it is more convenient to use one of the *foci* as the origin for the coordinate system. For example, the sun lies at the focus of the earth's orbit. Similarly, the light source of a parabolic reflector lies at its focus. In this section we will see that polar equations of conics take simple forms if one of the foci lies at the pole.

We begin with an alternative definition of a conic using the concept of eccentricity.

ALTERNATIVE DEFINITION OF CONIC

The locus of a point in the plane that moves so that its distance from a fixed point (focus) is in constant ratio to its distance from a fixed line (directrix) is a **conic.** The constant ratio is the **eccentricity** of the conic and is denoted by e. Moreover, the conic is an **ellipse** if $e < 1$, a **parabola** if $e = 1$, and a **hyperbola** if $e > 1$.

In Figure 11.56, note that for each type of conic, the pole corresponds to the fixed point (focus) given in the definition.

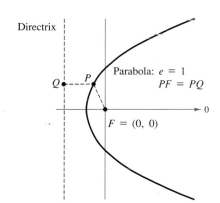

Parabola: $e = 1$
$PF = PQ$

$F = (0, 0)$

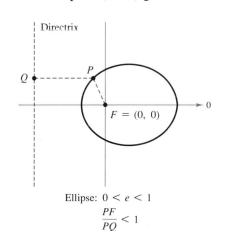

Ellipse: $0 < e < 1$
$$\frac{PF}{PQ} < 1$$

$F = (0, 0)$

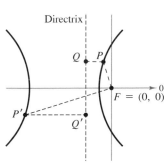

Hyperbola: $e > 1$
$$\frac{PF}{PQ} = \frac{P'F}{P'Q'} > 1$$

$F = (0, 0)$

FIGURE 11.56

Sketching a Plane Curve

When sketching a curve represented by a pair of parametric equations, we still plot points in the xy-plane. Each set of coordinates (x, y) is determined from a value chosen for the parameter t. By plotting the resulting points in the order of *increasing* values of t, we trace the curve in a specific direction. This is called the **orientation** of the curve.

EXAMPLE 1   Sketching a Curve

Sketch the curve described by the parametric equations

$$x = t^2 - 4 \quad \text{and} \quad y = \frac{t}{2}, \qquad -2 \le t \le 3.$$

Solution

Using values of t on the given interval, the parametric equations yield the points (x, y) shown in the table.

t	-2	-1	0	1	2	3
x	0	-3	-4	-3	0	5
y	-1	$-1/2$	0	$1/2$	1	$3/2$

By plotting these points in the order of increasing t, you obtain the curve C shown in Figure 11.63. Note that the arrows on the curve indicate its orientation as t increases from -2 to 3.

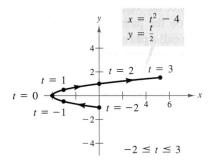

FIGURE 11.63

Note that the graph shown in Figure 11.63 does not define y as a function of x. This points out one benefit of parametric equations—they can be used to represent graphs that are more general than graphs of functions.

It often happens that two different sets of parametric equations have the same graph. For example, the set of parametric equations

$$x = 4t^2 - 4 \quad \text{and} \quad y = t, \qquad -1 \le t \le \frac{3}{2}$$

has the same graph as the set given in Example 1. However, by comparing the values of t in Figures 11.63 and 11.64, we see that this second graph is traced out more *rapidly* (considering t as time) than the first graph. Thus, in applications, different parametric representations can be used to represent various *speeds* at which objects travel along a given path.

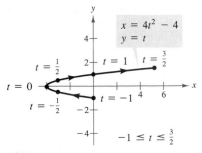

FIGURE 11.64

Eliminating the Parameter

In Example 1, we used simple point-plotting to sketch the given curve. This tedious process can sometimes be simplified by finding a rectangular equation (in x and y) that has the same graph. We call this process **eliminating the parameter.**

Parametric equations	$\rightarrow$	Solve for t in one equation	$\rightarrow$	Substitute into second equation	$\rightarrow$	Rectangular equation

$$x = t^2 - 4 \qquad t = 2y \qquad x = (2y)^2 - 4 \qquad x = 4y^2 - 4$$
$$y = t/2$$

Now we recognize that the equation $x = 4y^2 - 4$ represents a parabola with a horizontal axis and vertex at $(-4, 0)$.

One word of caution is in order when converting equations from parametric to rectangular form: the range of x and y implied by the parametric equations may be altered by the change to rectangular form. In such instances, it is necessary to adjust the domain of the rectangular equation so that its graph matches the graph of the parametric equations. Such a situation is demonstrated in the next example.

EXAMPLE 2   Adjusting the Domain after Eliminating the Parameter

Sketch the curve represented by the equations

$$x = \frac{1}{\sqrt{t + 1}} \quad \text{and} \quad y = \frac{t}{t + 1}$$

by eliminating the parameter and adjusting the domain of the resulting rectangular equation.

Solution

Solving for t in the equation for x, we have

$$x = \frac{1}{\sqrt{t + 1}} \quad \rightarrow \quad x^2 = \frac{1}{t + 1}$$

which implies that $t = (1 - x^2)/x^2$. Now, substituting into the equation for y, you obtain

$$y = \frac{t}{t + 1} = \frac{(1 - x^2)/x^2}{[(1 - x^2)/x^2] + 1} = 1 - x^2.$$

The rectangular equation, $y = 1 - x^2$, is defined for all values of x, but from the parametric equation for x we see that the curve is defined only when $-1 < t$. This implies that you should restrict the domain of x to positive values, as shown in Figure 11.65.

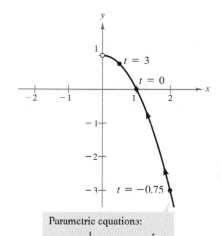

Parametric equations:

$$x = \frac{1}{\sqrt{t + 1}}, \quad y = \frac{t}{t + 1}$$

Rectangular equation:

$$y = 1 - x^2$$

FIGURE 11.65

It is not necessary for the parameter in a set of parametric equations to represent time. Our next example uses an *angle* as the parameter. In this example, we use *trigonometric identities* to eliminate the parameter.

EXAMPLE 3   Using a Trigonometric Identity to Eliminate a Parameter

Sketch the curve represented by

$$x = 3 \cos \theta \quad \text{and} \quad y = 4 \sin \theta, \qquad 0 \le \theta \le 2\pi$$

by eliminating the parameter and finding the corresponding rectangular equation.

Solution

We begin by solving for $\cos \theta$ and $\sin \theta$ in the given equations.

$$\cos \theta = \frac{x}{3} \quad \text{and} \quad \sin \theta = \frac{y}{4} \qquad \text{\textit{Solve for cos θ and sin θ}}$$

Make use of the identity $\sin^2 \theta + \cos^2 \theta = 1$ to form an equation involving only x and y.

$$\cos^2 \theta + \sin^2 \theta = 1 \qquad \text{\textit{Trigonometric identity}}$$

$$\cos^2 \theta + \sin^2 \theta = \left(\frac{x}{3}\right)^2 + \left(\frac{y}{4}\right)^2 = 1 \qquad \text{\textit{Substitute}}$$

$$\frac{x^2}{9} + \frac{y^2}{16} = 1 \qquad \text{\textit{Rectangular equation}}$$

From this rectangular equation, we see that the graph is an ellipse centered at (0, 0), with vertices at (0, 4) and (0, −4), and minor axis of length $2b = 6$, as shown in Figure 11.66. Note that the elliptic curve is traced out *counterclockwise* as θ varies from 0 to 2π.

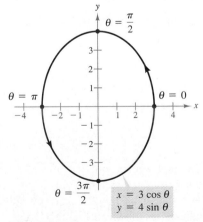

FIGURE 11.66

In Examples 2 and 3 it is important to realize that eliminating the parameter is primarily an *aid to curve-sketching*. If the parametric equations represent the path of a moving object, the graph alone is not sufficient to describe the object's motion. You still need the parametric equations to tell you the *position*, *direction*, and *speed* at a given time.

Finding Parametric Equations for a Graph

We have been looking at techniques for sketching the graph represented by a set of parametric equations. We now look at the reverse problem. How can we determine a set of parametric equations for a given graph or a given physical description? From the discussion following Example 1, we know that such a representation is not unique. This is further demonstrated in the following example in which we find two different parametric representations for a graph.

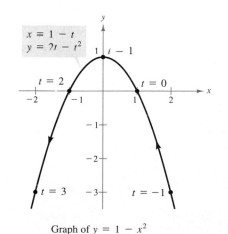

$x = 1 - t$
$y = 2t - t^2$

$t = 2$

$t = 0$

$t = 3$ $t = -1$

Graph of $y = 1 - x^2$

FIGURE 11.67

EXAMPLE 4   Finding Parametric Equations for a Given Graph

Find a set of parametric equations to represent the graph of $y = 1 - x^2$, using the following parameters.

a. $t = x$

b. $t = 1 - x$

Solution

a. Letting $t = x$, you obtain the parametric equations

$$x = t \quad \text{and} \quad y = 1 - x^2 = 1 - t^2.$$

b. Letting $t = 1 - x$, you obtain

$$x = 1 - t \quad \text{and} \quad y = 1 - (1 - t)^2 = 2t - t^2.$$

In Figure 11.67, note how the resulting curve is oriented by the increasing values of t. For part (a) the curve would have the opposite orientation.

EXAMPLE 5 Parametric Equations for a Cycloid

Determine the curve traced out by a point P on the circumference of a circle of radius a as the circle rolls along a straight line in a plane. Such a curve is called a **cycloid.**

Solution

As our parameter, let θ be the measure of the circle's rotation, and let the point $P = (x, y)$ begin at the origin. When $\theta = 0$, P is at the origin; when $\theta = \pi$, P is at a maximum point $(\pi a, 2a)$; and when $\theta = 2\pi$, P is back on the x-axis at $(2\pi a, 0)$. From Figure 11.68, you see that $\angle APC = 180° - \theta$. Hence, we have

$$\sin \theta = \sin(180° - \theta) = \sin(\angle APC) = \frac{AC}{a} = \frac{BD}{a}$$

$$\cos \theta = -\cos(180° - \theta) = -\cos(\angle APC) = \frac{AP}{-a}$$

which implies that $AP = -a \cos \theta$ and $BD = a \sin \theta$. Since the circle rolls along the x-axis, you know that $OD = \overset{\frown}{PD} = a\theta$. Furthermore, since $BA = DC = a$, we have

$$x = OD - BD = a\theta - a \sin \theta$$
$$y = BA + AP = a - a \cos \theta.$$

Therefore, the parametric equations are

$$x = a(\theta - \sin \theta) \quad \text{and} \quad y = a(1 - \cos \theta).$$

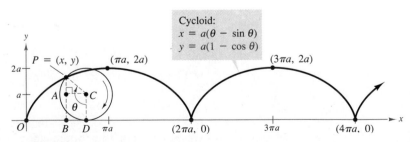

Cycloid:
$x = a(\theta - \sin \theta)$
$y = a(1 - \cos \theta)$

FIGURE 11.68

DISCUSSION

PROBLEM

Changing the Orientation of a Curve

The **orientation** of a curve refers to the direction in which the curve is traced as the values of the parameter increase. For instance, as t increases, the circle given by

$$x = \cos t \quad \text{and} \quad y = \sin t$$

is traced out *counterclockwise*. Find a parametric representation for which the circle is traced out *clockwise*.

WARM UP

The following warm-up exercises involve skills that were covered in earlier sections. You will use these skills in the exercise set for this section.

In Exercises 1–6, sketch the graph of the equation.

1. $y = -\frac{1}{4}x^2$

2. $y = 4 - \frac{1}{4}(x - 2)^2$

3. $16x^2 + y^2 = 16$

4. $-16x^2 + y^2 = 16$

5. $x + y = 4$

6. $x^2 + y^2 = 16$

In Exercises 7–10, simplify the expression.

7. $10 \sin^2 \theta + 10 \cos^2 \theta$

8. $5 \sec^2 \theta - 5$

9. $\sec^4 x - \tan^4 x$

10. $\dfrac{\sin 2\theta}{4 \cos \theta}$

EXERCISES for Section 11.9

In Exercises 1–20, sketch the curve represented by the parametric equations (indicate the direction of the curve), and write the corresponding rectangular equation by eliminating the parameter.

1. $x = t$
  $y = -2t$

2. $x = t$
  $y = \frac{1}{2}t$

3. $x = 3t - 1$
  $y = 2t + 1$

4. $x = 3 - 2t$
  $y = 2 + 3t$

5. $x = \frac{1}{4}t$
  $y = t^2$

6. $x = t$
  $y = t^3$

7. $x = t + 1$
  $y = t^2$

8. $x = \sqrt{t}$
  $y = 1 - t$

9. $x = t^3$
  $y = t/2$

10. $x = t - 1$
  $y = \dfrac{t}{t - 1}$

11. $x = 3 \cos \theta$
  $y = 3 \sin \theta$

12. $x = 4 \sin 2\theta$
  $y = 2 \cos 2\theta$

13. $x = \cos \theta$
  $y = 2 \sin^2 \theta$

14. $x = \sec \theta$
  $y = \cos \theta$

15. $x = 4 + 2 \cos \theta$
  $y = -1 + 4 \sin \theta$

16. $x = 4 \sec \theta$
  $y = 3 \tan \theta$

17. $x = e^{-t}$
  $y = e^{3t}$

18. $x = e^{2t}$
  $y = e^t$

19. $x = t^3$
  $y = 3 \ln t$

20. $x = \ln t$
  $y = t^2$

Appendix A
Graphing Utilities

Introduction

In Section 3.2, you studied the point-plotting method for sketching the graph of an equation. One of the disadvantages of the point-plotting method is that in order to get a good idea about the shape of a graph, you need to plot *many* points. With only a few points, you could badly misrepresent the graph. For instance, consider the equation

$$y = \frac{1}{30}x(39 - 10x^2 + x^4).$$

Suppose you plotted only five points: $(-3, -3)$, $(-1, -1)$, $(0, 0)$, $(1, 1)$, and $(3, 3)$, as shown in Figure A.1. From these five points, you might assume that the graph of the equation is a straight line. That, however, is not correct. By plotting several more points you can see that the actual graph is not straight at all! (See Figure A.2.)

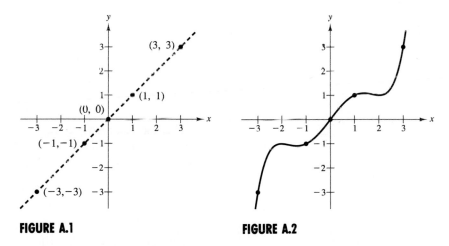

FIGURE A.1   **FIGURE A.2**

Thus, the point-plotting method leaves us with a dilemma. On the one hand, the method can be very inaccurate if only a few points are plotted. But, on the other hand, it is very time consuming to plot a dozen (or more) points. Technology can help us solve this dilemma. Plotting several (even several hundred) points in a rectangular coordinate system is something that a graphing utility can do easily.

The point-plotting method is the method used by *all* graphing packages for computers and *all* graphing calculators. Each computer or calculator screen is made up of a grid of hundreds or thousands of small areas called **pixels.** Screens that have many pixels per inch are said to have a higher **resolution** than screens that don't have as many. For instance, the screen shown in Figure A.3(a) has a higher resolution than the screen shown in Figure A.3(b). Note that the "graph" of the line on the first screen looks more like a line than the "graph" on the second screen.

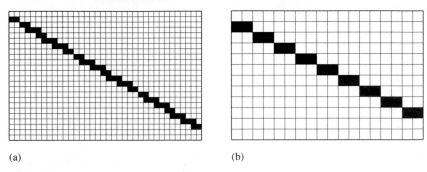

(a)   (b)

FIGURE A.3

Screens on most graphing calculators have 48 pixels per inch. Screens on computer monitors typically have between 32 and 100 pixels per inch.

EXAMPLE 1 Using Pixels to Sketch a Graph

Use the grid shown in Figure A.4 to sketch a graph of $y = \frac{1}{2}x^2$. Each pixel on the grid must be either on (shaded black) or off (unshaded).

Solution

To shade the grid, we use the following rule. If a pixel contains a plotted point of the graph, then it will be "on"; otherwise, the pixel will be "off." Using this rule, the graph of the curve looks like that shown in Figure A.5.

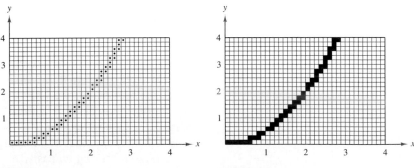

FIGURE A.4   **FIGURE A.5**

Basic Graphing

There are many different types of graphing utilities—graphing calculators and software packages for computers. The procedures used to draw a graph are similar with most of these utilities.

Basic Graphing Steps for a Graphing Utility

To draw the graph of an equation involving x and y with a graphing utility, use the following steps.

1. Rewrite the equation so that y is isolated on the left side of the equation.
2. Set the boundaries of the viewing rectangle by entering the minimum and maximum x-values and the minimum and maximum y-values.
3. Enter the equation in the form $y =$ (expression involving x). Read the user's guide that accompanies your graphing utility to see how the equation should be entered.
4. Activate the graphing utility.

EXAMPLE 2   Sketching the Graph of an Equation

Sketch the graph of $2y + x^3 = 4x$.

Solution

To begin, solve the given equation for y in terms of x.

$$2y + x^3 = 4x \qquad \text{\textit{Given equation}}$$

$$2y = -x^3 + 4x \qquad \text{\textit{Subtract } } x^3 \text{ \textit{from both sides}}$$

$$y = -\frac{1}{2}x^3 + 2x \qquad \text{\textit{Divide both sides by 2}}$$

Set the viewing rectangle so that $-10 \le x \le 10$ and $-10 \le y \le 10$. (On some graphing utilities, this is the default setting.) Next, enter the equation into the graphing utility.

$$Y = -X \wedge 3/2 + 2 * X$$

Finally, activate the graphing utility. The display screen should look like that shown in Figure A.6.

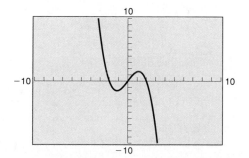

FIGURE A.6

In Figure A.6, notice that the calculator screen does not label the tick marks on the x-axis or the y-axis. To see what the tick marks represent, check the values in the utility's "range."

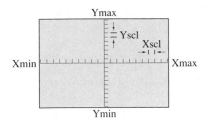

FIGURE A.7

Range

Xmin=−10   *The minimum x-value is −10.*
Xmax=10   *The maximum x-value is 10.*
Xscl=1   *The x-scale is 1 unit per tick mark.*
Ymin=−10   *The minimum y-value is −10.*
Ymax=10   *The maximum y-value is 10.*
Yscl=1   *The y-scale is 1 unit per tick mark.*
Xres=1   *The x-resolution is 1 plotted point per 1 pixel.*

These settings are summarized visually in Figure A.7.

EXAMPLE 3   Graphing an Equation Involving Absolute Value

Sketch the graph of $y = |x - 3|$.

Solution

This equation is already written so that y is isolated on the left side of the equation, so you can enter the equation as follows.

$$Y = \text{abs}(X - 3)$$

After activating the graphing utility, its screen should look like the one shown in Figure A.8.

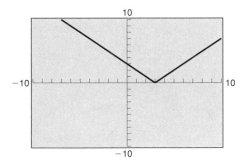

FIGURE A.8

Special Features

In order to be able to use your graphing calculator to its best advantage, you must be able to determine a proper viewing rectangle and use the zoom feature. The next two examples show how this is done.

EXAMPLE 4   Determining a Viewing Rectangle

Sketch the graph of $y = x^2 + 12$.

Solution

Begin as usual by entering the equation.

$$Y = x \wedge 2 + 12$$

Activate the graphing utility. If you used a viewing rectangle in which $-10 \le x \le 10$ and $-10 \le y \le 10$, then no part of the graph will appear on the screen, as shown in Figure A.9(a). The reason for this is that the lowest point on the graph of $y = x^2 + 12$ occurs at the point (0, 12). With the viewing rectangle in Figure A.9(a), the largest y-value is 10. In other words, none of the graph is visible on a screen whose y-values range between -10 and 10.

To be able to see the graph, change Ymax=10 to Ymax=30, Yscl=1 to Yscl=5. Now activate the graphing utility and you will obtain the graph shown in Figure A.9(b). On this graph, note that each tick mark on the y-axis represents 5 units because you changed the y-scale to 5. Also note that the highest point on the y-axis is now 30 because you changed the maximum value of y to 30.

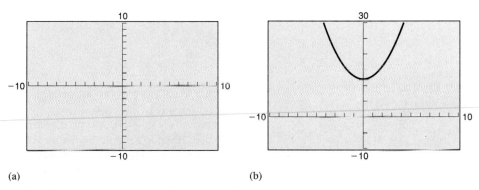

(a)   (b)

FIGURE A.9

EXAMPLE 5   Using the Zoom Feature

Sketch the graph of $y = x^3 - x^2 - x$. How many x-intercepts does this graph have?

Solution

Begin by drawing the graph on a "standard" viewing rectangle as shown in Figure A.10(a). From the display screen, it is clear that the graph has at least one intercept (just to the left of $x = 2$), but it is difficult to determine whether the graph has other intercepts. To obtain a better view of the graph near $x = -1$, you can use the zoom feature of the graphing utility. The redrawn screen is shown in Figure A.10(b). From this screen you can tell that the graph has three x-intercepts whose x-coordinates are approximately -0.6, 0, and 1.6.

FIGURE A.10

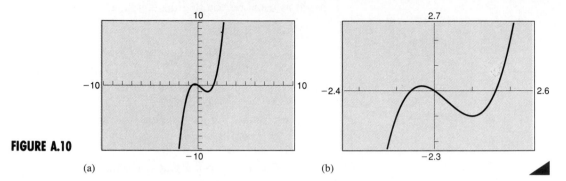

(a)   (b)

EXAMPLE 6   Sketching More Than One Graph on the Same Screen

Sketch the graphs of $y = -\sqrt{36 - x^2}$ and $y = \sqrt{36 - x^2}$ on the same screen.

Solution

To begin, enter both equations in the graphing utility.

$$Y = \sqrt{36 - X \wedge 2)}$$
$$Y = -\sqrt{(36 - X \wedge 2)}$$

Then, activate the graphing utility to obtain the graph shown in Figure A.11(a). Notice that the graph should be the upper and lower parts of the circle given by $x^2 + y^2 = 6^2$. The reason it doesn't look like a circle is that, with the standard settings, the tick marks on the x-axis are farther apart than the tick marks on the y-axis. To correct this, change the viewing rectangle so that $-15 \le x \le 15$. The redrawn screen is shown in Figure A.11(b). Notice that in this screen the graph appears to be more circular.

FIGURE A.11

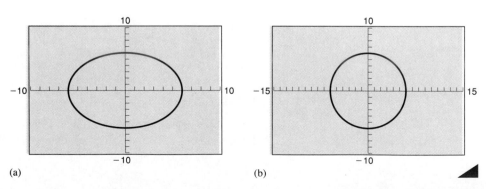

(a)   (b)

DISCUSSION

PROBLEM

A
Misleading
Graph

Sketch the graph of $y = x^2 - 12x$, using $-10 \le x \le 10$ and $-10 \le y \le 10$. The graph appears to be a straight line, as shown in Figure A.12. However, this is misleading because the screen doesn't show an important portion of the graph. Can you find a range setting that reveals a better view of this graph?

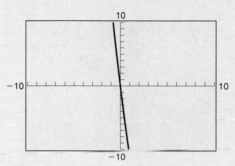

FIGURE A.12

WARM UP

In Exercises 1–10, solve for y in terms of x.

1. $3x + y = 4$

2. $x - y = 0$

3. $2x + 3y = 2$

4. $4x - 5y = -2$

5. $3x + 4y - 5 = 0$

6. $-2x - 3y + 6 = 0$

7. $x^2 + y - 4 = 0$

8. $-2x^2 + 3y + 2 = 0$

9. $x^2 + y^2 = 4$

10. $x^2 - y^2 = 9$

EXERCISES for Appendix A

In Exercises 1–20, use a graphing utility to sketch the graph of the equation. Use a setting on each graph of $-10 \le x \le 10$ and $-10 \le y \le 10$.

```
RANGE
Xmin=-10
Xmax=10
Xscl=1
Ymin=-10
Ymax=10
Yscl=1
Xres=1
```

1. $y = x - 5$

2. $y = -x + 4$

3. $y = -\frac{1}{2}x + 3$

4. $y = \frac{2}{3}x + 1$

5. $2x - 3y = 4$

6. $x + 2y = 3$

7. $y = \frac{1}{2}x^2 - 1$

8. $y = -x^2 + 6$

9. $y = x^2 - 4x - 5$

10. $y = x^2 - 3x + 2$

11. $y = -x^2 + 2x + 1$

12. $y = -x^2 + 4x - 1$

13. $2y = x^2 + 2x - 3$

14. $3y = -x^2 - 4x + 5$

15. $y = |x + 5|$

16. $y = \frac{1}{2}|x - 6|$

17. $y = \sqrt{x^2 + 1}$

18. $y = 2\sqrt{x^2 + 2} - 4$

19. $y = \frac{1}{5}(-x^3 + 16x)$

20. $y = \frac{1}{8}(x^3 + 8x^2)$

In Exercises 21–30, use a graphing utility to match the equation with its graph. [The graphs are labeled (a), (b), (c), (d), (e), (f), (g), (h), (i), and (j).]

21. $y = x$

22. $y = -x$

23. $y = x^2$

24. $y = -x^2$

25. $y = x^3$ **26.** $y = -x^3$

27. $y = |x|$ **28.** $y = -|x|$

29. $y = \sqrt{x}$ **30.** $y = -\sqrt{x}$

In Exercises 31–34, use a graphing utility to sketch the graph of the equation. Use the indicated setting.

31. $y = -2x^2 + 12x + 14$ **32.** $y = -x^2 + 5x + 6$

RANGE
Xmin=−5
Xmax=10
Xscl=1
Ymin=−5
Ymax=35
Yscl=5
Xres=1

RANGE
Xmin=−8
Xmax=4
Xscl=1
Ymin=−5
Ymax=15
Yscl=5
Xres=1

33. $y = x^3 + 6x^2$ **34.** $y = -x^3 + 16x$

RANGE
Xmin=−10
Xmax=5
Xscl=1
Ymin=−4
Ymax=36
Yscl=3
Xres=1

RANGE
Xmin=−6
Xmax=6
Xscl=1
Ymin=−25
Ymax=25
Yscl=5
Xres=1

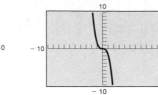

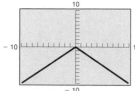
(a)

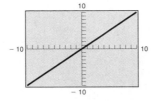
(b)

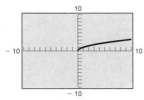
(c)

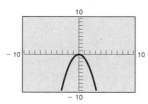
(d)

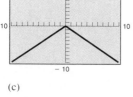
(e)

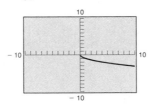
(f)

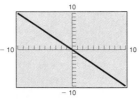
(g)

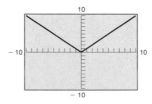
(h)

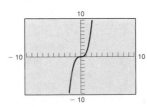
(i)

(j)

In Exercises 35–38, find a setting on a graphing utility so that the graph of the equation agrees with the graph shown.

35. $y = -x^2 - 4x + 20$ **36.** $y = x^2 + 12x - 8$

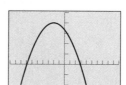

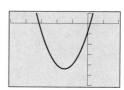

37. $y = -x^3 + x^2 + 2x$ **38.** $y = x^3 + 3x^2 - 2x$

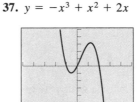

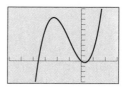

In Exercises 39–42, use a graphing utility to find the number of x-intercepts of the equation.

39. $y = \frac{1}{8}(4x^2 - 32x + 65)$

40. $y = \frac{1}{4}(-4x^2 + 16x - 15)$

41. $y = 4x^3 - 20x^2 - 4x + 61$

42. $y = \frac{1}{4}(2x^3 + 6x^2 - 4x + 1)$

In Exercises 43–46, use a graphing utility to sketch the graphs of the equations on the same screen. Using a "square setting," what geometrical shape is bounded by the graphs?

43. $y = |x| - 4$
    $y = -|x| + 4$

44. $y = x + |x| - 4$
    $y = x - |x| + 4$

45. $y = -\sqrt{25 - x^2}$
    $y = \sqrt{25 - x^2}$

46. $y = 6$
    $y = -\sqrt{3}x - 4$
    $y = \sqrt{3}x - 4$

Ever Been Married?   In Exercises 47–50, use the following models, which relate ages to the percentages of American males and females who have never been married.

$$y = \frac{0.36 - 0.0056x}{1 - 0.0817x + 0.00226x^2}, \quad \begin{array}{l} \text{Males} \\ 20 \le x \le 50 \end{array}$$

$$y = \frac{100}{8.944 - 0.886x + 0.249x^2}, \quad \begin{array}{l} \text{Females} \\ 20 \le x \le 50 \end{array}$$

In these models, y is the percent of the population (in decimal form) who have never been married and x is the age of the person. (*Source:* U.S. Bureau of the Census)

47. Use a graphing utility to sketch the graph of both equations giving the percentages of American males and females who have never been married. Use the following range settings.

```
RANGE
Xmin=20
Xmax=50
Xscl=5
Ymin=0
Ymax=1
Yscl=0.1
Xres=1
```

48. Write a short paragraph describing the relationship between the two graphs that were plotted in Exercise 47.

49. Suppose an American male is chosen at random from the population. If the person is 25 years old, what is the probability that he has never been married?

50. Suppose an American female is chosen at random from the population. If the person is 25 years old, what is the probability that she has never been married?

Earnings and Dividends   In Exercises 51–54, use the following model, which approximates the relationship between dividends per share and earnings per share for the Pall Corporation between 1982 and 1989.

$$y = -0.166 + 0.502x - 0.0953x^2, \quad 0.25 \le x \le 2$$

In this model, y is the dividends per share (in dollars) and x is the earnings per share (in dollars). (*Source:* Standard ASE Stock Reports)

51. Use a graphing utility to sketch the graph of the model that gives the dividend per share in terms of the earnings per share. Use the following range settings.

```
RANGE
Xmin=0
Xmax=2
Xscl=0.25
Ymin=0
Ymax=0.5
Yscl=0.1
Xres=1
```

52. According to the given model, what size dividend would the Pall Corporation pay if the earnings per share were $1.30?

53. Use a trace feature on your graphing utility to estimate the earnings per share that would produce a dividend per share of $0.25. The choices are labeled (a), (b), (c), and (d). (Find the y-value that is as close to 0.25 as possible. The x-value that is displayed will then be the approximate earnings per share that would produce a dividend per share of $0.25.)

   (a) $1.00   (b) $1.03   (c) $1.06   (d) $1.09

54. The *payout ratio* for a stock is the ratio of the dividend per share to earnings per share. Use the model to find the payout ratio for an earnings per share of (a) $0.75, (b) $1.00, and (c) $1.25.

Appendix B

Using Logarithmic Tables

Although it is more efficient to use calculators than tables in computations with logarithmic functions, it is instructive to see how to work with tables. Using base 10, note first that every positive real number can be written as a product $c \times 10^k$, where $1 \leq c < 10$ and k is an integer. For example, $1989 = 1.989 \times 10^3$, $5.37 = 5.37 \times 10^0$, and $0.0439 = 4.39 \times 10^{-2}$. Suppose you apply the properties of logarithms to the number 1989.

$$1989 = 1.989 \times 10^3$$

$$
\begin{aligned}
\log_{10} 1989 &= \log_{10}(1.989 \times 10^3) \\
&= \log_{10}(1.989) + \log_{10}(10^3) \\
&= \log_{10}(1.989) + 3 \log_{10}(10) \\
&= \log_{10}(1.989) + 3
\end{aligned}
$$

In general, for any positive real number x (expressible as $x = c \times 10^k$), its common logarithm has the **standard form**

$$\log_{10} x = \log_{10} c + \log_{10}(10^k) = \log_{10} c + k$$

where $1 \leq c < 10$. We call $\log_{10} c$ the **mantissa** and k the **characteristic** of $\log_{10} x$. Since the function $f(x) = \log_{10} x$ increases as x increases, and since $1 \leq c < 10$, it follows that

$$\log_{10} 1 \leq \log_{10} c < \log_{10} 10$$
$$0 \leq \log_{10} c < 1$$

which means that the *mantissa* of $\log_{10} x$ lies between 0 and 1.

The common logarithm table in Appendix E gives four-decimal-place approximations of the *mantissa* for the logarithm of every three-digit number between 1.00 and 9.99. The next example shows how to use the table in Appendix E to approximate common logarithms.

EXAMPLE 1   Approximating Common Logarithms with Tables

Use the tables in Appendix E to approximate the following.

a. $\log_{10} 85.6$ **b.** $\log_{10} 0.000329$

Solution

a. Since $85.6 = 8.56 \times 10^1$, the characteristic is 1. Using the common logarithm table, you can see that the mantissa is $\log_{10} 8.56 \approx 0.9325$. Therefore,

$$\log_{10} 85.6 = (\text{mantissa}) + (\text{characteristic})$$
$$= \log_{10} 8.56 + 1$$
$$\approx 0.9325 + 1$$
$$= 1.9325.$$

b. Since $0.000329 = 3.29 \times 10^{-4}$, the characteristic is -4. From the common logarithm table for the mantissa 3.29, you obtain

$$\log_{10} 0.000329 = \log_{10} 3.29 + (-4)$$
$$\approx 0.3598 - 4$$
$$= -3.6402.$$

The next example shows how to combine the use of properties of logarithms with tables to evaluate logarithms.

EXAMPLE 2   Combining Properties of Logarithms with Tables

Use the tables in Appendix E to approximate $\log_{10} \sqrt[3]{38.6}$.

Solution

$$\log_{10} \sqrt[3]{38.6} = \frac{1}{3} \log_{10} 38.6$$
$$= \frac{1}{3}(\log_{10} 3.86 + 1)$$
$$\approx \frac{1}{3}(0.5866 + 1)$$
$$\approx 0.5289$$

The table for common logarithms can be used in the *reverse* manner to find the number (called an **antilogarithm**) that has a given logarithm. We demonstrate this procedure in Example 3.

EXAMPLE 3   Finding the Antilogarithm of a Number

Use the tables in Appendix E to approximate the value of x in each of the following.

a. $\log_{10} x = 2.6571$ **b.** $x = 10^{-3.6364}$

Solution

a. You know that $\log_{10} x = 2.6571 = 0.6571 + 2$. Thus, the mantissa is 0.6571 and the characteristic is 2. From the table, you find that the mantissa 0.6571 corresponds approximately to $\log_{10} 4.54$. Since the characteristic is 2, it follows that x is given by

$$x \approx 4.54 \times 10^2 = 454.$$

b. In logarithmic form, this exponential equation can be written as $\log_{10} x = -3.6364$. To obtain the standard form, add and subtract 4 to obtain

$$\log_{10} x = (4 - 3.6364) - 4 = 0.3636 - 4.$$

Thus, the mantissa is 0.3636 and the characteristic is -4. From the table, you find that

$$x \approx 2.31 \times 10^{-4} - 0.000231.$$ ◢

For numbers with more than three nonzero digits, you can still use the common logarithm tables by applying a procedure called **linear interpolation.** This procedure is based on the fact that changes in $\log_{10} x$ are approximately proportional to the corresponding changes in x. We demonstrate the procedure in Example 4.

EXAMPLE 4   Linear Interpolation

Use linear interpolation and the tables in Appendix E to approximate the value of $\log_{10} 5.382$.

Solution

The three-digit x-values in the table that are closest to 5.382 are $x = 5.38$ and $x = 5.39$. Use the logarithms of these two values in the following arrangement.

$$0.01 \left\{ 0.002 \left\{ \begin{array}{l} \log_{10} 5.38 \approx 0.7308 \\ \log_{10} 5.382 \approx \ ? \\ \log_{10} 5.39 \approx 0.7316 \end{array} \right\} d \right\} 0.0008$$

Note that the differences between the x-values are beside the left braces and the differences between the corresponding logarithms are beside the right braces. From this arrangement, you can write the following proportion.

$$\frac{d}{0.0008} = \frac{0.002}{0.01}$$

$$d = (0.0008)\left(\frac{0.002}{0.01}\right) = 0.00016 \approx 0.0002$$

Therefore,

$$\log_{10} 5.382 \approx \log_{10} 5.38 + d \approx 0.7308 + 0.002 = 0.7310.$$ ◢

The next example shows how to perform numerical computations with logarithms.

EXAMPLE 5   Using Logarithms to Perform Numerical Computations

Use the tables in Appendix E to approximate the value of

$$x = \frac{(1.9)^3}{\sqrt{82.7}}.$$

Solution

Using the properties of logarithms, you can write

$$\log_{10} x = 3 \log_{10} 1.9 - \frac{1}{2} \log_{10} 82.7$$

$$\approx 3(0.2788) - \frac{1}{2}(1.9175) \approx -0.12235.$$

By adding and subtracting 1, you obtain the standard form

$$\log_{10} x \approx (1 - 0.12235) - 1 = 0.87765 - 1.$$

Finally, since the antilogarithm of 0.87765 is approximately 7.54, we find that

$$x \approx 7.54 \times 10^{-1} = 0.754.$$

EXERCISES for Appendix B

In Exercises 1–4, approximate the common logarithm of the given number by using the table in Appendix E.

1. (a) 417 (b) 0.0417
2. (a) 985 (b) 9.85
3. (a) 6300 (b) 1000
4. (a) 0.0001 (b) 41.3

In Exercises 5–8, approximate the common logarithm of the given quantity by using the table in Appendix E.

5. (a) $\dfrac{5.30}{21.5}$ (b) $(30500)(0.258)$
6. (a) $\sqrt[3]{5.33}$ (b) $(1.02)^{36}$
7. (a) $\sqrt[5]{7200}$ (b) $(3.4)^8$
8. (a) $\dfrac{(3.6)^6}{500}$ (b) $(0.245)^4(8.7)^3$

In Exercises 9–12, find N (antilogarithm) by using the table in Appendix E.

9. (a) $N = 10^{4.3979}$ (b) $N = 10^{-1.6021}$
10. (a) $\log_{10} N = 3.6702$ (b) $\log_{10} N = -2.3298$
11. (a) $\log_{10} N = 6.1335$ (b) $\log_{10} N = 8.1335 - 10$
12. (a) $\log_{10} N = 4.8420$ (b) $\log_{10} N = 7.8420 - 10$

In Exercises 13 and 14, use linear interpolation to approximate the common logarithm of the given number by using the table in Appendix E.

13. (a) 4385 (b) 0.6058
14. (a) 125.2 (b) 0.08675

In Exercises 15 and 16, use linear interpolation to approximate the antilogarithm N by using the table in Appendix E.

15. (a) $\log_{10} N = 5.6175$ (b) $\log_{10} N = -2.1503$

16. (a) $N = 10^{0.5743}$ (b) $N = 10^{9.9317}$

In Exercises 17–22, approximate the given quantity by using common logarithms.

17. $\dfrac{(86.4)(8.09)}{38.6}$

18. $\dfrac{1243}{(42.8)(67.9)}$

19. $\sqrt[3]{86.5}$

20. $\sqrt[4]{(4.705)(18.86)}$

21. $500(1.03)^{20}$

22. $(0.2313)^6$

In Exercises 23 and 24, approximate the natural logarithm of the given number by using the table in Appendix D.

23. (a) 6.24   (b) 9.55

24. (a) 2.605   (b) 3.005

In Exercises 25 and 26, approximate the antilogarithm N by using the table in Appendix D.

25. (a) $\ln N = 2.0096$ (b) $\ln N = 1.4422$

26. (a) $\ln N = 1.1233$ (b) $\ln N = 0.2271$

In Exercises 27 and 28, approximate the exponential by using the table in Appendix C.

27. (a) $e^{3.5}$ (b) $e^{-3.5}$

28. (a) $e^{6.2}$ (b) $e^{-6.2}$

Appendix C

Exponential Tables

x	e^x	e^{-x}	x	e^x	e^{-x}	x	e^x	e^{-x}
0.0	1.0000	1.0000	3.5	33.115	0.0302	7.0	1096.63	0.0009
0.1	1.1052	0.9048	3.6	36.598	0.0273	7.1	1211.97	0.0008
0.2	1.2214	0.8187	3.7	40.447	0.0247	7.2	1339.43	0.0007
0.3	1.3499	0.7408	3.8	44.701	0.0224	7.3	1480.30	0.0007
0.4	1.4918	0.6703	3.9	49.402	0.0202	7.4	1635.98	0.0006
0.5	1.6487	0.6065	4.0	54.598	0.0183	7.5	1808.04	0.0006
0.6	1.8221	0.5488	4.1	60.340	0.0166	7.6	1998.20	0.0005
0.7	2.0138	0.4966	4.2	66.686	0.0150	7.7	2208.35	0.0005
0.8	2.2255	0.4493	4.3	73.700	0.0136	7.8	2440.60	0.0004
0.9	2.4596	0.4066	4.4	81.451	0.0123	7.9	2697.28	0.0004
1.0	2.7183	0.3679	4.5	90.017	0.0111	8.0	2980.96	0.0003
1.1	3.0042	0.3329	4.6	99.484	0.0101	8.1	3294.47	0.0003
1.2	3.3201	0.3012	4.7	109.95	0.0091	8.2	3640.95	0.0003
1.3	3.6693	0.2725	4.8	121.51	0.0082	8.3	4023.87	0.0002
1.4	4.0552	0.2466	4.9	134.29	0.0074	8.4	4447.07	0.0002
1.5	4.4817	0.2231	5.0	148.41	0.0067	8.5	4914.77	0.0002
1.6	4.9530	0.2019	5.1	164.02	0.0061	8.6	5431.66	0.0002
1.7	5.4739	0.1827	5.2	181.27	0.0055	8.7	6002.91	0.0002
1.8	6.0496	0.1653	5.3	200.34	0.0050	8.8	6634.24	0.0002
1.9	6.6859	0.1496	5.4	221.41	0.0045	8.9	7331.97	0.0001
2.0	7.3891	0.1353	5.5	244.69	0.0041	9.0	8103.08	0.0001
2.1	8.1662	0.1225	5.6	270.43	0.0037	9.1	8955.29	0.0001
2.2	9.0250	0.1108	5.7	298.87	0.0033	9.2	9897.13	0.0001
2.3	9.9742	0.1003	5.8	330.30	0.0030	9.3	10938.02	0.0001
2.4	11.023	0.0907	5.9	365.04	0.0027	9.4	12088.38	0.0001
2.5	12.182	0.0821	6.0	403.43	0.0025	9.5	13359.73	0.0001
2.6	13.464	0.0743	6.1	445.86	0.0022	9.6	14764.78	0.0001
2.7	14.880	0.0672	6.2	492.75	0.0020	9.7	16317.61	0.0001
2.8	16.445	0.0608	6.3	544.57	0.0018	9.8	18033.74	0.0001
2.9	18.174	0.0550	6.4	601.85	0.0017	9.9	19930.37	0.0001
3.0	20.086	0.0498	6.5	665.14	0.0015	10.0	22026.47	0.0000
3.1	22.198	0.0450	6.6	735.10	0.0014			
3.2	24.533	0.0408	6.7	812.41	0.0012			
3.3	27.113	0.0369	6.8	897.85	0.0011			
3.4	29.964	0.0334	6.9	992.27	0.0010			

Appendix D

Natural Logarithmic Tables

	0.00	0.01	0.02	0.03	0.04	0.05	0.06	0.07	0.08	0.09
1.0	0.0000	0.0100	0.0198	0.0296	0.0392	0.0488	0.0583	0.0677	0.0770	0.0862
1.1	0.0953	0.1044	0.1133	0.1222	0.1310	0.1398	0.1484	0.1570	0.1655	0.1740
1.2	0.1823	0.1906	0.1989	0.2070	0.2151	0.2231	0.2311	0.2390	0.2469	0.2546
1.3	0.2624	0.2700	0.2776	0.2852	0.2927	0.3001	0.3075	0.3148	0.3221	0.3293
1.4	0.3365	0.3436	0.3507	0.3577	0.3646	0.3716	0.3784	0.3853	0.3920	0.3988
1.5	0.4055	0.4121	0.4187	0.4253	0.4318	0.4383	0.4447	0.4511	0.4574	0.4637
1.6	0.4700	0.4762	0.4824	0.4886	0.4947	0.5008	0.5068	0.5128	0.5188	0.5247
1.7	0.5306	0.5365	0.5423	0.5481	0.5539	0.5596	0.5653	0.5710	0.5766	0.5822
1.8	0.5878	0.5933	0.5988	0.6043	0.6098	0.6152	0.6206	0.6259	0.6313	0.6366
1.9	0.6419	0.6471	0.6523	0.6575	0.6627	0.6678	0.6729	0.6780	0.6831	0.6881
2.0	0.6931	0.6981	0.7031	0.7080	0.7129	0.7178	0.7227	0.7275	0.7324	0.7372
2.1	0.7419	0.7467	0.7514	0.7561	0.7608	0.7655	0.7701	0.7747	0.7793	0.7839
2.2	0.7885	0.7930	0.7975	0.8020	0.8065	0.8109	0.8154	0.8198	0.8242	0.8286
2.3	0.8329	0.8372	0.8416	0.8459	0.8502	0.8544	0.8587	0.8629	0.8671	0.8713
2.4	0.8755	0.8796	0.8838	0.8879	0.8920	0.8961	0.9002	0.9042	0.9083	0.9123
2.5	0.9163	0.9203	0.9243	0.9282	0.9322	0.9361	0.9400	0.9439	0.9478	0.9517
2.6	0.9555	0.9594	0.9632	0.9670	0.9708	0.9746	0.9783	0.9821	0.9858	0.9895
2.7	0.9933	0.9969	1.0006	1.0043	1.0080	1.0116	1.0152	1.0188	1.0225	1.0260
2.8	1.0296	1.0332	1.0367	1.0403	1.0438	1.0473	1.0508	1.0543	1.0578	1.0613
2.9	1.0647	1.0682	1.0716	1.0750	1.0784	1.0818	1.0852	1.0886	1.0919	1.0953
3.0	1.0986	1.1019	1.1053	1.1086	1.1119	1.1151	1.1184	1.1217	1.1249	1.1282
3.1	1.1314	1.1346	1.1378	1.1410	1.1442	1.1474	1.1506	1.1537	1.1569	1.1600
3.2	1.1632	1.1663	1.1694	1.1725	1.1756	1.1787	1.1817	1.1848	1.1878	1.1909
3.3	1.1939	1.1969	1.2000	1.2030	1.2060	1.2090	1.2119	1.2149	1.2179	1.2208
3.4	1.2238	1.2267	1.2296	1.2326	1.2355	1.2384	1.2413	1.2442	1.2470	1.2499
3.5	1.2528	1.2556	1.2585	1.2613	1.2641	1.2669	1.2698	1.2726	1.2754	1.2782
3.6	1.2809	1.2837	1.2865	1.2892	1.2920	1.2947	1.2975	1.3002	1.3029	1.3056
3.7	1.3083	1.3110	1.3137	1.3164	1.3191	1.3218	1.3244	1.3271	1.3297	1.3324
3.8	1.3350	1.3376	1.3403	1.3429	1.3455	1.3481	1.3507	1.3533	1.3558	1.3584
3.9	1.3610	1.3635	1.3661	1.3686	1.3712	1.3737	1.3762	1.3788	1.3813	1.3838
4.0	1.3863	1.3888	1.3913	1.3938	1.3962	1.3987	1.4012	1.4036	1.4061	1.4085
4.1	1.4110	1.4134	1.4159	1.4183	1.4207	1.4231	1.4255	1.4279	1.4303	1.4327
4.2	1.4351	1.4375	1.4398	1.4422	1.4446	1.4469	1.4493	1.4516	1.4540	1.4563
4.3	1.4586	1.4609	1.4633	1.4656	1.4679	1.4702	1.4725	1.4748	1.4770	1.4793
4.4	1.4816	1.4839	1.4861	1.4884	1.4907	1.4929	1.4951	1.4974	1.4996	1.5019
4.5	1.5041	1.5063	1.5085	1.5107	1.5129	1.5151	1.5173	1.5195	1.5217	1.5239
4.6	1.5261	1.5282	1.5304	1.5326	1.5347	1.5369	1.5390	1.5412	1.5433	1.5454
4.7	1.5476	1.5497	1.5518	1.5539	1.5560	1.5581	1.5602	1.5623	1.5644	1.5665
4.8	1.5686	1.5707	1.5728	1.5748	1.5769	1.5790	1.5810	1.5831	1.5851	1.5872
4.9	1.5892	1.5913	1.5933	1.5953	1.5974	1.5994	1.6014	1.6034	1.6054	1.6074
5.0	1.6094	1.6114	1.6134	1.6154	1.6174	1.6194	1.6214	1.6233	1.6253	1.6273
5.1	1.6292	1.6312	1.6332	1.6351	1.6371	1.6390	1.6409	1.6429	1.6448	1.6467
5.2	1.6487	1.6506	1.6525	1.6544	1.6563	1.6582	1.6601	1.6620	1.6639	1.6658
5.3	1.6677	1.6696	1.6715	1.6734	1.6752	1.6771	1.6790	1.6808	1.6827	1.6845
5.4	1.6864	1.6882	1.6901	1.6919	1.6938	1.6956	1.6974	1.6993	1.7011	1.7029

Natural Logarithmic Tables (Continued)

	0.00	0.01	0.02	0.03	0.04	0.05	0.06	0.07	0.08	0.09
5.5	1.7047	1.7066	1.7084	1.7102	1.7120	1.7138	1.7156	1.7174	1.7192	1.7210
5.6	1.7228	1.7246	1.7263	1.7281	1.7299	1.7317	1.7334	1.7352	1.7370	1.7387
5.7	1.7405	1.7422	1.7440	1.7457	1.7475	1.7492	1.7509	1.7527	1.7544	1.7561
5.8	1.7579	1.7596	1.7613	1.7630	1.7647	1.7664	1.7681	1.7699	1.7716	1.7733
5.9	1.7750	1.7766	1.7783	1.7800	1.7817	1.7834	1.7851	1.7867	1.7884	1.7901
6.0	1.7918	1.7934	1.7951	1.7967	1.7984	1.8001	1.8017	1.8034	1.8050	1.8066
6.1	1.8083	1.8099	1.8116	1.8132	1.8148	1.8165	1.8181	1.8197	1.8213	1.8229
6.2	1.8245	1.8262	1.8278	1.8294	1.8310	1.8326	1.8342	1.8358	1.8374	1.8390
6.3	1.8405	1.8421	1.8437	1.8453	1.8469	1.8485	1.8500	1.8516	1.8532	1.8547
6.4	1.8563	1.8579	1.8594	1.8610	1.8625	1.8641	1.8656	1.8672	1.8687	1.8703
6.5	1.8718	1.8733	1.8749	1.8764	1.8779	1.8795	1.8810	1.8825	1.8840	1.8856
6.6	1.8871	1.8886	1.8901	1.8916	1.8931	1.8946	1.8961	1.8976	1.8991	1.9006
6.7	1.9021	1.9036	1.9051	1.9066	1.9081	1.9095	1.9110	1.9125	1.9140	1.9155
6.8	1.9169	1.9184	1.9199	1.9213	1.9228	1.9242	1.9257	1.9272	1.9286	1.9301
6.9	1.9315	1.9330	1.9344	1.9359	1.9373	1.9387	1.9402	1.9416	1.9430	1.9445
7.0	1.9459	1.9473	1.9488	1.9502	1.9516	1.9530	1.9544	1.9559	1.9573	1.9587
7.1	1.9601	1.9615	1.9629	1.9643	1.9657	1.9671	1.9685	1.9699	1.9713	1.9727
7.2	1.9741	1.9755	1.9769	1.9782	1.9796	1.9810	1.9824	1.9838	1.9851	1.9865
7.3	1.9879	1.9892	1.9906	1.9920	1.9933	1.9947	1.9961	1.9974	1.9988	2.0001
7.4	2.0015	2.0028	2.0042	2.0055	2.0069	2.0082	2.0096	2.0109	2.0122	2.0136
7.5	2.0149	2.0162	2.0176	2.0189	2.0202	2.0215	2.0229	2.0242	2.0255	2.0268
7.6	2.0281	2.0295	2.0308	2.0321	2.0334	2.0347	2.0360	2.0373	2.0386	2.0399
7.7	2.0412	2.0425	2.0438	2.0451	2.0464	2.0477	2.0490	2.0503	2.0516	2.0528
7.8	2.0541	2.0554	2.0567	2.0580	2.0592	2.0605	2.0618	2.0631	2.0643	2.0656
7.9	2.0669	2.0681	2.0694	2.0707	2.0719	2.0732	2.0744	2.0757	2.0769	2.0782
8.0	2.0794	2.0807	2.0819	2.0832	2.0844	2.0857	2.0869	2.0882	2.0894	2.0906
8.1	2.0919	2.0931	2.0943	2.0956	2.0968	2.0980	2.0992	2.1005	2.1017	2.1029
8.2	2.1041	2.1054	2.1066	2.1078	2.1090	2.1102	2.1114	2.1126	2.1138	2.1150
8.3	2.1163	2.1175	2.1187	2.1199	2.1211	2.1223	2.1235	2.1247	2.1258	2.1270
8.4	2.1282	2.1294	2.1306	2.1318	2.1330	2.1342	2.1353	2.1365	2.1377	2.1389
8.5	2.1401	2.1412	2.1424	2.1436	2.1448	2.1459	2.1471	2.1483	2.1494	2.1506
8.6	2.1518	2.1529	2.1541	2.1552	2.1564	2.1576	2.1587	2.1599	2.1610	2.1622
8.7	2.1633	2.1645	2.1656	2.1668	2.1679	2.1691	2.1702	2.1713	2.1725	2.1736
8.8	2.1748	2.1759	2.1770	2.1782	2.1793	2.1804	2.1815	2.1827	2.1838	2.1849
8.9	2.1861	2.1872	2.1883	2.1894	2.1905	2.1917	2.1928	2.1939	2.1950	2.1961
9.0	2.1972	2.1983	2.1994	2.2006	2.2017	2.2028	2.2039	2.2050	2.2061	2.2072
9.1	2.2083	2.2094	2.2105	2.2116	2.2127	2.2138	2.2148	2.2159	2.2170	2.2181
9.2	2.2192	2.2203	2.2214	2.2225	2.2235	2.2246	2.2257	2.2268	2.2279	2.2289
9.3	2.2300	2.2311	2.2322	2.2332	2.2343	2.2354	2.2364	2.2375	2.2386	2.2396
9.4	2.2407	2.2418	2.2428	2.2439	2.2450	2.2460	2.2471	2.2481	2.2492	2.2502
9.5	2.2513	2.2523	2.2534	2.2544	2.2555	2.2565	2.2576	2.2586	2.2597	2.2607
9.6	2.2618	2.2628	2.2638	2.2649	2.2659	2.2670	2.2680	2.2690	2.2701	2.2711
9.7	2.2721	2.2732	2.2742	2.2752	2.2762	2.2773	2.2783	2.2793	2.2803	2.2814
9.8	2.2824	2.2834	2.2844	2.2854	2.2865	2.2875	2.2885	2.2895	2.2905	2.2915
9.9	2.2925	2.2935	2.2946	2.2956	2.2966	2.2976	2.2986	2.2996	2.3006	2.3016

Appendix E

Common Logarithmic Tables

	0.00	0.01	0.02	0.03	0.04	0.05	0.06	0.07	0.08	0.09
1.0	0.0000	0.0043	0.0086	0.0128	0.0170	0.0212	0.0253	0.0294	0.0334	0.0374
1.1	0.0414	0.0453	0.0492	0.0531	0.0569	0.0607	0.0645	0.0682	0.0719	0.0755
1.2	0.0792	0.0828	0.0864	0.0899	0.0934	0.0969	0.1004	0.1038	0.1072	0.1106
1.3	0.1139	0.1173	0.1206	0.1239	0.1271	0.1303	0.1335	0.1367	0.1399	0.1430
1.4	0.1461	0.1492	0.1523	0.1553	0.1584	0.1614	0.1644	0.1673	0.1703	0.1732
1.5	0.1761	0.1790	0.1818	0.1847	0.1875	0.1903	0.1931	0.1959	0.1987	0.2014
1.6	0.2041	0.2068	0.2095	0.2122	0.2148	0.2175	0.2201	0.2227	0.2253	0.2279
1.7	0.2304	0.2330	0.2355	0.2380	0.2405	0.2430	0.2455	0.2480	0.2504	0.2529
1.8	0.2553	0.2577	0.2601	0.2625	0.2648	0.2672	0.2695	0.2718	0.2742	0.2765
1.9	0.2788	0.2810	0.2833	0.2856	0.2878	0.2900	0.2923	0.2945	0.2967	0.2989
2.0	0.3010	0.3032	0.3054	0.3075	0.3096	0.3118	0.3139	0.3160	0.3181	0.3201
2.1	0.3222	0.3243	0.3263	0.3284	0.3304	0.3324	0.3345	0.3365	0.3385	0.3404
2.2	0.3424	0.3444	0.3464	0.3483	0.3502	0.3522	0.3541	0.3560	0.3579	0.3598
2.3	0.3617	0.3636	0.3655	0.3674	0.3692	0.3711	0.3729	0.3747	0.3766	0.3784
2.4	0.3802	0.3820	0.3838	0.3856	0.3874	0.3892	0.3909	0.3927	0.3945	0.3962
2.5	0.3979	0.3997	0.4014	0.4031	0.4048	0.4065	0.4082	0.4099	0.4116	0.4133
2.6	0.4150	0.4166	0.4183	0.4200	0.4216	0.4232	0.4249	0.4265	0.4281	0.4298
2.7	0.4314	0.4330	0.4346	0.4362	0.4378	0.4393	0.4409	0.4425	0.4440	0.4456
2.8	0.4472	0.4487	0.4502	0.4518	0.4533	0.4548	0.4564	0.4579	0.4594	0.4609
2.9	0.4624	0.4639	0.4654	0.4669	0.4683	0.4698	0.4713	0.4728	0.4742	0.4757
3.0	0.4771	0.4786	0.4800	0.4814	0.4829	0.4843	0.4857	0.4871	0.4886	0.4900
3.1	0.4914	0.4928	0.4942	0.4955	0.4969	0.4983	0.4997	0.5011	0.5024	0.5038
3.2	0.5052	0.5065	0.5079	0.5092	0.5105	0.5119	0.5132	0.5145	0.5159	0.5172
3.3	0.5185	0.5198	0.5211	0.5224	0.5237	0.5250	0.5263	0.5276	0.5289	0.5302
3.4	0.5315	0.5328	0.5340	0.5353	0.5366	0.5378	0.5391	0.5403	0.5416	0.5428
3.5	0.5441	0.5453	0.5465	0.5478	0.5490	0.5502	0.5514	0.5527	0.5539	0.5551
3.6	0.5563	0.5575	0.5587	0.5599	0.5611	0.5623	0.5635	0.5647	0.5658	0.5670
3.7	0.5682	0.5694	0.5705	0.5717	0.5729	0.5740	0.5752	0.5763	0.5775	0.5786
3.8	0.5798	0.5809	0.5821	0.5832	0.5843	0.5855	0.5866	0.5877	0.5888	0.5899
3.9	0.5911	0.5922	0.5933	0.5944	0.5955	0.5966	0.5977	0.5988	0.5999	0.6010
4.0	0.6021	0.6031	0.6042	0.6053	0.6064	0.6075	0.6085	0.6096	0.6107	0.6117
4.1	0.6128	0.6138	0.6149	0.6160	0.6170	0.6180	0.6191	0.6201	0.6212	0.6222
4.2	0.6232	0.6243	0.6253	0.6263	0.6274	0.6284	0.6294	0.6304	0.6314	0.6325
4.3	0.6335	0.6345	0.6355	0.6365	0.6375	0.6385	0.6395	0.6405	0.6415	0.6425
4.4	0.6435	0.6444	0.6454	0.6464	0.6474	0.6484	0.6493	0.6503	0.6513	0.6522
4.5	0.6532	0.6542	0.6551	0.6561	0.6571	0.6580	0.6590	0.6599	0.6609	0.6618
4.6	0.6628	0.6637	0.6646	0.6656	0.6665	0.6675	0.6684	0.6693	0.6702	0.6712
4.7	0.6721	0.6730	0.6739	0.6749	0.6758	0.6767	0.6776	0.6785	0.6794	0.6803
4.8	0.6812	0.6821	0.6830	0.6839	0.6848	0.6857	0.6866	0.6875	0.6884	0.6893
4.9	0.6902	0.6911	0.6920	0.6928	0.6937	0.6946	0.6955	0.6964	0.6972	0.6981
5.0	0.6990	0.6998	0.7007	0.7016	0.7024	0.7033	0.7042	0.7050	0.7059	0.7067
5.1	0.7076	0.7084	0.7093	0.7101	0.7110	0.7118	0.7126	0.7135	0.7143	0.7152
5.2	0.7160	0.7168	0.7177	0.7185	0.7193	0.7202	0.7210	0.7218	0.7226	0.7235
5.3	0.7243	0.7251	0.7259	0.7267	0.7275	0.7284	0.7292	0.7300	0.7308	0.7316
5.4	0.7324	0.7332	0.7340	0.7348	0.7356	0.7364	0.7372	0.7380	0.7388	0.7396

Common Logarithmic Tables (Continued)

	0.00	0.01	0.02	0.03	0.04	0.05	0.06	0.07	0.08	0.09
5.5	0.7404	0.7412	0.7419	0.7427	0.7435	0.7443	0.7451	0.7459	0.7466	0.7474
5.6	0.7482	0.7490	0.7497	0.7505	0.7513	0.7520	0.7528	0.7536	0.7543	0.7551
5.7	0.7559	0.7566	0.7574	0.7582	0.7589	0.7597	0.7604	0.7612	0.7619	0.7627
5.8	0.7634	0.7642	0.7649	0.7657	0.7664	0.7672	0.7679	0.7686	0.7694	0.7701
5.9	0.7709	0.7716	0.7723	0.7731	0.7738	0.7745	0.7752	0.7760	0.7767	0.7774
6.0	0.7782	0.7789	0.7796	0.7803	0.7810	0.7818	0.7825	0.7832	0.7839	0.7846
6.1	0.7853	0.7860	0.7868	0.7875	0.7882	0.7889	0.7896	0.7903	0.7910	0.7917
6.2	0.7924	0.7931	0.7938	0.7945	0.7952	0.7959	0.7966	0.7973	0.7980	0.7987
6.3	0.7993	0.8000	0.8007	0.8014	0.8021	0.8028	0.8035	0.8041	0.8048	0.8055
6.4	0.8062	0.8069	0.8075	0.8082	0.8089	0.8096	0.8102	0.8109	0.8116	0.8122
6.5	0.8129	0.8136	0.8142	0.8149	0.8156	0.8162	0.8169	0.8176	0.8182	0.8189
6.6	0.8195	0.8202	0.8209	0.8215	0.8222	0.8228	0.8235	0.8241	0.8248	0.8254
6.7	0.8261	0.8267	0.8274	0.8280	0.8287	0.8293	0.8299	0.8306	0.8312	0.8319
6.8	0.8325	0.8331	0.8338	0.8344	0.8351	0.8357	0.8363	0.8370	0.8376	0.8382
6.9	0.8388	0.8395	0.8401	0.8407	0.8414	0.8420	0.8426	0.8432	0.8439	0.8445
7.0	0.8451	0.8457	0.8463	0.8470	0.8476	0.8482	0.8488	0.8494	0.8500	0.8506
7.1	0.8513	0.8519	0.8525	0.8531	0.8537	0.8543	0.8549	0.8555	0.8561	0.8567
7.2	0.8573	0.8579	0.8585	0.8591	0.8597	0.8603	0.8609	0.8615	0.8621	0.8627
7.3	0.8633	0.8639	0.8645	0.8651	0.8657	0.8663	0.8669	0.8675	0.8681	0.8686
7.4	0.8692	0.8698	0.8704	0.8710	0.8716	0.8722	0.8727	0.8733	0.8739	0.8745
7.5	0.8751	0.8756	0.8762	0.8768	0.8774	0.8779	0.8785	0.8791	0.8797	0.8802
7.6	0.8808	0.8814	0.8820	0.8825	0.8831	0.8837	0.8842	0.8848	0.8854	0.8859
7.7	0.8865	0.8871	0.8876	0.8882	0.8887	0.8893	0.8899	0.8904	0.8910	0.8915
7.8	0.8921	0.8927	0.8932	0.8938	0.8943	0.8949	0.8954	0.8960	0.8965	0.8971
7.9	0.8976	0.8982	0.8987	0.8993	0.8998	0.9004	0.9009	0.9015	0.9020	0.9025
8.0	0.9031	0.9036	0.9042	0.9047	0.9053	0.9058	0.9063	0.9069	0.9074	0.9079
8.1	0.9085	0.9090	0.9096	0.9101	0.9106	0.9112	0.9117	0.9122	0.9128	0.9133
8.2	0.9138	0.9143	0.9149	0.9154	0.9159	0.9165	0.9170	0.9175	0.9180	0.9186
8.3	0.9191	0.9196	0.9201	0.9206	0.9212	0.9217	0.9222	0.9227	0.9232	0.9238
8.4	0.9243	0.9248	0.9253	0.9258	0.9263	0.9269	0.9274	0.9279	0.9284	0.9289
8.5	0.9294	0.9299	0.9304	0.9309	0.9315	0.9320	0.9325	0.9330	0.9335	0.9340
8.6	0.9345	0.9350	0.9355	0.9360	0.9365	0.9370	0.9375	0.9380	0.9385	0.9390
8.7	0.9395	0.9400	0.9405	0.9410	0.9415	0.9420	0.9425	0.9430	0.9435	0.9440
8.8	0.9445	0.9450	0.9455	0.9460	0.9465	0.9469	0.9474	0.9479	0.9484	0.9489
8.9	0.9494	0.9499	0.9504	0.9509	0.9513	0.9518	0.9523	0.9528	0.9533	0.9538
9.0	0.9542	0.9547	0.9552	0.9557	0.9562	0.9566	0.9571	0.9576	0.9581	0.9586
9.1	0.9590	0.9595	0.9600	0.9605	0.9609	0.9614	0.9619	0.9624	0.9628	0.9633
9.2	0.9638	0.9643	0.9647	0.9652	0.9657	0.9661	0.9666	0.9671	0.9675	0.9680
9.3	0.9685	0.9689	0.9694	0.9699	0.9703	0.9708	0.9713	0.9717	0.9722	0.9727
9.4	0.9731	0.9736	0.9741	0.9745	0.9750	0.9754	0.9759	0.9764	0.9768	0.9773
9.5	0.9777	0.9782	0.9786	0.9791	0.9795	0.9800	0.9805	0.9809	0.9814	0.9818
9.6	0.9823	0.9827	0.9832	0.9836	0.9841	0.9845	0.9850	0.9854	0.9859	0.9863
9.7	0.9868	0.9872	0.9877	0.9881	0.9886	0.9890	0.9894	0.9899	0.9903	0.9908
9.8	0.9912	0.9917	0.9921	0.9926	0.9930	0.9934	0.9939	0.9943	0.9948	0.9952
9.9	0.9956	0.9961	0.9965	0.9969	0.9974	0.9978	0.9983	0.9987	0.9991	0.9996

Appendix F

Trigonometric Tables

1 degree ≈ 0.01745 radians
1 radian ≈ 57.29578 degrees

For $0 \leqslant \theta \leqslant 45$, read from upper left.
For $45 \leqslant \theta \leqslant 90$, read from lower right.
For $90 \leqslant \theta \leqslant 360$, use the identities:

θ	Quadrant II	Quadrant III	Quadrant IV
sin θ	$\sin(180-\theta)$	$-\sin(\theta-180)$	$-\sin(360-\theta)$
cos θ	$-\cos(180-\theta)$	$-\cos(\theta-180)$	$\cos(360-\theta)$
tan θ	$-\tan(180-\theta)$	$\tan(\theta-180)$	$-\tan(360-\theta)$
cot θ	$-\cot(180-\theta)$	$\cot(\theta-180)$	$-\cot(360-\theta)$

Degrees	Radians	sin	cos	tan	cot			Degrees	Radians	sin	cos	tan	cot		
0° 00′	.0000	.0000	1.0000	.0000	–	1.5708	90° 00′	4° 00′	.0698	.0698	.9976	.0699	14.301	1.5010	86° 00′
10	.0029	.0029	1.0000	.0029	343.774	1.5679	50	10	.0727	.0727	.9974	.0729	13.727	1.4981	50
20	.0058	.0058	1.0000	.0058	171.885	1.5650	40	20	.0756	.0756	.9971	.0758	13.197	1.4952	40
30	.0087	.0087	1.0000	.0087	114.589	1.5621	30	30	.0785	.0785	.9969	.0787	12.706	1.4923	30
40	.0116	.0116	.9999	.0116	85.940	1.5592	20	40	.0814	.0814	.9967	.0816	12.251	1.4893	20
50	.0145	.0145	.9999	.0145	68.750	1.5563	10	50	.0844	.0843	.9964	.0846	11.826	1.4864	10
1° 00′	.0175	.0175	.9998	.0175	57.290	1.5533	89° 00′	5° 00′	.0873	.0872	.9962	.0875	11.430	1.4835	85° 00′
10	.0204	.0204	.9998	.0204	49.104	1.5504	50	10	.0902	.0901	.9959	.0904	11.059	1.4806	50
20	.0233	.0233	.9997	.0233	42.964	1.5475	40	20	.0931	.0929	.9957	.0934	10.712	1.4777	40
30	.0262	.0262	.9997	.0262	38.188	1.5446	30	30	.0960	.0958	.9954	.0963	10.385	1.4748	30
40	.0291	.0291	.9996	.0291	34.368	1.5417	20	40	.0989	.0987	.9951	.0992	10.078	1.4719	20
50	.0320	.0320	.9995	.0320	31.242	1.5388	10	50	.1018	.1016	.9948	.1022	9.788	1.4690	10
2° 00′	.0349	.0349	.9994	.0349	28.636	1.5359	88° 00′	6° 00′	.1047	.1045	.9945	.1051	9.514	1.4661	84° 00′
10	.0378	.0378	.9993	.0378	26.432	1.5330	50	10	.1076	.1074	.9942	.1080	9.255	1.4632	50
20	.0407	.0407	.9992	.0407	24.542	1.5301	40	20	.1105	.1103	.9939	.1110	9.010	1.4603	40
30	.0436	.0436	.9990	.0437	22.904	1.5272	30	30	.1134	.1132	.9936	.1139	8.777	1.4573	30
40	.0465	.0465	.9989	.0466	21.470	1.5243	20	40	.1164	.1161	.9932	.1169	8.556	1.4544	20
50	.0495	.0494	.9988	.0495	20.206	1.5213	10	50	.1193	.1190	.9929	.1198	8.345	1.4515	10
3° 00′	.0524	.0523	.9986	.0524	19.081	1.5184	87° 00′	7° 00′	.1222	.1219	.9925	.1228	8.144	1.4486	83° 00′
10	.0553	.0552	.9985	.0553	18.075	1.5155	50	10	.1251	.1248	.9922	.1257	7.953	1.4457	50
20	.0582	.0581	.9983	.0582	17.169	1.5126	40	20	.1280	.1276	.9918	.1287	7.770	1.4428	40
30	.0611	.0610	.9981	.0612	16.350	1.5097	30	30	.1309	.1305	.9914	.1317	7.596	1.4399	30
40	.0640	.0640	.9980	.0641	15.605	1.5068	20	40	.1338	.1334	.9911	.1346	7.429	1.4370	20
50	.0669	.0669	.9978	.0670	14.924	1.5039	10	50	.1367	.1363	.9907	.1376	7.269	1.4341	10
		cos	sin	cot	tan	Radians	Degrees			cos	sin	cot	tan	Radians	Degrees

TRIGONOMETRIC TABLES (Continued)

Degrees	Radians	sin	cos	tan	cot		
8°00'	.1396	.1392	.9903	.1405	7.115	1.4312	82°00'
10	.1425	.1421	.9899	.1435	6.968	1.4283	50
20	.1454	.1449	.9894	.1465	6.827	1.4254	40
30	.1484	.1478	.9890	.1495	6.691	1.4224	30
40	.1513	.1507	.9886	.1524	6.561	1.4195	20
50	.1542	.1536	.9881	.1554	6.435	1.4166	10
9°00'	.1571	.1564	.9877	.1584	6.314	1.4137	81°00'
10	.1600	.1593	.9872	.1614	6.197	1.4108	50
20	.1629	.1622	.9868	.1644	6.084	1.4079	40
30	.1658	.1650	.9863	.1673	5.976	1.4050	30
40	.1687	.1679	.9858	.1703	5.871	1.4021	20
50	.1716	.1708	.9853	.1733	5.769	1.3992	10
10°00'	.1745	.1736	.9848	.1763	5.671	1.3963	80°00'
10	.1774	.1765	.9843	.1793	5.576	1.3934	50
20	.1804	.1794	.9838	.1823	5.485	1.3904	40
30	.1833	.1822	.9833	.1853	5.396	1.3875	30
40	.1862	.1851	.9827	.1883	5.309	1.3846	20
50	.1891	.1880	.9822	.1914	5.226	1.3817	10
11°00'	.1920	.1908	.9816	.1944	5.145	1.3788	79°00'
10	.1949	.1937	.9811	.1974	5.066	1.3759	50
20	.1978	.1965	.9805	.2004	4.989	1.3730	40
30	.2007	.1994	.9799	.2035	4.915	1.3701	30
40	.2036	.2022	.9793	.2065	4.843	1.3672	20
50	.2065	.2051	.9787	.2095	4.773	1.3643	10
12°00'	.2094	.2079	.9781	.2126	4.705	1.3614	78°00'
10	.2123	.2108	.9775	.2156	4.638	1.3584	50
20	.2153	.2136	.9769	.2186	4.574	1.3555	40
30	.2182	.2164	.9763	.2217	4.511	1.3526	30
40	.2211	.2193	.9757	.2247	4.449	1.3497	20
50	.2240	.2221	.9750	.2278	4.390	1.3468	10
13°00'	.2269	.2250	.9744	.2309	4.331	1.3439	77°00'
10	.2298	.2278	.9737	.2339	4.275	1.3410	50
20	.2327	.2306	.9730	.2370	4.219	1.3381	40
30	.2356	.2334	.9724	.2401	4.165	1.3352	30
40	.2385	.2363	.9717	.2432	4.113	1.3323	20
50	.2414	.2391	.9710	.2462	4.061	1.3294	10
14°00'	.2443	.2419	.9703	.2493	4.011	1.3265	76°00'
10	.2473	.2447	.9696	.2524	3.962	1.3235	50
20	.2502	.2476	.9689	.2555	3.914	1.3206	40
30	.2531	.2504	.9681	.2586	3.867	1.3177	30
40	.2560	.2532	.9674	.2617	3.821	1.3148	20
50	.2589	.2560	.9667	.2648	3.776	1.3119	10
15°00'	.2618	.2588	.9659	.2679	3.732	1.3090	75°00'
10	.2647	.2616	.9652	.2711	3.689	1.3061	50
20	.2676	.2644	.9644	.2742	3.647	1.3032	40
30	.2705	.2672	.9636	.2773	3.606	1.3003	30
40	.2734	.2700	.9628	.2805	3.566	1.2974	20
50	.2763	.2728	.9621	.2836	3.526	1.2945	10
16°00'	.2793	.2756	.9613	.2867	3.487	1.2915	74°00'
10	.2822	.2784	.9605	.2899	3.450	1.2886	50
20	.2851	.2812	.9596	.2931	3.412	1.2857	40
30	.2880	.2840	.9588	.2962	3.376	1.2828	30
40	.2909	.2868	.9580	.2994	3.340	1.2799	20
50	.2938	.2896	.9572	.3026	3.305	1.2770	10
17°00'	.2967	.2924	.9563	.3057	3.271	1.2741	73°00'
10	.2996	.2952	.9555	.3089	3.237	1.2712	50
20	.3025	.2979	.9546	.3121	3.204	1.2683	40
30	.3054	.3007	.9537	.3153	3.172	1.2654	30
40	.3083	.3035	.9528	.3185	3.140	1.2625	20
50	.3113	.3062	.9520	.3217	3.108	1.2595	10
	cos	sin	cot	tan	Radians	Degrees	

Degrees	Radians	sin	cos	tan	cot		
18°00'	.3142	.3090	.9511	.3249	3.078	1.2566	72°00'
10	.3171	.3118	.9502	.3281	3.047	1.2537	50
20	.3200	.3145	.9492	.3314	3.018	1.2508	40
30	.3229	.3173	.9483	.3346	2.989	1.2479	30
40	.3258	.3201	.9474	.3378	2.960	1.2450	20
50	.3287	.3228	.9465	.3411	2.932	1.2421	10
19°00'	.3316	.3256	.9455	.3443	2.904	1.2392	71°00'
10	.3345	.3283	.9446	.3476	2.877	1.2363	50
20	.3374	.3311	.9436	.3508	2.850	1.2334	40
30	.3403	.3338	.9426	.3541	2.824	1.2305	30
40	.3432	.3365	.9417	.3574	2.798	1.2275	20
50	.3462	.3393	.9407	.3607	2.773	1.2246	10
20°00'	.3491	.3420	.9397	.3640	2.747	1.2217	70°00'
10	.3520	.3448	.9387	.3673	2.723	1.2188	50
20	.3549	.3475	.9377	.3706	2.699	1.2159	40
30	.3578	.3502	.9367	.3739	2.675	1.2130	30
40	.3607	.3529	.9356	.3772	2.651	1.2101	20
50	.3636	.3557	.9346	.3805	2.628	1.2072	10
21°00'	.3665	.3584	.9336	.3839	2.605	1.2043	69°00'
10	.3694	.3611	.9325	.3872	2.583	1.2014	50
20	.3723	.3638	.9315	.3906	2.560	1.1985	40
30	.3752	.3665	.9304	.3939	2.539	1.1956	30
40	.3782	.3692	.9293	.3973	2.517	1.1926	20
50	.3811	.3719	.9283	.4006	2.496	1.1897	10
22°00'	.3840	.3746	.9272	.4040	2.475	1.1868	68°00'
10	.3869	.3773	.9261	.4074	2.455	1.1839	50
20	.3898	.3800	.9250	.4108	2.434	1.1810	40
30	.3927	.3827	.9239	.4142	2.414	1.1781	30
40	.3956	.3854	.9228	.4176	2.394	1.1752	20
50	.3985	.3881	.9216	.4210	2.375	1.1723	10
23°00'	.4014	.3907	.9205	.4245	2.356	1.1694	67°00'
10	.4043	.3934	.9194	.4279	2.337	1.1665	50
20	.4072	.3961	.9182	.4314	2.318	1.1636	40
30	.4102	.3987	.9171	.4348	2.300	1.1606	30
40	.4131	.4014	.9159	.4383	2.282	1.1577	20
50	.4160	.4041	.9147	.4417	2.264	1.1548	10
24°00'	.4189	.4067	.9135	.4452	2.246	1.1519	66°00'
10	.4218	.4094	.9124	.4487	2.229	1.1490	50
20	.4247	.4120	.9112	.4522	2.211	1.1461	40
30	.4276	.4147	.9100	.4557	2.194	1.1432	30
40	.4305	.4173	.9088	.4592	2.177	1.1403	20
50	.4334	.4200	.9075	.4628	2.161	1.1374	10
25°00'	.4363	.4226	.9063	.4663	2.145	1.1345	65°00'
10	.4392	.4253	.9051	.4699	2.128	1.1316	50
20	.4422	.4279	.9038	.4734	2.112	1.1286	40
30	.4451	.4305	.9026	.4770	2.097	1.1257	30
40	.4480	.4331	.9013	.4806	2.081	1.1228	20
50	.4509	.4358	.9001	.4841	2.066	1.1199	10
26°00'	.4538	.4384	.8988	.4877	2.050	1.1170	64°00'
10	.4567	.4410	.8975	.4913	2.035	1.1141	50
20	.4596	.4436	.8962	.4950	2.020	1.1112	40
30	.4625	.4462	.8949	.4986	2.006	1.1083	30
40	.4654	.4488	.8936	.5022	1.991	1.1054	20
50	.4683	.4514	.8923	.5059	1.977	1.1025	10
27°00'	.4712	.4540	.8910	.5095	1.963	1.0996	63°00'
10	.4741	.4566	.8897	.5132	1.949	1.0966	50
20	.4771	.4592	.8884	.5169	1.935	1.0937	40
30	.4800	.4617	.8870	.5206	1.921	1.0908	30
40	.4829	.4643	.8857	.5243	1.907	1.0879	20
50	.4858	.4669	.8843	.5280	1.894	1.0850	10
	cos	sin	cot	tan	Radians	Degrees	

TRIGONOMETRIC TABLES (Continued)

Degrees	Radians	sin	cos	tan	cot		
28°00′	.4887	.4695	.8829	.5317	1.881	1.0821	62°00′
10	.4916	.4720	.8816	.5354	1.868	1.0792	50
20	.4945	.4746	.8802	.5392	1.855	1.0763	40
30	.4974	.4772	.8788	.5430	1.842	1.0734	30
40	.5003	.4797	.8774	.5467	1.829	1.0705	20
50	.5032	.4823	.8760	.5505	1.816	1.0676	10
29°00′	.5061	.4848	.8746	.5543	1.804	1.0647	61°00′
10	.5091	.4874	.8732	.5581	1.792	1.0617	50
20	.5120	.4899	.8718	.5619	1.780	1.0588	40
30	.5149	.4924	.8704	.5658	1.767	1.0559	30
40	.5178	.4950	.8689	.5696	1.756	1.0530	20
50	.5207	.4975	.8675	.5735	1.744	1.0501	10
30°00′	.5236	.5000	.8660	.5774	1.732	1.0472	60°00′
10	.5265	.5025	.8646	.5812	1.720	1.0443	50
20	.5294	.5050	.8631	.5851	1.709	1.0414	40
30	.5323	.5075	.8616	.5890	1.698	1.0385	30
40	.5325	.5100	.8601	.5930	1.686	1.0356	20
50	.5381	.5125	.8587	.5969	1.675	1.0327	10
31°00′	.5411	.5150	.8572	.6009	1.664	1.0297	59°00′
10	.5440	.5175	.8557	.6048	1.653	1.0268	50
20	.5469	.5200	.8542	.6088	1.643	1.0239	40
30	.5498	.5225	.8526	.6128	1.632	1.0210	30
40	.5527	.5250	.8511	.6168	1.621	1.0181	20
50	.5556	.5275	.8496	.6208	1.611	1.0152	10
32°00′	.5585	.5299	.8480	.6249	1.600	1.0123	58°00′
10	.5614	.5324	.8465	.6289	1.590	1.0094	50
20	.5643	.5348	.8450	.6330	1.580	1.0065	40
30	.5672	.5373	.8434	.6371	1.570	1.0036	30
40	.5701	.5398	.8418	.6412	1.560	1.0007	20
50	.5730	.5422	.8403	.6453	1.550	.9977	10
33°00′	.5760	.5446	.8387	.6494	1.540	.9948	57°00′
10	.5789	.5471	.8371	.6536	1.530	.9919	50
20	.5818	.5495	.8355	.6577	1.520	.9890	40
30	.5847	.5519	.8339	.6619	1.511	.9861	30
40	.5876	.5544	.8323	.6661	1.501	.9832	20
50	.5905	.5568	.8307	.6703	1.492	.9803	10
34°00′	.5934	.5592	.8290	.6745	1.483	.9774	56°00′
10	.5963	.5616	.8274	.6787	1.473	.9745	50
20	.5992	.5640	.8258	.6830	1.464	.9716	40
30	.6021	.5664	.8241	.6873	1.455	.9687	30
40	.6050	.5688	.8225	.6916	1.446	.9657	20
50	.6080	.5712	.8208	.6959	1.437	.9628	10
35°00′	.6109	.5736	.8192	.7002	1.428	.9599	55°00′
10	.6138	.5760	.8175	.7046	1.419	.9570	50
20	.6167	.5783	.8158	.7089	1.411	.9541	40
30	.6196	.5807	.8141	.7133	1.402	.9512	30
40	.6225	.5831	.8124	.7177	1.393	.9483	20
50	.6254	.5854	.8107	.7221	1.385	.9454	10
36°00′	.6283	.5878	.8090	.7265	1.376	.9425	54°00′
10	.6312	.5901	.8073	.7310	1.368	.9396	50
20	.6341	.5925	.8056	.7355	1.360	.9367	40
30	.6370	.5948	.8039	.7400	1.351	.9338	30
40	.6400	.5972	.8021	.7445	1.343	.9308	20
50	.6429	.5995	.8004	.7490	1.335	.9279	10
		cos	sin	cot	tan	Radians	Degrees

Degrees	Radians	sin	cos	tan	cot		
37°00′	.6458	.6018	.7986	.7536	1.327	.9250	53°00′
10	.6487	.6041	.7969	.7581	1.319	.9221	50
20	.6516	.6065	.7951	.7627	1.311	.9192	40
30	.6545	.6088	.7934	.7673	1.303	.9163	30
40	.6574	.6111	.7916	.7720	1.295	.9134	20
50	.6603	.6134	.7898	.7766	1.288	.9105	10
38°00′	.6632	.6157	.7880	.7813	1.280	.9076	52°00′
10	.6661	.6180	.7862	.7860	1.272	.9047	50
20	.6690	.6202	.7844	.7907	1.265	.9018	40
30	.6720	.6225	.7826	.7954	1.257	.8988	30
40	.6749	.6248	.7808	.8002	1.250	.8959	20
50	.6778	.6271	.7790	.8050	1.242	.8930	10
39°00′	.6807	.6293	.7771	.8098	1.235	.8901	51°00′
10	.6836	.6316	.7753	.8146	1.228	.8872	50
20	.6865	.6338	.7735	.8195	1.220	.8843	40
30	.6894	.6361	.7716	.8243	1.213	.8814	30
40	.6923	.6383	.7698	.8292	1.206	.8785	20
50	.6952	.6406	.7679	.8342	1.199	.8756	10
40°00′	.6981	.6428	.7660	.8391	1.192	.8727	50°00′
10	.7010	.6450	.7642	.8441	1.185	.8698	50
20	.7039	.6472	.7623	.8491	1.178	.8668	40
30	.7069	.6494	.7604	.8541	1.171	.8639	30
40	.7098	.6517	.7585	.8591	1.164	.8610	20
50	.7127	.6539	.7566	.8642	1.157	.8581	10
41°00′	.7156	.6561	.7547	.8693	1.150	.8552	49°00′
10	.7185	.6583	.7528	.8744	1.144	.8523	50
20	.7214	.6604	.7509	.8796	1.137	.8494	40
30	.7243	.6626	.7490	.8847	1.130	.8465	30
40	.7272	.6648	.7470	.8899	1.124	.8436	20
50	.7301	.6670	.7451	.8952	1.117	.8407	10
42°00′	.7330	.6691	.7431	.9004	1.111	.8378	48°00′
10	.7359	.6713	.7412	.9057	1.104	.8348	50
20	.7389	.6734	.7392	.9110	1.098	.8319	40
30	.7418	.6756	.7373	.9163	1.091	.8290	30
40	.7447	.6777	.7353	.9217	1.085	.8261	20
50	.7476	.6799	.7333	.9271	1.079	.8232	10
43°00′	.7505	.6820	.7314	.9325	1.072	.8203	47°00′
10	.7534	.6841	.7294	.9380	1.066	.8174	50
20	.7563	.6862	.7274	.9435	1.060	.8145	40
30	.7592	.6884	.7254	.9490	1.054	.8116	30
40	.7621	.6905	.7234	.9545	1.048	.8087	20
50	.7650	.6926	.7214	.9601	1.042	.8058	10
44°00′	.7679	.6947	.7193	.9657	1.036	.8029	46°00′
10	.7709	.6967	.7173	.9713	1.030	.7999	50
20	.7738	.6988	.7153	.9770	1.024	.7970	40
30	.7767	.7009	.7133	.9827	1.018	.7941	30
40	.7796	.7030	.7112	.9884	1.012	.7912	20
50	.7825	.7050	.7092	.9942	1.006	.7883	10
45°00′	.7854	.7071	.7071	1.0000	1.000	.7854	45°00′
		cos	sin	cot	tan	Radians	Degrees

Appendix G

Graphs of Inverse Trigonometric Functions

Domain: $[-1, 1]$
Range: $[-\pi/2, \pi/2]$

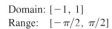

$y = \arcsin x$

Domain: $(-\infty, -1]$ and $[1, \infty)$
Range: $[-\pi/2, 0)$ and $(0, \pi/2]$

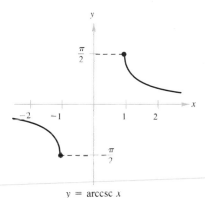

$y = \text{arccsc } x$

Domain: $(-\infty, \infty)$
Range: $(-\pi/2, \pi/2)$

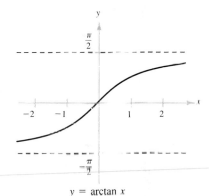

$y = \arctan x$

Domain: $[-1, 1]$
Range: $[0, \pi]$

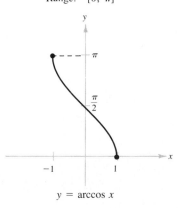

$y = \arccos x$

Domain: $(-\infty, -1]$ and $[1, \infty)$
Range: $[0, \pi/2)$ and $(\pi/2, \pi]$

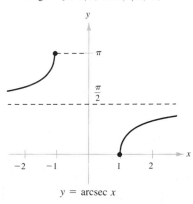

$y = \text{arcsec } x$

Domain: $(-\infty, \infty)$
Range: $(0, \pi)$

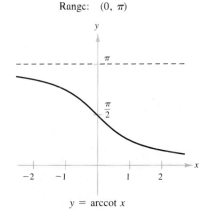

$y = \text{arccot } x$

Graphs of Inverse Trigonometric Functions

Definition of the Inverse Trigonometric Functions

Function	Domain	Range
$y = \arcsin x$ iff $\sin y = x$	$-1 \le x \le 1$	$-\pi/2 \le y \le \pi/2$
$y = \arccos x$ iff $\cos y = x$	$-1 \le x \le 1$	$0 \le y \le \pi$
$y = \arctan x$ iff $\tan y = x$	$-\infty < x < \infty$	$-\pi/2 < y < \pi/2$
$y = \operatorname{arccot} x$ iff $\cot y = x$	$-\infty < x < \infty$	$0 < y < \pi$
$y = \operatorname{arcsec} x$ iff $\sec y = x$	$|x| \ge 1$	$0 \le y \le \pi, \quad y \ne \pi/2$
$y = \operatorname{arccsc} x$ iff $\csc y = x$	$|x| \ge 1$	$-\pi/2 \le y \le \pi/2, \quad y \ne 0$

Answers to Warm Ups, Odd-Numbered Exercises, and Cumulative Tests

CHAPTER 1

Section 1.1 *(page 11)*

1. (a) 5, 1 **(b)** $-9, 5, 0, 1$ **(c)** $-9, -\frac{7}{2}, 5, \frac{2}{3}, 0, 1$
(d) $\sqrt{2}$ **3. (a)** $\frac{6}{3}$ **(b)** $\frac{6}{3}$ **(c)** $-\frac{1}{3}, \frac{6}{3}, -7.5$
(d) $-\pi, \frac{1}{2}\sqrt{2}$ **5.** Commutative (addition)
7. Inverse (multiplication) **9.** Distributive property
11. Associative (addition)
13. Associative (multiplication); Commutative (multiplication) **15.** 0
17. Division by 0 is undefined. **19.** 2 **21.** -14
23. $\frac{2}{7}$ **25.** $\frac{23}{24}$ **27.** $\frac{3}{10}$ **29.** 48
31. Given equation
Subtraction property of equality
Additive inverse property
Division property of equality
Multiplicative inverse property
33. $\frac{3}{2} < 7$ **35.** $-4 > -8$

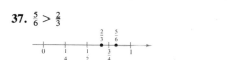

37. $\frac{5}{6} > \frac{2}{3}$

39. $x \le 5$ is the set of all real numbers less than or equal to 5.

41. $x < 2$ is the set of all real numbers less than 2.

43. $-1 \le x < 0$ is the set of all negative real numbers greater than or equal to -1 and less than 0.

45. $x < 0$ **47.** $y \le 25$ **49.** $3.5\% \le r \le 6\%$
51. (a) 10 **(b)** 0 **53. (a)** -1 **(b)** -6
55. (a) $|-3| > -|-3|$ **(b)** $|-4| = |4|$ **57.** 4
59. $\frac{5}{2}$ **61.** 51 **63.** 14.99 **65.** $|x - 5| \le 3$
67. $|7 - 18| = 11$ miles **69.** $|y| \ge 6$
71. $|\$113,356.52 - \$112,700| = \$656.52 > \$500$
$0.05(\$112,700) = \$5,635$
Since the actual expenses differ from the budget by more than \$500, there is failure to meet the budget variance test
73. $|\$37,335.80 - \$37,640| = \$304.20 < \$500$
$0.05(\$37,640) = \$1,882$
Since the difference between actual expenses and the budget is less than \$500 and less than 5% of the budgeted amount, there is compliance with the budget variance test.
75. $|77.8 - 92.2| = 14.4$
There was a deficit of \$14.4 billion.
77. $|520.0 - 590.2| = 70.2$
There was a deficit of \$70.2 billion.
79. $\frac{24}{35}$ **81.** $\frac{127}{90}, \frac{584}{413}, \frac{7071}{5000}, \sqrt{2}, \frac{47}{33}$ **83.** 0.625
85. $0.123123\ldots$
87. False. The reciprocal of 2 is $\frac{1}{2}$, which is rational.
89. True

Section 1.2 *(page 25)*

WARM UP **1.** $4 > -2$ **2.** $-\pi < -3$ **3.** 5
4. 4 **5.** 1 **6.** $\frac{1}{4}$ **7.** 0 **8.** $-\frac{1}{8}$ **9.** 4
10. 1

1. -24 **3.** $\frac{1}{2}$ **5.** 5 **7.** $-125z^3$ **9.** $24y^{10}$
11. $\frac{7}{x}$ **13.** $\frac{4}{3}(x + y)^2$ **15.** $-2x^3$ **17.** $\frac{x^2}{9z^4}$
19. $\frac{a^6}{64b^9}$ **21.** 1 **23. (a)** $\frac{3}{2}$ **(b)** $\frac{3}{2}$
25. (a) -125 **(b)** 562 **27. (a)** $2\sqrt{2}$ **(b)** $\frac{2\sqrt[3]{2}}{3}$

29. (a) $\dfrac{5|x|\sqrt{3}}{y^2}$ **(b)** $(x-y)\sqrt{5(x-y)}$

31. (a) $|x|y\sqrt{15}$ **(b)** $\dfrac{3\sqrt{3}}{|a|}$ **33. (a)** $2\sqrt{x}$

(b) $13\sqrt{2}$ **35. (a)** $8\sqrt{y}$ **(b)** $37\sqrt[3]{4a}$

37. (a) $\dfrac{\sqrt{10}}{2}$ **(b)** $3\sqrt{7}$ **39. (a)** $\dfrac{\sqrt[3]{5x}}{x}$ **(b)** $\dfrac{\sqrt[4]{3x}}{x}$

41. (a) $3(\sqrt{6}-\sqrt{5})$ **(b)** $-\dfrac{4(\sqrt{2}+2\sqrt{3})}{5}$

43. (a) $\dfrac{2}{\sqrt{2}}$ **(b)** $\dfrac{2}{3\sqrt{2}}$ **45. (a)** $\dfrac{1}{x(\sqrt{3}+\sqrt{2})}$

(b) $\dfrac{1}{\sqrt{15}-\sqrt{3}}$ **47.** $9^{1/2}=3$ **49.** $\sqrt{196}=14$

51. $(-216)^{1/3}=-6$ **53.** $\sqrt[3]{27^2}=9$ **55.** $81^{3/4}=27$
57. (a) 6   **(b)** 64   **59. (a)** $\frac{1}{16}$ **(b)** $\frac{2}{3}$
61. $\sqrt{x},\ x\ge 0$ **63.** $\sqrt[3]{(x+1)^2}$ **65.** $5\sqrt[6]{2^5}$
67. $\sqrt[6]{x}$ **69. (a)** 7.5498   **(b)** 3.5477   **(c)** 0.0270
(d) -2.3045 **71.** 5.75×10^7 **73.** 8.99×10^{-5}
75. 524,000,000   **77.** 0.00000000048
79. (a) 7697.125   **(b)** 954.448   **(c)** 1.479
(d) 111,369,991.292   **81.** $8\frac{1}{3}$ min

83.

Number of years	5	10	20
Balance	$910.97	$1659.73	$5509.41

Number of years	30	40	50
Balance	$18,288.29	$60,707.30	$201,515.59

85. 21.5%   **87.** 13.29   **89.** 1
91. When any positive integer is squared, the units digit is 0, 1, 4, 5, 6, or 9. Therefore, $\sqrt{5233}$ is not an integer.

Section 1.3   *(page 37)*

WARM UP   **1.** $42x^3$ **2.** $-20z^2$ **3.** $-27x^6$
4. $-3x^6$ **5.** $\frac{9}{4}z^3$ **6.** $4\sqrt{3}$ **7.** $\dfrac{9}{4x^2}$ **8.** 8
9. $\sqrt{2}$ **10.** $-3x$

1. $2x^2-x+1,\ 2,\ 2$ **3.** $-\frac{1}{2}x+1,\ 5,\ -\frac{1}{2}$
5. $-2x-10$ **7.** $3x^3-2x+2$
9. $8x^3+29x^2+11$ **11.** $12z+8$ **13.** $-15z^2+5z$
15. $30x^3+12x^2$ **17.** $x^4-5x^3-2x^2+11x-5$
19. x^3+27 **21.** x^4-1 **23.** $-xz+17z$
25. $x^3+4x^2-5x-20$ **27.** $4x^2-20xy+25y^2$
29. $x^2+2xy+y^2-6x-6y+9$ **31.** x^2-4y^2
33. m^2-n^2-6m+9 **35.** $4r^4-25$
37. x^3+3x^2+3x+1 **39.** $8x^3-12x^2y+6xy^2-y^3$
41. $2x(x^2-3)$ **43.** $(x-1)(x+5)$
45. $(4y+3)(4y-3)$ **47.** $(x+1)(x-3)$
49. $(x-2)^2$ **51.** $(5y-1)^2$ **53.** $(s-3)(s-2)$

55. $(x-20)(x-10)$ **57.** $(3z+1)(3z-2)$
59. $(5x+1)(x+5)$ **61.** $(x-2)(x^2+2x+4)$
63. $(3x+2)(9x^2-6x+4)$ **65.** $(x-1)(x^2+2)$
67. $(2x-1)(x^2-3)$ **69.** $(3+x)(2-x^3)$
71. $x^2(x-4)$ **73.** $(1-2x)^2$ **75.** $(9x+1)(x+1)$
77. $(2x-1)(6x-1)$ **79.** $-(x+1)(x-3)(x+9)$
81. $(3x+1)(x^2+5)$ **83.** $-z(z+10)$
85. $2(t-2)(t^2+2t+4)$
87. Total $=0.14x^2-3.33x+58.40$

x (mph)	Total
30	84.5 ft
40	149.2 ft
55	298.75 ft

89. $3x^3-\frac{135}{2}x^2+\frac{675}{2}x$

x	3	5	7
V	486	375	84

91. (a) $V=\pi h(R+r)(R-r)$ **(b)** $V=2\pi\left(\dfrac{R+r}{2}\right)(R-r)h$

93.

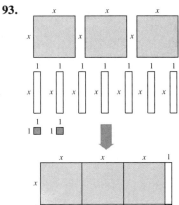

95.   **97.** $m+n$

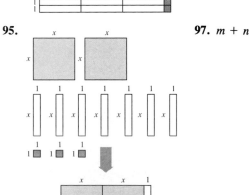

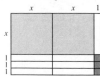

Section 1.4   *(page 48)*

WARM UP   **1.** $5x^2(1 - 3x)$ **2.** $(4x + 3)(4x - 3)$
3. $(3x - 1)^2$ **4.** $(2y + 3)^2$ **5.** $(z + 3)(z + 1)$
6. $(x - 5)(x - 10)$ **7.** $(3 - x)(1 + 3x)$
8. $(3x - 1)(x - 15)$ **9.** $(s + 1)(s + 2)(s - 2)$
10. $(y + 4)(y^2 - 4y + 16)$

1. All real numbers
3. All nonnegative real numbers
5. All real numbers x such that $x \neq 2$
7. All real numbers x such that $x \neq 0$ and $x \neq 4$
9. All real numbers x such that $x \geq -1$
11. $3x, \; x \neq 0$ **13.** $x - 2, \; x \neq 2$
15. $x + 2, \; x \neq -2$ **17.** $\dfrac{3x}{2}, \; x \neq 0$ **19.** $\dfrac{3y}{y + 1}, \; x \neq 0$
21. $-\dfrac{1}{2}, \; x \neq 5$ **23.** $\dfrac{x(x + 3)}{x - 2}, \; x \neq -2$
25. $\dfrac{y - 4}{y + 6}, \; y \neq 3$ **27.** $-(x^2 + 1), \; x \neq 2$
29. $z - 2$ **31.** $\dfrac{1}{5(x - 2)}, \; x \neq 1$
33. $-\dfrac{x(x + 7)}{x + 1}, \; x \neq 9$ **35.** $\dfrac{r + 1}{r}, \; r \neq 1$
37. $\dfrac{t - 3}{(t + 3)(t - 2)}, \; t \neq -2$ **39.** $\dfrac{x - y}{x(x + y)^2}, \; x \neq -2y$
41. $\dfrac{3}{2}, \; x \neq -y$ **43.** $x(x + 1), \; x \neq 0, -1$ **45.** $\dfrac{x + 5}{x - 1}$
47. $\dfrac{6x + 13}{x + 3}$ **49.** $-\dfrac{2}{x - 2}$ **51.** $\dfrac{x - 4}{(x + 2)(x - 2)(x - 1)}$
53. $-\dfrac{x^2 + 3}{(x + 1)(x - 2)(x - 3)}$ **55.** $\dfrac{2 - x}{x^2 + 1}, \; x \neq 0$
57. $\dfrac{1}{2}, \; x \neq 2$ **59.** $\dfrac{1}{x}, \; x \neq -1$ **61.** $\dfrac{(x + 3)^3}{2x(x - 3)}$
63. $-\dfrac{2x + h}{x^2(x + h)^2}, \; h \neq 0$ **65.** $\dfrac{2x - 1}{2x}, \; x > 0$
67. $-\dfrac{1}{t^2\sqrt{t^2 + 1}}$ **69.** $-\dfrac{1}{x^2(x + 1)^{3/4}}$ **71.** $\dfrac{1}{\sqrt{x + 2} + \sqrt{x}}$
73. (a) $\dfrac{1}{16}$ min   **(b)** $\dfrac{x}{16}$ min   **(c)** $\dfrac{60}{16} = \dfrac{15}{4}$ min   **75.** $\dfrac{11x}{30}$
77. (a) 12.65%   **(b)** $\dfrac{288(MN - P)}{N(MN + 12P)}$ **79.** $\dfrac{R_1 R_2}{R_1 + R_2}$

Section 1.5   *(page 61)*

WARM UP   **1.** $-3x - 10$ **2.** $5x - 12$ **3.** x
4. $x + 26$ **5.** $\dfrac{8x}{15}$ **6.** $\dfrac{3x}{4}$ **7.** $-\dfrac{1}{x(x + 1)}$ **8.** $\dfrac{5}{x}$
9. $\dfrac{7x - 8}{x(x - 2)}$ **10.** $-\dfrac{2}{x^2 - 1}$

1. Identity   **3.** Conditional   **5.** Conditional
7. (a) No   **(b)** No   **(c)** Yes   **(d)** No
9. (a) Yes   **(b)** Yes   **(c)** No   **(d)** No
11. (a) Yes   **(b)** No   **(c)** No   **(d)** No   **13.** 9
15. -4 **17.** 9   **19.** No solution   **21.** 10   **23.** 4
25. 3   **27.** 5   **29.** $\dfrac{11}{6}$ **31.** 0
33. $\dfrac{1 + 4b}{2 + a}, \; a \neq -2$ **35.** $0, -\dfrac{1}{2}$ **37.** $4, -2$
39. $-\dfrac{7}{4}$ **41.** $-\dfrac{3}{2}, 11$ **43.** $\pm 2\sqrt{3}$ **45.** $12 \pm 3\sqrt{2}$
47. $4, -8$ **49.** $1 \pm \dfrac{\sqrt{6}}{3}$ **51.** $\dfrac{1}{2}, -1$ **53.** $\dfrac{1}{4}, -\dfrac{3}{4}$
55. $1 \pm \sqrt{3}$ **57.** $\dfrac{2}{3} \pm \dfrac{\sqrt{7}}{3}$ **59.** $-\dfrac{1}{2} \pm \sqrt{2}$
61. $6 \pm \sqrt{11}$ **63.** $-\dfrac{1}{2} \pm \dfrac{\sqrt{21}}{6}$ **65.** $3, -1, 0$
67. $3, 1, -1$ **69.** ± 2 **71.** 0   **73.** 36   **75.** 3
77. $3, -2$ **79.** $\sqrt{3}, -3$ **81.** $\dfrac{1}{(x - 2)^2 - 16}$
83. 138.889   **85.** \$7600   **87.** $\approx$ 2121 ft
89. 14 in. sq   **91.** 400 mph   **93.** 200 units
95. 1 mi

Section 1.6   *(page 75)*

WARM UP   **1.** $-\dfrac{1}{2}$ **2.** $-\dfrac{1}{6}$ **3.** -3 **4.** $\dfrac{13}{2}$
5. $x \geq 0$ **6.** $-3 < z < 10$ **7.** $P \leq 2$
8. $W \geq 200$ **9.** $2, 7$ **10.** $0, 1$

1. $-1 \leq x \leq 3$; Bounded   **3.** $10 < x < \infty$; Unbounded
5. (a) Yes   **(b)** No   **(c)** Yes   **(d)** No
7. (a) Yes   **(b)** No   **(c)** No   **(d)** Yes
9. $x < 3$ **11.** $x > -4$

   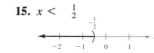

13. $x \geq 12$ **15.** $x < \dfrac{1}{2}$

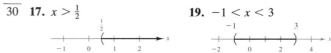

17. $x > \dfrac{1}{2}$ **19.** $-1 < x < 3$

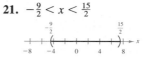   

21. $-\dfrac{9}{2} < x < \dfrac{15}{2}$ **23.** $-\dfrac{3}{4} < x < -\dfrac{1}{4}$

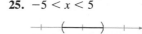   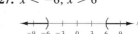

25. $-5 < x < 5$ **27.** $x < -6, \; x > 6$

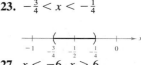

29. $16 \le x \le 24$

31. $x \le 16, x \ge 24$

33. $x \le -7, x \ge 13$

35. $4 < x < 5$

37. $x \le -\frac{29}{2}, x \ge -\frac{11}{2}$

39. No solution   **41.** $|x| \le 2$ **43.** $|x - 9| \ge 3$
45. $[-3, 3]$ **47.** $(-\infty, -2) \cup (2, \infty)$ **49.** $(-7, 3)$
51. $(-\infty, -5] \cup [1, \infty)$ **53.** $(-\infty, -1) \cup (1, \infty)$
55. $(-3, 1)$ **57.** $(-\infty, 0) \cup \left(0, \frac{3}{2}\right)$ **59.** $[-2, 0] \cup [2, \infty)$
61. $(-\infty, -1) \cup (0, 1)$ **63.** $(-\infty, -1) \cup (4, \infty)$
65. $\left(-5, -\frac{3}{2}\right) \cup (-1, \infty)$ **67.** $[5, \infty)$ **69.** $[-3, \infty)$
71. $[-2, 2]$ **73.** $(-\infty, 3] \cup [4, \infty)$
75. $(-3.51, 3.51)$ **77.** $(2.26, 2.39)$ **79.** $r > 12.5\%$
81. $x \ge 36$ units   **83.** $65.8 \le h \le 71.2$
85. Between 13.8 meters and 36.2 meters   **87.** $R_1 \ge 2$
89. $d \ge 3.83$ in.

Section 1.7   *(page 83)*

1. $2x - (3y + 4) = 2x - 3y - 4$
3. $5z + 3(x - 2) = 5z + 3x - 6$
5. $-\dfrac{x - 3}{x - 1} = \dfrac{3 - x}{x - 1}$ **7.** $a\left(\dfrac{x}{y}\right) = \dfrac{ax}{y}$
9. $(4x)^2 = 16x^2$ **11.** $\sqrt{x + 9}$ cannot be simplified.
13. $\dfrac{6x + y}{6x - y}$ cannot be simplified.   **15.** $\dfrac{1}{x + y^{-1}} = \dfrac{y}{xy + 1}$
17. $x(2x - 1)^2 = x(4x^2 - 4x + 1)$
19. $\sqrt[3]{x^3 + 7x^2}$ cannot be simplified.
21. $\dfrac{3}{x} + \dfrac{4}{y} = \dfrac{3y + 4x}{xy}$ **23.** $\dfrac{1}{2y} = \dfrac{1}{2} \cdot \dfrac{1}{y}$ **25.** $3x + 2$
27. $\frac{1}{3}$ **29.** $-\frac{1}{4}$ **31.** 2 **33.** $\frac{1}{2}$ **35.** $\dfrac{1}{2x^2}$
37. $1, 2$ **39.** $1 + x$ **41.** -1 **43.** $3x - 1$
45. $16x^{-1} - 5 - x$ **47.** $4x^{8/3} - 7x^{5/3} + x^{-1/3}$
49. $3x^{-1/2} - 5x^{3/2} - x^{7/2}$ **51.** $\dfrac{-2(21x^2 + 2x - 27)}{(x^2 - 3)^3(6x + 1)^4}$
53. $\dfrac{27x^2 - 24x + 2}{(6x + 1)^4}$ **55.** $\dfrac{-5}{(3x + 2)^{7/4}(2x + 3)^{2/3}}$
57. $\dfrac{4x - 3}{(3x - 1)^{4/3}}$

Chapter 1   Review Exercises   *(page 84)*

1. (a) 11 (b) $11, -14$ (c) $11, -14, -\frac{8}{9}, \frac{5}{2}, 0.4$
(d) $\sqrt{6}$ **3.** $|x - 7| \ge 4$ **5.** 25 **7.** $\frac{15,625}{729}$
9. 18 **11.** 9×10^8 **13.** 2.74×10^6
15. $483,300,000$ **17.** (a) $11,414.125$
(b) $18,380.160$ **19.** $\frac{1}{9}xy$ **21.** -1 **23.** $x^4 - 3x^2$
25. 5 **27.** $2x^2$ **29.** $2\sqrt{2}$ **31.** $2 + \sqrt{3}$
33. $x^5 - 2x^4 + x^3 - x^2 + 2x - 1$ **35.** $\dfrac{1}{x^2}$
37. $\dfrac{x(5x - 6)}{5}, x \ne -\dfrac{3}{2}, 0$ **39.** $\dfrac{3}{(x - 1)(x + 2)}$
41. $\dfrac{x^3 - x + 3}{(x + 2)(x - 1)}$ **43.** $\dfrac{x + 1}{x(x^2 + 1)}$
45. $\dfrac{2x^2 - 3x + 2}{(x + 2)(x - 2)^2}$ **47.** $-\dfrac{1}{xy(x + y)}, x \ne y$
49. $\dfrac{3ax^2}{(a^2 - x)(a - x)}, x \ne 0, a, a^2$ **51.** $(x - 1)(x^2 + 2)$
53. $(x - 1)(x^2 + x + 1)$ **55.** $\dfrac{1}{\sqrt{t + 1}}(-1)$ **57.** 20
59. $\frac{1}{5}$ **61.** $0, 2$ **63.** $\frac{4}{3}, -\frac{1}{2}$ **65.** $0, \frac{12}{5}$
67. $\pm\dfrac{\sqrt{2}}{2}$ **69.** 5 **71.** No solution   **73.** $-5, 15$
75. $\left(-\frac{5}{3}, \infty\right)$ **77.** $[-2, 2]$ **79.** $(-\infty, 3) \cup (5, \infty)$
81. $(-\infty, 0] \cup [3, \infty)$ **83.** $[5, \infty)$
85. $\pi(R + r)(R - r)$ **87.** 2.86 qt   **89.** 123 mi
91. 4 farmers   **93.** $x \ge 36$

CHAPTER 2

Section 2.1   *(page 96)*

WARM UP   **1.** 5 **2.** $3\sqrt{2}$ **3.** 1 **4.** -2
5. $3(\sqrt{2} + \sqrt{5})$ **6.** $2(\sqrt{3} + \sqrt{11})$ **7.** $-3, 11$
8. $9, 1$ **9.** 11 **10.** 4

1.

3.

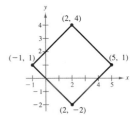

5. $(-1, 1), (3, 2), (0, 4)$ **7.** 8 **9.** 5
11. (a) $a = 4, b = 3, c = 5$ (b) 5
13. (a) $a = 10, b = 3, c = \sqrt{109}$ (b) $\sqrt{109}$

15. (a)

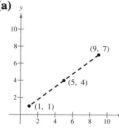

(b) 10
(c) (5, 4)

17. (a)

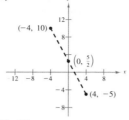

(b) 17
(c) $\left(0, \frac{5}{2}\right)$

19. (a)

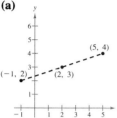

(b) $2\sqrt{10}$
(c) (2, 3)

21. (a)

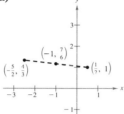

(b) $\dfrac{\sqrt{82}}{3}$

(c) $\left(1, \frac{7}{6}\right)$

23. (a)

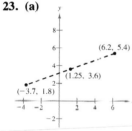

(b) $\sqrt{110.97}$
(c) (1.25, 3.6)

25. (a)

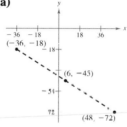

(b) $6\sqrt{277}$
(c) (6, −45)

27. $630,000   **29.** $(\sqrt{5})^2 + (\sqrt{45})^2 - (\sqrt{50})^2$
31. All sides have a length of $\sqrt{5}$.   **33.** $x = 6, -4$
35. $y = \pm15$ **37.** $3x - 2y - 1 = 0$
39. Quadrant IV   **41.** Quadrant I   **43.** Quadrant II
45. Quadrant III or IV   **47.** Quadrant III
49. $(2x_m - x_1, 2y_m - y_1)$
51. $\left(\dfrac{3x_1 + x_2}{4}, \dfrac{3y_1 + y_2}{4}\right), \left(\dfrac{x_1 + x_2}{2}, \dfrac{y_1 + y_2}{2}\right),$
$\left(\dfrac{x_1 + 3x_2}{4}, \dfrac{y_1 + 3y_2}{4}\right)$
53. $5\sqrt{74} \approx 43$ yd

55.

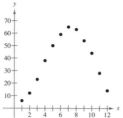

57. $14 per 100 lb of milk in 1989   **59.** ≈ 1782%
61.

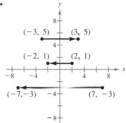

The points are reflected through the y-axis.

Section 2.2   *(page 107)*

WARM UP   **1.** $y = \dfrac{3x - 2}{5}$ **2.** $y = -\dfrac{(x - 5)(x + 1)}{2}$
3. 2   **5.** 0, ±3   **4.** 1, −5   **5.** 0, ±3   **6.** ±2
7. $y = x^3 + 4x$ **8.** $x^2 + y^2 = 4$ **9.** $y = 4x^2 + 8$
10. $y^2 = -3x^2 + 4$

1. (a) Yes   **(b)** Yes   **3. (a)** No   **(b)** Yes
5. (a) Yes   **(b)** Yes   **7.** 2   **9.** 4

11.

x	−4	−2	0	2	4
y	11	7	3	−1	−5
(x, y)	(−4, 11)	(−2, 7)	(0, 3)	(2, −1)	(4, −5)

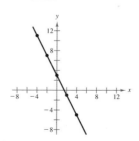

13. (5, 0), (0, −5)   **15.** (−2, 0), (1, 0), (0, −2)
17. (0, 0), (−2, 0)   **19.** (1, 0), $\left(0, \frac{1}{2}\right)$
21. y-axis symmetry   **23.** x-axis symmetry
25. Origin symmetry   **27.** Origin symmetry

31. $m = -\frac{7}{6}$, Intercept: $(0, 5)$

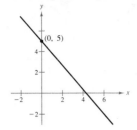

33. $3x + 5y - 10 = 0$ **35.** $x + 2y - 3 = 0$
37. $x + 8 = 0$ **39.** $2x - 5y + 1 = 0$
41. $3x - y - 2 = 0$

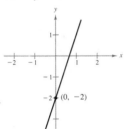

43. $2x + y = 0$

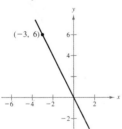

45. $x + 3y - 4 = 0$

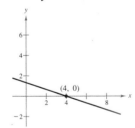

47. $x - 6 = 0$

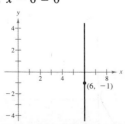

49. $2y - 5 = 0$

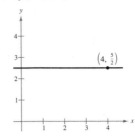

51. $3x + 2y - 6 = 0$ **53.** $12x + 3y + 2 = 0$
55. $x + y - 3 = 0$ **57. (a)** $2x - y - 3 = 0$
(b) $x + 2y - 4 = 0$ **59. (a)** $3x + 4y + 2 = 0$
(b) $4x - 3y + 36 = 0$ **61. (a)** $y = 0$
(b) $x + 1 = 0$ **63.** $V = 125t + 2{,}540$
65. $V = 2{,}000t + 20{,}400$ **67.** b   **69.** a
71. $F = \frac{9}{5}C + 32$ **73.** $39,500
75. $V = -175t + 875$ **77.** $S = 0.85L$
79. $W = 0.07S + 2500$ **81. (a)** $C = 16.75t + 36{,}500$
(b) $R = 27t$ **(c)** $P = 10.25t - 36{,}500$
(d) $t \approx 3{,}561$ hr   **83.** $y = 100 + 30t$

Section 2.4   *(page 131)*

WARM UP   **1.** -73 **2.** 13 **3.** $2(x + 2)$
4. $-8(x - 2)$ **5.** $y = \frac{7}{5} - \frac{2}{5}x$ **6.** $y = \pm x$
7. $x \le -2, x \ge 2$ **8.** $-3 \le x \le 3$
9. All real numbers   **10.** $x \le 1, x \ge 2$

1. (a) Function
   (b) Not a function, since the element 1 in A is matched
      with two elements, -2 and 1, in B
   (c) Function
   (d) Not a function, since not all elements of A are
      matched with an element in B
3. Not a function   **5.** Function   **7.** Function
9. Not a function
11. (a) $\dfrac{1}{4 + 1}$ **(b)** $\dfrac{1}{0 + 1}$ **(c)** $\dfrac{1}{4x + 1}$

   (d) $\dfrac{1}{(x + h) + 1}$
13. (a) -1 **(b)** -9 **(c)** $2x - 5$
15. (a) 0 **(b)** -0.75 **(c)** $x^2 + 2x$
17. (a) 1 **(b)** 2.5 **(c)** $3 - 2|x|$

19. (a) $-\frac{1}{9}$ **(b)** Undefined   **(c)** $\dfrac{1}{y^2 + 6y}$

21. (a) 1 **(b)** -1 **(c)** $\dfrac{|x - 1|}{x - 1}$

23. (a) -1 **(b)** 2 **(c)** 6 **25.** 5 **27.** ± 3
29. All real numbers x

31. All real numbers except $t = 0$
33. $y \geq 10$ **35.** $-1 \leq x \leq 1$
37. All real numbers except $x = 0, -2$
39. $(-2, 4), (-1, 1), (0, 0), (1, 1), (2, 4)$
41. $(-2, 0), (-1, 1), (0, \sqrt{2}), (1, \sqrt{3}), (2, 2)$
43. $2, -1$ **45.** $3, 0$ **47.** $3 + h$
49. $3x\Delta x + 3x^2 + (\Delta x)^2$ **51.** 3 **53.** $A = \dfrac{C^2}{4\pi}$
55. $A = \dfrac{x^2}{x - 1}, x > 1$
57. $V = 4x(6 - x)^2, 0 < x < 6$
59. $h = \sqrt{d^2 - 2000^2}, d \geq 2000$
61. (a) $C = 12.30x + 98,000$ (b) $R = 17.98x$
    (c) $P = 5.68x - 98,000$
63. (a) $R = \dfrac{240n - n^2}{20}$

(b)

n	90	100	110	120	130	140	150
$R(n)$	\$675	\$700	\$715	\$720	\$715	\$700	\$675

Section 2.5   (page 147)

WARM UP   **1.** 2   **2.** 0   **3.** $-\dfrac{3}{x}$ **4.** $x^2 + 3$
5. $0, \pm 4$ **6.** $\dfrac{1}{2}, 1$ **7.** All real numbers except $x = 4$
8. All real numbers except $x = 4, 5$ **9.** $t \leq \dfrac{5}{3}$
10. All real numbers

1. Domain: $[1, \infty)$, Range: $[0, \infty)$
3. Domain: $(-\infty, -2], [2, \infty)$, Range: $[0, \infty)$
5. Domain: $[-5, 5]$, Range: $[0, 5]$
7. Function   **9.** Not a function   **11.** Function
13. (a) Increasing on $(-\infty, \infty)$ (b) Odd function
15. (a) Increasing on $(-\infty, 0), (2, \infty)$, Decreasing on $(0, 2)$
    (b) Neither even nor odd
17. (a) Increasing on $(-1, 0), (1, \infty)$,
    Decreasing on $(-\infty, -1), (0, 1)$
    (b) Even function
19. (a) Increasing on $(-2, \infty)$, Decreasing on $(-3, -2)$
    (b) Neither even nor odd
21. Even   **23.** Odd   **25.** Neither even nor odd
27. Even   **29.** Neither even nor odd

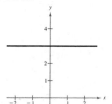

31. Odd

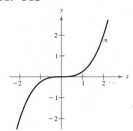

33. Neither even nor odd

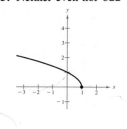

35. Neither even nor odd

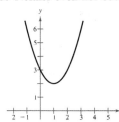

37. Neither even nor odd

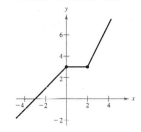

39. Neither even nor odd

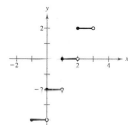

41. $(-\infty, 4]$

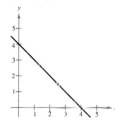

43. $(-\infty, -3], [3, \infty)$

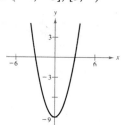

45. $[-1, 1]$

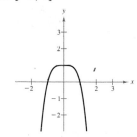

47. $(-\infty, \infty)$

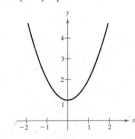

49. $f(x) < 0$ for all x

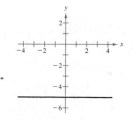

51. (a)

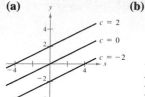

(b)

(c)

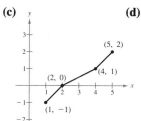

57. $C = 0.65 + 0.42[\![t]\!]$ **59.** 350,000 units

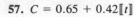

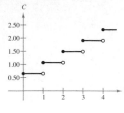

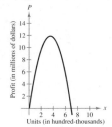

61. $h = (4x - x^2) - 3$ **63.** $h = 4x - 2x^2$
65. $L = (4 - y^2) - (y + 2)$
67. $f(-x) = a_{2n+1}(-x)^{2n+1} + a_{2n-1}(-x)^{2n-1} + \cdots +$
$$a_3(-x)^3 + a_1(-x)$$
$$= -(a_{2n+1}x^{2n+1} + a_{2n-1}x^{2n-1} + \cdots + a_3x^3 +$$
$$a_1x)$$
$$= -f(x)$$

69.

Interval	Intake Pipe	Drain Pipe 1	Drain Pipe 2
[0, 5]	Open	Closed	Closed
[5, 10]	Open	Open	Closed
[10, 20]	Closed	Closed	Closed
[20, 30]	Closed	Closed	Open
[30, 40]	Open	Open	Open
[40, 45]	Open	Closed	Open
[45, 50]	Open	Open	Open
[50, 60]	Open	Open	Closed

53. (a)

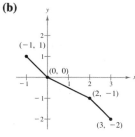

(b)

(c)

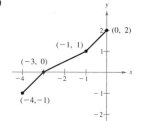

(d)

(e)

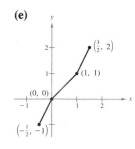

(f)

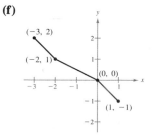

55. (a) $g(x) = (x - 1)^2 + 1$
   (b) $g(x) = -(x + 1)^2$

Section 2.6   *(page 156)*

WARM UP   **1.** $\dfrac{1}{x(1 - x)}$ **2.** $-\dfrac{12}{(x + 3)(x - 3)}$

3. $\dfrac{3x - 2}{x(x - 2)}$ **4.** $\dfrac{4x - 5}{3(x - 5)}$ **5.** $\sqrt{\dfrac{x - 1}{x + 1}}$

6. $\dfrac{x + 1}{x(x + 2)}$ **7.** $5(x - 2)$ **8.** $\dfrac{x + 1}{(x - 2)(x + 3)}$

9. $\dfrac{1 + 5x}{3x - 1}$ **10.** $\dfrac{x + 4}{4x}$

1. (a) $2x$ **(b)** 2 **(c)** $x^2 - 1$ **(d)** $\dfrac{x + 1}{x - 1}, x \neq 1$

3. (a) $x^2 - x + 1$ **(b)** $x^2 + x - 1$ **(c)** $x^2 - x^3$

   (d) $\dfrac{x^2}{1 - x}, x \neq 1$

5. (a) $x^2 + 5 + \sqrt{1 - x}$ **(b)** $x^2 + 5 - \sqrt{1 - x}$

   (c) $(x^2 + 5)\sqrt{1 - x}$ **(d)** $\dfrac{x^2 + 5}{\sqrt{1 - x}}, x < 1$

7. (a) $\dfrac{x + 1}{x^2}$ **(b)** $\dfrac{x - 1}{x^2}$ **(c)** $\dfrac{1}{x^3}$ **(d)** $x, x \neq 0$

9. 9   **11.** 5   **13.** $4t^2 - 2t + 5$ **15.** 0   **17.** 26

19. $\frac{3}{5}$ **21. (a)** $(x - 1)^2$ **(b)** $x^2 - 1$ **(c)** x^4

23. (a) $20 - 3x$ **(b)** $-3x$ **(c)** $9x + 20$

25. (a) $\sqrt{x^2 + 4}$ **(b)** $x + 4$

27. (a) $x - \frac{8}{3}$ **(b)** $x - 8$ **29. (a)** $\sqrt[4]{x}$ **(b)** $\sqrt[4]{x}$

31. (a) $|x + 6|$ **(b)** $|x| + 6$

33. (a) 3   **(b)** 0   **35. (a)** 0   **(b)** 4

37. $f(x) = x^2$, $g(x) = 2x + 1$

39. $f(x) = \sqrt[3]{x}$, $g(x) = x^2 - 4$

41. $f(x) = \dfrac{1}{x}$, $g(x) = x + 2$

43. $f(x) = x^2 + 2x$, $g(x) = x + 4$

45. (a) $x \geq 0$ **(b)** All real numbers

   (c) All real numbers

47. (a) All real numbers except $x = \pm 1$

   (b) All real numbers

   (c) All real numbers except $x = -2, 0$

49. $T = \frac{3}{4}x + \frac{1}{15}x^2$

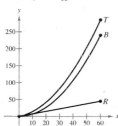

51. $(A \circ r)(t) = 0.36\pi t^2$

   $A \circ r$ represents the area of the circle at time t.

53. $(C \circ x)(t) = 3000t + 750$

   $C \circ x$ represents the cost after t production hours.

Section 2.7   (page 166)

WARM UP   **1.** All real numbers   **2.** $[-1, \infty)$

3. All real numbers except $x = 0, 2$

4. All real numbers except $x = -\frac{5}{3}$ **5.** x **6.** x

7. x **8.** x **9.** $x = \frac{3}{2}y + 3$ **10.** $x = \dfrac{y^3}{2} + 2$

1. $f^{-1}(x) = \frac{1}{8}x$ **3.** $f^{-1}(x) = x - 10$

5. $f^{-1}(x) = x^3$

7. (a) $f(g(x)) = f\left(\dfrac{x}{2}\right) = 2\left(\dfrac{x}{2}\right) = x$ **(b)**

   $g(f(x)) = g(2x) = \dfrac{(2x)}{2} = x$

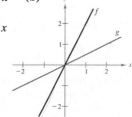

9. (a) $f(g(x)) = f\left(\dfrac{x - 1}{5}\right) = 5\left(\dfrac{x - 1}{5}\right) + 1 = x$

   $g(f(x)) = g(5x + 1) = \dfrac{(5x + 1) - 1}{5} = x$

(b)

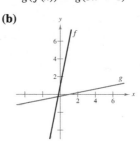

11. (a) $f(g(x)) = f(\sqrt[3]{x}) = (\sqrt[3]{x})^3 = x$

   $g(f(x)) = g(x^3) = \sqrt[3]{x^3} = x$

(b)

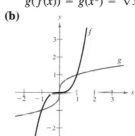

13. (a) $f(g(x)) = f(x^2 + 4)$, $x \geq 0$

   $= \sqrt{(x^2 + 4) - 4} = x$

   $g(f(x)) = g(\sqrt{x - 4})$

   $= (\sqrt{x - 4})^2 + 4 = x$

(b)

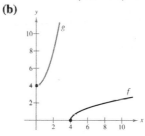

15. (a) $f(g(x)) = f(\sqrt[3]{1 - x})$

   $= 1 - (\sqrt[3]{1 - x})^3 = x$

   $g(f(x)) = g(1 - x^3)$

   $= \sqrt[3]{1 - (1 - x^3)} = x$

(b)

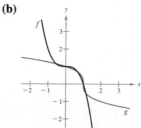

17. One-to-one   **19.** Not one-to-one   **21.** One-to-one
23. Not one-to-one   **25.** Not one-to-one

27. $f^{-1}(x) = \dfrac{x+3}{2}$ **29.** $f^{-1}(x) = \sqrt[5]{x}$

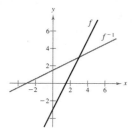 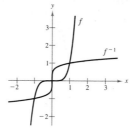

31. $f^{-1}(x) = x^2,\ x \ge 0$

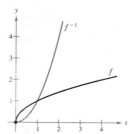

33. $f^{-1}(x) = \sqrt{4 - x^2},\ 0 \le x \le 2$

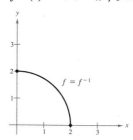

35. $f^{-1}(x) = x^3 + 1$

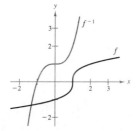

37. Not one-to-one   **39.** $g^{-1}(x) = 8x$
41. Not one-to-one   **43.** $f^{-1}(x) = \sqrt{x} - 3,\ x \ge 0$
45. $h^{-1}(x) = \dfrac{1}{x}$ **47.** $f^{-1}(x) = \dfrac{x^2 - 3}{2},\ x \ge 0$
49. Not one-to-one   **51.** $f^{-1}(x) = -\sqrt{25 - x},\ x \le 25$

53. $f^{-1}(x) = \sqrt{x} + 3,\ x \ge 0$ **55.** $f^{-1}(x) = x - 3,\ x \ge 0$

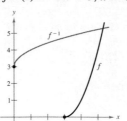 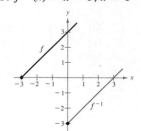

57.

x	0	1	2	3	4
$f^{-1}(x)$	-2	0	1	2	4

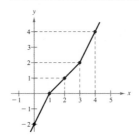

59. 32   **61.** 600   **63.** $2\sqrt[3]{x} + 3$

65. (a) $y = \dfrac{5\sqrt{6}}{3}\sqrt{2x - 509}$

     y: Percentage load; x: Exhaust temperature

     (b)

67. False   **69.** True

Section 2.8   (*page 174*)

WARM UP   **1.** $\frac{1}{3}$ **2.** $\frac{9}{16}$ **3.** $\frac{128}{3}$ **4.** 75   **5.** $\frac{275}{27}$
6. $\frac{105}{128}$ **7.** 27   **8.** $\frac{2}{9}$ **9.** $\frac{28}{13}$ **10.** 157.5

1. $A = kr^2$ **3.** $y = \dfrac{k}{x^2}$ **5.** $z = k\sqrt[3]{u}$ **7.** $z = kuv$

9. $F = \dfrac{kg}{r^2}$ **11.** $P = \dfrac{k}{V}$ **13.** $F = \dfrac{km_1 m_2}{r^2}$

15. The area of a triangle is jointly proportional to the magnitude of the base and the height.

17. The volume of a sphere varies directly as the cube of its radius.

19. Average speed is directly proportional to the distance and inversely proportional to the time.

21. $y = \frac{5}{2}x$ **23.** $A = \pi r^2$ **25.** $y = \dfrac{75}{x}$

27. $h = \dfrac{12}{t^3}$ **29.** $z = 2xy$ **31.** $F = 14rs^3$

33. $z = \dfrac{2x^2}{3y}$ **35.** $S = \dfrac{4L}{3(L-S)}$ **37. (a)** 2 in.

(b) 15 lb   **39.** 39.47 lb   **41.** 0.61 mph   **43.** 506 ft

45. 400 ft   **47.** No. The largest size is the best buy.

49. The illumination is one-fourth the original.

51. The velocity is increased by 1/3.

53.

x	2	4	6	8	10
$y = kx^2$	4	16	36	64	100

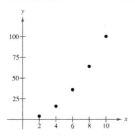

55.

x	2	4	6	8	10
$y = kx^2$	2	8	18	32	50

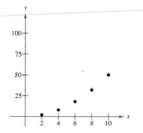

57.

x	2	4	6	8	10
$y = k/x^2$	$\frac{1}{2}$	$\frac{1}{8}$	$\frac{1}{18}$	$\frac{1}{32}$	$\frac{1}{50}$

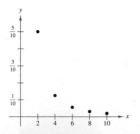

59.

x	2	4	6	8	10
$y = k/x^2$	$\frac{5}{2}$	$\frac{5}{8}$	$\frac{5}{18}$	$\frac{5}{32}$	$\frac{1}{10}$

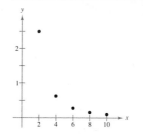

Chapter 2   Review Exercises   *(page 176)*

1. (a) 10   **(b)** $(0, 5)$ **(c)** $x = 0$

(d) $x^2 + (y - 5)^2 = 25$ **3. (a)** 13   **(b)** $\left(8, \frac{7}{2}\right)$

(c) $5x - 12y + 2 = 0$ **(d)** $(x - 8)^2 + \left(y - \frac{7}{2}\right)^2 = \frac{169}{4}$

5. (a) $\sqrt{53}$ **(b)** $\left(\frac{5}{2}, 1\right)$ **(c)** $2x - 7y + 2 = 0$

(d) $\left(x - \frac{5}{2}\right)^2 + (y - 1)^2 = \frac{53}{4}$ **7.** 725,000   **9.** $t = \frac{7}{3}$

11. $t = 3$

13. $d_1 = \sqrt{50}$ **15.** $d_1 = \sqrt{185}$
$d_2 = \sqrt{10}$ $d_2 = \sqrt{185}$
$d_3 = \sqrt{50}$ $d_3 = \sqrt{370}$
$d_4 = \sqrt{10}$ $d_1^2 + d_2^2 = d_3^2$
$d_1 = d_3$ and $d_2 = d_4$

17. Intercept: $(0, 0)$
Symmetry: x-axis

19. Intercepts: $(0, 0)$, $(-2\sqrt{2}, 0)$, $(2\sqrt{2}, 0)$
Symmetry: y-axis

21. Intercepts: $(0, 0)$, $(-2, 0)$, $(2, 0)$
Symmetry: Origin

23. Intercepts: $(0, 0)$, $(3, 0)$
No symmetry

25. Intercept: $(0, 0)$
Symmetry: x-axis

27. Center: $(6, 4)$ **29.** Center: $\left(\frac{1}{2}, 5\right)$
Radius: 3   Radius: $\frac{3}{2}$

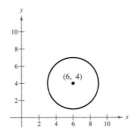

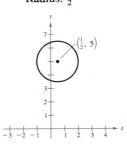

31.

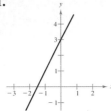

33.

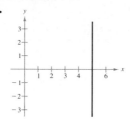

35.

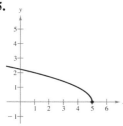

37.

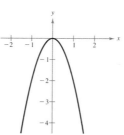

39.

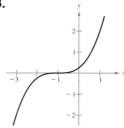

41.

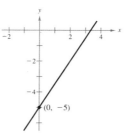

43.

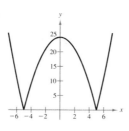

45.

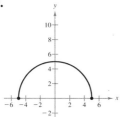

$3x - 2y - 10 = 0$

47.

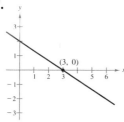

$2x + 3y - 6 = 0$

49. (a) $5x - 4y - 23 = 0$ **(b)** $4x + 5y - 2 = 0$

51. \$210,000   **53. (a)** 5   **(b)** 17   **(c)** $t^4 + 1$
(d) $-x^2 - 1$ **55. (a)** -14 **(b)** $-5x^2 - 30x - 39$
(c) -30 **(d)** $-10x - 5\Delta x$ **57.** $[-5, 5]$
59. All real numbers except $s = 3$
61. All real numbers except $x = -2, 3$
63. (a) $f^{-1}(x) = 2x + 6$
(b)

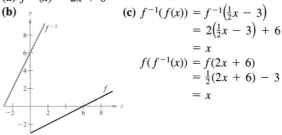

(c) $f^{-1}(f(x)) = f^{-1}\left(\frac{1}{2}x - 3\right)$
$= 2\left(\frac{1}{2}x - 3\right) + 6$
$= x$
$f(f^{-1}(x)) = f(2x + 6)$
$= \frac{1}{2}(2x + 6) - 3$
$= x$

65. (a) $f^{-1}(x) = x^2 - 1,\ x \ge 0$
(b)

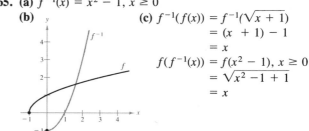

(c) $f^{-1}(f(x)) = f^{-1}(\sqrt{x + 1})$
$= (x + 1) - 1$
$= x$
$f(f^{-1}(x)) = f(x^2 - 1),\ x \ge 0$
$= \sqrt{x^2 - 1 + 1}$
$= x$

67. (a) $f^{-1}(x) = \sqrt{x + 5},\ x \ge -5$
(b)

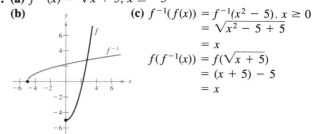

(c) $f^{-1}(f(x)) = f^{-1}(x^2 - 5),\ x \ge 0$
$= \sqrt{x^2 - 5 + 5}$
$= x$
$f(f^{-1}(x)) = f(\sqrt{x + 5})$
$= (x + 5) - 5$
$= x$

69. $x \ge 4,\ f^{-1}(x) = \sqrt{\dfrac{x}{2}} + 4,\ x \ge 0$

71. $x \ge 2,\ f^{-1}(x) = \sqrt{x^2 + 4},\ x \ge 0$ **73.** -7
75. 5   **77.** 23   **79.** 9   **81. (a)** 16 ft/sec
(b) 1.5 sec   **(c)** -16 ft/sec
83. $A = x(12 - x),\ (0, 6]$

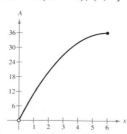

85. $F = \frac{1}{3}x\sqrt{y}$ **87.** $z = \dfrac{32x^2}{25y}$ **89.** 2,438.7 kilowatts

CHAPTER 3

Section 3.1   *(page 188)*

WARM UP   **1.** $\frac{1}{2}, -6$ **2.** $-\frac{3}{5}, 3$ **3.** $\frac{3}{2}, -1$

4. -10 **5.** $3 \pm \sqrt{5}$ **6.** $-2 \pm \sqrt{3}$ **7.** $4 \pm \dfrac{\sqrt{14}}{2}$

8. $-5 \pm \dfrac{\sqrt{3}}{3}$ **9.** $-\dfrac{3}{2} \pm \dfrac{\sqrt{3}}{2}i$ **10.** $-\dfrac{3}{2} \pm \dfrac{\sqrt{21}}{2}$

1. f   **3.** c   **5.** b   **7.** $f(x) = (x - 2)^2$
9. $f(x) = -(x + 2)^2 + 4$ **11.** $f(x) = -2(x + 3)^2 + 3$
13. Vertex: $(0, -5)$, Intercepts: $(\pm\sqrt{5}, 0), (0, -5)$

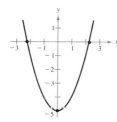

15. Vertex: $(0, 16)$, Intercepts: $(\pm 4, 0), (0, 16)$

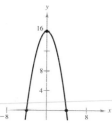

17. Vertex: $(-5, -6)$, Intercepts: $(-5 \pm \sqrt{6}, 0), (0, 19)$

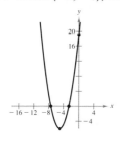

19. Vertex: $(4, 0)$, Intercepts: $(4, 0), (0, 16)$

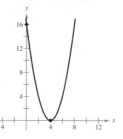

21. Vertex: $(-1, 4)$, Intercepts: $(1, 0), (-3, 0), (0, 3)$

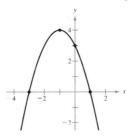

23. Vertex: $\left(\frac{1}{2}, 1\right)$, Intercept: $\left(0, \frac{5}{4}\right)$

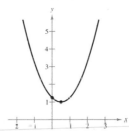

25. Vertex: $(1, 6)$, Intercepts: $(1 \pm \sqrt{6}, 0), (0, 5)$

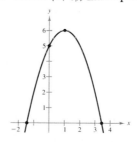

27. Vertex: $\left(\frac{1}{2}, 20\right)$, Intercept: $(0, 21)$

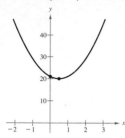

29. Vertex: $(4, -1)$, Intercepts: $\left(4 \pm \dfrac{\sqrt{2}}{2}, 0\right)$, $(0, 31)$

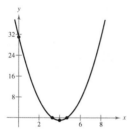

31. $f(x) = -\frac{1}{2}(x - 3)^2 + 4$

33. $f(x) = \frac{3}{4}(x - 5)^2 + 12$

35. $f(x) = x^2 - 2x - 3$
  $g(x) = -x^2 + 2x + 3$
  (The answer is not unique.)

37. $f(x) = x^2 - 10x$
  $g(x) = -x^2 + 10x$
  (The answer is not unique.)

39. $f(x) = 2x^2 + 7x + 3$
  $g(x) = -2x^2 - 7x - 3$
  (The answer is not unique.)

41. 55, 55   **43.** 12, 6

45. (a) $A = x(50 - x), 0 < x < 50$
  (b)

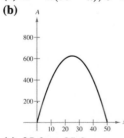

  (c) 25 ft × 25 ft

47. $x = 25$ ft
  $y = 33\frac{1}{3}$ ft

49. 4500 units

51. 20 fixtures

53. (a)

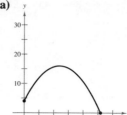

  (b) 4 ft
  (c) 16 ft
  (d) $12 + 8\sqrt{3} \approx 25.9$ ft

55. (a)

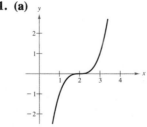

  (b) 166.7 board feet
  (c) 26.6 in.

57. $a\left(x + \dfrac{b}{2a}\right)^2 + \dfrac{4ac - b^2}{4a}$
  Vertex: $\left(-\dfrac{b}{2a}, -\dfrac{b^2 - 4ac}{4a}\right)$

59. $x = \dfrac{-b \pm \sqrt{b^2 - 4ac}}{2a}$ The average of these zeros is
  $x = -\dfrac{b}{2a}$.

Section 3.2   *(page 201)*

WARM UP   **1.** $(3x - 2)(4x + 5)$ **2.** $x(5x - 6)^2$
3. $z^2(12z + 5)(z + 1)$ **4.** $(y + 5)(y^2 - 5y + 25)$
5. $(x + 3)(x + 2)(x - 2)$ **6.** $(x + 2)(x^2 + 3)$
7. No real solution   **8.** $3 \pm \sqrt{5}$ **9.** $-\frac{1}{2} \pm \sqrt{3}$
10. ± 3

1. (a)

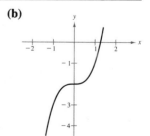

  (b)

(c) *y*

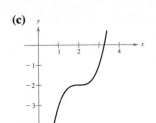

(d)

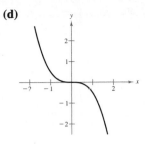

59.

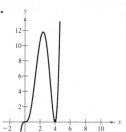

61.

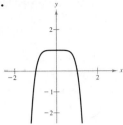

3. e **5.** b **7.** a **9.** d
11. Rises to the left. Rises to the right.
13. Falls to the left. Falls to the right.
15. Falls to the left. Rises to the right.
17. Rises to the left. Falls to the right.
19. Falls to the left. Falls to the right. **21.** ± 5
23. 3 **25.** 1, -2 **27.** $2 \pm \sqrt{3}$ **29.** 2, 0
31. ± 1 **33.** $\pm \sqrt{5}$ **35.** No real zeros
37. $f(x) = x^2 - 10x$ **39.** $f(x) = x^2 + 4x - 12$
41. $f(x) = x^3 + 5x^2 + 6x$
43. $f(x) = x^4 - 4x^3 - 9x^2 + 36x$
45. $f(x) = x^2 - 2x - 2$

47.

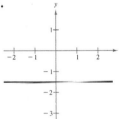

49.

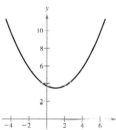

51.

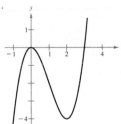

53.

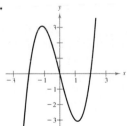

55.

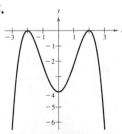

57.

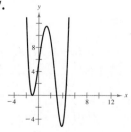

63. 0.7 **65.** 3.3
67. (b) Domain: $0 < x < 6$
(c) *V*

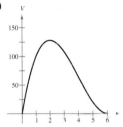

Maximum when $x = 2$
69. (200, 320)

Section 3.3 *(page 213)*

WARM UP **1.** $x^3 - x^2 + 2x + 3$
2. $2x^3 + 4x^2 - 6x - 4$
3. $x^4 - 2x^3 + 4x^2 - 2x - 7$
4. $2x^4 + 12x^3 - 3x^2 - 18x - 5$ **5.** $(x - 3)(x - 1)$
6. $2x(2x - 3)(x - 1)$ **7.** $x^3 - 7x^2 + 12x$
8. $x^2 + 5x - 6$ **9.** $x^3 + x^2 - 7x - 3$
10. $x^4 - 3x^3 - 5x^2 + 9x - 2$

1. $2x + 4$ **3.** $x^2 - 3x + 1$ **5.** $x^3 + 3x^2 - 1$
7. $7 - \dfrac{11}{x + 2}$ **9.** $3x + 5$ $\dfrac{2x - 3}{2x^2 + 1}$
11. $x^2 + 2x + 4 + \dfrac{2x - 11}{x^2 - 2x + 3}$
13. $2x - \dfrac{17x - 5}{x^2 - 2x + 1}$ **15.** $3x^2 - 2x + 5$
17. $4x^2 - 9$ **19.** $-x^2 + 10x - 25$
21. $5x^2 + 14x + 56 + \dfrac{232}{x - 4}$
23. $10x^3 + 10x^2 + 60x + 360 + \dfrac{1360}{x - 6}$
25. $x^2 - 8x + 64$
27. $-3x^3 - 6x^2 - 12x - 24 - \dfrac{48}{x - 2}$
29. $-x^2 + 3x - 6 + \dfrac{11}{x + 1}$ **31.** $4x^2 + 14x - 30$

33. $(x - 2)(x + 3)(x - 1)$ **35.** $(2x - 1)(x - 5)(x - 2)$
37. $(x + \sqrt{3})(x - \sqrt{3})(x + 2)$
39. $(x - 1)(x - 1 - \sqrt{3})(x - 1 + \sqrt{3})$
41. $f(x) = (x - 4)(x^2 + 3x - 2) + 3, f(4) = 3$
43. $f(x) = (x - \sqrt{2})[x^2 + (3 + \sqrt{2})x + 3\sqrt{2}] - 8,$
    $f(\sqrt{2}) = -8$
45. **(a)** 1   **(b)** 4   **(c)** 4   **(d)** 1954   **47.** **(a)** 97
(b) $-\frac{5}{3}$ **(c)** 17   **(d)** -199 **49.** **(a)** 72   **(b)** 0
(c) 37.648   **(d)** 30   **51.** $2x^2 - x - 1$
53. $x^2 + 2x - 3$ **55.** $x^2 + 3x$ **57.** 3300 rpm
59. (Answers are not unique.)
    (a) $f(x) = (x - 2)x^2 + 5 = x^3 - 2x^2 + 5$
    (b) $f(x) = -(x + 3)x^2 + 1 = -x^3 - 3x^2 + 1$

Section 3.4   *(page 223)*

WARM UP   **1.** $f(x) = 3x^3 - 8x^2 - 5x + 6$
2. $f(x) = 4x^4 - 3x^3 - 16x^2 + 12x$
3. $x^4 - 3x^3 + 5 + \dfrac{3}{x + 3}$ **4.** $3x^3 + 15x^2 - 9 - \dfrac{2}{x + \frac{2}{3}}$
5. $\frac{1}{2}, -3 \pm \sqrt{5}$ **6.** $10, -\frac{2}{3}, -\frac{3}{2}$ **7.** $-\frac{3}{4}, 2 \pm \sqrt{2}$
8. $\frac{2}{5}, -\frac{7}{2}, -2$ **9.** $\pm\sqrt{2}, \pm 1$ **10.** $\pm 2, \pm\sqrt{3}$

1. One negative zero   **3.** No real zeros
5. One positive zero   **7.** One or three positive zeros
9. Two or no positive zeros   **11.** $\pm 1, \pm 2, \pm 4$
13. $\pm 1, \pm 3, \pm\frac{1}{2}, \pm\frac{3}{2}, \pm\frac{1}{4}, \pm\frac{3}{4}$
15. $\pm 1, \pm 2, \pm 4, \pm 8, \pm\frac{1}{2}$ **17.** **(a)** Upper bound
(b) Lower bound   **(c)** Neither   **19.** **(a)** Neither
(b) Lower bound   **(c)** Upper bound   **21.** 1, 2, 3
23. $1, -1, 4$ **25.** $-1, -10$ **27.** 1, 2   **29.** $\frac{1}{2}, -1$
31. $1, -\frac{1}{2}$ **33.** $-\frac{3}{4}$ **35.** $\pm 1, \pm\sqrt{2}$ **37.** $-1, 2$
39. $0, -1, -3, 4$ **41.** $-2, 4, -\frac{1}{2}$
43. $0, 3, 4, \pm\sqrt{2}$
45. **(a)** $\pm 1, \pm 3, \pm\frac{1}{2}, \pm\frac{3}{2}, \pm\frac{1}{4}, \pm\frac{3}{4}, \pm\frac{1}{8}, \pm\frac{3}{8}, \pm\frac{1}{16}, \pm\frac{3}{16},$
    $\pm\frac{1}{32}, \pm\frac{3}{32}$
   (b)

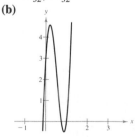

   (c) $1, \frac{3}{4}, -\frac{1}{8}$

47. **(a)** $\pm 1, \pm 2, \pm 3, \pm 6, \pm 9, \pm\frac{1}{2}, \pm\frac{3}{2}, \pm\frac{9}{2}, \pm\frac{1}{4}, \pm\frac{3}{4},$
    $\pm\frac{9}{4}, \pm 18$
   (b)

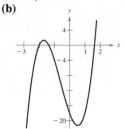

   (c) $-2, \dfrac{1}{8} \pm \dfrac{\sqrt{145}}{8}$
49. $\pm 2, \pm\frac{3}{2}$ **51.** $\pm 1, \frac{1}{4}$ **53.** d   **55.** b
57. 3.77 in. $\times$ 7.77 in. $\times$ 0.614 in.
59. 18 in. $\times$ 18 in. $\times$ 36 in.

Section 3.5   *(page 231)*

WARM UP   **1.** $2\sqrt{3}$ **2.** $10\sqrt{5}$ **3.** $\sqrt{5}$
4. $-6\sqrt{3}$ **5.** 12   **6.** 48   **7.** $\dfrac{\sqrt{3}}{3}$ **8.** $\sqrt{2}$
9. $\dfrac{1}{2} \pm \dfrac{\sqrt{5}}{2}$ **10.** $-1 \pm \sqrt{2}$

1. $a = -10, b = 6$ **3.** $a = 6, b = 5$ **5.** $4 + 3i$
7. $2 - 3\sqrt{3}i$ **9.** $5\sqrt{3}i$ **11.** $-1 - 6i$ **13.** 8
15. $0.3i$ **17.** $11 - i$ **19.** 4   **21.** $3 - 3\sqrt{2}i$
23. $-14 + 20i$ **25.** $\frac{1}{6} + \frac{7}{6}i$ **27.** $5 - 3i, 34$
29. $-2 + \sqrt{5}i, 9$ **31.** $-20i, 400$ **33.** $\sqrt{8}, 8$
35. $-2\sqrt{3}$ **37.** -10 **39.** $5 + i$ **41.** $12 + 30i$
43. 24   **45.** $-9 + 40i$ **47.** -10 **49.** $\frac{16}{41} + \frac{20}{41}i$
51. $\frac{3}{5} + \frac{4}{5}i$ **53.** $-7 - 6i$ **55.** $-\frac{9}{1681} + \frac{40}{1681}i$
57. $1 \pm i$ **59.** $-2 \pm \frac{1}{2}i$ **61.** $-\frac{3}{2}, -\frac{5}{2}$
63. $\dfrac{1}{8} \pm \dfrac{\sqrt{11}}{8}i$ **65.** $i, -1, -i, 1, i, -1, -i, 1, i,$
   $-1, -i, 1, i, -1, -i, 1$ **67.** $-1 + 6i$ **69.** $-5i$
71. $-375\sqrt{3}i$ **73.** i **75.** 8, 8, 8

Section 3.6   *(page 240)*

WARM UP   **1.** $4 - \sqrt{29}i, 4 + \sqrt{29}i$
2. $-5 - 12i, -5 + 12i$ **3.** $-1 + 4\sqrt{2}i, -1 - 4\sqrt{2}i$
4. $6 + \frac{1}{2}i, 6 - \frac{1}{2}i$ **5.** $-13 + 9i$ **6.** $12 + 16i$
7. $26 + 22i$ **8.** 29   **9.** i **10.** $-9 + 46i$

1. $\pm 5i, (x + 5i)(x - 5i)$
3. $2 \pm \sqrt{3}, (x - 2 - \sqrt{3})(x - 2 + \sqrt{3})$
5. $\pm 3, \pm 3i, (x + 3)(x - 3)(x + 3i)(x - 3i)$

7. $1 \pm i$, $(z - 1 + i)(z - 1 - i)$

9. $2, 2 \pm i$, $(x - 2)(x - 2 + i)(x - 2 - i)$

11. $-5, 4 \pm 3i$, $(t + 5)(t - 4 + 3i)(t - 4 - 3i)$

13. $-10, -7 \pm 5i$, $(x + 10)(x + 7 - 5i)(x + 7 + 5i)$

15. $-\frac{3}{4}, 1 \pm \frac{1}{2}i$, $(4x + 3)(2x - 2 + i)(2x - 2 - i)$

17. $-2, 1 \pm \sqrt{2}i$, $(x + 2)(x - 1 + \sqrt{2}i)(x - 1 - \sqrt{2}i)$

19. $-\frac{1}{5}, 1 \pm \sqrt{5}i$, $(5x + 1)(x - 1 + \sqrt{5}i)(x - 1 - \sqrt{5}i)$

21. $2, \pm 2i$, $(x - 2)^2(x + 2i)(x - 2i)$

23. $\pm i, \pm 3i$, $(x + i)(x - i)(x + 3i)(x - 3i)$

25. $-2, -\frac{1}{2}, \pm i$, $(x + 2)(2x + 1)(x + i)(x - i)$

27. $x^3 - x^2 + 25x - 25$ **29.** $x^3 - 10x^2 + 33x - 34$

31. $x^4 + 37x^2 + 36$ **33.** $x^4 + 8x^3 + 9x^2 - 10x + 100$

35. $16x^4 + 36x^3 + 16x^2 + x - 30$

37. (a) $(x^2 + 9)(x^2 - 3)$

(b) $(x^2 + 9)(x + \sqrt{3})(x - \sqrt{3})$

(c) $(x + 3i)(x - 3i)(x + \sqrt{3})(x - \sqrt{3})$

39. (a) $(x^2 - 2x - 2)(x^2 - 2x + 3)$

(b) $(x - 1 + \sqrt{3})(x - 1 - \sqrt{3})(x^2 - 2x + 3)$

(c) $(x - 1 + \sqrt{3})(x - 1 - \sqrt{3})(x - 1 + \sqrt{2}i) \cdot$
$(x - 1 - \sqrt{2}i)$ **41.** $-\frac{3}{2}, \pm 5i$ **43.** $\pm 2i, 1, -\frac{1}{2}$

45. $-3 \pm i, \frac{1}{4}$ **47.** $2, -3 \pm \sqrt{2}i$ **49.** $\frac{3}{4}, \frac{1}{2} \pm \frac{\sqrt{5}}{2}i$

51. Setting $h = 64$ and solving the resulting equation yields imaginary roots.

53. $x^2 + b$

Section 3.7   *(page 251)*

WARM UP   **1.** $(x - 5)(x + 2)$ **2.** $(x - 5)(x - 2)$

3. $x(x + 1)(x + 3)$ **4.** $(x^2 - 2)(x - 4)$

5.

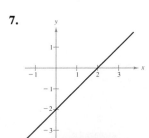

6.

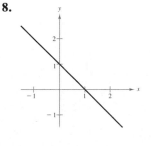

7.

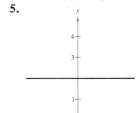

8.

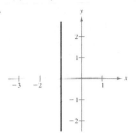

9. $x + 9 + \dfrac{42}{x - 4}$ **10.** $x + 1 + \dfrac{2}{x + 4}$

1. f   **3.** a   **5.** c   **7.** h

9. Domain: All $x \neq 0$
Vertical asymptote: $x = 0$
Horizontal asymptote: $y = 0$

11. Domain: All $x \neq 2$
Vertical asymptote: $x = 2$
Horizontal asymptote: $y = -1$

13. Domain: All $x \neq \pm 1$
Vertical asymptote: $x = \pm 1$
Slant asymptote: $y = x$

15. Domain: All reals
Horizontal asymptote: $y = 3$

17. Domain: All reals

19.

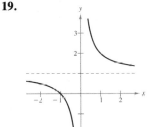

21.

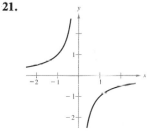

23.

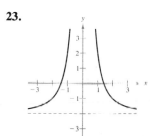

25.

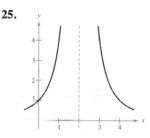

27.

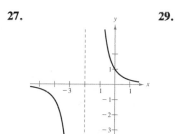

29.

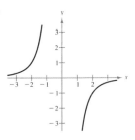

31.

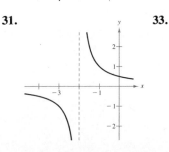

33.

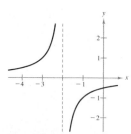

35.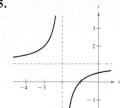

37.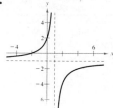

39.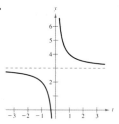

41.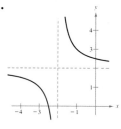

43.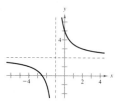

45.

47.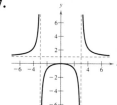

49.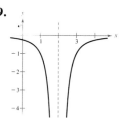

51.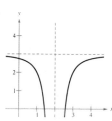

53.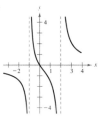

55.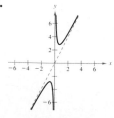

57.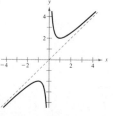

59.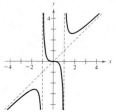

61.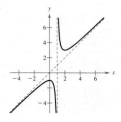

63.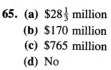

65. (a) $28\frac{1}{3}$ million
   (b) \$170 million
   (c) \$765 million
   (d) No

67. (a) 167, 250, 400
   (b) 750

69.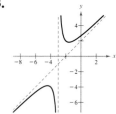

$150.25, $15.25, $1.75

71. Minimum area when $a \approx 4$

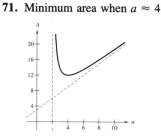

Section 3.8   *(page 264)*

WARM UP   **1.** $\dfrac{5x + 2}{x(x + 1)}$ **2.** $\dfrac{2(4x + 3)}{x(x + 2)}$

3. $\dfrac{11x - 1}{(x - 2)(2x - 1)}$ **4.** $-\dfrac{3x + 1}{(x + 5)(x + 12)}$

5. $\dfrac{x^2 - 3x - 5}{(x - 3)^3}$ **6.** $-\dfrac{5x + 6}{(x + 2)^2}$ **7.** $-\dfrac{x + 9}{x(x^2 + 3)}$

8. $\dfrac{4x^2 + 5x + 31}{(x + 1)(x^2 + 5)}$ **9.** $\dfrac{x(3x + 1)}{(x^2 + 1)^2}$ **10.** $\dfrac{x^3 + x^2 + 1}{(x^2 + x + 1)^2}$

1. $\dfrac{1}{2}\left(\dfrac{1}{x - 1} - \dfrac{1}{x + 1}\right)$ **3.** $\dfrac{1}{x} - \dfrac{1}{x + 1}$

5. $\dfrac{1}{x} - \dfrac{2}{2x + 1}$ **7.** $\dfrac{1}{x - 1} - \dfrac{1}{x + 2}$

9. $\dfrac{3}{2x - 1} - \dfrac{2}{x + 1}$ **11.** $-\dfrac{3}{x} - \dfrac{1}{x + 2} + \dfrac{5}{x - 2}$

13. $\dfrac{3}{x} - \dfrac{1}{x^2} + \dfrac{1}{x + 1}$ **15.** $\dfrac{2}{x} - \dfrac{1}{x^2} - \dfrac{2}{x + 1}$

17. $\dfrac{3}{x-3} + \dfrac{9}{(x-3)^2}$ **19.** $-\dfrac{1}{x} + \dfrac{2x}{x^2+1}$

21. $\dfrac{1}{3(x^2+2)} - \dfrac{1}{6(x+2)} + \dfrac{1}{6(x-2)}$

23. $\dfrac{1}{8(2x+1)} + \dfrac{1}{8(2x-1)} - \dfrac{x}{2(4x^2+1)}$

25. $\dfrac{1}{x^2+2} + \dfrac{x}{(x^2+2)^2}$ **27.** $\dfrac{1}{x+1} + \dfrac{2}{x^2-2x+3}$

29. $2x + \dfrac{1}{2}\left(\dfrac{3}{x-4} - \dfrac{1}{x+2}\right)$

31. $x + 3 + \dfrac{6}{x-1} + \dfrac{4}{(x-1)^2} + \dfrac{1}{(x-1)^3}$

33. $\dfrac{1}{2a}\left(\dfrac{1}{a+x} + \dfrac{1}{a-x}\right)$ **35.** $\dfrac{1}{L}\left(\dfrac{1}{y} + \dfrac{1}{L-y}\right)$

Chapter 3   Review Exercises   *(page 265)*

1.

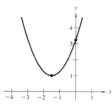

Vertex: $\left(-\frac{3}{2}, 1\right)$
Intercept: $\left(0, \frac{13}{4}\right)$

3.

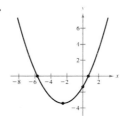

Vertex: $\left(-\dfrac{5}{2}, -\dfrac{41}{12}\right)$

Intercepts: $\left(0, -\dfrac{4}{3}\right)$, $\left(\dfrac{-5 \pm \sqrt{41}}{2}, 0\right)$

5. $f(x) = (x-1)^2 - 4$ **7.** Minimum: $(1, -1)$
9. Maximum: $(3, 9)$ **11.** Maximum: $(1, 3)$
13. Minimum: $\left(-\frac{5}{2}, -\frac{41}{4}\right)$ **15.** $\left(3, \frac{3}{2}\right)$ **17.** 4500 units
19. \$1029   **25.**
21. Falls to the left.
  Falls to the right.
23. Rises to the left.
  Rises to the right.

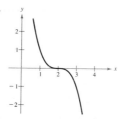

27.

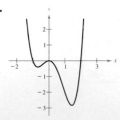

29.

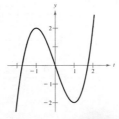

31.

33. $8x + 5 + \dfrac{2}{3x-2}$

35. $x^2 - x + 1$ **37.** $x^2 - 2$

39. $x^2 - 3x + 2 - \dfrac{1}{x^2+2}$ **41.** $-\sqrt{2}i$

43. $40 + 65i$ **45.** $-4 - 46i$ **47.** $1 - 6i$ **49.** $\frac{4}{3}i$

51. $0.25x^3 - 3.5x^2 - 7x - 14 - \dfrac{28}{x-2}$

53. $6x^3 - 27x$ **55.** $2x^2 - (3-4i)x + (1-2i)$
57. (a) No   (b) Yes   (c) Yes   (d) No
59. (a) No   (b) Yes   (c) Yes   (d) No
61. (a) 580   (b) 0   **63.** (a) -421 (b) 96
65. $f(x) = 6x^4 + 13x^3 + 7x^2 - x - 1$
67. $f(x) = 3x^4 - 14x^3 + 17x^2 - 42x + 24$ **69.** $1, \frac{3}{4}$
71. $\frac{5}{6}, \pm 2i$ **73.** $-1, \frac{3}{2}, 3, \frac{2}{3}$
75.

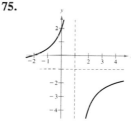

77.

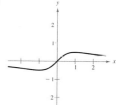

79.

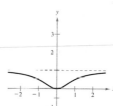

81.

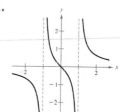

83.

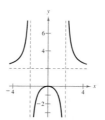

85. (a) \$176 million   (b) \$528 million
  (c) \$1584 million   (d) No   **87.** 0.35
89. $\dfrac{3}{x+2} - \dfrac{4}{x+4}$ **91.** $\dfrac{1}{2}\left(\dfrac{3}{x-1} - \dfrac{x-3}{x^2+1}\right)$
93. $\dfrac{3x}{x^2+1} + \dfrac{x}{(x^2+1)^2}$

Cumulative Test for Chapters 1–3 *(page 269)*

1. $\dfrac{4x^3}{15y^5}$ **3.** $x(1 - 6x)(1 + x)$ **5.** $\dfrac{1}{2\sqrt{x}(2x + 1)}$

7. $4, \frac{5}{2}$ **9.** 1, 2 **11. (a)** $3\sqrt{5}$

(b) $x + 2y - 5 = 0$

13.

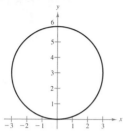

15. $(f \circ g)(x) = \sqrt{x^2 + 3}$ **17.** 1.80 gal

19. $3x^2 + 6x + 7 + \dfrac{18}{x - 2}$ **21.** 1.20

CHAPTER 4

Section 4.1 *(page 280)*

WARM UP **1.** 5^x **2.** 3^{2x} **3.** 4^{3x} **4.** 10^x
5. 4^{2x} **6.** 4^{10x} **7.** $\left(\frac{3}{2}\right)^x$ **8.** 4^{3x} **9.** 2^{-x}
10. $16^{x/4}$

1. 946.852 **3.** 747.258 **5.** 5.256
7. 472,369.379 **9.** 673.639 **11.** 7.389
13. 0.472 **15.** g **17.** b **19.** d **21.** f
23. **25.**

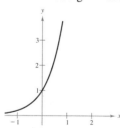

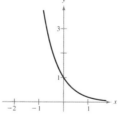

27. **29.**

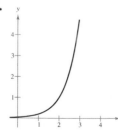

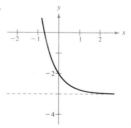

31.

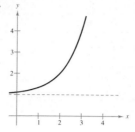

33.

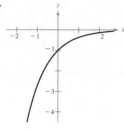

35.

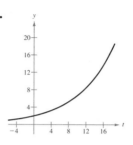

37.

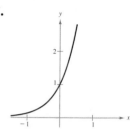

39.

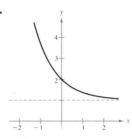

41.

n	1	2	4
A	$7,764.62	$8,017.84	$8,155.09

n	12	365	Continuous compounding
A	$8,250.97	$8,298.66	$8,300.29

43.

n	1	2	4
A	$24,115.73	$25,714.29	$26,602.23

n	12	365	Continuous compounding
A	$27,231.38	$27,547.07	$27,557.94

45.

t	1	10	20
P	$91,393.12	$40,656.97	$16,529.89

t	30	40	50
P	$6,720.55	$2,732.37	$1,110.90

47.

t	1	10	20
P	\$90,521.24	\$36,940.70	\$13,646.15

t	30	40	50
P	\$5,040.98	\$1,862.17	\$687.90

49. \$222,822.57   **51.** (a) \$472.70   (b) \$298.29

53. (a) 100   (b) 300   (c) 900

55. (a) 25 units   (b) 16.297 units

(c)

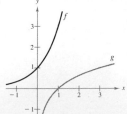

57. 80%

59. \$11,250

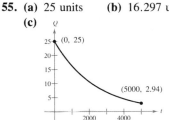

61. (a) $f(u + v) = a^{u+v} = a^u a^v = f(u) \cdot f(v)$

(b) $f(2x) = a^{2x} = (a^x)^2 = [f(x)]^2$

Section 4.2   (page 291)

WARM UP   **1.** 3   **2.** 0   **3.** −1   **4.** 1

5. 7.389   **6.** 0.368

7. Graph is shifted 2 units to the left.

8. Graph is reflected about the x-axis.

9. Graph is shifted down 1 unit.

10. Graph is reflected about the y-axis.

1. 4   **3.** −2   **5.** $\frac{1}{2}$ **7.** 0   **9.** −2   **11.** 3

13. −2   **15.** 2   **17.** $\log_5 125 = 3$ **19.** $\log_{81} 3 = \frac{1}{4}$

21. $\log_6 \frac{1}{36} = -2$ **23.** $\ln 20.0855 \ldots = 3$ **25.** $\ln 4 = x$

27. 2.538   **29.** −0.319   **31.** 2.913   **33.** 1.005

35.

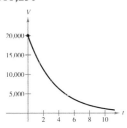

37.

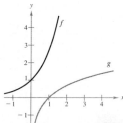

39. d   **41.** a   **43.** f

45. Domain: $(0, \infty)$

Vertical asymptote: $x = 0$

Intercept: $(1, 0)$

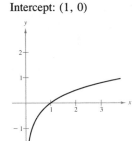

47. Domain: $(3, \infty)$

Vertical asymptote: $x = 3$

Intercept: $(4, 0)$

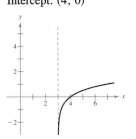

49. Domain: $(0, \infty)$

Vertical asymptote: $x = 0$

Intercept: $(9, 0)$

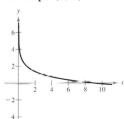

51. Domain: $(0, \infty)$

Vertical asymptote: $x = 0$

Intercept: $(5, 0)$

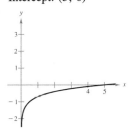

53. Domain: $(2, \infty)$

Vertical asymptote: $x = 2$

Intercept: $(3, 0)$

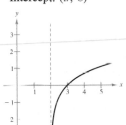

55. Domain: $(-\infty, 0)$

Vertical asymptote: $x = 0$

Intercept: $(-1, 0)$

57. (a) 80   (b) 68.1   (c) 62.3

59.

r	0.005	0.010	0.015	0.020	0.025	0.030
t	138.6 yr	69.3 yr	46.2 yr	34.7 yr	27.7 yr	23.1 yr

61. 17.658 ft^3/min   **63.** 20 yr   **65.** \$280,178.40

67. 21,357.023 ft-lb

69. (a)

x	1	5	10	10^2	10^4	10^6
$f(x)$	0	0.322	0.230	0.046	0.00092	0.0000138

(b) 0

Section 4.3   *(page 299)*

WARM UP   **1.** 2   **2.** -5 **3.** -2 **4.** -3
5. e^5 **6.** $\dfrac{1}{e}$ **7.** e^6 **8.** 1   **9.** x^{-2} **10.** $x^{1/2}$

1. $\dfrac{\log_{10} 5}{\log_{10} 3}$ **3.** $\dfrac{\log_{10} x}{\log_{10} 2}$ **5.** $\dfrac{\ln 5}{\ln 3}$ **7.** $\dfrac{\ln x}{\ln 2}$
9. 1.771   **11.** -2.000 **13.** -0.417 **15.** 2.633
17. $\log_{10} 5 + \log_{10} x$ **19.** $\log_{10} 5 - \log_{10} x$
21. $4 \log_8 x$ **23.** $\frac{1}{2} \ln z$ **25.** $\ln x + \ln y + \ln z$
27. $\frac{1}{2} \ln(a - 1)$ **29.** $\ln z + 2 \ln(z - 1)$
31. $\frac{1}{3} \ln x - \frac{1}{3} \ln y$
35. $2 \log_b x - 2 \log_b y - 3 \log_b z$ **37.** $\ln 2x$
39. $\log_4 \dfrac{z}{y}$ **41.** $\log_2(x + 4)^2$ **43.** $\log_3 \sqrt[3]{5x}$
45. $\ln \dfrac{x}{(x + 1)^3}$ **47.** $\ln \dfrac{x - 2}{x + 2}$ **49.** $\ln \dfrac{x}{(x^2 - 4)^2}$
51. $\ln \sqrt[3]{\dfrac{x(x + 3)^2}{x^2 - 1}}$ **53.** $\ln \dfrac{\sqrt[3]{y(y + 4)^2}}{y - 1}$
55. $\ln \dfrac{9}{\sqrt{x^2 + 1}}$ **57.** 0.9208   **59.** 0.2084
61. 1.6542   **63.** 0.1781   **65.** -0.7124
67. 0.91355   **69.** 2.0367   **71.** 2   **73.** 2.4
75. 4.5   **77.** $\frac{3}{2}$ **79.** $\frac{1}{2} + \frac{1}{2} \log_7 10$
81. $-3 - \log_5 2$ **83.** $6 + \ln 5$
85. $\beta = 10(\log_{10} I + 16)$,   60 db

Section 4.4   *(page 307)*

WARM UP   **1.** $\dfrac{\ln 3}{\ln 2}$ **2.** $1 + \dfrac{2}{\ln 4}$ **3.** $\dfrac{e}{2}$ **4.** $2e$
5. $2 \pm i$ **6.** $\frac{1}{2}, 1$ **7.** $2x$ **8.** $3x$ **9.** $2x$
10. $-x^2$

1. 2   **3.** -2 **5.** 3   **7.** 64   **9.** $\frac{1}{10}$ **11.** x^2
13. $5x + 2$ **15.** x^2 **17.** $\ln 10 \approx 2.303$
19. $\ln \frac{39}{2} \approx 2.970$ **21.** $\ln 15 \approx 2.708$ **23.** 0
25. $\dfrac{\ln 12}{3} \approx 0.828$ **27.** $\ln \frac{5}{3} \approx 0.511$
29. $\frac{2}{3} \ln \frac{962}{3} \approx 3.847$ **31.** $\ln 5 \approx 1.609$
33. $\frac{1}{2} \ln \frac{1}{3} \approx -0.549$ **35.** 0   **37.** $\log_{10} 42 \approx 1.623$
39. $\dfrac{\ln 80}{2 \ln 3} \approx 1.994$ **41.** 2   **43.** $\frac{1}{2} \log_{10} 36 \approx 0.778$
45. $1 + \dfrac{\ln 7}{\ln 5} \approx 2.209$ **47.** $\dfrac{\ln 25 + \ln 3}{\ln 9 - \ln 5} \approx 7.345$
49. $\dfrac{\ln 2}{12 \ln\left(1 + \frac{0.10}{12}\right)} \approx 6.960$ **51.** $e^5 \approx 148.413$

53. $\dfrac{e^{2.4}}{2} \approx 5.512$ **55.** $\frac{1}{4} = 0.250$
57. $e^2 - 2 \approx 5.389$ **59.** $1 + \sqrt{1 + e} \approx 2.928$
61. 103   **63.** $\dfrac{-1 + \sqrt{17}}{2} \approx 1.562$ **65.** 4
67. No solution   **69.** 3   **71.** 8.2 yr   **73.** 12.9 yr
75. (a) 1426 units   **(b)** 1498 units   **77. (a)** 29.3 yr
(b) 39.8 yr   **79.** Males: 69.71 in.;   Females: 64.51 in.

Section 4.5   *(page 316)*

WARM UP

1.   **2.**

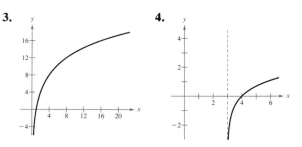

3.   **4.**

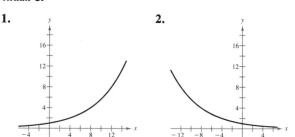

5.   **6.**

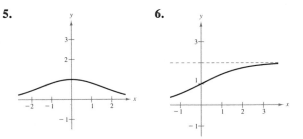

7. $\frac{1}{2} \ln \frac{7}{3} \approx 0.424$ **8.** $\dfrac{\ln(0.001)}{-0.2} \approx 34.539$
9. $\frac{1}{5} e^{7/2} \approx 6.623$ **10.** $\frac{1}{2} e^2 \approx 3.695$

Initial investment	Annual % rate	Effective yield	Time to double	Amount after 10 years
1. $1,000	12%	12.75%	5.78 yr	$3,320.12
3. $750	8.94%	9.35%	7.75 yr	$1,833.67
5. $500	9.5%	9.97%	7.30 yr	$1,292.85
7. $6,392.79	11%	11.63%	6.30 yr	$19,205.00
9. $5,000	8%	8.33%	8.66 yr	$11,127.70

11. $112,087.09   **13. (a)** 6.642 yr   **(b)** 6.330 yr
(c) 6.302 yr   **(d)** 6.301 yr

15.

r	2%	4%	6%	8%	10%	12%
t	54.93	27.47	18.31	13.73	10.99	9.16

Isotope	Half-life (years)	Initial quantity	Amount after 1,000 years	Amount after 10,000 years
17. Ra^{226}	1620	10 g	6.52 g	0.14 g
19. C^{14}	5730	6.70 g	5.95 g	2 g
21. Pu^{230}	24,360	2.16 g	2.1 g	1.63 g

23. $\frac{1}{4} \ln 10 \approx 0.5756$ **25.** $\frac{1}{4} \ln \frac{1}{4} \approx -0.3466$
27. 2013   **29.** $k \approx 0.0137$, 3288
31. $y = 4.22e^{0.0430t}$, 9.97 million   **33.** 3.15 hr
35. 96.1%   **37.** $9,281
39. (a) $S(t) = 100(1 - e^{0.6125t})$ **(b)** 55,629
41. (a) 1252   **(b)** 7.8 mo
43. (a) $S = 10(1 - e^{-0.0575x})$ **(b)** 3314   **45. (a)** 7.9
(b) 7.7   **47. (a)** 20 db   **(b)** 70 db   **(c)** 95 db
(d) 120 db   **49.** 95%   **51.** 4.64
53. 1.6×10^{-6} moles per liter   **55.** 10^7 **57.** 7:30 A.M.

15.

n	1	2	4
A	$9,499.28	$9,738.91	$9,867.22

n	12	365	Continuous compounding
A	$9,956.20	$10,000.27	$10,001.78

17.

t	1	10	20
P	$184,623.27	$89,865.79	$40,379.30

t	30	40	50
P	$18,143.59	$8,152.44	$3,663.13

19. $1,069,047.14   **21.** 229.2 units per mL

23.

Speed	50	55	60	65	70
Mi/gal	28	26.4	24.8	23.4	22.0

25. 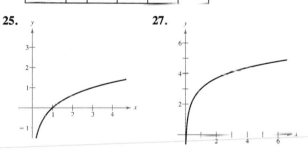   **27.**

29.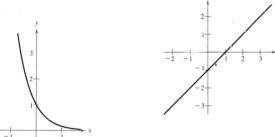

31. $\log_4 64 = 3$ **33.** 3   **35.** -2 **37.** 7   **39.** 0
41. 1.585   **43.** 2.132   **45.** $1 + 2\log_5 x$
47. $\log_{10} 5 + \frac{1}{2}\log_{10} y - 2\log_{10} x$
49. $\ln(x^2 + 1) + \ln(x - 1)$ **51.** $\log_2 5x$
53. $\ln \dfrac{\sqrt{|2x - 1|}}{(x + 1)^2}$ **55.** $\ln \dfrac{3\sqrt[3]{4 - x^2}}{x}$ **57.** False
59. False   **61.** 1.6542   **63.** 0.2823   **65.** 27.16 mi
67. $\ln 12 \approx 2.485$ **69.** $-\dfrac{\ln 44}{5} \approx -0.757$

Chapter 4 Review Exercises   *(page 320)*

1. d   **3.** a   **5.** c
7. 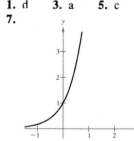   **9.**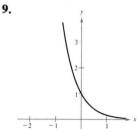

11. 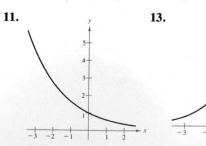   **13.**

71. $\ln 2 \approx 0.693$, $\ln 5 \approx 1.609$ **73.** $\frac{1}{3}e^{8.2} \approx 1{,}213.650$

75. $3e^2 \approx 22.167$ **77.** $y = 2e^{0.1014t}$

79. $y = 4e^{-0.4159t}$ **81. (a)** 1151 units   **(b)** 1325 units

83. (a) 8.94%   **(b)** $1833.67   **(c)** 9.35%

85. $10^{-3.5}$

CHAPTER 5

Section 5.1   *(page 333)*

WARM UP   **1.** 45   **2.** 70   **3.** $\frac{\pi}{6}$ **4.** $\frac{\pi}{3}$ **5.** $\frac{\pi}{4}$

6. $\frac{4\pi}{3}$ **7.** $\frac{\pi}{9}$ **8.** $\frac{11\pi}{6}$ **9.** 45   **10.** 45

1. (a) Quadrant I   **(b)** Quadrant III
3. (a) Quadrant IV   **(b)** Quadrant III
5. (a) Quadrant II   **(b)** Quadrant IV
7. (a)   **(b)**

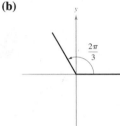

9. (a)   **(b)**

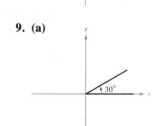
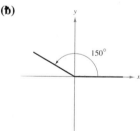

11. (a) $\frac{19\pi}{9}$, $-\frac{17\pi}{9}$ **(b)** $\frac{10\pi}{3}$, $-\frac{2\pi}{3}$
13. (a) $396°$, $-324°$ **(b)** $315°$, $-405°$
15. (a) $660°$, $-60°$ **(b)** $20°$, $-340°$

17. (a) Complement: $\frac{\pi}{6}$, Supplement: $\frac{2\pi}{3}$

(b) Complement: None, Supplement: $\frac{\pi}{4}$

19. (a) Complement: $72°$, Supplement: $162°$
(b) Complement: None, Supplement: $65°$ **21. (a)** $270°$

(b) $210°$ **23. (a)** $420°$ **(b)** $-66°$

25. (a) $\frac{\pi}{6}$ **(b)** $\frac{5\pi}{6}$

27. (a) $-\frac{\pi}{9}$ **(b)** $-\frac{4\pi}{3}$ **29. (a)** 2.007

(b) 1.525   **31. (a)** 9.285   **(b)** 0.009

33. (a) $25.714°$ **(b)** $81.818°$ **35. (a)** $-756°$

(b) $275.020°$ **37. (a)** $245.167°$ **(b)** $2.2°$

39. (a) $240°36'$ **(b)** $-145°48'$ **41. (a)** $143°14'22''$

(b) $-205°7'8''$ **43.** $\frac{4}{15}$ rad   **45.** 1.724 rad

47. 15π in.   **49.** 12 m   **51.** 591.7 mi

53. 1141.0 mi   **55.** $4.655°$ **57.** $\frac{1}{4}$ rad $\approx 14.324°$

59. (a) 560.2 rev/min   **(b)** 3520 rad/min

61. (a) 3400π rad/min, 1700π rad/min   **(b)** 850

63. (a) 80π rad/sec   **(b)** 78.54 ft/sec

Section 5.2   *(page 344)*

WARM UP   **1.** $-\frac{\sqrt{3}}{3}$ **2.** -1 **3.** $\frac{2\pi}{3}$ **4.** $\frac{7\pi}{4}$

5. $\frac{\pi}{6}$ **6.** $\frac{3\pi}{4}$ **7.** $60°$ **8.** $-270°$ **9.** 2π

10. π

1. $\left(\frac{\sqrt{2}}{2}, \frac{\sqrt{2}}{2}\right)$ **3.** $\left(-\frac{\sqrt{3}}{2}, \frac{1}{2}\right)$ **5.** $\left(-\frac{1}{2}, -\frac{\sqrt{3}}{2}\right)$

7. $(0, -1)$

9. $\sin \frac{\pi}{4} = \frac{\sqrt{2}}{2}$ **11.** $\sin -\frac{5\pi}{4} = \frac{\sqrt{2}}{2}$

$\cos \frac{\pi}{4} = \frac{\sqrt{2}}{2}$ $\cos -\frac{5\pi}{4} = -\frac{\sqrt{2}}{2}$

$\tan \frac{\pi}{4} = 1$ $\tan -\frac{5\pi}{4} = -1$

13. $\sin \frac{11\pi}{6} = -\frac{1}{2}$ **15.** $\sin \frac{4\pi}{3} = -\frac{\sqrt{3}}{2}$

$\cos \frac{11\pi}{6} = \frac{\sqrt{3}}{2}$ $\cos \frac{4\pi}{3} = -\frac{1}{2}$

$\tan \frac{11\pi}{6} = -\frac{\sqrt{3}}{3}$ $\tan \frac{4\pi}{3} = \sqrt{3}$

17. $\sin \frac{3\pi}{4} = \frac{\sqrt{2}}{2}$ **19.** $\sin \frac{\pi}{2} = 1$

$\cos \frac{3\pi}{4} = -\frac{\sqrt{2}}{2}$ $\cos \frac{\pi}{2} = 0$

$\tan \frac{3\pi}{4} = -1$ $\tan \frac{\pi}{2}$ is undefined

$\csc \frac{3\pi}{4} = \sqrt{2}$ $\csc \frac{\pi}{2} = 1$

$\sec \frac{3\pi}{4} = -\sqrt{2}$ $\sec \frac{\pi}{2}$ is undefined

$\cot \frac{3\pi}{4} = -1$ $\cot \frac{\pi}{2} = 0$

21. $\sin\left(-\dfrac{4\pi}{3}\right) = \dfrac{\sqrt{3}}{2}$

$\cos\left(-\dfrac{4\pi}{3}\right) = -\dfrac{1}{2}$

$\tan\left(-\dfrac{4\pi}{3}\right) = -\sqrt{3}$

$\csc\left(-\dfrac{4\pi}{3}\right) = \dfrac{2\sqrt{3}}{3}$

$\sec\left(-\dfrac{4\pi}{3}\right) = -2$

$\cot\left(-\dfrac{4\pi}{3}\right) = -\dfrac{\sqrt{3}}{3}$

23. $\sin \pi = 0$ **25.** $\cos\dfrac{2\pi}{3} = -\dfrac{1}{2}$

27. $\cos\dfrac{7\pi}{6} = -\dfrac{\sqrt{3}}{2}$ **29.** $\sin\dfrac{7\pi}{4} = -\dfrac{\sqrt{2}}{2}$

31. (a) $-\frac{1}{3}$ **(b)** -3 **33. (a)** $-\frac{7}{8}$ **(b)** $-\frac{8}{7}$

35. (a) $\frac{4}{5}$ **(b)** $-\frac{4}{5}$ **37.** 0.7071 **39.** -0.9900

41. -0.1288 **43.** 1.3940 **45. (a)** -1 **(b)** -0.4

47. (a) $0.25, 2.9$ **(b)** $1.8, 4.5$ **49. (a)** 0.2500 ft

(b) 0.0177 ft   **(c)** -0.2475 ft   **51.** 0.794

Section 5.3   *(page 354)*

WARM UP   **1.** $2\sqrt{5}$ **2.** $3\sqrt{10}$ **3.** 10 **4.** $3\sqrt{2}$

5. 1.24 **6.** 317.55 **7.** 63.13 **8.** 133.57

9. $2{,}785{,}714.29$ **10.** 28.80

1. $\sin\theta = \dfrac{1}{2}$

$\cos\theta = \dfrac{\sqrt{3}}{2}$

$\tan\theta = \dfrac{\sqrt{3}}{3}$

$\csc\theta = 2$

$\sec\theta = \dfrac{2\sqrt{3}}{3}$

$\cot\theta = \sqrt{3}$

3. $\sin\theta = \dfrac{\sqrt{161}}{15}$

$\cos\theta = \dfrac{8}{15}$

$\tan\theta = \dfrac{\sqrt{161}}{8}$

$\csc\theta = \dfrac{15\sqrt{161}}{161}$

$\sec\theta = \dfrac{15}{8}$

$\cot\theta = \dfrac{8\sqrt{161}}{161}$

5.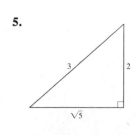

$\cos\theta = \dfrac{\sqrt{5}}{3}$

$\tan\theta = \dfrac{2\sqrt{5}}{5}$

$\csc\theta = \dfrac{3}{2}$

$\sec\theta = \dfrac{3\sqrt{5}}{5}$

$\cot\theta = \dfrac{\sqrt{5}}{2}$

7.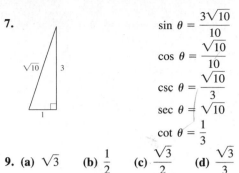

$\sin\theta = \dfrac{3\sqrt{10}}{10}$

$\cos\theta = \dfrac{\sqrt{10}}{10}$

$\csc\theta = \dfrac{\sqrt{10}}{3}$

$\sec\theta = \sqrt{10}$

$\cot\theta = \dfrac{1}{3}$

9. (a) $\sqrt{3}$ **(b)** $\dfrac{1}{2}$ **(c)** $\dfrac{\sqrt{3}}{2}$ **(d)** $\dfrac{\sqrt{3}}{3}$

11. (a) $\dfrac{1}{3}$ **(b)** $\dfrac{2\sqrt{2}}{3}$ **(c)** $\dfrac{\sqrt{2}}{4}$ **(d)** 3 **13. (a)** $\dfrac{1}{2}$

(b) $\dfrac{\sqrt{3}}{3}$ **15. (a)** 1 **(b)** $\dfrac{\sqrt{2}}{2}$ **17. (a)** 0.2815

(b) 3.5523 **19. (a)** 5.0273 **(b)** 0.1989

21. (a) 1.1884 **(b)** 1.1884 **23. (a)** $30°, \dfrac{\pi}{6}$

(b) $30°, \dfrac{\pi}{6}$ **25. (a)** $60°, \dfrac{\pi}{3}$ **(b)** $45°, \dfrac{\pi}{4}$

27. (a) $60°, \dfrac{\pi}{3}$ **(b)** $45°, \dfrac{\pi}{4}$

29. (a) $55°, 0.960$ radians   **(b)** $89°, 1.553$ radians

31. (a) $50°, 0.873$ radians   **(b)** $25°, 0.436$ radians

33. 57.74 **35.** 14.43 **37.** 15.56 **39.** 9.19

41. 15 ft   **43.** 19.32 ft   **45.** 2145 ft

47. $(10\sqrt{3}, 10), (10, 10\sqrt{3})$

49. $\sin 25° \approx 0.42$

$\cos 25° \approx 0.91$

$\tan 25° \approx 0.47$

$\csc 25° \approx 2.37$

$\sec 25° \approx 1.10$

$\cot 25° \approx 2.14$

51. True   **53.** False   **55.** False

Section 5.4   *(page 367)*

WARM UP   **1.** $\frac{1}{2}$ **2.** 1 **3.** $\dfrac{\sqrt{2}}{2}$ **4.** $\dfrac{\sqrt{3}}{3}$

5. $\dfrac{2\sqrt{3}}{3}$ **6.** $\sqrt{2}$

7. $\sin\theta = \dfrac{3\sqrt{13}}{13}$

$\cos\theta = \dfrac{2\sqrt{13}}{13}$

$\csc\theta = \dfrac{\sqrt{13}}{3}$

$\sec\theta = \dfrac{\sqrt{13}}{2}$

$\cot\theta = \dfrac{2}{3}$

8. $\sin\theta = \dfrac{\sqrt{5}}{3}$

$\tan\theta = \dfrac{\sqrt{5}}{2}$

$\csc\theta = \dfrac{3\sqrt{5}}{5}$

$\sec\theta = \dfrac{3}{2}$

$\cot\theta = \dfrac{2\sqrt{5}}{5}$

9. $\cos \theta = \dfrac{2\sqrt{6}}{5}$

$\tan \theta = \dfrac{\sqrt{6}}{12}$

$\csc \theta = 5$

$\sec \theta = \dfrac{5\sqrt{6}}{12}$

$\cot \theta = 2\sqrt{6}$

10. $\sin \theta = \dfrac{2\sqrt{2}}{3}$

$\cos \theta = \dfrac{1}{3}$

$\tan \theta = 2\sqrt{2}$

$\csc \theta = \dfrac{3\sqrt{2}}{4}$

$\cot \theta = \dfrac{\sqrt{2}}{4}$

---

1. (a) $\sin \theta = \frac{4}{5}$

$\cos \theta = \frac{3}{5}$

$\tan \theta = \frac{4}{3}$

$\csc \theta = \frac{5}{4}$

$\sec \theta = \frac{5}{3}$

$\cot \theta = \frac{3}{4}$

(b) $\sin \theta = -\frac{15}{17}$

$\cos \theta = \frac{8}{17}$

$\tan \theta = -\frac{15}{8}$

$\csc \theta = -\frac{17}{15}$

$\sec \theta = \frac{17}{8}$

$\cot \theta = -\frac{8}{15}$

3. (a) $\sin \theta = \dfrac{1}{2}$

$\cos \theta = -\dfrac{\sqrt{3}}{2}$

$\tan \theta = -\dfrac{\sqrt{3}}{3}$

$\csc \theta = 2$

$\sec \theta = -\dfrac{2\sqrt{3}}{3}$

$\cot \theta = -\sqrt{3}$

(b) $\sin \theta = -\dfrac{\sqrt{2}}{2}$

$\cos \theta = -\dfrac{\sqrt{2}}{2}$

$\tan \theta = 1$

$\csc \theta = -\sqrt{2}$

$\sec \theta = -\sqrt{2}$

$\cot \theta = 1$

5. (a) $\sin \theta = \frac{24}{25}$

$\cos \theta = \frac{7}{25}$

$\tan \theta = \frac{24}{7}$

$\csc \theta = \frac{25}{24}$

$\sec \theta = \frac{25}{7}$

$\cot \theta = \frac{7}{24}$

(b) $\sin \theta = -\frac{24}{25}$

$\cos \theta = \frac{7}{25}$

$\tan \theta = -\frac{24}{7}$

$\csc \theta = -\frac{25}{24}$

$\sec \theta = \frac{25}{7}$

$\cot \theta = -\frac{7}{24}$

7. (a) $\sin \theta = \dfrac{5\sqrt{29}}{29}$

$\cos \theta = -\dfrac{2\sqrt{29}}{29}$

$\tan \theta = -\dfrac{5}{2}$

$\csc \theta = \dfrac{\sqrt{29}}{5}$

$\sec \theta = -\dfrac{\sqrt{29}}{2}$

$\cot \theta = -\dfrac{2}{5}$

(b) $\sin \theta = -\dfrac{5\sqrt{34}}{34}$

$\cos \theta = \dfrac{3\sqrt{34}}{34}$

$\tan \theta = -\dfrac{5}{3}$

$\csc \theta = -\dfrac{\sqrt{34}}{5}$

$\sec \theta = \dfrac{\sqrt{34}}{3}$

$\cot \theta = -\dfrac{3}{5}$

9. (a) $c_1 = 5$

$b_2 = 12$

$c_2 = 15$

(b) $\sin \alpha_1 = \dfrac{a_1}{c_1} = \dfrac{3}{5} = \dfrac{a_2}{c_2} = \sin \alpha_2$

$\cos \alpha_1 = \dfrac{b_1}{c_1} = \dfrac{4}{5} = \dfrac{b_2}{c_2} = \cos \alpha_2$

$\tan \alpha_1 = \dfrac{a_1}{b_1} = \dfrac{3}{4} = \dfrac{a_2}{b_2} = \tan \alpha_2$

$\csc \alpha_1 = \dfrac{c_1}{a_1} = \dfrac{5}{3} = \dfrac{c_2}{a_2} = \csc \alpha_2$

$\sec \alpha_1 = \dfrac{c_1}{b_1} = \dfrac{5}{4} = \dfrac{c_2}{b_2} = \sec \alpha_2$

$\cot \alpha_1 = \dfrac{b_1}{a_1} = \dfrac{4}{3} = \dfrac{b_2}{a_2} = \cot \alpha_2$

11. (a) $b_1 = \sqrt{3}$

$a_2 = \dfrac{5\sqrt{3}}{3}$

$c_2 = \dfrac{10\sqrt{3}}{3}$

(b) $\sin \alpha_1 = \dfrac{a_1}{c_1} = \dfrac{1}{2} = \dfrac{a_2}{c_2} = \sin \alpha_2$

$\cos \alpha_1 = \dfrac{b_1}{c_1} = \dfrac{\sqrt{3}}{2} = \dfrac{b_2}{c_2} = \cos \alpha_2$

$\tan \alpha_1 = \dfrac{a_1}{b_1} = \dfrac{\sqrt{3}}{3} = \dfrac{a_2}{b_2} = \tan \alpha_2$

$\csc \alpha_1 = \dfrac{c_1}{a_1} = 2 = \dfrac{c_2}{a_2} = \csc \alpha_2$

$\sec \alpha_1 = \dfrac{c_1}{b_1} = \dfrac{2\sqrt{3}}{3} = \dfrac{c_2}{b_2} = \sec \alpha_2$

$\cot \alpha_1 = \dfrac{b_1}{a_1} = \sqrt{3} = \dfrac{b_2}{a_2} = \cot \alpha_2$

13. (a) Quadrant III   **(b)** Quadrant II

15. (a) Quadrant II   **(b)** Quadrant IV

17. $\sin \theta = \frac{3}{5}$

$\cos \theta = -\frac{4}{5}$

$\tan \theta = -\frac{3}{4}$

$\csc \theta = \frac{5}{3}$

$\sec \theta = -\frac{5}{4}$

$\cot \theta = -\frac{4}{3}$

19. $\sin \theta = -\frac{15}{17}$

$\cos \theta = \frac{8}{17}$

$\tan \theta = -\frac{15}{8}$

$\csc \theta = -\frac{17}{15}$

$\sec \theta = \frac{17}{8}$

$\cot \theta = -\frac{8}{15}$

21. $\sin \theta = \dfrac{\sqrt{3}}{2}$

$\cos \theta = -\dfrac{1}{2}$

$\tan \theta = -\sqrt{3}$

$\csc \theta = \dfrac{2\sqrt{3}}{3}$

$\sec \theta = -2$

$\cot \theta = -\dfrac{\sqrt{3}}{3}$

25. $\sin \theta = -\dfrac{2\sqrt{5}}{5}$

$\cos \theta = -\dfrac{\sqrt{5}}{5}$

$\tan \theta = 2$

$\csc \theta = \dfrac{-\sqrt{5}}{2}$

$\sec \theta = -\sqrt{5}$

$\cot \theta = \dfrac{1}{2}$

23. $\sin \theta = 0$

$\cos \theta = -1$

$\tan \theta = 0$

$\csc \theta$ is undefined

$\sec \theta = -1$

$\cot \theta$ is undefined

27. (a) $\theta' = 23°$ **(b)** $\theta' = 53°$

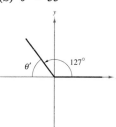

29. (a) $\theta' = 65°$ **(b)** $\theta' = 72°$

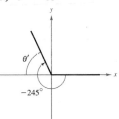

31. (a) $\theta' = \dfrac{\pi}{3}$ **(b)** $\theta' = \dfrac{\pi}{6}$

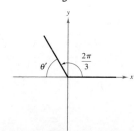

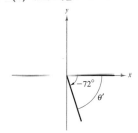

33. (a) $\theta' = 3.5 - \pi$ **(b)** $\theta' = 2\pi - 5.8$

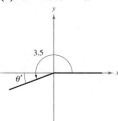

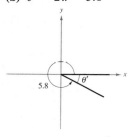

35. (a) $\sin 225° = -\dfrac{\sqrt{2}}{2}$

$\cos 225° = -\dfrac{\sqrt{2}}{2}$

$\tan 225° = 1$

(b) $\sin(-225°) = \dfrac{\sqrt{2}}{2}$

$\cos(-225°) = -\dfrac{\sqrt{2}}{2}$

$\tan(-225°) = -1$

37. (a) $\sin 750° = \dfrac{1}{2}$

$\cos 750° = \dfrac{\sqrt{3}}{2}$

$\tan 750° = \dfrac{\sqrt{3}}{3}$

(b) $\sin 510° = \dfrac{1}{2}$

$\cos 510° = -\dfrac{\sqrt{3}}{2}$

$\tan 510° = -\dfrac{\sqrt{3}}{3}$

39. (a) $\sin \dfrac{4\pi}{3} = -\dfrac{\sqrt{3}}{2}$

$\cos \dfrac{4\pi}{3} = -\dfrac{1}{2}$

$\tan \dfrac{4\pi}{3} - \sqrt{3}$

(b) $\sin \dfrac{2\pi}{3} = \dfrac{\sqrt{3}}{2}$

$\cos \dfrac{2\pi}{3} = -\dfrac{1}{2}$

$\tan \dfrac{2\pi}{3} = -\sqrt{3}$

41. (a) $\sin\left(-\dfrac{\pi}{6}\right) = -\dfrac{1}{2}$

$\cos\left(-\dfrac{\pi}{6}\right) = \dfrac{\sqrt{3}}{2}$

$\tan\left(-\dfrac{\pi}{6}\right) = -\dfrac{\sqrt{3}}{3}$

(b) $\sin \dfrac{5\pi}{6} = \dfrac{1}{2}$

$\cos \dfrac{5\pi}{6} = -\dfrac{\sqrt{3}}{2}$

$\tan \dfrac{5\pi}{6} = -\dfrac{\sqrt{3}}{3}$

43. (a) $\sin \dfrac{11\pi}{4} = \dfrac{\sqrt{2}}{2}$

$\cos \dfrac{11\pi}{4} = -\dfrac{\sqrt{2}}{2}$

$\tan \dfrac{11\pi}{4} = -1$

(b) $\sin\left(-\dfrac{13\pi}{6}\right) = -\dfrac{1}{2}$

$\cos\left(-\dfrac{13\pi}{6}\right) = \dfrac{\sqrt{3}}{2}$

$\tan\left(-\dfrac{13\pi}{6}\right) = -\dfrac{\sqrt{3}}{3}$

45. (a) 0.1736 **(b)** 5.7588 **47. (a)** -0.3420
(b) -0.3420 **49. (a)** 1.7321 **(b)** 1.7321
51. (a) 0.3640 **(b)** 0.3640

53. (a) $30° = \dfrac{\pi}{6},\ 150° = \dfrac{5\pi}{6}$

(b) $210° = \dfrac{7\pi}{6},\ 330° = \dfrac{11\pi}{6}$

55. (a) $60° = \dfrac{\pi}{3},\ 120° = \dfrac{2\pi}{3}$

(b) $135° = \dfrac{3\pi}{4},\ 315° = \dfrac{7\pi}{4}$

57. (a) $45° = \dfrac{\pi}{4},\ 225° = \dfrac{5\pi}{4}$

(b) $150° = \dfrac{5\pi}{6},\ 330° = \dfrac{11\pi}{6}$ **59. (a)** 54.99°, 125.01°.

(b) 195.00°, 345.00°   **61. (a)** 0.175, 6.109

(b) 2.201, 4.083   **63. (a)** 0.873, 4.014

(b) 1.693, 4.835   **65.** $\frac{4}{5}$ **67.** $-\sqrt{3}$.

69. $\sin^2 \theta + \cos^2 \theta = 1$
$\sin^2 2 + \cos^2 2 = 1$

71. (a) 25.2° F   **(b)** 65.1° F   **(c)** 50.8° F

73. (a) 10 mi   **(b)** 5.18 mi   **(c)** 5 mi

Section 5.5   *(page 378)*

WARM UP   **1.** 6π **2.** $\frac{1}{2}$ **3.** $\dfrac{\pi}{6}$ **4.** $\dfrac{7\pi}{6}$ **5.** -2

6. $-\frac{4}{3}$ **7.** 1   **8.** 0   **9.** 1   **10.** 0

1. Period: π, Amplitude: 2

3. Period: 4π, Amplitude: $\frac{3}{2}$

5. Period: 2, Amplitude: $\frac{1}{2}$

7. Period: 2π, Amplitude: 2

9. Period: $\dfrac{\pi}{5}$, Amplitude: 3

11. Period: 3π, Amplitude: $\frac{1}{2}$

13. Period: $\frac{1}{2}$, Amplitude: 3

15. *Shift* the graph of f π units to the right to obtain the graph of g.

17. *Reflect* the graph of f about the x-axis to obtain the graph of g.

19. The *period* of f is twice the period of g.

21. *Shift* the graph of f two units up to obtain the graph of g.

23.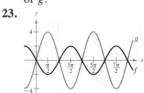

25.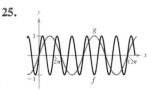

27.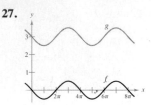

29.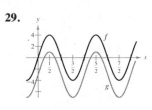

31.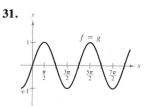

33.

35.

37.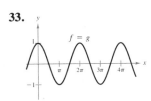

39.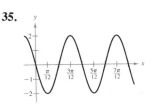

41.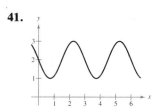

43.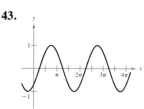

45.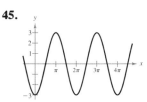

47.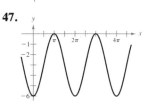

49.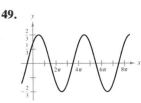

51.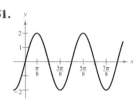

53.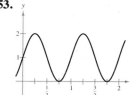

55.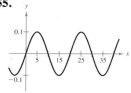

7.

8.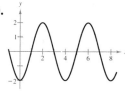

57.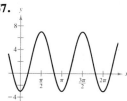

59.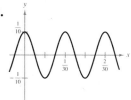

9.

10.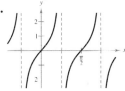

61. $-\dfrac{5\pi}{6}, -\dfrac{\pi}{6}, \dfrac{7\pi}{6}, \dfrac{11\pi}{6}$ **63.** $-\dfrac{7\pi}{4}, -\dfrac{\pi}{4}, \dfrac{\pi}{4}, \dfrac{7\pi}{4}$

1. c, π **3.** $e, 2\pi$ **5.** $d, 1$ **7.** $b, 2\pi$

65. $a = 2, b = 4, c = 0$ **67.** $a = 1, b = 2, c = -\dfrac{\pi}{2}$

9.

11.

69. **(a)** 6   **(b)** 10 cycles/min
(c)

13.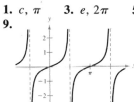

15.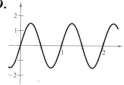

71. **(a)** $\frac{1}{440}$ **(b)** 440
(c)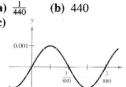

17.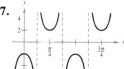

19.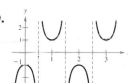

73.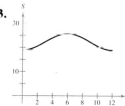

21.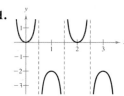

23.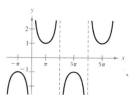

75. $g(x) = 2f(x)$ **77.** $g(x) = f(x - \pi)$

25.

27.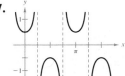

Section 5.6   *(page 388)*

WARM UP   **1.** 0   **2.** $\dfrac{\sqrt{2}}{2}$ **3.** 1   **4.** 0   **5.** 0
6. 0

29.

31.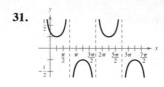

7.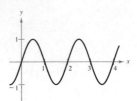

8.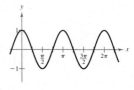

33.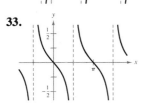

35.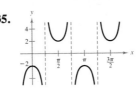

9. $0, \dfrac{\sqrt{3}\pi}{12}, \dfrac{\sqrt{2}\pi}{8}, \dfrac{\pi}{6}, 0$

10. $0, \dfrac{3+\pi}{6}, \dfrac{2\sqrt{2}+\pi}{4}, \dfrac{3\sqrt{3}+2\pi}{6}, \dfrac{\pi+2}{2}$

37.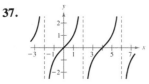

39.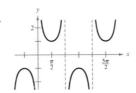

1.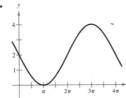

3.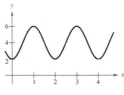

41. $-\dfrac{7\pi}{4}, -\dfrac{3\pi}{4}, \dfrac{\pi}{4}, \dfrac{5\pi}{4}$
43. $-\dfrac{4\pi}{3}, -\dfrac{2\pi}{3}, \dfrac{2\pi}{3}, \dfrac{4\pi}{3}$

45. $d = 6 \cot x$

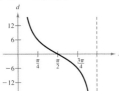

5.

7.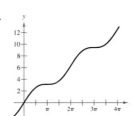

Section 5.7   *(page 395)*

WARM UP

1. $f(x) = -1: \dfrac{3\pi}{2}$
$\qquad f(x) = 0: 0, \pi, 2\pi$
$\qquad f(x) = 1: \dfrac{\pi}{2}$

2. $f(x) = -1: \pi$
$\qquad f(x) = 0: \dfrac{\pi}{2}, \dfrac{3\pi}{2}$
$\qquad f(x) = 1: 0, 2\pi$

3. $f(x) = -1: \dfrac{3\pi}{4}, \dfrac{7\pi}{4}$
$\qquad f(x) = 0: 0, \dfrac{\pi}{2}, \pi, \dfrac{3\pi}{2}, 2\pi$
$\qquad f(x) = 1: \dfrac{\pi}{4}, \dfrac{5\pi}{4}$

4. $f(x) = -1: 2\pi$
$\qquad f(x) = 0: \pi$
$\qquad f(x) = 1: 0$

9.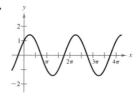

11.

13.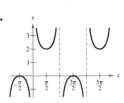

15.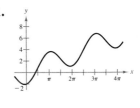

5.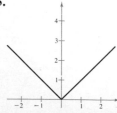

6.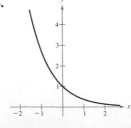

17.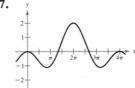

19.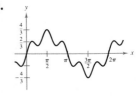

21.

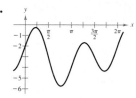

23.

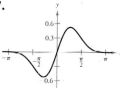

25.

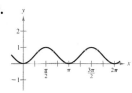

27.

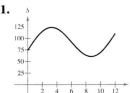

29.

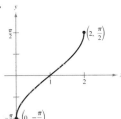

31.

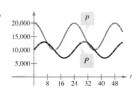

33.

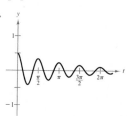

We can explain the cycles of this predator-prey population by noting the cause and effect pattern.

35.

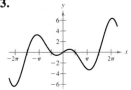

Section 5.8   (page 406)

WARM UP   **1.** -1 **2.** -1 **3.** -1 **4.** $\dfrac{\sqrt{2}}{2}$

5. 0   **6.** $\dfrac{\pi}{6}$ **7.** π **8.** $\dfrac{\pi}{4}$ **9.** 0   **10.** $-\dfrac{\pi}{4}$

1. $\dfrac{\pi}{6}$ **3.** $\dfrac{\pi}{3}$ **5.** $\dfrac{\pi}{6}$ **7.** $\dfrac{5\pi}{6}$ **9.** $-\dfrac{\pi}{3}$ **11.** $\dfrac{2\pi}{3}$

13. $\dfrac{\pi}{3}$ **15.** 0   **17.** 1.29   **19.** -0.85

21. -1.11 **23.** 0.32   **25.** 1.99   **27.** 0.74

29. 0.3   **31.** -0.1 **33.** 0   **35.** $\frac{3}{5}$ **37.** $\dfrac{\sqrt{5}}{5}$

39. $\frac{12}{13}$ **41.** $\dfrac{\sqrt{34}}{5}$ **43.** $\dfrac{1}{x}$ **45.** $\sqrt{1-4x^2}$

47. $\sqrt{1-x^2}$ **49.** $\dfrac{\sqrt{9-x^2}}{x}$ **51.** $\dfrac{\sqrt{x^2+2}}{x}$

53. $\arcsin\dfrac{9}{\sqrt{x^2+81}}$ **55.** $\arcsin\dfrac{|x-1|}{\sqrt{x^2-2x+10}}$

57.

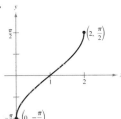

59.

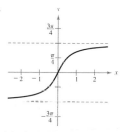

61. (a) $\beta \approx 40.6°$ **(b)** $\beta \approx 30.3°$ **63. (a)** 14.5°
(b) 30.0°

65.

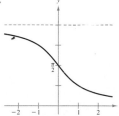

67.

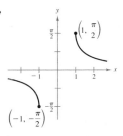

Section 5.9   (page 416)

WARM UP   **1.** 8.45   **2.** 78.99   **3.** 1.06   **4.** 1.24
5. 4.88   **6.** 34.14   **7.** 4; π **8.** $\frac{1}{2}$; 2   **9.** 3; $\frac{2}{3}$
10. 0.2; 8π

1. $a \approx 3.64$
$c \approx 10.64$
$B = 70°$
5. $a \approx 91.34$
$b \approx 420.70$
$B = 77°45'$
9. $a \approx 49.48$
$A \approx 72.08°$
$B \approx 17.92°$

3. $a \approx 8.26$
$c \approx 25.38$
$A = 19°$
7. $c \approx 11.66$
$A \approx 30.96°$
$B \approx 59.04°$

11. 2.56 in.   **13.** 121.2 ft   **15.** 15.4 ft
17. 56.3°   **19.** 12.68°   **21.** 5099 ft
23. 19.9 ft   **25.** 508 miles north; 650 miles east
27. N 56.3° W   **29. (a)** N 58° E   **(b)** 68.8 yd
31. 1657 ft   **33.** 17,054 ft $\approx$ 3.23 mi
35. 29.389 in.   **37.** $y = \sqrt{3}r$
39. $a \approx 7$, $c \approx 12.2$ **41. (a)** 4   **(b)** 4   **(c)** $\frac{1}{16}$
43. (a) $\frac{1}{16}$ **(b)** 60   **(c)** $\frac{1}{120}$ **45.** $\omega = 528\pi$

Chapter 5   Review Exercises   *(page 420)*

1.

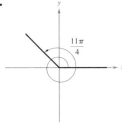

$\dfrac{3\pi}{4}, -\dfrac{5\pi}{4}$

3.

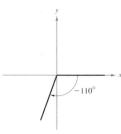

$250°, -470°$

5. 135.28°   **7.** 5.38°   **9.** 135°16'12"   **11.** −85°9'
13. 128.57°   **15.** −200.54°   **17.** 8.3776
19. −0.5890   **21.** 72°   **23.** $\dfrac{\pi}{5}$

25. $\sin \theta = \frac{4}{5}$
$\cos \theta = \frac{3}{5}$
$\tan \theta = \frac{4}{3}$
$\csc \theta = \frac{5}{4}$
$\sec \theta = \frac{5}{3}$
$\cot \theta = \frac{3}{4}$

27. $\sin \theta = \dfrac{2\sqrt{53}}{53}$
$\cos \theta = -\dfrac{7\sqrt{53}}{53}$
$\tan \theta = -\dfrac{2}{7}$
$\csc \theta = \dfrac{\sqrt{53}}{2}$
$\sec \theta = -\dfrac{\sqrt{53}}{7}$
$\cot \theta = -\dfrac{7}{2}$

29. $\sin \theta = -\dfrac{3\sqrt{13}}{13}$
$\cos \theta = -\dfrac{2\sqrt{13}}{13}$
$\tan \theta = \dfrac{3}{2}$
$\csc \theta = -\dfrac{\sqrt{13}}{3}$
$\sec \theta = -\dfrac{\sqrt{13}}{2}$
$\cot \theta = \dfrac{2}{3}$

31. $\sin \theta = -\dfrac{\sqrt{11}}{6}$
$\cos \theta = \dfrac{5}{6}$
$\tan \theta = -\dfrac{\sqrt{11}}{5}$
$\csc \theta = -\dfrac{6\sqrt{11}}{11}$
$\cot \theta = -\dfrac{5\sqrt{11}}{11}$

33. $\cos \theta = -\dfrac{\sqrt{55}}{8}$
$\tan \theta = -\dfrac{3\sqrt{55}}{55}$
$\csc \theta = \dfrac{8}{3}$
$\sec \theta = -\dfrac{8\sqrt{55}}{55}$
$\cot \theta = -\dfrac{\sqrt{55}}{3}$

35. $\sqrt{3}$ **37.** $-\dfrac{\sqrt{3}}{2}$ **39.** $-\dfrac{\sqrt{2}}{2}$ **41.** 0.65

43. 3.24   **45.** $135° = \dfrac{3\pi}{4}$, $225° = \dfrac{5\pi}{4}$

47. $210° = \dfrac{7\pi}{6}$, $330° = \dfrac{11\pi}{6}$

49. $57° \approx 0.9948$, $123° \approx 2.1468$

51. $165° \approx 2.8798$, $195° \approx 3.4034$ **53.** $\dfrac{\sqrt{-x^2 + 2x}}{-x^2 + 2x}$

55. $\dfrac{2\sqrt{4 - 2x^2}}{4 - x^2}$

57.

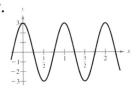

59.

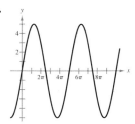

61.

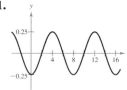

63.

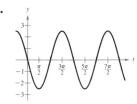

65.

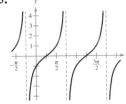

67.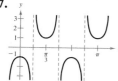

69.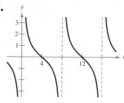

71.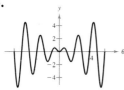

73.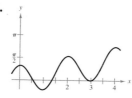

75.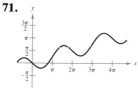

77.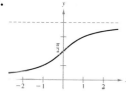

79.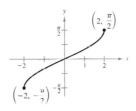

81. 7.66 m   **83.** 1.33 mi   **85.** 268.8 ft

Polynomial	Calculator
87. (a) 0.8415	0.8415
(b) 0.5403	0.5403
(c) 0.9079	0.9093
(d) 0.5403	0.5403
(e) 0.7071	0.7071
(f) 0.5000	0.5000

CHAPTER 6

Section 6.1   *(page 429)*

WARM UP

1. $\sin \theta = \dfrac{3\sqrt{13}}{13}$

$\cos \theta = \dfrac{2\sqrt{13}}{13}$

$\tan \theta = \dfrac{3}{2}$

$\csc \theta = \dfrac{\sqrt{13}}{3}$

$\sec \theta = \dfrac{\sqrt{13}}{2}$

$\cot \theta = \dfrac{2}{3}$

2. $\sin \theta = \dfrac{2\sqrt{2}}{3}$

$\cos \theta = \dfrac{1}{3}$

$\tan \theta = 2\sqrt{2}$

$\csc \theta = \dfrac{3\sqrt{2}}{4}$

$\sec \theta = 3$

$\cot \theta = \dfrac{\sqrt{2}}{4}$

3. $\sin \theta = -\dfrac{3\sqrt{58}}{58}$

$\cos \theta = \dfrac{7\sqrt{58}}{58}$

$\tan \theta = -\dfrac{3}{7}$

$\csc \theta = -\dfrac{\sqrt{58}}{3}$

$\sec \theta = \dfrac{\sqrt{58}}{7}$

$\cot \theta = -\dfrac{7}{3}$

4. $\sin \theta = \dfrac{\sqrt{5}}{5}$

$\cos \theta = -\dfrac{2\sqrt{5}}{5}$

$\tan \theta = -\dfrac{1}{2}$

$\csc \theta = \sqrt{5}$

$\sec \theta = -\dfrac{\sqrt{5}}{2}$

$\cot \theta = -2$

5. $\dfrac{1}{2}$

6. $\dfrac{5}{4}$

7. $\dfrac{\sqrt{73}}{8}$ **8.** $\dfrac{2}{3}$ **9.** $\dfrac{x^2 + x + 16}{4(x + 1)}$ **10.** $\dfrac{8x - 2}{1 - x^2}$

1. $\sin x = \dfrac{1}{2}$

$\cos x = \dfrac{\sqrt{3}}{2}$

$\tan x = \dfrac{\sqrt{3}}{3}$

$\csc x = 2$

$\sec x = \dfrac{2\sqrt{3}}{3}$

$\cot x = \sqrt{3}$

3. $\sin \theta = -\dfrac{\sqrt{2}}{2}$

$\cos \theta = \dfrac{\sqrt{2}}{2}$

$\tan \theta = -1$

$\csc \theta = -\sqrt{2}$

$\sec \theta = \sqrt{2}$

$\cot \theta = -1$

5. $\sin x = -\dfrac{5}{13}$

$\cos x = -\dfrac{12}{13}$

$\tan x = \dfrac{5}{12}$

$\csc x = -\dfrac{13}{5}$

$\sec x = -\dfrac{13}{12}$

$\cot x = \dfrac{12}{5}$

7. $\sin \phi = 0$

$\cos \phi = -1$

$\tan \phi = 0$

$\csc \phi$ is undefined

$\sec \phi = -1$

$\cot \phi$ is undefined

9. $\sin x = \dfrac{2}{3}$ **11.** $\sin \theta = -\dfrac{2\sqrt{5}}{5}$

$\cos x = -\dfrac{\sqrt{5}}{3}$ $\cos \theta = -\dfrac{\sqrt{5}}{5}$

$\tan x = -\dfrac{2\sqrt{5}}{5}$ $\tan \theta = 2$

$\csc x = \dfrac{3}{2}$ $\csc \theta = -\dfrac{\sqrt{5}}{2}$

$\sec x = -\dfrac{3\sqrt{5}}{5}$ $\sec \theta = -\sqrt{5}$

$\cot x = -\dfrac{\sqrt{5}}{2}$ $\cot \theta = \dfrac{1}{2}$

13. $\sin \theta = -1$
$\cos \theta = 0$
$\tan \theta$ is undefined.
$\csc \theta = -1$
$\sec \theta$ is undefined.
$\cot \theta = 0$

15. d   **17.** a   **19.** b   **21.** b   **23.** e   **25.** f
27. $\sec \phi$ **29.** $\sin \beta$ **31.** $\cos x$ **33.** 1
35. $-\tan x$ **37.** $\tan x$ **39.** $1 + \sin y$ **41.** $\sin^2 x$
43. $\sin^2 x \tan^2 x$ **45.** $\sec^4 x$ **47.** $\sin^2 x - \cos^2 x$
49. $1 + 2\sin x \cos x$ **51.** $\tan^2 x$ **53.** $2\csc^2 x$
55. $2\sec x$ **57.** $1 + \cos y$ **59.** $3(\sec x + \tan x)$
61. $5\cos \theta$ **63.** $3\tan \theta$ **65.** $5\sec \theta$ **67.** $\cos \theta$
69. $27\sec^3 \theta$ **71.** $0 \le \theta < \dfrac{\pi}{2}, \dfrac{3\pi}{2} < \theta < 2\pi$

73. Not an identity since $\dfrac{\sin k\theta}{\cos k\theta} = \tan k\theta$.

75. Identity since $\sin \theta \dfrac{1}{\sin \theta} = 1$.

77. (a) $\csc^2 132° - \cot^2 132° \approx 1.8107 - 0.8107 = 1$

     (b) $\csc^2 \dfrac{2\pi}{7} - \cot^2 \dfrac{2\pi}{7} \approx 1.6360 - 0.6360 = 1$

79. (a) $\cos(90° - 80°) = \sin 80° \approx 0.9848$

     (b) $\cos\left(\dfrac{\pi}{2} - 0.8\right) = \sin 0.8 \approx 0.7174$

81. $\cos \theta = \pm\sqrt{1 - \sin^2 \theta}$

$\tan \theta = \pm\dfrac{\sin \theta}{\sqrt{1 - \sin^2 \theta}}$

$\csc \theta = \dfrac{1}{\sin \theta}$

$\sec \theta = \pm\dfrac{1}{\sqrt{1 - \sin^2 \theta}}$

$\cot \theta = \pm\dfrac{\sqrt{1 - \sin^2 \theta}}{\sin \theta}$

Section 6.2   (page 436)

WARM UP   **1.** (a) $x^2(1 - y^2)$ (b) $\sin^4 x$
2. (a) $x^2(1 + y^2)$ (b) 1   **3.** (a) $(x^2 + 1)(x^2 - 1)$
(b) $\sec^2 x(\tan^2 x - 1)$ **4.** (a) $(z + 1)(z^2 - z + 1)$
(b) $(\tan x + 1)(\tan^2 x - \tan x + 1)$
   5. (a) $(x - 1)(x^2 + 1)$ (b) $(\cot x - 1)\csc^2 x$
6. (a) $(x^2 - 1)^2$ (b) $\cos^4 x$ **7.** (a) $\dfrac{y^2 - x^2}{x}$

(b) $\tan x$ **8.** (a) $\dfrac{x^2 - 1}{x^2}$ (b) $\sin^2 x$

9. (a) $\dfrac{y^2 + (1 + z)^2}{y(1 + z)}$ (b) $2\csc x$

10. (a) $\dfrac{y(1 + y) - z^2}{z(1 + y)}$ (b) $\dfrac{\tan x - 1}{\sec x(1 + \tan x)}$

1–55. Proofs.   **57.** $\sin \theta = \pm\sqrt{1 - \cos^2 \theta}$; $\dfrac{7\pi}{4}$

59. $\sqrt{\tan^2 x} = |\tan x|$; $\dfrac{3\pi}{4}$ **61.** Proof

---

Section 6.3   (page 446)

WARM UP   **1.** $\dfrac{2\pi}{3}, \dfrac{4\pi}{3}$ **2.** $\dfrac{\pi}{3}, \dfrac{2\pi}{3}$ **3.** $\dfrac{\pi}{4}, \dfrac{7\pi}{4}$

4. $\dfrac{7\pi}{4}, \dfrac{5\pi}{4}$ **5.** $\dfrac{\pi}{3}, \dfrac{4\pi}{3}$ **6.** $\dfrac{3\pi}{4}, \dfrac{7\pi}{4}$ **7.** $\dfrac{15}{8}$

8. $-3, \dfrac{5}{2}$ **9.** $\dfrac{2 \pm \sqrt{14}}{2}$ **10.** $-1, 3$

1–5. Proofs   **7.** $\dfrac{2\pi}{3} + 2n\pi, \dfrac{4\pi}{3} + 2n\pi$

9. $\dfrac{\pi}{3} + 2n\pi, \dfrac{2\pi}{3} + 2n\pi$ **11.** $\dfrac{\pi}{4} + \dfrac{n\pi}{2}$

13. $\dfrac{\pi}{6} + n\pi, \dfrac{5\pi}{6} + n\pi$ **15.** $n\pi, \dfrac{\pi}{4} + n\pi$

17. $n\pi, \dfrac{3\pi}{2} + 2n\pi$ **19.** $\dfrac{\pi}{3} + n\pi, \dfrac{2\pi}{3} + n\pi$

21. $\dfrac{\pi}{3}, \dfrac{5\pi}{3}$ **23.** $\dfrac{7\pi}{6}, \dfrac{3\pi}{2}, \dfrac{11\pi}{6}$ **25.** $0, \dfrac{\pi}{2}, \pi, \dfrac{3\pi}{2}$

27. $\dfrac{\pi}{3}, \dfrac{3\pi}{4}, \dfrac{4\pi}{3}, \dfrac{7\pi}{4}$ **29.** $\dfrac{\pi}{6}, \dfrac{5\pi}{6}, \dfrac{7\pi}{6}, \dfrac{11\pi}{6}$

31. No solution   **33.** $\dfrac{2\pi}{3}, \dfrac{5\pi}{6}, \dfrac{5\pi}{3}, \dfrac{11\pi}{6}$ **35.** $\dfrac{\pi}{2}$

37. π **39.** $\dfrac{\pi}{3}, \dfrac{5\pi}{3}$

41. $-5, \dfrac{3}{2}$
     $0.9828, 1.7682, 4.1244, 4.9098$
43. $\dfrac{1}{3}, \dfrac{3}{4}$
     $0.3398, 0.8481, 2.2935, 2.8018$

45. $\frac{2}{3}, \frac{3}{2}$
0.8411, 5.4421

47. $4 \pm \sqrt{3}$
1.1555, 1.3981, 4.2971, 4.5397

49. $-1 \pm \sqrt{2}$
0.4271, 2.7145

51. Maximum: $\left(\frac{\pi}{4}, \sqrt{2}\right)$, Minimum: $\left(\frac{5\pi}{4}, -\sqrt{2}\right)$

53. 0.04, 0.43, 0.83   **55.** 37° or 53°

Section 6.4   *(page 456)*

WARM UP   **1.** $\frac{\sqrt{10}}{10}$ **2.** $\frac{-5\sqrt{34}}{34}$ **3.** $-\frac{\sqrt{7}}{4}$

4. $\frac{2\sqrt{2}}{3}$ **5.** $\frac{\pi}{4}, \frac{3\pi}{4}$ **6.** $\frac{\pi}{2}, \frac{3\pi}{2}$ **7.** $\tan^3 x$

8. $\cot^2 x$ **9.** $\sec x$ **10.** $1 - \tan^2 x$

1. $\sin 75° = \frac{\sqrt{2}}{4}(1 + \sqrt{3})$

$\cos 75° = \frac{\sqrt{2}}{4}(\sqrt{3} - 1)$

$\tan 75° = \sqrt{3} + 2$

3. $\sin 105° = \frac{\sqrt{2}}{4}(\sqrt{3} + 1)$

$\cos 105° = \frac{\sqrt{2}}{4}(1 - \sqrt{3})$

$\tan 105° = -2 - \sqrt{3}$

5. $\sin 195° = \frac{\sqrt{2}}{4}(1 - \sqrt{3})$

$\cos 195° = -\frac{\sqrt{2}}{4}(\sqrt{3} + 1)$

$\tan 195° = 2 - \sqrt{3}$

7. $\sin \frac{11\pi}{12} = \frac{\sqrt{2}}{4}(\sqrt{3} - 1)$

$\cos \frac{11\pi}{12} = -\frac{\sqrt{2}}{4}(\sqrt{3} + 1)$

$\tan \frac{11\pi}{12} = -2 + \sqrt{3}$

9. $\sin \frac{17\pi}{12} = -\frac{\sqrt{2}}{4}(\sqrt{3} + 1)$

$\cos \frac{17\pi}{12} = \frac{\sqrt{2}}{4}(1 - \sqrt{3})$

$\tan \frac{17\pi}{12} = 2 + \sqrt{3}$

11. $\cos 40°$ **13.** $\sin 200°$ **15.** $\tan 239°$
17. $\sin 1.8$ **19.** $\tan 3x$ **21.** $\frac{33}{65}$ **23.** $-\frac{56}{65}$
25. $-\frac{3}{5}$ **27.** $\frac{44}{125}$ **29–45.** Proofs

47. (a) $\sqrt{2} \sin\left(\theta + \frac{\pi}{4}\right)$ (b) $\sqrt{2} \cos\left(\theta - \frac{\pi}{4}\right)$

49. (a) $13 \sin(3\theta + 0.3948)$ (b) $13 \cos(3\theta - 0.3948)$

51. $\sqrt{2} \sin \theta + \sqrt{2} \cos \theta$ **53.** 1   **55.** $\frac{\pi}{2}$

57. $\frac{\pi}{4}, \frac{7\pi}{4}$ **59.** $0, \frac{\pi}{3}, \pi, \frac{5\pi}{3}$ **61.** Proof

63. Proof

Section 6.5   *(page 466)*

WARM UP   **1.** $\sin x(2 + \cos x)$

2. $(\cos x - 2)(\cos x + 1)$ **3.** $0, \frac{\pi}{2}, \pi, \frac{3\pi}{2}$

4. $\frac{\pi}{4}, \frac{3\pi}{4}, \frac{5\pi}{4}, \frac{7\pi}{4}$ **5.** π **6.** 0   **7.** $\frac{2 - \sqrt{2}}{4}$

8. $\frac{3}{4}$ **9.** $\tan 3x$ **10.** $\cos x(1 - 4\sin^2 x)$

1. $0, \frac{\pi}{3}, \pi, \frac{5\pi}{3}$ **3.** $\frac{\pi}{12}, \frac{5\pi}{12}, \frac{13\pi}{12}, \frac{17\pi}{12}$

5. $0, \frac{2\pi}{3}, \frac{4\pi}{3}$ **7.** $\frac{\pi}{2}, \frac{\pi}{6}, \frac{5\pi}{6}, \frac{7\pi}{6}, \frac{3\pi}{2}, \frac{11\pi}{6}$

9. $0, \frac{\pi}{2}, \pi, \frac{3\pi}{2}$

11.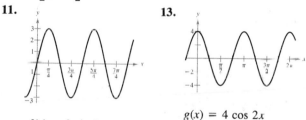

$f(x) = 3 \sin 2x$ $g(x) = 4 \cos 2x$

13.

15. $\sin 2u = \frac{24}{25}$ **17.** $\sin 2u = \frac{4}{5}$ **19.** $\sin 2u = -\frac{4\sqrt{21}}{25}$
$\cos 2u = \frac{7}{25}$ $\cos 2u = \frac{3}{5}$ $\cos 2u = -\frac{17}{25}$
$\tan 2u = \frac{24}{7}$ $\tan 2u = \frac{4}{3}$ $\tan 2u = \frac{4\sqrt{21}}{17}$

21. $\frac{1}{8}(3 + 4\cos 2x + \cos 4x)$ **23.** $\frac{1}{8}(1 - \cos 4x)$
25. $\frac{1}{32}(2 + \cos 2x - 2\cos 4x - \cos 6x)$
27. $\sin 105° = \frac{1}{2}\sqrt{2 + \sqrt{3}}$
$\cos 105° = -\frac{1}{2}\sqrt{2 - \sqrt{3}}$
$\tan 105° = -2 - \sqrt{3}$
29. $\sin 112°30' = \frac{1}{2}\sqrt{2 + \sqrt{2}}$
$\cos 112°30' = -\frac{1}{2}\sqrt{2 - \sqrt{2}}$
$\tan 112°30' = -1 - \sqrt{2}$

31. $\sin \dfrac{\pi}{8} = \dfrac{1}{2}\sqrt{2 - \sqrt{2}}$ **33.** $\sin \dfrac{u}{2} = \dfrac{5\sqrt{26}}{26}$

$\cos \dfrac{\pi}{8} = \dfrac{1}{2}\sqrt{2 + \sqrt{2}}$ $\cos \dfrac{u}{2} = \dfrac{\sqrt{26}}{26}$

$\tan \dfrac{\pi}{8} = \sqrt{2} - 1$ $\tan \dfrac{u}{2} = 5$

35. $\sin \dfrac{u}{2} = \sqrt{\dfrac{89 - 8\sqrt{89}}{178}}$ **37.** $\sin \dfrac{u}{2} = \dfrac{3\sqrt{10}}{10}$

$\cos \dfrac{u}{2} = -\sqrt{\dfrac{89 + 8\sqrt{89}}{178}}$ $\cos \dfrac{u}{2} = -\dfrac{\sqrt{10}}{10}$

$\tan \dfrac{u}{2} = \dfrac{8 - \sqrt{89}}{5}$ $\tan \dfrac{u}{2} = -3$

39. $|\sin 3x|$ **41.** $-|\tan 4x|$ **43.** π **45.** $\dfrac{\pi}{3}, \pi, \dfrac{5\pi}{3}$

47. $3\left(\sin \dfrac{\pi}{2} + \sin 0\right)$ **49.** $\dfrac{1}{2}(\sin 8\theta + \sin 2\theta)$

51. $\dfrac{5}{2}(\cos 8\beta + \cos 2\beta)$ **53.** $\dfrac{1}{2}(\cos 2y - \cos 2x)$

55. $\dfrac{1}{2}(\sin 2\theta + \sin 2\pi)$ **57.** $2 \sin 45° \cos 15°$

59. $-2 \sin \dfrac{\pi}{2} \sin \dfrac{\pi}{4}$ **61.** $2 \cos 4x \cos 2x$

63. $2 \cos \alpha \sin \beta$ **65.** $2 \cos(\phi + \pi) \cos \pi$

67. $0, \dfrac{\pi}{4}, \dfrac{\pi}{2}, \dfrac{3\pi}{4}, \pi, \dfrac{5\pi}{4}, \dfrac{3\pi}{2}, \dfrac{7\pi}{4}$ **69.** $\dfrac{\pi}{6}, \dfrac{5\pi}{6}$

71–87. Proofs

89.

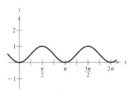

91. $2x\sqrt{1 - x^2}$ **93.** Proof

95. $f(x) = \sin x(2 \cos x + 1)$

$0, \dfrac{2\pi}{3}, \pi, \dfrac{4\pi}{3}$

97. (a) $A = 100 \sin \dfrac{\theta}{2} \cos \dfrac{\theta}{2}$

(b) $A = 50 \sin \theta$

The area is maximum when $\theta = \dfrac{\pi}{2}$.

Chapter 6   Review Exercises   (page 469)

1. $\sin^2 x$ **3.** $1 + \cot \alpha$ **5.** 1   **7.** 1

9. $\cos^2 2x$ **11–35.** Proofs   **37.** $\dfrac{\sqrt{2}}{4}(\sqrt{3} + 1)$

39. $-\dfrac{1}{2}\sqrt{2 + \sqrt{2}}$ **41.** $-\dfrac{3}{52}(5 + 4\sqrt{7})$

43. $\dfrac{1}{52}(36 + 5\sqrt{7})$ **45.** $\dfrac{1}{4}\sqrt{2(4 - \sqrt{7})}$

47. False; if $\dfrac{\pi}{2} < \theta < \pi$, then $\cos \dfrac{\theta}{2} > 0$.   **49.** True

51. $0, \pi$ **53.** $\dfrac{\pi}{3}, \dfrac{5\pi}{3}$ **55.** $0, \dfrac{3\pi}{4}, \pi, \dfrac{5\pi}{4}$

57. $0, \dfrac{\pi}{2}, \pi$ **59.** $\dfrac{\pi}{4}, \dfrac{5\pi}{4}$ **61.** $2 \cos \dfrac{5\theta}{2} \cos \dfrac{\theta}{2}$

63. $\dfrac{1}{2}(\cos \alpha - \cos 5\alpha)$ **65.** $8x^2 - 1$ **67.** Proof

69. (a) $y = \dfrac{1}{2}\sqrt{10} \sin\left(8t - \arctan \dfrac{1}{3}\right)$

(b) $\dfrac{1}{2}\sqrt{10}$ (c) $\dfrac{4}{\pi}$

CHAPTER 7

Section 7.1   (page 478)

WARM UP   **1.** $b = 3\sqrt{3}, A = 30°, B = 60°$
2. $c = 5\sqrt{2}, A = 45°, B = 45°$
3. $a = 8, A \approx 28.07°, B \approx 61.93°$
4. $b \approx 8.33, c \approx 11.21, B = 48°$
5. $a \approx 22.69, c \approx 23.04, A = 80°$
6. $a \approx 45.73, b \approx 142.86, A = 17° 45'$ **7.** 8.48
8. 12.94   **9.** 2.25   **10.** 91.06

1. $C = 105°, b \approx 14.14, c \approx 19.32$
3. $C = 110°, b \approx 22.44, c \approx 24.35$
5. $B \approx 21.55°, C \approx 122.45°, c \approx 11.49$
7. $B = 10°, b \approx 69.46, c \approx 136.81$
9. $B = 42° 4', a \approx 22.05, b \approx 14.88$
11. $A \approx 10° 11', C \approx 154° 19', c \approx 11.03$
13. $A \approx 25.57°, B \approx 9.43°, a \approx 10.5$
15. $B \approx 18° 13', C \approx 51° 32', c \approx 40.06$
17. No solution
19. Two solutions:
$B \approx 70.4°, C \approx 51.6°, c \approx 4.16$
$B \approx 109.6°, C \approx 12.4°, c \approx 1.14$
21. No solution

23. (a) $b \leq 5, b = \dfrac{5}{\sin 36°}$

(b) $5 < b < \dfrac{5}{\sin 36°}$ (c) $b > \dfrac{5}{\sin 36°}$

25. 10.4   **27.** 1675.2   **29.** 474.9   **31.** 6 ft
33. 77 yd   **35.** 5 mi   **37.** 26.1 mi, 15.9 mi
39. 4.55 mi   **41.** No solution

Section 7.2   (page 487)

WARM UP   **1.** $2\sqrt{13}$ **2.** $3\sqrt{5}$ **3.** $4\sqrt{10}$
4. $3\sqrt{13}$ **5.** 20   **6.** 48
7. $a \approx 4.62, c \approx 26.20, B = 70°$
8. $a \approx 34.20, b \approx 93.97, B = 70°$ **9.** No solution
10. $a \approx 15.09, B \approx 18.97°, C \approx 131.03°$

1. $A \approx 27.7°$, $B \approx 40.5°$, $C \approx 111.8°$
3. $B \approx 23.8°$, $C \approx 126.2°$, $a \approx 12.4$
5. $A \approx 36.9°$, $B \approx 53.1°$, $C \approx 90°$
7. $A \approx 92.9°$, $B \approx 43.55°$, $C \approx 43.55°$
9. $a \approx 11.79$, $B \approx 12.7°$, $C \approx 47.3°$
11. $A \approx 158° \, 36'$, $C \approx 12° \, 38'$, $b \approx 10.4$
13. $A = 27° \, 10'$, $B = 27° \, 10'$, $c \approx 56.9$

	a	b	c	d	θ	ϕ
15.	4	6	9.67	3.23	30°	150°
17.	10	14	20	13.86	68.2°	111.8°
19.	10	11.57	18	12	67.1°	112.9°

21. 16.25   23. 54   25. 96.82   27. 97,979.6 ft²
29. N 52° 37′ E, S 64° 40′ E   31. 43.3 mi
33. 1344 ft   35. 114.95°
37. $\overline{PQ} \approx 9.4$ ft
    $\overline{QS} \approx 5.0$ ft
    $\overline{RS} \approx 12.8$ ft
39. (a) N 58.3° W   (b) S 81.6° W
41. (a) 63.7 ft   (b) 47.6 ft   43. 3.26 ft
45. (a) 570.60   (b) 5910.68   (c) 177.09
47. Proof

Section 7.3   *(page 501)*

WARM UP   1. $7\sqrt{10}$ 2. $\sqrt{58}$
3. $3x + 5y - 14 = 0$ 4. $4x - 3y - 1 = 0$
5. $111.8°$ 6. $323.1°$ 7. $\dfrac{1}{2}, \dfrac{\sqrt{3}}{2}$ 8. $\dfrac{\sqrt{3}}{2}, -\dfrac{1}{2}$
9. $-\dfrac{\sqrt{3}}{2}, \dfrac{1}{2}$ 10. $-\dfrac{1}{2}, -\dfrac{\sqrt{3}}{2}$

1.
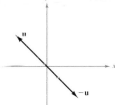

3.

5.
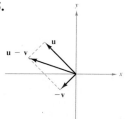

7. $v = \langle 3, 4 \rangle$, $\|v\| = 5$ 9. $v = \langle -3, 2 \rangle$, $\|v\| = \sqrt{13}$
11. $v = \langle 0, 5 \rangle$, $\|v\| = 5$
13. $v = \langle 16, -3 \rangle$, $\|v\| = \sqrt{265}$
15. $v = \langle 8, 4 \rangle$, $\|v\| = 4\sqrt{5}$ 17. (a) $\langle 4, 3 \rangle$
(b) $\langle -2, 1 \rangle$ (c) $\langle -7, 1 \rangle$ 19. (a) $\langle -4, 4 \rangle$
(b) $\langle 0, 2 \rangle$ (c) $\langle 2, 3 \rangle$ 21. (a) $\langle 4, -2 \rangle$
(b) $\langle 4, -2 \rangle$ (c) $\langle 8, -4 \rangle$ 23. (a) $3i - 2j$
(b) $-i + 4j$ (c) $-4i + 11j$ 25. (a) $2i + j$
(b) $2i - j$ (c) $4i - 3j$ 27. $\|v\| = 5$, $\theta = 30°$
29. $\|v\| = 6\sqrt{2}$, $\theta = 315°$

31. $v = \langle 3, 0 \rangle$
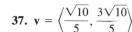

33. $v = \left\langle -\dfrac{\sqrt{3}}{2}, \dfrac{1}{2} \right\rangle$
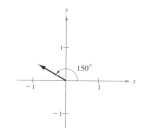

35. $v = \left\langle -\dfrac{3\sqrt{6}}{2}, \dfrac{3\sqrt{2}}{2} \right\rangle$ 37. $v = \left\langle \dfrac{\sqrt{10}}{5}, \dfrac{3\sqrt{10}}{5} \right\rangle$
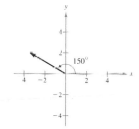
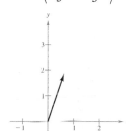

39. $v = \left\langle 3, -\dfrac{3}{2} \right\rangle$ 41. $v = \langle 4, 3 \rangle$

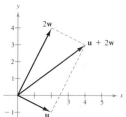

43. $\mathbf{v} = \left\langle \dfrac{7}{2}, -\dfrac{1}{2} \right\rangle$

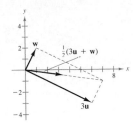

45. $\langle 5, 5 \rangle$ 　　**47.** $\langle (10\sqrt{2} - 50), 10\sqrt{2} \rangle$ 　　**49.** $\frac{4}{5}\mathbf{i} - \frac{3}{5}\mathbf{j}$
51. $\mathbf{j}$ 　　**53.** $90°$ 　　**55.** $63.4°$ 　　**57.** $62.7°$
59. $12.3°$, 82.2 lb 　　**61.** $71.3°$, 228.5 lb
63. Horizontal component: $80 \cos 50° \approx 51.42$ ft/sec
　　　Vertical component: $80 \sin 50° \approx 61.28$ ft/sec
65. $T_{AC} \approx 879.4$ lb
　　　$T_{BC} \approx 652.7$ lb
67. 3192.5 lb 　　**69.** N $25.2°$ E, 82.8 mph
71. 425 ft-lb

Section 7.4 　　*(page 511)*

WARM UP 　　**1.** $-5 - 10i$ 　　**2.** $7 + 3\sqrt{6}i$
3. $-1 - 4i$ 　　**4.** $-3i$ 　　**5.** $6 - 14i$ 　　**6.** $6 + 4\sqrt{2}i$
7. $-22 + 16i$ 　　**8.** 13 　　**9.** $-\frac{3}{2} + \frac{5}{2}i$ 　　**10.** $-\frac{5}{2} - \frac{3}{2}i$

1. 5

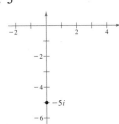

3. $4\sqrt{2}$

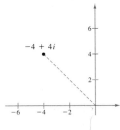

5. $\sqrt{85}$

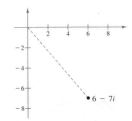

7. $4\left(\cos \dfrac{\pi}{2} + i \sin \dfrac{\pi}{2} \right)$ 　　**9.** $3\sqrt{2}\left(\cos \dfrac{5\pi}{4} + i \sin \dfrac{5\pi}{4} \right)$

11. $3\sqrt{2}\left(\cos \dfrac{7\pi}{4} + i \sin \dfrac{7\pi}{4} \right)$

13. $2\left(\cos \dfrac{\pi}{6} + i \sin \dfrac{\pi}{6} \right)$

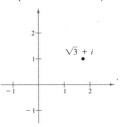

15. $4\left(\cos \dfrac{4\pi}{3} + i \sin \dfrac{4\pi}{3} \right)$ 　　**17.** $6\left(\cos \dfrac{\pi}{2} + i \sin \dfrac{\pi}{2} \right)$

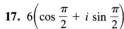
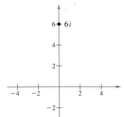

19. $\sqrt{65}(\cos 2.62 + i \sin 2.62)$

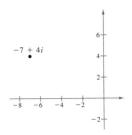

21. $7(\cos 0 + i \sin 0)$

23. $\sqrt{37}(\cos 1.41 + i \sin 1.41)$

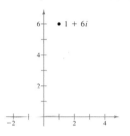

25. $\sqrt{10}(\cos 3.46 + i \sin 3.46)$

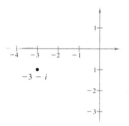

27. $-\sqrt{3} + i$

29. $\dfrac{3}{4} - \dfrac{3\sqrt{3}}{4}i$

31. $\dfrac{-15\sqrt{2}}{8} + \dfrac{15\sqrt{2}}{8}i$

33. $-4i$

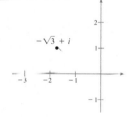

35. $2.8408 + 0.9643i$

37. $12\left(\cos \dfrac{\pi}{2} + i \sin \dfrac{\pi}{2}\right)$ **39.** $\dfrac{10}{9}(\cos 200° + i \sin 200°)$

41. $0.27(\cos 150° + i \sin 150°)$

43. $\dfrac{1}{2}(\cos 80° + i \sin 80°)$ **45.** $\cos \dfrac{2\pi}{3} + i \sin \dfrac{2\pi}{3}$

47. $4[\cos(-58°) + i \sin(-58°)]$

49. (a) $2\sqrt{2}(\cos 45° + i \sin 45°)$; $\sqrt{2}[\cos(-45°) + i \sin(-45°)]$

(b) $4(\cos 0° + i \sin 0°) = 4$

(c) 4

51. (a) $2[\cos(-90°) + i \sin(-90°)]$; $\sqrt{2}(\cos 45° + i \sin 45°)$

(b) $2\sqrt{2}[\cos(-45°) + i \sin(-45°)] = 2 - 2i$

(c) $-2i - 2i^2 = -2i + 2 = 2 - 2i$

53. (a) $5(\cos 0° + i \sin 0°)$; $\sqrt{13}(\cos 56.31° + i \sin 56.31°)$

(b) $\dfrac{5}{\sqrt{13}}[\cos(-56.31°) + i \sin(-56.31°)] \approx 0.7692 - 1.154i$

(c) $\dfrac{10}{13} - \dfrac{15}{13}i \approx 0.7692 - 1.154i$

55. Proof **57. (a)** r^2 **(b)** $\cos 2\theta + i \sin 2\theta$

59.

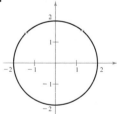

Section 7.5 *(page 518)*

WARM UP **1.** $3\sqrt[3]{2}$ **2.** $2\sqrt{2}$

3. $5\sqrt{2}(\cos 135° + i \sin 135°)$

4. $3(\cos 270° + i \sin 270°)$

5. $12(\cos 180° + i \sin 180°)$ **6.** $12(\cos 0° + i \sin 0°)$

7. $\cos \dfrac{3\pi}{4} + i \sin \dfrac{3\pi}{4}$ **8.** $\cos \dfrac{11\pi}{12} + i \sin \dfrac{11\pi}{12}$

9. $2\left(\cos \dfrac{\pi}{2} + i \sin \dfrac{\pi}{2}\right)$ **10.** $\dfrac{2}{3}(\cos 45° + i \sin 45°)$

---

1. $-4 - 4i$ **3.** $-32i$ **5.** $-128\sqrt{3} - 128i$

7. $\dfrac{125}{2} + \dfrac{125\sqrt{3}}{2}i$ **9.** i **11.** $608.02 + 144.69i$

13. (a) $3(\cos 60° + i \sin 60°)$
    $3(\cos 240° + i \sin 240°)$

(b)

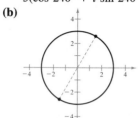

(c) $\dfrac{3}{2} + \dfrac{3\sqrt{3}}{2}i, \ -\dfrac{3}{2} - \dfrac{3\sqrt{3}}{2}i$

15. (a) $2\left(\cos \dfrac{\pi}{3} + i \sin \dfrac{\pi}{3}\right)$
    $2\left(\cos \dfrac{5\pi}{6} + i \sin \dfrac{5\pi}{6}\right)$
    $2\left(\cos \dfrac{4\pi}{3} + i \sin \dfrac{4\pi}{3}\right)$
    $2\left(\cos \dfrac{11\pi}{6} + i \sin \dfrac{11\pi}{6}\right)$

(b)

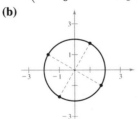

(c) $1 + \sqrt{3}i, \ -\sqrt{3} + i, \ -1 - \sqrt{3}i, \ \sqrt{3} - i$

17. (a) $5\left(\cos \dfrac{3\pi}{4} + i \sin \dfrac{3\pi}{4}\right)$
    $5\left(\cos \dfrac{7\pi}{4} + i \sin \dfrac{7\pi}{4}\right)$

(b)

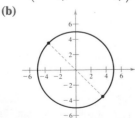

(c) $-\dfrac{5\sqrt{2}}{2} + \dfrac{5\sqrt{2}}{2}i, \ \dfrac{5\sqrt{2}}{2} - \dfrac{5\sqrt{2}}{2}i$

19. (a) $5\left(\cos \dfrac{4\pi}{9} + i \sin \dfrac{4\pi}{9}\right)$
    $5\left(\cos \dfrac{10\pi}{9} + i \sin \dfrac{10\pi}{9}\right)$
    $5\left(\cos \dfrac{16\pi}{9} + i \sin \dfrac{16\pi}{9}\right)$

(b)

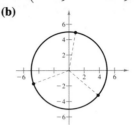

(c) $0.8682 + 4.924i, \ -4.698 - 1.710i,$
    $3.830 - 3.214i$

21. (a) $2(\cos 0 + i \sin 0)$
    $2\left(\cos \dfrac{2\pi}{3} + i \sin \dfrac{2\pi}{3}\right)$
    $2\left(\cos \dfrac{4\pi}{3} + i \sin \dfrac{4\pi}{3}\right)$

(b)

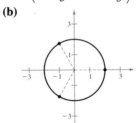

(c) $2, \ -1 + \sqrt{3}i, \ -1 - \sqrt{3}i$

23. (a) $\cos 0 + i \sin 0$
    $\cos \dfrac{2\pi}{5} + i \sin \dfrac{2\pi}{5}$
    $\cos \dfrac{4\pi}{5} + i \sin \dfrac{4\pi}{5}$
    $\cos \dfrac{6\pi}{5} + i \sin \dfrac{6\pi}{5}$
    $\cos \dfrac{8\pi}{5} + i \sin \dfrac{8\pi}{5}$

(b)

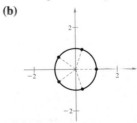

(c) $1, \ 0.3090 + 0.9511i, \ -0.8090 + 0.5878i,$
    $-0.8090 - 0.5878i, \ 0.3090 - 0.9511i$

25. $\cos \dfrac{\pi}{8} + i \sin \dfrac{\pi}{8}$

$\cos \dfrac{5\pi}{8} + i \sin \dfrac{5\pi}{8}$

$\cos \dfrac{9\pi}{8} + i \sin \dfrac{9\pi}{8}$

$\cos \dfrac{13\pi}{8} + i \sin \dfrac{13\pi}{8}$

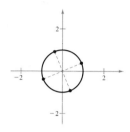

27. $3\left(\cos \dfrac{\pi}{5} + i \sin \dfrac{\pi}{5}\right)$

$3\left(\cos \dfrac{3\pi}{5} + i \sin \dfrac{3\pi}{5}\right)$

$3(\cos \pi + i \sin \pi)$

$3\left(\cos \dfrac{7\pi}{5} + i \sin \dfrac{7\pi}{5}\right)$

$3\left(\cos \dfrac{9\pi}{5} + i \sin \dfrac{9\pi}{5}\right)$

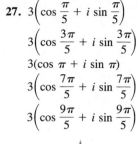

31. $\left\langle \dfrac{6}{\sqrt{61}}, -\dfrac{5}{\sqrt{61}} \right\rangle$

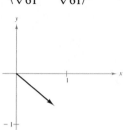

33. $\langle -26, -35 \rangle$

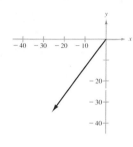

29. $4\left(\cos \dfrac{\pi}{2} + i \sin \dfrac{\pi}{2}\right)$

$4\left(\cos \dfrac{7\pi}{6} + i \sin \dfrac{7\pi}{6}\right)$

$4\left(\cos \dfrac{11\pi}{6} + i \sin \dfrac{11\pi}{6}\right)$

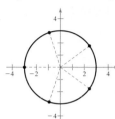

31. $\sqrt[6]{2}(\cos 105° + i \sin 105°)$

$\sqrt[6]{2}(\cos 225° + i \sin 225°)$

$\sqrt[6]{2}(\cos 345° + i \sin 345°)$

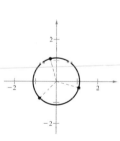

35. 92.3°, 117.0   **37.** 100 lb

39. 460.3 mph, N 32.2° E

41. $5\sqrt{2}(\cos 315° + i \sin 315°)$

43. $13(\cos 67.38° + i \sin 67.38°)$ **45.** $-50 - 50\sqrt{3}i$

47. 13

49. (a) $z_1 = 5(\cos \pi + i \sin \pi)$

$z_2 = 5\left(\cos \dfrac{\pi}{2} + i \sin \dfrac{\pi}{2}\right)$

(b) $z_1 z_2 = 25\left(\cos \dfrac{3\pi}{2} + i \sin \dfrac{3\pi}{2}\right)$

$\dfrac{z_1}{z_2} = \cos \dfrac{\pi}{2} + i \sin \dfrac{\pi}{2}$

51. (a) $z_1 = 3\sqrt{2}\left(\cos \dfrac{5\pi}{4} + i \sin \dfrac{5\pi}{4}\right)$

$z_2 = 4\left(\cos \dfrac{\pi}{6} + i \sin \dfrac{\pi}{6}\right)$

(b) $z_1 z_2 = 12\sqrt{2}\left(\cos \dfrac{17\pi}{12} + i \sin \dfrac{17\pi}{12}\right)$

$\dfrac{z_1}{z_2} = \dfrac{3\sqrt{2}}{4}\left(\cos \dfrac{13\pi}{12} + i \sin \dfrac{13\pi}{12}\right)$

53. $\dfrac{625}{2} + \dfrac{625\sqrt{3}}{2}i$ **55.** $2035 - 828i$

57. $3\left(\cos \dfrac{\pi}{4} + i \sin \dfrac{\pi}{4}\right)$

$3\left(\cos \dfrac{7\pi}{12} + i \sin \dfrac{7\pi}{12}\right)$

$3\left(\cos \dfrac{11\pi}{12} + i \sin \dfrac{11\pi}{12}\right)$

$3\left(\cos \dfrac{5\pi}{4} + i \sin \dfrac{5\pi}{4}\right)$

$3\left(\cos \dfrac{19\pi}{12} + i \sin \dfrac{19\pi}{12}\right)$

$3\left(\cos \dfrac{23\pi}{12} + i \sin \dfrac{23\pi}{12}\right)$

59. $\cos \dfrac{\pi}{3} + i \sin \dfrac{\pi}{3} = \dfrac{1}{2} + \dfrac{\sqrt{3}}{2}i$

$\cos \pi + i \sin \pi = -1$

$\cos \dfrac{5\pi}{3} + i \sin \dfrac{5\pi}{3} = \dfrac{1}{2} - \dfrac{\sqrt{3}}{2}i$

Chapter 7   Review Exercises   *(page 519)*

1. $A \approx 29.7°,\ B \approx 52.4°,\ C \approx 97.9°$

3. $C = 110°,\ b \approx 20.4,\ c \approx 22.6$

5. $A = 35°,\ C = 35°,\ b \approx 6.6$ **7.** No solution

9. $A \approx 25.9°,\ C \approx 39.1°,\ c \approx 10.1$

11. $B \approx 31.2°,\ C \approx 133.8°,\ c \approx 13.9$

$B \approx 148.8°,\ C \approx 16.2°,\ c \approx 5.39$

13. $A \approx 9.9°,\ C \approx 20.1°,\ b \approx 29.1$

15. $A \approx 40.9°,\ C \approx 114.1°,\ c \approx 8.6$

$A \approx 139.1°,\ C \approx 15.9°,\ c \approx 2.6$

17. 9.798   **19.** 9.08   **21.** 31 ft   **23.** 31.1 m

25. 1135 mi   **27.** $\langle 7, -7 \rangle$ **29.** $\langle -4, 4\sqrt{3} \rangle$

61. $3\left(\cos\dfrac{\pi}{4} + i\sin\dfrac{\pi}{4}\right) = \dfrac{3\sqrt{2}}{2} + \dfrac{3\sqrt{2}}{2}i$

$3\left(\cos\dfrac{3\pi}{4} + i\sin\dfrac{3\pi}{4}\right) = -\dfrac{3\sqrt{2}}{2} + \dfrac{3\sqrt{2}}{2}i$

$3\left(\cos\dfrac{5\pi}{4} + i\sin\dfrac{5\pi}{4}\right) = -\dfrac{3\sqrt{2}}{2} - \dfrac{3\sqrt{2}}{2}i$

$3\left(\cos\dfrac{7\pi}{4} + i\sin\dfrac{7\pi}{4}\right) = \dfrac{3\sqrt{2}}{2} - \dfrac{3\sqrt{2}}{2}i$

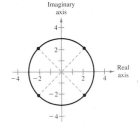

63. $\cos 0 + i\sin 0 = 1$

$\cos\dfrac{\pi}{2} + i\sin\dfrac{\pi}{2} = i$

$\cos\dfrac{2\pi}{3} + i\sin\dfrac{2\pi}{3} = -\dfrac{1}{2} + \dfrac{\sqrt{3}}{2}i$

$\cos\dfrac{4\pi}{3} + i\sin\dfrac{4\pi}{3} = -\dfrac{1}{2} - \dfrac{\sqrt{3}}{2}i$

$\cos\dfrac{3\pi}{2} + i\sin\dfrac{3\pi}{2} = -i$

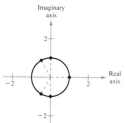

Cumulative Test for Chapters 4–7 *(page 522)*

1. (a)   **(b)**

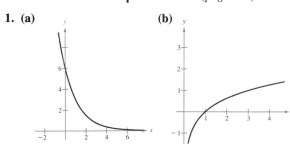

3. $\ln\dfrac{x^2}{\sqrt{x + 5}}$ **5.** $16,302.05   **7.** $134.6°$

9. $\sqrt{1 - 4x^2}$ **11.** Proof

13. (a) $B \approx 26.4°$, $C \approx 123.6°$, $c \approx 15.0$

(b) $a \approx 5.0$, $B \approx 52.5°$, $C \approx 97.5°$

15. $1, -\dfrac{1}{2} + \dfrac{\sqrt{3}}{2}i, -\dfrac{1}{2} - \dfrac{\sqrt{3}}{2}i$

17. N 32.6° E, 543.9 mph

CHAPTER 8

Section 8.1   *(page 532)*

WARM UP

1.   **2.**

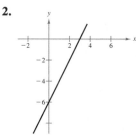

3.   **4.**

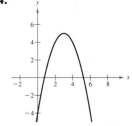

5. x **6.** $-37v$ **7.** $2x^2 + 9$ **8.** -1 **9.** $x = 6$

10. $y = 1$

1. $(1, 2)$ **3.** $(-1, 2), (2, 5)$ **5.** $(0, 5), (3, 4)$

7. $(0, 0), (2, 4)$ **9.** $(-1, 1), (8, 4)$ **11.** $(5, 5)$

13. $\left(\dfrac{1}{2}, 3\right)$ **15.** $\left(\dfrac{3}{2}, \dfrac{3}{10}\right)$ **17.** $\left(\dfrac{20}{3}, \dfrac{40}{3}\right)$ **19.** $(0, 0)$

21. $(1, 2)$ **23.** $\left(\dfrac{29}{10}, \dfrac{21}{10}\right), (-2, 0)$

25. $(-1, -2), (2, 1)$ **27.** $(-1, 0), (0, 1), (1, 0)$

29. $\left(\dfrac{1}{2}, 2\right), \left(-4, -\dfrac{1}{4}\right)$ **31.** $(2, 2), (4, 0)$

33. No points of intersection   **35.** $(3, \pm4)$ **37.** $(0, 1)$

39. $(0, 0), (1, 1)$ **41.** $(0, -13), (\pm12, 5)$

43. 193 units   **45.** 233,334 units   **47.** 6,400 units

49. $13,000 at 8%, $12,000 at 8.25%

51. More than $8,333.33   **53. (a)** 24.7 in

(b) Doyle Log Rule   **55.** 8 mi × 12 mi

57. (a) $y = 2x$ **(b)** $y = 0$ **(c)** $y = x - 2$

Section 8.2   *(page 542)*

WARM UP

1. 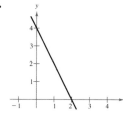   **2.**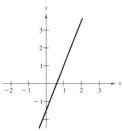

3. $x - y + 4 = 0$ **4.** $5x + 3y - 28 = 0$ **5.** $-\frac{1}{2}$
6. $\frac{7}{4}$ **7.** Perpendicular   **8.** Parallel
9. Neither parallel nor perpendicular   **10.** Perpendicular

1. (2, 0)   **3.** $(-1, -1)$

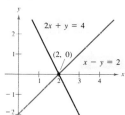   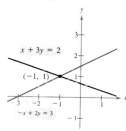

5. Inconsistent   **7.** All points (x, y) lying on the line $3x - 2y = 6$.

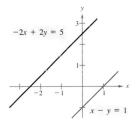   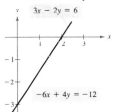

9. $\left(-\frac{1}{3}, -\frac{2}{3}\right)$ **11.** $\left(\frac{5}{2}, \frac{3}{4}\right)$ **13.** (3, 4)

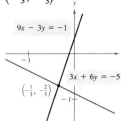

15. (4, −1)   **17.** (40, 40)   **19.** Inconsistent   **21.** $\left(\frac{18}{5}, \frac{3}{5}\right)$
23. (5, −2)   **25.** All points (x, y) lying on the line $x - 2y = 5$.
27. $\left(\frac{90}{31}, -\frac{67}{31}\right)$ **29.** $\left(-\frac{6}{35}, \frac{43}{35}\right)$
31. (79,400, 398)   It is necessary to change the scale on the axes to see the point of intersection of the lines.
33. 550 mph, 50 mph
35. $\frac{20}{3}$ gal of 20% solution, $\frac{10}{3}$ gal of 50% solution
37. $4,000 at 10.5%, $8,000 at 12%
39. 375 adults, 125 children   **41.** (80, 10)
43. (100, 200)   **45.** (2,000,000, 100)
47. 75 mi, 225 mi   **49.** $y = 0.97x + 2.10$
51. $y = 0.318 x + 4.061$ **53.** $y = \frac{3}{4}x + \frac{4}{3}$
55. $y = -2x + 4$ **57.** $y = -240x + 685$, 349 units
59. $x + 2y = 8$
    $x + 4y = 13$

Section 8.3   *(page 558)*

WARM UP   **1.** (15, 10)   **2.** $\left(-2, -\frac{8}{3}\right)$ **3.** (28, 4)
4. (4, 3)   **5.** Not a solution   **6.** Not a solution
7. Solution   **8.** Solution   **9.** $5a + 2$ **10.** $a + 13$

1. (1, 2, 3)   **3.** (2, −3, −2)   **5.** (5, −2, 0)
7. Inconsistent   **9.** $\left(1, -\frac{3}{2}, \frac{1}{2}\right)$
11. $(-3a + 10, 5a - 7, a)$ **13.** $\left(13 - 4a, \frac{45}{2} - \frac{15}{2}a, a\right)$
15. $(-a, 2a - 1, a)$ **17.** $\left(\frac{1}{2} - \frac{3}{2}a, 1 - \frac{2}{3}a, a\right)$
19. (1, 1, 1, 1)   **21.** Inconsistent   **23.** (0, 0, 0)
25. $\left(-\frac{3}{5}a, \frac{4}{5}a, a\right)$ **27.** $y = 2x^2 + 3x - 4$
29. $y - x^2 - 4x + 3$ **31.** $x^2 + y^2 - 4x = 0$
33. $x^2 + y^2 - 6x - 8y = 0$ **35.** $s = -16t^2 + 144$
37. $s = -16t^2 - 32t + 500$
39. $4,000 at 5%, $5,000 at 6%, $7,000 at 7%
41. $300,000 at 8%, $400,000 at 9%, $75,000 at 10%
43. $250,000 - \frac{1}{2}s$ in certificates of deposit
    $125,000 + \frac{1}{2}s$ in municipal bonds
    $125,000 - s$ in blue-chip stocks
    s in growth stocks
45. 20 gal of spray X, 18 gal of spray Y, 16 gal of spray Z
47. Use 4 medium trucks or use 2 large, 1 medium, and 2 small trucks
49. $t_1 = 96$ lb
    $t_2 = 48$ lb
    $a = -16$ ft/sec^2
51. $\frac{1}{2}\left(-\frac{2}{x} + \frac{1}{x - 1} + \frac{1}{x + 1}\right)$
53. $\frac{1}{2}\left(\frac{1}{x} - \frac{1}{x - 2} + \frac{2}{x + 3}\right)$
55. $y = -\frac{5}{24}x^2 - \frac{3}{10}x + \frac{41}{6}$ **57.** $y = x^2 - x$

1. $x = -4, y = 22$ **3.** $x = 2, y = 3$

5. (a) $\begin{bmatrix} 3 & -2 \\ 1 & 7 \end{bmatrix}$ **(b)** $\begin{bmatrix} -1 & 0 \\ 3 & -9 \end{bmatrix}$ **(c)** $\begin{bmatrix} 3 & -3 \\ 6 & -3 \end{bmatrix}$

(d) $\begin{bmatrix} -1 & -1 \\ 8 & -19 \end{bmatrix}$ **7. (a)** $\begin{bmatrix} 7 & 3 \\ 1 & 9 \\ -2 & 15 \end{bmatrix}$ **(b)** $\begin{bmatrix} 5 & -5 \\ 3 & -1 \\ -4 & -5 \end{bmatrix}$

(c) $\begin{bmatrix} 18 & -3 \\ 6 & 12 \\ -9 & 15 \end{bmatrix}$ **(d)** $\begin{bmatrix} 16 & -11 \\ 8 & 2 \\ -11 & -5 \end{bmatrix}$

9. (a) $\begin{bmatrix} 3 & 3 & -2 & 1 & 1 \\ -2 & 5 & 7 & -6 & -8 \end{bmatrix}$

(b) $\begin{bmatrix} 1 & 1 & 0 & -1 & 1 \\ 4 & -3 & -11 & 6 & 6 \end{bmatrix}$

(c) $\begin{bmatrix} 6 & 6 & -3 & 0 & 3 \\ 3 & 3 & -6 & 0 & -3 \end{bmatrix}$

(d) $\begin{bmatrix} 4 & 4 & -1 & -2 & 3 \\ 9 & -5 & -24 & 12 & 11 \end{bmatrix}$ **11. (a)** $\begin{bmatrix} 0 & 15 \\ 6 & 12 \end{bmatrix}$

(b) $\begin{bmatrix} -2 & 2 \\ 31 & 14 \end{bmatrix}$ **(c)** $\begin{bmatrix} 9 & 6 \\ 12 & 12 \end{bmatrix}$ **13. (a)** $\begin{bmatrix} 0 & -10 \\ 10 & 0 \end{bmatrix}$

(b) $\begin{bmatrix} 0 & -10 \\ 10 & 0 \end{bmatrix}$ **(c)** $\begin{bmatrix} 8 & -6 \\ 6 & 8 \end{bmatrix}$

15. (a) $\begin{bmatrix} 6 & -21 & 15 \\ 8 & -23 & 19 \\ 4 & 7 & 5 \end{bmatrix}$ **(b)** $\begin{bmatrix} 9 & 0 & 13 \\ 7 & -2 & 21 \\ 1 & 4 & -19 \end{bmatrix}$

(c) $\begin{bmatrix} 20 & 7 & -8 \\ 24 & 7 & -2 \\ 2 & -5 & 30 \end{bmatrix}$ **17.** Not possible

19. $\begin{bmatrix} -1 & 19 \\ 4 & -27 \\ 0 & 14 \end{bmatrix}$ **21.** $\begin{bmatrix} 1 & 0 & 0 \\ 0 & 1 & 0 \\ 0 & 0 & \frac{7}{2} \end{bmatrix}$ **23.** $\begin{bmatrix} 60 & 72 \\ -20 & -24 \\ 10 & 12 \\ 60 & 72 \end{bmatrix}$

25. $\begin{bmatrix} -6 & -9 \\ -1 & 0 \\ 17 & -10 \end{bmatrix}$ **27.** $\begin{bmatrix} 3 & 3 \\ -\frac{1}{2} & 0 \\ -\frac{13}{2} & \frac{11}{2} \end{bmatrix}$

29. $A = \begin{bmatrix} -1 & 1 \\ -2 & 1 \end{bmatrix}$ **31.** $A = \begin{bmatrix} 1 & -2 & 3 \\ -1 & 3 & -1 \\ 2 & -5 & 5 \end{bmatrix}$

$X = \begin{bmatrix} x \\ y \end{bmatrix}$

$B = \begin{bmatrix} 4 \\ 0 \end{bmatrix}$ $X = \begin{bmatrix} x \\ y \\ z \end{bmatrix}$

$x = 4, y = 8$ $B = \begin{bmatrix} 9 \\ -6 \\ 17 \end{bmatrix}$

$x = 1, y = -1, z = 2$

33. $\begin{bmatrix} -4 & 0 \\ 8 & 2 \end{bmatrix}$ **35.** $\begin{bmatrix} 0 & 0 & 0 \\ 0 & 0 & 0 \\ 0 & 0 & 0 \end{bmatrix}$

37. $AC = BC = \begin{bmatrix} 12 & -6 & 9 \\ 16 & -8 & 12 \\ 4 & -2 & 3 \end{bmatrix}$ **39.** $\begin{bmatrix} 72 & 48 & 24 \\ 36 & 108 & 72 \end{bmatrix}$

41. $AB = [\$1250 \quad \$1331.25 \quad \$981.25]$
The entries represent the profit from the two products at each of the three outlets.

43. (a) $18,300   **(b)** $21,260
(c) $\begin{bmatrix} \$15,770 & \$18,300 \\ \$26,500 & \$29,250 \\ \$21,260 & \$24,150 \end{bmatrix}$
The entries are the wholesale and retail price of the inventory at each outlet.

45. $\begin{bmatrix} 0.40 & 0.15 & 0.15 \\ 0.28 & 0.53 & 0.17 \\ 0.32 & 0.32 & 0.68 \end{bmatrix}$

Section 9.3   *(page 619)*

WARM UP   **1.** $\begin{bmatrix} 4 & 24 \\ 0 & -16 \\ 48 & 8 \end{bmatrix}$ **2.** $\begin{bmatrix} \frac{11}{2} & 5 & 24 \\ \frac{1}{2} & 0 & 8 \\ 0 & 1 & 4 \end{bmatrix}$

3. $\begin{bmatrix} -5 & -2 & -13 \\ 4 & -13 & -2 \end{bmatrix}$ **4.** $\begin{bmatrix} -13 & 11 \\ -19 & 21 \end{bmatrix}$ **5.** $\begin{bmatrix} 1 & 0 \\ 0 & 1 \end{bmatrix}$

6. $\begin{bmatrix} 6 & 5 \\ 3 & -2 \end{bmatrix}$ **7.** $\begin{bmatrix} 1 & 0 & 0 \\ 0 & 1 & 0 \\ 0 & 0 & 1 \end{bmatrix}$ **8.** $\begin{bmatrix} 1 & 0 & 0 \\ 0 & 1 & 0 \\ 0 & 0 & 1 \end{bmatrix}$

9. $\begin{bmatrix} 1 & 0 & 3 & -2 \\ 0 & 1 & 4 & -3 \end{bmatrix}$

10. $\begin{bmatrix} 1 & 0 & 0 & -6 & -4 & 3 \\ 0 & 1 & 0 & 11 & 6 & -5 \\ 0 & 0 & 1 & -2 & -1 & 1 \end{bmatrix}$

1–8. Proofs
9. $\begin{bmatrix} \frac{1}{2} & 0 \\ 0 & \frac{1}{3} \end{bmatrix}$ **11.** $\begin{bmatrix} -3 & 2 \\ -2 & 1 \end{bmatrix}$ **13.** $\begin{bmatrix} 1 & -1 \\ 2 & -1 \end{bmatrix}$
15. Does not exist   **17.** Does not exist
19. $\begin{bmatrix} 1 & 1 & -1 \\ -3 & 2 & -1 \\ 3 & -3 & 2 \end{bmatrix}$ **21.** $\frac{1}{2}\begin{bmatrix} -3 & 3 & 2 \\ 9 & -7 & -6 \\ -2 & 2 & 2 \end{bmatrix}$
23. $\frac{5}{11}\begin{bmatrix} 0 & -4 & 2 \\ -22 & 11 & 11 \\ 22 & -6 & -8 \end{bmatrix}$ **25.** $\begin{bmatrix} 1 & 0 & 0 \\ -0.75 & 0.25 & 0 \\ 0.35 & -0.25 & 0.2 \end{bmatrix}$
27. Does not exist   **29.** $\begin{bmatrix} -24 & 7 & 1 & -2 \\ -10 & 3 & 0 & -1 \\ -29 & 7 & 3 & -2 \\ 12 & -3 & -1 & 1 \end{bmatrix}$
31. $(5, 0)$ **33.** $(-8, -6)$ **35.** $(4, 8)$ **37.** $(10, 30)$
39. $(3, 8, -11)$ **41.** $(2, 1, 0, 0)$
43. $10,000 in AAA rated bonds, $5,000 in A rated bonds, $10,000 in B rated bonds
45. $9,000 in AAA rated bonds, $1,000 in A rated bonds, $2,000 in B rated bonds

47. $I_1 = -3$ amps
$I_2 = 8$ amps
$I_3 = 5$ amps

Section 9.4   (page 631)

WARM UP **1.** $\begin{bmatrix} 3 & 5 \\ 4 & 0 \end{bmatrix}$ **2.** $\begin{bmatrix} -2 & 8 \\ 2 & -4 \end{bmatrix}$

3. $\begin{bmatrix} 9 & -12 & 6 \\ 3 & 0 & -3 \\ 0 & 3 & -6 \end{bmatrix}$ **4.** $\begin{bmatrix} 0 & 8 & 12 \\ -4 & 8 & 12 \\ -8 & 4 & -8 \end{bmatrix}$ **5.** -22

6. 35   **7.** -15 **8.** $-\frac{1}{8}$ **9.** -45 **10.** -16

1. 5   **3.** 5   **5.** 27   **7.** -24 **9.** 6   **11.** 0
13. -0.002 **15.** 0   **17.** 0   **19.** -9 **21.** -18
23. $-7x + 3y - 8$
25. (a) $M_{11} = -5, M_{12} = 2, M_{21} = 4, M_{22} = 3$
    (b) $C_{11} = -5, C_{12} = -2, C_{21} = -4, C_{22} = 3$
27. (a) $M_{11} = 30, M_{12} = 12, M_{13} = 11, M_{21} = -36,$
    $M_{22} = 26, M_{23} = 7, M_{31} = -4, M_{32} = -42,$
    $M_{33} = 12$
    (b) $C_{11} = 30, C_{12} = -12, C_{13} = 11, C_{21} = 36,$
    $C_{22} = 26, C_{23} = -7, C_{31} = -4, C_{32} = 42, C_{33} = 12$
29. -75 **31.** 96   **33.** 170   **35.** -58 **37.** -30
39. -108 **41.** 0   **43.** 412   **45.** $x = -1, x = 4$
47. $8uv - 1$ **49.** e^{5r} **51.** $1 - \ln x$

Section 9.5   (page 639)

WARM UP **1.** $\begin{bmatrix} 1 & 3 \\ 0 & 1 \end{bmatrix}$ **2.** $\begin{bmatrix} 1 & -3 \\ 0 & 1 \end{bmatrix}$

3. $\begin{bmatrix} 1 & 3 & 4 \\ 0 & 1 & 1 \\ 0 & 0 & 0 \end{bmatrix}$ **4.** $\begin{bmatrix} 1 & 2 & 4 \\ 0 & 1 & \frac{10}{7} \\ 0 & 0 & 0 \end{bmatrix}$ **5.** -2 **6.** 0

7. -8 **8.** x^2 **9.** 8   **10.** 60

1. Column 2 is a multiple of Column 1.
3. Row 2 has only zero entries.
5. The interchange of Columns 2 and 3 results in a change of sign of the determinant.
7. Multiplying any row by a constant multiplies the value of the determinant by that constant.
9. Multiplying the entries of all three rows by 5 multiplies the value of the determinant by 5^3.
11. Adding -4 times the entries of Row 1 to the elements of Row 2 leaves the determinant unchanged.
13. Adding multiples of Column 2 to Columns 1 and 3 leaves the determinant unchanged.
15. 1   **17.** -26 **19.** -126 **21.** 0   **23.** 0
25. 236   **27.** 7441   **29.** 410   **31.** Not invertible

33. Invertible   **35.** Invertible   **37.** $k = -1, k = 4$
39. Proof   **41.** Proof   **43.** Proof
45. (a) -3 (b) -2 (c) $\begin{bmatrix} -2 & 0 \\ 0 & -3 \end{bmatrix}$ (d) 6

47. (a) 2   (b) -6 (c) $\begin{bmatrix} 1 & 4 & 3 \\ -1 & 0 & 3 \\ 0 & 2 & 0 \end{bmatrix}$ (d) -12

Section 9.6   (page 650)

WARM UP **1.** $(1, 1)$ **2.** $(1, 2)$ **3.** $(3, 0, -4)$
4. $(-2, 1, 1)$ **5.** 8   **6.** -49 **7.** -3 **8.** 20
9. 9   **10.** 35

1. $(1, 2)$ **3.** $(2, -2)$ **5.** $\left(\frac{3}{4}, -\frac{1}{2}\right)$
7. Cramer's Rule does not apply.   **9.** $\left(\frac{2}{3}, \frac{1}{2}\right)$ **11.** -1
13. 1   **15.** 0   **17.** Cramer's Rule does not apply.
19. 5
21. $I_1 = \frac{125}{22}$ amps
    $I_2 = \frac{93}{11}$ amps
    $I_3 = \frac{61}{22}$ amps
23. $y = 1.768 + 0.202t$; Maximum contribution is about $4200.   **25.** 7   **27.** 14   **29.** $\frac{33}{8}$ **31.** $\frac{5}{2}$
33. 28   **35.** 250 sq mi   **37.** Collinear
39. Not collinear   **41.** Collinear   **43.** $3x - 5y = 0$
45. $x + 3y - 5 = 0$ **47.** $2x + 3y - 8 - 0$
49. $1\ -25\ -65\ 17\ 15\ -9\ -12\ -62\ -119\ 27\ 51\ 48\ 43\ 67$
    $48\ 57\ 111\ 117$
51. $-5\ -41\ -87\ 91\ 207\ 257\ 11\ -5\ -41\ 40\ 80\ 84\ 76\ 177$
    227
53. SEND PLANES

Chapter 9   Review Exercises   (page 653)

1. $(10, -12)$ **3.** $(0.6, 0.5)$ **5.** $(2, -3, 3)$
7. $\left(\frac{1}{2}, -\frac{1}{3}, 1\right)$ **9.** $\left(-2a + \frac{3}{2}, 2a + 1, a\right)$
11. Inconsistent   **13.** $\begin{bmatrix} -13 & -8 & 18 \\ 0 & 11 & -19 \end{bmatrix}$

15. $\begin{bmatrix} 14 & -2 & 8 \\ 14 & -10 & 40 \\ 36 & -12 & 48 \end{bmatrix}$ **17.** $\begin{bmatrix} 44 & 4 \\ 20 & 8 \end{bmatrix}$

19. $\begin{bmatrix} 4 & 6 & 3 \\ 0 & 6 & -10 \\ 0 & 0 & 6 \end{bmatrix}$ **21.** $\begin{bmatrix} -14 & -4 \\ 7 & -17 \\ -17 & -2 \end{bmatrix}$

23. $\frac{1}{3}\begin{bmatrix} 9 & 2 \\ -4 & 11 \\ 10 & 0 \end{bmatrix}$
25. $5x + 4y = \quad 2$
    $-x + \ y = -22$

27. $\begin{bmatrix} \frac{1}{5} & -\frac{1}{5} \\ \frac{1}{10} & -\frac{1}{15} \end{bmatrix}$ **29.** $\begin{bmatrix} \frac{1}{2} & -1 & -\frac{1}{2} \\ \frac{1}{2} & -\frac{2}{3} & -\frac{5}{6} \\ 0 & \frac{2}{3} & \frac{1}{3} \end{bmatrix}$

31. 550 **33.** 279 **35.** $(-3, 1)$ **37.** $(1, 1, -2)$
39. $(2, -4, 6)$ **41.** Inconsistent **43.** 16 **45.** 7
47. $x - 2y + 4 = 0$ **49.** $2x + 6y - 13 = 0$
51. 8 carnations, 4 roses **53.** $y = x^2 + 2x + 3$
55. 128; Each of the three rows is multiplied by 4.

CHAPTER 10

Section 10.1   *(page 664)*

WARM UP **1.** $\frac{4}{5}$ **2.** $\frac{1}{3}$ **3.** $(2n + 1)(2n - 1)$
4. $(2n - 1)(2n - 3)$ **5.** $(n - 1)(n - 2)$
6. $(n + 1)(n + 2)$ **7.** $\frac{1}{3}$ **8.** 24 **9.** $\frac{13}{24}$ **10.** $\frac{3}{4}$

1. 3, 5, 7, 9, 11 **3.** 2, 4, 8, 16, 32
5. $-2, 4, -8, 16, -32$ **7.** $0, 1, 0, \frac{1}{2}, 0$
9. $\frac{5}{2}, \frac{11}{4}, \frac{23}{8}, \frac{47}{16}, \frac{95}{32}$ **11.** $1, \frac{1}{2^{3/2}}, \frac{1}{3^{3/2}}, \frac{1}{4^{3/2}}, \frac{1}{5^{3/2}}$
13. $3, \frac{9}{2}, \frac{9}{2}, \frac{27}{8}, \frac{81}{40}$ **15.** $-1, \frac{1}{4}, -\frac{1}{9}, \frac{1}{16}, -\frac{1}{25}$
17. 3, 4, 6, 10, 18 **19.** $\frac{1}{30}$ **21.** $n + 1$
23. $\dfrac{1}{2n(2n + 1)}$ **25.** $a_n = 3n - 2$ **27.** $a_n = n^2 - 1$
29. $a_n = \dfrac{(-1)^{n+1}}{2^n}$ **31.** $a_n = 1 + \dfrac{1}{n}$ **33.** $a_n = \dfrac{1}{n!}$
35. $a_n = (-1)^{n+1}$ **37.** 35 **39.** 40 **41.** 30
43. $\frac{9}{5}$ **45.** 238 **47.** 56 **49.** $\frac{47}{60}$ **51.** $\sum_{i=1}^{9} \dfrac{1}{3i}$
53. $\sum_{i=1}^{8} \left[2\left(\dfrac{i}{8}\right) + 3 \right]$ **55.** $\sum_{i=1}^{6} (-1)^{i+1} 3^i$
57. $\sum_{i=1}^{20} \dfrac{(-1)^{i+1}}{i^2}$ **59.** $\sum_{i=1}^{5} \dfrac{2^i - 1}{2^{i+1}}$
61. (a) $A_1 = \$5,100.00$, $A_2 = \$5,202.00$, $A_3 = \$5,306.04$,
  $A_4 = \$5,412.16$, $A_5 = \$5,520.40$, $A_6 = \$5,630.81$,
  $A_7 = \$5,743.43$, $A_8 = \$5,858.30$
  (b) $\$11,040.20$
63. $a_0 = 242.67$, $a_1 = 285.34$, $a_2 = 328.01$,
  $a_3 = 370.68$, $a_4 = 413.35$, $a_5 = 456.02$,
  $a_6 = 498.69$, $a_7 = 541.36$

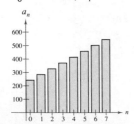

65. 16.02; Result of adding dividends in the figure is 16.11.

Section 10.2   *(page 674)*

WARM UP **1.** 36 **2.** 240 **3.** $\frac{11}{2}$ **4.** $\frac{10}{3}$
5. 18 **6.** 4 **7.** 143 **8.** 160 **9.** 430
10. 256

1. Arithmetic sequence, $d = 3$
3. Not an arithmetic sequence
5. Arithmetic sequence, $d = -\frac{1}{4}$
7. Not an arithmetic sequence
9. Arithmetic sequence, $d = 0.4$
11. 8, 11, 14, 17, 20; Arithmetic sequence, $d = 3$
13. $\frac{1}{2}, \frac{1}{3}, \frac{1}{4}, \frac{1}{5}, \frac{1}{6}$; Not an arithmetic sequence
15. 97, 94, 91, 88, 85; Arithmetic sequence, $d = -3$
17. 1, 1, 2, 3, 5; Not an arithmetic sequence
19. $a_n = 3n - 2$ **21.** $a_n = -8n + 108$
23. $a_n = 2xn - x$ **25** $a_n = -\frac{5}{2}n + \frac{13}{2}$
27. $a_n = \frac{10}{3}n + \frac{5}{3}$ **29.** $a_n = -3n + 103$
31. 5, 11, 17, 23, 29
33. $-2.6, -3.0, -3.4, -3.8, -4.2$ **35.** $\frac{3}{2}, \frac{5}{4}, 1, \frac{3}{4}, \frac{1}{2}$
37. 2, 6, 10, 14, 18 **39.** $-2, 2, 6, 10, 14$ **41.** 620
43. 4600 **45.** 265 **47.** 4000 **49.** 1275
51. 25,250 **53.** 355 **55.** 126,750 **57.** 520
59. 44,625 **61.** 9, 13 **63.** $\frac{15}{4}, \frac{9}{2}, \frac{21}{4}$ **65.** 10,000
67. (a) $\$35,000$ (b) $\$187,500$ **69.** 2340
71. 470 bricks

Section 10.3   *(page 685)*

WARM UP **1.** $\frac{64}{125}$ **2.** $\frac{9}{16}$ **3.** $\frac{1}{16}$ **4.** $\frac{5}{81}$ **5.** $6n^3$
6. $27n^4$ **7.** $4n^3$ **8.** n^2 **9.** $\dfrac{2^n}{81^n}$ **10.** $\dfrac{3}{16^n}$

1. Geometric sequence, $r = 3$
3. Not a geometric sequence
5. Geometric sequence, $r = -\frac{1}{2}$
7. Not a geometric sequence
9. Not a geometric sequence **11.** 2, 6, 18, 54, 162
13. $1, \frac{1}{2}, \frac{1}{4}, \frac{1}{8}, \frac{1}{16}$ **15.** $5, -\frac{1}{2}, \frac{1}{20}, -\frac{1}{200}, \frac{1}{2000}$
17. $1, e, e^2, e^3, e^4$ **19.** $3, \dfrac{3x}{2}, \dfrac{3x^2}{4}, \dfrac{3x^3}{8}, \dfrac{3x^4}{16}$
21. $\left(\frac{1}{2}\right)^7$ **23.** $-\dfrac{2}{3^{10}}$ **25.** $100e^{8x}$ **27.** $500(1.02)^{39}$
29. 9 **31.** $-\frac{2}{9}$ **33.** (a) $\$2,593.74$ (b) $\$2,653.30$
(c) $\$2,685.06$ (d) $\$2,707.04$ (e) $\$2,717.91$
35. $\$22,689.45$ **37.** 511 **39.** 43 **41.** ≈ 6.40
43. $\approx 29,921.31$ **45.** ≈ 2092.60 **47.** $\$7,808.24$
49. Proof **51.** (a) $\$26,198.27$ (b) $\$26,263.88$

53. (a) $637,678.02   **(b)** $645,861.43

55. $3,048.1 million   **57.** $3,623,993.23   **59.** 2

61. $\frac{2}{3}$ **63.** $\frac{16}{3}$ **65.** 32   **67.** $\frac{8}{3}$ **69.** 152.42 ft

Section 10.4   *(page 693)*

WARM UP   **1.** 24   **2.** 40   **3.** $\frac{77}{60}$ **4.** $\frac{7}{2}$

5. $\dfrac{2k + 5}{5}$ **6.** $\dfrac{3k + 1}{6}$ **7.** $8 \cdot 2^{2k} = 2^{2k+3}$ **8.** $\frac{1}{9}$

9. $\dfrac{1}{k}$ **10.** $\frac{4}{5}$

1. 210   **3.** 91   **5.** 225   **7.** 2275   **9.** 70

11. $\dfrac{5}{(k + 1)(k + 2)}$ **13.** $\dfrac{(k + 1)^2(k + 2)^2}{4}$

Section 10.5   *(page 701)*

WARM UP   **1.** $5x^5 + 15x^2$ **2.** $x^3 + 5x^2 - 3x - 15$

3. $x^2 + 8x + 16$ **4.** $4x^2 - 12x + 9$ **5.** $\dfrac{3x^3}{y}$

6. $-32z^5$ **7.** 120   **8.** 336   **9.** 720   **10.** 20

1. 10   **3.** 1   **5.** 15,504   **7.** 4950   **9.** 4950

11. $x^4 + 4x^3 + 6x^2 + 4x + 1$

13. $a^3 + 6a^2 + 12a + 8$

15. $y^4 - 8y^3 + 24y^2 - 32y + 16$

17. $x^5 + 5x^4y + 10x^3y^2 + 10x^2y^3 + 5xy^4 + y^5$

19. $r^6 + 18r^5s + 135r^4s^2 + 540r^3s^3 + 1215r^2s^4 + 1458rs^5 + 729s^6$

21. $x^5 - 5x^4y + 10x^3y^2 - 10x^2y^3 + 5xy^4 - y^5$

23. $1 - 6x + 12x^2 - 8x^3$

25. $x^8 + 20x^6 + 150x^4 + 500x^2 + 625$

27. $\dfrac{1}{x^5} + \dfrac{5y}{x^4} + \dfrac{10y^2}{x^3} + \dfrac{10y^3}{x^2} + \dfrac{5y^4}{x} + y^5$

29. $2x^4 - 24x^3 + 113x^2 - 246x + 207$ **31.** -4

33. $2035 + 828i$ **35.** 1

37. $32t^5 - 80t^4s + 80t^3s^2 - 40t^2s^3 + 10ts^4 - s^5$

39. $81 - 216z + 216z^2 - 96z^3 + 16z^4$ **41.** 1,732,104

43. 180   **45.** $-326,592$ **47.** 210

49. $\frac{1}{128} + \frac{7}{128} + \frac{21}{128} + \frac{35}{128} + \frac{35}{128} + \frac{21}{128} + \frac{7}{128} + \frac{1}{128}$

51. $\frac{1}{6561} + \frac{16}{6561} + \frac{112}{6561} + \frac{448}{6561} + \frac{1120}{6561} + \frac{1792}{6561} + \frac{1792}{6561} + \frac{1024}{6561} + \frac{256}{6561}$

53. $0.07776 + 0.25920 + 0.34560 + 0.23040 + 0.07680 + 0.01024$

55. 1.172   **57.** 510,568.785

59. $g(x) = -x^2 - 5x - 2$

61. $g(x) = x^3 - 15x^2 + 71x - 105$

63. $g(t) = 0.2187t^2 + 5.0455t + 55.255$

Section 10.6   *(page 713)*

WARM UP   **1.** 6656   **2.** 291,600   **3.** 7920

4. 13,800   **5.** 792   **6.** 2300

7. $n(n - 1)(n - 2)(n - 3)$ **8.** $n(n - 1)(2n - 1)$

9. $n!$ **10.** $n!$

1. 7   **3.** 12   **5.** 12   **7.** 6,760,000   **9.** 64

11. (a) 900   **(b)** 648   **(c)** 180   **(d)** 600

13. 64,000   **15. (a)** 720   **(b)** 48   **17.** 24

19. 336   **21.** 1,860,480   **23.** 9900   **25.** 120

27. ABCD, ABDC, ACBD, ACDB, ADBC, ADCB,
BACD, BADC, CABD, CADB, DABC, DACB,
BCAD, BDAC, CBAD, CDAB, DBAC, DCAB,
BCDA, BDCA, CBDA, CDBA, DBCA, DCBA

29. 120   **31.** 11,880   **33.** 420   **35.** 1260

37. 2520

39. AB, AC, AD, AE, AF, BC, BD, BE, BF, CD, CE, CF,
DE, DF, EF

41. 4845   **43.** 3,838,380   **45.** 3,921,225   **47.** 560

49. (a) 70   **(b)** 30   **51. (a)** 70   **(b)** 54   **(c)** 16

53. 5   **55.** 20   **57.** $n = 5$ or $n = 6$

Section 10.7   *(page 726)*

WARM UP   **1.** $\frac{9}{16}$ **2.** $\frac{8}{15}$ **3.** $\frac{1}{6}$ **4.** $\frac{1}{80,730}$

5. $\frac{1}{495}$ **6.** $\frac{1}{24}$ **7.** $\frac{1}{12}$ **8.** $\frac{135}{323}$ **9.** 0.366

10. 0.997

1. {(h, 1), (h, 2), (h, 3), (h, 4), (h, 5), (h, 6), (t, 1),
(t, 2), (t, 3), (t, 4), (t, 5), (t, 6)}

3. {ABC, ACB, BAC, BCA, CAB, CBA}

5. {AB, AC, AD, AE, BC, BD, BE, CD, CE, DE}

7. $\frac{3}{8}$ **9.** $\frac{7}{8}$ **11.** $\frac{3}{13}$ **13.** $\frac{5}{13}$ **15.** $\frac{1}{12}$ **17.** $\frac{7}{12}$

19. $\frac{1}{3}$ **21.** $\frac{1}{5}$ **23.** $\frac{2}{5}$ **25.** 0.3   **27.** 0.85

29. (a) $\frac{112}{209}$ **(b)** $\frac{97}{209}$ **(c)** $\frac{274}{627}$

31. $P(\{\text{Taylor wins}\}) = 0.50$, $P(\{\text{Moore wins}\}) = P(\{\text{Jenkins wins}\}) = 0.25$

33. (a) $\frac{21}{1292} \approx 0.016$ **(b)** $\frac{225}{646} \approx 0.348$

(c) $\frac{49}{323} \approx 0.152$ **35. (a)** $\frac{1}{3}$ **(b)** $\frac{5}{8}$ **37. (a)** $\frac{1}{120}$

(b) $\frac{1}{24}$ **39. (a)** $\frac{1}{169}$ **(b)** $\frac{1}{221}$ **41. (a)** $\frac{14}{55}$ **(b)** $\frac{12}{55}$

(c) $\frac{54}{55}$ **43. (a)** $\frac{1}{4}$ **(b)** $\frac{1}{2}$ **(c)** $\frac{9}{100}$ **(d)** $\frac{1}{30}$

45. (a) ≈ 0.9702 **(b)** ≈ 0.9998 **(c)** ≈ 0.0002

47. (a) $\frac{1}{1024}$ **(b)** $\frac{243}{1024}$ **(c)** $\frac{781}{1024}$ **49. (a)** $\frac{1}{16}$

(b) $\frac{1}{8}$ **(c)** $\frac{15}{16}$ **51.** 0.1024

15. Center: $(-2, 3)$, Foci: $(-2, 3 \pm \sqrt{5})$, Vertices: $(-2, 6)$, $(-2, 0)$, $e = \dfrac{\sqrt{5}}{3}$

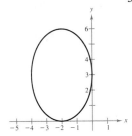

17. Center: $(1, -1)$, Foci: $\left(\frac{7}{4}, -1\right)$, $\left(\frac{1}{4}, -1\right)$, Vertices: $\left(\frac{9}{4}, -1\right)$, $\left(-\frac{1}{4}, -1\right)$, $e = \frac{3}{5}$

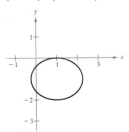

19. Center: $\left(\frac{1}{2}, -1\right)$, Foci: $\left(\frac{1}{2} \pm \sqrt{2}, -1\right)$, Vertices: $\left(\frac{1}{2} \pm \sqrt{5}, -1\right)$, $e = \dfrac{\sqrt{10}}{5}$

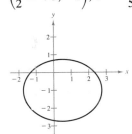

21. $\dfrac{x^2}{36} + \dfrac{y^2}{11} = 1$ **23.** $\dfrac{y^2}{4} + x^2 = 1$

25. $\dfrac{(y-4)^2}{64} + \dfrac{x^2}{48} = 1$ **27.** $\dfrac{(x-3)^2}{36} + \dfrac{(y-2)^2}{32} = 1$

29. Place tacks 1.5 feet from center. Length of string: $2a = 5$ feet

31.

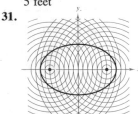

33.

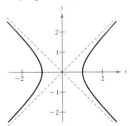

35.

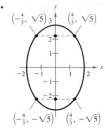

37. Least distance: $a - c \approx 91.377$ million miles; Greatest distance: $a + c \approx 94.537$ million miles

39. $e = 0.0543$ **41.** $e = 0.052$ **43.** Proof

Section 11.4   *(page 764)*

WARM UP   1. $\sqrt{61}$ **2.** $\sqrt{65}$

3.

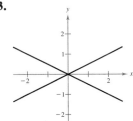

4.

5.

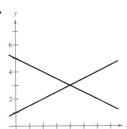

6.

7. Parabola   **8.** Ellipse   **9.** Circle   **10.** Parabola

1. e   **3.** f   **5.** d

7. Center: $(0, 0)$, Vertices: $(\pm 1, 0)$, Foci: $(\pm\sqrt{2}, 0)$, Asymptotes: $y = \pm x$

9. Center: $(0, 0)$, Vertices: $(0, \pm 5)$, Foci: $(0, \pm 13)$, Asymptotes: $y = \pm \frac{5}{12}x$

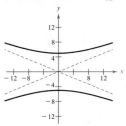

11. Center: $(0, 0)$, Vertices: $(0, \pm 2)$, Foci: $(0, \pm 3)$,

Asymptotes: $y = \pm \dfrac{2}{\sqrt{5}}x$

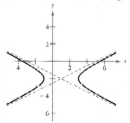

13. Center: $(1, -2)$, Vertices: $(-1, -2)$, $(3, -2)$, Foci: $(1 \pm \sqrt{5}, -2)$, Asymptotes: $y = -2 \pm \frac{1}{2}(x - 1)$

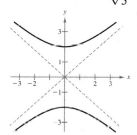

15. Center: $(2, -6)$, Vertices: $(2, -5)$, $(2, -7)$, Foci: $(2, -6 \pm \sqrt{2})$, Asymptotes: $y = -6 \pm (x - 2)$

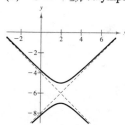

17. Center: $(1, -3)$, Vertices: $(1, -3 \pm \sqrt{2})$, Foci: $(1, -3 \pm 2\sqrt{5})$, Asymptotes: $y = -3 \pm \frac{1}{3}(x - 1)$

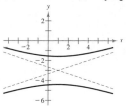

19. Degenerate hyperbola is two intersecting lines

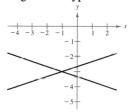

21. $\dfrac{y^2}{4} - \dfrac{x^2}{12} = 1$ **23.** $x^2 - \dfrac{y^2}{9} = 1$

25. $\dfrac{(x - 4)^2}{4} - \dfrac{y^2}{12} = 1$ **27.** $\dfrac{y^2}{9} - \dfrac{(x - 2)^2}{9/4} = 1$

29. $\dfrac{(x - 3)^2}{9} - \dfrac{(y - 2)^2}{4} = 1$ **31.** $(4400, -4290)$

33. $\left(\sqrt{216 - 72\sqrt{5}}, 0\right) \approx (7.42, 0)$ **35.** Circle

37. Hyperbola   **39.** Ellipse   **41.** Parabola

Section 11.5   *(page 773)*

WARM UP   **1.** h   **2.** e   **3.** d   **4.** a   **5.** f

6. c   **7.** $\dfrac{1}{2}x - \dfrac{\sqrt{3}}{2}y$ **8.** $-\dfrac{1}{2}x + \dfrac{\sqrt{3}}{2}y$

9. $\dfrac{4x^2 - 12xy + 9y^2}{13}$ **10.** $\dfrac{x^2 - 2\sqrt{2}xy + 2y^2}{3}$

1. $\dfrac{(y')^2}{2} - \dfrac{(x')^2}{2} = 1$ **3.** $\dfrac{(x')^2}{1/4} - \dfrac{(y')^2}{1/6} = 1$

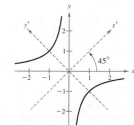

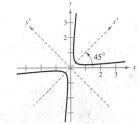

5. $\dfrac{(x' - 3\sqrt{2})^2}{16} - \dfrac{(y' - \sqrt{2})^2}{16} = 1$

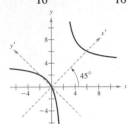

Section 11.6   *(page 779)*

WARM UP   **1.** $\dfrac{3\pi}{4}$ **2.** $\dfrac{7\pi}{6}$

3. $\sin \theta = \dfrac{\sqrt{5}}{5}$ **4.** $\sin \theta = -\dfrac{3}{5}$

$\cos \theta = \dfrac{2\sqrt{5}}{5}$ $\cos \theta = \dfrac{4}{5}$

5. $\dfrac{3\pi}{4}$ **6.** 0.5880   **7.** $-\dfrac{\sqrt{3}}{2}$ **8.** $-\dfrac{\sqrt{2}}{2}$

9. −0.3090   **10.** 0.9735

7. $\dfrac{(x')^2}{3} + \dfrac{(y')^2}{2} = 1$

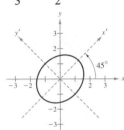

9. $4(y')^2 + 4x' = 0$, $x' = -(y')^2$

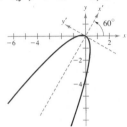

1. (0, 4)

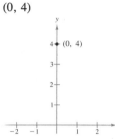

3. $\left(\dfrac{\sqrt{2}}{2}, \dfrac{\sqrt{2}}{2}\right)$

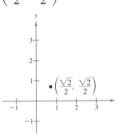

11. $(x' - 1)^2 = 4\left(\dfrac{3}{2}\right)\left(y' + \dfrac{1}{6}\right)$

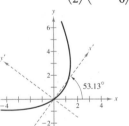

13. $\dfrac{(x')^2}{3} - \dfrac{(y')^2}{5} = 1$

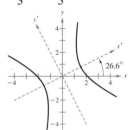

5. $(2, -2\sqrt{3})$

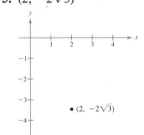

7. (0, 0)

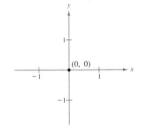

15. $\dfrac{(x')^2}{1.096} - \dfrac{(y')^2}{6.153} = 1$

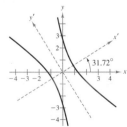

9. (−1.004, 0.996)

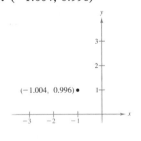

11. $\left(\sqrt{2}, \dfrac{\pi}{4}\right), \left(-\sqrt{2}, \dfrac{5\pi}{4}\right)$

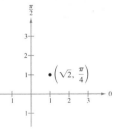

17. Parabola   **19.** Ellipse or circle   **21.** Hyperbola
23. Parabola   **25.** Proof

13. $(6, \pi), (-6, 0)$

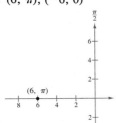

15. $(5, 2.214), (-5, 5.356)$

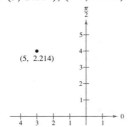

47. $x - y = 0$

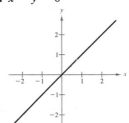

49. $x - 3 = 0$

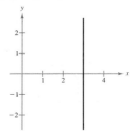

51. Proof

17. $\left(\sqrt{6}, \dfrac{5\pi}{4}\right), \left(-\sqrt{6}, \dfrac{\pi}{4}\right)$

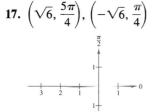

19. $(2\sqrt{13}, 0.983), (-2\sqrt{13}, 4.124)$

Section 11.7   (*page 787*)

WARM UP

1. Amplitude: 5
Period: $\pi/2$

2. Amplitude: 3
Period: 1

3. Amplitude: 5
Period: $\frac{4}{5}$

4. Amplitude: $\frac{1}{2}$
Period: 4π

5.

6.

7.

8.

9. $\dfrac{1}{2}(\sqrt{3}\,\sin x - \cos x)$

10. $\dfrac{\sqrt{2}}{2}(\cos x + \sin x)$

21. $r = 3$ **23.** $r = 2a\cos\theta$ **25.** $r = 4\csc\theta$

27. $r = 10\sec\theta$ **29.** $r = \dfrac{-2}{3\cos\theta - \sin\theta}$

31. $r^2 = 4\sec\theta\csc\theta - 8\csc 2\theta$ **33.** $r^2 = 9\cos 2\theta$

35. $x^2 + y^2 - 4y = 0$ **37.** $\sqrt{3}x - 3y = 0$

39. $y = 2$ **41.** $(x^2 + y^2)^2 = 6x^2y - 2y^3$

43. $4x^2 - 5y^2 - 36y - 36 = 0$

45. $x^2 + y^2 = 9$

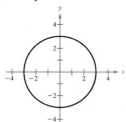

1. Polar axis   **3.** $\theta = \dfrac{\pi}{2}$ **5.** $\theta = \dfrac{\pi}{2}$, polar axis, pole

7. Maximum: $|r| = 5$ when $\theta = 0, \dfrac{\pi}{3}, \dfrac{2\pi}{3}$

Zero: $r = 0$ when $\theta = \dfrac{\pi}{6}, \dfrac{\pi}{2}, \dfrac{5\pi}{6}$

9. Maximum: $|r| = 20$ when $\theta = \dfrac{3\pi}{2}$

Zero: $r = 0$ when $\theta = \dfrac{\pi}{2}$

11.

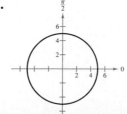

13.

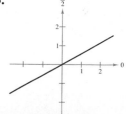

15.

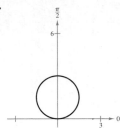

17.

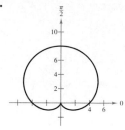

Section 11.8   *(page 794)*

WARM UP

1. $\left(\dfrac{3\sqrt{2}}{2}, -\dfrac{3\sqrt{2}}{2}\right)$

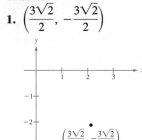

2. $(-2, -2\sqrt{3})$

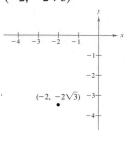

19.

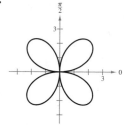

21.

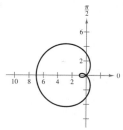

3. $\left(3, \dfrac{3\pi}{2}\right), \left(-3, \dfrac{\pi}{2}\right)$

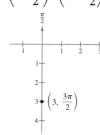

4. (13, 1.9656),
(−13, 5.1072)

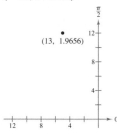

23.

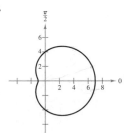

25.

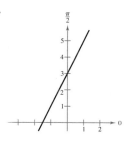

5. $r = 5$ **6.** $r^3 = 4 \sec^2 \theta \csc \theta$ **7.** $y = -4$
8. $x^2 + y^2 - 4x = 0$
9.

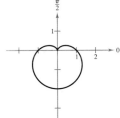

10.

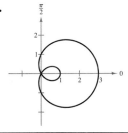

27.

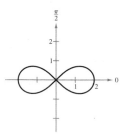

29.

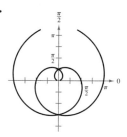

1. c   **3.** a   **5.** b
7.

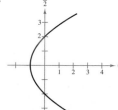

9.

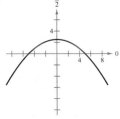

31. $y = \pm \left|\dfrac{x}{x+1}\right| \sqrt{3 - 2x - x^2}$ **33.** Proof

35. (a) $r = 2 - \dfrac{\sqrt{2}}{2}(\sin \theta - \cos \theta)$ **(b)** $r = 2 + \cos \theta$

(c) $r = 2 + \sin \theta$ **(d)** $r = 2 - \cos \theta$

37. (a)

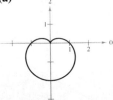

(b)

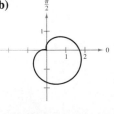

11.

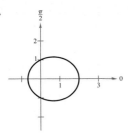

13.

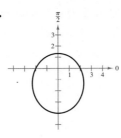

15.

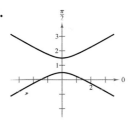

17.

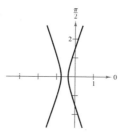

19. Parabola: $r = \dfrac{1}{1 - \cos \theta}$ **21.** Ellipse: $r = \dfrac{1}{2 + \sin \theta}$

23. Hyperbola: $r = \dfrac{2}{1 + 2 \cos \theta}$

25. Parabola: $r = \dfrac{2}{1 - \sin \theta}$

27. Parabola: $r = \dfrac{10}{1 - \cos \theta}$

29. Ellipse: $r = \dfrac{16}{5 + 3 \cos \theta}$

31. Ellipse: $r = \dfrac{20}{3 - 2 \cos \theta}$

33. Hyperbola: $r = \dfrac{9}{4 - 5 \sin \theta}$ **35.** Proof

37. $r^2 = \dfrac{24{,}336}{169 - 25 \cos^2 \theta}$ **39.** $r^2 = \dfrac{144}{25 \cos^2 \theta - 9}$

41. $r^2 = \dfrac{144}{25 \cos^2 \theta - 16}$

43.

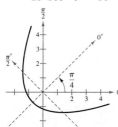

45. Proof

47. $r = \dfrac{9.2931 \times 10^7}{1 - 0.0167 \cos \theta}$ **49.** $r = \dfrac{8200}{1 + \sin \theta}$
   9.1405×10^7
   9.4509×10^7

Section 11.9   *(page 803)*

WARM UP

1.

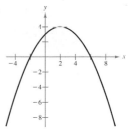

2.

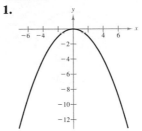

3.

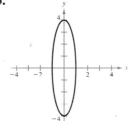

4.

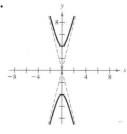

5.

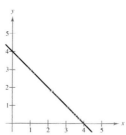

6.

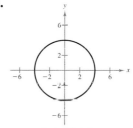

7. 10   **8.** $5 \tan^2 \theta$ **9.** $\sec^2 x + \tan^2 x$ **10.** $\frac{1}{2} \sin \theta$

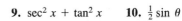

1. $y = -2x$ **3.** $2x - 3y + 5 = 0$

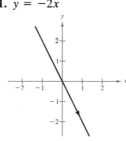

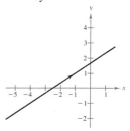

5. $y = 16x^2$ **7.** $y = (x - 1)^2$

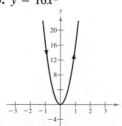

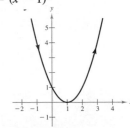

9. $y = \frac{1}{2}\sqrt[3]{x}$

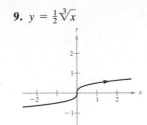

11. $x^2 + y^2 = 9$

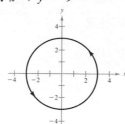

13. $y = 2 - 2x^2,\ -1 \le x \le 1$

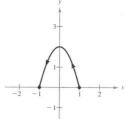

15. $\dfrac{(x-4)^2}{4} + \dfrac{(y+1)^2}{16} = 1$

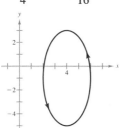

17. $\sqrt[3]{y} = \dfrac{1}{x},\ y = \dfrac{1}{x^3},\ x > 0,\ y > 0$

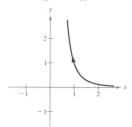

19. $y = \ln x$

21. Each curve represents a portion of the line $y = 2x + 1$.

	Domain	*Orientation*
(a)	$-\infty < x < \infty$	Up
(b)	$-1 \le x \le 1$	Oscillates
(c)	$0 < x < \infty$	Down
(d)	$0 < x < \infty$	Up

23. $y - y_1 = \dfrac{y_2 - y_1}{x_2 - x_1}(x - x_1)$

25. $\dfrac{(x-h)^2}{a^2} + \dfrac{(y-k)^2}{b^2} = 1$

27. $x = 5t$
   $y = -2t$
   Solution not unique

29. $x = 2 + 4\cos\theta$
   $y = 1 + 4\sin\theta$
   Solution not unique

31. $x = 5\cos\theta$
   $y = 3\sin\theta$
   Solution not unique

33. $x = 4\sec\theta$
   $y = 3\tan\theta$
   Solution not unique

35. *Examples:*
   $x = t,\ y = t^3$
   $x = \sqrt[3]{t},\ y = t$
   $x = \tan t,\ y = \tan^3 t$

37.

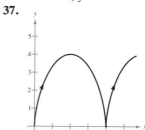

39.

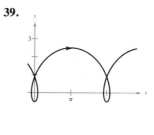

41.

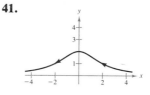

43. b   **45.** d

47. $x = a\theta - b\sin\theta$ and $y = a - b\cos\theta$.

Chapter 11   Review Exercises   *(page 808)*

1. $-\sqrt{3}$ **3.** $135°$ **5.** $2\sqrt{2}$

7. Circle   **9.** Hyperbola

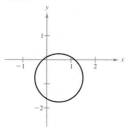   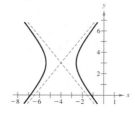

11. Ellipse   **13.** Parabola

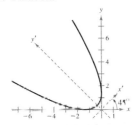   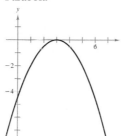

15. Parabola

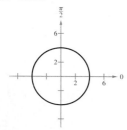

17. $(x - 4)^2 = -8(y - 2)$ **19.** $(y - 2)^2 = 12x$

21. $\dfrac{(x - 2)^2}{25} + \dfrac{y^2}{21} = 1$ **23.** $\dfrac{x^2}{9/2} + \dfrac{y^2}{36} = 1$

25. $y^2 - \dfrac{x^2}{8} = 1$ **27.** $\dfrac{(x - 4)^2}{16/5} - \dfrac{y^2}{64/5} = 1$

29. Focus: $(0, 50)$ **31.** $-2x + 3y = 25$

33. $\frac{2}{3}x - \sqrt{3}y = 1$

35. Circle   **37.** Rose curve

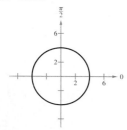   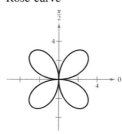

39. Cardioid   **41.** Dimpled limaçon

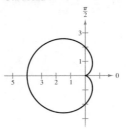   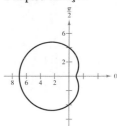

43. Rose curve   **45.** Lemniscate

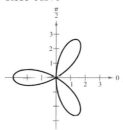   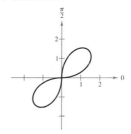

47. Line   **49.** Parabola

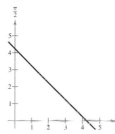   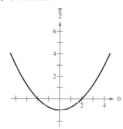

51. $x^2 + y^2 = 3x$ **53.** $x^2 + 4y - 4 = 0$

55. $(x^2 + y^2)^2 - x^2 + y^2 = 0$ **57.** $r = a \cos^2 \theta \sin \theta$

59. $r = 10 \sin \theta$ **61.** $r = \dfrac{4}{1 - \cos \theta}$

63. $r = \dfrac{5}{3 - 2 \cos \theta}$

65. $y = 2x$ **67.** $3x + 4y = 11$

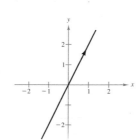   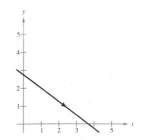

69. $y = \dfrac{1}{x^2}$

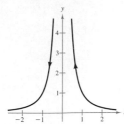

71. $\dfrac{x^2}{36} + \dfrac{y^2}{36} = 1$

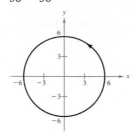

73. $x^{2/3} + \left(\dfrac{y}{4}\right)^{2/3} = 1$

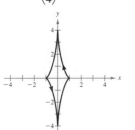

75. $xy = 1, x, y > 0$

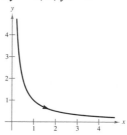

77. $x = -3 + 4 \cos \theta$
$y = 4 + 3 \sin \theta$
This solution is not unique.

79. Proof

81.

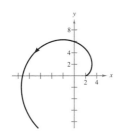

Cumulative Test for Chapters 8–11   (page 811)

1. $(1, 2), \left(-\dfrac{3}{2}, \dfrac{3}{4}\right)$ **3.** $(1, -2, 1)$

5. $\begin{bmatrix} 9 & 1 \\ 7 & -7 \\ 15 & -10 \end{bmatrix}$

7. 22   **9.** 6   **11.** $z^4 - 12z^3 + 54z^2 - 108z + 81$

13. $402,492.56   **15. (a)** $\dfrac{1}{6}$ **(b)** $\dfrac{1}{4}$

17. $\dfrac{(y - 2)^2}{4/5} - \dfrac{x^2}{16/5} = 1$ **19.** $x = 6 + 4t, y = 4 + 7t$
This solution is not unique.

APPENDIX A   (page A11)

WARM UP   **1.** $y = 4 - 3x$ **2.** $y = x$
3. $y = \frac{2}{3}(1 - x)$ **4.** $y = \frac{2}{5}(2x + 1)$
5. $y = \frac{1}{4}(5 - 3x)$ **6.** $y = \frac{2}{3}(-x + 3)$
7. $y = 4 - x^2$ **8.** $y = \frac{2}{3}(x^2 - 1)$
9. $y = \pm\sqrt{4 - x^2}$ **10.** $y = \pm\sqrt{x^2 - 9}$

1.

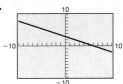

3.

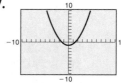

5.

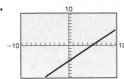

7.

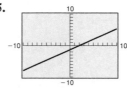

9.

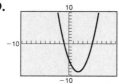

11.

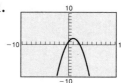

13.

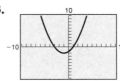

15.

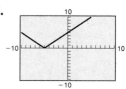

17.

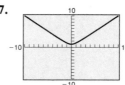

19.

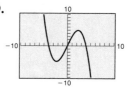

21. (d)   **23.** (a)   **25.** (i)   **27.** (j)   **29.** (e)
31.

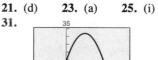

33.

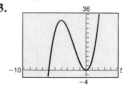

35. Xmin = −10
Xmax = 10
Xscl = 1
Ymin = −12
Ymax = 30
Yscl = 6
Xres = 1

37. Xmin = −10
Xmax = 10
Xscl = 1
Ymin = −10
Ymax = 10
Yscl = 1
Xres = 1

39. No intercepts   **41.** Three *x*-intercepts

43. Square   **45.** Circle

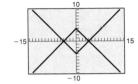

47.

49. 0.59

51.

53. (b)

Appendix B   *(page A18)*

1. **(a)** 2.6201   **(b)** −1.3799   **3.** **(a)** 3.7993
(b) 3   **5.** **(a)** −0.6081   **(b)** 3.8959
7. **(a)** 0.7715   **(b)** 4.2520   **9.** **(a)** 25,000
(b) 0.025   **11.** **(a)** 1,360,000   **(b)** 0.0136
13. **(a)** 3.6420   **(b)** −0.2176   **15.** **(a)** 414,500
(b) 0.007075   **17.** 18.10   **19.** 4.42   **21.** 901.5
23. **(a)** 1.8310   **(b)** 2.2565   **25.** **(a)** 7.46
(b) 4.23   **27.** **(a)** 33.115   **(b)** 0.0302

Index of Applications

U.S. Demographics Applications

Index

Z

FORMULAS FROM GEOMETRY

Triangle:

$h = a \sin\theta$

$\text{Area} = \dfrac{1}{2}bh$

(Law of Cosines)

$c^2 = a^2 + b^2 - 2ab \cos\theta$

Right Triangle:

(Pythagorean Theorem)

$c^2 = a^2 + b^2$

Equilateral Triangle:

$h = \dfrac{\sqrt{3}\,s}{2}$

$\text{Area} = \dfrac{\sqrt{3}\,s^2}{4}$

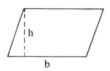

Parallelogram:

$\text{Area} = bh$

Trapezoid:

$\text{Area} = \dfrac{h}{2}(a+b)$

Circle:

$\text{Area} = \pi r^2$

$\text{Circumference} = 2\pi r$

Sector of Circle:

(θ in radians)

$\text{Area} = \dfrac{\theta r^2}{2}$

$s = r\theta$

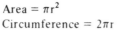

Circular Ring:

(p = average radius,
w = width of ring)

$\text{Area} = \pi(R^2 - r^2)$

$\quad\quad = 2\pi pw$

Sector of Circular Ring:

(p = average radius,
w = width of ring,
θ in radians)

$\text{Area} = \theta pw$

Ellipse:

$\text{Area} = \pi ab$

$\text{Circumference} \approx 2\pi \sqrt{\dfrac{a^2 + b^2}{2}}$

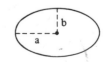

Cone:

(A = area of base)

$\text{Volume} = \dfrac{Ah}{3}$

Right Circular Cone:

$\text{Volume} = \dfrac{\pi r^2 h}{3}$

$\text{Lateral Surface Area} = \pi r \sqrt{r^2 + h^2}$

Frustum of Right Circular Cone:

$\text{Volume} = \dfrac{\pi(r^2 + rR + R^2)h}{3}$

$\text{Lateral Surface Area} = \pi s(R + r)$

Right Circular Cylinder:

$\text{Volume} = \pi r^2 h$

$\text{Lateral Surface Area} = 2\pi rh$

Sphere:

$\text{Volume} = \dfrac{4}{3}\pi r^3$

$\text{Surface Area} = 4\pi r^2$

Wedge:

(A = area of upper face,
B = area of base)

$A = B \sec\theta$

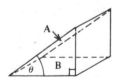

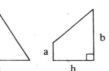

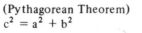